One-Stop Internet Resources

JUST FOR NEW YORK!

Log on to www.glencoe.com

ONLINE STUDY TOOLS

- InterActive Reading Practice
- ePuzzles and Games
- Fluency Activities
- Literature Library Study Guides
- Backpack Reader Study Guides

- Standardized Test Practice
- Study-to-Go™
- Study Central™
- Unit Self-Check Assessments
- Vocabulary eFlashcards

ONLINE RESEARCH

- Author Search
- Big Question Activities and Resources
- Interactive Literary Elements Handbook
- Interactive Writing Models

- Multi-Language Glossaries
- State Resources
- Web Resources

ONLINE STUDENT EDITION

- Complete Interactive Student Edition

- Textbook Updates

FOR TEACHERS

- Professional Development Resources
- State Correlations

- Teacher Forum
- Big Question Web Activity Lesson Plans

TEST-TAKING TIPS

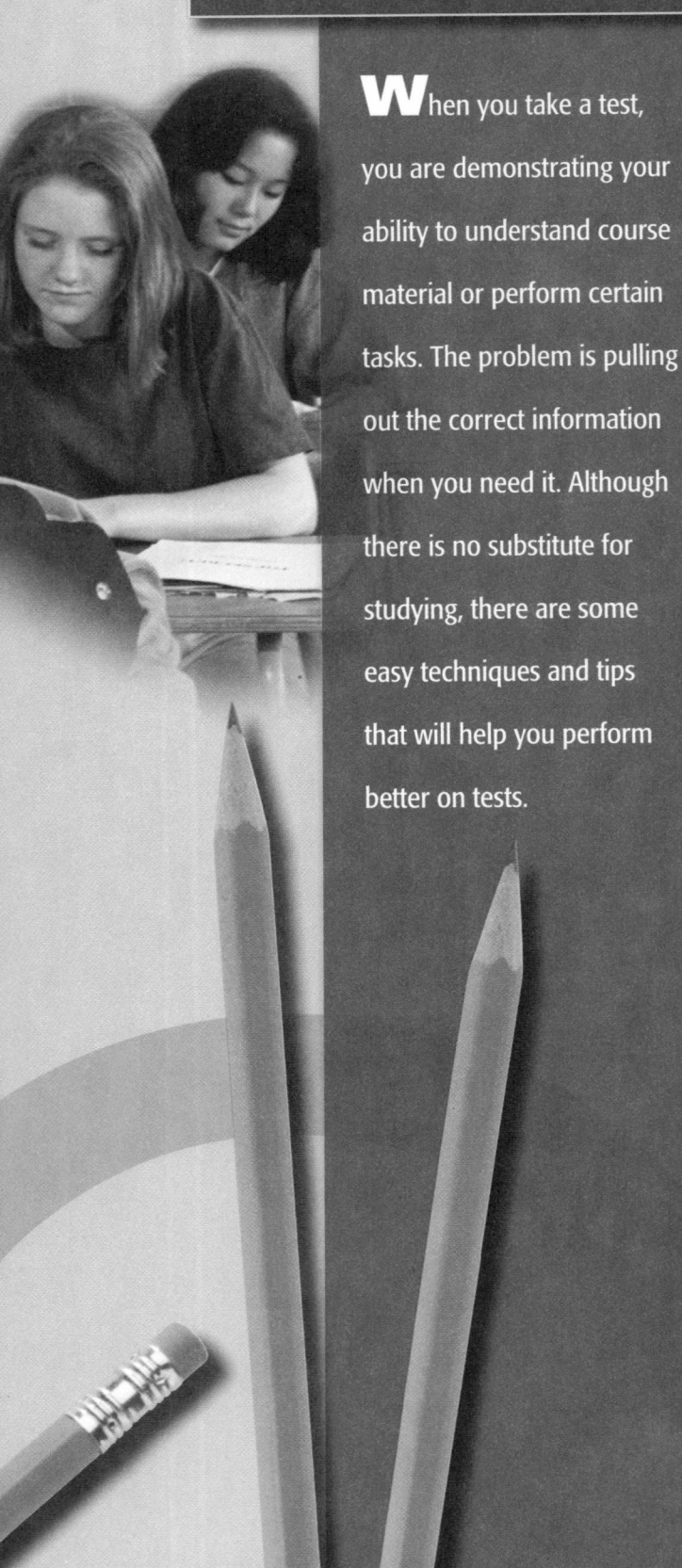

When you take a test, you are demonstrating your ability to understand course material or perform certain tasks. The problem is pulling out the correct information when you need it. Although there is no substitute for studying, there are some easy techniques and tips that will help you perform better on tests.

- Go to bed early the night before the test. You will think more clearly after a good night's rest.

- Bring a watch to the test with you so that you can better pace yourself.

- Read each question or problem carefully. Underline key words and think about the best way to approach the question before you start to write.

- Do the problems that have the greatest point values first.

- Write legibly. If the grader can't read what you wrote it will most likely be marked wrong.

- Always read the whole question carefully. Don't make assumptions about what the question might be.

- Answer the questions you are sure about first. If you do not know the answer to a question, skip it and go back to that question later. This will ensure that you will be able to answer the questions that you do know before time runs out.

- Think positively. Some questions may seem hard to you at first, but if you break it into steps or parts, you may be able to figure it out more easily.

- Make sure that the number of the question on the answer sheet matches the number of the question on which you are working in your test booklet (if you have been given one).

- Don't worry if others finish before you; focus on the test in front of you.

- Relax. Most people get nervous when taking a test. It's natural. Just do your best.

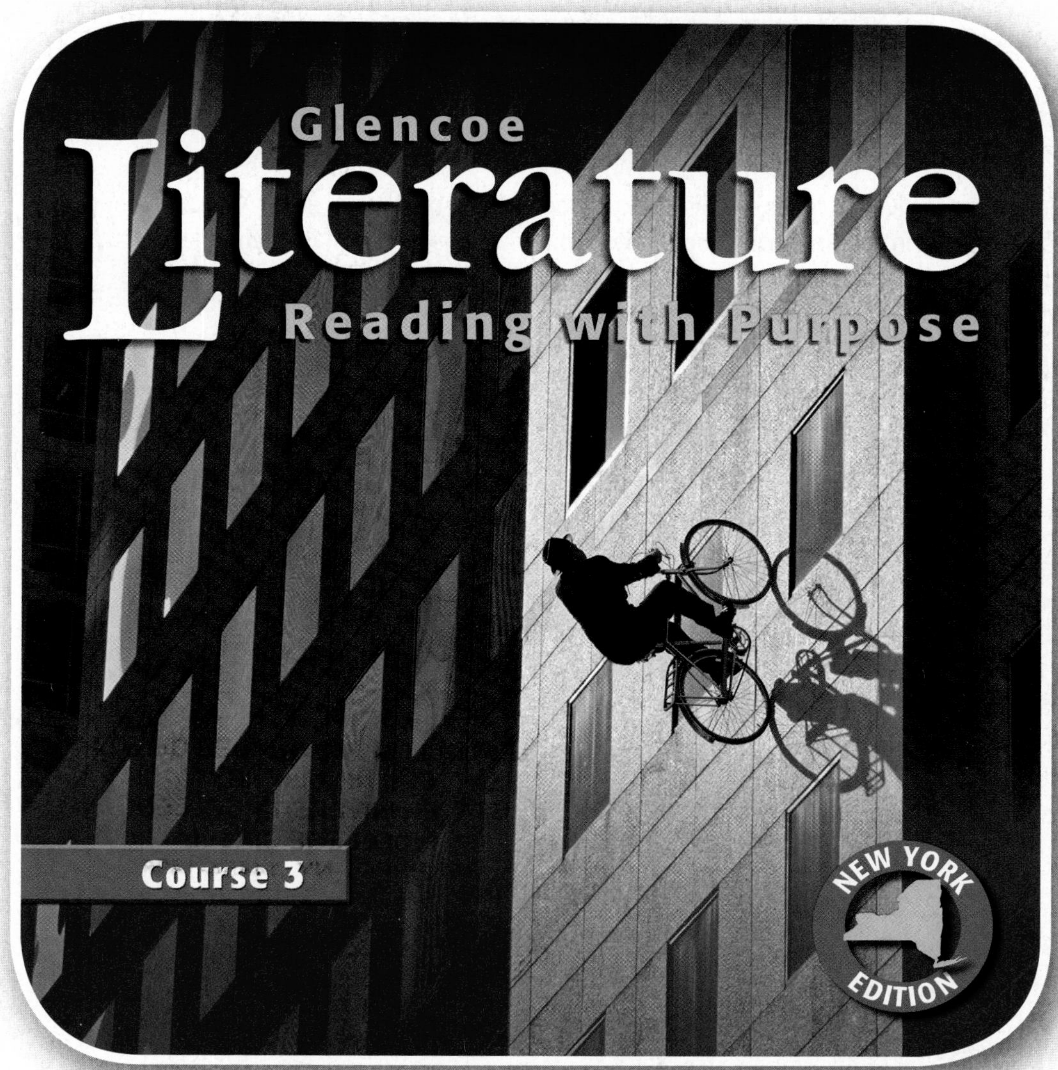

Glencoe Literature
Reading with Purpose

Course 3

New York Edition

Program Consultants

Jeffrey D. Wilhelm, PhD

Douglas Fisher, PhD

Kathleen A. Hinchman, PhD

David O'Brien, PhD

Taffy Raphael, PhD

Cynthia Hynd Shanahan, EdD

227380086

New York, New York   Columbus, Ohio   Chicago, Illinois   Peoria, Illinois   Woodland Hills, California

Acknowledgments

Grateful acknowledgment is given authors, publishers, photographers, museums, and agents for permission to reprint the following copyrighted material. Every effort has been made to determine copyright owners. In case of any omissions, the Publisher will be pleased to make suitable acknowledgments in future editions.

Acknowledgments continued on page R80.

Photo credits:

NY5 Photodisc/Getty Images, NY6 Henry Hobson Richardson/CORBIS, NY7 Photodisc/Getty Images, NY10 CORBIS

Glencoe

The McGraw·Hill Companies

Send all inquiries to:
Glencoe/McGraw-Hill
8787 Orion Place
Columbus, OH 43240-4027

ISBN-13 (student edition): 978-0-07-875744-0
ISBN-10 (student edition): 0-07-875744-0
ISBN-13 (teacher wraparound edition): 978-0-07-875745-7
ISBN-10 (teacher wraparound edition): 0-07-875745-2

Printed in the United States of America.

2 3 4 5 6 7 8 9 079/111 13 12 11 10 09 08 07 06

Program Consultants

Senior Program Consultants

Jeffrey D. Wilhelm, PhD Jeffrey Wilhelm is Professor of English Education at Boise State University. He specializes in reading and adolescent literacy and does research on ways to engage readers and writers. A middle and high school teacher for thirteen years, Wilhelm is author or coauthor of eleven books, including the award-winning works *You Gotta BE the Book* and *Reading Don't Fix No Chevys.*

Douglas Fisher, PhD Douglas Fisher is Professor of Language and Literacy Education at San Diego State University. He is also Director of the award-winning City Heights Educational Pilot, a project for improving urban adolescent literacy. Fisher has published many articles on reading and literacy and has coauthored *Improving Adolescent Literacy: Strategies that Work.*

Program Consultants

Kathleen A. Hinchman, PhD Kathleen Hinchman is Professor and Chair, Reading and Language Arts Center, School of Education, Syracuse University. A former middle school English and reading teacher, Hinchman researches social perspectives toward literacy. She is coauthor of three books on reading and literacy, including *Principled Practices of a Literate America: A Framework for Literacy and Learning in the Upper Grades.*

David O'Brien, PhD David O'Brien is Professor of Literacy Education at the University of Minnesota and a former classroom teacher. O'Brien's research explores reading in content areas as well as ways to motivate learners to engage in school-based literacy tasks. He is conducting studies on the use of technology-based literacy, using computers and related technology.

Taffy Raphael, PhD Taffy Raphael is Professor of Literacy Education at the University of Illinois at Chicago (UIC). She does literacy research on upper elementary and middle school students and has coauthored several books, including *Book Club: A Literature-Based Curriculum* and *Book Club for Middle School.* She has received the International Reading Association (IRA) Outstanding Educator Award and is in the IRA Hall of Fame.

Cynthia Hynd Shanahan, EdD Cynthia Hynd Shanahan is Professor in the Reading, Writing, and Literacy program at the University of Illinois at Chicago (UIC). She is also a consultant with the Center for Literacy at UIC. Hynd Shanahan has been a classroom teacher and has taught reading instruction to elementary-level through college-level teachers. She has authored a chapter in the book *Engaged Reading,* edited by John T. Guthrie and Donna Alverman.

New York Teacher Consultants and Reviewers

Consultants

Francine Stayter
Reading Specialist
State University of New York,
  College at Oneonta
Oneonta, New York

Trudy Walp
Instructor, Reading
  Department
University at Albany,
  State University of New York
Albany, New York

Christine Wylie
Orange-Ulster Board of
  Cooperative Educational
  Services
Goshen/Monroe, New York

Middle School Reviewers

Jennifer Dee
Reading Specialist and
  7th Grade Teacher
West Genesee Central
  School District
Camillus, New York

Donna Mahar
Adolescent Literary Specialist
  and 7th Grade Teacher
West Genesee Central
  School District
Camillus, New York

Sue Volo
English Language Arts
  Coordinator
Menands School
Menands, New York

High School Reviewers

Elizabeth Carson-Tompkins
Teacher of English/ELA
North Salem Central
  School District
North Salem, New York

Regina Derrico
English Department Team
  Leader
Williamsville Central School
  District
East Amherst, New York

John Harmon
Humanities Curriculum
  Coordinator
Skaneateles Central
  School District
Skaneateles, New York

The New York Edition

Welcome to the New York edition of *Glencoe Literature: Reading with Purpose.* We have written this text with several goals in mind. First, we want you to succeed in this course. We also want you to succeed in the New York English Language Arts Core Curriculum and in the New York State Testing Program. To help you, we have provided lessons for the Core Curriculum, which tells you what you are expected to learn throughout the school year. We have also included New York English Language Arts Test Practice at the end of every unit so that you can prepare for the state test. As you read the selections in this book and work through questions and activities, you will become a better reader, a better test-taker, and a more successful student!

Covers the New York Grade 8 Performance Indicators and Literacy Competencies

New York State Capitol

This section of your book contains the following:

New York State English Language Arts Core Curriculum

A Guide for Students and Parents

Why does the New York State Core Curriculum for Language Arts matter to me?

Success in school and in life is determined in large part by competence in language skills. Language is a central factor in learning in all disciplines. Thinking creatively, making informed and reasoned judgments, producing and inventing, critiquing and analyzing are all skills that depend upon our effective use of language.

Language is a lifelong skill, one that we use every day as young adults, as workers and parents, and as members of social and civic organizations. In fact, the skillful use of language is probably the single most important tool for success in the community and workplace.

Statue of Liberty

How do I succeed in the English Language Arts Core Curriculum?

Your textbook includes a variety of tools designed to help you be successful as you study English Language Arts and Literature. One of the most valuable of these is a list of objectives, or standards, that you will be expected to master by the end of the school year. This is called the New York English Language Arts Core Curriculum and you will find it on pages NY11–NY34 of this book.

Using the Standards

Knowing what you are expected to learn from the very beginning of the year will help focus your studies. It will also help you and your parents or caregivers see when you might need extra help in mastering the concepts of a particular unit of study. Such extra help will ensure that your study of literature and language arts will be both enjoyable and successful.

In addition to identifying objectives you need to master, every unit of *Reading with Purpose* ends with six pages of Skills and Strategies Assessment. These New York English Language Arts Test Practices will help you succeed on the state-mandated test for your grade level. See pages NY35–NY37 for more about these helpful test practice pages.

Core Curriculum The lessons in this book will help you succeed in the New York English Language Arts Core Curriculum.

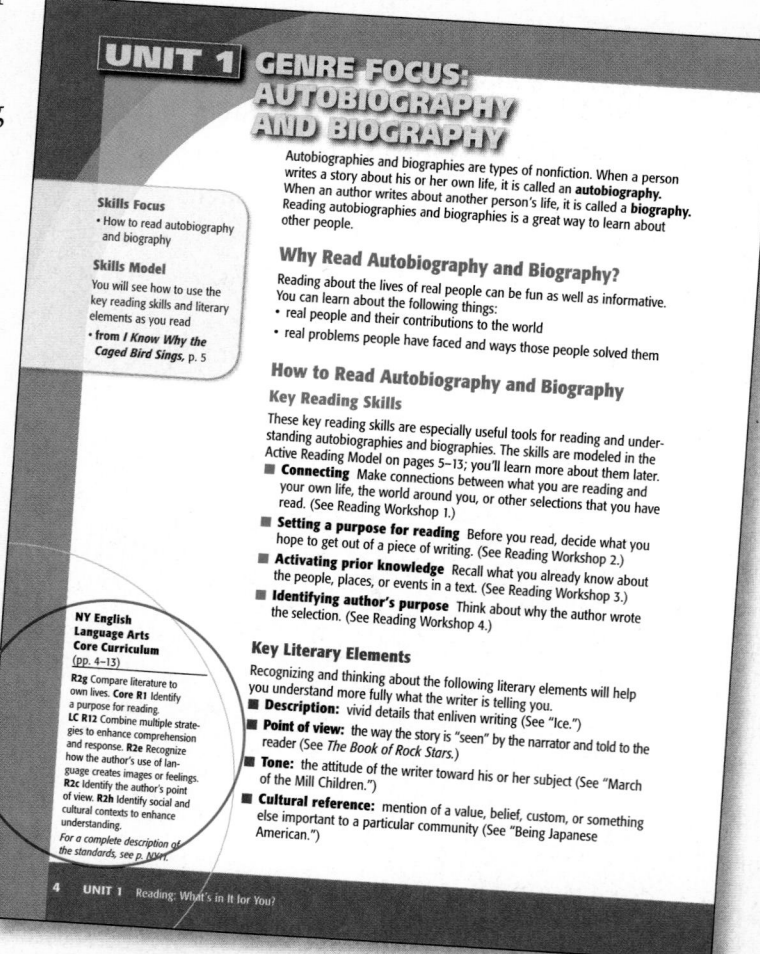

UNIT 1 GENRE FOCUS: AUTOBIOGRAPHY AND BIOGRAPHY

Autobiographies and biographies are types of nonfiction. When a person writes a story about his or her own life, it is called an **autobiography.** When an author writes about another person's life, it is called a **biography.** Reading autobiographies and biographies is a great way to learn about other people.

Skills Focus
• How to read autobiography and biography

Skills Model
You will see how to use the key reading skills and literary elements as you read
• from *I Know Why the Caged Bird Sings,* p. 5

Why Read Autobiography and Biography?
Reading about the lives of real people can be fun as well as informative. You can learn about the following things:
• real people and their contributions to the world
• real problems people have faced and ways those people solved them

How to Read Autobiography and Biography
Key Reading Skills

These key reading skills are especially useful tools for reading and understanding autobiographies and biographies. The skills are modeled in the Active Reading Model on pages 5–13; you'll learn more about them later.
■ **Connecting** Make connections between what you are reading and your own life, the world around you, or other selections that you have read. (See Reading Workshop 1.)
■ **Setting a purpose for reading** Before you read, decide what you hope to get out of a piece of writing. (See Reading Workshop 2.)
■ **Activating prior knowledge** Recall what you already know about the people, places, or events in a text. (See Reading Workshop 3.)
■ **Identifying author's purpose** Think about why the author wrote the selection. (See Reading Workshop 4.)

NY English Language Arts Core Curriculum (pp. 4–13)

R2g Compare literature to own lives. **Core R1** Identify a purpose for reading. **LC R12** Combine multiple strategies to enhance comprehension and response. **R2e** Recognize how the author's use of language creates images or feelings. **R2c** Identify the author's point of view. **R2h** Identify social and cultural contexts to enhance understanding.

For a complete description of the standards, see p. NY11.

Key Literary Elements
Recognizing and thinking about the following literary elements will help you understand more fully what the writer is telling you.
■ **Description:** vivid details that enliven writing (See "Ice.")
■ **Point of view:** the way the story is "seen" by the narrator and told to the reader (See *The Book of Rock Stars.*)
■ **Tone:** the attitude of the writer toward his or her subject (See "March of the Mill Children.")
■ **Cultural reference:** mention of a value, belief, custom, or something else important to a particular community (See "Being Japanese American.")

What is the New York State English Language Arts Core Curriculum?

The **English Language Arts Core Curriculum** is organized by the following grade-level clusters:

- Grades PreK–1
- Grades 2–4
- Grades 5–6
- Grades 7–8
- Grades 9–12

Each cluster is divided into four English Language Arts standards (listed below), and each standard is further divided by the purposes for language use: reading, writing, listening, and speaking.

Standard 1:

Students will read, write, listen, and speak for **information and understanding.**

As listeners and readers, students will collect data, facts, and ideas; discover relationships, concepts, and generalizations; and use knowledge generated from oral, written, and electronically produced texts. As speakers and writers, they will use oral and written language to acquire, interpret, apply, and transmit information.

Standard 2:

Students will read, write, listen, and speak for **literary response and expression.**

Students will read and listen to oral, written, and electronically produced texts and performances; relate texts and performances to their own lives; and develop an understanding of the diverse social, historical, and cultural dimensions the texts and performances represent. As speakers and writers, students will use oral and written language for self-expression and artistic creation.

Standard 3:

Students will read, write, listen, and speak for **critical analysis and evaluation.**

As listeners and readers, students will analyze experiences, ideas, information, and issues presented by others using a variety of established criteria. As speakers and writers, they will present, in oral and written language and from a variety of perspectives, their opinions and judgments on experiences, ideas, information and issues.

Standard 4:

Students will read, write, listen, and speak for **social interaction.**

Students will use oral and written language for effective social communication with a wide variety of people. As readers and listeners, they will use the social communications of others to enrich their understanding of people and their views.

What is included in the following pages?

New York English Language Arts Core Curriculum

- **Pages NY11-NY16** include a correlation of the Core Performance Indicators, Grades 7–8, to your textbook.

- **Pages NY16–NY23** include a correlation of the Grade 8 Reading Literacy Competencies and Grade-Specific Performance Indicators for the four core standards.

- **Pages NY23–NY27** include a correlation of the Grade 8 Writing Literacy Competencies and Grade-Specific Performance Indicators for the four core standards.

- **Pages NY27–NY30** include a correlation of the Grade 8 Listening Literacy Competencies and Grade-Specific Performance Indicators for the four core standards.

- **Pages NY30–NY34** include a correlation of the Grade 8 Speaking Literacy Competencies and Grade-Specific Performance Indicators for the four core standards.

Keys to Succeeding in the Grade 8 New York State Testing Program for English Language Arts

Turn to pages NY35–NY37 to learn how to use the Skills and Strategies Assessments that appear at the end of each unit in *Reading with Purpose.*

New York state flower

Correlation to the New York ELA Core Curriculum

Core Performance Indicators:

Throughout grades 7 and 8, students demonstrate the following core performance indicators in the key ideas of reading, writing, listening, and speaking.

Reading	
CORE PERFORMANCE INDICATORS	**PAGE NUMBERS**
Core R1 Identify a purpose for reading	Genre Focus: Key Reading Skills: Setting a Purpose for Reading 4
	Skill Lesson: Setting a Purpose for Reading 42–43
	Key Reading Skill: Setting a Purpose for Reading 45, 46, 53, etc.
	Setting Purposes for Reading 17, 31, 45, etc.
Core R2 Adjust reading rate according to the purpose for reading	Genre Focus: Key Reading Skills: Skimming and Scanning 292
	Skill Lesson: Skimming and Scanning 322–323
	Key Reading Skill: Skimming and Scanning 325, 326, 329, etc.
Core R3 Use word recognition and context clues to read fluently	Vocabulary Preview 16, 30, 44, etc.
	English Language Coach: Context Clues 16, 30, 44, etc.
Core R4 Determine the meaning of unfamiliar words by using context clues, a dictionary, or a glossary, and structural analysis (i.e., looking at roots, prefixes, and suffixes of words)	English Language Coach: Context Clues 16, 30, 44, etc.
	English Language Coach: Using Word References 388, 391, 393, etc.
	English Language Coach: Base Words, Suffixes, Prefixes 560, 572, 586, 1081, 1095, etc. . .
	Vocabulary Check: 763, 789, 1111, etc. . .
Core R5 Distinguish between dictionary meaning and implied meaning of the author's words	English Language Coach: Connotation and Denotation 932, 940, 942, 950, 958, 1020, 1026, etc. . .

Please note: The numbering system for the New York English Language Arts Core Curriculum has been created by Glencoe/McGraw-Hill for the reader's ease of reference. It is not intended to indicate any order of importance to the standards. Because of space limitations, the standards appearing on the student pages are abbreviations of the full-text standards and therefore do not reflect official New York state language. The full-text version of the standards text has been provided in this correlation of the New York English Language Arts Core Curriculum to *Reading with Purpose.*

Core Performance Indicators (continued)

Reading

CORE PERFORMANCE INDICATORS	PAGE NUMBERS
Core R6 Identify transitional words or phrases, such as *furthermore* or *in comparison,* that provide clues to organizational formats such as compare/contrast	Genre Focus: Key Reading Skill: Understanding Text Structure 292 Skill Lesson: Understanding Text Structure 336–337 Key Reading Skill: Understanding Text Structure 339, 341, 350, etc.
Core R7 Use knowledge of punctuation to assist in comprehension	Grammar Link 315, 593, 603, etc.
Core R8 Apply corrective strategies, such as discussing with others and monitoring for misunderstandings, to assist in comprehension	Genre Focus: Key Reading Skill: Monitoring Comprehension 546 Skill Lesson: Monitoring Comprehension 500–501 Key Reading Skill: Monitoring Comprehension 503, 504, 507, etc
Core R9 Seek opportunities for improvement in reading comprehension by choosing more challenging writers, topics, and texts	Reading on Your Own 138–139, 280–281, 434–435, etc.
Core R10 Maintain a personal reading list to reflect reading accomplishments	Keep Track of Your Ideas: Foldables Study Organizer 3, 149, 291, etc.

Writing

CORE PERFORMANCE INDICATORS	PAGE NUMBERS
Core W1 Understand the purpose for writing; the purpose may be to explain, describe, narrate, persuade, or express feelings	Assignment: Purpose 38, 92, 178, etc.
Core W2 Identify the intended audience	Assignment: Audience 38, 92, 178, etc.
Core W3 Use tone and language appropriate to audience and purpose	Applying Good Writing Traits: Voice 40, 865 Applying Good Writing Traits: Word Choice 466
Core W4 Use prewriting activities (e.g., brainstorming, note taking, freewriting, outlining, and paragraphing)	Writing Workshop: Prewriting 38–40, 92–93, 178–180, etc.
Core W5 Use the writing process (e.g., prewriting, drafting, revising, proofreading, and editing)	Writing Workshop 38–41, 92–93, 178–181, etc.
Core W6 Write clear, concise, and varied sentences, developing a personal writing style and voice	Applying Good Writing Traits: Voice 40, 865 Grammar Link: Compound and Complex Sentences 583 Applying Good Writing Traits: Fluency 994

Core Performance Indicators (continued)

Writing

CORE PERFORMANCE INDICATORS		PAGE NUMBERS
Core W7	Observe rules of punctuation, italicization, capitalization, and spelling as follows: • punctuate correctly simple/compound/complex sentences, undivided/divided direct quotations, exact words from sources (quotations), titles of articles/ literary works, and business letters • use italics and underlining for titles • capitalize proper nouns, such as geographical names, academic courses, and organizations • spell correctly commonly misspelled words, homonyms, and content-area vocabulary	Grammar Link 53, 61, 315, etc. Italics R40 Capitalization R32, R36–R37 Spelling R43–R44
Core W8	Use correct grammatical construction in • parts of speech, such as nouns; adjectives and adverbs (comparative/superlative); pronouns (indefinite/nominative/objective); conjunctions (coordinating/subordinating); prepositions and prepositional phrases; interjections; and conjunctions to connect ideas • simple/compound/complex sentences; note especially subject-verb agreement, infinitives and participles, clear antecedents for pronouns, placement of modifiers, and use active voice	Grammar Link 75, 91, 193, etc.
Core W9	Use signal/transitional words or phrases, such as *first, next,* and *in addition,* to produce organized, cohesive texts	Writing Workshop: Make a Plan 39 Writing Workshop: Check the Sequence 93 Applying Good Writing Traits: Organization 629
Core W10	Use dictionaries, thesauruses, and style manuals	English Language Coach: Using Word References 388, 391, 393, etc. Write to Learn 398
Core W11	Use computer software (e.g., word processing, import graphics) to support the writing process	Using a Computer for Writing R27
Core W12	Write for an authentic purpose, including publication	Writing Workshop: Publishing and Presenting 93, 235, 382, etc.

Core Performance Indicators (continued)

Listening

CORE PERFORMANCE INDICATORS	PAGE NUMBERS
Core L1 Adapt listening strategies to different purposes and settings	Listening, Speaking, and Viewing: Active Listening 94 Storytelling 237 Oral Presentation 382 Reading Poetry Aloud 499 Group Discussion 633 Dramatizing Literature—Performance 871 Understanding Persuasive Techniques 995 Conducting an Interview 1084 Talk About Your Reading 36, 60, 90, etc.
Core L2 Listen respectfully and responsively	Listening, Speaking, and Viewing: Active Listening 94 Storytelling 237 Oral Presentation 382 Reading Poetry Aloud 499 Group Discussion 633 Dramatizing Literature—Performance 871 Understanding Persuasive Techniques 995 Conducting an Interview 1084 Talk About Your Reading 36, 60, 90, etc.
Core L3 Identify own purpose for listening	Listening, Speaking, and Viewing: Active Listening 94 Storytelling 237 Oral Presentation 382 Reading Poetry Aloud 499 Group Discussion 633 Dramatizing Literature—Performance 871 Understanding Persuasive Techniques 995 Conducting an Interview 1084 Talk About Your Reading 36, 60, 90, etc.
Core L4 Recognize content-specific vocabulary or terminology	Listening, Speaking, and Viewing: Oral Presentation 382 Talk About Your Reading 36, 60, 90, etc.

Core Performance Indicators (continued)

Speaking

CORE PERFORMANCE INDICATORS	PAGE NUMBERS
Core S1 Respond respectfully	Listening, Speaking, and Viewing: Active Listening 94 Storytelling 237 Oral Presentation 382 Reading Poetry Aloud 499 Group Discussion 633 Dramatizing Literature—Performance 871 Understanding Persuasive Techniques 995 Conducting an Interview 1084 Talk About Your Reading 36, 60, 90, etc.
Core S2 Initiate communication with peers and adults in the school and local community	Talk About Your Reading 36, 60, 90, etc. Answering the Big Question 132, 276, 420, etc.
Core S3 Adapt language and presentational features for the audience and purpose	Listening, Speaking, and Viewing: Storytelling 237 Oral Presentation 382 Reading Poetry Aloud 499 Dramatizing Literature—Performance 871
Core S4 Use language and grammar appropriate to the purpose for speaking	Listening, Speaking, and Viewing: Active Listening 94 Storytelling 237 Oral Presentation 382 Reading Poetry Aloud 499 Group Discussion 633 Dramatizing Literature—Performance 871 Understanding Persuasive Techniques 995 Conducting an Interview 1084 Talk About Your Reading 36, 60, 90, etc.
Core S5 Use volume, tone, pitch, and rate appropriate to content and audience	Listening, Speaking, and Viewing: Storytelling 237 Oral Presentation 382 Reading Poetry Aloud 499 Dramatizing Literature—Performance 871

Core Performance Indicators (continued)

Speaking

CORE PERFORMANCE INDICATORS	PAGE NUMBERS
Core S6 Use effective nonverbal communication	Listening, Speaking, and Viewing: Storytelling 237 Dramatizing Literature—Performance 871
Core S7 Use visual aids to enhance the presentation	Listening, Speaking, and Viewing: Oral Presentation 382
Core S8 Establish and maintain eye contact with audience	Listening, Speaking, and Viewing: Storytelling 237 Oral Presentation 382 Reading Poetry Aloud 499

Grade 8 Reading

Literacy Competencies

The reading competencies common to all four ELA standards that students demonstrate during grade 8 are

Word Recognition

LITERACY COMPETENCIES	PAGE NUMBERS
LC R1 Recognize at sight a large body of high-frequency words and specialized content vocabulary	Vocabulary Preview 16, 30, 44, etc.
LC R2 Use a variety of word recognition strategies, such as letter-sound correspondence, syllable patterns, decoding by analogy, word structure, use of syntactic (grammar) cues, and use of semantic (meaning) cues, to read unfamiliar words quickly and accurately	English Language Coach: Base Words, Suffixes, Prefixes 560, 572, 586, etc. English Language Coach: Context Clues 16, 30, 44, etc. English Language Coach: Building Vocabulary: 240, etc. . .
LC R3 Use varied sources of information, including context, to monitor and self-correct for word-reading accuracy	English Language Coach 16, 30, 44, etc.

Background Knowledge and Vocabulary

LITERACY COMPETENCIES	PAGE NUMBERS
LC R4 Acquire grade-appropriate vocabulary by reading a variety of texts across subject areas	Vocabulary Preview 16, 30, 44, etc. Vocabulary Check 29, 37, 53, etc.
LC R5 Determine the meaning of unfamiliar words, terms, and idioms by using context, dictionaries, glossaries, and other print and electronic resources	English Language Coach: Context Clues 16, 30, 44, etc. English Language Coach: Using Word References 388, 391, 393, etc. English Language Coach: English as a Changing Language: 1066, 1074, 1088, 1096, 1100, etc. . .

Background Knowledge and Vocabulary

LITERACY COMPETENCIES	PAGE NUMBERS
LC R6 Determine the meaning of unfamiliar words, terms, and idioms by using word structure knowledge, such as roots (e.g., Greek and Latin), prefixes, and suffixes, to determine word meaning	English Language Coach: Base Words, Suffixes, Prefixes 560, 572, 586, 593, etc. . . English Language Coach: Greek Roots 848, 851, 1151; Latin Roots 870, 876
LC R7 Determine the meaning of unfamiliar words, terms, and idioms by using prior knowledge and context clues	English Language Coach: Context Clues 16, 30, 44, etc.
LC R8 Recognize grade-appropriate synonyms and antonyms and use a thesaurus to identify additional examples	English Language Coach: Synonyms and Antonyms 54, 56, 57, 169, 258, 274, etc. . .
LC R9 Recognize multiple meanings of words and connections among meanings of words	English Language Coach: Multiple-Meaning Words 298, 310, 324, 1016, 1073, etc. . .

Fluency

LITERACY COMPETENCIES	PAGE NUMBERS
LC R10 Read grade-appropriate texts with appropriate expression, phrasing, and pacing	Opportunities to practice this competency occur throughout the textbook.

Comprehension/Response

LITERACY COMPETENCIES	PAGE NUMBERS
LC R11 Respond to and comprehend various genres for student-selected and teacher-selected purposes	Opportunities to practice this competency occur throughout the textbook.
LC R12 Combine multiple strategies (e.g., predict/confirm, question, visualize, summarize, monitor, self-correct) to enhance comprehension and response	Key Reading Skill: Predicting 150, 207, 208, 210, etc. Skill Lesson: Predicting 204–205 Key Reading Skill: Questioning 546, 587, 588, 590, etc. Skill Lesson: Questioning 584–585 Key Reading Skill: Visualizing 712, 875, 876, 877, etc. Skill Lesson: Visualizing 868–869 Key Reading Skill: Paraphrasing and Summarizing 712, 849, 850, 853, etc. Skill Lesson: Paraphrasing and Summarizing 846–847

Literacy Competencies (continued)

Comprehension/Response

LITERACY COMPETENCIES	PAGE NUMBERS
LC R12 continued	Key Reading Skill: Monitoring Comprehension 446, 503, 504, 507, etc. Skill Lesson: Monitoring Comprehension 500–501
LC R13 Use text structure and literary devices to aid comprehension and response	Key Reading Skill: Understanding Text Structure 292, 339, 341, 350, etc. Skill Lesson: Understanding Text Structure 336–337 Key Literary Element: Figurative Language: Metaphor and Simile 446, 471, 472, 473, etc.
LC R14 Work collaboratively with peers to comprehend and respond to texts	Before You Read 16, 30, 44, etc. After You Read 28, 36, 52, etc.
LC R15 Analyze, contrast, support, and critique points of view in a wide range of genres	Opportunities to practice this competency occur throughout the textbook.
LC R16 Find, evaluate, and combine information from print and electronic sources for student-selected and teacher-selected inquiries	Writing Workshop: Research Report: Research Your Topic 316–321
LC R17 Demonstrate comprehension and response through a range of activities, such as writing, drama, oral presentation, and mixed media performance	After You Read: 52–53, 60–61, 74–75, 90–91, etc. . . Write About Your Reading 28, 52, 74, etc. Answering the Big Question 132, 276, 420, etc.

Motivation to Read

LITERACY COMPETENCIES	PAGE NUMBERS
LC R18 Show interest in reading a wide range of texts, topics, genres, and authors	Reading on Your Own 138–139, 280–281, 434–435, etc.
LC R19 Read voluntarily for a variety of personal and academic purposes	Reading on Your Own 138–139, 280–281, 434–435, etc.
LC R20 Be familiar with titles and authors of a wide range of grade-appropriate literature	Table of Contents NY40–NY55 Meet the Author 16, 30, 44, etc.
LC R21 Engage in independent silent reading for extended periods of time	Opportunities to practice this competency occur in every reading selection in this book.

Grade 8 Reading

Grade-Specific Performance Indicators

The grade-specific performance indicators that grade 8 students demonstrate as they learn to read include

GRADE-SPECIFIC PERFORMANCE INDICATORS	PAGE NUMBERS
Standard 1: Students will read, write, listen, and speak for **information and understanding.**	
R1a Locate and use school and public library resources, independently to acquire information	Research Report: Research Your Topic 317
R1b Apply thinking skills, such as define, classify, and infer, to interpret data, facts, and ideas from informational texts	**Unit 3: Informational Articles** After You Read: Critical Thinking 308, 328, 334, etc.
R1c Read and follow written multi-step directions or procedures to accomplish a task or complete an assignment	Filling Out the Application 7
R1d Preview informational texts to assess content and organization and select texts useful for the task	Genre Focus: Key Reading Skill: Skimming and Scanning 292 Skill Lesson: Skimming and Scanning 322–323 Key Reading Skill: Skimming and Scanning 325, 326, 331, etc.
R1e Use indexes to locate information and glossaries to define terms	Research Report: Research Your Topic 317
R1f Use knowledge of structure, content, and vocabulary to understand informational text	**Unit 3: Informational Articles** Genre Focus: Key Reading Skill: Understanding Text Structure 292 Skill Lesson: Understanding Text Structure 336–337 Key Reading Skill: Understanding Text Structure 339, 341, 350, etc. Genre Focus: Key Reading Skill: Identifying Main Idea and Supporting Details 292 Skill Lesson: Identifying Main Idea and Supporting Details 386–387 Key Reading Skill: Identifying Main Idea and Supporting Details 389, 390, 391, etc. Vocabulary Preview 298, 310, 324, etc.
R1g Distinguish between relevant and irrelevant information	Research Report: Choose a Topic and Focus Your Ideas 317

Grade-Specific Performance Indicators (continued)

GRADE-SPECIFIC PERFORMANCE INDICATORS	PAGE NUMBERS
R1h Identify missing, conflicting, or unclear information	Key Reading Skill: Questioning 546, 926, 967, 975, etc. . . Skill Lesson: Questioning 584–585
R1i Formulate questions to be answered by reading informational text	**Unit 3: Informational Articles** The Big Question: Set Purposes for Reading 299, 325, 331, etc.
R1j Compare and contrast information from a variety of different sources	Writing Workshop: Research Report: Research Your Topic 316, 380
R1k Condense, combine, or categorize new information from one or more sources	Writing Workshop: Research Report: Research Your Topic 316, 380
R1l Draw conclusions and make inferences on the basis of explicit and implied information	Key Reading Skill: Drawing Conclusions 712, 735, 738, 739, etc. Skill Lesson: Drawing Conclusions 732–733 Key Reading Skill: Making Inferences 150, 195, 197, 199, 637, 651, 652, 660, etc. . . Skill Lesson: Making Inferences 182–183, 634–635
R1m Make, confirm, or revise predictions	Key Reading Skill: Predicting 150, 207, 208, 210, 607, 619, 621, 626, etc. . . Skill Lesson: Predicting 204–205, 604–605
Standard 2: Students will read, write, listen, and speak for **literary response and expression.**	
R2a Read silently and aloud from a variety of genres, authors, and themes	Opportunities to practice this competency occur in every reading selection in this book.
R2b Interpret characters, plot, setting, theme, and dialogue, using evidence from the text	Skill Lesson: Interpreting: 794–795 Key Literary Element: Characterization 546, 561, 563, 564, etc. Key Literary Element: Plot 150, 195, 197, 198, etc.

Grade-Specific Performance Indicators (continued)

GRADE-SPECIFIC PERFORMANCE INDICATORS		PAGE NUMBERS
R2b	continued	Key Literary Element: Setting 546, 637, 638, 641, etc. Key Literary Element: Theme 150, 241, 244, 247, etc. Key Literary Element: Dialogue and Monologue 712, 765, 770, 772, etc.
R2c	Identify the author's point of view, such as first-person narrator and omniscient narrator	Key Literary Element: Point of View 4, 45, 46, 47, 966, 974, etc. . .
R2d	Determine how the use and meaning of literary devices, such as symbolism, metaphor and simile, illustration, personification, flashback, and foreshadowing, convey the author's message or intent	Literary Element: Symbol 311, 312, 313, etc. Key Literary Element: Figurative Language: Metaphor and Simile 446, 471, 472, 473, etc. Key Literary Element: Foreshadowing 357, 362, 363, etc.
R2e	Recognize how the author's use of language creates images or feelings	Key Literary Element: Imagery 1067, 1068, 1070, etc. Key Literary Element: Mood 712, 825, 831, 832, etc.
R2f	Identify poetic elements, such as repetition, rhythm, and rhyming patterns, in order to interpret poetry	Key Literary Element: Sound Devices 875, 877, 879, etc.
R2g	Compare motives of characters, causes of events, and importance of setting in literature to people, events, and places in own lives	Key Reading Skill: Connecting 4, 17, 18, 20, 37, etc. . . Skill Lesson: Connecting 14–15 Connect to the Reading 45, 55, 65, 106, 171, 185, 195, 207, 249, 299, 311, 399, 491, etc. . .
R2h	Identify social and cultural contexts and other characteristics of the time period in order to enhance understanding and appreciation of text	Build Background 17, 31, 45, etc. Key Literary Element: Cultural Reference 107, 108, 110, etc.
GRADE-SPECIFIC PERFORMANCE INDICATORS		**PAGE NUMBERS**
R2i	Compare a film, video, or stage version of a literary work with the written version	This competency is covered in the Teacher's Edition.

Grade-Specific Performance Indicators (continued)

Standard 3: Students will read, write, listen, and speak for **critical analysis and evaluation.**

R3a	Evaluate the validity and accuracy of information, ideas, themes, opinions, and experiences in texts: for example, • identify conflicting information • consider the background and qualifications of the writer • question the writer's assumptions, beliefs, intentions, and biases • evaluate examples, details, or reasons used to support ideas • identify fallacies of logic that lead to unsupported conclusions • discriminate between apparent messages and hidden agendas • identify propaganda and evaluate its effectiveness • identify techniques the author uses to persuade (e.g., emotional and ethical appeals) • identify differing points of view in texts and presentations • identify cultural and ethnic values and their impact on content • identify multiple levels of meaning	Key Reading Skill: Distinguishing Fact from Opinion 926, 933, 934, 935, etc. Skill Lesson: Distinguishing Fact from Opinion 930–931 Reading Across Texts 404–419 Key Literary Element: Persuasive Appeals 926, 933, 936, 937, etc. Key Literary Element: Author's Bias 926, 979, 981, 982, etc. Skill Lesson: Identifying Main Idea and Supporting Details: 386, 389 Key Reading Skill: Identifying Author's Purpose 1056, 1135, 1137, 1139, etc. Skill Lesson: Identifying Author's Purpose 1132–1133
R3b	Judge a text by using evaluative criteria from a variety of perspectives, such as literary, political, and personal	Key Reading Skill: Evaluating 446, 471, 472, 473, etc. Skill Lesson: Evaluating 468–469
R3c	Suspend judgment until all information has been presented	Opportunities to practice this standard occur throughout the textbook.

Standard 4: Students will read, write, listen, and speak for **social interaction.**

R4a	Share reading experiences with peers or adults; for example, read together silently or aloud with a partner or in small groups	After You Read 28, 36, 52, etc. Talk About Your Reading 36, 60, 90, etc.
R4b	Respect the age, gender, position, and traditions of the writer	Meet the Author 16, 30, 44, etc. Build Background 17, 31, 45, etc. Key Literary Element: Cultural Reference 107, 108, 110, etc.
GRADE-SPECIFIC PERFORMANCE INDICATORS		**PAGE NUMBERS**
R4c	Recognize the types of language (e.g., informal vocabulary, culture-specific terminology, jargon, colloquialisms, and email conventions) that are appropriate to social communication	This competency is covered in the Teacher's Edition.

Grade 8 Writing

Literacy Competencies

The writing competencies common to all four ELA standards that students demonstrate during grade 8 are

Spelling

LITERACY COMPETENCIES	PAGE NUMBERS
LC W1 Correctly spell most words in one's writing	Writing Workshop: Writing Tip: Spelling 93, 381, 630 Spelling R43–T44
LC W2 Use a variety of spelling resources, such as spelling dictionaries and spell-check tools, to spell words correctly	Writing Workshop: Writing Tip: Spelling 93, 381, 630 Spelling R43–T44

Text Production

LITERACY COMPETENCIES	PAGE NUMBERS
LC W3 Use legible print and/or cursive writing, or type	Writing Workshop: Writing Tip: Handwriting 93, 382

Composition

LITERACY COMPETENCIES	PAGE NUMBERS
LC W4 Compose mechanically grade-appropriate texts for a variety of student-selected and teacher-selected purposes	Writing Workshop 38, 92, 178, etc.
LC W5 Write with voice to address varied purposes, topics, and audiences across the curriculum	Applying Good Writing Traits: Voice 40, 865
LC W6 Organize writing effectively to communicate ideas to an intended audience	Write About Your Reading: 52, 168, etc. . . Make a Plan 39, 179 Create an Outline 319 Writing Tip: Sequence 581 Applying Good Writing Traits: Organization 629 Develop Your Draft 954 Organize Your Thoughts 1083

Literacy Competencies (continued)

Composition

LITERACY COMPETENCIES	PAGE NUMBERS
LC W7 Compose arguments to support points of view with relevant details from single and multiple texts	Writing Workshop: Persuasive Essay 948, 988
LC W8 Work collaboratively with peers to plan, draft, revise, and edit written work	Answering the Big Question 132, 276, 420, etc.
LC W9 Produce written and multimedia reports of inquiry, using multiple sources	Writing Workshop: Research Report: Research Your Topic 316–321

Motivation to Write

LITERACY COMPETENCIES	PAGE NUMBERS
LC W10 Engage in writing voluntarily for a variety of purposes, topics, and audiences	Answering the Big Question 132, 276, 420, etc.
LC W11 Publish writing in a variety of presentations or display media	Writing Workshop: Presenting 235, 497, 630, etc.

Grade 8 Writing

Grade-Specific Performance Indicators

The grade-specific performance indicators that grade 8 students demonstrate as they learn to write include

GRADE-SPECIFIC PERFORMANCE INDICATORS	PAGE NUMBERS
Standard 1: Students will read, write, listen, and speak for **information and understanding.**	
W1a Use several sources of information, in addition to an encyclopedia, to develop research reports	Writing Workshop: Research Report: Research Your Topic 317
W1b Identify appropriate format for sharing information with intended audience and comply with the accepted features of that format	Writing Workshop: Presenting 235, 497, 630, etc. Applying Good Writing Traits: Presentation 1123
W1c Take research notes, using a note-taking process	Research Report: Take Notes 318
W1d Use outlines and graphic organizers, such as semantic webs, to plan reports	Research Report: Choose a Topic and Focus Your Ideas 317 Create an Outline 319
W1e Include relevant and exclude irrelevant information	Research Report: Choose a Topic and Focus Your Ideas 317
W1f Use paraphrase and quotation correctly	Research Report: Take Notes 318

Grade-Specific Performance Indicators (continued)

GRADE-SPECIFIC PERFORMANCE INDICATORS	PAGE NUMBERS
W1g Connect, compare, and contrast ideas and information from one or more sources	Writing Workshop: Writing Tip: Evaluating Information 317 Comparing Literature Workshop 119, 131, 261, 665, etc.
W1h Support ideas with examples, definitions, analogies, and direct references to the text	Gather Ideas 316 Focus Your Ideas 317 Develop Your Draft 954 Organize Your Thoughts 1083
W1i Cite sources in notes and bibliography, using correct form	Writing Workshop: Research Report: Cite Your Sources 320
W1j Write accurate and complete responses to questions about informational material	**Unit 3: Informational Articles** After You Read 308, 314, 328, etc.
W1k Maintain a portfolio that includes informational writing	Writing Workshop: Research Report 316–321, 380–385
Standard 2: Students will read, write, listen, and speak for **literary response** and **expression**.	
W2a Write original literary texts to • develop a narrative, using an organizational plan such as chronology or flashback • sequence events to advance a plot; use action, conflict, climax, falling action, and resolution • maintain a consistent point of view that enhances the message and/or establishes the mood • select a genre and use appropriate conventions, such as dialogue, rhythm, and rhyme	Writing Workshop: Autobiographical Sketch 38–41, 92–95 Writing Workshop: Folktale 178–181, 234–237 Writing Workshop: Short Story 580–583, 628–633 Writing Workshop: Dramatic Scene 786–789, 864–867
W2b Write interpretive and responsive essays of approximately three pages to • express opinions and support them through specific references to the text • demonstrate an understanding of plot and theme • identify and describe characters and their motivations • analyze the importance of setting • identify and interpret how the use of literary devices, such as symbolism, metaphor and simile, alliteration, personification, flashback, and foreshadowing, affects meaning • draw conclusions and provide reasons for the conclusions • compare and contrast characters, setting, mood, and voice in more than one literary text or performance	Write About Your Reading 28, 52, 168, etc. Comparing Literature Workshop 116, 256, 886, etc. Reading Across Texts Workshop 407, 516, 665, etc.

Grade-Specific Performance Indicators (continued)

GRADE-SPECIFIC PERFORMANCE INDICATORS	PAGE NUMBERS
W2c Maintain a writing portfolio that includes literary, interpretive, and responsive writing	Writing Workshop: Autobiographical Sketch 38–41, 92–95 Writing Workshop: Folktale 178–181, 234–237 Writing Workshop: Short Story 580–583, 628–633 Writing Workshop: Dramatic Scene 786–789, 864–867 Writing Workshop: Poem 464–467, 496–499 Write About Your Reading 28, 52, 168, etc. Comparing Literature Workshop 116, 256, 886, etc. Reading Across Texts Workshop 407, 516, 665, etc.

Standard 3: Students will read, write, listen, and speak for **critical analysis and evaluation.**

W3a Present clear analyses, using examples, details, and reasons from text	Writing Workshop: Research Report 317–321, 380–385
W3b Present a hypothesis and predict possible outcomes from one or more perspectives	This competency is covered in the Teacher's Edition.
W3c Select content and choose strategies for written presentation on the basis of audience, purpose, and content	Assignment: Audience & Purpose 38, 92, 180, etc. Writing Workshop: Prewriting and Drafting 38, 92, 178, etc.
W3d Explain connections between and among texts to extend the meaning of each individual text	Writing: Compare the Literature 131, 275, 685, etc.
W3e Compare and contrast the use of literary elements in more than one genre, by more than one author	Writing: Compare the Literature 131, 275, 685, etc.
W3f Maintain a writing portfolio that includes writing for critical analysis and evaluation	Writing Workshop: Persuasive Essay 952–955, 992–997 Writing Workshop: Letter 1082–1085, 1128–1131

Standard 4: Students will read, write, listen, and speak for **social interaction.**

W4a Share the process of writing with peers and adults; for example, write a condolence note, get well-card, or thank-you letter with a writing partner or in small groups	Answering the Big Question: Group Activity 132, 276, 420, etc.

Grade-Specific Performance Indicators (continued)

GRADE-SPECIFIC PERFORMANCE INDICATORS	PAGE NUMBERS
W4b Respect the age, gender, social position, and cultural traditions of the recipient	Write About Your Reading 104, 314, 328, etc.
W4c Develop a personal voice that enables the reader to get to know the writer	Applying Good Writing Traits: Voice 40, 93, 865
W4d Write personal reactions to experiences, events, and observations, using a form of social communication	Write About Your Reading 104, 314, 328, etc.
W4e Identify and model the social communication techniques of published writers	Dear Exile 134–137 Letter to Senator Edwards 927–929
W4f Maintain a portfolio that includes writing for social communication	Write About Your Reading 104, 314, 328, etc.
W4g Use the conventions of email	Write About Your Reading 328

Grade 8 Listening
Literacy Competencies

The listening competencies common to all four ELA standards that students demonstrate during grade 8 are

Listening	
LITERACY COMPETENCIES	PAGE NUMBERS
LC L1 Listen with comprehension, for an extended period of time, to texts read aloud	Opportunities to practice this competency occur throughout the textbook.
LC L2 Listen with comprehension, for an extended period of time, to oral presentations	Listening, Speaking, and Viewing: Active Listening 94 Storytelling 237 Oral Presentation 382 Reading Poetry Aloud 499
LC L3 Listen with comprehension, for student-determined and teacher-determined purposes	Listening, Speaking, and Viewing: Active Listening 94 Storytelling 237 Oral Presentation 382 Reading Poetry Aloud 499 Group Discussion 633 Dramatizing Literature–Performance 871 Conducting an Interview 1084 Talk About Your Reading 36, 60, 90, etc.

Literacy Competencies (continued)

Listening

LITERACY COMPETENCIES	PAGE NUMBERS

LC L4 Respond appropriately to what is heard	Listening, Speaking, and Viewing:
	   Active Listening 94
	   Storytelling 237
	   Oral Presentation 382
	   Reading Poetry Aloud 499
	   Group Discussion 633
	   Dramatizing Literature—Performance 871
	   Conducting an Interview 1084
	 Talk About Your Reading 36, 60, 90, etc.

LC L5 Listen with comprehension and respect when others speak	Listening, Speaking, and Viewing:
	   Active Listening 94
	   Storytelling 237
	   Oral Presentation 382
	   Reading Poetry Aloud 499
	   Group Discussion 633
	   Dramatizing Literature—Performance 871
	   Conducting an Interview 1084
	 Talk About Your Reading 36, 60, 90, etc.

Grade 8 Listening

Grade-Specific Performance Indicators

The grade-specific performance indicators that grade 8 students demonstrate as they learn to listen include

GRADE-SPECIFIC PERFORMANCE INDICATORS	PAGE NUMBERS
Standard 1: Students will read, write, listen, and speak for **information and understanding.**	
L1a Recall significant ideas and details and the relationships between and among them	After You Read 28, 36, 52, etc. Talk About Your Reading 36, 60, 90, etc. Answering the Big Question 132, 276, 420, etc.

L1b Identify missing, conflicting, or unclear information	Listening, Speaking, and Viewing:
	   Active Listening 94
	   Group Discussion 633
	 Talk About Your Reading 36, 60, 90, etc.

L1c Draw conclusions and make inferences on the basis of explicit and implied information	After You Read 28, 36, 52, etc.

Grade-Specific Performance Indicators (continued)

GRADE-SPECIFIC PERFORMANCE INDICATORS	PAGE NUMBERS
L1d Recognize that the speaker's voice and delivery impact communication	Listening, Speaking, and Viewing: Storytelling 237 Oral Presentation 382 Reading Poetry Aloud 499 Dramatizing Literature—Performance 871 Understanding Persuasive Techniques 995
Standard 2: Students will read, write, listen, and speak for **literary response and expression.**	
L2a Listen to class lectures, and small group and classroom discussions, to comprehend, interpret, and critique literary text	Listening, Speaking, and Viewing: Group Discussion 633 After You Read 28, 36, 52, etc. Talk About Your Reading 36, 60, 90, etc.
L2b Identify how the author's choice of words, use of characterization, and use of other literary devices affect the listener's interpretation of the oral text	Listening, Speaking, and Viewing: Storytelling 237 Reading Poetry Aloud 499 Dramatizing Literature—Performance 871
L2c Identify how the poet's use of repetition, rhythm, and rhyming patterns affects the listener's interpretation of poetry	Listening, Speaking, and Viewing: Reading Poetry Aloud 499 Key Literary Element: Sound Devices 875, 877, 879, etc.
L2d Recognize social, historical, and cultural features in presentation of literary texts	Listening, Speaking, and Viewing Storytelling 237 Build Background 17, 31, 45, etc. Key Literary Element: Cultural Reference 107, 108, 110, etc.
Standard 3: Students will read, write, listen, and speak for **critical analysis** and **evaluation.**	
L3a Form an opinion or judgment about the validity and accuracy of information, ideas, opinions, issues, themes, and experiences	Listening, Speaking, and Viewing: Understanding Persuasive Techniques 995
L3b Recognize persuasive techniques, such as emotional and ethical appeals, in presentations	Listening, Speaking, and Viewing: Understanding Persuasive Techniques 995
L3c Consider the experience, qualifications, and possible biases of speakers in analyzing and evaluating presentations	Listening, Speaking, and Viewing: Understanding Persuasive Techniques 995
L3d Identify conflicting, missing, or unclear information	Listening, Speaking, and Viewing: Active Listening 94
L3e Suspend judgment until all information has been presented	Opportunities to practice this standard occur throughout the textbook.
L3f Evaluate the quality of the speaker's presentation style by using criteria such as voice quality, enunciation, and delivery	Listening, Speaking, and Viewing: Storytelling 237 Oral Presentation 382 Reading Poetry Aloud 499 Dramatizing Literature—Performance 871

Grade-Specific Performance Indicators (continued)

GRADE-SPECIFIC PERFORMANCE INDICATORS	PAGE NUMBERS
Standard 4: Students will read, write, listen, and speak for **social interaction.**	
L4a Participate as a listener in social conversation with one or more people who are friends or acquaintances	Small Group/Whole Class Discussion 13, 31, 55, etc. Partner Talk 31, 65, 76, etc.
L4b Respect the age, gender, social position, and cultural traditions of the speaker	Small Group/Whole Class Discussion 13, 31, 55, etc. Partner Talk 31, 65, 76, etc.
L4c Listen for more than one level of meaning, articulated and unspoken	Small Group/Whole Class Discussion 13, 31, 55, etc. Partner Talk 31, 65, 76, etc.
L4d Encourage the speaker with appropriate facial expressions and gestures	Small Group/Whole Class Discussion 13, 31, 55, etc. Partner Talk 31, 65, 76, etc.
L4e Withhold judgment	Small Group/Whole Class Discussion 13, 31, 55, etc. Partner Talk 31, 65, 76, etc.
L4f Appreciate the speaker's uniqueness	Small Group/Whole Class Discussion 13, 31, 55, etc. Partner Talk 31, 65, 76, etc.

Grade 8 Speaking
Literacy Competencies

The speaking competencies common to all four ELA standards that students demonstrate during grade 8 are

Speaking	
LITERACY COMPETENCIES	PAGE NUMBERS
LC S1 Speak to share responses to a variety of texts and performances	After You Read 28, 36, 52, etc. Answering the Big Question 132, 276, 420, etc.

LC S2 Use precise vocabulary to communicate ideas	Listening, Speaking, and Viewing:
	  Oral Presentation 382
	  Group Discussion 633
	  Conducting an Interview 1084
	After You Read 28, 36, 52, etc.
	Talk About Your Reading 36, 60, 90, etc.
	Answering the Big Question 132, 276, 420, etc.

Literacy Competencies (continued)

Speaking

LITERACY COMPETENCIES	PAGE NUMBERS
LC S3 Speak, using grammatical structures suited to particular audiences	Listening, Speaking, and Viewing: Oral Presentation 382 Group Discussion 633 Conducting an Interview 1084 Small Group/Whole Class Discussion 13, 31, 55, etc. Partner Talk 31, 65, 76, etc. After You Read 28, 36, 52, etc. Talk About Your Reading 36, 60, 90, etc. Answering the Big Question 132, 276, 420, etc.
LC S4 Speak to include details and examples relevant to the audience and purpose	Listening, Speaking, and Viewing: Oral Presentation 382 Group Discussion 633 Talk About Your Reading 36, 60, 90, etc.
LC S5 Communicate spoken ideas in an organized and coherent manner	Listening, Speaking, and Viewing: Oral Presentation 382 Group Discussion 633 Talk About Your Reading 36, 60, 90, etc.
LC S6 Speak with expression, volume, pace, and gestures appropriate to the topic, audience, and purpose of communication	Listening, Speaking, and Viewing: Storytelling 237 Oral Presentation 382 Reading Poetry Aloud 499 Dramatizing Literature–Performance 871
LC S7 Respond respectfully to others	Listening, Speaking, and Viewing: Active Listening 94 Group Discussion 633 Talk About Your Reading 36, 60, 90, etc. Small Group/Whole Class Discussion 13, 31, 55, etc. Partner Talk 31, 65, 76, etc.

Literacy Competencies (continued)

LITERACY COMPETENCIES	PAGE NUMBERS
LC S8 Participate in group discussions on a range of topics and for a variety of purposes	Listening, Speaking, and Viewing: Group Discussion 633 Small Group/Whole Class Discussion 13, 31, 55, etc. Partner Talk 31, 65, 76, etc. After You Read 28, 36, 52, etc. Talk About Your Reading 36, 60, 90, 494, etc. . . Answering the Big Question 132, 276, 420, etc.
LC S9 Offer verbal feedback to others in a respectful and responsive manner	Listening, Speaking, and Viewing: Group Discussion 633 Small Group/Whole Class Discussion 13, 31, 55, etc. Partner Talk 31, 65, 76, etc. After You Read 28, 36, 52, etc. Talk About Your Reading 36, 60, 90, etc. Answering the Big Question 132, 276, 420, etc.

Grade 8 Speaking

Grade-Specific Performance Indicators

The grade-specific performance indicators that grade 8 students demonstrate as they learn to speak include

GRADE-SPECIFIC PERFORMANCE INDICATORS	PAGE NUMBERS
Standard 1: Students will read, write, listen, and speak for **information and understanding.**	
S1a Prepare and give presentations on informational topics	Listening, Speaking, and Viewing: Oral Presentation 382
S1b Contribute to group discussions by offering comments to clarify and interpret ideas and information	Listening, Speaking, and Viewing: Group Discussion 633 Talk About Your Reading 36, 60, 90, etc.
S1c Present information to address audience needs and to anticipate questions	Listening, Speaking, and Viewing: Oral Presentation 382
S1d Present examples, definitions, analogies, and direct references to the text in support of ideas	After You Read 28, 36, 52, etc. Talk About Your Reading 36, 60, 90, etc.
S1e Connect, compare, and contrast ideas and information	Comparing Literature: Reading/Critical Thinking 131, 275, 531, etc.

Grade-Specific Performance Indicators (continued)

GRADE-SPECIFIC PERFORMANCE INDICATORS	PAGE NUMBERS
S1f Use the conventions of the presentational format for panel discussions, debates, and mock trials	Listening, Speaking, and Viewing: Group Discussion 633
S1g Ask and respond to questions to clarify information	Listening, Speaking, and Viewing: Active Listening 94 Group Discussion 633 After You Read 28, 36, 52, etc. Talk About Your Reading 36, 60, 90, etc.
Standard 2: Students will read, write, listen, and speak for **literary response and expression.**	
S2a Express interpretations and support them through specific references to the text	After You Read 28, 36, 52, etc.
S2b Present original, literary texts, using language and text structures that are inventive; for example, • use rhyme, rhythm, and repetition to create an emotional or aesthetic effect	Listening, Speaking, and Viewing: Storytelling 237 Reading Poetry Aloud 499
S2c Ask and respond to questions to clarify an interpretation or response to literary texts and performances	After You Read 28, 36, 52, etc.
Standard 3: Students will read, write, listen, and speak for **critical analysis and evaluation.**	
S3a Express opinions or judgments about information, ideas, opinions, issues, themes, and experiences	Listening, Speaking, and Viewing: Group Discussion 633 After You Read 28, 36, 52, etc. Talk About Your Reading 36, 60, 90, etc.
S3b State a hypothesis and predict possible outcomes from one or more perspectives	This competency is covered in the Teacher's Edition.
S3c Present content, using strategies designed for the audience, purpose, and context	Listening, Speaking, and Viewing: Storytelling 237 Oral Presentation 382 Reading Poetry Aloud 499 Dramatizing Literature—Performance 871
S3d Credit sources of information and opinions accurately in presentations and handouts	Listening, Speaking, and Viewing: Oral Presentation 382
Standard 4: Students will read, write, listen, and speak for **social interaction.**	
S4a Respect the age, gender, social position, and cultural traditions of the listener	Small Group/Whole Class Discussion 13, 31, 55, etc. Partner Talk 31, 65, 76, etc.
S4b Provide feedback by asking questions designed to encourage further conversation	Small Group/Whole Class Discussion 13, 31, 55, etc. Partner Talk 31, 65, 76, etc.

Grade-Specific Performance Indicators (continued)

GRADE-SPECIFIC PERFORMANCE INDICATORS	PAGE NUMBERS
S4c Use courtesy; for example, avoid sarcasm, ridicule, dominating the conversation, and interrupting	Small Group/Whole Class Discussion 13, 31, 55, etc. Partner Talk 31, 65, 76, etc.
S4d Use culture-specific language, jargon, colloquialisms, and gestures appropriate to the purpose, occasion, and listener	Small Group/Whole Class Discussion 13, 31, 55, etc. Partner Talk 31, 65, 76, etc.
S4e Respond to the listener's interests, needs, and reactions to social conversation	Small Group/Whole Class Discussion 13, 31, 55, etc. Partner Talk 31, 65, 76, etc.
S4f Adopt conventions of email to establish friendly tone in electronic-based social communication	Write About Your Reading 328

English Language Arts for Grade 8

Glencoe Literature: Reading with Purpose provides standardized test practice at the end of every unit. These tests are like the ones you will take during Grade 8. By practicing these tests now, you will be even better prepared to master the learning standards covered on the New York English Language Arts Test.

You will find some tips on this in the following pages that will help you become a better test-taker.

TIP **Always read the test directions carefully** before beginning any section of a test. The directions will often describe the general setting or plot of the story and will help you understand what is happening as you begin to read.

TIP **Read initially for the "big picture."** Read carefully, but don't try to memorize details at this time. If you don't understand a particular word, keep reading. The meaning may become clear from the context of later sentences.

UNIT 8 SKILLS AND STRATEGIES ASSESSMENT

New York English Language Arts Test Practice

Directions
Read this passage from a novel about Leona Vicario, a Mexican woman who helped Mexico earn its independence from Spain in the 19th century. Then answer questions 1 through 5.

from *Leona: A Love Story*
by Elizabeth Borton de Treviño

Doña Angela was reading Leona's latest composition, a four-page essay on the duties of government. It seemed a curious choice of subject, she reflected, but the girl had done her research well, and she wrote a clear and rhythmic Spanish. Still, the essay was dull.

She said so to the serious girl studying across the table from her.

"I know," agreed Leona, moving uneasily in her chair. "But I wanted to find out for myself and get it clear in my mind. That's why it is so factual, so unadorned."

Doña Angela was quick and intuitive. "Have you any doubts about the way our government here, under the Viceroy, is conducted?"

"No," protested Leona. "But sometimes I argue with Padre Anselmo. He thinks the King has too much power."

"Padre Anselmo should be reminded of his duties," said Doña Angela crisply, "which are to confess you and instruct you in religion, not to give you revolutionary ideas."

Leona wisely nodded in agreement and went on to a different subject.

"Lately," she told her chaperone, "I have been writing some poetry. Well, verse. I am not good enough to call my thoughts poetry."

Doña Angela gathered up the sheets of verses and said, "I will look these over later in my room. But meanwhile, Leona, you must be fitted for an evening dress." Don Agustín had specified a pale color, perhaps even white. But Leona was dark. Her golden-brown skin, glowing with health, showed a soft deep rose in the cheeks. Her hair, long and curly, was almost black, and with difficulty subjected to combs. Only her light brown eyes were not a part of her inheritance from native ancestors. Leona was descended on her father's side from the Mexican poet Netzahualcóyotl.

TIP **If there are fewer than 10 questions,** you may wish to read quickly through them before you begin reading the selection. This will alert you to important things to look for while you read.

SKILLS AND STRATEGIES ASSESSMENT **UNIT 8**

TIP **Pay attention to bolded words in the question itself.** These are often words like "best" or "first" or "most likely." They will help you decide between two answers that may both appear at first to be correct.

1 According to the passage, Doña Angela **most likely** disagrees with Padre Anselmo's opinions about
   A religion
   B Leona's education
   C government
   D Leona's duties

2 Which of these statements **best** describes Doña Angela's evaluation of Leona's essay?
   F The essay is simply boring.
   G Despite a few flaws, strong writing makes the essay interesting.
   H The unusual topic results in an interesting essay.
   J Although the content is not interesting, the essay is well written and well supported.

3 According to the passage, Leona's appearance
   A makes her seem mysterious
   B provides evidence that she is a descendent of Netzahualcóyotl's people
   C leads her to wish for darker eyes
   D is her only tie to her native ancestors

TIP **When a question is asking about a specific detail or fact** from the selection, it can be worth the time to go back to that particular point in the story to check your answer.

4 Leona's behavior toward Doña Angela shows that Leona **most likely**
   F is afraid of Doña Angela
   G thinks that Doña Angela is annoying
   H respects Doña Angela
   J is worried that Doña Angela doesn't like her

5 Read this sentence from the passage.
   "That's why it is so factual, so unadorned."
   In this sentence, the word "unadorned" means about the same as
   A interesting
   B plain
   C bad
   D detailed

TIP **When a quotation from the selection has been provided** to you in the question, you generally can answer from the quotation alone. You do not need to spend time going back to the selection to find it.

TIP When you have completed a section of the test and if you still have time, go back and review your choices. If you are sure you made a mistake in one of your choices, then change it to the correct answer. If you are not sure, then you are probably better off staying with your first response and not changing your initial answer.

SKILLS AND STRATEGIES ASSESSMENT **UNIT 6**

never cared to ask what lay beyond it, everything about me was beautiful. My courtiers called me the Happy Prince, and happy indeed I was, if pleasure be happiness. So I lived, and so I died. And now that I am dead they have set me up here so high that I can see all the ugliness and the misery of my city, and though my heart is made of lead yet I cannot choose but weep.

"Far away, far away in a little street there is a poor house. One of the windows is open, and through it I can see a woman seated on a table. Her face is thin and worn, and she has coarse, red hands, all pricked by the needle, for she is a seamstress. She is embroidering passion-flowers on a satin gown for the loveliest of the Queen's maids-of-honour to wear at the next Court-ball. In a bed in the corner of the room her little boy is lying ill. He has a fever and is asking for oranges. His mother has nothing to give him but river water, so he is crying. Swallow, Swallow, little Swallow, will you not bring her the ruby out of my sword-hilt? My feet are fastened to this pedestal and I cannot move."

TIP **Read through the answer options and eliminate the obvious.** Then compare what is left before making your choice.

9 Although the passage is a monologue, a speech for a single character (the Happy Prince), the swallow also plays a role in the story. In its role, the swallow serves as

A a messenger of goodwill

B a symbol of the people's misery

C an audience for the monologue

D a living thing in contrast to the statue

10 Why is the Happy Prince statue weeping?

F He misses the pleasures of his life as a prince.

G He sees the ugliness and misery of his city's people.

H His heart has turned into lead and his body into stone.

J His feet are attached to a pedestal, and he cannot move.

11 To the people who pass by his statue, the Happy Prince seems

A sad

B envious

C lonely

D content

12 Which emotion does the Happy Prince **most likely** feel that prompts him to send the ruby to the seamstress?

F loneliness

G reflection

H generosity

J compassion

13 What can you infer from the passage about the way the Happy Prince might view the use of power and wealth if he were alive today? Use details from the passage to support your answer.

TIP **You are given important clues to help you succeed** in this set of directions. You are told that the answer cannot be found directly in the reading passage. You will have to make an inference. An inference is a statement based on details from the passage and your own reasoning abilities.

Book Overview

UNIT 1 · Reading: What's in It for You? 1

Genre Focus:	Autobiography and Biography
Reading Skills:	Connecting, Setting a Purpose for Reading, Activating Prior Knowledge, Identifying Author's Purpose
Literary Elements:	Description, Point of View, Tone, Cultural Reference
Writing Product:	Autobiographical Sketch
English Language Coach:	Context Clues
Grammar:	Nouns, Pronouns

UNIT 2 · Which Is More Important, the Journey or the Destination? 146

Genre Focus:	Folktales
Reading Skills:	Analyzing, Making Inferences, Predicting, Comparing and Contrasting
Literary Elements:	Protagonist and Antagonist, Plot, Conflict, Theme
Writing Product:	Folktale
English Language Coach:	Vocabulary Building
Grammar:	Adjectives and Adverbs, Other Parts of Speech

UNIT 3 · When Is the Price Too High? 288

Genre Focus:	Informational Articles
Reading Skills:	Previewing, Skimming and Scanning, Understanding Text Structures, Identifying Main Idea and Supporting Details
Text Elements:	Tone, Evidence, Irony, Photographs
Writing Product:	Research Report
English Language Coach:	Multiple-Meaning Words, Word References
Grammar:	Sentences

UNIT 4 · What Do You Do When You Don't Know What to Do? . . 442

Genre Focus:	Poetry
Reading Skills:	Connecting, Evaluating, Interpreting, Monitoring Comprehension
Literary Elements:	Free Verse, Figurative Language: Metaphor and Simile, Alliteration, Rhyme
Writing Product:	Poem
English Language Coach:	Compound Nouns, Compound Adjectives, Word Choice, Dialect
Grammar:	Subject-Verb Agreement

Reference Section

Contents

UNIT 2

Which Is More Important, the Journey or the Destination?

Genre Focus: Folktales

Reading Skills Focus
Analyzing
Making Inferences
Predicting
Comparing and Contrasting

Literary Elements
Protagonist and
    Antagonist
Plot
Conflict
Theme

Vocabulary Skills
Building Vocabulary

Grammar
Adjectives and
    Adverbs
Other Parts
    of Speech

UNIT 3

?BIG Question: When Is the Price Too High? 288

Genre Focus: Informational Articles

Reading Skills Focus
Previewing
Skimming and Scanning
Understanding Text Structures
Identifying Main Idea and
   Supporting Details

Text Elements
Tone
Evidence
Irony
Photographs

Vocabulary Skills
Multiple-Meaning Words
Word References

Grammar
Sentences

Contents

UNIT 4

Genre Focus: Poetry

Reading Skills Focus
Connecting
Evaluating
Interpreting
Monitoring Comprehension

Vocabulary Skills
Compound Nouns
Compound Adjectives
Word Choice

Literary Elements
Free Verse
Figurative Language:
   Metaphor and Simile
Alliteration
Rhyme

Grammar
Subject-Verb
   Agreement

UNIT 5

 **How Do You Stay True to Yourself?** 542

Genre Focus: Short Story

Reading Skills Focus
Analyzing
Questioning
Predicting
Making Inferences

Literary Elements
Characterization
Plot
Theme
Setting

Vocabulary Skills
Structural Analysis

Grammar
Sentences
Sentence Structure

UNIT 6

 **How Do You Keep from Giving Up When Bad Things Happen?** 708

Genre Focus: Drama

Reading Skills Focus
Drawing Conclusions
Interpreting
Paraphrasing and
  Summarizing
Visualizing

Literary Elements
Act and Scene
Dialogue and
  Monologue
Stage Directions
Mood

Vocabulary Skills
Structural Analysis (Greek,
  Latin, and Anglo-Saxon
  word parts)

Grammar
Commas
Semicolons

UNIT 7

 **What's Worth Fighting For? What's Not?** . . 922

Genre Focus: Persuasive Writing

Reading Skills Focus
Distinguishing Fact from
Opinion
Questioning
Reviewing
Clarifying

Literary Elements
Persuasive Appeals
Author's Bias
Faulty Reasoning

Vocabulary Skills
Denotation
Connotation
Semantic Slanting
Extended Definition

Grammar
Punctuation

UNIT 8

What Is the American Dream? 1052

Genre Focus: Historical Text

Reading Skills Focus
Analyzing
Understanding Cause
 and Effect
Identifying Main Idea
 and Supporting Details
Identifying Author's Purpose

Vocabulary Skills
Word Origins
Impact of Historical Events
 on Language

Literary and Text Elements
Chronological Order
Style
Cultural Reference
Metaphor

Grammar
Spelling
Capitalization
Verbals
Misused/Confused Words

Selections by Genre

Drama

Folktales

Graphic Stories

Personal Essays

Biography, Autobiography, Memoirs, Letters

Informational Texts

Historical Documents

Functional Text

Skills Features

VOCABULARY SKILLS

English Language Coach

WRITING SKILLS

Writing Products

Writing Traits

GRAMMAR SKILLS

LISTENING, SPEAKING, AND VIEWING

How to Use *Reading with Purpose*

Wouldn't you like to read better—and understand more? That's what *Reading with Purpose* is all about. This book will help you bridge the gap between a writer's meaning and your understanding.

The next few pages will show you some of the ways *Reading with Purpose* can help you read, think, and write better.

What's in It for You?

Every unit in *Reading with Purpose* is built around a **Big Question,** a question that you will want to think about, talk about, maybe even argue about, and finally answer. The unit's reading selections will help you come up with your answers.

Organization

Each unit contains:

- A **Unit Warm-Up** that introduces the unit's Big Question
- Four **Reading Workshops,** each one containing reading selections that will help you think about the Big Question
  - **Literature** such as short stories, poems, plays, and biographies
  - **Informational texts** such as nonfiction, newspaper and magazine articles, reference books, and manuals
  - **Functional documents** such as signs, schedules, labels, and instructions
- A two-part **Writing Workshop** to help you put your ideas about the Big Question into writing
- A **Comparing Workshop** that will give you a chance to compare different pieces of writing
- A **Unit Wrap-Up** where you'll answer the Big Question

Reading and Thinking

Here are some of the ways *Reading with Purpose* will help you develop your reading and thinking skills.

Skills and Strategies The skills you need to become a better reader are related to your state's standards.

Consultant's Note

Standards tell what you are expected to do or learn—the learning objectives. They help teachers plan lessons and select reading and writing tasks. In addition, standards ensure that the content taught at one school will be similar to the content at other schools in the state. The standards also help you figure out what will be on tests. Standards help you figure out what you need to learn to do well in school!

—Doug Fisher

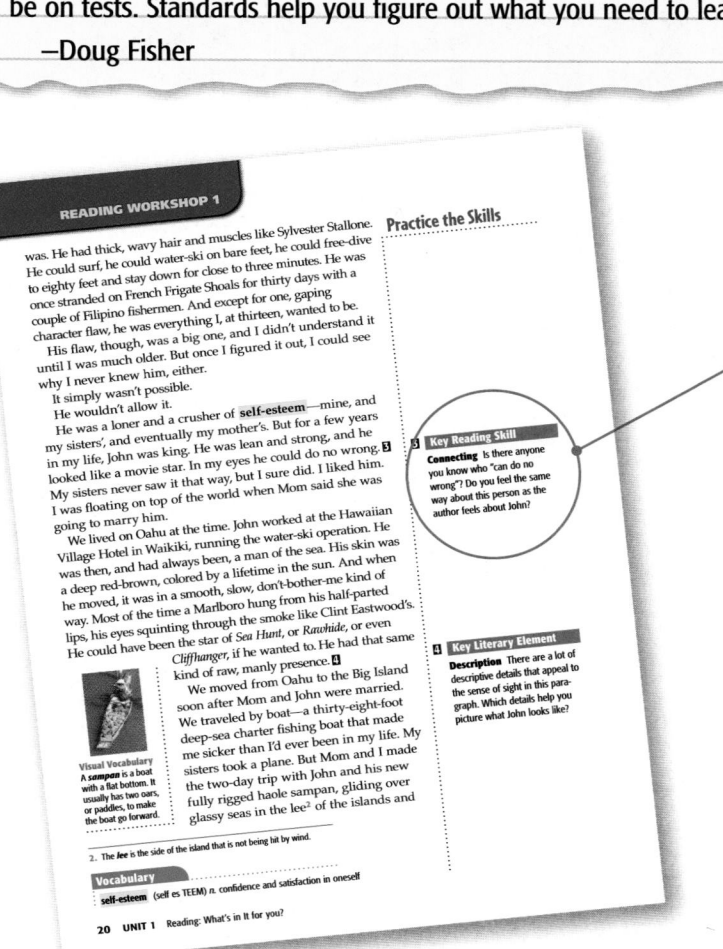

Margin Notes These notes will help you with a difficult passage, point out an important development, model a skill, or ask a question to get you thinking about what you are reading.

Question and Answer Relationship

Four types of questions are used on standardized tests:

1. **Right There Questions** The answer is "right there" on the page.

2. **Think and Search Questions** The answers to these questions are on the page (or pages), but you'll need to use information from different parts of the text.

3. **Author and Me Questions** Information from the text may help, but you'll put it together with your own ideas to answer a question.

4. **On My Own Questions** Answers do not come from the text. You'll base your answer on what you know.

Knowing how to deal with such questions can help improve your test scores. At the end of most Workshops is a set of questions. In the first two units, each question is followed by a tip to help you answer. For example:

• What promise does Victor make to himself about this school year?

   TIP **Right There** You will find the answer in the story.

Vocabulary

Vocabulary words may be difficult or new to you, but they're useful words.

Vocabulary Preview Vocabulary words are introduced on the Before You Read page. Each word is followed by its pronunciation, its part of speech, a definition, and a sample sentence.

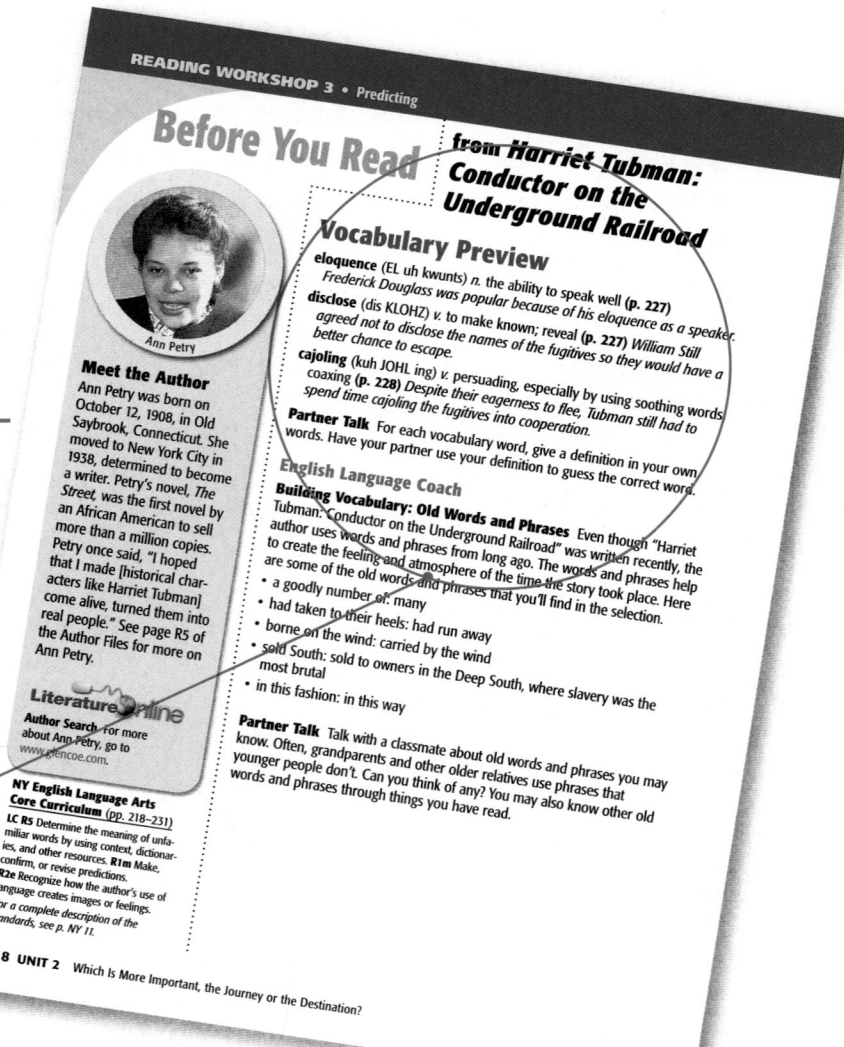

READING WORKSHOP 3

The elder[2] daughter said quickly: 'I shall go, of course, since I am the elder.'

'Very well,' replied the man. 'I shall call all my friends and bid the drummers lead you to your husband's home.'

'Indeed you will not,' said the girl haughtily. 'When I go to the home of my husband, I shall go alone.'

Now in that part of Africa it was unheard of for a bride to go to her wedding without a host of friends and relations all singing and dancing for joy. So the father was astonished when his daughter said she would go alone, even though he knew she had been proud and headstrong from childhood.

'But, my daughter,' he **pleaded**, 'no woman ever goes alone to her marriage. It is not the custom.' 2

'Then I shall start a new custom,' said the girl. 'Unless I go alone, I shall not go at all.'

At last the father, realizing that no amount of persuasion would **induce** the girl to change her mind, agreed to her going alone, and early the next morning she set out. He took her across the river and pointed out the way, then returned home unhappily. 3

The girl began her journey without looking back and after a little while she met a mouse on the path. It stood up on its hind-legs, and rubbing its two front paws together, asked politely:

'Would you like me to show you the way to the chief's village?'

The girl scarcely stopped walking and almost trod on the mouse as she replied:

'Get out of my sight! I want no help from you.'

Then she continued on her way while the mouse screeched after her:

'Bad luck to you!'

2. *Elder* means older.

Vocabulary

induce (in DOOS) *v.* convince to do something; influence

Practice the Skills

2 **English Language Coach**

Classification Charts The word **pleaded** describes how the father's voice sounds when he talks to his daughter. If you don't know what the word means, use context clues to figure out the definition or look it up. Add the word and definition to the classification chart you made earlier.

3 **Key Literary Element**

Conflict The unhappy father has an internal conflict. What external conflict with his daughter causes him to feel unhappy?

Homeward Bound, 2004. Tilly Willis. Oil on canvas. Private Collection.

Analyzing the Painting How does this painting help you visualize the story's setting?

The Snake Chief **209**

Vocabulary The word is in **bold** type when it first appears in the reading selection.

Vocabulary The word with its pronunciation, part of speech, and definition appear at the bottom of the same page.

● **English Language Coach** These notes help students whose first language is not English. For example, they help explain multiple-meaning words and also idioms—phrases that mean something other than what their individual words mean.

● **Footnotes** Selection footnote explains words or phrases that you may not know to help you understand the story.

READING WORKSHOP 1

Skills Focus

You will practice using these skills when you read the following selections:

• "Ice," p. 18
• "On Top of the World," p. 32

Reading
• Connecting

Literature
• Identifying use of description
• Identifying and using the title and subheads

Vocabulary
• Using context clues involves categories and explanation
• Academic Vocabulary: *texts*

Writing/Grammar
• Identifying and using concrete and abstract nouns
• Identifying and using personal and possessive pronouns and antecedents

NY English Language Arts Core Curriculum
(pp. 14–15)
R2g Compare literature to own lives. For a complete description of the standards, see p. NY1.

14 **UNIT 1**

Skill Lesson

Connecting

Learn It!

What Is It? **Connecting** is finding the links between things you read about and your own knowledge and experience.

• You can connect to the characters you read about. They may remind you of yourself, people you know, or people or characters from other **texts**.
• You can connect to the ideas in a text. You may agree or disagree with them.
• You can connect to the experiences described in a text. You may have had, read about, or heard about similar experiences.

Analyzing Cartoons
Clare enjoys reading *Walden* because she can connect what Thoreau writes to her own experiences in the woods.

Academic Vocabulary

texts (teksts) *n.* the words and forms of written or printed works

● **Academic Vocabulary** These are words you come across in your school work—in science, math, or social studies books as well as this book. The academic words are treated the same as regular vocabulary words.

Organizing Information

Foldables For every unit, you'll be shown how to make a *Foldable* that will help you keep track of your thoughts about the Big Question. See page NY68 for more about Foldables.

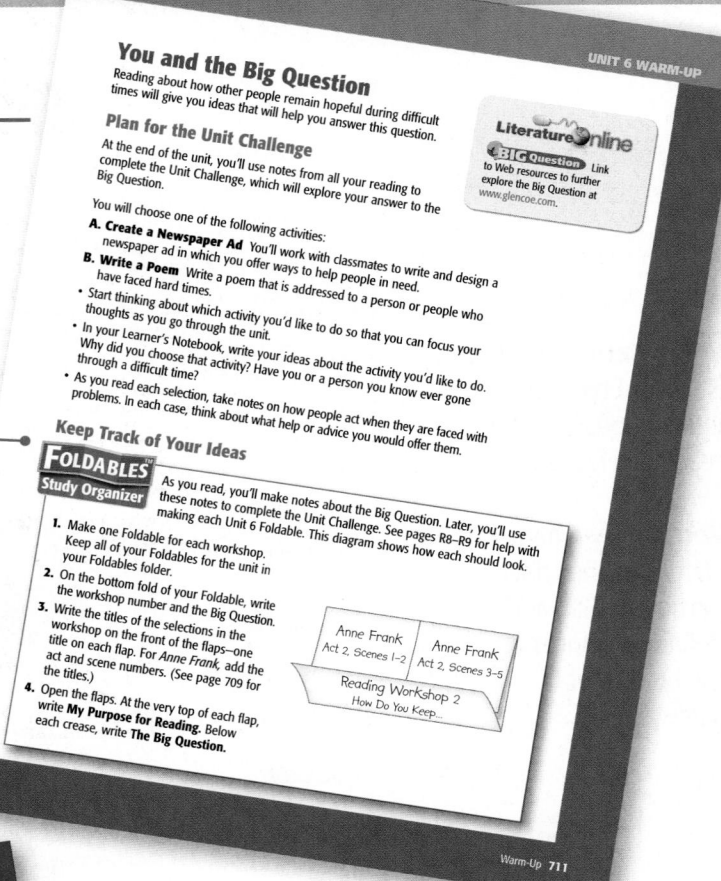

You and the Big Question

Reading about how other people remain hopeful during difficult times will give you ideas that will help you answer this question.

Plan for the Unit Challenge

At the end of the unit, you'll use notes from all your reading to complete the Unit Challenge, which will explore your answer to the Big Question.

You will choose one of the following activities:

A. Create a Newspaper Ad You'll work with classmates to write and design a newspaper ad in which you offer ways to help people in need.

B. Write a Poem Write a poem that is addressed to a person or people who have faced hard times.

- Start thinking about which activity you'd like to do so that you can focus your thoughts as you go through the unit.
- In your Learner's Notebook, write your ideas about the activity you'd like to do. Why did you choose that activity? Have you or a person you know ever gone through a difficult time?
- As you read each selection, take notes on how people act when they are faced with problems. In each case, think about what help or advice you would offer them.

Keep Track of Your Ideas

FOLDABLES™ Study Organizer As you read, you'll make notes about the Big Question. Later, you'll use these notes to complete the Unit Challenge. See pages R8–R9 for help with making each Unit 6 Foldable. This diagram shows how each should look.

1. Make one Foldable for each workshop. Keep all of your Foldables for the unit in your Foldables folder.
2. On the bottom fold of your Foldable, write the workshop number and the Big Question.
3. Write the titles of the selections in the workshop on the front of the flaps—one title on each flap. For *Anne Frank*, add the act and scene numbers. (See page 709 for the titles.)
4. Open the flaps. At the very top of each flap, write **My Purpose for Reading**. Below each crease, write **The Big Question**.

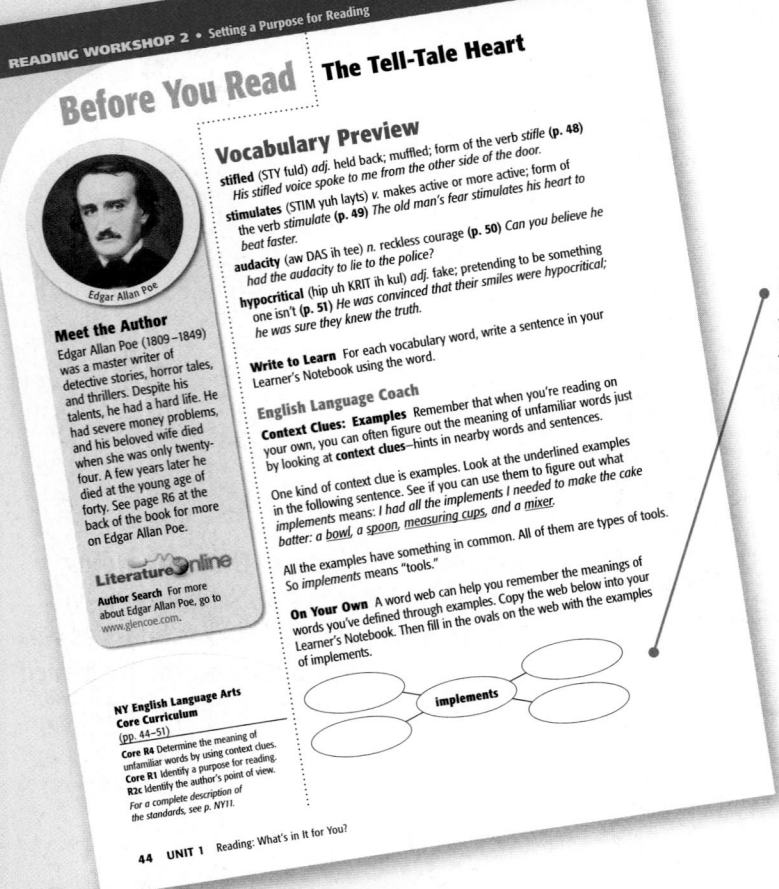

Before You Read — The Tell-Tale Heart

Meet the Author

Edgar Allan Poe (1809–1849) was a master writer of detective stories, horror tales, and thrillers. Despite his talents, he had a hard life. He had severe money problems, and his beloved wife died when she was only twenty-four. A few years later he died at the young age of forty. See page R6 at the back of the book for more on Edgar Allan Poe.

Literature Online
Author Search For more about Edgar Allan Poe, go to www.glencoe.com.

NY English Language Arts Core Curriculum
(pp. 44–51)
Core R4 Determine the meaning of unfamiliar words by using context clues. **Core R1** Identify a purpose for reading. **R2c** Identify the author's point of view.
For a complete description of the standards, see p. NY11.

Vocabulary Preview

stifled (STY fuld) *adj.* held back; muffled; form of the verb *stifle* (p. 48) *His stifled voice spoke to me from the other side of the door.*

stimulates (STIM yuh layts) *v.* makes active or more active; form of the verb *stimulate* (p. 49) *The old man's fear stimulates his heart to beat faster.*

audacity (aw DAS ih tee) *n.* reckless courage (p. 50) *Can you believe he had the audacity to lie to the police?*

hypocritical (hip uh KRIT ih kul) *adj.* fake; pretending to be something one isn't (p. 51) *He was convinced that their smiles were hypocritical; he was sure they knew the truth.*

Write to Learn For each vocabulary word, write a sentence in your Learner's Notebook using the word.

English Language Coach

Context Clues: Examples Remember that when you're reading on your own, you can often figure out the meaning of unfamiliar words just by looking at **context clues**—hints in nearby words and sentences.

One kind of context clue is examples. Look at the underlined examples in the following sentence. See if you can use them to figure out what *implements* means: *I had all the implements I needed to make the cake batter: a bowl, a spoon, measuring cups, and a mixer.*

All the examples have something in common. All of them are types of tools. So *implements* means "tools."

On Your Own A word web can help you remember the meanings of words you've defined through examples. Copy the web below into your Learner's Notebook. Then fill in the ovals on the web with the examples of *implements*.

implements

Graphic Organizers In *Reading with Purpose*, you will use different kinds of graphic organizers to help you arrange information. These graphic organizers include, among others, Venn Diagrams, Compare and Contrast Charts, Cluster Diagrams, and Chain-of-Events Charts.

Writing

In the selections in *Reading with Purpose,* you'll read many examples of excellent writing, and you'll explore what makes those pieces of writing so good.

Here are some other ways *Reading with Purpose* will help you become a better writer.

Writing to Learn As you learn new skills, you will sometimes complete a short writing assignment that will help you practice or think about your new skill.

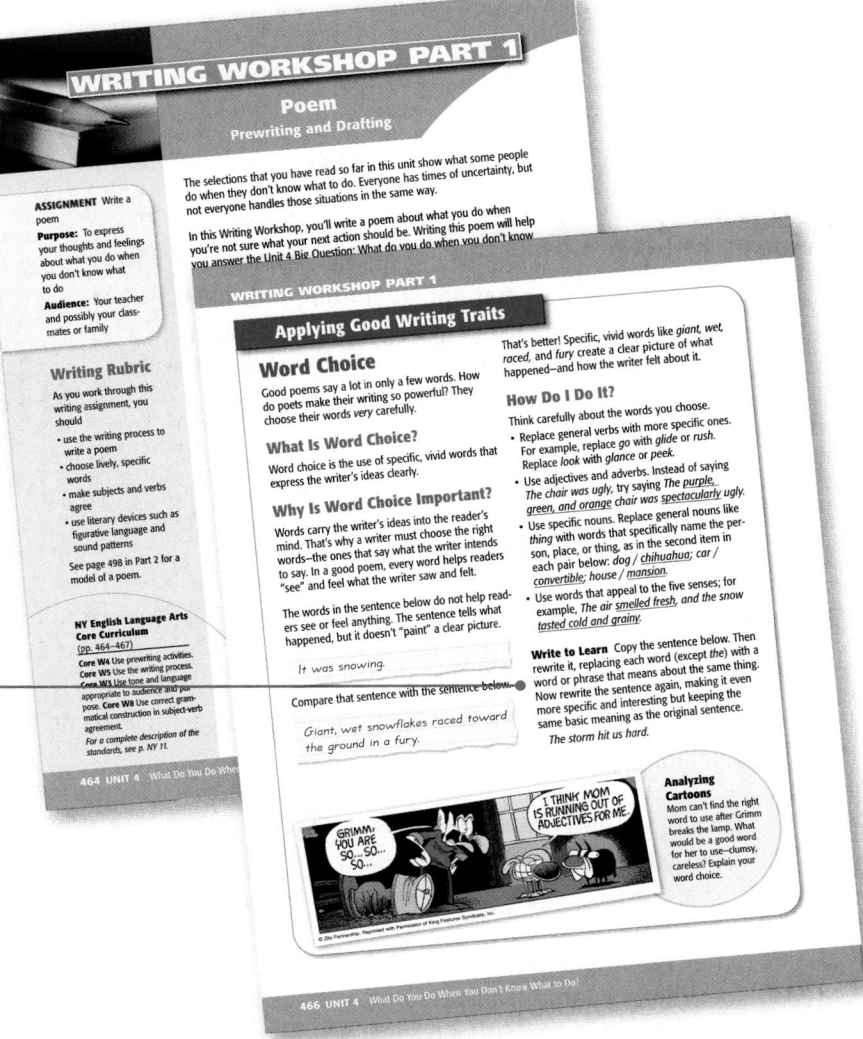

Test Preparation and Practice

Following each unit, there is a New York English Language Arts practice test. This simulated standardized test will help you become familiar with the content and the format of the state test so that you can succeed in New York's testing program.

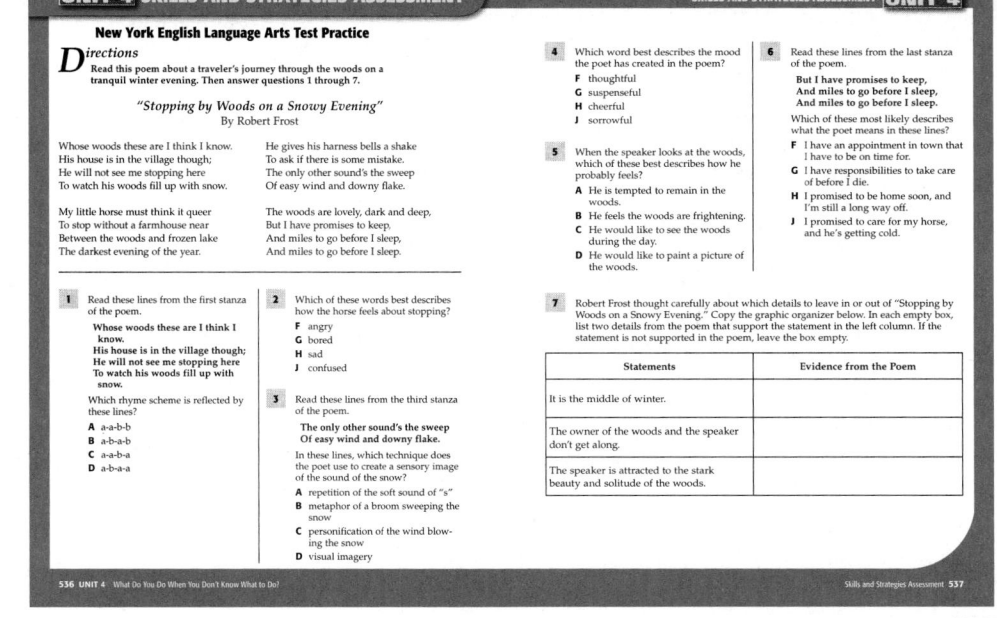

Foldables™

by Dinah Zike, M.Ed., Creator of Foldables™

Foldables™ are three-dimensional interactive graphic organizers for taking notes and organizing your ideas. They're also fun! You will fold paper, cut tabs, write, and manipulate what you have made in order to organize information; review skills, concepts, and strategies; and assess your learning.

Using Dinah Zike's Foldables in Reading and Literature Classes

Use Foldables before, during, and after reading selections in *Glencoe Literature: Reading With Purpose.*

- **Before you read:** Your unit Foldable will help you to focus on your purpose for reading by reminding you about the Big Question.

- **During reading:** Your unit Foldable will help you to stay focused and engaged. You will track key ideas and your thoughts about each selection and how it helps you answer the Big Question. It will also encourage you to use higher level thinking skills in approaching text.

- **After reading:** Your unit Foldable will help you to review your thoughts from your reading and to analyze, interpret, and evaluate various aspects of the Big Question. Your Foldable notes will also help you with your unit challenge. They also stimulate rich group discussions and inquiry.

As you read, you'll make notes about the Big Question. Later, you'll use these notes to complete the Unit Challenge. See pages R8–R9 for help with making each Unit 6 Foldable. This diagram shows how each should look.

1. Make one Foldable for each workshop. Keep all of your Foldables for the unit in your Foldables folder.

2. On the bottom fold of your Foldable, write the workshop number and the Big Question.

3. Write the titles of the selections in the workshop on the front of the flaps—one title on each flap. For *Anne Frank,* add the act and scene numbers. (See page 709 for the titles.)

4. Open the flaps. At the very top of each flap, write **My Purpose for Reading.** Below each crease, write **The Big Question.**

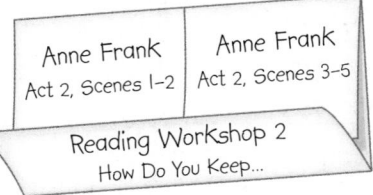

Anne Frank
Act 2, Scenes 1–2

Anne Frank
Act 2, Scenes 3–5

Reading Workshop 2
How Do You Keep...

Become an active reader, track and reorganize information so that you can better understand the selection.

Use the illustrations that make the directions easier to follow.

Practice reading and following step-by-step directions.

Scavenger Hunt

Reading with Purpose has a lot of information, excitement, and entertainment. This Scavenger Hunt will help you explore the book. You'll learn how to find what you need quickly. There are ten questions in your scavenger hunt. All the answers are in this book. Write your answers in your Learner's Notebook.

1. How many units are there in the book?

2. How many types of Workshops are in a unit and what are their names?

3. What is the genre focus of Unit 6?

4. How many short stories are in Unit 3?

5. Where can you find a list of all the poems in this book?

6. What's the fastest way to find a particular short story in the book?

7. Where in this book can you quickly find the correct pronunciation of the word *maneuvers?*

8. Where could you most quickly find the difference between a simile and a metaphor?

9. Where can you look for the answer to a question about grammar?

10. Name two places in the book where you can find biographical information about a writer.

After you answer all the questions, meet with a small group to compare answers.

READING HANDBOOK

You don't read a news article the way you read a novel. You read a news article mainly for information; you read a novel mainly for fun. To get the most out of your reading, you need to choose the right reading strategy to fit the reason you're reading. This handbook focuses on skills and strategies that can help you understand what you read.

Identifying Words and Building Vocabulary

What do you do when you come across a word you don't know as you read? Do you skip over the word and keep reading? If you're reading for fun or entertainment, you might. And that's just fine. But if you're reading for information, an unfamiliar word may get in the way of your understanding. When that happens, try the following strategies to figure out how to say the word and what it means. These strategies will help you better understand what you read. They will also help you increase the vocabulary you use in everyday speaking and reading.

Reading Unfamiliar Words

Sounding the Word Out

One way to figure out how to say a new word is to sound it out, syllable by syllable. Look carefully at the word's beginning, middle, and ending. Inside the new word, do you see a word you already know how to pronounce? What vowels are in the syllables? Use the following tips when sounding out new words.

▶ Ask Yourself

- What letters make up the beginning sound or beginning syllable of the word?

  Example: In the word *coagulate*, *co-* rhymes with *so.*

- What sounds do the letters in the middle part of the word make?

  Example: In the word *coagulate*, the syllable *ag* has the same sound as the *ag* in bag, and the syllable *u* is pronounced like the letter *u.*

- What letters make up the ending sound or syllable?

  Example: In the word *coagulate, late* is a familiar word you already know how to pronounce.

- Now try pronouncing the whole word: *co ag u late.*

Using Word Parts

Looking closely at the parts of a word is another way to learn it. By studying word parts—the root or base word, prefixes, and suffixes—you may discover more than just how to pronounce a word. You may also find clues to the word's meaning.

- **Roots and Base Words** The main part of a word is called its **root.** When the root is a complete word, it may be called the **base word.** Many roots in English come from an old form of English called Anglo-Saxon. You probably know many of these roots already. For example, *endearing* and *remarkable* have the familiar words *dear* and *mark* as their roots. Other roots come from Greek and Latin.

You may not be as familiar with them. For example, the word *spectator* contains the Latin root *spec,* which means "to look at." You can see that meaning in the word *spectator*, "one who looks."

When you come across a new word, check whether you recognize its root or base word. It can help you pronounce the word and figure out its meaning.

- **Prefixes** A prefix is a word part that can be added to the beginning of a root or base word to change the word's meaning. For example,

  the prefix *semi-* means "half" or "partial," so *semicircle* means "half a circle"

  un- means "not," so *unhappy* means "not happy"

- **Suffixes** A suffix is a word part that can be added to the end of a root or base word to change the word's meaning. Adding a suffix to a word can also change that word from one part of speech to another. For example,

  the word *joy* (which is a noun) becomes an adjective when the suffix *-ful* (meaning "full of") is added. *Joyful* means "full of joy"

Determining a Word's Meaning

Using Syntax

Languages have rules and patterns for the way words are arranged in sentences. The way a sentence is organized is called the **syntax** of the sentence. If English is your first language, you have known this pattern since you started talking in sentences. If you're learning English now, you may find the syntax is different from the patterns you know in your first language.

In a simple sentence in English, someone or something (the **subject**) does something (the **predicate** or **verb**) to or with another person or thing (the **object**).

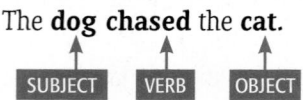

Sometimes adjectives, adverbs, and phrases are added to spice up the sentence.

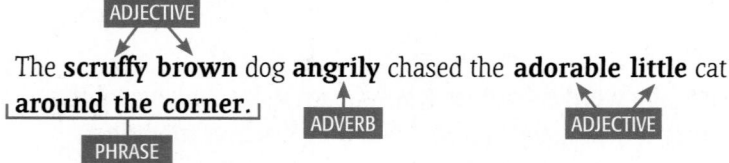

▶ **Check It Out**

Knowing about syntax can help you figure out the meaning of an unfamiliar word. Just look at how syntax can help you figure out the following nonsense sentence.

The blizzy kwarkles sminched the flerky broogs.

Your experience with English syntax tells you that the action word, or verb, in this sentence is *sminched.*

> **Who did the *sminching?*** The *kwarkles.*
>
> **What kind of *kwarkles* were they?** *Blizzy.*
>
> **Whom did they *sminch?*** The *broogs.*
>
> **What kind of *broogs* were they?** *Flerky.*

Even though you don't know the meaning of the words in the nonsense sentence, you can make some sense of the entire sentence by studying its syntax.

Using Context Clues

You can often figure out the meaning of an unfamiliar word by looking at its context (the words and sentences that surround it).

▶ Do It!

To learn new words as you read, follow these steps for using context clues.

1. Look before and after the unfamiliar word for
   - a definition or a synonym (another word that means the same as the unfamiliar word)

     Some outdoor plants need to be **insulated,** or shielded, against cold weather.
   - a general topic associated with the word

     The painter brushed **primer** on the walls before the first coat of paint.
   - a clue to what the word is similar to or different from

     Like a spinning top, the dancer **pirouetted** gracefully.
   - an action or a description that has something to do with the word

     The cook used a **spatula** to flip the pancakes.

2. Connect what you already know with what the author has written.

3. Predict a possible meaning.

4. Use the meaning in the sentence.

5. Try again if your guess does not make sense.

Using Reference Materials

Dictionaries and other reference sources can help you learn new words. Check out these reference sources:

- A **dictionary** gives the pronunciation and the meaning or meanings of a word. Some dictionaries also give other forms of words, their parts of speech, and synonyms. You might also find the historical background of a word, such as its Greek, Latin, or Anglo-Saxon origins.

- A **glossary** is a word list that appears at the end of a book or other written work. It includes only words that are in that work. Like dictionaries, glossaries have the pronunciation and definitions of words. However, the definitions in a glossary give just enough information to help you understand the words as they are used in that work.

- A **thesaurus** lists groups of words that have the same, or almost the same, meaning. Words with similar meanings are called **synonyms.** Seeing the synonyms of words can help you build your vocabulary.

Understanding Denotation and Connotation

Words can have two types of meaning.

Denotation is the literal meaning, the meaning you find in dictionaries.

Connotation is a meaning or feeling that people connect with the word.

For example, you may say that flowers have a *fragrance* but that garbage has a *stench.* Both words mean "smell," but *fragrance* has a pleasant connotation, while *stench* has a very unpleasant one. As you read, it's important to think about the connotation of a word to completely understand what a writer is saying.

Recognizing Word Meanings Across Subjects

Have you ever learned a new word in one class and then noticed it in your reading for other subjects? The word may not mean exactly the same thing in each class. But you can use what you know about the word's meaning to help you understand what it means in a different subject area.

Look at the following example from three subjects:

Social Studies: One major **product** manufactured in the South is cotton cloth. (something manufactured by a company)

Math: After you multiply those two numbers, explain how you arrived at the **product.** (the result of multiplying two numbers)

Science: One **product** of photosynthesis is oxygen. (the result of a chemical reaction)

In all three subject areas, a product is the result of something.

▶ **Practice It!**

1. Write each word below in your Learner's Notebook. Then underline the familiar word or root inside it. (Notice that the end of the familiar word or root may change in spelling a little when a suffix is added to it.)

   a. configuration   **d.** perspective

   b. contemporary   **e.** invaluable

   c. reformation

2. Try to pronounce each of the words. Then check your pronunciation against the pronunciation given in the Glossary at the back of this book.

3. The following sentences can all be completed by the same word or form of the word. Use context clues to find the missing word. Write the word in your Learner's Notebook.

   a. I took the ____ to the photo shop to have a large print made.

   b. Protons are positive; electrons are ____.

   c. You always think ____; can't you think positively for a change?

Reading Fluently

Reading fluently is reading easily. When you read fluently, your brain recognizes each word so you can read without skipping or tripping over words. If you're a fluent reader, you can concentrate on the ideas in your reading because you don't have to worry about what each word means or how to say it.

To develop reading fluency . . .

• **Read often!** The more, the better. Reading often will help you develop a good sight vocabulary—the ability to quickly recognize words.

• **Practice reading aloud.** Believe it or not, reading aloud does help you become a better silent reader.

  – Begin by reading aloud a short, interesting passage that is easy for you.

  – Reread the same passage aloud at least three times or until your reading sounds smooth. Make your reading sound like you are speaking to a friend.

  – Then move on to a longer passage or a slightly more difficult one.

▶ **Practice It!**

Practice reading the paragraph under the next heading. After you think you can read it fluently—without errors or unnecessary pauses—read it aloud to a partner. Ask your partner to comment on your fluency.

Reading for a Reason

Why are you reading that paperback mystery? What do you hope to get from your science textbook? And are you going to read either of these books in the same way that you read a restaurant menu?

The point is, you read for different reasons. The reason you're reading something helps you decide on the reading strategies you use with a text. In other words, how you read will depend on why you're reading.

Knowing Your Reason for Reading

In school and in life, you'll have many reasons for reading, and those reasons will lead you to a wide range of materials. For example,

- **To learn and understand new information,** you might read news magazines, textbooks, news on the Internet, books about your favorite pastime, encyclopedia articles, primary and secondary sources for a school report, instructions on how to use a calling card, or directions for a standardized test.

- **To find specific information,** you might look at the daily newspaper's sports section for the score of last night's game, a notice on where to register for a field trip, weather reports, bank statements, or television listings.

- **To be entertained,** you might read your favorite magazine, e-mails or letters from friends, the Sunday comics, or even novels, short stories, plays, or poems!

Adjusting How Fast You Read

How quickly or how carefully you should read a text depends on your purpose for reading it. Think about your purpose and choose a strategy that works best. Try out these strategies:

- **Scanning** means quickly running your eyes over the material, looking for **key words** or **phrases** that point to the information you're looking for. Scan when you need to find a particular piece or type of information. For example, you might scan a newspaper for movie show times or an encyclopedia article for facts to include in a research report.

- **Skimming** means quickly reading a piece of writing to **find its main idea** or to **get a general overview** of it. For example, you might skim the sports section of the daily newspaper to find out how your favorite teams are doing. Or you might skim a chapter in your science book to prepare for a test.

- **Careful reading** involves **reading slowly and paying attention** with a purpose in mind. Read carefully when you're learning new concepts, following complicated directions, or preparing to explain information to someone else. You definitely should read carefully when you're studying a textbook to prepare for class.

But you might also use this strategy when you're reading a mystery story and don't want to miss any details. Below are some tips you can use to help you read more carefully.

— **Take breaks** when you need them. There's no point in reading when you're sleepy. And if you're reading on the computer, give your eyes a break about every fifteen minutes by focusing on something more distant than your monitor screen.

— **Take notes** as you read. Write in your book if it's OK or use a notebook or sticky notes on the pages. Your notes may be just words or phrases that will jog your memory when you need to review. If you use a notebook, write page numbers from the book in the margin of your notes. That way you can quickly find the original material later if you need it.

— **Make graphic organizers** to help you organize the information from your reading. These can sort out ideas, clear up difficult passages, and help you remember important points. For example, **webs** can show a main idea and supporting details. A **flowchart** can help you keep track of events in a sequence. A **Venn diagram,** made up of overlapping circles, can help you organize how two characters, ideas, or events are alike and different.

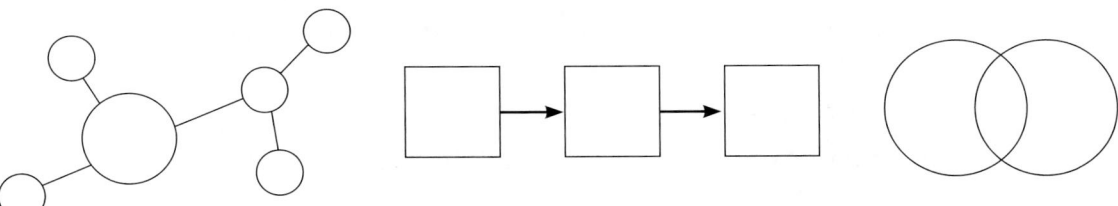

— **Review material** before stopping. Even a short review will help you remember what you've read. Try rereading difficult passages. They will be much easier to understand the second time.

▶ Practice It!

1. In your Learner's Notebook, write whether you would **skim, scan,** or **read carefully** in each of the following cases.

   a. a short story for your English class

   b. the school newspaper for your team's score in last week's game

   c. reviewing a chapter for tomorrow's social studies test

   d. a science book to find if it has information about nuclear waste

   e. to decide which stories and articles to read in a magazine

Becoming Engaged

In reading, *engagement* means relating to what you're reading in a way that makes it meaningful to you. It means finding links between the text and your own life. As you begin to read something, be ready to become engaged with the text. Then as you read, react to the text and relate it to your own experience. Your reading will be much more interesting, and you'll find it easier to understand and remember what you read.

Connect

You will become more involved with your reading and remember events, characters, and ideas better if you relate what you're reading to your own life. **Connecting** is finding the links between what you read and your own experience.

▶ Ask Yourself

- Have I been to places similar to the **setting** described by this writer?
- What **experiences** have I had that compare or contrast with what I am reading?
- What **opinions** do I already have about this topic?
- What **characters** from life or literature remind me of the characters or narrator in the selection?

Respond

Enjoy what you read and make it your own by **responding** to what's going on in the text. Think about and express what you like or don't like, what you find boring or interesting. What surprises you, entertains you, scares you, makes you angry, makes you sad, or makes you laugh out loud? The relationship between you and what you're reading is personal, so react in a personal way.

Understanding What You Read

Reading without understanding is like trying to drive a car on an empty gas tank. You can go through all the motions, but you won't get anywhere! Skilled readers adopt a number of strategies before, during, and after reading to make sure they understand what they read.

Previewing

If you were making a preview for a movie, you would want to let your audience know what the movie is like. When you **preview** a piece of writing, you're treating yourself like that movie audience. You're trying to get an idea about that piece of writing. If you know what to expect before reading, you will have an easier time understanding ideas and relationships. Follow these steps to preview your reading assignments.

▶ Do It!

1. **Look** at the title and any illustrations that are included.

2. **Read** the headings, subheadings, and anything in bold letters.

3. **Skim** over the passage to see how it is organized. Is it divided into many parts? Is it a long poem or short story? Don't forget to look at the graphics—pictures, maps, or diagrams.

4. **Set a purpose** for your reading. Are you reading to learn something new? Are you reading to find specific information?

Activating Prior Knowledge

Believe it or not, you already know quite a bit about what you're going to read. You don't know the plot or the information, of course, but keep in mind that you bring knowledge and unique personal experience to a selection. Drawing on your own background is called **activating prior knowledge,** and it can help you create meaning in what you read. Ask yourself, What do I already know about this topic? What do I know about related topics?

Predicting

You don't need a crystal ball to make **predictions** when you read. The predictions don't even have to be accurate! What's important is that you get involved in your reading from the moment you turn to page one. Take educated guesses before and during your reading about what might happen in the story. Follow these steps:

1. Use your prior knowledge and the information you gathered in your preview to predict what you will learn or what might happen in a selection. Will the hero ever get home? Did the butler do it?

2. As you read on, you may find that your prediction was way off base. Don't worry. Just adjust your predictions and go on reading.

3. Afterwards check to see how accurate your predictions were. You don't have to keep score. By getting yourself involved in a narrative, you always end up a winner.

Visualizing

Creating pictures in your mind as you read—called **visualizing**—is a powerful aid to understanding. As you read, set up a movie theater in your imagination.

- Imagine what a character looks like.
- Picture the setting—city streets, the desert, or the surface of the moon.
- Picture the steps in a process or the evidence that an author wants you to consider. If you can visualize what you read, selections will be more vivid, and you'll recall them better later on.

Identifying Sequence

When you discover the logical order of events or ideas, you are **identifying sequence.** Look for clues and signal words that will help you find the way information is organized.

Are you reading a story that takes place in chronological, or time, order? Do you need to understand step-by-step directions? Are you reading a persuasive speech with the reasons listed in order of importance? You'll understand and remember the information better when you know the organization the author has used.

Determining the Main Idea

When you look for the **main idea** of a selection, you look for the most important idea. The examples, reasons, or details that further explain the main idea are called supporting details.

Some main ideas are clearly stated within a passage—often in the first sentence of a paragraph, or sometimes in the last sentence of a passage.

Other times, an author doesn't directly state the main idea but provides details that help readers figure out what the main idea is.

▶ **Ask Yourself**

- What is each sentence about?
- Is there one sentence that tells about the whole passage or that is more important than the others?
- What main idea do the supporting details point out?

Questioning

Keep up a conversation with yourself as you read by **asking questions** about the text. Feel free to question anything!

- Ask about the importance of the information you're reading.
- Ask how one event relates to another or why a character acts a certain way.
- Ask yourself if you understand what you just read.
- As you answer your own questions, you're making sure that you understand what's going on.

Clarifying

Clear up, or **clarify,** confusing or difficult passages as you read. When you realize you don't understand something, try these techniques to help you clarify the ideas.

- Reread the confusing parts slowly and carefully.
- Diagram relationships between ideas.
- Look up unfamiliar words.
- Simply "talk out" the part to yourself.

Then read the passage once more. The second time through is often much easier and more informative.

Reviewing

You probably **review** in school every day in one class or another. You review what you learned the day before so the ideas stick in your mind. Reviewing when you read does the same thing.

Take time now and then to pause and review what you've read. Think about the main ideas and reorganize them for yourself so you can recall them later. Filling in study aids such as graphic organizers, notes, or outlines can help you review.

Monitoring Your Comprehension

Who's checking up on you when you read? You are! There's no teacher standing by to ask questions or to make sure that you're paying attention. As a reader, you are both the teacher and the student. It's up to you to make sure you accomplish a reader's most important task: understanding the material. As you read, check your understanding by using the following strategies.

- **Summarize** what you read by pausing from time to time and telling yourself the main ideas of what you've just read. When you **summarize,** include only the main ideas of a selection and only the useful supporting details. Answer the questions *Who? What? Where? When? Why?* and *How?* Summarizing tests your comprehension by encouraging you to clarify key points in your own words.

- **Paraphrase** Sometimes you read something that you "sort of" understand, but not quite. Use **paraphrasing** as a test to see whether you really got the point. Paraphrasing is retelling something in your own words. So shut the book and try putting what you've just read into your own words. If you can't explain it clearly, you should probably have another look at the text.

▶ Practice It!

Here are some strategies good readers use to understand a text. In your Learner's Notebook, tell which strategy is shown by each statement below.

connect   respond   predict   monitor comprehension
visualize   question   clarify   preview

1. I'm sure the doctor's going to be the main character in this story.

2. Why would this smart character make a dumb remark like that?

3. This woman reminds me of my mother when she's really mad.

4. This is a difficult passage. I'd better read it again and also look up the word malefactor in the dictionary.

5. Let's see if I've got this plot straight. So far, Greg's crazy about Donna, but she's hooked on Jesse, who seems interested in Sheila, who is Greg's date for the dance. And Dana's out to mess up everybody.

Thinking Critically About Your Reading

You've engaged with the text and used helpful reading strategies to understand what you've read. But is that all there is to it? Not always. Sometimes it's important to think more deeply about what you've read so that you can get the most out of what the author says. These critical thinking skills will help you go beyond what the words say and get at the important messages of your reading.

Interpreting

When you listen to your best friend talk, you don't just hear the words he or she says. You also watch your friend, listen to the tone of voice, and use what you already know about that person to put meaning to the words. In doing so, you are making meaning from what your friend says by using what you understand. You are **interpreting** what your friend says.

Readers do the same thing when they interpret as they read. Interpreting is more than just understanding the facts or story line you read. It's asking yourself, What's the writer really saying here? and then using what you know about the world to help answer that question. When you interpret as you read, you come to a much better understanding of the work.

Inferring

You may not realize it, but you **infer,** or make inferences, every day. Here's an example:

> You run to the bus stop a little later than usual. There's no one there. "I've missed the bus," you say to yourself. You may be wrong, but that's the way our minds work. We look at the evidence (you're late; no one's there) and come to a conclusion (you've missed the bus).

When you read, you go through exactly the same process because writers don't always directly state what they want you to understand. By providing clues and interesting details, they suggest certain information. Whenever you combine those clues with your own background and knowledge, you are making an inference.

Drawing Conclusions

Skillful readers are always **drawing conclusions,** or figuring out much more than an author says directly. The process is a little like a detective solving a mystery. You combine information and evidence that the author provides to come up with a statement about the topic, about a character, or about anything else in the work. Drawing conclusions helps you find connections between ideas and events and helps you have a better understanding of what you're reading.

Analyzing

Analyzing, or looking at separate parts of something to understand the entire piece, is a way to think critically about written work.

• In analyzing **fiction,** for example, you might look at the characters' values, events in the plot, and the author's style to figure out the story's theme.

• In analyzing persuasive **nonfiction,** you might look at the writer's reasons to see if they actually support the main point of the argument.

• In analyzing **informational text,** you might look at how the ideas are organized to see what's most important.

Distinguishing Fact from Opinion

Distinguishing between fact and opinion is one of the most important reading skills you can learn.

A **fact** is a statement that can be proved with supporting information.

An **opinion,** on the other hand, is what a writer believes on the basis of his or her personal viewpoint. An opinion is something that cannot be proved.

As you examine information, always ask yourself, Is this a fact or an opinion?

Don't think that opinions are always bad. Very often they are just what you want. You read editorials and essays for their authors' opinions. Reviews of movies and CDs can help you decide whether to spend your time and money on something. It's when opinions are based on faulty reasoning or prejudice or when they are stated as facts that they become troublesome.

For example, look at the following examples of fact and opinion.

Fact: California produces fruits and other agricultural products.

Opinion: California is a wonderful place for a vacation.

You could prove that fruits and other agricultural products are grown in California. It's a fact. However, not everyone might agree that California is a great vacation site. That's someone's opinion.

Evaluating

When you form an opinion or make a judgment about something you're reading, you are **evaluating.**

If you're reading **informational texts** or something on the Internet, it's important to evaluate how qualified the author is to write about the topic and how reliable the information that's presented is. Ask yourself whether

- the author seems biased.
- the information is one-sided.
- the argument presented is logical.

If you're reading **fiction,** evaluate the author's style or ask yourself questions such as

- Is this character interesting or dull?
- Are the events in the plot believable or realistic?
- Does the author's message make sense?

Synthesizing

When you **synthesize,** you combine ideas (maybe even from different sources) to come up with something new. It may be a new understanding of an important idea or a new way of combining and presenting information.

Many readers enjoy taking ideas from their reading and combining them with what they already know to come to new understandings. For example, you might

1. Read a manual on coaching soccer

2. Combine what you learn from that reading with your own experiences playing soccer

3. Add what you know about coaches you've had

4. Come up with a winning plan for coaching your sister's soccer team this spring.

Understanding Text Structure

Writers organize each piece of their writing in a specific way for a specific purpose. That pattern of organization is called **text structure.** When you know the text structure of a selection, you'll find it easier to locate and recall an author's ideas. Here are four ways that writers organize text, along with some signal words and phrases containing clues to help you identify their methods.

Comparison and Contrast

Comparison-and-contrast structure shows the similarities and differences between people, things, and ideas. When writers use comparison-and-contrast structure, often they want to show you how things that seem alike are different or how things that seem different are alike.

- **Signal words and phrases:** similarly, more, less, on the one hand, on the other hand, in contrast to, but, however

    Example: That day had been the best and worst of her life. **On the one hand,** the tornado had destroyed her home. **On the other hand,** she and her family were safe. Her face was full of cuts and bruises, **but** she smiled at the little girl on her lap.

Cause and Effect

Just about everything that happens in life is the cause or the effect of some other event or action. Sometimes what happens is pretty minor: You don't look when you're pouring milk (cause); you spill milk on the table (effect). Sometimes it's a little more serious: You don't look at your math book before the big test (cause); you mess up on the test (effect).

Writers use **cause-and-effect** structure to explore the reasons for something happening and to examine the results of previous events. A scientist might explain why the rain falls. A sports writer might explain why a team is doing badly. A historian might tell us why an empire rose and fell. Cause-and-effect structure is all about explaining things.

- **Signal words and phrases:** so, because, as a result, therefore, for the following reasons

    Example: The blizzard raged for twelve hours. **Because** of the heavy snow, the streets were clogged within an hour of being plowed. **As a result,** the city was at a standstill. Of course, we had no school that day, **so** we went sledding!

Problem and Solution

How did scientists overcome the difficulty of getting a person to the moon? How can our team win the pennant this year? How will I brush my teeth when I've forgotten my toothpaste? These questions may be very different in importance, but they have one thing in common: each identifies a problem and asks how to solve it. **Problems and solutions** are part of what makes life interesting.

By organizing their texts around that important question-word *how,* writers state the problem and suggest a solution. Sometimes they suggest many solutions. Of course, it's for you to decide if they're right.

- **Signal words and phrases:** how, help, problem, obstruction, overcome, difficulty, need, attempt, have to, must

    Example: A major **difficulty** in learning to drive a car with a standard shift is starting on hills. Students **need** to practice starting slowly and smoothly on a level surface before they graduate to slopes. Observing an experienced driver perform the maneuver will also **help**.

Sequence

Consider these requests: Tell us what happened at the picnic. Describe your favorite CD cover. Identify the causes of the Civil War. Three very different instructions, aren't they? Well, yes and no. They are certainly about different subjects. But they all involve **sequence,** the order in which thoughts are arranged. Take a look at three common forms of sequencing.

- **Chronological order** refers to the order in which events take place. First you wake up; next you have breakfast; then you go to school. Those events don't make much sense in any other order. Whether you are explaining how to wash the car, giving directions to a friend's house, or telling your favorite joke, the world would be a confusing place if people didn't organize their ideas in chronological order. Look for signal words such as *first, next, then, later,* and *finally.*

- **Spatial order** describes the order of things in space. For example, take a look at this description of an ice cream sundae:

    At the bottom of the dish are two scoops of vanilla. The scoops are covered with fudge and topped with whipped cream and a cherry.

    Your eyes follow the sundae from the bottom to the top. Spatial order is important in descriptive writing because it helps you as a reader to see an image the way the author does. Signal words include *above, below, behind, left, right,* and *next to.*

- **Order of importance** is going from most important to least important or the other way around. For example, a typical news article has a most-to-least-important structure. Readers who don't have the time to read the entire article can at least learn the main idea by reading the first few paragraphs. Signal words include *principal, central, important,* and *fundamental.*

Reading for Research

An important part of doing research is knowing how to get information from a wide variety of sources. The following skills will help you when you have a research assignment for a class or when you want information about a topic outside of school.

Reading Text Features

Researching a topic is not only about asking questions. It's about finding answers. Textbooks, references, magazines, and other sources provide a variety of **text features** to help you find those answers quickly and efficiently.

- **Tables of contents** Look at the table of contents first to see whether a resource offers information you need.

- **Indexes** An index is an alphabetical listing of significant topics covered in a book. It is found in the back of a book.

- **Headings and subheadings** Headings often tell you what information is going to follow in the text you're reading. Subheadings allow you to narrow your search for information even further.

- **Graphic features** Photos, diagrams, maps, charts, graphs, and other graphic features can communicate large amounts of information at a glance. They usually include captions that explain what they show.

Interpreting Graphic Aids

When you're researching a topic, be sure to read and interpret the graphic aids you find. **Graphic aids** explain information visually. When reading graphic aids, read the title first to see if you're likely to find information you want.

- **Reading a map** Maps are flat representations of land. A **compass rose** shows you directions—north, south, east, and west. A **legend,** or **key,** explains the map's symbols. A **scale** shows you how distances shown on the map relate to the actual distances.

- **Reading a graph** A graph shows you how two or more things relate. Graphs can use circles, dots, bars, or lines. For example, on the weather part of a TV newscast you might see a weather graph that predicts how the temperatures for the next five days will rise or fall.

- **Reading a table** A table groups numbers or facts and puts them into categories so you can compare what is in each category. The facts are organized in rows and columns. Find the row that has the category you're looking for. Then read across to the column that has the information you need.

Organizing Information

When researching a topic, you can't stop after you've read your sources of information. You also have to make sense of that information, organize it, and put it all together in ways that will help you explain it to someone else. Here are some ways of doing just that.

- **Record** information from your research and keep track of your resources on note cards.

- **Summarize** information before you write it on a note card. That way you'll have the main ideas in your own words.

- **Outline** ideas so you can see how subtopics and supporting information will fit under a main idea.

- **Make a table or graph** to compare items or categories of information.

The BIG Question

Reading: What's in It for You?

> " I could spend the rest of my life reading, just satisfying my curiosity. "
>
> –Malcolm X
> 20th-century African American leader

LOOKING AHEAD

The skill lessons and readings in this unit will help you develop your own answer to the Big Question.

UNIT 1 WARM-UP • Connecting to the Big Question
GENRE FOCUS: Autobiography and Biography

UNIT 1 WRAP-UP • Answering the Big Question

Connecting to The BIG Question Reading: What's in It for You?

Reading can take you new places and teach you new things. It can make you laugh out loud. It can send a shiver down your spine. It can widen your world and make you glad to be alive. Do you need adventure? Advice? Information? You can find these things—and more—by reading.

Real Kids and the Big Question

HECTOR belongs to a bike club. He even races a few times a year. Hector never misses a biking event because his local newspaper always has the information he needs. Hector reads. What's in it for him?

OKSANA loves stories. She likes being caught up in lives and problems that are different from her own. She loves mysteries that make her think and suspense stories that keep her turning the pages. She loves any story that seems real to her. Oksana reads. What's in it for her?

Warm-Up Activity

Think about the reasons that you read. Do you read to learn new things or just to have fun? Maybe you read to escape your daily life and experience new adventures. What's in it for you? Write your answers in your Learner's Notebook.

You and the Big Question

There are lots of reasons to read. In this unit you will explore some of those reasons. You will also think about your own reasons for reading to discover what is—or can be—in it for you.

Literature Online

BIG Question

Link to Web resources to further explore the Big Question at www.glencoe.com.

Plan for the Unit Challenge

At the end of the unit, you'll use notes from all your reading to complete the Unit Challenge.

You'll choose one of the following activities:

A. Write a Reading Plan Design a reading plan to help you learn about and do the things in your life that you want to do.

B. Reading Chart Create a reading chart to figure out what you read and why.

- Start thinking about which activity you'd like to do so that you can focus your thoughts as you go through the unit.

- In your Learner's Notebook, write your thoughts about the activity you'd like to do.

- Each time you make notes about the Big Question, think about how your ideas will help you with the Unit Challenge activity you chose.

Keep Track of Your Ideas

As you read, you'll make notes about the Big Question. Later, you'll use these notes to complete the Unit Challenge. See pages R8–R9 for help with making Foldable 1. This diagram shows how it should look.

1. Use this Foldable for all the selections in this unit. On the front cover, write the unit number and the Big Question.

2. Turn the page. Across the top, write the selection title. To the left of the crease, write **My Purpose for Reading.** To the right of the crease, write **the Big Question.**

3. Repeat step 2 until you have all the titles in your Foldable. (See page 1 for the titles.)

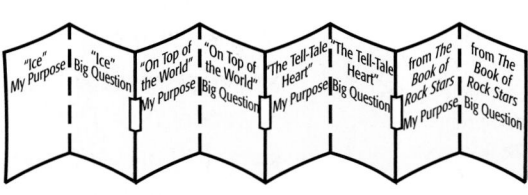

Skills Focus

- How to read autobiography and biography

Skills Model

You will see how to use the key reading skills and literary elements as you read

- **from *I Know Why the Caged Bird Sings,*** p. 5

Autobiographies and biographies are types of nonfiction. When a person writes a story about his or her own life, it is called an **autobiography.** When an author writes about another person's life, it is called a **biography.** Reading autobiographies and biographies is a great way to learn about other people.

Why Read Autobiography and Biography?

Reading about the lives of real people can be fun as well as informative. You can learn about the following things:
- real people and their contributions to the world
- real problems people have faced and ways those people solved them

How to Read Autobiography and Biography

Key Reading Skills

These key reading skills are especially useful tools for reading and understanding autobiographies and biographies. The skills are modeled in the Active Reading Model on pages 5–13; you'll learn more about them later.

■ **Connecting** Make connections between what you are reading and your own life, the world around you, or other selections that you have read. (See Reading Workshop 1.)

■ **Setting a purpose for reading** Before you read, decide what you hope to get out of a piece of writing. (See Reading Workshop 2.)

■ **Activating prior knowledge** Recall what you already know about the people, places, or events in a text. (See Reading Workshop 3.)

■ **Identifying author's purpose** Think about why the author wrote the selection. (See Reading Workshop 4.)

Key Literary Elements

Recognizing and thinking about the following literary elements will help you understand more fully what the writer is telling you.

■ **Description:** vivid details that enliven writing (See "Ice.")

■ **Point of view:** the way the story is "seen" by the narrator and told to the reader (See *The Book of Rock Stars.*)

■ **Tone:** the attitude of the writer toward his or her subject (See "March of the Mill Children.")

■ **Cultural reference:** mention of a value, belief, custom, or something else important to a particular community (See "Being Japanese American.")

**NY English
Language Arts
Core Curriculum**
(pp. 4–13)

R2g Compare literature to own lives. **Core R1** Identify a purpose for reading.
LC R12 Combine multiple strategies to enhance comprehension and response. **R2e** Recognize how the author's use of language creates images or feelings. **R2c** Identify the author's point of view. **R2h** Identify social and cultural contexts to enhance understanding.

For a complete description of the standards, see p. NY11.

from
I KNOW WHY THE CAGED BIRD SINGS

by Maya Angelou

The notes in the side columns model how to use the skills and elements you read about on page 4.

Autobiography and Biography
ACTIVE READING MODEL

1 Key Reading Skill
Setting a Purpose for Reading *I'd like to know more about Mrs. Flowers, and I want to find out what effect she'll have on the narrator.*

2 Key Reading Skill
Connecting *I've known people like Mrs. Flowers— people I respected so much that it made me happy if they smiled at me.*

Mrs. Bertha Flowers was the aristocrat of Black Stamps. She had the grace of control to appear warm in the coldest weather, and on the Arkansas summer days it seemed she had a private breeze which swirled around, cooling her. She was thin without the taut look of wiry people, and her printed voile[1] dresses and flowered hats were as right for her as denim overalls for a farmer. She was our side's answer to the richest white woman in town. **1**

Her skin was a rich black that would have peeled like a plum if snagged, but then no one would have thought of getting close enough to Mrs. Flowers to ruffle her dress, let alone snag her skin. She didn't encourage familiarity. She wore gloves too.

I don't think I ever saw Mrs. Flowers laugh, but she smiled often. A slow widening of her thin black lips to show even, small white teeth, then the slow effortless closing. When she chose to smile on me, I always wanted to thank her. The action was so graceful and inclusively benign.[2] **2**

---

1. **Voile** (voyl) is a light cotton fabric.
2. Here **benign** (bih NYN) means "kind."

Analyzing the Painting How does this image capture Mrs. Flowers' grace and style?

She was one of the few gentlewomen I have ever known, and has remained throughout my life the measure of what a human being can be. **3**

Momma had a strange relationship with her. Most often when she passed on the road in front of the Store, she spoke to Momma in that soft yet carrying voice, "Good day, Mrs. Henderson." Momma responded with "How you, Sister Flowers?"

Mrs. Flowers didn't belong to our church, nor was she Momma's familiar. Why on earth did she insist on calling her Sister Flowers? Shame made me want to hide my face. Mrs. Flowers deserved better than to be called Sister. Then, Momma left out the verb. Why not ask, "How *are* you, *Mrs.* Flowers?" With the unbalanced passion of the young, I hated her for showing her ignorance to Mrs. Flowers. It didn't occur to me for many years that they were as alike as sisters, separated only by formal education. **4**

Although I was upset, neither of the women was in the least shaken by what I thought an unceremonious greeting. Mrs. Flowers would continue her easy gait up the hill to her little bungalow, and Momma kept on shelling peas or doing whatever had brought her to the front porch.

Occasionally, though, Mrs. Flowers would drift off the road and down to the Store and Momma would say to me, "Sister, you go on and play." As I left I would hear the beginning of an intimate conversation. Momma persistently using the wrong verb, or none at all.

"Brother and Sister Wilcox is sho'ly the meanest—" "Is," Momma? "Is"? Oh, please, not "is," Momma, for two or more. But they talked, and from the side of the building where I waited for the ground to open up and swallow me, I heard the soft-voiced Mrs. Flowers and the textured voice of my grandmother merging and melting. They were interrupted from time to time by giggles that must have come from Mrs. Flowers (Momma never giggled in her life). Then she was gone. **5**

She appealed to me because she was like people I had never met personally. Like women in English novels who walked the moors (whatever they were) with their loyal

---

ACTIVE READING MODEL

3 Key Literary Element
Tone *The way the writer describes Mrs. Flowers—both the words she chooses and the details she includes—shows admiration and respect.*

4 Key Literary Element
Point of View *I know this selection is from an autobiography, so the narrator is a real person telling about her real life. All autobiographies are written in the first-person point of view. I don't know much more than that about the narrator . . . yet.*

5 Key Reading Skill
Connecting *Oh yes, yes, yes. I know that horrible, wanting-to-disappear feeling. I have felt exactly like that.*

dogs racing at a respectful distance. Like the women who sat in front of roaring fireplaces, drinking tea incessantly from silver trays full of scones and crumpets.[3] Women who walked over the "heath" and read morocco-bound books and had two last names divided by a hyphen. It would be safe to say that she made me proud to be Negro, just by being herself.

She acted just as refined as whitefolks in the movies and books and she was more beautiful, for none of them could have come near that warm color without looking gray by comparison.

It was fortunate that I never saw her in the company of powhitefolks. For since they tend to think of their whiteness as an evenizer, I'm certain that I would have had to hear her spoken to commonly as Bertha, and my image of her would have been shattered like the unmendable Humpty-Dumpty. 6

One summer afternoon, sweet-milk fresh in my memory, she stopped at the Store to buy provisions. Another Negro woman of her health and age would have been expected to carry the paper sacks home in one hand, but Momma said, "Sister Flowers, I'll send Bailey up to your house with these things."

She smiled that slow dragging smile, "Thank you, Mrs. Henderson. I'd prefer Marguerite, though." My name was beautiful when she said it. "I've been meaning to talk to her, anyway." They gave each other age-group looks.

Momma said, "Well, that's all right then. Sister, go and change your dress. You going to Sister Flowers's."

The chifforobe was a maze. What on earth did one put on to go to Mrs. Flowers' house? I knew I shouldn't put on a Sunday dress. It might be sacrilegious.[4] Certainly not a house dress, since I was already wearing a fresh one. I chose a school dress, naturally. It was formal without

6 Key Reading Skill
Activating Prior Knowledge
I know that African Americans used to face really obvious discrimination and that this was often most noticeable in the South.

Visual Vocabulary
A **chifforobe** is a type of dresser. It has drawers and a place to hang clothes.

---

3. A *moor* is a stretch of open rolling land. *Incessantly* means "constantly." A *scone* is a sweet biscuit, and a *crumpet* is an English muffin.

4. If something is *sacrilegious,* it shows disrespect for something sacred.

Somewhere in America, ca. 1933–34. Robert Brackman. Oil on canvas, 30⅛ x 25⅛ in. Smithsonian American Art Museum, Washington, D.C.

Analyzing the Painting What hopes and dreams might the girl in this painting share with Marguerite?

suggesting that going to Mrs. Flowers' house was equivalent to attending church.

I trusted myself back into the Store.

"Now, don't you look nice." I had chosen the right thing, for once. **7**

"Mrs. Henderson, you make most of the children's clothes, don't you?"

"Yes, ma'am. Sure do. Store-bought clothes ain't hardly worth the thread it take to stitch them."

"I'll say you do a lovely job, though, so neat. That dress looks professional."

Momma was enjoying the seldom-received compliments. Since everyone we knew (except Mrs. Flowers, of course) could sew competently, praise was rarely handed out for the commonly practiced craft.

7 Key Literary Element
Tone *I can tell that the tone is complimentary because the narrator says, "I had chosen the right thing, for once."*

"I try, with the help of the Lord, Sister Flowers, to finish the inside just like I does the outside. Come here, Sister."

I had buttoned up the collar and tied the belt, apronlike, in back. Momma told me to turn around. With one hand she pulled the strings and the belt fell free at both sides of my waist. Then her large hands were at my neck, opening the button loops. I was terrified. What was happening?

"Take it off, Sister." She had her hands on the hem of the dress.

"I don't need to see the inside, Mrs. Henderson, I can tell . . ." But the dress was over my head and my arms were stuck in the sleeves. Momma said, "That'll do. See here, Sister Flowers, I French-seams around the armholes." Through the cloth film, I saw the shadow approach. "That makes it last longer. Children these days would bust out of sheet-metal clothes. They so rough."

"That is a very good job, Mrs. Henderson. You should be proud. You can put your dress back on, Marguerite."

"No ma'am. Pride is a sin. And 'cording to the Good Book, it goeth before a fall."

"That's right. So the Bible says. It's a good thing to keep in mind."

I wouldn't look at either of them. Momma hadn't thought that taking off my dress in front of Mrs. Flowers would kill me stone dead. If I had refused, she would have thought I was trying to be "womanish" and might have remembered St. Louis. Mrs. Flowers had known that I would be embarrassed and that was even worse. I picked up the groceries and went out to wait in the hot sunshine. It would be fitting if I got a sunstroke and died before they came outside. Just dropped dead on the slanting porch. 🖪

There was a little path beside the rocky road, and Mrs. Flowers walked in front swinging her arms and picking her way over the stones.

She said, without turning her head, to me, "I hear you're doing very good school work, Marguerite, but that it's all written. The teachers report that they have trouble getting you to talk in class." We passed the triangular farm on our left and the path widened to allow us to walk together. I hung back in the separate unasked and unanswerable questions.

🖪 **Key Reading Skill**
Connecting *I've been embarrassed by my mom like this before—it's the worst feeling in the world. It makes you feel as if you're five years old!*

Analyzing the Photo How does this image help you create a mental picture of Stamps, Arkansas?

"Come and walk along with me, Marguerite." I couldn't have refused even if I wanted to. She pronounced my name so nicely. Or more correctly, she spoke each word with such clarity that I was certain a foreigner who didn't understand English could have understood her.

"Now no one is going to make you talk—possibly no one can. But bear in mind, language is man's way of communicating with his fellow man and it is language alone which separates him from the lower animals." That was a totally new idea to me, and I would need time to think about it. **9**

"Your grandmother says you read a lot. Every chance you get. That's good, but not good enough. Words mean more than what is set down on paper. It takes the human voice to infuse them with the shades of deeper meaning."

I memorized the part about the human voice infusing words. It seemed so valid and poetic.

She said she was going to give me some books and that I not only must read them, I must read them aloud. She suggested that I try to make a sentence sound in as many different ways as possible.

"I'll accept no excuse if you return a book to me that has been badly handled." My imagination boggled at the punishment I would deserve if in fact I did abuse a book of Mrs. Flowers'. Death would be too kind and brief.

9 Key Reading Skill
Connecting *I can relate to that. Sometimes my teacher says things that are new to me, and I don't quite get them until later.*

The odors in the house surprised me. Somehow I had never connected Mrs. Flowers with food or eating or any other common experience of common people. There must have been an outhouse, too, but my mind never recorded it.

The sweet scent of vanilla had met us as she opened the door.

"I made tea cookies this morning. You see, I had planned to invite you for cookies and lemonade so we could have this little chat. The lemonade is in the icebox." **10**

It followed that Mrs. Flowers would have ice on an ordinary day, when most families in our town bought ice late on Saturdays only a few times during the summer to be used in the wooden ice-cream freezers.

She took the bags from me and disappeared through the kitchen door. I looked around the room that I had never in my wildest fantasies imagined I would see. Browned photographs leered or threatened from the walls and the white, freshly done curtains pushed against themselves and against the wind. I wanted to gobble up the room entire and take it to Bailey, who would help me analyze and enjoy it.

"Have a seat, Marguerite. Over there by the table." She carried a platter covered with a tea towel. Although she warned that she hadn't tried her hand at baking sweets for some time, I was certain that like everything else about her the cookies would be perfect.

They were flat round wafers, slightly browned on the edges and butter-yellow in the center. With the cold lemonade they were sufficient for childhood's lifelong diet. Remembering my manners, I took nice little lady-like bites off the edges. She said she had made them expressly for me and that she had a few in the kitchen that I could take home to my brother. So I jammed one whole cake in my mouth and the rough crumbs scratched the insides of my jaws, and if I hadn't had to swallow, it would have been a dream come true. **11**

As I ate she began the first of what we later called "my lessons in living." She said that I must always be intolerant of ignorance but understanding of illiteracy. That some people unable to go to school were more

10 Key Reading Skill
Setting a Purpose for Reading *It looks as if Mrs. Flowers has gone out of her way to talk to Marguerite. I wonder what she wants to tell her. I wonder how Marguerite will respond.*

11 Key Literary Element
Description *This description helps me picture what's happening. I can just see the wafers and feel the scratching of the rough crumbs.*

educated and even more intelligent than college professors. She encouraged me to listen carefully to what country people called mother wit. That in those homely sayings was couched[5] the collective wisdom of generations.

When I finished the cookies she brushed off the table and brought a thick, small book from the bookcase. I had read *A Tale of Two Cities*[6] and found it up to my standards as a romantic novel. She opened the first page and I heard poetry for the first time in my life.

"It was the best of times and the worst of times . . ." **12** Her voice slid in and curved down through and over the words. She was nearly singing. I wanted to look at the pages. Were they the same that I had read? Or were there notes, music, lined on the pages, as in a hymn book? Her sounds began cascading gently. I knew from listening to a thousand preachers that she was nearing the end of her reading, and I hadn't really heard, heard to understand, a single word.

"How do you like that?"

It occurred to me that she expected a response. The sweet vanilla flavor was still on my tongue and her reading was a wonder in my ears. I had to speak.

I said, "Yes, ma'am." It was the least I could do, but it was the most also.

Visual Vocabulary
Wormwood is a sweet-smelling plant, but the word is often used to refer to something unpleasant.

"There's one more thing. Take this book of poems and memorize one for me. Next time you pay me a visit, I want you to recite."

I have tried often to search behind the sophistication of years for the enchantment I so easily found in those gifts. The essence escapes but its aura[7] remains. To be allowed, no, invited, into the private lives of strangers, and to share their joys and fears, was a chance to exchange the Southern bitter wormwood

12 Key Literary Element
Cultural Reference *A Tale of Two Cities is a very well-known English novel. The quotation "It was the best of times and the worst of times . . ." is one of the most famous lines in English literature. The fact that Mrs. Flowers knows the novel shows that she is an educated woman who is aware of life beyond the small town of Stamps.*

---

5. Here, ***homely*** means "ordinary." ***Couch,*** as a verb, means "to say."

6. ***A Tale of Two Cities*** is a novel by Charles Dickens that describes English people who get caught up in the French Revolution.

7. The ***essence*** of a thing is its most basic nature. An ***aura*** (OR uh) is the feeling or mood that surrounds a person, thing, or experience.

for a cup of mead with Beowulf or a hot cup of tea and milk with Oliver Twist.[8] When I said aloud, "It is a far, far better thing that I do, than I have ever done . . ." tears of love filled my eyes at my selflessness.

On that first day, I ran down the hill and into the road (few cars ever came along it) and had the good sense to stop running before I reached the Store.

I was liked, and what a difference it made. I was respected not as Mrs. Henderson's grandchild or Bailey's sister but for just being Marguerite Johnson.

Childhood's logic never asks to be proved (all conclusions are absolute). I didn't question why Mrs. Flowers had singled me out for attention, nor did it occur to me that Momma might have asked her to give me a little talking to. All I cared about was that she had made tea cookies for *me* and read to *me* from her favorite book. It was enough to prove that she liked me. **13** ○

---

8. ***Beowulf*** and ***Oliver Twist*** are famous characters from English literature.

13 Key Reading Skill
Identifying Author's Purpose *Angelou seems to want readers to know about a special person who made a difference in her life by believing in her and helping her believe in herself.*

Small-Group Discussion Talk with classmates about the relationship between Mrs. Flowers and Marguerite.
• How do you know that reading is important to Mrs. Flowers?
• What does Mrs. Flowers want to show or tell Marguerite about the value of reading good books aloud?

Write to Learn How does listening to Mrs. Flowers read affect Marguerite? What does Marguerite discover about the power of words? Use details from the selection to explain your answer. Think about your own experiences. When was the last time you felt excited or impressed by something you read?

Study Central Visit www.glencoe.com and click on Study Central to review autobiography and biography.

Skills Focus

You will practice using these skills when you read the following selections:

- "Ice," p. 18
- "On Top of the World," p. 32

Reading

- Connecting

Literature

- Identifying use of description
- Identifying and using the title and subheads

Vocabulary

- Using context clues involves categories and explanation
- Academic Vocabulary: *texts*

Writing/Grammar

- Identifying and using concrete and abstract nouns
- Identifying and using personal and possessive pronouns and antecedents

NY English Language Arts Core Curriculum
(pp. 14–15)

R2g Compare literature to own lives.

For a complete description of the standards, see p. NY11.

Skill Lesson

Connecting

Learn It!

What Is It? Connecting is finding the links between things you read about and your own knowledge and experience.

- You can connect to the characters you read about. They may remind you of yourself, people you know, or people or characters from other **texts.**
- You can connect to the ideas in a text. You may agree or disagree with them.
- You can connect to the experiences described in a text. You may have had, read about, or heard about similar experiences.

Lucky Cow © 2005 Mark Pett. Dist. By UNIVERSAL PRESS SYNDICATE. Reprinted with permission All rights reserved.

Analyzing Cartoons
Clare enjoys reading *Walden* because she can connect what Thoreau writes to her own experiences in the woods.

Academic Vocabulary

texts (tekts) *n.* the words and forms of written or printed works

Why Is It Important? You'll become more involved with your reading and remember characters, ideas, and events better if you relate what you're reading to your own life.

How Do I Do It? As you read, ask yourself questions like these:
- *Do I know anyone who acts or feels like these characters?*
- *Am I familiar with these ideas? Do I agree or disagree with them?*
- *What experiences from life or books are like the ones in this text?*

Below is a connection a student made to this passage from *I Know Why the Caged Bird Sings.*

> Occasionally . . . Mrs. Flowers would drift off the road and down to the Store and Momma would say to me, "Sister, you go on and play." As I left, I would hear the beginning of an intimate conversation. . . . [T]hey talked, and from the side of the building where I waited for the ground to open up and swallow me, I heard the soft-voiced Mrs. Flowers and the textured voice of my grandmother merging and melting.

> *I can relate to what the narrator is saying about being asked to go play. When my sister and I were really little, my parents always told us to go outside and play when they wanted to have a grown-up conversation.*

Practice It!

These are some of the topics you will read about in the selections:
- a fourteen-year-old boy who is trying to gain his stepfather's approval
- the desire to do something that is extremely difficult and dangerous

In your Learner's Notebook, make a list of experiences, ideas, and people or characters you can connect to these topics.

Use It!

As you read, connect to "Ice" and "On Top of the World" by using your list of ideas.

Before You Read : Ice

Graham Salisbury

Meet the Author

Graham Salisbury grew up in Hawaii. He has worked on boats and taught in an elementary school. He even had a rock 'n' roll band. He has written many short stories and novels for kids. Today Salisbury lives in Oregon with his family. See page R6 of the Author Files in the back of the book for more on Graham Salisbury.

Author Search For more about Graham Salisbury, go to www.glencoe.com.

NY English Language Arts Core Curriculum
(pp. 16–27)

Core R4 Determine the meaning of unfamiliar words by using context clues.
R2g Compare literature to own lives.
R2e Recognize how the use of language creates images.

For a complete description of the standards, see p. NY11.

Vocabulary Preview

minority (mih NOR uh tee) *n.* a smaller group **(p. 18)** *He was in the minority at school because unlike most kids, his ancestors were not from Hawaii.*

self-esteem (self es TEEM) *n.* confidence and satisfaction in oneself **(p. 20)** *He had low self-esteem because his stepfather constantly put him down.*

oblivious (uh BLIV ee us) *adj.* not aware **(p. 21)** *The boy's mother was so busy that she was oblivious to the boy's problems.*

relentlessly (ruh LENT lis lee) *adv.* without pity or mercy **(p. 21)** *John relentlessly ignored and scorned Graham.*

void (voyd) *n.* empty space **(p. 22)** *John thought Graham was brainless and had a void between his ears.*

On My Own Choose three vocabulary words. Use the words in a paragraph.

English Language Coach

Context Clues: Characteristics When you see a new word while reading, try to define it by using **context clues**—hints in nearby words and sentences. One kind of context clue involves characteristics, or details that tell you what something does, is made of, or looks like. The sentence below contains characteristics of a kelpie. Use them to figure out what a kelpie is. Then read the chart to see if you were right.

• The kelpie barked, wagged its tail, and brought us its favorite rubber ball.

Word	Characteristics	Definition
kelpie	barked, wagged tail, brought rubber ball	a type of dog

Partner Work With a classmate, find the characteristics of a *laceration* in the sentence below. Make a chart like the one shown, and complete it by filling in the characteristics and defining *laceration*. Then look the word up in a dictionary to see if you're right.

• The accident victim was bleeding heavily from a four-inch laceration caused by broken glass.

Skills Preview

Key Reading Skill: Connecting

"Ice" is about a boy's relationship with his stepfather. As you read, use these tips to connect to the story, and ask yourself the following questions:

- Think about adults in your life whom you admire. *Is your relationship similar to or different from the author's relationship with his stepfather?*
- Think about a time when you wanted someone's approval. *Why was it important to you?*

Write to Learn In your Learner's Notebook, explain whose approval you wanted and why.

Key Literary Element: Description

If you like to know what a character looks like or how he or she figures out he or she is in danger, you can thank the writer's **description**. Description tells you what things look, sound, and feel like. A writer describes smells and tastes that make the story or poem come alive. Almost everything in a story besides the characters' thoughts and words involves some description.

When you're reading, your imagination is more important than when you're watching television or a movie. A good description lets you see people and things you're reading about in your mind. But do your part. If the writer says that the character smells a charcoal grill, remember a time when you smelled a grill. If the writer says a balloon is the color of a red tulip, think of how red a tulip is.

The selection you are about to read is filled with description. As you read, ask yourself,

- *Which details are especially vivid and original?*
- *How do these details help me imagine what a person, place, or thing is like?*

Interactive Literary Elements Handbook
To review or learn more about the literary elements, go to www.glencoe.com.

Get Ready to Read

Connect to the Reading

Have you ever stubbornly tried to prove a point? For example, the boy in this story tries to carry ice with his bare hands, just to show how tough he can be.

Partner Talk With your partner, discuss times when you or another person tried too hard to prove something. Did the person finally give in? What was the outcome?

Build Background

The author grew up in Hawaii, a chain of islands located in the Central Pacific Ocean. Hawaii became a state in the United States in 1959. People from many different cultures live in Hawaii. More than half the population is Asian.

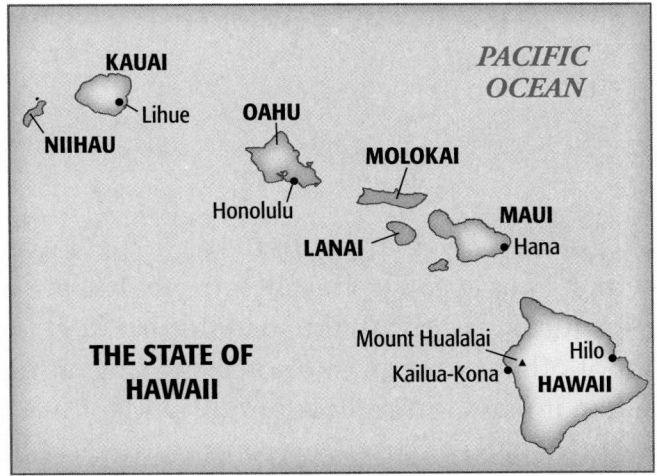

Set Purposes for Reading

BIG Question Read "Ice" to learn what a boy finds out about himself when he spends the summer working with his stepfather.

Set Your Own Purpose What else would you like to learn from the selection to help you answer the Big Question? Write your own purpose on the "Ice" page of Foldable 1.

Keep Moving

Use these skills as you read "Ice."

by Graham Salisbury

Practice the Skills

I got into my share of fights as a kid. I was short. And white. People called me shrimp, shahkbait, mongoose, pipsqueak, runt, hanakuso, half-pint, cock-a-roach, zit, and a lot of other more gross and disgusting things. That was okay when it was coming from my friends. I was a haole[1] boy. A **minority.** Fair game. My roots in the Hawaiian Islands went back to 1820, which meant exactly zero. But I was one of the boys. They liked me and I liked them. Race wasn't an issue. But coolness was, and I was cool enough. ◼ I could take whatever they dished out. I knew they were just doing their job. Besides, I called them worse things back. And we all laughed about it.

But sometimes boys who weren't my friends called me things I didn't want to be called.

◼ **Key Reading Skill**

Connecting Is it important at your school to be "cool" in order to fit in? Explain.

---

1. **Haole** (HOW lee) is the Hawaiian term for a white person.

Vocabulary

minority (mih NOR uh tee) *n.* a smaller group

Bok! Nobody was calling me a sissy. *Bok! Bok!* **2**

I even fractured my finger once, throwing a punch that missed and hit the school bus window. Hurt like fire for days, and I was sorry I'd gotten into that fight.

Even so, I believed it was good to be a fighter. It was healthy. Got stuff out of my system. I still believe it's good. But I've long since learned that you don't have to fight with your fists to be a fighter. In fact, it's better not to.

My problem was I never asked myself what *kind* of fighter I was. I never even thought about it, and I should have. But for much of my youth, thinking wasn't a primary character trait. I just did it—whatever it was—then paid the price. I should have thought about *why* I got into fights. Was I fighting for myself, or was I just trying to prove something to someone else? There's a difference, you know. A big difference. I learned that the hard way, mostly by fighting stupid fights.

But I learned it best from a block of ice.

I had three fathers, none of whom I knew.

My real father was a fighter pilot in the U.S. Navy. Lt. Commander Henry Forester Graham, VBF 83, USS *Essex*. He went down with his plane on my first birthday. The exact day. April eleventh. He was only twenty-seven years old. I never knew him, except through letters my mother received from his fellow officers after his death, letters which mostly said: "I only hope the boy grows up to be half the man Hank Graham was."

A year or so later my mother married another navy man, Guy Salisbury, who adopted me. He lived with us eight years, fathered my three sisters, then died of cancer at the age of thirty-three. He was a "sweetheart and a fine, fine man, just like your father was," my aunt told me. He was also a busy man, and I hardly ever saw him.

I didn't know him either, but at least I can remember what he looked like.

Two or three years after that my mother married again. A beachboy. A man named John, who was ten years younger than she

Practice the Skills

2 **Key Reading Skill**

Connecting Think about a time you were in a fight, either with fists or words. Did the argument feel as important after the fight as it did during the fight? Would you do it again?

Analyzing the Photo F6F fighter planes prepare for takeoff on the USS *Essex* in 1945. How does this photo help you visualize the selection's time period?

Ice **19**

was. He had thick, wavy hair and muscles like Sylvester Stallone. He could surf, he could water-ski on bare feet, he could free-dive to eighty feet and stay down for close to three minutes. He was once stranded on French Frigate Shoals for thirty days with a couple of Filipino fishermen. And except for one, gaping character flaw, he was everything I, at thirteen, wanted to be.

His flaw, though, was a big one, and I didn't understand it until I was much older. But once I figured it out, I could see why I never knew him, either.

It simply wasn't possible.

He wouldn't allow it.

He was a loner and a crusher of **self-esteem**—mine, and my sisters', and eventually my mother's. But for a few years in my life, John was king. He was lean and strong, and he looked like a movie star. In my eyes he could do no wrong. **3** My sisters never saw it that way, but I sure did. I liked him. I was floating on top of the world when Mom said she was going to marry him.

We lived on Oahu at the time. John worked at the Hawaiian Village Hotel in Waikiki, running the water-ski operation. He was then, and had always been, a man of the sea. His skin was a deep red-brown, colored by a lifetime in the sun. And when he moved, it was in a smooth, slow, don't-bother-me kind of way. Most of the time a Marlboro hung from his half-parted lips, his eyes squinting through the smoke like Clint Eastwood's. He could have been the star of *Sea Hunt*, or *Rawhide*, or even *Cliffhanger*, if he wanted to. He had that same kind of raw, manly presence. **4**

We moved from Oahu to the Big Island soon after Mom and John were married. We traveled by boat—a thirty-eight-foot deep-sea charter fishing boat that made me sicker than I'd ever been in my life. My sisters took a plane. But Mom and I made the two-day trip with John and his new fully rigged haole sampan, gliding over glassy seas in the lee[2] of the islands and

Visual Vocabulary
A **sampan** is a boat with a flat bottom. It usually has two oars, or paddles, to make the boat go forward.

3 **Key Reading Skill**

Connecting Is there anyone you know who "can do no wrong"? Do you feel the same way about this person as the author feels about John?

4 **Key Literary Element**

Description There are a lot of descriptive details that appeal to the sense of sight in this paragraph. Which details help you picture what John looks like?

---

2. The *lee* is the side of the island that is not being hit by wind.

Vocabulary

self-esteem (self es TEEM) *n.* confidence and satisfaction in oneself

battering through the channels between them, channels that threw the boat around like a cork in a hurricane. John was in heaven. My mother was **oblivious,** a newlywed caught up in the Big Bopper singing "Chantilly Lace" on the boat's radio. I was sickly green, dehydrated, and barely human.

Two days later we cruised into Kailua-Kona in the calm lee of Mount Hualalai. There, in the shade of groves of coconut trees that lined the shore, was my new home, a serene, turquoise-bayed fishing village where John was going to be a charter-boat skipper. The sun was more brilliant there than in any other place I'd ever been. It made the glassy water in the harbor sparkle. And it warmed the vast, mysterious ocean that **relentlessly** hissed along the shoreline, an ocean that reached out and put its arms around you, called you closer, like the sirens in *The Odyssey.*[3] You could have called it paradise, because it just about was. And there I stood on the pier, the heir apparent to all of John's great wealth of maritime[4] knowledge. **5**

Day after day I followed him around, watching, mimicking. I walked like John. I scowled like John. I made John remarks to my sisters, terse and scornful and sarcastic. I carried my T-shirt hanging from the back pocket of my shorts and squinted into the sun like I'd been on the ocean all my life.

At home, John did a multitude[5] of secret things in the garage. But mostly he made <u>lures</u> out of fiberglass resin. **6** Plugs, he called them. Tubular-shaped things about the size of the cardboard center of a roll of toilet paper. He'd put plastic eyes and pearl inlays into his mold. Then, when they'd dried, he'd fit them with flashy plastic and rubber skirts that

Analyzing the Photo Craftspeople at the Rapala Normark Group factory in Finland still paint fishing lures by hand. How does this image help you better understand John's hobby?

Practice the Skills

5 **Key Literary Element**

Description Which details in this paragraph help you picture what the ocean looks like?

6 **English Language Coach**

Context Clues: Characteristics Find the context clues that help you understand the meaning of **lures.** Look for characteristics of *lures* in the sentences that follow the word. Then define it.

---

3. *The Odyssey* is an ancient Greek story. In the story, the *sirens* are creatures that sing enchanting songs to lure sailors to their death.

4. *Maritime* means "having to do with the sea."

5. A *multitude* means "a great number."

Vocabulary ·

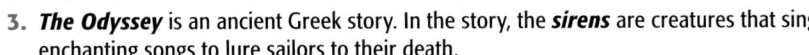

oblivious (uh BLIV ee us) *adj.* not aware

relentlessly (ruh LENT lis lee) *adv.* without pity or mercy

wiggled in the water. Finally he'd drill a hole down the center and thread through a wire leader and a hook big enough to handle a thousand-pound marlin. He made plugs in every color combination he could think of, trying to find the prize among them, the one that would *work*, the one that would catch the Big Fish.

On a technical level, I was privy[6] to none of this. I could only watch from a distance, could not touch anything, could not even ask a question. The one time I did, his answer was vague and totally useless. Fishermen, it seemed, guarded their secrets even from the ignorant.

Still, I watched him, like a cat watches a dove peck around in the grass. **7**

My mother practically begged him to let me work as his deck hand. John scowled and told her I was too small. He needed someone with muscle, and brains. But Mom persisted. Maybe she was worried that John was right and hoped that a summer on the boat would shape me up.

In the end, her wish was granted. I got the job. I was a deck hand on a deep-sea charter fishing boat, the youngest and smallest in the Kona fleet. All the other skippers and their first-rate deck hands were kind and supportive, always smiled and waved at me from the decks of their boats. One of them even told me I looked like a miniature Tarzan, which I loved to hear, because John looked like Tarzan.

The major part of my job, I soon found out, took place between getting up in the morning and heading out to sea three hours later. Then, for the next eight hours, I did little more than go for a boat ride . . . unless we caught a fish. Then I sat at the wheel and tried to keep the angler's line behind the boat. I was a spectator. Because that's when the muscle came in, and the brains . . . which, of course, I didn't have. John reminded me of the **void** between my ears almost daily, in all sorts of unspoken ways.

But who cared? I was working. On a boat. We caught *big* fish—up to a thousand pounds, sometimes. And we took out famous people, like Red Skelton, Spencer Tracy, and a football

Practice the Skills

7 Key Literary Element

Description Here, the author uses a comparison to help you "see" how carefully he watched his stepfather. Picture a cat watching a bird. That's how closely the boy watched John.

---

6. When you are *privy* to something, you know something that is hidden to others.

Vocabulary

void (voyd) *n.* empty space

player named Paul Hornung, the biggest human being I'd ever seen in my life. How many other fourteen-year-old boys could say that? **8**

I was to work an entire summer with John. That was the deal Mom had made for me. The first week I did nothing but handle the wharf lines, tying and untying the boat at the pier. Then I got to sponge the salt from the seats and windows at the beginning and end of each day. That, I began to realize, was all I was going to get. John was accommodating my mother, not training a deck hand.

Wanting to prove that I was good enough, and hoping to gain a small shot of approval from John, I dreamed up a set of duties for myself. I figured I could start by doing more to get the boat ready in the mornings.

I studied John's routine until it was as clear as the resin in his prize lures: the night before, check the two-gallon bucket of water in the freezer in the garage; get up at five in the morning and take the bucket out of the freezer and work the ice out, then put the ice on a burlap bag on the back seat of the Jeep; refill the bucket and put it back in the freezer; take a couple of six-packs of Coke and Budweiser from the storage closet and set them next to the ice; unscrew the five-horse Evinrude outboard engine from its sawhorse stand and throw it in the Jeep, too; drive to the harbor in silence; take the ice out of the Jeep and put it on your hand, like a waiter carrying a tray of dishes; grab the outboard with the other hand and walk slowly down to the skiff; set the outboard on the back of the **skiff**, fire it up, and buzz on out into the harbor to get the boat. **9**

This was what John did, day after day. It seemed simple enough. I could do all of that. All he'd have to do was have a first cup of coffee from his corroding silver Thermos.

I asked him if I could take over the job of the ice and the outboard.

John studied me a moment, smoke drifting off the end of his cigarette. Then he shrugged, and said, "I don't care." That's all he had to say about it, nothing more, nothing less.

Yes! I thought. I'll do it just like he did it. When I get that down, he'll ask me to do more. He'll see that I can be a good deck hand, that I have muscles and brains.

Practice the Skills

8 | **Key Reading Skill**

Connecting Can you connect to how the author feels here? Does he mind having little to do? Why?

9 | **English Language Coach**

Context Clues: Characteristics What is a **skiff**? Look for characteristics of a *skiff* in the paragraph; then define the word.

That night, I checked to be sure the water in the bucket was freezing up. Even got the drinks and put them in the garage near the outboard. Easy. No sweat.

John banged on my bedroom door at five the next morning, just like always. Boom! One time. That's all. No words. I heard it or I didn't. If I didn't, he'd leave me behind without a second thought. I got up instantly, a habit I developed then, and cling to even to this day.

I couldn't get the ice out of the bucket. I kicked it, I twisted it, I pounded it on the ground, I swore at it, but it wouldn't budge. John suddenly appeared at my side and pushed me out of the way. Without saying a word, he took an ice pick and chiseled an inch of ice off the top, all the way around, leaving a space between the lip of the bucket and the block of ice. Then he turned the bucket over and dropped it on the ground.

The ice popped out. **10**

You needed to leave a drop-space around the top of the bucket. Simple. Part of where the brains came in. John hadn't told me that, and I hadn't noticed. He picked up the ice and put it in the Jeep. Then the Evinrude and the drinks. When we got to the pier, he took both the ice and the engine down to the skiff himself.

The next day I did it right, got the ice out of the bucket and put it in the Jeep. Then the outboard engine. It was heavy. I wasn't sure I could carry both of them at the same time.

On the way to the pier, I decided I would only take the ice, at least until I could do that much without screwing up. I told that to John when we got there. He shook his head and grabbed the engine and started walking toward the skiff. No words had passed his lips since the night before, when he told me to do the ice right this time.

I took the ice off the back seat and, as John always did, raised it to my shoulder on the palm of my hand. I started following him, walking slowly, in the don't-bother-me way, which I had mastered. It wasn't far, maybe thirty or forty yards. When we got about halfway, my hand started feeling like it was on fire. It froze so badly it burned. I had to switch hands. I ended up carrying the ice cradled between both arms, nestled against my chest. When we got to the skiff, I dropped the ice down onto the floorboards and jammed my

10 **Key Reading Skill**

Connecting Think of a time when you had trouble doing a task that an adult did very easily. How did you feel? How do you think the author felt?

Analyzing the Photo Deep sea charter fishing boats idle in an Oahu harbor. What does this image suggest about the selection's setting?

hands into the warm ocean, and let them sting until I could move my fingers again.

John fired up the outboard and started out into the harbor to the boat, silent and sullen[7] as a flat tire. **11**

I spent the next eight hours being angry at myself, wondering how I was ever going to carry that blasted ice *and* the outboard from the Jeep to the skiff at the same time.

The ice was just too cold to carry in one hand that far, at John's impossibly slow pace. I didn't know how he could do it, except that his hands were thick and leathery from fishing all his life. Mine were lily-white and as soft as raw fish meat. Once, the ice burned me so badly that I had to set it down on the hood of a truck . . . just for a second . . . while I buried my hands in my armpits.

John stopped, and looked back at me, and said, "Tsk . . ."

---

7. Someone who is **sullen** is in a silent, bad mood.

Practice the Skills

11 **Key Literary Element**

Description Here, the author uses a comparison to help you picture how John looked. What two things are being compared?

And I knew I was losing ground.

After a couple of weeks of murdering my screaming hands, I came up with a solution. I put a canvas fish glove on . . . *then* carried the stupid ice. It worked. So simple, and well worth the scorn I figured John would pour all over me for being so sissy as to have to put on a glove.

But he didn't say a word about it.

Not one word.

In fact, I don't think he even noticed. I was trying so hard to be like him, trying to live up to this self-imposed manly goal of carrying ice with my bare hand, when the reality of it all suddenly hit me—*who cared?* **12**

Certainly not John. He didn't give a rat's you-know-what how I carried the ice, just as long as I got it to the boat.

Only I cared.

Why?

Because I didn't know any better. Because I was fighting for the wrong reason. I was being watched. Right? I was being

Practice the Skills

12 **Key Reading Skill**

Connecting Imagine how it feels to try hard to impress someone who doesn't even notice your efforts. How do you think the author felt?

Analyzing the Photo Today, many Hawaiians still make their living from the sea. Why might commercial fishing be challenging for a young boy?

watched by John, and all the other fishermen, and all their ace deck hands, and all the kids on shore who were rubbing their hands together to have my job if I couldn't do it. I had to live up to the code, the image, the machismo.[8] I *had* no choice in the matter. Right? **13**

Wasn't that right?

Carrying ice taught me a great lesson, though I didn't truly understand it until years later. But there it was, right in front of me, and I didn't see it. I *still* tried to carry the ice bare-handed a couple of times, and *still* failed. And I still felt as if I'd never live up to John's expectations.

I kicked myself around for a long time before I finally realized that John didn't *have* any expectations. He didn't seem to care much what I did, one way or the other.

Today, I thank John for letting me work on his boat. And I thank him for being the way he was. I learned a lot simply by being there. He truly was a wealth of knowledge. But most of all, I learned about how hard I tried, even into later years, to please *others* rather than myself, always searching for that elusive[9] outside approval. Long, hard, bumbling years dragged by before I finally understood how foolish, if not impossible, that search was.

Jeeze. To think back. How I would do all manner of stupid things in order to be accepted, to be seen as manly. Nobody was calling *me* a sissy, confonnit.

And nobody's calling *you* one, either. Right?

You're going with the bare hand. Grit it out until your fingers fall off.

Good. I understand that. You're a fighter. You gotta do what you gotta do.

But just one thing. Are you doing it for you? Or are you doing it for someone else? It's an important question. **14** ○

Practice the Skills

13 **Key Reading Skill**

Connecting Do you agree with the author? Have you ever felt as if you had no choice in doing something? Explain.

14 **BIG Question**

Did you enjoy reading this selection? Why or why not? Write your answer on the "Ice" page of Foldable 1. Your response will help you complete the Unit Challenge later.

---

8. **Machismo** (mah CHEEZ moh) is behavior that is meant to show how manly someone is.

9. When something is **elusive** (ee LOO siv), it is hard to catch.

After You Read : Ice

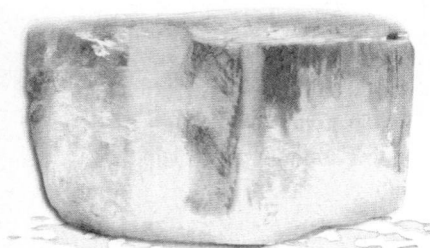

Answering the 🔵BIG Question

1. What did you get out of reading "Ice"? Explain.

2. **Recall** Why doesn't the author remember what his first (biological) father was like?

   TIP **Right There** The answer is in the selection.

3. **Recall** What happened to the author's second father?

   TIP **Right There** The answer is in the selection.

Critical Thinking

4. **Infer** Why do you think the author wanted to impress John?

   TIP **Think and Search** You will find this information in the text but not all in one place.

5. **Interpret** Now that the author is an adult, how does he feel about the way his stepfather treated him?

   TIP **Author and Me** You will find clues in the text, but you must also use the information in your head.

6. **Apply** How did the author deal with his problems? What, if anything, have you learned about dealing with problems in the future? Explain.

   TIP **Author and Me** You will find clues in the text, but you must also use the information in your head.

Write About Your Reading

Written Response Near the beginning of the selection, the author says, "Was I fighting for myself, or was I just trying to prove something to someone else? There's a big difference, you know. A big difference. I learned that the hard way, mostly by fighting stupid fights. But I learned it best from a block of ice."

In a few paragraphs explain what lesson the author learned from a block of ice and how the block of ice taught him that lesson. Back up your ideas with details from the selection.

NY English Language Arts Core Curriculum
(pp. 28–29)

LC R17 Demonstrate comprehension and response through a range of activities. **LC W4** Compose grade-appropriate texts for a variety of purposes. **R2g** Compare literature to own lives. **R2e** Recognize how the use of language creates images. **Core R4** Determine the meaning of unfamiliar words by using context clues. **Core W8** Use correct grammatical construction in parts of speech (nouns).

For a complete description of the standards, see p. NY11.

Skills Review

Key Reading Skill: Connecting

7. What part of the selection was easiest to connect to something else you have read—the setting, the people, or the author's experiences?

Key Literary Element: Description

8. Find examples in "Ice" of descriptive details that appeal to each of the following senses: sight, sound, and touch. Put your examples on a chart like the one pictured below. Also include the page number of each example on your chart.

Sense	Example	Page No.
sight		
sound		
touch		

Vocabulary Check

For each vocabulary word below, write a clue on an index card or a sheet of paper to hint at its definition. Shuffle the cards and give them to a partner. Have him or her guess which word goes with each clue.

9. minority

10. self-esteem

11. oblivious

12. relentlessly

13. void

14. Academic Vocabulary List three **texts** you have studied this month.

15. English Language Coach The sentence below contains characteristics of a *jacamar*. List the characteristics; then define what a *jacamar* is.

- The jacamar spread its shiny green wings and flew over the forest in search of insects.

Look up *jacamar* in the dictionary to see if you're right.

Grammar Link: Concrete and Abstract Nouns

Nouns are words that name people, places, things, feelings, or ideas. Nouns can be concrete or abstract.

Concrete nouns name things that you can see or touch. *Tree* and *shoe* are examples of concrete nouns.

Abstract nouns name ideas, qualities, and feelings—things you cannot see or touch. *Friendship, satisfaction,* and *freedom* are abstract nouns.

- <u>Waves</u> crashed against the <u>boat</u> as it headed for <u>shore</u>; the <u>captain</u> urged the <u>crew</u> to fight off <u>fear</u> and maintain <u>hope</u> that they would survive.

The nouns *waves, boat, shore, captain,* and *crew* are concrete. The nouns *fear* and *hope* are abstract.

Grammar Practice

Copy each sentence. Underline all the concrete nouns. Circle all the abstract nouns.

16. The civilians admired the soldier's courage.

17. The young man showed great maturity.

18. She wanted to make peace with her sister.

19. The doctor talked with the patient about good health.

20. The book was filled with wisdom.

Writing Application Review your Write About Your Reading activity. List five concrete nouns and two abstract nouns you used.

Literature Online

Web Activities For eFlashcards, Selection Quick Checks, and other Web activities, go to www.glencoe.com.

Before You Read : On Top of the World

Meet the Author

Martha Pickerill is the managing editor of *Time for Kids.* She has been writing for more than 18 years. She writes mostly nonfiction articles and has worked for the Children's Television Workshop.

Author Search For more about Martha Pickerill, go to www.glencoe.com.

Vocabulary Preview

feat (feet) *n.* remarkable action **(p. 32)** *Climbing the world's highest mountain is an amazing feat.*

trekked (trekd) *v.* walked or hiked a long distance; form of the verb *trek* **(p. 35)** *They trekked the many miles from Nepal to Tibet.*

expeditions (ek spuh DISH unz) *n.* groups that take trips for specific purposes **(p. 35)** *Many people who wanted to climb Mount Everest joined expeditions led by Sherpas.*

Write to Learn Work with a partner to write a one-paragraph story about a person who has an adventure. Use the vocabulary words above in your paragraph. Your story can be funny or serious. You decide.

English Language Coach

Context Clues: Explanatory Words and Phrases Sometimes authors will include an explanatory word or phrase to help you understand what an unfamiliar word means. Explanatory words and phrases are usually set off with certain marks of punctuation. Look at the chart below.

Punctuation	Example
pair of dashes	The people believed that genii—**friendly spirits who watch over places**—protected their village.
pair of commas	Down, **the fluffy feathers of geese and ducks,** is used to stuff pillows.
pair of parentheses	The frog's skin contains toxins **(poisons).**
pair of commas with *or*	The story's theme, **or main idea,** is that love conquers all.
pair of commas with *called*	These basic units of rhythm, **called feet,** make up a poem's meter.

On Your Own Use the explanatory words and phrases in the chart to define the following words: *genii, down, toxins, theme,* and *feet.* Write your definitions in your Learner's Notebook.

NY English Language Arts Core Curriculum
(pp. 30–35)

Core R4 Determine the meaning of unfamiliar words by using context clues. **R1j** Compare information from different sources. **R2g** Compare literature to own lives. **LC R13** Use text structure to aid comprehension and response.

For a complete description of the standards, see p. NY11.

Skills Preview

Key Reading Skill: Connecting

Imagine that you're about to climb the tallest mountain in the world. The weather will be very cold. What supplies and equipment will you bring on your journey and why?

Whole Class Discussion As a class, brainstorm a list of items you will take with you on your climb. You will have to carry whatever you bring. So make sure you pack only the most essential things.

Text Element: Title and Subheads

The **title,** or name, of a selection fulfills one or more of these purposes: (1) to let readers know what, in general, the selection will be about; (2) to capture readers' attention so that they want to read on; and (3) to introduce the main, or most important, idea in the selection.

Nonfiction selections may also contain **subheads**—titles that preview the content of each section of the article. Always read and think about the title and subheads of a selection. These elements contain helpful information that can make it easier for you to understand the selection. As you read "On Top of the World," ask yourself these questions:

- *What topic does the title say the selection will be about?*
- *From the subheads, what things about the topic will be discussed?*

Partner Talk The title "On Top of the World" is a **pun**—a phrase with a double meaning. With a classmate, see if you can figure out what the two meanings are. Why do you think the author used a pun in the title?

Literature Online

Interactive Literary Elements Handbook
To review or learn more about the literary elements, go to www.glencoe.com.

Get Ready to Read

Connect to the Reading

You will read about two people who faced an enormous challenge. What's the greatest challenge you've ever faced? What made it so challenging? How did you feel when you first faced the challenge? What finally happened and how did you feel about it?

Write to Learn In your Learner's Notebook, answer the questions above.

Build Background

About a half century ago, Edmund Hillary and Tenzing Norgay became the first people to climb to the top of Mount Everest, the tallest mountain in the world. Mount Everest is in the Himalayas, a mountain range on the border of Nepal and Tibet, China.

In interviews, Hillary has said that he was often frightened during the difficult climb—especially when he fell into a large crack in the ice—but that he kept on because "this is part of the challenge."

- Find Nepal and China on the map on the next page. Mount Everest is in the mountain range on the border of these two countries.
- Today's hikers use equipment and clothing that did not exist in 1953, when Hillary and Norgay made their climb. Most of what today's climbers use is strong or warm but light to carry. For example, hikers now wear fabrics that are warmer and thinner than the many layers of wool worn by Hillary and Norgay.

Set Purposes for Reading

BIG Question Read to find out what it's like to hike to the top of the world's highest mountain.

Set Your Own Purpose What else would you like to learn from the selection to help you answer the Big Question? Write your own purpose on the "On Top of the World" page of Foldable 1.

Keep Moving

Use these skills as you read "On Top of the World."

TIME

On TOP of the WORLD

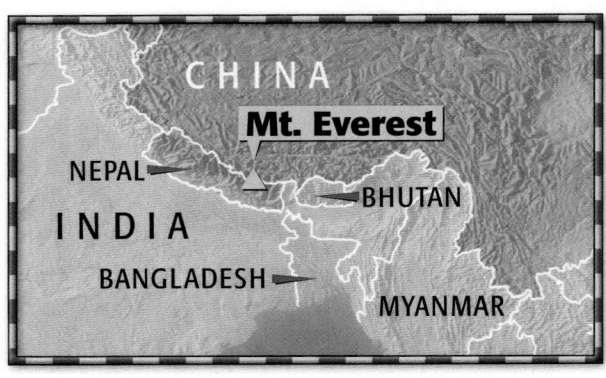

It has been more than 50 years since two adventurers first climbed Mount Everest.

By MARTHA PICKERILL

O n May 29, 1953, Edmund Hillary and his mountain-climbing companion, Tenzing Norgay, got a glimpse of Asia that no other human had ever enjoyed. They became the first to look down from the dizzying height of the world's tallest mountain, Mount Everest, while standing upon its snowy top. But it wasn't a time for celebrating.

"I didn't leap or throw my hands in the air or something," Hillary recalled in an interview. "We were tired, of course." But finally in May 2003, the long-delayed celebration took place. Hillary, who lives in New Zealand, joined his friends and fans in Kathmandu, Nepal, to honor the 50th anniversary of his towering **feat.**

The Quest for the Top ▪

Sir George Everest, a British surveyor who mapped India and part of the Himalayan range, probably never saw the big mountain. But his colleagues,[1] who measured the peak and declared it the world's tallest in 1852, wanted to honor Everest's work by naming it after him. The 29,035-foot-tall mountain straddles the border of Nepal and the Tibet region of China.

---

1. *Colleagues* are people who work in the same profession

Vocabulary . . . .

feat (feet) *n.* remarkable action

▪ **Text Element**

Titles and Subheads Reread the subhead. A *quest* is a difficult journey to reach a goal. What difficult journey do you think this section will be about?

Climbing to Mount Everest's summit became an irresistible goal for many adventurers. But people risked their lives to get to the top. Has the challenge been worth the serious risk? When a reporter asked George Mallory, a British mountaineer, why he wanted to climb Everest, he famously replied, "Because it is there." Mallory's final attempt in 1924 to climb to the top of Mount Everest ended in his death. At least 175 climbers are known to have died on Everest since 1920. Nearly 1,200 others have made it to the top. **2**

One Mean Mountain

Anyone who has climbed Everest can tell you that humans are not meant to hang around 5.5 miles above sea level. The ice, snow, freezing wind, deep ice cracks, called **crevasses,** and lack of oxygen are constant threats to climbers' safety and health. Because of the thin air, most climbers breathe from oxygen tanks. Some climbers have lost toes, ears, and fingers to frostbite.[2] All of these factors force climbers who do reach the top to turn around and scramble back down as quickly as possible. **3**

2 **Key Reading Skill**

Connecting Would you like to climb Mount Everest? Do you think climbing it is worth the risk? Why or why not?

3 **English Language Coach**

Context Clues What are **crevasses?** Use the explanatory phrase in the sentence to figure out the meaning of this word.

Sherpas carried tons of supplies for the 1953 climb.

Royal Geographic Society

---

2. ***Frostbite*** happens when a part of the body becomes so cold that the blood cannot circulate. Usually frostbite happens to fingers, toes, and ears.

"You cannot conquer Everest. It's not possible," says Norgay's son Jamling, who has climbed Everest with Hillary's son, Peter. "Everest will give you a chance to stand on the top for a few minutes, and that's it."

It's Still There ❹

The mountain is much less a mystery now than when Hillary and Norgay reached its peak in 1953. People have approached climbing it from all sides and have succeeded in getting to its top by 15 different routes. Satellite phones and other equipment keep adventurers in touch with the world below. Special clothes made for climbing are now made of high-tech thermal fabrics. Hillary and Norgay had only layers of wool and cotton and a simple cotton tent to keep them warm. They didn't have any high-tech equipment as safety nets.

Some modern climbers who are inexperienced pay a lot of money to have professional guides take them to the top. But even with guides, the climb can be risky. In 1996, tragedy struck. On one of the mountain's busiest days, a storm blew in, and eight climbers died in a single night.

❹ **Text Element**

Title and Subheads From the subhead and the other parts of the article that you've read, what do you think the section "It's Still There" will be about?

Climber Heidi Howkins uses a ladder to cross a crevasse in the Khumbu Ice Fall, a jumble of ice blocks on the path to the top. Inset: Hillary and Norgay have tea after their triumph in 1953.

Royal Geographic Society

Bobby

Hillary continued a life of achievement. After being knighted by Queen Elizabeth II, Sir Edmund Hillary led a team across Antarctica to the South Pole and climbed many mountains. He has worked for decades to build desperately needed schools and hospitals for Norgay's people, the Sherpas of Nepal. "That's how I'd like to be remembered," says Hillary. "Not for Everest but for the work I did and the cooperation I had with my Sherpa friends." **5**

—**Updated 2005, from *TIME For Kids*, May 9, 2003**

The Mountain's Keepers

Tenzing Norgay, who died in 1986, was a Sherpa. The Sherpas are one of about 30 ethnic groups[3] in Nepal. Sherpas, who are mainly farmers and herders, are believed to have **trekked** to Nepal from Tibet about 500 years ago.

Because many live in the Khumbu Valley at the foot of Everest, Sherpas work as porters and guides for outsiders who come to climb the mountain. On big **expeditions,** Sherpas may go ahead of official climbers to carry tons of gear to the few camps along the way. It's hard to imagine that many foreigners would have made it up Everest without help from Sherpas, who are used to working at high altitudes.

Sherpas follow the Buddhist religion, which holds deep respect for nature as a core belief. They call the mountain *Sagarmatha*, which means "goddess mother of the world."

Bobby Model

This Sherpa boy carried a heavy load in 1999.

5 🗨 **BIG** Question

What did you learn about Mount Everest from reading this article? What did you learn about people who set difficult goals for themselves? Write your answer on the "On Top of the World" page of Foldable 1. Your response will help you complete the Unit Challenge later.

---

3. *Ethnic groups* are groups of people that share a language, customs, and social ideas.

Vocabulary

trekked (trekd) *v.* walked or hiked a long distance

expeditions (ek spuh DISH unz) *n.* groups that take trips for specific purposes

After You Read

On Top of the World

Answering the **BIG** Question

1. Were you entertained by the article? Explain. If you were not entertained, explain what you got out of reading it.

2. **Recall** Where is Mount Everest located?

   TIP Right There The answer is in the article.

3. **List** What are some of the dangers people who climb Mount Everest must face? List at least three.

   TIP Right There The answer is in the article.

Critical Thinking

4. **Evaluate** Do you think George Mallory had a good reason for climbing the mountain? Why or why not?

   TIP Author and Me You will find clues in the text, but you must also use the information in your head.

5. **Interpret** Jamling Norgay has said, "you cannot conquer Everest." What do you think he meant?

   TIP Author and Me You will find clues in the text, but you must also use the information in your head.

6. **Infer** Edmund Hillary has said he wishes to be remembered for his friendship with the Sherpas rather than for climbing Mount Everest. What does this wish tell you about Hillary as a person?

   TIP On My Own Use your knowledge of people to answer.

Talk About Your Reading

Oral Report Imagine that you're writing a short biography of Hillary. With a small group of classmates, brainstorm a list of at least ten questions you feel you would need to answer about Hillary's life in order to write the biography. They could be questions you would like to ask Hillary in an interview or questions you might answer yourself by doing research on the Internet or in the library. Follow up by doing the research. Present your findings in an oral report to your class.

NY English Language Arts Core Curriculum
(pp. 36–37)

LC R17 Demonstrate comprehension and response through a range of activities. **S1a** Give presentations on informational topics. **R1j** Compare information from different sources. **R2g** Compare literature to own lives. **LC R13** Use text structure to aid comprehension and response. **Core W8** Use correct grammatical construction in parts of speech (pronouns).

For a complete description of the standards, see p. NY11.

Skills Review

Key Reading Skill: Connecting

7. What are some reasons that you have for trying new or difficult activities? How do these reasons help you relate to this story?

Text Element: Title and Subheads

8. Did the subheads help you preview the content of the article? Explain why or why not.

Vocabulary Check

Play a game with a group of three. Follow these steps:

• Write the words below on note cards.
• Turn the cards face down.
• On your turn, choose one card.
• Make up a sentence using the word on that card. Each sentence has to be different from the other ones that used the same word. Keep playing until you have all gone twice.

9. feat
10. trekked
11. expeditions

English Language Coach Each of the following sentences contains an underlined word that may be unfamiliar to you. Copy the sentences. Then circle the explanatory word or phrase that defines the underlined word.

12. Volcanoes are formed when <u>magma</u>, hot liquid rock beneath the earth's surface, breaks through a weak spot in the earth's crust.

13. <u>Daal bhaat</u> (rice with lentil beans) is a common meal for the Sherpas.

14. <u>Yaks</u>—large, shaggy animals that are similar to buffalo and oxen—are native to central Asia.

15. Roving bands of robbers, called <u>dacoits</u>, terrorized the countryside of India.

Grammar Link: Personal and Possessive Pronouns and Antecedents

Pronouns take the place of nouns.	
Personal pronouns refer to people or things	*I, me, you, he, she, him, her, it, we, us, they, them*
Possessive pronouns show ownership	*my, mine, our, ours, you, yours, his, her, hers, its, their, theirs, whose*

The words in dark type below are personal pronouns. The underlined words are possessive pronouns.

• When **I** slipped on ice, **she** put down <u>her</u> book to help **me** get on <u>my</u> feet. Then <u>our</u> friends came to find **us.**

An **antecedent** (an tuh SEE dunt) is the noun that a pronoun refers to. A pronoun must refer clearly to its antecedent.

<u>Cheryl Lynn</u> and <u>Tabitha</u> went to <u>her</u> house.
  antecedent   *antecedent*   *pronoun*

In the example above, the antecedent for *her* is unclear. Did the girls go to Cheryl Lynn's house or Tabitha's house? To fix the unclear pronoun reference, you can replace the pronoun with a noun.

• Cheryl Lynn and Tabitha went to <u>Tabitha's</u> house.

Grammar Practice

Circle the personal pronouns in the sentences below. Underline the possessive pronouns. Correct the sentence if the antecedent of a pronoun is unclear.

16. Juanita likes to tease her friends when she's in a bad mood.

17. I hit a branch with my head, and it broke off.

18. "Whose car is in front of your house?" he asked.

Web Activities For eFlashcards, Selection Quick Checks, and other Web activities, go to www.glencoe.com.

Autobiographical Sketch
Prewriting and Drafting

ASSIGNMENT Write an autobiographical sketch

Purpose: To describe an experience you've had that shaped your feelings about reading

Audience: Your teacher and your classmates

Writing Rubric

As you work through this writing assignment, you should follow these guidelines:

- develop a sequence of events
- use first-person point of view
- use well-chosen descriptions and details
- develop your writing voice

For a model of an autobiographical sketch, see page 95.

NY English Language Arts Core Curriculum (pp. 38–41)

Core W4 Use prewriting activities. **Core W5** Use the writing process. **W4c** Develop a personal voice. **W4d** Write personal reactions to experiences. **Core W8** Use correct grammatical construction.

For a complete description of the standards, see p. NY11.

Have you ever found yourself thinking about a special time or event in your life? Could you picture your surroundings in detail, remember the people who were there with you, and relive the feelings you had?

If you wrote this memory down, it could be the beginning of an autobiographical sketch. When a person writes the story of his or her life, it's called an autobiography. A sketch is a short scene that describes only the key details. So if you write an autobiographical sketch you describe one "scene," or event, in your life.

In this Writing Workshop you'll write an autobiographical sketch about a meaningful event in your life that involved reading. You'll explore how reading changed your outlook and share that experience with others.

Prewriting
Get Ready to Write

What do the following things have in common: stories, cereal boxes, street signs, schoolbooks, notes from friends? They're all things you've read, of course. Think about the different reading experiences you've had.

Gather Ideas and Choose a Topic

In your Learner's Notebook, write about the kinds of reading experiences you've had in your life. Here are some examples to get you started:

- being read to before going to bed at night
- reading your favorite magazine at the newsstand
- reading short stories or books assigned in school
- reading a postcard from traveling friends or family
- reading instructions on how to play a new video game

After you've thought of as many examples as possible, choose an experience from your list. Pick one that you think is interesting and important—one that helped shape how you feel about reading. (Don't worry about choosing the "perfect" experience. If your choice doesn't work out, you can change it later.)

Develop Your Ideas

Once you've chosen an experience to write about, recall specific details about your experience. These details are important because they will help your readers to understand how you felt at the time. If you have trouble coming up with details, think about the experience in terms of your five senses: sight, sound, taste, touch, and smell.

1. In your Learner's Notebook, jot down as many specific details about your topic as you can remember.

2. Make sure that your list includes when and where the experience happened and who else, if anyone, was there.

3. Ask yourself how the experience made you feel. How do you feel about it now?

If you don't have enough details or can't recall how you felt at the time, now is a good time to pick a different reading experience.

Make a Plan

After you've developed your ideas, decide what order you want to put them in, or how to **sequence** your sketch.

- You can describe the experience in **chronological order**—the order in which things actually happened. Start at the beginning of your experience and end by telling how it influenced how you feel about reading now—or how you hope to feel in the future.

- You may want to describe your experience in a **flashback**—an interruption in chronological order to describe the past. For example, you might begin by describing how you feel about reading now. Then you could flash back to the past experience that shaped your feelings. You could end by returning to the present.

To help organize your sketch, fill in a map like the one below.

> **Literature Online**
>
> **Writing Models** For models and other writing activities, go to www.glencoe.com.

> ◄ **Writing Tip**
>
> **Prewriting** Think about interesting ways to begin your autobiographical sketch. You may begin with a question, a dialogue, or a sentence that uses strong action verbs. These are good ways to capture your readers' attention.

When and Where Experience Occurred
a friend's party and my bedroom

People Involved
me, a few of my classmates, and my social studies teacher

Beginning
I come home from a party after having an awful time because people ignored me.

Middle
I read a couple of scenes in my Spanish book that I can relate to.

End
The characters in the book give me hope for the future.

Drafting

Start Writing!

Sometimes the hardest part of writing a first draft is getting down the first few words. You don't have to worry, though. You've already done that by writing notes and filling in a story map!

Get It on Paper

Writing Tip ▶

Conclusion Don't stop writing when you run out of ideas. Give your sketch a strong ending by telling what the experience meant to you.

Begin writing about your experience. Use your story map as a guide, but feel free to make changes as you go along. You are telling a story that happened to you, so use first-person point of view. Refer to yourself as *I* and *me.* Describe the other people in your story. Tell what they looked like, how they acted, and what they said.

Applying Good Writing Traits

Voice

One of the best parts about reading a story is discovering the writer's personality from the way he or she sounds on paper.

What is Voice?

When you speak, you don't sound like anyone else—your voice is yours alone. You want to have a one-of-a-kind voice when you write too.

Why Is Voice Important in My Writing?

Using a strong, individual voice in your writing will get your ideas and feelings across to the reader and make your writing more interesting.

How Do I Do It?

• Don't be afraid to show who you really are! Write with personality, as if you are telling close friends about your experience.

• Choose words that show what you really believe and feel.

• Vary the way that you structure sentences. Every sentence in your autobiographical sketch should not start with "I."

• Include details that will help your readers picture in their minds the events in your text.

Write to Learn Here's how you can strengthen the voice in your draft:

1. After you have written your first draft, read your sketch aloud.

2. Make changes when your writing doesn't sound like you.

3. Keep making changes through the rest of the sketch until you feel that your voice is consistent throughout.

Grammar Link

Verbs

Verbs are words that show action or a state of being.

What Are the Different Types of Verbs?

Action verbs show action.

- My sister <u>plays</u> on the basketball team.
- The bells ring in the church.

Many action verbs are obvious and easy to spot, but some are not. To find an action verb, look for what something or someone *does*.

> Netty <u>reads</u> to her sister Sara. Sara <u>listens</u> carefully. The baby, Patty, <u>bangs</u> on a pot and Sara <u>jumps</u>. Netty <u>closes</u> the book and <u>smiles</u> at Patty.

Some action verbs might be less obvious. Some action verbs show what someone or something is *thinking* or *feeling*.

> Netty <u>loves</u> her sisters. She <u>cares</u> about both of them very much. But she <u>wants</u> a brother, too.

Linking verbs show a state of being. They connect a person, place or thing with a word that *describes* it or *tells what it is*. The most common linking verb is the verb *to be*. Some forms of the *to be* verb are:

is, am, are, was, were, been

- The car <u>is</u> shiny.

  The verb *is* links *car* to *shiny*. *Shiny* describes *the car*.

- The athletes in the gym <u>were</u> all gymnasts.

  The verb *were* links *athletes* to *gymnasts*. *Gymnasts* names the kind of *athletes*.

Other Linking Verbs

Other common linking verbs are:

seem, look, feel, become, appear, grow, turn, taste, feel, smell, sound

- Milk <u>turns</u> sour out of the refrigerator.

  The verb *turns* links *milk* and *sour*. *Sour* describes the *milk*.

- After the show, Marita <u>seemed</u> sad.

  The verb *seemed* links *Marita* to *sad*. *Sad* describes *Marita*.

Writing Application Look back at your autobiographical sketch draft. Check that you correctly used action and linking verbs. Fix any errors that you find.

Looking Ahead

There's another part to this Writing Workshop. Keep the writing you did here. In the next part you'll learn how to turn your first draft into a great autobiographical sketch!

Skills Focus

You will practice using these skills when you read the following selections:
- "The Tell-Tale Heart," p. 46
- from *The Book of Rock Stars*, p. 56

Reading

- Setting a purpose for reading

Literature

- Identifying and analyzing the effects of narrative point of view

Vocabulary

- Using examples, synonyms, and antonyms to find the meaning of words
- Academic Vocabulary: *strategy*

Writing/Grammar

- Identifying and using common and proper nouns
- Correctly forming noun plurals

NY English Language Arts Core Curriculum
(pp. 42–43)

Core R1 Identify a purpose for reading.

For a complete description of the standards, see p. NY11.

Skill Lesson

Setting a Purpose for Reading

Learn It!

What Is It? Why are you reading that paperback mystery? What do you hope to get from your science textbook? The point is, you read for different reasons. You may read a mystery for entertainment or escape and a science text for knowledge. **Setting a purpose for reading** is deciding why you are reading. Here are some common purposes:

- to be entertained—for a good scare or a good laugh
- to learn and understand new information
- to find out more about a person you admire
- to explore an interest

BALDO© 2005 Baldo Partnership. Dist. By UNIVERSAL PRESS SYNDICATE. Reprinted with permission. All rights reserved.

Analyzing Cartoons
What purpose could you set for reading about people who lived a hundred years ago? What would you like to know about their lives?

Why Is It Important? Setting a purpose for reading helps you choose a reading strategy. If you're reading a mystery story, for example, you'll probably want to look for clues to solve the mystery. If you want to find the answer to a science question, you can read quickly to look for key words.

How Do I Do It? One way to set a purpose for reading is to read the title of the work. You can also look for subheads and pictures. You might even read the first paragraph or two. Then think about why you want to read. Are you curious about the main character? Do you want to answer a question? Here's how a student set a purpose for reading *I Know Why the Caged Bird Sings*. He began by reading the first paragraph:

> Mrs. Bertha Flowers was the aristocrat of Black Stamps. She had the grace and control to appear warm in the coldest weather, and on the Arkansas summer days it seemed she had a private breeze which swirled around, cooling her. She was thin without the taut look of wiry people, and her printed voile dresses and flowered hats were as right for her as denim overalls for a farmer. . . .

Mrs. Flowers sounds pretty interesting. The person describing her obviously admires her. I'd like to find out more about Mrs. Flowers as I read.

Literature Online

Study Central Visit www.glencoe .com and click on Study Central to review setting a purpose for reading.

Practice It!

In your Learner's Notebook, write a purpose for reading each of these:
- a short story about a man who has just committed a murder
- a biography of a famous musician
- want ads in the newspaper

Use It!

When you read the titles and the first few paragraphs of the selections in this workshop, list in your Learner's Notebook your purposes for reading. You can have more than one purpose for reading. As you read, set more purposes for reading and add them to your list.

Academic Vocabulary

strategy (STRA tuh jee) *n.* a careful method or plan

Before You Read : The Tell-Tale Heart

Edgar Allan Poe

Meet the Author

Edgar Allan Poe (1809–1849) was a master writer of detective stories, horror tales, and thrillers. Despite his talents, he had a hard life. He had severe money problems, and his beloved wife died when she was only twenty-four. A few years later he died at the young age of forty. See page R6 at the back of the book for more on Edgar Allan Poe.

Literature Online

Author Search For more about Edgar Allan Poe, go to www.glencoe.com.

NY English Language Arts Core Curriculum
(pp. 44–51)

Core R4 Determine the meaning of unfamiliar words by using context clues.
Core R1 Identify a purpose for reading.
R2c Identify the author's point of view.

For a complete description of the standards, see p. NY11.

Vocabulary Preview

stifled (STY fuld) *adj.* held back; muffled; form of the verb *stifle* **(p. 48)** *His stifled voice spoke to me from the other side of the door.*

stimulates (STIM yuh layts) *v.* makes active or more active; form of the verb *stimulate* **(p. 49)** *The old man's fear stimulates his heart to beat faster.*

audacity (aw DAS ih tee) *n.* reckless courage **(p. 50)** *Can you believe he had the audacity to lie to the police?*

hypocritical (hip uh KRIT ih kul) *adj.* fake; pretending to be something one isn't **(p. 51)** *He was convinced that their smiles were hypocritical; he was sure they knew the truth.*

Write to Learn For each vocabulary word, write a sentence in your Learner's Notebook using the word.

English Language Coach

Context Clues: Examples Remember that when you're reading on your own, you can often figure out the meaning of unfamiliar words just by looking at **context clues**—hints in nearby words and sentences.

One kind of context clue is examples. Look at the underlined examples in the following sentence. See if you can use them to figure out what *implements* means: *I had all the implements I needed to make the cake batter: a bowl, a spoon, measuring cups, and a mixer.*

All the examples have something in common. All of them are types of tools. So *implements* means "tools."

On Your Own A word web can help you remember the meanings of words you've defined through examples. Copy the web below into your Learner's Notebook. Then fill in the ovals on the web with the examples of implements.

implements

Skills Preview

Key Reading Skill: Setting a Purpose for Reading

One thing that can help you set a purpose for reading is information about the author. Edgar Allan Poe was a great writer of horror stories and thrillers, so you know a mystery or murder may be involved. The purpose you set could be to find out what the mystery is or simply to enjoy all the scary, gruesome stuff in the story. It's up to you!

Write to Learn Suppose you set yourself the purpose of learning how to *write* a horror story while you're reading "The Tell-Tale Heart." In your Learner's Notebook, write three things you would want to learn.

Key Literary Element: Point of View in Fiction

Every story has a storyteller, or **narrator.** The perspective from which the narrator tells the story is the **point of view.** In the **first-person point of view,** the narrator is a character in the story who refers to himself or herself as "I" or "me." The first-person narrator takes part in what happens and describes the events from his or her perspective. When a first-person narrator tells the story, you may feel as though he or she is talking directly to you.

In the **third-person point of view,** the narrator is not a character in the story and does not take part in events. He or she stands apart from the action and describes what is happening. When a third-person narrator tells the story, you may feel a sense of distance from the action.

To identify point of view, ask yourself, *Who is telling this story? Is he or she a character in the story (first-person) or a nameless voice (third-person)?*

On Your Own Read the first paragraph of "The Tell-Tale Heart." What is the point of view?

Get Ready to Read

Connect to the Reading

In your opinion, do most people see themselves as others see them? Explain.

Write to Learn In your Learner's Notebook, jot down your opinion. Back it up with a short example or two that supports your opinion.

Build Background

A superstition (soo per STIH shun) is a belief that is rooted in fear and fantasy rather than reason and evidence. One such superstition is the curse of the Evil Eye. According to this superstition, some people have the power to harm others just by looking at them. Who are these special people? The answer varies from culture to culture. In Mediterranean cultures—those in countries bordering the Mediterranean Sea—many people who believe in the Evil Eye say that blue-eyed individuals are the ones to fear. Other cultures have different ideas. In fact, in some cultures in the Middle East the color blue is believed to protect people from the Evil Eye.

Set Purposes for Reading

BIG Question Read "The Tell-Tale Heart" to find out why a man commits a murder and whether he gets away with it without being punished.

Set Your Own Purpose What else would you like to learn from the selection to help you answer the Big Question? Write your own purpose on "The Tell-Tale Heart" page of Foldable 1.

Literature Online

Interactive Literary Elements Handbook
To review or learn more about the literary elements, go to www.glencoe.com.

Keep Moving

Use these skills as you read "The Tell-Tale Heart."

The Tell-Tale Heart

by Edgar Allan Poe

True!—nervous—very, very dreadfully nervous I had been and am; but why *will* you say that I am mad? **1** The disease had sharpened my senses—not destroyed—not dulled them. Above all was the sense of hearing acute. I heard all things in the heaven and in the earth. I heard many things in hell. How, then, am I mad? Hearken![1] and observe how healthily—how calmly I can tell you the whole story. **2**

It is impossible to say how first the idea entered my brain; but once conceived,[2] it haunted me day and night. Object there was none. Passion there was none. I loved the old man. He had never wronged me. He had never given me insult. For his gold I had no desire. I think it was his eye! yes, it was this! One of his eyes resembled that of a vulture—a pale blue eye, with a film over it. Whenever it fell upon me, my blood ran cold; and so by degrees—very gradually—I made up my mind to take the life of the old man, and thus rid myself of the eye for ever.

Now this is the point. You fancy me mad. Madmen know nothing. But you should have seen *me*. You should have seen how wisely I proceeded—with what caution—with what foresight—with what dissimulation I went to work![3] I was

Practice the Skills

1 | **Key Literary Element**

Point of View The narrator refers to himself as "I." What is the point of view?

2 | **Key Reading Skill**

Setting a Purpose The narrator insists that he's not crazy and that he can calmly tell his story. So your purpose for reading might be to see whether the narrator really is in his right mind or what story he has to tell.

---

1. When the narrator says "***Hearken,***" he is asking the reader to listen.
2. Here, ***conceived*** means "thought of."
3. ***Foresight*** means "care or preparation for the future." ***Dissimulation*** means "the hiding or disguising of one's true feelings and intentions."

never kinder to the old man than during the whole week before I killed him. And every night, about midnight, I turned the latch of his door and opened it—oh, so gently! And then, when I had made an opening sufficient for my head, I put in a dark lantern, all closed, closed, so that no light shone out, and then I thrust in my head. Oh, you would have laughed to see how cunningly[4] I thrust it in! **3** I moved it slowly—very, very slowly, so that I might not disturb the old man's sleep. It took me an hour to place my whole head within the opening so far that I could see him as he lay upon his bed. Ha!—would a madman have been so wise as this? And then, when my head was well in the room, I undid the lantern cautiously—oh, so cautiously— cautiously (for the hinges creaked)—I undid it just so much that a single thin ray fell upon the vulture eye. And this I did for seven long nights—every night just at midnight—but I found the eye always closed; and so it was impossible to do the work; for it was not the old man who vexed[5] me, but his Evil Eye. And every morning, when the day broke, I went boldly into the chamber, and spoke courageously to him, calling him by name in a hearty tone, and inquiring how he had passed the night. So you see he would have been a very profound[6] old man, indeed, to suspect that every night, just at twelve, I looked in upon him while he slept.

Upon the eighth night I was more than usually cautious in opening the door. A watch's minute hand moves more quickly than did mine. Never before that night, had I *felt* the extent of my own powers—of my sagacity.[7] I could scarcely contain my feelings of triumph. To think that there I was, opening the door, little by little, and he not even to dream of my secret deeds or thoughts. I fairly chuckled at the idea; and perhaps he heard me; for he moved on the bed suddenly, as if startled. Now you may think that I drew back—but no. His room was as black as pitch with the thick darkness, (for the shutters were close fastened, through fear of robbers,) and so I knew that he could not see the opening of the door, and I kept pushing it on steadily, steadily. **4**

---

4. **Cunningly** means "cleverly."
5. Another way of saying **vexed** is "annoyed" or "made angry."
6. Here, **profound** means "very thoughtful and wise."
7. **Sagacity** (suh GAS uh tee) is wisdom and judgment.

Practice the Skills

3 **Key Literary Element**

Point of View Notice how Poe makes it seem as if the narrator is talking directly to you. This draws you into the story.

4 **Key Literary Element**

Point of View Though you are "seeing" what happened from the narrator's perspective, you don't have to agree with him. He talks about his *sagacity*, or wisdom. Would you call his actions wise? Why or why not?

I had my head in, and was about to open the lantern, when my thumb slipped upon the tin fastening, and the old man sprang up in the bed, crying out—"Who's there?"

I kept quite still and said nothing. For a whole hour I did not move a muscle, and in the meantime I did not hear him lie down. He was still sitting up in the bed, listening;—just as I have done, night after night, hearkening to the death watches[8] in the wall.

Presently I heard a slight groan, and I knew it was the groan of mortal terror. It was not a groan of pain or of grief— oh, no!—it was the low **stifled** sound that arises from the bottom of the soul when overcharged with awe. I knew the sound well. Many a night, just at midnight, when all the world slept, it has welled up from my own bosom, deepening, with its dreadful echo, the terrors that distracted me. I say I knew it well. I knew what the old man felt, and pitied him, although I chuckled at heart. I knew that he had been lying awake ever since the first slight noise, when he had turned in the bed. His fears had been ever since growing upon him. He had been trying to fancy them causeless, but could not. He had been saying to himself—"It is nothing but the wind in the chimney—it is only a mouse crossing the floor," or "it is merely a cricket which has made a single chirp." Yes, he has been trying to comfort himself with these **suppositions:** but he had found all in vain. *All in vain;* because Death, in approaching him, had stalked with his black shadow before him, and enveloped[9] the victim. **5** And it was the mournful influence of the unperceived shadow that caused him to feel—although he neither saw nor heard—to *feel* the presence of my head within the room.

When I had waited a long time, very patiently, without hearing him lie down, I resolved to open a little—a very, very little crevice in the lantern. So I opened it—you cannot imagine how stealthily, stealthily—until, at length, a single dim ray, like the thread of the spider, shot from out the crevice and fell upon the vulture eye.

---

8. ***Death watches*** are beetles that bore into wood, especially of old houses and furniture. Some people believe that the insects' ticking sounds warn that death is approaching.

9. Here, ***enveloped*** means "surrounded."

Vocabulary . . . .

stifled (STY fuld) *adj.* held back; muffled

Practice the Skills

5 | **English Language Coach**

Context Clues: Examples
What are **suppositions?** Reread the third paragraph on this page to find the three examples of *suppositions* that the old man makes. Using the examples and the rest of the context, define *suppositions*.

It was open—wide, wide open—and I grew furious as I gazed upon it. I saw it with perfect distinctness—all a dull blue, with a hideous veil over it that chilled the very marrow in my bones; but I could see nothing else of the old man's face or person: for I had directed the ray as if by instinct, precisely upon the damned spot.

And now have I not told you that what you mistake for madness is but overacuteness of the senses?—now, I say, there came to my ears a low, dull, quick sound, such as a watch makes when enveloped in cotton. I knew *that* sound well, too. It was the beating of the old man's heart. It increased my fury, as the beating of a drum **stimulates** the soldier into courage.

But even yet I refrained and kept still. I scarcely breathed. I held the lantern motionless. I tried how steadily I could maintain the ray upon the eye. Meantime the hellish tattoo[10] of the heart increased. It grew quicker and quicker, and louder and louder every instant. The old man's terror *must* have been extreme! It grew louder, I say, louder every moment!—do you mark me well? I have told you that I am nervous: so I am. And now at the dead hour of the night, amid the dreadful silence of that old house, so strange a noise as this excited me to uncontrollable terror. Yet, for some minutes longer I refrained and stood still. But the beating grew louder, louder! I thought the heart must burst. And now a new anxiety seized me—the sound would be heard by a neighbor! The old man's hour had come! With a loud yell, I threw open the lantern and leaped into the room. He shrieked once—once only. In an instant I dragged him to the floor, and pulled the heavy bed over him. I then smiled gaily, to find the deed so far done. ⑥ But, for many minutes, the heart beat on with a muffled sound. This, however, did not vex me; it would not be heard through the wall. At length it ceased. The old

---

10. The heart was making a drumming or rapping sound. (This *tattoo* comes from a Dutch word; the other *tattoo*, a design on the skin, comes from the language of Tahiti, a Pacific island.)

Vocabulary . . . .

stimulates (STIM yuh layts) *v.* makes active or more active

Practice the Skills

⑥ **Key Literary Element**

Point of View The narrator smiles gaily after the killing. What does this tell you about him?

Analyzing the Art How does this picture illustrate the mood of "The Tell-Tale Heart"?

man was dead. I removed the bed and examined the corpse. Yes, he was stone, stone dead. I placed my hand upon the heart and held it there many minutes. There was no pulsation. He was stone dead. His eye would trouble me no more.

If still you think me mad, you will think so no longer when I describe the wise precautions I took for the concealment of the body. The night waned, and I worked hastily, but in silence. First of all I **dismembered** the corpse. I cut off the head and the arms and the legs. **7**

I then took up three planks from the flooring of the chamber, and deposited all between the scantlings.[11] I then replaced the boards so cleverly, so cunningly, that no human eye—not even *his*—could have detected anything wrong. There was nothing to wash out—no stain of any kind—no blood-spot whatever. I had been too wary for that. A tub had caught all—ha! ha!

When I had made an end of these labors, it was four o'clock—still dark as midnight. As the bell sounded the hour, there came a knocking at the street door. I went down to open it with a light heart—for what had I *now* to fear? There entered three men, who introduced themselves, with perfect suavity,[12] as officers of the police. A shriek had been heard by a neighbor during the night; suspicion of foul play had been aroused; information had been lodged at the police office, and they (the officers) had been deputed[13] to search the **premises**. **8**

I smiled—for *what* had I to fear? I bade the gentlemen welcome. The shriek, I said, was my own in a dream. The old man, I mentioned, was absent in the country. I took my visitors all over the house. I bade them search—search *well*. I led them, at length, to *his* chamber. I showed them his treasures, secure, undisturbed. In the enthusiasm of my confidence, I brought chairs into the room, and desired them *here* to rest from their fatigues, while I myself, in the wild **audacity** of my perfect triumph, placed my own seat upon the very spot beneath which reposed the corpse of the victim.

---

11. The **scantlings** are the boards that hold up the floor planks.
12. **Suavity** (SWOV uh tee) is a smooth, polite, gracious manner.
13. The officers were assigned a duty, or **deputed**, by a superior.

Vocabulary

audacity (aw DAS ih tee) *n.* reckless courage

Practice the Skills

7 | **English Language Coach**

Context Clues: Examples Do you know the meaning of the word **dismembered?** There are context clues in the sentence immediately following the word.

8 | **English Language Coach**

Context Clues: Examples What does **premises** mean in this context? Read on for an example. Then define the word.

The officers were satisfied. My *manner* had convinced them. I was singularly at ease. They sat, and while I answered cheerily, they chatted of familiar things. But, ere long, I felt myself getting pale and wished them gone. My head ached, and I fancied a ringing in my ears: but still they sat and still chatted. The ringing became more distinct—it continued and became more distinct: I talked more freely to get rid of the feeling: but it continued and gained definitiveness—until, at length, I found that the noise was *not* within my ears.

No doubt I now grew *very* pale—but I talked more fluently,[14] and with a heightened voice. Yet the sound increased—and what could I do? It was *a low, dull, quick sound—much such a sound as a watch makes when enveloped in cotton.* I gasped for breath—and yet the officers heard it not. I talked more quickly—more vehemently; but the noise steadily increased. I arose and argued about trifles, in a high key and with violent gesticulations;[15] but the noise steadily increased. Why *would* they not be gone? I paced the floor to and fro with heavy strides, as if excited to fury by the observations of the men— but the noise steadily increased. Oh God! what *could* I do? I foamed—I raved—I swore! I swung the chair upon which I had been sitting, and grated it upon the boards, but the noise arose over all and continually increased. It grew louder— louder—*louder!* And still the men chatted pleasantly, and smiled. Was it possible they heard not? Almighty God!—no, no! They heard!—they suspected!—they *knew!*—they were making a mockery of my horror!—this I thought, and this I think. But anything was better than this agony! Anything was more tolerable than this derision![16] I could bear those **hypocritical** smiles no longer! I felt that I must scream or die!—and now—again!—hark! louder! louder! louder! *louder!*—

"Villains!" I shrieked, "dissemble[17] no more! I admit the deed!—tear up the planks!—here, here!—it is the beating of his hideous heart!" **9** ○

---

14. To speak **fluently** is to do so smoothly and effortlessly.

15. **Trifles** are unimportant things. Bold, expressive gestures are **gesticulations.**

16. To make a **mockery** of a thing is to make it seem stupid or worthless. **Derision** is ridicule.

17. Here, **dissemble** means "to disguise one's true thoughts or feelings; act in an insincere way."

Vocabulary

hypocritical (hip uh KRIT ih kul) *adj.* fake; pretending to be something one isn't

Practice the Skills

9 **BIG** Question
Would you recommend this story to others? Why or why not? Write your answer on "The Tell-Tale Heart" page of Foldable 1. Your response will help you complete the Unit Challenge later.

After You Read

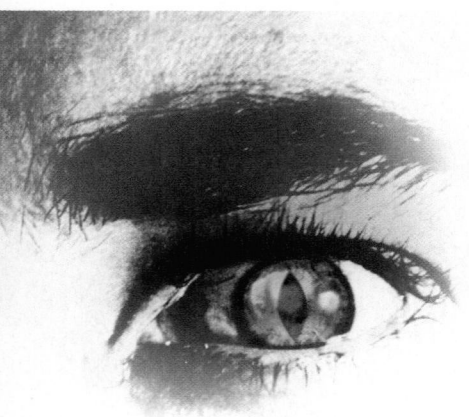

The Tell-Tale Heart

Answering the BIG Question

1. What parts of this story, if any, did you enjoy? Why?
2. **Recall** Why did the narrat ill the old man?
   TIP **Right There** The answer is found in the story.

3. **Summarize** Sum up how the narrator killed the old man.
   TIP **Right There** The answer is found in the story.

Critical Thinking

4. **Infer** What is making the "ticking" noise at the end of the story?
   TIP **Author and Me** You will find clues in the text, but you must also use the information in your head.

5. **Classify** Use evidence from the story to explain why it is called a thriller.
   TIP **Think and Search** The answer is in the text, but the details are not in one place.

6. **Evaluate** Do you think "The Tell-Tale Heart" is a good title for the story? Explain, using details from the story to support your opinion.
   TIP **Author and Me** You will find clues in the text, but you must also use the information in your head.

Write About Your Reading

Law Brief Imagine that the narrator is going to trial for the murder of the old man. With a small group of classmates, discuss whether you think the narrator should be held responsible for his actions:

- Is he innocent because he is not in his right mind and therefore unable to tell right from wrong?
- Or is he guilty because he is as perfectly sane as he insists?
- Build a case either for or against the narrator. Use specific evidence from the story to support your opinions.
- Then write a paragraph defending the narrator or sentencing him. Give convincing reasons for your defense or condemnation.

NY English Language Arts Core Curriculum
(pp. 52–53)

LC R17 Demonstrate comprehension and response through a range of activities.
LC S8 Participate in group discussions.
LC W6 Organize writing to communicate ideas. **Core R1** Identify a purpose for reading. **R2c** Identify the author's point of view.
Core W8 Use correct grammatical construction in parts of speech (nouns).

For a complete description of the standards, see p. NY11.

Skills Review

Key Reading Skill: Setting a Purpose for Reading

7. Review your purposes for reading this story. Did you get what you wanted out of reading it? Explain your thoughts.

Key Literary Element: Point of View in Fiction

8. How would the story change if it were told in the first-person point of view by one of the police officers?

Vocabulary Check

Fill in the blanks with the correct vocabulary word.

stifled   stimulates   audacity   hypocritical

9. Jogging _____ your heart and helps it grow stronger.

10. Monique had the _____ to talk back to the teacher.

11. Mona is so _____; she insists that I be on time, but she's always late.

12. I found my cat when I heard a _____ meow coming from inside the coat closet.

English Language Coach Write these sentences on a separate sheet of paper. Circle the examples in each sentence that help you figure out the meaning of the underlined word.

13. The thief was guilty of <u>dissimulation</u> when he pretended to be the old woman's friend and when he told her he was putting her retirement checks in the bank.

14. She took several <u>precautions</u> before leaving for vacation, including asking the police to check on her house, installing new locks on the front and back doors, and putting timers on several lamps.

15. **Academic Vocabulary** If your teacher asks you to choose a reading **strategy,** what is he or she asking you to do?

Grammar Link: Common and Proper Nouns

Nouns are words that name people, places, things, feelings, or ideas.

A **common noun** refers to *any* person, place, thing, or idea. A common noun is not capitalized unless it begins a sentence.

- Three students visited a museum.

  (The nouns *students* and *museum* do not refer to specific students or a specific museum. They are common nouns and are therefore not capitalized.)

A **proper noun** refers to a *specific* person, place, thing, or idea. Proper nouns are always capitalized.

- Ed, Alicia, and Al visited Harris Museum.

  (The nouns *Ed, Alicia,* and *Al* refer to specific students; the noun *Harris Museum* refers to a specific museum. The nouns are capitalized because they are proper nouns.)

Grammar Practice

There are five capitalization mistakes in the following paragraph. Copy the paragraph on a separate sheet of paper and fix the mistakes.

When my family and I visited Chicago last year, we went to Lincoln Park zoo. It is next to a beautiful park near lake Michigan. I hadn't been to a Zoo in years, so I had forgotten how much fun it can be to watch the animals. I especially liked watching the Monkeys play. I also enjoyed eating lunch at one of the outdoor Cafés.

Writing Application Check the nouns in the brief you wrote. Fix any capitalization errors.

Literature Online

Web Activities For eFlashcards, Selection Quick Checks, and other Web activities, go to www.glencoe.com.

Before You Read

from *The Book of Rock Stars*

Kathleen Krull

Meet the Author

Kathleen Krull has been interested in reading for most of her life. In fact, when she was only fifteen, she worked at a library. She has said that she spent so much time reading she didn't get her work done and got fired! Krull has written series of books about presidents, artists, and women. See page R3 of the Author Files in the back of the book for more on Kathleen Krull.

Author Search For more about Kathleen Krull, go to www.glencoe.com.

NY English Language Arts Core Curriculum
(pp. 54–59)

Core R4 Determine the meaning of unfamiliar words by using context clues.
LC R8 Recognize antonyms.
Core R1 Identify a purpose for reading.
R2c Identify the author's point of view.

For a complete description of the standards, see p. NY11.

Vocabulary Preview

oppressed (uh PRESD) *adj.* held down; held back; kept from making progress; form of the verb *oppress* **(p. 56)** *The oppressed people of Jamaica had little power to change their situation and improve their lives.*

premature (pree muh CHUR) *adj.* early; before the right time **(p. 57)** *At the age of thirty-six, he was too young to die; his death was premature.*

compassion (kom PASH un) *n.* the feeling of sorrow or pity caused by someone else's misfortunes; sympathy **(p. 59)** *Carlos Santana has compassion for the needy and helps charitable organizations.*

Partner Work Make flash cards. Write each of the vocabulary words on a separate card or sheet of paper. On the other side of the card or paper, write the meaning of the word. Use the flash cards to test a classmate's knowledge of the definitions of each word.

English Language Coach

Context Clues: Contrast Sometimes a context clue can show you what a word does *not* mean. That can be just as helpful.
*I decided to give up being **desolate** all the time and be happy instead.*

The contrasting word "happy" tells you that desolate means "unhappy." The words are antonyms. But sometimes, the contrasting clue is a word or phrase that is not an exact antonym.
*I was tired of the same old places and faces; I wanted something **exotic**.*

The contrasting phrase "same old" tells you that **exotic** means new and different.

On Your Own The chart below contains one word from the selection you are about to read. It also contains a contrasting clue to help you figure out the word's definition. Copy the chart and complete it by filling in the word's and definition.

Word	Contrasting Clue	Definition
rural	big city	

Skills Preview

Key Reading Skill: Setting a Purpose for Reading

The selection you are about to read consists of two short biographies of rock stars. In a biography an author tells someone else's life story. Think about the purposes that people might have for reading biographies.

Whole Class Discussion With your class, brainstorm a list of purposes for reading biographies.

Key Literary Element: Point of View in Nonfiction

Point of view in nonfiction is the perspective from which a factual story is told. In the **first-person point of view,** an author refers to himself or herself as "I" or "me" and describes actual events that he or she took part in or observed. Autobiographies and memoirs are two kinds of nonfiction told in the first person.

In the **third-person point of view,** the author does not refer to himself or herself. He or she is a nameless voice describing events, facts, or ideas. Biographies and newspaper reports are two of the many kinds of nonfiction told in the third person.

To identify the point of view of a nonfiction selection, ask yourself the following question:

• *Does the author refer to himself or herself as "I" or "me" (first-person), or is the author a nameless voice (third-person)?*

Write to Learn In your Learner's notebook, write a few sentences about yourself in the first-person. Then rewrite the sentences in the third-person.

Get Ready to Read

Connect to the Reading

What do you know about Bob Marley, reggae, Carlos Santana, and Latin-based rock? What would you like to know about these musicians and their music?

Write to Learn In your Learner's Notebook, write a list of questions you would like to ask these musicians.

Build Background

The following list of facts will help you understand the biographies you are about to read. Read the list carefully, and refer to it as you read.

• Jamaica is the third largest Caribbean island. It has a population of more than 2.7 million.

• The majority of Jamaicans are of African descent, but there are also small, well-established Indian, Chinese, Arab, and European communities.

• B. B. King plays the blues. John Lee Hooker and T-Bone Walker also were blues musicians.

• Woodstock was a rock concert held in New York state in 1969. The concert lasted three days and featured 31 bands. Around 500,000 people gathered.

Set Purposes for Reading

BIG Question Read to find out about the lives of two famous musicians.

Set Your Own Purpose What else would you like to learn from the selection to help you answer the Big Question? Write your own purpose on the *The Book of Rock Stars* page of Foldable 1.

Interactive Literary Elements Handbook
To review or learn more about the literary elements, go to www.glencoe.com.

Keep Moving

Use these skills as you read from *The Book of Rock Stars*.

from
The Book of Rock Stars

by Kathleen Krull

Bob Marley (b. 1945–d. 1981)

Few rock stars have national holidays in their honor. On the beautiful but poor Caribbean island of Jamaica, February 6 is National Bob Marley Day. **1**

He was born into **rural** poverty and left home at fourteen to pursue music in the big city of Kingston. **2** Three years later, he recorded his first single, called "Judge Not." With a catchy Jamaican rock beat—reggae—his fierce songs gave voice to the day-to-day struggles of **oppressed** people.

He teamed up with childhood friends and fellow singers to form a dynamic new reggae band, the Wailers. Members included Bunny Livingstone and Peter Tosh, as well as Rita Anderson, whom he later married. Marley was the hypnotic[1] lead singer, and audiences couldn't stop dancing. The music was infused[2] with devout spirituality, social commentary, and

---

1. *Hypnotic* means "in a way that holds the complete attention of someone."
2. Here, *infused* means "filled with."

Practice the Skills

1 | **Key Reading Skill**

Setting a Purpose for Reading Here's a possible purpose for reading. You can read to find out why there is a national holiday named after Bob Marley.

2 | **English Language Coach**

Context Clues: Contrast What does **rural** mean? Find the contrasting phrase in the sentence.

Vocabulary

oppressed (uh PRESD) *adj.* held down; held back; kept from making progress

encouragement to rebel. Plus it was pure fun. With tunes like "Stir It Up" and "No Woman, No Cry," Bob Marley and the Wailers could do no wrong in Jamaica. **3**

When their song "I Shot the Sheriff" became a hit for Eric Clapton, reggae went global. As the first Third World[3] superstar, Marley introduced Jamaican music to the world and laid the groundwork for much to follow.

Pulsing hits flowed—"Jamming," "Waiting in Vain," "One Love/People Get Ready," and "Is This Love?" They were wildly popular, not just in Jamaica, but also Africa, Great Britain, and Scandinavia. Yet the band made so little in royalties[4] that Marley once worked in a factory for a year to support his family.

His last haircut was in 1968. After that his hair stayed in dreadlocks, as part of the Rastafari faith, the Jamaican religion that was the keystone of his life.

As famous a rock star as Marley was outside Jamaica, those at home saw him as almost godlike. On political and religious issues, ordinary Jamaicans hung on his every word. He became such a national hero that some in power even took him as a threat. In 1976 he was wounded in an assassination attempt and had to leave Jamaica for his safety.

Five years later, while jogging in New York's Central Park, he collapsed. Doctors discovered that he had advanced cancer. He released his final album, *Uprising*, and died at age thirty-six. Fans went into shock at the **premature** loss of the freedom-fighting entertainer.

---

3. The ***Third World*** consists of (relatively) poor, developing countries.

4. Many artists and writers are paid ***royalties.*** These are fees paid to the artist each time his or her work is sold or used.

Practice the Skills

3 **Key Literary Element**

Point of View The author is not writing her own life story; she is writing the story of Bob Marley's life. What is the point of view: first-person or third-person?

Bob Marley wrote songs about politics, religion, and people's need to be free. He also introduced reggae music to the rest of the world.

Vocabulary

premature (pree muh CHUR) *adj.* early; before the right time

from *The Book of Rock Stars*   **57**

In 1999 Carlos Santana released the album *Supernatural* and made one of the greatest comebacks in rock history.

Carlos Santana (b. 1947)

Carlos Santana came from a Mexican village so tiny it had no running water or electricity. **4** His father, a traditional mariachi violinist, tried to teach him violin, but Carlos preferred guitar, especially the style of American greats B. B. King, John Lee Hooker, and T-Bone Walker. By age eleven, when his family moved to the border town of Tijuana, people were paying to see him playing in nightclubs.

Later, in San Francisco, he worked full-time as a restaurant dishwasher—playing guitar as a street musician during his off time. With some help from Jerry Garcia,[5] he formed a band. He was shy and not really the leader type, but the local musicians' union required paperwork that designated a leader. So he wrote down his name, Santana, which became the band's name.

4 **Key Reading Skill**

Setting a Purpose for Reading Though Carlos Santana was poor as a child, he later became a very successful musician. A possible purpose for reading about him is to see how he managed to become a success.

---

5. *Jerry Garcia* was the leader of the Grateful Dead, an influential rock band.

At age twenty-two, when he played for half a million people at the Woodstock festival, the group didn't even have an album yet. They knocked the audience out with "Soul Sacrifice," written just for the event. It was a whole new, Latin-based rock sound featuring an Afro-Cuban beat, mixing congas and timbales with Carlos's spicy lead guitar. Soon after they appeared on *The Ed Sullivan Show*, and surged onto radio with "Oye Como Va," "Evil Ways," "Jingo," "Black Magic Woman," "Everybody's Everything," and "No One to Depend On."

Visual Vocabulary
Congas are tall, single-headed drums played with the hands. They originated in Africa.

In 1973, influenced by Hinduism, he changed his name to Devadip (meaning "the light of the lamp of God") Carlos Santana. He released several albums with specifically spiritual themes, and always his music had humanitarian messages about peace, joy, acceptance, **compassion,** and understanding. Later he converted to Christianity.

The group earned devotion and steady sales with its soulful, heartfelt concerts, but had no radio hits after 1982. Musicians came and went, Carlos always zooming in the lead.

Then, in 1999, Santana made what is considered the greatest comeback in rock history. The album *Supernatural* sold more than ten million—by far the group's best-selling release—and won eight Grammy Awards, including best rock album of the year.

Famous all over again, Santana continues to support a wide range of causes, including United Farm Workers, Amnesty International, Doctors Without Borders, Rainforest Action Network, and the American Indian College Fund. **5** ○

Practice the Skills

5 🗸 **BIG Question**
What are the most interesting pieces of information you learned from these biographies? If you haven't already listened to Bob Marley and Carlos Santana's music, are you interested now? Why or why not? Write your answer on *The Book of Rock Stars* page of Foldable 1. Your response will help you complete the Unit Challenge later.

Vocabulary

compassion (kom PASH un) *n.* the feeling of sorrow or pity caused by someone else's misfortunes; sympathy

After You Read

from *The Book of Rock Stars*

Answering the 🗨 BIG Question

1. Did you enjoy reading about Bob Marley and Carlos Santana? Why or why not?

2. **Recall** Why did Bob Marley leave Jamaica?
   TIP **Right There** The answer is in the biography.

3. **Recall** What instrument did Carlos Santana like to play as a child?
   TIP **Right There** The answer is in the biography.

4. **Summarize** Sum up the story of how the band Santana got its name.
   TIP **Right There** The answer is in the biography.

Critical Thinking

5. **Interpret** The author says on page 59 that Santana made albums with "spiritual themes." What do you think that phrase means?
   TIP **Author and Me** There are clues in the biography, but you must also use the ideas in your head.

6. **Infer** Think about the reason that Bob Marley left Jamaica. What does this reason show about the downside of fame?
   TIP **Author and Me** You will find clues in the text, but you must also use the information in your head.

Talk About Your Reading

Small Group Comparison and Contrast In a small group, compare and contrast the childhoods of Bob Marley and Carlos Santana. Use the following questions to guide your discussion:

• In what ways were Marley's and Santana's childhoods alike?

• In what ways were their childhoods different?

• What, if anything, do you think their childhoods had to do with the music they played? Explain.

• What did you learn from comparing and contrasting?

NY English Language Arts Core Curriculum
(pp. 60–61)

R1b Apply thinking skills to interpret data from informational texts. **LC S8** Participate in group discussions. **Core R1** Identify a purpose for reading. **R2c** Identify the author's point of view. **Core R4** Determine the meaning of unfamiliar words by using context clues. **Core W8** Use correct grammatical construction in parts of speech (nouns).

For a complete description of the standards, see p. NY11.

Skills Review

Key Reading Skill: Setting a Purpose for Reading

7. What purpose did you set for reading biographies? How did it help you as you read?

Key Literary Element: Point of View in Nonfiction

8. Imagine that the life story of Carlos Santana that you just read was written in the first-person by Santana himself. In what ways do you think the story might change? Why?

Vocabulary Check

For each vocabulary word, write a sentence using the word. Leave a blank space where the word belongs. Trade your sentences with a partner. Fill in the blanks in each other's sentences.

9. oppressed

10. premature

11. compassion

English Language Coach Copy the following sentences on a separate sheet of paper. Circle the contrasting word or phrase in each sentence that helps define the underlined word. Then define the word.

12. The hot sun was so <u>enervating</u> that I jumped into the pool to get some energy.

13. The twins are so different: whereas Jack is <u>volatile</u>, Jake is laid back and even-tempered.

Grammar Link: Noun Plurals

A **singular noun** refers to one person, place, or thing. A **plural noun** refers to more than one person, place, or thing. To form the plural of most nouns, add an -s ending. There are four exceptions to the rule:

A. To form the plural of a noun that ends in a consonant + y, change the y to i and add -es.

Singular: one ci<u>ty</u>   **Plural:** two cit<u>ies</u>

B. To form the plural of most nouns that end in a consonant + o, add -es.

Singular: a he<u>ro</u>   **Plural:** many hero<u>es</u>

C. To form the plural of a noun that ends in -s, -sh, -ch, -x, or -z, add an -es ending.

Singular: that bru<u>sh</u>   **Plural:** those brush<u>es</u>

D. **Irregular nouns** are nouns that do not form the plural with an -s ending. If you are not sure how to spell the plural of an irregular noun, check a dictionary.

Singular: one m<u>a</u>n   **Plural:** several m<u>e</u>n

Grammar Practice

Each of the following sentences has a plural noun. Some of the plural nouns are correctly spelled. Others are not. Copy the sentences on another sheet of paper and fix any misspelled plurals.

14. The two attorneys formed a partnership.

15. Radioes are on sale this weekend.

16. Several deer were hit by cars last summer.

17. Please store the box's in the basement.

18. Why did the women complain to the manager?

Literature Online

Web Activities For eFlashcards, Selection Quick Checks, and other Web activities, go to www.glencoe.com.

Skills Focus

You will practice using the following skills when you read these selections:
- "The March of the Mill Children," p. 66
- "Filling Out the Application," p. 78
- "Exploring Careers," p. 86

Reading
- Activating prior knowledge

Literature
- Identifying tone
- Identifying and using text features

Vocabulary
- Using word categories and direct definitions to find word meanings
- Academic Vocabulary: *prior*

Writing/Grammar
- Identifying and using reflexive and intensive pronouns
- Identifying and using indefinite pronouns

NY English Language Arts Core Curriculum
(pp. 62–63)

LC R12 Combine multiple strategies to enhance comprehension.

For a complete description of the standards, see p. NY11.

Skill Lesson

Activating Prior Knowledge

Learn It!

What Is It? Activating **prior** knowledge means using what you already know. When you read, you bring your own life experiences and knowledge with you. You use this prior knowledge to help you better understand what you read.

- To *activate* something is to make it active, to get it going so it can be useful.
- Your prior *knowledge* is what you already know about a topic.
- *Activating prior knowledge* is using what you already know about a topic to help you understand new ideas.

Analyzing Cartoons
Jeremy is shocked to find how high his phone bill is. How does he activate prior knowledge to understand why the bill is so high?

© Zits Partnership, Reprinted with Permission of King Features Syndicate, Inc.

Academic Vocabulary

prior (PRY er) *adj.* earlier; coming before

Why Is It Important? Activating prior knowledge helps you understand the meanings of certain words and ideas. For example, if you've used a computer before, you might understand why a character who is having trouble moving the *cursor* with her *mouse* is frustrated.

How Do I Do It? Before you read, look at the title and quickly look for headlines and pictures. Ask yourself, *What do I already know about this topic?* As you read, look for new information and details that you can connect with your prior knowledge. Here is how a student activated her prior knowledge to understand part of the article "On Top of the World."

> On May 29, 1953, Edmund Hillary and his mountain-climbing companion, Tenzing Norgay . . . became the first to look down from the dizzying height of the world's tallest mountain, Mount Everest, while standing upon its snowy top.

> *I saw a show about Mount Everest on a cable TV science channel. The main thing I remember is how bad the weather can get near the top of Everest. It's really cold and windy. Snowstorms can strike with little warning.*

Practice It!

Make a three-column chart in your Learner's Notebook. Label the columns **Topics, Prior Knowledge,** and **New Information.** List the topics below in the **Topics** column. Fill in the second column with one or two things you know about each topic. Fill in the third column as you read.

- protest marches
- children in the workforce in the United States
- filling out a job application
- jobs in TV, firefighting, and emergency medicine

Use It!

As you read, keep your chart beside you. When you find information to relate to your prior knowledge, note it on your chart.

Before You Read

The March of the Mill Children

Judith Pinkerton Josephson

Meet the Author

Judith Pinkerton Josephson was inspired by her children to write poetry. This led to other writing for magazines, newspapers, and books. Josephson has taught writing to children and adults. She has coauthored grammar books, and she appears on radio shows to answer grammar questions.

Author Search For more about Judith Pinkerton Josephson, go to www.glencoe.com.

NY English Language Arts Core Curriculum
(pp. 64–73)

Core R4 Determine the meaning of unfamiliar words by using context clues. **LC R12** Combine multiple strategies to enhance comprehension. **R2e** Recognize how the author's use of language creates images or feelings.

For a complete description of the standards, see p. NY11.

Vocabulary Preview

treacherous (TRECH ur us) *adj.* dangerously untrustworthy **(p. 66)** *That treacherous piece of machinery is unsafe for small children to use.*

mutilated (MYOO tih lay tid) *adj.* damaged in a way that cannot be repaired; form of the verb *mutilate* **(p. 68)** *The copy machine jammed and the paper was mutilated.*

dormitory (DOR mih tor ee) *n.* a building with rooms for people to sleep in **(p. 70)** *The workers lived together in a dormitory that was located next to the factory.*

Small Group Work With two other students, make up a short story using the vocabulary words. Have each person contribute a sentence to the story. Use a vocabulary word in every sentence.

English Language Coach

Context Clues: Category Sometimes you can get an idea of what an unfamiliar word means by thinking about the category of items it belongs to. A **category** is a group of people, places, or things that have something in common. In the sentence below, the word *feverfew* may be unfamiliar to you. See if you can figure out what it refers to by thinking about the other, more familiar items it is grouped with. They are all in the same category.

• The prairie had Indian grass, clover, ragweed, goldenrod, and feverfew.

Feverfew is grouped with other plants. You can tell it is a plant, even though you don't know what kind of plant.

On Your Own Use category context clues to get an idea of what the underlined word in each sentence means. Then define the underlined word as well as you can.

• In the room were a bed, a dresser, night tables, and an <u>armoire</u>.

• The new zoo is home to gorillas, chimpanzees, orangutans, and <u>gibbons</u>.

• The X-ray showed that my wisdom teeth and molars are okay, but there is a cavity in each of the lower right <u>bicuspids</u>.

• Though they may be unfashionable, <u>oxfords</u> are more comfortable than high-heeled boots, ankle-strap heels, or loafers.

Skills Preview

Key Reading Skill: Activating Prior Knowledge

"The March of the Mill Children" is about child workers at the turn of the 20th century. Recall what you know about this topic.

Whole Class Discussion List facts and ideas you know about child labor, workers' rights, or the labor movement. Briefly discuss each item you list.

Key Literary Element: Tone

"That's a beautiful coat you're wearing" can be a compliment or a cutting remark. It all depends on your tone of voice when you say it. If you mean what you say, your positive attitude will show in your tone of voice, and you'll sound enthusiastic. But if you actually hate the coat and want the person to know it, your negative attitude will show in your sarcastic tone of voice. Just as tone of voice reveals a speaker's attitude, so the tone of a piece of writing reveals the author's attitude toward his or her subject. To tell the tone of a piece of writing, look at the words the author uses. Are they filled with admiration? Sarcasm? Anger? Laughter? "Listen" when you read to "hear" the author's tone. Ask yourself this question:

- *What attitude is reflected in the words the author chose to use?*

Partner Talk Describe the tone of each item below.

- Robin Hood was a true hero. He helped countless people by getting money, food, and other items from the rich and giving them to the needy.
- Robin Hood was nothing but a thief. He stole the treasures of good, upright citizens and gave the items to lazy good-for-nothings.

Get Ready to Read

Connect to the Reading

What do you think is the best part of being a kid? As you read, think about what the children described in the selection missed out on because they had to work.

Whole Class Discussion Brainstorm with your class a list of reasons children should or should not work. How old should someone be to get a job?

Build Background

The selection you are about to read describes the work of Mary Harris Jones, better known as Mother Jones. Born in Ireland in 1837, Jones and her family immigrated to Canada when she was a girl. When she was in her twenties, Jones moved to the United States, married, and began raising a family. Two tragedies changed the course of her life. In 1867 her husband and four children died in a yellow fever epidemic, and in 1871 she lost her home and all her possessions in the Great Chicago Fire. Forced to support herself, she began working and came into contact with the labor movement. She spent most of the rest of her long life fighting for workers' rights.

Set Purposes for Reading

BIG Question Read "The March of the Mill Children" to learn what life was like for children who worked in mills and marched with Mother Jones in the early 1900s.

Set Your Own Purpose What else would you like to learn from the selection to help you answer the Big Question? Write your own purpose on "The March of the Mill Children" page of Foldable 1.

Literature Online

Interactive Literary Elements Handbook
To review or learn more about the literary elements, go to www.glencoe.com.

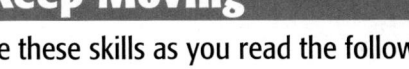

Keep Moving

Use these skills as you read the following selection.

The March of the Mill Children

by Judith Pinkerton Josephson

Practice the Skills

"I love children," Mother Jones once told a reporter. In countless shacks and shanties across the country, she had tied the shoes of children, wiped their noses, hugged them when they cried, scrambled to find food for them, fought for their rights. By the turn of the century, almost two million children under the age of sixteen worked in mills, factories, and mines. Images of the child workers Mother Jones had seen stayed with her—the torn, bleeding fingers of the breaker boys, the mill children living on coffee and stale bread. ▯

In June 1903, Mother Jones went to Philadelphia, Pennsylvania—the heart of a vast textile industry.[1] About one hundred thousand workers from six hundred different mills were on strike[2] there. The strikers wanted their workweek cut from sixty to fifty-five hours, even if it meant lower wages. About a sixth of the strikers were children under sixteen.

Nationwide, eighty thousand children worked in the textile industry. In the South, Mother Jones had seen how dangerous their jobs were. Barefooted little girls and boys reached their tiny hands into the **treacherous** machinery to repair snapped

▯ **Key Reading Skill**

Activating Prior Knowledge
How did your class discussion of child labor help prepare you for the introduction to this selection?

---

1. The **textile industry** includes all the businesses that make and use yarn and fabrics.
2. When workers go on **strike**, they stop working to protest unfair working conditions.

Vocabulary

treacherous (TRECH ur us) *adj.* dangerously untrustworthy

threads or crawled underneath the machinery to oil it. At textile union headquarters, Mother Jones met more of these mill children. Their bodies were bone-thin, with hollow chests. Their shoulders were rounded from long hours spent hunched over the workbenches. Even worse, she saw "some with their hands off, some with the thumb missing, some with their fingers off at the knuckles"—victims of mill accidents. **2**

Pennsylvania, like many other states, had laws that said children under thirteen could not work. But parents often lied about a child's age. Poor families either put their children to work in the mills or starved. Mill owners looked the other way, because child labor was cheap.

Mother Jones asked various newspaper publishers why they didn't write about child labor in Pennsylvania. The publishers told her they couldn't, since owners of the mills also owned stock in their newspapers.[3] "Well, I've got stock in these little children," she said, "and I'll arrange a little publicity."

Mother Jones, now seventy-three, gathered a large group of mill children and their parents. She led them on a one-mile march from Philadelphia's Independence Square to its courthouse lawn. Mother Jones and a few children climbed up on a platform in front of a huge crowd. She held one boy's arm up high so the crowd could see

Practice the Skills

2 Key Literary Element

Tone The author says the children are "bone-thin, with hollow chests." These words show the sympathy and concern she feels for them. The tone might be called compassionate and concerned.

Analyzing the Photo Children work in the spinning room of a South Carolina cotton mill in 1903. What does this picture reveal about working conditions there?

---

3. People who own **stock** in a company own part of the company. Because the mill owners were part owners of the newspapers, they could tell the papers what to print.

Practice the Skills

his **mutilated** hand. "Philadelphia's mansions were built on the broken bones, the quivering hearts,[4] and drooping heads of these children," she said. She lifted another child in her arms so the crowd could see how thin he was.

Mother Jones looked directly at the city officials standing at the open windows across the street. "Some day the workers will take possession of your city hall, and when we do, no child will be sacrificed on the altar of profit."[5] Unmoved, the officials quickly closed their windows.

Local newspapers and some New York newspapers covered the event. How, Mother Jones wondered, could she draw national attention to the evils of child labor? Philadelphia's famous Liberty Bell, currently on a national tour and drawing huge crowds, gave her an idea. She and the textile union leaders would stage their own tour. They would march the mill children all the way to the president of the United States— Theodore Roosevelt. Mother Jones wanted the president to get Congress to pass a law that would take children out of the mills, mines, and factories, and put them in school. **3**

When Mother Jones asked parents for permission to take their children with her, many hesitated. The march from Philadelphia to Sagamore Hill—the president's seaside mansion on Long Island near New York City—would cover 125 miles. It would be a difficult journey. But finally, the parents agreed. Many decided to come along on the march. Other striking men and women offered their help, too.

On July 7, 1903, nearly three hundred men, women, and children—followed by four wagons with supplies—began the long march. Newspapers carried daily reports of the march, calling the group "Mother Jones's Industrial Army," or "Mother Jones's Crusaders." The army was led by a fife-and-drum corps[6] of three children dressed in Revolutionary War uniforms. Mother Jones wore her familiar, lace-fringed black dress. The marchers sang and carried flags, banners, and

3 | **Key Reading Skill**

Activating Prior Knowledge
Have you seen other protest marches in movies or on TV? How does your knowledge of them help you understand the march described here?

---

4. When something is *quivering,* it is shaking. Mother Jones is describing the children as being really scared.

5. In a religious *sacrifice,* an animal is killed on an *altar.* Mother Jones is saying that she will not allow children to be harmed, or sacrificed, just so that people can make a lot of money.

6. This *fife-and-drum corps* was a small marching band that played drums and flutes.

Vocabulary

mutilated (MYOO tih lay tid) *adj.* damaged in a way that cannot be repaired

placards that read "We Want to Go to School!" "We Want Time to Play." "Prosperity Is Here, Where Is Ours?" "55 Hours or Nothing." "We Only Ask for Justice." "More School, Less Hospitals." **4**

The temperature rose into the nineties. The roads were dusty, the children's shoes full of holes. Many of the young girls returned home. Some of the marchers walked only as far as the outskirts of Philadelphia. For the hundred or so marchers who remained, this trip was an adventure in spite of the heat. They bathed and swam in brooks and rivers. Each of them carried a knapsack with a knife, fork, tin cup, and plate inside. Mother Jones took a huge pot for cooking meals on the way. Mother Jones also took along costumes, makeup, and jewelry so the children could stop in towns along the route and put on plays about the struggles of textile workers. The fife-and-drum corps gave concerts and passed the hat.

Practice the Skills

4 | **English Language Coach**

Context Clues: Category
Look at the words that come before **placards.** What do you think a *placard* is?

Analyzing the Photo Mother Jones's march from Philadelphia to New York began on July 7, 1903. Can you draw any conclusions about Mother Jones from her posture and facial expression in this photo?

The March of the Mill Children **69**

Practice the Skills

People listened and donated money. Farmers met the marchers with wagonloads of fruits, vegetables, and clothes. Railroad engineers stopped their trains and gave them free rides. Hotel owners served free meals.

On July 10, the marchers camped across the Delaware River from Trenton, New Jersey. They had traveled about forty miles in three days. At first, police told the group they couldn't enter the city. Trenton mill owners didn't want any trouble. But Mother Jones invited the policemen to stay for lunch. The children gathered around the cooking pot with their tin plates and cups. The policemen smiled, talked kindly to them, then allowed them to cross the bridge into Trenton. There Mother Jones spoke to a crowd of five thousand people. That night, the policemen's wives took the children into their homes, fed them, and packed them lunches for the next day's march.

By now, many of the children were growing weak. More returned home. Some adults on the march grumbled that Mother Jones just wanted people to notice *her*. They complained to reporters that Mother Jones often stayed in hotels while the marchers camped in hot, soggy tents filled with whining mosquitoes. **5** Sometimes Mother Jones did stay in hotels, because she went ahead of the marchers to arrange for lodging and food in upcoming towns and to get publicity for the march.

As the remaining marchers pushed on to Princeton, New Jersey, a thunderstorm struck. Mother Jones and her army camped on the grounds of former President Grover Cleveland's estate. The Clevelands were away, and the caretaker let Mother Jones use the big, cool barn for a **dormitory.**

Mother Jones got permission from the mayor of Princeton to speak opposite the campus of Princeton University. Her topic: higher education. She spoke to a large crowd of professors, students, and residents. Pointing to one ten-year-old boy, James Ashworth, she said, "Here's a textbook on economics." The boy's body was stooped from carrying seventy-five-pound bundles of yarn. "He gets three dollars a week and his sister, who is fourteen, gets six dollars. They work in a carpet factory ten hours a day while the children

5 **Key Literary Element**

Tone What is the tone of the first few sentences of this paragraph? Think about the following words, which appear in the paragraph. Then describe the tone.

- "grumbled"
- "complained"
- "hot, soggy tents"
- "whining mosquitoes"

Vocabulary

dormitory (DOR mih tor ee) *n.* a building with rooms for people to sleep in

of the rich are getting their higher education." Her piercing glance swept over the students in the crowd.

Mother Jones talked about children who could not read or write because they spent ten hours a day in Pennsylvania's silk mills. Those who hired these child workers used "the hands and feet of little children so they might buy automobiles for their wives and police dogs for their daughters to talk French to." She accused the mill owners of taking "babies almost from the cradle." **6**

The next night, the marchers slept on the banks of the Delaware River. In every town, Mother Jones drew on what she did best—speaking—to gather support for her cause. One reporter wrote, "Mother Jones makes other speakers sound like tin cans."

Battling heat, rain, and swarms of mosquitoes at night, the marchers arrived in Elizabeth. Socialist party members helped house and feed the weary adults and children. The next morning, two businessmen gave Mother Jones her first car ride. She was delighted with this new "contraption."[7]

On July 15, Mother Jones wrote a letter to President Roosevelt. She told him how these poor mill children lived, appealed to him as a father, and asked him to meet with her and the children. President Roosevelt did not answer Mother Jones's letter. Instead, he assigned secret service officers to watch her. They thought she might be a threat to the president. That made her furious.

On July 24, after more than two weeks on the road, the marchers reached New York City. By now, just twenty marchers remained. One of them was Eddie Dunphy, a child whose job was to sit on a high stool eleven hours a day handing thread to another worker. For this he was paid three dollars a week. Mother Jones talked about Eddie and about Gussie Rangnew, a child who packed stockings in a factory. She too worked eleven hours a day for pennies.

---

7. A ***contraption*** is a mechanical device.

Practice the Skills

6 **Key Literary Element**

Tone How would you describe Mother Jones's tone? Which words and phrases help you identify this tone?

At one meeting, a crowd of thirty thousand gathered. "We are quietly marching toward the president's home," she told the people. "I believe he can do something for these children, although the press declares he cannot."

One man wanted the children to have some fun while they were in New York City. Frank Bostick owned the wild animal show at Coney Island, an amusement park and resort. He invited the mill children to spend a day at the park. The children swam in the ocean and played along the beach.

When Frank Bostick's wild animal show ended that night, he let Mother Jones speak to the crowd that had attended. To add drama, she had some of the children crawl inside the empty cages. The smells of sawdust and animals hung in the air. But instead of lions and tigers, the cages held children. The children gripped the iron bars and solemnly stared out at the crowd while Mother Jones spoke. **7**

Practice the Skills

7 **Key Reading Skill**

Activating Prior Knowledge
Have you ever seen an animal in a cage? How did it make you feel about the animal? Use your experience to understand why Mother Jones asked the children to crawl into the cages. What effect did she hope it would have on the crowd?

Analyzing the Photo Not tall enough to operate these looms from the ground, two young boys climb the machines to do their jobs. What do you notice about the boy in the foreground? Why might this job be particularly risky for him?

"We want President Roosevelt to hear the wail of the children who never have a chance to go to school, but work eleven and twelve hours a day in the textile mills of Pennsylvania," she said, "who weave the carpets that he and you walk upon; and the lace curtains in your windows, and the clothes of the people."

She continued, "In Georgia where children work day and night in the cotton mills they have just passed a bill to protect songbirds. What about the little children from whom all song is gone?" After Mother Jones finished speaking, the crowd sat in stunned silence. In the distance, a lone lion roared.

The grueling walk had taken almost three weeks. Mother Jones had written the president twice with no answer. On July 29, she took three young boys to Sagamore Hill, where the president was staying. But the secret service stopped them at the mansion's gates. The president would not see them.

The group returned to New York City. Discouraged, Mother Jones reported her failure to the newspapers. Most of the marchers decided to return home. She stayed on briefly with the three children. Once more, she wrote President Roosevelt: "The child of today is the man or woman of tomorrow. . . . I have with me three children who have walked one hundred miles. . . . If you decide to see these children, I will bring them before you at any time you may set."

The president's secretary replied that the president felt that child labor was a problem for individual states to solve. "He is a brave guy when he wants to take a gun out and fight other grown people," said Mother Jones in disgust, "but when those children went to him, he could not see them."

In early August, Mother Jones finally took the last three children home. Soon after, the textile workers gave up and ended their strike. Adults and children went back to work, their working conditions unchanged.

Though she had not met with the president, Mother Jones had drawn the attention of the nation to the problem of child labor. She became even more of a national figure. Within a few years, Pennsylvania, New York, New Jersey, and other states did pass tougher child labor laws. The federal government finally passed a child labor law (part of the Fair Labor Standards Act) in 1938—thirty-five years after the march of the mill children. 8 ○

Practice the Skills

8 **BIG Question**

Was it interesting to learn about Mother Jones and the mill children? Explain. Write your answer on "The March of the Mill Children" page of Foldable 1. Your response will help you complete the Unit Challenge later.

After You Read

The March of the Mill Children

Answering the BIG Question

1. What did you get out of reading "The March of the Mill Children"? List at least three facts about Mother Jones, the labor movement, or child labor that you learned by reading the selection.

2. **Recall** Child labor laws of Mother Jones's time banned children under the age of thirteen from working. Why did parents sometimes break these laws and allow their children to work?

   TIP Right There The answer is in the text.

3. **Summarize** In a sentence or two, sum up the actions that Mother Jones took to protest child labor.

   TIP Think and Search The answer is in the text but not in one place.

Critical Thinking

4. **Compare and Contrast** How are working conditions different today from what they were in Mother Jones's day?

   TIP Author and Me You will find the answer in the text, but you must also use your own knowledge.

5. **Evaluate** Do you think Mother Jones should have put children in animal cages? Explain your answer.

   TIP On My Own You must use your own knowledge and experience to answer the question.

6. **Evaluate** Do you think the march was a failure or a success? Why?

   TIP Author and Me You will find the answer in the text, but you must also use your own knowledge.

Write About Your Reading

Persuasive Poster Mother Jones believed in a cause; she wanted child labor to end. What cause do you believe in? Create a poster asking people to march to support a cause. Include an appropriate picture. Make sure your poster has the following information:

- the name of the cause
- the ways in which the march will help the cause
- the time and location to meet before the start of the march
- the route of the march—where the march will start and finish

NY English Language Arts Core Curriculum
(pp. 74–75)

R1b Apply thinking skills to interpret data from informational texts. **LC W7** Compose arguments to support points of view. **LC R12** Combine multiple strategies to enhance comprehension. **R2e** Recognize how the author's use of language creates images or feelings. **Core R4** Determine the meaning of unfamiliar words by using context clues. **Core W8** Use correct grammatical construction in parts of speech (pronouns).

For a complete description of the standards, see p. NY11.

Skills Review

Key Reading Skill: Activating Prior Knowledge

7. What did you already know about child labor before you read the selection? How did this information help you understand the selection?

Key Literary Element: Tone

8. How would you describe the overall tone of "The March of the Mill Children"? Quote sentences from the selection to support your answer.

Vocabulary Check

Fill in the blank with the correct vocabulary word.

treacherous   mutilated   dormitory

9. Over one hundred students sleep in the _____ at my brother's college.

10. The sharp turn in the road is a _____ place to stop and change a tire.

11. The child's _____ hand horrified the crowd.

12. Academic Vocabulary What **prior** knowledge of child labor conditions made Mother Jones decide to go on her march?

13. English Language Coach Copy the following sentence. Circle the context clues you can use to infer the meaning of the underlined word.

There were outbreaks of the flu, yellow fever, chicken pox, and <u>diphtheria</u>.

Web Activities For eFlashcards, Selection Quick Checks, and other Web activities, go to www.glencoe.com.

Grammar Link: Reflexive and Intensive Pronouns

Reflexive and Intensive Pronouns	
Singular	**Plural**
myself, yourself, himself, herself, itself	ourselves, yourselves, themselves

Reflexive pronouns serve a special purpose. All pronouns refer back to another noun or pronoun, but we use reflexive pronouns when a pronoun that is *not possessive* refers back to the subject. Instead of "I pinched me," we say "I pinched myself." The pinched one *reflects* the pincher, so we use a reflexive pronoun.

- The machine stopped itself.

- Maria bought herself flowers.

Intensive pronouns have the same form as reflexive pronouns, but their purpose is to emphasize the subject.

- The principal herself introduced the speaker.

  (The intensive pronoun *herself* emphasizes that it was not just anyone who did the introduction. It was the principal.)

Look Out! These are not standard words: *theirselves, hisself.* Never use them.

Grammar Practice

Copy each sentence. Circle the correct pronoun.

14. Jake (himself, hisself) sent (her, herself) the letter.

15. They gave us the gift (themselves, theirselves).

16. I (my, myself) would rather trade with (her, herself).

17. Juan and (I, myself) went to the movies.

18. I reminded my little brother to wash (himself, hisself) before going to bed.

19. I got (me, myself) a new pair of boots yesterday.

20. Sara told her guests to help (themselves, theirselves) to chips and soda.

Writing Application Look back at your Write About Your Reading activity. Check to make sure that you used all pronouns correctly.

Before You Read

Filling Out the Application *and* Exploring Careers

Meet the Authors

Debby Hobgood and Cindy Pervola wrote "Filling Out the Application" as part of their book *How To Get A Job If You're A Teenager.* Hobgood has years of experience hiring young people for various companies. Pervola is a freelance writer and a counselor who works with teens.

The second selection, "Exploring Careers," comes from the *Young Person's Occupational Outlook Handbook,* published by JIST Works. It is based on information from the United States Department of Labor.

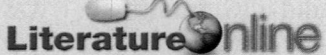

Author Search For more about Debby Hobgood and Cindy Pervola, go to www.glencoe.com.

Vocabulary Preview

prone (prohn) *adj.* likely to act or be a certain way **(p. 78)** *John never studies vocabulary, so he is prone to making spelling errors.*

residences (REZ uh dun suz) *n.* places where one lives **(p. 79)** *Junette lives with her mother during the week and her father on the weekend; she has two residences.*

Partner Work With a classmate, write a paragraph in which you correctly use the vocabulary words.

English Language Coach

Context Clues: Direct Definitions In articles that contain technical language that is specific to a particular field, authors sometimes define words for you directly. These words may be highlighted in boldface, or darker, type. Suppose, for example, you run across the following passage in a manual for Internet users. To signal that *bulletin board system* will be defined, the authors put it in boldface and then define it.

Internet Users' Handbook

A **bulletin board system** is an Internet function that allows users to carry on discussions, upload and download files, and post announcements without users being online at the same time.

Partner Talk With a classmate, quickly look over a chapter from a textbook you use for another class. Then answer the following questions:
- How many words are directly defined for you?
- Are these words in boldface type, or is a different type of signal used to indicate defined words?
- If a different type of signal is used, what is it?

NY English Language Arts Core Curriculum (pp. 76–89)

Core R4 Determine the meaning of unfamiliar words by using context clues. **LC R12** Combine multiple strategies to enhance comprehension. **LC R13** Use text structure to aid comprehension and response.

For a complete description of the standards, see p. NY11.

Skills Preview

Key Reading Skill: Activating Prior Knowledge

Before you read the selections, look at each title. Think about what you already know about these topics:

- ways to look for a job
- guidelines for filling out a job application
- the work of television and movie camera operators and editors
- the work of firefighters, emergency medical technicians, and paramedics

Whole Class Discussion As a class, discuss what jobs you might like to hold in the future and how you would apply for them. Talk about what you'd like to learn from the selections.

Text Element: Text Features

Text features are visual clues that help readers find and understand information. Common text features include the following elements:

- titles and subheads
- graphic aids such as charts and graphs
- visual aids such as maps and photographs
- numbered or bulleted lists
- boldface type and italic type

The selections you are about to read contain many of these text features. As you read, look for text features and ask yourself, *How does this feature help me find or understand the information in this article?*

Partner Work With a classmate, look over the selection that begins on the next page. In your Learner's Notebook, list all the text features used in the selection.

Interactive Literary Elements Handbook
To review or learn more about the literary elements, go to www.glencoe.com.

Get Ready to Read

Connect to the Reading

What kinds of application forms have you filled out during the past few years? An application for a library card? An application to take part in a school activity? Something else? Think about the forms.

Whole Class Discussion Together as a class, list the kinds of application forms that you have had experience filling out. What parts of each application, if any, did you find tricky to complete? Why?

Build Background

- Most employers require a person interested in working for them to fill out a job application. This form gives the employer personal and work information about the job applicant. Employers use this information to decide whether to interview the applicant.

- Minimum wage is an hourly rate of pay that is set by the federal government. In 2005 the minimum wage was $5.15 per hour. All companies have to pay at least this amount to their employees.

- Many laws protect children in the workplace. The legal age to get a job in most states is between 14 and 16 years of age. Some states require a person who is under 18 years of age to get a work permit.

Set Purposes for Reading

BIG Question Read to learn how to fill out a job application correctly and to learn about various careers.

Set Your Own Purpose What else would you like to learn from the selection to help you answer the Big Question? Write your own purpose on the "Filling Out the Application" and "Exploring Careers" page of Foldable 1.

Keep Moving

Use these skills as you read "Filling Out the Application" and "Exploring Careers."

INFORMATIONAL TEXT
REFERENCE BOOK
*How to Get a Job
If You're a Teenager*

Filling Out the Application

by Cindy Pervola and Debby Hobgood

The two most important things to keep in mind when filling out an application are to be **honest** and to fill it out **completely.** An application is a legal document, and you could get fired for lying on your application. **1**

Employers do not like to see any blank spaces on applications they receive. Every bit of information you can give them about yourself is extremely helpful, so do not leave any questions unanswered.

Complete the application in pen with black or blue ink and get a dictionary or use a spell checker to avoid misspelling. Print neatly and take your time. A sloppy application with words crossed out or misspelled turns off an employer right away, and your application will end up at the bottom of the stack. (You might even ask for two applications if you're **prone** to making mistakes.)

The following is a guide to filling out a typical application. Every application is a little different but all the basic information is the same.

Practice the Skills

1 **Key Reading Skill**

Activating Prior Knowledge
How might remembering applications you've filled out be helpful in understanding this selection?

Vocabulary

prone (prohn) *adj.* likely to act or be a certain way

Date: Write today's date. **2**

Name: Your full name as it appears on your birth certificate or driver's license. If you go by a nickname, you can put your nickname in parenthesis. For example, you can write, Jacob (Jake) Williams, if you wish to be called Jake.

Social Security Number: If you do not have a social security number, you can find out how to apply for one by calling 1-800-772-1213. You can also look in the phone book for Social Security under "United States Government" for an office close to you. Do not apply for a job until you have a Social Security Number.

- **SSN:** abbreviation for Social Security Number.

Address: Employers want your current address. For example, if you are in college, use your college address. Use your permanent address (or home address) for your tax information.

Telephone number: Write in your home telephone number. Be sure to include a second number if you have two **residences.** For instance, if your parents are divorced and you spend time with both of them, write in both telephone numbers.

- **applicant:** person applying for a job.

Under 18? The employer wants to know if you will need a work permit. If you are over 18, you don't need a work permit. If you're under 18, you might need one, but it varies with each state. A work permit tells the employer how many hours a day and a week you are allowed to work. Your high school will issue your work permit or tell you how to get one.

Are you a U.S. citizen? If you are not a U.S. citizen, the employer will need to see your alien card when you are hired.

Practice the Skills

2 **Text Element**

Text Features Why do you think the authors put the word *date* in darker type?

Vocabulary

residences (REZ uh dun suz) *n.* places where one lives

- **alien:** a person who is from another country.

Position applied for (or desired): They want to know if you are applying for a sales position, stock person, waiter/waitress, bus person, dishwasher, etc. If you are interested in anything that they have open, it's okay to put "any position available."

Full time, part time, seasonal: They want to know how many hours a week you would prefer to work. Full-time is usually 30–40 hours a week and part time is usually 0–30 hours per week. This will vary with each company. Seasonal refers to temporary work for under 90 days during a certain time of year, usually summer and winter holiday. **3**

Salary desired (or rate of pay requested): Put "minimum wage" if this is your first job. If you have worked before, put the rate of pay when you left your last job. If you feel you were underpaid at your last job or you need extra pay because you will need to use public transportation or have other expenses, add 5%–10% more per hour. Also, be sure you're ready to tell them why you feel you deserve that amount.

"I asked for $1 over minimum wage because I had to take the bus. I live about 45 minutes away but I needed full-time work for the summer and I said I could work any day of the week as long as the buses were running. They needed somebody with experience that could work any time, so they gave me more than minimum wage, but not as much as I requested."
—Maria, age 18.

Date available to start work: If you can start working tomorrow, write that date. If you're applying for a seasonal job, put in the date when you can start working. For example, if you are applying for a summer job but don't get out of school for three weeks, write in the date after the last day of school when you can actually begin working. Be specific.

Availability: Here, the employer wants to know specifically when you can work each day of the week. It doesn't necessarily mean that you will be scheduled to work at those

Practice the Skills

3 **Key Reading Skill**

Activating Prior Knowledge
Think of jobs that are seasonal. What jobs depend on the weather? What jobs last only through a holiday season, such as December?

times every day. It lets the employer know when or if you could work on those days, if needed.

It is very frustrating for employers when new-hires change their availability. One of the reasons you may have been hired was because you could work, say, on Saturdays. If after a month, you suddenly cannot work on Saturdays anymore, there's a good chance your employer will tell you they no longer need you. You may be back to square one, looking for a job again. So, be accurate as to which days and times you are available to work. ▉

The following chart can help you determine your availability. For example, if Jake gets out of school at 2 p.m., has basketball practice every Monday and Wednesday afternoons from 3–5 p.m., has to babysit his little brother every Saturday, and has to be home no later than 10:30 p.m., his availability worksheet would look like this:

Practice the Skills

4 **Reviewing Skills**

Connecting How do you feel when you try to make plans with someone who is always busy? Why do you think an employer needs to know your availability?

Jake's availability worksheet

	Sunday	Monday	Tuesday	Wednesday	Thursday	Friday	Saturday
7 am		School	School	School	School	School	X
8 am		"	"	"	"	"	X
9 am		"	"	"	"	"	X
10 am		"	"	"	"	"	X
11 am	Open	"	"	"	"	"	Not
12 pm	anytime	"	"	"	"	"	available
1 pm	all day	"	"	"	"	"	anytime
2 pm	7 am–10 pm	School ends	School ends	School ends	School ends	School ends	Saturdays
3 pm		Basketball		Basketball			X
4 pm		till		till			X
5 pm		5 pm		5 pm			X
6 pm							X
7 pm							X
8 pm							X
9 pm							
10 pm							

This worksheet makes it easy to see when Jake is available to work.

On the application, Jake's availability would look like this (N/A means not available):

Sunday	Monday	Tuesday	Wednesday	Thursday	Friday	Saturday
anytime	6–10	3–10	6–10	3–10	3–10	N/A

"I had to give up basketball to get my job at the computer store. I couldn't do it all. I think I made the right choice."
—Shane, age 17.

Work experience: List the jobs you have had in the past, beginning with your most recent position. Fill this out **completely.** You might need to make some phone calls or look in the phone book to get the information. You will need to know the date you started and ended those jobs, your supervisors' names, the addresses and telephone numbers of the places of business, your job title and duties, your starting and ending salary and the reason for leaving. **5**

Good Idea Don't forget jobs like babysitting, yard work, odd jobs, volunteer work and community service in this section. All that counts as work experience, too.

Dos and Don'ts . . .

There may be a section titled 'reason for leaving.' Do **not** leave this section blank. Be honest about why you left your last job and always try to turn it into something positive.

- **terminated:** to be let go from or fired from a job.

Do write: "I was <u>terminated</u> because I was late too often, but I have learned from this experience and now I make sure I'm at work five minutes before I'm scheduled to work." **6**
Don't write: "I got fired because I was late all the time."

Do write: "I want to work for a company that works as a team."
Don't write: "I didn't get along with my boss."

Do write: "I'm looking for a company with better opportunities."
Don't write: "I need more money."

Do write: "I needed more hours and they were only able to give me 10 hours a week."
Don't write: "I quit."

Practice the Skills

5 **Key Reading Skill**

Activating Prior Knowledge
What kinds of jobs have you had or work have you done for others? What information about these experiences would you add to a job application?

6 **English Language Coach**

Context Clues: Direct Definition What does **terminated** mean? Look at the definition above the word to understand its meaning. Then define it.

Do write: "I had a hard time getting to work but I am now applying to businesses within walking distance from my house."
Don't write: "Transportation problem."

Do write: "I had too many conflicts with school. I have learned to manage my time better and now I only work on weekends."
Don't write: "Left because of school."

Do write: "I had some family (or personal) problems that are now resolved."
Don't write: "Family problems."
or "Personal problems." **7**

May we contact your current employer? If you are working and you do not want your current employer to know you are looking for another job, put "no." But if the reason you are leaving is that you need more hours or better pay, you might want to let your current employer know that. Maybe they cannot give you any more hours or they won't be able to give you a raise for another six months. If that's the case, they'll probably understand your desire to look for another job and appreciate that you let them know you are leaving. It will give them time to look for a replacement for you.

"I was scared to tell my boss I was giving my two week notice. I thought he'd get mad. He didn't though. He asked if I was tired of taking orders and if I wanted to try making pizzas, instead. I got a raise, too."
—Michelle, age 17.

References: A reference is an adult, other than a relative, who knows you well and can say what kind of worker you are. A reference is not a friend, a relative or previous employer that

Practice the Skills

7 **Reviewing Skill**

Connecting Have you ever had to quit a job? How could you explain your reason for quitting in a positive way?

Analyzing the Photo Why might the young man in this photograph make a good impression on a potential employer?

you have already listed on the application. It can be an adult friend of the family, a teacher, a coach, a neighbor or religious leader. You will need to call and ask if you can use them as a reference on your job application before you name them, though. A good reference can get you the job, so it is a good idea to be careful who you ask.

"I put a friend of my Mom's down as a reference, but I didn't let her know. When they called her, she told them she had never heard of me. She couldn't think of any adults she knew named Monica. She felt really bad after she realized they were asking about me. I won't do that again."
—Monica, age 18.

Education: Be specific and fill this out completely. List your high school(s) and college(s) with their addresses and the number of years you have completed. Make sure you include any additional training, such as computer classes, first aid training, swimming instruction, foreign language, etc.

Analyzing the Photo The woman in this photograph smiles and makes eye contact with her interviewer. How do these actions show that she is confident?

Have you ever been convicted of a crime?[1] It might also say "Have you ever been convicted of a felony?" They are asking if you have been convicted of more serious crimes here, such as murder, assault, battery or rape. This does not refer to parking tickets or other minor traffic offenses.

The open-ended question: This is a question that cannot be answered with a "yes" or "no." It is usually the last question on the application before your signature and will be worded in different ways: **8**

- List any additional information you would like us to consider.

- Detail outstanding features of your last job.

8 **Key Reading Skill**

Activating Prior Knowledge
Think of an open-ended question you've answered recently for school. (Hint: Look at the *Big Questions* and the *responding* questions.) Can you think of any others, either from this book or another subject?

---

1. To be **convicted** of a crime is to be found guilty.

- Why do you want to work for our company?

- What strengths would you bring to our company?

- Indicate any skills or experience which you believe reflect on your capability to perform . . .

- List any hobbies or special interests you have.

- Applicant comments.

They are all looking for the same thing. **They want to know something about you.** They want you to tell them something about yourself that will make them want to hire you. (They will also be looking to see if you can write a complete sentence.) Be truthful, enthusiastic, positive and brag about yourself. Tell them what you are and not what you aren't. Tell them what you have accomplished. Think of words that best describe you and use those, but be honest about yourself. Remember that the employer will probably check your references.

"When I applied at the grocery store, I wrote that I was a hard worker and dependable. I also wrote that I had handled money in my last job and dealt with customers. I think I got the job because I said I was dependable. People call in sick here all the time."
—Eric, age 16.

When You're Done

Once you have completed the application and signed it, you may then take it back to the employer, following the same dress code you did when you obtained the application. The employer might want to do the interview when you return the application, so be prepared. 🔟 ○

Practice the Skills

🔟 **BIG Question**

What have you learned from this article that will help you apply for a job with confidence? Write your answer on the "Filling Out the Application" page of Foldable 1. Your response will help you complete the Unit Challenge later.

INFORMATIONAL TEXT
HANDBOOK
Young Person's Occupational Outlook Handbook

Exploring Careers

Television, Video & Motion Picture Camera Operators & Editors

On the Job [10]

Camera operators work behind the scenes on TV shows, documentaries,[1] motion pictures, and industrial films.

Visual Vocabulary
Scaffolding is a raised wooden frame on which workers sit or stand when doing things at heights above the ground.

They shoot the film you see on screen, sometimes from high up on scaffolding or flat on their bellies on the ground. They may work long, irregular hours in places all over the world. Film editors look at the hundreds of hours worth of film shot for a project and decide which scenes to include and which to cut.

Subjects to Study

English, journalism, photography, art, creative writing, business, accounting [11]

Discover More

Use a digital camcorder to make your own movie. These cameras let you load your movie onto a computer and then alter the images in countless ways. Give your leading lady green hair, drop in a few aliens, and you've got the ultimate in science fiction!

---

1. **Documentaries** are videos or films about real people and events.

Practice the Skills

[10] **Text Element**

Text Features How might the red subheads help you find information in the selection?

[11] **Key Reading Skill**

Activating Prior Knowledge What do you already know about the subjects listed under "Subjects to Study"? How could studying these subjects help a camera operator do his or her job?

Related Jobs

Artists and related workers, broadcast and sound engineering technicians and radio operators, designers, photographers

Something Extra

For a good view of what's possible in filmmaking today, rent the movie *Forrest Gump.* Among other tricks, the filmmakers spliced and altered vintage film to show their hero, Tom Hanks, shaking hands with John F. Kennedy, more than 30 years after Kennedy's death.

Education & Training

Short-term OJT to voc/tech[2] training

Earnings

$$$$

Job Outlook

Average increase[3]

Firefighting Occupations 🔢

On the Job

Firefighters protect people from the dangers of fires. They must stay physically fit and strong. At the scene of a fire, they rescue victims, perform emergency medical aid, and operate and maintain equipment. During their shifts, firefighters live at the fire station. Most work 50 hours a week or more. Forest firefighters may parachute into a fire area to put out fires and dig a fire line. Firefighting is one of the most dangerous jobs in the U.S. economy.

Subjects to Study

Physical science, chemistry, driver's education, physical education

Analyzing the Image A career in film editing requires technical and creative know-how. How might the men here use both types of skills?

🔢 **Key Reading Skill**

Activating Prior Knowledge List some facts that you already know about firefighters.

---

2. **OJT** is short for on-the-job training; **voc/tech,** vocational/technical.

3. **Average increase** means that this field should grow at an average rate.

Discover More

Tour the fire station in your neighborhood or at your local airport. Ask the firefighters about their jobs, the training they receive, and the risks of the job.

Related Jobs

Emergency medical technicians and paramedics, police and detectives

Something Extra

Firefighters who battle wildfires are a special breed. During the hot, dry months of late summer, they travel from state to state, helping local firefighters battle forest fires. They may jump from airplanes into a fire zone to dig fire lines. If a fire travels too quickly and they get trapped, they drop to the ground and cover themselves with a special fireproofed tent. They wait until the fire has passed over them, get up, and keep on fighting the flames. **13**

Education & Training

Voc/tech training

Earnings

$$$$–$$$$$

Job Outlook

Average increase

Emergency Medical Technicians & Paramedics

On the Job

Emergency medical technicians (EMTs) and paramedics drive ambulances and give emergency medical care. They determine a patient's medical condition at the scene, stabilize[4]

---

4. When an EMT **stabilizes** a patient, he or she makes sure that the patient is well enough to travel in an ambulance.

Practice the Skills

13 | **Reviewing Skills**

Connecting When you think of firefighters, what images come to mind? Did reading this description of the job change how you think about firefighting as a career? Explain.

Firefighters may have to run—or jump!— into fires like this one. They risk their lives to help other people.

the patient, then drive him or her to the hospital. They work outdoors in all kinds of weather, and the work can be very stressful. Some patients may become violent, and EMTs may be exposed to diseases. They work for fire departments, hospitals, and private ambulance services.

Subjects to Study

Driver's education, health, biology, chemistry, anatomy, English, foreign languages

Discover More

Check with the Red Cross in your area to register for a first-aid or CPR course. You can learn how to save another person's life and be helpful in different kinds of emergencies.

Related Jobs

Air traffic controllers, firefighting occupations, physician assistants, police and detectives, registered nurses

Something Extra

What's a typical day like for an EMT? There is no such thing! Because EMTs respond to emergencies, their jobs are never the same from day to day. They might be the first on the scene of a car accident in the morning, revive a heart attack victim at lunch, and deliver a baby in a taxicab by dinner. EMTs must be able to remain calm in any situation—because they never know what's around the next corner.

Education & Training

Voc/tech training

Earnings

$$$

Job Outlook

Above-average increase **14** ○

Practice the Skills

14 **BIG Question**

What did you learn about careers that you didn't know before you read this article? Write your answer on the "Filling Out the Application" and "Exploring Careers" page of Foldable 1. Your response will help you complete the Unit Challenge later.

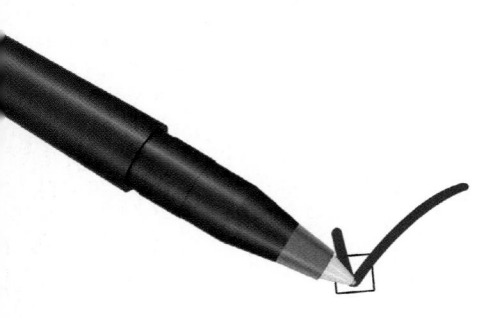

After You Read

Filling Out the Application *and* Exploring Careers

Answering the

1. How can you use what you learned from reading "Filling Out the Application" to help yourself get a job? How can you use what you learned from "Exploring Careers" to decide what career you want?

2. **Recall** Who would be a good reference to list on a job application?
   TIP **Right There** The answer is found in the text.

3. **Recall** Describe what an "open-ended question" is.
   TIP **Right There** The answer is found in the text.

Critical Thinking

4. **Apply** Are you interested in any of the careers described in "Exploring Careers"? Why? If your answer is no, describe a career that you are interested in.
   TIP **On My Own** Answer from your own ideas or experience.

5. **Evaluate** Do you feel ready to apply for a job after reading the selections? What more would you like to know?
   TIP **Author and Me** The answer is in the text, but you must also use your own knowledge.

6. **Infer** Why would a television camera operator need to study accounting? Why would a firefighter need to study chemistry? Why would a paramedic want to study foreign languages?
   TIP **Author and Me** The answer is in the text, but you must also use your own knowledge.

Talk About Your Reading

Interview Imagine that you could apply for your dream job. Tell your partner what the job is, and have him or her interview you for the position. Then switch roles and interview your partner. Use questions that could be found on a job application. Ask and answer at least five questions.

NY English Language Arts Core Curriculum
(pp. 90–91)

R1b Apply thinking skills to interpret data from informational texts. **LC S1** Speak to share responses to a variety of texts. **LC R12** Combine multiple strategies to enhance comprehension. **LC R13** Use text structure to aid comprehension and response. **Core R4** Determine the meaning of unfamiliar words by using context clues. **Core W8** Use correct grammatical construction in parts of speech (pronouns).

For a complete description of the standards, see p. NY11.

Skills Review

Key Reading Skill: Activating Prior Knowledge

7. List two things you already knew about job applications and two things you already knew about the careers described in "Exploring Careers." How did your prior knowledge help you understand the new information you learned?

Text Element: Text Features

8. Which text features did you find the most helpful when you were reading the selection? Why?

Reviewing Skills: Connecting

9. Think of the people you know who have interesting careers. After reading "Exploring Careers," what questions would you ask them about their jobs?

Vocabulary Check

Write *true* if the sentence is true or *false* if it is false.

10. If someone is <u>prone</u> to making grammar mistakes, he or she almost never makes any grammar errors when writing.

11. A family with many <u>residences</u> has more than one home.

12. **English Language Coach** Figure out the meaning of the underlined word by using contrast clues. Write your definition for the word.

The crowd at the basketball game fell silent as Jill shot a three-pointer with less than a second to go. But, as the ball swished through the hoop, <u>pandemonium</u> broke out among the crowd.

Web Activities For eFlashcards, Selection Quick Checks, and other Web activities, go to www.glencoe.com.

Grammar Link: Indefinite Pronouns and Agreement

An **indefinite pronoun** does *not* refer to a particular person, place, thing, or idea. Use indefinite pronouns to speak in general terms.

Examples of Singular Indefinite Pronouns

• Is <u>anyone</u> going to the library today?

• Is <u>everybody</u> here?

Examples of Plural Indefinite Pronouns

• <u>Both</u> were mistaken.

• <u>Few</u> have climbed Mount Everest to its top.

Examples of Indefinite Pronouns That Can Be Singular or Plural

• Is <u>some</u> left?

• <u>Most</u> are on the shelf, but <u>some</u> are on the table.

Look Out! Do not use plural pronouns to refer to singular indefinite pronouns. Pronouns must agree in number with their antecedents.

Wrong: <u>Nobody</u> remembered to bring <u>their</u> book. (The pronouns do not agree in number. *Nobody* is singular; *their* is plural.)

Right: <u>Nobody</u> remembered to bring <u>his or her</u> book. (Note that the pronouns agree in number. *Nobody* is singular and so are *his* and *her.*)

Grammar Practice

Copy the following paragraph on a separate sheet of paper. Find and fix the three agreement errors.

I judge people by their behavior, not by their clothes, grades, or anything else. If somebody is kind and friendly, I usually like them. On the other hand, if a person is mean to me, I avoid them. Nobody wants their feelings hurt, and I am no exception.

Autobiographical Sketch
Revising, Editing, and Presenting

ASSIGNMENT Write an autobiographical sketch

Purpose: To describe an experience you've had that shaped your feelings about reading

Audience: Your teacher and your classmates

Revising Rubric

Your revised sketch should have these elements:

• a clear focus
• interesting details and descriptions
• a clear point of view
• a logical organization
• a strong voice

NY English Language Arts Core Curriculum (pp. 92–95)

Core W5 Use the writing process. **Core W2** Identify the intended audience. **Core L2** Listen respectfully and responsively. **Core L3** Identify own purpose for listening. **Core S1** Respond respectfully.

For a complete description of the standards, see p. NY11.

You're off to a great start with your first draft! Now think about how to improve, edit, and present your sketch. Keep a copy of the final draft in a writing portfolio so you and your teacher can evaluate your writing progress.

Revising
Make It Better

Here are some things that you can do to make your first draft into something you'll be proud to share with someone else.

• Read your draft and write notes about things you want to change. Then go through the draft again, checking for items in the Revising Rubric.

• Remember to include vivid details in your sketch. Providing the "specifics" of a story helps make it memorable to readers.

• Make changes as you go. If you're not sure of the exact words to write, make notes to yourself so you can go back and make the changes later. Don't get stuck on one trouble spot—keep making progress.

needs more details

> *I got home from the party and started reading.*

Consider the Audience

Remember that your main audience is your teacher and classmates.

• What do you want to tell them about your reading experience?

• How can you help them understand what you want to say about reading?

> *I want my teacher and classmates to know that I've always liked relating to the characters in books.*

Check the Voice

Ask yourself these questions as you reread your draft.

- *Have I chosen an experience that I feel strongly about?*
- *Is the language lively?*
  Is the sentence structure varied?
- *Does my sketch express my unique point of view?*
- *How do I feel about the details and descriptions I've written? Did I include enough details and descriptions for the reader to understand my experience?*

Literature Online

Writing Models For models and other writing activities, go to www.glencoe.com.

Check the Sequence

Make sure the reader can follow the events in your sketch. Have you used sequence signal words like *first, next, then*? If the events have moved forward or backward in time, are the time shifts clear to the reader?

Editing

Finish It Up

For your final copy, read your autobiographical sketch aloud and use the Editing Checklist to help you spot errors. Use the proofreading symbols in the chart on page R19 to mark needed corrections.

Editing Checklist

☑ Proper nouns are correctly capitalized.
☑ Pronouns are in the correct form and agree with their antecedents.
☑ All sentences end with a punctuation mark.
☑ All words are correctly spelled.

◀ **Writing Tip**

Spelling Carefully check your work for words that sound the same but have different meanings, such as *too, to, two; their, they're, there; you're, your; its, it's; which, witch.* These are called **homophones.** Look for other words that you sometimes mix up. Make sure you use the correct spelling for the word you want.

Presenting

Show It Off

Make a clean final copy of your sketch. Read it to a small group of your classmates. Listen to them read their sketches. Then discuss any common ideas about reading that came up. Also talk about any surprising feelings about reading that people in the class might have expressed.

◀ **Writing Tip**

Handwriting Make your final draft easy to read. Use your best handwriting. Make each letter and punctuation mark clear for the reader.

Listening, Speaking, and Viewing

Active Listening

Many times we listen to what people are saying, but we don't focus only on listening to them. Sometimes we are thinking about what we want to say next. Or sometimes our minds wander to something else entirely. Active listening helps us to focus on what the speaker is saying.

What Is Active Listening?

Active listening is a way of being involved as a listener. You listen carefully to what the speaker says. Then you tell the speaker what you heard.

Why Is Active Listening Important?

To make your autobiographical sketch as good as it can be, you need feedback from others. When they share their thoughts about your writing, you need to listen carefully. Active listening will help you do many things, including these:

- understand what they are saying about your writing
- learn how they see your work
- get ideas about how to make your writing better

How Do I Do It?

When someone talks to you, listen to what he or she is saying. Do not think about what you want to say next. Don't try to immediately come up with answers to the person's questions. Don't let your mind wander.

When the person is done talking, tell him or her what you heard. Here are some phrases to get you started.

- So what I think you're saying is _____.
- What I heard you say was _____.

Small Group Discussion With two or three other students, talk about your autobiographical sketch and the benefits you got from reading it. The rest of the group should practice active listening. When you are done, each person should tell the group what he or she thinks you just said. Then have another person in the group speak. Now it's your turn to practice active listening. Take turns until everyone has a chance to be the speaker.

Analyzing Cartoons
What advice would you give Baldo on how to be a better listener?

Baldo © 2004 Baldo Partnership. Dist. by UNIVERSAL PRESS SYNDICATE. Reprinted with permission. All rights reserved.

Writer's Model

Comfort from a Book

Reading has always helped lift my spirits whenever I've felt sad. For example, there was the time I got home from a party at my friend Lisa's and felt really down. I went straight to my room and fell onto the bed. I felt more lonely than usual and wanted to forget about what happened that night. My Spanish book was on my small bedside table. I picked it up and opened it to the Escena de la Vida (Scene from Life), which we had been assigned to read over the weekend. In the scene, Estela was alone in her room, listening to a love song, while her "friends" were getting ready to go to a party without her. That's not too different from being at a party where your "friends" ignore you. That's what happened at Lisa's party. That's why I was feeling so sad.

I wanted to find out more about Estela, so I turned to the Escena de la Vida in the next chapter. Estela wasn't in that scene, but a guy named Ricardo was calling his English teacher "The Witch." He said he was sick of her jokes.

The teacher who told jokes reminded me of my social studies teacher, Ms. Carne. People call her a witch because she yells so much, but they think she's really funny, too. When she was a teenager on crutches, she must have had plenty of lonely times like Estela and me, but now she has a husband, a good job, and, most important, a positive, no-nonsense attitude. I can deal with being like Estela now if I can be like Ms. Carne when I grow up.

I've always known books could show me that other people have the same problems I do. Now I know reading can also remind me that someday my life will be better.

Active Writing Model

- The writer makes it clear that the events happened in the past. Here and throughout the sketch, the writer's use of time order makes it easy to follow the order of events.

- Details and descriptions help the readers share the writer's experience.

- The writer uses first-person point of view throughout the sketch.

- The writer's attitude toward the events comes through in the sketch.

- The sketch maintains a clear focus from the beginning to the end. Notice how the conclusion sums up the main idea of the sketch.

READING WORKSHOP 4

Skills Focus

You will practice using these skills when you read the following selections:
- from *Akiko in the Forbidden Foothills of Gozmaturk,* p. 100
- "Being Japanese American," p. 108

Reading
- Identifying author's purpose

Literature
- Identifying cultural references
- Identifying and analyzing sequence

Vocabulary
- Using visual and general context clues
- Academic Vocabulary: *visual, sequence*

Writing/Grammar
- Using the correct pronoun case

NY English Language Arts Core Curriculum
(pp. 96–97)

LC R12 Combine multiple strategies to enhance comprehension and response.

For a complete description of the standards, see p. NY11.

Skill Lesson

Identifying Author's Purpose

Learn It!

What Is It? The **author's purpose** is the reason that he or she wrote the text—his or her aim, or goal, for writing. Four common purposes are as follows:

- to entertain, such as with a comic strip, a short story, or a funny letter
- to persuade, such as with a commercial or a letter to the editor of a newspaper
- to inform, such as with a brochure that explains how to live a healthy lifestyle
- to express a feeling, such as with a love poem

I REALLY LIKE READING THE WORKS OF ISABEL ALLENDE...

SHE'S A GREAT WRITER.

BUT SOMETIMES I THINK SHE JUST MAKES A LOT OF THIS STUFF UP.

Baldo © 2005 Baldo Partnership. Dist. by UNIVERSAL PRESS SYNDICATE. Reprinted with permission. All rights reserved.

Analyzing Cartoons
The reader enjoys Allende's work even if it is "made up." Allende is a fiction writer. What might be her purpose in writing a novel?

Why Is It Important? When you know why an author wrote something, you can better understand and evaluate what you are reading.

How Do I Do It? To figure out the author's purpose, look at several things. Is the text fiction or nonfiction? Most fiction entertains or gives the reader insight into human life. Nonfiction often informs or persuades by using strong word choices and emotional appeals. Also, look to see if the text was written for a particular occasion or audience.

Study Central Visit www.glencoe .com and click on Study Central to review identifying the author's purpose.

Here's how a student described Maya Angelou's purpose in writing *I Know Why the Caged Bird Sings.* Read the passage from Angelou's work, below.

> She appealed to me because she was like people I had never met personally. Like women in English novels who walked the moors (whatever they were) with their loyal dogs racing at a respectful distance. Like the women who sat in front of roaring fireplaces, drinking tea incessantly from silver trays full of scones and crumpets. . . . It would be safe to say that she made me proud to be Negro, just by being herself.

I think Maya Angelou's purpose in this passage might be to entertain readers with her memories of Mrs. Flowers.

Practice It!

Every kind of writing has a purpose. In your Learner's Notebook, copy these two columns. Then draw lines from one column to another, matching the kind of writing to its most likely purpose.

kind of writing	purpose
article about a forest fire	to provide information about events
job application	to provide information about a person
advertisement	to express a feeling
patriotic song	to persuade someone to buy something

Use It!

As you read *Akiko* and "Being Japanese American," look for clues that will help you identify each author's purpose. Add these to your Learner's Notebook. Read each piece with that purpose in mind.

Before You Read

from *Akiko in the Forbidden Foothills of Gozmaturk*

Mark Crilley

Meet the Author

Mark Crilley began drawing at a young age. After college, he worked in Japan, where he invented the character Akiko. Since then, he has published more than 50 issues of the *Akiko* comic book series. He writes that "somewhere underneath all the silly drawings and slapstick humor lies a gentle reminder of the little 4th grader within us all . . . ."

Author Search For more about Mark Crilley, go to www.glencoe.com.

NY English Language Arts Core Curriculum (pp. 98–103)

Core R4 Determine the meaning of unfamiliar words by using context clues.
LC R12 Combine multiple strategies to enhance comprehension and response.
LC R13 Use text structure to aid comprehension and response.

For a complete description of the standards, see p. NY11.

Vocabulary Preview

wretched (RECH id) *adj.* very unpleasant or uncomfortable; terrible
  (p. 103) *The gooey, wretched stuff stuck to everything and everyone.*

coordinate (koh OR duh nayt) *v.* to make (things) work together smoothly
  (p. 103) *To avoid extra work, they decided to coordinate their efforts.*

Write to Learn Write a short paragraph using both vocabulary words.

English Language Coach

Context Clues: Visual Context Clues Usually, when you look for context clues to the meaning of a word, you look at the sentences and words around it. In a graphic novel, you have pictures that are **visual context clues**. The expressions on the characters' faces are clues. Suppose a character looks very sad and is saying, "I'm miserable." That's a very strong clue to the meaning of *miserable* (very sad). The characters' actions are clues. Suppose two characters are fighting. One says, "You will never triumph!" That's a clue to the meaning of *triumph* (win).

The setting of the story can contain clues, too. Suppose a character is looking at a very tall mountain and says, "It's too high to scale." That's a clue to the meaning of *scale* (climb). Or perhaps the characters are walking through a dark forest. The branches of the trees reach out like claws. There are eyes looking out from the darkness. One of the characters says, "What an eerie place!" You can be pretty sure that *eerie* has something to do with being weird and scary.

Visual clues can be very important in a graphic novel or cartoon. Often writers use words they make up, especially for noises. As you're reading the selection from *Akiko in the Forbidden Foothills of Gozmaturk,* look at the visual clues to identify the actions that go with words such as *skraw* and *shrlup.*

Partner Talk Without looking at the story, write meanings for *skraw* and *shrlup* in your Learner's Notebook. Don't try to write dictionary-style definitions. Instead, say each word aloud; then write a few notes about what the sound of the word suggests to you.

Academic Vocabulary

visual (VIZH oo ul) *adj.* meant to be viewed or seen

Skills Preview

Key Reading Skill: Identifying Author's Purpose

How can you tell Mark Crilley's purpose in *Akiko*? Use the following tips.

- Look at the pictures. Think about the mood, or feeling, they create and the story they tell.
- Think about the genre, or type of writing, of *Akiko* and the usual purpose of that genre.

On Your Own As you read *Akiko*, think particularly about the intended audience.

Literary Element: Sequence

A **sequence** is a regular order or arrangement. Text sequences commonly used to organize writing are as follows:

- **chronological order**—time order. This is often used in biographies and nonfiction, where it's important to know the order in which events actually happened.
- **spatial order**—the order within a certain space, such as left to right, top to bottom, foreground to background, and clockwise. Spatial order is best for describing people and places and giving directions.
- **order of importance**—going from most to least important or from least to most important. This form of sequence is often used in nonfiction.

Partner Talk What sequence would you expect in a graphic story? Talk it over with a partner.

Interactive Literary Elements Handbook
To review or learn more about the literary elements, go to www.glencoe.com.

Academic Vocabulary

sequence (SEE kwents) *n.* a regular order or arrangement in time, space, or importance

Get Ready to Read

Connect to the Reading

Your best friend has been kidnapped by a dragon! Yoiks! It will destroy your friend if you don't pay a ransom. Gadzooks! Do you reply "What's in it for me?" Of course not! Think about stories you've read or seen in which one character rescues another.

Write to Learn In *Akiko*, one of the characters is captured by a dragon. Jot down what you think that character's friends will do. Use your imagination!

Build Background

The selection you are about to read is from *Akiko in the Forbidden Foothills of Gozmaturk,* one of many graphic novels featuring Akiko and her friends. (The main characters live on the planet Smoo, but their adventures take them many places.) Here is a list of the main characters and a description of each:

- Akiko (the girl with pigtails)
- Spuckler Boach (the guy with spiky hair)
- Mr. Beeba (the bald creature with glasses)
- Gax (the one with the long neck)
- Poog (the floating head)

You'll read only the ending of this adventure, but all you need to know is that a dragon has captured Mr. Beeba, and his pals are trying to rescue him.

Set Purposes for Reading

BIG Question Read this story to learn how a group of friends tries to save one of their own, without worrying about reward or danger.

Set Your Own Purpose What would you like to learn from the story to help you answer the Big Question? Write your own purpose on the *Akiko* page of Foldable 1.

Keep Moving

Use these skills as you read the following selection.

from *Akiko in the Forbidden Foothills of Gozmaturk* **99**

from Akiko in the Forbidden Foothills of Gozmaturk

by **Mark Crilley**

Practice the Skills

1 **Key Reading Skill**

Identifying Author's Purpose
Notice the odd markings on the stones. Although we don't know what they represent, they're fun to look at. This may hint at Crilley's purpose.

2 **English Language Coach**

Context Clues The way Gax speaks (or sounds) looks different from the way the others speak. What are two differences?

Practice the Skills

3 **English Language Coach**

Context Clues Look at the visual context clues for *skraw* and *shrlup.* Do you think Crilley invented good words for the actions they represent?

Practice the Skills

4 Literary Element

Sequence Which of the patterns of organization described on page 99 is used in this selection?

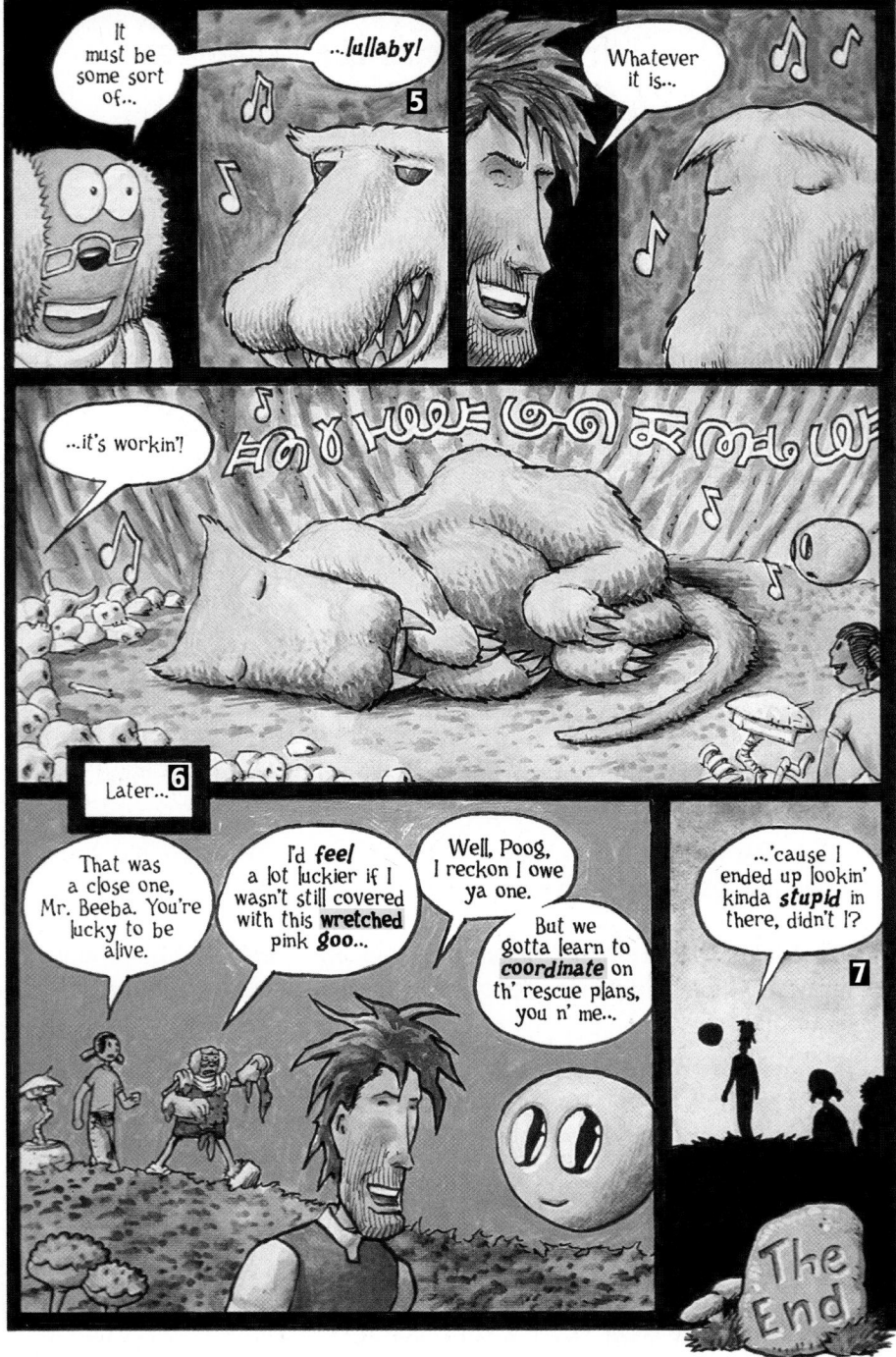

Practice the Skills

5 **Literary Element**

Sequence It's the sequence of what happens to the dragon that tells Mr. Beeba what kind of song Poog is singing.

6 **Literary Element**

Sequence Chronological order is often signaled by words such as *later, after, then,* and, of course, *The End.*

7 **BIG Question**

What did you get out of reading *Akiko*? Write your answer on the *Akiko* page of Foldable 1. Your response will help you complete the Unit Challenge later.

Vocabulary

wretched (RECH id) *adj.* very unpleasant or uncomfortable; terrible

coordinate (koh OR duh nayt) *v.* to make (things) work together smoothly

After You Read

from *Akiko in the Forbidden Foothills of Gozmaturk*

All right, gang. Jus' leave everything to me...

Answering the BIG Question

1. What do you get out of reading graphic stories that you might not get from reading a novel?
2. **Recall** What is Gax? How can you tell?
   TIP **Right There** You will find this information in the selection.

3. **Recall** How does Poog help Spuckler and Mr. Beeba escape?
   TIP **Right There** You will find this information in the selection.

Critical Thinking

4. **Infer** Why does Spuckler want a weapon when he enters the cave?
   TIP **Author and Me** You will find clues in the selection, but you must also use the information in your head.

5. **Infer** Based on Spuckler's actions, what kind of person do you think he is? How might he act during other adventures?
   TIP **Author and Me** You will find clues in the selection, but you must also use the information in your head.

6. **Evaluate** Do you think Crilley's drawings are effective? What about the story he tells? Explain, using examples from *Akiko* to support your answer.
   TIP **Author and Me** You will find clues in the selection, but you must also use the information in your head.

Write About Your Reading

Postcard Pretend you are Akiko. Write a postcard to your friends on your home planet, describing your adventure with the dragon. Draw a picture for the front of the postcard. Use the following questions as a guide to writing your message for the back of the card.

- What happened when you entered the cave?
- How did you feel when the dragon tied up Spuckler?
- How did you help your friends in the cave?
- How did you escape?
- Where are you off to next?

NY English Language Arts Core Curriculum
(pp. 104–105)

LC R17 Demonstrate comprehension and response through a range of activities.
LC W4 Compose grade-appropriate texts for a variety of purposes.
LC R12 Combine multiple strategies to enhance comprehension and response.
LC R13 Use text structure to aid comprehension and response. **Core W8** Use correct grammatical construction in parts of speech (pronouns).

For a complete description of the standards, see p. NY11.

Skills Review

Key Reading Skill: Identifying Author's Purpose

7. What do you think was the most important purpose Crilley had in creating the *Akiko* stories?

Explain your answer.

Literary Element: Sequence

8. What is the main form of sequence Crilley uses in his graphic story?

9. What happens before Spuckler, Akiko, Poog, and Gax enter the cave?

10. What happens after Poog begins to sing?

11. Look at the second-to-last drawing on page 103. Which form of sequence would be best for identifying the characters in this drawing?
- chronological order
- spatial order
- order of importance

Vocabulary Check

12. List three nouns that the word *wretched* might describe.

13. Think of a group of people who would need to **coordinate** their actions. Write two or three sentences explaining why. Be sure to use the word *coordinate* in at least one sentence.

14. Academic Vocabulary Which of the following would be a **visual** aid:

a spoken description or a photo?

15. English Language Coach Look at the pictures containing the words *scraw* and *shrlup.* Using visual context clues from the selection, rewrite the meaning for each word.

Grammar Link: Pronouns as Subjects and Objects

A **subject pronoun** is used as the subject of a sentence. The subject of a sentence is who or what the sentence is about.

An **object pronoun** is a pronoun that receives the action expressed by the verb in the sentence.

	Subject Pronouns	**Object Pronouns**
Singular	I, you, he, she, it	me, you, her, him, it
Plural	we, you, they	us, you, them

To figure out when to use a subject or object pronoun, get rid of the extra person (or people) in a sentence.
- ~~Maurice, Phil, and~~ (him? he?) agreed.
- They spoke to ~~Bianca and~~ (I? me?).

You would never say "Him agreed," so you should use "he" in the first example. You would never say "They spoke to I," so you should use "me" in the second example.

Grammar Practice

Rewrite each sentence, using the correct pronoun in parentheses.

16. My friends and (I, me) like mystery novels.

17. Tina, Ashley, or (she, her) will ask Mrs. Hill.

18. Please give Sandy and (I, me) a chance.

19. Guess what happened to Paul and (I, me)!

20. (Me and my brother, My brother and I) went shopping.

Writing Application Review the postcard you wrote for the Write About Your Reading activity. Make sure you correctly used subject and object pronouns. Fix any mistakes.

Literature Online

Web Activities For eFlashcards, Selection Quick Checks, and other Web activities, go to www.glencoe.com.

Before You Read

Being Japanese American

Yoshiko Uchida

Meet the Author

Yoshiko Uchida was born in 1921, in Alameda, California. During World War II, Uchida and her family were sent to an internment camp for Japanese American citizens. Uchida taught while in the camp and learned to love education. When she was released, she went on to write many books about Japanese American culture. Uchida died in 1992. See page R7 of the Author Files for more on Yoshiko Uchida.

Author Search For more about Yoshiko Uchida, go to www.glencoe.com.

NY English Language Arts Core Curriculum (pp. 106–113)

Core R4 Determine the meaning of unfamiliar words by using context clues.
LC R12 Combine multiple strategies to enhance comprehension and response.
R2g Compare literature to own lives.
R2h Identify social and cultural contexts to enhance understanding.
For a complete description of the standards, see p. NY11.

Vocabulary Preview

corresponded (kor uh SPON did) *v.* wrote letters to one another; form of the verb *correspond* **(p. 109)** *Yuri and Ko corresponded with their families while they were away at college.*

relish (REL ish) *n.* enjoyment or delight **(p. 109)** *Casey smiled as he played his favorite sport with much relish.*

humiliated (hyoo MIL ee ayt ud) *adj.* embarrassed; ashamed; form of the verb *humiliate* **(p. 110)** *Jonah felt humiliated when other kids made fun of him.*

Write to Learn Make a fill-in-the-blank worksheet. List each vocabulary word at the top of a sheet of paper. Then write a sentence for each vocabulary word. Leave a blank where the vocabulary word should go. Trade worksheets with a partner and try to complete each other's sentences.

English Language Coach

General Context Clues You've used all of the following kinds of clues: characteristics, explanatory words, examples, synonyms and antonyms, category, direct definition, and visual. But sometimes there are **general context clues** that don't fit into one of these types. They may require you to look at more than one sentence and make inferences. Look at this example.

- *It is not clear whether the dinosaurs cooperated in hunting, as wolves or lions do. They may have mobbed their quarry or just gathered around after one of them made a kill.*

It's pretty easy to figure out what *quarry* means. It's what the dinosaurs hunted. You must make some inferences, but they are not difficult.

Use the following tips for using context:

- Look before, at, and after the unfamiliar word for a general topic or action associated with the word.
- Connect what you know with what the author has written.
- Predict a possible meaning, and apply it in a sentence.
- Try again if your guess did not make any sense.

Partner Talk Get the front page of a newspaper. With a partner, search for a word that neither of you know the meaning of. Then try to figure out the meaning from the context. Talk it out together. Then look the word up in a dictionary to see if you were right.

Skills Preview

Key Reading Skill: Identifying Author's Purpose

As you read "Being Japanese American," think about everything you just read about Yoshiko Uchida. Use this information to identify what her purpose might be for writing this text.

Partner Talk Think of something that has happened in your life that you would like to write a story about. Talk with a partner about what happened and determine what the purpose of sharing your story should be.

Key Literary Element: Cultural Reference

A **reference** is a mention of a character, place, or situation from another work of art or literature, or from history. A **cultural reference** is a mention of a value, belief, tradition, or custom practiced in a certain culture. For example, you may read about a powwow in a Native American story. A powwow is a Native American cultural event where traditional dancing, drumming, and chanting are performed. Such cultural events are unique to Native Americans, and you most likely won't be reading about them in Japanese, Chinese, or Russian stories.

To identify cultural references, look for ideas or customs that are not practiced worldwide. When you read about events or beliefs, think about whether they are part of your culture or specific to another culture.

Small Group Work Imagine that a new student from another country is joining your class. In a small group, make a list of American customs to teach the new student about the culture.

Get Ready to Read

Connect to the Reading

Think about your family background. What are your roots, or heritage, and customs?

Whole Class Discussion Americans come from families with many different backgrounds. What do you think is good about this? Why is it hard sometimes? Talk about these questions with your class.

Build Background

This selection describes growing up in Berkeley, California, as a second generation Japanese American, or *Nisei*.

- During World War II, the United States fought against Japan.
- Many Japanese Americans living on the West Coast were imprisoned during World War II in crowded, badly built internment camps in the desert, mainly because they "looked like the enemy."

Set Purposes for Reading

BIG Question Read to find out how a young Japanese American girl struggles to accept and understand her heritage.

Set Your Own Purpose What would you like to learn about being Japanese American by reading this selection? Write your own purpose on the "Being Japanese American" page of Foldable 1.

Interactive Literary Elements Handbook
To review or learn more about the literary elements, go to www.glencoe.com.

Keep Moving

Use these skills as you read "Being Japanese American."

Being Japanese American

by Yoshiko Uchida

Superstitions were not the only Japanese things in my life. A lot more of me was Japanese than I realized, whether I liked it or not.

I was born in California, recited the Pledge of Allegiance to the flag each morning at school, and loved my country as much as any other American—maybe even more. **1**

Still, there was a large part of me that was Japanese simply because Mama and Papa had passed on to me so much of their own Japanese spirit and soul. Their own values of loyalty, honor, self-discipline, love, and respect for one's parents, teachers, and superiors were all very much a part of me.

There was also my name, which teachers couldn't seem to pronounce properly even when I shortened my first name to Yoshi. And there was my Japanese face, which closed more and more doors to me as I grew older.

Practice the Skills

1 | **Key Literary Element**

Cultural Reference The Pledge of Allegiance is a custom practiced in many schools across the country. By reciting the Pledge of Allegiance daily, Uchida shows her loyalty and involvement in American culture.

How wonderful it would be, I used to think, if I had blond hair and blue eyes like Marian and Solveig. Or a name like Mary Anne Brown or Betty Johnson.

If only I didn't have to ask such questions as, "Can we come swim in your pool? We're Japanese." Or when we were looking for a house, "Will the neighbors object if we move in next door?" Or when I went for my first professional haircut, "Do you cut Japanese hair?"

Still, I didn't truly realize how different I was until the summer I was eleven. Although Papa usually went on business trips alone, bringing back such gifts as silver pins for Mama or charm bracelets for Keiko and me, that summer he was able to take us along, thanks to a railroad pass.

We took the train, stopping at the Grand Canyon, Houston, New Orleans, Washington, D.C., New York, Boston, Niagara Falls, and on the way home, Chicago, to see the World's Fair.

Crossing the Mississippi River was a major event, as our train rolled onto a **barge** and sailed slowly over that grand body of water. ◙ We all got off the train for a closer look, and I was so impressed with the river's majesty, I felt impelled[1] to make some kind of connection with it. Finally, I leaned over the barge rail and spit so a part of me would be in the river forever.

For my mother, the high point of the trip was a visit to the small village of Cornwall, Connecticut. There she had her first meeting with the two white American pen pals with whom she had **corresponded** since her days at Doshisha University. She also visited one of her former missionary teachers, Louise DeForest, who had retired there. And it was there I met a young girl my age, named Cathy Sellew. We became good friends, corresponded for many years, and met again as adults when I needed a home and a friend.

Everyone in the village greeted us warmly, and my father was asked to say a few words to the children of the Summer Vacation Church School—which he did with great **relish.**

Practice the Skills

◙ **English Language Coach**

General Context Clues You can use context clues to figure out the meaning of **barge.** The train uses one to cross a river. Also, notice the word *sailed.* You know that boats sail. What do you think a *barge* is?

---

1. Here, to feel ***impelled*** means to feel a strong urge to make a connection.

Vocabulary

corresponded (kor uh SPON did) *v.* wrote letters to one another

relish (REL ish) *n.* enjoyment or delight

Analyzing the Photo Yoshiko Uchida, second from the left, is ten years old here. Her parents, grandmother, and older sister are also pictured. What does this photo suggest about Uchida's family?

Most of the villagers had never before met a Japanese American. One smiling woman shook my hand and said, "My, but you speak English so beautifully." She had meant to compliment me, but I was so astonished, I didn't know what to say. I realized she had seen only my outer self—my Japanese face—and addressed me as a foreigner. I knew then that I would always be different, even though I wanted so badly to be like my white American friends.

I hated having Mama stop on the street and greet a friend with a series of bows as was customary in Japan. "Come on, Mama," I would say impatiently tugging at her sleeve. I felt as though everyone was staring at us. **3**

I was **humiliated** when the post office called us one Sunday requesting that we pick up immediately a package of rotting food. Actually, it was just some pungent[2] pickled *daikon* (long white radish), sent by a friend who knew Papa loved eating it with rice and hot tea. But the man at the post office thrust it at us at arm's length, as though it were a piece of stinking garbage.

---

2. When something is *pungent*, it has a very strong smell.

Practice the Skills

3 | **Key Literary Element**

Cultural Reference In Japan, bowing is the traditional way to greet someone. Bows signify respect and are used both when meeting and parting. How does Uchida react to her mother's bowing? Who is more Americanized, Uchida or her mother?

Vocabulary

humiliated (hyoo MIL ee ayt ud) *adj.* embarrassed; ashamed

Keiko and I absolutely refused when Mama wanted us to learn how to read and write Japanese. We wanted to be *Americans*, not Japanese!

"Wouldn't it be nice to write to your grandmother in Japanese?" she asked.

"It's easier if you write her, Mama," we said.

"Don't you want to be able to read those nice storybooks from Japan?"

We didn't. Not really. We liked having Mama read them to us. We read our own favorites in English.

I loved going to the South Berkeley branch of the public library, where I would head for the children's corner. There I looked for the books with stars on their spines, which meant they were mysteries. I read such books as Augusta H. Seaman's *The Boarded Up House* and *The Mystery of the Old Violin*. I also liked Hugh Lofting's *Dr. Doolittle* books, and loved Louisa May Alcott's *Little Women* and *Little Men*. Other favorites were Anna Sewell's *Black Beauty* and Frances Hodgson Burnett's *The Secret Garden*.

Learning Japanese, Keiko and I felt, would only make us seem more different from our white classmates. So Mama didn't force us to go to Japanese Language School after regular school, as many of our Nisei (second-generation Japanese) friends did. **4**

We finally agreed, however, to let her teach us Japanese during summer vacations when she also taught us how to embroider. We loved learning how to make daisies and rosebuds on pillowcases, but we certainly didn't make it easy for Mama to teach us Japanese. Keiko and I grumbled endlessly as we tried to learn how to read and write the complicated Japanese characters,[3] and by the time each summer rolled around, we had forgotten most of what we had learned the year before.

Practice the Skills

4 **Key Reading Skill**

Identifying Author's Purpose
The author wanted to be more like her white classmates than her *Nisei* friends. Remember that the author is a *Nisei*. What does this tell you about her purpose for writing this selection?

Analyzing the Photo This picture of Yoshiko and Keiko was taken in Berkeley, California. Does this photo help you understand their relationship? Explain.

---

3. The Japanese language uses three different sets of *characters,* or letters: Kanji, Hiragana, and Katakana. These characters look nothing like the letters used by languages like English and Spanish.

Still, we managed to learn a lot of Japanese by osmosis. Our parents spoke Japanese to each other and to us, although we usually answered in English, sprinkling in a few Japanese words here and there.

Then there were many Japanese phrases we used every day. We always said, *"Itadaki masu,"* before each meal, and *"Gochiso sama"* afterward to thank Mama for preparing the food. The first thing we called out when we came home from school was *"Tadaima!* I'm home!"

The Japanese names Mama gave to the tools and implements around the house were the sounds they made. The vacuum cleaner was the *buhn-buhn.* The carpet sweeper was the *goro-goro.* Mama's little sewing scissors with the silver bell tied to it was the *chirin-chirin.*

Keiko and I often talked in a strange **hybrid** language. **5** "It's your turn to do the *goro-goro* today." Or, "Mama said to *buhn-buhn* the living room." And anytime Mama asked us to fetch the *chirin-chirin,* we knew exactly what she meant.

Every night when we were little, Keiko and I would climb into bed and wait for Mama to come sit between our two beds and read a Japanese story to us. I first heard such wonderful folktales as "The Old Man Who Made the Flowers Bloom" and "The Tongue-Cut Sparrow" from her.

Although Papa loved to sing American folk songs, he and Mama taught us many Japanese songs that still float through my memory today. Their prayers, too, were always in Japanese—Papa's grace before meals (nice and short) and Mama's prayers at bedtime (not so short). So when it came to praying, I always did it in Japanese, even after I grew up.

We always celebrated Doll's Festival Day[4] on March 3, as all girls did in Japan, displaying special dolls for the occasion. Mama would open the big brown trunk in the basement and bring up dozens of tiny wooden boxes containing her Japanese doll collection. These

Practice the Skills

5 | **English Language Coach**

General Context Clues The author uses examples of phrases that use a **hybrid** language. The phrases use both English and Japanese words. What do you think *hybrid* means?

On Doll's Festival Day, Japanese girls dress dolls like this one in ceremonial kimonos. Why are traditions like this one important? What traditions do you celebrate?

---

4. ***Doll's Festival Day*** is a holiday in Japan to pray for the growth and happiness of all young girls. On this day, girls display dolls in their homes and dedicate peach blossoms to them.

were not dolls to be played with, but to be treasured carefully and viewed only once a year.

A formal festival doll set consisted of an emperor and empress presiding over their court of musicians, guards, ladies-in-waiting, and so forth down to the lowliest member of the imperial court. **6**

But Mama's collection was different. She did have an emperor and empress, but the rest were tiny dolls or toys that had caught her fancy. There were good-luck charms on ivory rings, round-bottomed *daruma* dolls that always sprang up when pushed down, miniature tea sets and kitchen utensils, dolls that were characters from folktales or dolls she'd dressed herself as a child, balls made of colored silk thread, small clay bells from old temples, folk toy animals that brought good luck, and anything else Mama wanted to include. It was all sort of a pleasant, Mama-like jumble laid out on a table covered with a festive red felt cloth.

Visual Vocabulary
Daruma dolls are round dolls with red-painted bodies and white faces.

"Bring out your own dolls, too," she would tell us. "We don't want them to feel left out."

So Keiko and I would bring out our white baby dolls with brown hair and green glass eyes and place them around the table as well.

Until I was much older and wiser, the Japanese dolls didn't mean much to me. Mama seemed to enjoy them more than Keiko or I did, and she would often have friends to tea to share her pleasure in their yearly appearance.

As for me, it was my white baby doll and my Patsy doll that I loved, even though they didn't look anything like me. I suppose it was because I always thought of myself as being an American. I just didn't realize how much of me was Japanese as well. **7** ○

Practice the Skills

6 **Key Literary Element**
Cultural Reference What Japanese holiday is celebrated in the last two paragraphs? What aspects make it a uniquely Japanese holiday?

7 **BIG Question**
What did you learn about being Japanese American from reading this selection? Write your answer on the "Being Japanese American" page of Foldable 1. Your response will help you complete the Unit Challenge later.

After You Read

Being Japanese American

Answering the BIG Question

1. What have you learned about being an American after reading this selection?

2. **Recall** How old was the author when she first realized she was "different"?

   Tip **Right There** You will find the answer in the text.

3. **Summarize** The author wrote about some of the difficulties she faced being Japanese American. Summarize the situations she described where she felt different for being Japanese American.

   Tip **Think and Search** You will find the answer in the text, but you will need to search for it.

Critical Thinking

4. **Compare and Contrast** The author and her sister did not want to be like other *Nisei.* How were they different from other *Nisei?* How were they the same?

   Tip **Author and Me** Use information from the text plus your own knowledge.

5. **Analyze** Think about what happened when Yoshiko went to Connecticut. What did Yoshiko learn about the way other people saw her?

   Tip **Author and Me** Use information from the text plus your own knowledge.

6. **Analyze** How did Yoshiko's feelings about the Japanese dolls change as she got older?

   Tip **Author and Me** Use information from the text plus your own knowledge.

Talk About Your Reading

List of Details In the first paragraph Uchida directly states the main, or most important, idea of the selection: "A lot more of me was Japanese than I realized, whether I liked it or not." With a small group of classmates, list at least five specific details that Uchida gives to support the main idea. Then share your list with the rest of the class.

NY English Language Arts Core Curriculum
(pp. 114–115)

LC R17 Demonstrate comprehension and response through a range of activities. **S2a** Express interpretations and support them through specific references to the text. **LC R12** Combine multiple strategies to enhance comprehension and response. **R2h** Identify social and cultural contexts. **Core R4** Determine the meaning of unfamiliar words by using context clues. **Core W8** Use correct grammatical construction.

For a complete description of the standards, see p. NY11.

Skills Review

Key Reading Skill: Identifying Author's Purpose

7. Now that you have read the selection, why do you think Yoshiko Uchida wrote the text?

Key Literary Element: Cultural Reference

8. Give four examples of how members of the Uchida family still practice Japanese customs or traditions, even though they live in the United States.

9. What are Japanese "characters," and why does Uchida resist learning them?

Reviewing Skills: Activating Prior Knowledge

10. How does the author's experiences in the story remind you of experiences you know about or have read about second generation Americans?

Vocabulary Check

Choose the best word from the list to complete each sentence below. Rewrite each sentence with the correct word in place.

corresponded   relish   humiliated

11. He ate his wife's delicious cooking with great _____.

12. Sometimes Yoshiko felt _____ because of her family background.

13. The American children _____ with their friends who lived in Japan.

14. **English Language Coach** In your Learner's Notebook, write a sentence using a general context clue for the following words you learned while reading "Being Japanese American."

barge   osmosis   astonished   hybrid

Grammar Link: Pronouns as Objects of Prepositions

A **preposition** is a word that relates a noun or a pronoun to another word in a sentence. Examples of prepositions are *about, across, against, before, during, into, off, on, to, through, under,* and *with*. When a pronoun is the object of a preposition, use an object pronoun.

• Joel gave the computer <u>to</u> *her.*
• Hamal went <u>before</u> *me.*

Use the object pronoun *whom* after a preposition.
• <u>To</u> *whom* did you give the folder?
• The person <u>with</u> *whom* I'm going is Terrence.

Be careful when a preposition has a compound object with both a noun and a pronoun. It still takes an object pronoun.
• Alex will apologize <u>to</u> the teacher and *me.*
• Can you come to the movie <u>with</u> Joe and *us?*

Look out! Never use the pronoun *I* after the preposition <u>to</u>.

Grammar Practice

Copy each sentence. Underline each preposition. Then circle the correct form of the pronoun in parentheses.

15. To (who, whom) should Yoshiko send the package?

16. Oh, you arrived at class before (I, me).

17. This gift is from your grandmother and (we, us).

18. Give it to Marie and (I, me).

Writing Application Look back at your Write About Your Reading activity. Did you use pronouns as objects of prepositions correctly? Fix any mistakes.

Web Activities For eFlashcards, Selection Quick Checks, and other Web activities, go to www.glencoe.com.

from
A Gift of Laughter

by Allan Sherman

&

A Family Thing
by Jerry Spinelli

&

KNOXVILLE,
T E N N E S S E E

by Nikki Giovanni

What You'll Learn

- How to compare three pieces of literature
- How to identify tone

What You'll Read

- from *A Gift of Laughter*, p. 119
- "A Family Thing," p. 124
- "Knoxville, Tennessee," p. 129

Point of Comparison

- Tone

Purpose

- To compare the tone of two personal essays and a poem
- Academic Vocabulary: *analyze*

NY English Language Arts Core Curriculum (pp. 116–117)

R2e Recognize how the author's use of language creates images or feelings.

For a complete description of the standards, see p. NY11.

Have you ever wanted to taste a new food? You probably asked, "What does it taste like?" In other words, you wanted to know how it was similar to or different from something you've tried before. Making comparisons helps you understand new things and relate to new people.

How to Compare Literature: Tone

Before you compare anything—friends, food, or things you read—you need to choose a point of comparison. In this workshop, your point of comparison is tone.

Tone is the writer's attitude toward a subject as shown in the language he or she uses. Tone can be serious or lighthearted; it can be funny, scary, or even sarcastic.

As you read, use the tips below to find and understand the tone in a selection from *A Gift of Laughter,* and in "A Family Thing" and "Knoxville, Tennessee."

- Look at the words the author uses.
  Are they strong words that describe emotions, such as joy, anger, sadness, or love?

- Look at what the characters do.
  Do they laugh, scream, smile, or cry?

- Look at the details the author includes.
  Do they influence the way you feel about the topic? How?

After you read, compare the tone of the three selections.

Get Ready to Compare

As you read, use a chart like the one below for help in identifying tone. Copy three of these charts in your Learner's Notebook—one for each selection. As you look for tone, pay attention to the words and details the author uses. Notice the feelings you have as you respond to the words and details.

Title (from _A Gift of Laughter_)	My Response	Author's Attitude (Tone)
Words		
Details		
Actions or Events		

Making Your Comparison

Look at this selection from _A Gift of Laughter_ on page 119. Then use the steps below to understand the tone.

"Robbie, _please!_" I said. Then I appealed to my wife. "Can't we have just five minutes around here without kids screaming?"

Step 1: Look at how the narrator speaks to—or about—other characters.

- _How does the narrator speak to Robbie? How does he speak to his wife? Does he seem calm or flustered? How can you tell?_

Step 2: Look at the action the author includes.

- _The narrator requests five minutes "without kids screaming." What does this tell you about his attitude toward what's happening around him?_

Step 3: Look at punctuation marks and italics that show strong feeling.

- _The narrator says, "Robbie, please!" Does it seem as if he is shouting? If he is, what tone does this create?_

As you read the selections in this workshop, you will use these steps and others to compare the tone of the readings. You can also use the steps to analyze the tone in other selections.

Before You Read : from *A Gift of Laughter*

Allan Sherman

Meet the Author

Allan Sherman was born in Chicago in 1924. He is well known for his funny songs. His most famous song is "Hello Muddah, Hello Faddah." It's about a boy at summer camp. In 1965 he published his autobiography, *A Gift of Laughter.* He died in 1973 at age 48.

Author Search For more about Allan Sherman, go to www.glencoe.com.

NY English Language Arts Core Curriculum
(pp. 118–122)

Core R4 Determine the meaning of unfamiliar words by using context clues.
R2g Compare literature to own lives.
R2e Recognize how the author's use of language creates images or feelings.

For a complete description of the standards, see p. NY11.

Vocabulary Preview

appealed (uh PEELD) *v.* made a serious request **(p. 119)** *Ramone appealed to his teacher for a higher grade.*

bewilderment (bih WIL dur munt) *n.* confusion **(p. 119)** *Maria looked at her messy math notes with bewilderment.*

English Language Coach

Context Clue Review As you worked through Unit 1, you practiced using different kinds of context clues. They include looking for word characteristics, explanatory words and phrases, examples, synonyms, antonyms, and word categories. In this workshop you will practice applying some of these clues. Look at the sentences below, from "A Family Thing." What does *tend* mean, and how can you tell?

• *During the growing months, every day after work, he went to . . . **tend** his vegetables. [A]s he put hoe to earth, he sometimes reflected . . . .*

In this context, *tend* means "take care of." The context clue is "put hoe to earth." It gives an example of tending.

Get Ready to Read

Connect to the Reading

Recall a time when you were short-tempered with someone you care about. How did you feel afterward?

Build Background

• In this selection, Sherman recalls an event from his past.

• Sherman's grandmother has a thick Yiddish accent. Yiddish is a language that comes from German and Hebrew. It also borrows words from Slavic and Romance languages and from English. Yiddish developed in Europe hundreds of years ago.

Set Purposes for Reading

BIG Question Read to find out what lesson Allan Sherman learns from his grandmother and how he applies the lesson.

Set Your Own Purpose What else would you like to learn from the selection to help you answer the Big Question? Write your own purpose on the *Gift of Laughter* page of Foldable 1.

from *A Gift of Laughter*

by Allan Sherman

"DaddydaddyDADDY!" That's how it came out—one long, excited word. He started yelling it at the top of the stairs, and by the time he bounded into the living room he really had it going good. I'd been talking to his mother about a money problem, and it stopped me mid-sentence.

"Robbie, *please*!" I said. Then I **appealed** to my wife. "Can't we have just five minutes around here without kids screaming?"

Robbie had been holding something behind his back. Now he swung it around for me to see. "Daddy, *look*!"

It was a picture, drawn in the messy crayon of a seven-year-old. It showed a weird-looking creature with one ear three times as big as the other, one green eye and one red; the head was pear-shaped, and the face needed a shave.

I turned on my son. "Is *that* what you interrupted me for? Couldn't you wait? I'm talking to your mother about something *important*!" **1**

His face clouded up. His eyes filled with **bewilderment**, rage, then tears. "Awright!" he screamed, and threw the picture to the floor. "But it's *your* birthday Saturday!" Then he ran upstairs.

1 | **Comparing Literature**

Tone What is Sherman's attitude here? How can you tell? Make notes on your chart to tell what you know about Sherman so far.

Vocabulary

appealed (uh PEELD) *v.* made a serious request

bewilderment (bih WIL dur munt) *n.* confusion

I looked at the picture on the floor. At the bottom, in Robbie's careful printing, were some words I hadn't noticed: MY DAD by Robert Sherman.

Just then Robbie slammed the door of his room. But I heard a different door, a door I once slammed— 25 years ago—in my grandmother's house in Chicago.

It was the day I heard my grandmother say she needed a *football*. I heard her tell my mother there was going to be a party tonight for the whole family, and she had to have a football, for after supper.

I couldn't imagine *why* Grandmother needed a football. I was sure she wasn't going to play the game with my aunts and uncles.

She had been in America only a few years, and still spoke with a deep Yiddish accent. But Grandma wanted a football, and a football was something in *my* department. If I could get one, I'd be important, a contributor to the party. I slipped out the door.

There were only three footballs in the neighborhood, and they belonged to older kids. Homer Spicer wasn't home. Eddie Polonsky wouldn't sell or rent, at any price.

The last possibility was a tough kid we called Gudgie. It was just as I'd feared. Gudgie punched me in the nose. Then he said he would trade me his old football for my new sled, plus all the marbles I owned.

I filled Gudgie's football with air at the gas station. Then I sneaked it into the house and shined it with shoe polish. When I finished, it was a football worthy of Grandmother's party. All the aunts and uncles would be proud. When nobody was looking I put it on the dining-room table. Then I waited in my room for Grandma to notice it. **2**

But it was Mother who noticed it. "Allan!" she shouted.

I ran to the dining room.

Analyzing the Photo Can a photographer express a tone, or attitude, in a picture? Can you describe the photographer's tone in this picture? Explain.

Practice the Skills

2 Comparing Literature

Tone Here Sherman is talking about himself as a child. What words and phrases show you that, as a kid, Allan was eager to please his family? Record your answers on your chart.

"You know your grandmother's giving a party tonight. Why can't you put your things where they belong?"

"It's not mine," I protested.

"Then give it back to whoever it belongs to. Get it out of here!"

"But it's for Grandma! She said she needed a football for the party." I was holding back the tears.

Mother burst into laughter. "A *football* for the party! Don't you understand your own grandma?" Then, between peals of laughter, Mother explained: "Not football. Fruit bowl! Grandma needs a fruit bowl for the party." **3**

I was starting to cry, so I ran to my room and slammed the door. The worst part of crying was trying to stop. I can still feel it—the shuddering, my breath coming in little, **staccato** jerks. **4** And each sputtery breath brought back the pain, the frustration, the unwanted feeling that had made me cry in the first place. I was still trying to stop crying when the aunts and uncles arrived. I heard their voices (sounding very far away), and the clink-clink of Grandma's good china, and now and then an explosion of laughter.

After dinner, Mother came in. "Allan," she said, "come with me. I want you to see something." I followed her into the living room.

Grandma was walking around the room like a queen, holding out to each of the aunts and uncles the biggest, most magnificent cut-glass bowl I'd ever seen. There were grapes and bananas in it, red apples, figs and tangerines. And in the center of the bowl, all shiny and brown, was Gudgie's football.

Just then my Uncle Sol offered Grandma a compliment.[1]

"Esther," he said, "that's a beautiful *football*. Real *cott gless*."

Grandma looked at Uncle Sol with great superiority. "Sol," she said, "listen close, you'll learn something. This *cott gless* is called a *frutt boll*, not a *football*. This in the middle, *this* is a *football*."

Uncle Sol was impressed. "Very smot,"[2] he said. "Very nice. But, Esther, now tell me something. How come you got a *football* in your *frutt boll*?" He pronounced them both very carefully.

"Because," Grandma said, "today mine Allan brought me a nice present, this football. It's beautiful, no?"

---

1. A *compliment* is an expression of admiration or respect.

2. The author is writing the words so that you can hear how they sound. Uncle Sol is saying the word *smart*. With his accent, it sounds like *smot*.

Practice the Skills

3 | **Comparing Literature**

Tone The tone changes at this point. How would you describe Mother's tone? Why?

4 | **English Language Coach**

Context Clue Review The writer uses the word **staccato** to describe his breath. Look at the context clues in the sentence: *shuddering, little,* and *jerks.* What do you think *staccato* means?

Before Uncle Sol could answer, Grandma continued, "It's beautiful, yess—because from a child is beautiful, anything." **5**

. . . From a child is beautiful, anything.

I picked up Robbie's picture from the floor. It wasn't bad, at that. One of my ears *is* a little bigger than the other. And usually, when Robbie sees me at the end of the day, I *do* need a shave.

I went up to his room. "Hi, Rob," I said.

His breath was shuddering, and his nose was running. He was packing a cardboard box, as he always does when he Leaves Home. I held up the picture. "Say, I've been looking this over. It's very good."

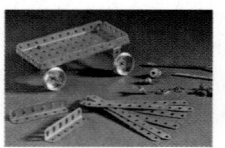

Visual Vocabulary
An **erector set** is a building toy made of small parts.

"I don't care," he said. He threw a comic book into the box and some Erector-set pieces. "Tear it up if you want to. I can't draw, anyhow."

He put on his cap and jacket, picked up the box and walked right past me. I followed him with the picture in my hand. **6**

When he got to the front door, he just stood there, his hand on the knob, the way he always does. I suppose he thinks of the same things I used to, whenever I Left Home. You stand there by the door, and pray *they* won't let you go, because you have no place to go, and if *they* don't want you, who does?

I got my coat and joined him. "Come on," I said. "I'm going with you." And I took him by the hand.

He looked up at me, very scared. "Where we going?"

"The shopping center is open tonight," I said. "We're going to buy a frame for this picture. It's a beautiful picture. We'll hang it in the living room. After we get the frame we're going to have an ice-cream soda and I'll tell you about something."

"About what?"

"Well, you remember that old football your great-grandma keeps in the cut-glass bowl on her dining-room table?"

"Yes."

"Well, I'm going to tell you how she got it." **7** ○

Practice the Skills

5 | **Comparing Literature**

Tone Sherman's grandma says his present is beautiful. How does this make him feel? What words and phrases tell you that this is a positive memory for him? Explain your answers on your chart.

6 | **Comparing Literature**

Tone What words and phrases does Sherman use to show that his attitude—and his tone—toward Robbie has changed? On your chart, make notes about the tone here.

7 | **BIG Question**

Sherman learned that every child's gift is valuable. What did you learn from reading this selection? Write your answer on the *Gift of Laughter* page of Foldable 1. Your response will help you complete the Unit Challenge later.

Before You Read

A Family Thing *and* Knoxville, Tennessee

Meet the Authors

Jerry Spinelli was born in Norristown, Pennsylvania, in 1941. He has written more than 20 books. "A Family Thing" is a chapter from his autobiography *Knots in My Yo-yo String*.

Nikki Giovanni was born in Knoxville, Tennessee, in 1943. She grew up in Ohio but spent many summers in Tennessee. Giovanni has written more than 24 books. She is committed to fighting for civil rights and equality.

Author Search For more about Jerry Spinelli and Nikki Giovanni, go to www.glencoe.com.

NY English Language Arts Core Curriculum

(pp. 123–129)

Core R4 Determine the meaning of unfamiliar words by using context clues. **R2g** Compare literature to own lives. **R2e** Recognize how the author's use of language creates images or feelings.

For a complete description of the standards, see p. NY11.

Vocabulary Preview

procedure (pro SEE jur) *n.* series of steps taken to do something **(p. 124)** *The students followed a safety procedure when the fire drill went off.*

recollections (rek uh LEK shuns) *n.* memories **(p. 125)** *Arnie's grandfather shared his recollections of the past.*

eclipsed (ee KLIPSD) *v.* made to seem unimportant; form of the verb *eclipse* **(p. 127)** *The team won the state championship and eclipsed its earlier losses.*

English Language Coach

Context Clue Review As you read, find the words below in "A Family Thing." Use context clues to understand their meanings. Remember to read the whole paragraph—and not just the sentence—as you hunt for context clues.

- triptych
- gauge

Get Ready to Read

Connect to the Reading

The authors of these selections write about places they love. Is there a place you love to go? Why is it meaningful to you? Write your answer in your Learner's Notebook.

Build Background

- The essay talks about holidays in the Spinelli household.
- The poem describes summers in Knoxville, Tennessee.
- Both the essay and the poem describe childhood memories.

Set Purposes for Reading

BIG Question Read "A Family Thing" and "Knoxville, Tennessee" to find out what the authors remember about the great family, food, and friends they had growing up.

Set Your Own Purpose What else would you like to learn from the story and poem to help you answer the Big Question? Write your own purpose on the "A Family Thing" and "Knoxville, Tennessee" page of Foldable 1.

A Family Thing

by Jerry Spinelli

On the night of May 16, 1936, my mother and father got married. This was three years after Lou Spinelli, nicknamed Poppy, had spotted pretty, dark-haired Lorna Bigler on the dance floor at the Orioles Lodge and said to his friend Babe Richards, "See that girl. That's who I'm going to marry." On the night of their wedding, they were on another dance floor, at the Little Ritz, a nightspot on Route 202 north of town. They were broke, so this was all the honeymoon they would have. **1**

At one point during the evening an announcement was made: A contest would determine the prettiest lady in attendance. My mother doesn't recall the contest **procedure,** only the result. The winner was the new Mrs. Lou Spinelli. Her prize was a gift certificate to have her portrait done at the Davis Photography Studio.

Four and a half years later, on February 1, 1941, I was born. My brother, Bill, came along four and a half years after that, on July 29, 1945. My mother's wedding-day prize, the framed

Practice the Skills

1 | **Comparing Literature**

Tone The author, Jerry Spinelli, begins with a story about his parents. Look at the words Spinelli has chosen and the details he includes. What's the tone of this part of the essay? Write your answer on your chart.

Vocabulary

procedure (pro SEE jur) *n.* series of steps taken to do something

portrait from Davis Studio, stands today on her bedroom dresser, the center of a **triptych** flanked by photo portraits of toddlers Bill and me. ❷

Mothers can get short-changed by memory. My **recollections**, for example, begin somewhere in my third year. By then some of my best experiences with my mother, some three years' worth of constant daily interaction, were already over. When my mind's recorder finally turned on, it was moments with my father that made the more memorable impressions: trips to high school ball games, backyard baseball, setting up the Christmas crèche. My mother's attentions continued, of course, but they tended to be less obvious, less noticed. They were the background of my life, the everyday care and support that at last came into full recognition when I acquired a family of my own.

Visual Vocabulary
A **crèche** (kresh) is a representation of Jesus's birth in a stable.

The marriage of Louis Anthony Spinelli and Lorna Mae Bigler brought together two heritages: Italian (my father) and Pennsylvania Dutch (my mother).

When I think of my Italian side, I think first of Sundays after church. The four of us would walk—or after 1954, when we got our first car, ride—the four blocks from First Presbyterian to my grandparents' home at 226 Chestnut. It was a row house with porches front and back and a rose arbor and dark polished furniture that made the living and dining rooms feel gloomy to me. The kitchen was where the light and the people and the food were.

Around the kitchen table sat aunts and uncles and cousins and, always at the head, my grandfather, Alessandro "Alex" Spinelli. In front of him was a small glass pitcher of red wine. Before each meal, including breakfast of cold spaghetti, he drew the wine from his own barrel in the cellar. He was bald and he did not speak English very well and his breath always smelled of garlic and he smoked thin black wicked stogies and his fingers were as thick as sausages. He had labored many years for the Pennsylvania Department of Highways. Later the Borough of Norristown employed him as a street

Practice the Skills

❷ **English Language Coach**

Context Clue Review What is a **triptych?** Use context clues to write a definition. (Hint: How many pictures are on the dresser?)

Vocabulary

recollections (rek uh LEK shuns) *n.* memories

sweeper. Sometimes, riding my bike, I would see him with other old men, pushing a broom along a curb.

That was his job. His love was the "farm," a small patch of vacant land that he rented in the East End. During the growing months, every day after work, he went to the farm to tend his vegetables. I like to think that, as he put hoe to earth, he sometimes reflected on what to me was the remarkable central fact of his life:

"He came over on a boat all by himself when he was only fourteen years old."

That's how I say it, even now, when describing my grandfather's coming to this country. He was an orphan in Italy. He worked in the olive groves around Naples. An aunt arranged for relatives to meet him in New York, handed him a one-way ticket on a steamship, and off he went, across the Atlantic Ocean, a black-haired teenager, alone, *solo*.

Fifty years later I, a nine-year-old American-born boy, sat at his kitchen table, eating the roast chicken with my fingers because that's how he did it, trying to imagine the bald old man at the head of the table with black hair.

The first course was always salad, as simple as salad gets: lettuce with oil and vinegar. Then came the chicken, then spaghetti and meatballs. My grandmother often made her own spaghetti, rolling out the dough and slicing it into strands with a device that reminded me of a harp. She would spend a whole day nursing the gravy at the stove. (To many Italians, spaghetti sauce is "gravy.") The dessert was often hot chestnuts, roasted on a second stove in the cellar. **3**

As with the Spinellis, a table stands in the center of my memory of the maternal relatives. In this case the table is not in a kitchen but on a sloping lawn under a huge oak tree. Made of planks laid over sawhorses, the table is very long and

Analyzing the Photo How does this image capture the "feel" of Spinelli's hometown?

Practice the Skills

3 | **Comparing Literature**

Tone Describe Spinelli's attitude toward the people and food he remembers. Write your answers on your chart.

is crowded with pickled eggs and cold cuts and potato salad and three-bean salad and lemon meringue pie and dozens of other goodies. The place is my Aunt Isabel and Uncle Ted's home in Phoenixville, Pennsylvania, about ten miles from Norristown. The occasion is the annual family reunion.

In my early years the reunion was, after Christmas, the biggest event on my calendar. It was the only time I got to see Aunt Lizzie and her gang from Highspire, some eighty miles away. Even their names seemed different. There was a Willard and a Juanita and a second cousin exotically named Kendra. **4**

One year there was even more excitement than usual: Uncle Elwood and Aunt Kay drove in from Michigan. I kept staring at my Midwestern cousins Bruce, Janey, and Suzie. They might as well have come from Mars. Alas for Aunt Margaret and Uncle Chet and their kids Cindy, George, JoAnne, and Patty, there was no magic of distance. They lived on Chain Street in Norristown, a mere block and a half from 802 George. I barely noticed them.

As a once-a-year event, the reunion became a **gauge** by which to measure my progress, both physical and social. **5** On the tennis court-size side yard, the uncles always got up a game of softball for the kids. I began as a tiny, grunting fumbler, swinging in vain at the slowest underhand tosses with a bat as big as I was. By the age of ten or eleven, I was clipping the grass with sharp grounders; then line drives to the garage; then, as a seasoned teenage shortstop, long flies into the strawberry patch beyond the trees. But by then the family reunion was no longer number two on my calendar. It had been **eclipsed** by such happenings as school dances and miniature golf with my friends. The year came when I felt myself too big to participate in the softball game. In college, some years, I did not even attend the reunion.

But home—home is a reunion daily. And I never felt too big for Christmas. Christmas was a Bible thing, of course, and a school-vacation thing and a wrapped-presents thing and a homemade-

Vocabulary

eclipsed (ee KLIPSD) *v.* made to seem unimportant

Practice the Skills

4 **Reviewing Skills**

Connecting Think about your favorite memory. How would you describe it to someone else? What details would you use to show how you feel about the people, places, and things you're describing?

5 **English Language Coach**

Context Clue Review What is a **gauge**? Use context clues to write a definition. (Hint: Spinelli says he uses the *gauge* "to measure.")

Analyzing the Photo What does Spinelli remember about the way his grandmother made spaghetti? How are his memories of food and family related?

cookies thing—but most of all, as I look back, it was a family thing.

My parents spent almost nothing on themselves. They bought only the clothes they needed. It was a big deal to treat themselves to a milkshake. They never went to the movies. And yet, for all they gave my brother and me, you'd have thought they were rich. My Christmas gifts came in piles. From Lincoln Logs to the inevitable walnut in the toe of my red felt stocking, I accepted the presents strictly as the objects they appeared to be. Only years later did I realize the truth: the gift was my parents' selfless love. **6**

One Christmas morning it bounced lightly off my chest as I came down the stairs, and I looked to see my first football wobbling at my feet. Another year it waited for me in the kitchen. I had unwrapped the last present from under the tree, and my father said, "Well, I guess that's it. Looks like you did pretty good this year." And then someone asked me to go to the kitchen for something, and there it was, in front of the sink: a spanking-new cream and green whitewall-tired Roadmaster bicycle. Love leaning on a kickstand. **7** ○

Analyzing the Photo
What does this photograph tell you about the way the Spinellis celebrated Christmas?

Practice the Skills

6 | **Comparing Literature**

Tone What words and phrases does Spinelli use in this paragraph to show that he loves and respects his parents? What tone do the words and phrases create? Write your answers on your chart.

7 **BIG Question**

What emotions did you feel as you read "A Family Thing"? Did reading about Spinelli's family cause you to think about your own? Write your answer on the "A Family Thing" page of Foldable 1. Your response will help you complete the Unit Challenge later.

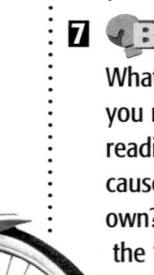

KNOXVILLE, TENNESSEE

by Nikki Giovanni

A Chat in the Road, 1991. Anna Belle Lee Washington. Oil on canvas, 20 x 30 in.

I always like summer
best
you can eat fresh corn
from daddy's garden
5 and okra*
and greens*
and cabbage*
and lots of
barbecue
10 and buttermilk
and homemade ice-cream
at the church picnic
and listen to
gospel music
15 outside
at the church
homecoming **1**
and go to the mountains with
your grandmother
20 and go barefooted
and be warm
all the time
not only when you go to bed
and sleep **2** ◯

5, 6, 7 *Okra, greens,* and *cabbage* are all vegetables commonly eaten in the South.

Practice the Skills

1 **Comparing Literature**

Tone What is the speaker's attitude toward summer and summer foods? What words and phrases tell you so? Put them on your chart.

2 **BIG Question**

What did you learn from reading "Knoxville, Tennessee"? Did the poem make you think about the place you come from in a new way? Explain. Write your answers on the "Knoxville, Tennessee" page of Foldable 1.

After You Read

from
A Gift of Laughter **&** **A Family Thing**

& KNOXVILLE, TENNESSEE

Vocabulary Check

In your Learner's Notebook, copy 1–10 below. For 1–5, cross out the word or phrase that does not belong with the others.

from *A Gift of Laughter* and **A Family Thing**

appealed   procedure   eclipsed   bewilderment   recollections

1. requested, appealed, asked for, denied
2. procedure, process, manual, method
3. eclipsed, moved beyond, outran, fell behind
4. confusion, astonishment, excitement, bewilderment
5. memories, thoughts, recollections, songs

Look at 6–10. If the boldfaced word is used correctly in the sentence, write *correct* above it. If not, rewrite the sentence using the boldfaced word correctly.

6. When Kip broke his ankle, he fell behind at school and **eclipsed** his classmates academically.

7. Following standard **procedure,** the paramedics responded to the call.

8. Feeling **bewilderment** about the material, Mario finished his French homework with ease.

9. Starla's grandparents loved to share their **recollections** of the past.

10. Calvin **appealed** for fewer working hours because he needed the money.

11. **English Language Coach** Read the following sentence from "A Family Thing." Use context clues to figure out what *solo* means; then define it.

    *An aunt . . . handed him a one-way ticket on a steamship, and off he went, across the Atlantic Ocean, a black-haired teenager, alone, **solo.***

NY English Language Arts Core Curriculum
(pp. 130–131)

Core R4 Determine the meaning of unfamiliar words by using context clues. **LC R17** Demonstrate comprehension through a range of activities. **R2e** Recognize how the author's use of language creates images or feelings. **W1g** Connect, compare, and contrast ideas.

For a complete description of the standards, see p. NY11.

Reading/Critical Thinking

from A Gift of Laughter

12. Recall Why did Robbie pack his bags and try to leave home?

Tip **Right There** The answer is in the text.

13. Draw Conclusions What lesson did Sherman learn from his grandmother?

Tip **Think and Search** The answer is in the text, but the details are not in one place.

14. Interpret What did Grandma mean when she said, "From a child is beautiful, anything"?

Tip **Author and Me** You will find clues in the text, but you must also use your ideas.

A Family Thing and
KNOXVILLE, TENNESSEE

15. Summarize Summarize Spinelli's main idea in "A Family Thing."

Tip **Think and Search** The answer is in the text, but the details are not in one place.

16. Analyze What did Spinelli's family mean to him when he was a child? What do you think his family means to him now?

Tip **Author and Me** You will find clues in the text, but you must also use your ideas.

17. Interpret What might the speaker in "Knoxville, Tennessee" mean when she says that summer is a time to "be warm / all the time / not only when you go to bed / and sleep"?

Tip **Author and Me** You will find clues in the text, but you must also use your ideas.

Writing: Compare the Literature

Use Your Notes
Follow these steps to compare the tones of the selection from *A Gift of Laughter* and "A Family Thing" and "Knoxville, Tennessee."

Step 1: Study the chart you made for each selection. Did you notice similar dialogue, descriptions, or events in any of the selections? Circle those details on your charts.

Step 2: Look at the notes you made in the "Writer's Attitude" column. Did you note any similarities among the three selections? Underline those details on your charts.

Step 3: Look at the notes you made in the "My Response" column. Do your responses to the selections have anything in common? Draw a box around those details on your charts.

Step 4: Look over all the similarities you just found. Use your notes and your own ideas to write responses to the questions below.

Get It on Paper
Remember that **tone** is a writer's attitude toward the subject he or she is writing about. Tone can be positive, negative, sentimental, playful, funny, or serious, among other things.

How are the tones of the selections alike? How are they different? Copy and complete these statements on a separate sheet of paper. Use the details from your comparison charts in your answers.

18. The tone of "Knoxville, Tennessee" is _____. These details support my statement: _____.

19. The tone of "A Family Thing" is _____. These details support my statement: _____.

20. The tone of *A Gift of Laughter* is _____. These details support my statement: _____.

21. "Knoxville, Tennessee," "A Family Thing," and *A Gift of Laughter* share a _____ tone. They share these similarities: _____.

UNIT 1 WRAP-UP

Answering The BIG Question — Reading: What's in It for You?

As you read the selections, you have been thinking about people's reasons for reading. Now use what you've learned to do the Unit Challenge.

The Unit Challenge

Follow the directions for the activity you've chosen.

A. Group Activity: Write a Reading Plan

With your group, you are going to make a Reading Plan for your own life. The plan will help you figure out what you can read to help you develop your interests and reach your goals. If you don't read a lot now, don't worry! This activity will help you think about how to read—with a sense of purpose—the things that relate to you.

1. **Brainstorm** Work with your group to make a list of goals you'd like to achieve. (Choose one person to be the note-taker for the group.) Do you want to go to college? What do you want to be when you grow up? Maybe you have a favorite hobby, such as drawing or playing music, and you dream of turning that hobby into a career someday.

2. **Create Diagrams** Review the notes you made on your Foldable, and think about how reading can help you reach these goals. For example, some books might show you how to do something, like make a sculpture or draw a still-life. Other books might tell you about people who share your interests. Use web diagrams to show the different things you might read. Make a separate web for

each of the goals you listed in Step 1. Look at this example:

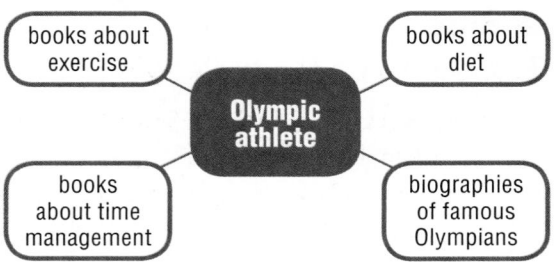

3. **Make Lists** Talk with your group about how reading can help you meet your goals and learn about interesting things. Think about the word webs you just made. Use the lists below to develop your reading plans.

Goal or Dream _____

What else do I need to know?	Where can I find out?
1. _____	1. _____
2. _____	2. _____

4. **Put It All Together** Staple together the lists and diagrams your group just made. If you can, make copies for everyone in the group. Display one copy for the class.

B. Solo Activity: Create a Reading Chart

The selections in this unit have helped you think about why you read. Now it's time to make a chart that will help you answer the Big Question. If you don't read a lot, use this activity to think about what you might like to read and why.

1. **What Do You Like to Read?** Maybe you like to read comic books, emails, and text messages from friends. Maybe you like to read books, magazines, and newspapers. Think about what you enjoy reading. What do you read often? List and explain your answers.

2. **Create a Chart** Draw a chart like the one on this page. Use the list you just made to fill it in. If there's something you've been meaning to read but haven't, write that down too. Think about why you read the things you listed.

   Maybe you read for reasons like these:
   • to find out what happened
   • to learn the facts for a test
   • for fun

   Think about what you got from reading each selection in Unit 1. Use the notes you made on your Foldable to help you.

   Maybe you gained benefits like these from reading the things on your chart.
   • learned to do something new
   • continued a friendship
   • had fun thinking about a far-off place

3. **Present Your Chart** In a small group, take turns presenting your charts. Tell group members what you read, and what you "got" from reading. Remember that not everything you read grabs your interest—sometimes you just read to get information you need. Use one or two examples from the chart to help explain why you read different things.

4. **Plan for the Future** Reading is like exercise for your brain. It helps keeps your mind in good shape. What do you want to read in the future to keep your mind in shape? Think about your hobbies, interests, and goals. With a partner, discuss topics that you'd like to know more about. Then, use your discussion to help your partner make a reading list of his or her own.

What I Read	Why I Read It	What I "Got" from Reading It
e-mails from my best friend	to find out what she did last weekend	exciting news from a person I care about

Big Question Link to Web resources to further explore the Big Question at www.glencoe.com.

Meet the Authors

Kate Montgomery grew up in Rhode Island. She went to Yale and Columbia University. She met Hilary Liftin at college. After college Montgomery went to Kenya with the Peace Corps. She and Liftin wrote letters back and forth to each other. This selection is a letter she wrote from Kenya.

Author Search For more about Hilary Liftin and Kate Montgomery, go to www.glencoe.com.

from
Dear Exile

by Hilary Liftin and
Kate Montgomery

Dear Hilary,

For the time being, Kenya has totally kicked both of our butts. Now we are full-time housewives, in a big way. Every day we have to go to market (most food spoils overnight), get water by bicycle, and sweep the red dust out of our house. Every day we cook over charcoal fires, burn the trash, bury the compost, pour our tea-colored water through a coffee filter to get out the chunks, boil it (yes, start the fire again), put it through a filter, and sometimes wash our clothes. Then perhaps a nice flour and water meal and a sponge bath by candlelight, and we try to sleep through the shrieks of the bush babies.[1] And now to be teaching too (well, not yet). (As Dave said, the term ends in April, so school probably has to start sometime before that, right?)

We finally met some of our students-to-be this week, and it got us more excited to start teaching because chatting with them was so much fun. They were really shy at first, but

---

1. A **bush baby** is a small African animal, somewhat like a monkey, that lives in trees.

when we spoke to them in Kiswahili[2] and were willing to make fools of ourselves doing it, they started to laugh and ask us questions. One boy wanted to know how many cows Dave had traded to marry me. I think he seriously damaged my credibility as a teacher by saying I was free. The kids thought it was very funny. Later, while having tea, Mr. Mbogo, the Islamic studies teacher, asked us if it was really true. When David confirmed it, Mr. Mbogo raised his hands to the sky and said, "Oh God, take me to America, where the women are free!" Anyway, we're hoping classes will begin in earnest next week.

About your vision of me having a face-off with a big spider in a mud hut: I don't live in a mud hut. It's made of concrete. (But there is usually a lot of mud in it tracked in by goats and chickens. The door doesn't close very well.) Upon seeing a spider I mostly walk away and assume she'll be gone by the time I come back. The house feels like home now, although because it's so big mostly the rooms are empty.

Already, Ramisi is starting to look different to me. At first I could only see the fallen down, ghost-town decay of the place. Then yesterday while coming back from market, I noticed that on some of the houses, the stoops were washed, the clotheslines taut, and the dirt around the front was packed down and its edges neatened. I thought, How clean! Some parts of Ramisi seem downright bright.

As for food, yesterday when I saw a shriveled up carrot for sale in the market I dove on it excitedly. We pick rocks out of the rice like we are supposed to but

never get them all, and it would increase your nightmares of losing your teeth. On the bright side, we can now add coconut milk to our short but growing list of ingredients. The other night we decided to make coconut rice. We had the coconut, a hammer, and a deadly, deer-gutting knife we got as a wedding present. I was holding the knife and the coconut while Dave tried to pound it open and hold the tin dish under it to catch the juice. There were a lot of hands and instruments and noise going on, and not a lot of coconut juice. To make it all that much more embarrassing, there were about twenty neighborhood kids staring at us from our doorway (as always since we're such a spectacle),[3] probably thinking we were trying to do a magic trick. To make conversation I said, Hey kids, I can't get the coconut open. Cute little Ali dashed off, and I figured I had scared him, but he soon came back bringing one of our neighbor women whom we hadn't met. She was carrying a huge double-edged sword and looked very determined. I was thinking, Sure, we're having a little trouble here, but you don't have to kill us for it. (Then I thought, Yes, maybe that would be best.) She walked right in, helped herself to our tortured coconut, and with one blow cracked it in half. It was a Wonder Woman moment. Dave is very excited that we will be buying such a manly kitchen instrument. Unfortunately, all the coconut juice went onto the floor when she did it, but who's going to argue with a woman with a *panga*?[4] (This incident has evolved into a friendship, and Mama Abdu has

---

2. **Kiswahili** is the language the people speak in Ramisi.

3. A **spectacle** is a strange sight.

4. A **Panga** is a large, swordlike knife.

Kate and a friend pose for a quick photo. The brightly colored cloth garment Kate wears is called a *khanga*.

since taught me many cooking tricks, like that coconut milk isn't the whitish water in the center of the nut, it's made from the meat. Who knew!)

It's amazing the different meals Mama Abdu taught me to cook out of just flour and water (and some lard): a hot, liquidy, Cream of Wheat thing for breakfast called *uji*, a lump like Play-Doh for lunch called *ugali*, and a flattened fried patty for dinner, called *chapati*. I felt like I was watching an infomercial for flour.

Last night Dave and I sat on our back stoop and watched the sunset. Yes, we sort

of have a wasteland in the backyard, but in the not-so-distant distance, beyond the burnt ground, is some greenery—trees and palmy things, and there's a palm tree right by the house, so we saw the pink and orange sunset, the silhouette[5] of a coconut palm, and a bright planet overhead. We were just sitting there by the charcoal fire, and occasionally a monkey or a jungle chicken would squawk or a sheep would wander over and nose through our compost. Then we had ourselves some warm, flat Coke, and Dave fried up some *chapati*, which he is very good at cooking, and we munched in the toxic[6] incense of mosquito-repellant smoke. Now and then a child running by would yell, "*Habari*, Daudi! *Jambo*, Katie!" Or a man returning from the next-door village would stop and chat with us about the day. We were thinking—hey, this is pretty okay.

But I don't think you need to prepare for us living here permanently. I miss you all too much, and it's too much work. Still, I am learning how to do things for the first time, with help from our neighbors, who teach us how to do everything because it's never done the way you might think (the Lesson of the Coconut). I can't just go to the store and get Scotch tape to fix things. If I need to make two items stick together, I have to figure out how to do that with whatever is around—spit, dirt, melted garbage, whatever. My students use thorns as pins to hold their papers together—when they want to hold their papers together. It's nice not to feel the

---

5. A *silhouette* is the dark outline of something against a light background. In this case, they could see the dark outline of the coconut palm against the bright sunset.

6. *Toxic* means "poisonous."

Analyzing the Photo Taking a midday break, Kate and some of her new neighbors pause for a photo. Living in Ramisi, what does Kate realize about the place she calls her "American world"?

slightest need for plastic wrap. Yes, Hilary, I know plastic wrap prevents a lot of very unsanitary[7] things from happening. But since a person doesn't die right away from eating food that hasn't been wrapped in plastic (usually), and because thorns seem to work rather well as paper fasteners (when you don't accidentally run your fingers over the corners of your students' papers, leaving a messy dribble of blood), it gives one a feeling of independence.

Of course, I can walk through a magical doorway any second I choose and be back in my American world of OfficeMax and plastic popper-pins-that-tell-you-when-the-turkey's-done-roasting. So my feeling of independence is really not from deprivation[8] but actually from privilege and wealth. I can feel lighter, relieved of

the load of a life of luxury. Poor American me. This is how I make myself sick in my free time—by making sure I realize that I'm lucky to have those things that I'm happy not to have.

Still unable to carry anything of consequence[9] atop my head,

Kate

Analyzing the Photo Study this picture of one of Kate's students. From the photo, what can you tell about this student's personality?

7. If something is ***unsanitary,*** it is unclean.

8. ***Deprivation*** is the condition of not having things you need.

9. Something of ***consequence*** is something large or important.

Reading on Your Own

To read more about the Big Question, choose one of these books from your school or local library. Work on your reading skills by choosing books that are challenging to you.

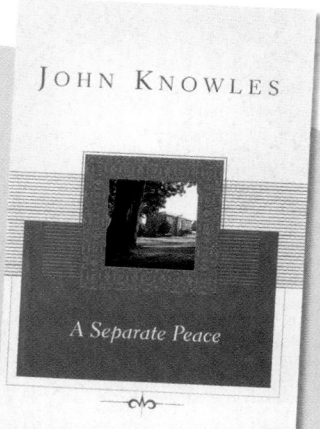

Fiction

A Separate Peace
by John Knowles

Gene is quiet, studious, and lonely. Finny is outgoing, athletic, and a daredevil. In the summer of 1942, the boys are roommates at a boarding school in New Hampshire. This is the story of their friendship and the tragic accident that changes their lives forever.

The Adventures of Huckleberry Finn
by Mark Twain

To escape his cruel father, thirteen-year-old Huckleberry Finn fakes his own death and runs away. With Jim, a runaway enslaved person, Huck travels on a raft down the Mississippi River. On shore they run into thieves, feuding families, and swindlers who kidnap Jim. To rescue him, Huck needs the help of his friend Tom Sawyer.

M. C. Higgins, the Great
by Virginia Hamilton

Sarah's Mountain has been home to fifteen-year-old Mayo Cornelius Higgins's family ever since his great-grandmother escaped from enslavement and settled there. Now their home is threatened by a pile of rubble from a mine. When two strangers arrive and offer a solution to the problem, M. C. learns about the importance of making good choices.

Shelf Life: Stories by the Book
edited by Gary Paulsen

A homeless teenager, a girl who has been brought up on Mars, and an eighth grader with a learning disability are among the characters featured in these ten short stories about how books can change lives. Authors who contributed to this collection include Joan Bauer, M.T. Anderson, and Margaret Peterson Haddix.

Nonfiction

I Know Why the Caged Bird Sings
by Maya Angelou

Maya Angelou is a well-known and highly respected writer of poetry and memoir. In this autobiography Angelou tells about her childhood in the deep South. She writes about her real experiences, even though many of them were painful. She also writes about some of the people who helped her along the way. (A selection from *I Know Why the Caged Bird Sings* is in the Genre Focus of Unit 1.)

Sitting Bull and His World
by Albert Marrin

This biography of a distinguished Native American describes not only the life and times of this influential leader but also the customs and beliefs that made him who he was. Sitting Bull's youth, his development into a brave and wise man, and his tragic death are all presented, along with helpful explanations of the culture of the Plains Indians.

Open Your Eyes: Extraordinary Experiences in Faraway Places
edited by Jill Davis

This collection of autobiographical stories reveals how being exposed to other cultures can change a young person's life. Ten writers describe their experiences in places as different as a boarding school in England and a small shop in Tokyo. In one of the two stories set in the United States, Piper Dellums writes about the foreign-exchange student who comes to live in her home and is shocked to discover that the African American Dellums are her host and not the household servants.

Guinea Pig Scientists: Bold Self-Experimenters in Science and Medicine
by Leslie Dendy and Mel Boring

Here are ten stories of real scientists who try their experiments on themselves. Their explorations of such things as digestion, deadly diseases, and safety gear are brave, often dangerous, and sometimes shocking. Each chapter ends with a description of what is learned from the scientist's work and what is now known about the subject.

New York English Language Arts Test Practice

*D*irections
Read this passage about the childhood of an author's father. Then answer questions 1 through 6.

from *Ornaments*
Ross's Angel
By Patricia C. and Fredrick McKissack, Jr.

When Grandmother Melinda was 18 years old, she married Daniel Ripley and the couple moved to Chicago. Ross Ripley, my father, was the youngest of their three children. His sister, Grace, was the oldest, and his brother, Thomas, was next.

The November Ross turned seven, Franklin Delano Roosevelt was elected president of the United States, and his daddy died. Times were hard, but Melinda knew they would be harder if she stayed in Chicago. Widowed and poor, she packed up her family and moved back to Thomasville, Tennessee. Grandmother Melinda's folks were still living then, and they welcomed their daughter and three grandchildren into the ancestral home.

By the following year, Melinda had met and married her second husband, Charles Bevels. He was a robust man with large hands and broad shoulders. He had a voice as large as his body, and when he laughed the chandelier tingled in the dining room. Everybody called him Big Dad; everybody was charmed by his warmth and generosity. All except Ross.

"He's not my daddy," Ross said defiantly. "And he'll never be my Daddy."

Nobody knew how much Ross was hurting inside. He missed his father, but he was unable to express his feelings. Instead, he chose not to talk much, because he had developed a stutter. Adding to his problems, Ross was clumsy and slow to smile. Beside his brother and sister, who had sunny dispositions, he became a gray child who would just blend into the scenery. That's where he stayed, thinking nobody really cared.

1 In this passage, a **conflict** is developing

A around Ross's feelings about his father and "Big Dad"

B between Ross and his mother

C between Ross and the children who make fun of him

D among the crowded family members

2 What is the author's **main** purpose in this passage?

F to show how brave Ross's mother is

G to explain how Ross's father died

H to show how Ross is reacting to his father's death

J to explain why Ross's mother was poor

3 The tone of this passage is **best** described as

A defiant toward "Big Dad"

B making fun of Ross

C sympathetic toward Ross

D remorseful about Ross's father

4 The description of "Big Dad" in the third paragraph shows

F why Ross doesn't like "Big Dad"

G why "Big Dad" married Ross's mother

H why most people like "Big Dad"

J why "Big Dad" is so funny

5 Based on this passage, choose the sentence that **most likely** describes why Ross doesn't like "Big Dad."

A "Big Dad" is mean to Ross.

B "Big Dad" likes Ross's brother and sister more.

C Ross is worried about his mother.

D Ross misses his father.

6 On a separate sheet of paper, copy the chart below and identify one of the problems Ross struggles with in the passage. Then explain how that problem affects Ross.

Ross's problem	How it affects him

Directions

Read this article about author Larry Woiwode. Then answer questions 7 through 11.

Meet Author Larry Woiwode

In his classroom at the University of North Dakota, author and professor Larry Woiwode passes along his lifetime of experience to another generation of writers. It is a fitting venue for Woiwode, whose fiction reflects his family's long history in North Dakota. Five generations of his family had lived on the state's western plains, and the writer and his work have close ties to the area.

In a discussion about regional writing, Woiwode said, "The more you enter your particular region, the area in which you live, or the place in which your characters are set, the more you must be accurate." This accuracy gives his own writing a strong sense of place and character that brings his stories to life.

North Dakota to New York...and Back

Woiwode was born in Carrington, North Dakota, on October 30, 1941. He spent his early childhood in the nearby town of Sykeston, where his parents were both schoolteachers and his father was also superintendent. When Woiwode was nine, his father uprooted the family and moved them to Illinois. A year after moving, his mother died from kidney problems, and the tragedy deeply affected the young Woiwode. At the age of eighteen, he began attending the University of Illinois and published his first fiction while he was still a student there. Woiwode soon left Illinois and moved to New York City, determined to succeed as either a writer or an actor.

In New York, Woiwode was mentored by the fiction editor of the *New Yorker* magazine, William Maxwell. Maxwell was famous for helping develop other great authors—such as John Updike and J. D. Salinger—and in the 1960s he helped Woiwode establish himself as one of the premier young writers of his generation. After publishing several stories and poems in the *New Yorker* and other major magazines, Woiwode published his acclaimed first novel, *What I'm Going to Do, I Think*, in 1969. His writing has received numerous awards over the years, and in 1995 he received the Award of Merit Medal from the American Academy of Arts and Letters. Woiwode eventually moved back to North Dakota and now teaches at the university in Grand Forks.

7 Based on this article, choose the sentence that best explains why moving to New York was good for Woiwode's career.

F Woiwode met his mentor in New York.

G William Maxwell introduced Woiwode to John Updike and J. D. Salinger in New York.

H New York was a big city with a broad audience.

J Woiwode wasn't being noticed in North Dakota.

8 The opening paragraph is **mainly** intended to

A explain why Woiwode became a professor

B provide Woiwode's family history

C show how Woiwode became a writer

D reveal Woiwode's connection to North Dakota

9 When Woiwode left for New York, what was **most likely** the reason for his confidence that he would succeed as a writer?

F He had received the Award of Merit Medal.

G Both his parents were schoolteachers.

H William Maxwell had been mentoring him.

J He had already been published.

10 Read these sentences from the passage.

It is a fitting venue for Woiwode, whose fiction reflects his family's long history in North Dakota. Five generations of his family had lived on the state's western plains, and the writer and his work have close ties to the area.

In this sentence, the word *venue* **most likely** means

A place

B profession

C attitude

D philosophy

11 Based on the article, choose the statement with which Woiwode would **most likely** agree.

F In regional writing, setting is more important than character.

G It is more difficult to be accurate when writing about a region.

H Accuracy is important when you write in depth about a place.

J An accurate setting is important for character development.

Directions

**Read this passage about the author's visit to his hometown.
Then answer questions 12 through 17.**

from *When We Were Colored*
By Clifton L. Taulbert

It was a beautiful October day in the 1970s. It was not quite like those other October days when I was a child growing up in this southern cotton community, but it was beautiful nonetheless. I had come home for my yearly pilgrimage to see Glen Allan, Mississippi, to remember the life I once knew and visit my older relatives. Somehow I always felt better after visiting those tired old people who had given me strength when I was a child. So many changes had taken place in Glen Allan. "Colored" people were now "black," soap operas had replaced quilting bees in their homes, and the schools their children attended were now integrated. But the land was the same; the rich delta land had not changed. And the cotton smelled as it did in the early '50s when I picked it as a way of life. Now, however, the quarter of a mile long cotton rows seemed shorter and instead of the bent backs were scores of big red machines harvesting the white fields. As always, the land was giving life, being faithful, fruitful and productive, providing stability and a sense of worth.

---

12 Which statement **best** explains why the author returns to visit his hometown?

 A because he feels guilty about leaving

 B because he cannot believe how much it has changed

 C because the town is beautiful and visiting it helps him remember his past

 D so he can show his family how successful he has become

13 Based on the passage, choose which of these things could **best** be described as "the foundation of the Glen Allan community."

 F the workers in the fields

 G the author's family

 H the schools and neighborhoods

 J the land

14 The author mentions the "big red machines" in order to show
  A how much has changed since he lived there
  B how much cotton there is to pick
  C how beautiful they were in the white fields
  D why he can never live there again

15 Based on the passage, choose the word that **best** describes how the author feels about his hometown.
  F disappointed
  G nostalgic
  H sad
  J angry

16 According to the passage, what is one of the things that have remained constant since the author's childhood?
  A the integrated schools
  B the smell of the cotton
  C the tired old people
  D the quilting bees

17 In the passage from *When We Were Colored*, the narrator describes how his hometown has changed since he was a child. On a separate sheet of paper, explain the significance of one of these changes. Use details from the article to support your answer.

UNIT 2

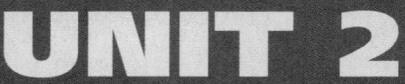

The BIG Question

Which Is More Important, the Journey or the Destination?

> "A journey of a thousand miles begins with a single step."
>
> —Lao Tzu
> 6th-century B.C. Chinese philosopher

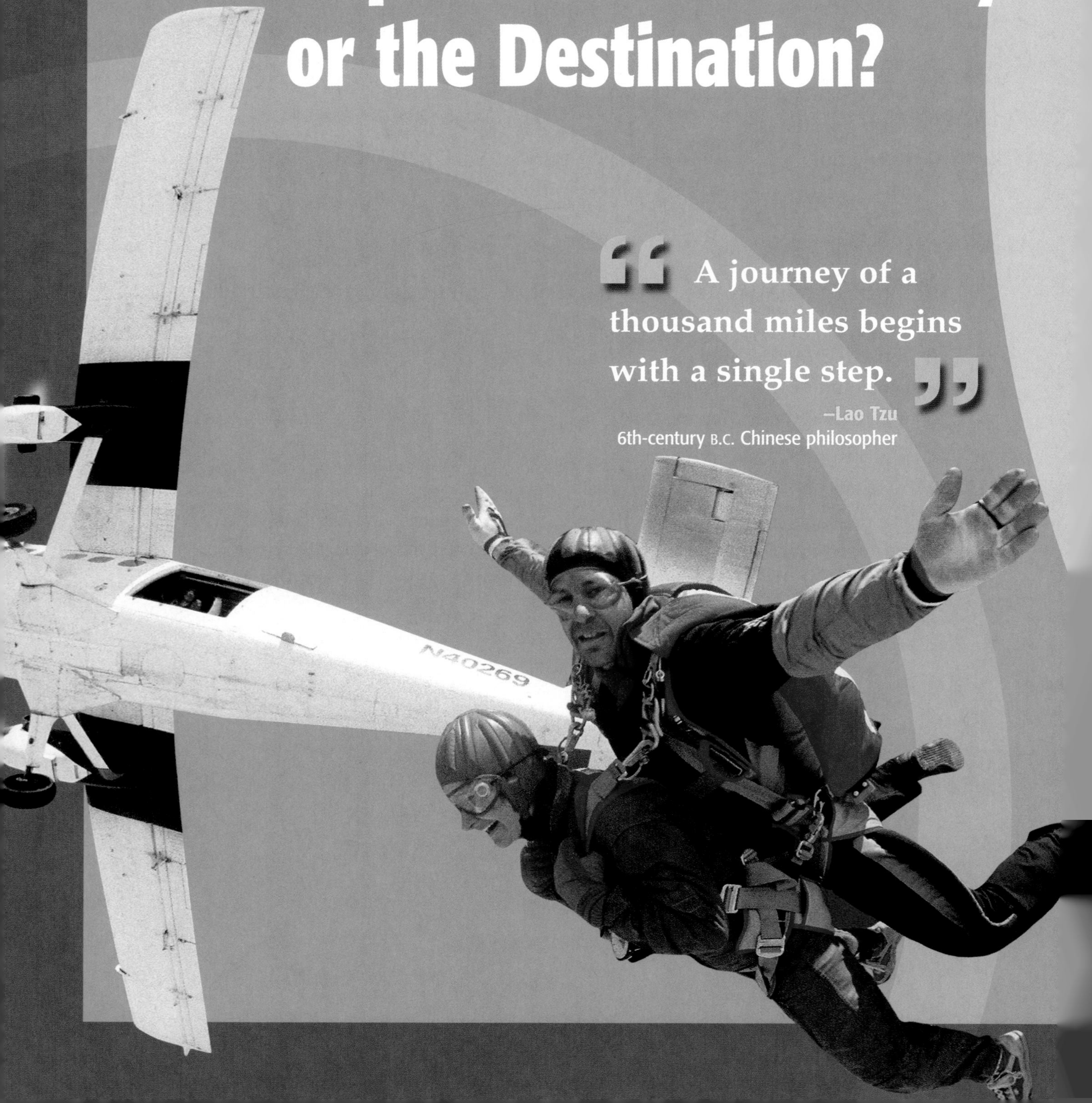

LOOKING AHEAD

The skill lessons and readings in this unit will help you develop your own answer to the Big Question.

UNIT 2 WRAP-UP • Answering the Big Question

Connecting to **BIG** *The Question* Which Is More Important, the Journey or the Destination?

It's important to have a destination, or a place where you want to go. But there is much more to life than just reaching your destination. Sometimes your efforts along the way are just as important as the end result. In this unit, you'll read about different people and their journeys.

Real Kids and the Big Question

JULIE and her friend Lelia walk home together every day after school. As they walk, they laugh, talk, and share secrets. Although there's a bus that stops near the girls' homes, they would rather walk home from school. Why do you think Julie and Lelia prefer the journey of walking home?

TAKESHI loves to ride his bike. He rides it to school every day and to the park on weekends. Most times, Takeshi likes riding to specific places. Other times, he enjoys riding just for fun, with no destination in mind. What do you think Takeshi would say is more important, the journey or the destination?

Warm-Up Activity

On your own, choose one of the questions above and answer it in a few sentences in your Learner's Notebook.

You and the Big Question

Reading about other people's journeys will help you think about and compare the importance of journeys and destinations.

Literature Online

BIG Question Link to Web resources to further explore the Big Question at www.glencoe.com.

Plan for the Unit Challenge

At the end of the unit, you'll use notes from all your reading to complete the Unit Challenge. You'll choose one of the following activities:

A. Trial TV You'll work with classmates to hold a made-for-TV trial in which you try to convince a jury that either journeys or destinations are more important.

B. Interview Interview a family member, neighbor, or friend about a journey that he or she made, and decide which part of it was most important.

- Start thinking about which activity you'd like to do so that you can narrow your focus as you read each selection. Do you usually enjoy working as part of a group or team? Do you like to act, role play, or perform in front of an audience of classmates? If your answer to these questions is "yes," then you would probably prefer to do Activity A, Trial TV. On the other hand, if you usually prefer working with just one other person, then Activity B may be more your style.

- In your Learner's Notebook, write your thoughts about the activity you'd like to do.

- Each time you make notes about the Big Question, think about how your ideas will help you with the Unit Challenge activity you chose.

Keep Track of Your Ideas

FOLDABLES™
Study Organizer

As you read, you'll make notes about the Big Question. Later, you'll use these notes to complete the Unit Challenge. See pages R8–R9 for help with making Foldable 2. This diagram shows how it should look.

1. Use this Foldable for all of the selections in this unit. Label the front flap with the unit number and the Big Question. Label the bottom of each flap below with a title, beginning with "The People Could Fly." (See page 147 for the titles.)

2. Open each flap. Near the top of each flap, write **My Purpose for Reading.**

3. Below each crease, write **The Big Question.**

Unit 2
Which Is More Important,
the Journey or the Destination?

Title	Title
Title	Title
Title	Title
Title	Title
Title	Title

Folktales are stories that have been told from one generation to the next before being written down. Aside from being entertaining, many of the tales also teach a lesson in life or express the beliefs of a group of people. In this unit, you'll read these and other kinds of folktales:

- **Legends**–stories about heroes and extraordinary events. The deeds and events in legends are usually based on fact but become exaggerated as generations of storytellers add to the stories
- **Cautionary Tales**–stories in which people are punished for breaking society's rules or misbehaving
- **Myths**–ancient stories about gods, goddesses, or other supernatural beings and their influence on people and nature

Why Read Folktales?

Throughout history, people have told stories to explain who they are, where they come from, and why things happen. Folktales can help you understand human society, connect the past and present, and pass on cultural ideals.

How to Read Folktales

Key Reading Skills

These reading skills are especially useful tools for reading and understanding folktales. You'll see these skills modeled in the Active Reading Model on pages 151–159, and you'll learn more about them later in this unit.

- **■ Analyzing** Identify the elements of a selection and their relationship to each other. (See Reading Workshop 1.)
- **■ Making Inferences** Use clues to figure out the meaning of ideas that are not directly stated. (See Reading Workshop 2.)
- **■ Predicting** Guess what will happen next in a tale, based on what you know and have read. (See Reading Workshop 3.)
- **■ Comparing and Contrasting** See how things are alike and different. (See Reading Workshop 4.)

Key Literary Elements

Recognizing and thinking about the following literary elements will help you understand more fully what the author is telling you.

- **■ Protagonist and Antagonist:** the main character and the person or force that stands in the way of his or her happiness (See "The People Could Fly.")
- **■ Plot:** events and the order in which they are arranged (See "The Oxcart.")
- **■ Conflict:** a struggle between opposing forces (See "The Snake Chief.")
- **■ Theme:** a story's main idea or life lesson (See "Daedalus and Icarus.")

Skills Focus

- Key skills for reading folktales
- Key literary elements of folktales

Skills Model

You will see how to use the key reading skills and elements as you read

- *Racing the Great Bear,* p. 151

Study Central Visit www.glencoe .com and click on Study Central to review folktales.

NY English Language Arts Core Curriculum (pp. 150–159)

LC R13 Use text structure and literary devices to aid comprehension and response. **R1l** Draw conclusions and make inferences on the basis of explicit and implied information. **R1m** Make, confirm, or revise predictions. **LC R12** Combine multiple strategies to enhance comprehension and response. **R2b** Interpret characters, plot, and theme, using evidence from the text.

For a complete description of the standards, see p. NY 11.

Racing THE GREAT BEAR

retold by Joseph Bruchac

The notes in the side columns model how to use the skills and elements you read about on page 150.

Folktale

ACTIVE READING MODEL

NE ONENDJI. Hear my story, which happened long ago. For many generations, the five nations of the Haudenosaunee, the People of the Longhouse, had been at war with one another. No one could say how the wars began, but each time a man of one nation was killed, his relatives sought revenge in the blood feud,[1] and so the fighting continued. Then the Creator took pity on his people and sent a messenger of peace. **1**

The Peacemaker traveled from nation to nation, convincing the people of the Five Nations—the Mohawk, the Oneida, the Onondaga, the Cayuga, and the Seneca[2]—that it was wrong for brothers to kill one another. It was not easy, but finally the nations agreed and the Great Peace began. Most welcomed that peace, though there were some beings with bad hearts who wished to see the return of war.

One day, not long after the Great Peace had been established, some young men in a Seneca village decided they would pay a visit to the Onondaga people.

"It is safe now to walk the trail between our nations," the young men said. "We will return after the sun has risen and set seven times."

Then they set out. They walked toward the east until they were lost from

1 **Key Reading Skill**
Analyzing *I know from the first few sentences that this story takes place a long time ago and that it is about Native Americans. I know that many Native American tales entertain and teach lessons, so I'll be on the lookout for the theme.*

Alabaster Bear with Heartline. Contemporary Zuni. Alabaster, 1⅝ x 2¾ in. Private collection.

---

1. A **feud** is a long, bitter quarrel between two individuals or groups.
2. **Oneida** (oh NY duh), **Onondaga** (aw nun DAW guh), **Cayuga** (ky OO guh), **Seneca** (SEN uh kuh)

sight in the hills. But many more than seven days passed, and those young men never returned. Now another group of young men left, wanting to find out where their friends had gone. They, too, did not return. **2**

The people grew worried. Parties were sent out to look for the vanished young men, but no sign was found. And the searchers who went too far into the hills did not return, either.

The old chief of the village thought long and hard. He asked the clan[3] mothers, those wise women whose job it was to choose the chiefs and give them good advice, what should be done.

"We must find someone brave enough to face whatever danger is out there," the clan mothers said.

So the old chief called the whole village to a council meeting. He held up a white strand of wampum beads made from quahog[4] clamshells as he spoke.

"Hear me," he said. "I am of two minds about what has happened to our people. It may be that the Onondaga have broken the peace and captured them. It may be there is something with an evil mind that wishes to destroy this new peace and so has killed our people. Now someone must go and find out. Who is brave enough? Who will come and take this wampum from my hand?"

Many men were gathered in that council. Some were known to speak of themselves as brave warriors. Still, though they muttered to one another, no man stepped forward to take the strand of wampum. The old chief began to walk about the circle, holding the wampum in front of each man in turn. But each man only lowered his eyes to the ground. No man lifted his hand to take the wampum. **3**

2 Key Reading Skill
Making Inferences *The author does not say for sure, but I think that something bad must have happened to the young men. Otherwise, they would have returned by now.*

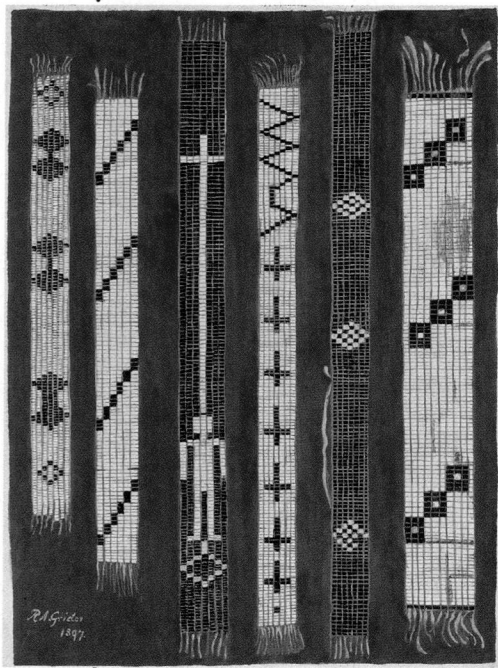

Iroquois Wampum Belts. Rufus Grider. Newberry Library, Chicago.

Wampum is a string of white shell beads. Some Native Americans used wampum as a form of money, and it was also used in tribal rituals and to record history.

3 Key Reading Skill
Predicting *I think that the person who goes after the young men will find that something evil has taken them. Most citizens of the Five Nations want peace, so the Onondaga are probably not behind the young men's disappearance.*

---

3. A *clan* is group of families who descend from a common ancestor.

4. The *quahog* (KOH hawg) is a type of clam found on the Atlantic coast of North America.

Just outside the circle stood a boy who had not yet become a man. His parents were dead, and he lived with his grandmother in her old lodge at the edge of the village. His clothing was always torn and his face dirty because his grandmother was too old to care for him as a mother would. The other young men made fun of him, and as a joke they called him Swift Runner—even though no one had ever seen him run and it was thought that he was weak and lazy. All he ever seemed to do was play with his little dog or sit by the fire and listen when the old people were talking.

"Our chief has forgotten our greatest warrior," one of the young men said to another, tilting his head toward Swift Runner.

"*Nyoh,*" the other young man said, laughing. "Yes. Why does he not offer the wampum to Swift Runner?"

The chief looked around the circle of men, and the laughing stopped. He walked out of the circle to the place where the small boy in torn clothes stood. He held out the wampum and Swift Runner took it without hesitating. 🔢

"I accept this," Swift Runner said. "It is right that I be the one to face the danger.

In the eyes of the people I am worthless, so if I do not return, it will not matter. I will leave when the sun rises tomorrow."

When Swift Runner arrived home at his grandmother's lodge, the old woman was waiting for him.

"Grandson," she said, "I know what you have done. The people of this village no longer remember, but your father was a great warrior. Our family is a family that has power."

Then she reached up into the rafters and took down a heavy bow. It was blackened with smoke and seemed so thick that no man could bend it.

"If you can string this bow, Grandson," the old woman said, "you are ready to face whatever waits for you on the trail."

🔢 Key Reading Skill
Comparing and Contrasting
This boy is different from the others. He seems braver because he takes the wampum instead of looking at the ground, but he also seems weaker because he is small.

Northeast Woodlands Pottery Vessel. Iroquois. 27 cm.

Swift Runner took the bow. It was as thick as a man's wrist, but he bent it with ease and strung it.

"Wah-hah!" said his grandmother. "You are the one I knew you would grow up to be. Now you must sleep. At dawn we will make you ready for your journey." **5**

It was not easy for Swift Runner to sleep, but when he woke the next morning, he felt strong and clearheaded. His grandmother was sitting by the fire with a cap in her hand.

"This was your grandfather's cap," she said. "I have sewed four hummingbird feathers on it. It will make your feet more swift."

Swift Runner took the cap and placed it on his head.

His grandmother held up four pairs of moccasins.

"Carry these tied to your waist. When one pair wears out, throw them aside and put on the next pair."

Swift Runner took the moccasins and tied them to his belt.

Next his grandmother picked up a small pouch. "In this pouch is cornmeal mixed with maple sugar," she said. "It is the only food you will need as you travel. It will give you strength when you eat it each evening."

Swift Runner took the pouch and hung it from his belt by the moccasins.

"The last thing I must give you," said the old woman, "is this advice. Pay close attention to your little dog. You have treated him well and so he is your great friend. He is small, but his eyes and nose are keen.[5] Keep him always in front of you. He will warn you of danger before it can strike you."

Then Swift Runner set out on his journey. His little dog stayed ahead of him, sniffing the air and sniffing the ground. By the time the sun was in the middle of the sky, they were far from the

ACTIVE READING MODEL

5 Key Literary Element
Protagonist and Antagonist
The tale is now focusing on Swift Runner. He must be the main character, or protagonist. I wonder whom the antagonist will turn out to be?

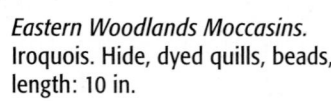

Eastern Woodlands Moccasins. Iroquois. Hide, dyed quills, beads, length: 10 in.

---

5. Something that is **keen** is highly sensitive or sharp.

village. The trail passed through deep woods, and it seemed to the boy as if something was following them among the trees. But he could see nothing in the thick brush.

The trail curved toward the left, and the boy felt even more the presence of something watching. Suddenly his little dog ran into the brush at the side of the trail, barking loudly. There were the sounds of tree limbs breaking and heavy feet running. Then out of the forest came a Nyagwahe, a monster bear. Its great teeth were as long as a man's arm. It was twice as tall as a moose. Close at its heels was Swift Runner's little dog.

"I see you," Swift Runner shouted. "I am after you. You cannot escape me."

Swift Runner had learned those words by listening to the stories the old people told. They were the very words a monster bear speaks when it attacks, words that terrify anyone who hears them. On hearing those words, the great bear turned and fled from the boy.

"You cannot escape me," Swift Runner shouted again. Then he ran after the bear.

The Nyagwahe turned toward the east, with Swift Runner and his dog close behind. It left the trail and plowed through the thick forest, breaking down great trees and leaving a path of destruction like that of a whirlwind. It ran up the tallest hills and down through the swamps, but the boy and the dog stayed at its heels. They ran past a great cave in the rocks. All around the cave were the bones of people the bear had caught and eaten.

"My relatives," Swift Runner called as he passed the cave, "I will not forget you. I am after the one who killed you. He will not escape me." 6

Throughout the day, the boy and his dog chased the great bear, growing closer bit by bit. At last, as the sun began to set, Swift Runner stopped at the head of a small valley and called his small dog to him.

"We will rest here for the night," the boy said. He took

Beaded Pouch. Iroquois. Velvet, metal, beads, cloth, length: 6 1/2 in.

6 Key Literary Element
Conflict *It looks as if trouble is ahead. There's a conflict brewing between Swift Runner and the monster bear, Nyagwahe. If that turns out to be true, then Nyagwahe is the antagonist, and Swift Runner is the protagonist.*

off his first pair of moccasins, whose soles were worn away to nothing. He threw them aside and put on a new pair. Swift Runner made a fire and sat beside it with his dog. Then he took out the pouch of cornmeal and maple sugar, sharing his food with his dog.

"Nothing will harm us," Swift Runner said. "Nothing can come close to our fire." He lay down and slept.

In the middle of the night, he was awakened by the growling of his dog. He sat up with his back to the fire and looked into the darkness. There, just outside the circle of light made by the flames, stood a dark figure that looked like a tall man. Its eyes glowed green.

"I am Nyagwahe," said the figure. "This is my human shape. Why do you pursue[6] me?"

"You cannot escape me," Swift Runner said. "I chase you because you killed my people. I will not stop until I catch you and kill you." **7**

The figure faded back into the darkness.

"You cannot escape me," Swift Runner said again. Then he patted his small dog and went to sleep.

As soon as the first light of the new day appeared, Swift Runner rose. He and his small dog took the trail. It was easy to follow the monster's path, for trees were uprooted and the earth torn by its great paws. They ran all through the morning. When the sun was in the middle of the sky, they reached the head of another valley. At the other end they saw the great bear running toward the east. Swift Runner pulled off his second pair of moccasins, whose soles were worn away to nothing. He put on his third pair and began to run again.

All through that day, they kept the Nyagwahe in sight, drawing closer bit by bit. When the sun began to set, Swift Runner stopped to make camp. He took off the third pair of moccasins, whose soles were worn away to nothing, and put on the last pair.

"Tomorrow," he said to his small dog, "we will catch the monster and kill it." He reached for his pouch of cornmeal and maple sugar, but when he opened it, he found it filled with worms. The magic of the Nyagwahe

7 Key Reading Skill

Predicting *From what I've seen of Swift Runner's personality, I think he'll keep this promise. I predict he won't stop until he catches Nyagwahe.*

---

6. **Pursue** means to chase after something.

had done this. Swift Runner poured out the pouch and said in a loud voice, "You have spoiled our food, but it will not stop me. I am on your trail. You cannot escape me."

That night, once again, he was awakened by the growling of his dog. A dark figure stood just outside the circle of light.

It looked smaller than the night before, and the glow of its eyes was weak.

"I am Nyagwahe," the dark figure said. "Why do you pursue me?"

"You cannot escape me," Swift Runner said. "I am on your trail. You killed my people. You threatened the Great Peace. I will not rest until I catch you."

"Hear me," said the Nyagwahe. "I see your power is greater than mine. Do not kill me. When you catch me, take my great teeth. They are my power, and you can use them for healing. Spare my life and I will go far to the north and never again bother the People of the Longhouse." 8

"You cannot escape me," Swift Runner said. "I am on your trail."

The dark figure faded back into the darkness, and Swift Runner sat for a long time, looking into the night.

At the first light of day, the boy and his dog took the trail. They had not gone far when they saw the Nyagwahe ahead of them. Its sides puffed in and out as it ran. The trail was beside a big lake with many alder trees close to the water. As the great bear ran past, the leaves were torn from the trees. Fast as the bear went, the boy and his dog came closer, bit by bit. At last, when the sun was in the middle of the sky, the giant bear could run no longer. It fell heavily to the earth, panting so hard that it stirred up clouds of dust.

Swift Runner unslung his grandfather's bow and notched an arrow to the sinewy[7] string.

Bear Claw Necklace. Native American. Bear claws, metal beads, otter or fisher tail, length: 57 1/2 in.

8 Key Reading Skill
Predicting *I'm not sure whether Swift Runner will let Nyagwahe go. It seems to me he wants to prove himself as a warrior, so I predict he won't.*

---

7. Something that is **sinewy** is tough and strong.

Analyzing the Photo A giant grizzly bares its teeth in a ferocious roar. Does this picture capture the Nyagwahe's enormous size and strength? Why or why not?

"Shoot for my heart," said the Nyagwahe. "Aim well. If you cannot kill me with one arrow, I will take your life."

"No," Swift Runner said. "I have listened to the stories of my elders. Your only weak spot is the sole of your foot. Hold up your foot and I will kill you."

The great bear shook with fear. "You have defeated me," it pleaded. "Spare my life and I will leave forever."

"You must give me your great teeth," Swift Runner said. "Then you must leave and never bother the People of the Longhouse again."

"I shall do as you say," said the Nyagwahe. "Take my great teeth."

Swift Runner lowered his bow. He stepped forward and pulled out the great bear's teeth. It rose to its feet and walked to the north, growing smaller as it went. It went over the hill and was gone. 🄰

Carrying the teeth of the Nyagwahe over his shoulder, Swift Runner turned back to the west, his dog at his side. He walked for three moons before he reached the place where the bones of his people were piled in front of the

🄰 **Key Literary Element**
Plot *This is an important time in the story. The conflict between Swift Runner and Nyagwahe reaches its peak, so this is the climax of the plot.*

monster's empty cave. He collected those bones and walked around them four times. "Now," he said, "I must do something to make my people wake up." He went to a big hickory tree and began to push it over so that it would fall on the pile of bones.

"My people," he shouted, "get up quickly or this tree will land on you."

The bones of the people who had been killed all came together and jumped up, alive again and covered with flesh. They were filled with joy and gathered around Swift Runner.

"Great one," they said, "who are you?"

"I am Swift Runner," he said.

"How can that be?" one of the men said. "Swift Runner is a skinny little boy. You are a tall, strong man."

Swift Runner looked at himself and saw that it was so. He was taller than the tallest man, and his little dog was bigger than a wolf.

"I am Swift Runner," he said. "I was that boy and I am the man you see before you."

Then Swift Runner led his people back to the village. He carried with him the teeth of the Nyagwahe, and those who saw what he carried rejoiced. The trails were safe again, and the Great Peace would not be broken. **10** Swift Runner went to his grandmother's lodge and embraced her.

"Grandson," she said, "you are now the man I knew you would grow up to be. Remember to use your power to help the people."

So it was that Swift Runner ran with the great bear and won the race. Throughout his long life, he used the teeth of the Nyagwahe to heal the sick, and he worked always to keep the Great Peace.

Da neho. I am finished. **11** ○

10 Key Literary Element
Plot *The action is winding down. The conflict is over, Swift Runner has met his goals, and peace is restored. This must be the falling action of the plot.*

11 Key Literary Element
Theme *After analyzing the characters and events in the story, I see a pattern. Swift Runner helps his village by getting rid of Nyagwahe. Then he also helps his relatives by bringing them back to life. Finally, his grandmother tells him he must always help the people, and he does. So a theme of the story must be that helping others can make you a true hero.*

Small Group Discussion With two or three other students, talk about a time that you have predicted the outcome of a TV show or movie. Share how you made inferences that led to your prediction.

Write to Learn In your Learner's Notebook, write the name of someone you think is a modern-day hero. What are some things this person has done that make him or her a hero? How is he or she like a hero in a folktale? Write your answers in your Learner's Notebook.

Skills Focus

You will practice these skills when you read the following selections:
"The People Could Fly," p. 164
"A Father's Daring Trek," p. 172

Reading

• Analyzing content and structure

Literature

• Identifying protagonists and antagonists
• Understanding how setting can influence plot

Vocabulary

• Using techniques for building vocabulary
• Academic Vocabulary: *analyzing*

Writing/Grammar

• Using adjectives and adverbs correctly

NY English Language Arts Core Curriculum
(pp. 160–161)

LC R13 Use text structure and literary devices to aid comprehension and response.

For a complete description of the standards, see p. NY 11.

Skill Lesson

Analyzing

Learn It!

What Is It? Analyzing is looking at the separate parts of a selection and thinking how they work together to express ideas. Just as you might take apart a watch to see how it works, so you can take apart a story or article to see what makes it "tick." When you analyze a story, you might look at parts, or elements, like these:
• plot
• conflict
• theme

When you analyze an article, you might think about these elements:
• main ideas
• reasons, examples, descriptions
• organization

BIG TOP © 2005 Harrell. Dist. by UNIVERSAL PRESS SYNDICATE. Reprinted with permission. All rights reserved

Analyzing Cartoons
The bear analyzes his relationship with food by considering his feelings about his sandwich.

Academic Vocabulary

analyzing (AN uh lyz ing) *n.* examining by separating into parts and identifying relationships between the parts

Why Is It Important? Analyzing helps you look carefully at a piece of writing. You'll understand it better, because you know the parts it is made of and the ways that the parts fit together.

How Do I Do It? First, decide what you want to analyze; then separate it into parts. Think about what each part is saying. Then see how the parts fit together to convey an overall idea. To see how this works, read the passage below. Then read to see how a student analyzed the conflict described in the passage.

Literature Online

Study Central Visit www.glencoe .com and click on Study Central to review analyzing.

> The stars and moon hid behind the clouds. Still the man walked on, his fingers grasping the handle of his silver sword. He knew he might need it at any moment. Suddenly, a streak of lightning flashed across the sky. In that instant, he saw it. It was waiting for him in the darkness. He held his breath and drew his sword.

> *Everything in the passage tells me a dangerous conflict, or struggle, is about to take place. The darkness and flash of lightning create a sense of danger, and so do the man's thoughts and actions. He holds onto his sword as he walks, so he must feel threatened by someone or something. Then he sees "it." I'm not sure what "it" is—maybe a monster?—but I am sure the man thinks that "it" is about to attack him, because he draws his sword.*

Practice It!

Think about a story you have recently read or a movie you have recently seen. Answer these questions.

- Who is the most important character in the story?
- What problem or challenge does that character face?
- How does the character solve the problem or overcome the challenge?
- What is the main message, or theme, of the story?

Use It!

As you read the selections, think about how you might analyze what they mean.

Before You Read | The People Could Fly

Virginia Hamilton

Meet the Author

Many of Virginia Hamilton's award-winning books celebrate her African American ancestry and culture. She once said, "In the background of much of my writing is the dream of freedom tantalizingly out of reach." This dream is the source of many folktales, including "The People Could Fly." See page R2 of the Author Files in the back of the book for more on Virginia Hamilton.

Author Search For more about Virginia Hamilton, go to www.glencoe.com.

NY English Language Arts Core Curriculum (pp. 162–167)

LC R8 Recognize grade–appropriate synonyms and antonyms. **LC R13** Use text structure and literary devices to aid comprehension and response. **R2b** Interpret characters and theme, using evidence from the text.

For a complete description of the standards, see p. NY 11.

Vocabulary Preview

scorned (skornd) *adj.* looked down upon by someone; form of the verb *scorn* **(p. 164)** *The scorned people longed for justice.*

snarled (snarld) *v.* made tangled or knotted; form of the verb *snarl* **(p. 166)** *The rope snarled around the young girl's ankle.*

English Language Coach

Vocabulary Building: Synonyms and Antonyms Every time you study the vocabulary words in a lesson, you're working on building your vocabulary. But how can you remember all the vocabulary words you study?

One way is to link "new" words with "old" ones you already know. Pair an unfamiliar word with a synonym—a word or phrase that means about the same thing—or an antonym, a word or phrase that means the opposite. Suppose, for example, that you want to remember the word *perplexing* (per PLEKS ing), which means "puzzling" or "confusing." Make a synonym-antonym chart like the one below to help yourself remember the word.

Word	Synonym	Antonym
perplexing	confusing	clear

With a Partner Get together with a classmate, and use a dictionary to look up the underlined words below. Make a synonym-antonym chart for the words.

- The stubborn child was very **exasperating**.
- The **towering** office building had 50 floors.
- That **arrogant** woman thinks she knows more than anybody else.

Word	Synonym	Antonym
exasperating		
towering		
arrogant		

Skills Preview

Key Reading Skill: Analyzing

As you read "The People Could Fly," you'll analyze ways it is like other folktales you've read. Before you read, spend a few minutes thinking about the tales.

Whole Class Discussion Brainstorm a list of folktales, like "Little Red Riding Hood," "Cinderella," and "Hansel and Gretel." Then discuss the following questions:

- Which tales have characters with magical powers?
- Which tales have at least one character who is very evil and one who is very good?
- In which tales do the good characters win out over the evil ones?
- What do your answers tell you about folktales?

Key Literary Element: Protagonist and Antagonist

The main character in a narrative, or story, is known as the **protagonist** (pro TAG oh nist). In traditional stories, like folktales, the protagonist is often a completely good person—someone you like or look up to, identify with, and hope will win in the end. In modern stories, the protagonist is often good *and* bad. Like real people, he or she may have faults and weaknesses.

The **antagonist** (an TAG oh nist) is the person, group of people, or force that stands in the way of the protagonist's happiness. The force might be bad luck or a force of nature. For example, a blinding snowstorm can be the antagonist in a story if the storm keeps the main character from reaching the safety of his or her home. To find the protagonist and antagonist in a story, ask yourself, *Who is this mainly about? Who or what is working against him or her?*

Literature Online

Interactive Literary Elements Handbook
To review or learn more about the literary elements, go to www.glencoe.com.

Get Ready to Read

Connect to the Reading

Imagine that you could fly on your own like a bird. When might you use your special ability and why?

Write to Learn In your Learner's Notebook, describe a situation in which you would want to fly and explain why.

Build Background

This story takes place on a plantation in North America during slavery times.

- The practice of kidnapping Africans and bringing them to North America as slaves began in 1619. Slavery was allowed to continue in parts of the United States until the end of the Civil War in 1865.
- "The People Could Fly" can be classified as a legend—a folktale about amazing people and events that are loosely based on fact. In the early 1800s a group of enslaved West Africans rose up against the slave agents that were carrying them from one part of Georgia to another by boat. The agents were killed; the enslaved people were never found. Local slave owners believed that the West Africans drowned themselves to escape bondage. But the enslaved people on their plantations had a very different explanation of what happened. That explanation is preserved in "The People Could Fly."

Set Purposes for Reading

BIG Question Read "The People Could Fly" to learn how some enslaved people were able to make an unusual journey toward freedom.

Set Your Own Purpose What else would you like to learn from the story to help yourself answer the Big Question? Write your own purpose on the "People Could Fly" flap of Foldable 2.

Keep Moving

Use these skills as you read the following selection.

THE PEOPLE COULD FLY

told by Virginia Hamilton

They say the people could fly. Say that long ago in Africa, some of the people knew magic. And they would walk up on the air like climbin up on a gate. And they flew like blackbirds over the fields. Black, shiny wings flappin against the blue up there.

Then, many of the people were captured for Slavery. The ones that could fly shed their wings. They couldn't take their wings across the water on the slave ships. Too crowded, don't you know. ∎

The folks were full of misery, then. Got sick with the up and down of the sea. So they forgot about flyin when they could no longer breathe the sweet scent of Africa.

Say the people who could fly kept their power, although they shed their wings. They kept their secret magic in the land of slavery. They looked the same as the other people from Africa who had been coming over, who had dark skin. Say you couldn't tell anymore one who could fly from one who couldn't.

One such who could was an old man, call him Toby. And standin tall, yet afraid, was a young woman who once had wings. Call her Sarah. Now Sarah carried a babe tied to her back. She trembled to be so hard worked and **scorned.**

The slaves labored in the fields from sunup to sundown. The owner of the slaves callin himself their Master. Say he was a hard lump of clay. A hard, glinty coal. A hard rock pile, wouldn't be moved. His Overseer[1] on horseback pointed out the slaves who were slowin down. So the one called

---

1. In times of slavery, the *overseer* directed the field workers.

Practice the Skills

1 **Key Reading Skill**

Analyzing The narrator uses dialect, or nonstandard English (like "climbin" and "flappin"), and conversational phrases. How do you think this would help a reader understand and enjoy this story?

Vocabulary

scorned (skornd) *adj.* looked down upon by someone

Driver cracked his whip over the slow ones to make them move faster. That whip was a slice-open cut of pain. So they did move faster. Had to.

Sarah hoed and chopped the row as the babe on her back slept.

Say the child grew hungry. That babe started up bawling too loud. Sarah couldn't stop to feed it. Couldn't stop to soothe and quiet it down. She let it cry. She didn't want to. She had no heart to croon[2] to it.

"Keep that thing quiet," called the Overseer. He pointed his finger at the babe. The woman scrunched low. The Driver cracked his whip across the babe anyhow. The babe hollered like any hurt child, and the woman fell to the earth. **2**

The old man that was there, Toby, came and helped her to her feet.

"I must go soon," she told him.

"Soon," he said.

Sarah couldn't stand up straight any longer. She was too weak. The sun burned her face. The babe cried and cried, "Pity me, oh, pity me," say it sounded like. Sarah was so sad and starvin, she sat down in the row. **3**

---

2. To *croon* is to sing or hum in a low, soft tone.

Practice the Skills

2 **Key Literary Element**

Protagonist and Antagonist
The Overseer and Driver whip a baby. That's about as mean as people can get. One or both of them must be the antagonist.

3 **Key Reading Skill**

Analyzing Think about the Overseer and Driver, their actions, and their effects on Sarah and her baby. What do those pieces of information say about slavery?

The People Could Fly, 1985. Leo & Diana Dillon. Pastel and watercolor. Private collection.

Practice the Skills

"Get up, you black cow," called the Overseer. He pointed his hand, and the Driver's whip **snarled** around Sarah's legs. Her sack dress tore into rags. Her legs bled onto the earth. She couldn't get up.

Toby was there where there was no one to help her and the babe.

"Now, before it's too late," panted Sarah. "Now, Father!"

"Yes, Daughter, the time is come," Toby answered. "Go, as you know how to go!"

He raised his arms, holding them out to her. *"Kum . . . yali, kum buba tambe,"* and more magic words, said so quickly, they sounded like whispers and sighs. **4**

The young woman lifted one foot on the air. Then the other. She flew clumsily at first, with the child now held tightly in her arms. Then she felt the magic, the African mystery. Say she rose just as free as a bird. As light as a feather.

The Overseer rode after her, hollerin. Sarah flew over the fences. She flew over the woods. Tall trees could not snag her. Nor could the Overseer. She flew like an eagle now, until she was gone from sight. No one dared speak about it. Couldn't believe it. But it was, because they that was there saw that it was. **5**

Say the next day was dead hot in the fields. A young man slave fell from the heat. The Driver come and whipped him. Toby come over and spoke words to the fallen one. The words of ancient Africa once heard are never remembered completely. The young man forgot them as soon as he heard them. They went way inside him. He got up and rolled over on the air. He rode it awhile. And he flew away.

Another and another fell from the heat. Toby was there. He cried out to the fallen and reached his arms out to them. *"Kum kunka yali, kum . . . tambe!"* Whispers and sighs. And they too rose on the air. They rode the hot breezes. The ones flyin were black and shinin sticks, wheelin above the head of the Overseer. They crossed the rows, the fields, the fences, the streams, and were away.

"Seize the old man!" cried the Overseer. "I heard him say the magic *words.* Seize him!"

4 Key Literary Element

Protagonist and Antagonist
Who do you think the main character, or protagonist, is: Sarah or Toby? (You could argue either way.)

5 Key Reading Skill

Analyzing How is this part of the tale similar to other folktales you know? Think about
- the way Sarah escapes
- the kind of person Sarah is
- the kind of people the Driver and Overseer are

Vocabulary

snarled (snarld) *v.* made tangled or knotted

The one callin himself Master come runnin. The Driver got his whip ready to curl around old Toby and tie him up. The slaveowner took his hip gun from its place. He meant to kill old, black Toby.

But Toby just laughed. Say he threw back his head and said, "Hee, hee! Don't you know who I am? Don't you know some of us in this field?" He said it to their faces. "We are ones who fly!"

And he sighed the **ancient** words that were a dark promise. **6** He said them all around to the others in the field under the whip, ". . . *buba yali . . . buba tambe. . . .*"

There was a great outcryin. The bent backs straighted up. Old and young who were called slaves and could fly joined hands. Say like they would ring-sing. But they didn't shuffle in a circle. They didn't sing. They rose on the air. They flew in a flock that was black against the heavenly blue. Black crows or black shadows. It didn't matter, they went so high. Way above the plantation, way over the slavery land. Say they flew away to *Free-dom*.

And the old man, old Toby, flew behind them, takin care of them. He wasn't cryin. He wasn't laughin. He was the seer.[3] His gaze fell on the plantation where the slaves who could not fly waited.

"Take us with you!" Their looks spoke it but they were afraid to shout it. Toby couldn't take them with him. Hadn't the time to teach them to fly. They must wait for a chance to run.

"Goodie-bye!" The old man called Toby spoke to them, poor souls! And he was flyin gone.

So they say. The Overseer told it. The one called Master said it was a lie, a trick of the light. The Driver kept his mouth shut.

The slaves who could not fly told about the people who could fly to their children. When they were free. When they sat close before the fire in the free land, they told it. They did so love firelight and *Free-dom,* and tellin.

They say that the children of the ones who could not fly told their children. And now, me, I have told it to you. **7** ○

---

3. A *seer* is a prophet or someone who is unusually wise.

Alexander Chandler, 1955. Andrew Wyeth. Drybrush, 21 1/4 x 14 1/2 in. Private collection. Photograph courtesy of the Wyeth collection. © Andrew Wyeth.

Analyzing the Painting Study the expression and pose of the man in this painting. What personal qualities might he have in common with Toby?

Practice the Skills

6 **English Language Coach**

Vocabulary Building: Synonyms and Antonyms
What does **ancient** mean? In your Learner's Notebook, make a synonym-antonym chart for the word.

7 **BIG Question**

Where is Toby going? What do you think is more important— the journey he is taking or his destination? Why? Write your answer on the "People Could Fly" flap of Foldable 2. Your response will help you complete the Unit Challenge later.

The People Could Fly **167**

After You Read : The People Could Fly

Answering the BIG Question

1. What is the importance of the journey the enslaved people take in this story?

2. **Recall** Why didn't the people in the story have wings?

   TIP **Right There** You will find this information in the story.

3. **Summarize** In a few sentences, sum up what happens in the story.

   TIP **Think and Search** The answer is in the story, but it is not all in one place.

Critical Thinking

4. **Infer** Why does Toby speak the magic words when he does?

   TIP **Author and Me** You will find clues in the story, but you must also use the information in your head.

5. **Interpret** When Toby speaks the words of Africa, the words go "way inside" a young enslaved man. What do you think this means?

   TIP **Author and Me** You will find clues in the story, but you must also use the information in your head.

6. **Infer** What message do you think this story may have had for enslaved people who heard it? Why?

   TIP **Author and Me** You will find clues in the story, but you must also use the information in your head.

Write About Your Reading

Story Sequel A sequel (SEE kwul) picks up where a story ends and adds new scenes and actions to it. Use your imagination to write a short sequel to "The People Could Fly." In your sequel, describe the journey Sarah and her baby took and the place they finally landed.

Try to make your sequel sound like the original folktale. For example, you might drop the letter -g from the endings of -ing words. And you might use conversational phrases like "don't you know" and "so they say."

NY English Language Arts Core Curriculum (pp. 168–169)

LC R17 Demonstrate comprehension and response through a range of activities. **W2a** Write original literary texts to sequence events, select a genre, and use appropriate conventions, such as dialogue. **LC R13** Use text structure and literary devices to aid comprehension and response. **R2b** Interpret characters and theme, using evidence from the text. **Core W8** Use correct grammatical construction in parts of speech. **LC R8** Recognize grade-appropriate synonyms and antonyms.

For a complete description of the standards, see p. NY 11.

Skills Review

Key Reading Skill: Analyzing

7. The following elements are often found in folktales. Which elements are in "The People Could Fly"? Support your answer with examples from the story.

- at least one character with magical powers
- at least one character who is very good and one who is very evil
- good characters who win out over evil ones

8. How did reading "The People Could Fly" add to your understanding of folktales and legends? Use details from the story to support your answer.

Key Literary Element: Protagonist and Antagonist

9. Is the antagonist in the story the Overseer, the Driver, the Master, or slavery itself? Give reasons for your answer.

10. While reading the story, you were asked to identify the protagonist. Now that you've read the story, who do you think the protagonist is—Sarah or Toby? Support your opinion with evidence from the story.

Vocabulary Check

Answer *true* or *false* to each statement. Rewrite each false statement to make it true.

11. A person who is **scorned** is someone whom others appreciate.

12. If your hair is **snarled,** it's full of knots.

13. **Academic Vocabulary** If your teacher asks you to analyze a story, what is he or she asking you to do?

14. **English Language Coach** Look up the word *freedom* in a thesaurus. Then make a synonym-antonym chart for the word *freedom*. List as many synonyms and antonyms for the word *freedom* as you can.

Grammar Link: Adjectives

Adjectives are words that describe, or modify, nouns and pronouns. Adjectives describe by answering one of these questions:

- *What kind?*   *happy* man, *stormy* weather
- *How many?*   *five* chairs, *several* months
- *How much?*   *more* work, *less* rain
- *Which one?*   *this* page, *that* day

Adjectives add specific detail to general ideas. Compare the sentences below. Which is better?

- The dogs chased the cats.
- Those enormous stray dogs chased five terrified cats.

The adjectives *those, enormous, stray, five,* and *terrified* make the second sentence clearer and more vivid than the first.

Grammar Practice

Copy the following sentences. Underline all the adjectives. For help in finding the adjectives, answer the questions in parentheses.

15. I like story problems. *(What kind of problems?)*

16. Did you do those equations yourself? *(Which equations?)*

17. My math teacher gave us ten problems to do. *(What kind of teacher? How many problems?)*

18. I prefer less homework. *(How much homework?)*

19. I need more free time. *(How much time? What kind of time?)*

20. I have many hours of homework. *(How many hours?)*

Writing Application Review the sequel you wrote for the Write About Your Reading activity. Add three adjectives to make your writing more vivid.

Web Activities For eFlashcards, Selection Quick Checks, and other Web activities, go to www.glencoe.com.

Before You Read : A Father's Daring Trek

Meet the Author

Julie K. L. Dam is a reporter and feature writer for publications such as *Time* and *People* magazines. She has written on a wide variety of topics, from celebrity interviews to theater reviews. She has also written a novel about a fashion-loving American girl who visits Paris, France, during Fashion Week.

 Literature Online

Author Search For more about Julie K. L. Dam, go to www .glencoe.com.

NY English Language Arts Core Curriculum (pp. 170–175)

LC R8 Recognize grade-appropriate synonyms. **LC R13** Use text structure and literary devices to aid comprehension and response. **R2b** Interpret setting, using evidence from the text. **R2g** Compare literature to own lives.

For a complete description of the standards, see p. NY 11.

Vocabulary Preview

exile (EG zyl) *n.* the state of living away from one's home country **(p. 172)** *The father and daughter chose to live in exile because life in their country was so hard.*

persecution (pur suh KYOO shun) *n.* violence and hostility directed toward people of a particular group **(p. 172)** *The Tibetan people suffered terrible persecution.*

destiny (DES tuh nee) *n.* a person's fate or fortune **(p. 175)** *It was Yangdol's destiny to live a good life in India.*

Sentence Challenge Write a sentence for each vocabulary word.

English Language Coach

Vocabulary Building: Collections of Synonyms Do you find yourself using the same words over and over? Use a thesaurus (thih SOR us)—a collection of synonyms—to find other words that mean about the same thing. Whether in book or electronic form, thesauruses are easy to use. Suppose that you want to find a synonym for the word *happy.* If you're using a thesaurus in book form, look up *happy* just as you would if you were using a dictionary. If you're using an online thesaurus, enter the word *happy* in the search box. Either way, you'll get an entry that looks something like this:

> **Main Word:** happy
> **Part of Speech:** adjective
> **Synonyms:** pleased, joyous, glad, contented

To help yourself remember all the synonyms, put them on a word web like the one below:

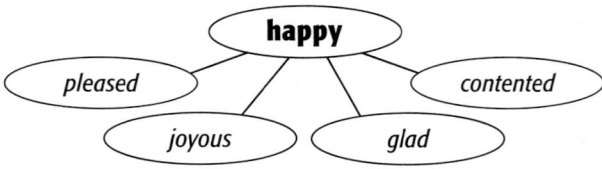

Partner Work With a classmate, look up the word *nice* in a thesaurus. Together, make a word web of synonyms that could be used in place of *nice* in this sentence: The weather was nice today.

Skills Preview

Key Reading Skill: Analyzing

As you read "A Father's Daring Trek," you'll analyze the parts of a magazine article and the order in which they appear. Think about articles you've read before. Most of them follow this pattern:

1. An **attention-getting device,** or interesting opener that makes you want to read on
2. **Main point or points,** a preview of the most important general ideas in the article
3. **Background,** or basic information you need to know about a topic to understand it. Not all topics require background information
4. **Details** that explain main point(s)
5. A **conclusion,** or ending, that wraps up the main point(s) in an interesting or inspiring way

Partner Talk Imagine that you're writing an article about one of the topics below. What would be an interesting way to begin your article? With a classmate come up with an idea or two.

• a game one of your school teams won in overtime
• a how-to-do-it article on a popular hobby
• an article about a new fad or fashion

Literary Element: Setting

The **setting** is the world of the story. Its details tell about the characters. The kind of house a character lives in tells you a great deal about that character. The part of the world a character lives in can tell you about his or her cultural beliefs and customs. Setting may even be a source of conflict for the characters.

Whole Class Discussion Discuss conflicts you think might occur in these settings:

• an 1800s pioneer trail across Native American country
• a space station on Mars during the 24th century

Get Ready to Read

Connect to the Reading

Imagine that it's winter in a cold part of the world. You're about to go on a long journey on foot through high mountains. What problems do you think you might face? Brainstorm a list of possible dangers.

Think-Pair-Share Pair up with a classmate and share your lists. Did you write down the same dangers or different ones? Combine your lists.

Build Background

• The article you are about to read takes place in Tibet, a region in southwest China and one of the world's highest places. For that reason, Tibet has been called "The Roof of the World."
• The Himalaya Mountains in southern Tibet are home to Mt. Everest, the world's tallest mountain.
• In general, the higher one climbs in the Himalayas, the harsher the weather conditions become. Winds of 50 to 60 miles an hour are common, as are below-zero temperatures.

Set Purposes for Reading

BIG Question Read "A Father's Daring Trek" to learn about a father and daughter who make a dangerous journey in hopes of beginning a better life.

Set Your Own Purpose What else would you like to learn from the story to help yourself answer the Big Question? Write your own purpose on the "Father's Daring Trek" flap of Foldable 2.

Interactive Literary Elements Handbook
To review or learn more about the literary elements, go to www.glencoe.com.

Keep Moving

Use these skills as you read the following selection.

TIME

A Father's Daring TREK

A Tibetan man takes his 6-year-old daughter on a dangerous journey through the world's highest, harshest mountains to give her a better life.

By JULIE K.L. DAM

After a weeklong march in the bitter, piercing cold and thin air of the Himalayan Mountains, the Tibetan father Kelsang and his daughter, Yangdol (not their real names), thought they had reached freedom. From the top of Nangapa La, a pass on the southern border of Chinese-occupied Tibet, a peaceful life in **exile** seemed only steps away. Their perilous journey was only half over, though, because the trip down the pass would be just as difficult as the way up. Still the courageous father and daughter struggled on, determined to reach their goal. **1**

For Tibetans, the trek[1] to freedom is filled with hardships, both physical and emotional. Many make the heart-wrenching decision to become refugees, people who are forced to leave their country of birth because of political or religious **persecution** or war. In 1951, Tibet lost its independence when Chinese troops invaded Lhasa, the Tibetan capital. The

1 Key Reading Skill

Analyzing What does the writer do to interest you in reading the rest of the article? Think about
- the description of the trek
- the people involved
- the reason for the trek

---

1. A *trek* is a long, often difficult journey.

Vocabulary

exile (EG zyl) *n.* the state of living away from one's home country

persecution (pur suh KYOO shun) *n.* the condition of being caused to suffer cruelty because of personal beliefs

Chinese government claimed the region as part of its territory. During the 1950s, Tibetans protested Chinese rule and fought for independence. In 1959, the Dalai Lama, the Tibetan spiritual leader, set up a government-in-exile in Dharmsala, a hill town in northern India, and the Tibetans who could escape began to gather to him.

To this day, Tibet's culture has suffered under Chinese rule. China doesn't allow Tibetans to practice their religion, Tibetan Buddhism, and much of Tibetan culture has been lost. Many Tibetans have been imprisoned, tortured, or killed for standing up for their beliefs. Each year, thousands of Tibetan families choose to escape to Dharmsala. Once Tibetans like Kelsang and Yangdol decide that life as a refugee in India would be better than life under Chinese rule, they begin the demanding journey across the Himalayan Mountains, into neighboring Nepal, and—finally—to Dharmsala. **2**

2 **Key Reading Skill**

Analyzing Why does the writer give the reader background information? How does it improve your understanding of the story?

Before heading into the mountains, Kelsang spreads yak butter on Yangdol's face to protect it from the sun and cold.

Manuel Bauer/Lookat

A Father's Daring Trek **173**

Manuel Bauer/Lookat

The mountain wind is so strong that Kelsang and Yangdol have to lie flat on the ground until it dies down.

When Swiss photographer Manuel Bauer first met Kelsang, the 46-year-old father had decided to take his daughter to live in Dharmsala. The father knew the trek across the mountains would be **challenging**, but he believed life in Dharmsala—even as an exile far from home—would be better for him and his child. **3**

The photographer persuaded Kelsang to let him join the father and daughter on their trip across the mountains. The three arranged a ride on the back of a truck and quietly left Lhasa one winter morning. However, their journey was soon delayed by snowstorms. Six days later, they got a lift to Tingri, Tibet, and began the achingly long march on foot across the Himalayas.

The determined threesome hiked higher and higher up the mountains, battling frostbite,[2] dehydration,[3] frigid

3 **English Language Coach**

Vocabulary Building: Collections of Synonyms
What are some synonyms for the word **challenging**? Jot them down on a word web in your Learner's Notebook.

2. *Frostbite* is a serious condition that occurs when a part of the body becomes too cold.

3. People suffer *dehydration* when they do not have enough water.

temperatures, and fierce winds. **4** They traveled over the icy ground in silence, sometimes 14 hours a day, and were often too tired to even stop and eat. "They kept me going," says Bauer, "their story, sacrifice, and **destiny**."

After 12 stressful days, the group crossed Nangapa La and wearily made their way down to Namche Bazaar, a Nepalese village near Mount Everest. At last the worst was over. They flew by helicopter to Kathmandu, Nepal's capital, where officials at the Tibetan Reception Center greeted them and arranged a bus ride—a luxury after the long mountain trek— to their journey's end in Dharmsala.

Three days later, the father and daughter reached their destination, where they celebrated the journey's end with 50 other newly arrived refugees, many of whom had made much the same trek. Three long weeks after leaving Lhasa, Yangdol finally met the Dalai Lama and, with his blessing, began a new life—at home in exile. **5**

—**Updated 2005, from TIME International, January 8, 1996**

Kelsang and Yangdol battled fierce winds and freezing temperatures during their trek to freedom.

Manuel Bauer/Lookat

4 | **Literary Element**

Setting What problems does the mountain setting cause for the travelers?

5 | **BIG** Question

How do you think Yangdol and her father might answer the question, Which is more important, the journey or the destination? Why? Write your answer on the "Father's Daring Trek" flap of Foldable 2. Your response will help you complete the Unit Challenge later.

Vocabulary

destiny (DES tuh nee) *n.* a person's fate or fortune

A Father's Daring Trek   **175**

After You Read : A Father's Daring Trek

Manuel Bauer/Lookat

Answering the BIG Question

1. What do you think people can learn about themselves by taking a difficult journey, such as the one in "A Father's Daring Trek"?

2. **Summarize** What events happened in Tibet that caused people to want to leave?

   TIP **Right There** The answer is in one place in the article.

3. **Recall** What dangers do Yangdol and her father face as they walk through the mountains?

   TIP **Think and Search** You will find this information in the article, but not all in one place.

Critical Thinking

4. **Infer** Why do you think Manuel Bauer joined Yangdol and her father on their journey?

   TIP **Author and Me** You will find clues in the selection, but you must also use the information in your head.

5. **Infer** Why is the journey to Dharmsala so important for Tibetan refugees?

   TIP **Author and Me** You will find clues in the selection, but you must also use the information in your head.

6. **Evaluate** Would you recommend this article to other eighth graders? Why or why not? Use specific examples from the article to support your opinion.

   TIP **On My Own** Answer from your own knowledge.

Write About Your Reading

Postcard Pretend that you have just completed a journey from Tibet to Dharmsala with a group of Tibetan refugees. Write a postcard to your parents that describes

- who you were with
- what you saw on your journey
- what difficulties you faced
- how you felt at the end of the journey

To write your postcard, use facts and details from the article, but also use your imagination.

NY English Language Arts Core Curriculum (pp. 176–177)

LC R17 Demonstrate comprehension and response through a range of activities. **LC W5** Write with voice to address varied purposes. **LC R13** Use text structure and literary devices to aid comprehension and response. **R2b** Interpret setting, using evidence from the text. **LC R8** Recognize grade-appropriate synonyms. **Core W8** Use correct grammatical construction in parts of speech.

For a complete description of the standards, see p. NY 11.

Skills Review

Key Reading Skill: Analyzing

7. Copy the map below; then analyze "A Father's Daring Trek." Fill in each box on the map with a short summary of the content of the article. The first boxes are filled in to help you start.

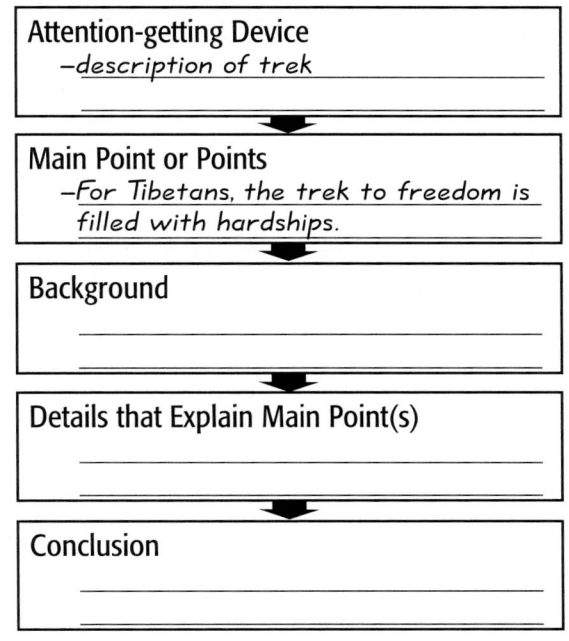

Attention-getting Device
—description of trek
_____

Main Point or Points
—For Tibetans, the trek to freedom is filled with hardships.

Background
_____

Details that Explain Main Point(s)
_____

Conclusion
_____

Literary Element: Setting

8. How are time and place sources of conflict for the father and daughter in the article?

Vocabulary Check

Each sentence below contains an underlined word. Use what you know about these words to tell whether each sentence is true or false. If a sentence is false, rewrite it to make it true.

9. People in <u>exile</u> live in their home country.

10. A person's <u>destiny</u> is the same as a person's fate.

11. <u>Persecution</u> makes people feel welcome in their home country.

12. **English Language Coach** Look back at the thesaurus entry for *happy* on page 170. Choose three of the synonyms, and use each one in a sentence that describes how the father and daughter feel once they reach freedom.

Grammar Link: Adverbs

Adverbs answer these questions: How? When? How often? Where? How much?

He <u>speaks</u> quickly.	How?	<u>quickly</u>
I studied <u>yesterday</u>.	When?	<u>yesterday</u>
She visits <u>weekly</u>.	How often?	<u>weekly</u>
He works <u>there</u>.	Where?	<u>there</u>
I am <u>too</u> busy.	How much?	<u>too</u> much

Adverbs can help you make your writing clearer and livelier. Compare the following two sentences. Which is clearer?

• Nadia said to her little sister, "Go to bed!"
• Yesterday Nadia angrily said to her little sister, "Go to bed NOW!"

The second sentence is clearer because the adverbs *yesterday, angrily,* and *now* tell you when and how actions occurred.

Grammar Practice

Copy the following sentences. Underline the adverbs. For help in finding the adverbs, answer the questions in parentheses.

13. Dad hurriedly left without his jacket. (*How did Dad leave?*)

14. It was too cold outside to be without a jacket. (*"How much" cold was it?*)

15. I quickly ran after him to give him his jacket. (*How did you run?*)

Writing Application Look back at the postcard you wrote for the Write About Your Reading activity. Find two sentences in which you describe something that happened. Add an adverb to each sentence to tell *how* or *when* the event happened.

Interactive Literary Elements Handbook
To review or learn more about the literary elements, go to www.glencoe.com.

Folktale
Prewriting and Drafting

ASSIGNMENT Write an entertaining folktale

Purpose: To create a folktale about a character who takes a journey

Audience: Your teacher and your classmates

Writing Rubric

As you work through this writing assignment, you should

- Write in the style of a folktale
- Develop a main character who has the qualities of a folktale protagonist
- Make a point or teach a lesson through your story

See page 236 in Part 2 for a model of a folktale.

NY English Language Arts Core Curriculum (pp. 178–181)

Core W4 Use prewriting activities. **Core W5** Use the writing process. **W2a** Write original literary texts to develop a narrative. **Core W8** Use correct grammatical construction in parts of speech.

For a complete description of the standards, see p. NY 11.

Folktales are traditional stories handed down from generation to generation. Most folktales have these basic ingredients:

- a main character (protagonist) who does good deeds and has special, perhaps even magical, powers
- an evil antagonist (which can be a person or a force of nature, like a storm)
- a storyline that ends with good overcoming evil

Many folktales also contain a journey, or quest, for something precious. (Think, for example, of the enslaved people who journey for freedom in "The People Could Fly.") Your folktale will also be about a journey. Writing the folktale will help you think about the Unit 2 Big Question: Which is more important, the journey or the destination?

Prewriting
Get Ready to Write

Before you start writing, think about your main character, the journey he or she will take, and the reason for the journey. Will your main character be young or old? Male or female? Magical or just talented?

You've probably read and seen many stories about characters that go on a journey in search of something precious. Remember the Greek myth about Jason and his journey to find golden fleece? How about Dorothy, the Tin Man, Cowardly Lion, and Scarecrow in *The Wonderful Wizard of Oz?* They, too, took a long and hard journey in quest of precious things. What journey will your character take? What will the character search for?

Partner Talk Discuss with a classmate the ideas you have so far for a main character and a journey. Jot down notes from your discussion, and use the notes as you work on your story.

Make a Plan

A story map can help you arrange your ideas into a plan.

Characters	Who is the main character? What's special (or even magical) about him or her? Who (or what) is the antagonist, or bad guy?
Reason for Journey	Why does the main character go on a journey?
Major Events of Journey	What difficulties does he or she face during the journey?
Outcome of Journey	How does the main character overcome the difficulties?
Point, or Central Message, of the Tale	What point, or lesson about life, do you want readers to get from your folktale?

Literature online

Writing Models For models and other writing activities, go to www.glencoe.com.

Applying Good Writing Traits

Ideas

Without ideas, you'd have nothing to write about or even to think about. Your brain would be a blank as you rode the bus or walked the dog. The good news is that you have dozens of ideas every day.

What Are Ideas?

In this case ideas are your thoughts about your folktale and the things it should include. You've already come up with some ideas about your main character, your antagonist, and the journey.

The main idea of any story is its message, or theme. The theme is not the subject of a story; it is the story's meaning. For example, you might say the main idea of "Little Red Riding Hood" is to be suspicious of "people" who act like something they're not.

Why Are Ideas Important?

Readers find fresh, original ideas entertaining and fun. What's more, a central idea that says something important and true about people will probably stay with readers for a long time to come.

How Do I Come Up with Ideas?

- Read other folktales. Notice the basic elements they share with yours.

- Talk over the assignment and your thoughts with classmates, friends, or family. Bounce ideas off each other.

- Pay attention to the people you see, experiences you have, and situations you observe. A particular person, a bit of conversation, or an ordinary event might spark ideas that you can use in your folktale or in other writing assignments.

- Keep story ideas in the back of your mind as you go through the day. Jot down ideas as they come to you.

Drafting

Start Writing!

Now it's time to start writing your folktale. Grab a pencil or pen and some blank paper or head to the computer.

Get It on Paper

Writing Tip ▶

Talk It Out If you're having trouble getting started, tell someone about your story. Talking about it can rev up your creativity.

- Start by describing who your main character is and what he or she is doing. Use the map as a writing guide, but don't let it get in the way of new ideas.
- Let your writing flow. Don't worry about correct spelling or punctuation.
- After fifteen minutes or so, read what you've written. If you have more ideas, keep going.
- Think about what you like and what you don't like about your folktale so far. Make notes about those things you want to change.

Develop Your Ideas

Here are some things that experienced writers do to go from general ideas to a lively and interesting story.

Writing Tip ▶

Picture Your People Think about how your characters look and sound. The better you know them, the more real they'll seem to your readers.

Use specific details. Pick just the right details to help your readers picture the characters and events in your folktale. Describe how people and things look, sound, smell, taste, and touch.

> *The queen waved a wand made of coral with a shell at its tip.*

Develop a main point. Make sure all parts of your tale add to the central message. For example, if the message is that courage is rewarded, the main character should act bravely.

> *Unafraid, Finny ran into the ocean and swam underwater, farther and farther from shore.*

Modifying Phrases and Clauses

You've identified one-word adjectives like *tall* and *happy,* and you've found one-word adverbs like *quickly* and *yesterday*. Now learn about adjectives and adverbs that are more than one word.

What Are Modifying Phrases and Clauses?

A **modifying phrase or clause** is a group of words that describes another word in a sentence. The phrase or clause works the same as one-word adjectives and adverbs do.

An **adjective phrase or clause** is a group of words that modifies a noun or a pronoun.

- The kids <u>at the front of the bus</u> are noisy.

  (Which kids? the kids at the front of bus)

- I like buses <u>that are air-conditioned</u>.

  (What kinds of buses? buses that are air-conditioned)

An **adverb phrase or clause** may modify an action verb, an adjective, or another adverb.

- I caught the bus <u>before it left</u>.

  (When did you catch it? before it left)

- We enter <u>through the front door</u>.

  (Where do you enter? through the front door)

- We exit the bus <u>in a hurry</u>.

  (How do you exit? In a hurry)

Why Are Modifying Phrases and Clauses Important?

Modifying clauses and phrases make a piece of writing more interesting and specific. The details they provide help paint a word picture in the reader's mind. Compare the following sentences.

No modifiers: Look at it.

Adjective modifiers: Look at <u>the red maple</u> tree.

Modifying adjective clause: Look at <u>the red maple</u> tree <u>that is growing next to the shed</u>.

The last sentence, with both one-word adjectives and an adjective clause, is clear and descriptive.

How Do I Use Modifying Phrases and Clauses?

Use an adjective phrase or clause to add detail to a noun or a pronoun. The adjective phrase or clause usually comes *after* the word it describes.

- The drivers <u>behind the bus</u> were impatient.

Sometimes, however, you can place an adjective phrase *before* the noun or pronoun it modifies.

- <u>Sweaty and breathless</u>, he caught the bus.

To use an adverb phrase or clause, describe a verb with a group of words. The adverb phrase or clause may come before *or* after the word it describes.

- <u>After dinner</u>, Anya does her homework.
- Anya does her homework <u>after dinner</u>.

Writing Application Carefully reread the draft of your folktale. Look for any sentences that are dull or unclear. Try adding a modifying phrase or clause to improve the sentences.

Keep Moving

Part 2 of this Writing Workshop is coming up later. Keep the writing you did here, and in Part 2 you'll learn how to improve it.

Skills Focus

You will practice these skills when you read the following selections:
- "Paul Revere's Ride," p. 186
- "The Oxcart," p. 196

Reading

- Making inferences

Literature

- Understanding and analyzing narrative poetry
- Identifying the parts of a plot

Vocabulary

- Building vocabulary with key words
- Recognizing and using compound words to expand vocabulary
- Academic Vocabulary: *inferring*

Writing/Grammar

- Using comparative and superlative adjectives and adverbs
- Using articles and demonstratives

NY English Language Arts Core Curriculum
(pp. 182–183)

R1I Make inferences on the basis of explicit and implied information.

For a complete description of the standards, see p. NY 11.

Skill Lesson

Making Inferences

Learn It!

What Is It? **Inferring** is using your knowledge and experience to figure out something that is not written or stated.

- When you make an inference, you act like a detective, using clues to make guesses about what might be true.
- For example, if you are watching a TV show and you see a character shaking and biting his nails, you might infer that he is nervous.

Analyzing Cartoons
What does the boy infer from the look on his mother's face?

THAT LOOK HAD "CHORE" WRITTEN ALL OVER IT!

© Zits Partnership, Reprinted with Permission of King Features Syndicate, Inc.

Academic Vocabulary

inferring (in FUR ing) *n.* using reason and experience to make an educated guess

Why Is It Important? In life, we never know everything we'd like to know about people and situations. So we make inferences about them. We decide what to think by making educated guesses based on what we do know. In literature, no author tells you *everything* you'd like to know. You make inferences based on what the author *does* say—and on your own experiences.

Literature online

Study Central Visit www.glencoe .com and click on Study Central to review making inferences.

How Do I Do It? As you read, look for clues. Combine these with what you know from your own experience. Then make an educated guess.

Read the following passage from a story. Then read to see how a student made an inference to answer the question, "How does Kathy feel?"

> A crowd gathered around Mrs. Kurstings' door almost the moment she posted the list. Brandi peeked around the door of an empty classroom, scanning the crowd for Kathy's face. Kathy had worked so hard to be a cheerleader. If she didn't make the squad, well . . . . Brandi didn't even want to think about it. Just then, Brandi spotted her friend walking slowly away from Mrs. Kurstings' door. Kathy's shoulders were slumped, and her eyes were on the floor.

I think Kathy feels disappointed. She must not have made the squad. The clues are in the way she walks. Based on experience, I know that people get excited when they are chosen to be cheerleaders. Kathy seems sad rather than excited.

Practice It!

How does Brandi feel about Kathy? Reread the passage; then make inferences about their relationship. Support your inferences with specific clues from the passage.

Use It!

Use the skill as you read "Paul Revere's Ride" and "The Oxcart."

Before You Read : Paul Revere's Ride

Henry Wadsworth Longfellow

Meet the Author

Henry Wadsworth Longfellow was a teacher and poet who lived from 1807 until 1882. He published his first poem when he was 13 years old. Some of his poems help shape what Americans think of their nation and their past. See page R4 of the Author Files for more on Henry Wadsworth Longfellow.

Author Search For more about Henry Wadsworth Longfellow, go to www.glencoe.com.

NY English Language Arts Core Curriculum (pp. 184–191)

LC R2 Use a variety of word recognition strategies to read unfamiliar words. **R1l** Make inferences on the basis of explicit and implied information. **R2f** Identify poetic elements to interpret poetry. **R2g** Compare literature to own lives.

For a complete description of the standards, see p. NY 11.

Vocabulary Preview

stealthy (STEL thee) *adj.* quiet and hidden **(p. 187)** *Paul's friend had to be stealthy to avoid being heard.*

somber (SAHM bur) *adj.* dark and gloomy **(p. 187)** *The atmosphere at the Old North Church was somber as the men prepared to fight.*

lingers (LING urz) *v.* waits or is slow in leaving; form of the verb *linger* **(p. 189)** *Paul decided to linger and watch for a second light.*

emerge (ee MURJ) *v.* to come out into view **(p. 191)** *Paul Revere's friend watched the British ships emerge from the darkness.*

defiance (dih FY unts) *n.* the act of challenging authority **(p. 191)** *The war began with defiance of British rule.*

Partner Talk Answer the following questions with a classmate.

• Which is more stealthy: a burglar or a salesperson?

• Which is somber: a funeral or a party?

• Who lingers at a party: people who are bored or people who are having fun?

• At dawn does the sun emerge from the dark or fade into it?

• Which act is an example of defiance: breaking rules or obeying them?

English Language Coach

Old Words A lot of great literature was written long ago. However, language changes over time. Some words that people knew one hundred years ago are no longer used.

When you come across an unfamiliar word in a story or poem that was written long ago, look first to see if there's a footnote. That's where old or unusual words are often defined. There might be information in a glossary at the end of the book. If not, you can use a dictionary to find the definition of the word. Here are some words you will see in *Paul Revere's Ride*.

• belfry: a tower where a bell hangs

• man-of-war: battleship

• grenadier: a soldier who threw hand grenades

• steed: a horse with a lot of spirit

• meeting-house: town hall

• musket: a gun with a long barrel that shot a lead ball

Partner Work With a classmate, talk about old words you have learned in your reading.

Skills Preview

Key Reading Skill: Making Inferences

An author doesn't always tell you why people do what they do or what the consequences of a person's actions will be. As you read "Paul Revere's Ride," think about why Paul Revere and his friend put themselves in danger to warn the colonists of the approach of the British soldiers. What were their motivations?

Write to Learn In your Learner's Notebook write a few sentences about what might have motivated Revere and his friends to take such a risk.

Literary Element: Narrative Poetry

Narrative poetry tells a story in verse. Like all stories, narrative poems have setting, characters, and conflict. Unlike other stories, a narrative poem contains rhythm, rhyme, and other sound devices. These "musical" elements add to the beauty of the language, support the storyline, and make the poem more memorable. As you read "Paul Revere's Ride," ask yourself these questions:

- *When and where does the story take place?*
- *Who is the protagonist, or main character?*
- *What is the protagonist's goal? What antagonist stands in the way?*
- *Does the protagonist reach his or her goal? Why or why not?*

Small Group Discussion With a group of classmates, recite a school cheer that you know. Together, rewrite the cheer in your own words. Do not use rhythm or rhyme. Read aloud each version of the cheer. Then answer the following questions:

- Which version is more stirring and why?
- Which version is easier to remember and why?

Interactive Literary Elements Handbook
To review or learn more about the literary elements, go to www.glencoe.com.

Get Ready to Read

Connect to the Reading

Paul Revere's fellow colonists were counting on him to warn them when British soldiers marched toward their villages. Think of a time when other people counted on you to do an important job.

Write to Learn In a few sentences describe the job and your feelings about doing it.

Build Background

- "Paul Revere's Ride" celebrates the patriotism of Paul Revere (1735–1818), a colonist who supported American independence from Great Britain. On April 18, 1775, Revere rode from Boston to Lexington, Massachusetts, to warn local leaders that British soldiers were preparing to advance. He was arrested before he could reach his final destination.

- Revere was not the only colonist who rode through the countryside sounding the alert that day. He is the best remembered, however, because of the popularity of "Paul Revere's Ride."

- "Paul Revere's Ride" was published in 1861, when the nation was headed toward civil war. In those dark days, some Americans looked to the past for heroes that both Northerners and Southerners could be proud of. Revere was just such a man.

Set Purposes for Reading

BIG Question Read the poem "Paul Revere's Ride" to find out what happened on the night that Paul Revere made his famous ride.

Set Your Own Purpose What else would you like to learn from the poem to help you answer the Big Question? Write your own purpose on the "Paul Revere's Ride" flap of Foldable 2.

Keep Moving

Use these skills as you read the following selection.

Paul Revere's *Ride*

by Henry Wadsworth Longfellow

Listen, my children, and you shall hear
Of the midnight ride of Paul Revere,
On the eighteenth of April, in Seventy-five;[1]
Hardly a man is now alive
5 Who remembers that famous day and year.
He said to his friend, "If the British march
By land or sea from the town to-night,
Hang a lantern aloft in the belfry arch
Of the North Church tower as a signal light,—
10 One, if by land, and two, if by sea;
And I on the opposite shore will be,
Ready to ride and spread the alarm
Through every Middlesex[2] village and farm,
For the country folk to be up and to arm." **1**

15 Then he said, "Good night!" and with muffled oar
Silently rowed to the Charlestown shore,
Just as the moon rose over the bay,
Where swinging wide at her moorings[3] lay
The Somerset, British man-of-war;

Practice the Skills

1 | **Literary Element**

Narrative Poetry In the first lines of the poem, Longfellow sets the scene by describing the time (April 18, 1775), the place (Middlesex county), and the basic storyline.

---

1. **Seventy-five** refers to 1775, the year of Paul Revere's ride.
2. The county of **Middlesex,** Massachusetts, includes the town of Concord, where the first shots of the Revolutionary War were fired on April 19, 1775.
3. The place where a ship is docked is called its **moorings.**

20 A phantom ship, with each mast and spar
Across the moon like a prison bar,
And a huge black hulk, that was magnified
By its own reflection in the tide.

Meanwhile, his friend, through alley and street,
25 Wanders and watches with eager ears,
Till in the silence around him he hears
The muster of men at the barrack door,
The sound of arms, and the tramp of feet,
And the measured tread of the grenadiers,[4]
30 Marching down to their boats on the shore.

Then he climbed the tower of the Old North Church,
By the wooden stairs, with **stealthy** tread,
To the belfry-chamber overhead,
And startled the pigeons from their perch
35 On the **somber** rafters, that round him made
Masses and moving shapes of shade,—
By the trembling ladder, steep and tall,
To the highest window in the wall,
Where he paused to listen and look down
40 A moment on the roofs of the town,
And the moonlight flowing over all. **2**

Beneath, in the churchyard, lay the dead,
In their night-encampment on the hill,
Wrapped in silence so deep and still
45 That he could hear, like a sentinel's[5] tread,
The watchful night-wind, as it went
Creeping along from tent to tent,
And seeming to whisper, "All is well!"

Practice the Skills

2 **Key Reading Skill**

Making Inferences How do you think Revere's friend feels as he climbs the tower? Think about these clues:
• his stealthy walk
• the startled pigeons
• the somber rafters
• the trembling ladder

---

4. The ***measured tread*** is a steady march or walk. In the British army, ***grenadiers*** (greh nuh DEERZ) were foot soldiers.

5. A ***sentinel*** (SENT nul) is a guard.

Vocabulary

stealthy (STEL thee) *adj.* quiet and hidden

somber (SAHM bur) *adj.* dark and gloomy

Paul Revere's Midnight Ride. Artist unknown.
Analyzing the Painting In what ways does this painting capture the drama of Paul Revere's late-night ride?

A moment only he feels the spell
50 Of the place and the hour, and the secret dread
Of the lonely belfry and the dead;
For suddenly all his thoughts are bent
On a shadowy something far away,
Where the river widens to meet the bay,—
55 A line of black that bends and floats
On the rising tide, like a bridge of boats. **3**

Meanwhile, impatient to mount and ride,
Booted and spurred, with a heavy stride
On the opposite shore walked Paul Revere.

Practice the Skills

3 Key Reading Skill

Making Inferences What do you think is the "line of black that floats and bends"? Think about why Revere's friend is in the tower and what he is looking for.

Practice the Skills

⁶⁰ Now he patted his horse's side,
Now gazed at the landscape far and near,
Then, impetuous, stamped the earth,
And turned and tightened his saddlegirth;⁶
But mostly he watched with eager search
⁶⁵ The belfry-tower of the Old North Church,
As it rose above the graves on the hill,
Lonely and spectral⁷ and somber and still.
And lo! as he looks, on the belfry's height
A glimmer, and then a gleam of light!
⁷⁰ He springs to the saddle, the bridle he turns,
But **lingers** and gazes, till full on his sight
A second lamp in the belfry burns!

A hurry of hoofs in a village street,
A shape in the moonlight, a bulk in the dark,
⁷⁵ And beneath, from the pebbles, in passing, a spark
Struck out by a steed flying fearless and fleet:⁸
That was all! And yet, through the gloom and the light,
The fate of a nation was riding that night; **4**
And the spark struck out by that steed, in his flight,
⁸⁰ Kindled the land into flame with its heat.

He has left the village and mounted the steep,⁹
And beneath him, tranquil and broad and deep,
Is the Mystic,¹⁰ meeting the ocean tides;
And under the alders¹¹ that skirt its edge,
⁸⁵ Now soft on the sand, now loud on the ledge,
Is heard the tramp of his steed as he rides.

4 | **Key Reading Skill**

Making Inferences Why does the nation's fate, or future, depend on Paul Revere? Think about what Revere saw in the belfry-tower of the church, what his friend saw and heard, and why Revere rides out of town in such a hurry.

---

6. Here **impetuous** means "acting suddenly." When Revere **tightened his saddlegirth,** he checked the belt that holds the saddle on a horse.
7. Something **spectral** is ghost-like.
8. Here, **fleet** means "very fast."
9. As a noun, **steep** means "a steep slope."
10. The **Mystic** is a short river that flows into Boston Harbor.
11. **Alders** are trees in the birch family.

Vocabulary

lingers (LING urz) *v.* waits or is slow in leaving

Midnight Ride of Paul Revere, 1931. Grant Wood. Oil on composition board, 30 x 40 in. The Metropolitan Museum of Art, NY.

It was twelve by the village clock,
When he crossed the bridge into Medford town.
He heard the crowing of the cock,
90 And the barking of the farmer's dog,
And felt the damp of the river fog,
That rises after the sun goes down.

It was one by the village clock,
When he galloped into Lexington.
95 He saw the gilded¹² weathercock
Swim in the moonlight as he passed,
And the meeting-house windows, blank and bare,
Gaze at him with a spectral glare,
As if they already stood aghast
100 At the bloody work they would look upon. **5**

Practice the Skills

5 | Literary Element

Narrative Poetry Paul Revere is the protagonist of the story. What is his goal, or mission? What antagonist might keep him from reaching it?

---

12. A *gilded* object has, or seems to have, a thin coating of gold.

It was two by the village clock,
When he came to the bridge in Concord town.
He heard the bleating of the flock,
And the twitter of birds among the trees,
105 And felt the breath of the morning breeze
Blowing over the meadows brown.
And one was safe and asleep in his bed
Who at the bridge would be first to fall,
Who that day would be lying dead,
110 Pierced by a British musket-ball. 6

You know the rest. In the books you have read,
How the British Regulars[13] fired and fled,—
How the farmers gave them ball for ball,
From behind each fence and farm-yard wall,
115 Chasing the red-coats down the lane,
Then crossing the fields to **emerge** again
Under the trees at the turn of the road,
And only pausing to fire and load.

So through the night rode Paul Revere;
120 And so through the night went his cry of alarm
To every Middlesex village and farm,—
A cry of **defiance** and not of fear,
A voice in the darkness, a knock at the door,
And a word that shall echo forevermore!
125 For, borne on the night-wind of the Past,
Through all our history, to the last,
In the hour of darkness and peril[14] and need,
The people will waken and listen to hear
The hurrying hoof-beats of that steed,
130 And the midnight message of Paul Revere. 7 ○

Practice the Skills

6 English Language Coach

Old Words If you don't remember what a musket is, look back at the English Language Coach on page 184. Does the context also help you understand what a musket-ball is?

7 BIG Question

Which do you think was more important: Paul Revere's destination or the journey he took to reach it? Why? Write your answer on the "Paul Revere's Ride" flap of Foldable 2. Your response will help you complete the Unit Challenge later.

---

13. ***Regulars*** are soldiers and officers belonging to a permanent professional army. ***Irregulars*** are those who are drafted for a short time.

14. ***Peril*** means "danger."

Vocabulary

emerge (ee MURJ) *v.* to come out into view

defiance (dih FY unts) *n.* the act of challenging authority

After You Read : Paul Revere's Ride

Answering the BIG Question

1. Why do you think Paul Revere's journey through the countryside helped make him an American legend?

2. **Recall** In the secret code Revere and his friend use, what is the meaning of the two lanterns hanging in the church tower?

   TIP **Right There** The answer is in one place in the poem.

3. **Summarize** In a few sentences sum up the story of Revere's ride as it is described in the poem.

   TIP **Think and Search** The answer is in the poem, but it is not all in one place.

Critical Thinking

4. **Interpret** Lines 79–80 say that "the spark struck out by [Revere's horse], in his flight, / Kindled the land into flame with its heat." What "land" is the poem referring to? How was it "kindled into flame"?

   TIP **Author and Me** Draw on your knowledge of American history and think about the poem.

5. **Evaluate** The poem says that Revere rode into Concord. In reality, he was arrested before he could get there. Do you think the poem would be improved if it were completely factual, rather than a mix of fact and fiction?

   TIP **Author and Me** Think about the poem and formulate your own opinion about it.

Write About Your Reading

Diary Entry Scan the poem for things that Paul Revere sees and hears. Write your examples in a copy of the chart below.

Sights	Sounds

Pretend that you are Paul Revere. Use information in your chart to write a diary entry dated April 19, 1775, that describes the events of the previous night. Explain how you feel about the night's events and what lies ahead.

NY English Language Arts Core Curriculum (pp. 192–193)

LC R17 Demonstrate comprehension and response through a range of activities. **LC W5** Write with voice to address varied purposes. **R1I** Make inferences on the basis of explicit and implied information. **R2f** Identify poetic elements, such as repetition, rhythm, and rhyming patterns, to interpret poetry. **Core W8** Use correct grammatical construction in parts of speech.

For a complete description of the standards, see p. NY 11.

Skills Review

Key Reading Skill: Making Inferences

6. In the first two lines of the poem, an adult asks a group of children to listen as he tells the tale of Revere's ride. How do these lines help set up the idea that Paul Revere is an American legend?

7. What do you think Longfellow wanted Americans to think of Paul Revere? Use details from the poem to support your opinion.

Literary Element: Narrative Poetry

8. Read aloud lines 73–86 and listen to the rhythm, or beat, of the poem. Try to picture the actions that are described. Why is it fitting that the actions are described in a regular pattern of rhythm?

9. What are the rhyming words in the first stanza (lines 1–14)? Copy the chart below. Then, in the bottom row, fill in the word or words that rhyme with each word above.

hear	-five	march	to-night	sea	alarm

Vocabulary Check

Write an antonym for each vocabulary word below. An antonym has the opposite meaning of a word. You may use a thesaurus to help you.

10. **stealthy** ____

11. **somber** ____

12. **linger** ____

13. **emerge** ____

14. **defiance** ____

15. **Academic Vocabulary** Imagine that a friend asks you what *inferring* means. Define the word and give an example that shows what it means.

16. **English Language Coach** Choose an old word from the poem and use it in a sentence.

Web Activities For eFlashcards, Selection Quick Checks, and other Web activities, go to www.glencoe.com.

Grammar Link: Comparative and Superlative

- The **comparative forms** of adjectives and adverbs are used to compare one person, place, thing, or action with another. The **superlative forms** are used to compare one person, place, thing, or action with more than one other.

- To form the comparative, add *–er* to the end of adjectives or adverbs of one syllable and to some with two syllables. To form the **superlative,** add *–est.*

- Carrie is <u>older</u> than Heba. (One person's age is compared to another person's.)

- Lou is the <u>oldest</u> of the eight children. (One person's age is compared to several others'.)

Use the word *more* or *less* to form the comparative of adjectives or adverbs of two syllables or more. Use the word *most* or *least* to form the superlative.

- Donna is the <u>most</u> <u>musical</u> of all the kids. (The word *most* is used instead of an *–est* ending because *musical* has three syllables.)

- Teddy runs the <u>least</u> <u>gracefully</u>. (The word *least* is used instead of an *–est* ending because *gracefully* has three syllables.)

Look out! Never use the ending *–er* or *–est* and *more* or *most, less* or *least* at the same time.
Wrong: He is the <u>most</u> <u>smartest</u> person I know.
Right: He is the <u>smartest</u> person I know.

Grammar Practice

On a separate piece of paper, write the comparative and superlative forms of each of these words: *loud, big, popular,* and *talented.*

Writing Application Look back at the diary entry you wrote for the Write About Your Reading activity. Check any comparatives and superlatives you used to make sure you formed them correctly.

Before You Read : The Oxcart

Eric A. Kimmel

Meet the Author

"The Oxcart" is a folktale that was told for hundreds of years before it was written down. Everyone who told it gave a slightly different version, so in a way the story has many authors. The person responsible for writing this version of the story is Eric A. Kimmel. He is well known for his stories about cultures from all over the world. See page R3 of the Author Files in the back of the book for more on Eric Kimmel.

Author Search For more about Eric A. Kimmel, go to www.glencoe .com.

NY English Language Arts Core Curriculum (pp. 194–201)

Core R4 Determine the meaning of words by using structural analysis. **R1l** Make inferences on the basis of explicit and implied information. **R2b** Interpret plot, using evidence from the text. **R2g** Compare literature to own lives.

For a complete description of the standards, see p. NY 11.

Vocabulary Preview

procession (proh SEH shun) *n.* a group of individuals walking forward together in a ceremony **(p. 197)** *People stopped to watch the procession of soldiers go by.*

elegant (EH lih gunt) *adj.* beautiful and tasteful **(p. 198)** *The queen had an elegant coach drawn by four horses.*

lurching (LURCH ing) *adj.* rolling or swaying in a jerky motion; form of the verb *lurch* **(p. 199)** *The lurching car made me sick.*

distinguished (dis TIN gwisht) *adj.* well-known for excellence and honor **(p. 201)** *The govenor was a distinguished member of the community.*

Partner Talk Answer the questions with a classmate. Give reasons for your answers.
- Which is a procession: bridesmaids walking down an aisle or people crossing the street?
- Which is likely to be elegant: a fast-food meal or a wedding feast?
- Which is a lurching object: a ship at sea during a storm or an airplane parked on a runway?
- Who is more distinguished: an infamous criminal or an award-winning scientist?

English Language Coach

Building Vocabulary: Compound Words Expand your vocabulary with **compound words**—words made up of two or more words. Divide a compound into the words of which it is made, think about what each word means, and use the meanings to understand other compounds. For example, if you know that a *high-level* official is one who has reached the upper ranks of his or her profession, you might guess that *highborn* (high + born) means "born into the upper (higher) class."

On Your Own Add the word *high* to the beginning of each of the following words to form a compound word. Then use each compound correctly in a sentence.
- **-energy**
- **-spirited**
- **-powered**

Skills Preview

Key Reading Skill: Making Inferences

"The Oxcart" is about three samurai who go on a journey. As you read, be on the lookout for clues that tell what society expected of samurai and of noblewomen. You may find clues in

- what the samurai and the women say
- what they do
- how others respond to them

Whole Class Discussion Preview the art in the selection. What inferences can you make about life in Japan in the days of the samurai?

Key Literary Element: Plot

Every story, novel, and play has a **plot**—a sequence of events that are set into motion by a conflict, or problem. Many plots follow this pattern:

1. **Exposition (eks puh ZIH shun):** description or dialogue that introduces the characters, the setting, and the situation
2. **Rising action:** events that complicate the situation by introducing a conflict
3. **Climax:** the moment of highest tension in the conflict, when a character takes decisive action or makes an important decision
4. **Falling action:** as the action winds down, the effects of the action or decision are revealed
5. **Resolution (rez uh LOO shun):** the final outcome of the conflict is described, and loose ends are tied up

Small Group Discussion Analyze the plot of a story, a TV show, or a movie you know. Discuss what happens during each of the five stages of plot.

Get Ready to Read

Connect to the Reading

Have you ever tried to take an easy way out of a situation and discovered that it wasn't so easy after all?

Write to Learn In a few sentences summarize what the situation was, what you did to try to get out of it, and what you learned from the experience.

Build Background

- "The Oxcart" takes place in Japan hundreds of years ago, when there were very strict rules about how people should behave. At that time, it was impossible to rise out of the working class. If a noble disgraced himself, he could be thrown out of his house and have everything taken from him by the ruler. People who were rich and powerful were expected to live up to the rules of their social level. No one had any pity for those who broke the rules and fell down the social ladder.

- "The Oxcart" can be classified as a **cautionary tale**—a story in which people are punished for breaking society's rules or misbehaving. Though the punishment in cautionary tales is usually harsh and heavy-handed, the punishment in "The Oxcart" is definitely light-hearted.

Set Purposes for Reading

BIG Question Read "The Oxcart" to find out what happens to the three samurai on their journey and what lesson they learn in the end.

Set Your Own Purpose What else would you like to learn from the story to help you answer the Big Question? Write your own purpose on the "Oxcart" flap of Foldable 2.

Literature Online

Interactive Literary Elements Handbook
To review or learn more about the literary elements, go to www.glencoe.com.

Keep Moving

Use these skills and strategies as you read the following selection.

From the Illustrations to 100 poems by 100 poets. Katsushika Hokusai (1760–1849). Japan.

THE OXCART

by Eric A. Kimmel

Old Japan had strict rules governing how people of all classes should behave. Highborn women were not allowed to have any contact with commoners. They could travel only in two-wheeled oxcarts. Small windows and heavy curtains hid the passengers from unwelcome stares. Although these carts were beautifully furnished and decorated, they were cramped, poorly ventilated, and extremely uncomfortable to ride in. The oxcarts were reserved for women. No male samurai could ride in one. If he did and was caught, he faced severe punishment, possibly even the loss of his samurai status. The three samurai in this story tried to cut corners. They learned a well-deserved lesson. ▮

The governor of Settsu had three outstanding samurai[1] in his service. Their names were Taira no Hidemichi, Taira no Suetake, and Sakata no Kintoki. Once in late fall, when the time of the Kamo festival was approaching, the three samurai

---

1. A *samurai* was a member of the Japanese military class, just below powerful nobles in importance. Samurai were expected to fight bravely and lead perfect lives.

Practice the Skills

▮ **Reviewing Skills**

Setting a Purpose for Reading The author gives background information to help readers understand the folktale. What can you expect to learn from reading this story? Write your answer in your Learner's Notebook.

wanted to go to Murasakino to watch the **procession**. 🔢 They looked forward to seeing the beautiful shrines[2] pulled through the streets on wagons while the great *taiko* drums filled the air with their pounding rhythm.

"How will we get to Murasakino?" Hidemichi asked.

"We'll ride our horses," Suetake suggested.

"That's not a good idea," said Kintoki. "The streets in Murasakino are going to be crowded. Our horses are trained for war. Once they find themselves in the middle of those crowds, they'll think they're on a battlefield. They'll start kicking and plunging. Someone's bound to get hurt, and it will be our fault. The governor will be very angry with us."

"Then we'll walk," said Hidemichi.

"Three samurai walking along on foot, like common peasants? We'd be disgraced," Suetake replied.

"We could cover our faces so no one would know who we are," Kintoki suggested.

Hidemichi argued against that idea. "The city guards would take us for bandits. We'd end up in jail, and the governor would have to get us out. Even if we could go by foot, it's a long walk to Murasakino and back. I don't want to do it."

"Neither do we," Kintoki and Suetake agreed.

"If we can't walk or ride, how will we get there?" Suetake asked.

"I have an idea," Kintoki said. "We'll go in an oxcart." 🔢

"What? A farmer's wagon?"

"No! I mean the kind of closed oxcart that the wives and daughters of highborn nobles ride in."

"Is that a good idea?" Hidemichi asked. "Samurai are warriors. We aren't allowed to ride in carts or wagons. If anyone sees us, we'll be disgraced."

"Nobody will see us," Kintoki assured him. "These oxcarts are completely enclosed. The windows are covered with heavy curtains so no one can see inside." 🔢

---

2. In this case, a **shrine** is a case or a box for sacred objects.

Vocabulary

procession (proh SEH shun) *n.* a group of individuals walking forward together in a ceremony

Practice the Skills

🔢 **Key Literary Element**

Plot Here, in the exposition, the three main characters and the setting are introduced.

🔢 **Key Literary Element**

Plot The exposition continues as the situation is introduced. Here is the situation in a nutshell: The samurai want to go to a festival, but the streets will be too crowded for them to ride their horses. They decide to ride in an oxcart instead.

🔢 **Key Reading Skill**

Making Inferences What can you infer about the lives of upper-class women in old Japan? Think about these clues:

- The women do not ride on horseback; they ride in carts and wagons.
- The windows of the carts and wagons are covered so no one can look in.
- The covers also prevent the women from looking out the windows.

The Oxcart **197**

"How will we get one?" Suetake asked. "Three samurai can't hire an oxcart without the whole town learning about it."

"I've thought of that already," said Kintoki. "My sister is lady-in-waiting[3] to the governor's wife. The governor has plenty of oxcarts. Some are hardly ever used. My sister can arrange for us to borrow one. We'll walk along beside it on the way through town, pretending we're an escort.[4] When no one is looking, we'll get in and ride all the way to Murasakino. Our servant, Akira, will lead the ox while we travel in comfort."

The plan worked perfectly—except for one unforeseen difficulty. The three samurai had never traveled in an oxcart. Although the vehicle looked **elegant,** it had no springs. Every bump in the road bounced them around like grains of rice pounded in a mortar. And there were many, many bumps, holes, and gullies along the way to Murasakino.

They had hardly gone a mile when Suetake turned pale. **5** "I feel sick. I think I'm going to throw up," he said. "Hurry! Open the door! Let me out!"

Kintoki and Hidemichi grabbed him. "You can't go out! The road is full of people. If they see us riding in this oxcart, we'll be in trouble!"

"I can't help it!" Suetake moaned. "You have to let me out. I'm going to be—"

Poor Suetake threw up all over the oxcart. Like a **seasick** traveler, he couldn't stop

Practice the Skills

5 | Key Literary Element

Plot Which stage of the plot begins here? Hint: The situation is complicated by a conflict—the bumpy ride makes Suetake sick.

Japanese samurai warriors, c. 1880. R.P. Kingston.

Analyzing the Photo How does this photograph capture the nobility of the Japanese samurai?

---

3. A **lady-in-waiting** was a noblewoman who was a servant to an even more rich and powerful woman, often a queen.

4. An **escort** is one who accompanies another person on a journey.

vomiting, even when his stomach was empty. **6** He lay helpless on the floor, moaning and coughing.

Hidemichi turned pale. "What a terrible stench! Open the curtains, Kintoki, or I'll be sick, too!"

"I can't open the curtains! No one must see us in here!" said Kintoki.

"Then I am going to be sick with Suetake!" Hidemichi clutched his stomach and threw up, too. Within minutes, Kintoki joined him. The three samurai lay in a heap, vomiting on each other, groaning in misery.

The people on the road to Murasakino heard terrible groans coming from the oxcart. "What is going on in there?" they asked Akira, the samurais' servant. "It sounds as if someone is dying. Open the door! The people inside need help."

"Don't touch that door!" Akira blurted out. He could not allow his masters to be discovered riding in a women's oxcart. "The governor's aunt is inside. She was suddenly stricken with a terrible disease. Oozing sores broke out all over her body. The doctors can't help her. She is going to the temple in Murasakino to pray for a cure. No one must go near that cart. She might have the plague."[5] **7**

Needless to say, no one approached the cart again. The opposite happened. People on the road ran away when they saw the oxcart coming. It continued on to Murasakino, **lurching** back and forth on the bumpy road, with the three miserable samurai tumbling around inside it. **8**

At last the cart stopped. "Masters, we are here. We've reached the outskirts of Murasakino," Akira whispered. He waited for a reply but heard nothing. Finally he said, "I'm going to find a pasture for the ox. Then I'm going to watch the procession. Come quickly. It will be starting soon."

Akira unhitched the ox and led it away. When he returned hours later, he found the oxcart door still shut, with no sign that his masters had ever emerged. Fearing they might be dead, Akira opened the door and peeped inside.

He saw the three samurai lying in a heap, too weak to stand or even groan. Akira lifted them out of the cart, one by one.

---

5. The *plague* is an infectious, deadly disease.

Vocabulary

lurching (LURCH ing) *adj.* rolling or swaying in a jerky motion

Practice the Skills

6 | **English Language Coach**

Compound Words What two words are in the compound word **seasick**? What does *seasick* mean?

7 | **Key Literary Element**

Plot When people hear groans coming from the oxcart, the conflict intensifies. Is this the climax of the plot? Who takes decisive action to protect the samurai, and what action does he take?

8 | **Key Reading Skill**

Making Inferences The samurai feel terrible, but they do not get out of the cart. Why are they so stubborn about not being seen riding in the oxcart?

"Ashida" from *Sixty-nine Stations on the Kisokaido Highway,* c. 1838. Ando or Utagawa Hiroshige. Woodblock color print. Brooklyn Museum of Art, New York. Frank L. Babbott Fund.

Analyzing the Painting What aspect of the samurai's journey to Murasakino does this picture depict?

"Masters, I am so sorry. I did not know you were so ill. Have you been here the whole time? Didn't you go to the festival?"

"How could we?" Kintoki answered. "We were so sick we could hardly lift our heads."

"How stupid we were to ride in that cart!" Suetake exclaimed.

Hidemichi agreed. "We suffered for nothing. We missed the whole festival."

Akira ran to an inn down the road. He returned with hot water, new clothes, and a kettle of hot soup. The samurai felt better after cleaning themselves and eating.

"Let's go home," Kintoki said, disgusted.

"Not in that cart," said Hidemichi and Suetake. "We'll walk beside it. We'll pretend we're an escort."

The three samurai walked all the way back to Settsu. It took a long time to get there. They walked slowly, holding their stomachs, dragging their swords in the dust. **9**

Kintoki's sister was waiting for them. "Where have you been? I was expecting you hours ago. Why do you look so pale? Why does the cart smell so bad?"

"You're lucky we brought it back at all. This cart should be burned!" Kintoki told her.

"The horrid vehicle nearly killed us!" Hidemichi added.

"I'd rather face slow death by torture than ride in an oxcart again!" said Suetake.

Practice the Skills

9 **Key Reading Skill**

Making Inferences From this description of how the samurai are walking, what can you infer about how they feel?

Kintoki's sister began to laugh. "You samurai are always telling your wives and sisters how tough you are! You only went to Murasakino. **10** One short ride in an oxcart and you come back looking like corpses. We women are tougher than you! We ride in these carts all the time. Ha, ha, ha!"

Kintoki, Suetake, and Hidemichi slunk away without a word.

The three samurai had long, **distinguished** careers. Kintoki climbed the walls of an enemy castle and opened the gate, all by himself. Suetake stood alone in the middle of a bridge and fought off an attacking army. Hidemichi, after losing his sword, pulled an enemy general off his horse and captured him with his bare hands. But brave as they were, not one of the three ever went near an oxcart again. **11**

"A samurai does not fear death," they would say. "But some things are worse than death. An oxcart is one of them." **12** ○

Vocabulary

distinguished (dis TIN gwisht) *adj.* well-known for excellence and honor

Practice the Skills

10 **Key Literary Element**

Plot The action is winding down, and the outcome of the conflict is becoming clear. The women think it's funny that the "tough" samurai got sick in the oxcart. At this point, what stage of the plot is the story in?

11 **Key Literary Element**

Plot The plot is now in the final stage—resolution. What is the final outcome of the conflict?

12 **BIG Question**

The samurai go on to be brave men, but they never go in an oxcart again. What do you think their journey taught them about themselves? Write your answer on the "Oxcart" flap of Foldable 2. Your response will help you complete the Unit Challenge later.

Mount Fuji viewed from the province of Hara in Suruga, 1860. Hiroshige II. Colour woodcut. Victoria and Albert Museum, London.

Analyzing the Painting Does this image capture the fun and festivity of the procession to Murasakino? Why or why not?

After You Read

The Oxcart

Answering the BIG Question

1. Was the samurai's destination an important part of the story? Why or why not?

2. **Recall** Why did the samurai decide to ride in an oxcart?

   TIP **Right There** You will find this information in the story.

3. **Summarize** In a few sentences sum up what happens in the story.

   TIP **Think and Search** You will find the answer in the story but not all in one place.

Critical Thinking

4 **Analyze** How are the samurai punished for breaking the rules of their society?

   TIP **Author and Me** To answer the question, combine your understanding of the story with your own knowledge and experience.

5. **Evaluate** In your opinion, does the samurai's punishment fit the "crime" the samurai committed? Explain why or why not.

   TIP **Author and Me** To answer the question, combine your understanding of the story with your own knowledge and experience.

6. **Infer** Why would people think it was funny for the samurai to be sick?

   TIP **Author and Me** To answer the question, combine your understanding of the story with your own knowledge and experience.

Talk About Your Reading

Interview Get together with another student and pretend one of you is a journalist and the other one is one of the samurai in the story. The journalist should interview the samurai about his ride in the oxcart and things he learned from the experience. Be sure to ask *Who, What, When, Where, How,* and *Why* questions. Here are some examples:

• Who were your traveling companions on your journey?

• What was the purpose of your journey?

• Where did you journey?

Jot down your questions and answers in your Learner's Notebook.

NY English Language Arts Core Curriculum (pp. 202–203)

LC R17 Demonstrate comprehension and response through a range of activities. **S2c** Ask and respond to questions to clarify an interpretation of literary texts. **R1l** Make inferences on the basis of explicit and implied information. **R2b** Interpret plot, using evidence from the text. **Core W8** Use correct grammatical construction in parts of speech.

For a complete description of the standards, see p. NY 11.

Skills Review

Key Reading Skill: Making Inferences

7. What did society in Old Japan expect of samurai? Write two rules that explain how samurai were supposed to behave. Support each rule with an example or other evidence from the story.

Key Literary Element: Plot

8. The pyramid diagram below shows the relationship among the parts of a plot. Copy the diagram and complete it by taking notes on what happens in each part of the story's plot.

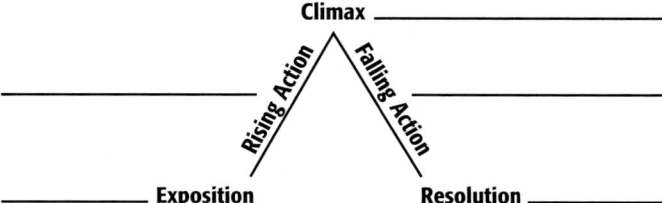

Reviewing Skills: Setting a Purpose for Reading

9. Read your Learner's Notebook notes about what you expected to learn from reading the story. Did you learn what you expected to learn? Explain.

Vocabulary Check

Answer *true* or *false* to each statement.

10. Soldiers marching in formation are an example of a **procession.**

11. A **lurching** rollercoaster car would jerk from side to side.

12. **Elegant** clothes are ugly and in bad taste.

13. A person who is **distinguished** is looked down upon by others.

14. **English Language Coach** While reading "The Oxcart," you analyzed the compound word *seasick.* Now apply what you learned. Define each of the following similar compound words:

• **heartsick** • **carsick**

Grammar Link: Articles and Demonstrative Adjectives

The adjectives *a, an,* and *the* are **articles.** Use the **definite article** *the* when writing about a specific person, place, thing, feeling or idea. Use the **indefinite articles** *a* and *an* with general nouns.

• **General:** I want to buy <u>a</u> book. *(Any book will do.)*

• **Specific:** <u>The</u> book I want is at the mall. *(The speaker wants a particular book.)*

Watch Out! Do not confuse *a* and *an*. The word *an* goes with a noun that begins with a vowel sound. *A* goes with a noun that begins with a consonant sound.

• <u>an</u> egg • <u>an</u> ~~h~~our (silent *h*) • <u>a</u> cottage

Demonstrative adjectives describe nouns by answering the question *which one*? or *which ones*?

Use the demonstratives *this* and *these* to refer to nearby people, places, and things. *This* is singular. *These* is plural. Use the demonstratives *that* and *those* to refer to people, places, and things that are farther away. *That* is singular. *Those* is plural.

Near: Do <u>this</u> one. / <u>These</u> bugs are cute.
Far away: I saw <u>that</u> movie. / I met <u>those</u> girls.

Grammar Practice

Copy the words below on another sheet of paper. Add an article or demonstrative adjective in front of each word. Use a different article or demonstrative adjective for each.

• **ant**
• **months**
• **honor**
• **idea**

Web Activities For eFlashcards, Selection Quick Checks, and other Web activities, go to www.glencoe.com.

Skills Focus

You will practice using these skills when you read the following selections:
- "The Snake Chief," p. 208
- from *Harriet Tubman: Conductor on the Underground Railroad* p. 220

Reading
- Predicting

Literature
- Identifying and analyzing conflicts
- Analyzing author's style

Vocabulary
- Classifying words to expand vocabulary
- Academic Vocabulary: *predicting*

Writing/Grammar
- Identifying and correcting double negatives
- Identifying and correcting dangling and misplaced modifiers

NY English Language Arts Core Curriculum (pp. 204–205)

R1m Make, confirm, or revise predictions.

For a complete description of the standards, see p. NY 11.

Skill Lesson

Predicting

Learn It!

What Is It? **Predicting** is making an educated guess about what will happen. You make predictions every day. For example, if you say that a ballplayer will win the game with a home run in the ninth inning, you are predicting, or guessing beforehand, how the game will end.

To predict when you're reading a story, you think about the events and details you've read about so far. Then you use them as clues to guess what might happen next. Once you make a prediction, you read on to see if you guessed right or whether the author surprises you.

To make good predictions:
- Pay attention to the details in the story.
- Use what you already know.

Analyzing Cartoons
What clues in Thomas's baby picture lead you to predict that he may become a circus performer?

© Reprinted with permission of King Features Syndicate, Inc.

Academic Vocabulary

predicting (pree DIKT ing) *n.* using clues to guess what will happen

Why Is It Important? Predicting gives you a reason to read and helps you get involved in your reading. For example, when you first start reading a story, you might predict what will happen next. The fun part is reading on to see whether your prediction comes true! As you read, adjust or change your predictions if they don't fit what you learn.

Literature online

Study Central Visit www.glencoe .com and click on Study Central to review predicting.

How Do I Do It? Think about the characteristics of the genre you're reading. For example, if you're reading a folktale, think about the kinds of characters, conflicts, and plots you usually find in folktales. Also look for patterns, or repeated ideas, as you read. The patterns and the genre characteristics are clues that will help you make good predictions. To see how a student made predictions using clues, read the model below.

> Once upon a time a beautiful maiden named Grace lived near a forest. Every day she walked through the woods to see the creatures and smell the flowers. She knew every animal and plant so well they were like family. Then one day a mysterious new plant appeared. Grace was strangely drawn to its velvety black flowers and blood-red thorns. She wanted to bring some flowers home, but she was afraid. The plant smelled so strange!

"Once upon a time" tells me this is a folktale. It also tells me this is the beginning of the tale. That's when the characters, setting, and situation are usually introduced. Since the mysterious plant is described at the beginning, it must have something to do with the situation. I predict that Grace will pick the flowers and that something bad will happen as a result. I think something bad will happen because if it didn't there wouldn't be any conflict.

Practice It!

Do you agree with the student's prediction? If so, predict what bad thing will happen in the folktale. If not, predict what will happen instead. Give reasons for your prediction.

Use It!

As you read "The Snake Chief" and from *Harriet Tubman*, make predictions about what will happen.

Before You Read : **The Snake Chief**

Meet the Author

Kathleen Arnott was born in England in 1914. She taught elementary school in Beckingham, Kent, England, and later in Nigeria. Arnott first started writing fiction for African children when she discovered that her students and other children in local schools had no Nigerian storybooks. When she returned to England, Arnott continued to write, alternating between writing more fiction for African children and retelling African folktales for British and American children.

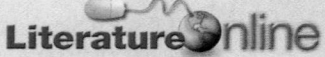

Author Search For more about Kathleen Arnott, go to www.glencoe.com.

NY English Language Arts Core Curriculum (pp. 206–215)

LC R9 Recognize connections among meaning of words. **R1m** Make, confirm, or revise predictions. **R2b** Interpret characters and plot, using evidence from the text. **R2g** Compare literature to own lives.

For a complete description of the standards, see p. NY 11.

Vocabulary Preview

induce (in DOOS) *v.* convince to do something; influence **(p. 209)** *Even a high salary would not induce the lazy man to work.*

quavered (KWAY verd) *v.* spoke in a shaky or trembling voice; form of the verb *quaver* **(p. 211)** *"I feel ill," the old woman quavered.*

incompetence (in KAHMP uh tunts) *n.* lack of ability or skill **(p. 212)** *Her failure to make good bread was a sign of her incompetence.*

reluctantly (ree LUK tunt lee) *adv.* against one's wishes **(p. 213)** *She reluctantly agreed to marry, although she thought she was too young.*

Write to Learn In your Learner's Notebook, write a definition in your own words for each of the vocabulary words.

English Language Coach

Building Vocabulary: Classification Charts A useful way to build your vocabulary is to make classification charts. These charts can help you remember words and their definitions by putting words that belong together into groups. For example, you might group *quavered* with other words that describe how voices may sound. All the words on the chart below are from "The Snake Chief."

Descriptions of Voices	
quavered	spoke in a shaky or trembling voice
screeched	cried out in a high, piercing voice
hissed	spat out words in an angry voice

As the different definitions show, the words are *not* synonyms, because they have different meanings. Yet they belong together because they all are ways of using your voice.

Partner Work Copy the classification chart on another sheet of paper. With a classmate, add two or three other words that describe how someone's voice might sound.

Skills Preview

Key Reading Skill: Predicting

"The Snake Chief" is a folktale about two sisters. One of them is stubborn, conceited, and rude. The other is gentle, courteous, and kind. Think about what you have learned about folktales and the characters in them. What do you think might happen to each sister?

Whole Class Discussion As a class, predict what will happen to each sister and why.

Key Literary Element: Conflict

Conflict is a struggle between opposing forces in a story or play.

- **External conflict** occurs when a main character, or protagonist, clashes with an outside force, or antagonist. The force might be another character; society; fate; or a natural event, such as a tornado.

- An **internal conflict** is a psychological or emotional struggle that takes place within a character. External conflicts often cause internal conflicts. For example, a character who continually argues with his parents (external conflict) may wonder if he's doing the right thing (internal conflict).

- To find the conflicts in "The Snake Chief," ask yourself questions like these: *With whom or what do the characters clash? Does this struggle cause psychological or emotional upset? If so, how?*

Write to Learn Classify the conflicts listed below. Which are external? Internal? Why? Jot down your thoughts in your Learner's Notebook.

- playing an opposing baseball team
- making a tough decision
- wanting to spend your money or to save it
- battling a storm while on a boat at sea

Interactive Literary Elements Handbook
To review or learn more about the literary elements, go to www.glencoe.com.

Get Ready to Read

Connect to the Reading

Think about a time when people tried to give you good advice, but you refused to take it.

Write to Learn In a few sentences sum up what the situation was, whose advice you ignored, and how the situation turned out.

Build Background

"The Snake Chief" is a folktale that was first told by the Xhosa (KO suh), a group of South African tribes.

Traditionally, the typical Xhosa village was close knit. Relatives lived in the same small, circular hut or built huts near each other. The cooking areas were outside the huts, making it easy and natural to share food. Cooking over open fires in cast-iron pots, Xhosa women welcomed their neighbors to sample their cooking. The Xhosa believed that it was important for people to cooperate, share, and help one another.

Storytelling was an important part of Xhosa life. Through stories, older members of the village taught the kids what their history was, what the Xhosa community valued most in life, and how to behave in ways that were true to Xhosa values. As you read "The Snake Chief," think about the values the story might have taught to kids.

Set Purposes for Reading

BIG Question Read "The Snake Chief" to find out what journeys lie ahead for two sisters—and where their journeys will take them.

Set Your Own Purpose What else would you like to learn from the story to help you answer the Big Question? Write your own purpose on the "Snake Chief" flap of Foldable 2.

Keep Moving

Use these skills as you read the following selection.

THE SNAKE CHIEF

retold by Kathleen Arnott

There were once two sisters who lived in a village beside a river. When they were old enough to be married, their father looked around for suitors,[1] but alas, none came, so he decided he must visit other villages and let it be known that he had two daughters ready to be wed.

One day, he took his small canoe and crossed the big river. Then he walked along a path until he came to a village. It appeared to be a happy place and the people greeted him kindly.

'Welcome!' they cried 'What news have you brought?'

'I have no news of importance,' he replied. 'Have you?'

'Our chief is looking for a wife,' the people replied, 'otherwise nothing we can think of is worth repeating.' ∎

Now the man had found out what he wanted to know, and he told the people that he would send a wife for the chief the next day.

He re-crossed the river and went to his house, smiling contentedly. When his daughters came back from their work in the fields he called them and said:

'At last I have found a man who is worthy to be the husband of one of my daughters. The chief in the village across the water is looking for a wife. Which of you shall I send?'

Practice the Skills

∎ Key Reading Skill

Predicting Think about what you've read about the father and his daughters. What do you think will happen next?

---

1. **Suitors** are men who wish to marry.

The elder[2] daughter said quickly: 'I shall go, of course, since I am the elder.'

'Very well,' replied the man. 'I shall call all my friends and bid the drummers lead you to your husband's home.'

'Indeed you will not,' said the girl haughtily. 'When I go to the home of my husband, I shall go alone.'

Now in that part of Africa it was unheard of for a bride to go to her wedding without a host of friends and relations all singing and dancing for joy. So the father was astonished when his daughter said she would go alone, even though he knew she had been proud and headstrong from childhood.

'But, my daughter,' he **pleaded,** 'no woman ever goes alone to her marriage. It is not the custom.' **2**

'Then I shall start a new custom,' said the girl. 'Unless I go alone, I shall not go at all.'

At last the father, realizing that no amount of persuasion would **induce** the girl to change her mind, agreed to her going alone, and early the next morning she set out. He took her across the river and pointed out the way, then returned home unhappily. **3**

The girl began her journey without looking back and after a little while she met a mouse on the path. It stood up on its hind-legs, and rubbing its two front paws together, asked politely:

'Would you like me to show you the way to the chief's village?'

The girl scarcely stopped walking and almost trod on the mouse as she replied:

'Get out of my sight! I want no help from you.'

Then she continued on her way while the mouse screeched after her:

'Bad luck to you!'

---

2. *Elder* means older.

Vocabulary . . . .

induce (in DOOS) *v.* convince to do something; influence

Practice the Skills

2 **English Language Coach**

Classification Charts The word **pleaded** describes how the father's voice sounds when he talks to his daughter. If you don't know what the word means, use context clues to figure out the definition or look it up. Add the word and definition to the classification chart you made earlier.

3 **Key Literary Element**

Conflict The unhappy father has an internal conflict. What external conflict with his daughter causes him to feel unhappy?

Homeward Bound, 2004. Tilly Willis. Oil on canvas. Private Collection.

Analyzing the Painting How does this painting help you visualize the story's setting?

The Snake Chief **209**

A little further on the girl met a frog, sitting on a stone at the side of the path.

'Would you like me to show you the way?' he croaked.

'Don't you speak to me!' answered the girl, tipping the frog off the stone with her foot. 'I am going to be a chief's wife and am far too important to have anything to do with a mere frog.'

'Bad luck to you then,' croaked the frog, as he picked himself up from where he had fallen and jumped off into the bush.

Analyzing the Photo These hand-woven baskets contain millet, a staple food for many African people. What aspect(s) of village life might this image represent?

Soon after this the girl began to feel tired and she sat down under a tree to rest. In the distance she could hear goats bleating[3] and presently a herd of them passed by, driven by a little boy.

'Greetings, sister,' he said politely. 'Are you going on a long journey?'

'What business is that of yours?' demanded the girl.

'I thought you might be carrying food with you,' replied the boy, 'and I hoped you might give me something to eat for I am so hungry.' **4**

'I have no food,' said the girl, 'and even if I had I should not dream of giving any to you.'

The boy looked disappointed and hurried after his goats, turning back to say over his shoulder:

'Bad luck to you then.'

Presently the girl got to her feet and continued her journey. Suddenly she found herself face to face with a very old woman.

'Greetings, my daughter,' she said to the girl. 'Let me give you some advice.

'You will come to some trees which will laugh at you, but do not laugh back at them.

'You will find a bag of thick, curdled[4] milk, but do not on any account drink it.

'You will meet a man who carries his head under his arm, but you must not drink water if he offers you any.'

Practice the Skills

4 **Key Reading Skill**

Predicting Do you think the daughter will share her food with the hungry boy? Think about
- how she treated her father
- how she treated the mouse
- how she treated the frog

---

3. **Bleating** is a sound that goats make, similar to whining or crying.
4. **Curdled milk** is similar to yogurt.

Practice the Skills

'Be quiet, you ugly old thing!' exclaimed the girl, pushing the old woman aside. 'If I want any advice from you, I'll ask for it.'

'You will have bad luck if you don't listen to me,' **quavered** the old woman, but the girl took no notice and went on her way.

Sure enough she soon came to a clump of trees which began to laugh loudly as she approached them.

'Stop laughing at me,' she **commanded,** and when they did not, she laughed noisily at them in return as she passed them by. **5**

A little further on, she saw a bag made from a whole goatskin, lying at her feet. On picking it up, she discovered it was full of curdled milk and since this was something she was particularly fond of, she drank it with relish, exclaiming:

'How lucky I found this! I was getting so thirsty with such a long journey.'

Then she threw the bag into the bush and continued on her way. As she walked through a shady grove, she was a little taken aback at the strange sight of a man coming towards her, carrying his head under one arm. The eyes in the head looked at her and the mouth spoke:

'Would you like some water to drink, my daughter?' it said, and the hand that was not carrying the head held out a calabash[5] of water to the girl. **6**

She was not really thirsty but decided to taste the water and see whether it was sweet, so she took a sip, found it delicious and drank the whole calabash full. Then she continued, without a word of thanks to the strange creature.

As she turned the next bend in the path, she saw in the distance the village she was seeking and knew that her journey was almost over. She had to cross a small stream and found a girl bending there, filling her water-pot.

She was about to pass on when the village girl greeted her and asked:

'Where are you going, pray?'

With scarcely a glance at her questioner she replied:

5 **English Language Coach**

Classification Charts How do you think a voice sounds when it has **commanded** something? Add the word to your classification chart.

6 **Key Reading Skill**

Predicting Do you think the daughter will go against the old woman's advice and drink the water? Think about
- whether she followed her father's advice
- how she treated the old woman
- whether she followed the other advice the old woman gave her

---

5. A *calabash* is a dried gourd that is used as a container.

Vocabulary

quavered (KWAY verd) *v.* spoke in a shaky or trembling voice

'I am going to that village to marry a chief. You have no right to speak to me, for I am older than you and far more important.'

Now the younger girl was the chief's sister, but she did not boast about this. She merely said:

'Let me give you some advice. Do not enter the village from this side. It is unlucky to do so. Go right round past those tall trees and enter it on the far side.'

The girl took no notice at all but just walked on to the nearest entrance with her head in the air. When she arrived, the women crowded round her to find out who she was and what she wanted.

'I have come to marry your chief,' she explained. 'Get away, and let me rest.' **7**

'How can you be a bride if you come alone?' they asked. 'Where is the bridal procession, and are there no drummers with you?'

The girl did not answer, but she sat down in the shade of a hut to rest her aching legs.

Presently some of the older women came over to her.

'If you are to be the wife of our chief,' they said, 'then you must prepare his supper, as all good wives do.'

The girl realized that this was true, so she asked:

Visual Vocabulary
Millet is a grass that produces seeds that can be eaten or crushed into flour.

'And from where shall I get the millet to cook my husband's supper?'

They gave her some millet and told her to grind it, showing her where the grinding-stones were, but unlike most women, she only ground the corn for a very short time, so that the flour was coarse and gritty. Then she made some bread, and when the other women saw it, they went away together and laughed at her **incompetence.**

As the sun set, a mighty wind blew up. The roof of the hut shook and shivered and the girl crouched against the mud walls in fear. But worse was to come. A huge snake with five heads suddenly appeared, and coiling itself up at the door of the hut, told her to bring it the supper she had cooked.

7 Key Reading Skill

Predicting The daughter assumes she will become the chief's wife. Do you think she will? Why or why not?

Vocabulary

incompetence (in KAHMP uh tunts) *n.* lack of ability or skill

Analyzing the Photo In the story, members of a community keep old traditions alive. How might the people in this photo be doing the same thing?

'Did you not know that I am the chief?' asked the snake, as it began to eat the bread. Then it uttered a fearful scream, spat the food from its mouth and hissed:

'This supper is so badly cooked, I refuse to have you for a wife! So I shall slay you!' and with a mighty blow from his tail, he killed her. **8**

When the news of her death at last reached her father, he still had not found a husband for his younger daughter, whose name was Mpunzanyana.

'Let me go to this chief,' she begged him. 'I am sure I could please him if I tried.'

Rather **reluctantly** the father called together all his relations and friends and asked them to make up a bridal procession for his second daughter. They were all delighted and went away to put on their best clothes, while the father summoned the musicians and drummers who were to lead the way.

They set off early in the morning, and crossing the big river, they sang joyfully as they went. They began the long journey along the same little path that the eldest daughter had taken not so long ago, and presently they met a mouse.

'Shall I tell you how to get there?' it asked of Mpunzanyana, as she stopped to avoid treading on it.

Practice the Skills

8 | **Key Literary Element**

Conflict What kind of conflict has just taken place between the chief and the daughter—internal or external? Explain.

Vocabulary

reluctantly (ree LUK tunt lee) *adv.* against one's wishes

'Thank you very much,' she replied, and listened courteously as the tiny animal told them which path to take.

On they went until they came to a deep valley and found a very old woman sitting beside a tree. The ugly old creature rose shakily to her feet to stand before the girl. Then she said:

'When you come to a place where two paths meet, you must take the little one, not the big one as that is unlucky.'

'Thank you for telling me, grannie,' Mpunzanyana answered. 'I will do as you say and take the little path.'

They journeyed on and on, meeting no one for some time, until suddenly a coney[6] stood on the path in front of them all. Stretching up its head, it looked at the girl and said:

'You are nearly there! But let me give you some advice. Soon you will meet a young girl carrying water from the stream. Mind you speak politely to her.

'When you get to the village they will give you millet to grind for the chief's supper. Make sure you do it properly.

'And finally, when you see your husband, do not be afraid. I beg you, have no fear, or at least, do not show it.' **9**

'Thank you for your advice, little coney,' said the girl. 'I will try to remember it all and do as you say.'

Sure enough, as they turned the last bend in the path, they caught sight of the village, and coming up from the stream they overtook a young girl carrying a pot of water on her head. It was the chief's sister, and she asked:

'Where are you bound for?'

'We are going to this village where I hope to be the chief's bride,' answered Mpunzanyana.

'Let me lead you to the chief's hut,' said the younger girl, 'and do not be afraid when you see him.'

Mpunzanyana followed the girl, and the bridal party followed Mpunzanyana, so that all the people came out of their huts to see what the joyful noise was about. They welcomed the visitors politely and gave them food to eat. Then the chief's mother brought millet to Mpunzanyana and said:

'If you are to be the wife of our chief, then you must prepare his supper, as all good wives do.'

So the girl set to work and ground the millet as finely as she could, then made it into light, delicious bread.

Practice the Skills

9 | **Key Reading Skill**

Predicting There is a pattern in the way the daughter treats animals and people. Based on this pattern, do you think the daughter will follow the coney's advice? Explain.

---

6. A *coney* is a type of rabbit.

As the sun set, a strong wind arose which shook the house and when Mpunzanyana heard the people saying: 'Here comes our chief,' she began to tremble. Then she remembered what she had been told and even when one of the poles which supported the roof fell to the ground, she did not run outside in a panic but stood quietly waiting for her husband to come home.

She almost cried out when she saw the huge snake, but when it asked her for food, she gave it the bread she had cooked and it ate it with obvious enjoyment.

'This bread is delicious,' said the snake. 'Will you be my wife?'

For one moment, Mpunzanyana was struck dumb, but she smiled bravely when she thought of all the advice she had had, and replied:

'Yes, O chief, I will marry you.'

At her words, the shining snake-skin fell from the chief and he rose up, a tall, handsome man.

'By your brave words, you have broken the spell,' he explained.

That night a feast was begun in the chief's village which lasted for twenty days. Oxen were slaughtered, beer was brewed and all the time the sound of music and drumming made the people's hearts glad.

So Mpunzanyana became the wife of a rich and splendid chief, and in course of time they had many sons, while the village prospered under her husband's wise rule. **10** ○

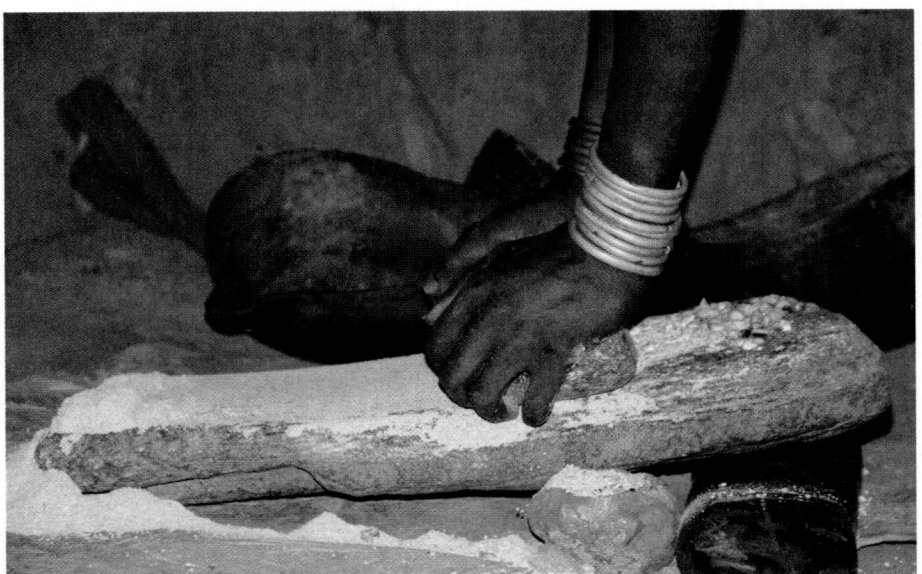

Practice the Skills

10 **BIG** Question
Which daughter do you think learned more from her journey—the older daughter or the younger? Explain. Write your answer on the "Snake Chief" flap of Foldable 2. Your response will help you complete the Unit Challenge later.

Analyzing the Photo How does this photo help you understand the difficulty of Mpunzanyana's task?

The Snake Chief **215**

After You Read

The Snake Chief

Answering the **BIG** Question

1. How do you think "The Snake Chief" answers the Big Question, "Which is more important, the journey or the destination?" Explain.

2. **Recall** Why does the elder sister set out on a journey?

   TIP **Right There** The answer is in the story.

3. **Summarize** How does the elder sister respond to those who try to help her?

   TIP **Think and Search** The answer is in the story, but it is not all in one place.

Critical Thinking

4. **Analyze** What is the elder sister's greatest weakness or flaw?

   TIP **Author and Me** To answer, think about the story and draw on your knowledge of people.

5. **Infer** Why might a chief want his future wife to first prepare a meal for him? What does this suggest about the role of women in Xhosa society?

   TIP **Author and Me** To answer, think about the story and your prior knowledge.

Write About Your Reading

RAFT Assignment Use the RAFT system to write about "The Snake Chief." A **RAFT** assignment provides four details:

   R is for your *role* as a writer—who or what you must pretend to be as you write.

   A stands for your *audience*—the person or group who will read what you write.

   F means *format*—the form for your writing, such as a letter or a speech.

   T means *topic*—what your writing should be about.

Role: the snake chief

Audience: the snake chief's future children

Format: narrative

Topic: Explain how you felt when you first met the person who would become your wife and how you felt about her older sister.

NY English Language Arts Core Curriculum (pp. 216–217)

LC R17 Demonstrate comprehension and response through a range of activities. **LC W5** Write with voice to address varied purposes, topics, and audiences. **R1m** Make, confirm, or revise predictions. **R2b** Interpret characters and plot, using evidence from the text. **LC R9** Recognize connections among meaning of words. **Core W8** Use correct grammatical construction.

For a complete description of the standards, see p. NY 11.

Skills Review

Key Lesson Skill: Predicting

6. Which of your predictions were right? Which were wrong? For each wrong prediction, figure out why you guessed wrong.

Key Literary Element: Conflict

7. The older daughter has external conflicts with several characters. Look back at the story, and make a list of all the people and animals with whom she clashes.

8. Do you think the older daughter's conflicts with other characters cause internal conflicts for her? Explain, using evidence from the story to back up your opinion.

Vocabulary Check

Choose the best word from the list to complete each sentence below. On a separate piece of paper, rewrite each sentence with the correct word in place.

> **incompetence**
> **reluctantly**
> **induce**
> **quavered**

9. Her ___ as a cook was clear when the Snake Chief spat out her bread.

10. ___, the father agreed to let his younger daughter make the dangerous journey.

11. No amount of persuasion could ___ her to follow the customs of the village.

12. "What was that sound?" the frightened child ___.

13. **Academic Vocabulary** Describe a time when you used *predicting* outside of school. Was your prediction right or wrong?

14. **English Language Coach** Review your classification chart. Choose four words, and use each one in a sentence.

Grammar Link: Double Negatives

Negative words express the idea of "no." Examples of negative words include *not, never, nobody, none, nothing,* and *nowhere.* Two negative words used together in the same sentence create an error called a *double negative.* Avoid using two negative words in the same sentence.

Incorrect: Mpunzanyana <u>didn't</u> have <u>no</u> fear when she faced the snake chief.

Correct: Mpunzanyana <u>didn't</u> have <u>any</u> fear when she faced the snake chief.

Correct: Mpunzanyana had <u>no</u> fear when she faced the snake chief.

Double negatives can make your writing awkward and confusing. Only one negative word is necessary to convey a negative meaning. Correct a sentence that has a double negative by removing one of the negative words or by replacing one of the negative words with an affirmative word, such as *always, anybody, all, any, someone, something,* and *some.*

Grammar Practice

Each sentence below contains a double negative. Underline the word or words in parentheses that best complete each sentence.

15. I didn't see (nothing, anything) that I wanted to buy.

16. I can't find my shoes (nowhere, anywhere).

17. We never have (no, any) good food around here.

Writing Application Look back at the RAFT assignment you wrote. Make sure that you haven't used any double negatives.

Web Activities For eFlashcards, Selection Quick Checks, and other Web activities, go to www.glencoe.com.

Before You Read

from *Harriet Tubman: Conductor on the Underground Railroad*

Ann Petry

Meet the Author

Ann Petry was born on October 12, 1908, in Old Saybrook, Connecticut. She moved to New York City in 1938, determined to become a writer. Petry's novel, *The Street,* was the first novel by an African American to sell more than a million copies. Petry once said, "I hoped that I made [historical characters like Harriet Tubman] come alive, turned them into real people." See page R5 of the Author Files for more on Ann Petry.

Author Search For more about Ann Petry, go to www.glencoe.com.

NY English Language Arts Core Curriculum (pp. 218–231)

LC R5 Determine the meaning of unfamiliar words by using context, dictionaries, and other resources. **R1m** Make, confirm, or revise predictions. **R2e** Recognize how the author's use of language creates images or feelings.

For a complete description of the standards, see p. NY 11.

Vocabulary Preview

eloquence (EL uh kwunts) *n.* the ability to speak well **(p. 227)** *Frederick Douglass was popular because of his eloquence as a speaker.*

disclose (dis KLOHZ) *v.* to make known; reveal **(p. 227)** *William Still agreed not to disclose the names of the fugitives so they would have a better chance to escape.*

cajoling (kuh JOHL ing) *v.* persuading, especially by using soothing words; coaxing **(p. 228)** *Despite their eagerness to flee, Tubman still had to spend time cajoling the fugitives into cooperation.*

Partner Talk For each vocabulary word, give a definition in your own words. Have your partner use your definition to guess the correct word.

English Language Coach

Building Vocabulary: Old Words and Phrases Even though "Harriet Tubman: Conductor on the Underground Railroad" was written recently, the author uses words and phrases from long ago. The words and phrases help to create the feeling and atmosphere of the time the story took place. Here are some of the old words and phrases that you'll find in the selection.

• a goodly number of: many
• had taken to their heels: had run away
• borne on the wind: carried by the wind
• sold South: sold to owners in the Deep South, where slavery was the most brutal
• in this fashion: in this way

Partner Talk Talk with a classmate about old words and phrases you may know. Often, grandparents and other older relatives use phrases that younger people don't. Can you think of any? You may also know other old words and phrases through things you have read.

Skills Preview

Key Reading Skill: Predicting

The selection you are about to read tells the true story of Harriet Tubman and her role in the underground railroad. Think about other nonfiction stories you have read about people from the past. Recall what you already know about the Underground Railroad.

Whole Class Discussion As a class, predict what kinds of facts and details you'll find in the selection.

Literary Element: Style

Style is the distinctive way an author writes. Elements of style include word choice, sentence type and length, "sound devices" like repetition, and description. To analyze an author's style, ask yourself questions like these:

- *Does the author mainly use short, simple words or longer, more difficult words?*
- *Does the author mainly use short, simple sentences or longer, complex ones?*
- *Does the author use repetition or other sound devices?*
- *Does the author use descriptive language?*

Partner Talk With a classmate, use the questions above to compare the style of the two passages below.

- It was cold. Very cold. At 20 degrees below zero, breathing is hard. The ice on a man's mustache grows thicker with every breath.
- How cold it was! Every time the man drew in his breath, icy needles pierced his lungs. When he exhaled, small icy clouds formed. Each breath left its frosty mark as drops of ice on his mustache.

Literature Online

Interactive Literary Elements Handbook
To review or learn more about the literary elements, go to www.glencoe.com.

Get Ready to Read

Connect to the Reading

Recall a time when you were a member of a group. If the group's task was difficult, there probably were times when the group members wanted to give up.

- How did you react when people stopped trying?
- Did you get angry or frustrated?
- Did you find ways to persuade them not to give up?

Write to Learn Write a few sentences about your experiences working in a group.

Build Background

The Underground Railroad wasn't really a railroad, and it wasn't really underground. It was a secret series of travel routes, hiding places, and safe houses where people who were against slavery helped hide people who had escaped from slavery on their way north.

- The people who guided the runaways along the Underground Railroad were called "conductors."
- Most enslaved people hid during the day and traveled during the night to avoid being caught.

Set Purposes for Reading

BIG Question Read the selection from *Harriet Tubman: Conductor on the Underground Railroad* to find out about the long and difficult journey that Harriet Tubman took to bring a group of escapees to freedom.

Set Your Own Purpose What else would you like to learn from the selection to help you answer the Big Question? Write your own purpose on the "Harriet Tubman" flap of Foldable 2.

Keep Moving

Use these skills as you read the following selection.

from

HARRIET TUBMAN:

Conductor on the Underground Railroad

by Ann Petry

Harriet Tubman, 1945. William H. Johnson. Oil on paperboard, 29³/₈ x 23³/₈ in. National Museum of American Art, Washington, DC.

Along the Eastern Shore of Maryland, in Dorchester County, in Caroline County, the masters kept hearing whispers about the man named Moses,[1] who was running off slaves. At first they did not believe in his existence. The stories about him were fantastic, unbelievable. Yet they watched for him. They offered rewards for his capture.

They never saw him. Now and then they heard whispered rumors to the effect that he was in the neighborhood. The woods were searched. The roads were watched. There was never anything to indicate his whereabouts. But a few days afterward, a goodly number of slaves would be gone from the plantation. Neither the master nor the overseer had heard or seen anything unusual in the quarter.[2] Sometimes one or the other would vaguely remember having heard a whippoorwill call somewhere in the woods, close by, late at night. Though it was the wrong season for whippoorwills. **1**

---

1. **Moses** was a Hebrew prophet who led his people out of slavery in Egypt. To enslaved persons, Biblical figures like Moses represented the hope of freedom.
2. Here, **quarter** refers to the area in which the enslaved people lived on a farm or plantation.

Practice the Skills

1 **Key Reading Skill**

Predicting In the context of the story, who do you think Moses will turn out to be? Use these clues to make your prediction:
- The first paragraph says that Moses is someone "who was running off slaves."
- The second paragraph says, "They never saw him."

Sometimes the masters thought they had heard the cry of a hoot owl, repeated, and would remember having thought that the intervals between the low moaning cry were wrong, that it had been repeated four times in succession instead of three. There was never anything more than that to suggest that all was not well in the quarter. Yet when morning came, they invariably discovered that a group of the finest slaves had taken to their heels.

Unfortunately, the discovery was almost always made on a Sunday. Thus a whole day was lost before the machinery of pursuit could be set in motion. The posters offering rewards for the fugitives could not be printed until Monday. The men who made a living hunting for runaway slaves were out of reach, off in the woods with their dogs and their guns, in pursuit of four-footed game, or they were in camp meetings[3] saying their prayers with their wives and families beside them.

Visual Vocabulary
The ***whippoorwill***, a North American bird, is active mainly at night; its name imitates the sound of its call.

Harriet Tubman could have told them that there was far more involved in this matter of running off slaves than signaling the would-be runaways by imitating the call of a whippoorwill, or a hoot owl, far more involved than a matter of waiting for a clear night when the North Star was visible. ②

In December, 1851, when she started out with the band of fugitives that she planned to take to Canada, she had been in the vicinity of the plantation for days, planning the trip, carefully selecting the slaves that she would take with her.

She had announced her arrival in the quarter by singing the forbidden spiritual[4]—"Go down, Moses, 'way down to Egypt Land"—singing it softly outside the door of a slave cabin, late at night. The husky voice was beautiful even when it was barely more than a murmur borne[5] on the wind.

Once she had made her presence known, word of her coming spread from cabin to cabin. The slaves whispered to

② Literary Element

Style Ann Petry uses long sentences in the second and third paragraphs on this page. Are lengthy sentences part of her writing style? To find out, look for other long sentences as you continue reading.

---

3. ***Camp meetings*** are religious meetings held in a tent or outdoors.

4. Many African American ***spirituals*** like "Go Down Moses," had secret references to the Underground Railroad. Certain songs were forbidden for fear that they might inspire enslaved people to escape or rebel.

5. ***Borne*** is the past participle of *to bear* and, here, means "carried."

from *Harriet Tubman: Conductor on the Underground Railroad* **221**

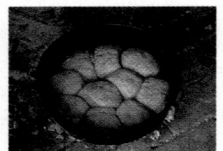

Visual Vocabulary
Ashcake is a cornmeal bread that's baked among the ashes at the back of a fireplace.

each other, ear to mouth, mouth to ear, "Moses is here." "Moses has come." "Get ready. Moses is back again." The ones who had agreed to go North with her put ashcake and salt herring in an old bandanna, hastily tied it into a bundle, and then waited patiently for the signal that meant it was time to start. **3**

There were eleven in this party, including one of her brothers and his wife. It was the largest group that she had ever conducted, but she was determined that more and more slaves should know what freedom was like.

She had to take them all the way to Canada. The Fugitive Slave Law[6] was no longer a great many incomprehensible words written down on the country's lawbooks. The new law had become a reality. It was Thomas Sims, a boy, picked up on the streets of Boston at night and shipped back to Georgia. It was Jerry and Shadrach, arrested and jailed with no warning.

She had never been in Canada. The route beyond Philadelphia was strange to her. But she could not let the runaways who accompanied her know this. As they walked along she told them stories of her own first **flight,** she kept painting vivid word pictures of what it would be like to be free.

But there were so many of them this time. She knew moments of doubt when she was half-afraid, and kept looking back over her shoulder, imagining that she heard the sound of pursuit. They would certainly be pursued. Eleven of them. Eleven thousand dollars' worth of flesh and bone and muscle that belonged to Maryland planters. If they were caught, the eleven runaways would be whipped and sold South, but she—she would probably be hanged. **4**

They tried to sleep during the day but they never could wholly relax into sleep. She could tell by the positions they assumed, by their restless movements. And they walked at night. Their progress was slow. It took them three nights of walking to reach the first stop. She had told them about the place where they would stay, promising warmth and good

Practice the Skills

3 | **Key Reading Skill**

Predicting Here, you learn that "Moses" was a code name for Harriet Tubman. Did you correctly predict who Moses would turn out to be?

4 | **English Language Coach**

Old Words and Phrases Do you remember the meaning of the phrase "sold South"? If not, look back on page 218.

---

6. The 1850 *Fugitive Slave Law* allowed owners to get back escaped slaves, even if the slaves had reached free states.

Underground Railroad, c. 1945. William H. Johnson. Oil on paperboard, 33 3/8 x 36 3/8 in. National Museum of American Art, Washington, DC.

food, holding these things out to them as an incentive to keep going.

When she knocked on the door of a farmhouse, a place where she and her parties of runaways had always been welcome, always been given shelter and plenty to eat, there was no answer. She knocked again, softly. A voice from within said, "Who is it?" There was fear in the voice.

She knew instantly from the sound of the voice that there was something wrong. She said, "A friend with friends," the password on the Underground Railroad. **5**

The door opened, slowly. The man who stood in the doorway looked at her coldly, looked with unconcealed astonishment and fear at the eleven disheveled runaways who were standing near her. Then he shouted, "Too many, too many. It's not safe. My place was searched last week. It's not safe!" and slammed the door in her face.

She turned away from the house, frowning. She had promised her passengers food and rest and warmth, and instead of that, there would be hunger and cold and more walking over the frozen ground. Somehow she would have to instill courage into these eleven people, most of them

Practice the Skills

5 **Key Reading Skill**

Predicting After reading this paragraph, what do you think might happen to Tubman and the fugitives?

Practice the Skills

strangers, would have to feed them on hope and bright dreams of freedom instead of the fried pork and corn bread and milk she had promised them.

They stumbled along behind her, half-dead for sleep, and she urged them on, though she was as tired and as discouraged as they were. She had never been in Canada but she kept painting wondrous word pictures of what it would be like. She managed to dispel[7] their fear of pursuit, so that they would not become hysterical, panic-stricken. Then she had to bring some of the fear back, so that they would stay awake and keep walking though they drooped with sleep.

Yet during the day, when they lay down deep in a thicket, they never really slept, because if a twig snapped or the wind sighed in the branches of a pine tree, they jumped to their feet, afraid of their own shadows, shivering and shaking. It was very cold, but they dared not make fires because someone would see the smoke and wonder about it. **6**

She kept thinking, eleven of them. Eleven thousand dollars' worth of slaves. And she had to take them all the way to Canada. Sometimes she told them about Thomas Garrett, in Wilmington. She said he was their friend even though he did not know them. He was the friend of all fugitives. He called them God's poor. He was a Quaker and his speech was a little different from that of other people. His clothing was different, too. He wore the wide-brimmed hat that the Quakers wear.

She said that he had thick white hair, soft, almost like a baby's, and the kindest eyes she had ever seen. He was a big man and strong, but he had never used his strength to harm anyone, always to help people. He would give all of them a new pair of shoes. Everybody. He always did. Once they reached his house in Wilmington, they would be safe. He would see to it that they were. **7**

She described the house where he lived, told them about the store where he sold shoes. She said he kept a pail of milk and a loaf of bread in the drawer of his desk so that he would have food ready at hand for any of God's poor who should suddenly appear before him, fainting with hunger. There was a hidden room in the store. A whole wall swung open, and behind it was a room where he could hide fugitives. On the wall there were shelves filled with small boxes—boxes of

---

7. To ***dispel*** something is to make it go away or disappear.

6 Reviewing Skills

Connecting Think of a time when you were so frightened or anxious that you couldn't sleep. How did you feel the next morning? Now think about what it must have been like for the fugitives to stay awake for the long night walks, often with little rest.

7 Literary Element

Style Ann Petry uses a lot of description in this paragraph. Is description part of her style? Read on to see.

shoes—so that you would never guess that the wall actually opened.

While she talked, she kept watching them. They did not believe her. She could tell by their expressions. They were thinking, New shoes, Thomas Garrett, Quaker, Wilmington—what foolishness was this? Who knew if she told the truth? Where was she taking them anyway? **8**

That night they reached the next stop—a farm that belonged to a German. She made the runaways take shelter behind trees at the edge of the fields before she knocked at the door. She hesitated before she approached the door, thinking, suppose that he, too, should refuse shelter, suppose— Then she thought, Lord, I'm going to hold steady on to You and You've got to see me through—and knocked softly.

She heard the familiar guttural[8] voice say, "Who's there?"

She answered quickly, "A friend with friends."

He opened the door and greeted her warmly. "How many this time?" he asked.

"Eleven," she said and waited, doubting, wondering.

He said, "Good. Bring them in."

He and his wife fed them in the lamp-lit kitchen, their faces glowing, as they offered food and more food, urging

Practice the Skills

8 **Key Reading Skill**

Predicting Notice how Tubman describes Thomas Garrett and his house to the fugitives. They do not seem to believe her. Do you? Predict whether Tubman's story is true or just meant to motivate the people to keep walking.

In this undated photo, Harriet Tubman *(left)* poses with some of the people she helped escape from slavery.

Analyzing the Photo How might these individuals be similar to those in the selection?

---

8. A *guttural* (GUT ur ul) voice has a rough, harsh sound.

from *Harriet Tubman: Conductor on the Underground Railroad* **225**

Practice the Skills

them to eat, saying there was plenty for everybody, have more milk, have more bread, have more meat.

They spent the night in the warm kitchen. They really slept, all that night and until dusk the next day. When they left, it was with reluctance. They had all been warm and safe and well-fed. It was hard to exchange the security offered by that clean warm kitchen for the darkness and the cold of a December night.

Harriet had found it hard to leave the warmth and friendliness, too. But she urged them on. For a while, as they walked, they seemed to carry in them a measure of contentment; some of the serenity and the cleanliness of that big warm kitchen lingered on inside them. But as they walked farther and farther away from the warmth and the light, the cold and the darkness entered into them. They fell silent, sullen, suspicious. She waited for the moment when some one of them would turn mutinous.[9] It did not happen that night. 🔳

Two nights later she was aware that the feet behind her were moving slower and slower. She heard the irritability in their voices, knew that soon someone would refuse to go on.

She started talking about William Still and the Philadelphia Vigilance Committee. No one commented. No one asked any questions. She told them the story of William and Ellen Craft and how they escaped from Georgia. Ellen was so fair that she looked as though she were white, and so she dressed up in a man's clothing and she looked like a wealthy young planter. Her husband, William, who was dark, played the role of her slave. Thus they traveled from Macon, Georgia, to Philadelphia, riding on the trains, staying at the finest hotels. Ellen pretended to be very ill—her right arm was in a sling, and her right hand was bandaged, because she was supposed to have rheumatism. Thus she avoided having to sign the register at the hotels for she could not read or write. They finally arrived safely in Philadelphia, and then went on to Boston.

No one said anything. Not one of them seemed to have heard her.

🔳 **Key Reading Skill**

Predicting Tubman expects one of the fugitives to "turn mutinous," but nothing happens that night. After reading this paragraph, predict what might happen later in the selection.

---

9. To turn **mutinous** (MYOO tun us) means to become openly rebellious.

She told them about Frederick Douglass, the most famous of the escaped slaves, of his **eloquence,** of his magnificent appearance. Then she told them of her own first vain effort at running away, evoking[10] the memory of that miserable life she had led as a child, reliving it for a moment in the telling.

But they had been tired too long, hungry too long, afraid too long, footsore too long. One of them suddenly cried out in despair, "Let me go back. It is better to be a slave than to suffer like this in order to be free."

She carried a gun with her on these trips. She had never used it—except as a threat. Now as she aimed it, she experienced a feeling of guilt, remembering that time, years ago, when she had prayed for the death of Edward Brodas, the Master, and then not too long afterward had heard that great wailing cry that came from the throats of the field hands, and knew from the sound that the Master was dead.

One of the runaways said, again, "Let me go back. Let me go back," and stood still, and then turned around and said, over his shoulder, "I am going back."

She lifted the gun, aimed it at the despairing slave. She said, "Go on with us or die." The husky low-pitched voice was grim. **10**

He hesitated for a moment and then he joined the others. They started walking again. She tried to explain to them why none of them could go back to the plantation. If a runaway returned, he would turn traitor, the master and the overseer would force him to turn traitor. The returned slave would **disclose** the stopping places, the hiding places, the cornstacks they had used with the full knowledge of the owner of the farm, the name of the German farmer who had fed them and sheltered them. These people who had risked their own security to help runaways would be ruined, fined, imprisoned.

She said, "We got to go free or die. And freedom's not bought with dust." **11**

---

10. Tubman is *evoking,* or calling up, this memory.

Vocabulary

eloquence (EL uh kwunts) *n.* the ability to speak well

disclose (dis KLOHZ) *v.* to make known; reveal

Practice the Skills

10 | **Literary Element**

Style What are a few of the descriptive words that Petry uses on this page? Would you say that description is part of her writing style? Explain.

11 **BIG Question**

Judging from this quotation, which do you think Harriet Tubman feels is more important, the journey or the destination? Write your answer on the "Harriet Tubman" flap of Foldable 2.

from *Harriet Tubman: Conductor on the Underground Railroad* **227**

This time she told them about the long agony of the Middle Passage[11] on the old slave ships, about the black horror of the holds, about the chains and the whips. **12** They too knew these stories. But she wanted to remind them of the long hard way they had come, about the long hard way they had yet to go. She told them about Thomas Sims, the boy picked up on the streets of Boston and sent back to Georgia. She said when they got him back to Savannah, got him in prison there, they whipped him until a doctor who was standing by watching said, "You will kill him if you strike him again!" His master said, "Let him die!"

Thus she forced them to go on. Sometimes she thought she had become nothing but a voice speaking in the darkness, **cajoling**, urging, threatening. Sometimes she told them things to make them laugh, sometimes she sang to them, and heard the eleven voices behind her blending softly with hers, and then she knew that for the moment all was well with them.

She gave the impression of being a short, muscular, indomitable[12] woman who could never be defeated. Yet at any moment she was liable to be seized by one of those curious fits of sleep,[13] which might last for a few minutes or for hours.

Even on this trip, she suddenly fell asleep in the woods. The runaways, ragged, dirty, hungry, cold, did not steal the gun as they might have, and set off by themselves, or turn back. They sat on the ground near her and waited patiently until she awakened. They had come to trust her implicitly,[14] totally. They, too, had come to believe her repeated statement, "We got to go free or die." She was leading them into freedom, and so they waited until she was ready to go on. **13**

---

11. The ***Middle Passage*** was the sea route followed by slave traders between Africa and the Americas.

12. ***Indomitable*** (in DAHM it uh bul) means "cannot be conquered," or "unbeatable."

13. Tubman's ***curious fits of sleep*** were occasional unexplained spells of dizziness or unconsciousness.

14. To trust ***implicitly*** (im PLIS it lee) is to have complete faith, with no question, doubt, or hesitation.

Vocabulary

cajoling (kuh JOHL ing) *v.* persuading, especially by using soothing words; coaxing

Practice the Skills

12 **Literary Element**

Style In this sentence Petry repeats the word *about.* Repetition helps unify the ideas in the sentence and create rhythm in the prose. Is repetition part of Petry's style? To find out, look for repeated words and phrases as you continue reading.

13 **Key Reading Skill**

Predicting Use the information in this paragraph to predict whether Harriet Tubman will succeed in bringing the fugitive slaves to freedom. Explain your answer.

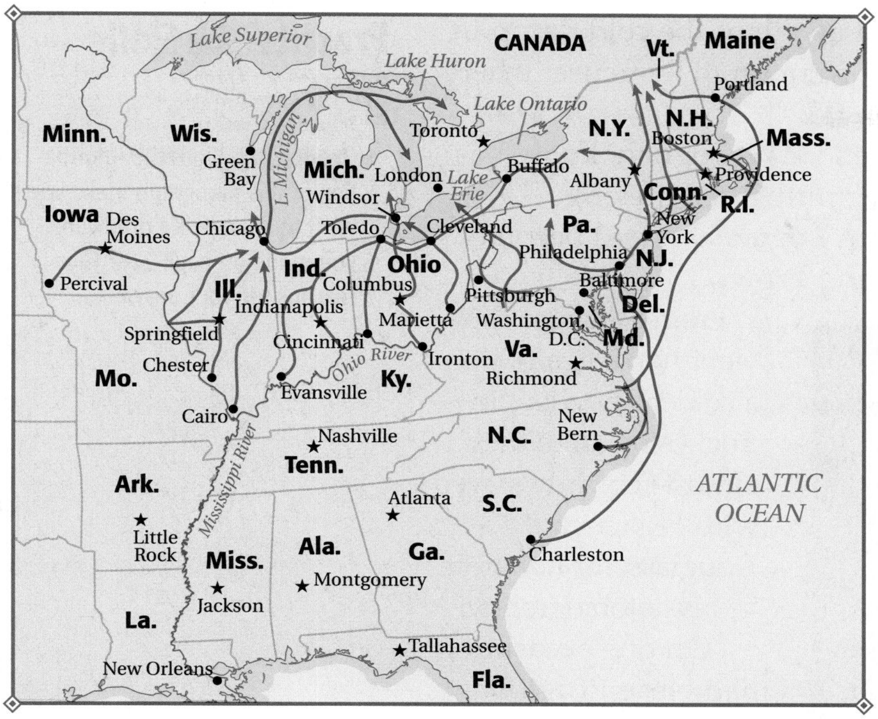

Underground Railroad routes traveled by people escaping slavery during the 1800s.

Finally, they reached Thomas Garrett's house in Wilmington, Delaware. Just as Harriet had promised, Garret gave them all new shoes, and provided carriages to take them on to the next stop.

By slow stages they reached Philadelphia, where William Still hastily recorded their names, and the plantations **whence** they had come, and something of the life they had led in slavery. **14** Then he carefully hid what he had written, for fear it might be discovered. In 1872 he published this record in book form and called it *The Underground Railroad*. In the foreword to his book he said: "While I knew the danger of keeping strict records, and while I did not then dream that in my day slavery would be blotted out, or that the time would come when I could publish these records, it used to afford me great satisfaction to take them down, fresh from the lips of fugitives on the way to freedom, and to preserve them as they had given them."

William Still, who was familiar with all the station stops on the Underground Railroad, supplied Harriet with money and sent her and her eleven fugitives on to Burlington, New Jersey.

Harriet felt safer now, though there were danger spots ahead. But the biggest part of her job was over. As they went farther and farther north, it grew colder; she was aware of

Practice the Skills

14 English Language Coach

Can you figure out the meaning of the old word **whence** in the second line of this paragraph? If not, look it up in the dictionary.

the wind on the Jersey ferry and aware of the cold damp in New York. From New York they went on to Syracuse, where the temperature was even lower. **15**

In Syracuse she met the Reverend J. W. Loguen, known as "Jarm" Loguen. This was the beginning of a lifelong friendship. Both Harriet and Jarm Loguen were to become friends and supporters of Old John Brown.

Practice the Skills

15 | **Key Reading Skill**

Predicting Does the information in this paragraph make you want to change the prediction you made on page 228? Give reasons for your answer.

John Brown, pictured here, was a leader of the American antislavery movement. In 1859 he led an unsuccessful raid of a federal weapons storehouse in Virginia, hoping to inspire a slave rebellion.

From Syracuse they went north again, into a colder, snowier city—Rochester. Here they almost certainly stayed with Frederick Douglass, for he wrote in his autobiography:

"On one occasion I had eleven fugitives at the same time under my roof, and it was necessary for them to remain with me until I could collect sufficient money to get them to Canada. It was the largest number I ever had at any one time, and I had some difficulty in providing so many with food and shelter, but, as may well be imagined, they were not very fastidious[15] in either direction, and were well content with very plain food, and a strip of carpet on the floor for a bed, or a place on the straw in the barnloft."

Late in December, 1851, Harriet arrived in St. Catharines, Canada West (now Ontario), with the eleven fugitives. It had taken almost a month to complete this journey; most of the time had been spent getting out of Maryland.

That first winter in St. Catharines was a terrible one. Canada was a strange frozen land, snow everywhere, ice everywhere, and a bone-biting cold the like of which none of

---

15. If the fugitive slaves had been **fastidious** (fas TIH dee us), they would have been difficult to please or satisfy.

them had ever experienced before. Harriet rented a small frame house in the town and set to work to make a home. The fugitives boarded with her. They worked in the forests, felling trees, and so did she. Sometimes she took other jobs, cooking or cleaning house for people in the town. She cheered on these newly arrived fugitives, working herself, finding work for them, finding food for them, praying for them, sometimes begging for them.

Often she found herself thinking of the beauty of Maryland, the mellowness of the soil, the richness of the plant life there. The climate itself made for an ease of living that could never be duplicated in this bleak, barren countryside. **16**

In spite of the severe cold, the hard work, she came to love St. Catharines, and the other towns and cities in Canada where black men lived. She discovered that freedom meant more than the right to change jobs at will, more than the right to keep the money that one earned. It was the right to vote and to sit on juries. It was the right to be elected to office. In Canada there were black men who were county officials and members of school boards. St. Catharines had a large colony of ex-slaves, and they owned their own homes, kept them neat and clean and in good repair. They lived in whatever part of town they chose and sent their children to the schools.

When spring came she decided that she would make this small Canadian city her home—as much as any place could be said to be home to a woman who traveled from Canada to the Eastern Shore of Maryland as often as she did.

In the spring of 1852, she went back to Cape May, New Jersey. She spent the summer there, cooking in a hotel. That fall she returned, as usual, to Dorchester County, and brought out nine more slaves, conducting them all the way to St. Catharines, in Canada West, to the bone-biting cold, the snow-covered forests—and freedom.

She continued to live in this fashion, spending the winter in Canada, and the spring and summer working in Cape May, New Jersey, or in Philadelphia. She made two trips a year into slave territory, one in the fall and another in the spring. She now had a definite crystallized[16] purpose, and in carrying it out, her life fell into a pattern which remained unchanged for the next six years. **17** ○

---

16. Here, ***crystallized*** (KRIS tuh lyzd) means "having a clear, specific form."

Practice the Skills

16 **Literary Element**

Style On this page Petry uses a lot of descriptive words. In your opinion, which descriptions are the most original? Which are the most effective?

17 **BIG Question**

What did you learn from reading about the journey Tubman and the fugitives took? Write your answer on the "Harriet Tubman" flap of Foldable 2. Your response will help you complete the Unit Challenge later.

from *Harriet Tubman: Conductor on the Underground Railroad* **231**

After You Read

from *Harriet Tubman: Conductor on the Underground Railroad*

Answering the BIG Question

1. After reading the selection from *Harriet Tubman: Conductor on the Underground Railroad,* which do you think was more important, the fugitives' destination or the journey they took to get there? Explain.

2. **Recall** Why does Tubman have to take the fugitives all the way to Canada rather than just to a northern state?

   TIP **Right There** The answer is in one place in the text.

3. **Summarize** Why was it so important that the Underground Railroad be kept a secret?

   TIP **Think and Search** The answer is in the text, but it is not all in one place.

Critical Thinking

4. **Infer** What do you think motivated Tubman to risk her own life to help others? Use details from the selection to support your ideas.

   TIP **Author and Me** To answer the question, apply your understanding of what Tubman was like.

5. **Infer** When Tubman fell asleep, none of the fugitives left, even though they were doubtful of where she was taking them. Why do you think they remained with Tubman?

   TIP **Author and Me** To answer the question, combine your understanding of the text with your understanding of human nature.

6. **Interest** What did Tubman mean when she said, "We got to go free or die. And freedom's not bought with dust"?

   TIP **Author and Me** Think about the text and about Tubman's experiences.

Talk About Your Reading

Role Play Imagine that you are the German farmer who allowed the eleven fugitives to eat and sleep in your house. A friend has recently written you a letter, telling you to stop helping people who were enslaved escape to freedom because you are taking too much of a risk. How would you respond to your friend's concerns? With a partner or small group, explain why you have chosen to risk your own safety to help others escape and how you feel about your choice.

NY English Language Arts Core Curriculum (pp. 232–233)

LC R17 Demonstrate comprehension and response through a range of activities.
S2a Express interpretations and support them through references to the text.
R1m Make, confirm, or revise predictions.
R2e Recognize how the author's use of language creates images or feelings.
LC R5 Determine the meaning of unfamiliar words by using context, dictionaries, and other resources. **Core W8** Use correct grammatical construction in placement of modifiers.

For a complete description of the standards, see p. NY 11.

Skills Review

Key Reading Skill: Predicting

7. Review the predictions you made with your class before reading. State whether your predictions were accurate and explain why.

Literary Element: Style

8. What is Petry's writing style like? Use the questions on page 219 to analyze her style. Then write a few sentences that describe her style.

Reviewing Skills: Connecting

9. Were there any feelings or thoughts in the story that you could connect to? Have you ever felt tired or afraid? Have you ever accomplished something you weren't sure you could? Explain.

Vocabulary Check

Match the words in Column A with the correct definition in Column B.

Column A	Column B
10. disclose ____	(a) to make known
11. cajoling ____	(b) ability to speak well
12. eloquence ____	(c) persuading

13. Academic Vocabulary What does *predicting* mean? Define it in your own words.

14. English Language Coach Does the following sentence use the underlined phrase correctly? If you need to, go back to the ELC on page 218. People escaping from slavery dreaded the thought of being <u>sold South</u>.

Web Activities For eFlashcards, Selection Quick Checks, and other Web activities, go to www.glencoe.com.

Grammar Link: Misplaced and Dangling Modifiers

Adjectives and adverbs should point clearly to the words they modify. A **misplaced modifier** describes, or modifies, the wrong word or group of words. Misplaced modifiers are a problem because they can cause readers to misunderstand the meaning of sentences.

• Sam went home to eat lunch on his skates. (It sounds as if Sam ate *on his skates!*)

To fix a misplaced modifier, bring the modifier closer to the word it describes.

• Sam went home <u>on his skates</u> to eat lunch.

(The phrase "on his skates" tells how Sam went home. By moving the phrase closer to "went home," the writer fixed the misplaced modifier.)

A **dangling modifier** makes it unclear *who* is doing *what* in a sentence. To correct a dangling modifier, add a clear subject for the modifier to describe.
Wrong: Wiggling, Mom held my little brother.
(Is Mom wiggling? Is the little brother wiggling?)
Right: Mom held my little brother, who was wiggling.

Grammar Practice

On a separate sheet of paper, copy each pair of sentences below. For each pair, underline the correct placement or form of modifier.

15. I went to the field to play hockey on my bike./ I went to the field on my bike to play hockey.

16. Running in circles, Ivanna watched the dog./ Ivanna watched the dog running in circles.

17. While walking to school, a thunderstorm struck the neighborhood. / A thunderstorm struck the neighborhood while I was walking to school.

18. After reading the review, I think the movie seems unappealing. / After reading the review, the movie seems unappealing.

Folktale
Revising, Editing, and Presenting

ASSIGNMENT Write an entertaining folktale

Purpose: To create a folktale about a character who takes a journey

Audience: Your teacher and your classmates

Revising Rubric

Your revised folktale should have

• The major elements of a folktale
• A major character who is trying to do good
• A central message
• Correct spelling, grammar, and punctuation

See page 236 for a model of a folktale.

NY English Language Arts Core Curriculum (pp. 234–237)

Core W5 Use the writing process. **LC W4** Compose mechanically grade-appropriate texts for a variety of purposes. **LC W8** Work collaboratively with peers to plan, draft, revise, and edit written work. **S2b** Present original, literary texts, using language and text structures that are inventive.

For a complete description of the standards, see p. NY 11.

In Writing Workshop 1, you drafted an original folktale about a character on a journey. Now it's time to make changes. You can add a new story event, leave out something you don't like, add a new character (good or evil!), or change the ending. You'll also keep a copy in a writing portfolio so that you and your teacher can evaluate your writing progress over time.

Make It Better

When story writers revise, they ask themselves, "Does my story make sense?" To make sure your story will be clear to readers, ask yourself these questions:

• Is it clear what my characters are like? Will readers recognize my protagonist, or main character, as a good person? Will they recognize the antagonist as a bad person? Put a checkmark next to any words or phrases that show good or evil actions.

• Is it clear why my character went on a journey? Did I explain that early in the story? Put a checkmark next to the paragraph that tells why the journey was necessary.

• Is it clear what difficulties my main character faced and overcame during the journey? Did I make sure the character's personality traits or special powers helped him or her solve those problems? Put a checkmark next to each paragraph that shows the character overcoming an obstacle.

• Is the outcome of the journey clear? Will readers understand what happened to the main character and why? Put a checkmark next to the paragraph that tells the journey's result.

• Did various parts of the story add to the main idea? Put a checkmark next to any detail that helps support the central message.

If you're missing any checkmarks, you may need to revise parts of your folktale. Make sure that your story describes events in the order that they happen. Include story events that support the message and help move the story toward a satisfying ending.

Editing and Proofreading
Trade Papers

1. After you have revised your draft, trade it with a partner. Ask your partner to underline any sentences in your draft that he or she finds confusing. Circle any spelling or punctuation mistakes. Pay close attention to your use of adjectives and adverbs.
   - Did you use adjectives and adverbs well?
   - Did you use the correct forms for comparative and superlative adjectives?
   - Are there any double negatives in the draft?

2. Ask your partner to return your draft, and look at what he or she has circled on your paper. Use a dictionary, the Grammar Links in this book, or Glencoe's *Grammar and Composition Handbook* to see how to fix your spelling and grammar mistakes.

3. Look at the underlined parts of your story. Ask your partner why he or she found these parts confusing. Brainstorm ways to make these details clearer.

4. When you're finished editing and proofreading, read your folktale aloud to your partner or just to yourself. If there's any place where you stumble as you read, you may need to revise that section a little bit more.

5. Make sure the title of your folktale fits the story and will attract readers' attention.

6. Take one last quick look through your folktale before you hand it in. Ask yourself, *Is this as good as I can make it? Did I miss anything?*

Publishing and Presenting
Show It Off

Consider sending your folktale out for other people to read.

- You and your classmates might put together a collection of all the folktales your class has written. Bind your stories in a three-ring binder or post them on a school bulletin board.

- Your class might give copies of your folktales to your school library or the children's room of your community library so that other readers can enjoy them.

- You might send your folktale to an appropriate print or online magazine. For instructions on how to do so, check the Web sites of magazines you like, or ask a librarian for help. Make sure the magazine you choose publishes folktales.

> **Writing Tip**
>
> **Spelling** When you proofread, double-check your spelling. Sometimes words that sound the same are spelled differently, but a computer spellchecker may not catch these mistakes.

> **Writing Tip**
>
> **Publishing and Presenting** When you have edited and proofread your folktale, rewrite it or enter it on a computer that has a wordprocessing program. Make your paper as neat as possible.

Literature Online

Writing Models For models and other writing activities, go to www.glencoe.com.

Active Writing Model

Writer's Model

Finny Thinks Fast

Long ago a girl lived along the seacoast. She was called Finny because she could swim like a fish and hold her breath for hours. Finny's parents carved beautiful bowls. The bowls were so beautiful the wicked Sea Queen wanted them all for herself. One night she turned Finny's parents into stone and took their bowls.

The next morning Finny ran into the ocean and swam deep underwater. She had to find the Sea Queen. "Oh, Sea Queen, where are you?" she cried.

Suddenly a creature that was half human, half fish swam up to her. "It's a long journey to the palace," he said. He took her hand, and they swam farther into the depths. Mile after mile, they swam. Just when Finny's lungs were about to burst, she saw the palace. It was a giant seashell guarded by sharks! "I must leave you here," the creature said.

"Please, sharks, do not hurt me," Finny cried. "I have to help my parents! The Sea Queen has cast a spell on them!"

The sharks felt sorry for her. "We will take you to her," they said.

They swam into the giant seashell and up to the Sea Queen's throne. Finny said, "I beg you to lift the spell from my parents!"

"Why should I?" asked the Sea Queen.

Finny thought fast. "If you make my parents well, they can carve more bowls. Every year on this day, we'll leave them on the shore for you."

The queen lovingly ran her fingers over one of the bowls she had stolen. "All right," she said. She waved a coral wand tipped with a shell. "You'll find your parents back to normal when you return."

The Sea Queen kept her word, and they all lived happily ever after.

Like many main characters in folktales, Finny has a special talent. She can hold her breath underwater for hours at a time.

Finny is a good person. She goes on a dangerous journey to help her parents.

The evil Sea Queen is the antagonist. Finny saves the day by offering her gifts.

The central message is that goodness and courage are rewarded. Finny was selfless and brave enough to make the journey to help her parents, and the Sea Queen granted her request.

Listening, Speaking, and Viewing

Storytelling

Long before books, radio, movies, or TV, people entertained each other by telling stories. Storytelling is almost as old as humankind itself.

What Is Storytelling?

A storyteller presents a story to listeners rather than readers. Many stories were never written down. Instead they were passed along by word of mouth. Each person told a story a little differently, changing details to suit his or her style and audience. As a result, the story changed over time.

Why Is Storytelling Important?

Stories can be both entertaining and educational. Storytelling provides people with a way to preserve and pass along their history, beliefs, and culture. In the time of slavery, the folktale that's now called "The People Could Fly" was an entertainment, but it also gave enslaved people hope and a sense of pride in their African roots.

Storytelling also provides older people with a way to teach younger people how to behave. In the folktale "The Snake Chief," the selfish and headstrong daughter is punished, and the kind and obedient daughter is rewarded.

How Do I Tell a Story?

Like all kinds of public speaking, storytelling becomes easier with practice. Here are some basic steps you can follow to get you started.

Step 1: Know Your Story Unless you are experienced at making up stories on the spot, your first step should be to learn your story. Do not try to memorize it word for word. Your goal should be to *tell* a story, not *recite* it. Read your story several times until you know the storyline well.

Step 2: Rehearse Alone Practice telling your story without an audience. Don't be afraid to act

parts out! In general, the more you liven up your storytelling, the more your audience will enjoy it. Use your voice and your body to make the story come alive.

- Speak clearly and with expression. Vary the speed of your voice and the pitch (high or low) to show different emotions and characters.
- Remember that pauses can be powerful. Pausing after an important point can give it emphasis.
- Use facial expressions, gestures, and movements to support dialogue and action.

Step 3: Rehearse with an Audience Practice telling your story to an audience of family members, classmates, or friends. Apply the guidelines in the bulleted list above. Also practice making eye contact with audience members. Do not look above their heads or at their feet. Briefly make eye contact with different people at different times.

Step 4: Ask for Feedback Ask your rehearsal audience to evaluate your storytelling. Here's a checklist you can use.

- Could you hear me clearly?
- Did I speak too quickly or too slowly?
- Did I vary my expression enough to help you picture each character in the story?
- Did I pause for emphasis?
- Did I use appropriate facial expressions?
- Did I use gestures effectively?
- What could I do to improve my storytelling?

Use audience feedback to improve how you tell your story. Then practice some more.

Tell Your Tales Work with a few classmates to practice telling your folktale. Do not *read* your story; practice *telling* it. Ask your classmates to use the checklist above to give you feedback on your storytelling. Give them feedback on their stories too. When you all feel ready, tell your stories to the whole class.

Skills Focus

You will practice using these skills when you read the following selections:

- "Icarus and Daedalus," p. 242
- "A Dose of Medicine," p. 250

Reading

- Comparing and contrasting within and across texts

Literature

- Identifying the theme

Vocabulary

- Using systematic methods to build vocabulary
- Academic Vocabulary: *similar*

Writing/Grammar

- Identifying and using prepositional phases
- Identifying and using interjections

NY English Language Arts Core Curriculum (pp. 238–239)

LC R12 Combine multiple strategies to enhance comprehension and response.

For a complete description of the standards, see p. NY 11.

Skill Lesson

Comparing and Contrasting

Learn It!

What Is It? When you **compare,** you notice how two things are **similar,** or alike. When you **contrast,** you notice how they are different. For example, if you want to buy a new bike, being able to compare and contrast features, price, and quality will help you get the best bike for the best price. Comparing the ingredients on the label of a snack can help you pick the healthiest snack. Comparing and contrasting is also useful when you read:

- You can compare and contrast characters, settings, and events within a selection.
- You can also compare and contrast characters, plots, and themes across different reading selections.
- You can even compare how authors organize and present information in reading selections.

BALDO © 2004 Baldo Partnership. Dist. By UNIVERSAL PRESS SYNDICATE. Reprinted with permission. All rights reserved.

Analyzing Cartoons

One character compares bike riding to studying and reaching a goal. Can you compare the lipstick case to a problem you might face while studying?

Academic Vocabulary

similar (SIM uh lur) *adj.* alike, but not exactly the same

Why Is It Important? As your reading takes you across a variety of sources, it is helpful to compare and contrast the similarities and differences within and among your reading selections. That way you'll gain a better understanding of all the material you've read. You'll also learn to read more critically and get more out of each selection.

How Do I Do It? As you read a selection, think about the characters' thoughts, words, and actions. Ask yourself, *In what ways are the characters alike and different?* As you read more than one selection, ask yourself what was included in one selection that might have been left out of another and why might that be.

Here's how a student compared and contrasted main characters in "The Snake Chief" and "Icarus and Daedalus."

Study Central Visit www.glencoe. com and click on Study Central to review comparing and contrasting.

> The older sister in "The Snake Chief" is stubborn and self-centered, and she refuses to take good advice. In "Icarus and Daedalus," Icarus has some of the same faults. Though he is not stubborn and self-centered like the older sister, he is similar in that he does not follow his father's advice. In both stories, not following the advice of other people causes serious problems for the characters.

Practice It!

Make a list of your favorite after-school activities and hobbies, and have a partner do the same. Then compare your lists. Which activities are alike? Which are different? What can you learn about each other by comparing and contrasting the activities you like to do?

Use It!

As you read "Icarus and Daedalus" and "A Dose of Medicine," look for ways that the characters' thoughts, words, and actions are alike and different. Also notice how each story is told and what details are given. Write your notes in your Learner's Notebook.

Before You Read : Icarus and Daedalus

Josephine Preston Peabody

Meet the Author

Josephine Preston Peabody was born in Brooklyn, New York, in 1874 and died in Cambridge, Massachusetts, in 1922. She published her first poem when she was fourteen years old. Six years later, the publication of her poems in magazines helped her attend Radcliffe College. See page R5 of the Author Files in the back of the book for more on Josephine Preston Peabody.

Author Search For more about Josephine Preston Peabody, go to www.glencoe.com.

NY English Language Arts Core Curriculum (pp. 240–245)

LC R2 Use a variety of word recognition strategies to read unfamiliar words.
LC R12 Combine multiple strategies to enhance comprehension and response.
R2b Interpret theme, using evidence from the text.

For a complete description of the standards, see p. NY 11.

Vocabulary Preview

veered (veerd) *v.* suddenly changed direction; form of the verb *veer* **(p. 242)** *The young boy veered off course and headed off the sidewalk.*

wavered (WAY vurd) *v.* became unsteady; form of the verb *waver* **(p. 243)** *The first time he tried to fly, Daedalus wavered a bit before he was able to steady himself.*

rash (rash) *adj.* reckless; done without thought or concern **(p. 243)** *Icarus was young and inexperienced and therefore made many rash decisions that worried his father.*

quench (kwench) *v.* to satisfy a need **(p. 244)** *He flew as high as he could in an attempt to quench his need to reach the sun.*

Write to Learn In your Learner's Notebook, write a sentence for each of the vocabulary words above.

English Language Coach

Building Vocabulary: Parts of Speech One way to build your vocabulary is to build on the words you already know. When you're reading, you may see a word that looks familiar. Often, you can use the meaning of the word you already know to help you figure out the new word.

In "Icarus and Daedalus," one of the words you'll find is *cunning*. Cunning means "clever and skillful." But another word in the story is *cunningly*. You can tell from the way the word is used in the sentence that it is an adverb. It describes the way something was done. So you know right away that it means "in a clever and skillful way."

Another sentence in the story is "he gathered a store of feathers." You know that *store* can be a verb that means "to put away for later use." *Store* in this sentence is a noun, and it makes sense that it means "a supply of things put away for future use."

Partner Work With another student, come up with a list of adjectives. Then see whether you can turn them into adverbs by adding *-ly*. After you do, try using them in sentences.

Skills Preview

Key Reading Skill: Comparing and Contrasting

As you read "Icarus and Daedalus," look for ways in which Icarus and Daedalus are alike and different.

Write to Learn Use a Venn diagram like the one below to record similarities and differences between Icarus and Daedalus as you read.

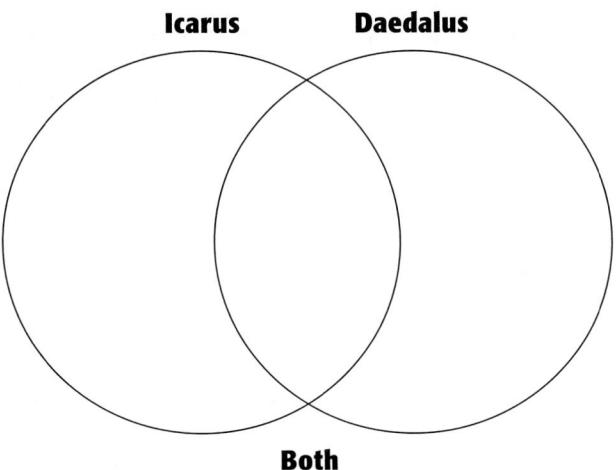

Icarus   Daedalus

Both

Key Literary Element: Theme

A **theme** is the main message of a literary work. Most themes are "lessons in life"–things that characters learn from the conflicts they experience. In a **directly stated theme,** the author sums up the lesson in a general statement, such as "Slow but steady wins the race," the moral at the end of the fable "The Tortoise and the Hare." Most literary works have **implied themes**–lessons in life that are hinted at rather than stated. To find an implied theme, think about the central conflict, or the problem the main character struggles to overcome. Ask yourself what he or she learns from the experience. That lesson is a theme of the work.

Whole Class Discussion Think of a story or movie in which a reckless young person does not heed warnings about avoiding danger. What was the theme of the work? Put it in your own words.

Get Ready to Read

Connect to the Reading

Have you ever wanted something so badly that you went about getting it in a reckless way? Have you ever wished that you could "do it over" so that the outcome would be different?

Write to Learn Write a few sentences about a time when you or someone you know would have liked to relive a situation in order to change it.

Build Background

"Icarus and Daedalus" is an ancient Greek myth that has been retold many times over the centuries. The story is set "once upon a time" in Greece when, supposedly, humans and gods lived on the island of Crete. A **myth** is an ancient story about gods, goddesses, or other supernatural beings and their influence on people and nature. When people in myths overstep their bounds and try to act like supernatural beings, they usually learn a hard lesson in life.

Set Purposes for Reading

BIG Question Read "Icarus and Daedalus" to learn what happens to a boy on a dangerous mythological journey when he doesn't behave with caution.

Set Your Own Purpose What else would you like to learn from the story to help you answer the Big Question? Write your own purpose on the "Icarus and Daedalus" flap of Foldable 2.

Literature Online

Interactive Literary Elements Handbook
To review or learn more about the literary elements, go to www.glencoe.com.

Keep Moving

Use these skills as you read the following selections.

Icarus and Daedalus

by Josephine Preston Peabody

Practice the Skills

Among all those mortals[1] who grew so wise that they learned the secrets of the gods, none was more cunning[2] than Daedalus.[3] **1**

He once built, for King Minos of Crete, a wonderful Labyrinth of winding ways so cunningly tangled up and twisted around that, once inside, you could never find your way out again without a magic clue. But the king's favor **veered** with the wind, and one day he had his master architect imprisoned in a tower. Daedalus managed to escape from his cell; but it seemed impossible to leave the island, since every ship that came or went was well guarded by order of the king.

At length, watching the sea gulls in the air—the only creatures that were sure of liberty—he thought of a plan for himself and his young son Icarus,[4] who was captive with him.

Visual Vocabulary
The *Labyrinth* was a huge maze in which a complicated, twisted path enclosed by high walls made it nearly impossible for people to find their way out.

1 | **Key Reading Skill**

Comparing and Contrasting
When you contrast, you show how two things are different. The author contrasts Daedalus to other mortals in the first paragraph. How is Daedalus different?

---

1. Humans are *mortals,* which means that they die. Greek gods were believed to be immortal.
2. *Cunning* (KUH ning) means "clever and skillful."
3. *Daedalus* (DED uh lus)
4. *Icarus* (IK uh rus)

Vocabulary

veered (veerd) *v.* suddenly changed direction

Practice the Skills

Little by little, he gathered a store of feathers great and small. He fastened these together with thread, molded them in with wax, and so fashioned[5] two great wings like those of a bird. When they were done, Daedalus fitted them to his own shoulders, and after one or two efforts, he found that by waving his arms he could winnow the air and cleave[6] it, as a swimmer does the sea. He held himself aloft, **wavered** this way and that with the wind, and at last, like a great fledgling,[7] he learned to fly.

Without delay, he fell to work on a pair of wings for the boy Icarus, and taught him carefully how to use them, bidding him beware of **rash** adventures among the stars. "Remember," said the father, "never to fly very low or very high, for the fogs about the earth would weigh you down, but the blaze of the sun will surely melt your feathers apart if you go too near."

For Icarus, these cautions went in at one ear and out by the other. Who could remember to be careful when he was to fly for the first time? Are birds careful? Not they! And not an idea remained in the boy's head but the one joy of escape. **2**

The day came, and the fair wind that was to set them free. The father bird put on his wings, and, while the light urged them to be gone, he waited to see that all was well with Icarus, for the two could not fly hand in hand. Up they rose, the boy after his father. The hateful ground of Crete sank beneath them; and the country folk, who caught a glimpse of them when they were high above the treetops, took it for a vision of the gods—Apollo, perhaps, with Cupid[8] after him. **3**

At first there was a terror in the joy. The wide vacancy of the air dazed them—a glance downward made their brains reel. But when a great wind filled their wings, and Icarus felt

2 | **Key Reading Skill**

Comparing and Contrasting Compare and contrast Icarus's and Daedalus's attitude toward flight. Which one of them is cautious? Which one seems more reckless? How do you know? Remember to include these ideas on your Venn diagram.

3 | **Reviewing Skills**

Predicting What do you think will happen to Icarus? To Daedalus? Think about what usually happens in myths to people who try to act like gods.

---

5. Here, **fashioned** means "made" or "constructed."

6. **Winnow** and **cleave** both mean "to separate or divide."

7. A **fledging** is a young bird that has recently grown the feathers it needs to fly.

8. In mythology, **Apollo** is the god of the sun, and **Cupid** is the god of love.

Vocabulary

wavered (WAY vurd) *v.* became unsteady

rash (rash) *adj.* reckless; done without thought or concern

himself sustained, like a halcyon-bird[9] in the hollow of a wave, like a child uplifted by his mother, he forgot everything in the world but joy. He forgot Crete and the other islands that he had passed over: he saw but **vaguely** that winged thing in the distance before him that was his father Daedalus. He longed for one draft[10] of flight to **quench** the thirst of his captivity: he stretched out his arms to the sky and made toward the highest heavens. **4 5**

Alas for him! Warmer and warmer grew the air. Those arms, that had seemed to uphold him, relaxed. His wings wavered, drooped. He fluttered his young hands vainly— he was falling—and in that terror he remembered. The heat of the sun had melted the wax from his wings; the feathers were falling, one by one, like snowflakes; and there was none to help.

Practice the Skills

4 | Key Literary Element

Theme Icarus seems to be forgetting his father's warning. Be on the lookout for the lesson in life that Icarus learns from this mistake. It is a theme of the story.

5 | English Language Coach

Building Vocabulary: Parts of Speech If you know that the word *vague* means "unclear," what does *vaguely* mean in this paragraph?

Mountains in the Fog. Cindy Kassab.

Analyzing the Painting Does this painting help you understand how Icarus felt as he flew over Crete? Explain your answer.

---

9. Here, **sustained** means "to be kept from sinking or falling." The **halcyon-bird**, or kingfisher, glides slowly and smoothly near the water's surface as it hunts for fish.

10. Here, **draft** means "taste."

Vocabulary

quench (kwench) *v.* to satisfy a need

The Fall of Icarus, 1975. Marc Chagall. Private collection.

Analyzing the Painting How does this painting illustrate the action described in the paragraph below?

He fell like a leaf tossed down the wind, down, down, with one cry that overtook Daedalus far away. When he returned, and sought high and low for the poor boy, he saw nothing but the bird-like feathers afloat on the water, and he knew that Icarus was drowned. **6**

The nearest island he named Icaria, in memory of the child; but he, in heavy grief, went to the temple of Apollo in Sicily, and there hung up his wings as an offering. Never again did he attempt to fly. **7** ○

Practice the Skills

6 **Key Reading Skill**

Comparing and Contrasting
What similarities can you find between the flight of Icarus and the flight of Daedalus? What is the main difference in the outcome of their flights?

7 **BIG Question**

What is the destination of Icarus and Daedalus? What prevents them both from reaching it? Write your answer on the "Icarus and Daedalus" flap of Foldable 2. Your response will help you complete the Unit Challenge later.

Icarus and Daedalus **245**

After You Read

Icarus and Daedalus

Answering the BIG Question

1. What do you think was more important to Daedalus, the journey or the destination? What do you think was more important to Icarus? Why?

2. **Recall** What does King Minos do to keep Daedalus and Icarus from escaping Crete?

   TIP **Right There** The answer is in one place in the story.

3. **Quote** What warning does Daedalus give his son about flying? Copy it word for word from the story.

   TIP **Right There** The warning is in one place in the story.

Critical Thinking

4. **Infer** Why do the people of Crete think that Daedalus and Icarus are gods when they see the father and son flying overhead?

   TIP **Author and Me** Use your understanding of the myth and of the beliefs of people long ago.

5. **Interpret** In your own words, tell what the following sentence means: "Icarus felt himself sustained, like a halcyon-bird in the hollow of a wave, like a child uplifted by his mother, he forgot everything in the world but joy." (pages 243–244).

   TIP **Author and Me** To answer the question, use the footnotes and your understanding of how Icarus feels.

6. **Evaluate** Do you think Daedalus is a concerned father? Do you think he feels responsible for what happens to his son? Why or why not?

   TIP **On My Own**

Write About Your Reading

NY English Language Arts Core Curriculum (pp. 246–247)

LC R17 Demonstrate comprehension and response through a range of activities. **W2a** Write original texts. **LC R12** Combine multiple strategies to enhance comprehension and response. **R2b** Interpret theme, using evidence from the text. **Core W8** Use correct grammatical construction in parts of speech (prepositions).

For a complete description of the standards, see p. NY 11.

Newspaper Article Imagine that you have been assigned to write a news story about Daedalus, Icarus, and their flight to freedom. Write a short news report about what happened. Make sure you answer the following questions in your story:

- *What* happened?
- *Who* was involved?
- *When* did it happen?
- *Where* did it happen?
- *Why* did it happen?
- *How* did it happen?

Skills Review

Key Reading Skill: Comparing and Contrasting

7. How were Daedalus and Icarus alike and how were they different? Use the notes you made on your Venn diagram to help you answer the question.

Key Literary Element: Theme

8. Think about the theme of the story. Write the theme in one sentence in your own words.

9. How might the theme of "Icarus and Daedalus" apply to life today? Give an example of a situation that could happen in today's world, and explain how the theme might apply to it.

Reviewing Skills: Predicting

10. Did you predict what would happen to Daedalus and Icarus? Did you get close? Did knowing about myths help you? Explain.

Vocabulary Check

Match the words below to their definitions.

11. veered   a. to satisfy

12. rash   b. without caution

13. quench   c. became unsteady

14. wavered   d. changed direction

15. Academic Vocabulary What is a synonym for *similar?*

16. English Language Coach Building Vocabulary: Parts of Speech See if you can figure out the meaning of *fueled* used as a verb in the following sentence. Use your knowledge of the meaning of *fuel* as a noun and any context clues in the sentence.

   • The story of Daedalus and Icarus was so interesting to me that it **fueled** my imagination.

Grammar Link: Prepositions

A **preposition** connects a noun or pronoun to another word in a sentence. Some common prepositions are *above, after, as, at, before, behind, during, for, from, inside, in, near, over, since, under,* and *with.* In the sentence below, the preposition *on* shows the relationship between *bus* and *boy.*

   • The boy <u>on</u> the bus looks happy.

A **prepositional phrase** is a group of words that begins with a preposition and ends with a noun or pronoun, called the **object of the preposition.**

   • Jamilla ran [<u>beside</u> his best <u>friend</u>].

   (The prepositional phrase in brackets begins with the preposition beside *and ends with the noun* friend.*)*

   • Jamilla ran [beside him].

   (The prepositional phrase in brackets begins with the preposition beside *and ends with the pronoun* him.*)*

Compound prepositions consist of more than one word. Some compound prepositions are *along with, because of, in front of, instead of,* and *on top of.*

   • Yoshi stood <u>in front of</u> his locker.

Grammar Practice

Copy the prepositional phrase in each sentence.

17. The athletes raced to the finish line.

18. Carlita jumped into the pool.

19. Can I come along with you?

20. The books on the table are mine.

Writing Application Review your news story. Make sure you used prepositions correctly.

Web Activities For eFlashcards, Selection Quick Checks, and other Web activities, go to www.glencoe.com.

Before You Read : A Dose of Medicine

Charlotte Foltz Jones

Meet the Author

Charlotte Foltz Jones was born in 1945. She has written many science books for young readers to try to make the subject interesting for young people. Aside from *Mistakes That Worked,* she has written *Accidents May Happen* and *Fingerprints and Funny Bones: How Real-Life Crimes are Solved.* See page R3 of the Author Files in the back of the book for more information on Charlotte Foltz Jones.

Author Search For more about Charlotte Foltz Jones, go to www .glencoe.com.

NY English Language Arts Core Curriculum (pp. 248–253)

Core R4 Determine the meaning of unfamiliar words by using context, dictionaries, and other resources. **LC R12** Combine multiple strategies to enhance comprehension and response. **LC R13** Use text structure and literary devices to aid comprehension and response. **R2g** Compare literature to own lives.

For a complete description of the standards, see p. NY 11.

Vocabulary Preview

prospect (PRAH spekt) *n.* that which is expected **(p. 250)** *The prospect of having a tooth pulled is usually very unpleasant.*

hilarious (hih LAR ee us) *adj.* very funny **(p. 251)** *Everything seemed hilarious to the comedians.*

deaden (DEH dun) *v.* to make weak or dull **(p. 251)** *The shot will deaden the pain in my tooth.*

consciousness (KAHN shus nes) *n.* the state of being fully awake or alert **(p. 251)** *The injury to his head knocked him flat and made him lose consciousness.*

publicized (PUB lih syzd) *v.* made the public aware of something; form of the verb *publicize* **(p. 252)** *People knew about the doctor's discovery after it was publicized in the morning paper.*

Small Group Work With a small group of classmates, write a paragraph with sentences that include each of the vocabulary words above.

English Language Coach

Building Vocabulary: Preview List The selection "A Dose of Medicine" contains words and phrases from science and medicine that may be unfamiliar to you. As you learned in Reading Workshop 3, you can make it easier to understand selections with unfamiliar vocabulary by creating your own personalized list of key terms.

On Your Own Quickly look over "A Dose of Medicine" before you read it. As you look, jot down at least three key terms that are new to you. Use context clues, a dictionary, footnotes, or other aids to define the words on your list. Keep the list nearby when you read the selection, and add other terms to your list if you need to. Here's a sample to help you get started.

1. nitrous oxide (page 250): laughing gas

2. cholera (page 252): deadly disease

3. contracted (page 252): caught

4. organism (page 252): living thing

Skills Preview

Key Reading Skill: Comparing and Contrasting

Before you read the selection, think about how advances in science and medicine have improved our lives.

Write to Learn List some of the discoveries that have been made in your lifetime. Next to each discovery, tell how the discovery has made your life different.

Text Element: Chronological Order

When an author presents events in the order in which they actually happened, he or she is using **chronological order,** or time order.

- This sequence is useful for nonfiction narratives such as biographies and autobiographies, history articles, and newspaper stories.
- Chronological order is also often used in fictional narratives, such as short stories and novels.

To help readers understand what happened first, next, and so on, authors may include **time-order signal words,** which are transitions that tell when something happened.

Whole Class Discussion As a class, brainstorm a list of time-order transition words and phrases. Try to list at least ten different words. The following examples will help you get started.

- then
- later
- after
- before
- yesterday
- today

Interactive Literary Elements Handbook
To review or learn more about the literary elements, go to www.glencoe.com.

Get Ready to Read

Connect to the Reading

How do you feel about going to the doctor to get a shot or a vaccination? Think about your experiences getting shots.

Write to Learn In your Learner's Notebook jot down a few sentences describing how you feel about shots and why.

Build Background

Until Louis Pasteur discovered that a bacteria caused cholera, that disease and others killed thousands of people each year.

- Between the 1840s and 1860s, many major cities experienced severe outbreaks of cholera. Immigrants traveling to America on unsanitary and crowded boats brought cholera to the cities in which they settled.

- In 1849 678 people died from cholera in Chicago. About half of these deaths happened between July 25 and August 28. Though Pasteur had not yet completed his work, people in Chicago thought that there had to be a relationship between dirty drinking water and the spread of cholera. After an 1854 outbreak killed 1,424 people, pipes were built into Lake Michigan to bring fresh water to the city. This system reduced the amount of drinking water people got from buckets and wells and greatly cut the number of cholera deaths in the coming years.

Set Purposes for Reading

BIG Question Read "A Dose of Medicine" to find out how both Dr. Wells and Louis Pasteur worked hard to discover ways to make peoples' lives better.

Set Your Own Purpose What else would you like to learn from the selection to help you answer the Big Question? Write your own purpose on the "Dose of Medicine" flap of Foldable 2.

Keep Moving

Use these skills as you read the following selections.

A Dose of Medicine

by Charlotte Foltz Jones

"All the world is a laboratory to the inquiring mind."
—Martin H. Fischer

Tooth Extraction Caricature,
1773. John Collier.

ETHER AND NITROUS OXIDE

Do you need to have a tooth pulled, an appendix removed, or a cut stitched up? A couple of centuries ago surgery was a pretty grim **prospect.**

If you couldn't stand the pain (and who could?), there were several options. You could be:

frozen,
beaten senseless,
asphyxiated,[1]
pumped full of alcohol,
or given a piece of wood to bite down on. ∎

But in the 1800s things changed.

New gases had been discovered—ether and nitrous oxide, which was called laughing gas because it made people who inhaled it sing, laugh, act silly, or fight. At first these two gases were mainly used for entertainment at parties called ether frolics or laughing gas parties.

Practice the Skills

1 Key Reading Skill

Comparing and Contrasting
Contrast the pain-relieving methods used before the discovery of modern pain medicine to what is used today. How are they different?

---

1. To be *asphyxiated* (as FIK see ayt id) means to be deprived of oxygen.

Vocabulary

prospect (PRAH spekt) *n.* that which is expected

Also, so-called professors traveled from town to town giving public lectures. They administered ether or nitrous oxide to a volunteer, and that person's **hilarious** behavior made the audience laugh. **2**

At one of these **demonstrations** an accident occurred. In 1844 in Hartford, Connecticut, a "professor" named Colton asked for someone to inhale nitrous oxide. **3** Samuel Cooley volunteered, but he soon became violent, tripped, and fell. When he went back to his seat, someone noticed that Cooley was bleeding from his fall.

Horace Wells, a dentist, had come to the demonstration with Cooley. He realized that Cooley felt no pain from his fall, and he reasoned that the gas might **deaden** patients' pain while he performed dental work.

Wells began testing the gases. He breathed some nitrous oxide and had a fellow dentist pull one of his teeth. The procedure went so well that Wells decided to give a demonstration at a university. He was probably excited and eager to prove the success of the gas. After giving a patient some gas, Wells began to remove the patient's tooth. The gas had not taken effect, and the patient screamed out in pain. The audience of students hissed and drove Wells away in disgrace.

Wells, however, still felt confident that the gas would be effective, and he continued to use it in his practice.

Another dentist, William T. G. Morton, learned of Wells's use of nitrous oxide. He tried some on his patients. Then his partner, Charles T. Jackson, suggested using ether. So Morton extracted[2] a tooth from a patient on September 30, 1846, using ether.

Still another physician, Dr. Crawford W. Long of Jefferson, Georgia, said he had seen a slave lose **consciousness**—yet breathe normally—after

---

2. *Extracted* (eks TRAKT id) means "pulled out."

Vocabulary ....

hilarious (hih LAR ee us) *adj.* very funny

deaden (DEH dun) *v.* to make weak or dull

consciousness (KAHN shus nes) *n.* the state of being fully awake or alert

Practice the Skills
....

2 **Text Element**

Chronological Order Notice the time-order clues that the author gives you at the beginning of this article. She states when the events began (the 1800s) and includes the time-order signal words *at first.*

3 **English Language Coach**

Building Vocabulary: Preview List Did you put the word **demonstrations** on your preview list? Can you tell from the context what it means, or do you need to look it up?

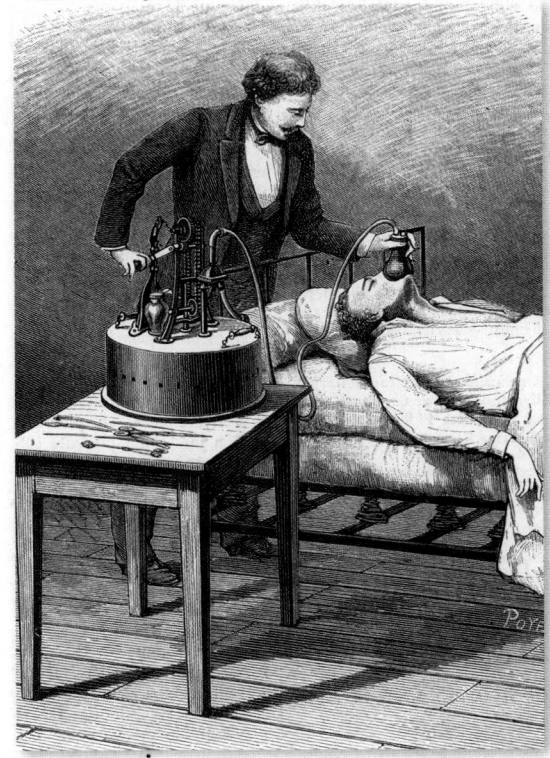

Illustration in *La Nature,* March 21, 1885.

Analyzing the Painting How does this scene compare to a modern-day doctor's office?

A Dose of Medicine **251**

inhaling ether. Long claimed that on March 30, 1842, he used ether as an anesthesia[3] while removing a tumor from a patient's neck. He continued using ether on patients but never **publicized** his discovery.

So four doctors claimed to have first used ether or nitrous oxide to dull pain. The U.S. Congress offered $100,000 to the person who discovered anesthesia. But since it could not decide who should receive the award, Congress never paid the money.

The American Dental Association and the American Medical Association finally decided that Horace Wells was the discoverer of anesthesia in the United States. 4

INOCULATION[4]

Louis Pasteur was one of the most brilliant chemists of the nineteenth century. In 1880 he helped the French chicken industry battle chicken cholera. It was a terrible disease. Chickens that contracted it soon had drooping wings, feathers standing on end, and tottery legs. A chicken would stagger around until it collapsed, flutter its wings, and die.

Pasteur grew the organism that caused the cholera and stored the germs in bottles. One day he fed some of the germs to a few chickens. He expected them to get sick and die. The chickens acted a little sickly for a while, but then they recovered.

Practice the Skills

4 | **Key Reading Skill**

Comparing and Contrasting
Notice that the author explains how four different doctors tried to use ether or nitrous oxide to deaden pain. Compare and contrast the different techniques that the four doctors used.

Curly-Haired Cockerel, c. 1767-1776. Hand colored engraving. Private collection, The Stapleton Collection/ Bridgeman Art Library.

---

3. Here, ***anesthesia*** (an uh STEE zhuh) is a substance that causes a loss of feeling in order to numb or block pain.

4. ***Inoculation*** (ih nawk yoo LAY shun) is the process of injecting the body with medicine to prevent disease.

Vocabulary

publicized (PUB lih syzd) *v.* made the public aware of something

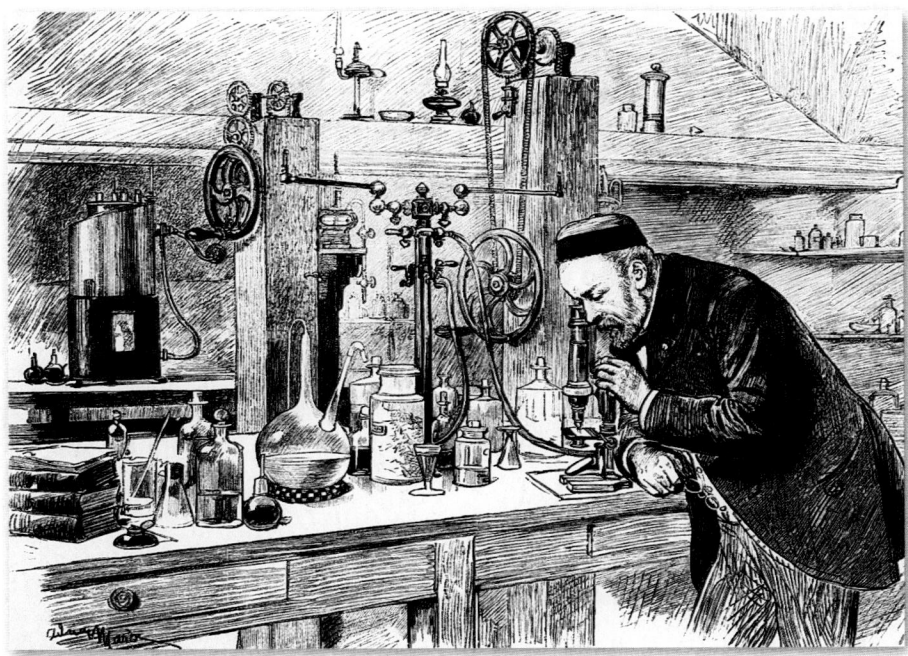

Analyzing the Art What does this picture tell you about the nature of scientific research in Pasteur's time?

The germs had been growing for about six weeks, and Pasteur figured they must be stale. So he fed a fresh crop of the germs to the same birds.

Nothing happened.

Pasteur fed some of the same fresh crop of germs to a different set of chickens. All of those birds got sick and died, as he had expected. **5**

Pasteur had discovered by accident that the "old" crop of germs had somehow changed. They no longer caused serious disease, and they protected the chickens from getting the disease later, even when the chickens were exposed to fresh germs.

Pasteur quickly realized that the same thing would happen with bacteria[5] affecting humans, and in 1881 he developed the anticholera vaccine.[6] **6** ○

5 **Key Reading Skill**

Comparing and Contrasting
How was Pasteur's approach different from that of the dentists and doctors who experimented with anesthesia?

6 **BIG Question**

What lessons about the methods of scientific discovery can we learn from this selection? Explain. Write your answer on the "Dose of Medicine" flap of Foldable 2. Your response will help you complete the Unit Challenge later.

---

5. ***Bacteria*** (bak TEER ee uh) are tiny one-celled organisms. Some bacteria help digest food, while others cause diseases.

6. A ***vaccine*** (vak SEEN) is medicine given to people or animals to protect them from a specific disease.

A Dose of Medicine **253**

After You Read

A Dose of Medicine

Answering the BIG Question

1. What is more important—the journeys that scientists take toward making discoveries or the discoveries themselves? Explain.

2. **Recall** What happened when Louis Pasteur first fed the cholera germs to chickens?

   TIP **Right There** The answer is in the selection.

3. **Summarize** How did the use of anesthesia help dental patients?

   TIP **Think and Search** The answer is in the selection, but it is not all in one place.

Critical Thinking

4. **Infer** What do you think people thought of Louis Pasteur?

   TIP **Author and Me** Use your understanding of the selection and of people.

5. **Evaluate** Which of the four doctors do you think made the biggest contribution to the development of anesthesia? Explain your answer.

   TIP **Author and Me** Use your own judgment.

6. **Infer** How does the author feel about the "mistakes" scientists make?

   TIP **Author and Me** Use your understanding of the selection and your own judgment.

Talk About Your Reading

Round Table Working in a group of six classmates, jot down questions that you might ask each of these people mentioned in the article:

- Horace Wells
- Charles T. Jackson
- Louis Pasteur
- William T. G. Morton
- Crawford W. Long

Write questions that can be answered only by reading "A Dose of Medicine." For example, you might ask Wells, "How did you figure out that nitrous oxide would deaden pain?" When you have at least one question for each person, assign roles to group members—the five people listed plus a "host." Then hold a roundtable discussion, with the host asking the questions and group members answering them in character.

NY English Language Arts Core Curriculum (pp. 254–255)

LC R17 Demonstrate comprehension and response through a range of activities. **S1b** Contribute to group discussions by offering comments to clarify and interpret ideas and information. **LC R12** Combine multiple strategies to enhance comprehension and response. **LC R13** Use text structure and literary devices to aid comprehension and response. **Core W8** Use correct grammatical construction in parts of speech (interjections).

For a complete description of the standards, see p. NY 11.

Skills Review

Key Reading Skill: Comparing and Contrasting

7. Compare a visit to the dentist today with a visit to the dentist in the 1800s. Use information from the selection and information from your own personal experience.

8. Think about the ways Pasteur and Wells went about their experiments. How were their methods alike? How were they different? Explain.

Text Element: Chronological Order

9. What are some time-order signal words that the author uses in the article? List at least three.

10. Make a time line that begins with 1842 and ends with 1846. On your time line, list in chronological order the major events that led to the discovery of anesthesia.

Vocabulary Check

Rewrite each sentence on a separate sheet of paper, using the correct vocabulary word.

**prospect   publicized   consciousness
hilarious   deaden**

11. The ____ antics of people who used nitrous oxide made people who were watching them laugh.

12. One way doctors tried to ____ pain was to knock their patients out.

13. The discovery of a new vaccine is usually well ____.

14. Anesthesia allowed patients to have surgery without losing ____.

15. In the early 1800s, the ____ of recovery from major surgery was not very good.

16. **English Language Coach** Choose any three words from your personalized preview list, and use them correctly in a paragraph.

Grammar Link: Interjections

An **interjection** is a word or group of words that expresses emotion or attracts attention. It has no grammatical connection to the rest of the sentence, so it is set off by an exclamation point or a comma.

An interjection that expresses strong emotion may stand alone. Though not a sentence, it begins with a capital letter and ends with an exclamation point.

• <u>Ouch!</u> You are stepping on my foot!

• <u>Good grief!</u> I'm going to sit somewhere else.

An interjection that expresses mild emotion is set off from the sentence with commas.

• <u>No,</u> I'm not hungry.

• <u>Well,</u> maybe I am hungrier than I thought I was.

Some Common Interjections		
aha	hey	oops
gee	hooray	ouch
good grief	my	well
great	no	wow
ha	oh	yes

Grammar Practice

On a separate sheet of paper, copy each sentence below. Underline the interjections.

17. I took the test, and, oh, it was hard.

18. Well! It's about time you showed up.

19. Yes, I would love some more carrots.

20. Oh, no, here we go again!

Web Activities For eFlashcards, Selection Quick Checks, and other Web activities, go to www.glencoe.com.

Kamau's Finish

by Muthoni Muchemi

& The Bunion Derby

by Leone Castell Anderson

Skills Focus

You will use these skills as you read and compare the following selections:

- "Kamau's Finish," p. 259
- "The Bunion Derby," p. 268

Reading

- Making connections across texts
- Comparing and contrasting information in different texts

Literature

- Recognizing and analyzing theme

Writing

- Using comparison and contrast to understand author's use of theme

NY English Language Arts Core Curriculum (pp. 256–257)

R2b Interpret theme, using evidence from the text.

Literature For a complete description of the standards, see p. NY 11.

Have you ever tried to describe a new song to a friend? Maybe you compared the song to other songs you know. Making comparisons is a great way to understand—and help others understand—new things.

When you compare two pieces of writing, you look at certain elements, or points of comparison, to see how they are similar or different. Points of comparison may be setting, conflict, or other elements that you use to understand what you read.

How to Compare Literature: Theme

In this workshop, your point of comparison is **theme.** Theme is the main idea or message of what you read. A theme is often stated directly, such as "Be honest" or "Respect your elders." But sometimes a theme is not stated directly, and you must figure it out by looking closely at the characters and events. Themes that are not stated directly are **implied** themes.

As you read "Kamau's Finish" and "The Bunion Derby," you'll notice that the subject of both selections is running. Don't confuse subject with theme. Subject is what the selection is about. Theme is the selection's message, or main idea. As you look for theme, ask yourself

- what problems do the characters in these selections face?
- do they meet their goals?
- how would they answer the Big Question?

Academic Vocabulary

implied (im PLYD) *adj.* expressed indirectly; suggested rather than said plainly

Get Ready to Compare

In your Learner's Notebook, make a chart like the one below. As you read, answer the questions in the chart. If the answer is "yes," put a check mark in the column for that story. Briefly explain your answer in the "Notes" column. If the answer is "no," leave the space blank. After you read, you'll use the checklist and notes to help you compare the theme of "Kamau's Finish" and "The Bunion Derby."

"Kamau's Finish" & "The Bunion Derby"

Does the runner...	Kamau's Finish	The Bunion Derby	Notes
love running?			
want support from family and friends?			
run for a prize?			
face obstacles while racing?			
try his best?			
value winning above everything else?			
win the race?			
learn something?			

Use Your Comparison

Think about this unit's Genre Focus selection, "Racing the Great Bear." What is its theme? The theme is implied in the selection—you must find it by thinking about the characters and events. When you look at *how* Swift Runner accepts the task and faces the great bear, you might answer, "It takes courage, wisdom, and determination to conquer challenges."

As you read the following selections, pay attention to what the characters think and say about the things that happen to them. Look for themes that are stated directly or implied. Compare how the characters in each selection deal with events. Ask yourself the questions below and keep track of your thoughts in the chart you just made.

1. Does the narrator or a character directly state the theme?
   - *Are there any messages or lessons stated in a sentence?*
   - *Is there a statement about life or human nature?*
2. Is the theme implied throughout the selection?
   - *Do the events teach a character something valuable?*
   - *Does a character's attitude toward a subject or event hint at a larger message?*

Before You Read : Kamau's Finish

Muthoni Muchemi

Meet the Author

Muthoni Muchemi lives in Kenya with her husband, four children, and two dogs. She has been published in the United States and Africa. "Kamau's Finish" is based on her childhood memories of school races—races in which her parents encouraged her to run like a famous Kenyan runner.

Author Search For more about Muthoni Muchemi, go to www .glencoe.com.

NY English Language Arts Core Curriculum (pp. 258–266)

LC R8 Use a thesaurus to identify synonyms. **R2b** Interpret theme, using evidence from the text.

For a complete description of the standards, see p. NY 11.

Vocabulary Preview

financial (fy NAN chul) *adj.* concerning money **(p. 261)** *Mami worries about her family's financial problems because she has three children to feed.*

distracted (dih STRAK tid) *adj.* losing attention easily **(p. 261)** *Since Kamau is distracted in school, he doesn't get good grades.*

dramatic (druh MA tik) *adj.* showing strong emotion **(p. 266)** *When the runner crossed the finish line, he gave a dramatic cry of relief.*

sheepishly (SHEEP ish lee) *adv.* with embarrassment **(p. 266)** *Kamau smiled sheepishly as the crowd shouted his name.*

English Language Coach

Vocabulary Building: Collections of Synonyms You can use synonyms to help you understand an unfamiliar word. As you read, look up words and make a word web of synonyms like the one below.

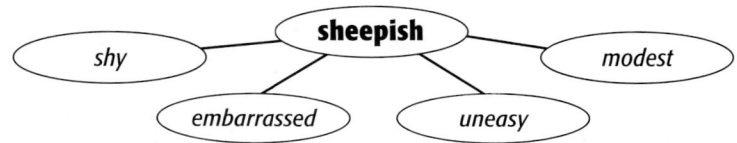

Get Ready to Read

Connect to the Reading

Think about a time when you wanted to prove something about yourself to others. What did you want to prove and why?

Build Background

This story takes place in Nairobi, the capital of Kenya, a country in East Africa. In Kenya, English is the official language used in business and law, and Kiswahili is the common language spoken on the streets and in homes. Two Kiswahili words you'll see, *Baba* and *Mami*, mean father and mother.

Set Purposes for Reading

BIG Question Read to find out what Kamau learns on the way to the finish line.

Set Your Own Purpose What else would you like to learn from the selection to help you answer the Big Question? Write your own purpose on the "Kamau's Finish" Flap of Foldable 2.

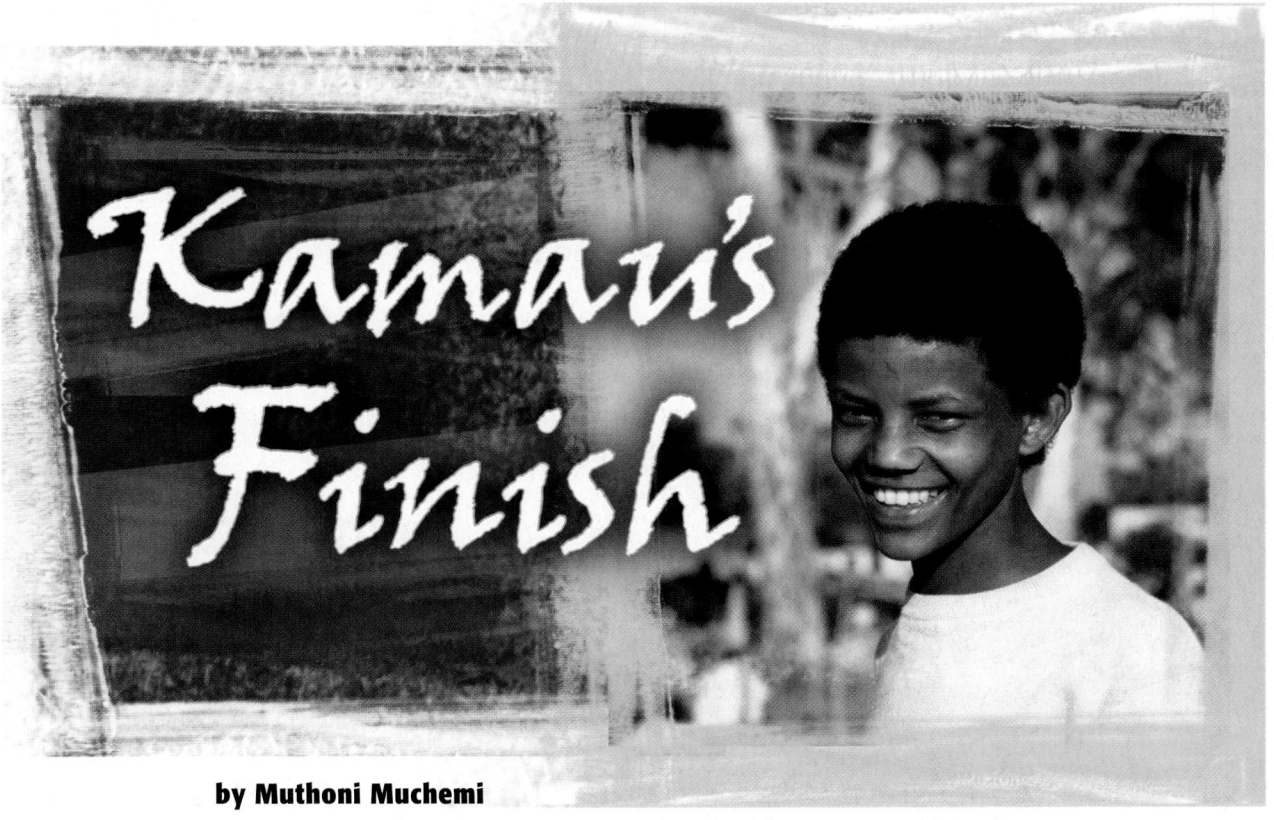

Kamau's Finish

by Muthoni Muchemi

"**W**ooyay, please with sugarcane juice," I silently pray. "Let me be one of the lucky ones today." Although Kenyatta Primary Academy in Nairobi has almost four hundred students, not many parents have showed up for Sports Day. I don't care about other parents so long as Baba is there for me.

While the headmistress <u>screeches</u> something or other on the squeaky microphone, I scan the group standing on the other side of the track. Baba is not among them. He's tall and big like Meja Rhino the champion wrestler, so you can't miss him. ∎

My team is the Red House, and we're squashed between the Yellow and Blue House teams. Immediately across is the three-step winners' podium.[1] I cross my eyes three times in its direction, shooting lucky *uganga*[2] rays.

But Chris and Daudi pull my T-shirt and break my concentration. I bat their hands away and crouch down. We're

Practice the Skills

∎ **English Language Coach**

Vocabulary Building Use a dictionary or a thesaurus to look up the verb **screech.** Then make a word web of synonyms.

---

1. A *podium* (POH dee um) is a raised structure for giving speeches or receiving awards.
2. *Uganga* (yoo GAWNG uh) is a Swahili word that means "magic" or "charms."

sitting on the ground right in front of the track. Mr. Juma, our sports master, let us sit here because we helped him mark the track into lanes with white chalk. Murram³ dust will fly in our face during the races, but we'll still have the best view.

Suddenly I see a tall figure approaching from a distance and shoot up again. But Baba is half bald, and this man has tight clumps that look like sleeping safari ants scattered about his head.

"Down, Kamau!" barks Mr. Juma.

My race will start in a few minutes. I close my eyes and slowly mouth the secret word. *Ndigidigimazlpixkarumbeta!* Please let Baba be here by the end of this blink. But I open my eyes too soon, way too soon.

Still, I will not lose faith. **2**

Analyzing the Photo What aspect of the story's setting does this photograph capture?

Practice the Skills

2 Comparing Literature

Theme Think about what you've learned about Kamau. Is he determined? What does he seem to want most? Begin filling in your chart.

---

3. A *murram* (MUR um) road is made of hard soil and stones.

Just this morning, I pressed my thumb into the fleshy pad of Baba's thumb. He didn't pull away.

"I have an important business meeting, Kamau, so we'll just have to see." His dark brown eyes seemed full of heavy thoughts.

I pushed my thumb in harder to drill my way into focus. "Please, Baba . . ." **3**

Mami butted in, "Stop pestering your father. Only thinking about yourself. How selfish can you be?" She is hugely pregnant and can scold until your head vibrates. "Your father has to work. Do you think the money we use to educate you is donated by foreign aid?[4] Maybe you think we can feed on saliva like bacteria, or live on yesterday's skin like fleas? You have no idea about the **financial** problems—"

Baba coughed. Mami stopped talking, and for a moment they stared at each other. Mami lashed at me again. "What's that mashing thumbs *uganga* anyway?"

My eight-year-old sister, Wanja, laughed, giving us all a good long look at the mushy stuff in her mouth. Neither of my parents said anything about her bad manners. She had just shown them her report card and, as vomit usual, she was first in her class. Of course, they then asked for mine, and I had to dig it out of the bottom of my bag.

"Kamau needs to concentrate. He is easily **distracted** . . ." Mami had waved the report at Baba. "Didn't I tell you that all this boy does night and day is dream? If they tested a subject called dreaming, Kamau's grades would burst through the ceiling and pierce the cover of the sky!"

Baba had nodded his head in Mami's direction. Did he agree with Mami?

"Kamau's head is full of nonsense!" She'd prodded my head. I let it bob up and down like a rubber ball on a string. "He needs to knuckle down. I want him to succeed. Achievement is what matters. Maybe he dreams he'll be the next president of this country. President Kamau? Heh!"

---

4. **Foreign aid** is money or other help given from one country to another.

Practice the Skills

3 **Reviewing Skills**

Connecting Kamau admires Baba and wants his attention. Who have you looked up to like Kamau looks up to Baba? Explain your answer in your Learner's Notebook.

Vocabulary

financial (fy NAN chul) *adj.* concerning money

distracted (dih STRAK tid) *adj.* losing attention easily

Practice the Skills

Kamau, get serious. Even future kings need to work."

It was no use telling her I try.

My friend Chris once told me his mother said babies in the belly kick. So I squinted and sent mega-*uganga* rays to the baby in Mami's belly to make its legs stronger. She stopped talking and placed a hand over her side.

Maybe my *uganga* rays were too strong.

I held my breath in awe of my powers, but nothing else happened.

Then Njau, my four-year-old brother, had piped up in his high voice, "Baba said effort is what matters."

Baba rumbled, "And problems help us grow." 🄣

Mami had scrunched her face as though a mountain of firewood pressed her head and waddled off to pack my special energy lunch—sweet potato slices, *maziwa lala,*[5] boiled egg, two carrots, and an orange.

I bite into the pad of my thumb. It's tingling. *Ndigidigimazlp-ixkarumbeta!*

"Sit down, Kamau, how many times do I have to tell you?" Mr. Juma's voice rises up and whips me back down.

I glance over at the Yellows and silently chant, "Yellow, yellow, dirty fellow," when my eyes lock with Kip's. He points his index finger and cocks his thumb at me. I duck the imaginary bullet, but he's laughing, trading high-fives with his mates, and doesn't notice. Kip is ten, a year younger than most of my class, and usually the fastest. But twice during

🄣 **Comparing Literature**

Theme Mami says that achievement matters most. But Baba thinks that effort is what matters. Both of these direct statements could be themes. Which one do you think is more important?

Analyzing the Photo Which line from the story would be a good caption for this photo? Explain your choice.

5. *Maziwa lala* (mah ZEE wah lah lah) is a kind of thick milk, similar to yogurt.

practice runs this term, I beat him. He spat at me and sulked off. Everyone else clapped me on the back, even Mr. Juma.

When I told Baba, he said, "Well done, son," and "Good for you."

Now if only Baba would get here, I'd show him how I did it. I'd prove to him that I'm not just a hopeless dreamer. **5**

Our 800-meter race is announced over the screechy microphone. I stare desperately at the parents' side of the track as we file to the starting block. He isn't there.

Three runners from each team stand at attention. Mr. Juma calls for silence.

"Good luck," says Chris in a hoarse voice.

"Same to you," I whisper as we crouch down in starting position.

"On your marks!"

Daudi is in the farthest lane. His lips are moving in silent prayer. Kip calls him *mkiha,* the last carriage of a train. Of course, Kip sees himself as the engine, the one that always gets to its destination first.

I look past Daudi. No sign of Baba, only other parents jostling[6] to get a better view of their sons at the starting line.

Mami said I was selfish to need Baba here today, but I so want to prove to him and Mami that I can be a winner. If he comes just this once, I'll never ask him again.

"Get set!"

I look down at my hands splayed on the ground and feel such a sharp tingling in my thumb that I glance up.

And there he is! My thumb never lies. There is Baba, pushing his way through the throng[7] of parents along the track. There is no mistaking that huge shining head floating above the rest, hurrying in my direction.

Boom! The gun goes off.

I want to burst with happiness. But a blur of bodies has already bolted forward. They have a head start.

I have to concentrate on the race instead of thinking about the miracle of Baba being here. I glue my eyes on the nearest

Practice the Skills

5 | **Comparing Literature**

Theme Kamau wants to prove that he's a winner to Baba. Use this information to continue filling in your chart.

---

6. The parents are *jostling,* or pushing and shoving lightly, to get a better view.

7. A *throng* is a large group.

Analyzing the Photo How is the man in this photo similar to or different from the Baba you've imagined?

runner, a blue T-shirt. I concentrate on catching up with him. I run like Ananse[8] the hungry hare on his way to Mr. Elephant's feast. I overtake him.

Concentration, concentration, concentration now begins. To that beat, I run faster. I run in long hard strides that bounce off the ground and pull on the backs of my thighs. My legs feel strong. I set my sights on a yellow back. A surge of warmth **floods** my body as I overtake him. **6**

I can tell it's Daudi directly in front of me, because he runs with his head facing the sky. He's already slowing. I pound past him with my eyes locked on Kip's yellow shirt.

He's in a cluster, but I know Kip always goes for the flashy sprint finish. I have to catch up with him now if I'm to have a chance. Concentration, concentration, concentration now begins.

Amid all the crowd noises, I think I hear Baba yell, "Run, son!"

A new energy tingles from my feet, up along my legs, loosens my hips, and expands my chest. I tear past Chris, who is panting like a horse. *Uganga* magic is with me!

Practice the Skills

6 **English Language Coach**

Vocabulary Building Some synonyms for **floods,** as it is used here, are *rushes through* and *pours through*. Do you think either of them works as well as *floods* to communicate what Kamau is feeling?

---

8. Known for his tricks, ***Ananse*** (ah NAWN see) is a character found in many African folktales.

The cluster is breaking up. Kip is racing ahead. My heart hammers in my ribs. I open my mouth wider to take in more air. I'm catching up. I'm in the dispersing cluster. I overtake one, two, three boys.

I'm flying, my feet almost slapping my bottom, half a step behind Kip.

When I win this race, Mami will never scold me again. When I win this race, Wanja will swallow her snickering. Best of all, Baba will look in my eyes to congratulate me. Baba will finally see me.

Everything feels slow motion. The noise, the people, and the track float away into the great *uganga*-land of dreams. I hear only distant echoes. "Win, win, win!"

I'm neck and neck with Kip, matching him stride for stride. He leans in my direction as though to draw strength from me. The finish-line ribbon flutters red maybe fifty meters ahead.

I'm going to win! I'm going to win! My teammates will carry me on their shoulders, shouting, "Hero! Hero!" When I climb the winner's podium to collect my medal, I won't even punch the air or do a show-off dance. Baba will already know I'm a hero. Baba will— **7**

An unexpected shove jolts me out of my dream and back to the moment. Then I'm wobbling, fighting for control. I fall.

Unbelievable!

I swallow the grit on my tongue and shake my head to clear the ringing in my ears. I feel confused. Not quite on this earth. My hands are grazed with white track chalk mixed with brown soil and smudges of blood. I shape them into fists and press hard to force the pain away. A blue shirt whizzes by, kicking dust in my face.

While I was in my dream, Kip must have pushed me with his elbow. Mami would be proud of a son like Kip, who knows winning is what matters.

Legs zoom past me in a whir of hot air and dust. I glance toward the side of the track. The crowd probably thinks Kip and I touched accidentally.

A cheer goes up and I realize Kip must have crossed the red ribbon. Kip has won my race. No. Kip has stolen my race.

Practice the Skills

7 **Comparing Literature**

Theme Think about what is most important to Kamau right now. Do you think he agrees with Mami that winning is what matters? Or does he agree with Baba that effort is most important? Look back at your chart and see which questions you can answer.

I want to call to Baba that I should have won. Will he believe that Kip tripped me?

Most of the runners are finishing. Daudi rushes past me, his tongue lolling out of his mouth, probably elated not to be the *mkiha* for once.

I look back and see Baba's shiny face. He is running alongside the track, gesturing wildly—up, up, up—pointing to the finish line. But how will getting up help me? I'll pretend my leg is broken. I'll give a **dramatic** cry for help. I'll— 8

I become aware of the noise, the cheering. They're chanting my name. "KA-MA-UU! KA-MA-UU! KA-MA-UU!" They're shouting for me to finish. I feel like shouting back, "Whatever for? All I'm good for is dreaming."

Then I notice their eyes are not on me, but on my lumbering Baba, who has crossed onto the track behind me. He is wearing a black suit and shiny lizard shoes he bought donkey years ago that usually make me cringe.

My ears buzz, but I think I hear him shout, "Run, son! Get up and run!"

Uncertain, I scramble up and gape at Baba. Sweat streams down his face, and he holds a hand over his chest. Is he having a heart attack?

He can't be. His eyes are shining. I can see every tooth in his mouth.

Baba is beaming!

So I wipe my nose with my wrist and laugh through the tears. It sounds like I am crying. But Baba is beaming.

I keep my eyes on him and trot **sheepishly** alongside to the finish. So much noise, so many people crowding the finish area. Mr. Juma is probably shouting for order.

But I only have ears for Baba. 9 ○

Practice the Skills

8 Comparing Literature

Theme Kamau doesn't want to finish the race. Why does he feel that it's useless to keep going? Think about Mami's definition of what matters, and how that might influence Kamau.

9 BIG Question

What has Kamau learned about running, and finishing, a race? Finish filling in your chart and write your answer on the "Kamau's Finish" flap of Foldable 2. Your response will help you complete the Unit Challenge later.

Vocabulary

dramatic (druh MA tik) *adj.* showing strong emotion

sheepishly (SHEEP ish lee) *adv.* with embarrassment

Before You Read

The Bunion Derby

Leone Castell Anderson

Meet the Author

Leone Castell Anderson has written many stories for young people, including two historical novels titled *Sean's War* and *Sean's Quest*. She lives in an old schoolhouse in Illinois, but she travels the country giving writing workshops for children of all ages.

Author Search For more about Leone Castell Anderson, go to www.glencoe.com.

NY English Language Arts Core Curriculum (pp. 267–273)

LC R8 Use a thesaurus to identify synonyms and antonyms. **R2b** Interpret theme, using evidence from the text.

For a complete description of the standards, see p. NY 11.

Vocabulary Preview

furnished (FUR nisht) *v.* supplied; given **(p. 270)** *Mr. Pyle furnished the runners with food and water.*

promoter (pruh MOH tur) *n.* a person who organizes and pays the costs of a sporting event **(p. 271)** *The promoter of the race made sure the runners had a place to sleep.*

grimacing (GRIM us ing) *adj.* making a face that shows discomfort or disgust **(p. 273)** *The runner was grimacing after he twisted his ankle.*

English Language Coach

Vocabulary Building: Synonyms A great way to remember an unfamiliar word is to pair it with a synonym or two. Use a synonym chart like the one below to help you remember unfamiliar words.

Word	Synonym	Synonym
furnish	provide	supply

Get Ready to Read

Connect to the Reading

Think about a goal you've set for yourself. What did you do to reach it?

Build Background

Imagine running more than 26 miles in one day! That's what marathon runners do. Marathoners don't just run for good times, though. They run for personal pride—and money. For example, the winner of the Boston marathon, one of the country's most popular marathons, can expect to win a $100,000 prize.

Set Purposes for Reading

BIG Question Read to find out how Andy Payne, a young man from Oklahoma, ran an amazing race across the United States.

Set Your Own Purpose What else would you like to learn from the selection to help you answer the Big Question? Write your own purpose on the "Bunion Derby" flap of Foldable 2.

The Bunion Derby

by Leone Castell Anderson

Practice the Skills

What would your mom say if you wore out a pair of shoes and had to get a new pair every 17 days? Too many shoes?

That's what Andy Payne did, and his mother never scolded him.

Andrew Hartley Payne, who was part Cherokee, grew up on his parents' farm near the town of Foyil, just up the road from Claremore, Oklahoma. From the time he was a kid, he loved to run. He ran the five miles to grade school, practiced running in the fields and hills, and ran the mile at Foyil High School, where he could never be beaten. **1**

After graduation in 1927, he went west to Los Angeles, California, seeking to make his fortune. One day as Andy searched the want ads, he saw a notice about "runners wanted" for an International Trans-Continental Foot Race. His heart pounded as he read on. Runners were to cross the country from Los Angeles to Chicago, on the new Route 66, and then go on to Madison Square Garden in New York City. The winner's prize would be $25,000.

Twenty-five thousand! Andy later told an interviewer, "I knew I was strong and could run. And I just concluded that I would stand as good a chance as any." He dreamed about how he would use the winnings. He'd help pay off the

1 **Reviewing Skills**

Connecting Think about your hobbies—maybe you draw, skateboard, write poetry, or dance. What do you love to do as much as Andy loves to run? In your Learner's Notebook, explain your answer.

mortgage on his family's farm. And his fame and fortune would help him convince Vivian Shaddox, his high-school sweetheart, to marry him.

Andy soon learned about the $25 entry fee and the $100 deposit for a return ticket from New York. He didn't let that stop him. Making his way back to Oklahoma, Andy went first to Claremore's chamber of commerce. He asked the members to sponsor[1] him in the race. They hemmed and hawed. They looked at the slender 20-year-old, with his dark wavy hair and his good looks. They weren't sure, they told him.

Andy persisted. He was young, he was strong, he'd been a runner all his life, he'd made records at running, he told them. The chamber finally came through with some of the money. **2**

Andy's father, Andrew Lane Jackson Payne, was more confident. He borrowed enough to cover Andy's entry fee and expenses.

After signing up to enter the race, Andy knew he needed to get back in shape for running. Throughout the winter months, then, he ran. Up and down the rolling hills of southern California he ran. Tom Young, a high-school coach from Los Angeles, spurred him on. Andy felt his legs getting stronger, his wind improving, his staying power returning. He spent three weeks in the training camp at the Ascot Speedway in Los Angeles "for final conditioning[2] for the race," as the runners were required to do.

Now the big day arrived: 4 March 1928. Andy took his place on the track of the Ascot Speedway, his number 43 on his athletic undershirt. He felt the jostling of the other runners as they vied for the best starting positions. Over 240 of them, he'd been told. He saw the crowd . . . thousands of people. He heard their wild cheering.

Practice the Skills

2 | **Comparing Literature**

Theme What have you learned about Andy so far? Fill in your chart.

Andy Payne leads the pack in this 1928 photo.

---

1. A ***chamber of commerce*** is an association that promotes a community. To ***sponsor*** someone means to support his or her effort, usually with money.

2. ***Conditioning*** (kun DIH shun ing) is a kind of training to get in shape.

Andy waited for the signal from Red Grange, the famous football player known as the Galloping Ghost. He flexed his muscles. He bounced lightly on his canvas sneakers. He took a deep breath. Suddenly a loud boom sounded. Andy sprang forward, sensing the other runners beside and behind him. He was on his way to New York, just 3,422.3 miles away.

On that first day, a cool cloudy one, Andy kept up a steady pace, covering the assigned daily route. He knew his time would be noted. Each day's time would be added to his total. Winning the race depended on having the lowest time over the entire course. **3**

As he ran, Andy was aware of his competitors. Some were close to his age. Some were older. Andy stepped along. He knew there were some well-known runners, from places like Germany and Italy and England. And from Canada and the States, too. There were Finns and Greeks and Hopi Indians offering Andy tough competition.

Andy stared at a passing runner. He'd seen some in overalls or BVDs or even a sheet, wearing boots or moccasins.[3] But that last one was running in his bare feet!

Andy knew newspaper reporters were calling the race the Bunion Derby. He'd never had any bunions.[4] But he had taken time to break in his running shoes. He was sure they'd need replacing before the race was over.

He arrived at the first scheduled checkpoint in Puente, California, by noon, having made about six miles an hour, a good average. He enjoyed the first of the meals **furnished** the runners. Later, after exercising to keep in shape, Andy ate a tasty dinner with the other competitors. He soon headed for his cot in the tent housing arranged for them by the organizer of the race, Mr. C. C. Pyle. His personal belongings and blanket, all marked with his number 43, were there. The rule was lights out at 9 P.M., and Andy slept.

Practice the Skills

3 **Comparing Literature**

Theme Andy must keep a steady pace and not tire himself out if he wants to win the race. From what you've read, can you think of a theme for this selection?

---

3. **BVD** is a brand of underwear, and **moccasins** (MAWK uh sinz) are soft, leather shoes.

4. **Bunions** are swollen areas on the joint of the big toe.

Vocabulary

furnished (FUR nisht) *v.* supplied; given

As days went by, Andy struggled along with the others. Heavy rains slashed at his face and soaked his jersey. They made the ground underfoot sticky with mud that pulled at his shoes. He struggled up Cajon Pass, the first of the steep slopes he knew he'd have to climb, and noticed other runners dropping back. As he shuffled across the hot sands of the Mojave Desert, the blazing sun blistered his nose and ears, and the gritty sand wore down the soles of his sneakers. He stumbled through sandstorms with his hands in front of his face. But he just kept "stepping along," as he told reporters later.

Adding to his problems, Andy learned that C. C. Pyle was a pinchpenny **promoter.** The promised "deluxe" food was replaced with a daily tasteless mulligan stew.[5] With Pyle's 35-cent allowance given the runners for each meal, then, Andy bought himself sandwiches and other more passable food in the towns they ran through. The tent housing proved hot, the blankets unwashed. Sometimes the caravan carrying the tents, cots, blankets, and belongings didn't make it to the checkpoints in time. Andy and the other runners were sometimes put up in stables or barns, even chicken houses.

By the time the runners reached northern Arizona, many had begun dropping out from exhaustion, sore feet, sprains, shin splints, and other ailments. Andy himself, his throat sore and running a fever from tonsillitis,[6] was not racing well. But Arthur Newton, the front runner, unable to breathe in the thin air of the high elevation of 6,000 feet, dropped out of the race on the road into Winslow, Arizona. The coordinators announced, "The totals thus far show Andy Payne is in first place." Andy took a deep breath and grinned. But he knew there were miles to go. He replaced his worn-out shoes and kept running. **4**

---

5. *Mulligan stew* is a soup made of meat, vegetables, and broth.
6. *Tonsillitis* (tawn sul EYE tus) is an irritation of the tonsils, or part of the throat.

Practice the Skills
....

John Salo and Peter Garrizzi run nearly neck and neck in this 1929 photo.

4 Comparing Literature

Theme In "Kamau's Finish," Kamau's main obstacle is another runner. What obstacles does Andy face during his race? Remember to fill in your chart.

The race went on, across New Mexico and Texas. Sometimes cheering town residents lined the streets as the runners went by. Schools along the route would excuse children from class so they could watch the race, and the kids would sometimes run alongside Andy and the others. Sometimes enthusiastic drivers would try to follow them. A Finnish runner endured broken ribs from a collision with a car, but got up and kept running. Two other runners left the race after similar encounters. But Andy just kept "stepping along."

On 15 April Governor Henry S. Johnston of Andy's home state and a cheering crowd met the race leaders at the fairgrounds in Oklahoma City. Invited to the speaker's stand, Andy said, "Hello, home folks. I'm glad to be back. Hope to see you in New York."

But it was in Claremore, Oklahoma, on 17 April that the biggest and most enthusiastic crowd welcomed Andy, and a squad of cadets from the military academy ran on either side of him. It was the exact halfway point of the race. Andy smiled and greeted everyone, but he kept on running, knowing he had to maintain his time. However, the next day he did take some moments to visit with his family and friends, especially Vivian, when he entered his hometown of Foyil. He assured them he was going to make it—and replaced his shoes with still another pair. **5**

Andy was aware of the runners who were trying to match and **surpass** his time. John Salo of New Jersey was close. Salo had adopted one of the dogs who had begun following the runners, naming him Blisters and taking care of him. Another challenger was Phillip Granville, a tall Jamaican from Canada, who changed his strategy of walking to running in an effort to catch Andy. **6**

But Andy learned he had a strong rival for first place as the course took the runners across the Midwest. He befriended the bearded Englishman, Peter Gavuzzi, who was two years older and an experienced marathon runner. They often ran side by side. Through a corner of Kansas, across Missouri, and into Illinois they went, until they reached Chicago, the

Practice the Skills

Clouds Over Seligman, September 1, 1947. Andreas Feininger. Silver gelatin photograph.

The race wound through arid Arizona (above), where cumulus clouds billow over a flat, dry landscape.

5 Reviewing Skills

Connecting The people in Andy's hometown cheer him on when he races through. Think about the people who cheer you on. Why is it important to have the support of others as you work toward your goals?

6 English Language Coach

Vocabulary Building Look up the word **surpass** in a dictionary or a thesaurus. Make a synonym chart to help you remember what the word means.

end of Route 66. They headed for New York, still keeping pace with each other, although Andy knew Peter had a lead over him by several hours.

As they were crossing Indiana, Andy saw his friend **grimacing,** and when he asked what his problem was, Peter told him it was an abscessed[7] tooth. Peter Gavuzzi kept doggedly[8] on until they reached Wauseon, Ohio, when the pain proved too much for him, and he dropped out of the race. Andy reluctantly left his friend behind. But he knew he was now the only front runner.

On 26 May 1928, wearing pair number five of his Bunion Derby shoes, Andy Payne was one of 55 weary runners who arrived at New York's Madison Square Garden track. Over the daily routes, varying in length from 15 to 75 miles, it had taken Andy 573 hours, 4 minutes, and 34 seconds and 84 consecutive days to run the 3,422.3 miles of "C. C. Pyle's First Annual International Trans-Continental Foot Race: Los Angeles to New York City."

Andy Payne was declared the winner of the $25,000 prize. John Salo placed second, with a prize of $10,000. Phillip Granville finished in third place, which paid $5,000. **7**

With a tired smile on his face, Andy the Bunion Derby winner pointed to his feet. "No bunions," he said. **8**

Author's Note

Andy did pay off the mortgage on his family farm and built his folks a new home. He married Vivian in 1929. Six years later, he hung up his racing shoes for good and entered a political race. He was elected clerk of the Supreme Court of Oklahoma in 1934 and served for 38 years. He died at age 69 in 1977.

On 16 May 1992, the Cherokee Heritage Center in Tahlequah, Oklahoma, dedicated a life-sized statue of Andy Payne, honoring him as a notable member of the tribe. ○

---

7. If something is *abscessed* (AB sest), it is infected.
8. *Doggedly* means in a stubborn or determined way.

Vocabulary

grimacing (GRIM us ing) *adj.* making a face that shows discomfort or disgust

Practice the Skills

7 **Comparing Literature**

Theme The theme of this selection is implied. We learn about Andy by his actions. What makes Andy a successful runner? What doesn't he do?

8 **BIG Question**

Which would Andy Payne say is more important, running his best race or winning the prize? Write your answer on the "Bunion Derby" flap of Foldable 2. Your response will help you complete the Unit Challenge later.

After You Read

Kamau's Finish & *The* **Bunion** *Derby*

Vocabulary Check

Rewrite the sentences below. Replace the word in parentheses ( ) with the vocabulary word that means about the same thing.

Kamau's Finish

financial   distracted   sheepishly   dramatic

1. The game's score was tied, promising a (thrilling) finale.
2. Waylon tried to think about homework, but he kept getting (sidetracked) watching TV.
3. "I've never flown on an airplane," Gabrielle told her friend (self-consciously).
4. Loretta asked her banker for (money-related) advice.

The **Bunion** *Derby*

furnished   promoter   grimacing

5. Not even the (event coordinator) could believe the boxing match went twelve rounds.
6. The dancer tripped, (wincing), and knew she'd sprained her foot.
7. The chef (supplied) his guests with cake and other desserts.
8. **Academic Vocabulary** What is an **implied** theme?
9. **English Language Coach** In 1992 Andy Payne was honored as a **notable** member of his tribe. What does *notable* mean? Copy the synonym chart below, and use a dictionary or a thesaurus to fill in the chart.

Word	Synonym	Synonym
notable		

NY English Language Arts Core Curriculum (pp. 274–275)

LC R8 Use a thesaurus to identify synonyms. **R2b** Interpret theme, using evidence from the text.

For a complete description of the standards, see p. NY 11.

Reading/Critical Thinking

On a separate sheet of paper, answer the following questions.

Kamau's Finish

10. **Compare** Compare Kamau's attitude about winning at the beginning of the story with his attitude about winning at the end of the story.

    Tip **Author and Me**

11. **Infer** What does Kamau want to prove to Mami and Baba by winning?

    Tip **Think and Search**

12. **Analyze** Why is it important to Baba that Kamau finish the race?

    Tip **Author and Me**

The Bunion *Derby*

13. **Evaluate** How does Andy treat his competitors?

    Tip **Think and Search**

14. **Identify** What is Andy's strategy, or plan, for running the race? Does it work?

    Tip **Think and Search**

15. **Analyze** Do you think Andy's personal characteristics and habits helped him later in his life? Why or why not?

    Tip **Think and Search**

Writing: Compare the Literature

Use Your Notes

16. Follow these steps to compare the themes in "Kamau's Finish" and "The Bunion Derby."

    Step 1: Look at your completed chart. You probably answered "yes" in both columns for a few questions, which means that Kamau and Andy Payne are alike in some ways. They may also have similar experiences. Circle the questions to which you answered "yes" about both selections.

Step 2: Reread the notes you made about those questions in your chart. Use those notes to write a few sentences about how both selections are alike. Then write one or two sentences describing how they are different.

Step 3: Use your chart to identify the themes of the selections. You may find different themes for each selection. Or you may find that one theme works for both selections. (Hint: Think about why Kamua and Andy run and what they learn from competing.)

Step 4: Make a table like the one below. Label one column "Kamau's Finish" and the other column "The Bunion Derby." Then write the theme or themes of the selections.

"Kamau's Finish"	"The Bunion Derby"
Theme:	Theme:
1:	1:
2:	2:
3:	3:

Step 5: Go back to the selections and look for details that support the theme or themes you've chosen. Look closely at what Kamau, Andy, and other people say and do. Then list at least three details in your chart for each selection.

Get It On Paper

To show your understanding of theme in "Kamau's Finish" and "The Bunion Derby," answer the questions below on a separate sheet of paper.

17. What obstacles do Kamau and Andy Payne face as they run?

18. What do Kamau and Andy Payne hope to achieve by running in a race?

19. What lessons do Kamau and Andy Payne learn about doing their best?

BIG Question

20. What did Kamau and Andy Payne learn about working hard to achieve a goal? What did they learn about winning? How would Kamau and Andy Payne answer the Big Question?

Answering  Which Is More Important, the Journey or the Destination?

You've just read about people who made journeys in pursuit of a destination. Now use what you've learned to do the Unit Challenge.

The Unit Challenge

Choose Activity A or Activity B and follow the directions for that activity.

A. Group Activity: Trial TV

This week's case on Trial TV seeks to answer the question "Is the journey or the destination more important?" Two teams, one representing "Journey" and the other "Destination," will try to convince a panel of peers which is more important, the journey or the destination.

1. Discuss the Assignment

- Form your teams. Assign sides.
- Together, choose a selection from this unit that you believe clearly shows that either the journey or the destination is more important. To choose your selection, review and discuss the notes you took on your unit Foldables.
- Once you've chosen your selection, discuss how it supports your side. Look for details that help you argue either that the journey is more important or that the destination is more important.
- Choose two students from each team to act as lead "lawyers." The lawyers' job is to argue the group's position. Choose another student to represent one of the characters from your selection and act as the "witness."

- Team members should be prepared to discuss details of the character's journey and destination with emphasis on what was more important.
- Other class members serve as the jury.

2. Review Your Notes and Prepare
The lawyers should prepare an opening argument. In your teams, review the notes you took in your Foldable. The "witnesses" from the unit should reread parts of their selections and review notes to back up their testimony. The jury may wish to prepare a list of questions that they need to have answered to come up with a verdict.

3. Make a Decision
After the cases have been presented, the jury should meet privately to discuss which argument is more convincing. When each jury reaches a final decision, a jury member should announce the answer to the Big Question: Which is more important, the journey or the destination?

4. Meet as a Class
As a class, discuss whether you agree or disagree with the decision.

B. Solo Activity: Interview

You'll interview a family member, family friend, or neighbor who has taken a major journey in his or her life. Your purpose is to see which was more important, the journey or the destination.

1. **Prepare** After you have chosen which person you are going to interview, you should prepare for the interview by making a list of questions. Use the notes on your Foldable to help you think of interview questions. For example:

   - What was your destination?
   - When did the journey take place? Why did you decide to take this journey?
   - What happened when you reached your destination?
   - How did you feel at the end of the journey?
   - Which was more important: your destination or the journey to get there?

2. **Interview and Organize** Ask your questions, and write down the person's answers. If possible, record the interview on tape so that you can listen to it later. On a separate sheet of paper, fill in a graphic organizer like the one shown below to record your answers.

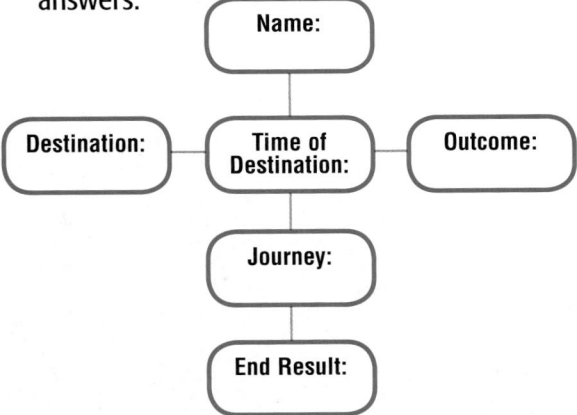

Name:

Destination: — Time of Destination: — Outcome:

Journey:

End Result:

3. **Reflect and Write** Look at your chart. Based on the person's answers, write a short paper explaining which was more important, the journey or the destination. Begin your paper with an introductory paragraph. In the paragraph, tell whom you interviewed, when, and why. End the paragraph with a sentence that states what you learned from the interview. The sentence should explain whether the journey or the destination is more important.

   In the next paragraph or two of your paper, give reasons why you believe the journey or destination is more important. Your reasons should be based on the answers you received from the person you interviewed.

   End your paper with a short paragraph describing how you felt about the interview and what, if anything, you would differently the next time you interview someone.

4. **Review** Look over your paper before you hand it in. Check to make sure that your paper is complete and that your writing is clear. You may want to ask another student to look over your paper to see whether it needs improving. Also check to make sure there aren't any spelling errors or other kinds of mistakes. Then give your paper to your teacher.

Edna St. Vincent Millay

Meet the Author

Throughout her life, Edna St. Vincent Millay was one of the most successful and respected poets in the United States. Millay dreamed of becoming a concert pianist, but her music teacher said that Millay's hands were too small. Millay then threw her energies into writing. She wrote not only poetry, but also plays, and a libretto (lyrics) for an opera. Millay received many awards for her poetry, including the Gold Medal of the Poetry Society and a Pulitzer Prize. See page R4 of the Author Files for more on Edna St. Vincent Millay.

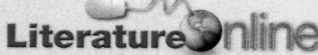

Author Search For more about Edna St. Vincent Millay go to www.glencoe.com.

TRAVEL

by Edna St. Vincent Millay

The railroad track is miles away,
    And the day is loud with voices speaking,
Yet there isn't a train goes by all day
    But I hear its whistle shrieking.

5 All night there isn't a train goes by,
    Though the night is still for sleep and dreaming
But I see its cinders* red on the sky,
    And hear its engine steaming.

My heart is warm with the friends I make,
10   And better friends I'll not be knowing,
Yet there isn't a train I wouldn't take,
    No matter where it's going.

---

7 *Cinders* are hot coals without flames.

278 UNIT 2   Which Is More Important, the Journey or the Destination?

(l)Library of Congress/Corbis, (r)Ace Stock Limited/Alamy

Reading on Your Own

To read more about the Big Question, choose one of these books from your school or local library. Work on your reading skills by choosing books that are challenging to you.

Fiction

Banner in the Sky
by James Ramsey Ullman

When Rudi's father dies in his attempt to scale a mountain in the Alps, Rudi decides that he must conquer the peak that killed his father. Read to find out more as the author, an experienced climber, adds detailed information to a tense tale of courage and determination.

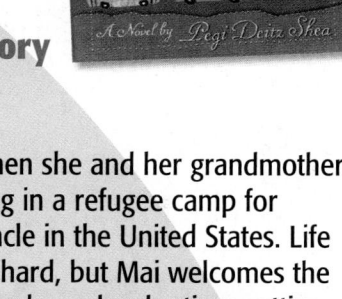

Tangled Threads: A Hmong Girl's Story
by Pegi Dietz Shea

Mai was a young girl when she and her grandmother escaped Laos. After living in a refugee camp for years, they join Mai's uncle in the United States. Life in a new culture can be hard, but Mai welcomes the change. Her grandmother has a harder time getting used to life in the United States.

After the War
by Carol Matas

Ruth is fifteen when she is freed from a Nazi concentration camp and fears that she is the only surviving member of her family. She joins an underground organization to make a dangerous and illegal journey to Palestine. Read to learn how she rediscovers her inner strength and finds reasons for hope along the way.

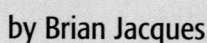

Redwall
by Brian Jacques

The creatures living at Redwall Abbey are a peaceful group until the king of vermin declares war against them. Read about Matthias, an apprentice mouse, who sets out to find a magic sword that can save Redwall. This is the first book in a series of more than ten tales of quests and fights between good and evil.

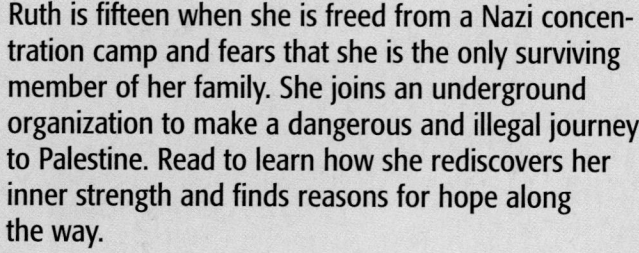

Nonfiction

Laborers for Liberty: American Women 1865–1890
by Harriet Sigerman

From after the Civil War to the end of the 19th century, women in the United States faced a new set of challenges even as they enjoyed new freedoms and new work and education opportunities. This book looks at the lives of women from every corner of the country, including sharecroppers, frontier dwellers, and champions of causes, such as getting the right to vote.

Curse of the Pharaohs: My Adventures with Mummies
by Zahi Hawass

Zahi Hawass, head of Egypt's Supreme Council of Antiquities, tells of his adventures and close calls while searching for pieces of Egypt's ancient civilization. Read to find out whether Hawass experiences the effects of the pharaoh's curse.

Escape from Saigon: How a Vietnam War Orphan Became an American Boy
by Andrea Warren

Living in an orphanage in Saigon at the end of the Vietnam War, the young Amerasian boy Hoang Van Long did not know what his future would hold. Read to learn about his dangerous journey to find a new life and join a new family in the United States.

His Promised Land: The Autobiography of John P. Parker, Former Slave and Conductor on the Underground Railroad
edited by Stuart Seely Sprague

John P. Parker is born enslaved, but he purchases his own freedom after teaching himself to read. As a free man, Parker becomes an important member of the Underground Railroad. Read to learn how Parker risks his life time and again to help hundreds of people who were enslaved escape to freedom.

New York English Language Arts Test Practice

*D*irections
Read this folktale from India. Then answer questions 1 through 3.

"The Brahman's Clothes"
A Folktale from India
Retold by D.L. Ashliman

There once was a Brahman who had two wives. Like many Brahmans he lived by begging and was very clever at wheedling money out of people. One day the fancy took him to go to the marketplace dressed only in a small loincloth such as the poorest laborers wear and see how people treated him. So he set out, but on the road and in the marketplace and in the village no one salaamed to him or made way for him and when he begged no one gave him alms.

He soon got tired of this and hastened home and, putting on his best *pagri* and coat and *dhoti*, went back to the marketplace. This time everyone who met him on the road salaamed low to him and made way for him, and every shopkeeper to whom he went gave him alms and the people in the village who had refused before gladly made offerings to him.

The Brahman went home smiling to himself and took off his clothes and put them in a heap and prostrated himself before them three or four times, saying each time, "O source of wealth! O source of wealth! It is clothes that honored the world and nothing else."

Brahman = a wise or spiritual man	
salaamed = bowed	
alms = food or money	
pagri = turban	
dhoti = waistcloth	

---

1 The Brahman is treated unkindly because he

  A lacks common sense

  B looks ragged and tattered

  C takes food from others

  D does not have good manners

2 When the Brahman "prostrated himself" before the clothes, he was acting like

  F he didn't like the clothes

  G he was praying to the clothes

  H he was cleaning the clothes

  J he was ripping the clothes

3 Read this sentence from "The Brahman's Clothes."

> **Like many Brahmans he lived by begging and was very clever at wheedling money out of people.**

In this sentence, the phrase "wheedling money out of people" means about the same as

A urging people to give him money

B cheating people out of money

C forcing people to give him money

D stealing money from people

Directions
Read this story from Africa about how the cat became a household pet. Then answer questions 4 through 7.

"The Cat Who Came Indoors"
Retold by Hugh Tracey

Once upon a time, there was a cat, a wild cat, who lived all by herself out in the bush. After a while she got tired of living alone and took herself a husband, another wild cat who she thought was the finest creature in all the jungle.

One day, as they strolled together along the path through the tall grass, *swish*, out of the grass jumped Leopard, and Cat's husband was bowled over, all fur and claws, into the dust.

"O-oh!" said Cat. "I see my husband is covered in dust and is not the finest creature in all the jungle. It is Leopard." So Cat went to live with Leopard.

They lived together very happily until one day, as they were hunting in the bush, suddenly—*whoosh*—out of the shadows leapt Lion right onto Leopard's back and ate him all up.

"O-o-oh!" said Cat. "I see Leopard is not the finest creature in all the jungle. It is Lion."

So Cat went to live with Lion.

They lived together very happily until one day, as they were stalking through the forest, a large shape loomed overhead, and—*fu-chu*—Elephant put one foot on top of Lion and squashed him flat.

"O-o-o-oh!" said Cat. "I see that Lion is not the finest creature in all the jungle. It is Elephant."

So Cat went to live with Elephant. She climbed up onto his back and sat purring on his neck, right between his two ears.

They lived together very happily until one day, as they were moving through the tall reeds down by the river—*pa-wa!*—there was a loud bang, and Elephant sat down onto the ground.

Cat looked around and all she could see was a small man with a gun.

"O-o-o-o-oh!" said Cat. "I see Elephant is not the finest creature in all the jungle. It is Man."

So Cat walked after Man, all the way to his home, and jumped up onto the thatch of his hut.

thatch = roof

"At last," said Cat, "I have found the finest creature in all the jungle."

She lived up in the thatch of the hut very happily and began to catch mice and rats that lived in that village. Until one day, as she sat on the roof warming herself in the sun, she heard a noise inside the hut. The voices of Man and his wife grew louder and louder until—*wara-wara-wara . . . yo-we!*— out came Man, tumbling head over heels into the dust.

"Aha!" said Cat. "Now I *do* know who is truly the finest creature in all the jungle. It is Woman."

She came down from the thatch, went inside the hut, and sat by the fire.

And that is where she has been ever since.

---

4 "The Cat Who Came Indoors" is an example of a

A fantasy
B folktale
C trickster tale
D fairy tale

5 Read this sentence from the beginning of the folktale.

> **Once upon a time, there was a cat, a wild cat, who lived all by herself out in the bush.**

The opening sentence of this folktale is similar to the beginning of a

F myth
G fable
H legend
J fairy tale

6 In telling what happens during Cat's encounters, the storyteller interjects words in *italic* type. What effect do these words have on the tale?

A They add suspense to the plot.
B They slow the pace of the story.
C They indicate the sounds of the actions.
D They show that the folktale is from Africa.

7 In this story, the cat feels that the "finest creature in all the jungle" is the one who is

F the most powerful creature
G the handsomest creature
H the smartest creature
J the friendliest creature

*D*irections

By the time this folktale was published in 1875, it was already quite old. Read the tale, and then answer questions 8 through 12.

"The Gingerbread Boy"

A Folktale from the United States
Retold by D. L. Ashliman

Now you shall hear a story that somebody's great-great-grandmother told a little girl ever so many years ago:

There was once a little old man and a little old woman, who lived in a little old house in the edge of a wood. They would have been a very happy old couple but for one thing—they had no little child, and they wished for one very much. One day, when the little old woman was baking gingerbread, she cut a cake in the shape of a little boy, and put it into the oven.

Presently she went to the oven to see if it was baked. As soon as the oven door was opened, the little gingerbread boy jumped out, and began to run away as fast as he could go.

The little old woman called her husband, and they both ran after him. But they could not catch him. And soon the gingerbread boy came to a barn full of threshers. He called out to them as he went by, saying:

> I've run away from a little old woman,
> A little old man,
> And I can run away from you, I can!

Then the barn full of threshers set out to run after him. But, though they ran fast, they could not catch him. And he ran on till he came to a field full of mowers. He called out to them:

> I've run away from a little old woman,
> A little old man,
> A barn full of threshers,
> And I can run away from you, I can!

Then the mowers began to run after him, but they couldn't catch him. And he ran on till he came to a cow. He called out to her:

> I've run away from a little old woman,
> A little old man,
> A barn full of threshers,
> A field full of mowers,
> And I can run away from you, I can!

But, though the cow started at once, she couldn't catch him. And soon he came to a pig. He called out to the pig:

> I've run away from a little old woman,
> A little old man,
> A barn full of threshers,
> A field full of mowers,
> A cow,
> And I can run away from you, I can!

But the pig ran, and couldn't catch him. And he ran till he came across a fox, and to him he called out:

> I've run away from a little old woman,
> A little old man,
> A barn full of threshers,
> A field full of mowers,
> A cow and a pig,
> And I can run away from you, I can!

Then the fox set out to run. Now foxes can run very fast, and so the fox soon caught the gingerbread boy and began to eat him up.

Presently the gingerbread boy said, "Oh dear! I'm quarter gone!" And then, "Oh, I'm half gone!" And soon, "I'm three-quarters gone!" And at last, "I'm all gone!" and never spoke again.

---

8 According to the story, the sequence of dangers from which the gingerbread boy escapes is

A man, threshers, mowers, cow, pig, fox

B man, woman, threshers, mowers, cow, pig

C woman, man, threshers, mowers, cow, pig

D woman, man, threshers, mowers, cow, pig, fox

9 The folktale is told from the point of view of

F the gingerbread boy

G the little old woman

H a storyteller who knows the thoughts of all the characters

J a storyteller who knows the thoughts of only one character

10 In the story, the old man and woman most likely wanted to catch the gingerbread boy because

A they wanted to eat the gingerbread boy

B they were angry with the gingerbread boy for running away

C they wanted to sell the gingerbread

D they wanted a child of their own

11 In the story, "threshers" are most likely

F medium-size birds

G people who do a certain type of farm work

H crops that have been harvested

J old men and women

12 Read these sentences from the end of the folktale.

> **Presently the gingerbread boy said, "Oh dear! I'm quarter gone!" And then, "Oh, I'm half gone!" And soon, "I'm three-quarters gone!" And at last, "I'm all gone!" and never spoke again.**

For most of the tale, the gingerbread boy speaks in a songlike rhyme that keeps growing as the story goes on. Why does the storyteller shift from rhyme to direct quotation at the end of the story? Explain the effect of the use of direct quotation at the end of the folktale.

The BIG Question

When Is the Price Too High?

" What you risk reveals what you value. "

—Jeanette Winterson,
contemporary British novelist

LOOKING AHEAD

The skill lessons and readings in this unit will help you develop your own answer to the Big Question.

UNIT 3 WRAP-UP • Answering the Big Question

Connecting to ❓ The BIG Question — When Is the Price Too High?

When is a decision worth its price, when is the price too high, and how do you know? In this unit you'll read about what prices people pay for their decisions and what they think about their decisions later on.

Real Kids and the Big Question

DORI and Charise have been friends since they were little girls. Dori wants to be friends with a popular group of girls that don't like Charise. Now, Dori has been avoiding Charise. Do you think that becoming part of a popular group is worth the price of friendship? Why or why not?

RAUL likes to play the piano. He spends hours practicing. His friends think he should spend more time with them, just hanging out and having fun. But Raul says he wants to play in an orchestra someday, and he has to practice if he wants to be good. For him practicing the piano is fun. Is what Raul wants to do worth not being with his friends? Why or why not?

Warm-Up Activity

What would you be willing to pay a price to do? Write your answer in your Learner's Notebook. Then give an example of something you wouldn't do because the price would be too high.

You and the Big Question

The question of whether the price is too high comes up in many situations. As you read the selections in this unit, think about how you would answer the Big Question. That will help guide your thinking throughout this unit.

Literature Online

BIG Question

Link to Web resources to further explore the Big Question at www.glencoe.com.

Plan for the Unit Challenge

At the end of the unit, you'll use notes from all your reading to complete the Unit Challenge.

You'll choose one of the following activities:

A. What's the Ending? Write a story with two different endings.

B. Is It Worth It? Create a chart that lists the pros and cons of a decision.

- Start thinking about which activity you'd like to do so that you can focus your thoughts as you go through the unit.

- In your Learner's Notebook write your thoughts about the activity you'd like to do and why.

- Each time you make notes about the Big Question, think about how your ideas will help you with the Unit Challenge activity you chose.

Keep Track of Your Ideas

As you read, you'll make notes about the Big Question. Later, you'll use these notes to complete the Unit Challenge. See pages R8–R9 for help with making each Unit 3 Foldable. This diagram shows how each should look.

1. Make one Foldable for each workshop. Keep all of your Foldables for the unit in your Foldables folder.

2. On the bottom fold of your Foldable, write the workshop number and the Big Question.

3. Write the titles of the selections in the workshop on the front of the flaps—one title on each flap. (See page 289 for the titles.)

4. Open the flaps. At the very top of each flap, write **My Purpose for Reading.** Below each crease, write **The Big Question.**

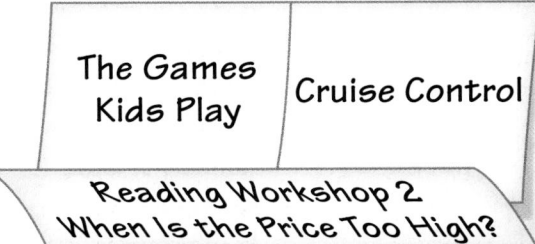

What Are Informational Articles?

Informational articles present information, facts, and explanations of topics. They are found in textbooks as well as newspapers, magazines, and Web sites.

Why Read Informational Articles?

When you want information about an unfamiliar topic or something you're interested in learning about, you can often find it in informational articles. For example, you can use informational articles to get the latest news, find interesting facts, and learn how to make something.

How to Read Informational Articles

Key Reading Skills

These key reading skills are useful for reading and understanding informational articles. You'll see these skills modeled in the Active Reading Model on pages 293–295, and you'll learn more about them in this unit.

- ■ **Previewing** Look over a selection before you read it to see what it is about. (See Reading Workshop 1.)
- ■ **Skimming and scanning** Skim a selection by reading through quickly for a general overview. Scan to find key words and phrases. (See Reading Workshop 2.)
- ■ **Understanding text structures** Look at how the writing is organized. (See Reading Workshop 3.)
- ■ **Identifying main idea and supporting details** Find the most important idea and the details that help support it. (See Reading Workshop 4.)

Key Literary and Text Elements

Recognizing and thinking about the following literary elements will help you understand informational articles better.

- ■ **Tone:** the writer's attitude toward a subject (See "Gymnasts in Pain.")
- ■ **Evidence:** facts, expert opinion, studies, and other types of details used to support an idea or an opinion (See "The Games Kids Play.")
- ■ **Irony:** the difference between what is expected and what actually happens or exists (See "Flowers for Algernon," Part 1.)
- ■ **Photographs:** pictures that explain, clarify, or add more information to an informational article (See "Tattoos: Fad, Fashion, or Folly?")

Skills Focus

- How to read informational articles

Skills Model

You will see how to use the key reading skills and literary elements as you read

- **"A Tremendous Trade,"** p. 293

NY English Language Arts Core Curriculum (pp. 292–295)

R1d Preview informational texts to assess content and organization. **LC R12** Combine multiple strategies to enhance comprehension and response. **R1f** Use knowledge of structure to understand informational text. **R1b** Apply thinking skills to interpret data, facts, and ideas from informational texts. **R2d** Determine how the use and meaning of literary devices convey the author's message or intent.

For a complete description of the standards, see p. NY11.

TIME

The notes in the side columns model how to use the reading skills and literary elements you read about on page 292.

Informational Articles

ACTIVE READING MODEL

A Tremendous TRADE

A superstar swap had baseball fans buzzing. **1**

By JEREMY CAPLAN

In early 2004, the New York Yankees rocked the baseball world by trading two players, second baseman Alfonso Soriano and a minor league player, to get Alex Rodriguez, who is widely considered the game's best player. It was the first time in Major League Baseball history that the current most valuable player had been traded. "I think the coolest thing in the world is being a Yankee and having the opportunity to win consistently," said Rodriguez, whose nickname is A-Rod. His former team, the Texas Rangers, had finished in last place for the last three seasons that A-Rod was with them. **2**

A-Rod played shortstop with the Rangers but plays third base for the Yankees because the team already has an all-star shortstop in Derek Jeter. When A-Rod first joined the Yankees, he was the highest paid player in the Major Leagues. His contract with the Yankees will earn him $252 million over 10 years. **3**

Timothy A. Clary/AFP/Getty Images

$25,200,000
In his first New York press conference, **ALEX RODRIGUEZ** says he feels honored and proud to be a Yankee.

1 Key Reading Skill
Previewing *Glancing at the title and subtitle, I see that the article is about baseball teams trading players. The graphics show how much money the players make. It's amazing how high their salaries are.*

2 Key Reading Skill
Skimming and Scanning *As I skim the article, I see that it names Alex Rodriguez several times. I'm going to scan to find out how much he makes.*

3 Key Literary Element
Irony *It's ironic that the team with the most valuable player ended up as the last-place team for three years. I would expect it to win with such a great player.*

Many fans celebrated A-Rod's switch to New York, saying that his presence on the team would make baseball more exciting. Other fans say he's overpaid.

You Get What You Pay For

Some people say the league should limit players' salaries. They argue that some salaries are so high that teams with smaller budgets simply cannot afford to compete with richer teams. "We have a spending limit, and the Yankees apparently don't," said John Henry, owner of the rival Boston Red Sox. Henry's attempt to get Rodriguez to play for his team failed. 4

Other people question why baseball players earn so much more than people in other professions who may struggle to make a living. For example, how is it that a baseball player can earn more than 800 times what some teachers earn in one year? 5

It might not seem fair, but in every profession, workers earn whatever people are willing to pay them. Baseball is no exception. Teams compete to offer as much money as they can to players who are among the league's best, like Rodriguez. Because baseball is such a popular sport, watched by ticket-buying fans at stadiums and on television by millions, a team can earn many millions of dollars each season. Teams use much of their earnings to pay their stars' salaries because the best players attract the most fans to games. For example, soon after the Yankees announced that A-Rod would be coming to town, the team sold $2 million worth of tickets. 6

4 Key Reading Skill
Identifying Main Idea and Supporting Details *The main idea of this paragraph seems to be that all teams cannot compete for the same players because they don't all have the same amount of money. The quotation from John Henry and the fact that his team couldn't hire A-Rod are details that support the main idea.*

5 Key Text Element
Evidence *The author states that a player may make 800 times as much as a teacher. He uses this statistic as evidence that players may be paid too much.*

6 Key Reading Skill
Understanding Text Structures *The word* because *shows up twice in this paragraph. I see that this cause-and-effect text structure explains why teams can pay players so much.*

$53,000,000
Pitcher PEDRO MARTINEZ helped the Boston Red Sox win the 2004 World Series. Can he do the same for the New York Mets?

Lou Cappozola/Sports Illustrated

Can Money Buy a Winner?

Now that the Yankees have A-Rod, New York fans have high hopes for future success. But Rodriguez alone won't guarantee his new team championships. "If you're a team with more money, you get to hire better players, but it doesn't mean you're going to win," says Andrew Zimbalist, a top sports economist.[1] Injuries, batting slumps, a lack of teamwork, and even bad luck can get in the way.

Even though the baseball world buzzed about the big trade and star players' soaring salaries, A-Rod and his teammates will be expected to catch, throw, and swing their way to success for years to come. After all, when the World Series rolls around each October, it will be skills, not salaries, that count. **7 8**

—Updated 2005,
from *TIME FOR KIDS*,
February 27, 2004

David N. Seelig/Icon SMI

$20,000,000
Boston Red Sox slugger **MANNY RAMIREZ** has averaged more than 40 homers a year over the last seven seasons.

$18,900,000
New York Yankees' captain, sure-handed shortstop **DEREK JETER**, has helped guide the team to the World Series at least four times.

7 Key Text Element
Photographs *The photos of players on these pages are exciting action shots. They help me understand why baseball players get huge salaries.*

8 Key Literary Element
Tone *The words* buzzed *and* soaring *make me think of action and excitement. I can almost hear the crowd at a game. The writer's tone seems fair and friendly, but he's also excited about baseball.*

---

1. An *economist* is someone who studies money and the ways things of value are made, bought, and sold.

Write to Learn Answer the following question in your Learner's Notebook. Imagine that you are going to write a letter to the editor of a sports magazine on the subject of salaries earned by professional athletes. What would you say about the very large amounts of money they earn?

Study Central Visit www.glencoe.com and click on Study Central to review informational articles.

Skills Focus

You will practice using these skills when you read the following selections:
- "Gymnasts in Pain: Out of Balance," p. 300
- "In Response to Executive Order 9066," p. 312

Reading

- Previewing to understand texts, their structures, and their purposes

Literature

- Understanding tone

Vocabulary

- Understanding multiple-meaning words in context
- Academic Vocabulary: *available*

Writing/Grammar

- Identifying types of sentences
- Correctly using end marks of punctuation

NY English Language Arts Core Curriculum (pp. 296–297)

R1d Preview informational texts to assess content and organization.

For a complete description of the standards, see p. NY11.

Skill Lesson

Previewing

Learn It!

What Is It? **Previewing** is looking over something to see what it's like in order to find out what you can expect from it. You probably preview often without even realizing it. For example, when you rent a movie, you preview it by reading the title and the description on the back of the case. Previewing helps you make good use of **available** information.

Analyzing Cartoons
Peter previews the book and learns, to his dismay, that the text is tiny. What else can you learn about a selection from looking over it before you read?

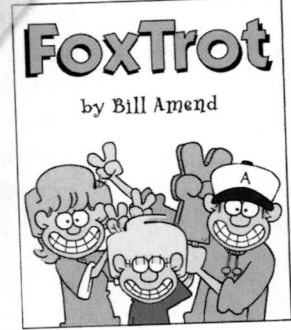

FOXTROT © 2001 Bill Amend. Reprinted with permission of UNIVERSAL PRESS SYNDICATE. All rights reserved.

Academic Vocabulary

available (uh VAY luh bul) *adj.* at hand; easily obtained

Why Is It Important? Previewing a reading selection saves you time by giving you a head start with your reading. Previewing helps you do all these things:

- understand what the text is about
- decide whether you want or need to read it
- plan a strategy for reading the text

How Do I Do It? Before you read a selection, follow these steps:

1. Look at the title, headlines, or anything in bold (heavy, dark) letters.
2. Look over pictures, charts, captions, and other text features.
3. Read the first paragraph and the first lines or sentences of other paragraphs. Try to find the most important information.
4. Quickly describe for yourself what the selection is about.
5. Decide whether to read the selection and how you'll read it.

Here's what one student learned from previewing "A Tremendous Trade."

Study Central Visit www.glencoe .com and click on Study Central to review previewing.

1. I can tell from the title, subheads, and graphics that this story is about baseball, money, and winning games.
2. The graphics show how much money some players make.
3. From reading the first lines of several paragraphs, I think the most important part is the section "You Get What You Pay For."
4. This article seems to be about how much money baseball players make and why they can get so much.

Practice It!

Pretend you haven't already worked through pages 296–297. Go back and preview this skill lesson. Follow steps 1–4 above. Write your preview notes in your Learner's Notebook.

Use It!

Before you read the next two selections, preview them. After you preview each text, write in your Learner's Notebook two things you learned from previewing.

Before You Read

Scott M. Reid

Meet the Author

Scott M. Reid is a sports reporter for the *Orange County Register* newspaper. Before joining the *Register* in 1996, Reid worked at the *Atlanta Journal Constitution* and at the *Dallas Times Herald.*

Author Search For more about Scott M. Reid, go to www.glencoe.com.

NY English Language Arts Core Curriculum (pp. 298–307)

LC R9 Recognize multiple meanings of words. **R1d** Preview informational texts to assess content and organization. **R2d** Determine how the use and meaning of literary devices convey the author's message or intent. **R2g** Compare literature to own lives.

For a complete description of the standards, see p. NY11.

Gymnasts in Pain: Out of Balance

Vocabulary Preview

expectations (ek spek TAY shunz) *n.* what someone thinks is likely to happen **(p. 301)** *People have the same high expectations of gymnasts as they do of other professional athletes.*

maneuvers (muh NOO vurs) *n.* clever or skillful moves or actions **(p. 301)** *Gymnasts must learn a complicated set of maneuvers to compete on gymnastics equipment.*

elite (eh LEET) *adj.* best, or most skilled **(p. 302)** *The most elite gymnasts compete in the Olympics.*

decades (DEK aydz) *n.* periods of ten years **(p. 306)** *Most gymnasts compete for only a few years of their lives before they retire, but the pain from injury lasts for many decades.*

Partner Talk With a partner write a paragraph about athletes in professional sports. Use all the vocabulary words above in your paragraph.

English Language Coach

Multiple-Meaning Words You already know that words can have many, or multiple, meanings. For example, you probably know the word *pool* as it relates to a swimming pool and even to the game of pool. But what does it mean in the following sentence?

• The students added their money to the *pool* for a new school flag.

You need to know another definition for the word *pool* to understand what the sentence means. A *pool* can be a supply or collection shared by a group. In the sentence above, then, *pool* is the collection of money that students are gathering, not a body of water or a game.

Watch for this word and other multiple-meaning words when you read "Gymnasts in Pain: Out of Balance." Use context clues or a dictionary to figure out what the words mean.

Write to Learn How many different meanings do you know for each word listed below? Write the words and their meanings in your Learner's Notebook. Then look up each word in a dictionary. If you left out definitions, add them.

1. break
2. deal
3. senior
4. tumble

Skills Preview

Key Reading Skill: Previewing

Remember that previewing gives you a head start in understanding what you read. To preview, read the title and headings. Examine photographs, charts, and other illustrations, and read their captions.

Partner Talk What might you learn by previewing an article before you read it closely? Talk it over.

Key Literary Element: Tone

Tone is an author's attitude toward the subject he or she is writing about. Any word that can be used to describe an attitude can also be used to describe a tone. Some examples are *objective, serious, sarcastic, lighthearted, sad,* and *angry.*

The tone of a selection is shown in the words that the author uses. When you read, look for the emotion behind the words. That emotion reveals the tone.

Here is the way three different people might talk about a job they're doing.
- We have a few problems that we will work out easily.
- It's going to be hard to get through this.
- This job is a real mess.

To identify the tone of "Gymnasts in Pain: Out of Balance," ask yourself these questions:
- *Why did the author choose certain words and details?*
- *What feeling, if any, do these words communicate?*

Partner Work Tell the plot of the story "Goldilocks and the Three Bears" in two different tones. First tell the story as if the narrator is angry with Goldilocks and thinks she's a little jerk. Then tell it with Goldilocks being a very sweet girl.

Interactive Literary Elements Handbook
To review or learn more about the literary elements, go to www.glencoe.com.

Get Ready to Read

Connect to the Reading

Think about a goal that was really important to you. How hard were you willing to work for it? As you read about the gymnasts, think about how their experiences compare to your own.

Write to Learn Describe your experiences with having a goal and the effort it took to reach it.

Build Background

The information in this article comes from a survey the writer did of more than 100 members of the United States women's national gymnastics teams.

- In the sport today, female gymnasts reach their peak before age sixteen, which means they are competing when their bodies are still growing and have less strength than that of an adult.
- More than a half-million kids take part in U.S. school-sponsored gymnastics competitions.
- Every year more than 25,000 children under the age of fifteen are treated in U.S. hospital emergency rooms for injuries related to gymnastics. Most of these injuries are mild to moderate. The most common injuries are sprains, strains, and stress fractures. However, serious injuries also occur.

Set Purposes for Reading

BIG Question Read "Gymnasts in Pain: Out of Balance" to find out what some girls experience as they try to become the best gymnasts in the world. What do they gain? What do they lose?

Set Your Own Purpose What else would you like to learn from this article to help you answer the Big Question? Write your own purpose on the "Gymnasts in Pain" flap of the Foldable for Workshop 1.

Keep Moving

Use these skills as you read "Gymnasts in Pain: Out of Balance."

INFORMATIONAL TEXT
NEWSPAPER
Orange County Register

Gymnasts in Pain: Out of Balance

by Scott M. Reid
December 19, 2004

By the time Alyssa Beckerman arrived for a U.S. national team training camp at Bela Karolyi's Texas ranch, three months before the 2000 Olympic Games, she wasn't sure what hurt worse. The year-old break in her wrist that hadn't been allowed to heal? Or her stomach burning from nerves and a daily diet of anti-inflammatory[1] drugs? ◻1

The 19-year-old U.S. champion broke her wrist a year earlier, but she continued to compete and train 40 hours a week—pressured, she said, by an often-screaming coach who accused her of faking the injury and driven by her own desire to win Olympic gold.

"That's what you've been dreaming about since you were a little girl," she said.

By the time she retired from international gymnastics later that year, Beckerman had broken nine bones and undergone two surgeries. ◻2

---

1. *Anti-inflammatory* (an tye in FLAM uh tor ee) drugs make swelling go down.

Practice the Skills

◻1 **Key Reading Skill**

Previewing To preview the article, read the title and subtitle. Look at the pictures and read the headings. Reread the first paragraph. What do you think the main idea of the article is?

◻2 **Key Literary Element**

Tone So far, the tone is disapproving. Here are some words and phrases that reveal this tone:

- Alyssa Beckerman says she was "pressured . . . by an often-screaming coach."

- The article says the coach "accused [Beckerman] of faking the injury."

The *Orange County Register* interviewed nearly half of the **roughly** 300 women who competed on the U.S. junior or senior national teams from 1982 to 2004. **3** More than 93 percent of the women interviewed suffered broken bones or had injuries that required surgery.

Current and former U.S. national team members—almost all girls in their early and mid-teens—describe a way of life that repeatedly places girls in danger. They train year-round as much as twelve hours a day, often living thousands of miles from home and away from other teens.

Like Beckerman, they do so often with broken bones or torn muscles and almost always without regular, if any, medical care. At the same time, they must deal with pressures and **expectations** similar to those for highly paid pro athletes.

The *Register* also found:

The rate of injuries has almost doubled since 1966 as women train longer and try more daring and dramatic **maneuvers.**

Nine out of every ten gymnasts interviewed said that they had continued to train on injuries that resulted in broken bones or surgery or that they had begun training again without getting a doctor's OK.

The sport's obsession with weight and diet, especially within the U.S. national team program, often has led to eating disorders. U.S. gymnasts competing in the 2001 World Championships said they were provided so little food that family members smuggled snacks into the team hotel by stuffing them inside teddy bears.

Three out of four gymnasts interviewed continue to experience health problems related to gymnastics.

Top gymnastics officials downplayed the *Register's* finding. Robert V. Colarossi, chief executive officer of USA Gymnastics, insisted his sport is no different from any other.

Practice the Skills

3 | English Language Coach

Multiple-Meaning Words
Roughly comes from the word *rough*. One meaning of *rough* is "not smooth." Another is "approximately, or about." Which definition of *roughly* makes sense here?

Vocabulary

expectations (ek spek TAY shunz) *n.* what someone thinks is likely to happen

maneuvers (muh NOO vurs) *n.* clever or skillful moves or actions

"**Elite** athletes in every sport push themselves to the limit," he said. He noted that the 22 years covered in the *Register*'s survey was a time of change in the sport. "It's unfair to draw an analysis over that many years," Colarossi continued. "The kids are doing skills that are more and more difficult. The equipment is getting better but still has a ways to go. The (scoring) is more difficult. In the past the sport was based more on artistry, and now it's based a lot more on skill. The one thing that hasn't changed is gravity. That's the constant."

Colarossi acknowledged gymnastics has "a lot more (physical) impact than other sports." Don Peters, head coach of the 1984 U.S. Olympic team, said he didn't believe the sports injury rates were as high as the *Register* found but said the comparison between gymnastics and the NFL is valid. "We're both contact sports," said Peters, owner of Scats Gymnastics Academy in Huntington Beach. "But in gymnastics we're dealing with very fragile athletes who don't wear protective gear. We're doing really dangerous things. We're flying through the air . . . . I think you have to remember whatever goes up has to come down. And every time something comes down, there's a chance somebody's going to get hurt. Considering everything, I think we do an amazing job."

Record numbers of Americans tune in every four years to what has become the Summer Olympics' most popular event. But behind the sparkly outfits, smiles and perfect 10's is a sport that has left a generation of young American women bearing physical and emotional scars that many will carry for the rest of their lives. **4**

Doctors discovered 22 stress fractures[2] on the spine of Olympian Kelly Garrison. Double Olympic medalist Kathy Johnson said she took so many anti-inflammatory drugs to deal with her injuries that she had to wash down the pills with Maalox. Melinda Baimbridge, a U.S. team member in

Practice the Skills

4 **Key Literary Element**

Tone Think about the image the author is creating here. Is it a clue to the author's tone? Explain.

---

2. A ***stress fracture*** is a very thin break in a bone, usually from putting too much pressure (stress) on the bone.

Vocabulary

elite (eh LEET) *adj.* best, or most skilled

Analyzing the Photo Spotted by her coach Bela Karolyi, Dominique Moceanu practices a difficult move. How does this picture capture the intensity of Karolyi's—and Moceanu's—concentration?

the late 1990s, trained with a fractured back even though her legs turned numb.

"People don't see the real sport," said Sierra Sapunar, a recent U.S. team member. "They see what looks pretty and elegant on the surface, but they don't realize what really goes on. All the nerves and pain and emotion and fear and abuse."

And too often, Johnson said, the sport has forgotten who the gymnasts are. "I think we have to remember," Johnson said, "yes, these are world-class athletes, but they're also little girls." **5**

Demands, injuries rise

American girls are being pushed harder than ever to reach the Olympic dream. As the sport has become more difficult—and dangerous—the demands of training have increased. An estimated 3.4 million girls participate in gymnastics in the United States—many of whom got their start in tumbling classes as toddlers. About 80,000 athletes today are registered with USA Gymnastics.

Practice the Skills

5 **Key Literary Element**

Tone How do the quotations from Sapunar and Johnson affect the tone of this article? Jot down words or phrases that support your answer.

At the very top of the sport in this country are the 120 women who compete at what is known as the elite level. It is from this group that U.S. national junior and senior teams and, finally, the Olympic team are selected. This deep talent **pool** has provided the foundation for perhaps the most successful period in USA Gymnastics' history. **6**

But, along with that success has come a sharp rise in injuries, the *Register* found in its interviews with 122 elite gymnasts. Women whose participation on the U.S. national team ended in 1994 or earlier averaged 2.75 broken bones or injuries that required surgery. Women who competed for the United States after 1996 averaged four such injuries. Overall, more than 68 percent of the gymnasts interviewed by the *Register* said they had needed surgery. **7**

Analyzing the Photo Carly Patterson focuses on her next event at a 2004 competition at Madison Square Garden. How would you describe Patterson's posture and facial expression?

Practice the Skills

6 **English Language Coach**

Multiple-Meaning Words Think about the definitions for the word **pool** that you learned in the "Before You Read" section. What is the meaning of *pool* as it is used here? How do you know?

7 **Reviewing Skills**

Fact and Opinion Does this paragraph state facts or the author's opinion? Do these facts support the opinion that seems clear from the author's tone?

Visual Vocabulary
The *uneven bars* are two horizontal bars set a distance apart from each other and raised off of the floor. A gymnast flips between the bars.

Karolyi, the well-known coach, dismissed the *Register*'s findings. "A **gross** exaggeration," he said. "There are no problems with our sport. We have an action-packed sport, and from time to time people get injured." **8**

But Carly Patterson, who won Olympic gold in 2004, acknowledged the risks. "It's a dangerous sport," said Patterson, who competed in the 2003 Worlds with a fractured elbow that would require two screws to hold it together. "It's really tough on your muscles and joints and bones. It's a lot of pounding every day."

How much pounding? Consider this: A gymnast can reach a height of 10 feet on her dismount from the uneven bars. Imagine standing on a basketball rim and jumping onto a mat less than 8 inches thick, several times a day, seven days a week. **9**

Coaches in control

At the center of the gymnast's universe is the coach. Too often, athletes said, many coaches push girls too hard even when it's clear that they're hurt.

Michelle Hilse, a U.S. team member in the 1980s, said she was struck in the head by a well-known coach after breaking her hand while training. "He yelled, 'Get out of my face,'" Hilse recalled. "Then he slapped my head and yelled, 'Stop your crying.'"

In 1998, U.S. champion Beckerman, then 17, left her family in New Jersey to train at the Cincinnati Gymnastics Academy. By the next year, her coach had her training as much as 10 hours a day, Beckerman said, while consuming fewer calories than the number recommended for a 2-year-old, 25-pound toddler. Beckerman, in fact, said she was swallowing anti-inflammatory drugs more often than she was eating.

According to Beckerman, when her training shifted to the pre-Olympic camp, her wrist throbbed constantly, and the combination of drugs and nervousness left her in so much stomach pain that she could barely stand.

Similar problems for other gymnasts have been met with yelling, scorn, disbelief, swearing, threats and even physical

Practice the Skills

8 | **English Language Coach**

Multiple-Meaning Words
You probably know that **gross** can refer to something disgusting. But there are other definitions: *adj.* huge, enormous; and *v.* to earn money. What is the meaning of *gross* as it is used here? How do you know?

9 | **Reviewing Skills**

Comparing and Contrasting
Does the comparison the author uses here help make his point?

abuse, according to dozens of gymnasts. Sixty percent of the gymnasts interviewed said they were either verbally abused by their coaches when they told them or were afraid to raise the subject with the coaches.

"The first thing they do is accuse you of making it up," said Sheehan Lemley, a U.S. team member in the late 1990s. "That's the last thing I wanted them to think. So you hold it in until it gets really bad, until you can't walk."

Lemley trained so long on an injured ankle that six operations haven't been able to repair it. "I basically ruined my ankle," she said.

Yet many gymnasts said that, even when faced with training for months on a broken bone and the almost daily verbal abuse, they didn't walk away because they had long been trained to accept injuries and pain as the price they had to pay for Olympic glory. **10**

Analyzing the Photo Coach Bela Karolyi carries injured gymnast Kerri Strug at the 1996 Olympic Games in Atlanta, Georgia. What emotions do you think Strug feels?

Legacy of pain

While a gymnast's career might be brief, her pain often lasts a lifetime. Injuries suffered as teenagers continue to affect many gymnasts **decades** later. Fifty-two percent of retired U.S. team members who spoke to the *Register* have had surgery for injuries related to gymnastics.

"I've been in constant pain since 1985," said Lisa McVay, a U.S. team member in the 1980s who broke her back at age 15. "I live with it daily. I deal with it constantly."

Double Olympic medalist Johnson has had five knee surgeries since winning her medals in 1984. Sunja Knapp, a U.S. team member in the 1980s, fractured her back three times between ages 12 and 14. Today, at 31, she sometimes needs a half-hour to get out of bed in the morning.

Practice the Skills

10 **Reviewing Skills**

Author's Purpose What do you think the author's purpose was in this article?

Vocabulary

decades (DEK aydz) *n.* periods of ten years

Former Olympian Garrison is facing knee surgery and hip replacement at age 37.

In 1991, Michelle Campi won a silver medal at the World Championships. By 1994, she was training 10 hours a day, six days a week. "I was emotionally tired," she said. "I was exhausted. I was an accident waiting to happen."

The crash came late in a workout while Campi was working on a move on the uneven bars. She lost her grip, fell and landed on her back.

"I don't think she broke anything," Campi recalled her coach telling her mother, Celi Campi, who was in the gym at the time.

"My mother said, 'She needs to take a break. She needs a break,'" Campi continued. "He said, 'No, we'll soak her in an ice bath after practice. She'll be fine.' So he made me climb back up on the bar. It was really painful. I dropped down and had this sensation that I was going to throw up."

Celi Campi finally took her daughter to the emergency room. Campi had fractured her back. Rods had to be inserted to support her spine. None of it seemed to matter to Campi as she lay in a hospital bed that night.

"It was really weird," she said. "Life as I knew it was over. I was lying there in bed, and I wasn't thinking about whether I was going to be able to walk again. I wasn't thinking about what was going to happen to my life—was I going to be crippled? I don't know if relieved is the right word, but I kept thinking, 'At least I don't have to go into the gym tomorrow. I don't have to go back into the gym.'" **11** ○

Practice the Skills

11 🗨**BIG** Question
Why do you think girls and young women pay such a high price to compete in international gymnastics? After reading this article, do you think the price is too high? Write your answers on the "Gymnasts in Pain" flap of the Foldable for Workshop 1. Your response will help you complete the Unit Challenge later.

Analyzing the Photo Gymnast Kathy Johnson competes on the balance beam in the 1984 Olympics.

After You Read

Gymnasts in Pain: Out of Balance

Answering the ⬤ BIG Question

1. The gymnasts in the article suffered pain and damage to their bodies while trying to become the best gymnasts in the world. Do you think the price they and other athletes pay to be the best is too high? Explain.

2. **Recall** Besides physical injuries, what other serious health problems might gymnasts experience?

   TIP Think and Search

3. **Summarize** What kind of negative response have some gymnasts received from their coaches after reporting their injuries?

   TIP Think and Search

Critical Thinking

4. **Analyze** Why do you think young gymnasts are being pushed so hard to reach the Olympic dream?

   TIP Author and Me

5. **Analyze** Why would the gymnast Michelle Campi have felt relief while she was lying in the hospital bed? Have you ever felt the same way about something? Explain.

   TIP Author and Me

6. **Evaluate** Do you think the writer presented a fair picture of training for international gymnastic competition? Why or why not? Use specific details from the article to support your opinion.

   TIP Author and Me

Talk About Your Reading

Class Debate Divide into two teams and debate the positive and negative sides of training for international gymnastic competition.

- Start with a statement about whether or not you support international gymnastics competition.
- Explain your position.
- Give specific reasons to support your position.
- Respond to at least one point the other team makes.

**NY English Language Arts
Core Curriculum** (pp. 308–309)

LC R17 Demonstrate comprehension and response through a range of activities.
LC S8 Participate in group discussions.
R1d Preview informational texts to assess content and organization. **R2d** Determine how the use and meaning of literary devices convey the author's message or intent. **LC R9** Recognize multiple meanings of words. **Core W8** Use correct grammatical construction in sentences.

For a complete description of the standards, see p. NY11.

Skills Review

Key Reading Skill: Previewing

7. What did you do to preview the selection before you read it? Which previewing skill helped you the most to understand the reading? Explain.

Key Literary Element: Tone

8. What does the phrase "out of balance" in the title tell readers about the writer's attitude?

9. What is the overall tone of this article? Support your answer with specific details from the article.

Reviewing Skills: Fact and Opinion

10. The author of this article has very strong opinions about the practices of women's gymnastics. Does he support these opinions with facts? Write a few sentences about what you think the author's opinion is and how he does or does not support them. Be sure to consider the statements of the athletes themselves.

Vocabulary Check

Match each word to its correct definition. Then use each word in a sentence.

11. expectations		**a.**	clever or skillful moves or actions
12. elite		**b.**	periods of ten years
13. decades		**c.**	what someone thinks is likely to happen
14. maneuvers		**d.**	best, most skilled

15. **English Language Coach** Write two sentences using a different meaning of the word *pool* in each sentence. Then do the same for the word *gross.*

16. **Academic Vocabulary** If your teacher asks you to find out what kinds of resources are **available** in the neighborhood library, what is he or she asking you to do?

Grammar Link: Sentence Types

A sentence is a group of words that expresses a complete thought. There are four types of sentences.

A **declarative sentence** makes a statement or tells something about the subject of the sentence.

• Sonya is practicing. • I like popsicles.

An **interrogative sentence** asks a question.

• Did Hanna soak her foot? • What is your address?

An **imperative sentence** gives a command. In other types of sentences, the subject is stated. In imperative sentences, the subject is the word *you.* However, *you* isn't written down or spoken in commands—it's just "understood" that the subject is *you.* For example, in the sentence *Sit down,* the speaker means *(You) sit down.*

• Pick up your socks now! • Come back at 3:00.

An **exclamatory sentence** expresses strong feeling.

• We won the competition! • That book was funny!

Grammar Practice

Copy each sentence below. Then write whether the sentence is *declarative, interrogative, imperative,* or *exclamatory.*

17. Do you like scary movies?

18. Juan skated all afternoon.

19. Stop!

20. I want to go now!

Web Activities For eFlashcards, Selection Quick Checks, and other Web activities, go to www.glencoe.com.

Before You Read

Dwight Okita

Meet the Author

Dwight Okita was born in 1958 in Chicago, where he still lives. He started writing poems in first grade and published his first book of poems in 1992. His mother's experience at a relocation camp during World War II inspired Mr. Okita to write "In Response to Executive Order 9066." For more about Dwight Okita, see page R5 of the Author Files in the back of this book.

Author Search For more about Dwight Okita, go to www.glencoe.com.

NY English Language Arts Core Curriculum (pp. 310–313)

LC R9 Recognize multiple meanings of words. **LC R13** Use text structure and literary devices to aid comprehension and response. **R2f** Identify poetic elements to interpret poetry. **R2g** Compare literature to own lives.

For a complete description of the standards, see p. NY11.

In Response to Executive Order 9066

Vocabulary Preview

descent (dih SENT) *n.* the family relation of a person to his or her ancestors; ancestry **(p. 312)** *Many people of Japanese descent live along the west coast of the United States.*

ripened (RYPE und) *v.* became ready to eat; form of the verb *ripen* **(p. 313)** *She knew the tomatoes had ripened when they turned completely red.*

Write to Learn With a partner, write a sentence for each word in the Vocabulary Preview.

English Language Coach

Multiple-Meaning Words While reading, you may find that a familiar word has unfamiliar meanings. When this happens, try to figure out the unfamiliar meaning by using context clues. If that doesn't work, use a dictionary to look up all the meanings of the word. Then choose the meaning that makes sense in context. Suppose, for example, that you see the word *mules* used in an unusual way:

• The woman sat on the edge of her bed and slipped into her mules.

You can tell that mules are not animals in the context of the sentence. So what are they? Look below at the sample dictionary entry for the word. Which definition makes the most sense?

---

mule (myool) *n.* [Middle English, from Old French *mul,* from Latin *mulus*] **1.** a cross between a horse and a donkey **2.** an unusually inflexible or stubborn person **3.** machinery that twists fiber into thread **4.** a slip-on shoe or slipper

---

Definition 4—a slip-on shoe or slipper—makes the most sense in the context of the sentence.

Partner Talk Discuss the different meanings of each word below. How many meanings for each word can you think of?

1. race
2. recall
3. round
4. run
5. sentence

Skills Preview

Key Reading Skill: Previewing

Before you read the poem, read the Build Background information on this page. Then preview the poem by looking at its title, its shape, and the first two or three lines. Quickly look at the rest of the poem.

Whole Class Discussion What do you think the poem will be about? Why?

Literary Element: Symbol

A **symbol** is a person, place, or thing that stands for, or represents, something else. Sometimes writers use common symbols, such as a dove to represent peace or the colors red, white, and blue to represent the United States. Other times writers create special symbols for particular stories or poems. Use these tips to find and understand symbols:

- Look for common symbols you've seen in other selections, such as a rose representing love.
  Do any familiar symbols appear in the selection?

- Notice which objects seem to be especially meaningful to the narrator or a character.
  Is there an object that has special importance to one of the characters?

- Think about qualities, emotions, or ideas that are associated with the meaningful objects.
  What does the object make you think of?

Whole Class Discussion What do you think each of the following objects symbolizes? As a class, discuss your ideas.

wedding ring • American flag • snake

Literature Online

Interactive Literary Elements Handbook
To review or learn more about the literary elements, go to www.glencoe.com.

Get Ready to Read

Connect to the Reading

Recall a time when you were accused of doing something that you didn't do. How did you feel? As you read the poem, imagine how the speaker feels.

Partner Talk Discuss what it's like to be unfairly accused of something. Then talk about why this can happen to a whole group of people. What can be done to prevent it?

Build Background

- As used in the poem's title, the term "executive order" refers to a rule or order issued by the President of the United States. An executive order has the same force and effect as a law that has been passed by Congress.

- In December 1941 Japanese planes attacked the U.S naval base at Pearl Harbor, Hawaii. The United States then declared war on Japan and entered World War II. A wave of fear and prejudice against Japanese Americans swept over the U.S.

- In February 1942 President Franklin D. Roosevelt signed Executive Order 9066. Under that order, Japanese Americans who lived along the West Coast were forced to leave their homes and move to "internment camps," or "relocation centers." More than 100,000 people had to live in these camps until the end of the war.

Set Purposes for Reading

BIG Question Read "In Response to Executive Order 9066" to learn about the sacrifice an American teenager had to make during World War II.

Set Your Own Purpose What else would you like to learn from this poem to help you answer the Big Question? Write your own purpose on the "In Response to Executive Order 9066" flap of the Foldable for Workshop 1.

Keep Moving

Use these skills as you read "In Response to Executive Order 9066."

In Response to Executive Order 9066

All Americans of Japanese **Descent** Must **Report** to Relocation Centers **1**

by Dwight Okita

2 Dear Sirs:

  Of course I'll come. I've packed my galoshes*
and three packets of tomato seeds. Denise calls them
love apples. My father says where we're going
5 they won't grow. **3**

  I am a fourteen-year-old girl with bad spelling
and a messy room. If it helps any, I will tell you
I have always felt funny using chopsticks
and my favorite food is hot dogs.
10 My best friend is a white girl named Denise—
we look at boys together. She sat in front of me
all through grade school because of our names:
O'Connor, Ozawa. I know the back of Denise's head
very well.

  I tell her she's going bald. She tells me I copy on tests.
15 We are best friends.

---

2. *Galoshes* (gah LAH shez) are waterproof covers for shoes that protect them from rain or snow.

Vocabulary

descent (dih SENT) *n.* the family relation of a person to his or her ancestors; ancestry

Practice the Skills

1 **English Language Coach**

Multiple-Meaning Words
What is the correct meaning of the word **report** as it is used in the subtitle?

2 **Key Reading Skill**

Previewing Look quickly at the structure of the poem. Why do you think the poet wrote in the form of a letter? Explain.

3 **Literary Element**

Symbol The tomato seeds must be important to the speaker because they're one of only two objects she packs. Also, it's unusual to call tomato seeds "love apples." These clues hint that tomato seeds may be a symbol in the poem.

I saw Denise today in Geography class.
She was sitting on the other side of the room.
"You're trying to start a war," she said, "giving secrets
away to the Enemy. Why can't you keep your big
20   mouth shut?"

I didn't know what to say.
I gave her a packet of tomato seeds
and asked her to plant them for me, told her
when the first tomato **ripened**
25   she'd miss me. **4 5** ○

4 | **Literary Element**

Symbol The speaker asks Denise to plant tomato seeds. Think about all the feelings and ideas that might be associated with planting seeds. What do you think the tomato seeds represent?

5 **BIG Question**

What does the speaker of the poem lose because of Executive Order 9066? What does Denise lose? Do you think they pay too high a price? Write your answers on the "In Response to Executive Order 9066" flap of the Foldable for Workshop 1. Your response will help you complete the Unit Challenge later.

Vocabulary

ripened (RYPE und) *v.* became ready to eat

After You Read

Early Tomato Seed 29¢

In Response to Executive Order 9066

Answering the 🐦 BIG Question

1. Putting Japanese Americans in relocation centers was intended to make other Americans feel safer. Do you believe in security at any cost, or would you draw the line at relocation centers? Explain.

2. **Recall** How do Denise's feelings toward the speaker change as a result of Executive Order 9066?

   TIP Think and Search

3. **Recall** What does the speaker ask Denise to do for her?

   TIP Right There

Critical Thinking

4. **Interpret** In lines 3–5 the speaker says love apples won't grow where the family is going. What do you think these lines say about the relocation camp they're going to?

   TIP Author and Me

5. **Infer** Why do you think Denise accuses her best friend of trying to start a war? Where do you think she got that idea?

   TIP Author and Me

6. **Evaluate** The poet chose to write his poem as a letter written by a young girl. How does that choice affect your understanding of the poem? Do you think it's a good choice? Explain.

   TIP Author and Me

Write About Your Reading

Letter Imagine that you are the speaker's friend Denise. Write a letter that apologizes for the way you acted. Explain why you were mean and what you miss about the speaker.

NY English Language Arts Core Curriculum (pp. 314–315)

LC R17 Demonstrate comprehension and response through a range of activities. **LC W5** Write with voice to address varied purposes. **LC R13** Use text structure and literary devices to aid comprehension and response. **R2f** Identify poetic elements to interpret poetry. **LC R9** Recognize multiple meanings of words. **Core W7** Observe rules of punctuation.

For a complete description of the standards, see p. NY11.

Skills Review

Key Reading Skill: Previewing

7. How did previewing the poem help you understand it? Explain.

Literary Element: Symbol

8. What does Denise call tomatoes? What do you think the speaker wants Denise to realize about their friendship when Denise sees a ripened tomato?

Vocabulary Check

Choose the word that best completes each sentence. Write the sentences on a separate sheet of paper.

descent • ripened

9. My ancestors came from Norway, so I am of Norwegian _____.

10. The fruit _____ because the weather conditions were perfect.

11. **English Language Coach** The sample dictionary entry below shows different meanings for the word *report.* Choose the meaning that makes sense in the subtitle of the poem. Then choose two other meanings. On a separate sheet of paper, write a sentence for each of the different meanings of *report,* for a total of three sentences.

---

report *v.* [Middle English, from Old French *reportare,* from Latin *re-* + *portare,* to carry] **1.** to relate, as a story **2.** to serve as a messenger **3.** to act as a newspaper reporter **4.** to complain about to authorities **5.** to let one's superiors know of one's arrival, as in soldiers reporting for duty **6.** to announce a problem to the proper authorities, as in reporting an accident or fire

---

Grammar Link: End Punctuation

When you talk, you change your tone of voice to indicate your emotions and you pause to separate your ideas. When you write, punctuation expresses your emotions and indicates pauses.

Use a question mark (**?**) to ask a question.

• What are you wearing to the band concert?

Use an exclamation point (**!**) to express strong feelings. Exclamatory sentences *always* end with an exclamation point.

• We won the championship!

An imperative sentence, or command, may end with an exclamation point or a period. An exclamation point is ordinarily used only when the command expresses strong emotion.

• Please lower your voice.   • Look out!

Use a period (**.**) whenever you don't need a question mark or an explanation point.

• Tired, she decided to go to bed.

Grammar Practice

Copy each sentence below, adding correct punctuation.

12. The hawk flew overhead

13. Hurry up

14. Did you see the rainbow this afternoon

15. I wonder where George went

Web Activities For eFlashcards, Selection Quick Checks, and other Web activities, go to www.glencoe.com.

Research Report
Prewriting and Drafting

ASSIGNMENT Write a research report

Purpose: To research a subject and write a report on what you find

Audience: Your teacher and your classmates

Writing Rubric

As you work through this writing assignment, you should

• write a thesis statement that clearly states what you are reporting

• support your thesis with evidence and details

• effectively organize and present the information

• cite sources correctly

• write an effective introduction and conclusion

• effectively use simple sentences

See pages 383–385 in Part 2 for a model of a research report.

NY English Language Arts Core Curriculum (pp. 316–321)

LC W4 Compose texts for a variety of purposes. **W1c** Take research notes. **W1a** Use several sources of information. **W1i** Cite sources in notes and bibliography, using correct form. **Core W8** Use correct grammatical construction in sentences.

For a complete description of the standards, see p. NY11.

In this unit you will research and write about a topic that has positive and negative sides—a person, action, or event that may have good aspects but "costs" a high price. Your research report will present your thoughts about this topic, and you will back up your ideas with factual information from expert sources. Writing a research report will help you think about the Big Question: When is the price too high? As you write your report, refer to the **Writing Handbook,** pp. R17–R27.

Prewriting
Get Ready to Write

Prewriting is an important part of writing a research report. When you prewrite, you explore ideas for topics, choose one, and research information about that topic. The following directions will guide you through the prewriting process.

Gather Ideas

Ask yourself these questions to think of possible ideas to research.

• *What do I want to learn about?*

• *What do I care about?*

• *What have I (or people I know) paid a high price for?*

Work with a partner to brainstorm a list of possible topics. Write your list in your Learner's Notebook. Both of you don't have to write down the same ideas, but one of your partner's ideas may trigger an idea of your own. For example, your partner might suggest the history of baseball, which might make you think about all the hours your sister puts in training for soccer. That might make you wonder about the trade-offs student athletes make.

Here are some topic ideas to get you started.

• space exploration—is learning about space worth risking human lives?

• violent video games—are they worth the violence they might cause?

• global warming—are daily conveniences worth harming our planet?

Choose a Topic and Focus Your Ideas

1. Choose one topic to research.

2. Do some general research to help you focus on a specific aspect, or part, of your topic.

• If your topic is too narrow, you won't be able to find enough information to write your report.

• If your topic is too broad, you'll find too much information, and your report may be too general.

One student decided to report on the history of unfair treatment against Native Americans. This chart shows examples of topics that are too broad, too narrow, and just right.

Too Broad	Still Too Broad	Just Right	Too Narrow	Way Too Narrow
Native Americans	the treatment of Native Americans in the 1800s	how and why the U.S. government relocated the Cherokee people in the 1800s	the Cherokee people and the U.S. Supreme Court	Cherokee Chief John Ross's child-hood

Keep your mind open as you research. The amount and type of information you uncover may lead you to change or reshape your topic.

Research your Topic

Begin your research by writing four or five questions about the topic you've chosen. If you have trouble thinking of questions, ask *who, what, where, when, why,* and *how.* If you were researching the relocation of the Cherokee tribe, you might ask questions like the ones below.

> Where did the Cherokees live in the 1800s?
> Who or what made them leave their homeland?
> What happened when they left?
> Who benefited from the Cherokees' leaving?
> What effects did the relocation have on the
>   Cherokee people?
> Where are the Cherokees today?

Look for answers to your questions in books, magazines, newspapers, and reliable Web sites. Library indexes and databases may be helpful. Depending on your topic, you may want to use primary sources, such as letters or diaries.

Literature Online

Writing Models For models and other writing activities, go to www.glencoe.com.

◀ **Writing Tip**

Sources Encyclopedias and textbooks are good general reference books for early research.

◀ **Writing Tip**

Evaluating Information
Not all Web sites deserve your trust. Find out who maintains the site you're using. Check facts you find against facts from another, reliable source. If they don't agree, find a third source for comparison.

Make Source Cards

In a research report, you must cite, or name, the source of your information. To keep track of your sources, write the author, title, publication information, and location of each source on a separate note card. Give each source card a number, and write it in the upper right corner. These cards will be useful for writing a bibliography.

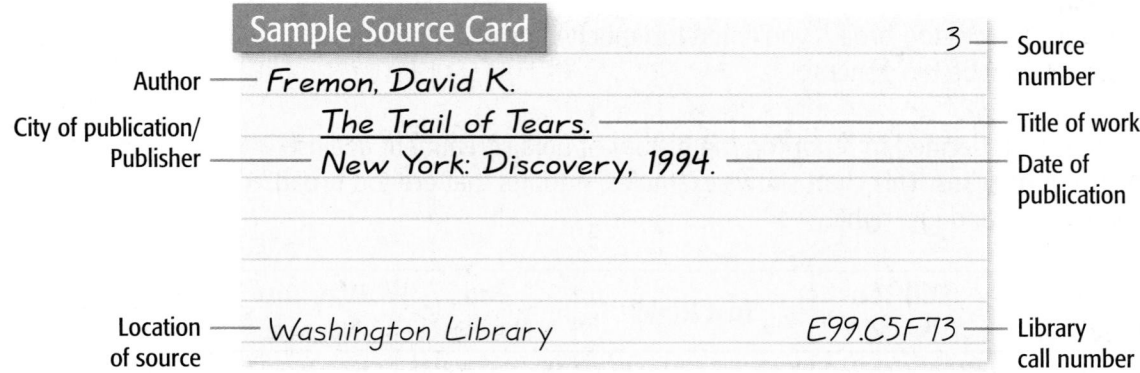

		Sample Source Card		3	Source number
Author	—	*Fremon, David K.*			
City of publication/ Publisher	—	*The Trail of Tears.*			Title of work
		New York: Discovery, 1994.			Date of publication
Location of source	—	*Washington Library*	*E99.C5F73*		Library call number

Take Notes

Writing Tip ▶

Taking Notes When you take notes, write important facts and details on separate note cards. It is useful to organize note cards into categories.

As you research, write down useful information on note cards. Keep track of the source of the information.

- At the top of each card, write a key word or phrase that tells you about the information. Also, write the number of the source you used.
- Write only the details and ideas that relate to your topic.
- Be careful to summarize information in your own words.
- Write down a phrase or a quotation only when the words are especially interesting or come from an important source. If you quote directly, copy the words exactly and place them in quotation marks to show that they are not your own words. That will help you avoid making mistakes later.

This sample note card shows information to include.

		Sample Note Card	3	Write the source number from your source card.
Write a key word or phrase that tells you what the information is about.	—	*Reasons the Cherokees were pushed from their homeland*		
		Gold was discovered in Georgia in 1830.		
		Thousands of settlers went there to get rich.		Write the number of the page on which you found the information.
		p. 56		

Create an Outline

When you have finished taking notes, sort your note cards and write a rough outline of your paper. (You can revise your outline later.)

1. Group together note cards on similar topics. Use each group as a main topic in your outline. (Main topics are noted on outlines with Roman numerals.)

2. Within each group of note cards, cluster similar note cards into subgroups that support and explain the larger and more general main topic. Use these subgroups as the subtopics in your outline (the capital letters).

3. Organize your piles of note cards in an order that makes sense for your topic.

4. Set aside note cards that don't fit under any heading.

The Trail of Tears
I. Background
    A. Cherokee life in their homeland
    B. White settlers' demand for more land
    C. Treaty of Echota
II. Forced removal
    A. Rounding up the Cherokees
    B. March to Oklahoma
III. Effect on Cherokee life
    A. Life in Oklahoma
    B. Life for Cherokees who escaped the roundup

> **Writing Tip**
>
> **Text Structure** You may want to organize your report in chronological order or cause-and-effect order.

Drafting
Start Writing!

With your outline and your note cards by your side, write your first draft. It should have an introduction, a body, and a conclusion.

- The introduction grabs readers' attention, presents the topic, and makes a **thesis statement,** or statement of the paper's main ideas.
- The body supports the thesis with evidence found during research.
- The conclusion summarizes main points and restates the thesis.

> **Writing Tip**
>
> **Drafting** Many writers like to write the body of the report and then go back and write the introduction and thesis statement. Others like to write a thesis statement and then write the body. Wherever you start, focus on getting your ideas down on paper.

Cite Your Sources

In your report, you need to give your readers information about any words, facts, or ideas that are not your own. If you use another writer's ideas or words without citing your source, you are plagiarizing. It is illegal and unethical to plagiarize! Your teacher may tell you how to cite your sources. Here are some guidelines for a common method called parenthetical documentation.

- Give the source in parentheses at the end of the sentence, paragraph, or passage that contains the information.
- For many print sources, you can simply give the author's last name and the page number where you found the information. If you mention the author in the sentence, include only the page number in parentheses at the end of the sentence.
- If the source doesn't give the author's name, give the source's title instead.
- See pages R23–R24 of the **Writing Handbook** or search the Internet for more information on citing sources and creating a Works Cited list.

The chart below shows two ways to cite works in your research report.

Type	Explanation	Example
Author cited in text	Page number in parentheses	According to Brown . . . (172).
Book with one author	Name of author followed by page number(s)	(Downing 15).

Use these examples and models as you make your list of works cited.

Type	Example
Article in a magazine	Johnson, Sally A. "A Beekeeper's Year." *Apiculture* (Sept. 1999): 40–44.
Article in a newspaper	Bertram, Jeffrey. "African Bees: Fact or Myth?" *Orlando Sentinel* 18 Aug. 1999: D2.
Book with one author	Stelley, Diane G. *Beekeeping: An Illustrated Handbook.* Blue Ridge Summit, PA: Tab, 1993.
Web site	Sanford, Malcolm T. "Small Hive Beetle." *Bee Culture* (Feb. 1999). 13 Feb. 2001 <http://www.bee.airoot.com/beeculture/99feb4.html>.

Writing Tip

Researching *The Reader's Guide to Periodical Literature* can help you find magazine articles on your topic.

Writing Tip

Text Features Save time by using the title page, table of contents, index, and appendix to judge whether a source will be useful and to find specific information within a book.

Grammar Link

Simple Sentences

Simple sentences are some of the most important pieces of your paragraphs. They are simple but powerful because they convey your ideas clearly, so that your readers can easily understand you.

What Is a Simple Sentence?

A **simple sentence** has one complete subject and one complete predicate. The **complete subject** tells who or what a sentence is about. The **complete predicate** tells what the subject is, does, or has.

- <u>Arturo and his sister</u> / <u>play basketball</u>.

(Who plays basketball? Arturo and his sister. The complete subject is "Arturo and his sister." What do Arturo and his sister do? They play basketball. The complete predicate is "play basketball.")

Complete Subject	Complete Predicate
Ali	danced.
Ali and Leila	danced.
Ali and Leila	danced and sang.

In the examples, the sentences were made up of nouns and verbs and a few other words. Simple sentences are more interesting when you add elements like modifiers, verb phrases, or prepositional phrases.

Complete Subject	Complete Predicate
Ali	danced joyfully around the room.
Ali and Leila	danced across the stage.
The handsome, charming Ali	danced and sang.

Why Are Simple Sentences Important in My Writing?

Simple sentences are important because they allow you to say what you need to say without a lot of extra words. They also allow you to communicate with a larger audience because they are easier for some people to follow.

How Do I Do It?

- Decide on the subject of your sentence. Which noun or pronoun will you use?
- Decide on what the subject will do or think or feel. Which verb will you use?

Write to Learn Write three or four simple sentences—one about each main point you plan to make in your research report.

Looking Ahead

Part 2 of this Writing Workshop is coming up later. Keep the writing you did here. In Part 2, you'll learn how to turn it into a clear, well-written research report!

Skills Focus

You will practice using these skills when you read the following selections:
- "The Games Kids Play," p. 326
- "Cruise Control," p. 332

Reading

- Skimming and scanning

Literature

- Identifying and evaluating text evidence

Vocabulary

- Understanding multiple-meaning words
- Academic Vocabulary: *identify*

Writing/Grammar

- Recognizing and correcting fragments

Skill Lesson

Skimming and Scanning

Learn It!

What Is It? Skimming and scanning are two ways to read a text.

- When you **skim** a text, you look it over quickly to get a general idea of what the whole thing is about. (When you previewed text in Reading Workshop 1 of this unit, you were skimming the text.)
- When you **scan** a text, you read it quickly to **identify,** or find, specific information. You also scan to find key words or phrases that point to the information you're looking for.

FOXTROT © 2003 Bill Amend. Reprinted with permission of UNIVERSAL PRESS SYNDICATE. All rights reserved.

Analyzing Cartoons

If Peter thinks one page is a lot to read, he'd better learn to skim and scan! How might skimming and scanning help you understand what you read?

NY English Language Arts Core Curriculum (pp. 322–323)

LC R12 Combine multiple strategies to enhance comprehension and response.

For a complete description of the standards, see p. NY11.

Academic Vocabulary

identify (eye DEN tuh fy) *v.* find; recognize

Why Are They Important? Skimming and scanning save you time while helping you read.

- Skimming text tells you quickly what a reading selection is about.
- Scanning helps you quickly find specific information.
- Skimming and scanning also help you remember what you've read.

How Do I Do Them?

To skim, follow these steps:

1. Read the title of the selection and quickly look over the entire piece.

2. Read headings, captions, and part of the first paragraph.

3. Look at summaries, lists, subheadings, and illustrations.

To scan, follow these steps:

1. Decide what information you're looking for.

2. Move your eyes quickly over the lines of text, looking for key words or phrases that will help you locate that information.

3. Try not to read; just focus on finding the key words.

Here's what a student learned from skimming and scanning the article "Gymnasts in Pain: Out of Balance" in Reading Workshop 1.

> *From skimming this article I see right away that it's about girls who suffer injuries from gymnastics training. The photos and heads are about girls with injuries, and each paragraph talks about injuries, pain, and training.*
>
> *I scanned to find names of gymnasts I admire: Alyssa Beckerman, Kelly Garrison, and my favorite, Carly Patterson.*

Literature Online

Study Central Visit www.glencoe .com and click on Study Central to review skimming and scanning.

Practice It!

1. Skim the poem "In Response to Executive Order 9066" on pages 312–313. Then write a quick summary of the poem in your Learner's Notebook.

2. Scan the Looking Ahead page for Unit 3 (p. 289) to find the skill lesson topic for Reading Workshop 3. Write it in your Learner's Notebook.

Use It!

Before you read the next two selections, skim them to see what they're about. For the After You Read questions, scan the selections to find answers.

Before You Read : The Games Kids Play

NY English Language Arts Core Curriculum (pp. 324–327)

LC R9 Recognize multiple meanings of words. **LC R12** Combine multiple strategies to enhance comprehension and response. **R3a** Evaluate examples, details, or reasons used to support ideas.

For a complete description of the standards, see p. NY11.

Vocabulary Preview

gory (GOR ee) *adj.* bloody; involving a lot of bloodshed **(p. 326)** *Some people like to play gory video games that show lots of physical violence.*

clamor (KLAH mor) *v.* to demand something in a noisy way **(p. 326)** *Kids and teenagers clamor for action-packed video games.*

modified (MOD i fyd) *adj.* changed; altered; form of the verb *modify* **(p. 327)** *Sometimes teens play modified video games that are more violent than the original.*

portray (por TREY) *v.* to show or represent someone or something **(p. 327)** *Many people do not approve of the glamorous way that video games portray gun violence.*

conclusive (kun KLOO siv) *adj.* definite; proven without doubt **(p. 327)** *The researchers thought they found conclusive evidence that the video games were harmful to kids.*

Write to Learn In your Learner's Notebook, rewrite the definition for each vocabulary word in your own words.

English Language Coach

Multiple-Meaning Words It is not unusual for a word to have many meanings. Remember to use the right definition for a word when you look it up in a dictionary. Pick the meaning that makes sense in the context in which you found the word while reading a selection. Below are four definitions for the word *conflict.* Read the definitions.

> **conflict** (KON flikt) *n.* **1.** a military struggle or battle; **2.** a clash between people or ideas; **3.** tension between characters in a story
> **conflict** (kun FLIKT) *v.* to be in disagreement with a person or thing

Partner Talk With a partner, read the following sentences. Then, using the definitions above and context clues in each sentence, decide which definition for **conflict** is correct.

1. My brother and I had a <u>conflict</u> over who would choose the TV show.

2. My ideas about what I should wear to school <u>conflict</u> with my mother's.

3. The <u>conflict</u> between the two countries resulted in many deaths.

Skills Preview

Key Reading Skill: Skimming and Scanning

Before you read "The Games Kids Play," do the following:

- skim the title, subtitle, headings, and illustrations.
- scan the pages to identify, or find, sections that describe the effects of playing video games.

Write to Learn After you skim and scan the article, write down a few notes about what stands out in the article and what you want to learn from it.

Key Text Element: Evidence

To support their ideas and opinions, authors present **evidence**—details that help prove that an idea, position, or opinion is correct. There are many kinds of evidence. They include the following kinds of details:

- **Statistics,** or numbers, such as the number of people who attend baseball games each year or the yearly salary a baseball player makes.
- **Expert opinion,** or the beliefs of a person who has studied a subject carefully or is part of a profession important to the subject. For example, a quotation from the Surgeon General about the effects of smoking would be an expert opinion.
- **Results of studies,** or conclusions based on research. For example, if a university does a study of the effects of violence on kids, the conclusions of that study might be used as evidence.

Whole Class Discussion As a class, discuss the kinds of evidence that you find the most convincing.

Get Ready to Read

Connect to the Reading

Do you ever watch movies or TV shows that have violence in them? Have you played violent video games? How do you think being exposed to violence in entertainment affects you?

Whole Class Discussion As a class, discuss how you react to watching violence in movies, on television, or in video games. Discuss whether you think movies, shows, or games might cause people to be more violent.

Build Background

- The first video games were developed in the 1950s and 1960s. They ran on huge computers.
- In the 1970s coin-operated game machines were built, which led to video arcades—public places where people can play video games. Later, video game equipment was developed that allowed people to play the games in their homes.
- Even early in the history of video games, people worried about the violence in the games. Some studies suggest that people who play violent video games are less upset by real-life violence than people who don't play the games.

Set Purposes for Reading

BIG Question Read the article "The Games Kids Play" to learn more about the effects of playing violent video games. Then decide whether the price the players and society pay is too high.

Set Your Own Purpose What else would you like to learn from the article to help you answer the Big Question? Write your own purpose on the "Games Kids Play" flap of the Reading Workshop 2 Foldable.

Interactive Literary Elements Handbook
To review or learn more about the literary elements, go to www.glencoe.com.

Keep Moving

Use these skills as you read "The Games Kids Play."

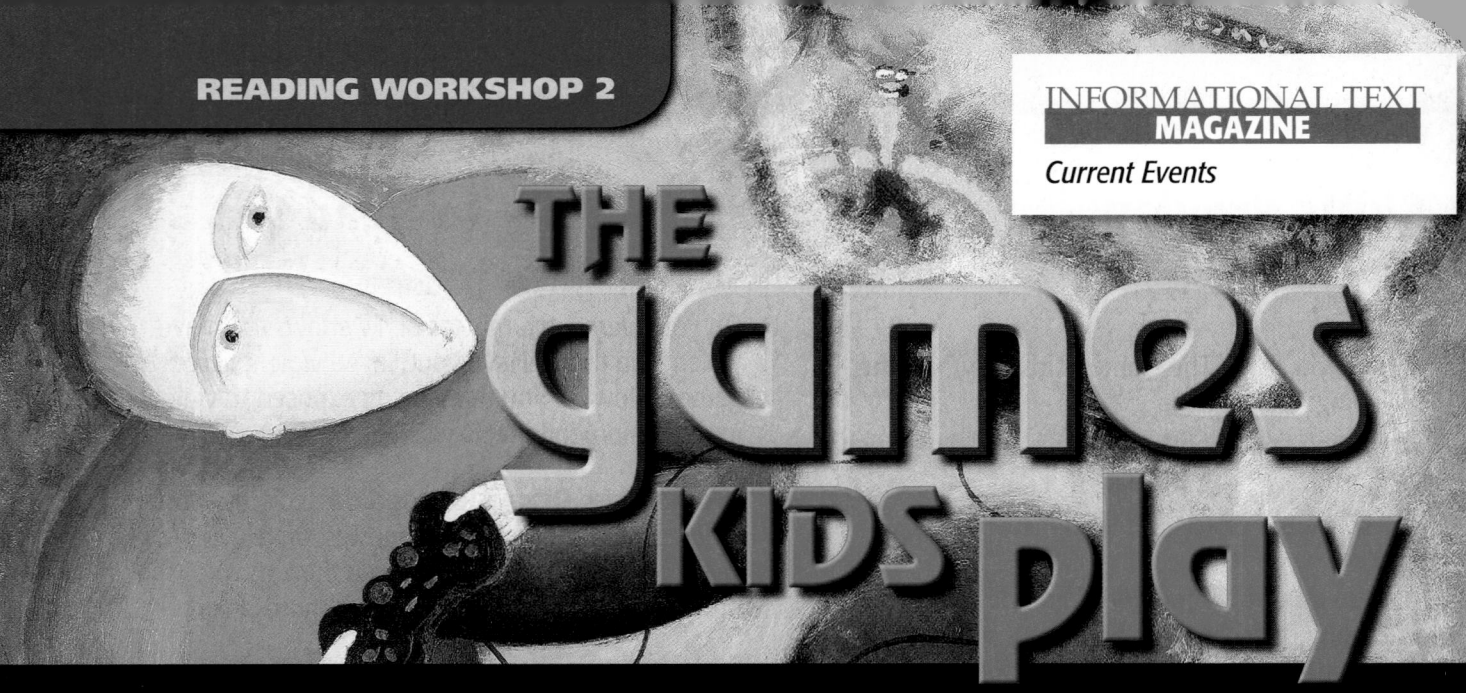

INFORMATIONAL TEXT
MAGAZINE
Current Events

THE games KIDS play

Are mature video games too violent for teens?

Press START and you become Tommy Vercetti, an ex-convict with nothing to lose. You race down the streets of Vice City, scoring points by stealing cars, robbing banks, dealing drugs, and killing women. **1**

The deadly gun battles and wild car chases are all part of the action of *Grand Theft Auto: Vice City*, one of the hottest video games around. But is the **gory** game harmless fun?

Some people aren't so sure.

Vice City and a few other popular video games have mature ratings, meaning they might contain violent content, strong language, and nudity. M-rated games are recommended for people seventeen and up.

Even though M-rated games are meant for adults, their popularity often extends all the way down to elementary schools. And as kids and teens **clamor** to play the games, the debate is heating up over whether those kids are old enough to walk the violent streets of Vice City.

Real Life Vice? Researchers say playing M-rated games could spark violent behavior. They say studies have shown

Practice the Skills

1 **Key Reading Skill**

Skimming and Scanning Before you read this selection, skim the article to get a general idea of what it is about. What do the title, the subtitle, and the first paragraph tell you about the main topic of the article?

Vocabulary

gory (GOR ee) *adj.* bloody; involving a lot of bloodshed

clamor (KLAH mor) *v.* to demand something in a noisy way

that people who play violent video games are more aggressive. "It increases the likelihood youngsters are going to react to **conflict** with aggression instead of cooperation," Iowa State University professor Craig Anderson told the *Star Tribune*. **2**

Experts point to Eric Harris as an example. Harris was one of two teens who opened fire in Columbine High School in Littleton, Colorado, in 1999, killing thirteen people before shooting himself. Harris had a **modified** version of *Doom*, an M-rated video game, on his Web site. His version resembled the Columbine shootings—two shooters, unlimited ammunition, and victims who couldn't shoot back. **3**

Some people say games like Vice City should be taken off the shelves because of the way they **portray** women. "I'm really offended that anybody would sell a [game] that has this kind of violence in it, that kicking a woman to death is a game, is fun," father Howard Winkler told the *Olympian*.

Just Fantasy Many parents and teens argue that no normal kid would be transformed by a video game's violence.

They say teens are smart enough to tell the difference between reality and fantasy.

"The guns, the weapons, blowing stuff up—it's just got something you can't do in real life," said 15-year-old Bryce Conley of Springfield, Missouri. "You might go shoot the cops in the game, but I'm not going to go out and shoot a cop in real life," he told newspapers.

The Interactive Digital Software Association[1] says there is no **conclusive** link between video games and violent behavior. They point out that as video games increase in popularity, youth violence in the United States declines.

What do you think? Should teens be allowed to play mature video games? **4** ○

---

1. The *Interactive Digital Software Association*, now called the Entertainment Software Association, works with companies that make and sell video games.

Vocabulary ....

modified (MOD i fyd) *adj.* changed; altered

portray (por TREY) *v.* to show or represent someone or something

conclusive (kun KLOO siv) *adj.* definite; proven without doubt

Practice the Skills

2 **English Language Coach**

Multiple-Meaning Words
Look back at the definitions that you learned in the Before You Read section. What is the correct definition of the word **conflict** as it is used here? Write it in your Learner's Notebook.

3 **Key Text Element**

Evidence Whose expert opinion does the author quote as evidence that playing violent games may spark violent acts? What example do experts point to as evidence?

4 **BIG Question**

What do people gain from playing violent video games? What might they lose? What is the possible price society pays for violent video games? Write your answers on the "Games Kids Play" flap of the Reading Workshop 2 Foldable. Your response will help you complete the Unit Challenge later.

After You Read

The Games Kids Play

Answering the BIG Question

1. In your opinion, which is more important: a) the enjoyment that young people get from playing violent video games, or b) the risk that these young people might become more aggressive?

2. **Recall** What does the Iowa State University professor say about the effects of M-rated video games on people?
   TIP Right There

3. **Summarize** In the article, what arguments do people make against M-rated video games? What are the arguments in support of the games?
   TIP Think and Search

Critical Thinking

4. **Evaluate** In your opinion, how old should someone be to play M-rated video games with wild car chases and deadly gun battles? Why?
   TIP On My Own

5. **Analyze** How could you remove the violence from a game like *Grand Theft Auto: Vice City* but still keep it exciting? Explain.
   TIP On My Own

6. **Evaluate** If you knew for sure that children who play M-rated video games would become more violent, what advice would you give parents who have children your age?
   TIP On My Own

Write About Your Reading

Write an E-mail Use the RAFT system to write about "The Games Kids Play." The RAFT assignment provides four details:

Role: Write as if you are a parent, grandparent, or other adult.

Audience: You

Format: An e-mail

Topic: M-rated video games. Write what the adult would say to you about playing these games. Use details from the article to support your points.

NY English Language Arts Core Curriculum (pp. 328–329)

LC R17 Demonstrate comprehension and response through a range of activities. **W4g** Use the conventions of email. **LC R12** Combine multiple strategies to enhance comprehension and response. **R3a** Evaluate examples, details, or reasons used to support ideas. **Core W8** Use correct grammatical construction in sentences.

For a complete description of the standards, see p. NY11.

Skills Review

Key Reading Skill: Skimming and Scanning

7. How did skimming and scanning before you read help you understand the information discussed in "The Games Kids Play"? Explain.

Key Text Element: Evidence

8. What evidence does the Interactive Digital Software Association present to support its opinion that there is no conclusive link between video games and violent behavior?

9. What possible biases might the Digital Software Association have?

Vocabulary Check

Choose the best word from the list to complete each sentence below. Rewrite each sentence with the correct word in place.

gory   clamor   modified   portray   conclusive

10. Every year kids _____ for more and more action-filled video games.

11. Some people say that M-rated video games should be banned because of the way the games _____ women.

12. There are many nonviolent video games, but kids seem to like the really _____ ones.

13. The Video Game Association states that there is no _____ evidence that shows video games make kids more aggressive.

14. Some people say that games would be more acceptable if they were _____ to show less violence.

15. **Academic Vocabulary** Which arguments for or against M-rated video games would you **identify** as most reasonable?

16. **English Language Coach** Look up *game* in a dictionary. Write three sentences, each one using a different definition of the word.

Grammar Link: Fragments That Lack a Subject or a Verb

A **fragment** is an incomplete sentence. A sentence may be incomplete because it is missing a subject or because it is missing a verb.

- **Fragment:** <u>Lila and Nathan</u>.

  (What about Lila and Nathan? The verb is missing. To fix the fragment, add a verb.)

- **Complete:** <u>Lila and Nathan</u> <u>have arrived</u>.

- **Fragment:** <u>Sold</u> her scooter.

  (Who or what sold? The subject is missing. To fix the fragment, add a subject.)

- **Complete:** <u>Emily</u> <u>sold</u> her scooter.

Grammar Practice

Copy each item below. Write *subject* next to the item if the subject is missing. Write *verb* if the verb is missing. If the item is a complete sentence, write *C*.

17. Played games for a while.

18. I wanted to see whether I could get to the next level.

19. The loud, pounding sound effects.

20. Levels three and four.

21. Feeling the excitement of the game.

22. I played for several minutes.

23. No one else playing.

24. Everyone else had stopped.

Writing Application Review your Write About Your Reading activity. Check to make sure that you do not have any sentence fragments. Fix any mistakes.

Web Activities For eFlashcards, Selection Quick Checks, and other Web activities, go to www.glencoe.com.

Before You Read : Cruise Control

Did You Know?

More than forty states now have graduated driver licensing. Under this system young drivers must get driving experience before they receive full driving rights. In general, graduated driver licensing consists of these steps:

- **Learner** During this step the young driver cannot drive alone. A fully licensed driver who is at least twenty-one years old must be in the car with the driver.

- **Intermediate** During this step the young driver can drive alone but only during certain hours. Late-night driving is generally banned, and the number of teens who can be in the car with the driver is limited.

- **Full Licensure** During this last step the driver is given full driving privileges.

  Statistics show that graduated drivers licensing programs save lives. Though many teenagers dislike the programs, all drivers are safer because of them.

NY English Language Arts Core Curriculum (pp. 330–333)

LC R9 Recognize multiple meanings of words. **LC R12** Combine multiple strategies to enhance comprehension and response. **R3a** Identify techniques the author uses to persuade.

For a complete description of the standards, see p. NY11.

Vocabulary Preview

restrictions (ree STRIK shunz) *n.* limits to things one can and can't do **(p. 332)** *Many states are placing driving restrictions on teenagers.*

perceives (pur SEEVZ) *v.* understands something in a particular way **(p. 333)** *The father said his daughter will start to drive better if she perceives that someone will report her driving errors.*

Write to Learn Using each vocabulary word correctly, write a few sentences about yourself or someone you know.

English Language Coach

Multiple-Meaning Words Below are definitions for two multiple-meaning words that you will read in "Cruise Control." As you read, watch for these words and use context clues to choose the correct meaning of each word.

> **trend** (trend) *n.* **1.** a general tendency, movement, or direction toward something; **2.** a current fashion or style

> **trend** (trend) *v.* to show a general movement toward something

> **sentence** (SEN tens) *n.* **1.** a group of words with a verb and subject; **2.** a punishment from a court

> **sentence** (SEN tens) *v.* to give a punishment for a crime

Partner Talk With a partner, read these sentences. Talk about which definition of the underlined word makes the most sense in each sentence.

1. Designer sunglasses are the latest <u>trend</u>.

2. "Write a complete <u>sentence</u> using all the vocabulary words," said Ms. Adams.

3. It's always a problem when gas prices <u>trend</u> up.

4. Jake was given a five-year prison <u>sentence</u> for stealing money from the store.

5. The judge will <u>sentence</u> Jake's brother next week.

Skills Preview

Key Reading Skill: Skimming and Scanning

Before you read "Cruise Control," do these things:

- Scan the selection to get a general idea of what it is about. Look for the title, subtitle, headings, and any photos or illustrations in the selection.
- Skim the paragraphs to get an idea of the topic of the article.
- Plan how you will read this selection. For example, will you read the graphics first or read the text and then check the graphics?

Write to Learn In your Learner's Notebook, write a list of the things you learned by skimming and scanning this article. To get more out of your reading, refer to this list as you read the article.

Literary Element: Humor

Some informational articles use humor to engage readers and make a point. One way that writers create humor is unexpected silly twists of language. Two techniques are hyperbole and puns.

Hyperbole (hy PER buhl ee) is making huge exaggerations about something to emphasize a point–for example, *Her eyes were as big as saucers.*

A **pun** is a play on words–for example, *Joe: "My grammar's not so good." Pete: "Well I hope she feels better soon!"*

As you read the following article, use these tips to recognize the humor.

- Watch for hyperbole, or exaggeration of ideas.
  Notice words that seem out of place, or too strong for the situation being described.
- Look for puns used to bring attention to a point.
  Think about what the writer might be trying to say with the pun.

Partner Talk Express the following idea as a hyperbole: He is very, very tall.

Get Ready to Read

Connect to the Reading

Think about a time you thought about breaking a rule or were caught breaking a rule. Are you more likely to follow the rules if you think you will get caught? Why or why not?

Write to Learn In a few sentences describe a time when you or someone you know got caught breaking rules. What happened? Who caught you? Were there any consequences?

Build Background

- Teenage drivers are more likely than older drivers to speed, run red lights, and make illegal turns. Teenagers are also less likely to wear seatbelts.
- Teenagers are four times more likely to be involved in driving accidents than older drivers.
- The risk of a car crash is greatest during the first year a driver has his or her license.

Set Purposes for Reading

BIG Question Read "Cruise Control" to find out how some parents use a creative way to help their teenagers practice better driving habits.

Set Your Own Purpose What else would you like to learn from the article to help you answer the Big Question? Write your own purpose on the "Cruise Control" flap of the Reading Workshop 2 Foldable for Unit 3.

Literature Online

Interactive Literary Elements Handbook
To review or learn more about the literary elements, go to www.glencoe.com.

Keep Moving

Use these skills as you read "Cruise Control."

INFORMATIONAL TEXT
MAGAZINE

Teen People

CRUISE CONTROL **1**

New Teen Driving **Restrictions** Put Parents in the Rear Window

by Kevin O'Leary

Anne Rekerdres likes to call it "the everlasting punishment." When the 17-year-old North Dallas senior came home with a speeding ticket in March, her dad, Randy, 47, slapped the back bumper of her beloved '92 red Ford Explorer with a sticker that read: "How's my driving? 1-866-2-TELLMOM." "It was humiliating," says Anne. But there was nothing she could do. "I told her, 'If the sticker comes off,'" recalls Randy, "'there go your keys.'"

Tattletale bumper stickers, which publicize where to call to notify parents about bad driving, are a trend that won't end soon. Besides the Web site on which Anne's dad bought hers, two other services—the San Diego-based Dad's Eyes (877-DADS-EYES) and 800-4-MYTEEN of Arlington, Texas— also allow strangers to play Big Mother. **2** The stickers have even become popular in Texas's municipal court[1] system, where several judges regularly **sentence** speeding teens to six months with the embarrassing banners. **3**

---

1. A **municipal court** manages court cases for a city.

Vocabulary . . . .

restrictions (ree STRIK shunz) *n.* limits to things one can and can't do

Practice the Skills

1 **Key Reading Skill**

Skimming and Scanning
Before you read, skim and scan the selection to get an idea of what the article is about. What words and other features tell you what the topic of the article is?

2 **Literary Element**

Humor: Pun "Big Mother" is a pun referring to the novel *1984* by George Orwell. In that novel, set in the future, Big Brother watches over everything that happens. "Big Brother" came to mean someone who has complete control over people's lives. How does this pun help you understand the author's attitude toward his subject?

3 **English Language Coach**

Multiple-Meaning Words
Review the definitions you learned for the word *sentence.* What is the meaning of *sentence* as it is used here? Write the meaning in your Learner's Notebook.

But do the stickers actually make teens drive more safely? "As long as she **perceives** she can be reported," says Randy, "it works." His attitude is exactly what angers Anne. "What if someone called and said, 'I saw your daughter run a red light,' and I didn't? Who's he going to believe? It's a trust-breaker." **4** ○

You Are So Busted!

"I got a ticket for doing 45 in a 30 zone,[2] and the judge ordered me to have a sticker for six months. My mom thought it was unfair too. I haven't tried to cover it or anything, but it came off when I washed my car. I had to get another one."

—**Missy Leavell, 19, Cleburne, Texas**

"I always think about the sticker when I'm driving. When [other drivers] do something stupid, sometimes I feel like I want to cut them off, but then I remember the sticker is there, and I stay calm. When I first got it, people were like, 'What's that?' But then it just got old. I don't get teased anymore." **5**

—**Stephanie Collins, 16, Green Bay, Wis.**

Practice the Skills

4 **Reviewing Skills**

Connecting How do you think it would feel to be driving alone for the first time? Do you think a "How's My Driving" bumper sticker would make you a better driver? Explain.

5 **BIG Question**

Do you think putting bumper stickers on the cars teenagers drive is worth the embarrassment the teens might feel? Explain. Write your answer on the "Cruise Control" flap of the Reading Workshop 2 Foldable for Unit 3.

---

2. Here, **zone** refers to the speed zone, which was 30 miles per hour. Leavell was driving 15 miles above the limit.

Vocabulary

perceives (pur SEEVZ) *v.* understands something in a particular way

After You Read

Cruise Control

CRUISE CONTROL

Answering the **BIG** Question

1. Do you think the teens interviewed would say the bumper stickers were too high a price to pay for breaking traffic regulations? Why or why not? Use specific details from the article to support your views.

2. Recall Name two places mentioned in the article where parents can get bumper stickers for their teenagers' cars.
TIP Right There

Critical Thinking

3. Infer How do you think the author of the article feels about the bumper sticker programs? List words or phrases from the article to support your answer.
TIP Author and Me

4. Evaluate How do *you* feel about the bumper sticker program? Use what you learned from reading the article and your own experiences to support your opinion.
TIP Author and Me

5. Apply Imagine that you are riding in a car when another car suddenly swerves in front of you and almost causes an accident. The car has a "Tell Mom" or "Dad's Eyes" bumper sticker on it and a telephone number. Would you call the number to report the driver? Why or why not?
TIP On My Own

6. Evaluate Many governments protect their citizens by limiting what individuals can do. Examples include laws about the legal driving age and laws against speeding. Do you think these laws are useful? Why or why not?
TIP On My Own

Talk About Your Reading

Small Group Discussion In small groups, talk about other ways to help people become safer drivers. Do you think a bumper sticker program would work well for adults too? Why or why not? Have someone in the group jot down everyone's ideas, then present them to the class.

NY English Language Arts Core Curriculum (pp. 334–335)

LC R17 Demonstrate comprehension and response through a range of activities.
LC S8 Participate in group discussions on a range of topics and for a variety of purposes. **LC R12** Combine multiple strategies to enhance comprehension and response. **R3a** Identify techniques the author uses to persuade. **Core W8** Use correct grammatical construction in parts of speech.

For a complete description of the standards, see p. NY11.

Skills Review

Key Reading Skill: Skimming and Scanning

7. How did skimming and scanning this article help you get more out of reading it?

Literary Element: Humor

8. In the first sentence of this article, Anne Rekerdres calls the bumper stickers "everlasting punishment." Later you learn that these bumper stickers last only a short time, so the word *everlasting* is a huge exaggeration. How does this hyperbole, or exaggeration, add to your understanding of the article?

Reviewing Skills: Connecting

9. After reading "Cruise Control," how do you feel about getting your driver's license? Will you get one as soon as you are old enough? Explain.

Vocabulary Check

Match each vocabulary word with a word or phrase that means the same thing or nearly the same thing. Each word will be used more than once.

restrictions   perceives

10. controls
11. recognizes
12. sees
13. believes
14. understands
15. limitations
16. realizes
17. rules

English Language Coach

18. The author of the article uses the multiple-meaning word *trend.* Look back at the definitions for *trend* listed on page 330 and write sentences correctly using the definitions.

Grammar Link: Dependent Clauses as Sentence Fragments

As you've learned, a sentence may be a **fragment,** or incomplete, because it is missing a subject or a verb. Another type of fragment is a dependent clause punctuated as if it were a complete sentence. A dependent clause has a subject and a verb, but it does not express a complete thought, so it cannot stand alone as a sentence.

• After <u>we</u> <u>study</u>.

(What should we do after we study? The sentence has a subject and verb, but it does not express a complete thought.)

To fix the fragment, connect it to an independent clause, or complete thought.

• After <u>we</u> <u>study</u>, **we will watch a movie.**

Grammar Practice

The following paragraph has four fragments. Two are dependent-clause fragments and two are fragments that lack a subject and verb. Copy the paragraph. Then underline and revise the fragments. (There is more than one right way to fix them.)

I am learning to play the drums. I really like it. Pounding on the drums is fun and helps me relax. Though my family sometimes complains about the noise. I try to practice everyday anyway. Also, I meet every Wednesday afternoon with a music teacher. For an hour-long lesson. I plan to try out for the band. When I start high school next year. By then I think I will be able to read music well enough. To play with other musicians.

Literature Online

Web Activities For eFlashcards, Selection Quick Checks, and other Web activities, go to www.glencoe.com.

READING WORKSHOP 3

Skills Focus

You will practice using these skills when you read the following selections:
- "Flowers for Algernon," Part 1, p. 340
- "Flowers for Algernon," Part 2, p. 358

Reading

- Recognizing and understanding text structures

Literature

- Understanding irony
- Analyzing the effects of foreshadowing

Vocabulary

- Understanding multiple-meaning words in context
- Academic Vocabulary: *structure*

Writing/Grammar

- Correcting run-on sentences
- Understanding compound subjects and predicates

NY English Language Arts Core Curriculum
(pp. 336–337)

LC R13 Use text structure and literary devices to aid comprehension and response.

For a complete description of the standards, see p. NY11.

Skill Lesson

Understanding Text Structures

Learn It!

What Is It? What do you think of when you hear the word **structure?** You probably think of something that you can see, like a house or a bridge. But writing has structure too. Authors organize their writing in a specific way for a specific purpose. These patterns of organization are called **text structures.** Here are some common text structures:

- **Comparison and contrast** shows how things are the same and different.
- **Cause and effect** shows how events are related.
- **Problem and solution** describes a problem and offers solutions.
- **Chronological order** presents events in time order.

Analyzing Cartoons
Why isn't this a logical solution? What else could they do to solve their money problem?

© 2005 King Features Syndicate, Inc. Reprinted with special permission.

Academic Vocabulary

structure (STRUK chur) *n.* the arrangement or organization of parts in a body or system

Why Is It Important? Recognizing, or identifying, the text structure in a reading selection helps you locate the writer's important points and understand how ideas relate to each other.

LiteratureOnline

Study Central Visit www.glencoe .com and click on Study Central to review using text structures.

How Do I Do It? When you read, watch for signal words and phrases that tell you the text structure. Study the lists below.

- **Comparison and contrast:** like, as, however, similarly, on the other hand, but, in contrast
- **Cause and effect:** because, has led to, as a result, so, therefore
- **Problem and solution:** so, need, answer, issue
- **Chronological order:** first, second, then, last, finally, earlier, later

Here's how a student figured out the cause-and-effect structure of this paragraph from "Gymnasts in Pain: Out of Balance."

> The sport's obsession with weight and diet, especially within the U.S. national team program, often has led to eating disorders. U.S. gymnasts competing in the 2001 World Championships said they were provided so little food that family members smuggled snacks into the team hotel by stuffing them inside teddy bears.

> *The phrase "has led to" makes me think what comes before the phrase is a cause and what comes after is the effect. The sport's obsession with weight and diet is the cause of eating disorders (the effect). The paragraph also says the gymnasts get so little food that family members sneak them snacks. That's cause and effect too.*

Practice It!

With a partner, decide which text structure is indicated by each of these signal words and phrases.

next • as a result • solve • in contrast

Use It!

As you read "Flowers for Algernon," look for clues that can help you figure out the text structures in the story.

Before You Read

Flowers for Algernon, Part 1

Daniel Keyes

Meet the Author

Daniel Keyes was born in 1927 in New York. In college he studied psychology. He has said that he loves to explore the "complexities of the human mind," and his writing shows his interest in personality and intelligence. Mr. Keyes has won literary awards for "Flowers for Algernon." See page R3 of the Author Files in the back of the book for more on Daniel Keyes.

Author Search For more about Daniel Keyes, go to www.glencoe.com.

NY English Language Arts Core Curriculum (pp. 338–353)

LC R9 Recognize multiple meanings of words. **LC R13** Use text structure and literary devices to aid comprehension and response. **R2d** Determine how the use and meaning of literary devices convey the author's message or intent.

For a complete description of the standards, see p. NY11.

Vocabulary Preview

You probably know most of the words in this part of "Flowers for Algernon," but you might not recognize the spelling. That's because the story is written as if the main character, Charlie, is keeping a diary or journal. Charlie misspells many of the words.

English Language Coach

Multiple-Meaning Words Remember that if you read a word you know but it doesn't make sense in context, the word has multiple meanings.

Look at the two words below. Study the meanings that are given. You'll see these words in "Flowers for Algernon."

Decide which definition makes sense for each word when you see it in context as you read the story.

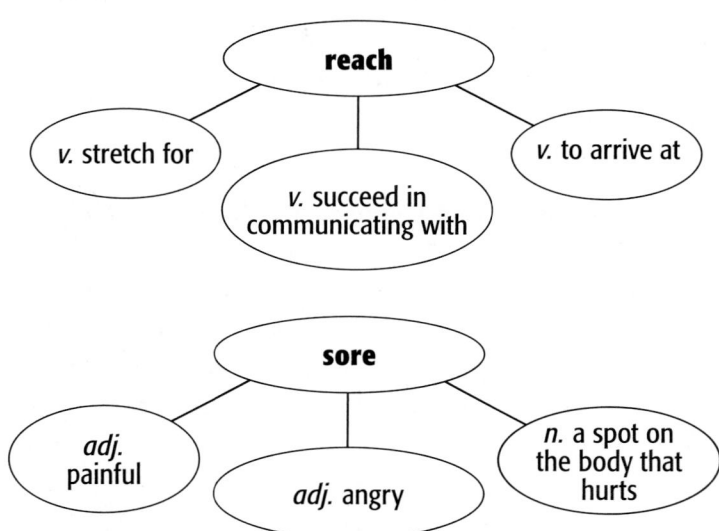

Partner Talk Read these sentences. Work with a partner to decide which meaning given above is the right one for each sentence.

1. I was <u>sore</u> at my older brother because he wouldn't let me play ball with him.
2. I tried to <u>reach</u> the cookies on the top shelf, but I was too short.
3. My arm is <u>sore</u> after throwing so many pitches.
4. Did you <u>reach</u> the student who needed help?

Skills Preview

Key Reading Skill: Understanding Text Structures

These signal words and phrases can tell you how the parts of a text are related.

- **Comparison and Contrast:** similarly, on the other hand, in contrast to, but, however
- **Cause and Effect:** so, because, as a result
- **Problem and Solution:** need, issue, solve
- **Chronological Sequence:** first, next, then, later

Think-Pair-Share Write two sentences with signal words that show one of the text structures listed above. Then exchange papers with a partner and see whether he or she can tell what text structure you used.

Key Literary Element: Irony

You probably already know about **verbal irony.** "Nice job," someone says, when they really mean you messed it up. There's a different kind of irony that you will find when you read. It's called **dramatic irony** and it happens when you, as a reader, know something a character doesn't. For example, suppose the narrator has just told you that there's a fire-breathing dragon around the next corner and the main character says, "This looks like a nice safe path." That's dramatic irony.

As you read, use these tips to understand irony.

- Pay attention to a character's thoughts about himself or herself or about a situation.

  Do you have knowledge that he or she doesn't?

Get Ready to Read

Connect to the Reading

Have you ever wished your life would change overnight? What would you wish to change? What would happen if your wish for change really came true?

Write to Learn If you could make one wish to change your life, what would it be? In your Learner's Notebook, describe something you'd like to change and tell how that change would make your life better.

Build Background

- Psychologists study how people behave, think, learn, and feel about things.
- There are many tests to measure human intelligence. The Intelligence Quotient, or IQ, is one such measure.
- In recent years, scientists have come to think that people have "multiple intelligences"—special abilities in language, music, art, and physical coordination, for example.

Set Purposes for Reading

BIG Question Read "Flowers for Algernon" to find out what happens to Charlie Gordon and his dream of growing smart.

Set Your Own Purpose What else would you like to learn from the selection to help you answer the Big Question? Write your own purpose on the "Flowers for Algernon," Part 1, flap of the Reading Workshop 3 Foldable.

Literature Online

Interactive Literary Elements Handbook
To review or learn more about the literary elements, go to www.glencoe.com.

Keep Moving

Use these skills as you read "Flowers for Algernon," Part 1.

Flowers for Algernon

by Daniel Keyes

progris riport 1—martch 5 1965

Dr. Strauss says I shud rite down what I think and evrey thing that happins to me from now on. I dont know why but he says its importint so they will see if they will use me. I hope they use me. Miss Kinnian says maybe they can make me smart. I want to be smart. My name is Charlie Gordon. I am 37 years old and 2 weeks ago was my birthday. I have nuthing more to rite now so I will close for today. ∎

progris riport 2—martch 6

I had a test today. I think I faled it. and I think that maybe now they wont use me. What happind is a nice young man was in the room and he had some white cards with ink

Practice the Skills

1 **Reviewing Skills**

Making Inferences You can learn a lot about Charlie from the way he writes. For instance, you can tell from his spelling and difficulty understanding other people that he finds it hard to do things most other people do easily.

spillled all over them. He sed Charlie what do you see on this card. I was very skared even tho I had my rabits foot in my pockit because when I was a kid I always faled tests in school and I spillled ink to.

I told him I saw a inkblot. He said yes and it made me feel good. I thot that was all but when I got up to go he stopped

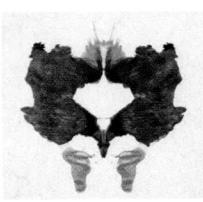

Visual Vocabulary
An *inkblot* is an ink mark made by dropping ink on a piece of paper and then folding the paper in half to make an interesting picture.

me. He said now sit down Charlie we are not thru yet. **Then** I dont remember so good but he wantid me to say what was in the ink. I dint see nuthing in the ink but he said there was picturs there other pepul saw some picturs. I coudnt see any picturs. I reely tryed to see. I held the card close up and then far away. Then I said if I had my glases I coud see better I usally only ware my glases in the movies or TV but I said they are in the closit in the hall. I got them. Then I said let me see that card agen I bet Ill find it now. **2**

I tryed hard but I still coudnt find the picturs I only saw the ink. I told him maybe I need new glases. He rote somthing down on a paper and I got skared of faling the test. I told him it was a very nice inkblot with littel points al around the eges. He looked very sad so that wasnt it. I said please let me try agen. Ill get it in a few minits becaus Im not so fast somtimes. Im a slow reeder too in Miss Kinnians class for slow adults but I'm trying very hard.

He gave me a chance with another card that had 2 kinds of ink spilled on it red and blue.

He was very nice and talked slow like Miss Kinnian does and he explained it to me that it was a *raw shok*.[1] He said pepul see things in the ink. I said show me where. He said think. I told him I think a inkblot but that wasnt rite eather. He said what does it remind you—pretend something. I closd my eyes for a long time to pretend. I told him I pretned a fowntan pen with ink leeking all over a table cloth. Then he got up and went out.

I dont think I passd the *raw shok* test.

Practice the Skills

2 **Key Reading Skill**

Understanding Text Structures Notice how many times Charlie uses the word <u>then</u> in this paragraph. What does this tell you about the text structure of the selection?

---

1. When Charlie says *raw shok,* he is talking about the *Rorschach* (ROR shok) test, which gathers information about personality and intelligence.

progris report 3—martch 7

Practice the Skills

Dr Strauss and Dr Nemur say it dont matter about the inkblots. I told them I dint spill the ink on the cards and I coudnt see anything in the ink. They said that maybe they will still use me. I said Miss Kinnian never gave me tests like that one only spelling and reading. They said Miss Kinnian told that I was her bestist pupil in the adult nite scool becaus I tryed the hardist and I reely wantid to lern. They said how come you went to the adult nite scool all by yourself Charlie. How did you find it. I said I askd pepul and sumbody told me where I shud go to lern to read and spell good. They said why did you want to. I told them becaus all my life I wantid to be smart and not dumb. But its very hard to be smart. They said you know it will probly be tempirery. I said yes. Miss Kinnian told me. I dont care if it herts.

Later I had more crazy tests today. The nice lady who gave it me told me the name and I asked her how do you spellit so I can rite it in my progris riport. THEMATIC APPERCEPTION TEST.[2] I dont know the frist 2 words but I know what *test* means. You got to pass it or you get bad marks. This test lookd easy becaus I coud see the picturs. Only this time she dint want me to tell her the picturs. That mixd me up. I said the man yesterday said I shoud tell him what I saw in the ink she said that dont make no difrence. She said make up storys about the pepul in the picturs.

I told her how can you tell storys about pepul you never met. I said why shud I make up lies. I never tell lies any more becaus I always get caut.

She told me this test and the other one the raw-shok was for getting personalty. I laffed so hard. I said how can you get that thing from inkblots and fotos. She got **sore** and put her picturs away. I dont care. It was sily. I gess I faled that test too. **3**

Later some men in white coats took me to a difernt part of the hospitil and gave me a game to play. It was like a race with a white mouse. They called the mouse Algernon. Algernon was in a box with a lot of twists and turns like all kinds of walls and they gave me a pencil and a paper with

3 | **English Language Coach**

Multiple-Meaning Words
Which meaning of **sore** makes the most sense here? Write the meaning in your Learner's Notebook.

---

2. A **Thematic Apperception** (thee MAT ik ap ur SEP shun) **Test** asks people to look at a few pictures and then make up a story about the pictures.

lines and lots of boxes. On one side it said START and on the other end it said FINISH. They said it was *amazed*[3] and that Algernon and me had the same *amazed* to do. I dint see how we could have the same *amazed* if Algernon had a box and I had a paper but I dint say nothing. Anyway there wasnt time because the race started.

One of the men had a watch he was trying to hide so I woudnt see it so I tryed not to look and that made me nervus.

Anyway that test made me feel worser than all the others because they did it over 10 times with difernt *amazeds* and Algernon won every time. I dint know that mice were so smart. Maybe thats because Algernon is a white mouse. Maybe white mice are smarter then other mice.

progris riport 4—Mar 8

Their going to use me! Im so exited I can hardly write. Dr Nemur and Dr Strauss had a argument about it first. Dr Nemur was in the office when Dr Strauss brot me in. Dr Nemur was worryed about using me but Dr Strauss told him Miss Kinnian rekemmended me the best from all the people who she was teaching. **4** I like Miss Kinnian becaus shes a very smart teacher. And she said Charlie your going to have a second chance. If you volenteer for this experament you mite get smart. They dont know if it will be perminint but theirs a chance. Thats why I said ok even when I was scared because she said it was an operashun. She said dont be scared Charlie you done so much with so little I think you deserv it most of all.

So I got scaird when Dr Nemur and Dr Strauss argud about it. Dr Strauss said I had something that was very good. He said

Practice the Skills

4 | **Key Literary Element**

Irony Charlie is excited that the scientists are going to use him. He thinks of the experiment as a reward for being a good student. Think about what you've learned about Charlie and the doctors so far. What information do you have that Charlie does not have? What's the irony in this passage?

Charly, 1967. Selmur Productions. Movie still.

Analyzing the Image What does this scene from the film show you about Charlie's struggle at this point in the story?

---

3. Charlie says *amazed,* but he means "a maze," which is a confusing set of paths that are easy to get lost in.

I had a good *motor-vation*.[4] I never even knew I had that. I felt proud when he said that not every body with an eye-q[5] of 68 had that thing. I dont know what it is or where I got it but he said Algernon had it too. Algernons *motor-vation* is the cheese they put in his box. But it cant be that because I didnt eat any cheese this week.

Then he told Dr Nemur something I dint understand so while they were talking I wrote down some of the words.

He said Dr Nemur I know Charlie is not what you had in mind as the first of your new brede of intelek** (coudnt get the word) superman. But most people of his low ment** are host** and uncoop** they are usualy dull apath** and hard to **reach**. He has a good natcher hes intristed and eager to please. **5**

Dr Nemur said remember he will be the first human beeng ever to have his intelijence trippled by surgicle meens.

Dr Strauss said exakly. Look at how well hes lerned to read and write for his low mentel age its as grate an acheve** as you and I lerning einstines therey of **vity[6] without help. That shows the intenss motorvation. Its comparat** a tremen** achev** I say we use Charlie.

I dint get all the words and they were talking to fast but it sounded like Dr Strauss was on my side and like the other one wasnt.

Then Dr Nemur nodded he said all right maybe your right. We will use Charlie. When he said that I got so exited I jumped up and shook his hand for being so good to me. I told him thank you doc you wont be sorry for giving me a second chance. And I mean it like I told him. After the operashun Im gonna try to be smart. Im gonna try awful hard.

Practice the Skills

5 | **English Language Coach**

Multiple-Meaning Words
Which meaning of **reach** makes the most sense here? How do you know? Write your answer in your Learner's Notebook.

---

4. Charlie means *motivation* (moh tih VAY shun). When people have motivation to do something, they feel that they want very much to do it.

5. When Charlie says *eye-q* he means IQ, which stands for "intelligence quotient" (KWOH shent). An IQ is the score a person gets on an intelligence test, which is supposed to measure a person's ability to learn.

6. When Charlie says *einstines therey of **vity,* he is talking about the theory of relativity developed by the scientist Albert Einstein which changed the way people understand the world.

progris ript 5—Mar 10

Im skared. Lots of people who work here and the nurses and the people who gave me the tests came to bring me candy and wish me luck. I hope I have luck. I got my rabits foot and my lucky penny and my horse shoe. Only a black cat crossed me when I was comming to the hospitil. Dr Strauss says dont be supersitis Charlie this is sience. Anyway Im keeping my rabits foot with me.

I asked Dr Strauss if Ill beat Algernon in the race after the operashun and he said maybe. If the operashun works Ill show that mouse I can be as smart as he is. Maybe smarter. Then Ill be abel to read better and spell the words good and know lots of things and be like other people. I want to be smart like other people. If it works perminint they will make everybody smart all over the wurld.

They dint give me anything to eat this morning. I dont know what that eating has to do with getting smart. Im very hungry and Dr Nemur took away my box of candy. That Dr Nemur is a grouch. Dr Strauss says I can have it back after the operashun. You cant eat befor a operashun . . .

Progress Report 6—Mar 15

The operashun dint hurt. He did it while I was sleeping. They took off the bandijis from my eyes and my head today so I can make a PROGRESS REPORT. Dr Nemur who looked at some of my other ones says I spell PROGRESS wrong and he told me how to spell it and REPORT too. I got to try and remember that.

I have a very bad memary for spelling. Dr Strauss says its ok to tell about all the things that happin to me but he says I shoud tell more about what I feel and what I think. When I told him I dont know how to think he said try. All the time when the bandijis were on my eyes I tryed to think. Nothing happened. I dont know what to think about. Maybe if I ask him he will tell me how I can think now that Im suppose to get smart. What do smart people think about. **Fancy** things I suppose. I wish I knew some fancy things alredy. 6

Practice the Skills

6 English Language Coach

Multiple-Meaning Words
Look up **fancy** in a dictionary. How many meanings of *fancy* are there? What does it mean in the context of the selection? (Hint: What part of speech is *fancy* in the selection?)

Progress Report 7—mar 19

Nothing is happining. I had lots of tests and different kinds of races with Algernon. I hate that mouse. He always beats me. Dr Strauss said I got to play those games. And he said some time I got to take those tests over again. Thse inkblots are stupid. And those pictures are stupid too. I like to draw a picture of a man and a woman but I wont make up lies about people.

I got a headache from trying to think so much. I thot Dr Strauss was my frend but he dont help me. He dont tell me what to think or when Ill get smart. Miss Kinnian dint come to see me. I think writing these progress reports are stupid too. **7**

Progress Report 8—Mar 23

Im going back to work at the factery. They said it was better I shud go back to work but I cant tell anyone what the operashun was for and I have to come to the hospitil for an hour evry night after work. They are gonna pay me mony every month for lerning to be smart.

Im glad Im going back to work because I miss my job and all my frends and all the fun we have there.

Dr Strauss says I shud keep writing things down but I dont have to do it every day just when I think of something or something speshul happins. He says dont get discoridged because it takes time and it happins slow. He says it took a long time with Algernon before he got 3 times smarter than he was before. Thats why Algernon beats me all the time because he had that operashun too. That makes me feel better. I coud probly do that *amazed* faster than a reglar mouse. Maybe some day Ill beat Algernon. Boy that would be something. So far Algernon looks like he mite be smart perminent.

Mar 25   (I dont have to write PROGRESS REPORT on top any more just when I hand it in once a week for Dr Nemur to read. I just have to put the date on. That saves time)

We had a lot of fun at the factery today. Joe Carp said hey look where Charlie had his operashun what did they do Charlie put some brains in. I was going to tell him but I remembered Dr Strauss said no. Then Frank Reilly said what

Practice the Skills

7 **Reviewing Skills**

Making Inferences Notice the change in Charlie's personality from earlier in the story. Why do you think he's getting cranky and calling everything "stupid"?

did you do Charlie forget your key and open your door the hard way. That made me laff. Their really my friends and they like me. **8**

Sometimes somebody will say hey look at Joe or Frank or George he really pulled a Charlie Gordon. I dont know why they say that but they always laff. This morning Amos Borg who is the 4 man at Donnegans used my name when he shouted at Ernie the office boy. Ernie lost a packige. He said Ernie for godsake what are you trying to be a Charlie Gordon. I dont understand why he said that. I never lost any packiges. **9**

Mar 28   Dr Strauss came to my room tonight to see why I dint come in like I was suppose to. I told him I dont like to race with Algernon any more. He said I dont have to for a while but I shud come in. He had a present for me only it wasnt a present but just for lend. I thot it was a little television but it wasnt. He said I got to turn it on when I go to sleep. I said your kidding why shud I turn it on when Im going to sleep. Who ever herd of a thing like that. But he said if I want to get smart I got to do what he says. I told him I dint think I was going to get smart and he put his hand on my sholder and said Charlie you dont know it yet but your getting smarter all the time. You wont notice for a while. I think he was just being nice to make me feel good because I dont look any smarter.

Oh yes I almost forgot. I asked him when I can go back to the class at Miss Kinnians school. He said I wont go their. He said that soon Miss Kinnian will come to the hospitil to start and teach me speshul. I was mad at her for not comming to see me when I got the operashun but I like her so maybe we will be frends again.

Practice the Skills

8 **Key Literary Element**

Irony What is the dramatic irony here? (Hint: What are Charlie's thoughts about his friends' behavior? How do his thoughts about his friends differ from yours?)

9 **Reviewing Skills**

Making Inferences What do you think it means when someone says, "He really pulled a Charlie Gordon"? Support your inference with story details.

Charly, 1967. Selmur Productions. Movie still.

Analyzing the Image Can you see Charlie's determination in this photograph?

Flowers for Algernon, Part 1   **347**

Mar 29   That crazy TV kept me up all night. How can I sleep with something yelling crazy things all night in my ears. And the nutty pictures. Wow. I dont know what it says when Im up so how am I going to know when Im sleeping.

Dr Strauss says its ok. He says my brains are lerning when I sleep and that will help me when Miss Kinnian starts my lessons in the hospitl (only I found out it isnt a hospitil its a labatory). I think its all crazy. If you can get smart when your sleeping why do people go to school. That thing I dont think will work. I use to watch the late show and the late late show on TV all the time and it never made me smart. Maybe you have to sleep while you watch it. **10**

PROGRESS REPORT 9—April 3

Dr Strauss showed me how to keep the TV turned low so now I can sleep. I dont hear a thing. And I still dont understand what it says. A few times I play it over in the morning to find out what I lerned when I was sleeping and I dont think so. Miss Kinnian says Maybe its another langwidge or something. But most times it sounds american. It talks so fast faster then even Miss Gold who was my teacher in 6 grade and I remember she talked so fast I coudnt understand her.

I told Dr Strauss what good is it to get smart in my sleep. I want to be smart when Im awake. He says its the same thing and I have two minds. Theres the *subconscious*[7] and the *conscious* (thats how you spell it). And one dont tell the other one what its doing. They dont even talk to each other. Thats why I dream. And boy have I been having crazy dreams. Wow. Ever since that night TV. The late late late late late show.

I forgot to ask him if it was only me or if everybody had those two minds.

(I just looked up the word in the dictionary Dr Strauss gave me. The word is *subconscious. adj. Of the nature of mental operations yet not present in consciousness; as, subconscious conflict of desires.*) Theres more but I still don't know what it means. This isnt a very good dictionary for dumb people like me.

---

7. A person is not aware of the thoughts and feelings in the ***subconscious*** (sub KON shus) part of his or her mind.

Practice the Skills

10   **Reviewing Skills**

Making Inferences What has changed about Charlie? (Hint: How does Charlie feel about Dr. Strauss's television idea?)

Analyzing the Art How does this image help you understand the idea of a *subconscious* mind?

Anyway the headache is from the party. My frends from the factery Joe Carp and Frank Reilly invited me to go with them to Muggsys Saloon for some drinks. I dont like to drink but they said we will have lots of fun. I had a good time.

Joe Carp said I shoud show the girls how I mop out the toilet in the factory and he got me a mop. I showed them and everyone laffed when I told that Mr Donnegan said I was the best janiter he ever had because I like my job and do it good and never come late or miss a day except for my operashun.

I said Miss Kinnian always said Charlie be proud of your job because you do it good.

Everybody laffed and we had a good time and they gave me lots of drinks and Joe said Charlie is a card when hes potted.[8] I dont know what that means but everybody likes me and we have fun. I cant wait to be smart like my best frends Joe Carp and Frank Reilly. **11**

I dont remember how the party was over but I think I went out to buy a newspaper and coffe for Joe and Frank and when I came back there was no one their. I looked for them all over till late. Then I dont remember so good but I think I got sleepy or sick. A nice cop brot me back home. Thats what my landlady Mrs Flynn says.

But I got a headache and a big lump on my head and black and blue all over. I think maybe I fell but Joe Carp says it was the cop they beat up drunks some times. I don't think so. Miss Kinnian says cops are to help people. Anyway I got a bad headache and Im sick and hurt all over. I dont think Ill drink anymore.

April 6 I beat Algernon! I dint even know I beat him until Burt the tester told me. Then the second time I lost because I got so exited I fell off the chair before I finished. But after that I beat him 8 more times. I must be getting smart to beat a smart mouse like Algernon. But I dont *feel* smarter.

I wanted to race Algernon some more but Burt said thats enough for one day. They let me hold him for a minit. Hes not so bad. Hes soft like a ball of cotton. He blinks and when he opens his eyes their black and pink on the eges.

---

8. *Charlie is a card when he's potted* is a slang way of saying that Charlie is funny when he drinks too much alcohol.

Practice the Skills

11 **Key Literary Element**

Irony This scene is an example of dramatic irony. What do you, the reader, know that Charlie does not know? How does this bit of irony make you feel about Charlie and his situation?

Charly, 1967. Selmur Productions. Movie still.
Analyzing the Image How would you describe Charlie's feelings toward Algernon?

I said can I feed him because I felt bad to beat him and I wanted to be nice and make frends. Burt said no Algernon is a very specshul mouse with an operashun like mine, and he was the first of all the animals to stay smart so long. He told me Algernon is so smart that every day he has to solve a test to get his food. Its a thing like a lock on a door that changes every time Algernon goes in to eat so he has to lern something new to get his food. That made me sad because if he coudnt lern he woud be hungry.

I dont think its right to make you pass a test to eat. How woud Dr Nemur like it to have to pass a test every time he wants to eat. I think Ill be frends with Algernon. **12**

April 9 Tonight after work Miss Kinnian was at the laboratory. She looked like she was glad to see me but scared. I told her dont worry Miss Kinnian Im not smart yet and she laffed. She said I have confidence in you Charlie the way you struggled so hard to read and right better than all the others. At werst you will have it for a littel wile and your doing somthing for sience.

12 **Key Reading Skill**

Understanding Text Structures Most selections have more than one text structure. Reread the first two paragraphs on this page. The text structure in these paragraphs is cause and effect. What causes and effects can you find here?

We are reading a very hard book. I never read such a hard book before. Its called *Robinson Crusoe* about a man who gets merooned on a dessert Iland. Hes smart and figers out all kinds of things so he can have a house and food and hes a good swimmer. Only I feel sorry because hes all alone and has no frends. But I think their must be somebody else on the iland because theres a picture with his funny umbrella looking at footprints. I hope he gets a frend and not be lonly.

April 10   Miss Kinnian teaches me to spell better. She says look at a word and close your eyes and say it over and over until you remember. I have lots of truble with *through* that you say *threw* and *enough* and *tough* that you dont say *enew* and *tew*. You got to say *enuff* and *tuff*. Thats how I use to write it before I started to get smart. Im confused but Miss Kinnian says theres no reason in spelling.

April 14   Finished *Robinson Crusoe.* I want to find out more about what happens to him but Miss Kinnian says thats all there is. *Why*

April 15   Miss Kinnian says Im lerning fast. She read some of the Progress Reports and she looked at me kind of funny. She says Im a fine person and Ill show them all. I asked her why. She said never mind but I shoudnt feel bad if I find out that everybody isnt nice like I think. She said for a person who god gave so little to you done more then a lot of people with brains they never even used. I said all my frends are smart people but there good. They like me and they never did anything that wasnt nice. Then she got something in her eye and she had to run out to the ladys room. **13**

April 16   Today, I lerned, the *comma,* this is a comma (,) a period, with a tail, Miss Kinnian, says its importent, because, it makes writing, better, she said, sombeody, could lose, a lot of money, if a comma, isnt, in the, right place, I dont have, any money, and I dont see, how a comma, keeps you, from losing it,

But she says, everybody, uses commas, so Ill use, them too,

April 17   I used the comma wrong. Its punctuation. Miss Kinnian told me to look up long words in the dictionary to lern to spell them. I said whats the difference if you can read it anyway. She said its part of your education so now on Ill

Practice the Skills

13   Key Literary Element

Irony Charlie thinks Miss Kinnian has run out of the room because she got something in her eye. What is the real reason she leaves? (Hint: How do you think she feels about the way Charlie's friends treat him?)

look up all the words Im not sure how to spell. It takes a long time to write that way but I think Im remembering. I only have to look up once and after that I get it right. Anyway thats how come I got the word *punctuation* right. (Its that way in the dictionary). Miss Kinnian says a period is punctuation too, and there are lots of other marks to lern. I told her I thot all the periods had to have tails but she said no.

You got to mix them up, she showed? me" how. to mix! them(up,. and now; I can! mix up all kinds" of punctuation, in! my writing? There, are lots! of rules? to lern; but Im gettin'g them in my head.

One thing I? like about, Dear Miss Kinnian: (thats the way it goes in a business letter if I ever go into business) is she, always gives me' a reason" when—I ask. She's a gen'ius! I wish! I cou'd be smart" like, her;

(Punctuation, is; fun!)

April 18 What a dope I am! I didn't even understand what she was talking about. I read the grammar book last night and it explanes the whole thing. Then I saw it was the same way as Miss Kinnian was trying to tell me, but I didn't get it. I got up in the middle of the night, and the whole thing straightened out in my mind.

Miss Kinnian said that the TV working in my sleep helped out. She said I reached a plateau. Thats like the flat top of a hill.

After I figgered out how punctuation worked, I read over all my old Progress Reports from the beginning. Boy, did I have crazy spelling and punctuation! I told Miss Kinnian I ought to go over the pages and fix all the mistakes but she said, "No, Charlie, Dr. Nemur wants them just as they are. That's why he let you keep them after they were photostated,[9] to see your own progress. You're coming along fast, Charlie."

That made me feel good. After the lesson I went down and played with Algernon. We don't race any more. **14**

---

9. Anything that is ***photostated*** (FOH toh stat ud) has been photocopied onto specially treated paper.

Practice the Skills

14 **Key Reading Skill**

Understanding Text Structures The author organizes the text in time order. How does the text structure help you see how quickly changes are happening to Charlie?

April 20   I feel sick inside. Not sick like for a doctor, but inside my chest it feels empty like getting punched and a heartburn at the same time.

I wasn't going to write about it, but I guess I got to, because it's important. Today was the first time I ever stayed home from work.

Last night Joe Carp and Frank Reilly invited me to a party. There were lots of girls and some men from the factory. I remembered how sick I got last time I drank too much, so I told Joe I didn't want anything to drink. He gave me a plain Coke instead. It tasted funny, but I thought it was just a bad taste in my mouth.

We had a lot of fun for a while. Joe said I should dance with Ellen and she would teach me the steps. I fell a few times and I couldn't understand why because no one else was dancing besides Ellen and me. And all the time I was tripping because somebody's foot was always sticking out. **15**

Then when I got up I saw the look on Joe's face and it gave me a funny feeling in my stomack. "He's a **scream,**" one of the girls said. Everybody was laughing. **16**

Frank said, "I ain't laughed so much since we sent him off for the newspaper that night at Muggsy's and ditched him."

"Look at him. His face is red."

"He's blushing. Charlie is blushing."

"Hey, Ellen, what'd you do to Charlie? I never saw him act like that before."

I didn't know what to do or where to turn. Everyone was looking at me and laughing and I felt naked. I wanted to hide myself. I ran out into the street and I threw up. Then I walked home. It's a funny thing I never knew that Joe and Frank and the others liked to have me around all the time to make fun of me.

Now I know what it means when they say "to pull a Charlie Gordon."

I'm ashamed. **17**

Practice the Skills

15 **Key Reading Skill**

Understanding Text Structures Charlie's writing is improving. Look at how he uses signal words for chronological order in the first four paragraphs on this page. What signal words can you find?

16 **English Language Coach**

Multiple-Meaning Words What does **scream** mean here? Write its definition in your Learner's Notebook. Use a dictionary if you need help.

17 **BIG Question**

What price does Charlie pay for getting smarter? Is the price too high? Write your answer on the "Flowers for Algernon," Part 1, flap of the Reading Workshop 3 Foldable. Your response will help you complete the Unit Challenge later.

After You Read

Flowers for Algernon, Part 1

Answering the BIG Question

1. How has Charlie changed since his operation? What has he gained and what has he lost?

2. **Recall** How did Charlie see himself before his operation? How did he feel toward other people?
   TIP Right There

Critical Thinking

3. **Analyze** What makes Charlie feel so ashamed at the end of Part 1?
   TIP Author and Me

4. **Analyze** Charlie ends the April 14 Progress Report with the word *Why.* How does this word show that Charlie's thinking has changed?
   TIP Author and Me

5. **Evaluate** What is your opinion so far about the experiment that Charlie is part of? Do you think it is a good thing or is it too dangerous for human beings? Explain your reasons for your opinion.
   TIP Author and Me

Write About Your Reading

Written Report The author presents "Flowers for Algernon" as a series of progress reports or journal entries written by Charlie. Write a brief report that compares Charlie before the operation with the person he's becoming since the operation. Write in your own voice and style, not in Charlie's. Follow this plan for your report:

- In the first paragraph, describe (a) how Charlie was before the operation and (b) the ways in which he's still the same at the end of Part 1.

- In the second paragraph, explain how Charlie has changed since the operation. Give examples.

- In the third paragraph, tell whether the changes that you noted are good or bad for Charlie. Give details from the story to support your opinion.

NY English Language Arts Core Curriculum (pp. 354–355)

LC R17 Demonstrate comprehension and response through a range of activities.
LC W4 Compose mechanically grade-appropriate texts for a variety of purposes.
LC R13 Use text structure and literary devices to aid comprehension and response.
R2d Determine how the use and meaning of literary devices convey the author's message or intent. **Core W8** Use correct grammatical construction in sentences.

For a complete description of the standards, see p. NY11.

Skills Review

Key Reading Skill: Understanding Text Structures

6. What is the main text structure of the selection? Why do you think the story is organized this way? Write the answer in your Learner's Notebook.

7. Name at least one other text structure, besides chronological order, that you noticed in Part 1 of the story. In your Learner's Notebook, write down the page number and a description of the passage with that text structure.

Key Literary Element: Irony

8. What example of irony in Part 1 stands out most for you? How does it affect the way you feel about Charlie and other characters?

9. You only have the information Charlie gives you in this story. There is no narrator to tell you anything else. So how do you know the things that Charlie doesn't?

Reviewing Skills: Making Inferences

10. Why do the doctors want Charlie to keep his operation a secret from his coworkers?

Vocabulary Check

11. English Language Coach Review the meanings of the words *sore* and *reach* on page 338. In your Learner's Notebook, write a sentence for each word that explains one of its meanings.

12. Academic Vocabulary What is a synonym for the word **structure?**

Web Activities For eFlashcards, Selection Quick Checks, and other Web activities, go to www.glencoe.com.

Grammar Link: Run-ons

Never run two or more independent clauses together. This mistake is called a **run-on sentence.**

Wrong: Jeremy has two brothers he is the oldest of the three boys.

There are two kinds of run-ons. In the above example, two independent clauses are jammed together with no conjunction or punctuation to separate the ideas. In a second kind of run-on, only a comma separates the two clauses.

Wrong: Jeremy has two brothers, he is the oldest of the three boys.

One way to fix a run-on is to separate the two ideas by making each one a complete sentence. Just insert the proper end punctuation and capitalization.

Right: Jeremy has two brothers. He is the oldest of the three boys.

You can also separate the two ideas with a comma and coordinating conjunction to make a compound sentence. (Use the conjunction that makes the sentence mean what you want it to mean.)

Right: Jeremy has two brothers, but he is the oldest of the three boys.

Grammar Practice

On another piece of paper, copy these sentences and correct each run-on error.

13. Estela can't wait for spring it is her favorite season.

14. Otto loves to draw, he is very artistic.

15. Juanita missed school today she has a fever.

16. My dog's name is Otis, he likes to jump and chew toys.

17. Carrie went to the store she bought milk, cereal, and eggs.

18. The rain stopped the sun came out.

Writing Application Review your Write About Your Reading activity. Fix any run-on sentences.

Before You Read

Flowers for Algernon, Part 2

Vocabulary Preview

tangible (TAN juh bull) *adj.* able to be seen, touched, or felt **(p. 364)**
The doctor wants to see tangible results that he can measure.

invariably (in VAYR ee ub lee) *adv.* constantly; always **(p. 367)** *Invariably,
when a waiter breaks a glass in a restaurant, customers laugh.*

cowered (KOW erd) *v.* moved away in fear; form of the verb *cower*
(p. 367) *The new dishwasher cowered when the owner yelled at him.*

obscure (ub SKYOOR) *v.* to hide **(p. 371)** *The success of the operation
cannot obscure the fact that it is not practical.*

stimulus (STIM yoo luss) *n.* something that causes a response **(p. 371)**
Food was the stimulus that caused the mouse to learn.

Whole Class Discussion As a class, talk about the following questions.

- What are three things that are tangible?
- What invariably happens when you get to school in the morning?
- Why would a person cower?
- What might a used car salesperson seek to obscure?
- What stimulus might cause you to squint?

English Language Coach

Multiple-Meaning Words When you come across a multiple-meaning
word, use context clues to figure out which meaning makes sense.

Look at these two words and some of their meanings. You'll see these
words in Part 2 of "Flowers for Algernon."

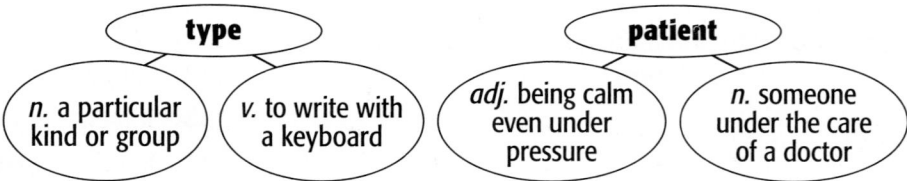

Write to Learn For each word above, write a sentence correctly using
one of the meanings of the word.

**NY English Language Arts
Core Curriculum** (pp. 356–377)

LC R9 Recognize multiple meanings of
words. **LC R13** Use text structure and literary devices to aid comprehension and
response. **R2d** Determine how the use
and meaning of literary devices convey
the author's message or intent.

*For a complete description of the
standards, see p. NY11.*

Skills Preview

Key Reading Skill: Understanding Text Structures

When you read Part 2 of the story, look for signal words and phrases that help identify how the writer has organized ideas.

Remember the signal words that show these text structures: cause and effect, comparison and contrast, problem and solution, and chronological order.

Write to Learn Think back to Part 1 of the story. The main text structure for that part is chronological order, but other text structures appear also. In your Learner's Notebook, describe one point in Part 1 in which Charlie uses a different kind of text structure in his own writing.

Literary Element: Foreshadowing

Foreshadowing is the planting of clues to prepare readers for events that will happen later. Foreshadowing can add suspense to a story, get readers involved in a story, and warn them that the story is going to take a different turn. Use these tips to recognize foreshadowing in "Flowers for Algernon."

- Pay attention to what Charlie and other characters say about future hopes, dreams, and fears.
  What possibilities for the future does the author want you to know about?

- Think about what the characters' actions tell you.
  Do the characters' actions hint at future events?

- When something new happens, think about what you read earlier that warned you this would happen.

Partner Talk Make a list of the statements and actions in Part 1 that might foreshadow what will happen next in the story. Share your list with a classmate and then discuss what you think might happen in Part 2. Write your predictions in your Learner's Notebook.

Get Ready to Read

Connect to the Reading

How would your life change if you woke up ten times smarter than you are now? What would you do with your new intelligence? When you read the rest of the story, compare what you would do with what Charlie Gordon does when he becomes very smart.

Partner Talk With a partner, talk about the changes in Charlie after his operation in Part 1 of the story. Include changes in his abilities to read, write, and think. Then talk about the changes in his feelings toward other people.

Build Background

- Psychologists rate someone who scores 140 or above on an IQ test a genius.

- Some geniuses can see connections between things that are not obvious to other people.

- There is debate over whether people are born geniuses, become geniuses because of their experiences, or both.

Set Purposes for Reading

BIG Question Read Part 2 of "Flowers for Algernon" to find out what happens to Charlie and Algernon and what prices they pay.

Set Your Own Purpose What else would you like to learn from the story to help you answer the Big Question? Write your own purpose on the "Flowers for Algernon," Part 2, flap of the Reading Workshop 3 Foldable.

Literature Online

Interactive Literary Elements Handbook
To review or learn more about the literary elements, go to www.glencoe.com.

Keep Moving

Use these skills as you read "Flowers for Algernon," Part 2.

Flowers for Algernon

by Daniel Keyes

PROGRESS REPORT 11

April 21   Still didn't go into the factory. I told Mrs. Flynn my landlady to call and tell Mr. Donnegan I was sick. Mrs. Flynn looks at me very funny lately like she's scared of me.

I think it's a good thing about finding out how everybody laughs at me. I thought about it a lot. It's because I'm so dumb and I don't even know when I'm doing something dumb. People think it's funny when a dumb person can't do things the same way they can. **1**

Anyway, now I know I'm getting smarter every day. I know punctuation and I can spell good. I like to look up all the hard words in the dictionary and I remember them. I'm reading a lot now, and Miss Kinnian says I read very fast. Sometimes I even understand what I'm reading about, and it stays in my mind. There are times when I can close my eyes and think of a page and it all comes back like a picture.

Besides history, geography, and arithmetic, Miss Kinnian said I should start to learn a few foreign languages. Dr. Strauss gave me some more tapes to play while I sleep. I still don't understand how that conscious and unconscious mind works, but Dr. Strauss says not to worry yet. He asked me to promise that when I start learning college subjects next week I wouldn't read any books on psychology—that is, until he gives me permission.

Practice the Skills

1 **Key Reading Skill**

Understanding Text Structures Charlie begins a new progress report here, but it's only one day after the last entry (in Part 1). What changes do you notice in Charlie from the last report entry to this one?

I feel a lot better today, but I guess I'm still a little angry that all the time people were laughing and making fun of me because I wasn't so smart. When I become intelligent like Dr. Strauss says, with three times my I.Q. of 68, then maybe I'll be like everyone else and people will like me and be friendly. **2**

I'm not sure what an I.Q. is. Dr. Nemur said it was something that measured how intelligent you were—like a scale in the drugstore weighs pounds. But Dr. Strauss had a big argument with him and said an I.Q. didn't weigh intelligence at all. He said an I.Q. showed how much intelligence you could get, like the numbers on the outside of a measuring cup. You still had to fill the cup up with stuff.

Then when I asked Burt, who gives me my intelligence tests and works with Algernon, he said that both of them were wrong (only I had to promise not to tell them he said so). Burt says that the I.Q. measures a lot of different things including some of the things you learned already, and it really isn't any good at all.

So I still don't know what I.Q. is except that mine is going to be over 200 soon. I didn't want to say anything, but I don't see how if they don't know *what* it is, or *where* it is—I don't see how they know *how much* of it you've got.

Dr. Nemur says I have to take a *Rorshach Test* tomorrow. I wonder what *that* is.

April 22 I found out what a *Rorshach* is. It's the test I took before the operation—the one with the inkblots on the pieces of cardboard. The man who gave me the test was the same one.

I was scared to death of those inkblots. I knew he was going to ask me to find the pictures and I knew I wouldn't be able to. I was thinking to myself, if only there was some way of knowing what kind of pictures were hidden there. Maybe there weren't any pictures at all. Maybe it was just a trick to see if I was dumb enough to look for something that wasn't there. Just thinking about that made me sore at him.

Practice the Skills

2 **Reviewing Skills**

Predicting Charlie thinks that once he is smarter he'll be like everyone else and people will like him. What do you predict will happen? Why? Read on to see if your prediction matches what happens.

"All right, Charlie," he said, "you've seen these cards before, remember?"

"Of course I remember."

The way I said it, he knew I was angry, and he looked surprised. "Yes, of course. Now I want you to look at this one. What might this be? What do you see on this card? People see all sorts of things in these inkblots. Tell me what it might be for you—what it makes you think of." **3**

I was shocked. That wasn't what I had expected him to say at all. "You mean there are no pictures hidden in those inkblots?"

He frowned and took off his glasses. "What?"

"Pictures. Hidden in the inkblots. Last time you told me that everyone could see them and you wanted me to find them too."

He explained to me that the last time he had used almost the exact same words he was using now. I didn't believe it, and I still have the suspicion that he misled me at the time just for the fun of it. Unless—I don't know any more—could I have been *that* feeble-minded?[1]

We went through the cards slowly. One of them looked like a pair of bats tugging at something. Another one looked like two men fencing with swords. I imagined all sorts of things. I guess I got carried away. But I didn't trust him any more, and I kept turning them around and even looking on the back to see if there was anything there I was supposed to **catch.** While he was making his notes, I peeked out of the corner of my eye to read it. But it was all in code that looked like this: **4**

WF+A DdF-Ad orig. WF-A SF+obj

The test still doesn't make sense to me. It seems to me that anyone could make up lies about things that they didn't really see. How could he know I wasn't making a fool of him by mentioning things that I didn't really imagine? Maybe I'll understand it when Dr. Strauss lets me read up on psychology. **5**

April 25 I figured out a new way to line up the machines in the factory, and Mr. Donnegan says it will save him ten thousand dollars a year in labor and increased production. He gave me a twenty-five-dollar bonus.

---

1. Learning and understanding can be very difficult for a ***feeble-minded*** person.

3 **Reviewing Skills**

Predicting How do you think Charlie will react to the inkblots this time? Why? Read on to find out what happens and if your prediction comes true.

4 **English Language Coach**

Multiple-Meaning Words Look up the verb **catch** in a dictionary and a thesaurus. Decide which meaning of the word matches how it is used in the selection. Then find a synonym that could replace *catch* in the story.

5 **Reviewing Skills**

Predicting Does Charlie's reaction to the inkblot test match your prediction? Why or why not?

I wanted to take Joe Carp and Frank Reilly out to lunch to celebrate, but Joe said he had to buy some things for his wife, and Frank said he was meeting his cousin for lunch. I guess it'll take a little time for them to get used to the changes in me. Everybody seems to be frightened of me. When I went over to Amos Borg and tapped him on the shoulder, he jumped up in the air.

People don't talk to me much any more or kid around the way they used to. It makes the job kind of lonely. **6**

April 27 I got up the nerve today to ask Miss Kinnian to have dinner with me tomorrow night to celebrate my bonus.

At first she wasn't sure it was right, but I asked Dr. Strauss and he said it was okay. Dr. Strauss and Dr. Nemur don't seem to be getting along so well. They're arguing all the time. This evening when I came in to ask Dr. Strauss about having dinner with Miss Kinnian, I heard them shouting. Dr. Nemur was saying that it was *his* experiment and *his* research, and Dr. Strauss was shouting back that he contributed just as much, because he found me through Miss Kinnian and he performed the operation. Dr. Strauss said that someday thousands of neurosurgeons[2] might be using his technique all over the world.

Dr. Nemur wanted to publish the results of the experiment at the end of this month. Dr. Strauss wanted to wait a while longer to be sure. Dr. Strauss said that Dr. Nemur was more interested in the Chair of Psychology at Princeton[3] than he was in the experiment. Dr. Nemur said that Dr. Strauss was nothing but an opportunist[4] who was trying to ride to glory on *his* coattails. **7**

When I left afterwards, I found myself trembling. I don't know why for sure, but it was as if I'd seen both men clearly for the first time. I remember hearing Burt say

Visual Vocabulary
Coattails are the back flaps of a man's dress coat. (They are also called simply "tails.")

If you "ride on someone's coattails," you use, or take advantage of, that person's power to gain power for yourself.

Practice the Skills

6 ✓ **BIG Question**
So far, what has Charlie gained and what has he lost since his operation? Write your answer on the "Flowers for Algernon," Part 2, flap of the Reading Workshop 3 Foldable. Your response will help you complete the Unit Challenge later.

7 **Key Reading Skill**

Understanding Text Structures In this paragraph about the two doctors, the text structure is comparing and contrasting. In your Learner's Notebook, jot down differences between the two doctors.

---

2. ***Neurosurgeons*** are doctors who study and operate on the brain.

3. The ***Chair of Psychology*** is the head of a psychology department at a college or university. ***Princeton*** is a famous university in New Jersey.

4. An ***opportunist*** is someone who takes advantage of every opportunity, regardless of consequences.

that Dr. Nemur had a shrew[5] of a wife who was pushing him all the time to get things published so that he could become famous. Burt said that the dream of her life was to have a big-shot husband.

Was Dr. Strauss really trying to ride on his coattails?

April 28   I don't understand why I never noticed how beautiful Miss Kinnian really is. She has brown eyes and feathery brown hair that comes to the top of her neck. She's only thirty-four! I think from the beginning I had the feeling that she was an unreachable genius—and very, very old. Now, every time I see her she grows younger and more lovely.

We had dinner and a long talk. When she said that I was coming along so fast that soon I'd be leaving her behind, I laughed.

"It's true, Charlie. You're already a better reader than I am. You can read a whole page at a glance while I can take in only a few lines at a time. And you remember every single thing you read. I'm lucky if I can recall the main thoughts and the general meaning."

"I don't feel intelligent. There are so many things I don't understand."

She took out a cigarette and I lit it for her. "You've got to be a *little* **patient.** You're accomplishing in days and weeks what it takes normal people to do in half a lifetime. That's what makes it so amazing. You're like a giant sponge now, soaking things in. Facts, figures, general knowledge. And soon you'll begin to connect them, too. You'll see how the different branches of learning are related. There are many levels, Charlie, like steps on a giant ladder that take you up higher and higher to see more and more of the world around you. 🔳

"I can see only a little bit of that, Charlie, and I won't go much higher than I am now, but you'll keep climbing up and up, and see more and more, and each step will open new worlds that you never even knew existed." She frowned. "I hope . . . I just hope to God—"

"What?"

"Never mind, Charles. I just hope I wasn't wrong to advise you to go into this in the first place." 🔳

5. Here, **shrew** means "a bad-tempered, nagging woman."

8 | **English Language Coach**

Multiple-Meaning Words
Use the definitions given earlier to decide which meaning of **patient** makes sense here.

9 | **Literary Element**

Foreshadowing Why do you think Miss Kinnian is worried about getting Charlie involved in the project? What events might this foreshadow?

I laughed. "How could that be? It worked, didn't it? Even Algernon is still smart."

We sat there silently for a while and I knew what she was thinking about as she watched me toying with the chain of my rabbit's foot and my keys. I didn't want to think of that possibility any more than elderly people want to think of death. I *knew* that this was only the beginning. I knew what she meant about levels because I'd seen some of them already. The thought of leaving her behind made me sad. **10**

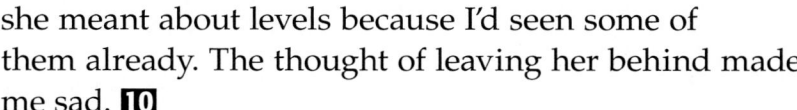

I'm in love with Miss Kinnian.

PROGRESS REPORT 12

April 30 I've quit my job with Donnegan's Plastic Box Company. Mr. Donnegan insisted that it would be better for all concerned if I left. What did I do to make them hate me so?

The first I knew of it was when Mr. Donnegan showed me the petition. Eight hundred and forty names, everyone connected with the factory, except Fanny Girden. Scanning the list quickly, I saw at once that hers was the only missing name. All the rest demanded that I be fired.

Joe Carp and Frank Reilly wouldn't talk to me about it. No one else would either, except Fanny. She was one of the few people I'd known who set her mind to something and believed it no matter what the rest of the world proved, said, or did—and Fanny did not believe that I should have been fired. She had been against the petition on principle and despite the pressure and threats she'd held out.

"Which don't mean to say," she remarked, "that I don't think there's something mighty strange about you, Charlie. Them changes. I don't know. You used to be a good, dependable, ordinary man—not too bright maybe, but honest. Who knows what you done to yourself to get so smart all of a sudden. Like everybody around here's been saying, Charlie, it's not right."

Practice the Skills

10 Literary Element

Foreshadowing What is Charlie worried about? Explain how his concern could be a foreshadowing clue.

"But how can you say that, Fanny? What's wrong with a man becoming intelligent and wanting to acquire knowledge and understanding of the world around him?"

She stared down at her work and I turned to leave. Without looking at me, she said: "It was evil when Eve listened to the snake and ate from the tree of knowledge. It was evil when she saw that she was naked. If not for that none of us would ever have to grow old and sick, and die."

Once again now I have the feeling of shame burning inside me. This intelligence has driven a wedge between me and all the people I once knew and loved. Before, they laughed at me and despised me for my ignorance and dullness; now, they hate me for my knowledge and understanding. What in God's name do they want of me? **11**

They've driven me out of the factory. Now I'm more alone than ever before . . .

May 15 Dr. Strauss is very angry at me for not having written any progress reports in two weeks. He's justified because the lab is now paying me a regular salary. I told him I was too busy thinking and reading. When I pointed out that writing was such a slow process that it made me impatient with my poor handwriting, he suggested that I learn to **type.** It's much easier to write now because I can type nearly seventy-five words a minute. Dr. Strauss continually reminds me of the need to speak and write simply so that people will be able to understand me. **12**

I'll try to review all the things that happened to me during the last two weeks. Algernon and I were presented to the American Psychological Association sitting in convention with the World Psychological Association last Tuesday. We created quite a sensation. Dr. Nemur and Dr. Strauss were proud of us.

I suspect that Dr. Nemur, who is sixty—ten years older than Dr. Strauss—finds it necessary to see **tangible** results of his work. Undoubtedly the result of pressure by Mrs. Nemur.

Contrary to my earlier impressions of him, I realize that Dr. Nemur is not at all a genius. He has a very good mind, but it struggles under the spectre[6] of self-doubt. He wants people to

---

6. A *spectre* is something that haunts or troubles your mind a lot.

Practice the Skills

11 Key Reading Skill

Understanding Text Structures How does the compare-and-contrast text structure in this passage help you understand what Charlie is going through?

12 English Language Coach

Multiple-Meaning Words The word **type** has several meanings. Which meaning from page 356 makes sense here?

Vocabulary

tangible (TAN juh bull) *adj.* able to be seen, touched, or felt

Charly, 1967. Selmur Productions. Movie still.

Analyzing the Image How does this photo show that Charlie has changed?

take him for a genius. Therefore, it is important for him to feel that his work is accepted by the world. I believe that Dr. Nemur was afraid of further delay because he worried that someone else might make a discovery along these lines and take the credit from him.

Dr. Strauss on the other hand might be called a genius, although I feel that his areas of knowledge are too limited. He was educated in the tradition of narrow specialization;[7] the broader aspects of background were neglected far more than necessary—even for a neurosurgeon. **13**

I was shocked to learn that the only ancient languages he could read were Latin, Greek, and Hebrew, and that he knows almost nothing of mathematics beyond the elementary levels of the calculus of variations.[8] When he admitted this to

13 **Key Reading Skill**

Understanding Text Structures What is the text structure of this paragraph and the one above it? Look for signal words and phrases.

---

7. Most people who get a PhD, a type of advanced university degree, are educated *in the tradition of narrow specialization,* which means they learn only one subject.

8. *Calculus* is a branch of advanced mathematics. The *calculus of variations* is even more complicated than simple calculus.

me, I found myself almost annoyed. It was as if he'd hidden this part of himself in order to deceive me, pretending—as do many people I've discovered—to be what he is not. No one I've ever known is what he appears to be on the surface. **14**

Dr. Nemur appears to be uncomfortable around me. Sometimes when I try to talk to him, he just looks at me strangely and turns away. I was angry at first when Dr. Strauss told me I was giving Dr. Nemur an inferiority complex.[9] I thought he was mocking me and I'm oversensitive at being made fun of.

How was I to know that a highly respected psychoexperimentalist like Nemur was unacquainted with Hindustani[10] and Chinese? It's absurd when you consider the work that is being done in India and China today in the very field of this study.

I asked Dr. Strauss how Nemur could refute[11] Rahajamati's attack on his method and results if Nemur couldn't even read them in the first place. That strange look on Dr. Strauss' face can mean only one of two things. Either he doesn't want to tell Nemur what they're saying in India, or else—and this worries me—Dr. Strauss doesn't know either. I must be careful to speak and write clearly and simply so that people won't laugh.

May 18   I am very disturbed. I saw Miss Kinnian last night for the first time in over a week. I tried to avoid all discussions of intellectual concepts[12] and to keep the conversation on a simple, everyday level, but she just stared at me blankly and asked me what I meant about the mathematical variance equivalent in Dorbermann's *Fifth Concerto*.

When I tried to explain she stopped me and laughed. I guess I got angry, but I suspect I'm approaching her on the wrong level. No matter what I try to discuss with her, I am unable to communicate. I must review Vrostadt's equations on *Levels of Semantic Progression*. I find that I don't communicate with people much any more. Thank God for books and music and things I can think about. I am alone in my apartment at Mrs. Flynn's boardinghouse most of the time and seldom speak to anyone.

---

9. Someone with an *inferiority complex* feels less worthy or valuable than others.
10. *Hindustani* (hin dew STAHN ee) is a dialect spoken in India.
11. To *refute* the attack would be to prove that the criticism is false or incorrect.
12. *Intellectual concepts* are ideas that relate to learning and thinking.

Practice the Skills

14   Reviewing Elements

Irony Before the operation, there were things Charlie didn't know about the people around him. That helped to create dramatic irony. Are there things he doesn't know now?

May 20   I would not have noticed the new dishwasher, a boy of about sixteen, at the corner diner where I take my evening meals if not for the incident of the broken dishes.

They crashed to the floor, shattering and sending bits of white china under the tables. The boy stood there, dazed and frightened, holding the empty tray in his hand. The whistles and catcalls from the customers (the cries of "hey, there go the profits!" . . . "*Mazeltov!*"[13] . . . and "well, *he* didn't work here very long . . ." which **invariably** seem to follow the breaking of glass or dishware in a public restaurant) all seemed to confuse him.

When the owner came to see what the excitement was about, the boy **cowered** as if he expected to be struck and threw up his arms as if to ward off the blow.

"All right! All right, you dope," shouted the owner, "don't just stand there! Get the broom and sweep that mess up. A broom . . . a broom, you idiot! It's in the kitchen. Sweep up all the pieces."

The boy saw that he was not going to be punished. His frightened expression disappeared and he smiled and hummed as he came back with the broom to sweep the floor. A few of the rowdier customers kept up the remarks, amusing themselves at his expense.

"Here, sonny, over here there's a nice piece behind you . . ."
"C'mon, do it again . . ."
"He's not so dumb. It's easier to break 'em than to wash 'em . . ."

As his vacant eyes moved across the crowd of amused onlookers, he slowly mirrored their smiles and finally broke into an uncertain grin at the joke which he obviously did not understand.

I felt sick inside as I looked at his dull, vacuous smile, the wide, bright eyes of a child, uncertain but eager to please. They were laughing at him because he was mentally retarded. **15**

And I had been laughing at him too.

Suddenly, I was furious at myself and all those who were smirking at him. I jumped up and shouted, "Shut up! Leave

---

13. ***Mazeltov*** or ***mazel tov*** (MAH zul tov) means "congratulations" in the Hebrew language.

Vocabulary

invariably   (in VAYR ee ub lee) *adv.* constantly; always

cowered   (KOW erd) *v.* moved away in fear

Practice the Skills

15   **Key Reading Skill**

Understanding Text Structures The dishwasher dropping dishes sets off a chain of causes and effects that leads Charlie to this understanding. Quickly scan the May 20 journal entry to find the causes and effects that lead Charlie to this point.

him alone! It's not his fault he can't understand! He can't help what he is! But for God's sake . . . he's still a human being!"

The room grew silent. I cursed myself for losing control and creating a scene. I tried not to look at the boy as I paid my check and walked out without touching my food. I felt ashamed for both of us.

How strange it is that people of honest feelings and sensibility, who would not take advantage of a man born without arms or legs or eyes—how such people think nothing of abusing a man born with low intelligence. It infuriated me to think that not too long ago I, like this boy, had foolishly played the clown. **16**

And I had almost forgotten.

I'd hidden the picture of the old Charlie Gordon from myself because now that I was intelligent it was something that had to be pushed out of my mind. But today in looking at that boy, for the first time I saw what I had been. *I was just like him!*

Only a short time ago, I learned that people laughed at me. Now I can see that unknowingly I joined with them in laughing at myself. That hurts most of all.

I have often reread my progress reports and seen the illiteracy, the childish naiveté,[14] the mind of low intelligence peering from a dark room, through the keyhole, at the dazzling light outside. I see that even in my dullness I knew that I was inferior, and that other people had something I lacked—something denied me. In my mental blindness, I thought that it was somehow connected with the ability to read and write, and I was sure that if I could get those skills I would automatically have intelligence too.

Even a feeble-minded man wants to be like other men.

A child may not know how to feed itself, or what to eat, yet it knows of hunger.

This then is what I was like, I never knew. Even with my gift of intellectual awareness, I never really knew.

This day was good for me. Seeing the past more clearly, I have decided to use my knowledge and skills to work in the field of increasing human intelligence levels. Who is better equipped for this work? Who else has lived in both worlds? These are my people. Let me use my gift to do something for them.

Practice the Skills

16 **BIG Question**

Charlie realizes that he was once laughed at by others. The pain he feels is a price he has to pay for becoming smarter. Is the price too high? Discuss your answer with a partner. Then write your ideas on the "Flowers for Algernon," Part 2, flap of the Reading Workshop 3 Foldable.

---

14. *Naiveté* (nah EVE tay) is innocence, or lack of worldly knowledge and experience.

Tomorrow, I will discuss with Dr. Strauss the manner in which I can work in this area. I may be able to help him work out the problems of widespread use of the technique which was used on me. I have several good ideas of my own.

There is so much that might be done with this technique. If I could be made into a genius, what about thousands of others like myself? What fantastic levels might be achieved by using this technique on normal people? On *geniuses?*

There are so many doors to open. I am impatient to begin.

PROGRESS REPORT 13

May 23   It happened today. Algernon bit me. I visited the lab to see him as I do occasionally, and when I took him out of his cage, he snapped at my hand. I put him back and watched him for a while. He was unusually disturbed and vicious. **17**

May 24   Burt, who is in charge of the experimental animals, tells me that Algernon is changing. He is less cooperative; he refuses to run the maze any more; general motivation has decreased. And he hasn't been eating. Everyone is upset about what this may mean.

May 25   They've been feeding Algernon, who now refuses to work the shifting-lock problem. Everyone identifies me with Algernon. In a way we're both the first of our kind. They're all pretending that Algernon's behavior is not necessarily significant for me. But it's hard to hide the fact that some of the other animals who were used in this experiment are showing strange behavior.

Dr. Strauss and Dr. Nemur have asked me not to come to the lab any more. I know what they're thinking but I can't accept it. I am going ahead with my plans to carry their research forward. With all due respect to both of these fine scientists, I am well aware of their limitations. If there is an answer, I'll have to find it out for myself. Suddenly, time has become very important to me. **18**

May 29   I have been given a lab of my own and permission to go ahead with the research. I'm on to something. Working day and night. I've had a cot moved into the lab. Most of my writing time is spent on the notes which I keep in a separate folder, but from time to time I feel it necessary to put down my moods and my thoughts out of sheer habit.

Practice the Skills

17 **Literary Element**

Foreshadowing What might this event foreshadow? Remember, Charlie has had the same operation as Algernon.

18 **Literary Element**

Foreshadowing Why has time all of a sudden become so important to Charlie? What does he feel is going to happen?

I find the *calculus of intelligence* to be a fascinating study. Here is the place for the application of all the knowledge I have acquired. In a sense it's the problem I've been concerned with all my life.

May 31   Dr. Strauss thinks I'm working too hard. Dr. Nemur says I'm trying to cram a lifetime of research and thought into a few weeks. I know I should rest, but I'm driven on by something inside that won't let me stop. I've got to find the reason for the sharp regression[15] in Algernon. I've got to know *if* and *when* it will happen to me.

June 4 🔟

LETTER TO DR. STRAUSS (*copy*)

Dear Dr. Strauss:

Under separate cover I am sending you a copy of my report entitled, "The Algernon-Gordon Effect: A Study of Structure and Function of Increased Intelligence," which I would like to have you read and have published.

As you see, my experiments are completed. I have included in my report all of my formulae, as well as mathematical analysis in the appendix. Of course, these should be verified.

Because of its importance to both you and Dr. Nemur (and need I say to myself, too?) I have checked and rechecked my results a dozen times in the hope of finding an error. I am sorry to say the results must stand. Yet for the sake of science, I am grateful for the little bit that I here add to the knowledge of the function of the human mind and of the laws governing the artificial increase of human intelligence.

I recall your once saying to me that an experimental *failure* or the *disproving* of a theory was as important to the advancement of learning as a success would be. I know now that this is true. I am sorry, however, that my own contribution to the field must rest upon the ashes of the work of two men I regard so highly.

Yours truly,

Charles Gordon
encl.: rept.

---

15. When something returns to an earlier stage, it shows ***regression*** (ree GREH shun).

Practice the Skills

🔟 **Key Reading Skill**

Understanding Text Structures The story continues in chronological order. Why do you think the author chose to use chronological order? How does following events in order add to the impact of the story?

June 5 I must not become emotional. The facts and the results of my experiments are clear, and the more sensational aspects of my own rapid climb cannot **obscure** the fact that the tripling of intelligence by the surgical technique developed by Drs. Strauss and Nemur must be viewed as having little or no practical applicability (at the present time) to the increase of human intelligence. **20**

As I review the records and data on Algernon, I see that although he is still in his physical infancy, he has regressed mentally. Motor activity is impaired; there is a general reduction of glandular activity; there is an accelerated loss of co-ordination.

There are also strong indications of progressive[16] amnesia.

As will be seen by my report, these and other physical and mental deterioration syndromes[17] can be predicted with statistically significant results by the application of my formula.

The surgical **stimulus** to which we were both subjected has resulted in an intensification and acceleration of all mental processes. The unforeseen development, which I have taken the liberty of calling the *Algernon-Gordon Effect,* is the logical extension of the entire intelligence speed-up. The hypothesis[18] here proven may be described simply

Conversion. Diana Ong. Computer generated.

Analyzing the Art How might this face show what is happening to Charlie?

20 | **Reviewing Elements**

Style How has Charlie's style of writing changed in the last few entries?

---

16. ***Progressive amnesia*** is a loss of memory that is getting worse.

17. ***Deterioration*** is a worsening, and ***syndromes*** are groups of symptoms that, together, indicate disease. The combined term refers to diseases that result in a lessening of some ability or strength.

18. A ***hypothesis*** is an unproven idea or theory.

Vocabulary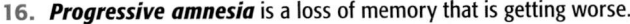

obscure (ub SKYOOR) *v.* to hide

stimulus (STIM yoo luss) *n.* something that causes a response

Flowers for Algernon, Part 2 **371**

in the following terms: Artificially increased intelligence deteriorates at a rate of time directly proportional to the quantity of the increase.

I feel that this, in itself, is an important discovery.

As long as I am able to write, I will continue to record my thoughts in these progress reports. It is one of my few pleasures. However, by all indications, my own mental deterioration will be very rapid. **21**

I have already begun to notice signs of emotional instability and forgetfulness, the first symptoms of the burnout.

June 10   Deterioration progressing. I have become absentminded. Algernon died two days ago. Dissection shows my predictions were right. His brain had decreased in weight and there was a general smoothing out of cerebral convolutions as well as a deepening and broadening of brain fissures.

I guess the same thing is or will soon be happening to me. Now that it's definite, I don't want it to happen.

I put Algernon's body in a cheese box and buried him in the back yard. I cried.

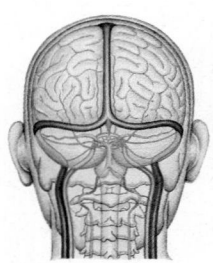

Visual Vocabulary
Charlie cuts up Algernon's brain to study it *(dissection)*. A healthy brain surface would have many irregular folds *(convolutions)* and cracks *(fissures)* that are long, narrow, and shallow.

June 15   Dr. Strauss came to see me again. I wouldn't open the door and I told him to go away. I want to be left to myself. I have become touchy and irritable. I feel the darkness closing in. It's hard to throw off thoughts of suicide. I keep telling myself how important this introspective[19] journal will be.

It's a strange sensation to pick up a book that you've read and enjoyed just a few months ago and discover that you don't remember it. I remembered how great I thought John Milton was, but when I picked up *Paradise Lost* I couldn't understand it at all. I got so angry I threw the book across the room.

I've got to try to hold on to some of it. Some of the things I've learned. Oh, God, please don't take it all away.

---

19. ***Introspective*** means "looking into or examining your own feelings and thoughts."

Practice the Skills

21 **Key Reading Skill**

Understanding Text Structures How has comparing his situation with Algernon's allowed Charlie to make this prediction?

June 19 Sometimes, at night, I go out for a walk. Last night I couldn't remember where I lived. A policeman took me home. I have the strange feeling that this has all happened to me before—a long time ago. I keep telling myself I'm the only person in the world who can describe what's happening to me.

June 21 Why can't I remember? I've got to fight. I lie in bed for days and I don't know who or where I am. Then it all comes back to me in a flash. Fugues of amnesia. Symptoms of senility[20]—second childhood. I can watch them coming on. It's so cruelly logical. I learned so much and so fast. Now my mind is deteriorating rapidly. I won't let it happen. I'll fight it. I can't help thinking of the boy in the restaurant, the blank expression, the silly smile, the people laughing at him. No— please—not that again . . . **22**

June 22 I'm forgetting things that I learned recently. It seems to be following the classic pattern—the last things learned are the first things forgotten. Or is that the pattern? I'd better look it up again . . .

I reread my paper on the *Algernon-Gordon Effect* and I get the strange feeling that it was written by someone else. There are parts I don't even understand.

Motor activity impaired. I keep tripping over things, and it becomes increasingly difficult to type.

Visual Vocabulary
This is an old-style manual *typewriter.* People used typewriters before computers were invented.

June 23 I've given up using the typewriter completely. My coordination is bad. I feel that I'm moving slower and slower. Had a terrible shock today. I picked up a copy of an article I used in my research, Krueger's *Uber psychische Ganzheit,* to see if it would help me understand what I had done. First I thought there was something wrong with my eyes. Then I realized I could no longer read German. I tested myself in other languages. All gone.

Practice the Skills

22 | **Reviewing Skills**

Predicting Do you think Charlie will be able to keep his mind from deteriorating? Why or why not?

---

20. **Fugues** (FYOOGS) **of amnesia** (am NEE zha) are times when a person seems to be aware of his or her actions but can't recall them later. **Senility** refers to the loss of physical and mental abilities that can accompany old age.

June 30   A week since I dared to write again. It's slipping away like sand through my fingers. Most of the books I have are too hard for me now. I get angry with them because I know that I read and understood them just a few weeks ago.

I keep telling myself I must keep writing these reports so that somebody will know what is happening to me. But it gets harder to form the words and remember spellings. I have to look up even simple words in the dictionary now and it makes me impatient with myself.

Dr. Strauss comes around almost every day, but I told him I wouldn't see or speak to anybody. He feels guilty. They all do. But I don't blame anyone. I knew what might happen. But how it hurts. **23**

July 7   I don't know where the week went. Todays Sunday I know because I can see through my window people going to church. I think I stayed in bed all week but I remember Mrs. Flynn bringing food to me a few times. I keep saying over and over Ive got to do something but then I forget or maybe its just easier not to do what I say Im going to do.

I think of my mother and father a lot these days. I found a picture of them with me taken at a beach. My father has a big ball under his arm and my mother is holding me by the hand. I dont remember them the way they are in the picture. All I remember is my father drunk most of the time and arguing with mom about money.

He never shaved much and he used to scratch my face when he hugged me. My mother said he died but Cousin Miltie said he heard his mom and dad say that my father ran away with another woman. When I asked my mother she slapped my face and said my father was dead. I dont think I ever found out which was true but I don't care much. (He said he was going to take me to see cows on a farm once but he never did. He never kept his promises . . .)

July 10   My landlady Mrs Flynn is very worried about me. She says the way I lay around all day and dont do anything I remind her of her son before she threw him out of the house. She said she doesnt like loafers. If Im sick its one thing, but if Im a loafer thats another thing and she wont have it. I told her I think Im sick.

I try to read a little bit every day, mostly stories, but sometimes I have to read the same thing over and over again

Practice the Skills

23 **Reviewing Skills**

Making Inferences Why do you think Dr. Strauss and all the others feel guilty?

because I dont know what it means. And its hard to write. I know I should look up all the words in the dictionary but its so hard and Im so tired all the time.

Then I got the idea that I would only use the easy words instead of the long hard ones. That saves time. I put flowers on Algernons grave about once a week. Mrs Flynn thinks Im crazy to put flowers on a mouses grave but I told her that Algernon was special.

July 14 Its sunday again. I dont have anything to do to keep me busy now because my television set is broke and I dont have any money to get it fixed. (I think I lost this months check from the lab. I dont remember) **24**

I get awful headaches and asperin doesnt help me much. Mrs Flynn knows Im really sick and she feels very sorry for me. Shes a wonderful woman whenever someone is sick.

July 22 Mrs Flynn called a strange doctor to see me. She was afraid I was going to die. I told the doctor I wasnt too sick and that I only forget sometimes. He asked me did I have any friends or relatives and I said no I dont have any. I told him I had a friend called Algernon once but he was a mouse and we used to run races together. He looked at me kind of funny like he thought I was crazy.

He smiled when I told him I used to be a genius. He talked to me like I was a baby and he winked at Mrs Flynn. I got mad and chased him out because he was making fun of me the way they all used to.

July 24 I have no more money and Mrs Flynn says I got to go to work somewhere and pay the rent because I havent paid for over two months. I dont know any work but the job I used to have at Donnegans Plastic Box Company. I dont want to go back there because they all knew me when I was smart and maybe theyll laugh at me. But I dont know what else to do to get money.

July 25 I was looking at some of my old progress reports and its very funny but I cant read what I wrote. I can make out some of the words but they dont make sense.

Miss Kinnian came to the door but I said go away I dont want to see you. She cried and I cried too but I wouldnt let her in because I didnt want her to laugh at me. I told her I didn't like her any more. I told her I didnt want to be smart any

Practice the Skills

24 **Key Reading Skill**

Understanding Text Structures What has Charlie done over the past week? Why do you think the author organizes information in chronological order? How does this help you understand the changes that are happening to Charlie?

more. Thats not true. I still love her and I still want to be smart but I had to say that so shed go away. She gave Mrs Flynn money to pay the rent. I dont want that. I got to get a job.

Please . . . please let me not forget how to read and write . . .

July 27 Mr Donnegan was very nice when I came back and asked him for my old job of janitor. First he was very suspicious but I told him what happened to me then he looked very sad and put his hand on my shoulder and said Charlie Gordon you got guts.

Everybody looked at me when I came downstairs and started working in the toilet sweeping it out like I used to. I told myself Charlie if they make fun of you dont get **sore** because you remember their not so smart as you once thot they were. And besides they were once your friends and if they laughed at you that doesnt mean anything because they liked you too. **25**

One of the new men who came to work there after I went away made a nasty crack he said hey Charlie I hear your a very smart fella a real quiz kid. Say something intelligent. I felt bad but Joe Carp came over and grabbed him by the shirt and said leave him alone you lousy cracker or Ill break your neck. I didnt expect Joe to take my part so I guess hes really my friend.

Later Frank Reilly came over and said Charlie if anybody bothers you or trys to take advantage you call me or Joe and we will set em straight. I said thanks Frank and I got choked up so I had to turn around and go into the supply room so he wouldnt see me cry. Its good to have friends.

July 28 I did a dumb thing today I forgot I wasnt in Miss Kinnians class at the adult center any more like I use to be. I went in and sat down in my old seat in the back of the room and she looked at me funny and she said Charles. I dint remember she ever called me that before only Charlie so I said hello Miss Kinnian Im redy for my lesin today only I lost my reader that we was using. She startid to cry and run out of the room and everybody looked at me and I saw they wasnt the same pepul who used to be in my class.

Then all of a suddin I rememberd some things about the operashun and me getting smart and I said holy smoke I reely pulled a Charlie Gordon that time. I went away before she come back to the room.

Practice the Skills

25 Key Reading Skill

Understanding Text Structures The author uses a comparing and contrasting text structure when Charlie returns to the factory. What is the difference between the way the other workers treat him in the beginning of the story and the way they treat him now?

Practice the Skills

Thats why Im going away from New York for good. I dont want to do nothing like that agen. I dont want Miss Kinnian to feel sorry for me. Evry body feels sorry at the factery and I dont want that eather so Im going someplace where nobody knows that Charlie Gordon was once a genus and now he cant even reed a book or rite good.

Im taking a cuple of books along and even if I cant reed them Ill practise hard and maybe I wont forget every thing I lerned. If I try reel hard maybe Ill be a littel bit smarter than I was before the operashun. I got my rabits foot and my luky penny and maybe they will help me.

If you ever reed this Miss Kinnian dont be sorry for me Im glad I got a second chanse to be smart becaus I lerned a lot of things that I never even new were in this world and Im grateful that I saw it all for a littel bit. I dont know why Im dumb agen or what I did wrong maybe its becaus I dint try hard enuff. But if I try and practis very hard maybe Ill get a littl smarter and know what all the words are. I remember a littel bit how nice I had a feeling with the blue book that has the torn cover when I red it. Thats why Im gonna keep trying to get smart so I can have that feeling agen. Its a good feeling to know things and be smart. I wish I had it rite now if I did I would sit down and reed all the time. Anyway I bet Im the first dumb person in the world who ever found out something important for sience. I remember I did somthing but I dont remember what. So I gess its like I did it for all the dumb pepul like me. **26**

Good-by Miss Kinnian and Dr. Strauss and evreybody. And P.S. please tell Dr Nemur not to be such a grouch when pepul laff at him and he woud have more frends. Its easy to make frends if you let pepul laff at you. Im going to have lots of frends where I go.

P.P.S. Please if you get a chanse put some flowrs on Algernons grave in the bak yard . . . ○

26 **BIG Question**

What price did Charlie pay to have the operation? Do you think that he was sorry he had the operation? Why or why not? Write your answers on the "Flowers for Algernon," Part 2, flap of the Reading Workshop 3 Foldable. Your response will help you complete the Unit Challenge later.

After You Read

Flowers for Algernon, Part 2

Answering the BIG Question

1. Knowing what happened to Charlie Gordon, would you pay the price he paid for the experience that he had? Why or why not?

2. **List** How does the author show you that Charlie is becoming smarter? List examples.

   TIP Think and Search

3. **Recall** What are some of the first things that Charlie loses when the experiment starts to fail? What does he fear losing the most?

   TIP Right There

Critical Thinking

4. **Infer** When Charlie goes back to Miss Kinnian's class, why does she start to cry and then run out of the room?

   TIP Author and Me

5. **Draw Conclusions** At the end of the story, why does Charlie decide to move away from New York?

   TIP Author and Me

Write About Your Reading

Cause-and-Effect Chart Even though the main text structure in this story is chronological order, many parts are organized in the cause-and-effect text structure. Copy and complete the following cause-and-effect chart. The first entry is done for you.

Cause	→	Effect
Because Charlie has a strong desire to learn,	→	Miss Kinnian recommends him for the operation.
1. Because Charlie's operation is a success,	→	
2.	→	the factory workers demand that Charlie be fired.
3. Because he loses his job,	→	

NY English Language Arts Core Curriculum (pp. 378–379)

LC R17 Demonstrate comprehension and response through a range of activities.
LC W4 Compose mechanically grade-appropriate texts for a variety of purposes.
LC R13 Use text structure and literary devices to aid comprehension and response.
R2d Determine how the use and meaning of literary devices convey the author's message or intent. **Core W8** Use correct grammatical construction in sentences.

For a complete description of the standards, see p. NY11.

Skills Review

Key Reading Skill: Understanding Text Structures

6. Think of four ways that Charlie changed after his operation. Write them in chronological order. Write a paragraph about these changes, using chronological order as the text structure.

Literary Element: Foreshadowing

7. Look over the story and list the clues that foreshadow the failure of the experiment. How would the story have been different if the failure had come as a complete surprise?

8. After Charlie starts to lose his intelligence, the friends who once laughed at him defend him (see the July 27 Progress Report). What earlier event foreshadows their defense of Charlie?

Reviewing Elements: Irony

9. One of the things the reader knows at the end is that Charlie completed an important scientific report on artificially-increased intelligence. Charlie only remembers that he did something. Is this dramatic irony? Explain.

Vocabulary Check

Answer *true* or *false* to the statements below.

10. Apples and oranges are **tangible.**

11. A sudden noise might be a **stimulus** that makes someone jump.

12. If something happens **invariably,** nobody can predict it.

13. If you want to **obscure** something, you should let everyone see it.

14. If a boy **cowered** when his teacher spoke to him, he might have been afraid of her.

15. **English Language Coach** Review the word **type** on page 356. Then write two sentences, each using a different meaning of the word.

Grammar Link: Compound Subjects and Predicates

A **compound subject** is made up of two or more simple subjects that have the same predicate. When the subjects are joined by *and* or by *both . . . and,* the plural form of the verb is used.

• <u>Keisha</u>, <u>Hala</u>, *and* <u>Saba</u> are sisters.

(The subjects <u>Keisha</u>, <u>Hala</u>, and <u>Saba</u> are joined by *and.* The compound subject is *Keisha, Hala,* and *Saba.*)

When two simple subjects are joined by *or, either . . . or,* or *neither . . . nor,* the verb must agree with the simple subject closer to it.

• Neither Keisha nor *Saba* likes country music.
• Neither her sisters nor *Keisha* likes country music.
• Neither Keisha nor her *sisters* like country music.

A **compound predicate** is made up of two or more verbs that have the same subject. They are joined by *and, or, but, both . . . and, either . . . or,* or *neither . . . nor.*

• The rabbit <u>ran</u> quickly and <u>dashed</u> into the hole.

(The verbs *ran* and *dashed* are joined by *and.*)

Grammar Practice

Copy the sentences below on a separate sheet of paper. Underline compound subjects. Circle compound predicates.

16. The monkeys and chimps screech from the tree.

17. Neither he nor I can go.

18. My dad and my uncles were sitting and resting.

19. Aunt Sherry fries or bakes her own potato chips.

Web Activities For eFlashcards, Selection Quick Checks, and other Web activities, go to www.glencoe.com.

Research Report
Revising, Editing, and Presenting

ASSIGNMENT Write a research report

Purpose: To research a subject and write a report on what you find

Audience: Your teacher and your classmates

Revising Rubric

Your revised research report should have

- a clear thesis statement that states what you are reporting
- evidence and details that support your thesis
- effective organization
- accurately cited sources and a works cited list
- a strong introduction and conclusion
- effective simple sentences

NY English Language Arts Core Curriculum (pp. 380–385)

LC W4 Compose mechanically grade-appropriate texts for a variety of purposes. **Core W5** Use the writing process. **Core W9** Use transitional words to produce cohesive texts. **Core W8** Use correct grammatical construction in parts of speech. **Core W7** Observe rules of punctuation. **S1a** Prepare and give presentations.

For a complete description of the standards, see p. NY11.

In Part 2, you'll revise and edit your research report draft. Revising and editing can be hard work, but the hard work pays off in the end. Your final draft will be much easier to read and understand than your first draft. When you're finished, you'll keep a copy of your report in a writing portfolio so that you and your teacher can evaluate your writing progress over time.

Revising
Make It Better

Reread your first draft carefully and ask yourself the questions below. Write your answers in your Learner's Notebook. Then use the suggestions to revise.

Question	Suggestion
Does my introduction grab readers' attention and include a thesis statement?	If not, begin with a surprising statement or question to get readers interested in your topic. Make sure your thesis statement is near the end of your introduction.
Is my thesis, or main idea, clearly stated?	If not, rewrite it until it says exactly what your report is about.
Does each paragraph have a clear main idea supported by details?	If not, rewrite the topic sentence. Add supporting details that relate directly to the topic sentence. Remove details that aren't necessary.
Do I stick to my topic throughout my report?	If not, make sure the topic sentence of each paragraph supports your thesis statement. Delete off-track sentences and paragraphs.
Does my conclusion restate my thesis and say what I think about the topic?	If not, rewrite sentences that summarize your topic. Add one or two sentences that state your final thoughts about your topic.
Have I correctly cited my sources?	If not, review Writing Workshop Part 1 and see the **Writing Handbook** for help.

After you read and comment on your draft, give it to a peer reviewer (a classmate). Have your reviewer read it and answer the questions. His or her comments may be helpful, but you decide what changes to make. See page R18 of the **Writing Handbook** for more on peer reviewers.

Editing

Finish It Up

It's time to get your report ready to share with others. Use the **Editing Checklist** below to help you spot errors.

Editing Checklist

- ☑ Verb forms are correct, and verb tenses are consistent.
- ☑ Pronouns agree with antecedents.
- ☑ All sentences are complete, begin with a capital letter, and end with correct punctuation.
- ☑ All words are spelled correctly.
- ☑ All citations and the works cited list are in correct form.

Literature Online

Writing Models For models and other writing activities, go to www.glencoe.com.

◀ **Writing Tip**

Spelling If you are using a computer to write your report, you can use the Spell Check feature to check your spelling. But the only way to be completely sure of a word's spelling is to look it up.

Applying Good Writing Traits

Conventions

Conventions make your writing easier to read and understand. It can be difficult to master all the writing conventions at once, but don't worry! You probably know more than you think you do.

What Are Conventions?

Conventions are the rules of language: spelling, capitalization, punctuation, grammar and usage, and paragraphing. Formal Standard English—the kind you speak and write in school and most businesses—has many conventions.

Why Are Conventions Important?

When you use conventions, your writing is clearer. Readers can pay attention to your ideas instead of struggling to figure out what you are trying to say. You can bend some rules when you write stories or poems. But when you write formal papers, such as research reports, you must follow the rules of Standard English.

Look at how conventions can affect meaning:

- Did you see that weasel?
- Did you see that, weasel?

The punctuation makes a big difference in the meanings of the sentences. In the first, the speaker is pointing out a weasel to a listener. In the second, the speaker is calling the listener a weasel!

How Do I Use Conventions?

Read your final draft carefully. Be sure to see the words as they appear on the page, not as they're *supposed* to appear. Then read your paper several times and look for one kind of error each time.

1. Check the spellings of difficult words.
2. Check for proper capitalization. Each sentence should start with a capital letter. Proper nouns and proper adjectives should be capitalized.
3. Make sure that each sentence ends with the correct punctuation mark and that commas are in the right places.
4. Fix errors in grammar and usage. Reading your paper aloud may help.
5. Make sure the first line of every paragraph is indented.

Partner Work Follow the steps above to spot and correct errors in conventions. Trade papers with a partner and circle any errors in the paper.

Presenting

Show It Off

Writing Tip ▶

Handwriting Make your final draft easy to read. Use your best handwriting. Make each letter and punctuation mark clear for the reader.

Rewrite or print out a clean copy of your report. Then follow these steps to write a summary and share it with some of your classmates.

1. Reread your report and write down your thesis in one sentence.
2. Write three to four sentences that help you prove and support your thesis.
3. Read your summary to a small group. Then share and explain the most interesting thing you learned from your research.

Listening, Speaking, and Viewing

Oral Presentation

The final step of a research report is sharing what you've learned with others. An oral presentation gives you this opportunity.

What Is an Oral Presentation?

An oral presentation is a formal speech given to a group of people.

Why Is It Important?

An oral presentation gives the speaker a chance to share interesting and important information with others. It also gives listeners a chance to learn about a topic without having to research it.

How Do I Give an Oral Presentation?

When you prepare an oral presentation, you use the writing process to develop the content of your presentation. Your presentation should have a thesis statement that is supported with evidence. It should also have three main parts—an introduction, a body, and a conclusion. The tips below will help you prepare and give a great oral presentation.

- Think about your purpose and audience. Choose your words carefully and explain any terms or ideas that your audience might not know.

- Write your main points on note cards. You will glance at these notes while you are speaking to keep track of where you are in your speech.

- Prepare a visual aid (a graphic) that shows something you are going to talk about. Make sure your visual aid is big enough for your audience to see. You may use a slide projector or PowerPoint presentation, or you may make copies of your graphic and hand them out to your audience.

- Practice and practice again! Give your speech in front of a mirror or a family member. Ask your family member how you can improve your presentation. Make sure your presentation is within the time limit that your teacher assigned.

- Relax! When you give your presentation, try to stay calm. Speak slowly and clearly and make eye contact with your listeners.

Write and Speak to Learn Use the tips above to prepare and give an oral presentation based on your research report. Be sure to organize your ideas and include a visual aid, so your listeners can easily understand your points.

As you listen to other presentations, take notes about what makes a good presentation and how you might improve your own presentation skills.

Writer's Model

America's Betrayal and the Trail of Tears

Why would one group of people remove another group from their homeland by force? Could the moved group ever recover? In 1838 Cherokee people living in Georgia were rounded up by federal troops and forced to walk eight hundred miles to land in Oklahoma. The Cherokees call the journey the "Trail Where They Cried." Some historians call it the "Trail of Tears." The events surrounding the Trail of Tears reveal a story of betrayal, unfair treatment, and great sacrifice.

The Cherokees had very old and strong ties to their homeland. Their territory covered a large area, including what is now the state of Georgia. When European explorers arrived during the mid-1500s, the Cherokees were the largest Native American group in North America.

Over time, the white settlers wanted more and more Cherokee land. The Cherokees and the settlers struggled for control. By 1827 the Cherokees had written and adopted a constitution declaring themselves their own nation. White Georgians who felt threatened claimed that the Cherokee Constitution went against the U.S. Constitution. The governor of Georgia asked President John Quincy Adams to support this position, and the state legislature took steps to force the Cherokees from Georgia.

In 1830 the discovery of gold in Georgia drew thousands of settlers who were looking to make their fortunes (Fremon 56). Also, white settlers and Southern cotton planters pressured the tribe to trade their rich land for land in the West. But the Cherokees refused to give in.

The Cherokees asked the U.S. Supreme Court to defend Native Americans' rights in the Southeast. Georgia claimed the right to make laws for the Cherokees. The Cherokees claimed that federal agreements and the U.S. Constitution protected their group as a self-ruling nation. In 1832, the Supreme Court declared that Georgia's

Notice how the introductory paragraph grabs your attention. The first two sentences help you connect to the Cherokees' experience. The third sentence tells you the paper's topic, and the final sentence is the thesis statement.

The writer organizes this report in chronological order (time order). The paragraphs move forward in time from the mid-1500s to 1827 and then to 1830. As you read on, the paper will discuss events that occurred throughout the 1830s leading up to the Trail of Tears in 1838.

The writer cites sources for two pieces of information: the background about the treaty and the quotation from John Quincy Adams. Both citations have the effect of making readers trust what the writer says.

The writer uses a quotation to strengthen a point. The quotation also supports the thesis statement.

actions against the Cherokees were unconstitutional. But President Jackson still sided with Georgia.

While the Supreme Court had been thinking about the Cherokee Nation's claim to its land, Jackson pushed the Indian Removal Act of 1830 through Congress. This act gave the federal government the power to negotiate treaties with Native Americans in the Southwest. The goal of these treaties was to make Native Americans move west. The moving was supposed to be "voluntary and peaceful," but if tribes resisted, Jackson forced them to move ("Indian").

In 1835 the federal government persuaded a small group of Cherokees to sign the Treaty of New Echota, which gave them $5 million to exchange their lands in the East for lands in the West. Most Cherokees did not sign the treaty, so Cherokee law considered it invalid (Bealer 64). Even former president John Quincy Adams, who was not always kind to the Cherokees, said the treaty "brings eternal disgrace upon the country" (Fremon 71). This unfair treaty became the justification for removing the Cherokees from their homeland.

The principal chief of the Cherokees appealed to the country's leaders one last time. The new president, Martin Van Buren, agreed to let the Cherokees remain on their land for two more years, but then he changed his mind. On May 23, 1838, army troops stormed into Cherokee land, invaded homes, and dragged people from their fields. Thousands of Cherokees were put into stockades to wait for the long march to their new lands ("Trail" screens 1, 3). The forced march began during October and November of 1838. The conditions of the eight-hundred-mile journey were terrible, and more than 4,000 Cherokees died. Army private John Burnett said, "The sufferings of the Cherokees were awful.... They had to sleep in the wagons and on the ground without fire. And I have known as many as twenty-two of them to die in one night of pneumonia due to ill treatment, cold, and exposure" ("Trail" screens 1-2).

In Oklahoma, there were more problems. The Cherokees who had opposed the Treaty of New Echota were still angry with those who had signed it. In fact, two of the men who had helped create the treaty were murdered by an anti-treaty group. Also, the new arrivals had to get along with another Native American group who had moved from the East many years earlier. For several years, the new Cherokee land was the scene of violent conflicts.

The Cherokees' claim to their land was respected by many people, including several U.S. senators. The Cherokees placed their trust in the American legal system, but that trust was betrayed. President Jackson's and President Van Buren's administrations used unfair strategies to force the Cherokees from their land. In order to have more land for settlers, the U.S. government crossed the line and paid too high a price—the loss of thousands of Cherokees and a unique culture.

This conclusion restates the writer's thesis. The writer ties up the paper and tells what he or she thinks of the events surrounding the Trail of Tears.

Works Cited

Bealer, Alex W. _Only the Names Remain_. New York: Little, Brown, 1996.

"Brief History of the Trail of Tears." _Cherokee Messenger_. 1995. The Cherokee Cultural Society of Houston. 11 Nov. 2005 <http://www.powersource.com/cherokee/history.html>.

Fremon, David K. _The Trail of Tears_. New York: New Discovery, 1994.

"Indian Removal." PBS Online. 11 Nov. 2005 <http://www.pbs.org/wgbh/aia/part4/4h1567.html>.

"The Trail of Tears." Cherokee Publishing. 11 Oct. 2000 <http://www.chota.com/cherokee/trail.html>.

The list of works cited gives all the information that readers need to check the writer's sources: authors, titles, dates, and Web sites.

Skills Focus

You will practice using these skills when you read the following selections:

- "Tattoos: Fad, Fashion, or Folly?" p. 390
- "We Real Cool," p. 400
- "The Market Economy," p. 401

Reading

- Identifying main idea and supporting details

Literature

- Understanding graphics and other visual aids
- Understanding and using alliteration

Vocabulary

- Using word references
- Academic Vocabulary: *implied*

Writing/Grammar

- Understanding and using direct objects and indirect objects

NY English Language Arts Core Curriculum (pp. 386–387)

R1b Apply thinking skills to interpret data, facts, and ideas from informational texts. **R3a** Evaluate details or reasons used to support ideas.

For a complete description of the standards, see p. NY11.

Skill Lesson

Identifying Main Idea and Supporting Details

Learn It!

What Is It? The **main idea** is the general point of a selection—the "big idea" that the author wants you to understand and remember.

Supporting details are the specific details that explain the main idea. They may be examples, descriptions, facts, reasons—any specifics that make the point. The main idea of a selection may be directly stated, or it may be **implied,** or suggested, through details.

Analyzing Cartoons

Jeremy got "the picture," or main idea, about Pierce's weekend. When you identify the main idea, you find the most important thought in what you read or hear. What main idea does Pierce communicate?

© Zits Partnership, Reprinted with Permission of King Features Syndicate, Inc.

Academic Vocabulary

implied (im PLYD) *adj.* expressed indirectly; suggested

Why Is It Important? Identifying main idea helps you figure out what's really important in a selection. It also helps you understand and remember what you read.

How Do I Do It? To find the main idea, ask yourself these questions:
- What is this generally about?
- What sentence or sentences state the general point?
- If the general point is not stated, what do the supporting details have in common?

Study Central Visit www.glencoe .com and click on Study Central to review identifying main idea and supporting details.

Here is how one student identified the main idea of this passage from the article "A Tremendous Trade."

> Now that the Yankees have A-Rod, New York fans have high hopes for future success. But Rodriguez alone won't guarantee his new team championships. "If you're a team with more money, you get to hire better players, but it doesn't mean you're going to win," says Andrew Zimbalist, a top sports economist. Injuries, batting slumps, a lack of teamwork, and even bad luck can get in the way.

I see the writer's point—money can buy good players, but there's no guarantee that a team will do well. The main idea is stated in the quotation. The last sentence gives specific examples of what can get in the way of winning championships. Those are supporting details.

Practice It!

The statements below are about the next selection. Copy them into your Learner's Notebook. Then underline the one that is most likely the main idea. Remember that a main idea is a *big* idea—not a specific detail.
- People from the Stone Age (35,000 to 10,000 B.C.) practiced tattooing.
- Tattooing is not just a passing fad.
- Mummies found in Egypt show that tattooing existed 4,000 years ago.

Use It!

As you read the next selection, write the main idea of each section in your Learner's Notebook. After you've finished reading, use your notes to identify the main idea of the whole article.

Before You Read

Tattoos: Fad, Fashion, or Folly?

Linda Bickerstaff

Meet the Author

Linda Bickerstaff is a retired surgeon, who found dealing with tattoos in her medical practice to be quite challenging. A regular contributor to *Odyssey: Adventures in Science* and other publications, she writes about health, medical, and teen issues.

Author Search For more about Linda Bickerstaff, go to www.glencoe.com.

NY English Language Arts Core Curriculum (pp. 388–395)

Core W10 Use dictionaries, thesauruses, and style manuals. **R1b** Apply thinking skills to interpret data, facts, and ideas from informational texts. **R3a** Evaluate details or reasons used to support ideas.

For a complete description of the standards, see p. NY11.

Vocabulary Preview

migrated (MY gray tud) *v.* moved from one place to another; form of the verb *migrate* **(p. 391)** *When a group of people migrated from one area to another, they held on to their traditions.*

indelible (in DEL ih bul) *adj.* impossible to erase, remove, or blot out **(p. 391)** *Tattoos are made with indelible ink, which leaves a permanent stain.*

compiled (kum PY uld) *v.* collected into a book or list; form of the verb *compile* **(p. 392)** *The student gathered the facts and compiled a book about the history of tattooing.*

Write to Learn Copy the following clues into your Learner's Notebook. Next to each clue, write the vocabulary word it describes.

- Someone who puts together a collection of information has done this.
- This describes something that cannot be removed.
- Someone who has done this has lived in more than one place.

English Language Coach

Word References What should you do when you can't figure out what a word means, you aren't sure how to spell it, or you can't decide which word works best in your writing? Use one of these resources about words!

- A **glossary** will help you understand the vocabulary words in your school books. You'll find glossaries in the backs of many of your textbooks.
- A **general dictionary** gives pronunciations, parts of speech, spellings, and definitions as well as the histories, or origins, of words.
- A **specialized dictionary** or **glossary** gives pronunciations, parts of speech, spellings, and definitions of words used in a specific subject area, such as medicine or automobile mechanics.
- A **thesaurus** gives synonyms and antonyms for words.

Partner Talk Copy the chart below into your Learner's Notebook. With a partner, use a dictionary and thesaurus to complete the chart.

This has...	definitions	synonyms	antonyms	word origins	pronun- ciations
a dictionary	yes				
a thesaurus			yes		

Skills Preview

Key Reading Skill: Identifying Main Idea and Supporting Details

"Tattoos: Fad, Fashion, or Folly?" has directly stated main ideas. Look for sentences in the first paragraph that sum up the "big ideas" in the article. As you read the rest of the article, pay special attention to the subheads. Each subhead sums up what a section of the article is about. Notice how each section supports the main ideas.

Key Text Element: Photographs

Photographs can add a lot to your reading experience. For example, you might not ever climb Mount Everest, but you can get an idea of what it's like to be on the mountain by looking at a photo of it. To get the most out of a photo, do these things:

- Read the caption—the words printed above, beside, or below the photo.

  Who took the photograph? Where was it shot? What exactly does it show?

- Look closely at the details.

  How do they help you understand the article?

- Think about why this particular photo was included with the selection.

  Does the photograph show something that's described in the article? Does it add information? Or is it just for decoration?

Write to Learn Choose an interesting photograph from this textbook. Spend one minute making a list of what you see in the photo. Answer these questions:

- Who or what is in the photo?
- What is happening in the photo?
- When and where was the photo taken?

Get Ready to Read

Connect to the Reading

Think about tattoos you have seen on people or in pictures. What did you think of the tattoos?

Partner Talk With a partner, discuss possible reasons someone might get a tattoo. List the reasons in your Learner's Notebook. Then add to your list as you read the selection.

Build Background

- Tattoos are designs created on a person's skin. Permanent tattoos are made by inserting dye under the top layer of skin.
- Our skin is made up of a sensitive inner layer and a thin outer layer. When the cells of the outer layer die, they flake off. A tattoo is made by punching a tiny hole and inserting dye into the *inner* layer of skin, underneath the layer that flakes off. That way the color is permanent.
- Archaeologists have long known that ancient peoples practiced the art of tattooing. Archaeologists learn about ancient civilizations by digging into the earth to find the remains of people and evidence of how they lived.

Set Purposes for Reading

BIG Question Read "Tattoos: Fad, Fashion, or Folly?" to learn about some of the hidden dangers that people face when they get tattoos.

Set Your Own Purpose What else would you like to learn from the article to help you answer the Big Question? Write your own purpose on the "Tattoos" flap of the Reading Workshop 4 Foldable for Unit 3.

Literature Online

Interactive Literary Elements Handbook
To review or learn more about the literary elements, go to www.glencoe.com.

Keep Moving

Use these skills as you read "Tattoos: Fad, Fashion, or Folly?"

INFORMATIONAL TEXT
MAGAZINE
Odyssey

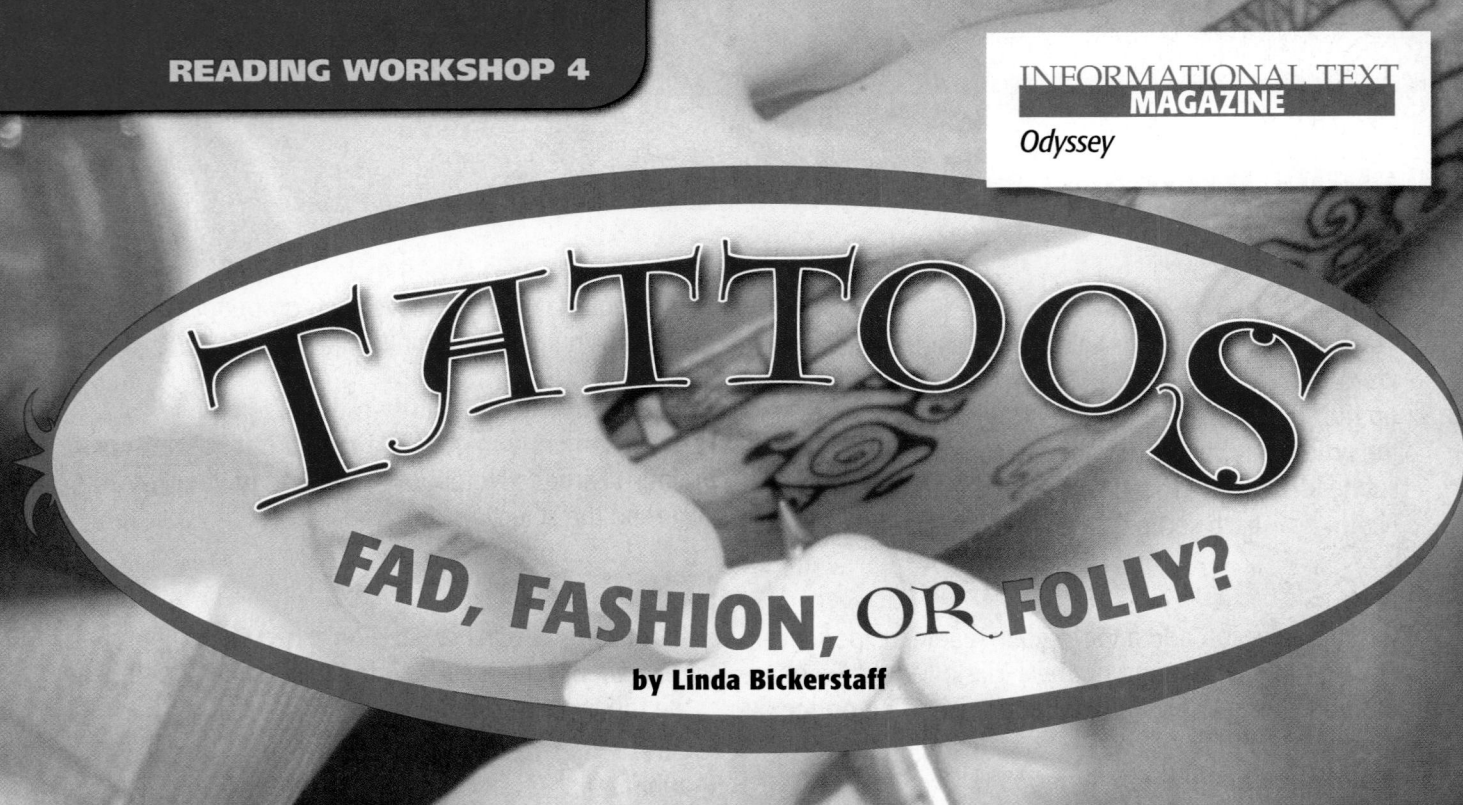

TATTOOS
FAD, FASHION, OR FOLLY?
by Linda Bickerstaff

From a tiny butterfly hiding behind a knee to an elaborate, multicolored, geometric design **emblazoning** muscular arms—tattoos are cropping up everywhere. Just take a look at some of the famous tattoo canvases.[1] **1**

For instance, professional snowboarder Tara Dakides has a dragon tattooed on her left side and Cat-in-the-Hat adorns her right calf. The three Dixie Chicks have small chick footprints tattooed on their feet, and Whoopi Goldberg sports Woodstock from *Peanuts* on her skin.[2] But it isn't just the famous who sport tattoos. Even some teachers, librarians, and other professionals proudly wear them. Is tattooing a passing fad? Or is it a fashion statement that's here to stay? And then there's the most important question of all: Is getting a tattoo a fashion mistake? **2**

Tattoo Time Line

Although today's tattooing techniques are high-tech, the practice is ancient. Archaeological evidence from Europe indicates that tattooing was practiced in the Stone Age or upper Paleolithic

---

1. Here, *canvases* refers to the skin on people's bodies.
2. The *Dixie Chicks* are a top-selling, all-girl country music group. *Whoopi Goldberg* is a comedian and actress. *Woodstock* is the name of a bird character in *Peanuts,* a popular comic strip that ran in thousands of newspapers from 1950–2000.

Practice the Skills

1 English Language Coach

Word References Use a word reference to look up the meaning of the word *emblazon* in order to understand the meaning of **emblazoning**.

2 Key Reading Skill

Identifying Main Idea and Supporting Details Do these questions give you a sense of what the main idea will be?

tattooing was practiced in the Stone Age or upper Paleolithic period (35,000 to 10,000 B.C.). In 1991, the body of a hunter, estimated to be 5,300 years old, was discovered in the Austrian Alps. Called the "Iceman," the mummy was so well preserved that the tattoo of a cross on the inside of his knee was still visible. Fifty-seven other simple tattoos were found on his body. Mummies found in Egypt and archaeological discoveries in China, Russia, and Japan indicate that tattooing was widespread there 4,000 years ago. As people **migrated,** they carried the practice of tattooing with them.

The modern history of tattooing and the word "tattoo" date to 1769 when Captain James Cook first saw tattooed South Sea islanders. In the *Endeavor*'s ship log, Captain Cook wrote: "They stain their bodies by indenting or pricking the skin with a small instrument made of bone, cut into short teeth; which indenting they fill up with a dark-blue or black mixture prepared from the smoke [soot] of an oily nut. . . . This operation, which is called by the natives 'tattaw,' leaves an **indelible** mark on the skin. It is usually performed when they are about 10 or 12 years of age, and on different parts of the body." The Tahitian word "tattau," meaning "to mark," is the origin of the modern word, tattoo. **3**

Why Tattoo?

Why do people as different as the Iceman, President Franklin Delano Roosevelt, and members of the Dixie Chicks get tattoos? The earliest people probably used tattooing as a means of expressing bereavement.[3] When a member of their band died, they slashed themselves with sharp implements and rubbed ashes from a fire into their wounds. Permanent carbon deposits were left under their skin. Professor Konrad Spindler of Innsbruck University in Austria thinks that the Iceman's tattoos were applied to cure pain and other ailments.[4] President Roosevelt's tattoo was a family **crest**. **4** The Dixie Chicks' chick print tattoos reinforce the group's identity and are good publicity.

---

3. **Bereavement** means "deep sadness over death."

4. **Ailments** are illnesses or physical problems.

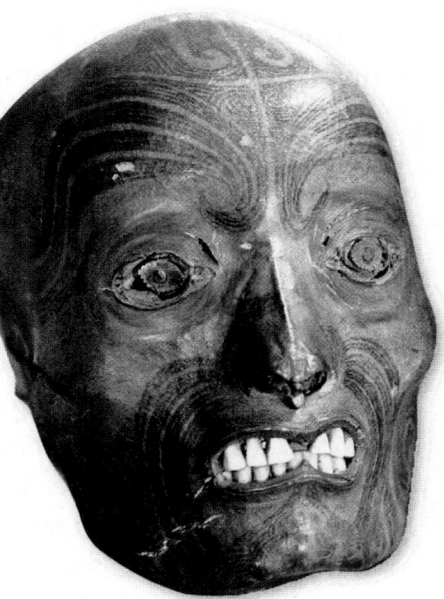

Analyzing the Image This mid-19th century Maori skull is covered with shell inlay and inked designs. Why might this tribe have used tattoos?

Practice the Skills

3 | **Key Reading Skill**

Identifying Main Idea and Supporting Details In the section titled "Tattoo Time Line," the author gives examples of different groups of people from long ago who had tattoos. What is the main idea of this section? Where in the section is the main idea directly stated?

4 | **English Language Coach**

Word References What does **crest** mean in this context? Look up the word in a dictionary. Define it in your own words.

Vocabulary . . . .

migrated (MY gray tud) *v.* moved from one place to another

indelible (in DEL ih bul) *adj.* impossible to erase, remove, or blot out

Katherine Krcmarik, a graduate art student at the University of Michigan, who recently **compiled** *The History of Tattooing*, says: "The practice of tattooing means different things in different cultures. In early practice, decoration appears to have been the most common motive for tattooing, and that still holds true today." Krcmarik points out that in some cultures tattoos had many purposes: to identify a wearer's rank in society, to mark special events in the wearer's life, to identify a person as belonging to a particular clan or family, or as evidence of a wearer's adventures. **5**

In 2002, Myrna L. Armstrong, a professor at Texas Tech University Health Sciences Center, surveyed 520 college students about their interests and attitudes toward tattooing. Ninety-seven of the students had tattoos. When asked why they got a tattoo, the most common answer was, "I just wanted one." Other answers included "To help me express myself" and "To feel unique." Armstrong concluded that for many teens, getting a tattoo is a means of self-expression or a nonviolent form of rebellion.

Tattooing also has been and continues to be used to mark people as inferior. In ancient Greece, tattooing was used to identify slaves. Romans marked criminals with tattoos. During World War II, one of the ways that Nazis dehumanized[5] prisoners taken to Auschwitz, the largest Nazi concentration camp in Europe, was to tattoo a registration number on the arm of each person. By 1942, most of the people at Auschwitz were Jewish. Most were killed before the war's end. Although only used at Auschwitz, the arm tattoo has become a symbol of the horrors of the Holocaust.

Today, neo-Nazis, racist skinheads, white supremacists, and others in the "hate" movement use symbols such as swastikas, Nazi "SS" thunderbolts, and ancient runes,[6] tattooed on various parts of their bodies, to instill a sense of fear and insecurity in those around them.

---

5. To **dehumanize** is to take away someone's human qualities, personality, or spirit.

6. **Runes** are characters of an alphabet used by the Germanic peoples from about the 3rd to the 13th centuries.

Practice the Skills

5 **Key Text Element**

Photographs How can you connect the text in this paragraph to what you see in the photo on this page? How do you think the man feels about his tattoos?

A Tahitian chief wears traditional tattoos in French Polynesia.

Vocabulary

compiled (kum PY uld) *v.* collected into a book or list

not involved in the gang's activities, a member tattooed with its symbol shares the gang's reputation. **6**

You Decide

Tattooing is certainly not a fad, as it has been practiced for over 35,000 years. Today, over 40 million Americans (16 percent of the population) **sport** at least one tattoo. According to *U.S. News and World Report*, tattooing was the sixth fastest growing retail venture[8] in the United States in the 1990s. **7**

So, is a tattoo for you? Getting even a tiny one is a BIG decision to make. Take the Tattoo Test . . . . Perhaps it will help you decide if a tattoo would be fashion or folly for you.

Is a Tattoo for You?
Take the Tattoo Test!

Never make an important decision that could affect your health or well-being before weighing all the information. See if you know the straight facts about tattoos. Answer True or False to the following questions:

1. Thomas Alva Edison contributed to the development of the first tattoo machine.
2. Modern tattooing techniques are painless.
3. Once done, a tattoo will remain the same forever.
4. Tattooing is risk-free and available to anyone who can pay for it.
5. It costs more to have a tattoo removed than to get one.

Tattoo Test Answers:

1. **True.** Prior to 1891, tattooing was done by piercing or cutting the skin with a variety of instruments, ranging from sharpened bones to metal awls and needles. The wounds were then rubbed with some type of pigment.[9] Samuel O'Reilly patented the first tattoo machine in 1891. It was a modification of a stencil transfer machine invented by Edison. Today, electrically driven, handheld machines move a needle up and down at a rate of several hundred vibrations per minute, injecting ink about a millimeter deep into the dermis of the skin.

---

7. An *initiate* is a new member of a group.
8. A *venture* is a new, often risky, business.
9. A *pigment* is a substance that gives colors to things.

Practice the Skills

6 **Key Reading Skill**

Identifying Main Idea and Supporting Details
Sometimes people choose to get tattoos. Sometimes people are tattooed against their will by others. These are some of the supporting details in this section. What is the main idea?

7 **English Language Coach**

Word References Here, **sport** is used as a verb. Use a thesaurus to find another word that means about the same thing as *sport*.

2. **False.** Individual pain tolerance, the size and location of a tattoo, and the skill and experience of the tattoo artist influence the amount of pain experienced by an individual.

3. **False.** Tattoo inks are injected into the dermis of the skin so that the design will not be lost due to the sloughing[10] of epidermal cells. Over time, however, the color of pigments may fade—especially if heavily exposed to the sun. Weight gain or loss, pregnancies, and injuries with scar formation at tattoo sites all can change the look of tattoos.

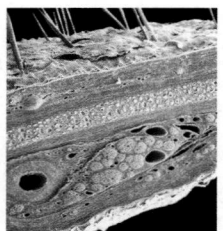

Visual Vocabulary
The skin is made up of a sensitive inner layer, called the **dermis,** and a thin outer layer, called the **epidermis.**

4. **False.** Bacteria from the skin surface may cause infection if carried into the dermis by tattoo needles. In some instances, although less common today, hepatitis B and C as well as syphilis and tuberculosis have been transmitted to tattoo recipients. To date, no documented cases of AIDS have been transmitted by tattooing. Mild to life-threatening allergic reactions to tattoo inks may occur. In most states and Canada, kids under the age of 18 must have parental consent for professional tattooing.

5. **True.** The cost of a small tattoo (less than a square inch) is about $100. The cost of a custom tattoo covering a large area is more than $1,000. The real cost comes, however, with tattoo removal. Dermatologic surgeons use at least three types of high-tech lasers for tattoo removal. Getting rid of even the smallest tattoo can require several treatments, each costing $300 to $400, depending on where you live. Removal of larger tattoos may cost thousands of dollars. Removal is considered cosmetic surgery, so few insurance plans will cover the cost. Tattoo removal is quite painful, has a 5 percent chance of leaving a permanent scar, and may fail to completely obliterate[11] the tattoo. In spite of this, with improvement in results, tattoo removal is in big demand. Several studies have shown that by age 40, over 50 percent of people with tattoos wish they did not have them. Many are seeking to have them removed. ⓼

---

10. **Sloughing** means "separating dead tissue from living tissue." This is how our skin gets rid of dead skin cells.

11. To **obliterate** something is to remove or destroy it completely.

Practice the Skills

⓼ **BIG Question**
The author describes the different kinds of costs, financial as well as personal, that go with getting tattoos. Do you think these prices are too high? Write your answers on the "Tattoos" flap of the Reading Workshop 4 Foldable. Your response will help you complete the Unit Challenge later.

United States Olympic Basketball Team member Allan Iverson sports several tattoos during a 2004 game in Athens, Greece.

Henna: The Tattoo Temp 🔟

Do you secretly yearn for just a *tiny* tattoo, but know that your parents would never allow it? Do you think a mouse might look cool tattooed on your ankle, but you aren't really sure? Does the idea of having your skin pierced by needles make you feel faint? If you answered "yes" to these questions, your solution might be a tattooing technique used for many thousands of years in India and other parts of the world—henna tattooing.

Henna is the Arabic name for the shrub *Lawsonia inermis* or *L. alba.* Its leaves are harvested, dried, and then crushed into a powder that is mixed with oil, lemon, and other ingredients to form a paste.

When the paste is applied to skin, reddish-brown pigments from the paste are transferred to the epidermis of the skin. The longer the henna is in contact with the skin, the darker the pigment transfer will be. Henna is usually left on the skin for 6 to 12 hours for the best results, then washed off.

Henna tattooing should really be called henna appliqué or henna painting. Henna tattoos differ from real tattoos in several ways: They are temporary, lasting only a few weeks; they are painless to apply; and they are relatively inexpensive to obtain. They are also an excellent way to get your tattoo without upsetting your parents.

The cells of the skin that are pigmented by the henna are epidermal cells. Over the course of several weeks, these cells die and are sloughed off the surface of the skin. As this happens, the henna tattoo fades and eventually disappears altogether. Depending on where the tattoo is placed on the body, it may last for one to three weeks.

Pre-prepared, do-it-yourself henna tattoo kits are available commercially. They contain patterns as well as instructions for applying.

Is a henna tattoo for you? Maybe, but be sure to check with Mom and Dad first.

CAUTION: Do not buy a kit or use any product containing "black henna." Black henna has a chemical compound called paraphenylenediamine (PPD) that is mixed with classic henna. The purpose of the PPD is to speed up the process of pigment transfer to the skin and to make the tattoo black instead of reddish-brown. PPD causes severe contact dermatitis in many people. People who are sensitive to it have a reaction similar to a bad case of poison ivy. They are miserable for many days. ○

Practice the Skills

🔟 **Key Reading Skill**

Identifying Main Idea and Supporting Details The main idea of this section is that henna tattoos can be a safer alternative to permanent tattoos. As you read, watch for the supporting details the author includes.

After You Read

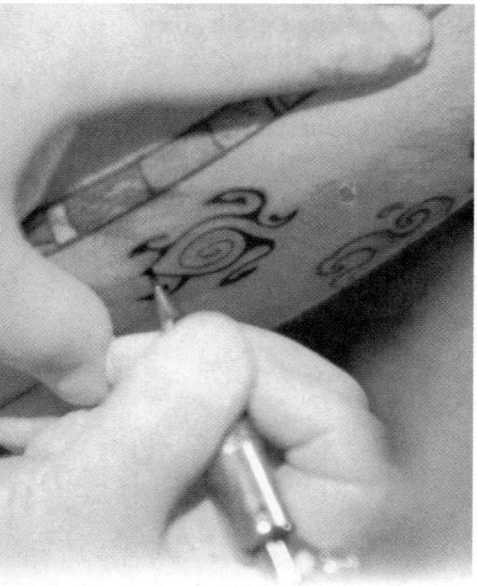

Tattoos: Fad, Fashion, or Folly?

Answering the **BIG Question**

1. What are some of the prices that people pay for getting tattoos? Think about the dollar cost of tattoos and also about intangible costs, such as the pain and permanence of tattoos.

2. **Recall** How long has tattooing been around?
   TIP Right There

3. **Recall** What physical problems or illnesses are related to getting and living with tattoos?
   TIP Think and Search

Critical Thinking

4. **Analyze** Many people get tattoos to decorate their bodies or to identify themselves as part of a group. What other ways do people in your school and community identify themselves as part of a group?
   TIP On My Own

5. **Infer** Why do you think tattooing has been around for so long? Do you think people will stop using tattoos some day? Explain your answer.
   TIP Author and Me

6. **Evaluate** Did this article sway you to be in favor of tattoos or against them? Explain your response.
   TIP Author and Me

Write About Your Reading

Newspaper Article Imagine that there are a lot of students at your school who are thinking about getting tattoos. Write an article for your school newspaper that tells them what you know about tattoos. The article should end with advice.

- Discuss the popularity of tattoos.
- Discuss the possible costs of getting a tattoo.
- End with your own advice to students who want to get a tattoo.

NY English Language Arts Core Curriculum (pp. 396–397)

LC R17 Demonstrate comprehension and response through a range of activities.
LC W4 Compose mechanically grade-appropriate texts for a variety of purposes.
R1b Apply thinking skills to interpret data, facts, and ideas from informational texts.
R3a Evaluate details or reasons used to support ideas. **Core W8** Use correct grammatical construction in sentences.

For a complete description of the standards, see p. NY11.

Skills Review

Key Reading Skill: Identifying Main Idea and Supporting Details

7. What is the author's main idea about tattoos?

8. List three supporting details from the article that support the main idea you wrote for question 7.

Key Text Element: Photographs

9. How could a photo of a henna tattoo be useful if you were deciding whether one is right for you?

10. If you could add a photo to this selection, what would you choose to show readers? Why?

Reviewing Skills: Making Inferences

11. What can you infer about the writer's attitude toward tattoos? Is she in favor of people getting tattoos? Is she against it? Or is she neutral, not caring either way? Use evidence from the article to support your inference.

Vocabulary Check

Choose the best word from the list to complete each sentence below. Rewrite each sentence with the correct word.

migrated • indelible • compiled

12. The birds _____ south to spend the winter months in warmer climates.

13. At the end of the year, Juanita _____ a book of poems written by her classmates.

14. I hope that's not _____ ink. That's one of my favorite sweaters.

15. **English Language Coach** What type of reference book would you use to learn more about *tuberculosis* and *dermatitis?* Explain your choice.

16. **Academic Vocabulary** If a main idea is **implied,** is it stated or only hinted at?

Grammar Link: Direct Objects

A **direct object** is the noun or pronoun in a sentence that receives the action of the verb. In fact, the direct object is located *after* the action verb. You can usually find it by asking *what?* or *whom?* The answer will be the direct object.

• After lunch, Cynthia always eats an apple.

First, find the verb in the sentence: *eats.* Then ask the question "*What* does Cynthia always eat?" The answer is an *apple.* So in this sentence, apple is the direct object.

A sentence may have more than one direct object. This is referred to as a **compound direct object.**

• Jenell helped Ryan and Lee with their project.

First, find the verb in the sentence: *helped.* Then ask the question, "*Whom* did Jenell help?" The answer is *Ryan* and *Lee.* So in this sentence, Ryan and Lee is the compound direct object.

Grammar Practice

Underline the verb and circle the direct object in each of the following sentences.

17. Ramona teaches history.

18. Nan watched the artist paint.

19. Mr. Delmar took the students on a field trip.

20. Victor spent time and money at the mall today.

21. He bought shoes, socks, and a shirt.

22. Victor also bought a new video game.

Web Activities For eFlashcards, Selection Quick Checks, and other Web activities, go to www.glencoe.com.

Before You Read

We Real Cool *and* The Market Economy

Meet the Authors

Gwendolyn Brooks

Poet Gwendolyn Brooks was the first African American writer to win the Pulitzer Prize. Brooks was born in 1917 in Topeka, Kansas and raised in Chicago, where she died in 2000. See page R1 of the Author Files for more on Gwendolyn Brooks.

Marge Piercy

Marge Piercy is a poet, novelist, and essayist. Piercy was born in Detroit, Michigan, in 1936. She has published fifteen books of poetry. See page R6 of the Author Files for more on Marge Piercy.

Literature Online

Author Search For more about these poets, go to www.glencoe.com.

NY English Language Arts Core Curriculum (pp. 398–401)

Core R4 Determine the meaning of words by using a dictionary. **LC R12** Combine multiple strategies to enhance comprehension and response. **R2f** Identify poetic elements to interpret poetry. **R2g** Compare literature to own lives.

For a complete description of the standards, see p. NY11.

Vocabulary Preview

Previewing these words and phrases from "We Real Cool" and "The Market Economy" will help you recognize and understand them when you read the poems.

- The word **lurk** means to hang around trying not to be seen. You might lurk outside your sister's bedroom door to find out her secrets.
- In a **market economy,** the things and services people buy are priced according to what people are willing to pay for them.
- **Polyvinyl cups** and **wash and wear suits** are products made from types of plastic (polyvinyl and polyester fibers). These plastic products are cheaper and easier to care for than similar products made from natural materials, such as glass, cotton, or wool. However, polyvinyl can cause cancer, and the production of plastics causes dangerous pollution.
- **Fine print** is the section of an agreement that describes the risks involved in the agreement. This section is often printed in tiny type, or "fine print."

English Language Coach

Using Word References Dictionaries and glossaries are reference sources that can help you learn the meanings of words. Thesauruses can help you find synonyms and antonyms for words. All these resources are available in print and online. Words are listed in alphabetical order.

Here's how the word *flower* appears in a dictionary. A glossary entry would be similar to this.

> **flower** *n.* [ME *flour*, fr. AF *flur, flour,* fr. L *flor-*] **1.** the blossom of a plant. **2.** a flowering plant. **3.** full bloom. **4.** the best or greatest part or time of something.
> *v.* **1.** to form flowers; to bloom. **2.** to come into full development; reach the peak or best time. flowered, flowering

Write to Learn Using a dictionary and a thesaurus, write one definition and one synonym for each word below.

1. conflict

2. test

3. smart

4. vacation

5. cold

Skills Preview

Key Reading Skill: Identifying Main Idea and Supporting Details

Reading a poem is different from reading an article. The main idea of a poem may not be directly stated as it usually is in an article. Poets often use images and emotions to communicate their main ideas. To determine the main idea of a poem, ask yourself these questions:

- What are the main images and symbols in this poem?
- What emotions do I feel when I read this poem?
- What is the poet saying about the topic?

Partner Talk Discuss your experiences reading poetry with a partner. Do you enjoy reading poetry? How is it different from reading articles or short stories?

Literary Element: Alliteration

Alliteration is the repetition of consonant sounds at the beginnings of words. A consonant is any letter of the alphabet except the vowels, *a, e, i, o,* and *u.* Poets use alliteration to create a musical effect, to emphasize meaning, or to draw attention to particular words.

Use these tips to think about alliteration in a poem.

- Read the poem aloud, exaggerating the pronunciation of words.

  Do you hear any repeated consonant sounds?

- How does the alliteration help the poem flow?

  Does the alliteration give you a sense of rhythm? Can you "hear" the speaker saying the words?

Small Group Work Form a group of four students and play this card game.

1. Write these words on separate index cards: *check, shoes, guzzle, put.* Then shuffle the cards.

2. Take turns picking a card and creating a sentence or phrase that repeats the consonant sound that begins the word on your card. For example, if you pick *guzzle,* you might come up with this sentence: *The gross green goblin grows giggles in his garden.*

Get Ready to Read

Connect to the Reading

When you read the poems "We Real Cool" and "The Market Economy," think about your hopes for the future and the decisions that lie ahead of you.

Partner Talk With two or three classmates, talk about some of the decisions you will have to make in your future. Which decisions do you think will be easy? Which ones do you think will be harder?

Build Background

- A pool hall is a place where people get together to play pool. Pool is a game played on a table by hitting balls with a long, thin stick into holes at the corners of the table.
- In "We Real Cool," the Golden Shovel is the name of a pool hall.
- Smog is a type of pollution. Smog is caused when the smoke and waste products from factories and automobiles combine with sunlight. The chemical reaction creates a thick, fine dust that looks like yellow fog.

Set Purposes for Reading

BIG Question Read "We Real Cool" and "The Market Economy" to learn how the choices people make can put their lives at risk.

Set Your Own Purpose What else would you like to learn from these poems to help you answer the Big Question? Write your own purpose in the Reading Workshop 4 Foldable for Unit 3.

Literature Online

Interactive Literary Elements Handbook
To review or learn more about the literary elements, go to www.glencoe.com.

Keep Moving

Use these skills as you read "We Real Cool" and "The Market Economy."

We Real Cool

by Gwendolyn Brooks

THE POOL PLAYERS.
SEVEN AT THE GOLDEN SHOVEL.

We real cool. We
Left school. We

Lurk late. We
Strike straight. We

Sing sin. We
Thin gin. We

Jazz June. We
Die soon. **1** ○

Practice the Skills

1 Literary Element

Alliteration There is alliteration in almost every line of this poem. How does it affect the rhythm of the poem?

The Market Economy

by Marge Piercy

Suppose some peddler offered
you can have a color TV
but your baby will be
born with a crooked spine;
5 you can have polyvinyl cups
and wash and wear
suits but it will cost
you your left lung
rotted with cancer; suppose
10 somebody offered you
a frozen precooked dinner
every night for ten years
but at the end
your colon dies
15 and then you do,
slowly and with much pain.

You get a house in the suburbs
but you work in a new plastics
factory and die at fifty-one
20 when your kidneys turn off.

But where else will you
work? Where else can
you rent but Smog City?
The only houses for sale
25 are under the yellow sky.
You've been out of work for
a year and they're hiring
at the plastics factory.
Don't read the fine
30 print, there isn't any. **2 3** ○

Practice the Skills

2 **Key Reading Skill**

Determining Main Idea and Supporting Details Summarize both poems. What is the main idea of each poem? How are they related?

3 **BIG Question**

In both poems, people choose one way to live and then pay the price. On the Reading Workshop 4 Foldable, write the choices the people make, what they gain, and what they lose in each poem. Then note whether you think the prices they pay are too high or not.

After You Read

We Real Cool *and* The Market Economy

Answering the BIG Question

1. Both poems talk about the prices people pay for their decisions. Do you think these people thought about costs before they made their decisions? Explain.

2. **Recall** Who are the "We" in "We Real Cool"?
   TIP Right There

3. **Recall** What are some of the conveniences of modern life mentioned in "The Market Economy"?
   TIP Right There

Critical Thinking

4. **Interpret** The speaker of "The Market Economy" speaks directly to the reader by using "you" and "your." What effect does this have on you as a reader?
   TIP Author and Me

5. **Compare** How is the decision to leave school in "We Real Cool" different from the decision to work at a plastics factory in "The Market Economy"?
   TIP Author and Me

6. **Evaluate** The poet who wrote "The Market Economy" seems to think that in a market economy some people do not have a choice about where they can work and live. Do you think this is true? Why or why not?
   TIP Author and Me

Talk About Your Reading

Role Play Imagine you are one of the people referred to in the poem "We Real Cool" or "The Market Economy." You could be one of the kids hanging out at the pool hall or a person who lives in Smog City. Tell the class about yourself—how old you are, the kind of place where you grew up, what your family is like, what you're interested in—and talk about whether you agree or disagree with the poet's message.

NY English Language Arts Core Curriculum (pp. 402–403)

LC R17 Demonstrate comprehension and response through a range of activities. **S3a** Express opinions or judgments about information, ideas, opinions, issues, themes, and experiences. **LC R12** Combine multiple strategies to enhance comprehension and response. **R3a** Evaluate details or reasons used to support ideas. **R2f** Identify poetic elements to interpret poetry. **Core W8** Use correct grammatical construction in sentences.

For a complete description of the standards, see p. NY11.

Skills Review

Key Reading Skill: Identifying Main Idea and Supporting Details

7. What do you think the main idea of "The Market Economy" is? State it in your own words and explain why you do or don't think it's true.

8. What are some of the images and examples Piercy uses to support the main idea of the poem?

Literary Element: Alliteration

9. Give examples of the alliteration Brooks uses in "We Real Cool." How does alliteration make the poem sound—like a song, a rap, or a riddle? Explain.

10. Give examples of the alliteration Piercy uses in "The Market Economy." Is it as obvious as in "We Real Cool"? How are the sounds of the two poems different?

Vocabulary Check

Answer the following questions about these words and phrases from "We Real Cool" and "The Market Economy."

11. In a **market economy,** why is a gold bracelet more expensive than one made of glass beads?

12. Why would people buy **polyvinyl cups** instead of glass ones?

13. If your shirt is **wash and wear,** would it be made of wool?

14. Who would be better at **lurking**—an active, noisy three-year-old child or a burglar?

15. Give an example of a document that is likely to include **fine print.**

16. **English Language Coach** Use a thesaurus to find synonyms for *cost.*

Web Activities For eFlashcards, Selection Quick Checks, and other Web activities, go to www.glencoe.com.

Grammar Link: Indirect Objects

An **indirect object** answers the question *to what? to whom? for what?* or *for whom?* It always comes between the verb and the direct object in a sentence. You will **never** find an *indirect* object in a sentence that doesn't have a *direct* object.

Susan gave Mrs. Monroe a flower.
    verb   *indirect*   *direct*
          object   *object*

(Susan gave a flower to *whom?* She gave it to *Selma.*)

A word is an indirect object only if *to* or *for* is **not** stated. If *to* or *for* is there, it's the object of a preposition. These two sentences contain prepositional phrases, not indirect objects:

My cat brought her toy to me.

Mike sent an e-mail to his boss.

Here are the same sentences with indirect objects:

My cat brought me her toy.

Mike sent my boss an e-mail.

Grammar Practice

Copy the following sentences. Underline the indirect object and circle the direct object.

17. The soccer coach gave Michael an award.

18. My brother sent his girlfriend a love letter.

19. Did you give your grandmother her birthday gift yet?

20. Lorenzo threw his dog a treat.

21. When will you tell Sari the truth?

22. Sandi gave the bus driver one dollar and one quarter.

23. After dinner, we wrote Aunt Louisa a letter.

24. Please give James his jacket.

25. Show me your favorite game.

26. My mother baked me a birthday cake.

Wearing Hijab: Veil of Valor
by Emilia Askari

&

from ZOYA'S STORY

by Zoya with John Follain
and Rita Cristofari

Skills Focus

You will use these skills as you read and compare the following selections:

- "Wearing Hijab: Veil of Valor," p. 407
- from *Zoya's Story: An Afghan Woman's Struggle for Freedom*, p. 414

Reading

- Read and understand texts representing a variety of authors, subjects, and genres
- Clarify understanding of texts by creating a graphic organizer
- Analyze author's qualifications and sources.

In this unit, you've read about the trade-offs people make. You've thought about what can happen when events and experiences cost people and communities too much. But who or what affects how you think and feel about a subject? Many times, writers help you decide when the price is too high.

How to Read Across Texts

When you read across two texts, you look at what subjects the writers discuss and how they communicate their ideas to readers. You think like a detective, asking questions about the writers and their subjects. That way, you learn more about the subject by evaluating how and why each writer writes about it.

As a reader, you need to think about the following questions:

- What are the writer's **qualifications?** Does he or she know about this topic from formal education, research, or personal experience?
- What are the writer's **sources?** Was the writer a witness to the events? If not, does he or she identify where the information came from?

NY English Language Arts Core Curriculum (pp. 404–405)

LC R15 Analyze, contrast, support, and critique points of view in a wide range of genres.

For a complete description of the standards, see p. NY11.

Academic Vocabulary

sources (SOR sez) *n.* books, articles or people that supply information

Get Ready to Compare

In your Learner's Notebook, draw a graphic organizer like the one below. Use your organizer to keep track of details about the writers as you read the following selections. Your notes will help you better understand the subject and compare the selections.

Writer	Emilia Askari	Zoya
Writer's Qualifications		
Writer's Sources		

Use Your Comparison

The two selections you will read in this workshop have something in common. They are both about the clothing many Muslim women wear. But the writers explore the issue in very different ways. One writer shares the stories of three women through a newspaper article, while the other writer draws upon her own experience.

As you read, use the information you add to your chart to think about how each writer approaches the issue.

- How does each writer share information and experiences? How does her approach make you think and feel as you read?
- What do you learn from one writer that you don't learn from the other?
- How does each selection make you, the reader, think about the issue in different ways?

Before You Read

Wearing Hijab: Veil of Valor

Emilia Askari

Meet the Author

Emilia Askari is a prize-winning journalist who has covered environmental and public health issues for more than a decade. She lives in the Detroit area and is a former president of the Society of Environmental Journalists. She works for the *Detroit Free Press*.

Author Search For more about Emilia Askari, go to www.glencoe.com.

NY English Language Arts Core Curriculum (pp. 406–412)

LC R9 Recognize multiple meanings of words. **R3a** Consider the background and qualifications of the writer.

For a complete description of the standards, see p. NY11.

Vocabulary Preview

valor (VAL or) *n.* courage **(p. 407)** *In Arthurian legend, the Knights of the Round Table are known for their valor.*

intercede (in tur SEED) *v.* to help settle differences between others **(p. 410)** *The teacher decided to intercede when the vote for class president ended in a tie.*

tolerance (TOL ur uns) *n.* the ability to recognize and respect different beliefs **(p. 410)** *Samir's grandfather was a devout Hindu, but he encouraged the tolerance of other faiths.*

English Language Coach

Multiple-Meaning Words Many words have more than one meaning. To discover the correct meaning of a word, you can look at context clues.

For example, the word *case* can mean:

(a) a container; (b) an occurrence; (c) someone who is being helped or treated by a professional

In "Wearing Hijab: Veil of Valor," you will find the word *case*. Use context clues to decide which meaning of *case* makes sense.

Get Ready to Read

Connect to the Reading

Have you ever stood up for something you believed in, even though doing so made you unpopular? How did that feel?

Build Background

First published in November 2001, this article is about women who follow the Muslim practice of covering their heads with scarves, called *hijab*. Many Muslim women choose to wear *hijab* as an expression of their faith.

Set Purposes for Reading

BIG Question Read to find out why women decide to wear *hijab* and what it can cost them.

Set Your Own Purpose What else would you like to learn from the selection to help you answer the Big Question? Write your own purpose on your Reading Across Texts Foldable.

INFORMATIONAL TEXT
NEWSPAPER
Detroit Free Press

Wearing Hijab:
Veil of Valor

by Emilia Askari

Practice the Skills

Alya Kazak had been thinking about wearing *hijab,* a scarf that would publicly identify her as Muslim, for a long time.

It was just a rectangle of cloth, plain and black. But it was heavy with symbolism—a reminder of her faith, her modesty, her wish that strangers would be attracted by her personality and not her physical beauty. **1**

So what if she worked in a Victoria's Secret selling cosmetics? Sure, there was a conflict there. But the life of an American Muslim is punctuated with cultural clashes. This one didn't seem any bigger than most.

Or did it?

The first day Kazak took up the veil, tears were pouring down her face as she drove toward the Somerset Collection.

She pulled over to the side of the road, daubed her eye makeup and prayed.

1 **Reviewing Elements**

Photographs How does the photograph above add to the author's description of *hijab?*

Vocabulary

valor (VAL or) *n.* courage

Please make this an easy transition for me. Please make me strong.

Today, about two and a half years later, Kazak is among tens of thousands of Muslim women in Michigan who wear *hijab*—pronounced hee-JAHB—in public. The practice often is misunderstood by non-Muslims, who may associate it with female oppression. But most *hijabis,* as women who wear the scarves are called, say that covering their hair was a personal choice. They credit the veils with improving their relationships with people and God. **2**

Here are the stories of three Muslim females in metro Detroit and their experiences with *hijabs.* They share faith in Islam and believe that publicly identifying themselves as Muslims is more important since Sept. 11.

Wearing *hijab* "clarified for me my identity as a Muslim woman," says Kazak, who left her part-time job at Victoria's Secret when her schedule of Oakland University classes changed. Now that she's graduated, she works full-time as a **case** manager for refugees at ACCESS, the Arab Community Center for Economic and Social Services in Dearborn. **3**

The scarf she wraps around her head each morning has liberated Kazak from the coquettish[1] games other people play, she says. "I notice a different level of respect, and I just love that. Self-esteem . . . I just feel so much better about myself, so much more respectable. I feel my personality come out with my scarf."

She burbles with confidence, happy to demonstrate how she pins the scarf after matching its color to her day's outfit. "It's like a declaration: Hello, I am Muslim," says Kazak, 22. She lives with her parents and sister in Bloomfield Hills, driving to work in a car sporting a vanity license and floor mats emblazoned[2] with her nickname, Princess. **4**

Kazak, who is of Palestinian descent, says taking up the veil was "the most positive decision I have made in my life."

With the world's attention focused on Muslims in the wake of the attacks, Kazak says she feels people staring a bit longer at her veil, giving her a wider berth[3] as she passes them on the street or in the mall. Still, she has been lucky. No one has

Practice the Skills

2 Reading Across Texts

Writer's Sources The writer does not tell you the source of this information, but newspaper editors usually verify, or check, that the information is correct.

3 English Language Coach

Multiple-Meaning Words Think about the three meanings of **case** on page 406. Now look at the context clues in this sentence. What does *case* mean here?

4 Reading Across Texts

Writer's Qualifications What can you learn from a writer who interviews others? Do you think you can learn more or less from someone who only writes about his or her own experiences?

---

1. When people are *liberated* (LIH bur ay tid), they are set free. *Coquettish* (koh KET ish) means "playful" or "flirtatious."

2. *Emblazoned* (em BLAY zund) means "decorated with bold words or colors."

3. *Giving a wider berth* means "giving someone a lot of room."

bothered her because she follows the religion that's also claimed by the killers of thousands of Americans.

Another story

Zaiba Lateef has not been so lucky. Perhaps that's because she is 15 and immersed in a peer culture where teasing and showing off are huge preoccupations.

The first shove came out of nowhere on Sept. 11, hours after the 5,000 or so students in the adjoining campuses of Plymouth-Canton and Salem high schools had watched the twin towers collapse on television.

Lateef, whose parents immigrated to Michigan from India, had just finished her American Literature class.

Then from the crowd of people filling the hallway came a boy's voice hissing an expletive,[4] followed by "terrorist." And someone's shoulder slammed Lateef into the wall of lockers.

"It was such a blackout," Lateef recalls. "I was so confused. I was so scared." She turned to see who had pushed her. But it was impossible to tell. **5**

Three young Arab women dance in a circle at a festival in Dearborn, Michigan.

Lateef has worn *hijab* since she was nine. All girls in fifth grade and up are required to cover their hair at the Crescent School, a private Muslim elementary school in Canton that Lateef attended.

Despite the fact that *hijab* was part of her school uniform, Lateef says she never felt forced to wear it. "It was more like a reward" for being old enough and mature enough, she says.

After the incident in the hallway, some of Lateef's relatives suggested that perhaps it would be best if the slim, analytical girl stopped wearing *hijab* for a while. But Lateef wouldn't hear of it. "I want to keep wearing *hijab* to show people that Islam is a true and beautiful religion," she says. "I'm proud to be a Muslim. This is a time when I need to be strong."

Practice the Skills

5 | **Reading Across Texts**

Writer's Sources How does the writer (Emilia Askari) know about Kazak's experiences—through education, research, or personal experience? Write your answer in your chart.

---

4. An **expletive** (EK spluh tiv) is a disrespectful word or phrase.

Weeks passed before it happened again. Then, in early October, she was standing in the second floor Spanish hall a few minutes before school was scheduled to start. A heavy shoe kicked her hard in the shin as a boy called out the same insult, laughing.

This time it wasn't as much of a shock. She turned and made a mental note of the boy's face, his green nylon ski jacket, and the bright orange fleece jacket worn by the girl who was with him, laughing.

Then Lateef says she saw a friend walking down the hall and broke down in tears. "I couldn't even talk," she says. "I couldn't walk. I just kept crying." **6**

A week later, she says that she and another friend were walking in a breezeway between two school buildings. A group of boys came up from behind them. One yelled, "Can I have one of those?" He reached for Lateef's *hijab.* Another put an arm around her friend and grabbed at the bun of hair beneath her veil.

6 Reviewing Skills

Making Inferences Why did Lateef break down in tears?

Visual Vocabulary
A *mosque* is a place of Muslim worship.

Lateef and her friend ran for an open door, choking back tears. She had trouble breathing. She was scared and angry and sad all at once. She leaned against a wall of lockers, caught her breath and went to her next class with a lump in her throat.

At Lateef's mosque, it seemed like everyone was talking of the young girl's troubles. The news eventually reached Haaris Ahmad, executive director of the Council on American Islamic Relations' Michigan office. He decided to **intercede** among the Lateef family, the school, and the families of the boys.

In the end, the boy in the green jacket apologized for kicking Lateef. Lateef forgave him. School officials agreed to enhance their efforts to teach cultural **tolerance,** developing what Ahmad calls a model program for other schools. Among the school's first actions was to encourage all of its students to attend an open house at a nearby mosque for extra credit.

Vocabulary

intercede (in tur SEED) *v.* to help settle differences between others
tolerance (TOL ur uns) *n.* the ability to recognize and respect different beliefs

The boy was there with his family. He appeared delighted when a woman wrote his first name in Arabic script, noting that it was the name of an Islamic prophet.

Although wearing *hijab* in public and while praying is encouraged by Islamic teachings, many Muslim women regard the practice as optional. There was a time, perhaps a decade or so ago, when professional, educated women were less likely to wear *hijab* than their Muslim sisters who were less educated or whose lives centered more on the home. **7**

In fact, some countries with large Muslim populations such as Turkey have tried to discourage or even forbid women from wearing *hijab* in an effort to modernize.

In the last 10 or 15 years, however, it has become less unusual in this country and many others around the world to see women like Dr. Razan Kadry wearing *hijab* as they see patients and consult with other physicians at Detroit Medical Center.

Kadry is a dermatology resident born in Pontiac of Syrian-American parents.

She has no recollection of the exact day, when she was 14, she made the decision to wear *hijab*. But in retrospect,[5] Kadry sees it as a turning point. "I was a very timid person," she says. "I was good in school, but I wasn't stellar." Covering her hair gave her the confidence to excel.

"It opened doors of opportunity," she says. "I was able to focus not so much on my appearance and social things but on what I needed to do at school. My grades shot through the roof. Everything fell into place."

She wound up skipping three grades and entering Oakland University at 15, then graduated from Wayne State's medical school.

Kadry feels that wearing *hijab* around the hospital makes it easier for her to do her job.

"People deal with me on a much more professional and friendly level because I veil," she explains.

Because she wears *hijab*—perhaps also because she is married and a mother—men treat Kadry, 27, as a comrade, barely noticing her physical appearance.

Practice the Skills

7 | **Reviewing Skills**

Making Inferences Why might women who worked outside of the home have been less likely to wear *hijab*?

---

5. If you think about things *in retrospect* (REH troh spekt), you think about the past.

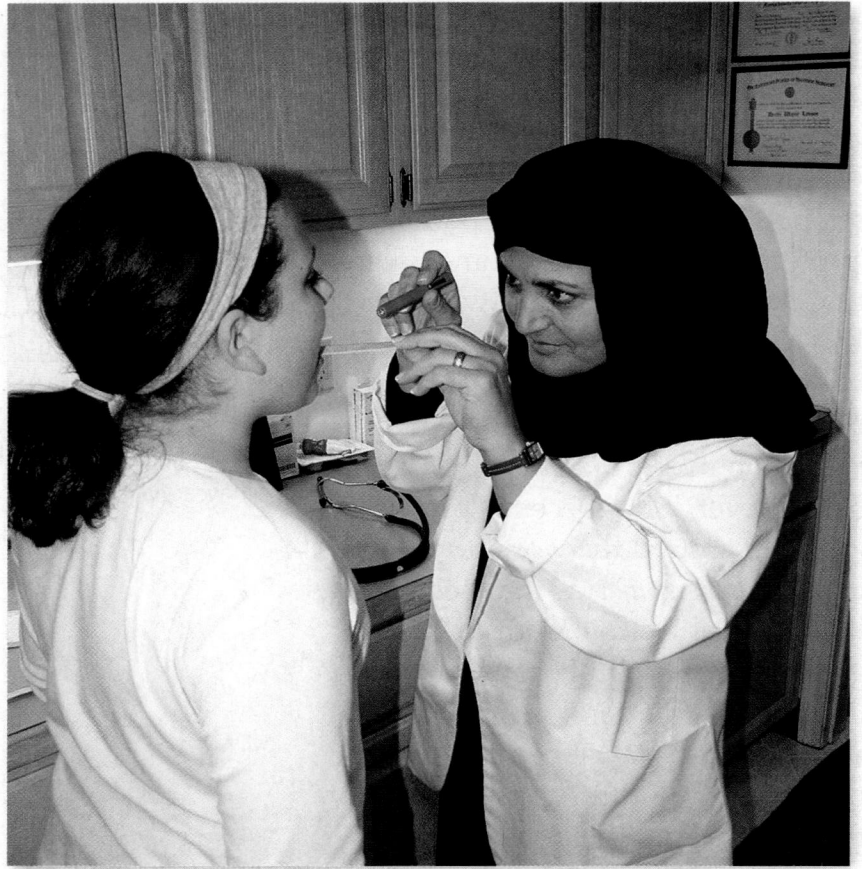

Analyzing the Photo Like the woman in this photo, Kadry practices medicine while wearing *hijab*. How might Kadry's experience as a doctor differ from the experiences of other doctors who don't wear *hijab*?

That camaraderie[6] abruptly faded on Sept. 11 as news of the attacks spread. "For a moment I felt there was a huge wall around me," Kadry says. "Then I started speaking, saying that the people who did this could not have been real Muslims."

The mood changed as everyone realized that she was just as shocked and horrified as they were by the attacks.

Her boss went out of his way to speak with her in private, expressing concern for her safety and suggesting that perhaps she might want to remove her *hijab* until feelings cooled down.

"I told him that was like asking a black person to bleach the color out of their skin," Kadry said. "Now more than ever I have to stay steadfast. I must wear *hijab* and be a better example." **9 10** ○

Practice the Skills

9 Reviewing Skills

Connecting How do you think you would feel in Kadry's place? Would you be afraid of violence if you wore *hijab*? Would you feel like a coward if you didn't?

10 BIG Question

What price were these three women willing to pay to wear *hijab*? Was that price too high? Write your answer in your Reading Across Texts Foldable.

---

6. ***Camaraderie*** (kawm RAH dur ee) is another word for "friendship."

Before You Read : from *Zoya's Story*

Meet the Author

Because Zoya must hide her true identity to protect her family and friends, two other people helped her write her story. John Follain lives and works in Rome. He writes mostly about the Vatican and the Mafia in Italy. Rita Cristofari has worked as a press officer for the United Nations, Médecins Sans Frontières, and France 2 television.

Literature Online

Author Search For more about these authors, go to www.glencoe.com.

NY English Language Arts Core Curriculum (pp. 413–417)

LC R9 Recognize multiple meanings of words. **R3a** Consider the background and qualifications of the writer.

For a complete description of the standards, see p. NY11.

Vocabulary Preview

instinctively (in STINK tiv lee) *adv.* resulting from or caused by a natural response **(p. 415)** *When he saw the car coming, Maleek instinctively jumped out of the way.*

perpetrated (PUR pih tray tid) *v.* was responsible for something harmful; form of the verb *perpetrate* **(p. 416)** *The police vowed to catch those who perpetrated the crime.*

English Language Coach

Multiple-Meaning Words *Treatment* is a multiple-meaning word that can mean

(a) a method for helping a person who is ill

(b) the way someone behaves toward you

Watch for the word *treatment* in *Zoya's Story.*

Get Ready to Read

Connect to the Reading

The person in the story you are about to read is treated negatively because she is female. How does it feel to be treated unfairly?

Build Background

- The Taliban (TAL ih ban) is the group that ruled Afghanistan from 1996–2001.
- The Taliban follow a strict form of Islamic law. Under this law, women must cover themselves completely with a *burqa,* a large piece of cloth that covers them from head to toe, including their face and hands.
- This story is told by a woman who was born in Afghanistan but moved away when the Taliban gained control of her country. This selection is about her return to Afghanistan when the Taliban were still in control.

Set Purposes for Reading

BIG Question Read to discover why Zoya returned to Afghanistan and how she felt about wearing a *burqa.*

Set Your Own Purpose What else would you like to learn from the selection to help you answer the Big Question? Write your own purpose on your Reading Across Texts Foldable.

ZOYA'S STORY

by Zoya

with John Follain and Rita Cristofari

Prologue

At the head of the Khyber Pass, when we reached the border with Afghanistan at Torkham,[1] our car stopped short of the Taliban checkpoint. Before getting out of the car, my friend Abida helped me to put the *burqa* on top of my shirt and trousers and adjusted the fabric until it covered me completely. I felt as if someone had wrapped me in a bag. As best I could in the small mountain of cheap blue polyester, I swung my legs out of the car and got out. 1

The checkpoint was a hundred yards away, and I stared for a moment at my homeland beyond it. I had been living in exile in Pakistan[2] for five years, and this was my first journey back to Afghanistan. I was looking at its dry and dusty mountains through the bars of a prison cell. The mesh of tiny holes in front of my eyes chafed against my eyelashes. I tried to look up at the sky, but the fabric rubbed against my eyes.

---

1. The **Khyber Pass** is a 33-mile passage that connects Pakistan with **Afghanistan,** which is a mountainous country in central Asia. **Torkham** is a town on the border between Pakistan and Afghanistan.

2. **Pakistan** (PA kih stan) is a country in south Asia that shares borders with India, China, Iran, and Afghanistan.

Practice the Skills

1 **Reading Across Texts**

Writer's Qualifications How does the writer know about these events? How can you tell?

The *burqa* weighed on me like a shroud.[3] I began to sweat in the June sunshine and the beads of moisture on my forehead stuck to the fabric. The little perfume—my small gesture of rebellion—that I had put on earlier at once evaporated. Until a few moments ago, I had breathed easily, **instinctively,** but now I suddenly felt short of air, as if someone had turned off my supply of oxygen. **2**

I followed Javid, who would pretend to be our *mahram,* the male relative without whom the Taliban refused to allow any woman to leave her house, as he set out for the checkpoint. I could see nothing of the people at my side. I could not even see the road under my feet. I thought only of the Taliban edict[4] that my entire body, even my feet and hands, must remain invisible under the *burqa* at all times. I had taken only a few short steps when I tripped and nearly fell down.

When I finally neared the checkpoint, I saw Javid go up to one of the Taliban guards, who was carrying his Kalashnikov rifle slung jauntily over his shoulder. He looked as wild as the Mujahideen, the soldiers who claimed to be fighting a "holy war," whom I had seen as a child: the crazed eyes, the dirty beard, the filthy clothes. I watched him reach to the back of his head, extract what must have been a louse, and squash it between two fingernails with a sharp crack. I remembered what Grandmother had told me about the Mujahideen: "If they come to my house, they won't even need to kill me. I'll die just from seeing their wild faces."

I heard the Taliban ask Javid where he was going, and Javid replied, "These women are with me. They are my daughters. We traveled to Pakistan for some **treatment** because I am sick, and now we are going back home to Kabul." **3** No one asked

---

3. A cloth placed over a dead body is called a ***shroud*** (shrowd).

4. An ***edict*** (EE dikt) is a rule or an order.

Vocabulary

instinctively (in STINK tiv lee) *adv.* resulting from or caused by a natural response

Practice the Skills

2 | **Reviewing Elements**

Description Which details in this paragraph help you to imagine what it feels like to wear a *burqa*?

Analyzing the Photo Taliban fighters sit outside of the American embassy in Kabul, Afghanistan, in 2001. How do the men in this picture compare to Zoya's description of Taliban members?

3 | **English Language Coach**

Multiple-Meaning Words Look at the two meanings of **treatment** on page 413. Which meaning of *treatment* makes sense here?

from *Zoya's Story* **415**

me to show any papers. I had been told that for the Taliban, the *burqa* was the only passport they demanded of a woman. **4**

If the Taliban had ordered us to open my bag, he would have found, tied up with string and crammed at the bottom under my few clothes, ten publications of the clandestine[5] association I had joined, the Revolutionary Association of the Women of Afghanistan. They documented, with photographs that made my stomach churn no matter how many times I looked at them, the stonings to death, the public hangings, the amputations performed on men accused of theft, at which teenagers were given the job of displaying the severed limbs to the spectators, the torturing of victims who had fuel poured on them before being set alight, the mass graves the Taliban forces left in their wake.

These catalogs of the crimes **perpetrated** by the Taliban guard's regime had been compiled on the basis of reports from our members in Kabul. Once they had been smuggled to the city, they would be photocopied thousands of times and distributed to as many people as possible.

But the Taliban made no such request. Shuffling, stumbling, my dignity suffocated, I was allowed through the checkpoint into Afghanistan.

As women, we were not allowed to speak to the driver of a Toyota minibus caked in mud that was waiting to set out for Kabul, so Javid went up to him and asked how much the journey would cost. Then Abida and I climbed in, sitting as far to the back as we could with the other women. We had to wait for a Taliban to jump into the minibus and check that there was nothing suspicious about any of the travelers before we could set off. For him, even a woman wearing white socks would have been suspicious. Under a ridiculous Taliban rule, no one could wear them because white was the color of their flag and they thought it offensive that it should be used to cover such a lowly part of the body as the feet.

The longer the drive lasted, the tighter the headband on the *burqa* seemed to become, and my head began to ache. The cloth stuck to my damp cheeks, and the hot air that I was

---

5. A *clandestine* (klan DES tin) association is a secret organization.

Vocabulary

perpetrated (PUR pih tray tid) *v.* was responsible for something harmful

Practice the Skills

4 **Reviewing Skills**

Making Inferences What does the last sentence in this paragraph tell you about how the Taliban view women?

breathing out was trapped under my nose. My seat was just above one of the wheels, and the lack of air, the oppressive heat, and the smell of gasoline mixed with the stench of sweat and the unwashed feet of the men in front of us made me feel worse and worse until I thought I would vomit. I felt as if my head would explode.

We had only one bottle of water between us. Every time I tried to lift the cloth and take a sip, I felt the water trickle down my chin and wet my clothes. I managed to take some aspirin that I had brought with me, but I didn't feel any better. I tried to fan myself with a piece of cardboard, but to do so I had to lift the fabric off my face with one hand and fan myself under the *burqa* with the other. I tried to rest my feet on the back of the seat in front of me so as to get some air around my legs. I struggled not to fall sideways as the minibus swung at speed around the hairpin bends, or to imagine what would happen if it toppled from a precipice[6] into the valley below.

I tried to speak to Abida, but we had to be careful what we said, and every time I opened my mouth the sweat-drenched fabric would press against it like a mask. She let me rest my head on her shoulder, although she was as hot as I was.

It was during this journey that I truly came to understand what the *burqa* means. As I stole glances at the women sitting around me, I realized that I no longer thought them backward, which I had as a child. These women were forced to wear the *burqa*. Otherwise they face lashings, or beatings with chains. The Taliban required them to hide their identities as women, to make them feel so ashamed of their sex that they were afraid to show one inch of their bodies. The Taliban did not know the meaning of love.

The mountains, waterfalls, deserts, poor villages, and wrecked Russian tanks that I saw through the *burqa* and the mud-splattered window made little impression on my mind. I could only think ahead to when my trip would end. For the six hours that the journey lasted, we women were never allowed out. The driver stopped only at prayer time, and only the men were allowed to get out of the minibus to pray at the roadside. Javid got out with them and prayed. All I could do was wait. **5** ○

---

6. A *precipice* (PREH sih pis) is the edge of a steep cliff.

Practice the Skills

5 **BIG Question**
Zoya faces many dangers, including death, when she returns to Afghanistan. What price would you pay to help others? Write your answer on your Reading Across Texts Foldable. Your response will help you complete the Unit Challenge.

After You Read

Wearing Hijab: Veil of Valor & from *Zoya's Story*

Vocabulary Check

For items 1–5, copy the sentences, filling in the blanks with the correct words.

Wearing Hijab: Veil of Valor

intercede   tolerance   valor

1. Showing great _____, the fireman rushed into the burning house.
2. The school board wanted to _____ between the families and the school.
3. The principal encouraged students to learn about Islam and to show _____ for all religious beliefs.

from ZOYA'S STORY

perpetrated   instinctively

4. Finding out who _____ the crime would take a lot of detective work.
5. The young bird _____ flapped its wings as it left the nest and began to fly.

Academic Vocabulary

6. What kinds of **sources** might you use for a history report?

English Language Coach

7. Using context clues and what you know from reading "Wearing Hijab: Veil of Valor," decide which meaning of *descent* makes sense in the sentence below.

   Kazak, who is of Palestinian descent, says taking up the veil was "the most positive decision I have made in my life."
   - a downward slant
   - one's line of ancestors
   - a sudden raid or assault

8. Using context clues and what you know from reading *Zoya's Story*, decide which meaning of *louse* makes sense in the sentence below.

   I watched him reach to the back of his head, extract what must have been a louse, and squash it between two fingernails with a sharp crack.
   - a small insect that lives on warm-blooded animals
   - a mean person

NY English Language Arts Core Curriculum (pp. 418–419)

LC R17 Demonstrate comprehension and response through a range of activities. **Core R4** Determine the meaning of unfamiliar words by using context clues. **LC R15** Analyze, contrast, support, and critique points of view in a wide range of genres. **R3a** Consider the background and qualifications of the writer.

For a complete description of the standards, see p. NY11.

Reading/Critical Thinking

On a separate sheet of paper, answer the following questions.

Wearing Hijab: Veil of Valor

9. **Infer** Alya Kazak says that she cried the first day she wore *hijab*. Why might she have been nervous about her decision?

   TIP **Author and Me**

10. **Analyze** Lateef describes three of her conflicts with other students. How do you think these conflicts affected Lateef's determination to wear *hijab?*

    TIP **Author and Me**

11. **Evaluate** Did the author succeed in showing you why these three women wear *hijab?* Explain your answer with examples from the article.

    TIP **Author and Me**

from ZOYA'S STORY

12. **Interpret** Zoya says that she is looking at the "dry and dusty mountains as through the bars of a prison cell." What is Zoya's prison?

    TIP **Right There**

13. **Evaluate** Think about Zoya's reason for returning to Afghanistan. Do you find her courageous? Why or why not?

    TIP **Author and Me**

14. **Evaluate** Do you think Zoya is taking too much of a risk by doing what she believes in? Why or why not?

    TIP **Author and Me**

Writing: Reading Across Texts

Use Your Notes

15. Follow these steps to find similarities and differences between "Wearing Hijab: Veil of Valor" and *Zoya's Story.*

    Step 1: Look at the notes in your chart. Consider each writer's qualifications and sources of information.

    Step 2: In a paragraph, write about how each writer approaches the issue. Explain the similarities and differences among each writer's qualifications and sources.

    Step 3: Jot down a few notes about what each writer shares with readers. How do the women in the selections feel about wearing *hijab* and the *burqa*?

    Step 4: Explain what you learned from reading each selection.

Get It on Paper

To show how you compare the writers of the selections and the experiences of Muslim women, copy the following statements on a separate sheet of paper. Then complete the statements with your own thoughts.

16. In "Wearing Hijab: Veil of Valor," the writer explores the topic of *hijab* by _____.

17. After reading "Wearing Hijab: Veil of Valor," my thoughts about wearing *hijab* are _____.

18. In *Zoya's Story,* the writer explores the topic of the *burqa* by _____.

19. After reading *Zoya's Story,* my thoughts about wearing the *burqa* are _____.

BIG Question

20. The women in each selection pay a price for their beliefs. What do you think they learn about taking risks for things they care about? How do you think they would answer the Big Question?

Answering The BIG Question

When Is the Price Too High?

You've just read several different selections and you have thought about when the price is too high. Now use what you've learned to do the Unit Challenge.

The Unit Challenge

Choose Activity A or Activity B and follow the directions for that activity.

A. Group Activity: What's the Ending?

Work with your group to write and present a story. In the story, one of the characters must decide if what he or she wants or gets is worth the price it takes to get it. The situation can be either real or imaginary.

1. **Discuss the Assignment** With your group, brainstorm ideas for the story. Don't be afraid to use your imagination. You can use the notes you wrote in your Foldable for ideas, too. Write your ideas in your Learner's Notebook.

2. **Review Your Notes and Make a Decision** Now it's time to choose your story line. Choose the idea you think will be the most fun to write about or the idea that will best illustrate whether or not the goal is worth the price.

3. **Write the Story** After you have chosen a story line, write a draft of the story. Remember it's a draft, so it doesn't have to be perfect. You just want to get your ideas down on paper.

   • Write the title of the story.

   • Describe the character and the situation the character is facing.

   • Then describe the decision the person has to make. Write it as an either-or choice: The person can choose to do *X* or to do *Y*.

   • Write one ending for choice *X* (worth it) and another ending for choice *Y* (not worth it).

4. **Revise and Edit the Story** Make sure each member of the group reviews the draft of the story separately. Each member should take notes about what revisions to make.

   • Make sure the story introduces the character and his or her decision or goal.

   • Make sure the either-or choice is clear and easy to understand.

   • Make sure the consequences of both decisions are clearly illustrated in both endings.

   • Proofread and correct any mistakes in spelling, grammar, and punctuation.

5. **Present the Story** Now you're ready to present your story to the class. At the end of the story, have the class vote on which ending they like best.

B. Solo Activity: Is It Worth It?

Some decisions are easy, but others are difficult. When something is very important to you, it's often hard to make a decision about it. In this activity, you'll use a chart to decide if a decision you have to make is worth the cost or not.

1. **What's Your Decision?** Think of a difficult or important decision such as
   - deciding what group of friends to hang out with
   - choosing how to spend your time after school
   - showing who you really are, even if it shows how you are different from others
   - doing something other people might disapprove of

2. **Draw a Chart** Draw a chart like the one shown below. Then brainstorm the good and bad sides of the decision. Use the notes from your Foldables. Think about the good and the bad sides of the decisions people made in the selections you read.

Write the good things about your own decision in the **Worth It** column. Write the bad things about the decision in the **Not Worth It** column. List as many things as you can think of.

3. **Is It Worth It?** Look over your chart. When you look at the two columns, which column is more important? Is the decision worth the costs?

4. **Think About Your Chart** Write a paragraph that explains which decision you chose. Be sure to write what you learned from making the chart. How could a chart like the one you made help you make good decisions in the future?

5. **Present Your Decision** Copy your chart onto poster board. Use different colors to highlight the "Worth It" and "Not Worth It" columns. Then write or paste your paragraph below your chart. Hand your poster in to your teacher.

My Decision: I want to hang out with a group of kids my mom doesn't like because they get in trouble a lot.	
WORTH IT	**NOT WORTH IT**
1. I like this group of kids.	My mom will get really mad at me.
2. I have fun with them.	I might get in trouble with them.
3. They are really popular.	My other friends won't like me if I hang out with this other group.

Literature Online

BIG Question Link to Web resources to further explore the Big Question at www.glencoe.com.

Your Turn: Read and Apply Skills

O. Henry

Meet the Author

O. Henry was born William Sidney Porter in 1862 in North Carolina and, as a young man, went through some hard times, including three years in jail. Upon release he moved to New York City and began writing for magazines. In 1884 he took the pen name O. Henry. He soon became America's favorite short story writer. See page R2 of the Author Files for more on O. Henry

Tom Pomplun, who adapted the story, is also an editor and graphic artist. He chose Johnny Ryan to illustrate this story partly because Ryan wants comics to be "fun and crazy and weird and gross."

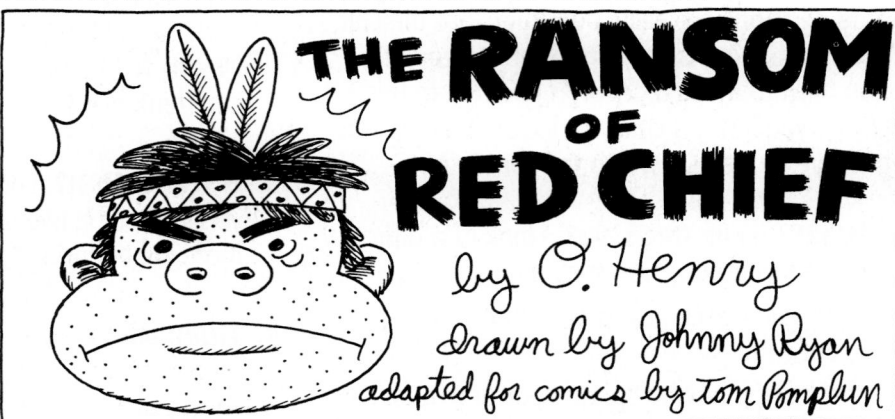

THE RANSOM OF RED CHIEF
by O. Henry
drawn by Johnny Ryan
adapted for comics by Tom Pomplun

WE WERE DOWN SOUTH, IN ALABAMA—BILL DRISCOLL & MYSELF—WHEN THIS KIDNAPPING IDEA STRUCK US.

THERE WAS A TOWN CALLED SUMMIT, WHICH WE KNEW COULDN'T GET AFTER US WITH ANYTHING STRONGER THAN A CONSTABLE & SOME LACKADAISICAL[1] BLOODHOUNDS. SO IT LOOKED GOOD.

WE SELECTED FOR OUR VICTIM THE ONLY CHILD OF A PROMINENT CITIZEN NAMED EBENEZER DORSET, A RESPECTABLE MORTGAGE FANCIER AND FORECLOSER.

THE KID WAS A BOY OF TEN, WITH BAS-RELIEF[2] FRECKLES & FIERY RED HAIR. WE FIGURED THAT EBENEZER WOULD MELT DOWN FOR A RANSOM OF $2000.

---

1. When someone is *lackadaisical* (lak uh DAZE ih kul) he or she is lazy and slow.
2. A *bas-relief* (bah rih LEEF) is when something is raised off the surface.

ABOUT TWO MILES FROM SUMMIT WAS A LITTLE MOUNTAIN, COVERED WITH DENSE CEDARS. ON THE REAR ELEVATION OF THIS MOUNTAIN WAS A CAVE. THERE WE STORED OUR PROVISIONS.

ONE EVENING, WE DROVE PAST DORSET'S HOUSE. THE KID WAS BUSY THROWING ROCKS AT A KITTEN.

WAP!

HEY, LITTLE BOY! WOULD YOU LIKE A BAG OF CANDY?

WAP!!

THAT WILL COST THE OLD MAN AN EXTRA FIVE HUNDRED DOLLARS.

THAT BOY PUT UP A NASTY FIGHT, BUT AT LAST WE GOT HIM INTO THE BUGGY AND DROVE AWAY.

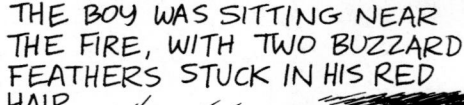

THEN WE HAD SUPPER; AND HE FILLED HIS MOUTH FULL OF BACON & BREAD & GRAVY, AND BEGAN TO TALK:

I LIKE THIS FINE. I NEVER CAMPED OUT BEFORE; BUT I HAD A PET 'POSSUM ONCE, AND I WAS NINE LAST BIRTHDAY. I HATE TO GO TO SCHOOL. ARE THERE ANY REAL INDIANS IN THESE WOODS? I WANT SOME MORE GRAVY. DOES THE TREES MOVING MAKE THE WIND BLOW? WHAT MAKES YOUR NOSE SO RED, BILL? ARE THE STARS HOT? I DON'T LIKE GIRLS. WHY ARE ORANGES ROUND? HOW MANY DOES IT TAKE TO MAKE TWELVE?...

HE JABBERED ON, BUT EVERY FEW MINUTES HE WOULD REMEMBER THAT HE WAS A PESKY REDSKIN, AND HE WOULD LET OUT A WAR-WHOOP THAT MADE BILL SHIVER. THAT BOY HAD HIM TERRORIZED FROM THE START.

WHOOOP!

WE WENT TO BED ABOUT ELEVEN O'CLOCK. WE SPREAD DOWN SOME BLANKETS AND PUT RED CHIEF BE-TWEEN US. WE WEREN'T AFRAID HE'D RUN AWAY.

HE KEPT US AWAKE FOR THREE HOURS, SCREECHING IN OUR EARS, BUT AT LAST I FELL INTO A TROUBLED SLEEP.

AT DAYBREAK, I WAS AWAKENED BY A SERIES OF AWFUL SCREAMS FROM BILL.

AIEEE!! SAM, HELP ME!!

THE KID HAD THE KNIFE WE USED FOR SLICING BACON, AND HE WAS ATTEMPTING TO TAKE BILL'S SCALP.

I GOT THE KNIFE AWAY FROM THE KID AND MADE HIM LIE DOWN AGAIN.

BUT, FROM THAT MOMENT, BILL'S SPIRIT WAS BROKEN. HE NEVER CLOSED AN EYE AGAIN AS LONG AS THAT BOY WAS WITH US.

I DOZED OFF FOR A WHILE, BUT ALONG TOWARD SUN-UP I REMEMBERED THAT RED CHIEF HAD SAID I WAS TO BE BURNED AT THE STAKE.

I WASN'T AFRAID; BUT I SAT UP AND LIT MY PIPE AND LEANED AGAINST A ROCK.

WHAT YOU GETTING UP SO SOON FOR, SAM?

YOU WAS TO BE BURNED TODAY AT SUNRISE, AND YOU WAS AFRAID HE'D REALLY DO IT!

AND HE WOULD, TOO, IF HE COULD FIND A MATCH. DO YOU THINK ANYBODY WILL PAY OUT MONEY TO GET A LITTLE IMP[3] LIKE THAT BACK?

SURE. A ROWDY KID LIKE THAT IS JUST THE KIND THAT PARENTS DOTE ON.[4]

NOW, YOU AND THE CHIEF COOK BREAKFAST, WHILE I GO UP THE MOUNTAIN & RECONNOITER.[5]

I WENT UP ON THE PEAK AND RAN MY EYE OVER THE VICINITY. I EXPECTED TO SEE THE VILLAGERS ARMED WITH PITCH FORKS BEATING THE COUNTRYSIDE FOR THE DASTARDLY KIDNAPPERS.

BUT WHAT I SAW WAS A PEACEFUL LANDSCAPE AND ONE MAN PLOUGHING WITH A MULE. PUZZLED, I WENT BACK TO THE CAVE.

AFTER BREAKFAST THE KID TAKES A TOY OUT OF HIS POCKET & GOES OUTSIDE THE CAVE.

WHAT'S HE UP TO NOW? YOU DON'T THINK HE'LL RUN AWAY, DO YOU, SAM?

NO FEAR OF IT, HE DON'T SEEM TO BE MUCH OF A HOMEBODY.[6]

BUT TONIGHT WE MUST GET A MESSAGE TO HIS FATHER DEMANDING THE RANSOM.

---

3. An ***imp*** is a mischievous, annoying person.

4. To ***dote on*** is to show a lot of attention toward someone.

5. ***Reconnoiter*** (ree kuh NOY tur) means "to look around an area."

6. A ***homebody*** is someone who likes to stay at home.

JUST THEN WE HEARD A WILD WAR-WHOOP. IT WAS A SLINGSHOT THAT RED CHIEF HAD PULLED OUT OF HIS POCKET.

WHOOP! WHOOP! WHOOP!

I DODGED, AND HEARD A HEAVY THUD.

A STONE HAD CAUGHT BILL JUST BEHIND HIS LEFT EAR, AND HE FELL ACROSS THE FIRE.

I DRAGGED HIM OUT AND POURED COLD WATER ON HIS HEAD FOR HALF AN HOUR.

THEN I CAUGHT THAT BOY AND SHOOK HIM UNTIL HIS FRECKLES RATTLED.

YOU'D BETTER BEHAVE, OR I'LL TAKE YOU STRAIGHT HOME!

I WAS ONLY FUNNING. I'LL BEHAVE, SNAKE-EYE, IF YOU'LL LET ME PLAY THE BLACK SCOUT TODAY.

BILL BEGGED ME TO MAKE THE RANSOM FIFTEEN HUNDRED DOLLARS INSTEAD OF TWO THOUSAND.

> Ebenezer Dorset, Esq.:——
>
> We have your boy. It is useless for you to attempt to find him. We demand $1500 in cash for his return; the money to be left at midnight tonight. If you agree to these terms, send your answer in writing tonight at eight. On the road to Poplar Cove, there are three large trees on the right side. At the bottom of the fence-post, opposite the third tree, is a small box. Your messenger will place the answer in this box. If you attempt any treachery,[7] you will never see your boy again.
>
> —Two Desperate Men

AW. SNAKE-EYE, YOU SAID I COULD PLAY THE BLACK SCOUT TODAY!

MR. BILL WILL PLAY WITH YOU. I NEED TO GO INTO TOWN.

WHAT AM I SUPPOSED TO DO?

YOU ARE A HOSS. I MUST RIDE TO THE STOCKADE.

YOU'D BETTER KEEP HIM AMUSED, 'TIL WE GET THE SCHEME GOING.

FOR HEAVEN'S SAKE, HURRY BACK. I WISH WE HADN'T MADE THE RANSOM MORE THAN A THOUSAND.

---

7. **Treachery** (TREH chur ee) means "underhanded, tricky behavior."

I WALKED OVER TO POPLAR COVE AND QUIETLY POSTED MY LETTER

WHEN I GOT BACK, BILL STUMBLED OUT OF THE CAVE, LOOKING EXHAUSTED.

WHAT'S THE TROUBLE, BILL?

I WAS RODE THE NINETY MILES TO THE STOCKADE. THEN I HAD TO EXPLAIN WHY THERE WAS NOTHIN' IN HOLES, HOW A ROAD CAN RUN BOTH WAYS AND WHAT MAKES THE GRASS GREEN.

I TELL YOU, SAM, A HUMAN CAN ONLY STAND SO MUCH!

I TOLD HIM THAT WE WOULD GET THE RANSOM BY MIDNIGHT. SO BILL BRACED UP ENOUGH TO GIVE THE KID A PROMISE TO PLAY RUSSIAN/JAPANESE WAR WITH HIM, AS SOON AS HE FELT A LITTLE BETTER.

THAT EVENING, EXACTLY ON TIME, A MESSENGER RODE UP THE ROAD ON A BICYCLE, LOCATED THE BOX AT THE FOOT OF THE FENCEPOST, SLIPPED A PIECE OF PAPER INTO IT, AND PEDALLED BACK TOWARD SUMMIT.

I SLID DOWN THE TREE I WAS HIDING IN, GOT THE NOTE, AND WAS BACK AT THE CAVE IN ANOTHER HALF AN HOUR.
I OPENED THE NOTE AND READ IT TO BILL:

Gentlemen:

In regard to the ransom you ask for the return of my son, I think you are a little high in your demands. I hereby make you a counter proposition, which I am inclined to believe you will accept. You bring Johnny home and pay me two hundred and fifty dollars in cash, and I agree to take him off your hands. You had better come at night, for the neighbors believe he is lost, and I couldn't be responsible for what they would do to anybody they saw bringing him back.

Very respectfully
Ebenezer Dorset.

SPEECHLESS, WE BOTH STARED AT EACH OTHER, THEN THE KID.

SAM... WHAT'S TWO HUNDRED AND FIFTY DOLLARS, AFTER ALL? I THINK MR. DORSET IS A THOROUGH GENTLEMAN FOR MAKING US SUCH A LIBERAL OFFER.

WE TOOK HIM HOME THAT NIGHT. IT WAS JUST TWELVE O'CLOCK WHEN WE KNOCKED AT EBENEZER'S FRONT DOOR.

JUST AT THE MOMENT WHEN WE SHOULD HAVE BEEN CLEARING FIFTEEN HUNDRED DOLLARS, BILL WAS COUNTING OUT TWO HUNDRED AND FIFTY INTO DORSET'S HAND.

WHEN THE KID FIGURED OUT WE WERE GOING TO LEAVE HIM AT HOME HE STARTED UP A HOWL LIKE A CALLIOPE[8] AND FASTENED HIMSELF AS TIGHT AS A LEECH TO BILL'S LEG.

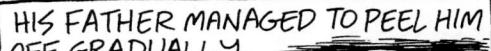

HIS FATHER MANAGED TO PEEL HIM OFF GRADUALLY.

HOW LONG CAN YOU HOLD HIM?

I'M NOT AS STRONG AS I USED TO BE, BUT I THINK I CAN PROMISE YOU TEN MINUTES.

ENOUGH—IN TEN MINUTES I SHALL BE NEARING THE CANADIAN BORDER.

AND AS FAT AS BILL WAS, AND AS GOOD A RUNNER AS I AM, HE WAS A MILE OUT OF SUMMIT BEFORE I COULD CATCH UP WITH HIM.

end.

---

8. A *calliope* (kuh LY uh pee) is an instrument you see at amusement parks; it looks a bit like an organ, but sounds very different.

Reading on Your Own

To read more about the Big Question, choose one of these books from your school or local library. Work on your reading skills by choosing books that are challenging to you.

Fiction

Bud, Not Buddy
by Christopher Paul Curtis

This story is set in the 1930s during the Great Depression. On the run from foster homes, ten-year-old Bud sets out to walk from Flint to Grand Rapids, Michigan, determined to find a musician who he thinks must be his father. Bud takes with him a cardboard suitcase filled with mysteriously labeled rocks, a blanket, a few flyers advertising bands, and his own list of rules.

Nightjohn
by Gary Paulsen

Sarny, an enslaved girl living on the Waller plantation, tells the story of how she learned to read. Even after she is caught and severely punished, Sarny continues to pursue her studies. Her inspiration is Nightjohn, a young man who gives up his freedom and risks torture to teach other enslaved people to read. Based on true events.

A Taste of Salt:
A Story of
Modern Haiti
by Frances Temple

In a hospital in Haiti, seventeen-year-old Djo tells his story to Jeremie, a young woman who entered a convent school in order to escape the slums. Djo left home at a young age, taught reading to young boys at a shelter, and was then kidnapped and sold into slavery as a sugar cane worker.

Julie of the Wolves
by Jean Craighead George

To escape traditional life in an Inuit village, thirteen-year-old Julie tries to run away to San Francisco, where her pen pal lives. When she becomes lost in the Arctic tundra, a wolf pack takes her in. Julie learns how to survive in the wild and develops an appreciation for her Inuit heritage, but she knows she must eventually leave the wilderness and choose between the old ways and the new.

Nonfiction

To Destroy You Is No Loss
by Joan Criddle

Told by 15-year-old Teeda, this book recounts the frightening experience of life in Cambodia during the rule of the Khmer Rouge. Teeda and her family are driven out of their home and find a way to survive and make it to the United States.

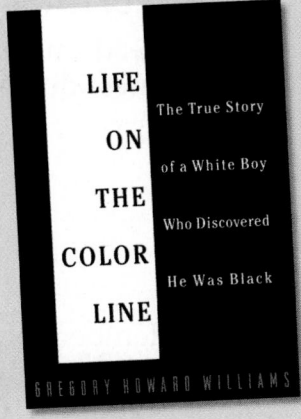

Life on the Color Line
by Gregory Williams

Gregory Williams tells his story about growing up white and finding out his father is African American. When his mother abandons him, Williams learns about his father's side of the family and his African American heritage.

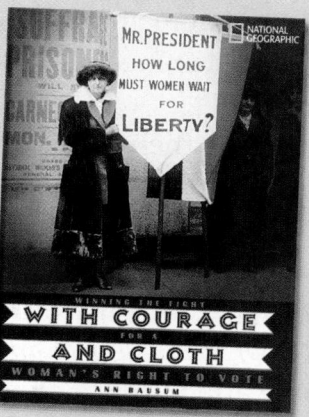

With Courage and Cloth: Winning the Fight for a Woman's Right to Vote
by Ann Bausum

From 1906 to 1920, a new and contentious group of suffragists emerged. Ann Bausum takes a close look at the women of the National Woman's Party and at others who shaped the fight for women's right to vote. Read Bausum's book to learn more about the people—passionate, determined, and utterly fearless— who paid a high price for equality.

The Great Hispanic Heritage: César Chávez
by Hal Marcovitz

The Great Depression affected many farm families in the Southwest. César Chávez was ten when his family lost their farm in Arizona and left to find jobs in California. As migrant workers, the family moved often from farm to farm across the state. Chávez's experience in the fields led to a lifetime of fighting for the fair treatment of migrant workers.

New York English Language Arts Test Practice

*D*irections

Read this passage from an article about wildlife. Then answer questions 1 through 6.

from Living with Wildlife
The Deer Family
By the California Center for Wildlife

Members of the deer family (Cervidae) native to North America include the mule, or black-tailed, deer, the white-tailed deer, the reindeer (known as caribou in North America), the wapiti (better known as elk), and the moose (whose true name is actually elk). Their common North American names are used for descriptions here.

Enemies and Defenses

Natural predators of black-tailed deer are mountain lions, occasionally coyotes, and, in Canada, wolves. However, like white-tailed deer and other large wildlife, their chief enemy is humans. Deer meat and rawhide fed and clothed many pioneers as they settled the West. The destruction of habitat through logging and clearing for farms played a large part in the decrease of deer. Today, hunters and automobiles destroy an estimated 400,000 deer annually. Also, domestic dog packs often kill deer.

Though bucks can use their antlers as weapons, their main defense is their hooves, powered by strong forelegs. White-tailed deer use their tails to give warning signals. Black-tailed deer, when threatened, bounce stiff-legged with their small, ropelike tail down. All deer become more excitable during the mating season and males can be particularly dangerous then. Does will go to great lengths to defend their young. *Never approach a deer at any time of the year, because humans are seen as a threat.* Deer can attack, and serious injury or death can result.

How to Observe

The secret to observing deer is choosing the right time of day: dawn or dusk, because deer feed in the open around those times. Position yourself near a good browsing area where there is enough cover, and make sure you are downwind of the site so the deer cannot detect your smell. Deer in the wild will probably not stay around long once they have noticed you. Do not attempt direct contact (deer can be carriers of Lyme disease ticks), and let the animals leave on their own.

1 This article would be **most** useful to someone who

A needs to treat an injured deer

B is planning to feed deer during the winter

C is trying to control the local deer population

D wants to photograph deer in their natural habitat

2 From the article, you can conclude that the largest single reason for the decline in the deer population has been

F automobiles and hunting for sport

G an increase in natural predators

H the expansion of human settlement on the continent

J the demand for deer meat

3 According to the article, what is the **main** reason people should not approach deer?

A because deer can attack and seriously injure people

B because people usually do not understand deer warning signs

C because deer mating season can occur at any time of the year

D because deer are not afraid of people

4 Based on the article, which of these attributes would be **most** useful to a male deer that is being attacked by another animal?

F large and strong antlers

G sharp teeth

H sharp back hooves and fast legs

J powerful front legs

5 According to the article, the best way to improve your chances of observing deer in the wild is to

A leave the deer alone

B cover your scent with pine leaves

C use food to attract them

D be near their feeding area at the right time of day

6 On a separate piece of paper, copy the chart below and name the **two** members of the deer family described in the "Enemies and Defenses" section. Then, for each type of deer, list one of its enemies and one of its warning signals.

Type of Deer	Enemy	Warning Signal

Directions

Read this passage about the city of Philadelphia at the end of the 18th century. Then answer questions 7 through 12.

from *Brotherly Love*
By the Public Broadcasting System

At the end of the 18th century, Philadelphia was a city of hope for African Americans. Pennsylvania had passed the first gradual abolition act, and Philadelphia was home by 1790 to some 2,000 free blacks. Some had bought their freedom after working during the Revolutionary War, some had been freed by slaveholders moved by revolutionary ideals. All had hopes for the future in the new country built on the ideals of independence, but doubts as to whether the declarations of liberty would apply to them.

Black migration into the city was heavy from the end of the Revolution until about 1815. People came from rural areas in a hundred-mile radius around Philadelphia, as well as from the South, attracted by job prospects and the promise of living among other free black people. Refugees from the revolution in St. Domingue (later Haiti) and fugitive slaves added to the influx of blacks in the city. Philadelphia was over 90 percent white, but its black community helped buffer the hostility of whites and provided an alternative to rural isolation. Many blacks were able to find work as mariners, day laborers and domestic servants. Many also worked as entrepreneurs, often serving a predominantly black clientele. Both men and women often worked to support their families. While some destitute blacks lived near the river, a few prospered and were able to invest in income-producing property. By 1796, black communities were growing along the northern and southern borders of the city. By 1830, all of the city's 14,500 black people were free, while the white population had grown to 150,000.

---

7 The tone of the passage can **best** be described as

  F angry

  G patriotic

  H sensitive toward African Americans

  J supportive of slaveholders

8 For the refugees from the revolution in St. Domingue and fugitive slaves, Philadelphia was **most likely** a symbol of

  A democracy

  B poverty

  C justice

  D hope

9 Although the new country was "built on the ideals of independence," America continued to allow slavery. This is ironic because

- **F** America no longer allows slavery
- **G** slavery would eventually cause the Civil War
- **H** slavery is the opposite of independence
- **J** some slaves had fought during the Revolutionary War

10 Which of the following was **most likely** used as one source for this article?

- **A** passenger lists from slave ships arriving in America
- **B** census reports from the early 1800s
- **C** historical articles about the Revolutionary War
- **D** a chart comparing the number of slaves in the North with the number of slaves in the South in 1830

11 According to the article, some of the most successful black families

- **F** earned their wealth during the Revolutionary War
- **G** started their own communities in the center of the city
- **H** were able to earn a living from the property they owned
- **J** were allowed special freedoms

12 On a separate sheet of paper, copy the chart below and list **two** places or areas that Philadelphia's black population migrated from. Then list **two** reasons blacks migrated to Philadelphia.

Where they came from	Why they came

Directions

Read this article about sea turtles. Then answer questions 13 through 17.

from **Sea Turtles**
Diet and Eating Habits
from the SeaWorld Web site

A. Food preferences and resources

Diet varies with species. Sea turtles may be *carnivorous* (meat eating), *herbivorous* (plant eating), or *omnivorous* (eating both meat and plants). The jaw structure of many species indicates their diet.

1. Green and black sea turtles have finely serrated jaws adapted for a vegetarian diet of sea grasses and algae. In adulthood, they are the only herbivorous sea turtles, but in an aquarium environment all sea turtle species can be maintained on a carnivorous diet.

2. Loggerheads' and ridleys' jaws are adapted for crushing and grinding. Their diet consists primarily of crabs, mollusks, shrimps, jellyfish, and vegetation.

3. A hawksbill has a narrow head with jaws meeting at an acute angle, adapted for getting food from crevices in coral reefs. They eat sponges, tunicates, shrimps, and squid.

4. Leatherbacks have delicate scissorlike jaws that would be damaged by anything other than their normal diet of jellyfish, tunicates, and other soft-bodied animals. The mouth cavity and throat are lined with *papillae* (spinelike projections) pointed backward to help them swallow soft foods.

5. Researchers continue to study the feeding habits of flatbacks. There is evidence that they are opportunistic feeders that eat seaweeds, cuttlefish, and sea cucumbers.

B. Eating habits

Some species change eating habits as they age. For instance, green sea turtles are mainly carnivorous from hatchling until juvenile size; they then progressively shift to a herbivorous diet.

Grammar

13 By quickly previewing the article, you could determine

A that not all turtles live in the sea

B that some turtles use *papillae* for swallowing

C that section A is divided into five parts

D that the article does not discuss how turtles find their food

14 Which of these statements **best** describes the main idea of item 4 in section A?

F Leatherbacks have delicate scissorlike jaws.

G Leatherbacks are designed to eat soft food.

H Leatherbacks' jaws would be damaged by eating anything other than soft food.

J Diet varies with species.

15 Study the index from a book about sea animals.

Sea Turtles	77–92
Dietary Content	81–83
crabs	81
plants	81–82
shrimps	82
squid	83
Jaws	77–79
crushing	77–78
serrated	78–79
scissorlike	79

Which page or pages would **most likely** mention loggerheads, ridleys, and hawksbills together?

A 81

B 82

C 77–78

D 79

16 This type of text structure allows the writer to

F list facts that cover a wide variety of topics

G create a narrative from specific details

H divide a topic into subtopics

J organize details into chronological order

17 Which of these statements **best** supports the main idea of the article's last paragraph?

A Green sea turtles become herbivorous as they age into adulthood.

B All sea turtle hatchlings are carnivorous.

C Sea turtles have adapted jaws that allow them to have specific diets.

D Flatbacks live in the sea.

The BIG Question

What Do You Do When You Don't Know What to Do?

" What you can do or think you can do, begin it. For boldness has magic, power, and genius in it. "

—Johann Wolfgang von Goethe,
German poet and playwright
(1749–1833)

LOOKING AHEAD

The skill lessons and readings in this unit will help you develop your own answer to the Big Question.

UNIT 4 WRAP-UP • Answering the Big Question

Connecting to The BIG Question

What Do You Do When You Don't Know What to Do?

It's one of the worst feelings in the world. You don't know what to do, and you feel alone and lonely. Whether the issue is large or small, it can make you feel tiny and helpless. So what *do* you do? What *should* you do? In this unit, you'll read about what other people have done when they didn't know what to do. Maybe one of their ideas will give you an idea for a strategy, or plan, of your own.

Real Kids and the Big Question

DARREN doesn't know what to do. A friend of his got into some trouble and told Darren about it. He made Darren promise not to tell anyone. Darren thinks that his friend should tell his parents. Darren wants to help his friend, but he doesn't want to break his promise not to tell anyone. What do you think Darren should do?

NICOLE is having a rough time understanding math. She is too embarrassed to raise her hand and ask questions. So she just pretends she understands. At night, she almost cries over the math homework because she can't figure out the problems. She doesn't know what to do. What would you advise her to do?

Warm-Up Activity

In a small group, discuss times when you felt you didn't know what to do. How did it make you feel? Talk about what you did to improve the situation. Which solutions worked best?

You and the Big Question

Reading about what other people did when they didn't know what to do will help you think about what you can do when you face a tough problem.

Literature Online

Big Question Link to Web resources to further explore the Big Question at www.glencoe.com.

Plan for the Unit Challenge

At the end of the unit, you'll use notes from all your reading to complete the Unit Challenge.

You will choose one of the following activities:

A. Advice Column You'll work with a group to write an advice column. You'll write a letter asking for advice about what to do. Then you'll answer a letter from the perspective of one of the speakers or characters in this unit.

B. Award for Best Supporting Role You'll create an award to honor the person who plays a supporting role in your life by helping you or someone else solve problems.

• Start thinking about which activity you'd like to do so that you can narrow your focus as you read each selection.

• In your Learner's Notebook, write your thoughts about which activity you'd like to do.

• Each time you make notes about the Big Question, think about how your ideas will help you complete the Unit Challenge.

Keep Track of Your Ideas

As you read, you'll make notes about the Big Question. Later, you'll use these notes to complete the Unit Challenge. See pages R8–R9 for help with making Foldable 4. The diagram below shows how it should look.

1. Use this Foldable for all of the selections in this unit. Label the stapled edge with the unit number and the Big Question.

2. Label each flap with a selection title. (See page 443 for the titles.)

3. Open each flap. Near the top of the page, write **My Purpose for Reading.** Below the crease, write **The Big Question.**

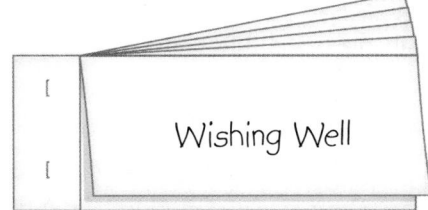

Wishing Well

You know poetry when you see it, even if you really can't explain what it is. **Poetry** looks and sounds different from stories and other kinds of literature. Poetry is organized into lines and stanzas instead of sentences and paragraphs. And in poetry how words sound is often as important as what they mean. In poetry the sounds of words support their meanings.

Why Read Poetry?

Poetry can help you see everyday things—and life in general—in new ways. It can make you feel less alone when you're lonely. It can inspire you when you're in a rut. It can help you smile when you're sad and work through hard times when the going gets tough. Poetry can also help you sharpen your thinking skills. Like riddles, poems contain clues to meaning that you can understand by thinking in fresh, creative ways.

How to Read Poetry

Key Reading Skills

These reading skills are especially useful tools for reading and understanding poetry. You'll see some of these skills modeled in the Active Reading Model, and you'll learn more about all of them later in this unit.

- ■ **Connecting** Link what you read to events in your own life or to other selections you've read. (See Reading Workshop 1.)
- ■ **Evaluating** Make a judgment or form an opinion about what you read. (See Reading Workshop 2.)
- ■ **Interpreting** Use your own understanding of the world to decide what the events or ideas in a selection mean. (See Reading Workshop 3.)
- ■ **Monitoring Comprehension** Pause from time to time to sum up the main idea and important details. Try putting these ideas into your own words. (See Reading Workshop 4.)

Key Literary Elements

Recognizing and thinking about the following literary elements will help you understand poetry more fully.

- ■ **Free verse:** poetry without regular patterns of rhyme or rhythm (See "Wishing Well.")
- ■ **Figurative language—metaphor and simile:** figures of speech that compare seemingly unlike things (See "Mother to Son" and "Harlem.")
- ■ **Alliteration:** the repetition of consonant sounds at the beginning of words (See "Fable for When There's No Way Out.")
- ■ **Rhyme:** the repetition of sounds, usually at the end of lines (See "O Captain! My Captain!")

Skills Focus

- Key reading skills for reading poetry
- Key literary elements of poetry

Skills Model

You will see how to use the key reading skills and literary elements as you read

- **"The Road Not Taken,"** p. 447

**NY English
Language Arts
Core Curriculum** (pp. 446–447)

R2g Compare causes of events to events in own lives. **R3a** Evaluate the validity and accuracy of information, ideas, themes, opinions, and experiences in texts. **R2b** Interpret characters, plot, setting, theme, and dialogue, using evidence from the text. **LC R12** Combine multiple strategies (monitor) to enhance comprehension and response. **R2d** Determine how the use and meaning of literary devices (metaphor and simile) convey the author's message or intent. **R2f** Identify poetic elements, such as repetition, rhythm, and rhyming patterns, to interpret poetry.

For a complete description of the standards, see p. NY 11.

THE ROAD NOT TAKEN

by Robert Frost

The notes in the side column model how to use some of the skills and elements you read about on page 446.

Poetry

Two roads diverged* in a yellow wood,
And sorry I could not travel both **1**
And be one traveler, long I stood
And looked down one as far as I could
5 To where it bent in the undergrowth; **2**

Then took the other, as just as fair,
And having perhaps the better claim,
Because it was grassy and wanted wear;
Though as for that the passing there
10 Had worn them really about the same,

And both that morning equally lay
In leaves no step had trodden* black. **3**
Oh, I kept the first for another day!
Yet knowing how way leads on to way,
15 I doubted if I should ever come back. **4**

I shall be telling this with a sigh
Somewhere ages and ages hence:
Two roads diverged in a wood, and I—
I took the one less traveled by,
20 And that has made all the difference.

1 Key Reading Skill
Connecting *The speaker has to make a decision. Sometimes I have a hard time making decisions.*

2 Key Literary Element
Rhyme *There seems to be a regular pattern of rhyme. Lines 1, 3, and 4 rhyme; and so do lines 2 and 5.*

3 Key Literary Element
Alliteration *I like the way the "l" sound is repeated in "lay" and "leaves."*

4 Key Reading Skill
Interpreting *This is interesting! The speaker seems to be saying you always think you'll come back to something even when you know you probably won't.*

---

1 To **diverge** means to split and go in two directions.

12 **Trodden** is the past tense of the old-fashioned verb *to tread.*

Write to Learn In your Learner's Notebook, write a poem about a time when you had to make a difficult decision about something. Include some descriptive details. What might you compare this situation to?

Study Central Visit www.glencoe.com and click on Study Central to review poetry.

Skills Focus

You will practice these skills when you read the following selections:

- "Wishing Well," p. 452
- "Signed, Sealed, Undelivered," p. 458

Reading

- Connecting to poems

Literature

- Identifying characteristics of free verse
- Finding and analyzing examples

Vocabulary

- Understanding compound nouns and adjectives
- Academic Vocabulary: *illustrates*

Writing/Grammar

- Understanding how to make subjects and verbs agree

Skill Lesson

Connecting

Learn It!

What Is It? You're watching a movie. During a funny scene, you think, *I know just how that character feels. I've been in the same situation, and I felt the same way.* When you relate a movie to your own life, you're **connecting** with the movie. You can connect what you read to your own life in the same way.

- Compare your experiences to those you read about.
- Think about similarities between different selections you've read.

Analyzing Cartoons
Curtis connects the lessons he's learned from scary movies to his own life. Do you think he understands and likes the movie he's watching better because he connects to it?

NY English Language Arts Core Curriculum
(pp. 448–449)

R2g Compare motives of characters, causes of events, and importance of setting to people, events, and places in own lives.

For a complete description of the standards, see p. NY 11.

Why Is It Important? When you connect with a reading selection, you become more involved in it. It's more interesting to you, and so you get more out of it.

How Do I Do It? As you read, ask yourself

• *Does someone I know remind me of this character?*

• *Have I ever felt this way?*

• *What else have I read or experienced that's similar to this selection?*

Here's how a student connected to part of a poem by A. E. Housman. Read the selection from the poem; then read what the student had to say.

> ### *from* Yonder See the Morning Blink
>
> Oh often have I washed and dressed
>   And what's to show for all my pain?
> Let me lie abed and rest:
> Ten thousand times I've done my best
>   And all's to do again.

> I can definitely relate to what the speaker in the poem is saying. It sounds as if the speaker is tired and in a rut. I know how that feels. Some mornings I don't feel like rushing to get dressed or working hard in school all day. I think the speaker wishes he could take a day off. Sometimes I do too.

Practice It!

Below are topics that relate to the selections in this Workshop. What connections can you make with each topic? Jot down some notes in your Learner's Notebook.

• not being able to sleep

• making a wish

• writing a letter to tell someone exactly how you feel

Use It!

As you read "Wishing Well" and "Signed, Sealed, Undelivered," remember the connections you made to the topics. If you make more connections as you read, add to your notes.

Before You Read : Wishing Well

Kate Schmitt

Meet the Author

Kate Schmitt's poems have been published in many collections. She believes that "by sharing our thoughts and experiences, writers . . . create relationships with readers, make connections between ideas, and illuminate our world." Schmitt is also a bookmaker and a teacher of writing.

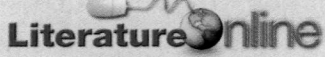

Author Search For more about Kate Schmitt, go to www.glencoe.com.

NY English Language Arts Core Curriculum (pp. 450–453)

LC R6 Determine the meaning of unfamiliar words, terms, and idioms by using word structure knowledge. **R2g** Compare causes of events to events in own lives. **R2f** Identify poetic elements, such as repetition, rhythm, and rhyming patterns, to interpret poetry.

For a complete description of the standards, see p. NY 11.

Vocabulary Preview

mesh (mesh) *n.* the weblike pattern of fibers in woven or knitted items **(p. 453)** *Large holes formed in the mesh of the old blanket.*

arc (ark) *n.* a curved line between two points **(p. 453)** *The arc of the fly ball made it easy for the baseball player to catch.*

On Your Own The following words refer to items that have mesh. Use each word in its own sentence that also contains the word *mesh*.

basketball net • knitted scarf

The following words refer to items that can form an arc when they are tossed into the air. Use each word in its own sentence that also contains the word *arc*.

volleyball • crumpled wad of paper

English Language Coach

Compound Nouns A **compound noun** is a combination of two or more words, such as *classroom (class + room)*. When you see an unfamiliar compound that's made up of words you already know, use your knowledge and context clues to figure out the meaning of the compound word. Try it now. See if you can figure out what the compound noun *passerby* means in the following sentence:

- A passerby who was shopping in the neighborhood saw a man running from the bank just after it was robbed.

By dividing *passerby* into the words it is made up of–*passer* and *by*–and thinking about the context, you can tell that *passerby* means "someone passing by, or walking past, a particular place."

Think-Pair-Share Find the two words in each compound noun below. Then guess what the compound means. Copy the chart in your Learner's Notebook, and write a definition for each compound. Then share your definitions with another student.

Compound Noun	Your Definition
pacesetter	
overcoat	
outgrowth	
paperback	

Skills Preview

Key Reading Skill: Connecting

As you read a selection, ask yourself questions such as: *Have I ever had the feeling the author describes? Have I ever known anyone like this character? Does this make sense to me?* The best readers ask themselves such questions. You can understand better if you relate what's new in what you're reading to what you've already learned by experience.

Partner Talk Practice connecting with a partner. Say something you think or feel about a selection in this book. Have your partner say something from his or her own experience that connects to your thoughts or feelings about that selection. Then do it the other way around.

Key Literary Element: Free Verse

Free verse is a type of poetry that is based on the rhythms of spoken language rather than on traditional patterns of rhythm. Free verse may or may not rhyme. As you read the following unrhymed free verse, notice how words are grouped together. Each line groups words together the way a person in a conversation might group them.

> Seeing the plates piled high
> with turkey, sweet potatoes,
>   mashed potatoes,
> cranberry relish, green beans,
>   cornbread, and more,
> I'm full
> before I've had
> a single bite
> to eat.

Think about how the rhythm of the lines supports the meaning. The last four lines of the poem force you to pause three times. That slows you down, much as feeling full slows you down. As you read "Wishing Well," ask yourself, *How does the rhythm of the poem help support the meaning?*

Get Ready to Read

Connect to the Reading

Before you read the selection, think about times when you had the following experiences:

- not being able to sleep because of a problem
- hoping that something good will happen
- making a wish

Write to Learn Make a list of wishes you have made and write down whether they came true.

Build Background

The poem you are about to read is about making wishes by throwing a coin into a wishing well. How did this custom begin? In the past, many people believed that wells were sacred places because of the much-needed water they provided. Some people even drank or bathed in the well water in the hopes of having their wishes granted.

Set Purposes for Reading

BIG Question   Read "Wishing Well" to see what someone does when she doesn't know what to do.

Set Your Own Purpose What else would you like to learn from the selection to help you answer the Big Question? Write your own purpose on the "Wishing Well" page of Foldable 4.

Interactive Literary Elements Handbook
To review or learn more about the literary elements, go to www.glencoe.com.

Keep Moving

Use these skills as you read the following selection.

Wishing Well

by Kate Schmitt

The **mesh** of the blanket tangles
and lumps of comforter*
two-toned flannel* and bedspread
twist and slip. **1**

5 I haven't slept in a week
so I wear my brown hooded
sweatshirt with the hoodstrings
pulled tightly around my face. **2** **3**

I picture a wishing well
10 with edges of greening minerals
and coins dull with old water.
I throw my wish in a copper **arc**.

After I've thrown it I lie
unconcerned. These things take time. **4**

Practice the Skills

1 | **Key Literary Element**

Free Verse Read this stanza aloud. How can you tell that this poem is written in free verse?

2 | **Key Reading Skill**

Connecting How would you feel if you didn't sleep for a week?

3 | **English Language Coach**

Compound Nouns Which words in this stanza are compound nouns?

4 | **BIG Question**

According to this poem, what can you do when you can't sleep? How effective do you think this technique is? Why? Write your answer on the "Wishing Well" page of Foldable 4. Your response will help you complete the Unit Challenge later.

---

2 A **comforter** is a bed covering that is often stuffed with feathers.

3 **Flannel** is a kind of warm fabric.

Vocabulary

mesh (mesh) *n.* the weblike pattern of fibers in woven or knitted items

arc (ark) *n.* a curved line between two points

After You Read : Wishing Well

Answering the BIG Question

1. What does "Wishing Well" say about the power of wishing?
2. **Recall** How long has it been since the speaker of the poem has slept?
   TIP Right There
3. **Summarize** In your own words, summarize the poem.
   TIP Think and Search

Critical Thinking

4. **Analyze** The speaker describes her blankets and bedsheets in detail in the first stanza. How does this description prepare you for the sleepless-ness she describes later?
   TIP Author and Me
5. **Infer** Why does the speaker pull the hoodstrings of her sweatshirt tightly around her face?
   TIP Author and Me
6. **Interpret** In line 12 the speaker says she throws her wish in a "copper arc." What do you think the copper arc is? Explain.
   TIP Author and Me
7. **Infer** Why is the speaker "unconcerned" after "throwing" her wish?
   TIP Author and Me

Talk About Your Reading

Literature Groups With a small group of classmates, discuss the **structure,** or organization, of the poem. Use the following questions to guide your discussion.
- What is the first stanza mainly about?
- What new idea is the second stanza about?
- Why did the poet begin a new stanza after line 8?
- What is the effect of tying the last two lines together in a stanza?

NY English Language Arts Core Curriculum (pp. 454–455)

LC R17 Demonstrate comprehension and response through a range of activities. **S2c** Ask and respond to questions to clarify an interpretation or response to literary texts and performances. **R2g** Compare causes of events to events in own lives. **R2f** Identify poetic elements, such as repetition, rhythm, and rhyming patterns, to interpret poetry. **Core W8** Use correct grammatical construction in subject-verb agreement.

For a complete description of the standards, see p. NY 11.

Skills Review

Key Reading Skill: Connecting

8. How did the activities on pages 450–451 help you connect to this selection? Rank the activities in order of helpfulness, with 1 being the most helpful and 3 the least helpful. Explain your rankings.

   - Connecting to what you already knew about having a problem that keeps you awake at night, hoping that something good would happen, and making a wish
   - Reading the facts in **Build Background**
   - Reading about Kate Schmitt in **Meet the Author**

Key Literary Element: Free Verse

9. You've read several poems in this book that have regular patterns of rhythm and rhyme. Some of those poems might be good as songs or raps. Would this poem work well as a song or rap? Explain your answer.

10. Do you think free verse is a good form for the topic of this poem? Explain your answer.

Vocabulary Check

On a separate piece of paper, write "T" if a sentence is true or "F" if it is false. Rewrite any false sentence to make it true.

11. Mesh is produced by weaving or knitting fibers or metals.

12. An arc is a straight line.

13. **English Language Coach** Divide each of the following compound nouns from "Wishing Well" into the two words it is made of.

    bedspread   sweatshirt   hoodstrings

Grammar Link: Subject-Verb Agreement

Subject-verb agreement is using the verb form that matches, or agrees with, the subject. There are two basic rules to remember when writing the present tense of a verb.

A. If the subject of a sentence is the pronoun *he, she,* or *it,* the verb must end in *-s.*

   - He cooks well.
   - She cooks even better.
   - It cooks quickly.

B. If the subject of a sentence is the pronoun *I, you, we,* or *they,* the verb does not end in *-s.*

   - I love cooking.
   - You cook well.
   - We cook together.
   - They cook at home.

Here are the rules in chart form.

Singular Pronoun Subjects	Plural Pronoun Subjects
I run.	*We* run.
You run.	*You* run.
He, she, it runs.	*They* run.

Grammar Practice

In the following sentences, the subject and verb might not agree. Copy the sentences on a separate sheet of paper. If a sentence is correct as is, write "C" after the sentence. If there is an error in the subject-verb agreement, revise the sentence by fixing the verb.

14. He practice the guitar everyday.

15. It sounds great!

16. She love his music.

Literature Online

Web Activities For eFlashcards, Selection Quick Checks, and other Web activities, go to www.glencoe.com.

Before You Read

Signed, Sealed, Undelivered

Did You Know?

In ancient Egypt, there was a tradition of writing letters to dead relatives. The Egyptians believed that the dead had the power to prevent bad luck. In letters to family members who had recently died, such as husbands, wives, or parents, Egyptians asked for help with problems such as ill health or arguments over property.

Vocabulary Preview

neglected (nuh GLEK tid) *adj.* given little attention or respect; form of the verb *neglect* **(p. 458)** *Writing letters is a neglected form of communication that more people should practice.*

humiliation (hyoo mih lee AY shun) *n.* something that makes a person feel ashamed or foolish **(p. 459)** *Ridiculing her in class is a form of humiliation.*

offensive (uh FEN siv) *adj.* unpleasant or disagreeable; causing anger **(p. 460)** *She wrote an offensive letter expressing her anger, but she knew better than to mail it.*

petty (PEH tee) *adj.* having or displaying a small, narrow-minded attitude **(p. 460)** *His petty comments were upsetting but not worth fighting over.*

Write to Learn For each word, write a sentence using the word correctly.

English Language Coach

Compound Adjectives A **compound adjective** is a describing word made up of two or more words.

• That <u>well-known</u> actor likes to eat at my dad's restaurant.

> (He is not a *well* actor or a *known actor*. He is a *well-known* actor. The hyphen shows that the words go together.)

• Hector's favorite food is <u>chocolate-chip</u> cookies.

> (They are not *chocolate* cookies or *chip* cookies. They are *chocolate-chip* cookies. The words go together to describe the noun.)

When a compound adjective comes *after* the noun it modifies, it doesn't have a hyphen.

• Hector's favorite cookies are chocolate chip.

There are some other compound adjectives that don't have hyphens. You can recognize them because the words work together to modify the noun. Taking out either one changes the meaning completely

• She is a member of the United States Senate.

On Your Own Copy the following sentences on a separate sheet of paper. Underline the compound adjective in each sentence.

• How many short-sleeved shirts do you own?

• His long-term goal is to run a marathon.

• Ana's little brother likes to watch Saturday morning cartoons.

• My sister is well liked at school.

NY English Language Arts Core Curriculum (pp. 456–461)

Core W8 Use correct grammatical construction in parts of speech (adjectives). **R2g** Compare causes of events to events in own lives. **R2d** Determine how the use and meaning of literary devices, such as illustration, convey the author's message or intent.

For a complete description of the standards, see p. NY 11.

Skills Preview

Key Reading Skill: Connecting

The title of the article, "Signed, Sealed, Undelivered," refers to letters that do not get sent, so nobody reads them. The writer of this article describes how free she feels when she writes whatever she wants to say without worrying about what people think.

As you read this selection, connect the descriptions and points the writer makes to your own experiences.

Text Element: Examples

An **example** is a specific instance that **illustrates,** or explains, a general statement. Suppose that a writer makes the following statement:

• My brother is messy.

To illustrate what he means, the writer might give examples like these:

• For instance, he throws his dirty socks on the floor, and he leaves banana peels on the kitchen table.

As you read "Signed, Sealed, Undelivered," ask yourself, *What general statements does the author make? What examples does she give to illustrate them?*

Small Group Work With a small group of classmates, take turns adding examples that illustrate the general statements below. Each group member should provide at least one example for each statement.

• Many kinds of music are played on the radio.

• Many sports are played using a ball.

Interactive Literary Elements Handbook
To review or learn more about the literary elements, go to www.glencoe.com.

Academic Vocabulary

illustrates (IL us trayts) *v.* shows clearly through examples

Get Ready to Read

Connect to the Reading

Think about times when you were upset with a friend but didn't feel you could tell him or her. What did you do? Why?

Write to Learn In your Learner's Notebook, write a few sentences about what upset you and what you did.

Build Background

There's a Stevie Wonder song called "Signed, Sealed, Delivered, I'm Yours." In the lyrics, the speaker asks his former girl friend to take him back and regrets "that time I went and said goodbye."

This guy might be in a better situation if he had read the article you're going to read next. It discusses writing letters—that you don't intend to send—to express your angry, upset feelings.

Recent studies have shown that writing about your deepest thoughts and feelings can improve your physical health. Holding in bad feelings causes stress. Expressing them can reduce it.

However, the article warns, keep those letters to yourself. Store them in a safe, private place or, better yet, destroy them. Sending such letters could bring new stress to both you and those you send them to.

Set Purposes for Reading

BIG Question Read "Signed, Sealed, Undelivered" to learn a good technique for dealing with difficult feelings, without bad consequences.

Set Your Own Purpose What else would you like to learn from the selection to help you answer the Big Question? Write your own purpose on the "Signed, Sealed, Undelivered" page of Foldable 4.

Keep Moving

Use these skills as you read the following selection.

TIME

Signed, Sealed, Undelivered

Writing a brutally honest letter feels good. But sending it probably isn't a good idea.

By KATHARINE WEBER

The summer I was 7, my 11-year-old brother was at the Mayo Clinic in Rochester, Minnesota, for heart surgery. I was sent to stay with my aunt and uncle in Evanston, Illinois. The day of his operation, I wrote a note to God on a tiny scrap of paper and then instantly shredded it into my cousin's guinea pig's cage. It was a five-word question—"Is he going to die?"—one that I didn't dare ask grown-ups.**1** The guinea pig died later that summer; my brother lived.

Unsent letters are a marvelous and far too **neglected** form of communication, one that I have been practicing for most of my life. Writing letters that will never be read is emotionally satisfying. I am free to express my deepest feelings without holding back. And by not mailing them, I have saved myself the real-life consequences that deeply felt letters can, for better or worse, cause.

In this age of e-mail and instant messaging, we all know stories about unfortunate messages sent too quickly, too

1 **English Language Coach**

Compound Adjectives Identify the compound adjective in this sentence.

Vocabulary ....

neglected (nuh GLEK tid) *adj.* given little attention or respect

angrily, too carelessly. The typed or handwritten letter (which can be revised for hours) is nearly a thing of the past. Letting an important letter slip and then vanish beyond reach into the belly of a mailbox has been replaced for most of us by watching the blip of the Send icon, clicked almost involuntarily. We think, *Oh, no, did I really say that? Did I really mean that? Did I accidentally hit Reply All?* **2**

When I was in the fifth grade, I wrote a series of despairing letters to my teacher, Mrs. Jacobson. I was convinced that her dislike for me caused her to seek out new forms of **humiliation** on a daily basis. ("Why do you hate me, Mrs. Jacobson? Is it because I finish my assignments before I'm supposed to? Is it because my hair is messy?")

I folded them into tight squares and mailed the first few down the storm drain on my way home from school. But after a classmate named Billy saw me pushing something through the grate and tried to fish it out, I began my collection of unsent letters in a shoe box in my closet. First lesson of unsent letters: Keep them safe.

My secret shoe box of unsent letters filled. There was a shy letter to a boy I liked. There was a pleading letter to a girl who had been unaccountably[1] mean on a field trip. There was a nasty letter to the grouch down the street who would pop out of his house to yell at the neighborhood children. **3**

"Writing letters that will never be read frees you to say anything at all."

Steve Mason/Photodisc/Getty Images

---

1. **Unaccountably** means "for no reason."

Vocabulary . . . .

humiliation (hyoo mih lee AY shun) *n.* something that makes a person feel ashamed or foolish

2 **Key Reading Skill**

Connecting Have you ever had this experience when sending an instant message or an e-mail? How did you feel?

3 **Text Element**

Examples The writer lists examples of the kinds of letters she wrote. How do these examples help you understand what kinds of feelings you can express in unsent letters?

When I left home for college, I took my shoe box with me. Second rule of unsent letters: They should be read only by the person who writes them. Then late in my college years, I decided to start my grown-up life and mailed the entire collection, one letter at a time, into an incinerator chute. And so they vanished from my life.

After having my first novel published in 1995, I once again wrote an unsent letter. A well-known critic[2] gave my novel an unfavorable review. And so I wrote Mr. Famous Literary Critic an angry three-page letter, flinging back at him some remarks he'd made. I was on my way to the mailbox when, fortunately, I thought about the possible consequences of mailing such an **offensive** letter. It had felt good to write it, but what would it feel like to receive it? So I kept it. For no particular reason, I stashed this ugly letter in a beautiful wooden box. **4**

4 | **Reviewing Skills**

Comparing and Contrasting
Compare and contrast this example of the writer's adult feelings towards a critic with her childhood feelings about Mrs. Jacobson. How are they the same? Different?

Malcolm Piers/Photographer's Choice/Getty Images

For Katharine Weber, an antique seal and wax add the final comforting touch to a letter she never intends to send.

2. A *critic* is a person whose job it is to write an opinion about the strengths and weaknesses of a book, movie, or other work of art.

3. To *rave* means to praise with great enthusiasm.

Vocabulary

offensive (uh FEN siv) *adj.* unpleasant or disagreeable; causing anger

petty (PEH tee) *adj.* having or displaying a small, narrow-minded attitude

By writing but not mailing a letter, Weber saves herself the real-life consequences that a deeply felt letter can cause.

In the years since, I have read the letter to the book critic a few times, and each time I have been aware that I was totally correct in every single word I wrote and that it was really a wise move to have kept the letter. Wiser than I could have imagined. Years later, when my third novel was published, the same critic gave it a rave[3] review—the kind of review novelists dream about.

Writing letters that will never be read frees you to say anything at all. You can write to those people whose **petty** meannesses stung you or whose significant cruelties really hurt you. It's open season[4] on expressing as much rage or sadness or wonder as your heart can desire and your sentences can contain. You can write yourself out of a mood or into a mood. You can even reveal your deepest feelings about a troubled relationship that haunts you. You just might find the peace you've been searching for. And you can do it all without having to spend the price of a stamp. **5**

—Updated 2005, from *Real Simple*, May 2004

5 **BIG Question**

What does the writer say about how to deal with difficult relationships? Write your answer on the "Signed, Sealed, Undelivered" page of Foldable 4. Your response will help you complete the Unit Challenge later.

4. The expression *open season* usually refers to a period of time when hunting is legally permitted. Here, the writer is saying that an unsent letter gives you total freedom to express your most honest, brutal feelings.

Signed, Sealed, Undelivered **461**

After You Read

Signed, Sealed, Undelivered

Steve Mason/Photodisc/Getty Images

Answering the **BIG** Question

1. According to the article "Signed, Sealed, Undelivered," what is one way to deal with fear, anger, or embarrassment?
2. **Recall** When did the writer compose her first undelivered letter?
   TIP Right There
3. **List** What are the writer's two rules about undelivered letters?
   TIP Think and Search

Critical Thinking

4. **Infer** What might have happened if the writer had mailed her letter to the critic? Explain.
   TIP Author and Me
5. **Evaluate** Do you think the writer's ideas about unsent letters are good ones? Explain.
   TIP On My Own

Write About Your Reading

Advice Column Imagine that you write an advice column for a school newspaper. Today you received the following letter from a student:

> Dear Advisor,
>   I am a member of one of the sports teams here at school, but you'd never know it. That's because the coach never lets me play. I know I am smaller than most of the other players, but I play hard. I'm really upset because the only thing holding me back is my coach. I am thinking of telling the coach exactly how I feel. Do you think I should?
>   Signed,
>   Bench Warmer

**NY English Language Arts
Core Curriculum** (pp. 462–463)

LC R17 Demonstrate comprehension and response through a range of activities.
LC W5 Write with voice to address varied purposes and audiences. **R2g** Compare causes of events to events in own lives.
R2d Determine how the use and meaning of literary devices, such as illustration, convey the author's message or intent. **Core W8** Use correct grammatical construction in subject-verb agreement.

For a complete description of the standards, see p. NY 11.

Use what you learned from reading "Signed, Sealed, Undelivered." Write a short letter giving advice to "Bench Warmer." In your letter include advice, examples, or other information from the article.

Skills Review

Key Reading Skill: Connecting

6. How can you link your experiences to Weber's?

Text Element: Examples

7. At the beginning of paragraph 2, Weber makes the following general statement: "Unsent letters are a marvelous and far too neglected form of communication . . . ." List five specific examples she gives to illustrate that general statement.

Reviewing Skills: Comparing and Contrasting

8. Compare and contrast the author's reason for writing a note to a boy she liked to her reason for writing a letter to a girl who had been mean to her. How were the reasons the same? Different?

Vocabulary Check

Write a sentence to answer each of the following questions.

9. How would you feel if someone made an **offensive** remark to you?

10. What form of **humiliation** might a bully subject someone to?

11. What would you do for a **neglected** puppy if you found one?

12. Would a **petty** comment make you feel happy or irritated?

13. **Academic Vocabulary** Give an **example** of each of the following:
  • music you like
  • sounds you hate
  • people you admire

14. **English Language Coach** Write a few sentences describing a friend or relative. Use at least one compound adjective in each sentence.

Grammar Link: Subject-Verb Agreement with Noun Subjects

In the last Grammar Link, you learned that a present tense verb must end in -s to agree with the pronoun subjects *he, she,* and *it.* Not all subjects are in pronoun form, however. How can you tell what verb form to use with a noun subject? "Translate" the noun into the pronoun that could take its place. Then check to make sure that the verb form is correct.

Read the following sentence. The verb in the sentence is *like.* The subject is the noun *Linda.* What pronoun could take the place of *Linda?*

• <u>Linda</u> <u>like</u> to dance.

The pronoun *she* could replace *Linda.* Now check the verb. Notice that it should end in -s because the subject *Linda* is equal to *she.* Here is the corrected sentence:

• <u>Linda</u> <u>likes</u> to dance.

Grammar Practice

The subject and verb are underlined in each sentence below. Translate each noun subject into a pronoun. Then check to make sure the verb agrees with the subject. If it doesn't, fix the verb.

15. <u>Linda and her sister</u> <u>take</u> dance lessons.

16. Her <u>sister</u> <u>enjoy</u> modern dance.

17. Linda's <u>brother</u> <u>prefer</u> sports to dance.

Writing Application Reread the letter you wrote for the Write About Your Reading activity. Make sure all subjects and verbs agree. Fix any mistakes.

Literature Online

Web Activities For eFlashcards, Selection Quick Checks, and other Web activities, go to www.glencoe.com.

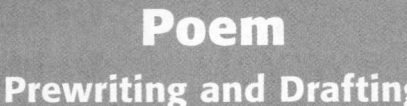

WRITING WORKSHOP PART 1

Poem
Prewriting and Drafting

ASSIGNMENT Write a poem

Purpose: To express your thoughts and feelings about what you do when you don't know what to do

Audience: Your teacher and possibly your class-mates or family

Writing Rubric

As you work through this writing assignment, you should

- use the writing process to write a poem
- choose lively, specific words
- make subjects and verbs agree
- use literary devices such as figurative language and sound patterns

See page 498 in Part 2 for a model of a poem.

NY English Language Arts Core Curriculum
(pp. 464–467)

Core W4 Use prewriting activities.
Core W5 Use the writing process.
Core W3 Use tone and language appropriate to audience and pur-pose. **Core W8** Use correct gram-matical construction in subject-verb agreement.

For a complete description of the standards, see p. NY 11.

The selections that you have read so far in this unit show what some people do when they don't know what to do. Everyone has times of uncertainty, but not everyone handles those situations in the same way.

In this Writing Workshop, you'll write a poem about what you do when you're not sure what your next action should be. Writing this poem will help you answer the Unit 4 Big Question: What do you do when you don't know what to do?

Prewriting
Get Ready to Write

Vivid memories and strong feelings can help you write a good poem. For this writing assignment, be sure to think of a situation that you remember clearly. Your poem can be serious, lighthearted, or anything in between.

Come Up with Ideas

In your Learner's Notebook, make a list of times when you were confused or troubled because you didn't know what to do. Don't worry yet about what experiences will or won't work. Just write.

- *I didn't turn in my science report on time.*
- *My friend wouldn't talk to me*

When your list has three or four good ideas, choose one that you remember clearly and that you want to write about.

Gather Details

You most likely have some general ideas about the situation you chose from your list. Now you need to come up with some specific details to use in your poem. The steps below will help you gather details.

1. Clear your mind and focus only on the situation you will write about. Bring to mind all the feelings and thoughts you had. You may even remember specific sights, sounds, smells, tastes, or feelings connected to the experience. Make notes about these details as they come to mind. You may want to try one of the approaches described on the next page.

- Quickly write what you remember for ten minutes. Don't edit your writing—just let your ideas flow.
- Make a web or cluster map of details. In the middle of a piece of paper, describe the situation and circle it. As you think of details, add them in circles connected to the center circle.

Writing Models For models and other writing activities, go to www.glencoe.com.

2. When you're finished generating ideas, underline details that you might want to include in your poem. Circle your favorite ideas—the ones you definitely want to use.

Make a Plan

Making a plan will help you start your draft and stay on track as you write. Answer the following questions in your Learner's Notebook.

- *What are the most important ideas I want to express?*
- *How do I want my poem to sound? Sad? Funny? Angry? Calm?*

> Last Friday was a really bad day. Everything went wrong, from losing my lunch pass to realizing I hadn't studied for a math test. I want to list what went wrong and the way I felt. The poem will have rhythm—maybe a hip-hop beat—and be funny (I hope!).

▶ **Writing Tip**

Purpose and Audience Your main purpose is to express your thoughts and feelings in a poem. Another purpose might be to share your thoughts and feelings with a friend or a family member. Think about who will read your poem. You may need to adjust your topic and word choice for your audience.

Drafting

Start Writing!

There's no right or wrong way to start drafting your poem. Just get something down on paper or computer screen. You can always revise later.

Get It on Paper

Reread your prewriting notes. Use them to start drafting your poem. You can use regular patterns of rhythm and rhyme, or you can write free verse (see page 451). The choice is yours. If words don't come when you sit down to write, set your poem aside. Then try again. Don't be too picky, and don't give up! Just write. Later, you can improve the wording of your poem.

On the next page you'll take a closer look at how to find the right words.

Applying Good Writing Traits

Word Choice

Good poems say a lot in only a few words. How do poets make their writing so powerful? They choose their words *very* carefully.

What Is Word Choice?

Word choice is the use of specific, vivid words that express the writer's ideas clearly.

Why Is Word Choice Important?

Words carry the writer's ideas into the reader's mind. That's why a writer must choose the right words—the ones that say what the writer intends to say. In a good poem, every word helps readers "see" and feel what the writer saw and felt.

The words in the sentence below do not help readers see or feel anything. The sentence tells what happened, but it doesn't "paint" a clear picture.

> *It was snowing.*

Compare that sentence with the sentence below.

> *Giant, wet snowflakes raced toward the ground in a fury.*

That's better! Specific, vivid words like *giant, wet, raced,* and *fury* create a clear picture of what happened—and how the writer felt about it.

How Do I Do It?

Think carefully about the words you choose.

- Replace general verbs with more specific ones. For example, replace *go* with *glide* or *rush.* Replace *look* with *glance* or *peek.*

- Use adjectives and adverbs. Instead of saying *The chair was ugly,* try saying *The <u>purple, green, and orange</u> chair was <u>spectacularly</u> ugly.*

- Use specific nouns. Replace general nouns like *thing* with words that specifically name the person, place, or thing, as in the second item in each pair below: *dog / <u>chihuahua</u>; car / <u>convertible</u>; house / <u>mansion</u>.*

- Use words that appeal to the five senses; for example, *The air <u>smelled fresh</u>, and the snow <u>tasted cold and grainy</u>.*

Write to Learn Copy the sentence below. Then rewrite it, replacing each word (except *the*) with a word or phrase that means about the same thing. Now rewrite the sentence again, making it even more specific and interesting but keeping the same basic meaning as the original sentence.

The storm hit us hard.

© Zits Partnership, Reprinted with Permission of King Features Syndicate, Inc.

Analyzing Cartoons

Mom can't find the right word to use after Grimm breaks the lamp. What would be a good word for her to use—clumsy, careless? Explain your word choice.

Grammar Link

Subject-Verb Agreement with Compound Subjects

What Is It?

Subject-verb agreement is using the verb form that matches, or agrees with, the subject.

Compound subjects are two or more persons, places, or things joined by *and, neither/nor, or,* or *either/or*.

Subjects joined by *and:* Kurt and I like burritos.

Subjects joined by *neither/nor:* Neither the restaurant nor the cafeteria serves enchiladas.

Subjects joined by *or:* Beef or pork goes well with beans.

Why Is It Important?

Many readers (and listeners) notice errors in subject-verb agreement. To be clear and correct, you need to know and follow standard rules of subject-verb agreement.

How Do I Do It?

Find the compound subject, see what word joins the subjects, and then apply the right rule.

1. **Subjects joined by *and:*** If the subjects joined by *and* refer to different people, places, or things, the subject is plural, or equal to *they*.
   - Grammar and spelling count.

     (*Grammar and spelling* are two different things. The compound subject is plural, or equal to *they*, so the verb should not end in –*s*.)

If the subjects joined by *and* refer to the same person, place, or thing, the compound subject is singular, or equal to *he, she,* or *it*.
   - The winner and new champion speaks three languages!

     (Both *winner* and *new champion* refer to the same person. The compound subject is singular, or equal to *he* or *she*, so the verb must end in –*s*.)

2. **Subjects joined by *neither/nor, or, either/ or:*** The verb agrees with the subject that is closer to it.
   - Neither Ellie nor her sisters speak Spanish.

     (*Sisters* is the subject that is closer to the verb. *Sisters* is equal to *they*, so the verb should not end in –*s*.)
   - Neither the sisters nor Ellie speaks Spanish.

     (Now *Ellie* is the subject that is closer to the verb. *Ellie* is equal to *she*, so the verb should end in –*s*.)

Grammar Practice

On a separate sheet of paper, write the compound subject and the correct verb form for each sentence.

1. Mariah and her brother (is, are) throwing an anniversary party for their parents.
2. Neither their mother nor their father (knows, know) about it.
3. Pizza and ice cream (is, are) on the menu.
4. Strawberries and cream (is, are) their favorite flavor of ice cream.
5. You or I (am, is, are) in charge of decorations.

Writing Application Look over the subjects and verbs in your poem. Make sure they all agree.

Looking Ahead

You'll use what you've written and learned in Part 2!

Skills Focus

You will practice these skills when you read the following selections:

- "Mother to Son," p. 472
- "Harlem," p. 473
- "Sittin' on the Dock of the Bay," p. 478

Reading

- Evaluating poems and song lyrics

Literature

- Understanding similes and metaphors
- Understanding song lyrics

Vocabulary

- Learning to recognize dialect and levels of diction
- Academic Vocabulary: *evaluate*

Writing/Grammar

- Understanding subject-verb agreement

NY English Language Arts Core Curriculum (pp. 468–469)

R3a Evaluate the validity and accuracy of information, ideas, themes, opinions, and experiences in texts.

For a complete description of the standards, see p. NY 11.

Skill Lesson

Evaluating

Learn It!

What Is It? To **evaluate** something is to look at it carefully in order to judge its value, or strengths and weaknesses. Before you buy a new CD, you might listen to some of the songs or discuss them with your friends. That way you can form an opinion about the quality of the CD beforehand. In much the same way, you can evaluate something you read.

For example, you might evaluate

- how believable the characters in a selection are
- whether the way characters speak rings true
- whether an author gives convincing reasons to share his or her opinions

Analyzing Cartoons
The kids in this cartoon evaluate, or make a judgment about, the book they just read. What influenced the opinion they formed?

© King Features Syndicate, Inc. Reprinted with permission.

Academic Vocabulary

evaluate (ih VAL yoo ayt) *v.* form an opinion or make a judgment

Why Is It Important? Making judgments and forming your opinions help you get more out of what you read. When you evaluate, you also pay attention to how well the selection was written.

How Do I Do It? Set standards for judgment, called *criteria.* For example, you might use these criteria to judge a poem.

- **Language:** Does the poet use descriptive words and phrases that appeal to your senses? Does the poet use figurative language, such as similes or metaphors? Are these figures of speech fresh and imaginative?
- **Sound Effects:** Does the poet use rhythm and rhyme well? What other sound effects are in the poem? Are they effective?
- **Theme and Content:** Did you enjoy the poem? Did it make you think about the subject in a different way? Why or why not?

Here's how a student evaluated part of an Emily Dickinson poem about the first steam-engine trains. Read it and the student's evaluation of it.

> *from* **I Like to See It**
> I like to see it lap the miles,
> And lick the valleys up,
> And stop to feed itself at tanks;
> And then, prodigious, step

> *I like how the poem makes the train seem alive. That makes me see trains in a whole new way. I also like the "music" in the poem. "Step" and "stop" sound good together because they begin and end with the same sounds; and "like," "lap," and "lick" go together because they all start with the sound of "l."*

Practice It!

Use the criteria to form your own judgment about the selection from the Emily Dickinson poem.

Use It!

As you read "Mother to Son," "Harlem," and "Sittin' on the Dock of the Bay," use the criteria to evaluate the selections.

Before You Read

Mother to Son *and* Harlem

Langston Hughes

Meet the Author

Langston Hughes was born in Joplin, Missouri, in 1902. As a young man, he traveled around the world and held many jobs. He drew on his experiences when he wrote. But it was his experience as an African American that allowed him to create powerful poems, short stories, and plays about African American life. See page R3 of the Author Files for more on Hughes.

Literature Online

Author Resources For more about Langston Hughes, go to www.glencoe.com.

NY English Language Arts Core Curriculum (pp. 470–473)

R2e Recognize how the author's use of language creates images or feelings. **R3a** Evaluate the validity and accuracy of information, ideas, themes, opinions, and experiences in texts. **R2d** Determine how the use and meaning of literary devices (metaphor and simile) convey the author's message or intent.

For a complete description of the standards, see p. NY 11.

Vocabulary Preview

deferred (dih FURD) *adj.* set aside or put off until a later time **(p. 473)** *Because the store didn't allow deferred payments, she had to pay for the new chair right away.*

fester (FES tur) *v.* to become infected; to decay **(p. 473)** *Carefully wash and wrap the cut so that it does not fester.*

Write to Learn In your Learner's Notebook, write a sentence for each vocabulary word.

English Language Coach

Dialect Have you ever listened closely to the way people speak in different parts of the country? Or even in different neighborhoods? Even when we all speak English, sometimes the *way* we speak it differs from place to place. These differences make up dialects.

A **dialect** is the special form of language spoken by a particular group of people. Dialects sound different from Standard English. To imitate a dialect, writers may drop letters in words (*nothin'* for *nothing*), respell words (*ole* for *old*), or combine words (*don'tcha* for *don't you*). A dialect may suggest where a character comes from, what social group he or she belongs to, and what kind of education he or she has had.

You'll see the following examples of dialect in "Mother to Son." Notice the differences between the dialect and Standard English.

Dialect	Standard English
I'se been a-climbin' on	I've been climbing
And reachin' landin's	And reaching landings

Small Group Talk With a small group of classmates, talk about ways in which people in your part of the country talk. What distinguishes your way of talking from the way people in other parts of the country talk? Try to write a sentence or two in a local dialect.

Skills Preview

Key Reading Skill: Evaluating

To evaluate poetry, you need criteria—standards by which to judge whether the poem is effective. A list of criteria for judging poetry is on page 469.

Whole-Class Discussion What criteria would you add, subtract, or rewrite? As a class, review the list on page 469. Tailor it to your interests and needs.

Key Literary Element: Figurative Language—Metaphor and Simile

Figurative language is descriptive language that is not to be taken literally. Suppose that a friend says, "That test was a piece of cake." You know that the test was not *actually* a piece of cake. Your friend is using a **metaphor** (MEH tuh for)—a direct comparison between very different things that are similar in some important way. Just as eating a piece of cake is easy, so is taking a test that is not difficult.

If the friend had said, "Taking that test was as easy as eating a piece of cake," she would be using a **simile** (SIM uh lee)—an indirect comparison that contains the word *like* or *as.*

As you read "Mother to Son" and "Harlem," look for metaphors and similes. Ask yourself, *What comparisons are being made? Which are direct? Which contain the words* like *or* as?

Partner Talk With a classmate, analyze the metaphor and simile below. For each, figure out what two things are compared and how they are similar.

Metaphor: Her smile was sunshine.

Simile: It was as cold as a snowman's toes.

Interactive Literary Elements Handbook
To review or learn more about the literary elements, go to www.glencoe.com.

Get Ready to Read

Connect to the Reading

Think about a dream you have for your future or a goal you've set for yourself. Now imagine that you meet with all sorts of problems that make it hard for you to achieve your dream or goal. Will you keep trying? If not, how do you think giving up would affect you? As you read "Mother to Son" and "Harlem," think about what each speaker says about dreams and goals.

Partner Talk With a partner, list qualities you think people must have to reach their goals.

Build Background

- Many of Langston Hughes's poems are about the African American experience in the first half of the 20th century. Though slavery had long been banned, African Americans still did not have the same rights as other U.S. citizens. Hughes addressed this inequality in his poetry. Sometimes he celebrates the strength and beauty of African American life. Other times he expresses frustration over the obstacles African Americans had to overcome.

- Hughes is often associated with Harlem, an African American community in New York City. During the 1920s, Harlem was at the center of African American life in the United States. Hughes gave the title "Harlem" to a poem you'll read. It's also published with the title "Dream Deferred."

Set Purposes for Reading

BIG Question Read the selections "Mother to Son" and "Harlem" to find out the importance of holding fast to your dreams despite obstacles in your path.

Set Your Own Purpose What else would you like to learn from these selections to help you answer the Big Question? Write your own purpose on the "Mother to Son" and "Harlem" page of Foldable 4.

Keep Moving

Use these skills as you read the following selections.

Mother to Son

by Langston Hughes

Survivor, 1978. Elizabeth Catlett. Linocut, 10⅞ x 9⅞ in. Armistad Research Center, Tulane University, New Orleans.

Well, son, I'll tell you:
Life for me ain't been no crystal stair. **1**
It's had tacks in it,
And splinters,
5 And boards torn up,
And places with no carpet on the floor—
Bare.
But all the time
I'se been a-climbin' on,
10 And reachin' landin's,
And turnin' corners,
And sometimes goin' in the dark
Where there ain't been no light. **2**
So, boy, don't you turn back.
15 Don't you set down on the steps
'Cause you finds it kinder hard.
Don't you fall now—
For I'se still goin', honey,
I'se still climbin',
20 And life for me ain't been no crystal stair. **3** ○

Practice the Skills

1 **Key Literary Element**

Figurative Language— Metaphor and Simile What is life being compared to? If life were a crystal stair, what would life be like?

2 **English Language Coach**

Dialect Do you have any trouble understanding the dialect? If so, read it aloud.

3 **Key Reading Skill**

Evaluating Is the mother's advice to her son believable? Do you think it's something a mother might actually say to her son? Why or why not?

HARLEM

by Langston Hughes

What happens to a dream **deferred**?

Does it dry up
like a raisin in the sun? **1**
Or **fester** like a sore—
5 And then run?
Does it stink like rotten meat?
Or crust and sugar over—
like a syrupy sweet?

Maybe it just sags
10 like a heavy load. **2**

Or does it explode? **3** ○

Analyzing the Painting This painting of Langston Hughes shows what he looked like as a young man. How would you describe the mood of the painting? Why?

Portrait of Langston Hughes, 1902–1967, Poet. Winold Reiss (1886–1953). Pastel on artist board, 76.3 x 54.9 cm. National Portrait Gallery, Washington, DC.

Practice the Skills

1 Key Literary Element

Figurative Language– Metaphor and Simile Reread the first three lines of the poem. What two things are being compared? In what way are they similar?

2 Key Reading Skill

Evaluating In your opinion, does the poem effectively express what it's like to have to set aside your dreams? Explain.

3 BIG Question

Imagine that you don't know what to do with your life. You ask the speakers of "Mother to Son" and "Harlem" for advice. What do you think they would tell you? Write your answer on the "Mother and Son" and "Harlem" page of Foldable 4. Your response will help you answer the Unit Challenge later.

Vocabulary

deferred (dih FURD) *adj.* set aside or put off until a later time

fester (FES tur) *v.* to become infected; to decay

Mother to Son *and* Harlem **473**

After You Read

Mother to Son *and* Harlem

Answering the  BIG Question

1. After reading "Mother to Son" and "Harlem," do you think you should follow a dream that seems impossible? Explain.

2. **Recall** What advice does the mother give in "Mother to Son"?
   TIP Right There

3. **Restate** In your own words, restate the first three lines of "Harlem."
   TIP On My Own

Critical Thinking

4. **Infer** What is the mother in "Mother to Son" like? Describe her, using evidence from the poem to back up your ideas.
   TIP Author and Me

5. **Compare and Contrast** How are the speakers in each poem alike? How are they different?
   TIP Author and Me

6. **Apply** Think about the mother's advice to her son. If he follows the advice, how will he act when the going gets tough?
   TIP Author and Me

7. **Analyze** Why do you think Hughes put the last line of "Harlem" in italics? How would the poem change if the italics were left out?
   TIP On My Own

8. **Synthesize** What do you think the mother in "Mother to Son" might say to the speaker in "Harlem"? Explain.
   TIP On My Own

Talk About Your Reading

Literature Groups With a small group of students, discuss the tone of "Harlem." If you could hear Langston Hughes read the poem, how do you think his voice would sound? Happy? Sad? Excited? Scared? Sarcastic? Angry? Something else? Take turns reading the poem with different tones of voice. Then decide as a group which tone best fits the poem. Support your opinion with evidence from the poem.

NY English Language Arts Core Curriculum (pp. 474–475)

LC R17 Demonstrate comprehension and response through a range of activities. **S2c** Ask and respond to questions to clarify an interpretation or response to literary texts and performances. **R3a** Evaluate the validity and accuracy of information, ideas, themes, opinions, and experiences in texts. **R2d** Determine how the use and meaning of literary devices (metaphor and simile) convey the author's message or intent. **Core W8** Use correct grammatical construction in subject-verb agreement.

For a complete description of the standards, see p. NY 11.

Skills Review

Key Reading Skill: Evaluating

9. Did you enjoy reading "Mother to Son" and "Harlem"? Why or Why not?

10. Did the poems make you look at life in a new way? Explain.

Key Literary Element: Figurative Language—Metaphor and Simile

11. In "Mother to Son," stairs are a metaphor for life. In what way are stairs and life alike?

12. There are five similes in "Harlem." List three of the five things that a "dream deferred" is compared to, and explain what each simile means.

Vocabulary Check

On a separate piece of paper, write "T" if a sentence is true or "F" if it is false. Rewrite any false sentence to make it true.

13. When you defer an action, you do it immediately.

14. When sores fester, they are healed.

15. **Academic Vocabulary** What does it mean to evaluate something you are reading?

16. **English Language Coach** Rewrite lines 15–20 of "Mother to Son" in Standard English. Look at the two versions—your Standard English version and Hughes's version in dialect. Which do you think is better and why?

Web Activities For eFlashcards, Selection Quick Checks, and other Web activities, go to www.glencoe.com.

Grammar Link: Agreement When Subjects Are Separated from Verbs

Subject-verb agreement can be tricky when the subject and verb of a sentence are separated from each other. In cases like this, you may wonder what the real subject of the sentence is. For example, in the sentence below is the subject *one* or *books?*

• One of the books (is, are) missing.

Here's a hint: *Subjects and predicates do not appear in prepositional phrases.* If you mentally leave out the prepositional phrase from the sentence, the real subject becomes easier to find.

One ~~of the books~~ (is, are) missing.
prepositional phrase

Once the prepositional phrase is omitted, it's easy to see that the subject is *one.* Because the subject is *one,* the right verb form is *is.*

Grammar Practice

On a separate piece of paper, copy the sentences below. Cross out the prepositional phrase that separates the subject and verb in each sentence. Underline the subject once and the correct verb form twice.

17. The presents for my grandmother (is, are) on the table in the back of the dining room.

18. One of the gifts (is, are) handmade.

19. The gifts from my sister (has, have) red bows.

20. The cookies on the tray (is, are) for Grandma.

21. The card with all the signatures (is, are) from the whole family.

22. The cupcakes with chocolate icing (tastes, taste) the best.

23. My grandmother's friends in Arizona always (calls, call) her on her birthday.

Before You Read

Sittin' on the Dock of the Bay

Otis Redding

Meet the Author

Otis Redding was a talented soul singer. He was born in Dawson, Georgia, in 1941. Redding wrote many of his own songs, but sometimes he collaborated with Steve Cropper of the band Booker T and the MGs. His most famous song, "Sittin' on the Dock of the Bay," which he wrote with Cropper, was recorded three days before he died in a plane crash. He was only 26.

Author Search for more about Otis Redding, go to www.glencoe.com.

NY English Language Arts Core Curriculum (pp. 476–479)

R2e Recognize how the author's use of language creates images or feelings. **R3a** Evaluate the validity and accuracy of information, ideas, themes, opinions, and experiences in texts. **R2f** Identify poetic elements, such as repetition, rhythm, and rhyming patterns, to interpret poetry.

For a complete description of the standards, see p. NY 11.

Vocabulary Preview

dock (dok) *n.* a platform where boats land at the edge of a body of water **(p. 479)** *He sat on the dock waiting for the boat to return from the sea.*

roamed (rohmd) *v.* wandered; went from place to place without purpose or direction; form of the verb *roam* **(p. 479)** *He roamed the United States just looking and dreaming.*

Write to Learn In your Learner's Notebook, write a sentence for each vocabulary word. Be sure to use the words correctly.

English Language Coach

Dialect and Word Choice A **dialect** is a form of language spoken by the people in a particular group. Dialect influences not only how a person pronounces words but also what words he or she uses. For example, in the northeastern part of the United States some people say that they sit on their front *stoop* in the summer. In the Midwest, however, most people would say that they sit on their front *porch.* Of course, not everyone in the same region of the United States speaks exactly the same dialect.

Many other factors go into a person's dialect and word choice. How old a person is, what kind of education the person has had, which social groups the person belongs to—all these factors and many others shape how a person talks and what words he or she uses. Authors are aware of differences in dialects and use those differences to help show what characters are like.

Partner Talk Do teens express themselves the same way as their parents? Do they use different words? With a classmate discuss some of these differences. Then write a short conversation between a teenager and a parent in which each person's choice of words reflects who he or she is. Here are some ideas for conversations:

• a talk in which a parent and a teenager describe the kind of music each of them likes best

• a chat between a parent and a teenager about the latest video games

• a discussion in which a parent and a teenager talk about their favorite movies

Skills Preview

Key Reading Skill: Evaluating

Although you may not have thought of it, song lyrics are closely tied to poetry. How would you go about evaluating lyrics to a song?

On Your Own What do you think a good song should communicate to listeners? Write your ideas in your Learner's Notebook.

Literary Element: Lyrics

Lyrics are words set to music. In fact, the word *lyrics* is tied to music. The term comes from the ancient Greek word *lyra,* which refers to a musical instrument that is similar to a harp. Lyrics also have much in common with poetry. Like poetry, lyrics may have these elements:

• repeated lines
• rhyming words
• a set rhythm, or "beat"
• figurative language such as similes and metaphors

As you read the lyrics to "Sittin' on the Dock of the Bay," pay attention to the rhythm of the lines, and look to see which phrases and lines are repeated. Ask yourself, *What is the "beat"? Which lines are repeated and to what effect?*

Small Group Discussion With a small group of classmates, think of the lyrics to a song that everyone knows and that is appropriate to discuss in class. What "poetic" elements do the lyrics contain: Rhythm? Figurative language? Rhyme? Repetition? Make a list of elements, give an example from the lyrics of each element, and then discuss what the elements add to the lyrics.

Get Ready to Read

Connect to the Reading

"I don't know what to do." Think about a time in your life when you felt that way. Did you get different advice from your family and friends? How did you decide which advice to follow? As you read "Sittin' on the Dock of the Bay," think about how it feels not to have a clear direction in life.

Write to Learn In your Learner's Notebook, jot down some notes about a time you couldn't figure out what to do. Explain what you finally decided to do and why.

Build Background

The song lyrics you are about to read tell about a man who travels from his home in Georgia to California. Traditionally, California is a place where people go to start over or make their fortunes.

• Otis Redding wrote the lyrics on a houseboat in Sausalito, California, a beautiful city located in the San Francisco Bay Area near the north end of the Golden Gate Bridge.

• Sausalito has one of the few ungated marinas in the Bay area, so people can feel free to relax there and enjoy the view.

Set Purposes for Reading

BIG Question Read the selection "Sittin' on the Dock of the Bay" to find out how it feels for someone who doesn't know what to do.

Set Your Own Purpose What else would you like to learn from this selection for help in answering the Big Question? Write your own purpose on the "Sittin' on the Dock of the Bay" page of Foldable 4.

Literature Online

Interactive Literary Elements Handbook
To review or learn more about the literary elements, go to www.glencoe.com.

Keep Moving

Use these skills as you read the following selection.

Sittin' on the Dock of the Bay

by Steve Cropper and Otis Redding

Sittin' in the morning sun,
I'll be sittin' when the evening comes,
Watching the ships roll in.
Then I watch 'em roll away again, yeah.
5 I'm sittin' on the **dock** of the bay,
Watching that tide* roll in,
Just sittin' on the dock of the bay wastin'
  time. **1**

I left my home in Georgia; **2**
Headed for the Frisco* Bay.
10 I had nothing to live for.
Looks like nothing's gonna come my way,
So I'm just sittin' on the dock of the bay,
Watching the tide roll in.
I'm sittin' on the dock of the bay
    wastin' time. **3**

15 Looks like nothing's gonna change;
Everything still remains the same.
I can't do what ten people tell me to do,
So I guess I'll remain the same.
Just sittin' here resting my bones.
20 And this loneliness won't leave me alone;
This 2,000 miles I **roamed**, just to make this dock my home
Now I'm sittin' on the dock of the bay,
Watching the tide roll in. **4**
Sittin' on the dock of the bay wastin' time. **5** ○

---

6 The *tide* is the rise and fall of the ocean that occurs about every twelve hours.

9 *Frisco* is short for San Francisco.

Vocabulary

dock (dok) *n.* a platform where boats land at the edge of a body of water

roamed (rohmd) *v.* wandered; went from place to place without purpose or direction

Practice the Skills

1 **English Language Coach**

Dialect and Word Choice
This song is not written in dialect, but it spells out many elements of pronunciation that are found in American dialects. Make notes of some of them in your Learner's Notebook.

2 **Reviewing Skills**

Connecting Have you ever left a place you were familiar with to try something new? How did it feel? Explain.

3 **Literary Element**

Lyrics Which lines in the lyrics are repeated? What does the repetition add to the lyrics?

4 **Key Reading Skill**

Evaluating How successful is the song at getting a message across and creating a mood?

5 **BIG Question**

Think about how the speaker of these lyrics feels about his life. What do you think he would say about the importance of choosing a direction even if you don't exactly know what to do with your life? Write your answer on the "Sittin' on the Dock of the Bay" page of Foldable 4. Your response will help you complete the Unit Challenge later.

After You Read

Sittin' on the Dock of the Bay

Answering the 🗨BIG Question

1. How do the lyrics to "Sittin' on the Dock of the Bay" help you think about the Big Question: What do you do when you don't know what to do?

2. **Recall** What does the speaker watch from the dock?

   Tip Right There

3. **Summarize** How has the speaker felt since he left home?

   Tip Right There

Critical Thinking

4. **Infer** Why do you think the speaker decided to travel so far from home? Explain.

   Tip Author and Me

5. **Compare** In what way is the speaker's life like the rolling tide that comes in and goes out again? Explain.

   Tip On My Own

6. **Infer** Do you think the speaker is satisfied with his decision to leave home? Why or why not?

   Tip On My Own

Write About Your Reading

Character Sketch Write a character sketch of the speaker of "Sittin' on the Dock of the Bay." Follow these steps.

Step 1: Your sketch should convey a main impression of the character. What one character trait stands out the most to you?

Step 2: Find specific details in the song lyrics to support the trait you wish to emphasize. How do the speaker's words, actions, thoughts, or feelings support the trait you have chosen to convey?

Step 3: Decide on the most effective order for presenting your details. Do you want to present your most important details first? Or do you want to start with the less important details and work your way up to the more important ones?

Step 4: Write your character sketch.

Step 5: Proofread your sketch for errors in grammar, usage, and mechanics. Fix any mistakes.

NY English Language Arts Core Curriculum (pp. 480–481)

LC R17 Demonstrate comprehension and response through a range of activities. **LC W5** Write with voice to address varied purposes, topics, and audiences. **R3a** Evaluate the validity and accuracy of information, ideas, themes, opinions, and experiences in texts. **R2f** Identify poetic elements, such as repetition, rhythm, and rhyming patterns, to interpret poetry. **Core W8** Use correct grammatical construction in subject-verb agreement.

For a complete description of the standards, see p. NY 11.

Skills Review

Key Reading Skill: Evaluating

7. Think about how you would evaluate the lyrics. Would you recommend that other eighth-graders read them? Why or why not?

Literary Element: Lyrics

8. Reread the second verse of the lyrics (lines 8–14). Which words rhyme?

9. What is the effect of the rhymes?

Reviewing Skills: Connecting

10. Think of situations in which you wasted time because you weren't sure what to do next. How do your experiences compare to those of the speaker in the poem?

Vocabulary Check

Answer "true" if a statement is true or "false" if it is false. Rewrite any false statement to make it true.

11. If a boat is near a dock, it is near a shore.

12. If someone roamed away from home, he or she went directly to a preplanned destination.

13. **Academic Vocabulary** How did evaluating help you understand the song lyrics?

14. **English Language Coach** Do you think the speaker's pronunciation and word choice are appropriate to the kind of person he is? Explain.

Grammar Link: Agreement in Inverted Sentences

Usually the subject comes before the verb in a sentence. However, in some sentences all or part of the verb comes before the subject. These sentences are in inverted, or reverse, order. Two common types of inverted sentences are:

A. Questions In many questions all or part of the verb comes before the subject.

- <u>Do</u> <u>you and your family</u> <u>have</u> a car?

  helping verb / subject / main verb

To make it less tricky to find the subject and verb, turn the question into a statement.

- <u>You and your family</u> <u>do have</u> a car.

B. Sentences that Begin with *Here/There* The words *here* and *there* cannot be subjects. To find the subject of a sentence that begins with *here* or *there,* omit the word. Find the verb; then ask yourself, who or what ____?

Example: There is a new girl in our class.

Omit *there;* then find the verb.

~~There~~ <u>is</u> a new girl in our class.

Ask, who or what <u>is</u>? *Girl* is.

There <u>is</u> a new <u>girl</u> in our class.

    verb   subject

Grammar Practice

Copy each sentence on a separate sheet of paper. Underline the subject of each sentence once and the verb twice. If the subject and verb do not agree, fix the verb.

15. Is my brother and you going to the party?

16. Here is his jacket and his books.

17. Are you and Janice invited?

18. There is a few items missing from my locker!

Writing Application Review your character sketch. Look for questions and for sentences that begin with *here* or *there.* Make sure that the subjects and verbs in all these sentences agree.

READING WORKSHOP 3

Skills Focus

You will practice these skills when you read the following selections:

- *from* "To the Democratic National Convention," p. 486
- "Fable for When There's No Way Out," p. 492

Reading

- Interpreting speeches and poems

Literature

- Identifying the sound devices alliteration and repetition and their effects

Vocabulary

- Understanding how word choice is affected by the author's purpose and audience
- Academic Vocabulary: *interpret*

Writing/Grammar

- Making verbs agree with indefinite pronoun subjects
- Making verbs agree with collective nouns

NY English Language Arts Core Curriculum
(pp. 482–483)

R2b Interpret characters, plot, setting, theme, and dialogue, using evidence from the text.

For a complete description of the standards, see p. NY 11.

Skill Lesson

Interpreting

Learn It!

What Is It? When you **interpret** as you read, you use your own understanding of the world to decide what the events or ideas in a selection mean. For example, when you read the poem "The Road Not Taken" (page 447), you were asked to think about how you have made decisions when you didn't know what to do. You used what you know about making choices to understand how the speaker in the poem reached a decision. Now learn to interpret every time you read.

Analyzing Cartoons

The kids in this cartoon respond to the mother in their own creative way. How do they interpret—or misinterpret—the mother's order?

FOXTROT © 2004 Bill Amend. Reprinted with permission of UNIVERSAL PRESS SYNDICATE. All rights reserved.

Academic Vocabulary

interpret (in TUR prit) *v.* to find the meaning of events or ideas

Why Is It Important? When you interpret text, you increase your understanding by using what you have learned through experience. You make sense of the text by bringing your own knowledge and experience to it.

How Do I Do It? As you read, think about what you already know about yourself and the world. To interpret the meaning of text, ask yourself, *What point is the author trying to make? Which details and examples make this point?* While you read, take notes to record your ideas. Here are notes a student took after reading part of the poem in this unit's Genre Focus.

Literature Online

Study Central Visit www.glencoe.com and click on Study Central to review interpreting.

> *from* **The Road Not Taken**
> I shall be telling this with a sigh
> Somewhere ages and ages hence:
> Two roads diverged in a wood, and I—
> I took the one less traveled by,
> And that has made all the difference.

> When the speaker says that he took the less-traveled road, I think he's saying that he didn't follow the crowd and do what everyone else does. He doesn't seem sorry about the decision, so I interpret that to mean he thinks it's good to take the road less traveled by. After all, he ends the poem by saying, "That has made all the difference." To me, that means his decision changed his life.

Practice It!

Below are some lines and sentences from the selections you will read in this Workshop. How would you interpret each one? Jot down some thoughts in your Learner's Notebook.

- "Keep hope alive."
- "Character breeds faith."
- "Rage works if reason won't."

Use It!

As you read from "To the Democratic National Convention" and "Fable for When There's No Way Out," remember the notes you made to practice interpreting. When you find a detail that helps you discover meaning, add it to your notes.

Before You Read

from To the Democratic National Convention

Jesse Jackson

Meet the Author

Jesse Jackson was born in 1941, a time when the United States did not recognize equality among the races. During the 1960s, Jackson became involved in the Civil Rights movement. In 1968 he was ordained as a Baptist minister. Jackson has also played an important role in American politics, founding the Rainbow Coalition and traveling around the world on peace-making missions.

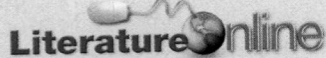

Author Search For more about Jesse Jackson, go to www.glencoe.com.

NY English Language Arts Core Curriculum (pp. 484–487)

R2e Recognize how the author's use of language creates images or feelings. **R2b** Interpret characters, plot, setting, theme, and dialogue, using evidence from the text. **R2d** Determine how the use and meaning of literary devices convey the author's message and intent.

For a complete description of the standards, see p. NY 11.

Vocabulary Preview

abandonment (uh BAN dun mint) *n.* the state of being deserted or left alone without help **(p. 486)** *Antoine's sense of abandonment when his father left was overwhelming.*

nomination (nah min NAY shun) *n.* the state of being a candidate for an office or honor **(p. 487)** *She placed Rodriguez in nomination for governor of her state.*

surrender (suh REN dur) *v.* to give up **(p. 487)** *When the fight gets tough, you may want to surrender.*

Write to Learn Write a one-paragraph story that uses all three vocabulary words. With the whole class, take turns reading your stories aloud. Discuss how these vocabulary words affected each story and added to its meaning.

English Language Coach

Word Choice and Audience Good writers and speakers tailor their word choice to their audiences. Jackson is a well-educated man with a very large vocabulary. But in the speech you're about to read, he uses simple, informal language because he wants to reach out to people who may not have had the opportunity to get a good education. He uses simple language for many reasons:

• so his audience will understand his message
• so his audience will see that he is one of them
• so his audience will share his feelings

The words on the left come from Jackson's speech. The words on the right are words he might have used to appeal to a different audience.

Informal Diction	Formal Diction
mama	mother
the projects	low-income housing
make it	be successful

Partner Talk With a partner, read the sentences below. Rewrite them to appeal to a more formal audience (of parents or teachers).

1. That movie was so cool.
2. I was like, "Why'd you do that?"
3. Ryan's excuse was way lame.

Skills Preview

Key Reading Skill: Interpreting

In "To the Democratic National Convention," Jesse Jackson says, "Wherever you are tonight you can make it. Hold your head high, stick your chest out. You can make it. It gets dark sometimes, but the morning comes."

What do you think the last sentence means?

Partner Talk Discuss the statement with a classmate. Together, interpret what it means. Put your interpretation in your own words.

Literary Element: Repetition

Repetition is the repeating of sounds, words, phrases, or whole sentences for emphasis. Repetition can also give a sense of unity and continuity to writing. Repetition is especially effective in spoken forms like speeches. Jackson uses repetition several times in the speech that you are about to read.

As you read, use these tips to learn about repetition.

- Look for words and phrases the writer uses again and again. Try reading aloud to find them.
  Which words and phrases does the writer repeat?

- Consider why Jackson chose these particular words and phrases to repeat.
  What is the effect of the repeated words or phrases?

Write to Learn Read the second paragraph of Jackson's speech (on page 486). What words are repeated? Why do you think Jackson repeats them? Jot down your thoughts in your Learner's Notebook.

Interactive Literary Elements Handbook
To review or learn more about the literary elements, go to www.glencoe.com.

Get Ready to Read

Connect to the Reading

Think about a time when you felt that you would never reach an important goal or see a dream come true. Why did this goal mean so much to you? Did you find a way to reach it? As you read Jackson's speech, notice how he explains how he helped himself when his path was not clear. What might you have done in his place?

Small Group Discussion With a small group of classmates, talk about the kinds of problems that are hard to solve. Brainstorm some ways that people can make decisions and act when they are not sure what to do. What powers within you might help at such a time? Where else could you turn for help?

Build Background

The speech you are about to read was made by Jesse Jackson at the Democratic National Convention in August 1988.

- A *convention* is a formal meeting of members of a group, such as a political group.

- The *Democratic National Convention* is the official meeting of the Democratic Party every four years for the purpose of nominating, or choosing, someone in the party to run for president of the United States.

Set Purposes for Reading

BIG Question Read this excerpt from "To the Democratic National Convention" to learn how Jesse Jackson's upbringing prepared him to help others find solutions to their problems.

Set Your Own Purpose What else would you like to learn from the speech to help you answer the Big Question? Write your own purpose on the "To the Democratic National Convention" page of Foldable 4.

Keep Moving

Use these skills as you read the following selection.

from To the Democratic National Convention

by Jesse Jackson

I have a story. I wasn't always on television. Writers were not always outside my door. When I was born late one afternoon, October 8th, in Greenville, South Carolina, no writers asked my mother her name. Nobody chose to write down our address. My mama was not supposed to make it. And I was not supposed to make it. You see, I was born to a teen-age mother who was born to a teen-age mother. **1**

I understand. I know **abandonment** and people being mean to you, and saying you're nothing and nobody, and can never be anything. I understand. Jesse Jackson is my third name. I'm adopted. When I had no name, my grandmother gave me her name. My name was Jesse Burns until I was twelve. So I wouldn't have a blank space, she gave me a name to hold me over. I understand when nobody knows your name. I understand when you have no name. I understand.

I wasn't born in the hospital. Mama didn't have insurance. I was born in the bed at home. I really do understand. Born in a three-room-house, bathroom in the backyard,[1] slop jar by the bed, no hot and cold running water. I understand. Wallpaper used for decoration? No. For a windbreaker. I understand. I'm a working person's person, that's why I understand you whether you're black or white. **2**

I understand work. I was not born with a silver spoon in my mouth. **3** I had a shovel programmed for my hand. My mother, a working woman. So many days she went to work early with runs in her stockings. She knew better, but she

---

1. ***Bathroom in the backyard*** means an outhouse without water or electricity.

Practice the Skills

1 **English Language Coach**

Word Choice and Audience Think about Jackson's choice of words in this paragraph. How does he tailor his word choice to fit the needs of the audience he most wants to reach?

2 **Literary Element**

Repetition What words does Jackson repeat in this paragraph? What is the effect of that repetition?

3 **Key Reading Skill**

Interpreting How do you interpret what Jackson has said so far? Write a sentence in your Learner's Notebook that sums up what you think he says in the first three paragraphs.

Vocabulary

abandonment (uh BAN dun mint) *n.* the state of being deserted or left alone without help

wore runs in her stockings so that my brother and I could have matching socks and not be laughed at at school.

Visual Vocabulary
Cranberries are bright red berries that have a sour taste.

I understand. At 3 o'clock on Thanksgiving Day we couldn't eat turkey because mama was preparing someone else's turkey at 3 o'clock. We had to play football to entertain ourselves and then around 6 o'clock she would get off the Alta Vista bus; then we would bring up the leftovers and eat our turkey—leftovers, the carcass, the cranberries around 8 o'clock at night. I really do understand.

Every one of these funny labels they put on you, those of you who are watching this broadcast tonight in the projects, on the corners, I understand. Call you outcast, low down, you can't make it, you're nothing, you're from nobody, subclass, underclass—when you see Jesse Jackson, when my name goes in **nomination,** your name goes in nomination. **4**

I was born in the slum, but the slum was not born in me. **5** And it wasn't born in you, and you can make it. Wherever you are tonight you can make it. Hold your head high, stick your chest out. You can make it. It gets dark sometimes, but the morning comes. Don't you **surrender.** Suffering breeds character. Character breeds faith. In the end faith will not disappoint.

You must not surrender. You may or may not get there, but just know that you're qualified and you hold on and hold out. We must never surrender. America will get better and better. Keep hope alive. Keep hope alive. Keep hope alive. On tomorrow night and beyond, keep hope alive. **6**

I love you very much. I love you very much. ○

Vocabulary

nomination (nah mih NAY shun) *n.* the state of being a candidate for an office or honor

surrender (suh REN dur) *v.* to give up

Practice the Skills

4 English Language Coach

Word Choice and Audience
How would you describe Jackson's word choice in this sentence? Which members of his audience do you think he's trying to reach?

5 Key Reading Skill

Interpreting What does Jackson mean when he says, "the slum was not born in me"?

Analyzing the Photo The Rev. Jesse Jackson hugs his mother, Helen Burns, at a 1988 Atlanta speech. What does Jackson say to connect with his audience?

6 BIG Question

What is Jackson saying to people who feel confused and hopeless? Write your answer on the "To the Democratic National Convention" page of Foldable 4. Your response will help you complete the Unit Challenge later.

After You Read

from To the Democratic National Convention

Answering the BIG Question

1. What advice does Jesse Jackson's speech give about what to do when you don't know what to do?
2. **Recall** What reason does Jackson give for being born at home instead of in a hospital?

   Tip Right There
3. **List** What are some of the obstacles Jackson had to overcome to be successful? List at least three.

   Tip Think and Search

Critical Thinking

4. **Infer** What do you think Jackson's mother did for a living when he was a child? Give details from the speech to support your answer.

   Tip Think and Search
5. **Infer** Near the end of his speech, Jackson says, "We must never surrender. America will get better and better." In what way or ways do you think Jackson hopes America will improve? Explain your reasoning.

   Tip Author and Me
6. **Evaluate** How powerful do you think Jackson's speech is? Do you think it affected listeners? Explain your answer.

   Tip On My Own

Talk About Your Reading

Oral Response Imagine yourself as a member of the audience at the convention where Jesse Jackson delivered his speech. Prepare a response to it. You can write it out word for word or just take notes, whichever you prefer. Tell Jackson how you felt about what he said. Could you identify or connect with his story? Mention any points in the speech that you agree or disagree with, and tell how his speech affected you. Rehearse your response and deliver your speech to the class.

NY English Language Arts Core Curriculum (pp. 488–489)

LC R17 Demonstrate comprehension and response through a range of activities. **S3a** Express opinions or judgments about information, ideas, and experiences. **R2b** Interpret characters, plot, setting, theme, and dialogue, using evidence from the text. **R2d** Determine how the use and meaning of literary devices convey the author's message and intent. **Core W8** Use correct grammatical construction in subject-verb agreement.

For a complete description of the standards, see p. NY 11.

Skills Review

Key Reading Skill: Interpreting

7. At the beginning of his speech, Jackson says, "I have a story. I wasn't always on television. Writers were not always outside my door." What is Jackson saying about himself in these sentences? Interpret what he means. Put your interpretation in your own words.

Literary Element: Repetition

8. When Jackson repeats the sentence "I understand," what is he saying he understands? How can you tell?

9. If you were giving this speech, how would you say "Keep hope alive"? Would it sound the same each time you said it? Explain.

Vocabulary Check

Read each word in column A. On a separate sheet of paper, write the letter of the correct definition from column B.

Column A	Column B
10. nomination	a. to give up control
11. surrender	b. state of being deserted or left alone
12. abandonment	c. act of proposing a candidate for office

13. Academic Vocabulary What do you do when you interpret a piece of literature?

14. English Language Coach Find three words and phrases from the selection that you think are especially well chosen for the audience. Write these words and phrases in your Learner's Notebook. Then explain why you think they are good examples.

Grammar Link: Agreement with Indefinite Pronouns

Indefinite pronouns are noun substitutes that do not refer to a particular person, place, or thing. Certain indefinite pronouns are always singular, or equal to *he, she,* or *it.* Study the list below.

anybody	everybody	no one
anyone	everyone	nothing
anything	everything	somebody
each	neither	someone
either	nobody	something

See if you can make the subject and verb agree in the sentences below. (Use the list above for help.)

• No one (is, are) to blame for the accident.

If you chose *is*, you're right. *No one* is singular, or equal to *he, she,* or *it.* So the right verb form is *is.*

• Neither of the cars (has, have) bad brakes.

If you chose *has,* you're right. The subject is *neither,* which is singular. (If you thought *cars* was the subject, remember that prepositional phrases do not contain subjects and verbs. *Cars* is in the phrase *of the cars,* so it can't be the subject.)

Grammar Practice

Write the correct verb form for each sentence.

15. Each of the CDs (sounds, sound) good.

16. There (is, are) nothing wrong with any of them.

17. Everyone (wants, want) a copy of that new CD.

18. Someone (needs, need) to see how good they are.

19. Neither of the musicians (is, are) nominated for an award.

Web Activities For eFlashcards, Selection Quick Checks, and other Web activities, go to www.glencoe.com.

Before You Read

May Swenson

Meet the Author

Many people consider May Swenson (1913–1989) one of the best American poets of the 20th century. Swenson once said her poetry came from "a craving to get through the curtains of things as they *appear*, to things as they *are*, and then into the larger, wilder space of things as they *are becoming*." See page R7 of the Author Files at the back of the book for more on May Swenson.

Author Search For more about May Swenson, go to www.glencoe.com.

NY English Language Arts Core Curriculum (pp. 490–493)

R2e Recognize how the author's use of language creates images or feelings. **R2b** Interpret theme using evidence from the text. **R2g** Compare literature to own lives. **R2f** Identify poetic elements to interpret poetry.

For a complete description of the standards, see p. NY 11.

Fable for When There's No Way Out

Vocabulary Preview

instinct (IN stinkt) *n.* unlearned knowledge that a person or animal is born with **(p. 492)** *A mother hen knows by instinct how to care for her chicks.*

ambition (am BIH shun) *n.* a strong drive or desire to succeed **(p. 492)** *Meg's ambition is to be an astronaut.*

despair (dih SPAIR) *n.* a complete loss of hope **(p. 493)** *Despair overcame Susan when she realized her cat was gone forever.*

rage (rayj) *n.* a feeling of great anger or fury **(p. 493)** *Jen's rage when her brother stepped on her artwork was overwhelming.*

Write to Learn For each of the above vocabulary words, write a sentence that shows what the word means.

English Language Coach

Word Choice, Purpose, and Audience Writers choose words that further their purpose and communicate best with their readers. For example:

- If a friend who doesn't know much about technology asks you to explain what instant messaging is, you might say, "With instant messaging, you communicate in real time. You send the message and the person gets it and answers you right away, almost as if you're having a phone conversation. But with e-mail, you may not get the message right away."

- An article in a magazine for technology experts might explain the same idea in very different words, like these: "Virtual communication in cyberspace may be characterized as either synchronous or asynchronous. In synchronous communication like IM, conversations happen in real time; in asynchronous communication, there's often a time lag."

Which explanation is better? It depends on the author's purpose and audience. If an author's purpose is to explain something to an audience that's probably unfamiliar with her subject, she'll use simple, informal words. But if the purpose is to communicate with specialists in a field, she'll use the technical language they understand.

On Your Own Rewrite the sentence below by replacing the big words with shorter, simpler ones. Use a dictionary.

- Music is aesthetically pleasing vocal or instrumental sounds having some degree of melody, harmony, or rhythm.

Skills Preview

Key Reading Skill: Interpreting

Sometimes a poem seems to be only about something in nature. But when you think about it, you realize you can interpret it differently. You can see how that animal or bird is like you. You can look at that storm or earthquake or process of nature and see how it's like your life. When you interpret that way, poetry comes alive!

Write to Learn As you read "Fable for When There's No Way Out," try to interpret the poem in two ways—as the story of a chick breaking out of an egg and as a story about life. Write your conclusions in your Learner's Notebook.

Key Literary Element: Alliteration

Poetry was originally a way for important stories and lessons to be passed from person to person. Poetic techniques like **alliteration** were used to make the poems easier to remember. Poets and audiences realized that the sounds of poems were also beautiful, like music in words.

Alliteration was the main sound device in the oldest of English poetry, even more important than rhyme. It is the repetition of sounds at the beginnings of words. Most often, the repeated sounds are consonants. Here is a famous example of alliteration from the poet Alexander Pope. (A zephyr is a "breeze.")

> Soft is the strain when Zephyr gently blows,
>
> And the smooth stream in smoother numbers flows.

Very smooth. But alliteration isn't always smooth. This is from a poem by Vachel Lindsay:

> Beat an empty barrel with the handle of a broom,
>
> Hard as they were able,/ Boom, boom, BOOM.

Small Group Discussion Together with some classmates, make up some riddles using alliteration. Here's a sample: What do you call a short novel? A brief book.

Get Ready to Read

Connect to the Reading

Have you ever worked really hard at something but still felt you were getting nowhere? If so, remember that feeling as you read this poem.

Partner Talk Talk with a classmate about what it means to give up. Are there situations where that's okay? Are there situations where giving up is not possible?

Build Background

You are going to read a poem about a chick's struggle to break through its shell and hatch.

- It takes a chick about 21 days to hatch. By Day 16, the chick turns around so that its head is close to the air cell at the larger end of the egg.

- Around Day 17, the chick uses its beak to break the inner membrane of the eggshell.

- The chick uses its sharp egg tooth to cut away at the shell. After it makes a hole in the shell, the chick must rest for three to eight hours before it succeeds in cracking the shell by pushing and pecking at it. The chick is then very tired.

Set Purposes for Reading

BIG Question Read "Fable for When There's No Way Out" to explore what happens when the will to live is tested against a life-or-death situation.

Set Your Own Purpose What else would you like to learn from the poem that will help you answer the Big Question? Write your own purpose on the "Fable for When There's No Way Out" page of Foldable 4.

Literature Online

Interactive Literary Elements Handbook
To review or learn more about the literary elements, go to www.glencoe.com.

Keep Moving

Use these skills as you read the following selection.

by May Swenson

In The Interior of Sight. Max Ernst (1891-1976). Oil on canvas. Mus
National d'Art Moderne, Centre Georges Pompidou, Paris.

Grown too big for his skin,
and it grown hard,

without a sea and atmosphere— **1**
he's drunk it all up—

5 his strength's inside him now,
but there's no room to stretch.

He pecks at the top
but his beak's too soft;

though **instinct** and **ambition** shoves,
10 he can't get through.

Barely old enough to bleed
and already bruised! **2**

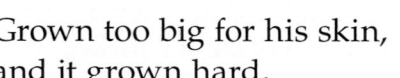

: **instinct** (IN stinkt) *n.* unlearned knowledge that a person or animal is born with
: **ambition** (am BIH shun) *n.* a strong drive or desire to succeed

Practice the Skills

1 **Key Reading Skill**

Interpreting What does the phrase "without a sea and atmosphere" mean? Think about what it's like inside an egg once a chick is ready to hatch.

2 **Key Literary Element**

Alliteration What alliteration do you see in this stanza of the poem?

In a case this tough
what's the use

15 if you break your head
instead of the lid?

Despair tempts him
to just go limp:

Maybe the cell's
20 already a tomb,* **3**

and beginning end
in this round room.

Still, stupidly he pecks
and pecks, as if from under

25 his own skull—
yet makes no crack . . .

No crack until
he finally cracks,

and kicks and stomps. **4**
30 What a thrill

and shock to feel
his little gaff* poke

through the floor!
A way he hadn't known or meant.

35 **Rage** works if reason won't. **5**
When locked up, bear down. **6** ○

---

20 A *tomb* is a room or chamber where a dead body is placed.
32 A *gaff* is a sharp metal spur on the leg of a fighting bird.

Vocabulary

despair (dih SPAIR) *n.* a complete loss of hope
rage (rayj) *n.* a feeling of great anger or fury

Practice the Skills

3 | **Key Reading Skill**

Interpreting What does the speaker compare to a cell and a tomb? What do you think this comparison means?

4 | **English Language Coach**

Word Choice, Purpose, and Audience Do you get a chuckle out of the double meaning of *crack*? Picture the tiny chick going nuts, kicking and stomping and finally cracking through the shell. How does the poet achieve this effect?

5 | **Key Literary Element**

Alliteration What words in this line begin with the same sound?

6 | **BIG Question**

What do you think the poet wants you to learn from the chick's struggle? Write your answer on the "Fable for When There's No Way Out" page of Foldable 4. Your response will help you complete the Unit Challenge later.

After You Read

Fable for When There's No Way Out

Answering the BIG Question

1. What does the chick's behavior in the poem teach you about what to do when you don't know what to do?
2. **Summarize** In lines 7–25, what does the chick do to try to hatch?
   TIP Think and Search
3. **Recall** How does the chick finally succeed in breaking the shell?
   TIP Right There

Critical Thinking

4. **Infer** Do you think the chick knows it must break the shell in order to survive? Why or why not?
   TIP Author and Me
5. **Analyze** Why do you think the poet uses the word "stupidly" in line 23 instead of "blindly," "instinctively," or a synonym?
   TIP On My Own
6. **Evaluate** How well does the poem help you imagine what it's like to be a hatching chick? Explain.
   TIP On My Own

Talk About Your Reading

Class Discussion Like many poems, "Fable for When There's No Way Out" has two different interpretations. One is a description of a chick pecking its way out of an egg. Another is about life and how to live it. As a class, discuss the second interpretation of the poem. First, several different students should give their view of the poem. Then everyone should talk about what message Swenson may be trying to get across. Try to think of situations in which that message might be helpful.

**NY English Language Arts
Core Curriculum** (pp. 494–495)

LC R17 Demonstrate comprehension and response through a range of activities.
LC S8 Participate in group discussions.
R2b Interpret theme using evidence from the text. **R2f** Identify poetic elements to interpret poetry. **Core W8** Use correct grammatical construction in subject-verb agreement.

For a complete description of the standards, see p. NY 11.

Skills Review

Key Reading Skill: Interpreting

7. The last two lines of the poem suggest that there's a lesson to be learned from the chick's experience. In your own words, how would you explain that lesson?

Key Literary Element: Alliteration

8. Which words are alliterative in lines 5–6?

9. What does alliteration add to the last lines of the poem?

Vocabulary Check

Choose the best word from the list to answer each question below.

instinct   ambition   despair   rage

10. What kind of knowledge are you born with?

11. What is a strong feeling of anger?

12. What helps a person do well and succeed?

13. What does a person feel who has no more hope?

14. Academic Vocabulary Write the academic vocabulary word that means "to figure out the meaning of what you read."

15. English Language Coach Review the discussion of word choice and author's purpose on page 490. Then choose a sentence from the poem and rewrite it in your Learner's Notebook using more formal diction, as if for an audience of scientists.

Web Activities For eFlashcards, Selection Quick Checks, and other Web activities, go to www.glencoe.com.

Grammar Link: Subject-Verb Agreement with Collective Nouns

Collective nouns name a group made up of a number of people or things.

Common Collective Nouns

audience	committee	family	swarm
class	crowd	flock	team

Collective nouns present special subject-verb agreement problems because they can have either a singular or a plural meaning.

If you are speaking about a group as a unit, then the noun has a singular meaning.

• The jury is refusing to speak to the press.

If you are referring to the individual members of the group, then the noun has a plural meaning.

• The jury are arguing about the case.

Grammar Practice

Rewrite each sentence below, using the correct verb from the pair in parentheses.

16. The audience (is, are) not all in their seats yet.

17. The herd (spend, spends) every summer in the far pasture.

18. The class (take, takes) their lunch at different periods.

19. The team (is, are) taking showers and getting dressed.

20. Every spring the whole family (takes, take) a vacation together.

Poem

Revising, Editing, and Presenting

ASSIGNMENT Write a poem

Purpose: To express your thoughts and feelings about what you do when you don't know what to do

Audience: Your teacher and possibly your classmates or family

Revising Rubric

Your revised poem should

- describe a situation clearly
- use lively, specific words
- use literary devices such as figurative language and sound patterns
- make subjects and verbs agree in number

See page 498 for a model of a poem.

NY English Language Arts Core Curriculum
(pp. 496–499)

Core W5 Use the writing process.
Core W3 Use tone and language appropriate to audience and purpose. **S2b** Present original, literary texts, using language and text structures that are inventive.

For a complete description of the standards, see p. NY 11.

In Writing Workshop Part 1, you gathered ideas and details and developed a draft. Now you'll revise and edit your draft to improve your poem. When you've finished polishing your poem, you'll share it with classmates and possibly friends or family members. Remember to keep a copy of it in your writing portfolio so that you and your teacher can evaluate your writing progress.

Revising

Make It Better

Skilled writers know that revising their work makes it better. Some even think it's the most important step in the writing process. Revising can take your poem from *blah* to *okay* to *fantastic*. Let's begin.

Improve Your Poem

Read the draft of your poem, looking especially for words that are boring, unclear, or too general. Now's your chance to replace them with more colorful and specific words. Use these tips to help you revise your poem.

Your poem should have . . .	Tip
action verbs	Read the verbs in your poem. Are they the most descriptive ones? Replace a few with words that *sound* like the idea you're describing (zoom, buzz, crackle).
adjectives and adverbs	Add to the word picture by telling exactly what things look like: Leon *proudly* placed the *blue wool* cap on his head.
specific nouns	Replace general nouns (like *music*) with ones that paint a more detailed picture (like *reggae*).
words that appeal to the senses	As you read your poem, do your senses come alive? Add words that help readers smell, taste, touch, hear, or see your poem.
figurative language, such as similes and metaphors	Read your poem as if you were someone else. Are your ideas easy to picture? If not, add similes or metaphors to compare them to things readers can easily picture. Example: Their laughter beat against my brain like a million fists.

What else in your poem might you need to revise or strengthen?

Title

Think of a title as an invitation that makes people want to read the poem.

1. Read your poem aloud and ask yourself
- *Does my title grab a reader's attention?*
- *Does it suggest the feelings and ideas that I want?*
- *Does it give a hint without giving away all the surprises?*

2. Keep editing your title until it sounds right.

> Original title: Funny Poem
> Alternate titles: Bad Day

Writing Tip

Title Trick If you have trouble thinking up a title for your poem, try taking the central word or phrase from your cluster web (page 465) and using alliteration.

How Does Your Poem Sound?

Good poets often use sound devices to make their poems memorable.

- **Rhyme** is the repetition of vowel sounds and succeeding sounds. For example, *game* rhymes with *fame* and *lame*.
- **Rhythm** is the pattern of sound created by stressed and unstressed syllables.
- **Repetition** of words, phrases, or lines can emphasize important ideas and give a sense of unity to a poem.
- **Alliteration** is the repetition of sounds at the beginnings of words. Example: "The <u>s</u>iren <u>s</u>plit the <u>s</u>ilence of the night."

Writing Tip

Repetition Choose a favorite line from your poem and repeat it, maybe just once or twice, or maybe as the last line of every stanza.

Editing
Finish It Up

Use the Editing Checklist as you read your poem one last time.

Proofreading Checklist
- ☑ Words are spelled correctly.
- ☑ Punctuation is correctly used.
- ☑ Subjects and verbs agree.

Presenting
Show It Off

Literature **O**nline

Writing Models For models and other writing activities, go to www.glencoe.com.

If you handwrite your poem, write legibly. If you type it, consider using a presentation program and illustrating it with clip art or magazine photos. Add your poem to your classmates' to create a class computer presentation.

Active Writing Model

Writer's Model

Bad Day

The questions involve readers in the poem and directly relate to the unit Big Question.

What do you do,
What should you do,
What can you do
When you don't know what to do?

When you've gone and lost your lunch pass,
And your empty stomach knows it,
And it's growling like a pit bull,
And you have no bone to throw it.

Notice the way the speaker compares her stomach to a pit bull. Does this simile paint a mental picture for you?

And it's almost time for math class,
And you know you didn't study,
And your mathless brain keeps moaning
One plus one plus one makes four.

The poet uses a made-up word to express a specific idea. Do you know what it feels like to have a "mathless" brain?

And your best friend came and told you
That this guy you like in soc class
Has a girlfriend who's a model
And is rich and smart and more.

The poet uses end rhymes (rhymes at the ends of lines), like *four* and *more*. She also uses a slant rhyme (where the words almost but don't quite rhyme): *bone* and *throw* in line 8.

What do you do,
What should you do,
What can you do?
(I guess you write a poem!)

Listening, Speaking, and Viewing

Reading Poetry Aloud

What Is It?

Poems are meant to be read aloud. They began as a form of spoken entertainment thousands of years ago. Rhyme and repetition made them easier to remember. We read and listen to poetry differently from other genres of literature.

Why Is It Important?

Reading poems aloud and listening to others read them helps you understand and appreciate the poets' craft. Good reading and listening skills make poems come alive.

How Do I Do It?

Use these tips as you get ready to read aloud.

- First read the poem to yourself. Do you understand it? Are there words you don't know or can't pronounce? Look them up or ask for help.

- Reread the poem to yourself, this time focusing on the feelings and mental pictures the poet creates. At different points in the poem, stop to close your eyes and "feel" each image.

- Practice reading the poem aloud to yourself. Look for punctuation. Pause at the ends of sentences, *not* at the end of every line. Pauses help listeners make sense of words. They also encourage your audience to think about what you've read and what will come next.

- Use your voice well. Don't read too fast, and don't use the same tone of voice the whole way through. Speak louder during important moments. Speak faster as you read action scenes. Use a higher voice for some characters and a lower one for others.

- Make eye contact with listeners. Make them feel as if *you* are the poet, sharing *yourself* as you read. Like any performer, gauge how you are doing by your audience's reaction.

Listening to Poetry

Follow these tips when you listen to poetry.

- What words or lines jumped out at you? Think about why they caught your attention. Did you connect them to experiences or feelings you've had? Could you feel what the poet felt?

- What word pictures did the descriptive details paint? What did you see in your mind?

- Which senses could you use as you listened to the poem? Did the poet make you almost taste or smell or touch something?

- Can you connect the message of the poem to your life? Even when you don't agree with the message, you can often find something in it that relates to your own life.

- Which words *sounded* just right? Did the author make the poem more fun with alliteration and other sound devices?

Perform In a small group, take turns reading poems aloud. You can read the poem you wrote or you can find another poem to read. Either way, practice reading the poem several times so you can perform it smoothly and easily for your audience.

"LORETTA, LORETTA, LORETTA MY LOVE, YOUR SKIN IS AS SOFT AS A NEW BASEBALL GLOVE. YOUR EYES ARE LIKE MARBLES, YOUR HAIR LIKE SPAGHETTI. WHEN I LOOK AT YOU, MY PALMS GET ALL SWEATY." .... GEE. YOU SURE KNOW HOW TO MAKE A GIRL FEEL SPECIAL.

THANKS, I WROTE IT MYSELF.

NO KIDDING.

Maybe making your own greeting cards isn't such a hot idea.

REAL LIFE ADVENTURES (c) 1998 GarLanco. Reprinted with permission of UNIVERSAL PRESS SYNDICATE. All rights reserved.

Analyzing Cartoons
Loretta doesn't find this poem very romantic. Why not? What feelings is her husband trying to express? Does he succeed or fail?

Skills Focus

You will practice using these skills when you read these selections:
- "O Captain! My Captain!" p. 504
- "Scorched! How to Handle Different Types of Burns," p. 510

Reading

- Monitoring comprehension of text

Literature

- Identifying types of rhyme and their effects
- Following instructions

Vocabulary

- Explaining how purpose, audience, and occasion influence word choice
- Academic Vocabulary: *comprehension*

Writing/Grammar

- Using correct subject-verb agreement

NY English Language Arts Core Curriculum
(pp. 500–501)

LC R12 Combine multiple strategies (monitor) to enhance comprehension and response.

For a complete description of the standards, see p. NY 11.

Skill Lesson

Monitoring Comprehension

Learn It!

What Is It? You finish reading several pages of a book. You look up, and suddenly it dawns on you. You've gotten almost nothing out of what you read. In fact, you can hardly remember it. Sound familiar?

Reading is more than moving your eyes over print. It's making sense of what the print says. To make sure you "get" what you read, you need to monitor, or keep track of, your **comprehension**.

- Check to make sure you understand what you're reading *while you're reading it.*
- If you don't understand something, stop and strategize.

© Zits Partnership. Reprinted with Permission of King Features Syndicate, Inc.

Analyzing Cartoons

Is Jeremy going to remember *David Copperfield* later? If not, why? Why is it important to think carefully about what you read?

Academic Vocabulary

comprehension (kahm prih HEN shun) *n.* the fact or power of understanding

Why Is It Important? When you monitor your comprehension, you make reading more meaningful. You become a more effective reader because you understand and remember more of what you read.

How Do I Do It? Recognize when your understanding breaks down. Pause from time to time to ask yourself, *Does this make sense to me? Could I explain it to somebody else?* If your answers are *no,* use one or more of the following strategies:

- Carefully reread what you've already read. Look for clues.
- Read on to see if your questions are answered later.
- Ask your teacher or a classmate for help.
- Paraphrase the hard parts by putting them in your own words.

Read on to see how a student applied some of the strategies to monitor her comprehension of a poem.

Literature Online

Study Central Visit www.glencoe .com and click on Study Central to review monitoring comprehension.

The Eagle

He clasps the crag with crooked hands;
Close to the sun in lonely lands,
Ring'd with the azure world, he stands.
The wrinkled sea beneath him crawls;
He watches from his mountain walls,
And like a thunderbolt, he falls.

Who's "he" in line 1? I'll reread the title to see if it gives clues. Hmmm. The title is "The Eagle." So I guess "he" may be a bird. I'll read on to see. I know that <u>clasps</u> means "hold tightly." Birds hold onto their perches tightly. And I know that crags are stony cliffs. I saw on a TV nature show that eagles sometimes nest on cliffs. So "he" probably is an eagle.

Practice It!

Discuss "The Eagle" with a small group of classmates. Then put the poem in your own words. Write your paraphrase in your Learner's Notebook.

Use It!

As you read "O Captain! My Captain!" and "Scorched! How to Handle Different Types of Burns," monitor your comprehension. Use at least two of the strategies above.

Before You Read

O Captain! My Captain!

Walt Whitman

Meet the Author

Walt Whitman (1819–1892) brought a fresh voice to American poetry. His most famous book of poems, *Leaves of Grass,* is an American classic. Whitman is best known for his free verse, in which he writes in the rhythms of spoken language. However, some of his most popular poems are in a more traditional style. See page R7 of the Author Files in the back of the book for more on Walt Whitman.

Author Search For more about Walt Whitman, go to www.glencoe.com.

NY English Language Arts Core Curriculum (pp. 502–505)

R2e Recognize how the author's use of language creates images or feelings. **LC R12** Combine multiple strategies (summarize, monitor) to enhance comprehension and response. **R2f** Identify poetic elements (rhyming patterns) in order to interpret poetry.

For a complete description of the standards, see p. NY 11.

Vocabulary Preview

grim (grim) *adj.* gloomy; somber **(p. 504)** *The team looked grim after losing the game.*

victor (VIK tor) *n.* winner; one who defeats an opponent **(p. 505)** *Al gets the prize money because he was the victor.*

mournful (MORN ful) *adj.* expressing sadness or grief **(p. 505)** *We were mournful after our dog ran away.*

Think-Pair-Share Think about the words and definitions above. What do you think a poem that has these words in it might be about? Discuss your thoughts with a classmate.

English Language Coach

Word Choice and Occasion What clothes would you wear to watch a baseball game? Would you wear the same clothes to a wedding? If you're like most people, you dress to fit the occasion, or event. Just as you match your clothing style to the occasion, so authors and public speakers match their choice of words to the event. For formal occasions, authors and speakers might "dress up" their language and use formal words. For everyday events, they might choose informal words. Compare:

Formal Occasion	Informal Occasion
automobile	car
children	kids
dine	eat
father	dad

Write to Learn Below is part of a speech a student has written for graduation. The language he used is too informal for the occasion. In your Learner's Notebook, rewrite the speech. Make the words fit the occasion.

• Hey, I'm here this p.m. to say "Congrats!" to y'all 'cause you're almost outta here!

Skills Preview

Key Reading Skill: Monitoring Comprehension

Poems pack a lot of meaning in very few words. You can't skip over too many hard parts in a poem, or you'll get lost. That's why it's especially important to monitor your comprehension when you read poetry.

On Your Own As you read "O Captain! My Captain!" stop after every stanza, or set of lines, and ask yourself whether you "get" what it says. To be sure that you do, sum up the stanza in your own words.

Key Literary Element: Rhyme

The rhymes that you are most familiar with are those that repeat the vowel and consonant sounds (like *moon* and *loon,* or *happy* and *sappy*) at the end of the line. In most poetry, the rhyming words appear at the ends of the lines

Hickory-dickory dock, / the mouse ran up the clock.

But there are other kinds of rhymes. One is called **slant rhyme** or **near rhyme.** In a slant rhyme, the vowel sounds are repeated or the consonant sounds are repeated, but not both.

feet and *seen*   *mine* and *sight*

ball and *fill*   *tick* and *tock*

In a slant rhyme, the effect is like an end-of-a-line rhyme but not quite as strong. Many poets use slant rhymes to make their poetry musical without the sing-song quality that rhymed poetry can have.

Partner Talk Together with a classmate, choose a nursery rhyme and change the rhymes to slant rhymes. Talk about how the slant rhymes change the verse.

Literature Online

Interactive Literary Elements Handbook
To review or learn more about the literary elements, go to www.glencoe.com.

Get Ready to Read

Connect to the Reading

Think of a time when your feelings were different from those of the people around you. For example, you may have felt sad at a time when it seemed as if the whole world was happy. Or you may have been upbeat when everyone else was down.

Write to Learn In your Learner's Notebook, jot down what you were feeling and why.

Building Background

- "O Captain! My Captain!" is an **elegy** (EL uh jee)—a poem written to honor someone who has died. As you might expect, elegies are usually solemn and sad. They praise the person who has died, and they express a sense of loss over the person's death.

- Whitman's elegy honors President Abraham Lincoln. Like most Americans, Whitman was shocked and saddened by Lincoln's death. After leading the United States through the long, dark days of the Civil War, Lincoln was shot and killed by John Wilkes Booth, a Southern sympathizer. Lincoln's greatest hope—that the nation would reunite—was realized when the war drew to a close and the South rejoined the Union. Soon after, Lincoln was killed.

- Have you ever heard someone refer to a nation or its government as a "ship of state"? Whitman uses this metaphor in "O Captain, My Captain." Throughout the poem, he compares post-war America to a ship returning from a difficult journey.

Set Purposes for Reading

BIG Question   Read "O Captain! My Captain!" to see how a poet honored a fallen leader.

Set Your Own Purpose What else would you like to learn from the selection to help you answer the Big Question? Write your own purpose on the "O Captain! My Captain!" page of Foldable 4.

Keep Moving

Use these skills as you read the following selection.

O Captain! My Captain!

by Walt Whitman

O Captain! my Captain! our fearful trip is done;
The ship has weather'd every rack,* the prize we sought
   is won; ❶
The port is near, the bells I hear, the people all exulting,*
While follow eyes the steady keel,* the vessel **grim** and
   daring:
5 But O heart! heart! heart!
    O the bleeding drops of red,
      Where on the deck my Captain lies,
        Fallen cold and dead. ❷

   O Captain! my Captain! rise up and hear the bells;
10 Rise up—for you the flag is flung—for you the bugle
   trills; ❸
For you bouquets and ribbon'd wreaths—for you the shores
   a-crowding;

---

2 Here, *rack* means "storm" or "jolt."

3 People who are *exulting* are filled with joy.

4 The keel is the main timber that runs along the bottom of a boat. So a *steady keel* is a straight, even course.

Vocabulary

grim (grim) *adj.* gloomy; somber

Practice the Skills

❶ **Reviewing Skills**

Symbol In this poem, the ship is a symbol for the country, the United States of America. Who would the captain of the ship be?

❷ **Key Reading Skill**

Monitoring Comprehension Stop and think about the first stanza. Could you explain it in your own words? If not, reread it and discuss it with someone.

❸ **Key Literary Element**

Rhyme Reread lines 9–10. What word does each line end with? What type of rhyme do these two words create?

For you they call, the swaying mass, their eager faces
 turning:
Here, Captain! dear father!
 This arm beneath your head;
15
 It is some dream that on the deck,
 You've fallen cold and dead. **4**

My Captain does not answer, his lips are pale and still;
My father does not feel my arm, he has no pulse nor will;
The ship is anchor'd safe and sound, its voyage closed
 and done;
20 From fearful trip, the **victor** ship comes in with object won:
 Exult, O shores, and ring, O bells!
 But I, with **mournful** tread,
 Walk the deck my Captain lies,
 Fallen cold and dead. **5** ○

Practice the Skills

4 **English Language Coach**

Word Choice and Occasion
Whitman uses formal language
in the poem. Why is that type of
language fitting for an elegy?

5 **BIG Question**

What does the speaker do to
cope with the "captain's" death?
Write your answer on the "O
Captain! My Captain!" page of
Foldable 4. Your response will
help you complete the Unit
Challenge later.

Flying Cloud, 1852. Currier and Ives. Private collection.

Vocabulary

victor (VIK tor) *n.* winner; one who defeats an opponent

mournful (MORN ful) *adj.* expressing sadness or grief

After You Read

O Captain! My Captain!

Answering the BIG Question

1. After reading "O Captain! My Captain!" what are your thoughts about what to do when you don't know what to do?

2. **Recall** Where is the ship headed at the beginning of the poem?
   TIP Right There

3. **Recall** Where are the people who are waiting for the ship to return?
   TIP Think and Search

Critical Thinking

4. **Interpret** In line 1, what "fearful trip" has the "ship of state" completed? What made the trip so fearful?
   TIP Author and Me

5. **Interpret** In line 2, what "prize" has the "captain" won?
   TIP Author and Me

6. **Evaluate** In your opinion, is the comparison between post-war America and a ship returning home an effective one? Explain.
   TIP On My Own

Talk About Your Reading

Literature Groups With a small group of classmates, compare and contrast the speaker's feelings with those of the other people in the poem.

- *In what ways are his feelings the same as theirs?*
- *In what ways are his feelings different?*
- *Why are his feelings different?*

Back up your ideas with specific details from the poem. Keep track of your ideas on a Venn diagram like the one pictured below.

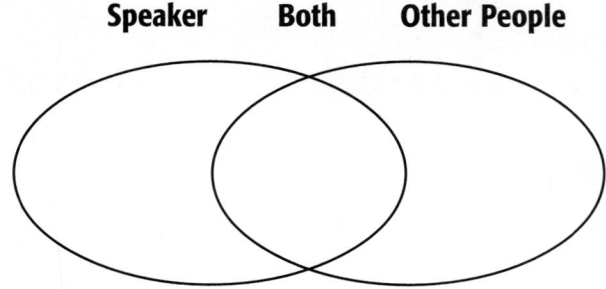

NY English Language Arts Core Curriculum (pp. 506–507)

LC R17 Demonstrate comprehension and response through a range of activities. **S2a** Express interpretations and support them through specific references to the text. **LC R12** Combine multiple strategies (monitor) to enhance comprehension and response. **R2f** Identify poetic elements (rhyming patterns) to interpret poetry. **Core W8** Use correct grammatical construction in subject-verb agreement.

For a complete description of the standards, see p. NY 11.

Skills Review

Key Reading Skill: Monitoring Comprehension

7. a. What strategies did you use to monitor your comprehension as you read the poem?

b. Will you use these strategies when you read poetry again? Why or why not?

Key Literary Element: Rhyme

8. What end rhymes can you find in the third stanza? List them in pairs, like this: still/will

9. What is the slant rhyme in the third stanza? Fill in the blanks: ___ / ___

10. a. How does rhyme help unify the ideas in the poem?

b. How does rhyme add to the "music" of the poem?

Vocabulary Check

Choose the best word from the list to complete each sentence below. Rewrite each completed sentence on a separate sheet of paper.

grim   victor   mournful

11. If you're filled with sadness and grief, you're ___.

12. If you've won a game or contest, you are the ___.

13. If a situation is very serious, it is ___.

14. Academic Vocabulary Define *comprehension* in your own words.

15. English Language Coach Change the language below to make the phrases sound less formal.
- "the prize we sought is won"
- "the people [are] all exulting"
- "the vessel [is] grim and daring"

16. English Language Coach If your word changes were put in the first stanza of the poem, how would the poem change? Do you think the changed poem would still fit the occasion? Explain.

Grammar Link: Agreement in Relative Clauses

Relative pronouns refer to nouns. The five relative pronouns are *that, which, who, whom,* and *whose.*

A **relative clause** is a group of words that begins with a relative pronoun followed by a noun and a verb or a verb only.

- The bike <u>that Collin wants</u> is expensive.
  (The relative pronoun *that* refers to the noun *bike.* The relative clause begins with *that* followed by the noun *Collin* and the verb *wants.*)

- This bike, <u>which is on sale</u>, costs a lot less.
  (The relative clause begins with the relative pronoun *which* followed by the verb *is.*)

Be careful to choose the correct verb form for relative clauses. A relative pronoun may be singular or plural, depending on the noun it refers to.

- The boy <u>who runs the bike club</u> owns a racer.
  (The relative pronoun *who* refers to the noun *boy.* Because boy is singular, or equal to *he,* the present tense verbs that go with *boy* must end in *-s.* Both *runs* and *owns* end in *-s,* so they are correct.)

- Two boys <u>who race for the club</u> win awards.
  (The relative pronoun *who* refers to the noun *boys.* Because *boys* is plural, or equal to *they,* the present tense verbs that go with *boys* should not end in *-s.* Neither *race* nor *win* ends in *-s,* so both verbs are correct.)

Grammar Practice

Underline the relative clause in each sentence. Then choose the correct verb form.

17. The girl who (wants, want) a bike (is, are) here.

18. The model that we (sells, sell) (is, are) the best.

Literature Online

Web Activities For eFlashcards, Selection Quick Checks, and other Web activities, go to www.glencoe.com.

Before You Read

Scorched! How to Handle Different Types of Burns

NY English Language Arts Core Curriculum (pp. 508–513)

LC R1 Recognize at sight a large body of high-frequency words and specialized content vocabulary. **LC R12** Combine multiple strategies (monitor) to enhance comprehension and response. **R1c** Read multistep directions.

For a complete description of the standards, see p. NY 11.

Vocabulary Preview

hobbled (HAH buld) *v.* walked with difficulty; limped; form of the verb *hobble* **(p. 510)** *Xavier hobbled to school on his sprained ankle.*

severity (suh VAIR ih tee) *n.* state of being very dangerous or harmful **(p. 510)** *Because of the severity of her injury, we called for an ambulance to rush her to the hospital.*

minor (MY nur) *adj.* of little importance; not serious **(p. 511)** *Minor injuries can be treated at home.*

sterile (STAIR ul) *adj.* free from germs; very clean **(p. 512)** *Cover the cut with a sterile bandage.*

Write to Learn For each of the above vocabulary words, write a sentence that shows what the word means.

English Language Coach

Word Choice and Subject To write about some subjects, authors must use specialized terms—words that are specific to the particular subjects. For example, authors writing about cooking might use the specialized terms *sauté, blanch,* and *fricassee,* while authors writing about football might use the terms *down, snap,* and *sack.* Authors do not define specialized terms if they are writing for readers who already know their subjects. When writing for general audiences who may not know the terms, the authors explain what the words mean. Specialized terms are useful because they allow people to communicate about a subject clearly and precisely.

Whole Class Discussion Which of the above specialized terms can class members define? As a class, write a definition for each term. Your definition should explain the terms clearly to people who know nothing about cooking or football. Copy the chart below into your Learner's Notebook. Fill in the right column with the definitions you write.

Subject	Specialized Term	Definition
cooking	sauté	
	blanch	
	fricasee	
football	down	
	snap	
	sack	

Skills Preview

Key Reading Skill: Monitoring Comprehension

When you monitor your comprehension, pause from time to time to make sure you understand what you are reading. If you don't understand, strategize.

Whole Class Discussion As a class, list and discuss strategies that can help readers improve their comprehension. Review the strategies on page 501, and add strategies of your own.

Text Element: Instructions

Instructions are explanations of how to perform a process. Recipes that explain how to cook something, on-screen commands that tell how to program a DVD player, and a teacher's directions on how to do homework are all examples of instructions. Instructions are usually written in **chronological order,** or time order, so that the first step in the process is presented first, the next step is presented second, and so on. When you read instructions, follow these tips:

- Quickly read through all the instructions before you begin to follow them. Get an overview.
- Remember that numbered, step-by-step instructions are usually the easiest to read and follow. If instructions are not in that format, take notes. In your notes, break the process into steps and number each step.
- As you read, picture yourself doing each step. Visualizing will help you understand and follow the instructions successfully.

Partner Work With a partner, jot down instructions on how to perform a simple process, such as brushing your teeth or washing a car. Then give your instructions to another pair of students for evaluation.

Interactive Literary Elements Handbook To review or learn more about the literary elements, go to www.glencoe.com.

Get Ready to Read

Connect to the Reading

As you read "Scorched! How to Handle Different Types of Burns," try to remember everything you know about taking care of a burn.

Small Group Discussion What do you know about taking care of skin after a burn? When might you be able to take care of a burn by yourself? When would you need to call a doctor right away? See how much your class already knows about first aid for this kind of injury.

Build Background

The selection you are about to read tells you how to begin to treat a burn.

- The most common types of burns come from fire, boiling water, or too much time in the sun.
- Chemicals can also cause burns and should be handled carefully.

Set Purposes for Reading

BIG Question Read the selection "Scorched! How to Handle Different Types of Burns" to find out about how to deal with burns—from mild to serious.

Set Your Own Purpose What else would you like to learn from the selection to help you answer the Big Question? Write your own purpose on the "Scorched!" page of Foldable 4.

Keep Moving

Use these skills as you read the following selection.

INFORMATIONAL TEXT
MAGAZINE
Current Health

SCORCHED!

How to Handle Different Types of Burns

by Stephen Fraser

Practice the Skills

Bryant Rice, 14, of Ravenna, Neb., was home alone one day when he decided to burn a stump in the yard. First he tried lighting the stump with a match. When that failed, he poured gasoline onto it and made a gas trail leading away from the stump, thinking the trail would act as a fuse.

Suddenly, the gasoline caught fire. Bryant's clothing went up in flames. Fortunately, he remembered a technique from a fire-safety class in school, namely, stop-drop-roll. He did just that: He dropped to the ground and rolled on the grass, which put out the flames. **1**

After sustaining burns on 20 percent of his body, he **hobbled** indoors, drew a cool bath, and sat in it while he called his mom. When Bryant's mother arrived home, she took one look at her peeling son and called 911.

Burns are classified according to the degree of **severity** of skin damage as follows: first degree, second degree, and third degree. That day, Bryant messed with fire and experienced the worst kind of burn—third degree. If you were in Bryant's shoes, would you know what to do? Get the burn basics. **2**

If your clothes catch fire, don't run! Stop where you are, drop to the ground, cover your face with your hands, and roll over and over to smother the flames.

1 | **Text Element**

Instructions The author gives simple instructions here. What are the three steps in the process?

2 | **English Language Coach**

Word Choice and Subject "Third-degree burn" is a specialized term. Here, the author defines it very simply. Later, he will define it in detail.

Vocabulary

hobbled (HAH buld) *v.* walked with difficulty; limped

severity (suh VAIR ih tee) *n.* state of being very dangerous or harmful

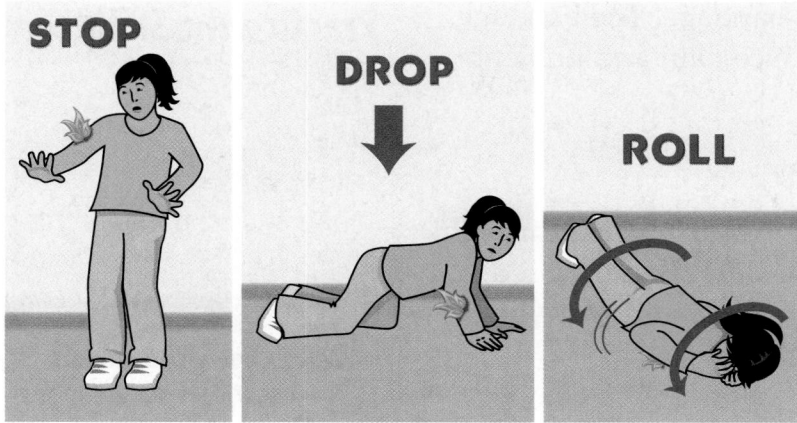

What It Is: First-degree burn

What It Looks Like Only the top layer of skin is damaged, resulting in redness, swelling, and pain. For example, most sunburns are first-degree burns. The healing time for a first-degree burn is about three to six days.

How Serious Is It?

If the burn is large or involves the face, feet, groin, or buttocks, see a doctor. If not, the burn should be treated as minor. See treatment for **minor** burns, below.

What to Do

Cool it! Hold the burned area under cool (not cold) running water for about 15 minutes, or apply a cold compress[1] to it. Cooling reduces swelling by conducting heat away from the skin. *Never* put ice on a burn; frostbite could result.

Visual Vocabulary
Aloe vera is a plant whose leaves contain a jellylike material which is often used to make lotions that soothe the skin.

Moisturize. To prevent drying, apply an aloe vera lotion, an antibiotic ointment,[2] or a moisturizer. Avoid home remedies, such as butter or olive oil. Those can do harm by mixing with bacteria on the skin and causing infection. **3**

3 | **Key Reading Skill**

Monitoring Comprehension
Do you understand now what to do for a minor burn? If not, reread this section.

---

1. A ***compress*** is a pad or cloth that can be used to apply cold, heat, or medicine.
2. ***Ointment*** is an oily substance put on the skin to heal or protect it.

Vocabulary

minor (MY nur) *adj.* of little importance; not serious

Cover the burn with a **sterile** gauze[3] bandage. The bandage, placed loosely over the burn, will reduce pain and prevent blistering.

What It Is: Second-degree burn

What It Looks Like The top layer of skin is burned through, and the second layer is damaged. The skin takes on a red, blotchy look, and blisters form. **4** Severe pain and swelling may occur, and healing can take weeks.

How Serious Is It?

If the burn involves the face, feet, groin, or buttocks, or is more than 2 inches wide, see a doctor. Otherwise, treat the burn as minor. You may need to add the steps listed below.

What to Do

Take an over-the-counter pain reliever. Watch for signs of infection—increased pain, redness, fever, swelling, or oozing. If any of those signs appear, seek medical help.

Don't pierce blisters; they protect against infection. If a blister accidentally breaks, wash the area with soap and water, then apply an antibiotic ointment and a gauze bandage.

What It Is: Third-degree burn

What It Looks Like All layers of skin and the underlying tissue are permanently damaged. The burned area may be dry and leathery or charred with black or white patches. Because nerve damage may occur, a third-degree burn can be painless. Healing is slow, and new skin has difficulty forming, except on the edges of the burn.

How Serious Is It?

Very serious. Seek immediate medical help.

---

3. *Gauze* is a light-weight cloth used as a bandage for a wound.

Vocabulary

sterile (STAIR ul) *adj.* free from germs; very clean

Practice the Skills

4 | **English Language Coach**

Word Choice and Subject
The author does not use specialized language in his description of second-degree burns. Why do you think he uses simple, everyday language?

What to Do

- Dial 911 for emergency medical assistance.

- Make sure the victim is not in contact with burning material or exposed to either heat or smoke.

- Make sure the victim is breathing, and perform cardiopulmonary resuscitation (CPR) if necessary.

- Don't remove burned clothing or apply ointments to the burn.

- Cover the burn with a cool, moist bandage or a clean cloth. **5** ○

Practice the Skills

5 **BIG Question**
Why do you think the writer of "Scorched!" gives readers such careful instructions for treating burns? Do you think most people could tell the difference between a mild burn and a more serious one? Do you think this article can help readers deal with burns in the future? Write your answers on the "Scorched!" page of Foldable 4. Your response will help you complete the Unit Challenge later.

After You Read

Scorched! How to Handle Different Types of Burns

Answering the **BIG Question**

1. What are your thoughts about what you do when you don't know what to do after reading the selection "Scorched! How to Handle Different Types of Burns"?

2. **Recall** When Bryant realized that his clothing had caught fire, how did he save himself from further harm?
   TIP Right There

3. **Summarize** What can you do if you or someone around you is burned?
   TIP Think and Search

Critical Thinking

4. **Infer** Why do you think the stop-drop-roll method is a good one to use?
   TIP Author and Me

5. **Infer** Why do you suppose it is important to get medical treatment for a burn on the face or feet?
   TIP On My Own

6. **Evaluate** How important is it to recognize the degree of a burn injury?
   TIP On My Own

Write about Your Reading

Step-by-Step Instructions Apply what you learned from reading "Scorched! How to Handle Different Types of Burns." Write numbered, step-by-step instructions on how to recognize and treat a first-degree burn.

Follow these guidelines as you write your instructions.

- Think through what you would do to treat a first-degree burn. Refer to the article if you need a reminder of what to do.

- Clearly explain each step. These are important instructions. Readers must be able to understand them.

- Use chronological order to sequence the steps.

- Be sure to write your instructions in your own words.

**NY English Language Arts
Core Curriculum** (pp. 514–515)

LC R17 Demonstrate comprehension and response through a range of activities.
LC W6 Organize writing effectively to communicate ideas to an intended audience.
R2g Compare literature to own lives.
LC R12 Combine multiple strategies (monitor) to enhance comprehension and response. **LC R13** Use text structure to aid comprehension and response.
Core W8 Use correct grammatical construction in subject-verb agreement.
For a complete description of the standards, see p. NY 11.

Skills Review

Key Reading Skill: Monitoring Comprehension

7. As you read "Scorched!" how did you monitor your comprehension?

8. What reading strategies did you use to improve your comprehension as you read?

Text Element: Instructions

9. In your opinion which of the following text features in "Scorched!" was the most helpful aid to reading the instructions? Explain your choice.

- the red subheads
- the black subheads
- the pictures of the stop-drop-roll process
- the bulleted list

Vocabulary Check

Answer *true* or *false* to each statement.

10. Getting dirt in a burn or other wound helps to keep it sterile.

11. If someone hobbled to school, he or she walked gracefully.

12. A description of the severity of a burn would tell how serious the burn is.

13. A minor problem is small and easily solved.

14. **English Language Coach** How does using specialized terms, or words that are specific to a particular subject, help you communicate more clearly? List three specialized terms that you know, and the subjects to which they apply.

Web Activities For eFlashcards, Selection Quick Checks, and other Web activities, go to www.glencoe.com.

Grammar Link: Agreement with Special Singulars

Usually a noun that ends in *-s* is plural, or more than one in number. To make a verb agree with *-s* ending plural nouns, you must use the form that goes with plural subjects (which are equal to *they*).

- Three <u>teachers</u> <u>are</u> absent today.
- Two <u>homes</u> <u>need</u> new roofs.
- Those <u>books</u> <u>include</u> maps.

There are a few exceptions to the *-s* ending plural noun rule. Some nouns that always end in *-s* are singular in meaning. These nouns generally refer to specialized fields and diseases.

Always Singular

- mumps
- measles
- mathematics
- civics
- physics
- economics

- The <u>mumps</u> usually <u>lasts</u> only a few days.
- <u>Mathematics</u> <u>is</u> my favorite subject.

Look out! A few nouns that always end in *-s* are plural in number: *pants, trousers, scissors* are common examples.
- His <u>pants</u> <u>have</u> unusual cuffs.

Grammar Practice

Write the correct form of the verb in parentheses.

15. Physics (is, are) the study of matter and energy.

16. The measles sometimes (lingers, linger) for days.

17. Civics (is, are) an interesting subject,

18. The scissors (needs, need) sharpening.

Writing Application Look over the Write About Your Reading assignment you completed. Make sure you used the right verb form with all subjects.

from
Thura's Diary & ESCAPING

by Thura Al-Windawi

by Zdenko Slobodnik

Skill Focus

You will use these skills as you read and compare the following selections:

- from *Thura's Diary*, p. 519
- "Escaping," p. 526

Reading

- Making connections across texts
- Comparing/contrasting internal and external conflict in different texts

Literature

- Identifying and analyzing internal and external conflicts in nonfiction texts

Writing

- Writing to compare and contrast

NY English Language Arts Core Curriculum (pp. 516–517)

R1j Compare and contrast information from a variety of different sources.

For a complete description of the standards, see p. NY 11.

Have you ever fought with a friend, or wrestled with a tough decision? If so, you've experienced conflict. Conflict is struggle between opposing forces. Conflict can be internal (something you worry about on the inside), or external (a problem you have with other people or forces). However, most conflicts—even the small ones—are both.

Great stories are full of conflict. Characters who struggle with their feelings or beliefs face **internal conflict.** Characters who struggle with other people or forces—like nature or society—face **external conflict.**

How to Read Across Texts: Internal and External Conflict

As you look for conflict in this part of *Thura's Diary* and "Escaping," pay attention to the people you're reading about. What worries them? What keeps them from being healthy and happy? Are they forced to make any painful decisions? If so, what are the results? How do they solve—or try to solve—their problems?

Also, think about how internal conflicts cause external conflicts for the people in these selections. Pay attention to the way in which external conflicts lead to internal conflicts as well. Just remember that internal conflict and external conflict—in stories and real life—are a two-for-one special. Order one, and you'll probably get the other, too.

Get Ready to Compare

In your Learner's Notebook, copy a chart like the one below for both of the selections in this workshop. As you read, use these charts to keep track of conflict in the selection from *Thura's Diary* and "Escaping."

Selection Title (Example: from <u>Thura's Diary</u>)			
Character	Problem, Obstacle, or Tough Decision	Conflict: Internal, External, or Both?	Resolution?

Use Your Comparison

The people in the selections you are about to read experienced similar forms of conflict. For example, people in both selections were forced to leave home as a result of war or political persecution. The details of their experiences differ, though. So do their internal conflicts.

As you read, look for specific similarities and differences between the characters' internal and external conflicts. Do the characters resolve all of their conflicts? If so, how? If not, why?

For help comparing and contrasting conflict in *Thura's Diary* and "Escaping," take detailed notes in the charts you just made.

Before You Read : from *Thura's Diary*

Thura Al-Windawi

Meet the Author

Thura Al-Windawi began keeping a diary to deal with her feelings about the war in Iraq, her home country. She says she found strength in writing about her family's experiences. Al-Windawi now attends college at the University of Pennsylvania, but hopes to return to Iraq someday. In the meantime, she hopes her diary spreads a message of peace.

Author Search For more about Thura Al-Windawi, go to www.glencoe.com.

NY English Language Arts Core Curriculum (pp. 518–524)

R2e Recognize how the author's use of language creates images or feelings.
R2h Identify social and cultural contexts to enhance understanding and appreciation of text.

For a complete description of the standards, see p. NY 11.

Vocabulary Preview

extinguished (ek STING wisht) *adj.* put out; form of the verb *extinguish* **(p. 520)** *The extinguished candle filled the room with smoke.*

rations (RASH unz) *n.* portions of needed items **(p. 521)** *During wartime, many people survive on small rations of food, water, and other supplies.*

bombardment (bom BARD mint) *n.* an attack **(p. 522)** *Outside Thura's home, gunshots and explosions signaled the neighborhood's bombardment.*

English Language Coach

Diction The writer's word choice is called **diction.** Diction can be formal or informal, depending on the writer's audience and purpose. Look at this sentence from *Thura's Diary:* "I'll get myself to America one day—not to take revenge, but to study and live and love like anyone else." Thura's diction is informal. Still, it sincerely conveys her hope for a better life.

Get Ready to Read

Connect to the Reading

The people in this selection faced fear and uncertainty when their country went to war. Think about a time when you felt uncertain about something. Did you also feel afraid? How did you resolve your feelings?

Build Background

In 2003 the United States invaded Iraq and removed its president, Saddam Hussein, from power. In Hussein's Iraq, people did not have the right to say negative things about the government in public. If they did, they could be jailed or killed. Thura wrote much of her diary while Hussein was still in power. The part of her diary you are about to read describes life in Baghdad, Iraq's capital, a few days after the invasion began. Thura and her family have been staying with her grandmother.

Set Purpose for Reading

BIG Question Read to find out what Thura Al-Windawi did when her way of life was in danger and she didn't know what to do.

Set Your Own Purpose What else would you like to learn about how Thura handled the conflicts in her life? Write your own purpose on the Reading Across Texts page of Foldable 4.

from Thura's Diary

by Thura Al-Windawi

Monday, 24 March 2003

Dear Diary,

Today I briefly went back home to get phone numbers of friends.[1] Lina and Wathika are in Adhamiya, where there is a lot of bombing. They said the bombing hit the Mukhabarat,[2] and that glass is everywhere.

Another friend, Abir, called me. She said all our group of friends are gone—some went to suburbs outside Baghdad, some went to their relatives' houses.

We're worried about another friend in Mosul. I'm most worried about Abir—she lives near Saddam International Airport. **1**

Tuesday, 25 March 2003

Dear Diary,

At last we are back home. I am going to be in my bedroom again. It's so nice to be home sweet home. I think I'll be able to sleep, now that I've calmed down a bit. Some of the young guys who live around here have volunteered to defend the neighbourhood, and they're taking it in turns to keep watch around the clock. They've put sandbag defences at the street corners, and the Baath Party has supplied them with Kalashnikovs.[3] But all the same, they won't be able to

---

1. Thura and her family have been staying with Thura's grandmother.
2. The equivalent of the CIA and the FBI rolled into one, the **Mukhabarat** was Iraq's main intelligence agency.
3. The **Baath Party** is a political party in Iraq and Syria. The **Kalashnikov** is an assault rifle designed by Russian military general M.T. Kalashnikov.

Practice the Skills

1 Reading Across Texts

Internal and External Conflict Thura is afraid for her friends. At the same time, she needs to go on with her life. Do you think her feelings are in conflict?

do anything about the noise of the planes and the bombs. It has become like a weird, disturbing kind of music to me. **2**

Wednesday, 26 March 2003

Dear Diary,

During the last few days there have been freak sandstorms here—it's as though Mother Nature's showing us how angry and hurt she is about the war. The weather's been chopping and changing, and the air has been so thick with red dust from the desert that you can only see a few metres in front of you. **3**

What's made matters worse is that the government's been burning huge amounts of oil inside Baghdad itself, because they think that by sending up clouds of black smoke they can affect the aim of the American missiles. They did the same thing in 1991, except that then they burnt piles of used tyres [tires] instead. This time they've dug dozens of ditches in and around the city, then filled them with crude oil and set the oil alight. The air is covered with thick, black smoke. The smell reminds me of the smoke trail that comes off a freshly **extinguished** match. I can't stand the smell or the way it pollutes the air. At night, as the sun goes down, the sky turns a combination of shades, from deep purples to fire-engine red.

Breathing is so difficult. It feels like you are stuck in a burning building, choking on the fumes. There is no fresh air any more. The leaves on the trees start to wilt. How will we get rid of all this dust and black smoke? Even if it rains, it will rain black drops of water. And it will hurt the soil. Every single living cell will be harmed by this

Practice the Skills

2 **Reading Across Texts**

Conflict Thura feels a little safer with the sandbags and the neighborhood guys with guns. But she can't forget the war and her fears. How do you think this causes an internal conflict?

3 **English Language Coach**

Diction Look at the words Thura uses to describe the sights and smells of her surroundings. How does her diction convey meaning? What imagery does this diction create?

On March 22, 2003, smoke rises from oil fires burning in trenches around Baghdad.

Analyzing the Photo How does this photo illustrate Thura's description of her environment?

Vocabulary

extinguished (ek STING wisht) *adj.* put out

weather. There are no sounds from the birds. Mother Nature is depressed and in pain.

This pollution is what causes lung cancer. I smell the dust and I go to the bathroom to wash my face, hoping maybe I will breathe fresh air. But it doesn't help. Poor Aula and Mum, they are sensitive to the dust. Every two minutes they must blow their noses with tissue. It looks like they are sick. They carry tissues with them wherever they walk. We are drowning in this polluted, black, dusty world. **4**

Mum has finished cleaning the living room that we watch TV in. She also cleaned the kitchen. She had to sponge everything down with a bucket of water to wipe away all the dust, and she had to clean the glasses by hand. We all helped. Each of us has a certain amount of water to use for cleaning. We have a three-gallon bucket each, filled halfway to the top. It came from our **rations** stored in the bathroom.

Sama was sitting and straightening up her Barbie dolls and teddy bears. We could not clean the whole house, only the ground floor and the bathrooms.

Friday, 28 March 2003

Dear Diary,

Today relatives and friends came to visit us. They are starting to visit a lot because they are worried about us and want to know if we are OK. The phone lines have been cut because the telephone exchange has been bombed. It is getting harder and harder to contact each other and find out exact news.

Saturday, 29 March 2003

Dear Diary,

My dad's friend Saad Al-Adamy and his wife and three children came to visit us. One of the children is only seven months old—just a baby. We tried to stop him being afraid of the noise from the bombs. We took him in our arms and comforted him. His sister Assal is twelve years old, but she is

Practice the Skills

4 **Reading Across Texts**

Internal and External Conflict Sometimes people struggle against forces outside of themselves. What outside forces do Baghdad residents face here? Think about what is preventing them from leading healthy, happy lives. Write your answer in your chart.

Vocabulary

rations (RASH unz) *n.* portions of needed items

from *Thura's Diary* **521**

just as scared. I don't want her to be afraid because the bombs are everywhere all the time. And it is getting worse. She is starting to understand that, and she is better than when I last spoke with her on the phone. Her older brother, Sayef, is sixteen and understands the whole situation. But they are still children. And it's difficult to take care of children during war. It's hard to control them at night, and during the day they like to go out; they like to play. Now they have to stay inside the house. They cannot play, they cannot see friends a lot—it's not easy. **5**

Just as every other day, the dust is everywhere. It's as if we didn't do any cleaning yesterday. But today there is more. I feel sorry for Aula and Mum—they are still sneezing. We didn't clean the whole house today, just the living room, kitchen and sitting room. Mum said we would have to wait to get rid of all of it.

Although I took my shower yesterday, I feel the dust all over me, on my hair, on my body. And because water is so precious, it's important that I only use a little amount of it, just to wash over myself to get off this dust. I would usually have a good bath, but not now. I use a quarter of the water I would normally use. Mum has difficulty washing the dishes. There are so many guests and visitors coming to our house and she hardly has any water to wash up after them.

How I wish all this dust would stop. It's getting boring, so boring. I just hope that it will stop soon.

Granny came. She was very worried about us after she heard from my aunt that we still hadn't left Baghdad. The troops are getting closer all the time. Granny's face was full of panic. She and my uncle Haydar came as fast as they could to see how we were. They couldn't call because the phones aren't working. She was relieved that she had come and that we hadn't been harmed.

Because they were here, and because there was no water at their house, they had a bath. Granny told us it was a very good thing that we had left her apartment because the **bombardment** there was very heavy and very frightening. The Al-Alwiya Maternity Hospital, where I was born, was damaged; it must have been terrifying for the mothers and

Practice the Skills

5 | **Reading Across Texts**

Internal and External Conflict Could fear be one of the forces the Iraqi children are struggling with? Does fear cause an external or internal conflict?

Vocabulary

bombardment (bom BARD mint) *n.* an attack

babies inside. In some way, somehow, it is quieter here.

Dad decided we should go and see my uncle Khalil who lives in our neighbourhood in an area called Al-Shamisiya, which is one of the oldest parts of Baghdad. Our families are very close. Uncle Khalil and his family have decided that they're not leaving their house under any circumstances, even though they're in an incredibly dangerous position, because a lot of weapons have been hidden in nearby palm groves.

Analyzing the Photo Smoke billows up in a Baghdad neighborhood. What conclusions can you draw from this photo about war's effect on a city?

My three cousins, Omar, Mounaf and Senan, are all teenagers but they were obviously terrified. Omar is older than me, and when I look at him I see a very strong man, but he and his brothers have in some way been affected by the storming bombardment near their house. Now, every time there is the slightest noise outside, they think it is a missile or a plane coming. The family all sleep in the dining room because it'll be the safest place if the windows get broken in an explosion. But Omar doesn't sleep, he lies awake waiting for the nightmare to begin; the coming of tons of missiles. But my uncle's not the sort to fuss about things like that, and he insists on sleeping in his own bedroom upstairs. The real problem is his wife, Afaaf; she gets into a complete panic if so much as a cockroach gets into the house. She was beside herself with worry[4] when the bombing started—because of the insects that might come into the house if the windows broke! Dad advised her to go to the shelter in her neighbours' basement, but her reply was hilarious. 'I can face the American missiles,' she said, 'but I couldn't sleep in that shelter if there was an insect in it.' **6**

Uncle Khalil told Dad that their elder brother Kadhim, who's seventy years old now, has decided not to leave his house, even though the rest of his family have all gone to

Practice the Skills

6 **Reading Across Texts**

Internal and External Conflict What conflict does Afaaf experience? Is it internal or external? Explain.

4. The phrase **beside herself with worry** is a figure of speech. Thura means that her aunt is anxious and distracted.

Syria. The problem is that his house is only a stone's throw away from some palaces belonging to Saddam's family and his half-brother Barzan. If Kadhim really does stay in his house it's sure to be the end of him; the palace complex has already come under attack, and it's bound to again. Kadhim refuses to go to the shelter under his house because he's convinced there won't be anyone to get him out if he does. So, instead, he's decided to take shelter in his garden, under a roofed area made out of concrete. 'If you don't find me, you'll know I've died over in that corner,' he said to my uncle. So far he's all right, thank God.

This evening we came back home again. Like my cousins, we were fed up with all the nationalistic[5] songs they keep repeating on Iraqi TV. The Iraqi army leaders only ever talk about their victories, but I don't believe a word of it—their propaganda's[6] just the same as it was during the first Gulf War, even though things are completely different now. This time it's a battle for the control of Iraq by the greatest power the world has ever known, with all the latest technology at its disposal. I keep wondering: *What will happen in the end?* ○ **7**

Practice the Skills

7 ◆**BIG** Question
What does Thura do when she doesn't know how to handle the problems she faces? How does she deal with the conflicts that define her life in Iraq? Write your answer on the *Thura's Diary* page of Foldable 4.

Analyzing the Photo Flanked by soldiers, a young Iraqi girl pauses in Baghdad. What does this photo tell you about her environment?

---

5. If something is *nationalistic*, it promotes a nation's independence and unity.
6. *Propaganda* is information, often false or one-sided, that is used to promote a cause.

Before You Read : Escaping

Meet the Author

Zdenko Slobodnik was born in communist Czechoslovakia. His family escaped to America when he was very young, and he wrote this account when he was eighteen. Slobodnik has a black belt in Tae Kwan Do. He also sings, acts, and plays guitar. He has dedicated his writing to his parents, for whose sacrifices he is very grateful.

Author Search For more about Zdenko Slobodnik, go to www.glencoe.com.

NY English Language Arts Core Curriculum (pp. 525–527)

R2e Recognize how the author's use of language creates images or feelings.
R2h Identify social and cultural contexts to enhance understanding and appreciation of text.

For a complete description of the standards, see p. NY 11.

Vocabulary Preview

perseverance (pur suh VEER ens) *n.* continuing steadily in some action **(p. 526)** *Perseverance is the key to success.*

glistened (GLIH sund) *v.* shone brightly; form of the verb *glisten* **(p. 527)** *The lights of the city glistened in the valley.*

indomitable (in DAH mih tuh bul) *adj.* unable to be conquered or overcome **(p. 527)** *Despite the harsh conditions, the refugees had indomitable hope.*

English Language Coach

Diction Writers choose their words carefully. Use the chart below to better understand the differences between formal and informal diction.

Formal: *Leaving Czechoslovakia at that point was very difficult, however.*
The writer's word choice tells readers that this is a serious subject.
Informal: *Getting out of there was tough, though.*
The casual diction doesn't effectively show that the writer is serious about the subject.

Get Ready to Read

Connect to the Reading

The family in this selection left home to make a new home in America. What does home mean to you? Is it a place, a group of people, or both?

Build Background

Zdenko Slobodnik was born in the former Czechoslovakia, a communist country in central Europe. Under communism, economic conditions were poor and people had few rights. In 1993 Czechoslovakia split into two countries: the Czech Republic and Slovakia. Today, citizens of the Czech Republic are governed by a parliamentary democracy.

Set Purpose for Reading

BIG Question Read to find out how one family triumphed over conflict to build a better life.

Set Your Own Purpose What else would you like to learn about the selection to help you answer the Big Question. Write your purpose on the Reading Across Texts page of Foldable 4.

ESCAPING

by Zdenko Slobodnik

Practice the Skills

I learned about **perseverance** when my parents decided that they wanted a better life for their children, their three-year-old son and their six-year-old daughter. We had been living in communist Czechoslovakia and were tired of the life we were living and the system.[1] At first they had doubts, as anyone might, but they would not let their children grow up as prisoners. ▌1

Leaving Czechoslovakia at that point was very difficult, however. They had to figure out a way to get to Austria, which was a free country. At first the plan was simple: They would claim I needed to see a doctor there for my ear infection. Their spirits were crushed when a border guard[2] gave their request a stern "No." As we approached a second border crossing, they hoped for a different response. However, as we sat in our car, the guard reached in, yanked out the keys and ordered my parents to turn themselves in to the police. ▌2

Feeling hopeless, they decided to take one last chance, which would be difficult. We would hike across the Alps[3] into Austria, leaving behind everything we could not carry.

---

1. The **system** refers to all the rules, punishments, and hardships connected to living under communist rule.
2. A **border guard** is a soldier who prevents people from illegally crossing a country's border.
3. The **Alps** is a large mountain range in Europe. It stretches through many countries, including Austria, Italy, France, and Germany.

Vocabulary

perseverance (pur suh VEER ens) *n.* continuing steadily in some action

1 Reading Across Texts

Internal and External Conflict What large external conflict do the Slobodniks face? Who or what stands between them and their happiness? Write your answer in your chart.

2 Reading Across Texts

Internal and External Conflict Sometimes people struggle against a general force, like nature or society. Sometimes they struggle against a specific person or situation. Is the Slobodniks' conflict general, specific, or both? Explain your answer in your chart.

It was extremely dangerous, and getting caught meant prison or even death. Yet we marched on because the freedom of America **glistened** in our souls. As my parents saw the sign welcoming us to Austria, they knew they had succeeded. **3**

Once in Austria, they found a refugee center[4] and then a hotel. We lived in this overcrowded, infested, dirty hotel for over a year. They often wondered if they had made the right decision leaving their homeland. However, once their time came to go to America and begin new, free lives, their question was answered. **4**

Even in America, life was very hard at first. We lived in slums in Boston where my parents had to fight with the landlord to give us heat, and waking up every day was a hard realization. My parents' perseverance was strong, though, and within a few years my father had gained recertification[5] of his medical degree and my mother, foreign accent and all, finished first in her dental-assistant school.

Perseverance is a valuable law of life, imperative to reaching one's dreams. My parents had little when we lived under Communism, yet they were willing to live with nothing. Realizing that I cannot fully appreciate my parents' perseverance and **indomitable** spirit that brought us here, I remain thankful for the chance to live a wonderful life, in which I had boundless opportunities. In my parents' case, "Perseverance [made] the difference between success and defeat," and I am glad it did. **5** ○

Practice the Skills

3 | **English Language Coach**

Diction How does diction help you understand and connect to the Slobodniks' struggle?

4 | **Reading Across Texts**

Internal and External Conflict What internal conflicts might the Slobodniks have faced about leaving their homeland? Think about the life they left behind, and the risks they took to reach their goal.

5 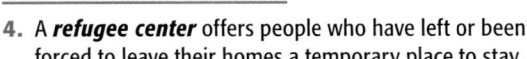 **BIG Question**

After two failed attempts to leave Czechoslovakia, the Slobodniks probably felt like they didn't know what to do. What did they do then? What would you have done? Write your answer on the "Escaping" page of Foldable 4. Your response will help you complete the Unit Challenge later.

---

4. A **refugee center** offers people who have left or been forced to leave their homes a temporary place to stay.

5. Although the writer's father was a doctor in Czechoslovakia, he had to pass tests, or gain **recertification,** in the United States before he could work as a doctor here.

Vocabulary

glistened (GLIH sund) *v.* shone brightly

indomitable (in DAH mih tuh bul) *adj.* unable to be conquered or overcome

Analyzing the Photo This sign, posted on the Austria–Czechoslovakia border, points the way for the refugees. What part of the writer's life does this image represent?

After You Read

from
Thura's Diary
by Thura Al-Windawi

& ESCAPING
by Zdenko Slobodnik

Vocabulary Check

Copy the sentences below. If the boldfaced vocabulary word is used correctly, write *correct* next to the sentence. If not, rewrite the sentence to show the boldfaced word's true meaning.

Thura's Diary

extinguished   rations   bombardment

1. Lighting a match, Andre **extinguished** the flame.
2. When camping, people often take **rations** of food and water.
3. During the **bombardment,** the neighborhood was still and quiet.

ESCAPING

perseverance   glistened   indomitable

4. The wet pavement **glistened** in the streetlight.
5. Because it was **indomitable,** Hector's spirit had broken.
6. The runners showed true **perseverance** when they quit the race early.
7. **English Language Coach** Rewrite the sentence below using informal diction.

   Realizing that I cannot fully appreciate my parents' perseverance, I remain thankful for the chance to live a wonderful life.

NY English Language Arts Core Curriculum (pp. 528–529)

R1j Compare and contrast information from a variety of different sources.
R2b Interpret characters, plot, setting, and theme using evidence from the text.
W1g Connect, compare, and contrast ideas and information from one or more sources.

For a complete description of the standards, see p. NY 11.

Reading/Critical Thinking

On a separate sheet of paper, answer the following questions. Read the tips to find the information that you need.

Thura's Diary

8. **BIG Question** What does Thura do when she doesn't know what to do? How does she express her thoughts and feelings?

9. **Recall** What physical problems do Thura's mother and sister, Aula, deal with, and why?

    Tip Think and Search

10. **Analyze** Who or what are Thura and her family mainly in conflict with? Explain.

    Tip Author and Me

ESCAPING

11. **BIG Question** Despite the obstacles in their path, the Slobodniks made it to the United States. What did they do when they didn't know what to do? What does Zdenko believe is necessary for success?

    Tip Right There

12. **Recall** How did the Slobodniks finally escape Czechoslovakia?

    Tip Right There

13. **Summarize** In one sentence, summarize Zdenko's message to others whose goals seem impossible to reach.

    Tip Author and Me

Writing: Reading Across Texts

Use Your Notes

14. Follow these steps to compare internal and external conflict in *Thura's Diary* and "Escaping."

    Step 1: Look at the notes in the charts you just completed. Circle the external conflicts shared by people in both selections.

Step 2: Did the people in both selections experience similar internal struggles? If so, underline those conflicts in your charts.

Step 3: Now think about the differences between the selections. In your Learner's Notebook, list three differences between the external conflicts faced by the families in both selections. For help, use the notes in your charts.

Step 4: Finally, think about the differences between internal conflicts in the selections you read. No two people's thoughts are ever *exactly* alike—so how were Thura's internal conflicts different from Zdenko's parents' internal conflicts? *Hint: The selections are told from different points of view. Do you know as much about the Slobodniks' inner thoughts as you do about Thura's? If not, why might this be?*

Get It on Paper

To show that you understand conflict in *Thura's Diary* and "Escaping," copy the following statements in your Learner's Notebook. Leave yourself plenty of room to write. Complete the statements with your own thoughts.

15. Thura's largest external conflict is with ____.

16. This conflict results in the following internal conflict(s): ____.

17. These conflicts are resolved/are not resolved/are resolved in part (circle one).

18. The Slobodnik family's largest external conflict is with ____.

19. This conflict results in the following internal conflict(s): ____.

20. These conflicts are resolved/are not resolved/are resolved in part (circle one).

21. Seeking ____, both families experienced ____.

BIG Question

22. In both selections, ordinary people take extraordinary risks in order to survive. How far would *you* go to reach a goal? What would you do if you didn't know what else to do?

Answering The BIG Question

What Do You Do When You Don't Know What to Do?

You've just read several selections and you have thought about what to do when you don't know what to do. Now use what you've learned to complete the Unit Challenge.

The Unit Challenge

Choose Activity A or Activity B and follow the directions for that activity.

A. Group Activity: Advice Column

Sometimes when you don't know what to do you could use a little advice to help point you in the right direction. Your group has been chosen to write an advice column called "What to Do When You Don't Know What to Do."

1. Discuss the Assignment

- Choose one group member to be the note-taker for the discussion.

- Review any notes that you wrote in your Learner's Notebook and your Foldable for the selections you read in the unit.

- Discuss some of the decisions that characters or speakers in the selections made. For example, the speaker in the poem "The Road Less Traveled" decided to take a path that differed from other people's paths. The speaker in the poem "Wishing Well" decides to wait to see if her wish will come true.

2. Ask for Advice

- Advice columnists need something to give advice about. So you and the members of your group will write letters seeking advice.

- You can write about a real or an imaginary problem that you just can't decide how to solve. Sign your letter with an amusing name, such as "Confused in Columbus."

- When each member is done writing, put the letters in a box or a bag.

3. Give Advice

- Have each member draw a letter from the box to answer.

- Imagine you are writing the answer to the problem as one of the speakers or characters from a selection you read. Write your advice from the perspective of that speaker or character.

4. Share the Letters When you're done, read aloud the letter asking for advice and your "character's" or "speaker's" response. Select the best ones, and consider publishing them in a school newspaper or newsletter.

B. Solo Activity: Award for Best Supporting Role

In life, it's usually the main character that gets all the glory. Now is your chance to change all that by honoring someone in the best supporting role. Follow these steps to create your award.

1. Create a List of Nominees

- List characters or speakers from the selections who played an important supporting role in helping someone solve a problem. Use the notes from your Foldables to help you.
- Add to the list the name of someone you know who has helped other people.
- Beside each name, jot down a few notes about the problem he or she helped solve. Now review your list, and choose the person or character you wish to honor.

2. Designing Your Award
Design and create your award. Here are some suggestions:

- Research award designs on the Internet or make up your own.
- Include a photo, drawing, or painting of the honoree.
- Get the correct spelling of the person's name.
- Write the text that will appear on the award, such as:

> _____
> *is hereby honored with the*
> _____ *Award*
> *for his/her supporting role*
> *in helping* _____
> *solve* _____ *problem.*

- Choose an unusual font or add a border to make your award look special.

3. Call the Press!
No award is complete without a press release, or announcement to the public.

- In your release include a headline at the top telling the name of the award and the person receiving it. Be sure to include the date and a person to contact for more information (you).
- Include a brief paragraph explaining the meaning or significance of the award and the reason why this person is receiving it.

4. And the Winner Is . . . .
Roll out the red carpet. It's Award Time. You've got a few options here:

- If your award is going to a fictional character, consider getting a friend to play that role. You play the presenter, and you can interview the winner right after you present the award.
- If your award is going to a real person, consider inviting him or her to the classroom to accept your award. Do everything to make the person feel comfortable and honored.
- If you don't care to make a big scene, simply post your press release and award side-by-side in your classroom. You may wish to read them aloud to the class.

Literature Online

BIG Question Link to Web resources to further explore the Big Question at www.glencoe.com.

Your Turn: Read and Apply Skills

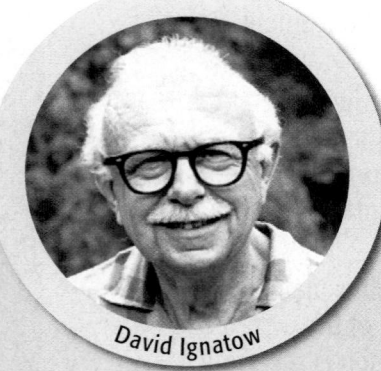

David Ignatow

Meet the Author

David Ignatow is remembered as a poet who wrote popular verse about the common man and the issues that all people encounter in daily life. Before becoming a writer, Ignatow worked as a butcher, a hospital admitting-clerk, and a paper salesman. It was only later in his career that he received acclaim for his writing. Ignatow once said that he admired poetry "where you can feel the mind running like an electrical current through the muscles." See page R3 of the Author Files for more information about Ignatow.

Literature Online

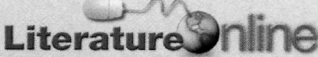

Author Search For more about David Ignatow, go to www.glencoe.com.

Analyzing the Photo How does this image represent the poem's message?

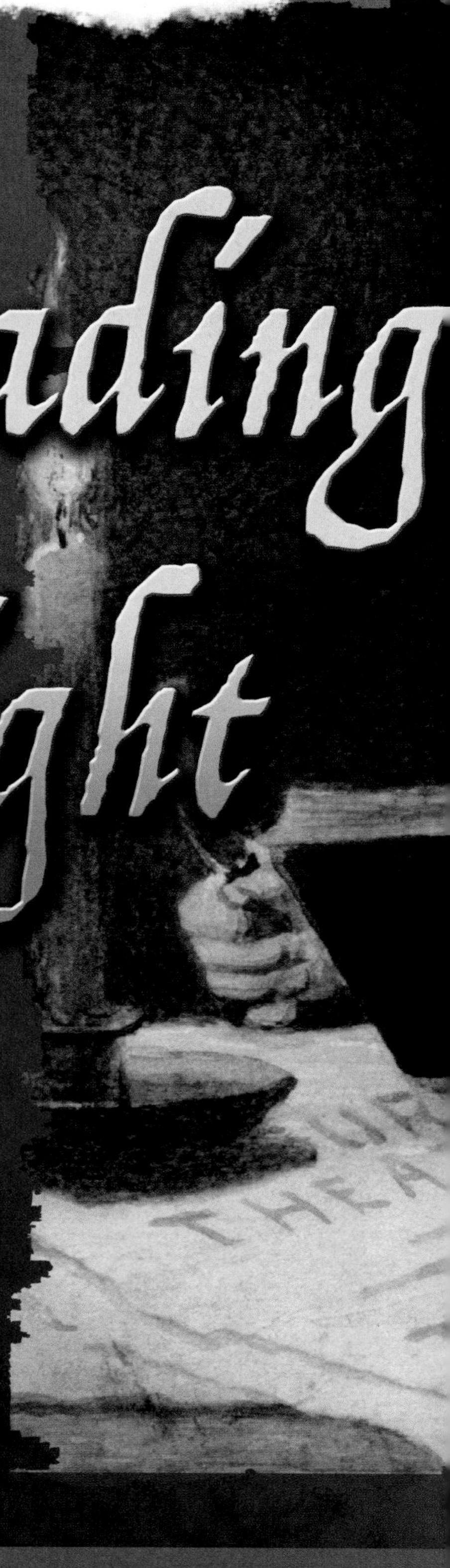

from Reading at Night

by David Ignatow

The Ghost Story. Frederick Smallfield
(1829-1915). Watercolor.

What have I learned that can keep me
from the simple fact of my dying?
None of the ideas I read stay
with me for long, I find the dark
closed in about me as I close
the book and I hurry to open it
again to let its light shine
on my face.

Reading on Your Own

To read more about the Big Question, choose one of these books from your school or local library. Work on your reading skills by choosing books that are challenging to you.

Fiction

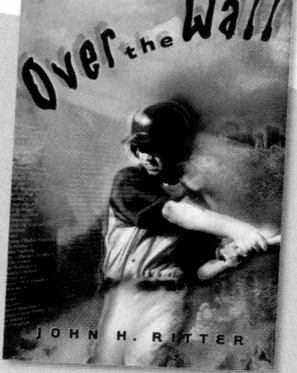

Over the Wall
by John H. Ritter

Thirteen-year-old Tyler is spending the summer with his aunt, uncle, and cousins in New York. This time away from his father, who has serious problems of his own, gives Tyler a chance to deal with his explosive temper and to begin to understand his family's past.

The Art of Keeping Cool
by Janet Taylor Lisle

During World War II, thirteen-year-old Robert discovers family secrets and his community's wartime fears. Themes of prejudice and loss emerge as Robert, his cousin, and their artist friend discover how destructive even a faraway war can be.

The Princess of Pop
by Cathy Hopkins

Squidge dares her friend Becca to enter the Prince and Princess of Pop competition, an *American Idol* type contest. Accepting the challenge forces Becca to face her fear of failure. The tension grows as she advances in the competition and struggles to find her true self.

Chu Ju's House
By Gloria Whelan

In China, where fourteen-year-old Chu Ju lives with her parents in a small village, families are allowed only two children, and girls are often considered inferior. When Chu Ju's mother gives birth to a second daughter, the parents decide to put the baby up for adoption so that they can try again to have a boy. To save her sister from this fate, Chu Ju decides to run away so that her family will have only one daughter.

534 UNIT 4 What Do You Do When You Don't Know What to Do?

(tl)Eclipse Studio, (bl)Eclipse Studio, (tr)Eclipse Studio, (br)Eclipse Studio

Nonfiction

Chinese Cinderella
by Adeline Yen Mah

Adeline Yen Mah's autobiography, like the fairy-tale Cinderella, tells of a childhood dominated by a cruel stepmother. It is only when she wins a writing contest that her father finally notices Yen Mah and grants her wish to attend college. The book includes the legend of the original Chinese Cinderella.

Teens with the Courage to Give: Young People Who Triumphed Over Tragedy and Volunteered to Make a Difference
by Jackie Waldman

This book profiles thirty young people who overcame great personal odds to reach out and help others. With their stories, these teens take us to the depths of their struggles and the heights of their newfound sense of purpose and peace.

The 7 Habits of Highly Effective Teens
by Sean Covey

Here is a collection of stories about real teens from all over the world who have overcome obstacles to succeed. Covey includes cartoons, quotes, clever ideas, and step-by-step guides to help readers reach their full potential.

Remember: The Journey to School Integration
by Toni Morrison

This powerful blend of photography and narrative tells about the fight of African Americans for integrated schooling. Packed with facts and photos, Morrison's book is also a tribute to those who risked, and lost, so that others could enjoy a more equal society. Read to learn more about those individuals—and about the courage and conviction that won the fight for integration.

New York English Language Arts Test Practice

*D*irections

Read this poem about a traveler's journey through the woods on a tranquil winter evening. Then answer questions 1 through 7.

"Stopping by Woods on a Snowy Evening"
By Robert Frost

Whose woods these are I think I know.
His house is in the village though;
He will not see me stopping here
To watch his woods fill up with snow.

My little horse must think it queer
To stop without a farmhouse near
Between the woods and frozen lake
The darkest evening of the year.

He gives his harness bells a shake
To ask if there is some mistake.
The only other sound's the sweep
Of easy wind and downy flake.

The woods are lovely, dark and deep,
But I have promises to keep,
And miles to go before I sleep,
And miles to go before I sleep.

---

1 Read these lines from the first stanza of the poem.

> **Whose woods these are I think I know.**
> **His house is in the village though;**
> **He will not see me stopping here**
> **To watch his woods fill up with snow.**

Which rhyme scheme is reflected by these lines?

A a-a-b-b

B a-b-a-b

C a-a-b-a

D a-b-a-a

2 Which of these words best describes how the horse feels about stopping?

F angry

G bored

H sad

J confused

3 Read these lines from the third stanza of the poem.

> **The only other sound's the sweep**
> **Of easy wind and downy flake.**

In these lines, which technique does the poet use to create a sensory image of the sound of the snow?

A repetition of the soft sound of "s"

B metaphor of a broom sweeping the snow

C personification of the wind blowing the snow

D visual imagery

4 Which word best describes the mood the poet has created in the poem?

F thoughtful

G suspenseful

H cheerful

J sorrowful

5 When the speaker looks at the woods, which of these best describes how he probably feels?

A He is tempted to remain in the woods.

B He feels the woods are frightening.

C He would like to see the woods during the day.

D He would like to paint a picture of the woods.

6 Read these lines from the last stanza of the poem.

**But I have promises to keep,
And miles to go before I sleep,
And miles to go before I sleep.**

Which of these most likely describes what the poet means in these lines?

F I have an appointment in town that I have to be on time for.

G I have responsibilities to take care of before I die.

H I promised to be home soon, and I'm still a long way off.

J I promised to care for my horse, and he's getting cold.

7 Robert Frost thought carefully about which details to leave in or out of "Stopping by Woods on a Snowy Evening." Copy the graphic organizer below. In each empty box, list two details from the poem that support the statement in the left column. If the statement is not supported in the poem, leave the box empty.

Statements	Evidence from the Poem
It is the middle of winter.	
The owner of the woods and the speaker don't get along.	
The speaker is attracted to the stark beauty and solitude of the woods.	

Directions

Read this poem about the thoughts of a child who is about to turn ten years old. Then answer questions 8 through 12.

"On Turning Ten"
By Billy Collins

The whole idea of it makes me feel
like I'm coming down with something,
something worse than a stomach ache
or the headaches I get from reading in bad light—
a kind of measles of the spirit,
a mumps of the psyche,
a disfiguring chicken pox of the soul.

You tell me it is too early to be looking back,
but that is because you have forgotten
the perfect simplicity of being one
and the beautiful complexity introduced by two.
But I can lie on my bed and remember every digit.
At four I was an Arabian wizard.
I could make myself invisible
by drinking a glass of milk a certain way.
At seven I was a soldier, at nine a prince.

But now I am mostly at the window
watching the late afternoon light.
Back then it never fell so solemnly
against the side of my tree house,
and my bicycle never leaned against the garage
as it does today,
all the dark blue speed drained out of it.

This is the beginning of sadness, I say to myself,
as I walk through the universe in my sneakers.
It is time to say good-bye to my imaginary friends,
time to turn the first big number.

It seems only yesterday I used to believe
there was nothing under my skin but light.
If you cut me I could shine.
But now when I fall upon the sidewalk of life,
I skin my knees. I bleed.

8 Which word **best** describes how the child feels about turning "the first big number"?

A excited

B anxious

C angry

D depressed

9 Read these lines from the poem.

> The whole idea of it makes me feel
> like I'm coming down with
>   something,
> something worse than a stomach
>   ache
> a kind of measles of the spirit,
> a mumps of the psyche,
> a disfiguring chicken pox of the
>   soul.

In these lines, the poet uses a recurring metaphor to express the speaker's feelings about leaving childhood. Which of these expressions most closely matches the meaning of this metaphor?

F down and out

G a babe in the woods

H sick at heart

J caught in a sinking ship

10 Read these lines from the poem.

> At four I was an Arabian wizard.
> I could make myself invisible
> by drinking a glass of milk a certain
>   way.

Based on these lines, a reader can infer that the speaker

A had traveled to other lands

B wanted to be a magician

C had heard tales of fantasy

D wanted to hide from others

11 The speaker in the poem believes that childhood is a period of

F imagination

G illness

H fear

J reality

12 Read these lines from the end of the poem.

> It seems only yesterday I used to
>   believe
> there was nothing under my skin
>   but light.
> If you cut me I could shine.
> But now when I fall upon the
>   sidewalk of life,
> I skin my knees. I bleed.

In these lines, how does the speaker view "the sidewalk of life" before and after age ten? Use details expressed through the images in these lines to support your answer.

Directions

Read this poem about a young prairie girl's relationship with a schoolmate. Then answer questions 13 through 17.

"The Difference"
By Laura Ingalls

My neighbor and I
Can never agree
Kind reader be judge
Between her and me.

I go to the school
Which she attends
In which I have "chums"
And she has "friends."

She works "difficult problems"
While I do "hard sums"
She says it "continues"
While I say it "runs."

She thinks things are self-evident
That I think are true
I say it is "boss"
She says "too-too"

But this is the strangest of all
You will own
And shows quite a difference
When taken alone

That she bangs her hair
While I bang my head
She "retires for the night"
While I "go to bed."

> **boss** = slang for excellent, first-rate

13 Based on information in the poem, the reader can infer that the speaker's neighbor is

    A friendlier than the speaker

    B more formal than the speaker

    C not as smart as the speaker

    D meaner than the speaker

14 Which word **best** describes the speaker of the poem?

    F chummy

    G agreeable

    H bossy

    J too-too

15 Read these lines from the poem.

> **She "retires for the night"**
> **While I "go to bed."**

In these lines, the speaker is **most likely** expressing

    A hostility

    B affection

    C anxiety

    D annoyance

16 Which word **best** characterizes the tone of the poem?

    F kidding

    G angry

    H serious

    J ironic

17 Read these lines from the poem.

> **My neighbor and I**
> **Can never agree**
> **Kind reader be judge**
> **Between her and me.**

You be the judge about the difference between the speaker and her neighbor. Explain how they are different. Use details from the poem to support your answer.

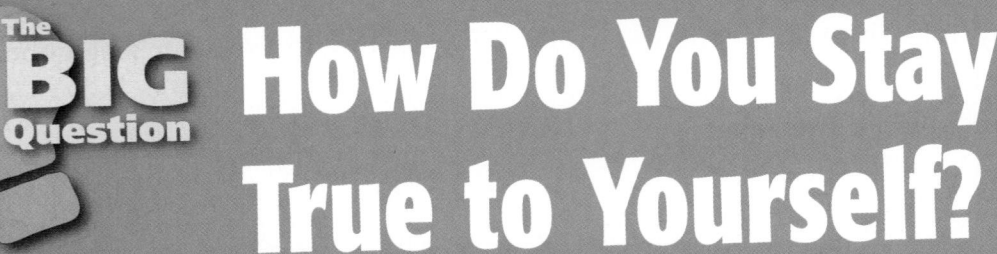

The **BIG** Question

How Do You Stay True to Yourself?

> "Be who you are and say what you feel, because those who mind don't matter, and those who matter don't mind."
>
> —Dr. Seuss
> pen name of Theodor Geisel (1904–1991), author of *The Cat in the Hat*

LOOKING AHEAD

The skill lessons and readings in this unit will help you develop your own answer to the Big Question.

UNIT 5 WRAP-UP • Answering the Big Question

Connecting to The BIG Question
How Do You Stay True to Yourself?

To be true to yourself, you have to be true to your own values and beliefs. They affect what you do. Sometimes it's hard to figure out what you should do, but as you gain more experience, strong beliefs and values can help you make good choices. In this unit you'll explore how to stay true to yourself and to your values.

Real Kids and the Big Question

RASHAD was walking home from school when he found a wallet. He wants to return the wallet to the person who owns it, but his friends are trying to talk him into keeping the money. Rashad could use the money, but he doesn't feel it's right to keep it. What should Rashad do to be true to himself?

SARA has been invited to James's party. She finds out later that James's parents won't be home during the get-together. She wants to go, but she knows that her parents won't approve. What should Sara do to stay true to herself?

Warm-Up Activity
With a partner, make a list of different ways Rashad and Sara can solve their problems. Decide on a solution that best helps Rashad and Sara stay true to themselves.

You and the Big Question

Reading about how other people stayed true to themselves will help you work out your own answer to the Big Question.

Literature Online

BIG Question

Link to Web resources to further explore the Big Question at www.glencoe.com.

Plan for the Unit Challenge

At the end of the unit, you'll use notes from all your reading to complete the Unit Challenge.

You'll choose one of the following activities:

A. Videotape a Soap Opera With a group you will role-play ways a teen can be true to herself, her friends, and her parents.

B. Values Chart Make a chart for help in ranking your own values.

- As you read the selections, think about the problems faced by the characters and people you read about. How did the problems challenge the people? How did they manage to stay true to themselves?

- In your Learner's Notebook, you'll write down what the characters and people did to stay true to themselves.

- You'll also comment on whether the people solved their problem, learned to live with it, or handled it in some other way.

Keep Track of Your Ideas

FOLDABLES™
Study Organizer

As you read, you'll make notes about the Big Question. Later you'll use these notes to complete the Unit Challenge. See pages R8–R9 for help with making Foldable 5. The diagram below shows how it should look.

1. Use this Foldable for all the selections in this unit. On the front cover, write the unit number and the Big Question.

2. Turn the page. Across the top, write the selection title. To the left of the crease, write **My Purpose for Reading.** To the right of the crease, write **The Big Question.**

3. Repeat step 2 until you have all the titles in your Foldable. (See page 543 for the titles.)

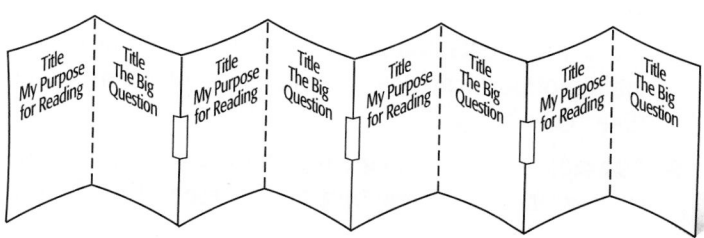

A **short story** is a brief fictional, or made-up, narrative about people, places, and events. Unlike a **novel,** or book-length story, a short story usually focuses on one incident and its effects on one or a few characters.

Why Read Short Stories?

Short stories are entertaining. Some stories make you laugh, and others stretch your imagination. Stories make you think about the challenges people face and ways that people stay true to themselves. When you read short stories, you'll not only enjoy yourself but also discover things like these:

- how characters deal with problems similar to yours
- how characters find ways to stay true to themselves

How to Read Short Stories

Key Reading Skills

These reading skills are especially useful tools for reading and understanding short stories. You'll see these skills modeled in the Active Reading Model on pages 547–557, and you'll learn more about them later in this unit.

- **Analyzing** Looking at the separate parts of a selection to discover how they work together to express ideas. (See Reading Workshop 1.)
- **Questioning** Asking yourself 5 Ws and an H questions about the plot, characters, setting, and the point of view of a story to make sure you understand it. (See Reading Workshop 2.)
- **Predicting** Making educated guesses about the characters and events in a story as you learn more about them. (See Reading Workshop 3.)
- **Making Inferences** Using clues and "reading between the lines" to figure out ideas that an author has not directly stated. (See Reading Workshop 4.)

Key Literary Elements

Recognizing and thinking about the following literary elements will help you understand more fully what the writer is telling you.

- **Characterization:** methods authors use to show what characters are like, such as describing what they think and do (See "Cream Puff.")
- **Plot:** the events in a story and the order in which they are arranged; main plot parts include exposition, rising action, climax, and falling action. (See "One Throw.")
- **Theme:** the lesson in life the characters learn through experience, such as "honesty is the best policy" (See "The Medicine Bag.")
- **Setting:** the time and place in which the events in a story happen, including the culture of that time and place (See "The Fire Pond.")

Skills Focus

- Key skills for reading short stories
- Key literary elements of short stories

Skills Model

You will see how to use the key reading skills and literary elements as you read

- **"Born Worker,"** p. 547

NY English Language Arts Core Curriculum (pp. 546–557)

LC R13 Use text structure and literary devices to aid comprehension and response. **LC R12** Combine multiple strategies (question, predict/confirm) to enhance comprehension and response. **R2b** Interpret characters, plot, setting, and theme, using evidence from the text.

For a complete description of the standards, see p. NY11.

The notes in the side columns model how to use the reading skills and literary elements you read about on page 546.

Short Story

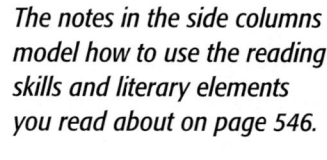

BORN WORKER

by Gary Soto

They said that José was born with a ring of dirt around his neck, with grime under his fingernails, and skin calloused from the grainy twist of a shovel. They said his palms were already rough by the time he was three, and soon after he learned his primary colors, his squint was the squint of an aged laborer. They said he was a born worker. By seven he was drinking coffee slowly, his mouth pursed the way his mother sipped. He wore jeans, a shirt with sleeves rolled to his elbows. His eye could measure a length of board, and his knees genuflected[1] over flower beds and leafy gutters.

They said lots of things about José, but almost nothing of his parents. His mother stitched at a machine all day, and his father, with a steady job at the telephone company, climbed splintered, sun-sucked poles, fixed wires and looked around the city at tree level. **1**

"What do you see up there?" José once asked his father. "Work," he answered. "I see years of work, *mi'jo*."[2] **2**

José took this as a truth, and though he did well in school, he felt destined to labor. His arms would pump, his legs would bend, his arms would carry a world of earth. He believed in hard work, believed that his strength was as ancient as a rock's. **2**

---

1. To **genuflect** is to kneel respectfully, as in church.
2. The contraction **mi'jo** stands for the Spanish phrase *mi hijo,* which means "my son."

1 Key Reading Skill
Making Inferences *The author doesn't say it straight out, but I can guess that "they" are the people in the community. From my own experience in life I can also guess that they approve of Jose.*

2 Key Literary Element
Characterization *Early in the story I learned that José is a hard worker and acts grown-up for his age. I learned these things about José from the narrator.*

"Life is hard," his father repeated from the time José could first make out the meaning of words until he was stroking his fingers against the grain of his sandpaper beard.

His mother was an example to José. She would raise her hands, showing her fingers pierced from the sewing machines. She bled on her machine, bled because there was money to make, a child to raise, and a roof to stay under.

Analyzing the Photo Which character in the story might this woman be? Why do you say so?

One day when José returned home from junior high, his cousin Arnie was sitting on the lawn sucking on a stalk of grass. José knew that grass didn't come from his lawn. His was cut and pampered, clean.

"José!" Arnie shouted as he took off the earphones of his CD Walkman.

"Hi, Arnie," José said without much enthusiasm. He didn't like his cousin. He thought he was lazy and, worse, spoiled by the trappings[3] of being middle class. His parents had good jobs in offices and showered him with clothes, shoes, CDs, vacations, almost anything he wanted. Arnie's family had never climbed a telephone pole to size up the future. **3**

Arnie rose to his feet, and José saw that his cousin was wearing a new pair of high-tops. He didn't say anything.

"Got an idea," Arnie said cheerfully. "Something that'll make us money."

José looked at his cousin, not a muscle of curiosity twitching in his face.

Still, Arnie explained that since he himself was so clever with words, and his best cousin in the whole world was good at working with his hands, that maybe they might start a company. **4**

"What would you do?" José asked.

---

3. The ***trappings*** of middle class are the things Arnie's family owns that show they have a comfortable life.

ACTIVE READING MODEL

3 Key Literary Element
Plot *During this first part of the plot, I learned about the setting, the characters, and possible conflicts. I can tell there might be a conflict between José and Arnie, because their lifestyles and values are so different.*

4 Key Reading Skill
Predicting *Arnie is a fast talker. He could create a problem for José if they go into business together.*

"Me?" he said brightly. "Shoot, I'll round up all kinds of jobs for you. You won't have to do anything." He stopped, then started again. "Except—you know—do the work."

"Get out of here," José said.

"Don't be that way," Arnie begged. "Let me tell you how it works."

The boys went inside the house, and while José stripped off his school clothes and put on his jeans and a T-shirt, Arnie told him that they could be rich.

"You ever hear of this guy named Bechtel?"[4] Arnie asked.

José shook his head.

"Man, he started just like us," Arnie said. "He started digging ditches and stuff, and the next thing you knew, he was sitting by his own swimming pool. You want to sit by your own pool, don't you?" Arnie smiled, waiting for José to speak up. **5**

"Never heard of this guy Bechtel," José said after he rolled on two huge socks, worn at the heels. He opened up his chest of drawers and brought out a packet of Kleenex.

Arnie looked at the Kleenex.

"How come you don't use your sleeve?" Arnie joked.

José thought for a moment and said, "I'm not like you." He smiled at his retort.

"Listen, I'll find the work, and then we can split it fifty-fifty."

José knew fifty-fifty was a bad deal.

"How about sixty-forty?" Arnie suggested when he could see that José wasn't going for it. "I know a lot of people from my dad's job. They're waiting for us."

José sat on the edge of his bed and started to lace up his boots. He knew that there were agencies that would find you work, agencies that took a portion of your pay. They're cheats, he thought, people who sit in air-conditioned offices while others work.

"You really know a lot of people?" José asked.

"Boatloads," Arnie said. "My dad works with this millionaire—honest—who cooks a steak for his dog every day."

5 Key Literary Element
Characterization *I can tell what Arnie is like by thinking about what he says. From what he says here, Arnie is the kind of guy who wants to make a lot of money without working hard for it.*

---

4. **Bechtel** is probably Stephen D. Bechtel (1900–1989), who was president of a large and famous construction and engineering company.

He's a liar, José thought. No matter how he tried, he couldn't picture a dog grubbing[5] on steak. The world was too poor for that kind of silliness.

"Listen, I'll go eighty-twenty," José said.

"Aw, man," Arnie whined. "That ain't fair."

José laughed.

"I mean, half the work is finding the jobs," Arnie explained, his palms up as he begged José to be reasonable.

José knew this was true. He had had to go door-to-door, and he disliked asking for work. He assumed that it should automatically be his since he was a good worker, honest, and always on time. 6

"Where did you get this idea, anyhow?" José asked.

"I got a business mind," Arnie said proudly.

"Just like that Bechtel guy," José retorted.

"That's right."

José agreed to a seventy-thirty split, with the condition that Arnie had to help out. Arnie hollered, arguing that some people were meant to work and others to come up with brilliant ideas. He was one of the latter. Still, he agreed after José said it was that or nothing.

In the next two weeks, Arnie found an array of jobs. José peeled off shingles from a rickety garage roof, carried rocks down a path to where a pond would go, and spray-painted lawn furniture. And while Arnie accompanied him, most of the time he did nothing. He did help occasionally. He did shake the cans of spray paint and kick aside debris so that José didn't trip while going down the path carrying the rocks. He did stack the piles of shingles, but almost cried when a nail bit his thumb. But mostly he told José what he had missed or where the work could be improved. José was bothered because he and his work had never been criticized before.

But soon José learned to ignore his cousin, ignore his comments about his spray painting, or about the way he lugged rocks, two in each arm. He didn't say anything, either, when they got paid and Arnie rubbed his hands like a fly, muttering, "It's payday."

6 **Key Reading Skill**
Making Inferences *José doesn't like the way Arnie is trying to take advantage of him. But he knows that Arnie will save him the trouble of finding jobs, a kind of work he does not like to do.*

Analyzing the Photo Which characters do these people remind you of? Why?

---

5. *Grub* is slang for food, so **grubbing** is eating.

Then Arnie found a job scrubbing a drained swimming pool. The two boys met early at José's house. Arnie brought his bike. José's own bike had a flat that grinned like a clown's face.

"I'll pedal," José suggested when Arnie said that he didn't have much leg strength. **7**

With Arnie on the handlebars, José tore off, his pedaling so strong that tears of fear formed in Arnie's eyes.

"Slow down!" Arnie cried.

José ignored him and within minutes they were riding the bike up a gravel driveway. Arnie hopped off at first chance.

"You're scary," Arnie said, picking a gnat from his eye. José chuckled. **8**

When Arnie knocked on the door, an old man still in pajamas appeared in the window. He motioned for the boys to come around to the back.

"Let me do the talking," Arnie suggested to his cousin. "He knows my dad real good. They're like this." He pressed two fingers together.

José didn't bother to say OK. He walked the bike into the backyard, which was lush with plants—roses in their last bloom, geraniums, hydrangeas, pansies with their skirts of bright colors. José could make out the splash of a fountain. Then he heard the hysterical yapping of a poodle. From all his noise, a person might have thought the dog was on fire. **9**

"Hi, Mr. Clemens," Arnie said, extending his hand. "I'm Arnie Sanchez. It's nice to see you again."

José had never seen a kid actually greet someone like this. Mr. Clemens said, hiking up his pajama bottoms, "I only wanted one kid to work."

"Oh," Arnie stuttered. "Actually, my cousin José really does the work and I kind of, you know, supervise."

Mr. Clemens pinched up his wrinkled face. He seemed not to understand. He took out a pea-sized hearing aid, fiddled with its tiny dial, and fit it into his ear, which was surrounded with wiry gray hair.

"I'm only paying for one boy," Mr. Clemens shouted. His poodle click-clicked and stood behind his legs. The dog bared its small crooked teeth.

7 Key Reading Skill
Analyzing It's just like Arnie to say something to get out of doing the hard work of pedaling. That fits in with his other comments and actions. You can tell that he believes he shouldn't have to work hard.

8 Key Reading Skill
Making Inferences José rides fast because he's disgusted with Arnie for pretending that his legs don't have much strength. José laughs because he got back at Arnie.

9 Key Literary Element
Setting This part of the story is set at a home where the family is well off. You can tell because the back yard is "lush with plants" and has a fountain. Also, the owner of the house has a poodle. Poodles are sometimes seen as dogs for rich people.

"That's right," Arnie said, smiling a strained smile. "We know that you're going to compensate[6] only one of us." **10**

Mr. Clemens muttered under his breath. He combed his hair with his fingers. He showed José the pool, which was shaped as round as an elephant. It was filthy with grime. Near the bottom some grayish water shimmered and leaves floated as limp as cornflakes.

"It's got to be real clean," Mr. Clemens said, "or it's not worth it."

"Oh, José's a great worker," Arnie said. He patted his cousin's shoulders and said that he could lift a mule.

Mr. Clemens sized up José and squeezed his shoulders, too.

"How do I know you, anyhow?" Mr. Clemens asked Arnie, who was aiming a smile at the poodle.

"You know my dad," Arnie answered, raising his smile to the old man. "He works at Interstate Insurance. You and he had some business deals."

Mr. Clemens thought for a moment, a hand on his mouth, head shaking. He could have been thinking about the meaning of life, his face was so dark.

"Mexican fella?" he inquired.

"That's him," Arnie said happily.

José felt like hitting his cousin for his cheerful attitude. **11** Instead, he walked over and picked up the white plastic bottle of bleach. Next to it were a wire brush, a pumice stone, and some rags. He set down the bottle and, like a surgeon, put on a pair of rubber gloves.

"You know what you're doing, boy?" Mr. Clemens asked.

José nodded as he walked into the pool. If it had been filled with water, his chest would have been wet. The new hair on his chest would have been floating like the legs of a jellyfish.

Analyzing the Photo What does this photograph of an empty pool suggest about the job José has to do?

ACTIVE READING MODEL

10 **Key Reading Skill**
Predicting *Arnie probably won't help José clean the pool. Arnie is very lazy, and all he does is talk. I'll keep reading to see if my prediction is right.*

11 **Key Reading Skill**
Questioning *Why is José so annoyed with Arnie's cheerful attitude? Maybe José thinks Arnie should be upset about Mr. Clemens's identifying Arnie's father as a "Mexican fella."*

---

6. To **compensate** is to pay someone for his or her work.

"Oh, yeah," Arnie chimed, speaking for his cousin. "José was born to work."

José would have drowned his cousin if there had been more water. Instead, he poured a bleach solution into a rag and swirled it over an area. He took the wire brush and scrubbed. The black algae[7] came up like a foamy monster. **12**

"We're a team," Arnie said to Mr. Clemens.

Arnie descended into the pool and took the bleach bottle from José. He held it for José and smiled up at Mr. Clemens, who, hands on hips, watched for a while, the poodle at his side. He cupped his ear, as if to pick up the sounds of José's scrubbing.

"Nice day, huh?" Arnie sang.

"What?" Mr. Clemens said.

"Nice day," Arnie repeated, this time louder. "So which ear can't you hear in?" Grinning, Arnie wiggled his ear to make sure that Mr. Clemens knew what he was asking.

Mr. Clemens ignored Arnie. He watched José, whose arms worked back and forth like he was sawing logs.

"We're not only a team," Arnie shouted, "but we're also cousins."

Mr. Clemens shook his head at Arnie. **13** When he left, the poodle leading the way, Arnie immediately climbed out of the pool and sat on the edge, legs dangling.

"It's going to be blazing," Arnie complained. He shaded his eyes with his hand and looked east, where the sun was rising over a sycamore, its leaves hanging like bats.

José scrubbed. He worked the wire brush over the black and green stains, the grime dripping like tears. He finished a large area. He hopped out of the pool and returned hauling a garden hose with an attached nozzle. He gave the cleaned area a blast. When the spray got too close, his cousin screamed, got up, and, searching for something to do, picked a loquat from a tree.

Visual Vocabulary
A *loquat* is a small, yellowish fruit that is juicy and tart. It grows in bunches.

---

7. **Algae** are plants, such as pond scum, that grow in water.

12 Key Literary Element
Plot *The tension between José and Arnie is growing here. This must be the rising action of the plot.*

13 Key Reading Skill
Questioning *What is Mr. Clemens thinking about Arnie? Maybe he, too, is disgusted with Arnie's laziness.*

"What's your favorite fruit?" Arnie asked.

José ignored him.

Arnie stuffed a bunch of loquats into his mouth, then cursed himself for splattering juice on his new high-tops. He returned to the pool, his cheeks fat with the seeds, and once again sat at the edge. He started to tell José how he had first learned to swim. "We were on vacation in Mazatlán.[8] You been there, ain't you?"

José shook his head. He dabbed the bleach solution onto the sides of the pool with a rag and scrubbed a new area.

"Anyhow, my dad was on the beach and saw this drowned dead guy," Arnie continued. "And right there, my dad got scared and realized I couldn't swim."

Arnie rattled on about how his father had taught him in the hotel pool and later showed him where the drowned man's body had been.

"Be quiet," José said.

"What?"

"I can't concentrate," José said, stepping back to look at the cleaned area.

Arnie shut his mouth but opened it to lick loquat juice from his fingers. He kicked his legs against the swimming pool, bored. He looked around the backyard and spotted a lounge chair. He got up, dusting off the back of his pants, and threw himself into the cushions. He raised and lowered the back of the lounge. Sighing, he snuggled in. He stayed quiet for three minutes, during which time José scrubbed. His arms hurt but he kept working with long strokes. José knew that in an hour the sun would drench the pool with light. He hurried to get the job done. **14**

Arnie then asked, "You ever peel before?"

José looked at his cousin. His nose burned from the bleach. He scrunched up his face.

"You know, like when you get sunburned."

"I'm too dark to peel," José said, his words echoing because he had advanced to the deep end. "Why don't you be quiet and let me work?"

Arnie babbled on that he had peeled when on vacation in Hawaii. He explained that he was really more French

14 Key Reading Skill
Analyzing *Here, the author shows the two cousins side by side, inviting readers to contrast Arnie with José. While Arnie lies around eating and talking, José works so hard his arms hurt.*

---

8. **Mazatlán** is a seaport in western Mexico. It is popular with tourists who like beaches and fishing.

than Mexican, and that's why his skin was sensitive. He said that when he lived in France, people thought that he could be Portuguese or maybe Armenian, never Mexican. **15**

José felt like soaking his rag with bleach and pressing it over Arnie's mouth to make him be quiet.

Then Mr. Clemens appeared. He was dressed in white pants and a flowery shirt. His thin hair was combed so that his scalp, as pink as a crab, showed.

"I'm just taking a little rest," Arnie said.

Arnie leaped back into the pool. He took the bleach bottle and held it. He smiled at Mr. Clemens, who came to inspect their progress.

"José's doing a good job," Arnie said, then whistled a song.

Mr. Clemens peered into the pool, hands on knees, admiring the progress.

"Pretty good, huh?" Arnie asked.

Mr. Clemens nodded. Then his hearing aid fell out, and José turned in time to see it roll like a bottle cap toward the bottom of the pool. It leaped into the stagnant water with a plop. A single bubble went up, and it was gone.

"Dang," Mr. Clemens swore. He took shuffling steps toward the deep end. He steadied his gaze on where the hearing aid had sunk. He leaned over and suddenly, arms waving, one leg kicking out, he tumbled into the pool. He landed standing up, then his legs buckled, and he crumbled, his head striking against the bottom. He rolled once, and half of his body settled in the water. **16**

"Did you see that!" Arnie shouted, big-eyed.

José had already dropped his brushes on the side of the pool and hurried to the old man, who moaned, eyes closed, his false teeth jutting from his mouth. A ribbon of blood immediately began to flow from his scalp.

"We better get out of here!" Arnie suggested. "They're going to blame us!"

José knelt on both knees at the old man's side. He took the man's teeth from his mouth and placed them in his shirt pocket. The old man groaned and opened his eyes, which were shiny wet. He appeared startled, like a newborn.

15 Key Reading Skill
Making Inferences *It seems as if Arnie may be prejudiced against Mexicans, even though he himself has Mexican roots. He seems to think that having a skin tone lighter than José's somehow makes him special.*

16 Key Literary Element
Plot *A terrible thing has happened that José has to deal with. This must be the climax of the story because the action of the story has reached a high point.*

"Sir, you'll be all right," José cooed, then snapped at his cousin. "Arnie, get over here and help me!"

"I'm going home," Arnie whined.

"You punk!" José yelled. "Go inside and call 911."

Arnie said that they should leave him there.

"Why should we get involved?" he cried as he started for his bike. "It's his own fault."

José laid the man's head down and with giant steps leaped out of the pool, shoving his cousin as he passed. He went into the kitchen and punched in 911 on a telephone. He explained to the operator what had happened. When asked the address, José dropped the phone and went onto the front porch to look for it.

"It's 940 East Brown," José breathed. He hung up and looked wildly about the kitchen. He opened up the refrigerator and brought out a plastic tray of ice, which he twisted so that a few of the cubes popped out and slid across the floor. He wrapped some cubes in a dish towel. When he raced outside, Arnie was gone, the yapping poodle was doing laps around the edge of the pool, and Mr. Clemens was trying to stand up.

"No, sir," José said as he jumped into the pool, his own knees almost buckling. "Please, sit down."

Mr. Clemens staggered and collapsed. José caught him before he hit his head again. The towel of ice cubes dropped from his hands. With his legs spread to absorb the weight, José raised the man up in his arms, this fragile man. He picked him up and carefully stepped toward the shallow end, one slow elephant step at a time. **17**

"You'll be all right," José said, more to himself than to Mr. Clemens, who moaned and struggled to be let free.

The sirens wailed in the distance. The poodle yapped, which started a dog barking in the neighbor's yard.

"You'll be OK," José repeated, and in the shallow end of the pool, he edged up the steps. He lay the old man in the lounge chair and raced back inside for more ice and

17 Key Reading Skill
Analyzing *It's interesting that José lifts up the old man. José's actions show just how grown-up José really is. Here he's literally carrying a man's weight, even though he is not yet a man.*

another towel. He returned outside and placed the bundle of cubes on the man's head, where the blood flowed. Mr. Clemens was awake, looking about. When the old man felt his mouth, José reached into his shirt pocket and pulled out his false teeth. He fit the teeth into Mr. Clemens's mouth and a smile appeared, something bright at a difficult time. **18**

"I hit my head," Mr. Clemens said after smacking his teeth so that the fit was right.

José looked up and his gaze floated to a telephone pole, one his father might have climbed. If he had been there, his father would have seen that José was more than just a good worker. He would have seen a good man. He held the towel to the old man's head. The poodle, now quiet, joined them on the lounge chair.

A fire truck pulled into the driveway and soon they were surrounded by firemen, one of whom brought out a first-aid kit. A fireman led José away and asked what had happened. He was starting to explain when his cousin reappeared, yapping like a poodle.

"I was scrubbing the pool," Arnie shouted, "and I said, 'Mr. Clemens, you shouldn't stand so close to the edge.' But did he listen? No, he leaned over and . . . Well, you can just imagine my horror."

José walked away from Arnie's jabbering. He walked away, and realized that there were people like his cousin, the liar, and people like himself, someone he was getting to know. **19** He walked away and in the midmorning heat boosted himself up a telephone pole. He climbed up and saw for himself what his father saw—miles and miles of trees and houses, and a future lost in the layers of yellowish haze. ○

18 Key Literary Element
Characterization *You can tell a lot about José from his actions. He calmly does what has to be done to help Mr. Clemens. José is a responsible, caring young man.*

19 Key Literary Element
Theme *It looks as if José has learned something from his experiences with Arnie and Mr. Clemens. José seems to think he did the right thing. So the theme of the story may be that it is more important to be responsible and caring than rich.*

Partner Talk With a partner, take turns retelling parts of the story. Choose a particular event and give all the important details.

Write to Learn Answer these questions in your Learner's Notebook: Why does José walk away and let Arnie tell lies to the firemen? How was José being true to himself?

 **Study Central** Visit www.glencoe.com and click on Study Central to review short stories.

Skills Focus

You will practice using these skills when you read the following selections:
- "Cream Puff," p. 562
- "The Question of Popularity," p. 574

Reading

- Analyzing fiction and informational text

Literature

- Identifying character traits
- Analyzing characters
- Identifying and analyzing attention-getting devices

Vocabulary

- Recognizing and using base words to infer meaning
- Academic Vocabulary: *significant*

Writing/Grammar

- Identifying clauses and phrases

NY English Language Arts Core Curriculum
(pp. 558–559)

LC R13 Use text structure and literary devices to aid comprehension and response.

For a complete description of the standards, see p. NY11.

Skill Lesson

Analyzing

Learn It!

What Is It? You might remember from Unit 2 that when you analyze you take a close look at the **significant** elements that make up a story or a work of nonfiction. For example, you might look at plot, characters, point of view, text structure, and supporting details. You then figure out how these elements contribute to the meaning of a selection.

LUCKY COW © 2004 Mark Pett. Dist. By UNIVERSAL PRESS SYNDICATE. Reprinted with permission. All rights reserved.

Analyzing Cartoons
Did these kids analyze the characters or the look of the book?

Academic Vocabulary

significant *adj.* having meaning; having much importance

Why Is It Important? Analyzing helps you gain a deeper understanding of the selections you read and the ways that authors put the selections together.

How Do I Do It? To analyze fiction, determine which elements are significant and why. Some questions you can ask yourself are as follows:

- What is each character in the story like?

- How can you tell? Through dialogue? Action? The narrator's descriptions?

- What, if anything, do the characters learn from their experiences?

- Which characters, if any, change as a result of their experiences?

When analyzing nonfiction, pay attention to text structure and the details that support the writer's main idea.

- How does the organization of the text help make the writer's points clear?

- What kinds of details does the writer include?

Here's how a student analyzed a passage from a short story.

> Tom and Maddy stared out the window of their log cabin. The blizzard had not let up for two days. Maddy shivered. A tear ran down her cheek. Tom looked grim. What if Maddy had their baby before the storm was over? His horse would never be able to make the ride to Dr. May's in deep snow.

> *You can tell from Maddy's actions that she is sad and worried. She shivers, and a tear runs down her cheek. Tom, on the other hand, is worried and grim. You can tell by the way he looks and also by the thoughts that are going through his head. The setting adds to Tom and Maddy's problem. The location of their cabin makes it hard to get a doctor.*

Literature Online

Study Central Visit www.glencoe.com and click on Study Central to review analyzing.

Practice It!

Analyze the setting of the passage. When and where do you think the story takes place? What details make you think so?

Use It!

As you read "Cream Puff," analyze what the characters are like.

Before You Read : Cream Puff

Linnea Due

Meet the Author

Linnea Due is the author of many short stories, novels, and magazine articles. She began playing sports as a young child and quickly became a fan of basketball, baseball, and other sports. Her novel *High and Outside* is about a teen softball player. *See page R1 of The Author Files in the back of the book for more on Linnea Due.*

Author Search For more about Linnea Due, go to www.glencoe.com.

NY English Language Arts Core Curriculum (pp. 560–569)

LC R6 Determine the meaning of unfamiliar words by using word structure knowledge. **LC R13** Use text structure and literary devices to aid comprehension and response. **R2b** Interpret characters, using evidence from the text.

For a complete description of the standards, see p. NY11.

Vocabulary Preview

swaggered (SWAG urd) *v.* walked boldly or showed off; form of the verb *swagger* **(p. 568)** *It was clear that Jinx had plenty of confidence when she swaggered onto the basketball court.*

barreling (BAYR ul ing) *v.* moving or traveling fast and hard, like a rolling barrel; form of the verb *barrel* **(p. 568)** *Jen stepped aside when Jinx came barreling toward her.*

On Your Own In your Learner's Notebook, answer these questions.

1. If a boy swaggered past you, would you think he was shy or bold?

2. Which is more likely to go barreling across a field, a horse or a fly?

English Language Coach

Word Analysis To understand the meaning of a word, it may help to look at its parts. For example, the word *unhappy* is formed by the prefix *un* and the word *happy*. Happy is called the **base word.** Letter combinations added to the front of a base word are called **prefixes.** Letter combinations added to the end of a base word are called **suffixes.** Sometimes there is a slight spelling change when a suffix is added.

You can sometimes figure out the meaning of an unfamiliar word by analyzing its parts. Look below at the word *unsinkable.*

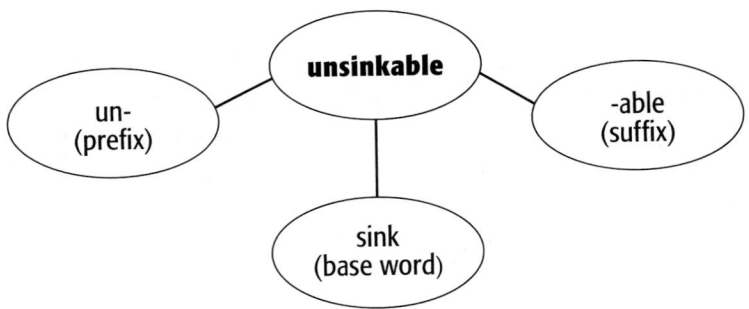

What does *unsinkable* mean? If you know that *un-* means "not" and *-able* means "can be done," you can guess *unsinkable* means "cannot be sunk."

Partner Work For each word below, make a word web like the one above.

- **disrespectful**
- **unbeatable**
- **preapproval**

Skills Preview

Key Reading Skill: Analyzing

As you read "Cream Puff," you'll be asked to analyze the conflicts that Jen, the main character, has. You've already learned that there can be **external conflict** between the main character and

- another person
- nature, in the form of animals or floods and so forth
- a person and society

There can also be **internal conflict,** a struggle of emotions going on within the character. As you're reading "Cream Puff," watch for signs of both kinds of conflict.

Key Literary Element: Characterization

A **character** is an individual in a story or other literary work. The qualities that make up a character's personality are **character traits.** A character might be greedy or generous, cowardly or courageous, kind or mean, and so on. The author reveals these traits through **characterization.** Methods of characterization include describing what a character looks like, says, thinks, and does and what other characters say about the character.

- Characters with several sides to their personalities are **dynamic** (dye NAM ik) **characters.** They grow and change as a result of their experiences.
- Characters with only one or two traits are **static** (STAT ik) **characters.** They don't change during the course of the story.

The main character of a story is usually dynamic. Minor characters are usually static.

Small Group Discussion With a small group of classmates, make a list of main characters from recent movies or TV shows you've seen. Together, label each character on the list either "dynamic" or "static." Give reasons for each label you use.

Literature Online

Elements Handbook To review or learn more about the literary elements, go to www.glencoe.com.

Get Ready to Read

Connect to the Reading

Think of a time when you had a problem and turned to others for advice. Did their suggestions help or did you have to figure out a solution on your own?

Write to Learn In a few sentences in your Learner's Notebook, explain how you solved the problem.

Build Background

Women first played basketball at the college level in the 1890s. Both on the court and off, women wore long dresses because it was thought to be in bad taste for a woman to show more than her head, neck, and hands in public. Players sometimes tripped over the hems of their long skirts, hurting themselves. Uniforms changed in the late 1890s, when female players began wearing bloomers—baggy shorts gathered at the knee.

"Cream Puff" takes place at a fictional basketball camp for teens. At basketball camps, kids work to improve their playing skills.

The narrator in "Cream Puff" uses real basketball terms:

- *drove for the basket* (ran quickly and aggressively toward the basket)
- *pump-faked* (pretended to throw)
- *possession* (control of the ball)
- *turnover* (when one team loses the ball and the other team takes possession)

Set Purposes for Reading

BIG Question Read "Cream Puff" to find out how the main character stays true to herself.

Set Your Own Purpose What else would you like to learn from the selection to help you answer the Big Question? Write your own purpose on the "Cream Puff" page of Foldable 5.

Keep Moving

Use these skills as you read "Cream Puff."

CREAM PUFF

by Linnea Due

Practice the Skills

Okay, I stepped aside. Wait a minute—*step* is too big a word. My big toe shifted a half inch to the left. Maybe my heel. I couldn't believe Coach Brandt could even notice, but she did, and she's been screaming at me ever since. *Wuss. Cream puff. Scared of your own shadow.* Things that make you laugh in real life or get up in someone's face just to show you can. In basketball, when the coach says those things, you're dead meat. The other kids stopped looking at me. I could smell the shame. **1**

That huge girl was caroming[1] down the court like a three-foot-wide brick wall on Rollerblades. Who wouldn't slide south? Only that's exactly what you can't do. You have to stand in there, take the hit. Dad's told me, over and over. "I'm small, Jen," he points out, and at six feet, he is, for basketball anyway. "These big guys'd come and bust me up. I had bruises up and down my arms, on my chest . . . even my neck! But you gotta take the hits if you're gonna play."

He was mad 'cause I'd told him I'd had it with basketball. When I used to play with the little kids, we didn't bust each other up on purpose. Then I got into the city league when I was eight and learned how real kids play. Rough. They muscle you out of the way and they stomp on your foot and they jab you with their elbows. Mom wanted me to quit the first day. I might have if I'd thought of it first. Every time I

1 **Key Reading Skill**

Analyzing Jen says that she is "dead meat" and that she could "smell the shame." From these descriptions, you can tell that she's having an internal conflict, or troubling feelings.

1. *Caroming* is hitting and bouncing off like a ball. The big girl was pushing off the other players on her way down the court.

wanted to quit **afterward**, what came up in my head was a picture of Mom saying, "I told you so," or Dad with a really disappointed look on his face. ▤ Four years after that first day at city league, I still don't like getting hit.

When the coach ran out of stuff to call me, I slunk off the court and sat on the bench. Nobody came near me; nobody wanted to catch what I had. I could see everybody on the floor tighten up and start popping each other good—it looked like the WWF[2] out there. Still, if you had to choose between getting smashed in the nose and having Coach Brandt call you a cream puff, what would you pick? There's no shame in a broken nose.

Keisha swung down next to me. "Whatcha scared of her for?" she asked. "She's just a big slow white girl." Then she giggled. "You're a big *fast* white girl, and that gives you the edge." ▤

Keisha was one of my roommates back in the dorm at San Francisco State. All of us had been chosen by our schools or city leagues to come to Bay Eagles coach Katherine Brandt's weeklong basketball camp. It was a huge honor, and now I was worried that Sharon Demming should have been picked instead of me. I felt like a pretend Rising Young Star, not a real one. And I sure didn't like how that slow white girl— her name tag read JINX—kept catching my eye just so I wouldn't miss her sneering at me. She reminded me of my uncle Robert, who can always find something mean to say about anybody.

---

2. The *WWF* is the World Wrestling Federation.

Analyzing the Photo What does the photo add to your understanding of the relationship between Jen and her coach?

Practice the Skills

▤ **English Language Coach**

Word Analysis The word **afterward** has two parts: the base word *after* and the suffix -*ward*, which means "in the direction of." Other words that have this suffix are *toward, forward,* and *backward.*

▤ **Key Literary Element**

Characterization From what Keisha says, you can tell two of her character traits. She is supportive of her friends, and she has a sense of humor.

By the time we got back to the dorm, my roommates had teased me so much, I felt better. Evelyn told me that Coach Brandt had a reputation for being really hard on people. I said I figured every coach has that reputation, but Evelyn said no, that her coach in Long Beach was really sweet and gave everybody candy. Keisha said she'd never heard of coaches giving out candy and was her coach a dirty old man? Evelyn laughed for a whole minute, and then Keisha turned to me and said, "That girl was *big*! I woulda got out of her way, too."

But that night, when the others were asleep, I started worrying again. What if it turned out I was a fraidy-cat? What if being scared was something I couldn't make go away? I love basketball. I love it more than eating and TV and video games and even swimming, which is what I love second best. I'm already five-seven, and like Keisha says, I'm fast and I can jump, too. I've got a chart on my wall at home that lists the top teams—the Tennessee Lady Vols, LSU, UConn, the Georgia Bulldogs, and closer to home, Stanford and Cal. The chart measures my height, so I can look at it and see I've gained two inches this year alone. I think about how everything's coming together: my desire, my body, my ability. I can't be afraid! **4**

To get to sleep, I pictured myself shooting baskets, keeping my wrist loose and letting the ball trail off my fingers like I'm caressing a baby. I run it through my head so often, I can make it happen for real—it's called visualizing. That doesn't mean I don't practice 24/7. I spend so much time shooting baskets that Mr. Ashton next door asked Mom to put up a sound wall. He was joking, I think. **5**

The next day, Jinx was waiting near the basket, a slight smile on her face. Even though we're the same height, she outweighs me by twenty pounds, and it was easy for her to muscle me aside. Keisha looked worried. "Stick it to her, Suburban. Make her back off." I tried to stay in front of her when she drove for the basket, but I was concentrating so much on sticking to my spot that I forgot to defend. Coach Brandt was on me in a heartbeat. "You're not in the game, Jennifer," she warned. "If you didn't come to play, you might as well get on the bus back to Sacramento." I could feel my face turning red and my eyes going black, which they always do when I'm mad.

Practice the Skills

4 | **Key Reading Skill**

Analyzing State the internal conflict that is bothering Jen. Think about these things:

- She doesn't want to disappoint her father.
- She doesn't like being hit.
- She says she loves basketball more than anything.
- She says she thought that everything was "coming together" for her.

5 | **Key Literary Element**

Characterization Jen practices "24/7." What does this tell you about her personality?

But a minute later I was back to chewing on my bottom lip. What *could* I do about Jinx? She was standing by the bench with a couple of other girls, and the three of them kept glancing over at me and rolling their eyes. Keisha stayed right on my shoulder, but I didn't want her fighting my fights. What would Dad do? He wouldn't let some big old player get up over his head every other minute, no matter how short he was. No answer came. Trying to figure out what my dad would do made me more nervous 'cause I didn't know, and that was even worse than not being able to handle Jinx in the first place. **6**

All that practice, I kept trying to show her up, but instead everything I did played into her hands. If I stood still, she went up over me. When she pump-faked, I jumped, and then she shot as I was coming down. Every mistake made me more upset, and the more upset I got, the more mistakes I made.

Practice the Skills

6 **Key Reading Skill**

Analyzing Jen's internal conflict is getting more complicated. Why does thinking about her dad make her even more nervous?

Analyzing the Photo What aspect of Jennifer's experience at basketball camp might this photo illustrate?

Practice the Skills

"She's rattled you," Evelyn said. She was the pretty one in our little group—her mother was Filipino and her dad African American. "Forget Keisha and her gang banging. Just play your own game."

But that was the problem—I didn't have one. I felt blank, like a window that opened onto nothing.

As we were leaving that afternoon, Coach Brandt called me over. "There will always be bullies, Jennifer," she said **quietly**. "At some point you'll have to learn to deal with them." **7**

As she walked away, my eyes went black again, and this time I couldn't stop myself. "Wait a second," I called to her, knowing I was stepping over the line and not caring. "You have to say more than that. You're the coach!"

She turned back with a laugh. "You want me to motivate you? Okay, here's the best advice I can give: Motivate yourself or get out. This game is too demanding to depend on a coach or your parents or your teammates to keep you in. You've got the ability to go all the way—and that's not something I say to many kids. But you need more than ability to make it. You even need more than wanting it so badly you can taste it." She could see the surprise cross my face, and she nodded as if it confirmed something she already knew. She took a deep breath and said, "You need *drive* to make it work. You can have the best engine on the face of this planet, and if you don't have a starter,[3] you'll never go an inch. That's what drive is, and it's what you're missing, Jennifer. I hope you find it." **8**

That night I called my mother. "What's wrong?" she asked. She could always tell when I had a problem. I said, "I keep thinking about Dad. He never gave up, and he was so small."

She waited for me to go on, and when I didn't, I could hear her sigh. "Jen, I know you won't believe this, but basketball isn't very important to your father. It never was."

"But that can't be true," I sputtered. "All he ever does is talk about it." I started to say more, but what was the point in arguing when I knew she was wrong? After a moment, she sighed again and asked me if I'd worn holes in any more socks and was my hair still in my eyes. Thanks, Mom.

7 **English Language Coach**

Word Analysis What is the suffix that makes the word **quietly** an adverb instead of an adjective?

8 **Key Literary Skill**

Characterization Coach Brandt has been giving Jen a hard time all week. Do you think what the coach says here shows more of the same or a different attitude toward Jen? Explain.

---

3. The *starter* is the part of a car engine that turns it on.

But when I went back to the room, Evelyn started talking about how her dad always goes to the playground with her, and I suddenly felt like somebody had dumped a bucket of ice-cold water on my head. Dad was too busy to come to my games, much less play in the driveway with me. The couple of times I'd gotten him to play, I was surprised at how bad he was. He blustered about how he'd lost his edge and did a lot of shoving and jumping around, but now that I was looking close, I could see how maybe that edge had never been sharp. **9**

Analyzing the Photo Jennifer's coach tells her that she needs *drive* in order to succeed. How does the girl in this photo exhibit that quality?

I didn't want to get out of bed the next morning. Here I was, at the statewide camp, finding out I'm a cream puff and my dad all talk and no help at all, and this girl Jinx was going to make me look even worse than I did yesterday, 'cause yesterday I had Dad to help and today I didn't. When I pulled the pillow over my head, Keisha told me she was going to jump on me, so I had to get up or risk broken ribs on top of a broken heart. How could my dad have pretended like that to me?

While I warmed up, I pictured my dad scrimmaging[4] with the starters season after season, knowing he wouldn't get into the games. I knew the other guys liked him, 'cause they'd call when they came through Sacramento, and Dad would have them over to the house. Maybe what Dad really missed was being on a team. **10**

---

4. *Scrimmaging* is playing practice games.

Practice the Skills

9 | **Reading Skill Review**

Monitoring Comprehension Jen realizes something important about her dad here. Do you "get" what it is? Make sure by putting it in your own words.

10 | **Key Literary Element**

Characterization What character trait does Jen's thinking in this paragraph reveal about her? Think about how angry she was with her father and how she feels about him now.

Visual Vocabulary
A *comet* is a bright heavenly body made mostly of ice and dust. It develops a cloudy tail when it orbits near the sun.

When Jinx came pounding down the court at me during the drills, I stood in there and took hit after hit. I felt so bad, I didn't care if I got hurt. But here's the terrible part: all my blocking didn't stop her making the shots. Oh, a couple of times I tipped away the ball, but I could tell I wasn't playing good, and I just didn't know what else to do. My Rising Young Star was blinking out like a dying comet. **11**

By the time Coach Brandt called lunch, I was so low, I could have crawled across the floor. Why was I even here? For Mom? She'd wanted me to quit the first day. For Dad? Mom was right; he really didn't care about basketball. He talked it all the time 'cause he wanted to connect with me, and he knew there was no better way to do that than talk basketball. Besides, now that I was seeing the awful truth, I realized that Dad couldn't have helped me much anyway—we were very different players. I was tall and he was short, I was fast and cagey, and he was more like a battering ram.[5] I didn't have anybody's footsteps to walk in, except maybe my own. And that's when it really hit me—basketball was *my* game, not Dad's, not Mom's, not even Keisha's or Evelyn's. When Evelyn told me to play my own game, she meant to burrow deep under the surface of what basketball looked like and find out where *I* lived. **12**

After lunch, when Jinx **swaggered** back onto the court for scrimmages, I was ready for her. On the first possession, when she came **barreling** toward me, I sidestepped her easily and snagged the ball as she came past. I could see Keisha's eyes widen—would Coach Brandt yell at me 'cause I'd moved aside? But she didn't say a word—she stood near the bench, her eyes narrowed in concentration. In the next five minutes, I trailed two shots over Jinx's shoulder, and the coach made a note on her clipboard. Why challenge Jinx head-to-head? She

---

5. In the Middle Ages, a ***battering ram*** was a big, heavy log used to break down the gates of a castle.

Practice the Skills

11 Key Reading Skill

Analyzing Jen repeats the phrase "Rising Young Star." What part of her internal conflict does this represent?

12 Key Reading Skill

Analyzing What do you learn from the way Jen finally resolves her internal conflict?

Vocabulary

swaggered (SWAG urd) *v.* walked boldly or showed off

barreling (BAYR ul ing) *v.* moving or traveling fast and hard, like a rolling barrel

Analyzing the Photo Going up for a rebound, these four girls compete for the win. What did Jennifer learn at basketball camp about competition? What does this photo show about competition?

was heavier and slower, and that made her easy to beat. She tried to run right over me a few times, and I avoided her like a matador[6] teases a bull. I could see the worry lines start in her forehead, and I felt sorry for her. A big smile was building on Evelyn's face, and Keisha had begun to laugh. **13**

The third time I forced a turnover, Keisha shouted, "Go-o-o, Cream Puff!" I could tell the name was going to stick, and it has, even after me and Evelyn and Keisha came back this year for our second camp. The kids that go to the camp all know each other, and word travels fast.

I still don't like getting hit. Nobody does—it's just part of the game. But I love being called Cream Puff. It reminds me of that summer I figured out who was missing from the court: me. ○

6. In bullfighting, the **matador,** or bullfighter, teases the bull by making it chase after his cape.

Practice the Skills

13 **BIG Question**

Jen has found a way to stay true to herself. What is it? Write your answer on the "Cream Puff" page of Foldable 5. Your response will help you complete the Unit Challenge later.

After You Read

Cream Puff

Answering the BIG Question

1. Do you think Jen would have stayed true to herself if she had quit basketball? Why or why not?

2. **Recall** What advice does Coach Brandt give Jen about how to succeed at basketball?

   Tip Right There

3. **Summarize** What does Jen learn about her dad from her mother? Sum it up in a sentence.

   Tip Right There

Critical Thinking

4. **Infer** Why doesn't Jen want Keisha to fight her fights?

   Tip Author and Me

5. **Evaluate** Do you think Coach Brandt is right to call Jen a "cream puff" in order to motivate her? Why or why not?

   Tip On My Own

Talk About Your Reading

Small Group Discussion What is Jen like? With a small group of class-mates, discuss Jen's character traits. Each person should name a different character trait, then name the method of characterization the author uses to reveal the trait. Record your group's responses on a chart like the one pictured below. An example has been filled in to help you start.

NY English Language Arts Core Curriculum (pp. 570–571)

LC R17 Demonstrate comprehension and response through a range of activities.
LC S8 Participate in group discussions.
LC R13 Use text structure and literary devices to aid comprehension and response. **R2b** Interpret characters, using evidence from the text. **LC R6** Determine the meaning of words by using word structure knowledge. **Core W8** Use correct grammatical construction.

For a complete description of the standards, see p. NY11.

Character Trait	Method(s) of Characterization
1. *insecure*	*what Jen says about feeling ashamed (p. 562) and what she thinks about late at night (p. 564)*
2.	
3.	

Skills Review

Key Reading Skill: Analyzing

6. Why does Jen fail several times before figuring out how to motivate herself? Support your answer with specific details from the story.

7. What do you think the story says about what it takes to succeed? Why do you say so? Use examples from the story to back up your answer.

Key Literary Element: Characterization

8. Which characters in the story are static? Which are dynamic? How can you tell? Using the list of characters that follows, label each character either "static" or "dynamic." Explain each choice.

Jen • Keisha • Coach Brandt • Jinx

9. Did you learn more about Jen from what she said or from what she did? Explain.

Vocabulary Check

Copy the following sentences on a separate sheet of paper. Then fill in each blank correctly with either *swaggered* or *barreling.*

10. The cart got loose and went _____ down the path.

11. In his new leather jacket, Manny _____ into the room.

English Language Coach As you read "Cream Puff," you analyzed the words *afterward* and *quietly.* Use what you learned to define the words below.

12. seaward

13. skyward

14. secretly

15. thoughtfully

16. **Academic Vocabulary** Are **significant** details in a story the most or least important ones?

Grammar Link: Clauses and Phrases

A **clause** is a group of words that work together to express meaning and that contain a subject and a predicate. A **phrase** is a group of words that work together but do not contain a subject and predicate.

Earlier, you learned that an **independent clause** can stand alone as a simple sentence. That's because an independent clause expresses a complete thought. A **dependent clause** cannot stand alone as a complete sentence. It does not express a complete thought. It "depends on" an independent clause to make its meaning complete.

Dependent Clause: when she is happy
Independent Clause: Mom sings
Dependent Clause + Independent Clause:
When she is happy, Mom sings.

A **phrase** does not express a complete thought. Types of phrases include (a) modifying phrases, (b) noun phrases, and (c) verb phrases.

(a) <u>Early Tuesday morning</u>, we will leave.

(b) <u>My brother, sister, and I</u> have packed.

(c) For two weeks we <u>will be traveling</u>.

Grammar Practice

On a separate sheet of paper, identify whether the underlined words are a *phrase* or a *clause.*

17. <u>The drama teacher watched the rehearsal</u>.

18. I'm going to the school dance <u>with my friends</u>.

19. <u>When the movie ends</u>, we can go shopping.

20. If I get a part in the school play, <u>I will be happy</u>.

Literature Online

Web Activities For eFlashcards, Selection Quick Checks, and other Web activities, go to www.glencoe.com.

Before You Read

The Question of Popularity

Meet the Author
Tamara Eberlein has written many articles about mental and physical health as well as parenting. She is also the author of books on child development. Eberlein is the mother of twins.

Literature Online

Author Search For more about Tamara Eberlein, go to www.glencoe.com.

Vocabulary Preview

factor (FAK tur) *n.* something that produces or contributes to a certain result **(p. 574)** *The amount of time people spend studying is very frequently a factor in their grades.*

obnoxious (ub NOCK shus) *adj.* very unpleasant and unlikeable **(p. 574)** *The boys in that "in" crowd are obnoxious and often put others down.*

majority (muh JOR ih tee) *n.* more than half; the greater part **(p. 575)** *The majority of people are nice; only a few cause problems.*

Think-Pair-Share Use the three vocabulary words in a paragraph. Leave blanks where the vocabulary words go. Then pair up with a classmate and trade paragraphs. Fill in the blanks in the paragraph.

English Language Coach

Word Families A **word family** is a group of words that have the same base word. For example, all the words on the web below are in the same family because they all have *use* as their base word. In each case, either a prefix *(mis-, re-)* or a suffix *(-able, -less)* has been added to the base word to form a new word. Take a few minutes to study the chart.

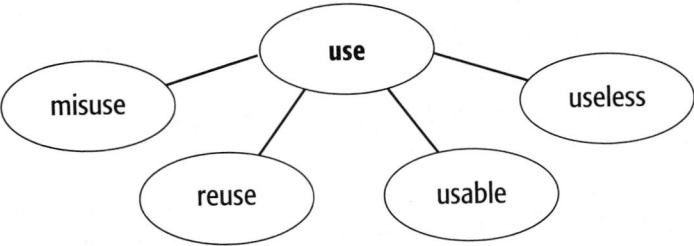

Whole Class Discussion Brainstorm a list of words in the same word family as *act.* Come up with at least two words created with prefixes and two words created with suffixes. Record your list on a web.

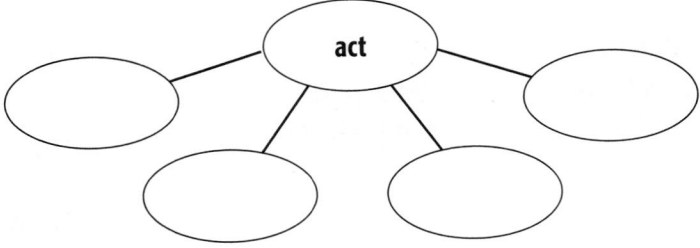

NY English Language Arts Core Curriculum (pp. 572–577)

LC R6 Determine the meaning of words by using word structure knowledge.
LC R13 Use text structure and literary devices to aid comprehension and response.

For a complete description of the standards, see p. NY11.

Skills Preview

Key Reading Skill: Analyzing

As you read "The Question of Popularity," you'll be asked to analyze the main idea and supporting details. To prepare for the analysis, look over the article.

Whole Class Discussion As a class, discuss which paragraphs on the first page of the article form the introduction and what you think the main idea of the article is. What details do you think the author might present to support that main idea?

Text Element: Direct Quotations

Direct quotations tell exactly what people said in their own words. Authors of nonfiction use direct quotations for many reasons:

- to develop a main idea
- to add vivid details to writing
- to analyze what someone said
- to persuade the reader to agree with them by quoting experts who share their opinion

As you read "The Question of Popularity," notice when the author quotes someone. Then ask yourself these questions:

- *Why does the author quote this person?*
- *What does this quotation add to the article?*

Partner Talk Interview a classmate in order to write a one-paragraph biography of him or her. To add vivid detail to the biography, directly quote the person at least once. Be sure to put quotation marks both before (") and after (") the quotation.

Get Ready to Read

Connect to the Reading

Think about the importance of popularity in your school. How much does popularity matter to you and your friends? To most kids at your school?

Write to Learn In your Learner's Notebook, list the advantages and disadvantages of being popular.

Build Background

People of all ages like to form social groups. Some groups are carefully organized; others are informal. Cliques are small, snobbish, informal associations. Clique members try to hang on to a special advantage—such as a leadership position—by refusing to let "non-members" join.

Studies show that most kids who make bad decisions are with their friends at the time. They're giving in to peer pressure—pressure from members of their social group to act certain ways in order to "fit in." Of course, peers can be good role models too. They can encourage good values, healthy behaviors, and teamwork—if kids choose the right peers to listen to.

Set Purposes for Reading

BIG Question Read "The Question of Popularity" to find out what other kids in middle school think about popularity.

Set Your Own Purpose What else would you like to learn from the selection to help you answer the Big Question? Write your own purpose on "The Question of Popularity" page of Foldable 5.

Interactive Literary Elements Handbook
To review or learn more about the literary elements, go to www.glencoe.com.

Keep Moving

Use these skills as you read "The Question of Popularity."

The Question of Popularity **573**

TIME

The Question of Popularity

How much does popularity matter?

By TAMARA EBERLEIN

Being popular isn't as important as having a few close friends who accept you for who you are.

Sean Murphy/Stone/Getty Images

Being popular means that other kids think you're cool. It doesn't mean (as many parents may think) that the cool kids are especially well liked or nice or admired for their smarts. Popular kids may be envied for their cool **factor,** but they may not have a lot of close friends.

   If you're like most middle schoolers, you've probably thought about how much (or perhaps how little) popularity matters to you. It's not unusual to want to fit in. But it's more important to have a few close friends, accept yourself for who you are, and be comfortable with the people you do hang out with. **1**

The In Crowd

Kids know that in most schools there is an "in crowd" of kids who are the most popular. Emily Kaplan, a middle schooler in Larchmont, New York, describes her school's in crowd this way: "The girls are kind of snobby, the boys **obnoxious.** If

1 | **Key Reading Skill**

Analyzing What opinion is the writer stating in the final sentence of this paragraph? Does that opinion give you a clue about the article's main idea? Explain.

Vocabulary

factor (FAK tur) *n.* something that produces or contributes to a certain result

obnoxious (ub NOCK shus) *adj.* very unpleasant and unlikeable

you laugh at something, they just go, 'That's not funny.' [But] when you're alone together, the popular girls are really nice." Emily's friend Liana Diamond adds, "When they're with their other friends, they don't talk to you."

Who is popular varies from place to place. And of course, not every popular kid is obnoxious or a snob or unfriendly. Believe it or not, for some kids who are popular, it's hard work to stay that way. Trying to stay on top can cause stress and insecurity because who's popular and who's not can change daily. 2

The Middle Group

The **majority** of kids fall somewhere in between the top and the bottom—and many adults say that kids in the middle group may be happiest and best off. "These kids have several close friends and are also part of a larger group that explores their interests, like soccer or music. They aren't overly caught up in the popularity game," says Sandy Sheehy, who has written a book about friendships. "What's important is not [if you get] invited to the 'right' sleepovers. It's whether [you have] a few close friends."

Margaret Sagarese, coauthor of a book about cliques, has a tip for kids who are trying to figure out where they belong. She suggests that you keep a list of what you like about yourself. "Social acceptance and personal acceptance are two very different things. [You] need to see that liking [yourself] is more important than being part of the in crowd," she says. 3 If being a part of the in group means acting in ways that you wouldn't normally act or want to act, then stay true to yourself. Make decisions according to your own values. Don't be afraid to be you.

2 Key Reading Skill

Analyzing How does this paragraph help support the main idea that "it's more important to have a few close friends . . . and be comfortable with the people you do hang out with"?

3 Text Element

Direct Quotations Explain how the quotations in this paragraph help support the idea that "it's more important to have a few close friends . . . and be comfortable with the people you do hang out with."

Michael Newman/PhotoEdit

Having several close friends and being part of a larger group may make kids happiest and best off.

Vocabulary

majority (muh JOR ih tee) *n.* more than half; the greater part

The Free Thinkers

What makes a kid less than popular? Sometimes it's the "wrong" clothes. Sometimes it's an embarrassing incident that a young person can't live down. And sometimes there's just no way of knowing.

"My friends and I are kind of the geeky group," says Zach McGraw,* a middle schooler in South Bend, Indiana. "I've wished I could be popular millions of times. But I've managed to find a good group to hang out with."

Kids like Zach might find a new friend or a group to hang out with outside of school—at church, synagogue,[1] martial arts classes, book clubs, or summer camps. Seeking out others with similar interests is often a good place to start trying to fit in and to develop relationships.

Having one good friend whom you can connect with makes a world of difference. When you like who that person is and can trust that person—then you have a true friendship that will last. Good friends build us up and help us feel confident about ourselves. They will most likely be around long after the in crowd is just a memory. **4**

IN THEIR OWN WORDS:

Kids Talk About Popularity
Want to know what other teens really think about cliques, geeks, and being cool? Read on for the innermost thoughts of middle schoolers.

BABYJOHN: "At my old school I didn't have many friends. When I moved, I was suddenly accepted into the in crowd. But I have bad memories of being unpopular, and I sometimes worry that my closest friends will exclude me."

RIVERRUNNER: "I had no real friends for about one-third of the year. When I finally thought I had found a true friend, she said to me that a different girl we hang out with was 'popular,' that she was '**semipopular**,' and that 'no offense, but you're a total geek.' **5** Now we just don't ever talk, and I am more happy with the not-so-popular group. And I have a few friends outside of school that I hang out with."

4 | **Key Reading Skill**

Analyzing In these two paragraphs the writer is giving advice. How does that advice support the idea that "it's more important to have a few close friends . . . and be comfortable with the people you do hang out with"?

5 | **English Language Coach**

Word Families The words *unpopular* and **semipopular** belong to the same word family. What is their base word?

---

* Name and location have been changed to protect privacy.

1. A *synagogue* is a Jewish house of worship.

CHERRY-COLA: "Lately, I have been feeling so unhip. I buy clothes and jewelry that make me seem more like everyone else. I feel as though I have to keep updating myself so that other people won't think I'm a loser. How you dress has everything to do with who you are."

TESTSCHIK182: "My best friend of five years was put in classes with all of the popular people. She'll do anything to be in the in crowd. I am definitely not a dork, but I'm not popular. [My best friend] has started to ignore me in the hall. How can I talk to her without feeling like an idiot? Her new friends aren't true friends at all."

MARISSA: "At the beginning of this year, the most popular guy in school liked me. I had tons of friends. But toward the middle of the year, Mr. Popular dumped me. Now I'm really lonely, I get made fun of a lot, and most kids don't like me."

HAPPY DUDE: "I get teased, hit, punched. I don't know if I should hit them back or just run away; I feel that rips apart my courage and self-confidence. I don't know what to do." **6**

SHORTY11: "During the school year, I was rejected and not invited to parties, movies, etc. But once the summer began, I met new people who accepted me for who I was, not for the clothing I wore or for my looks. So my advice to other kids is to hang on to the friends you've got and make an effort to meet new people." **7**

—**Updated 2005, from *Family Life*, August 2001**

6 **Text Element**

Direct Quotations Everybody quoted in this section is a kid. What makes the kids experts on this topic?

7 **BIG Question**

Why do some kids find it difficult to stay true to themselves when making friends? Write your answer on "The Question of Popularity" page of Foldable 5. Your response will help you complete the Unit Challenge later.

After You Read

The Question of Popularity

Answering the  BIG Question

1. In your opinion, is staying true to yourself more important than being popular? Why or why not?

2. **Recall** According to the writer of the article, what three groups do middle school students fall into?

     **Think and Search**

3. **Summarize** Sum up the article's main idea and most important supporting details in a few sentences.

    TIP **Think and Search**

Critical Thinking

4. **Infer** What two or three qualities would the writer say make a good friend? Why?

    TIP **Author and Me**

5. **Connect** Review the quotations at the end of the article. Do they help you connect to the article? Give reasons for your answer.

    TIP **Author and Me**

6. **Evaluate** Did the writer succeed in convincing you of her opinion? Why or why not? Support your answer with details from the article.

    TIP **Author and Me**

Write About Your Reading

Essay Write a short essay to express your opinion about social groups in your school. Consider these questions before you begin to write.

- Are social groups important to most kids in middle school?
- Is there any advantage to belonging to a particular social group?
- What are the different social groups in your school?

Be sure to state your opinion clearly in your introduction. Give convincing supporting details to explain and elaborate on your opinion.

Sean Murphy/Stone/Getty Images

NY English Language Arts Core Curriculum (pp. 578–579)

LC R17 Demonstrate comprehension and response through a range of activities.
LC W4 Compose grade-appropriate texts for a variety of purposes. **LC R13** Use text structure and literary devices to aid comprehension and response.
LC R6 Determine the meaning of words by using word structure knowledge.
Core W8 Use correct grammatical construction.

For a complete description of the standards, see p. NY11.

Skills Review

Key Reading Skill: Analyzing

7. When you analyzed the selection, what evidence did you find to support that main idea? Did your analysis make you think there should be more evidence? Explain your answer.

Text Element: Direct Quotations

8. What do the student quotations add to the article? Give examples from the article to support your answer.

Vocabulary Check

Answer each sentence *true* or *false*. Rewrite every false statement to make it true.

9. Watching too much TV can be a factor in the grades a student receives.

10. An obnoxious person is friendly and helpful.

11. A majority is always less than half of the total.

12. **English Language Coach** Find at least three words in the article that belong to the same word family as *friend.* Create a word web like the one below for this word family.

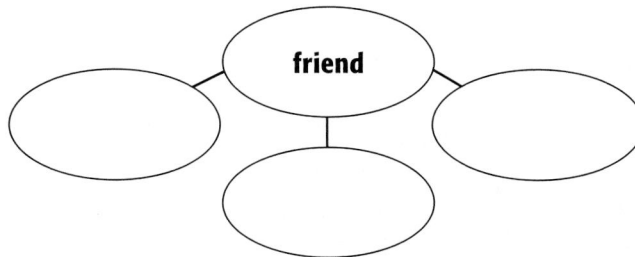

13. **Academic Vocabulary** Is the main idea of an article the most or least **significant** idea in the whole selection? Explain.

Web Activities For eFlashcards, Selection Quick Checks, and other Web activities, go to www.glencoe.com.

Grammar Link: Clauses and Phrases as Parts of Speech

A clause can take the place of a one-word part of speech in a sentence. A phrase also can take the place of a one-word part of speech.

Noun clauses take the place of nouns.
• Whoever scores the next point wins.

Adjective clauses take the place of adjectives.
• The ball, which he had hit hard, soared high.

Adverb clauses take the place of adverbs.
• When he hit it, the ball soared over our heads.

Prepositional phrases begin with a preposition and end with a noun or pronoun. They take the place of adjectives or adverbs.
• The chapter about the rescue was exciting.

(The prepositional phrase *about the rescue* functions as an adjective to describe the noun *chapter.*)

• The rescue team pulled the dog from the river.

(The prepositional phrase *from the river* functions as an adverb to describe the verb *pulled.*)

Verbal phrases act as nouns, adjectives, or adverbs.
As Noun: Bicycling in the mountains is hard work.
As Adjective: Staring outside, she saw rain.
As Adverb: We will hike to exercise.

Grammar Practice

Copy the underlined phrases on a separate sheet of paper. Write which part of speech each one is.

14. We built a feeder to feed wild birds.

15. However, squirrels climbed into the feeder.

16. They ate all the seeds that we placed there.

17. Stopping the squirrels was hard.

Writing Application Underline two clauses or phrases you used as parts of speech in your essay.

When you read a short story, you have the opportunity to connect to the characters, learn something about the world, and learn something about yourself. When you write a short story, you do the same thing, except *you* get to decide what happens in the story.

Writing about a character's personal struggle, or conflict, will help you think about the Unit 5 Big Question: How do you stay true to yourself? As you write your short story, refer to the **Writing Handbook,** pp. R17–R27.

Your story should have the basic elements you find in short stories.

• **Characters** are the actors in the story. They are *who* the story is about.

• **Conflict** is the struggle or problem your main character must solve. It's *what* the story is about. Conflict is developed through plot, which is the sequence of events that occurs in the story.

• **Setting** is the place and time in which the story happens. It's *where* and *when* the events take place, and it is usually conveyed through descriptive details.

• **Resolution** is the story's final outcome. It tells *how* the conflict is solved.

• **Dialogue** is conversation between characters. It helps readers understand what the characters are like and moves the plot forward.

Prewriting
Get Ready to Write

The following guidelines can help you plan and write your story, but you don't have to follow them word for word. Remember that you're in charge of your own writing process. You already know your story will be about a character's struggle to stay true to herself or himself, but you'll need to think about the character and the conflict before you start writing.

Gather Ideas

At this stage, start picturing whom and what you want to write about. Character and conflict affect each other. For example, if your main character is a thirteen-year-old boy, the conflict should be something that someone his age would be likely to experience.

Characters Think about the people in your story, starting with the main character. Picture each character in detail. What does he or she look like? How does he or she act? What is important to him or her? Take notes in a format that you find helpful. For example, you might list each character's traits, write a paragraph about each one, or make a word web for each one.

Literature Online

Writing Models For models and other writing activities, go to www.glencoe.com.

> My protagonist will be Marisol, a teenager with long black hair and gentle eyes. She is a great soccer player and plays for her school team. She is very close to her grandmother, who lives with the family.

Conflict List the events of your story in the order they'll happen. Or if you prefer, start by writing a scene that reveals the conflict.

- What causes the conflict?
- How will the main character stay true to himself or herself?
- How will the conflict be resolved?

If you don't know what to write about, think about your own experiences with trying to stay true to yourself. Or think about people you know and their struggles. Then use your imagination to add fictional details. For example, your main character might not want to go to an event with his family, or friends might be pressuring her to do something, or a brother or sister might ask him to help cover up a mistake they made.

> Marisol didn't know what to do. She didn't want to quit the soccer team, but she wanted to spend more time with her grandmother because she knew her grandmother wouldn't be around much longer.

Setting Describe where and when your story will take place. Use sensory imagery, such as descriptions of sights, smells, and sounds.

> Part of the story will take place at Marisol's school, and part will take place at her house, which will smell like her abuela's wonderful cooking.

> **Writing Tip**
>
> **Sequence** Most stories are told in chronological order: first this happened, then that happened, and then the next thing happened. That form of organization is usually easiest for readers to follow.

> **Writing Tip**
>
> **Vivid Details** Details that paint pictures in readers' minds include sensory imagery that appeals to the senses (the *sweet, crunchy tang* of honey chicken), vivid verbs (*ambled* instead of *walked*), specific nouns (*tulip,* not *flower*), and effective modifiers (*rusted-out* car with a *crumpled fender*).

Drafting
Start Writing!

Now that you have ideas about the basic elements of your story, it's time to start writing the first draft—your first version of your story.

Get It on Paper

To draft your short story, use the notes you made. Some of the decisions you made about your story may change as you write. That's OK. Just keep writing. If you're not sure how to begin your story, try these tips.

- Reread your prewriting. Underline words, phrases, or sentences you like.
- Start with dialogue. Have two characters start talking, and see what they have to say. Dialogue can tell you a lot about the characters as well as the conflict. Writing dialogue is a good way to get ideas flowing.

Develop Your Draft

Writers do a lot of different things to make their writing exciting to read. Look at the writing you've done so far. Use these tips to develop your draft.

1. Use details and descriptions to *show* your readers the characters, setting, and events. Specific and vivid details help to bring readers into the story and create a clear picture in their minds.

> Tears came into Marisol's eyes. Her grandmother looked so small and weak. Marisol pushed back her hair, pulled her jean jacket tighter, and ran to catch the bus.

2. Short stories keep readers interested by building suspense—making the reader wonder what is going to happen next. Help readers understand the conflict so they are interested in how the conflict is resolved.

> What was she going to do? She loved playing soccer, but she loved her grandmother more. If she didn't play, would she lose all her friends?

Writing Tip ▶

Getting Started Writing a short story should be fun. Don't make it into work. Relax and use your imagination. If your imagination runs dry, talk to friends or family members about your story.

Writing Tip ▶

Show; Don't Tell To make your writing more vivid, don't tell what characters feel. Show their reactions instead. Don't write "She felt angry." Write "She slammed her fist into her hand. Her face grew red."

Grammar Link

You have learned that a **simple sentence** is an independent clause. **Compound** and **complex sentences** are made up of a combination of independent and dependent clauses.

What Are Compound and Complex Sentences?

A **compound sentence** contains two or more simple sentences (independent clauses) joined by a comma and a coordinating conjunction (*and, but, or, nor, for, so,* and *yet*). In the following compound sentence, the independent clauses are underlined.

• The pears were ripe, but the plum was rotten.

A **complex sentence** contains at least one independent clause and one dependent clause. In the following complex sentences, the independent clause is underlined.

• Though the pears were ripe, the plum was rotten.

• When I picked it up, I could see that the plum was rotten from sitting in the sun.

Why Are Compound and Complex Sentences Important?

Using a variety of sentence types makes your writing more interesting. A series of simple sentences can be choppy and awkward to read. Combining different types of sentences creates a more natural flow. Compare the following:

Simple sentences only: I had so much fun at the zoo last Saturday. The panda bears were very playful. Tonya and I watched them for over an hour. The cub climbed on his mother. She sent him tumbling to the ground.

Simple, compound, and complex: I had so much fun at the zoo last Saturday. The panda bears were very playful, and Tonya and I watched them for over an hour. When the cub climbed on his mother, she sent him tumbling to the ground.

How Do I Use Compound and Complex Sentences?

Use a **compound sentence** to combine two ideas that are equally important.

• *The music was great.* + *The cake was delicious.* = The music was great, and the cake was delicious.

Use a **complex sentence** to combine ideas when one idea "depends on" another to make sense. Put the main idea in the independent clause. Put the idea that "depends on" the main idea in the dependent clause. The independent clause is underlined.

• *I slept in.* + *My alarm didn't go off.* = Because my alarm didn't go off, I slept in.

Write to Learn Reread your draft. Add variety and make your short story flow more smoothly by combining sentences to form compound and complex sentences.

Looking Ahead

Keep the writing you did here, and in Part 2 you'll learn how to turn it into a short story that you'll be proud of.

Skills Focus

You will practice using these skills when you read the following selections:

- "an african american," p. 588
- "One Throw," p. 596

Reading

- Questioning in order to improve comprehension

Literature

- Interpreting the effects of literary devices
- Analyzing features and styles of poetry
- Identifying and analyzing the plot elements in a story
- Explaining how conflict is related to the plot

Vocabulary

- Using suffixes to determine meaning
- Academic Vocabulary: *conversation*

Writing/Grammar

- Using commas in compound and complex sentences

NY English Language Arts Core Curriculum (pp. 584–585)

LC R12 Combine multiple strategies (question) to enhance comprehension and response.

For a complete description of the standards, see p. NY11.

Skill Lesson

Questioning

Learn It!

What Is It? **Questioning** is asking yourself questions about what you are reading. By asking and answering your own questions, you keep a **conversation** with yourself—a conversation that helps you better understand what you read. You might ask about people or characters in a selection. You might ask about the importance of what you're reading. Or you might ask about anything that puzzles you. Here are some sample questions.

- Who are the people or characters?
- How does one event relate to another?
- What is the main idea or theme?

Analyzing Cartoons
To find out about vultures, Barry questions his brother. To better understand the cartoon, you might ask yourself, *How does Barry's first question lead to his second question?*

Academic Vocabulary

conversation (kahn ver SAY shun) *n.* a talk between people

Why Is It Important? By asking questions, you make sure you understand what you are reading. As you answer your questions, you also keep track of important ideas and details.

How Do I Do It? As you read, stop from time to time and ask yourself questions. Many helpful questions begin with the 5Ws and an H: Who? What? When? Where? Why? How?

Literature Online

Study Central Visit www.glencoe.com and click on Study Central to review questioning.

Look at how a student used questions to understand the following passage.

> Dad pedaled like mad, flapped his paper wings, and . . . nothing happened. Unless, of course, riding into the pond counts.
>
> As I ran to help him, I heard Grandma shout, "You're going to break your fool head riding that contraption of yours, Sam McKenzie!"
>
> She hates Dad's inventions. I love them—and Dad. When he finally manages to build the first successful flying machine, we'll be rich.
>
> I can hardly wait for that day, because right now, to be perfectly honest, we're poor. We might not have a roof over our head if it weren't for Grandma.
>
> Dad spends most of his time and money on his inventions. The old barn is filled with metal parts.

What is the father in the story riding? I think it must be some kind of bike, because it says he "pedaled like mad." But it also says he "flapped his paper wings." Hmmm. The narrator says they'll be rich when his dad invents a successful flying machine. So the "contraption" must be a kind of flying machine with wheels, pedals, and wings.

Practice It!

Who do you think is telling the story? When do you think it takes place? Write your answers in your Learner's Notebook.

Use It!

As you read the selections, ask yourself 5Ws and an H questions. Answer your questions in your Learner's Notebook.

Before You Read : an african american

Meet the Author

Meri Nana-Ama Danquah was born in Ghana, West Africa, and raised in Washington, D.C. In addition to being an accomplished actress, poet, playwright, and performance artist, she is the author of a memoir, *Willow Weep for Me,* and the editor of two anthologies: *Becoming American* and *Shaking the Tree.* She divides her time between Los Angeles, California, and Accra, Ghana.

Author Search For more about Meri Nana-Ama Danquah, go to www.glencoe.com.

Vocabulary Preview

mimicked (MIH mikt) *v.* copied; imitated; form of the verb *mimic* **(p. 589)** *Keesha mimicked the girls' laughter, hoping they would include her in their conversation.*

unison (YOO nih sun) *n.* one voice **(p. 590)** *The chorus sang in perfect unison at the school assembly.*

anthem (AN thum) *n.* the official song of a country, school, or group **(p. 590)** *The band plays its school's anthem before every game.*

Write to Learn Write a paragraph using all the vocabulary words.

English Language Coach

Introduction to Suffixes A **suffix** is a word part that is added to the end of a root or base word. If you think about the meaning of the root or base and the suffix, you may be able to figure out the meaning of the word. Suppose, for example, that you see the word *flutist* in the following sentence: *Donna is an excellent flutist.* If you know that the suffix *-ist* means "person who," you can guess that a *flutist* is a person who plays the flute.

A suffix may change more than a word's meaning. It may also change the word's part of speech. For example, adding the suffix *-er* to the verb *teach* makes the word *teacher,* which is a noun. Look at the suffixes listed on the chart below. You'll see some of them in "an african american." When any of these suffixes is added to a word, the word usually becomes a noun.

Suffix	Meaning	Word Example
-an, -ian	"person who"	music<u>ian</u>
-ance,	"action or process of"	perform<u>ance</u>
-ence	"quality or state of"	exist<u>ence</u>
-ation, -ion	"action of or result of"	invent<u>ion</u>
-ist	"person who"	art<u>ist</u>
-ness	"state, quality, or condition of"	sad<u>ness</u>

Write to Learn Make each word below a noun by adding one of the suffixes above to it. Use a dictionary if you need help.

dark • **reflect** • **assist** • **special**

NY English Language Arts Core Curriculum (pp. 586–591)

LC R6 Determine the meaning of words by using word structure knowledge.
LC R12 Combine multiple strategies (question) to enhance comprehension and response. **R2e** Recognize how the author's use of language creates images or feelings.

For a complete description of the standards, see p. NY11.

Skills Preview

Key Reading Skill: Questioning

The selection you are about to read is a poem. Think about the questions you might have as you read a poem. Here are some examples:

- Who is the speaker?
- What is the speaker describing?

Write to Learn In your Learner's Notebook, write three other questions you might ask about a poem.

Literary Element: Sensory Imagery

Artists use colors, shapes, and patterns to pull you into their paintings. One way that writers pull you into their work is by using **sensory imagery,** or descriptions that appeal to the five senses.

Sensory imagery helps readers imagine how something looks, sounds, feels, smells, and tastes. Poets use sensory imagery to make their poems come alive and help readers connect to people, places, events, and ideas. As you read poetry, use these tips to find and understand sensory imagery.

- Notice descriptions of sights, sounds, textures, odors, and tastes. Ask yourself, *What do these details add to the selection?*
- Think about the speaker in the poem who makes the descriptions. Ask yourself, *What do the speaker's descriptions tell me about him or her?*

Partner Talk With a partner, discuss which senses the following sentences appeal to.

- When Ted bit into the shiny red apple, the fruit was so crisp that it snapped. With every crunchy bite he savored its sweetness.

Interactive Literary Elements Handbook
To review or learn more about the literary elements, go to www.glencoe.com.

Get Ready to Read

Connect to the Reading

Have you ever moved to a new neighborhood, city, or country? Think of what it would be like to adjust to life in a new place. How would you try to fit in? Would you act differently, or would you try to stay the same?

Partner Talk With a partner, list some things you might have to get used to if you moved someplace new.

Build Background

In the poem, the speaker mentions places in Africa and places in the United States.

- Washington, D.C., the capital of the United States, is on the east coast between Maryland and Virginia. The initials *D.C.* stand for District of Columbia. According to the last government census, or "head count," more than 5.5 million people live in Washington, D.C. More than half the population identifies itself as African American or black.
- Atlanta is the capital of Georgia, a southern U.S. state. States that border Georgia are North Carolina, South Carolina, Florida, Alabama, and Tennessee. About 400,000 people live in Atlanta. More than 60 percent of the population identifies itself as African American or black.

Set Purposes for Reading

BIG Question Read "an african american" to learn what values are important to the speaker in the poem and whether she is determined to stay true to herself.

Set Your Own Purpose What else would you like to learn from the poem to help you answer the Big Question? Write your own purpose on "an african american" page of Foldable 5.

Keep Moving

Use these skills as you read "an african american."

an african american

by Meri Nana-Ama Danquah

i wanna tell you a story
of washington, dc
of atlanta, georgia
of addis abbaba
5 of tangier, soweto and lagos*

i wanna shed some light
on the dark continent*
i wanna tell you a story
of me ◻1

10 i stand before you
dark and proud
asante princess
african queen
born and bred
15 on black soil
in a black nation
they call ghana

i spoke the language
of my ancestors
20 i ate the food
planted by our mothers' hand
i danced the drumbeats
of our animist* gods

Practice the Skills

◻1 Key Reading Skill

Questioning Ask yourself these questions after reading the first few lines of the poem:

• *What is the title of the poem?*

• *How does the title relate to the places mentioned in the first nine lines? To the speaker?*

Then answer the questions.

---

5 ***Addis Abbaba*** is the capital of Ethiopia in East Africa. ***Tangier*** is a city in Morocco in North Africa. ***Soweto*** is a group of townships in the country of South Africa. ***Lagos*** is a city in Nigeria in West Africa.

7 Europeans called Africa the ***dark continent*** in the nineteenth century because parts of it were so difficult for them to explore that they didn't know a lot about it.

23 An ***animist*** believes that all things in nature have a spirit or soul within them.

an asante princess
25 an african queen
who crossed the middle passage*
arrived in america
speaking very little english
with thick lips
30 and thick accent

unable to pronounce my name
people called me
the foreigner
the african girl
35 i went to school
with your daughters and sons
your cousins and friends
mimicked their speech
dressed their style
40 seemingly became one of them ❷

i wove my **blackness**
my **africanness** ❸
chameleon-like*
into the red, the white and the blue
45 which is the fabric of this nation
wanting desperately to belong

when i sleep
i snore with the lions and tigers
in the safari land
50 i snore with the sounds
of the noontime traffic on georgia avenue
in the district of columbia

Analyzing the Photo How does the teenager in this photo illustrate one important aspect of the speaker's identity?

Practice the Skills

❷ **Literary Element**

Sensory Imagery Which descriptions in lines 24–40 appeal to the sense of sight?

❸ **English Language Coach**

Suffixes Adding the suffix -*ness* to the adjectives *black* and *african* changes them into nouns. Review the meaning of -*ness;* then define the two nouns.

---

26. The *Middle Passage* was the journey that many slave ships took from West Africa across the Atlantic Ocean to the Americas.

43. A *chameleon* is a type of lizard that changes the color of its skin to fit in with its surroundings.

Vocabulary

mimicked (MIH mikt) *v.* copied; imitated

when i dream
the voices of jomo kenyatta, patrice lumumba
55 and dr. martin luther king, jr.*
speak to me in **unison**
when i cry
rain falls on the sahara
and the potomac river overflows* ◼4
60 i sway to alpha blondy*
as easily as i do stevie wonder

open your ears
my children
and listen to this griot*
65 talk of history
being made
i wanna tell you this story
of my life

the blood which flows
70 through the left side of my body
is the mississippi river
every day i wake it croons
"lift every voice and sing"
the **anthem** of the american negro

75 the blood which flows
through the right side of my body
is the nile river
every day i rise it screams out loud
"africa, oh africa, cry freedom
80 for all your children" ◼5

Analyzing the Photo In 1960 Patrice Lumumba became the first prime minister of the Democratic Republic of the Congo. He was assassinated in 1961. What do you learn about him in this photo?

Practice the Skills

◼4 **Literary Element**

Sensory Imagery A person crying doesn't really create rain in the desert or make a river overflow. What idea is the author trying to get across here?

◼5 **Key Reading Skill**

Questioning To what does the speaker compare the blood flowing through her body? Reread lines 69–80 to help yourself answer this question.

---

55. Here, two African leaders are paired with an African American leader: *Jomo Kenyatta* was the first president of Kenya; *Patrice Lumumba* was the first prime minister of the Democratic Republic of the Congo; *Dr. Martin Luther King Jr.* led the civil rights movement in the United States during the 1950s and 1960s.

59. The *Sahara* is a desert in North Africa, and the *Potomac* is a river that runs through Washington, D.C.

60. *Alpha Blondy* is a popular reggae musician from Ivory Coast in Africa.

64. A *griot* is a West African storyteller and musician who shares the history of his or her people.

Vocabulary

unison (YOO nih sun) *n.* one voice

anthem (AN thum) *n.* the official song of a country, school, or group

don't think me confused
because i don't know
where home is anymore
i just know
85 that the veins
in the body from the right and the left
flow to the heart
and become one love

if i die on african soil
90 bury me in jeans and sneakers
let my tombstone read in english
"native **washingtonian**"
and sing an old negro spiritual for me please ⑥

if i die on american soil
95 pour libation* on the ground
lay a flag of red, green and gold
with a black star*
on my coffin
let the talking drums spread the news
100 let the words on my tombstone
be multi-lingual and let them scream
asante princess
african queen ⑦

let no one question my origin
105 let me live and die in peace
as who i am
because you see
i have broken all barriers
of love and unity
110 i am
in the truest sense of the word
an african american ⑧ ○

---

95. To **pour libation** is to pour wine or oil on the ground as an offering to the gods in a religious ceremony.

97. The flag of Ghana has **red, green, and gold bands with a black star.**

Practice the Skills

⑥ **English Language Coach**

Suffixes Washington is a place. How does adding the suffix *-ian* change the meaning? What is a **Washingtonian**?

⑦ **Literary Element**

Sensory Imagery What sound imagery is in lines 100–104?

⑧ **BIG Question**

In this poem, the speaker defines who she is. How does she stay true to herself? Write your answer on "an african american" page of Foldable 5. Your response will help you complete the Unit Challenge later.

After You Read

an african american

Answering the **BIG** Question

1. How does the speaker of this poem remain true to herself?
2. **Recall** What part of Africa is the speaker from?
   TIP Right There

3. **Recall** What does the speaker want if she dies on African soil?
   TIP Right There

Critical Thinking

4. **Interpret** To what does the speaker compare her journey to America, and how is that important?
   TIP Author and Me

5. **Analyze** In lines 41–44 the speaker compares herself to a chameleon, saying, "i wove my blackness / my africanness / chameleon-like / into the red, the white and the blue." In what way or ways do you think that the speaker is like a chameleon?
   TIP Author and Me

6. **Evaluate** In your opinion, is the title "an african american" a good one for the poem? Back up your opinion with details from the poem.
   TIP On My Own

Talk About Your Reading

Whole Class Discussion Throughout the poem, the speaker describes the "African side" of her and the "American side" of her. As a class, reread the poem to find all the examples she gives of her "Africanness" and all the examples she give of her "Americanness." Record your findings on a chart like the one pictured below. Then discuss how identifying the examples helps you understand the poem.

African Side	American Side

**NY English Language Arts
Core Curriculum** (pp. 592–593)

LC R17 Demonstrate comprehension and response through a range of activities.
LC S8 Participate in group discussions on a range of topics and for a variety of purposes. **LC R12** Combine multiple strategies (question) to enhance comprehension and response. **R2e** Recognize how the author's use of language creates images or feelings. **LC R6** Determine the meaning of words by using word structure knowledge. **Core W8** Use correct grammatical construction.

For a complete description of the standards, see p. NY11.

Skills Review

Key Reading Skill: Questioning

7. How did questioning help you understand the speaker and the poem? Write two questions that you wrote in your Learner's Notebook and explain how they helped you.

Literary Element: Sensory Imagery

8. The poem contains a lot of imagery that appeals to the senses of sight and sound. List at least five examples of each. Include a line number for each image you list.

Vocabulary Check

Fill in each blank with the word that makes sense in the sentence.

mimicked • unison • anthem

9. The dancers performed in _____ and won first prize at the competition.

10. When the apes _____ human expressions, the people were amazed.

11. Many countries have their own national _____.

12. Academic Vocabulary If you are having a **conversation,** what are you doing?

English Language Coach For each noun below, write its base word and the suffix that makes it a noun.

13. flirtation

14. fairness

15. European

16. clearance

Literature Online

Web Activities For eFlashcards, Selection Quick Checks, and other Web activities, go to www.glencoe.com.

Grammar Link: Commas in Compound Sentences

The most basic kind of **compound sentence** contains two or more simple sentences (independent clauses) joined by a comma and a coordinating conjunction (*and, but, for, nor, or* and sometimes *so* and *yet*).

• Uma couldn't come to our get-together, and Joanne missed it, too.

  (The first simple sentence is "Uma couldn't come to our get-together." The second simple sentence is "Joanne missed it, too." The comma and conjunction *and* join the simple sentences.)

• I like watching martial arts like karate, but I do not want to learn them myself.

  (The first simple sentence is "I like watching martial arts like karate." The second simple sentence is "I do not want to learn them myself." The comma and conjunction *but* join the simple sentences.)

Look Out! If both simple sentences in a compound sentence are short—five words or less—you can omit the comma. In all other compound sentences, put a comma before the coordinating conjunction.

• Uma performs well <u>and</u> she enjoys learning.

  (Both simple sentences are three words long. Because they are short, the comma can be omitted.)

• Uma performs well in her karate class, <u>and</u> she enjoys learning new moves.

  (The comma is needed because the first simple sentence is more than five words long.)

Grammar Practice

Add a comma to each compound sentence that needs one.

17. I like to fly kites and I like to skateboard.

18. Ellie has had the chicken pox but she has never had the measles.

19. I finished cutting the grass so now I can go out.

Before You Read : One Throw

W. C. Heinz

Meet the Author

W. C. Heinz worked as a reporter in Europe during World War II and afterward became a sports editor. Besides articles he has written fiction and nonfiction books about sports. He is also the coauthor of the novel *MASH,* which inspired a movie and a TV series. *See page R2 of The Author Files in the back of the book for more on W. C. Heinz.*

Author Search For more about W. C. Heinz, go to www.glencoe.com.

NY English Language Arts Core Curriculum (pp. 594–601)

LC R6 Determine the meaning of words by using word structure knowledge.
LC R12 Combine multiple strategies (question) to enhance comprehension and response. **R2b** Interpret plot, using evidence from the text.

For a complete description of the standards, see p. NY11.

Vocabulary Preview

egging (EHG ing) *adj.* urging; encouraging to take action; form of the verb *egg* **(p. 600)** *The boys said, "Do it!" egging their brother on until he finally took the dare.*

needle (NEE duhl) *v.* cause to take action by repeated stinging comments **(p. 601)** *Your teasing remarks will not needle me into doing anything.*

English Language Coach

Other Common Suffixes You've already learned that adding a suffix to a word can change the word's meaning and part of speech. Remember that learning what common suffixes mean can help you unlock the meaning of unfamiliar words—especially in conjunction with context.

Study the common suffixes and their meanings below. You'll see some of these suffixes in the selection you are about to read, "One Throw."

Suffix	Meaning	Word Example
-er, -or	"that which" or "person who"	bak<u>er</u>, sail<u>or</u>
-hood	"state, condition, or quality of"	neighbor<u>hood</u>
-ment	"action or process of" or "result of"	arrange<u>ment</u>
-ship	"state, condition, or quality of"	friend<u>ship</u>

Partner Talk Which suffixes from the chart above could be added to the words below? With a classmate, find the suffix that goes with each word. Use a dictionary if necessary. Discuss how adding the suffix changes the word's meaning.

1. enjoy

2. child

3. speak

4. citizen

Skills Preview

Key Reading Skill: Questioning

Before you read "One Throw," think about questions you might ask yourself to understand the plot, characters, and theme of the short story. Here are some sample questions you might ask:

- *Who are the main characters?*
- *What causes a character to act a certain way?*
- *How does one event lead to another?*

Partner Talk With a partner, add questions to the list that you could ask yourself as you read. Write your questions in your Learner's Notebook. Refer to them as you read the story, and jot down answers to them.

Key Literary Element: Plot

Plot is the sequence of events in a fictional story in which a problem is explored and then solved. Plot is created through **conflict**—a struggle within or between people or forces. A plot has these parts:

1. **exposition**—the beginning that introduces the characters, setting, and conflict
2. **rising action**—the complications that arise as the protagonist faces the conflict
3. **climax**—the most emotional or suspenseful point in the story
4. **falling action**—the events that show how the conflict will probably work out
5. **resolution**—the outcome of the conflict

Whole Class Discussion "One Throw" is about a young baseball player who plays in the minor leagues. From this situation, what conflicts do you think you might find in the story? Make a list. Then read the story to see whether you guessed right.

Interactive Literary Elements Handbook
To review or learn more about the literary elements, go to www.glencoe.com.

Get Ready to Read

Connect to the Reading

Recall a time when a friend gave you advice that you thought was bad. Did you follow the advice?

Write to Learn In your Learner's Notebook, jot down a few sentences describing what the advice was, whether you followed it, and why.

Build Background

To understand "One Throw," you need to know a little about baseball's minor leagues and major leagues. Here is some background on those subjects.

- A *league* is a group of teams that play each other.
- The different minor leagues have groups of teams that play at different levels. Players who have good skills and who show promise are often moved up to a higher-level minor-league team.
- The best minor-league players are asked to join major-league teams. There, the players are the most skilled, and the competition is tough.
- These are the highest levels of the minor leagues:
  —Class AAA, sometimes called the "parking lot" because so many good players are "parked," or held on reserve, there
  —Class AA, home to many experienced players hoping to enter U.S. baseball from foreign leagues
  —Class A, where many promising young players work on improving their skills

Set Purposes for Reading

BIG Question Read "One Throw" to discover how a ballplayer stays true to himself.

Set Your Own Purpose What else would you like to learn from the story to help you answer the Big Question? Write your own purpose on the "One Throw" page of Foldable 5.

Keep Moving

Use these skills as you read "One Throw."

Baseball at Night, 1934.
Morris Kantor. Oil on
linen. Smithsonian
American Art Museum.

One Throw

by W. C. Heinz

I checked into a hotel called the Olympia, which is right on the main street and the only hotel in the town. After lunch I was hanging around the lobby, and I got to talking to the guy at the desk. I asked him if this wasn't the town where that kid named Maneri played ball.

"That's right," the guy said. "He's a pretty good **ballplayer.**" **1**

"He should be," I said. "I read that he was the new Phil Rizzuto."[1]

"That's what they said," the guy said.

"What's the matter with him?" I said. "I mean if he's such a good ballplayer what's he doing in this league?"

"I don't know," the guy said. "I guess the Yankees[2] know what they're doing."

"He's a nice kid," the guy said. "He plays good ball, but I feel sorry for him. He thought he'd be playing for the Yankees soon, and here he is in this town. You can see it's got him down." **2**

---

1. *Phil Rizzuto* was the star shortstop for the New York Yankees in the 1940s.
2. The *Yankees* were the dominant baseball team in the major leagues in the 1940s and 1950s.

Practice the Skills

1 **English Language Coach**

More Common Suffixes A **ballplayer** is someone who plays ball. Look at how the word *ballplayer* is formed: ball (noun) + play (verb) + er (suffix).

2 **Key Literary Element**

Plot In this beginning part of the plot, called *exposition,* you learn a little about the setting, the characters, and a possible conflict to come.

"He lives here in this hotel?"

"That's right," the guy said. "Most of the older ballplayers stay in rooming houses,[3] but Pete and a couple other kids live here."

He was leaning on the desk, talking to me and looking across the hotel lobby. He nodded his head. "This is a funny thing," he said. "Here he comes now."

The kid had come through the door from the street. He had on a light gray sport shirt and a pair of gray flannel slacks.

I could see why, when he showed up with the Yankees in spring training,[4] he made them all think of Rizzuto. He isn't any bigger than Rizzuto, and he looks just like him.

"Hello, Nick," he said to the guy at the desk.

"Hello, Pete," the guy at the desk said. "How goes it today?"

"All right," the kid said but you could see he was exaggerating.

"I'm sorry, Pete," the guy at the desk said, "but no mail today." **3**

"That's all right, Nick," the kid said. "I'm used to it."

"Excuse me," I said, "but you're Pete Maneri?"

"That's right," the kid said, turning and looking at me.

"Excuse me," the guy at the desk said, introducing us. "Pete, this is Mr. Franklin."

"Harry Franklin," I said.

"I'm glad to know you," the kid said, shaking my hand.

"I recognize you from your pictures," I said.

"Pete's a good ballplayer," the guy at the desk said.

"Not very," the kid said.

"Don't take his word for it, Mr. Franklin," the guy said.

"I'm a great ball fan," I said to the kid. "Do you people play tonight?"

"We play two games," the kid said.

"The first game's at six o'clock," the guy at the desk said. "They play pretty good ball."

"I'll be there," I said. "I used to play a little ball myself."

"You did?" the kid said.

"With Columbus," I said. "That's twenty years ago."

"Is that right?" the kid said. . . .

Practice the Skills

3 | **Key Reading Skill**

Questioning What do you think Pete is hoping will come in the mail? Why do you think so?

---

3. **Rooming houses** are private houses where the owners rent out rooms.

4. **Spring training** is a period in late winter and early spring when baseball players prepare for the regular playing season.

#71 *Minor League,* 1946. Clyde Singer. Oil on canvas. Butler Museum of American Art, Youngstown, OH.

Analyzing the Painting How does this picture capture the "feel" of a minor-league baseball game?

That's the way I got to talking with the kid. They had one of those pine-paneled taprooms[5] in the basement of the hotel, and we went down there. I had a couple and the kid had a Coke, and I told him a few stories and he turned out to be a real good **listener.** **4**

"But what do you do now, Mr. Franklin?" he said after a while.

"I sell hardware,"[6] I said. "I can think of some things I'd like better, but I was going to ask you how you like playing in this league."

"Well," the kid said, "I suppose it's all right. I guess I've got no kick coming." **5**

"Oh, I don't know," I said. "I understand you're too good for this league. What are they trying to do to you?"

"I don't know," the kid said. "I can't understand it."

"What's the trouble?"

"Well," the kid said, "I don't get along very well here. I mean there's nothing wrong with my playing. I'm hitting .365 right now. I lead the league in stolen bases. There's nobody can field with me, but who cares?" **6**

"Who manages this ball club?"

"Al Dall," the kid said. "You remember, he played in the outfield for the Yankees for about four years."

Practice the Skills

4 **English Language Coach**

Suffixes *Listen* is a verb. What happens when you add the suffix *-er* to this verb? Define **listener.**

5 **Skill Review**

Making Inferences What do you think Pete means when he says, "I guess I've got no kick coming"? Write your answer in your Learner's Notebook.

6 **Key Literary Element**

Plot Pete seems to be experiencing an inner conflict. What do you think that conflict is?

---

5. A *pine-paneled taproom* is a bar with pinewood paneling on the walls.

6. In this context, *hardware* is tools and equipment made from metal.

"I remember."

"Maybe he is all right," the kid said, "but I don't get along with him. He's on my neck all the time."

"Well," I said, "that's the way they are in the minors sometimes. You have to remember the guy is looking out for himself and his ball club first. He's not worried about you."

"I know that," the kid said. "If I get the big hit or make the play he never says anything. The other night I tried to take second on a loose ball and I got caught in the run-down. He bawls me out in front of everybody. There's nothing I can do."

"Oh, I don't know," I said. "This is probably a guy who knows he's got a good thing in you, and he's looking to keep you around. You people lead the league, and that makes him look good. He doesn't want to lose you to Kansas City or the Yankees." **7**

"That's what I mean," the kid said. "When the Yankees sent me down here they said, 'Don't worry. We'll keep an eye on you.' So Dall never sends a good report on me. Nobody ever comes down to look me over. What chance is there for a guy like Eddie Brown or somebody like that coming down to see me in this town?"

"You have to remember that Eddie Brown's the big shot," I said, "the great Yankee scout."[7]

"Sure," the kid said. "I never even saw him, and I'll never see him in this place. I have an idea that if they ever ask Dall about me he keeps knocking me down."

"Why don't you go after Dall?" I said. "I had trouble like that once myself, but I figured out a way to get attention."

"You did?" the kid said.

"I threw a couple of balls over the first baseman's head," I said. "I threw a couple of games away, and that really got the **manager** sore. **8** I was lousing up his ball club and his record. So what does he do? He blows the whistle[8] on me, and what happens? That gets the brass[9] curious, and they send down to see what's wrong."

"Is that so?" the kid said. "What happened?"

"Two weeks later," I said, "I was up with Columbus."

"Is that right?" the kid said.

---

7. A **scout** is someone who looks for new, talented sports players.

8. To **blow the whistle** is to give information about wrongdoing to someone in charge.

9. Here, **brass** means people in high positions.

Practice the Skills

7 Key Reading Skill

Questioning Why does the narrator takes an interest in Pete?

8 English Language Coach

Suffixes The suffix -er changes the verb *manage* into a noun. Notice that the base word ends in an *e*, so you add only the *r* of the suffix.

"Sure," I said, **egging** him on. "What have you got to lose?"

"Nothing," the kid said. "I haven't got anything to lose." **9**

"I'd try it," I said.

"I might try it," the kid said. "I might try it tonight if the spot comes up."

I could see from the way he said it that he was madder than he'd said. Maybe you think this is mean to steam a kid up like this, but I do some strange things.

"Take over," I said. "Don't let this guy ruin your career."

"I'll try it," the kid said. **10** "Are you coming out to the park tonight?"

"I wouldn't miss it," I said. "This will be better than making out route sheets and sales orders."

It's not much ballpark in this town—old wooden bleachers and an old wooden fence and about four hundred people in the stands. The first game wasn't much either, with the home club winning something like 8 to 1.

The kid didn't have any hard chances, but I could see he was a ballplayer, with a double and a couple of walks and a lot of speed.

The second game was different, though. The other club got a couple of runs and then the home club picked up three runs in one, and they were in the top of the ninth with a 3–2 lead and two outs when the pitching began to fall apart and they loaded the bases.

I was trying to wish the ball down to the kid, just to see what he'd do with it, when the batter drives one on one big bounce to the kid's right.

Visual Vocabulary
A **backhand** catch is very difficult because the player's arm is twisted and the body is turned away from the ball.

The kid was off for it when the ball started. He made a backhand stab and grabbed it. He was deep now, and he turned in the air and fired. If it goes over the first baseman's head, it's two runs in and a panic—but it's the prettiest throw you'd want to see. It's right on a line, and the runner is out by a step, and it's the ball game. **11**

Practice the Skills

9 **Key Reading Skill**

Questioning What does Pete actually have to lose?

10 **Key Reading Skill**

Questioning What is the "it" that Pete says he will try?

11 **Key Literary Element**

Plot This is the climax, or moment of highest tension, when Pete makes an important decision. Did he decide to follow the narrator's advice? Explain.

Vocabulary

egging (EHG ing) *adj.* urging; encouraging to take action

Practice the Skills

$\mathbf{I}$ walked back to the hotel, thinking about the kid. I sat around the lobby until I saw him come in, and then I walked toward the elevator like I was going to my room, but so I'd meet him. And I could see he didn't want to talk.

"How about a Coke?" I said.

"No," he said. "Thanks, but I'm going to bed."

"Look," I said. "Forget it. You did the right thing. Have a Coke."

We were sitting in the taproom again. The kid wasn't saying anything.

"Why didn't you throw that ball away?" I said.

"I don't know," the kid said. "I had it in my mind before he hit it, but I couldn't." **12**

"Why?"

"I don't know why."

"I know why," I said.

The kid didn't say anything. He just sat looking down.

"Do you know why you couldn't throw that ball away?" I said.

"No," the kid said.

"You couldn't throw that ball away," I said, "because you're going to be a major-league ballplayer someday."

The kid just looked at me. He had that same sore expression.

"Do you know why you're going to be a major-league ballplayer?" I said.

The kid was just looking down again, shaking his head. I never got more of a kick out of anything in my life.

"You're going to be a major-league ballplayer," I said, "because you couldn't throw that ball away, and because I'm not a hardware salesman and my name's not Harry Franklin."

"What do you mean?" the kid said.

"I mean," I explained to him, "that I tried to **needle** you into throwing that ball away because I'm Eddie Brown." **13** ○

12 Key Literary Element

Plot This is the falling action of the plot, when you begin to see how the resolution to the conflict will probably work out. The resolution is that Pete couldn't throw the ball away. Why couldn't Pete do it?

13 BIG Question

What do Pete's actions tell you about how he stays true to himself? Write your answer on the "One Throw" page of Foldable 5. Your response will help you complete the Unit Challenge later.

Vocabulary

needle (NEE duhl) *v.* cause to take action by repeated stinging comments

After You Read

One Throw

Answering the BIG Question

1. How did Pete stay true to himself?

2. **Recall** Whom does the narrator pretend to be?
   TIP Right There

3. **Recall** What is the narrator's real name and job?
   TIP Right There

Critical Thinking

4. **Infer** Why does the narrator keep his real identity a secret until his last conversation with Pete?
   TIP Author and Me

5. **Infer** Why does the narrator try to get Pete to throw a game?
   TIP Author and Me

6. **Interpret** The title "One Throw" has a double meaning. What are the two meanings of "throw" in this context?
   TIP Author and Me

7. **Analyze** Think about how Pete resolves his conflict and what happens to him at the end of the story. What theme, or message, do you think the story is trying to get across?
   TIP Author and Me

Write About Your Reading

Press Release Imagine that you work in the New York Yankees publicity office. You want to announce that Pete Maneri has just been signed by the team. In a small group, discuss how you would introduce the new player.

- Identify who Pete is. Include his age, the position he plays, and other personal information. Use facts from the story and your imagination.

- Describe his experience. Mention where he played before, what his statistics are as a player, and what his abilities are.

- Explain what the team's expectations are for his future.

When you are finished, write your press release and share it with the class.

NY English Language Arts Core Curriculum (pp. 602–603)

LC R17 Demonstrate comprehension and response through a range of activities. **LC W8** Work collaboratively with peers to plan, draft, revise, and edit written work. **LC R12** Combine multiple strategies (question) to enhance comprehension and response. **R2b** Interpret plot, using evidence from the text. **LC R6** Determine the meaning of words by using word structure knowledge. **Core W8** Use correct grammatical construction.

For a complete description of the standards, see p. NY11.

Skills Review

Key Reading Skill: Questioning

8. Think back to the questions that you asked your-self while you were reading "One Throw." Did any of them prepare you for the surprise ending? Explain your answer.

Key Literary Element: Plot

9. What happens in each part of the plot of "One Throw"? Copy the graphic organizer below. Under each heading, list the events from the story that make up that part.

exposition	rising action	climax	falling action	resolution

Vocabulary Check

10. The verbs *egg* and *needle* are similar in meaning as slang words. Write a sentence using one of them. Then replace it with the other. Did you have to change anything else in the sentence?

English Language Coach Find the noun in each sentence below that was made by adding a suffix to a base word. On a separate sheet of paper, write the base word and the suffix for each sentence.

11. Joe hired a builder to make the kitchen larger.

12. The U.S. government has three main branches.

13. Part of a team's success depends on its leadership.

14. Juan was my favorite actor in the school play.

Grammar Link: Commas in Complex Sentences

A **complex sentence** contains at least one independent clause and one dependent clause. The clauses are joined by a subordinating conjunction, such as *after, although, because, before, if, since, unless, until, when,* and *while.*

When a complex sentence begins with an *independent* clause, it does not need a comma.

- We will have dinner when Curtis arrives.
   independent   dependent

When a complex sentence begins with a *dependent* clause, put a comma **after** the dependent clause.

- When Curtis arrives, we will have dinner.
   dependent   independent

Look Out! Do not put a comma after a subordinating conjunction. Put the comma after the whole dependent clause.

Wrong: Although, I studied I didn't do well on the quiz.

Right: Although I studied, I didn't do well on the quiz.

Grammar Practice

On a separate sheet of paper, copy the complex sentences below. Add commas where needed.

15. Eduardo has loved camping since he was a child.

16. When he was little he always pretended to camp out.

17. Once he is older he will save to buy a camper.

Web Activities For eFlashcards, Selection Quick Checks, and other Web activities, go to www.glencoe.com.

Skills Focus

You will practice using these skills when you read the following selections:
- "The Medicine Bag," p. 608
- "A Year of Living Bravely," p. 622

Reading

- Predicting future events and behaviors in a story
- Predicting the content of a nonfiction selection

Literature

- Identifying and interpreting theme
- Identifying attention-getting devices

Vocabulary

- Using prefixes to determine meaning
- Academic Vocabulary: *relevant*

Writing/Grammar

- Combining sentences

NY English Language Arts Core Curriculum
(pp. 604–605)

LC R12 Combine multiple strategies (predict/confirm) to enhance comprehension and response. **R1m** Make, confirm, or revise predictions.

For a complete description of the standards, see p. NY11.

Skill Lesson

Predicting

Learn It!

Predicting is making an educated guess about what will happen in a story or what a nonfiction text will be about. Use your knowledge, your experience, and **relevant** information in a selection to predict things like these:

- what events will happen next in a story
- how characters will behave
- how conflicts will be resolved
- what you will find in a nonfiction text

Analyzing Cartoons

Hobbes makes a prediction based on what he knows he is going to do to Calivn. Do you think he is going go push Calvin into the mud? Your answer will be a prediction.

CALVIN AND HOBBES © 1987 Watterson. Dist. By UNIVERSAL PRESS SYNDICATE. Reprinted with permission. All rights reserved.

Academic Vocabulary

relevant (REH luh vunt) *adj.* important to the subject at hand; significant; pertinent

Why Is It Important? Making predictions keeps you involved in a selection because it's fun to guess and see whether your guesses are right. Predicting also helps you think critically about the selection. As you predict, you are actually analyzing the events, the characters, and the content.

How Do I Do It? Combine your knowledge of people and the world with the information in the story to predict what will happen. Make guesses that fit the characters' personalities, their situation, and their surroundings. Don't worry if a prediction is wrong. Analyze where you went wrong. (For example, did you misunderstand why a character was acting a particular way?) Then read on and revise your predictions to fit new information. Here's what a student predicted while reading a story about a family that has a dog and gets a new kitten.

Study Central Visit www.glencoe .com and click on Study Central to review predicting.

> Holding the kitten in her arms, Josie knelt down in front of the big brown dog. "Rover, this is Andy," she said. Rover sniffed Andy and began to growl.

I don't think Rover will welcome the new kitten. In fact, I think he's seconds away from biting Andy. Most dogs I know don't growl when they are being friendly.

Practice It!

In your Learner's Notebook, write your own prediction about what Andy will do. Then read the next paragraph of the story:

> Andy began licking the dog's head. Rover looked surprised and stopped growling. Soon he was licking back. It looked as if the two were becoming friends.

Was your prediction right? Why or why not? Do you think the author was trying to surprise you?

Use It!

As you read the selections in this workshop—"The Medicine Bag" and "A Year of Living Bravely"—make predictions about how the main characters will handle the problems they face.

Before You Read : The Medicine Bag

Virginia Driving Hawk Sneve

Meet the Author

Virginia Driving Hawk Sneve grew up on the Rosebud Reservation in South Dakota. She is a teacher, school counselor, and editor. Sneve has written many books about the history and culture of Native American peoples. She says her grandmothers gave her a love of Indian traditions and storytelling. *See page R6 of The Author Files in the back of the book for more on Virginia Driving Hawk Sneve.*

Author Search For more about Virginia Driving Hawk Sneve, go to www.glencoe.com.

NY English Language Arts Core Curriculum (pp. 606–617)
LC R6 Determine the meaning of words by using word structure knowledge.
LC R12 Combine multiple strategies (predict/confirm) to enhance comprehension and response. **R1m** Make, confirm, or revise predictions. **R2b** Interpret theme, using evidence from the text. **R2g** Compare literature to own lives.

For a complete description of the standards, see p. NY11.

Vocabulary Preview

authentic (aw THEN tik) *adj.* real; genuine **(p. 608)** *Martin and his sister got authentic Sioux gifts from their great-grandfather.*

stately (STAYT lee) *adj.* grand; impressive; dignified **(p. 608)** *The banquet was held at a stately mansion.*

commotion (kum OH shun) *n.* noisy, confused activity **(p. 609)** *There was so much commotion in the lunchroom she couldn't hear herself think.*

descendants (duh SEN dunts) *n.* people who are related to an earlier generation **(p. 611)** *Martin and his sister are the descendants of their grandfather.*

sacred (SAY krid) *adj.* holy; having to do with religion **(p. 615)** *Sage is part of a sacred ritual.*

Partner Talk With a classmate, talk about the vocabulary words and their definitions. Based on them, what do you think might happen in the story?

English Language Coach

Prefixes That Mean "Not" Breaking a word down into its parts can help you understand its meaning. A **prefix** is a syllable added to the beginning of a base word or root word. Just like suffixes, prefixes change or add to the meaning of the base word or root word. Here are some common prefixes that turn words into their opposites. You will see several of the prefixes in "The Medicine Bag." Look for them as you read.

Prefix	Word Examples	Meaning
dis-	disbelieve	"not believe"
il-	illegal	"not legal"
im-	imperfect	"not perfect"
in-	invisible	"not visible"
ir-	irregular	"not regular"
un-	unhappy	"not happy"

On Your Own Write a sentence using each of these words from the chart.

1. disbelieve
2. imperfect
3. invisible
4. unhappy

Skills Preview

Key Reading Skill: Predicting

When you read fiction, start making predictions early in the story. Look at the following elements:

- title
- Meet the Author and Build Background
- illustrations and captions
- first paragraph

Whole Class Discussion Before you read "The Medicine Bag," look at all the elements listed above. Then make these predictions:

- who the main characters will be
- what the subject of the story will be
- what the title means

Key Literary Element: Theme

The main message of a short story or other work of fiction is its **theme.** Themes are usually lessons in life about right (or wrong) ways to solve problems, such as "Violence only brings more violence." Themes may also be comments about human nature, such as "Everybody makes mistakes."

The theme of the "The Medicine Bag" is **implied,** which means it is not directly stated. You have to figure out what it is. To do so, think about the conflicts in the story. As you read, ask yourself:

- *What internal and external conflicts do the characters experience?*
- *How are the conflicts resolved?*
- *What life lesson does the main character learn from his experiences?*

Write to Learn Think about a conflict you and a friend resolved in the past. How did you resolve the conflict? What did you learn from it? If you wrote a story about your experience, what would the theme be? Answer in your Learner's Notebook.

Get Ready to Read

Connect to the Reading

In this selection, Martin's great-grandfather gives Martin a family treasure. Think of an object you would like to pass down to your children someday. Pick something that you think represents your family.

Write to Learn In your Learner's Notebook, write a few sentences about the family treasure you would pick. Explain its history and why it is important to your family. How does it represent who you are?

Build Background

In this selection Martin, the narrator, calls his great-grandfather "Grandpa." Grandpa is Sioux, a Native American who belongs to a group made up of seven tribes of the Great Plains. The plains are prairie land that covers the area from North Dakota to Wisconsin, south through Iowa and Missouri, and west into Wyoming.

Grandpa lives on a reservation—a limited area which the U.S. government set aside for Native Americans to live on after they were forced from their land.

Set Purposes for Reading

BIG Question Read "The Medicine Bag" to find out how Martin learns to appreciate the values of the Sioux side of his family and bring them into his suburban life.

Set Your Own Purpose What else would you like to learn from the story to help you answer the Big Question? Write your own purpose on "The Medicine Bag" page of Foldable 5.

Literature Online

Interactive Literary Elements Handbook
To review or learn more about symbols, go to www.glencoe.com.

Keep Moving

Use these skills as you read "The Medicine Bag."

THE Medicine Bag

by Virginia Driving Hawk Sneve

My kid sister Cheryl and I always bragged about our Sioux grandpa, Joe Iron Shell. Our friends, who had always lived in the city and only knew about Indians from movies and TV, were impressed by our stories. Maybe we exaggerated and made Grandpa and the reservation sound glamorous, but when we'd return home to Iowa after our yearly summer visit to Grandpa we always had some exciting tale to tell.

We always had some **authentic** Sioux article to show our listeners. One year Cheryl had new moccasins that Grandpa had made. On another visit he gave me a small, round, flat, rawhide drum which was decorated with a painting of a warrior riding a horse. He taught me a real Sioux chant[1] to sing while I beat the drum with a leather-covered stick that had a feather on the end. Man, that really made an impression. **1**

We never showed our friends Grandpa's picture. Not that we were ashamed of him, but because we knew that the glamorous tales we told didn't go with the real thing. Our friends would have laughed at the picture, because Grandpa wasn't tall and **stately** like TV Indians. His hair wasn't in braids, but hung in stringy, gray strands on his neck and he

---

1. A *chant* is a simple song that has several syllables or words sung to the same note.

Practice the Skills

1 **Key Reading Skill**

Predicting The narrator spends a lot of time describing his Sioux roots. From this, you might predict that his Sioux heritage will be important to the story.

Vocabulary

authentic (aw THEN tik) *adj.* real; genuine

stately (STAYT lee) *adj.* grand; impressive; dignified

Visual Vocabulary
A *tipi* is made of animal skins—usually buffalo—and supported by poles.

was old. He was our great-grandfather, and he didn't live in a tipi, but all by himself in a part log, part tar-paper shack on the Rosebud Reservation in South Dakota. So when Grandpa came to visit us, I was so ashamed and embarrassed I could've died.

There are a lot of yippy poodles and other fancy little dogs in our neighborhood, but they usually barked singly at the mailman from the safety of their own yards. Now it sounded as if a whole pack of mutts were barking together in one place.

I got up and walked to the curb to see what the **commotion** was. About a block away I saw a crowd of little kids yelling, with the dogs yipping and growling around someone who was walking down the middle of the street. ◨

I watched the group as it slowly came closer and saw that in the center of the strange procession was a man wearing a tall black hat. He'd pause now and then to peer at something in his hand and then at the houses on either side of the street. I felt cold and hot at the same time as I recognized the man. "Oh, no!" I whispered. "It's Grandpa!"

I stood on the curb, **unable** to move even though I wanted to run and hide. ◪ Then I got mad when I saw how the yippy dogs were growling and nipping at the old man's baggy pant legs and how wearily he poked them away with his cane. "Stupid mutts," I said as I ran to rescue Grandpa.

When I kicked and hollered at the dogs to get away, they put their tails between their legs and scattered. The kids ran to the curb where they watched me and the old man.

"Grandpa," I said and felt pretty dumb when my voice cracked. I reached for his beat-up old tin suitcase, which was tied shut with a rope. But he set it down right in the street and shook my hand.

"*Hau, Takoza*, Grandchild," he greeted me formally in Sioux.

All I could do was stand there with the whole neighborhood watching and shake the hand of the leather-brown old man. I saw how his gray hair straggled from under his big

Practice the Skills

◨ **Key Reading Skill**

Predicting This is a good point in the story to guess what will happen next. Think about what you've learned so far. Who do you think is walking down the street?

◪ **English Language Coach**

Prefixes That Mean "Not"
Break the word **unable** into its parts. The prefix *un-* means "not." The base word *able* means "can do." From this, you can see *unable* means "cannot do."

Vocabulary

commotion (kum OH shun) *n.* noisy, confused activity

black hat, which had a drooping feather in its crown. His rumpled black suit hung like a sack over his stooped frame. As he shook my hand, his coat fell open to expose a bright-red, satin shirt with a beaded bolo tie under the collar. His getup wasn't out of place on the reservation, but it sure was here, and I wanted to sink right through the pavement.

"Hi," I muttered with my head down. I tried to pull my hand away when I felt his bony hand trembling, and looked up to see fatigue in his face. I felt like crying. I couldn't think of anything to say so I picked up Grandpa's suitcase, took his arm, and guided him up the driveway to our house.

Mom was standing on the steps. I don't know how long she'd been watching, but her hand was over her mouth and she looked as if she couldn't believe what she saw. Then she ran to us.

"Grandpa," she gasped. "How in the world did you get here?"

She checked her move to embrace Grandpa and I remembered that such a display of affection is unseemly to the Sioux and would embarrass him.

"*Hau*, Marie," he said as he shook Mom's hand. She smiled and took his other arm.

As we supported him up the steps the door banged open and Cheryl came bursting out of the house. She was all smiles and was so obviously glad to see Grandpa that I was ashamed of how I felt.

"Grandpa!" she yelled happily. "You came to see us!"

Grandpa smiled and Mom and I let go of him as he stretched out his arms to my ten-year-old sister, who was still young enough to be hugged. ◼4

"*Wicincala*, little girl," he greeted her and then collapsed.

He had fainted. Mom and I carried him into her sewing room, where we had a spare bed.

After we had Grandpa on the bed Mom stood there helplessly patting his shoulder.

"Shouldn't we call the doctor, Mom?" I suggested, since she didn't seem to know what to do.

"Yes," she agreed with a sigh. "You make Grandpa comfortable, Martin."

I reluctantly moved to the bed. I knew Grandpa wouldn't want to have Mom undress him, but I didn't want to, either.

Analyzing the Image
How does this bolo tie help you picture what the grandfather is wearing?

Practice the Skills

◼4 **Key Reading Skill**

Predicting Why do you think Grandpa has come to visit?

He was so skinny and frail that his coat slipped off easily. When I loosened his tie and opened his shirt collar, I felt a small leather pouch that hung from a thong[2] around his neck. I left it alone and moved to remove his boots. The scuffed old cowboy boots were tight and he moaned as I put pressure on his legs to jerk them off.

I put the boots on the floor and saw why they fit so tight. Each one was stuffed with money. I looked at the bills that lined the boots and started to ask about them, but Grandpa's eyes were closed again. **5**

Mom came back with a basin of water. "The doctor thinks Grandpa is suffering from heat exhaustion,"[3] she explained as she bathed Grandpa's face. Mom gave a big sigh, "*Oh hính*, Martin. How do you suppose he got here?"

We found out after the doctor's visit. Grandpa was angrily sitting up in bed while Mom tried to feed him some soup.

"Tonight you let Marie feed you, Grandpa," spoke my dad, who had gotten home from work just as the doctor was leaving. "You're not really sick," he said as he gently pushed Grandpa back against the pillows. "The doctor said you just got too tired and hot after your long trip."

Grandpa relaxed, and between sips of soup he told us of his journey. Soon after our visit to him Grandpa decided that he would like to see where his only living **descendants** lived and what our home was like. Besides, he admitted sheepishly, he was lonesome after we left.

I knew everybody felt as guilty as I did—especially Mom. Mom was all Grandpa had left. So even after she married my dad, who's a white man and teaches in the college in our city, and after Cheryl and I were born, Mom made sure that every summer we spent a week with Grandpa.

I never thought that Grandpa would be lonely after our visits, and none of us noticed how old and weak he had become. But Grandpa knew and so he came to us. He had ridden on buses for two and a half days. When he arrived

Practice the Skills

5 | **Key Reading Skill**

Predicting Why do you think Grandpa has stuffed his boots with money?

---

2. A ***thong*** is a narrow strap of leather or similar material.

3. ***Heat exhaustion*** is dizziness and faintness from being in the sun too long.

Vocabulary ....

descendants (duh SEN dunts) *n.* people who are related to an earlier generation

in the city, tired and stiff from sitting for so long, he set out, walking, to find us.

He had stopped to rest on the steps of some building downtown and a policeman found him. The cop, according to Grandpa, was a good man who took him to the bus stop and waited until the bus came and told the driver to let Grandpa out at Bell View Drive. After Grandpa got off the bus, he started walking again. But he couldn't see the house numbers on the other side when he walked on the sidewalk so he walked in the middle of the street. That's when all the little kids and dogs followed him.

I knew everybody felt as bad as I did. Yet I was proud of this 86-year-old man, who had never been away from the reservation, having the courage to travel so far alone.

"You found the money in my boots?" he asked Mom.

"Martin did," she answered, and roused herself to scold. "Grandpa, you shouldn't have carried so much money. What if someone had stolen it from you?"

Grandpa laughed. "I would've known if anyone tried to take the boots off my feet. The money is what I've saved for a long time—a hundred dollars—for my funeral. But you take it now to buy groceries so that I won't be a burden to you while I am here." **6**

"That won't be necessary, Grandpa," Dad said. "We are honored to have you with us and you will never be a burden. I am only sorry that we never thought to bring you home with us this summer and spare you the **discomfort** of a long trip." **7**

Grandpa was pleased. "Thank you," he answered. "But do not feel bad that you didn't bring me with you for I would not have come then. It was not time." He said this in such a way that no one could argue with him. To Grandpa and the Sioux, he once told me, a thing would be done when it was the right time to do it and that's the way it was.

"Also," Grandpa went on, looking at me, "I have come because it is soon time for Martin to have the medicine bag."

We all knew what that meant. Grandpa thought he was going to die and he had to follow the tradition of his family to pass the medicine bag, along with its history, to the oldest male child.

Practice the Skills

6 | **Key Reading Skill**

Predicting Was your prediction about the money in Grandpa's boots correct?

7 | **English Language Coach**

Prefixes That Mean "Not" Divide the word **discomfort** into its two parts—its prefix and its base word. What does *discomfort* mean?

"Even though the boy," he said still looking at me, "bears a white man's name, the medicine bag will be his."

I didn't know what to say. I had the same hot and cold feeling that I had when I first saw Grandpa in the street. The medicine bag was the dirty leather pouch I had found around his neck. "I could never wear such a thing," I almost said aloud. I thought of having my friends see it in gym class, at the swimming pool, and could imagine the smart things they would say. But I just swallowed hard and took a step toward the bed. I knew I would have to take it.

But Grandpa was tired. "Not now, Martin," he said, waving his hand in dismissal, "it is not time. Now I will sleep."

So that's how Grandpa came to be with us for two months. My friends kept asking to come see the old man, but I put them off. I told myself that I didn't want them laughing at Grandpa. But even as I made excuses I knew it wasn't Grandpa that I was afraid they'd laugh at. **8**

Nothing bothered Cheryl about bringing her friends to see Grandpa. Every day after school started there'd be a crew of giggling little girls or round-eyed little boys crowded around the old man on the patio, where he'd gotten in the habit of sitting every afternoon.

Grandpa would smile in his gentle way and patiently answer their questions, or he'd tell them stories of brave warriors, ghosts, animals, and the kids listened in awed silence. Those little guys thought Grandpa was great.

Finally, one day after school, my friends came home with me because nothing I said stopped them. "We're going to see the great Indian of Bell View Drive," said Hank, who was supposed to be my best friend. "My brother has seen him three times so he oughta be well enough to see us."

When we got to my house Grandpa was sitting on the patio. He had on his red shirt, but today he also wore a fringed leather vest that was decorated with beads. Instead of his usual cowboy boots he had solidly beaded moccasins on his feet that stuck out of his black trousers. Of course, he had his old black

Practice the Skills

8 ▎ **Key Literary Element**

Theme To understand the theme of this story, think about the conflicts in it.

- Martin is afraid of being embarrassed by his grandfather and the medicine bag.
- Martin doesn't want to hurt his grandfather's feelings.
- Martin has mixed feelings about his grandfather and his Sioux heritage.

A Singing Indian. W. Ufer. Oil on canvas, 30 x 25¼ in.
Analyzing the Painting What items in this painting reflect the man's Native American heritage? What details about Grandpa reveal his identity as a Sioux?

The Medicine Bag **613**

hat on—he was seldom without it. But it had been brushed and the feather in the beaded headband was proudly erect, its tip a brighter white. His hair lay in silver strands over the red shirt collar.

I stared just as my friends did and I heard one of them murmur, "Wow!" **9**

Grandpa looked up and when his eyes met mine they twinkled as if he were laughing inside. He nodded to me and my face got all hot. I could tell that he had known all along I was afraid he'd embarrass me in front of my friends.

"*Hau, hoksilas*, boys," he greeted and held out his hand.

My buddies passed in a single file and shook his hand as I introduced them. They were so polite I almost laughed. "How, there, Grandpa," and even a "How-do-you-do, sir."

"You look fine, Grandpa," I said as the guys sat on the lawn chairs or on the patio floor.

"*Hanh*, yes," he agreed. "When I woke up this morning it seemed the right time to dress in the good clothes. I knew that my grandson would be bringing his friends."

"You guys want some lemonade or something?" I offered. No one answered. They were listening to Grandpa as he started telling how he'd killed the deer from which his vest was made.

Grandpa did most of the talking while my friends were there. I was so proud of him and amazed at how respectfully quiet my buddies were. **10** Mom had to chase them home at supper time. As they left they shook Grandpa's hand again and said to me:

"Martin, he's really great!"

"Yeah, man! Don't blame you for keeping him to yourself."

"Can we come back?"

But after they left, Mom said, "No more visitors for a while, Martin. Grandpa won't admit it, but his strength hasn't returned. He likes having company, but it tires him."

That evening Grandpa called me to his room before he went to sleep. "Tomorrow," he said, "when you come home, it will be time to give you the medicine bag."

Sioux vest, Plains Indian. British Museum, London.
Analyzing the Photo How is the vest in this photograph like the one Martin describes?

Practice the Skills

9 | **Key Reading Skill**

Predicting Do you think Martin will be embarrassed in front of his friends by his grandfather? Why or why not?

10 | **Key Reading Skill**

Predicting Did you correctly predict how Martin's friends would react to his grandfather? If not, why not?

I felt a hard squeeze from where my heart is supposed to be and was scared, but I answered, "OK, Grandpa."

All night I had weird dreams about thunder and lightning on a high hill. From a distance I heard the slow beat of a drum. When I woke up in the morning I felt as if I hadn't slept at all. At school it seemed as if the day would never end and, when it finally did, I ran home. **11**

Grandpa was in his room, sitting on the bed. The shades were down and the place was dim and cool. I sat on the floor in front of Grandpa, but he didn't even look at me. After what seemed a long time he spoke.

"I sent your mother and sister away. What you will hear today is only for a man's ears. What you will receive is only for a man's hands." He fell silent and I felt shivers down my back.

"My father in his early manhood," Grandpa began, "made a vision quest[4] to find a spirit guide for his life. You cannot understand how it was in that time, when the great Teton Sioux[5] were first made to stay on the reservation. There was a strong need for guidance from *Wakantanka*, the Great Spirit. But too many of the young men were filled with despair and hatred. They thought it was hopeless to search for a vision when the glorious life was gone and only the hated confines of a reservation lay ahead. But my father held to the old ways.

Visual Vocabulary
A ***butte*** (byoot) is a steep, flat-topped hill that stands alone.

"He carefully prepared for his quest with a purifying sweat bath and then he went alone to a high butte top to fast and pray. After three days he received his **sacred** dream—in which he found, after long searching, the white man's iron. He did not understand his vision of finding something belonging to the white people, for in that time they were the enemy. When he came down from the butte to cleanse himself at the stream below, he found the remains of a campfire and the broken shell of an iron kettle. This was a sign which

4. A ***vision quest*** was a special trip made by young Sioux men to receive a dream that gave them a song or an object that protected and guided them in life.

5. The ***Teton Sioux*** are the largest Sioux tribe. They were traditionally buffalo hunters.

Vocabulary

sacred (SAY krid) *adj.* holy; having to do with religion

Practice the Skills

11 | **Key Reading Skill**

Predicting How do you think Martin will react when Grandpa gives him the medicine bag? Why do you think so?

reinforced his dream. He took a piece of the iron for his medicine bag, which he had made of elk[6] skin years before, to prepare for his quest.

"He returned to his village, where he told his dream to the wise old men of the tribe. They gave him the name *Iron Shell,* but neither did they understand the meaning of the dream. This first Iron Shell kept the piece of iron with him at all times and believed it gave him protection from the evils of those unhappy days.

"Then a terrible thing happened to Iron Shell. He and several other young men were taken from their homes by the soldiers and sent far away to a white man's boarding school.[7] He was angry and lonesome for his parents and the young girl he had wed before he was taken away. At first Iron Shell resisted the teachers' attempts to change him and he did not try to learn. One day it was his turn to work in the school's blacksmith[8] shop. As he walked into the place he knew that his medicine had brought him there to learn and work with the white man's iron.

"Iron Shell became a blacksmith and worked at the trade when he returned to the reservation. All of his life he treasured the medicine bag. When he was old, and I was a man, he gave it to me, for no one made the vision quest any more." **12**

Grandpa quit talking and I stared in disbelief as he covered his face with his hands. His shoulders were shaking with quiet sobs and I looked away until he began to speak again.

"I kept the bag until my son, your mother's father, was a man and had to leave us to fight in the war across the ocean. I gave him the bag, for I believed it would protect him in battle, but he did not take it with him. He was afraid that he would lose it. He died in a faraway place."

Again Grandpa was still and I felt his grief around me.

"My son," he went on after clearing his throat, "had only a daughter and it is not proper for her to know of these things."

He unbuttoned his shirt, pulled out the leather pouch, and lifted it over his head. He held it in his hand, turning it over and over as if memorizing how it looked.

12 **BIG Question**

How might the story of the vision quest help Martin understand his true self?

---

6. An *elk* is a very large type of deer with broad antlers.

7. A *boarding school* is a school where students live together as well as go to school.

8. A *blacksmith* makes iron objects, such as horseshoes, kettles, and door hinges.

"In the bag," he said as he opened it and removed two objects, "is the broken shell of the iron kettle, a pebble from the butte, and a piece of the sacred sage."[9] He held the pouch upside down and dust drifted down.

"After the bag is yours you must put a piece of prairie sage within and never open it again until you pass it on to your son." He replaced the pebble and the piece of iron, and tied the bag.

I stood up, somehow knowing I should. Grandpa slowly rose from the bed and stood upright in front of me holding the bag before my face. I closed my eyes and waited for him to slip it over my head. But he spoke.

"No, you need not wear it." He placed the soft leather bag in my right hand and closed my other hand over it. "It would not be right to wear it in this time and place where no one will understand. Put it safely away until you are again on the reservation. Wear it then, when you replace the sacred sage."

Grandpa turned and sat again on the bed. Wearily he leaned his head against the pillow. "Go," he said, "I will sleep now."

"Thank you, Grandpa," I said softly and left with the bag in my hands. **13**

That night Mom and Dad took Grandpa to the hospital. Two weeks later I stood alone on the lonely prairie of the reservation and put the sacred sage in my medicine bag. **14** ○

Boy on Edge of Chasm, 1993 (detail). Kam Mak. Oil on panels, 14 x 10½ in. Collection of the artist.

Analyzing the Painting How does this painting capture the seriousness of the moment when Martin receives the medicine bag?

Practice the Skills

13 | **Key Literary Element**

Theme Martin's internal conflict about his grandfather is resolved. What did Martin learn from the experience? The answer to that question is the theme of the story.

14 **BIG Question**

How does accepting the medicine bag help Martin stay true to himself? Write your answer on "The Medicine Bag" page of Foldable 5. Your response will help you complete the Unit Challenge later.

---

9. *Sage* is a sweet-smelling plant. Different varieties are used as medicine or spice.

After You Read

The Medicine Bag

Answering the BIG Question

1. What do you think is Martin's true self, the way he is with his friends or with his family—or both? Explain.

2. **Recall** How does Martin feel about his Sioux background at the start of the story, when his grandfather first comes to visit?
   TIP Right There

3. **Summarize** In a sentence or two, sum up the reasons that Grandpa has come to visit Martin and his family.
   TIP Think and Search

Critical Thinking

4. **Infer** Why do you think Grandpa cries after he tells Martin how Iron Shell gave him the medicine bag?
   TIP Author and Me

5. **Interpret** A symbol is a person, place, or thing that stands for something more than what it is. For example, a red rose can represent, or symbolize, love. What do you think the medicine bag symbolizes in the story? Give details from the story to support your answer.
   TIP Author and Me

6. **Analyze** The story is told in the first-person from Martin's point of view. How might your feelings toward Martin change if the story were told in the third-person by an outsider watching what happens?
   TIP On My Own

Write About Your Reading

Diary Entry Imagine that you are Martin. Write a diary entry about the day Grandpa gave you the medicine bag. Be sure to include the following ideas:

• your feelings about the history of the medicine bag
• your feelings about owning the medicine bag
• how owning the medicine bag has changed you

NY English Language Arts Core Curriculum (pp. 618–619)

LC R17 Demonstrate comprehension and response through a range of activities. **LC W4** Compose grade-appropriate texts for a variety of purposes. **LC R12** Combine multiple strategies (predict/confirm) to enhance comprehension and response. **R1m** Make, confirm, or revise predictions. **R2b** Interpret theme, using evidence from the text. **Core W8** Use correct grammatical construction.

For a complete description of the standards, see p. NY11.

Skills Review

Key Reading Skill: Predicting

7. Explain how making predictions as you read helped you understand the story. Discuss the predictions you made about the characters and the plot.

Key Literary Element: Theme

8. In a sentence or two, state the theme of "The Medicine Bag."

9. How did understanding the conflicts in the story help you figure out the theme?

Vocabulary Check

Write *T* for each true statement and *F* for each false one.

10. An **authentic** medicine bag is made of plastic.

11. A group of government officials on their way to an important meeting would probably walk in a **stately** fashion.

12. A quiet, orderly exit from school is a **commotion.**

13. Your children will be your **descendants.**

14. A **sacred** object is likely to be holy to people.

15. **Academic Vocabulary** Why is an understanding of Martin's Sioux heritage **relevant** to a discussion of "The Medicine Bag"?

English Language Coach On a separate sheet of paper, write the prefix and the base word that make up the listed word. Then write a definition of the word. If you need help, use a dictionary.

16. disappear

17. unclean

18. immaterial

19. disbelieve

20. disinfect

21. unafraid

Grammar Link: Combining Sentences

Too many short, simple sentences can make writing sound choppy. Vary the lengths and kinds of sentences you use by combining simple sentences.

Method A: Compound Sentences Combine two simple sentences (independent clauses) to form a compound sentence. Form it with a comma and a coordinating conjunction (*and, but, nor, or, for, so, yet*).

- The sky darkened. It started to rain big drops.
- The sky darkened, **and** it started to rain big drops.

Method B: Complex Sentences Combine two simple sentences (independent clauses) to form a complex sentence. Add a subordinating conjunction to one of the independent clauses to make it a dependent clause.

Common subordinating conjunctions include *after, although, as, because, before, if, since, though, unless, until, when, whether,* and *while.*

- **After** the sky darkened, it started to rain big drops.

Grammar Practice

Combine sentences to vary the sentence patterns in the paragraph below. Include at least one compound sentence and one complex sentence. (There's more than one right way to revise the paragraph.)

Spring is here. The weather is warm. The beach will reopen soon. Baseball is back. You and your family will visit. We can catch up on old times.

Writing Application Review the diary entry you wrote for the Write About Your Reading activity. Make sure it contains at least one compound sentence and one complex sentence.

Web Activities For eFlashcards, Selection Quick Checks, and other Web activities, go to www.glencoe.com.

Before You Read : A Year of Living Bravely

Emily Costello

Meet the Author

Emily Costello was born in 1966. She has written many books and articles for young adults, including fiction and biography, and articles on science topics. Costello tells young people who want to write, "Keep a diary. Record what's happening in your life and practice explaining how you're feeling each day."

Author Search For more about Emily Costello, go to www.glencoe.com.

NY English Language Arts Core Curriculum (pp. 620–625)

LC R6 Determine the meaning of words by using word structure knowledge. **LC R12** Combine multiple strategies (predict/confirm) to enhance comprehension and response. **Rlm** Make, confirm, or revise predictions. **LC R13** Use text structure and literary devices to aid comprehension and response.

For a complete description of the standards, see p. NY11.

Vocabulary Preview

confesses (kun FES ses) *v.* tells a truth that one rarely talks about; form of the verb *confess* **(p. 623)** *Bethany confesses to being afraid sometimes.*

exotic (ig ZAH tik) *adj.* strangely beautiful and foreign **(p. 624)** *Bethany goes to exotic places to surf with her family and friends.*

hardships (HARD ships) *n.* things that cause pain or suffering; misfortunes **(p. 625)** *In spite of the hardships the fire caused, the family was happy because no one was hurt.*

Partner Talk With a partner, look over the vocabulary words. Then write down a synonym and an antonym for each word. (Remember that synonyms share almost the same meaning; antonyms have opposite meanings.)

English Language Coach

Prefixes That Show Relationships A prefix is a syllable added to the beginning of a word to change the word's meaning. If you know the meaning of common prefixes, you can unlock the meaning of words that begin with prefixes. The chart below lists prefixes that show relationships.

Prefix	Word Example	Meaning
co- means "with," "together," or "partner"	<u>co</u>worker	"one who works with another person"
	<u>co</u>exist	"to exist together"
	<u>co</u>author	"an author who writes as a partner of another"
pre- means "before"	<u>pre</u>season	"before the regular season"
post- means "after"	<u>post</u>season	"after the regular season"

Think-Pair-Share Use a dictionary to find three words that begin with the prefixes *co-, pre-,* or *post-*. Make a two-column chart in your Learner's Notebook, and write the words in the first column. In the second column, write a sentence using the word. Challenge a classmate to guess the meanings of the words by using word analysis and context clues.

Skills Preview

Key Reading Skill: Predicting

"A Year of Living Bravely" is about Bethany Hamilton, a teenaged surfer who was badly hurt in a shark attack in 2003. From this information and the title of the article, predict what the article will say about Bethany.

Whole Class Discussion As a class, guess what kinds of facts and details you will find in the article. To get started, think about the 5Ws and an H.

Text Element: Attention-Getting Device

Many nonfiction writers begin their articles with a statement intended to capture readers' attention and make them want to read on. This kind of beginning is an **attention-getting device.** Types of attention-getting devices include the following:

- a statement that presents interesting information
  Example: Bees have been producing honey for more than 100 million years.
- a **rhetorical** (reh TOR ih kul) **question**—a question that readers are not expected to answer
  Example: Did you know that bees have been producing honey for more than 100 million years?
- a surprising fact
  Example: A single bee colony has a lot of worker bees—in fact, more than 50,000!

Partner Talk With a classmate, read the first paragraph of a magazine or newspaper feature article. What type of attention-getting device does the writer use? Discuss whether it makes you want to read on.

Interactive Literary Elements Handbook
To review or learn more about author's purpose, go to www.glencoe.com.

Get Ready to Read

Connect to the Reading

Bethany Hamilton loves to surf. Being a surfer is a big part of who she is. What is your favorite activity or hobby? What would you do if an injury stopped you from doing it? Would you substitute a different activity?

Write to Learn In your Learner's Notebook, jot down a few sentences describing what your hobby is. Tell what you think you might do if you couldn't enjoy it anymore and why you think you would do that.

Build Background

Surfing dates back to prehistoric times. It is believed to have originated in the South Pacific among Polynesian sailors. During the 1800s, missionaries banned surfing in the South Pacific. Hawaiian Duke Kahanamoku revived the sport of surfing in the early 1900s. He started Waikiki's first surf club and introduced surfing to Australia. Today surfing is a popular sport in many parts of the world.

- The surfboards of the early 1900s were made of wood. They were eight to ten feet long. They were also heavy, weighing in at 100 pounds.
- Modern boards are made of plastic and are only about six feet long. They weigh five or six pounds and have fins on the bottom so the rider can steer.

Set Purposes for Reading

BIG Question Read "A Year of Living Bravely" to learn how Bethany stays true to herself in spite of her injury.

Set Your Own Purpose What would you like to learn from the selection to help you answer the Big Question? Write your own purpose on the "A Year of Living Bravely" page of Foldable 5.

Keep Moving

Use these skills as you read "A Year of Living Bravely."

A Year of Living Bravely

by Emily Costello

Bethany Hamilton had a horrifying experience last Halloween. A tiger shark attacked her while she was surfing off the coast of Hawaii. The shark chewed off Bethany's left arm just below the shoulder. By the time she reached the hospital, she'd lost half the blood in her body. She was near death. Bethany had two surgeries to close the wound. She spent eight days in the hospital. **1**

Nobody would have blamed Bethany if she'd never surfed again. Instead, she recovered with surprising speed. Less than a month after the attack, she was surfing again. On January 10, she entered a major competition. She took fifth place out of 24.

What helped Bethany recover so quickly? She loves to surf, and she wanted to start again. "Desire is the answer," she says, "and I had that." **2**

Practice the Skills

1 **Text Element**

Attention-Getting Device
By opening with interesting statements, the author tries to interest you in reading the rest of the article. Do the facts make you want to read on? Explain.

2 **Key Reading Skill**

Predicting To predict what the article will say about Bethany, think about these facts:

• The title of the selection is "A Year of Living Bravely."

• Bethany says she recovered fast to return to surfing.

From these facts, you can guess that the article will tell in more detail what Bethany did during the year after the shark attack.

Cool Accessories

Bethany isn't self-conscious about her missing arm. She calls what's left of her left arm "Stumpy." She rarely covers Stumpy with long-sleeved shirts. Instead, she wears what she's always liked to wear—tank tops and bathing suits.

Her new arm, which is made of plastic and metal, has a nickname too. She calls it "Haole Girl." Haole (HOWLee) means "white." It's a word Hawaiians use for non-natives. The name fits. Originally the arm was much paler than Bethany's own skin. It was recently dyed darker.

The arm was a gift from the manufacturer. It cost $45,000 to make! Still, the arm is mostly for looks. Bethany has to move it with her good arm. She **confesses** that she rarely takes it out of the closet.

"I'm complete without it," Bethany says. "I can paddle and balance on a surfboard. I can cut an orange by holding it between my feet. And I like my new look."

Suddenly Famous 3

Bethany has adjusted to a one-armed life without much trouble. But other parts of her new life have been challenging. "I'm learning how to balance my life—schooling, surfing, and my career," Bethany says.

Bethany is in the eighth grade. She's home-schooled[1]—although "on-the-road-schooled" might be more accurate.

During the past year, Bethany has had little time at home. She appeared on the TV news-magazine show *20/20.* She was on the cover of

---

1. Someone who is **home-schooled** is taught school subjects outside of school by a parent or a tutor rather than in school by a teacher.

Vocabulary

confesses (kun FES ses) *v.* tells a truth that one rarely talks about

Practice the Skills

3 **Key Reading Skill**

Predicting What do you think this section will be about? Think about these things:

- what you've learned so far about Bethany
- what the subtitle, or subhead, "Suddenly Famous" tells you.

Analyzing the Photo Hamilton smiles on arriving for the 2004 premier of the film *Open Water.* How does this photograph convey her confidence?

Analyzing the Photo Hamilton appears with Damien Fahey, veejay of MTV's *Total Request Live,* in 2003. How might Hamilton's story encourage other teens who face setbacks?

People and *Teen Vogue.* She <u>**co-wrote**</u> a book called *Soul Surfer.* **4** She has a movie in the works. The ESPN sports network gave her an Espy Award. She made an appearance at the Teen Choice Awards. She threw out the first pitch at the Oakland A's season opener. She has done hundreds of interviews for magazines.

Of course, being famous isn't all hard work. For Bethany, one of the perks² is going to **exotic** places to surf. Bethany traveled to Nicaragua and Portugal earlier this year, and loved it. "She wakes me up at 5 a.m. and screams, 'Let's go

---

2. *Perks* is short for *perquisites,* which are special privileges.

Vocabulary

exotic (ig ZAH tik) *adj.* strangely beautiful and foreign

Practice the Skills

4 **English Language Coach**

Prefixes That Show Relationships The prefix *co-* means "with," "together," or "partner." What does <u>**co-wrote**</u> mean?

surfing!'" her best friend, Alana Blanchard, told *USA Today*. "She just always wants to surf."

The Hard Part

Bethany is always training to become a better surfer. She plans to surf for the rest of her life.

But she admits that sometimes being in the ocean feels weird. She gets a little scared. When that happens, she calls to friends surfing nearby. Or she sings a song to herself.

"I have nightmares," Bethany confesses. When the nightmares come, she says it helps to think about other people's problems. This summer, Bethany hopes to raise $50,000 for disabled kids through a charity called World Vision.

Bethany notes that there are 120 million disabled kids worldwide. Landmines[3] injured many of them. In poor countries, few disabled kids get to go to school. Some poor families abandon disabled kids. Thinking about such **hardships,** Bethany knows how lucky she really is.

"Why shouldn't I be happy?" she asks. "I'm surfing and traveling and really doing all I ever wanted." **5** ○

Practice the Skills

5 **BIG Question**

Do you think it was important for Bethany to surf after her accident? Explain why or why not. Write your answer on the "A Year of Living Bravely" page of Foldable 5. Your response will help you complete the Unit Challenge later.

---

3. **Landmines** are explosive devices that are placed on or beneath the ground.

Vocabulary

hardships (HARD ships) *n.* things that cause pain or suffering; misfortunes

After You Read

A Year of Living Bravely

Answering the **BIG** Question

1. From reading "A Year of Living Bravely," what have you learned about how someone stays true to himself or herself?

2. **Recall** How did Bethany lose her left arm?
   TIP Right There

3. **Recall** What does Bethany say she does to get over her nightmares?
   TIP Right There

Critical Thinking

4. **Interpret** What does Bethany mean when she says, "I am complete without [the plastic arm]"?
   TIP Author and Me

5. **Analyze** What is the main idea of the article? Write it in your own words. Then explain which facts, details, and other clues in the article helped you find the main idea.
   TIP Author and Me

6. **Evaluate** Would you recommend this article to other eighth-graders? Why or why not? Use details from the article to support your answer.
   TIP On My Own

Talk About Your Reading

Whole Class Discussion Bethany Hamilton has been in the news a lot. She has been interviewed by TV, magazine, and newspaper reporters. She has won awards. She has written a book, and she is working on a movie about her life. As a class, discuss why Bethany has gotten so much publicity, or news coverage, and what more you'd like to know about her.

- Why do you think people are interested in her story?
- Why do you think she wants to tell others her story?
- If you could meet Bethany, what would you like to ask her? Why?

NY English Language Arts Core Curriculum (pp. 626–627)

LC R17 Demonstrate comprehension and response through a range of activities. **LC S8** Participate in group discussions on a range of topics and for a variety of purposes. **LC R12** Combine multiple strategies (predict/confirm) to enhance comprehension and response. **RIm** Make, confirm, or revise predictions. **LC R13** Use text structure and literary devices to aid comprehension and response. **Core W8** Use correct grammatical construction.

For a complete description of the standards, see p. NY11.

Skills Review

Key Reading Skill: Predicting

7. Look back at the predictions you made before you read "A Year of Living Bravely" and while you read it. Which of your predictions were correct? Did anything in the story surprise you? Explain.

Text Element: Attention-Getting Device

8. The author begins her article with interesting statements about Bethany's accident. Use a different attention-getting device, such as a rhetorical question or surprising facts, to write a new first paragraph for the selection. Then tell which introduction you think is better and why.

Vocabulary Check

Answer *true* or *false* to each statement. If a statement is false, rewrite it to make it true.

9. Someone who **confesses** to a crime admits to doing an illegal act.

10. An **exotic** place is a familiar location.

11. **Hardships** often cause unhappiness.

12. **Academic Vocabulary** If your teacher tells you to pick **relevant** details, what kind of details will you look for as you read?

English Language Coach On a separate sheet of paper, write the prefix and the base word that make up each of the words below. Then write a definition of the word. If you need help, use a dictionary.

13. cohost

14. preview

15. copilot

16. postgame

17. prerecord

Web Activities For eFlashcards, Selection Quick Checks, and other Web activities, go to www.glencoe.com.

Grammar Link: More Sentence Combining

Combining sentences is a useful way to avoid repeating ideas. Notice the repetition in the following paragraph. Repeated words and ideas are underlined.

- I often have to babysit <u>my twin brothers</u>. <u>My twin brothers</u> are Sam and Danny. They never sit still. <u>They like</u> to run around the house. <u>They like</u> to chase the dog. <u>They like</u> to throw baseballs at each other.

To fix repeated words and phrases, try combining sentences by using one or more of the following methods.

Method A: Explanatory Phrase Make the repeated idea into an explanatory phrase.

- Repetitious: I often have to babysit <u>my twin brothers</u>. <u>My twin brothers</u> are Sam and Danny.
- Better: I often have to babysit my twin brothers, <u>Sam and Danny</u>.

Method B: Series of Items Combine the repeated ideas in a series.

- Repetitious: <u>They like</u> to run around the house. <u>They like</u> to chase the dog. <u>They like</u> to throw baseballs at each other.
- Better: <u>They like</u> to run around the house, chase the dog, and throw baseballs at each other.

Grammar Practice

Use a method described above to combine each pair of repetitious sentences below. Write your sentences on a separate sheet of paper.

18. We like to visit Middletown Ocean View. Middletown Ocean View is a beautiful aquarium.

19. On our vacation we went swimming. We went boating. We also went hiking.

20. My little brother borrowed my favorite book. My favorite book is *Tuck Everlasting.*

21. The Tucks are the family described in the book. The Tucks have found the secret of eternal life.

22. They go into the forest. They drink water from a magic fountain. They never grow old.

Short Story
Revising, Editing, and Presenting

ASSIGNMENT Write a short story

Purpose: To tell a story about a character who struggles to stay true to himself or herself

Audience: Your teacher and your classmates

Revising Rubric

Your revised short story should have

- a clear focus and effective organization
- well-developed characters
- a plot with a clear beginning, conflict, and resolution
- a setting that fits your plot
- realistic dialogue

NY English Language Arts Core Curriculum (pp. 628–633)

Core W5 Use the writing process. **W2a** Write original literary texts to sequence events to advance a plot; use conflict and resolution. **Core W9** Use transitions to produce cohesive texts. **Core W8** Use correct grammatical construction. **Core W7** Observe rules of punctuation, capitalization, and spelling. **LC S8** Participate in group discussions on a range of topics and for a variety of purposes.

For a complete description of the standards, see p. NY11.

In Writing Workshop Part 1 you wrote a draft of your short story. Now it's time to improve it. Keep a copy of your story in your writing portfolio so that you and your teacher can evaluate your writing progress over time.

Revising
Make It Better

Take a fresh look at your draft. This is your chance to improve it.

1. Read your draft quickly and put it aside. Then think about the general impression you get from your story. Ask yourself these questions.

- *Does my writing tell the story I want to tell? Does everything in it contribute to one overall effect without wandering away from the point?*
- *Are there any parts that are awkward or confusing?*
- *Do my characters seem like real people?* (See the next section for help in developing your characters.)
- *Is the conflict understandable?*
- *Is the resolution satisfying?*
- *Do I describe the setting well enough that readers can picture it?*
- *Does my story have a consistent point of view? Is everything seen through the same character's eyes?*

2. Reread the draft slowly. Mark places where you want to rewrite.

Develop Believable Characters

Good characters are lifelike people your readers can care about. Characterization is how you bring them to life. You can develop characters by describing how they look, how they talk, how they act, and how they feel. You can also reveal what other characters say about them. Dialogue is another good way to develop your characters. Reread your story, looking for opportunities to further develop your characters.

Applying Good Writing Traits

Organization

Good short stories are well organized and focused. They have a point. They move clearly from the beginning to the middle to the end. The writing is smooth, and the conclusion makes sense.

What Is Organization?

Organization is the inner structure of a piece of writing–the order in which the ideas are arranged. The organization of a story guides readers through a sequence of events.

Why Is Organization Important in My Writing?

- Organizing your ideas can help you get them down on paper more quickly and easily.
- Clear organization guides readers through your ideas and makes your writing easier to follow.
- Strong organization gives readers a sense of direction while they read.

How Do I Organize My Writing?

Different types of writing are organized in different ways. The following guidelines will help you strengthen the organization of narratives, or stories.

- Organize the events of your story in a logical order. Set up the conflict clearly before you try to resolve it. Use transition words (*then, next, finally*) to link ideas and events.

- Write a satisfying end to your story. Show how the conflict is resolved and what the main character learns. Don't leave readers feeling as if you got up to answer the door and forgot to come back. Also avoid overused endings such as "and then I woke up" or "we lived happily ever after."

Organization Practice Check the organization of your story by making a story map like this one. Do the three stages of your story do their jobs?

Beginning
Introduce characters, conflict, setting.

Middle
Develop characters and conflict.

End
Resolve conflict. Tell what protagonist learned.

Analyzing Cartoons
This boy could sure use some help getting organized! If you wrote to a friend about your opinion of this cartoon, how would you organize your writing?

PICK UP **WHAT** JUNK?

© Zits Partnership. Reprinted with Permission of King Features Syndicate, Inc.

Editing

Finish It Up

When you are satisfied with your story, look carefully to see whether there are any errors in grammar, usage, and mechanics.

Use the Editing Checklist to spot and correct errors. Get rid of any words that aren't needed. If you have trouble recognizing your mistakes, try reading your story aloud. Hearing the words may help you catch mistakes that you miss when you only see the words on the page.

Editing Checklist

☑ Pronouns agree with their antecedents.

☑ The writing is free of sentence fragments and run-ons.

☑ All verbs agree with their subjects.

☑ Punctuation is correct.

☑ Spelling and capitalization are correct.

Take one last quick look through your short story before you hand it in. Ask yourself, *Is this as good as I can make it? Did I miss anything?*

Presenting

Show It Off

Stories are meant to be read! With your classmates, make a book of short stories that you can share with other classes. Your character's struggle to stay true may help readers handle something they are going through.

1. Neatly copy your story or, if possible, use a word-processing program to enter and print out a final copy of your story.

2. If you want to, add pictures to your story to help readers visualize a character, setting, or mood (the general feeling of your story). You can draw an illustration, find a picture in a magazine or newspaper, or search the Internet for an image you can use. Be sure that the image you choose captures an event or mood from your story.

3. Put all of the stories and pictures together in a binder. Now you have a collection of short stories about many different characters and situations but about the same theme (staying true to oneself in a difficult situation).

4. Finally, work together as a class to brainstorm possible titles for your collection. Vote to choose one of them.

▶ Writing Tip

Spelling If you are using a computer, you can use the Spell Check feature, but the only way to be 100 percent sure of a word's spelling is to look it up in a dictionary.

Literature Online

Writing Models For models and other writing activities, go to www .glencoe.com.

▶ Writing Tip

Read Aloud Another way to present your story is to read it to your class. You can act out scenes, use different voices for different characters—whatever you feel like doing. Have fun performing!

Being There for Abuela

Marisol finished getting ready for school. She went into the kitchen and grabbed her lunch, tuna fish and wheat bread, from the counter. She walked into the living room, where her grandmother sat on the couch knitting a blue sweater. "Abuela, how are you feeling today?"

"I am feeling better, Marisol. Are you leaving for school?" her grandmother asked.

"Yes, I have a math test. I will see you after school."

"Good, I will make us some asopao for dinner. I know it's your favorite."

Marisol walked out of the house into the cold morning. The tears came into her eyes. Her grandmother looked so small and weak. Marisol pushed back her hair and pulled her jean jacket more tightly together. She ran to catch the bus.

All day in school she thought about her grandmother. They had all moved so far to get to the United States. Her mom, dad, and brother were doing great. But her grandmother was dying. She was really old, and she did less and less every day. Marisol loved her so much. The thought of losing her broke Marisol's heart. She tried to finish writing her essay in English class, the last period of the day, but she couldn't concentrate. Finally, the bell rang, and she was free to go home.

Marisol went to her locker to get her books for homework. Her three best friends were there waiting for her. Julie, Tracy, and Sam had been there for Marisol since she moved to the new school. They were all on the soccer team and hung out together.

"Hey, Marisol, you ready for practice?" Julie yelled down the hallway.

"I can't go today," Marisol yelled back as she ran to her locker. "I have to get home and see my grandmother. She's not doing so well."

The beginning of the story introduces you to Marisol and her grandmother.

Dialogue and description show you what the main character acts like and looks like.

The writer uses third-person point of view ("she," "her") here and throughout the story. The words "I" and "my" appear only in dialogue.

Dialogue shows you the relationship between characters and gives you information about the conflict.

Active Writing Model

"Coach isn't going to like it. That's three practices you've missed, and we have a game tomorrow," said Sam.

"I know, but I can't help it." Marisol got her books and shut her locker door. "See you later," she said to her friends. They all looked at her.

Tracy smiled. "Tell your grandma we hope she feels better. See you tomorrow." The three of them turned and walked away toward the soccer field. Marisol walked down the other hall.

The writer moves the story's setting to the kitchen to give readers a better sense of the relationship between Marisol and her grandmother. Concrete details help readers imagine sights and sounds.

When she got home, she could smell the garlic from the asopao. She ran into the kitchen to see her grandmother, who stood at the stove. Her grandmother turned and smiled at her. Marisol knew then that not going to soccer practice was the right decision.

"Just in time," said her grandmother as she ladled the meat and vegetables into a bowl and placed it on the table. "Sit and eat."

Marisol sat down and put her books on the floor. Her grandmother sat across from her, straightening her red dress around her as she got comfortable. "Tell me about your day," she said, and Marisol began to talk. They sat there for hours as the sun went down and the rest of the family came home from work and school.

This paragraph focuses on the main conflict: Marisol's decision about whether to stay on the soccer team or spend time with her dying grandmother.

After dinner, Marisol went into her room. She sat on her bed and spread her books out. What should she do? She loved playing soccer, but she loved her grandmother more. If she didn't play, would she lose all her friends? What about college? Without a soccer scholarship, she didn't think she would be able to go. Marisol sat in her room and thought about her grandmother dying. How long did she have? Marisol knew it wasn't long.

The resolution of the story shows Marisol making her decision and being true to herself when she realizes that soccer will always be there, but her grandmother will not.

As Marisol started her homework, she made her decision. She would quit the soccer team this year. She could always play next year, but her grandmother might not be here then. With her decision made, Marisol finished her homework with no problem. Her mom came in to say good night. Marisol went to bed and slept better than ever.

Listening, Speaking, and Viewing

Group Discussion

Do you enjoy a good talk with your friends? In a group discussion you can try to persuade classmates to share your opinions.

What Is Group Discussion?

A group discussion is a gathering of three or more students to talk about a piece of writing. You might discuss one specific question (for example, What is the main conflict? Is the protagonist's behavior believable?), or you might cover several elements of a story. It's usually a good idea to take notes on the group's ideas so you can share them with the entire class.

Why Is Group Discussion Important?

In a group discussion students help each other learn. You voice and support your own opinions and listen to other people's. You develop skills in listening, dealing with conflict, and making decisions. When you share information and debate its meaning, you can learn new ideas and teach them. You also get a chance to see things from other people's perspectives and appreciate their different ways of communicating.

How Do I Take Part in Group Discussion?

Use the tips that follow to participate effectively in group discussion.

- Think before you speak, but then speak up. Volunteer your ideas and opinions.
- Use the skills of inferring and drawing conclusions in your discussion. Bring your own prior knowledge and experience to the conversation.
- Listen to what others have to say. Give everyone a chance to talk. Be encouraging.
- If you don't understand the point someone is making, ask for more information.
- It's okay to disagree with a classmate, but be polite. You might say, "But have you considered . . ." not "That doesn't make any sense."
- Build on other group members' comments.
- Help the group summarize its progress. Stop every few minutes and say, "This is what we've figured out so far. What else do we need to know or figure out?"
- Identify missing information in the group's answer. Help the other members fill in blanks.

Try It Out Use the guidelines on conducting a group discussion when you discuss these questions: **(1)** Did Marisol do the right thing to resolve her conflict? **(2)** Is there some way she could have handled it better? Be prepared to support your opinions with examples from the text and from life.

Analyzing Cartoons
Would Calvin have found Tommy's story funny if he had read it in a book?

Skills Focus

You will practice using these skills when you read the following selections:

- "The Fire Pond," p. 638
- from *Savion!: My Life in Tap,* p. 654

Reading

- Inferring unstated ideas in text

Literature

- Analyzing the setting of a story
- Recognizing how setting affects characters and conflicts
- Analyzing tone

Vocabulary

- Using prefixes to infer word meaning
- Academic Vocabulary: *imply*

Writing/Grammar

- Avoiding run-on sentences

NY English Language Arts Core Curriculum
(pp. 634–635)

LC R12 Combine multiple strategies to enhance comprehension and response. **RII** Make inferences on the basis of explicit and implied information.

For a complete description of the standards, see p. NY11.

Skill Lesson

Making Inferences

Learn It!

What Is It? Inferring is like being a detective. It's using your knowledge and information you gather from a text to make a good guess. Writers often **imply,** or hint at, an idea without stating it outright. To make inferences, you "read between the lines" and use what you know to figure out what the hints mean. For instance, while reading fiction you might make inferences about the following:

- why a character does something
- what a character is feeling
- how setting affects conflicts and characters

© Zits Partnership. Reprinted with Permission of King Features Syndicate, Inc.

Analyzing Cartoons
What clue tells Jeremy's dad that the phone call was for Jeremy?

Academic Vocabulary

imply (im PLY) to indicate or suggest without stating directly

Why Is It Important? In life you often do not have complete information about people or situations. You must use the information you *do* have to make inferences. Likewise, texts you read may not spell out every idea for you. You must use the information authors *do* give you.

How Do I Do It? As you read, pay attention to details. They are clues that will help you make inferences. Combine the clues with your own knowledge and experience. Then make inferences to figure out implied ideas. Read the following passage from a story. Then read to see how a student inferred what a character was like.

> My brother is eight years older than I am. But he seems to be twenty years wiser. Though I wouldn't say I'm jealous of him, exactly, I do sort of feel as if I live in the shadow of a giant. He seems to have it all—brains, looks, a great sense of humor, kindness. He's quarterback of his college football team, and girls are continually e-mailing and calling him. My aunt calls him Mr. Amourica because *amour* means "love" in French. I'll never get that kind of attention.

I think the narrator has mixed feelings about his brother. On the one hand, he seems to admire "Mr. Amourica," because he talks about all his great qualities. On the other hand, the narrator seems to want to be his own person. He may feel pressured to be like his brother. I've seen situations like that. I have a friend whose older sister did well in everything—school, sports, work, you name it. My friend had trouble in school. She hated being compared to her sister. She just wanted to be liked for who she was.

Practice It!

Do you agree with the student's inferences? List positive things the narrator says about his brother. Then jot down notes about anything negative about their relationship. Think about similar brother or sister relationships you've seen or experienced. Write a few sentences describing the relationship between the narrator and his brother.

Use It!

As you read "The Fire Pond" and from *Savion!: My Life in Tap,* make inferences based on details and descriptions in the texts.

Before You Read : The Fire Pond

Michael J. Rosen

Meet the Author

Michael J. Rosen writes, edits, and illustrates books. He lives in the country and loves nature. He works hard for the humane treatment of dogs. Rosen believes that to succeed at any task takes persistent effort. He says, "Inspiration's overrated. Strike until the iron is hot."

Author Search For more about Michael J. Rosen, go to www.glencoe.com.

NY English Language Arts Core Curriculum (pp. 636–649)
LC R6 Determine the meaning of words by using word structure knowledge.
LC R12 Combine multiple strategies to enhance comprehension and response.
RII Make inferences on the basis of explicit and implied information.
R2b Interpret setting, using evidence from the text.

For a complete description of the standards, see p. NY11.

Vocabulary Preview

fortune (FOR chun) *n.* luck; riches **(p. 639)** *When he won the lottery, the old man could not believe his good fortune.*

recedes (ree SEEDS) *v.* moves or pulls back; form of the verb *recede* **(p. 641)** *Whenever we have hot, dry weather for several days, the water in the pond recedes.*

salvaged (SAL vujd) *v.* saved from ruin; rescued; form of the verb *salvage* **(p. 641)** *We salvaged a few pieces of furniture and some pictures from our home after the flood.*

calculating (KAL kyoo layt ing) *v.* using math or logic to figure out something; form of the verb *calculate* **(p. 646)** *My sister is calculating how long it will take her to save for a new bicycle.*

On Your Own In your Learner's Notebook, write a sentence for each of the vocabulary words. Be sure to use each word correctly.

English Language Coach

Prefixes That Show Position Knowing what common prefixes mean will help you unlock the meaning of many words. Look at the chart below. All the prefixes on the chart show position. As you read "The Fire Pond," look for words that begin with these and other prefixes that show position.

Prefix	Meaning	Word Examples
out-	"outside" or "beyond"	<u>out</u>field, <u>out</u>building
sub-	"beneath"	<u>sub</u>marine, <u>sub</u>way
under-	"less than" or "below"	<u>under</u>pay, <u>under</u>ground
over-	"on top of" or "too much"	<u>over</u>coat, <u>over</u>shoot

Partner Work For each prefix, write a word that begins with the prefix. (Do not repeat the words on the chart.) Then use the word in a sentence. Work with a classmate, and use a dictionary if you need to.

Skills Preview

Key Reading Skill: Making Inferences

Authors rarely say exactly what a character values or believes. But you can usually infer what a character values. While you are reading "The Fire Pond," make inferences about the characters' values. Pay special attention to these points:

- what or whom the characters respect
- what the characters do
- how the characters treat each other

Whole Class Discussion How can you tell what a person values? List ideas.

Key Literary Element: Setting

Setting is the time and the place in which the events of a story occur. Setting includes the ideas, customs, values, and beliefs of the people who live in a particular time and place. For example, suppose that a story takes place now, in your neighborhood. The values and beliefs of the characters may be different from those of people in a story set in ancient Greece.

Setting may also influence the conflicts developed in a story. For example, if a story is set in a place often hit by tornadoes, then an external conflict—people against a force of nature—may arise from that setting.

To understand the setting and its effects on "The Fire Pond," ask yourself questions like these as you read: *When and where does the action take place? What is the relationship between the characters and their setting? Does conflict arise from the setting? If so, how does that affect the characters?*

Small Group Discussion "The Fire Pond" is set in the country. Before you read the story, get together with a small group of classmates and discuss possible similarities and differences between country life and city life. Take notes on a Venn diagram.

Get Ready to Read

Connect to the Reading

What makes you happy? Your idea of happiness may be different from that of your parents, your classmates, or your friends.

Write to Learn In a few sentences describe what makes you happy and why. Then briefly describe how you act when you're happy.

Build Background

People who live in the country may not have access to public water pipes and fire hydrants as people in cities do. So how do farm people find water to put out a fire?

- Many farms have ponds that can supply the thousands of gallons of water needed to put out a fire. Rural fire departments have special pumps that move the water from a pond into the hoses.
- Many rural fire departments are staffed by volunteer firefighters. They train together but do not stay at the fire station. When a fire is reported, the firefighters must rush to the fire station from their homes or jobs to pick up the equipment and fire trucks before they can get to the fire to extinguish it.

Set Purposes for Reading

BIG Question Read "The Fire Pond" to discover how the narrator of the story learns by example to stay true to himself.

Set Your Own Purpose What else would you like to learn from the story to help you answer the Big Question? Write your purpose on "The Fire Pond" page of Foldable 5.

Literature Online

Interactive Literary Elements Handbook To review or learn more about the literary elements, go to www.glencoe.com.

Keep Moving

Use these skills as you read "The Fire Pond."

The Fire Pond

by Michael J. Rosen

Practice the Skills

We stock the fire pond with rainbows. "Fire pond's" a thing I've said for fourteen years and never once thinking what it means besides this lake that Grandpa and friends dug behind the barn before I was born—before Dad was born. It's perfect for swimming, if you're not afraid of snakes (which you shouldn't be since snakes are more scared of you), and it's clear, so you can see your legs treading water[1] underneath. The pond's large enough to row around in a boat, and good for skating, too, unless you're hotdogging and trying those Olympic-medal spins. It's a place the cows and horses will drink—deer, too, though we'd rather they hang out at another farm and leave our crops alone. **1**

The rainbows are Grandpa's. A few times a summer, we fish out half a dozen for supper. **2** Sometimes we'll catch them on these hooks that don't have barbs, so we can measure the trout and release them again. But the rainbows aren't really for eating, just like the pond's not really for raising fish.

On the ride back from school, I stop and pick up loaves of two-day-old bread that Angela at the bakery holds for Grandpa (her mom was Grandpa's girlfriend before he met Grandma) and, every now and then, a piece of lung the butcher saves. Then Grandpa chops it all up and showers

1 Key Literary Element

Setting The following details in the story tell you that it takes place in the country.
- There's a lake behind a barn.
- There are snakes.
- Cows, horses, and deer drink from the lake.
- There's a farm and crops.

2 Key Reading Skill

Making Inferences What are rainbows in the context of the story? The narrator says several things about them. Here are some clues:
- "We stock the pond with rainbows."
- "We fish out half a dozen for supper."

---

1. **Treading water** is staying upright in the water by moving the feet up and down, as if walking.

handfuls around the dock so the rainbows surface, blurring Grandpa's reflection until it's gone and, looking down, the fish are all you can see.

He talks to the fish whether I'm there or not. Tells them stuff the way I guess I talk to the cats when they follow me around the barn.

"I do all the talking," Grandpa says. "I'm not expecting them to answer."

We have two farm cats—and also this Lab-shepherd mix that's owned by Mrs. Collins, except he spends all day across the road at our place following whoever of us is on the tractor. Grandpa never takes much notice of them. The rainbows are what he's got instead of pets—instead of lots of things. He walks the edge of the fire pond every day, just looking, just admiring what he's got there. It's like the story about the king—or was it the thief?—who has to count his riches every day because, well, I guess he can't believe his **fortune** or his luck. Not that Grandpa's really lucky or fortunate. Not that a bunch of fish swimming around a fire pond is something you count on. **3**

"That one's big as a railroad tie!"[2] he'll shout to me, if I'm walking with him, which I do, especially since Grandma died.

"At least," I answer.

"I don't go in for exaggerating and you know that. Don't need to when they're this beautiful big. But you're my witness, just in case someone doubts."

Practice the Skills

3 **Key Reading Skill**

Making Inferences What do you think the fish mean to Grandpa? Think about these clues:

- He talks to them.
- He has them instead of pets or other interests.
- He admires them everyday.

Analyzing the Photo The narrator's grandpa spends a lot of time at the pond. Why might this be? What is it about the pond that he seems to love most?

2. A *railroad tie* is a piece of wood that joins the two rails on which trains run and holds them in place.

Vocabulary

fortune (FOR chun) *n.* luck; riches

The Fire Pond **639**

Analyzing the Photo How does this picture illustrate the changed landscape that the narrator describes?

Rainbow's the only fish that Grandpa will eat. "No other fish worth catching, neither," he says. Me, I like tuna fish better. (Only fish Mom and Dad love is the perch on those all-you-can-eat nights at the lodge.) I like trawling[3] for bluefish, too, which I've done twice, on visits with Mom's family in Maryland. So I think I like what all the fish mean to Grandpa more than what the fish mean to me. Mainly, it's cool to watch their shiny bodies darting like the sun's shine on the water, only under. **4**

The day the Allegheny[4] floods, all hell breaks loose. That's how Grandpa calls it: "See, even that devil creature is loose." And he means the rattlers, which take to moving from the riverbanks toward higher ground near Salamanca. They're hanging from the elderberries[5] along the road. Who even knew snakes could drown. **5**

---

3. *Trawling* is fishing from the side of a boat by using a bag-shaped net.
4. The *Allegheny* is a large river in western Pennsylvania.
5. *Elderberries* are large shrubs that have white flowers and purple berries used in cooking.

Practice the Skills

4 **Reviewing Elements**

Sensory Imagery Have you ever seen the sun shining on a lake or pond? The slightest bit of wind causes the water to ripple and the sun's reflection to break up. Use that image to help you see what the rainbows looked like just under the surface of the water.

5 **Key Literary Element**

Setting How has the setting become part of the plot?

Every house I visit is filled with rainwater to the doors—inside and outside. Creek water. Pond water. Lots of farms are worse than ours, but to see our place, it looks like another country, like you're looking down from an airplane and seeing these islands in an ocean—like Hawaii—except it's all just our two hundred acres. Our whole farm is all pond except for the stables across the road, and the highest spots in the meadow, and the animal buildings, which were built on higher ground just for a time like now that was never supposed to happen. The fire pond connects with the creeks, and it's deep enough for powerboats, and there are some, too, trying to save the washed-away things—ours, and stuff from nearby houses—that float or bob to the surface. So much lost and stranded livestock,[6] too, that take weeks to return to their farms. And drowned ones, too. **6**

Over and over Mom says things like, "No matter what we lost, we're still blessed." **7**

As for the rainbows, they're spilled like oil spots down the highway.

It's hard to know if any are left in our pond when the water **recedes**—when the banks of the fire pond are where I remember them, when the rain stops long enough to pump the water from the buildings. We start two lists: what's been ruined or lost, and what can be **salvaged.** It's months, really, before the house feels dry, and then the winter cold seeps in, freezing all that extra water into frost and ice—at least, that's how it feels.

It's more months before the check arrives from the insurance people, which doesn't pay for hardly anything, and the check from the state and federal governments on account of our being declared a disaster area. Almost every day I remember some little thing I used to have and didn't realize the flood had swept it away. But our damages are minor compared with some people we meet, compared with families in Knapp Creek, or nearer the Allegheny.

---

6. *Livestock* are farm animals, such as cows and sheep, which farmers raise for profit.

Practice the Skills

6 Key Literary Element

Setting At the beginning of the story, the fire pond was a very peaceful place. How does the flood cause problems for the characters living in this setting?

7 Key Reading Skill

Making Inferences After the problems the flood causes, why might the mother think the family is still blessed?

Vocabulary

recedes (ree SEEDS) *v.* moves or pulls back

salvaged (SAL vujd) *v.* saved from ruin; rescued

With the start of winter, the fire pond's dark gets lighter and lighter as ice heals over the surface like a scar. No one goes there much. We just stare at the pond and it stares back—that is, when it isn't covered with fresh snow. I hardly skate at all. A few times at my friend Troy's pond. But it's like I've lost my appetite for skating or for the pond, but I don't know if that's possible. As for Grandpa, he has no reason to trudge through the drifts and walk to the pond. He heads to North Carolina for a month to visit his sister. And he spends two weeks in Atlanta, staying with Uncle Miles and his family. And the other thing is, Grandpa comes back tired, though vacations are supposed to be for rest. **8**

Around about Mother's Day, it's finally warm enough for Grandpa to stock the pond again, even though Dad tries to suggest in a nice way that maybe the pond's better left on its own. Grandpa won't hear of that. A truck arrives with fingerlings[7] I can't believe will grow as large as the rainbows we lost. Same day, Grandpa calls Angela and the butcher to start saving up treats for his fish. And that night, after dinner, out of the clear blue, Grandpa reaches into his shirt pocket as he leaves the table, and places his driver's license beside the centerpiece[8] like he's presenting us with the check. "I'm done driving," he says, and then he points to me: "You'll need a car soon anyway."

He's already out of the room when Mom and Dad are saying things like, don't be silly, and why on earth, and Pop, come back in here.

Come to find out from Uncle Miles, Grandpa's had an accident—just a fender bender—in Atlanta. Afterward, he insisted on going to an optometrist or ophthalmologist[9]—whatever—who told him he had the eyes of a teenager. He did suggest glasses to help reduce the glare at night. But as soon as he got home, Grandpa decided he wasn't going out on the road. "First and last accident in my life," he said, when we tried to talk some sense into him, which is something

Practice the Skills

8 **Key Reading Skill**

Making Inferences What do you think is making Grandpa feel so tired? (Hint: What is missing from his life?)

---

7. A **fingerling** is a small fish about as long as a person's finger.

8. A **centerpiece** is a decoration that goes in the center of the dinner table.

9. An **optometrist** examines the eyes and prescribes glasses to correct eyesight problems. An **ophthalmologist** treats diseases of the eyes.

only Grandma could do—and once in a blue moon, she could actually succeed. It's a year before I can get my license.

Early summer's one of the driest on record, but the pond's its normal size. Except for sleeping later than six o'clock, which is when I get up for morning chores during school, I do what work everyone else does: putting in the crops, mowing, moving the animals out to pasture and back in, repairing the grain auger[10] and the tractors with Dad. Most of my school friends do the same at their farms, and after supper, we meet at the quarry to swim or bike over to DeWitt's for ice cream. **9**

In no time flat it's halfway through summer vacation, August first. Grandpa is reading after the rest of us are in bed. He reads more than he sleeps at night. "Don't much like closing my eyes," he says. "At my age, seeing's a kind of being proud." So Grandpa goes to make some tea, and he sees smoke rising near the barn. If he'd been asleep—if it hadn't been a clear night with an almost full moon—I don't see how any one of us would be alive now. **10**

Grandpa shouts as he runs up the stairs. He pounds on our bedroom doors. He's the one who phones the head firefighter from Hinsdale—they're the closest, still about twelve minutes away—and they start the chain of calls to rally the volunteers and summon Mr. Tyler at the general store to sound the siren, which we can't hear from here, but I know is blaring from when I bike near town.

Until they come, there's just the four of us, and Mrs. Collins and her son, Dean, who live across the road. We all know what to do though, as if we've had fire drills every month, like at school. We start moving the animals, and then the machines. It's like a parade marching out into the middle of the field, but jumbled and scattered and in the dark. The cows and pigs are so frightened, they'd trample a person without even knowing it.

When the volunteers from Hinsdale arrive, it's no one but Grandpa who drags the fire truck's pump hose to the pond and lowers it, hand over hand, like an anchor. Even these

---

10. A *grain auger* is a farm machine with a long tube that lifts grain from a truck to the top of a tall storage building.

Practice the Skills

9 **Key Literary Element**

Setting How does having to do chores on a farm bring the family closer together?

10 **Reviewing Skills**

Interpreting What do you think Grandpa means when he says that "seeing's a kind of being proud"?

new fish have learned the sound of his boots on the dock, the scattering of food on the water that follows. From faraway as the front yard, I can see how the glassy surface of the moonlight shatters into ripples by the dock where the rainbows are chomping at the empty air.

I help strap the Indian fire pumps on a few of the volunteers, and they join the truck at the barn to do what they can. The fire's already spread to the corn crib, where Grandpa's stationed himself.

Now, after a whole year, Grandpa will laugh if someone makes a joke about the fire. "If only we'd have grown *popping* corn, the fire would have popped enough corn to serve all the whole crowd! It looked like a drive-in movie with all those cars." But that night, the dried field-corn burns so fast and hot that the sweat steams beneath Grandpa's rubber coat—but he won't turn away except until he passes out from the heat, and the smoke, too. **11**

A man I don't know carries Grandpa to the house, where he checks his breathing, his eyes, and his pulse. (All the volunteers—Dad's one, too—take first-aid courses.)

"Your grandpa's fine. Long as he stays inside and rests," he tells me, and *I* believe him, though Grandpa won't: He is going to catch his breath and head back out. I learn the man's name is Hawkins when he phones to tell some doctor that he's needed here.

Mom makes me stay with Grandpa. Her voice is so serious, I think even Grandpa might listen for once.

"Tell them to let the barn burn!" he orders Hawkins before he leaves the house. "No barn's going to stand on a half-burnt frame. And move the horses."

"But the stables are across the road . . ." I start to say, and then answer my own question. The twelve horses have got to be spooked. And even if they're safe for now, they'll get to panicking and kick through their stalls, break a bone or tear themselves up on the wire.

Grandpa gives me a reason I hadn't thought of. "Look out there. Too much wind."

Even though the fire's around the other side, from the back door that faces the stables and the corral, I see them **outlined** like by moonlight, only it's orange because of the flames. **12** I see Mom shove the gates free. She slides open the stable's door,

Practice the Skills

11 | **Reviewing Skills**

Clarifying Notice that the sequence, or order, of events shifts during this part of the story. How much time has passed since the fire occurred? Reread the paragraph if you're not sure.

12 | **English Language Coach**

Prefixes The word **outlined** contains the prefix *out-*, which means "outside" or "beyond." It means "to make a line around the outside" of something. Does that make sense in this sentence?

jumping clear since the horses charge out instantly and all at once. The horses are pitch-black, but the fire's light gives them even darker shadows, however that's possible. A few horses bolt along the fence to the entrance of the meadow, and some of them leap the rails as though it weren't the fence at all that kept them here every day, but something else. We've lost a horse before, accidentally, but never all of them at once, and never in a panicking herd. But now isn't the time for asking how we'll find them. We will. People around here know us even if we are spread out far from one another. **13**

Then there's a new sound, louder, closer than the fire. Before I can turn to ask Grandpa the question, he tells me, "It's all right," which suddenly makes me think it's not. A spray of water bursts on the picture window. The jet runs across the wall and back, back and forth, across and back, as though it were erasing something.

"That means the house's caught fire?" I ask.

"No, no. Just preventing it," he says, but his voice is too faint; it's a whisper like a part of the farm already gone up in smoke.

Which makes me say and ask at the same time (that has to be possible): "Grandpa, we're going to be okay."

His nodding means yes and at the same time I don't know.

The one hose pounds the roof and wall and doesn't stop. It's like our own storm: one thunderbolt rumbling right against the house, but more like heat lightning since it's bright in all the windows. Water pours down the panes in sheets, and the view is blurred and wobbly, like looking through the sheer curtains when the window's cracked open in Grandpa's room. But even so, I know what's out there: I watch the embers float, slower than pennies in a wishing well, from the barn to the stables, to the milk house, to the grain elevator that's thirty-six feet tall—the tallest thing for miles—and over to one and then the other silo.

Behind me, from the couch where Grandpa's supposed to be lying still, I hear him talking like he's talking to the rainbows, or like he's giving directions and he's still out there fighting the flames. I can see the fire outside in his eyes, which must mean it's reflected in my eyes, too, if Grandpa looks up to see it.

Practice the Skills

13 Key Literary Element

Setting The narrator and his family don't stop to look for the horses because they believe the animals will be returned to them. What does that tell you about the community where the story takes place?

"The pond's not deep enough," Grandpa tells me, as if he'd just remembered how deep they'd dug it. I bring him some juice from the fridge. I don't know why I can't be doing something more than watching Grandpa—though if I weren't here, he wouldn't be either. **14**

There's so much light, I keep forgetting it's night. Besides the flames, there's the white flash of cameras: someone from the insurance company and a photographer for the *Journal*. And probably people just wanting to shoot some cool pictures. And then, even at the farther-away dark edges, there are yellower lights, and red ones—new ones: headlights and taillights of cars pulling in. (The *Journal*, which only comes out once a week, will say that two thousand people attended the fire—drove from nearby towns like we were some kind of county fair that opened after midnight. There should have been another story to say how people kept coming for days— not thousands, but more than just people we know by name—strangers coming to drop off things they had extra of, like a milking machine or a bridle, and, of course, things to eat, as though the fire had burned the kitchen, too, but it didn't—only whatever it is inside a person that's supposed to make us want to eat or want to wake up.) **15**

When I crack the front door just to see something clearly, a burst of smoke slips in before my eyes can really make out much.

"Seems like maybe there's even more firemen now, Grandpa," I tell him, and he nods, as though he'd been **calculating** how long it'd take the volunteers from each of the neighboring villages to make their way here.

"Probably. Probably be at least three fire trucks by now." And then, after too long a pause, he finishes. "Look at it go. Fire's just like trout heading upstream: slow and certain of where it's going."

That's when Mom comes in again with one of the cats, bringing not only the smell but also the heat of the fire in her clothes and hair. She confirms what Grandpa guessed: "There's three trucks pumping water now. And so many other people wanting to help, they've got two men just

Practice the Skills

14 **Key Reading Skill**

Making Inferences Grandpa says that the pond "isn't deep enough." What isn't it deep enough for?

15 **Reviewing Skills**

Connecting Sometimes disasters bring out the best in people. Strangers go out of their way to help others in need. What real-life examples of this can you give?

Vocabulary

calculating (KAL kyoo layt ing) *v.* using math or logic to figure out something

keeping the crowd back." Her eyes leak tears down her cheek—maybe it's just from the smoke—her talk has more important things to do than sob. We fill bottles and jugs of water at the sink to take to the firefighters.

The seven thousand hay bales blaze all night, glowing right alongside the dawn, when all that's left of the barn is an arch that frames the sunrise. It's quiet, then, suddenly, like an alarm clock went off, but one that wakes you with silence since the night was so loud. The firemen coil their hoses half-filled with pond sludge, and the last of the crowds drive home to Portville, Ischua, and Knapp Creek. **16**

Friends in Olean, and farther south than Hinsdale, smell the smoke at sunup, the dead fish at dusk. The phone is always ringing. One call is from the Luthers, who have managed to pen the four horses that escaped. They'll hold them as long as we need them to.

It's three days before the coals lose heat, before Mom and Dad are done meeting the insurance people and the county agents. Grandpa and I comb the property after supper. The machines are still clustered in the pasture like cows, as though the only job they had was to wait. Since nothing else stands but the house and the woods—and the stables across the road, which were unharmed, after all—we watch the ground as if something were left here and we had to come to look. Instead of grass or dirt it's ashes, wet wherever we step. Across the meadow where the fire pond was, there's a mud valley now that's like a mirage of water, shimmering the way a highway in the summer heat looks wet until you get closer and see it's not. The pond shimmers, but closer up, it's the silt rippling where the tails are flaring beneath.

Practice the Skills

16 Key Reading Skill

Making Inferences How do you think Grandpa feels about having all the water drained from the pond? Why do you think so?

Analyzing the Photo How does this picture illustrate changes in the pond?

When Grandpa takes off his shoes and socks, I take off mine. We set them on the dock and climb down to the muck of the bottom. Forty years ago, I think to myself, Grandpa stood on the bottom like this.

We start off walking, our feet sinking into the clay, then popping free with a suction sound.

"It's raining," Grandpa announces to me, or maybe he's just used to talking to himself at the pond. He's smiling, even though no amount of water—not from clouds, not from our springs or our well, not from tanker trucks with nothing better to do than to cart water here—nothing will save the rainbows. The ones at the shallow end are dead. These last few that move have already drowned in the air.

Grandpa says, "I already hear them talking."

"Who, Grandpa?" I ask. I know he doesn't mean the fish.

"Just people. I hear them. 'You'd think that old fool'd have learnt that first time never to stock a fire pond.'" **17**

"No, they're not, Grandpa," I answer him, "they won't," though this is just another thing I don't know. I don't know if Grandpa's thinking about restocking the pond, or if I should plead with him not to if only so he'll slap me hard enough to let me cry. I don't know even why I think this, because he'd never do that. **18**

Practice the Skills

17 **Key Reading Skill**

Making Inferences Do you think Grandpa cares whether other people think he's a fool? Why or why not?

18 **Reviewing Skills**

Predicting Do you think Grandpa will restock the pond with rainbows? Explain.

"I'm going to tell you something," he says, "and I don't care if you're old enough to think you should start ignoring advice."

I do know I should tell him I'm not, that I'm listening, to go ahead, to keep walking—*something*. So I take a step forward. Grandpa's planted there like he's a boot that just slipped off your foot and stuck there. So I have to step back.

"You stock your life with what all makes you happy, you hear me? You put rainbows anyplace you like, not excepting your young heart."

And then it's Grandpa who turns, ready to complete our tour, if that's what we're doing, drawing a circle with footstep dashes around the fire pond like it's something you could cut out. But before I can say anything like I'm sorry or I believe you, he adds: "I'm not expecting you to answer."

Grandpa's footprints are the size of mine (the size of the fingerlings—grown a lot, of course, since May): They're little ponds the coming rain will fill, then flood, then wash away. **19** ○

Practice the Skills

19 **BIG** Question
How does Grandpa stay true to himself? Write your answer on "The Fire Pond" page of Foldable 5. Your response will help you answer the Unit Challenge later.

Analyzing the Photo Look closely at the water. How does the photo help you picture what the rainbows in the fire pond look like?

The Fire Pond **649**

After You Read | The Fire Pond

Answering the BIG Question

1. What did you learn about staying true to yourself from reading the story?

2. **Recall** What is the first natural disaster in the story?
   TIP Right There

3. **Summarize** In two or three sentences, sum up what happens to the fire pond during the course of the story.
   TIP Think and Search

Critical Thinking

4. **Analyze** How does the narrator feel about Grandpa at the end of the story? Give evidence from the story to back up your answer.
   TIP Author and Me

5. **Analyze** What do you think the narrator learns from his experiences? Support your answer with evidence from the story.
   TIP Author and Me

6. **Evaluate** Do you think Grandpa would be foolish to restock the pond with rainbows? Explain why or why not.
   TIP On My Own

Write About Your Reading

Letter What do you think happens next? Write a letter from the narrator to a friend telling what happens during the year after the story ends. Use your imagination to "fill in the blanks," but make the characters behave in ways that are consistent with the story. Use the questions below to get started.

• What does the family do about the farm?

• What happens to Grandpa? Does he restock the pond?

• What happens to the narrator? Does he change? If so, how?

NY English Language Arts Core Curriculum (pp. 650–651)
LC R17 Demonstrate comprehension and response through a range of activities.
LC W4 Compose grade-appropriate texts for a variety of purposes.
LC R12 Combine multiple strategies to enhance comprehension and response.
R11 Make inferences on the basis of explicit and implied information.
R2b Interpret setting, using evidence from the text. **Core W8** Use correct grammatical construction.

For a complete description of the standards, see p. NY11.

Skills Review

Key Reading Skill: Making Inferences

7. At the beginning of the story, Grandpa says he talks to the trout even though he doesn't expect them to answer. When he talks to the narrator at the end of the story, why doesn't Grandpa expect the narrator to answer him either?

Key Literary Element: Setting

8. Grandpa dug the fire pond years before the story begins. How else has he influenced the setting?

9. How might the story change if it were set in a big city? Identify at least two events that would turn out differently, and explain the differences.

Reviewing Skills: Connecting

10. What part of the story could you most easily relate to, or connect with? Why?

11. How did making the connection help you better understand or enjoy the story?

Reviewing Skills: Interpreting

12. What does Grandpa mean when he says, "You put rainbows anyplace you like, not excepting your young heart"? Support your answer with details from the story.

Vocabulary Check

Match each word with the word or phrase that means the opposite.

13. salvaged   **a.** destroyed

14. recedes   **b.** using instincts

15. fortune   **c.** advances

16. calculating   **d.** poverty

17. English Language Coach Copy the following words on another sheet of paper. Circle the prefix on each word. Then define the word. Check your definitions in a dictionary.

> **outpatient** • **subtitle** • **undersea** • **overreach**

18. Academic Vocabulary If a theme is **implied**, is it directly stated? Explain why or why not.

Grammar Link: Run-on Sentences

A **run-on sentence** is two or more independent clauses run together without correct punctuation or conjunctions. Run-on sentences are mistakes that make it hard for readers to understand where one thought ends and the next begins.

Run-On: Estela loves to play the piano it relaxes her.

To fix a run-on sentence, put a period between the two independent clauses, or simple sentences. The period shows readers where one thought ends and the next begins.

Correct: Estela loves to play the piano. It relaxes her.

Another way to fix a run-on sentence is to separate the independent clauses with a comma and a coordinating conjunction.

Correct: Estela loves to play the piano, <u>and</u> it relaxes her.

You can also correct a run-on sentence by adding a subordinating conjunction to one of the clauses.

Correct: Estela loves to play the piano <u>because</u> it relaxes her.

Grammar Practice

On another sheet of paper, copy and fix the following run-on sentences, using each of the ways listed above.

19. She practices every day she doesn't mind.

20. She wants to be a music teacher someday she must learn to play different instruments.

Writing Application Review your Write About Your Reading activity. Find and fix any run-on sentences.

Web Activities For eFlashcards, Selection Quick Checks, and other Web activities, go to www.glencoe.com.

Before You Read

from *Savion!: My Life in Tap*

Meet the Authors

Savion Glover was born in 1973. He is an award-winning dancer and actor who has performed on stage and in the movies. He also choreographs, or works out dance moves, for other dancers. He says, "My class . . . is an opportunity to pick up some of the knowledge and experience that I learned from the people who taught me."

Bruce Weber reports on culture and the arts for *The New York Times*. He also writes for many magazines.

Author Search For more about Savion Glover and Bruce Weber, go to www.glencoe.com.

NY English Language Arts Core Curriculum (pp. 652–659)

LC R6 Determine the meaning of words by using word structure knowledge.
LC R12 Combine multiple strategies to enhance comprehension and response.
RII Make inferences on the basis of explicit and implied information.
R2e Recognize how the author's use of language creates images or feelings.

For a complete description of the standards, see p. NY11.

Vocabulary Preview

askew (uh SKYOO) *adj.* turned or twisted to one side **(p. 654)** *He wore his baseball cap askew as a fashion statement.*

hygiene (HY jeen) *n.* cleanliness; habits that lead to good health **(p. 655)** *To maintain good personal hygiene, he takes a shower every day.*

translates (TRANZ laytz) *v.* changes successfully into another form or language; form of the verb *translate* **(p. 658)** *Savion feels his dancing translates into life lessons.*

Partner Talk Without saying the definitions, give clues to help your partner guess what each vocabulary word is. Give ideas and activities associated with the words. Then switch and have your partner give you clues.

English Language Coach

Adjective and Adverb Suffixes Knowing what common suffixes mean can help you figure out the meaning of many unfamiliar words. Recall that a **suffix** is a combination of letters added to the end of a word. Adding a suffix may change the word's meaning and part of speech. For example, adding the suffix *-ous* to the noun *glamor* makes the adjective *glamorous*. Look at the suffixes on the chart below.

Suffix	Part of Speech	Word Example
-ly	adverb	quick<u>ly</u>
-ic	adjective	poet<u>ic</u>
-ive	adjective	select<u>ive</u>
-ful	adjective	play<u>ful</u>
-ous	adjective	marvel<u>ous</u>

Partner Work With a classmate, look at each word below and decide what part of speech it is. Then separate the word into its base word and suffix. Decide what part of speech the base word is. Then use both the word and suffix in a sentence.

- gruffly
- heroic
- protective
- sorrowful

Skills Preview

Key Reading Skill: Making Inferences

In *Savion!: My Life in Tap,* Savion Glover talks about his experiences as a youngster and an adult working on stage. What inferences can you make about the content of the article? What do you think he might talk about in the article?

Whole Class Discussion As a class, discuss what kinds of information you think you might find.

Literary Element: Tone

Tone is an author's attitude toward a subject as shown in the language he or she uses. The tone of a selection may be admiring, sarcastic, angry, joyous, funny, ironic, neutral—any word that you can use to describe an attitude can be used to describe tone. To identify the tone of *Savion!: My Life in Tap,* ask yourself the following questions:

• *How does Savion feel about the person, place, or thing he is describing? How can I tell?*

• *If I were reading this aloud with expression, what feelings would I try to show in my voice? Why?*

Partner Talk Read the following passage from *Savion!: My Life in Tap.* With a classmate, identify the tone. Give reasons for your ideas.

> "[J]ust a few years ago, in *Tap,* I was hangin' with Sammy Davis, Jr., and he was on the set drinking Kool-Aid and wearing a do-rag. It was red Kool-Aid, I remember, and he drank it in a big mug. Like regular folks. Sammy Davis, man!
>
> And then I was on *Sesame Street*, which was also cool, a nice vibe. That's when people started recognizing me on the street . . ."

Get Ready to Read

Connect to the Reading

Savion Glover talks about older people whom he admired as he was growing up. Are there people in your life you feel that way about? It could be your parents, teachers, or coaches. Perhaps it's a neighbor. Think about how you feel when that person pays attention to you and helps you.

Partner Talk With a partner, discuss someone you admire.

Build Background

• Tap dancing developed in the nineteenth century. It mixed steps from jigs and reels danced by Irish and Scottish immigrants with African steps danced by African Americans. Irish dancers contributed the use of shoes with wooden soles that increased the sound. African Americans contributed the stress on rhythm, contrasting beats, and improvisation.

• By the 1920s, metal taps under the heels and toes began replacing wooden soles.

• Challenges are contests between dancers during jam sessions. Each dancer tries to outdo the previous one by using trickier or faster steps.

Set Purposes for Reading

BIG Question Read the selection from *Savion!: My Life in Tap* to find out how Savion learned to be true to himself as a dancer and as a human being.

Set Your Own Purpose What else would you like to learn from the selection to help you answer the Big Question? Write your purpose on the *Savion!: My Life in Tap* page of Foldable 5.

Literature Online

Interactive Literary Elements Handbook
To review or learn more about the literary elements, go to www.glencoe.com.

Keep Moving

Use these skills as you read from *Savion!: My Life in Tap.*

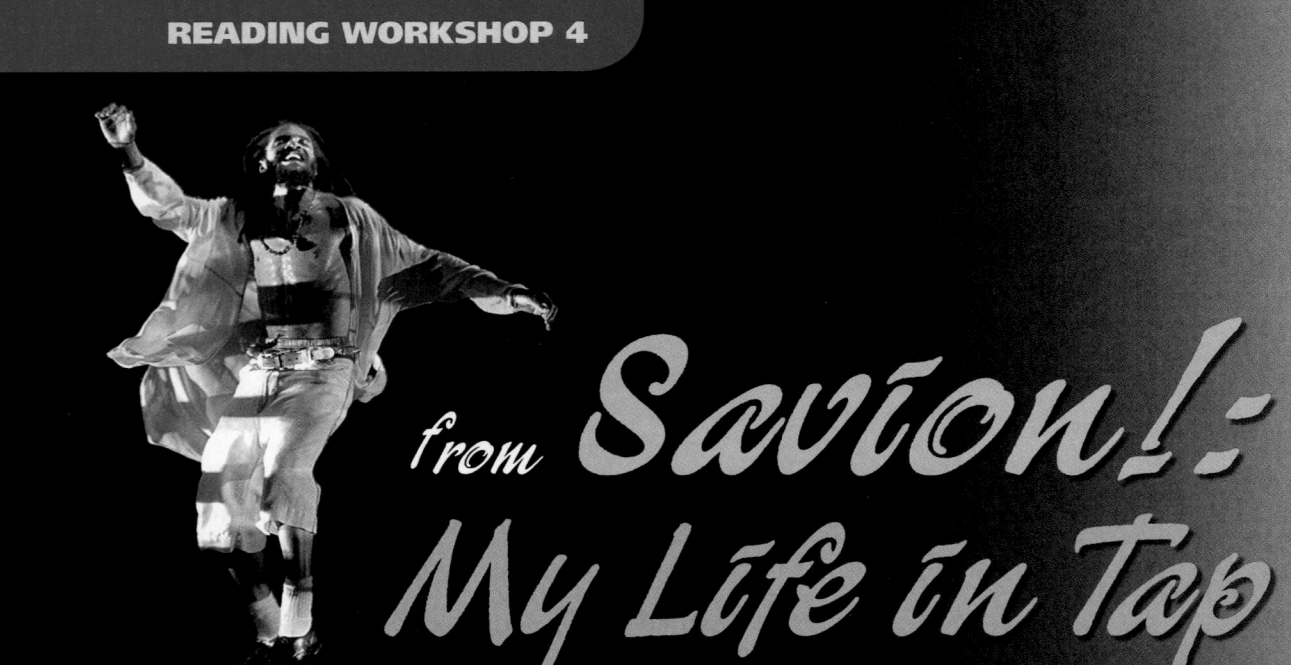

from *Savion!:*
My Life in Tap

by Savion Glover and Bruce Weber

I look back on it now, and it seems like everything happened so fast. It's hard to believe all that has happened since I was twelve years old and getting ready to go onstage for the first time in *Tap Dance Kid*. I mean, just a few years ago, in *Tap*, I was hangin' with Sammy Davis, Jr.,[1] and he was on the set drinking Kool-Aid and wearing a do-rag. It was red Kool-Aid, I remember, and he drank it in a big mug. Like regular folks. Sammy Davis, man!

And then I was on *Sesame Street*, which was also cool, a nice vibe. That's when people started recognizing me on the street. Kids. And I noticed a lot of them were wearing their hats **askew,** like I did on the show. I liked Elmo; he was my favorite, so innocent even when he was doing wrong stuff. ▪

Anyway, looking back to *Tap Dance Kid*, I can see I knew nothing, nothing. I went through all the rehearsals, all the

---

1. **Sammy Davis Jr.** became a big star in the 1950s. He was an all-around performer, working in theater, movies, and television as a singer, dancer, and actor.

Vocabulary

askew (uh SKYOO) *adj.* turned or twisted to one side

Practice the Skills

1 Literary Element

Tone Remember that tone is the attitude a writer takes toward a subject. Savion's tone is enthusiastic. Look at the details he mentions:

• He hung out with celebrities when he was a kid.

• He was on *Sesame Street.*

• People started recognizing him on the street.

understudy's rehearsals, and what did I know about scripts and scenes and blocking and upstaging and cues[2] and exit lines and all that? I had no idea how to change clothes between scenes in time to get back on. Someone's going to change me? Whoa! Hinton Battle,[3] the star, he was always on us kids about warming up, getting ready. And other stuff too, like **hygiene.** I can remember him pulling me aside and saying, "Yo, man, I don't know if you're using any deodorant, but you better get some." And he was right. I *was* funky that day.

My opening night I was <u>**nervous,**</u> out of my mind nervous. **[2]** Butterflies in my stomach and everywhere else. I'm not that great a singer to begin with, but that night my voice was shaky as milk. The only thing that saved me was my family. There was a scene in the show on the Roosevelt Island tram, and I rode across the stage on this tram, and while I was riding it, I saw my mom for the first time, and this relaxing feeling came over me. I saw her face, and it was, like, relief. I was comfortable from then on.

What I learned from *The Tap Dance Kid* was the basics, really the basics. The basic basics. Familiarity with the stage. How to position myself. How to prepare. How to listen. How to react to the audience. I took it on myself to learn the theater, walked around it as if I were working there, went up on the catwalks[4] to see what the guys do up there, backstage, all that. It was, like, I'm here to perform, but I'm also interested in what's behind the secret door. I guess I was ready for it to be real, not so magical anymore. You know, I was part of it. The magician has to know what the explanation for his magic is.

Anyway, that was why *Tap Dance Kid* was important for me. As for my performance, I didn't really feel like I was

Practice the Skills

[2] English Language Coach

Adjective and Adverb Suffixes What is the base word of <u>**nervous?**</u> How does adding the suffix change the part of speech?

---

2. An **understudy** is an actor who knows another performer's part and can substitute if needed. **Blocking** is working out the places on stage where the actors should stand during the different scenes. **Upstaging** is drawing attention to oneself and taking it away from another actor. A **cue** is the action or line that tells an actor to enter the stage or give a speech.

3. **Hinton Battle** won a Tony award for Best Actor for *Tap Dance Kid.* He learned to tap to play the role and has been known as a dancer ever since.

4. A **catwalk** is a narrow bridge above a stage from where the stage crew works the sets and lights.

Vocabulary

hygiene (HY jeen) *n.* cleanliness; habits that lead to good health

Analyzing the Photo A tap sensation, Savion dances opposite Gregory Hines in the Broadway musical *Jelly's Last Jam.* What does Savion learn about performing from his fellow dancers?

performing. That was *my* life up there, and being onstage was just like sitting around the kitchen table telling a story about what happened to me that day. And every night, when we'd take our solo bow, I felt like: These people aren't clapping for me, for Savion; they're clapping for Willie, the Tap Dance Kid. I never felt like Savion was taking that bow.

It was after I got started on *Black and Blue* that I began to understand it didn't have to be that way. During the show I'd go out and do double times,[5] big steps, trying to please the audience, and then afterward I was hanging out with Slyde and Chaney, and just by watching them, I saw it wasn't about pleasing the audience; it was about expressing yourself. **3** It didn't happen right away. You don't just wake up and find your voice, your style. It has to develop. But during *Black and*

---

5. Dancing **double time** is dancing very fast by doing twice the number of steps that the beat calls for.

Practice the Skills

3 **Key Reading Skill**

Making Inferences What do you think the difference is between pleasing the audience and expressing oneself?

Blue was when I started realizing I could create my own kind of dance. Up to that point all I was doing was dancing.

It wasn't anything they told me, not really. It was just being there every day. During rehearsals in New York I'd just be looking—at Slyde, at Chaney,[6] at Chuck, even at the women, like Dianne[7]—and I'd be watching them, saying to myself: This is nothing like what I was taught in dance class. The sounds, their bodies, the way they handled themselves. Once we got over to Paris, I'm in the wings watching them, I'm in Chaney's back pocket when he comes offstage. I was like that with all of them. I just wanted to follow them around. I don't know why; they were interesting, is all. This was a club I wanted to join.

I was learning how to hang out, to enjoy. People think I hung out with them and only learned dance. But remember, I had no father image in my life. And these cats were men, and they were accepting me, and I was just this little kid running around, and they let me hang out with them everywhere. We went out. We went to clubs. You ask what they taught me? Everything. About life. About being a man. About how to be. The point is I still spend time conversating with myself about these men. It doesn't matter where I am, something one of them said'll hit me, mad things, like footnotes—"Make sure you put the right foot first, even if it's the left one," or "If you can't flow with it, don't go with it"— and I'll have to ask myself: Are you talking about the dance or life? ◼4

Slyde would drop info on me. He's such a wise man. Through the dance he'd tell me, "Swing a little, sing the song." I would always come out and do double time, all the time fast, fast, and Slyde told me, "You should try swinging." And the first time I tried it, I danced for seven minutes, and my breathing was different. I was relaxed, not tense, not holding my breath. I felt like I was singing what I was dancing. So that was something he told me that helped my dancing. But he was always telling me, "Stay comfortable." Now is that about just dancing?

---

6. Jimmy **Slyde** has been a tap dancer since the 1940s. His stage name comes from his style of dancing that makes him appear to slide across the stage. Lon **Chaney** is part of Slyde's generation of tap dancers and has influenced many younger artists.

7. **Chuck Green** began dancing as a child in the 1920s. Audiences loved him for his graceful style. **Dianne Walker** is known as an elegant dancer. Her dance students call her "Aunt Dianne."

Practice the Skills

◼4 Literary Element

Tone What is Savion's attitude towards the men who helped him learn about dancing and life? Does that attitude come across clearly in the tone of this paragraph?

And Chaney would tell me, "Hit it! Put it *down*, young man!" and I understand that as a dancer and as a man. I can take that information about the dance and use it in my everyday life. It **translates.** You see what I'm saying? And I remember Chuck telling me, "Keep on the cardboard." What does that mean? I have no idea. "Keep on the cardboard." But I remember it, and I know, like twenty years from now, it'll come to me. That's what Chuck meant!

When we came back to Broadway, I was really trying to find myself as a tap dancer. My performance began to change, and even my mom noticed. I wasn't smiling as much, not trying to *please* so much. It wasn't, like, Hey, I'm here, it's show time! anymore. It was more, like, Hey, let's go out and dance! Forget what *they* think they want to see. Chaney, Slyde, those cats—they saw my progress. It was real. I was finally asking, Why am I performing?

And then came *Jelly's*,[8] which was really the turning point, the first time I ever performed in a show and felt like it was me. Savion, up there, getting the applause and not the character I was pretending to be. But mostly *Jelly's* was important to me because of Gregory.[9] He took me under his wing after *Tap*, and it was Gregory who made sure I got cast in *Jelly's*.

He wasn't like Slyde, who's more a grandfather type, with all the mysterious wisdom he lays on me. For me, knowing Gregory is like knowing you have a pops but not meeting him until you're twenty years old, and it turns out he's been very cool all this time. We met in Paris when he came to see *Black and Blue*, and little did I know he was setting up this audition for *Tap*. Right away he was calling me Save, which only my brothers call me. After that we just started hanging out. We'd go to Knicks games; he'd come over to family barbecues. **5**

Practice the Skills

5 **Literary Element**

Tone Describe Savion's tone. What words and sentences does he use to describe Slyde and Gregory Hines?

---

8. The full name of the musical is **Jelly's Last Jam.**

9. **Gregory Hines** began dancing as a child in the 1950s. He was also an actor, and many of his movies included dancing.

Vocabulary

translates (TRANZ laytz) *v.* changes successfully into another form or language

Savion rehearses his steps at New York's Joyce Theater in January 2005.

Analyzing the Photo How does this photo capture Savion's love of dance?

Anyway, that relationship made it easy for me to, like, complete my education as a tap dancer, putting the finishing touches on all the stuff that Slyde and them had begun to teach me. And in *Jelly's*, I was playing the kid and he was playing the adult, and it seemed perfect to me that we were just there being two sides of the same person. And that number in the second act, Jelly's Isolation Dance, that was the highlight. I would do everything he did, right away, right away, keep spitting back to him what he was handing me, and we'd really be laying it down some nights. It was supposed to be a five-minute number, but it went on longer and longer and longer, we'd go on and on, jamming, and some nights people would just gather in the wings and watch. It was six, seven, eight minutes of joy every performance. And yeah, it felt like he was passing the torch down to me every night. **6**

It was humbling. Still is. ○

Practice the Skills

6 **BIG Question**

How does Savion stay true to himself? Write your answer on the *Savion!: My Life in Tap* page of Foldable 5. Your response will help you answer the Unit Challenge later.

After You Read

from *Savion!: My Life in Tap*

Answering the **BIG** Question

1. What did Savion learn from his mentors about dance?

2. **Summarize** What was Savion's life like as a child?

   TIP Think and Search

3. **Recall** Why did Savion need mentors to help him figure out how to dance and live?

   TIP Right There

Critical Thinking

4. **Evaluate** Do you think Savion had the right attitude and work ethic to become successful as a tap dancer?

   TIP Author and Me

5. **Analyze** In what ways did Savion's role models set positive examples for him? Give details from the article to support your answer.

   TIP Author and Me

6. **Analyze** Savion says that when he watched older performers he thought, "This is nothing like what I was taught in dance class." Do you think Savion feels his classes were not useful? How is what he learned from the performers different from what he learned in his classes?

   TIP On My Own

Talk About Your Reading

Small Group Discussion Savion uses a lot of **slang,** or informal language that is specific to a particular group of people. With a small group of classmates, find and list at least ten examples of slang in the selection. You may include single words or whole expressions. Then discuss how the slang affects your understanding of Savion and the selection. Use the following questions to guide your discussion.

• What does Savion's use of slang tell you about him?

• How would the selection change if the author had translated Savion's slang into standard English?

• Is the slang Savion uses still in fashion? Explain.

NY English Language Arts Core Curriculum (pp. 660–661)

LC R17 Demonstrate comprehension and response through a range of activities.
LC W5 Write with voice to address varied purposes, topics, and audiences.
LC R12 Combine multiple strategies to enhance comprehension and response.
R11 Make inferences on the basis of explicit and implied information.
R2e Recognize how the author's use of language creates images or feelings.
Core W7 Observe the rules of punctuation, capitalization, and spelling.

For a complete description of the standards, see p. NY11.

Skills Review

Key Reading Skill: Making Inferences

7. We know what Savion thought about working with the men who were his role models, but what do you think these men thought about him? What makes you say so?

Literary Element: Tone

8. How would you describe the overall tone of the article? Why? Quote specific words or phrases that illustrate the tone.

Vocabulary Check

Copy the sentences below on another sheet of paper. Then fill in the blank in each sentence with the correct vocabulary word from the list below.

askew • hygiene • translates

9. To avoid infecting patients, the doctors and nurses practiced good _____.

10. After the toddler slept on the rug, he left it lying _____ on the floor.

11. Studying hard often _____ into good grades.

English Language Coach Use one of the suffixes below to make each word listed either an adjective or an adverb. You may use a dictionary if you need to.

-ly • -ic • -ive • -ful • -ous

12. Change the verb *thank* into an adjective.

13. Change the verb *ponder* into an adjective.

14. Change the noun *electron* into an adjective.

15. Change the adjective *sincere* into an adverb.

16. Change the verb *obsess* into an adjective.

Literature Online

Web Activities For eFlashcards, Selection Quick Checks, and other Web activities, go to www.glencoe.com.

Grammar Link: More Run-on Sentences

In the last Grammar Link you saw one kind of run-on sentence—two independent clauses that run together.

Run-on: I like soccer I like hockey even more.

A second kind of run-on sentence occurs when two independent clauses are separated by just a comma.

Run-on: I like soccer, I like hockey even more.

A comma alone is not strong enough to separate independent clauses, or simple sentences. Fix this type of run-on, which is sometimes called a **comma splice,** by using any of these methods:

A. Separate the sentences with a period.

• I like soccer. I like hockey even more.

B. Put a comma and a coordinating conjunction between the independent clauses.

• I like soccer, but I like hockey even more.

C. Add a subordinating conjunction to one of the clauses to make it a dependent clause.

• Though I like soccer, I like hockey even more.

Grammar Practice

Copy the following paragraph on another sheet of paper. Then find and fix the three run-on sentences. Use any of the methods shown above.

Last fall my family and I went to the beach. I had never seen the ocean before, it was quite an experience. At first my little brother was a little nervous about getting in the water the waves were big and noisy. Everyone else was having fun, so he finally decided to try going in. He went in the water up to his knees, a wave knocked him over. Instead of being afraid, he started laughing. After that, we had so much fun! I can hardly wait to go back to the beach.

A RETRIEVED REFORMATION
by O. Henry

A RETRIEVED REFORMATION
adapted by Gary Gianni

Skills Focus

You will use these skills as you read and compare the following selections:
- "A Retrieved Reformation," p. 665
- Adaptation of "A Retrieved Reformation," p. 675

Reading

- Comparing and contrasting literary elements in texts

Literature

- Comparing and contrasting characterization in stories

Vocabulary

- Using word analysis
- Academic Vocabulary: *reveal*

NY English Language Arts Core Curriculum
(pp. 662–663)

LC R15 Analyze, contrast, support, and critique points of view in a wide range of genres. **R2b** Interpret characters, using evidence from the text.
For a complete description of the standards, see p. NY11.

Have you ever watched a movie that was based on a book? If so, you've seen an adaptation. The word *adapt* means "change." An **adaptation** is a changed, or new, version of an existing literary work.

Adaptations tell the same story in different ways. In this workshop, you will read a short story and its illustrated, graphic story adaptation. As you read, pay attention to the similarities and differences between the two versions of the story. Notice what things you are told in words in the print version of the story and what things you are told in pictures in the graphic story version.

How to Compare Literature: Characterization

Characterization refers to the methods that an author uses to show what characters are like. An author may **reveal** what a character does, says, and thinks as well as what other characters or the narrator says. In print stories authors often reveal character through descriptions of actions and thoughts. In graphic stories authors often reveal character through dialogue and pictures.

As you read, think about how the author reveals character in each selection. What does O. Henry tell you about the main character? What does Gary Gianni show you?

Academic Vocabulary

reveal (rih VEEL) *v.* show

Get Ready to Compare

In your Learner's Notebook, make a chart like the one below. Use your chart to record details that characterize—tell you about—Jimmy Valentine. Pay attention to the differences between the two versions. When you're finished reading, you will use your chart to compare Jimmy's characterization in the original story and in the graphic story adaptation.

Jimmy Valentine's character is revealed through . . .	Examples from the original story	Examples from the graphic story
his speech		
his actions		
his thoughts		
his appearance		
other characters' reactions to him		

Use Your Comparison

Who are the characters in your life? Perhaps you have a cousin who is just as funny as your best friend, or a teacher who has a lot of the same caring qualities as a favorite aunt. Choose two people you know or that you've read about and tell about each of them in a few paragraphs. Discuss how each person is alike and different.

You also may decide to illustrate a storyboard about the characters you've chosen. (A storyboard is a panel of drawings that shows a story's action.) For example, one frame may show the mother from a story you've read talking with her child, and the other may show your mother talking with you. Keep it brief—use four to six frames.

Before You Read

A Retrieved Reformation
by O. Henry

O. Henry

Meet the Author

O. Henry's real name was William Sydney Porter. He was born in 1862. He began writing stories while serving a short prison sentence for stealing money from a bank where he had worked. When he left prison in 1901, Porter began writing under the pen name O. Henry, partly to hide his past. Porter lived in New York City until his death in 1910.

Author Search For more about O. Henry, go to www.glencoe.com.

NY English Language Arts Core Curriculum (pp. 664–673)

LC R6 Determine the meaning of words by using word structure knowledge.
R2b Interpret characters, using evidence from the text.

For a complete description of the standards, see p. NY11.

Vocabulary Preview

compulsory (kum PUL suh ree) *adj.* required **(p. 666)** *The final exam was compulsory for everyone in the course.*

retribution (re trih BYOO shun) *n.* punishment for crimes **(p. 668)** *The judge believed that all crimes deserved stiff retribution.*

simultaneously (sye mul TAYN ee us lee) *adv.* at the same time **(p. 671)** *Both doors slammed simultaneously, creating a loud noise.*

English Language Coach

Multiple Affixes Did you know that more than one prefix and suffix can be added to the same base word? Look at the words *villainously* and *immovable* on the chart below. Then complete the chart by jotting down, in the last column, what you think the words mean. Use the chart to understand some of the prefixes and suffixes in "A Retrieved Reformation."

Word	Base Word	Prefixes or Suffixes	Meaning
villainously	*villain* = an evil person	*-ous* = full of *-ly* = in a particular way	
immovable	*move* = to change places	*im-* = not *-able* = capable	

Get Ready to Read

Connect to the Reading

Think of a time when you did the wrong thing. How did you feel afterward?

Build Background

O. Henry is known for his plots—and plot twists. A **plot twist** is an unexpected turn of events in a story.

Set Purposes for Reading

BIG Question Read to find out what Jimmy Valentine, the main character of "A Retrieved Reformation," risks to stay true to himself.

Set Your Own Purpose What else would you like to learn from the selection to help you answer the Big Question? Write your own purpose on the "A Retrieved Reformation" page of Foldable 5.

A RETRIEVED REFORMATION

by O. Henry

A guard came to the prison shoe shop, where Jimmy Valentine was assiduously stitching uppers,[1] and escorted him to the front office. There the warden handed Jimmy his pardon, which had been signed that morning by the governor. Jimmy took it in a tired kind of way. He had served nearly ten months of a four-year sentence. He had expected to stay only about three months, at the longest. When a man with as many friends on the outside as Jimmy Valentine had is received in the "stir"[2] it is hardly worthwhile to cut his hair. 🔳

"Now, Valentine," said the warden, "you'll go out in the morning. Brace up, and make a man of yourself. You're not a bad fellow at heart. Stop cracking safes, and live straight."

"Me?" said Jimmy, in surprise. "Why, I never cracked a safe in my life."

"Oh, no," laughed the warden. "Of course not. Let's see, now. How was it you happened to get sent up on that Springfield job? Was it because you wouldn't prove an alibi for fear of compromising somebody in extremely high-toned society? Or was it simply a case of a mean old jury that had it in for you? It's always one or the other with you innocent victims." 🔳

"Me?" said Jimmy, still blankly virtuous. "Why, warden, I never was in Springfield in my life!"

Practice the Skills

🔳 Comparing Literature

Characterization The narrator means that Jimmy has a lot of important friends—friends who will make sure that Jimmy doesn't stay in prison for very long.

🔳 Comparing Literature

Characterization Does the warden believe that Jimmy is telling the truth? Think about the warden's
• words
• tone
• facial expressions and gestures

---

1. If you do something **assiduously,** you do it steadily and with care. Jimmy was busy sewing the **uppers**—the top part of shoes—onto the soles.
2. The **"stir"** is another name for prison.

"Take him back, Cronin," smiled the warden, "and fix him up with outgoing clothes. Unlock him at seven in the morning, and let him come to the bull-pen. Better think over my advice, Valentine."

At a quarter past seven on the next morning Jimmy stood in the warden's outer office. He had on a suit of the villain-ously fitting, ready-made clothes and a pair of stiff, squeaky shoes that the state furnishes to its discharged **compulsory** guests.

The clerk handed him a railroad ticket and the five-dollar bill with which the law expected him to rehabilitate himself into good citizenship and prosperity. The warden gave him a cigar, and shook hands. Valentine, 9762, was chronicled on the books "Pardoned by Governor," and Mr. James Valentine walked out into the sunshine.

Disregarding the song of the birds, the waving green trees, and the smell of the flowers, Jimmy headed straight for a restaurant. There he tasted the first sweet joys of liberty in the shape of a broiled chicken and a bottle of white wine— followed by a cigar a grade better than the one the warden had given him. From there he proceeded leisurely to the depot. He tossed a quarter into the hat of a blind man sitting by the door, and boarded his train. Three hours set him down in a little town near the state line. He went to the café of one Mike Dolan and shook hands with Mike, who was alone behind the bar. **3**

"Sorry we couldn't make it sooner, Jimmy, me boy," said Mike. "But we had that protest from Springfield to buck against, and the governor nearly balked. Feeling all right?"

"Fine," said Jimmy. "Got my key?"

He got his key and went upstairs, unlocking the door of a room at the rear. Everything was just as he had left it. There on the floor was still Ben Price's collar-button that had been torn from that eminent detective's shirt-band when they had overpowered Jimmy to arrest him. **4**

Pulling out from the wall a folding-bed, Jimmy slid back a panel in the wall and dragged out a dust-covered suitcase. He opened this and gazed fondly at the finest set of burglar's

3 | **Comparing Literature**

Characterization What does Jimmy's behavior reveal about his character? Keep in mind the time of the story. With only five dollars, Jimmy was able to buy a broiled chicken, a bottle of wine, and a good cigar. But he wouldn't have much more left than the quarter he gave the blind man.

4 | **Comparing Literature**

Characterization In this one sentence, the author introduces a new character. How much does that sentence tell you about Ben Price?

Vocabulary

compulsory (kum PUL suh ree) *adj.* required

tools in the East. It was a complete set, made of specially tempered steel, the latest designs in drills, punches, braces and bits, jimmies, clamps, and augers, with two or three novelties invented by Jimmy himself, in which he took pride. Over nine hundred dollars they had cost him to have made at _____, a place where they make such things for the profession.

In half an hour Jimmy went downstairs and through the café. He was now dressed in tasteful and well-fitting clothes, and carried his dusted and cleaned suitcase in his hand. **5**

"Got anything on?" asked Mike Dolan, genially.

"Me?" said Jimmy, in a puzzled tone. "I don't understand. I'm representing the New York Amalgamated Short Snap Biscuit Cracker and Frazzled Wheat Company."

This statement delighted Mike to such an extent that Jimmy had to take a seltzer-and-milk on the spot. He never touched "hard" drinks.

A week after the release of Valentine, 9762, there was a neat job of safe-burglary done in Richmond, Indiana, with no clue to the author. A scant eight hundred dollars was all that was secured. Two weeks after that a patented, improved, burglar-proof safe in Logansport was opened like a cheese to the tune of fifteen hundred dollars, currency; securities and silver[3] untouched. That began to interest the rogue catchers. Then an old-fashioned bank safe in Jefferson City became active and threw out of its crater an eruption of banknotes amounting to five thousand dollars. The losses were now high enough to bring the matter up into Ben Price's class of work. By comparing notes, a remarkable similarity in the methods of the burglaries was noticed. Ben Price investigated the scenes of the robberies, and was heard to remark: "That's Dandy Jim Valentine's autograph. He's resumed business. Look at that combination knob—jerked out as easy as pulling up a radish in wet weather. He's got the only clamps that can do it. And look how clean those tumblers were punched out! Jimmy never has to drill but one hole. Yes, I guess I want Mr. Valentine. He'll do his bit next time without any short-time or clemency foolishness."

Practice the Skills

5 | **Comparing Literature**

Characterization How do the author's descriptions help you picture Jimmy? Make notes on your chart about the way O. Henry describes Jimmy's appearance.

---

3. **Currency** is paper money, **securities** are stocks and bonds, and **silver** is silver coins. Valentine is careful not to steal securities that could be difficult to sell or silver that could be heavy and attention-getting. He doesn't want to get caught.

Ben Price knew Jimmy's habits. He had learned them while working up the Springfield case. Long jumps, quick get-aways, no confederates,[4] and a taste for good society—these ways had helped Mr. Valentine to become noted as a successful dodger of **retribution.** It was given out that Ben Price had taken up the trail of the elusive cracksman, and other people with burglar-proof safes felt more at ease. **6**

One afternoon Jimmy Valentine and his suitcase climbed out of the mailhack[5] in Elmore, a little town five miles off the railroad down in the blackjack country of Arkansas. Jimmy, looking like an athletic young senior just home from college, went down the board sidewalk toward the hotel.

A young lady crossed the street, passed him at the corner, and entered a door over which was the sign "The Elmore Bank." Jimmy Valentine looked into her eyes, forgot what he was, and became another man. She lowered her eyes and colored slightly. Young men of Jimmy's style and looks were scarce in Elmore. **7**

Jimmy collared a boy that was loafing on the steps of the bank as if he were one of the stockholders, and began to ask him questions about the town, feeding him dimes at intervals. By and by the young lady came out, looking royally unconscious of the young man with the suitcase, and went her way.

"Isn't that young lady Miss Polly Simpson?" asked Jimmy, with specious guile.[6]

"Naw," said the boy. "She's Annabel Adams. Her pa owns this bank. What'd you come to Elmore for? Is that a gold watch-chain? I'm going to get a bulldog. Got any more dimes?"

Jimmy went to the Planters' Hotel, registered as Ralph D. Spencer, and engaged a room. He leaned on the desk and declared his platform to the clerk. He said he had come to

6 Comparing Literature

Characterization Make notes on your chart about Jimmy's characteristics as a thief.

7 Comparing Literature

Characterization Based on what you know about Jimmy so far, do you think he can change and become a good person? Why or why not?

---

4. **Confederates,** here, are friends or accomplices.

5. The **mailhack** was a horse-drawn carriage that delivered mail and carried passengers.

6. **Guile** is deceit. If something is **specious,** it seems true but isn't. Jimmy wants to look as if he's asking an innocent question, even though he's not.

Vocabulary

retribution (re trih BYOO shun) *n.* punishment for crimes

Elmore to look for a location to go into business. How was the shoe business, now, in the town? He had thought of the shoe business. Was there an opening?

The clerk was impressed by the clothes and manner of Jimmy. He, himself, was something of a pattern of fashion to the thinly gilded youth of Elmore, but he now perceived his shortcomings. While trying to figure out Jimmy's manner of tying his four-in-hand[7] he cordially gave information. **8**

Yes, there ought to be a good opening in the shoe line. There wasn't an exclusive shoe store in the place. The dry-goods and general stores handled them. Business in all lines was fairly good. Hoped Mr. Spencer would decide to locate in Elmore. He would find it a pleasant town to live in, and the people very sociable.

Mr. Spencer thought he would stop over in the town a few days and look over the situation. No, the clerk needn't call the boy. He would carry up his suitcase, himself; it was rather heavy.

Mr. Ralph Spencer, the phoenix that arose from Jimmy Valentine's ashes—ashes left by the flame of a sudden and **alterative** attack of love—remained in Elmore, and prospered. He opened a shoe store and secured a good run of trade. **9**

Socially he was also a success and made many friends. And he accomplished the wish of his heart. He met Miss Annabel Adams, and became more and more captivated by her charms.

At the end of a year the situation of Mr. Ralph Spencer was this: he had won the respect of the community, his shoe store was flourishing, and he and Annabel were engaged to be married in two weeks. Mr. Adams, the typical, plodding, country banker, approved of Spencer. Annabel's pride in him almost equaled her affection. He was as much at home in the family of Mr. Adams and that of Annabel's married sister as if he were already a member.

Analyzing the Image These are the kinds of shoes men and women wore in Jimmy Valentine's day. How do they differ from the shoes people wear today?

Practice the Skills

8 **Comparing Literature**

Characterization Do most people respond positively or negatively to Jimmy? How can you tell? Write your answer on your chart.

9 **English Language Coach**

Multiple Affixes If you alter something, you change it. The suffix *-ive* means "having the quality of." What do you think the word **alterative** means?

---

7. A *four-in-hand* is a necktie.

One day Jimmy sat down in his room and wrote this letter, which he mailed to the safe address of one of his old friends in St. Louis:

DEAR OLD PAL:

I want you to be at Sullivan's place, in Little Rock, next Wednesday night, at nine o'clock. I want you to wind up some little matters for me. And, also, I want to make you a present of my kit of tools. I know you'll be glad to get them—you couldn't duplicate the lot for a thousand dollars. Say, Billy, I've quit the old business—a year ago. I've got a nice store. I'm making an honest living, and I'm going to marry the finest girl on earth two weeks from now. It's the only life, Billy—the straight one. I wouldn't touch a dollar of another man's money now for a million. After I get married I'm going to sell out and go West, where there won't be so much danger of having old scores brought up against me. I tell you, Billy, she's an angel. She believes in me; and I wouldn't do another crooked thing for the whole world. Be sure to be at Sally's, for I must see you. I'll bring along the tools with me.

Your old friend,
JIMMY 🔟

🔟 Comparing Literature

Characterization You've learned a lot about Jimmy from narrative description. This letter, however, contains Jimmy's own words. What does the letter reveal about Jimmy's personality? How do you picture Jimmy now?

Visual Vocabulary
A *livery buggy* is a hired horse-drawn carriage.

On the Monday night after Jimmy wrote this letter, Ben Price jogged unobtrusively into Elmore in a livery buggy. He lounged about town in his quiet way until he found out what he wanted to know. From the drugstore across the street from Spencer's shoe store he got a good look at Ralph D. Spencer.

"Going to marry the banker's daughter are you, Jimmy?" said Ben to himself, softly. "Well, I don't know!"

The next morning Jimmy took breakfast at the Adamses. He was going to Little Rock that day to order his wedding suit and buy something nice for Annabel. That would be the first time he had left town since he came to Elmore. It had been more than a year now since those last professional "jobs," and he thought he could safely venture out.

After breakfast quite a family party went down together— Mr. Adams, Annabel, Jimmy, and Annabel's married sister with her two little girls, aged five and nine. They came by the hotel where Jimmy still boarded, and he ran up to his room and brought along his suitcase. Then they went on to the bank. There stood Jimmy's horse and buggy and Dolph Gibson, who was going to drive him over to the railroad station.

All went well inside the high, carved oak railings into the banking room—Jimmy included, for Mr. Adams's future son-in-law was welcome anywhere. The clerks were pleased to be greeted by the good-looking, agreeable young man who was going to marry Miss Annabel. Jimmy set his suitcase down. Annabel, whose heart was bubbling with happiness and lively youth, put on Jimmy's hat and picked up the suitcase. "Wouldn't I make a nice drummer?" said Annabel. "My! Ralph, how heavy it is. Feels like it was full of gold bricks."

Analyzing the Photo This bank vault is from the same time period as the story. How does the photo help you understand the actions that occur on this page?

"Lot of nickel-plated shoehorns in there," said Jimmy, coolly, "that I'm going to return. Thought I'd save express charges by taking them up. I'm getting awfully economical."

The Elmore Bank had just put in a new safe and vault. Mr. Adams was very proud of it, and insisted on an inspection by everyone. The vault was a small one, but it had a new patented door. It fastened with three solid steel bolts thrown **simultaneously** with a single handle, and had a time lock. Mr. Adams beamingly explained its workings to Mr. Spencer, who showed a courteous but not too intelligent interest. The two children, May and Agatha, were delighted by the shining metal and funny clock and knobs. **11**

Practice the Skills

11 **Comparing Literature**

Characterization Why does Jimmy show little interest in the vault? Do you believe that he has really changed?

Vocabulary

simultaneously (sye mul TAYN ee us lee) *adv.* at the same time

While they were thus engaged Ben Price sauntered in and leaned on his elbow, looking casually inside between the railings. He told the teller that he didn't want anything; he was just waiting for a man he knew.

Suddenly there was a scream or two from the women, and a commotion. Unperceived by the elders, May, the nine-year-old girl, in a spirit of play, had shut Agatha in the vault. She had then shot the bolts and turned the knob of the combination as she had seen Mr. Adams do.

The old banker sprang to the handle and tugged at it for a moment. "The door can't be opened," he groaned. "The clock hasn't been wound nor the combination set."

Agatha's mother screamed again, hysterically.

"Hush!" said Mr. Adams, raising his trembling hand. "All be quiet for a moment. Agatha!" he called as loudly as he could. "Listen to me." During the following silence they could just hear the faint sound of the child wildly shrieking in the dark vault in a panic of terror.

"My precious darling!" wailed the mother. "She will die of fright! Open the door! Oh, break it open! Can't you men do something?"

"There isn't a man nearer than Little Rock who can open that door," said Mr. Adams, in a shaky voice. "My God! Spencer, what shall we do? That child—she can't stand it long in there. There isn't enough air, and, besides, she'll go into convulsions from fright."

Agatha's mother, frantic now, beat the door of the vault with her hands. Somebody wildly suggested dynamite. Annabel turned to Jimmy, her large eyes full of anguish, but not yet despairing. To a woman nothing seems quite impossible to the powers of the man she worships.

"Can't you do something, Ralph—try, won't you?"

He looked at her with a queer, soft smile on his lips and in his keen eyes. **12**

"Annabel," he said, "give me that rose you are wearing, will you?"

Hardly believing that she had heard him aright, she unpinned the bud from the bosom of her dress, and placed it in his hand. Jimmy stuffed it into his vest pocket, threw off his coat and pulled up his shirt sleeves. With that act

12 Comparing Literature

Characterization Why does Jimmy give a strange smile when Annabel asks him to do something?

Ralph D. Spencer passed away and Jimmy Valentine took his place.

"Get away from the door, all of you," he commanded, shortly.

He set his suitcase on the table, and opened it out flat. From that time on he seemed to be unconscious of the presence of anyone else. He laid out the shining, queer implements swiftly and orderly, whistling softly to himself as he always did when at work. In a deep silence and immovable, the others watched him as if under a spell.

In a minute Jimmy's pet drill was biting smoothly into the steel door. In ten minutes—breaking his own burglarious record—he threw back the bolts and opened the door. **13**

Agatha, almost collapsed, but safe, was gathered into her mother's arms.

Jimmy Valentine put on his coat, and walked outside the railings toward the front door. As he went he thought he heard a faraway voice that he once knew call "Ralph!" But he never hesitated. At the door a big man stood somewhat in his way.

"Hello, Ben!" said Jimmy, still with his strange smile. "Got around at last, have you? Well, let's go. I don't know that it makes much difference, now."

And then Ben Price acted rather strangely.

"Guess you're mistaken, Mr. Spencer," he said. "Don't believe I recognize you. Your buggy's waiting for you, ain't it?"

And Ben Price turned and strolled down the street. **14** ○

Practice the Skills ·······························

13 | **Comparing Literature**

Characterization Are you surprised that Jimmy is willing to "burglarize" the safe to save Agatha? Why or why not?

14 **BIG Question**

Jimmy risks losing his new life when he decides to crack the safe. Do you think he stays true to himself by making that decision? Explain. Write your answer on the first "A Retrieved Reformation" page of Foldable 5. Your response will help you complete the Unit Challenge later.

This postcard image shows a typical main street around the year 1900.

Analyzing the Image In what ways is the town shown here similar to the town in the story?

Before You Read

A Retrieved Reformation
adapted by Gary Gianni

Gary Gianni

Meet the Author

Gary Gianni spends months—and sometimes years—creating all the pen and ink drawings and oil paintings needed to illustrate a book. The work is often painstaking. In addition to his two graphic novel adaptations, Gianni has written and drawn for Dark Horse Comics. Gary Gianni is also the creator of *The Monstermen Mysteries*.

Author Search For more about Gary Gianni, go to www.glencoe.com.

NY English Language Arts Core Curriculum (pp. 674–683)

LC R6 Determine the meaning of words by using word structure knowledge.
R2b Interpret characters, using evidence from the text.

For a complete description of the standards, see p. NY11.

Vocabulary Preview

eminent (IH muh nint) *adj.* of outstanding rank or quality **(p. 676)** *In an effort to fully understand her condition, the patient consulted several eminent physicians.*

flourishing (FLUR ish ing) *v.* thriving; doing extremely well; form of the verb *flourish* **(p. 680)** *The flowers Sharma planted were flourishing in the summer sun.*

sauntered (SAWN turd) *v.* walked leisurely; form of the verb *saunter* **(p. 682)** *Looking cool and relaxed, Julio sauntered into the library.*

English Language Coach

Multiple Affixes Some words have both prefixes and suffixes. Study the chart below. Look for words in "A Retrieved Reformation" that follow a pattern similar to the word *unperceived*.

Word	Base Word	Prefix	Suffix
unperceived	*perceive* = to see	*un-* = not	*-ed* = past tense

Get Ready to Read

Connect to the Reading

Jimmy Valentine's life changed for the better when he fell in love with Annabel. What other forces can change people's lives in a positive way? Think of the people and things that influence you.

Set Purposes for Reading

BIG Question Read Gary Gianni's version to help you think further about what Jimmy Valentine risked to stay true to himself.

Set Your Own Purpose What would you like to learn from the selection to help you answer the Big Question? Write your own purpose on the "A Retrieved Reformation" page of Foldable 5.

Practice the Skills

1 **Comparing Literature**

Characterization Notice Jimmy's facial expressions and posture in the first nine frames. Look at the warden's gestures toward Jimmy. Make notes on your chart about your impression of Jimmy in this story so far. Did you have the same impression of him at the beginning of the print version? Why or why not?

Practice the Skills

TAKE HIM BACK, CRONIN, AND FIX HIM UP WITH OUTGOING CLOTHES. UNLOCK HIM AT SEVEN IN THE MORNING.

BETTER THINK OVER MY ADVICE, VALENTINE.

THE NEXT MORNING, THE CLERK HANDED HIM A RAILROAD TICKET AND THE FIVE-DOLLAR BILL WITH WHICH THE LAW EXPECTED HIM TO REHABILITATE HIMSELF INTO GOOD CITIZENSHIP AND PROSPERITY. DISREGARDING THE SONG OF THE BIRDS, JIMMY HEADED STRAIGHT FOR A RESTAURANT. THERE HE TASTED THE FIRST JOYS OF LIBERTY IN THE SHAPE OF A BROILED CHICKEN AND A BOTTLE OF WINE.

FROM THERE HE PROCEEDED LEISURELY TO THE DEPOT. HE TOSSED A QUARTER INTO THE HAT OF A BLIND MAN, AND BOARDED HIS TRAIN.

THREE HOURS SET HIM DOWN IN A LITTLE TOWN WHERE HE WENT TO THE CAFÉ OF ONE MIKE DOLAN.

JIMMY GOT HIS KEY AND WENT UPSTAIRS.

SORRY WE COULDN'T MAKE IT SOONER, JIMMY, ME BOY. BUT WE HAD THAT PROTEST FROM SPRINGFIELD.

EVERYTHING WAS JUST AS HE HAD LEFT IT.

THERE ON THE FLOOR WAS STILL BEN PRICE'S COLLAR-BUTTON THAT HAD BEEN TORN FROM THAT EMINENT DETECTIVE'S SHIRT WHEN THEY HAD OVERPOWERED JIMMY TO ARREST HIM.

JIMMY SLID BACK A PANEL IN THE WALL AND DRAGGED OUT A SUITCASE. HE GAZED FONDLY AT THE FINEST SET OF BURGLAR'S TOOLS IN THE EAST. IT WAS A COMPLETE SET, MADE OF TEMPERED STEEL, THE LATEST DESIGNS IN DRILLS, PUNCHES, BRACES AND BITS, JIMMIES, CLAMPS AND AUGERS...

...WITH TWO OR THREE NOVELTIES INVENTED BY JIMMY HIMSELF.

2 Comparing Literature

Characterization What do you think Jimmy feels when he looks at the button?

3 Comparing Literature

Characterization How does this picture make Jimmy—and his profession—seem more menacing?

Vocabulary

eminent (IH muh nint) *adj.* of outstanding rank or quality

IN HALF AN HOUR, JIMMY WENT DOWNSTAIRS.

GOT ANYTHING ON?

ME? I'M REPRESENTING THE NEW YORK AMALGAMATED SHORT SNAP BISCUIT CRACKER AND FRAZZELED WHEAT COMPANY.

A WEEK AFTER THE RELEASE OF VALENTINE, THERE WAS A NEAT JOB OF SAFEBURGLARY DONE IN RICHMOND, INDIANA, WITH NO CLUE TO THE AUTHOR.

TWO WEEKS AFTER THAT, A PATENTED, IMPROVED, BURGLAR-PROOF SAFE IN LOGANSPORT WAS OPENED LIKE A CHEESE.

THEN A BANK IN JEFFERSON CITY THREW OUT OF ITS CRATER AN ERUPTION OF BANK-NOTES AMOUNTING TO FIVE THOUSAND DOLLARS.

THE LOSSES WERE NOW HIGH ENOUGH TO BRING THE MATTER UP TO BEN PRICE'S CLASS OF WORK.

BEN PRICE

IT HAD BEEN GIVEN OUT THAT HE HAD TAKEN UP THE TRAIL OF THE ELUSIVE CRACKSMAN, AND PEOPLE WITH BURGLAR-PROOF SAFES FELT MORE AT EASE.

THAT'S DANDY JIM'S AUTOGRAPH. HE'S RESUMED BUSINESS.

LOOK AT THAT COMBINATION KNOB-- JERKED OUT AS EASY AS PULLING UP A RADISH IN WET WEATHER.

YES, I GUESS I WANT MISTER VALENTINE. HE'LL DO HIS BIT NEXT TIME WITHOUT ANY SHORT-TIME OR CLEMENCY[1] FOOLISHNESS.

Practice the Skills

4 Comparing Literature

Characterization Notice Jimmy's height and size compared to Mike Dolan's. Who appears to be the more powerful person? How does this drawing add to or change your perception of Jimmy Valentine?

5 Comparing Literature

Characterization In your opinion, does this illustrated version of the story leave out important parts of the original? Do you think this version is true to O. Henry's descriptions? Explain your answers on your chart.

---

1. **Clemency** is mercy or forgiveness for wrongdoing.

A Retrieved Reformation **677**

Practice the Skills

6 **Comparing Literature**

Characterization How does Gianni illustrate Jimmy's change? On your chart, list the items in this frame that stand for feelings of peace and love.

7 **Comparing Literature**

Characterization On your chart describe Jimmy's posture. Does he seem confident or uncertain? Serious or relaxed? How does this picture affect what you know or think about Jimmy?

Practice the Skills

8 **Comparing Literature**

Characterization In these two frames Gianni leaves out several sentences from the original story. He also changes Jimmy's dialogue with the hotel clerk. How might this shortened scene affect your understanding of Jimmy's character? What is gained or lost in this adaptation? Make notes on your chart about the way Gianni reveals Jimmy's character here.

9 **Comparing Literature**

Characterization Notice Jimmy's facial expression and gesture. How does this Jimmy Valentine seem different from the one who arrived in Elmore? How do the other drawings in this frame show other people's views of Jimmy?

2. A ***phoenix*** is a bird in Greek mythology that burns up when it dies and is reborn from its own ashes.

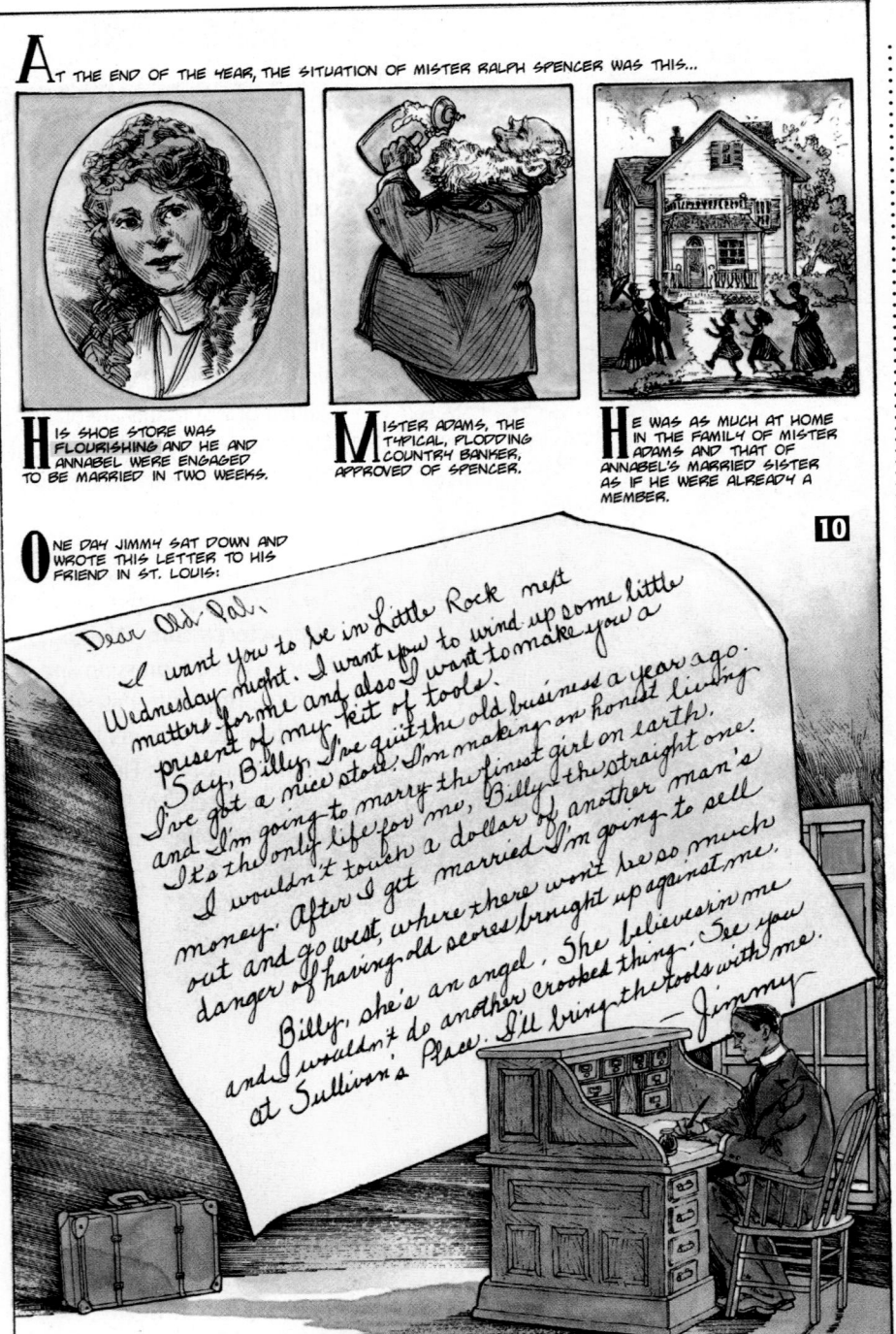

AT THE END OF THE YEAR, THE SITUATION OF MISTER RALPH SPENCER WAS THIS...

HIS SHOE STORE WAS FLOURISHING AND HE AND ANNABEL WERE ENGAGED TO BE MARRIED IN TWO WEEKS.

MISTER ADAMS, THE TYPICAL, PLODDING COUNTRY BANKER, APPROVED OF SPENCER.

HE WAS AS MUCH AT HOME IN THE FAMILY OF MISTER ADAMS AND THAT OF ANNABEL'S MARRIED SISTER AS IF HE WERE ALREADY A MEMBER.

10

ONE DAY JIMMY SAT DOWN AND WROTE THIS LETTER TO HIS FRIEND IN ST. LOUIS:

Dear Old Pal,

I want you to be in Little Rock next Wednesday night. I want you to wind up some little matters for me, and also I want to make you a present of my kit of tools. Say, Billy, I've quit the old business a year ago. I've got a nice store. I'm making an honest living, and I'm going to marry the finest girl on earth. It's the only life for me, Billy, the straight one. I wouldn't touch a dollar of another man's money. After I get married I'm going to sell out and go west, where there won't be so much danger of having old scores brought up against me. Billy, she's an angel. She believes in me, and I wouldn't do another crooked thing. See you at Sullivan's Place. I'll bring the tools with me.

— Jimmy

Practice the Skills

10 Comparing Literature

Characterization Imagine that this page of the story did not include words. From the sketches in this frame, what would you say Jimmy values most now?

Vocabulary

flourishing (FLUR ish ing) *adj.* thriving; doing extremely well

ONE MONDAY NIGHT AFTER JIMMY WROTE THIS LETTER, BEN PRICE JOGGED UNOBTRUSIVELY INTO ELMORE.

11

HE LOUNGED ABOUT THE TOWN IN HIS QUIET WAY UNTIL HE FOUND OUT WHAT HE WANTED TO KNOW.

GOING TO MARRY THE BANKER'S DAUGHTER ARE YOU, JIMMY? WELL, I DON'T KNOW.

JIMMY WAS GOING TO LITTLE ROCK THAT DAY TO ORDER HIS WEDDING-SUIT. QUITE A FAMILY PARTY WENT DOWNTOWN TOGETHER WHERE JIMMY'S HORSE AND BUGGY STOOD READY TO TAKE HIM TO THE RAILROAD STATION.

ALL WENT INSIDE THE BANK-- MISTER ADAMS, ANNABEL AND ANNABEL'S MARRIED SISTER WITH HER TWO LITTLE GIRLS. JIMMY WAS INCLUDED, FOR MISTER ADAMS' FUTURE SON-IN-LAW WAS WELCOME ANYWHERE.

MY! RALPH, HOW HEAVY THIS SUITCASE IS.

LOTS OF NICKEL-PLATED SHOE-HORNS IN THERE.

THE BANK HAD JUST PUT IN A NEW SAFE. MISTER ADAMS WAS VERY PROUD OF IT, AND INSISTED ON AN INSPECTION BY EVERYONE.

THIS VAULT IS A SMALL ONE, BUT IT HAS A NEW PATENTED DOOR. IT FASTENS WITH THREE SOLID STEEL BOLTS...

...AND IT HAS A TIME-LOCK.

12

Practice the Skills

11 English Language Coach

Multiple Affixes The word **unobtrusively** contains one prefix and two suffixes. The prefix -un means "not." The suffix -ive changes words into adjectives. The suffix -ly means "in the manner of." If something obtrudes, it becomes noticeable. Ben Price jogged into Elmore *unobtrusively*, or in a way that was not noticeable.

12 Comparing Literature

Characterization Does this version of the story show that Jimmy is trying to look uninterested in the safe? Do the sketches create a strong sense of danger about the vault? If so, how? Write your answers in your chart.

Practice the Skills

13 **Comparing Literature**

Characterization How does Gianni show Jimmy's transformation? Look at Jimmy's posture, gestures, and facial expression. Also, pay attention to the shape of Jimmy's face. Does it seem harder or more angular than in previous frames? Why might this be? Make notes in your chart.

Vocabulary

saundered (SAWN turd) *v.* walked leisurely

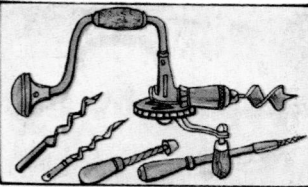

Practice the Skills

14 **Comparing Literature**

Characterization Jimmy hangs his head in shame or sorrow in this version, but not in the original. Why might Gianni have added this gesture? How could it affect your impression of Jimmy?

15 **BIG Question**

What did Jimmy have to do to stay true to himself? What did he risk? Do you think he's glad that he stayed true to himself? Write your answer on the second "A Retrieved Reformation" page of Foldable 5. Your response will help you complete the Unit Challenge later.

After You Read

A Retrieved Reformation
adapted by Gary Gianni

Vocabulary Check

In your Learner's Notebook, answer questions 1–3 below.

0. Henry's A RETRIEVED REFORMATION

1. Give an example of something that is **compulsory.**
2. How might being grounded be a form of **retribution?**
3. If two things happen **simultaneously,** do they happen **a)** at the same time, **b)** at different times, or **c)** in the same way?

Copy the sentences below. Draw a line through the italicized word or phrase; then replace it with the vocabulary word that fits.

Gary Gianni's *A RETRIEVED REFORMATION*

eminent   flourishing   sauntered

4. The reception honored a group of *distinguished* scientists.
5. Mel *strolled* in ten minutes late.
6. Students were *doing well* under the new teacher's instruction.
7. **English Language Coach** What does the word *burglarious* mean? Use what you have learned to fill in the chart below.

Word	Base Word	Suffix	Meaning
burglarious	*burgle* = to thieve	*-ous* = full of	

8. **Academic Vocabulary** Which of the following comes closest to the meaning of **reveal?**

• complain
• show
• listen

**NY English Language Arts
Core Curriculum** (pp. 684–685)

LC R17 Demonstrate comprehension and response through a range of activities.
R2b Interpret characters, using evidence from the text.

For a complete description of the standards, see p. NY11.

Reading/Critical Thinking

On a separate sheet of paper, answer the following questions.

O. Henry's A RETRIEVED REFORMATION

9. **BIG Question** How does Jimmy stay true to himself by saving Agatha?

   Tip Author and Me

10. **Recall** How does Ben Price know that Jimmy has "resumed business"?

    Tip Right There

11. **List** Jimmy gained several things when he moved to Elmore. List three of them.

    Tip Right There

Gary Gianni's _A RETRIEVED REFORMATION_

12. **Analyze** When Agatha gets locked in the vault, Jimmy must make a choice. Explain that choice and its possible consequences.

    Tip Author and Me

13. **Interpret** Look at the picture of a keyhole on the first page of the graphic story. What could it symbolize, or mean?

    Tip Think and Search

14. **Evaluate** How does Jimmy change by the end of the story?

    Tip Author and Me

Writing: Compare the Literature

Use Your Notes

15. Follow these steps to compare Jimmy Valentine's characterization in the original and graphic versions of "A Retrieved Reformation."

    Step 1: Look at the first column of your Comparison Chart. Underline examples of O. Henry's narrative description.

    Step 2: Look at the second column of your chart. When does Gianni choose to draw, or show, details that O. Henry describes, or tells? Underline examples.

Step 3: Compare both columns of your chart. What important dialogue or description (from O. Henry's version) does Gianni change or leave out? Underline these differences.

Step 4: Circle the stories' similarities that you noted on your chart. Think about why Gianni left original dialogue and description in some parts, but did not choose to leave them in others.

Get It On Paper

Answer these questions on a separate sheet of paper. Use examples from the chart and the notes you just made to explain your answers.

16. After reading O. Henry's story, how did you picture Jimmy Valentine in your mind?

17. Did your mental picture of Jimmy change after you read Gianni's version? If so, how?

18. Do you think Gianni's version of Jimmy is accurate? Would you have drawn Jimmy the same way? Why or why not?

19. Which version is more descriptive? Which version is more interesting? Did you learn more about Jimmy Valentine from O. Henry's description or Gianni's drawings?

20. Why might someone read a graphic story instead of a text story? What did O. Henry's story gain in graphic form? Lose in graphic form?

BIG Question

21. Jimmy stays true to himself by helping someone else. What does this tell you about the "self" to whom he stays true? Think about the change Jimmy undergoes in Elmore.

Literature Online

Web Activities For eFlashcards, Selection Quick Checks, and other Web activities, go to www.glencoe.com.

Answering The BIG Question: How Do You Stay True to Yourself?

You have read about people who worked to figure out how to stay true to themselves. Now use what you learned to do the Unit Challenge.

The Unit Challenge

Choose Activity A or Activity B and follow the directions for that activity.

A. Group Activity: Videotape a Soap Opera

With a group of students, read the following situation. Prepare to turn it into a TV show.

It's Friday, and Chris has a big test on Monday in English. English is the hardest subject for her. Chris started studying on Wednesday but still doesn't feel ready to take the test. Chris will need to study all weekend if she wants to do well on the test, which she needs to do to pass English this year. Late Friday afternoon, Chris learns that one of her friends, Steve, is having a party Saturday night. Steve really wants Chris to come to his party. Chris should stay home and study, but she really wants to go to the party too. Chris's parents have left it up to her to decide about Saturday night. What should Chris do?

1. **Role Play the Situation** Have group members take the parts of Chris, Chris's friends, and Chris's parents. Act out the situation several times, making sure everyone has a turn. Each time the group role plays, come up with a different way of handling the situation. Look at your Foldable for ideas about how characters in similar situations stayed true to themselves.

2. **Discuss the Different Role Plays** As a group, talk about which parts of the different role plays worked best. Decide which of Chris's values are being challenged in each situation. Figure out how Chris can deal with her dilemma in a way that (1) does not upset her parents, or (2) jeopardize her future, yet (3) allows Chris to be true to herself.

3. **Write a Script** Use your role plays to write a script for your soap opera. End your script with the best solution you came up with for Chris. Show why this course of action is best.

4. **Videotape and Present Your Soap** Have each group member, except the camera person, take a role and rehearse. Then videotape your show. Afterward, show your soap to the class.

B. Solo Activity: Values Chart

It's important to think clearly when making major decisions. Sometimes it's helpful to put things on paper to clarify your thoughts. Make a chart like this one to figure out the things you need to keep in mind to stay true to yourself.

Very Important	Less Important	Rank

1. **Determine Your Values** On the chart list the things that are very important to you and those that are less important. You might include such things as having time alone, respecting your parents' opinions, and figuring out solutions to problems for yourself.

   • Look over your notes in your Foldable and your Learner's Notebook to get ideas for your chart. Think about what was important to each main character.

2. **Consider Your Values** After you fill in your values, review them. Think about why you listed the different items in each column. You may want to make changes.

3. **Rank Your Values** Rank your values. Put a number next to each value in the "very important" column. Make number 1 the most important. You may want to give the same number to more than one value. Then do the same for the "less important" column.

4. **Write a Reflection** Think about what your values say about you. Write a paper describing yourself and your values. Consider the following questions:

   • What do your values show about you?

   • What do you value most and why?

   • What do you value least and why?

   • Where do you think your values come from? Parents? Family? Friends?

   • Are there values you would change? Are there values you would like to have that you don't right now?

   Finish your paper by discussing how you think your values will shape the way you live.

5. **Revise and Present Your Values** Review your chart and your paper. Make sure there are no mistakes in grammar, usage, or mechanics. Then share your work with a partner. Do you have values that are the same? What values do you have that are different? When you are done sharing, hand in your chart and reflection paper.

Literature Online

Big Question Link to Web resources to further explore the Big Question at www.glencoe.com.

Naomi Shihab Nye

Meet the Author

Naomi Shihab Nye is an Arab American. Her father is Palestinian, and her mother is American. She has published many books of poetry as well as a novel called *Habibi.* When she was a child, books were her escape. As an adult, she feels words help people discover the things that are important in their lives. Nye writes poems about little things that are an important part of people's lives. She says, "Familiar sights, sounds, smells have always been my necessities." See page R4 of the Author Files for more on Naomi Shihab Nye.

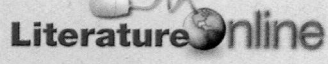

Author Search For more about Naomi Shihab Nye, go to www.glencoe.com.

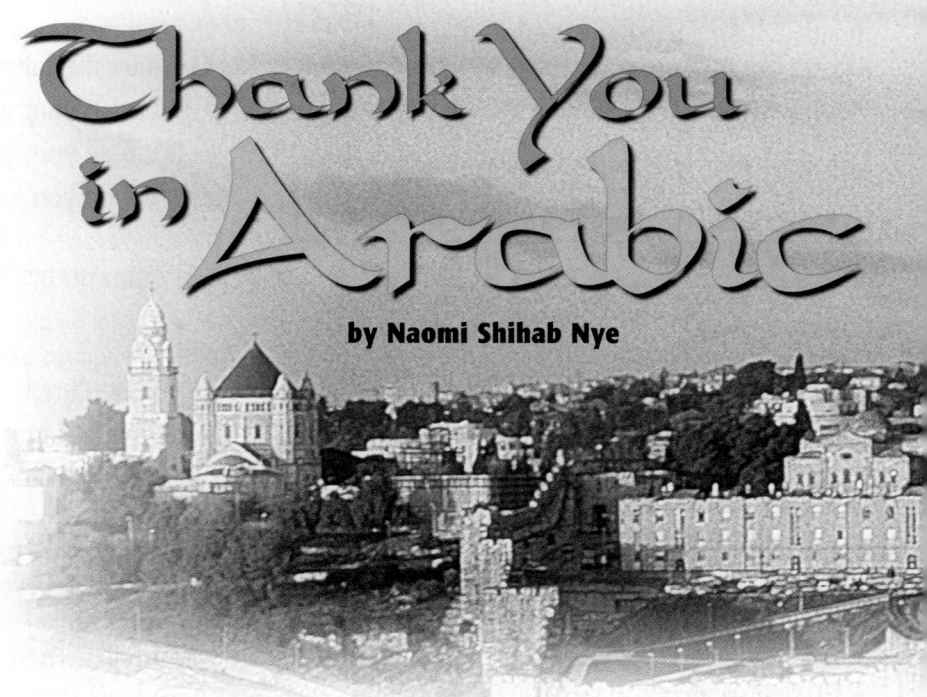

Thank You in Arabic

by Naomi Shihab Nye

Shortly after my mother discovered my brother had been pitching his vitamin C tablets behind the stove for years, we left the country. Her sharp alert, "Now the truth be known!" startled us at the breakfast table as she poked into the dim crevice with the nozzle of her vacuum. We could hear the pills go click, click, up the long tube.

My brother, an obedient child, a bright-eyed, dark-skinned charmer who scored high on all his tests and trilled a boy's sweet soprano, stared down at his oatmeal. Four years younger than I, he was also the youngest and smallest in his class. Somehow he maintained an intelligence and dignity more notable than those of his older, larger companions, and the pills episode was really a pleasant surprise to me.

Companions in mischief are not to be underestimated, especially when everything else in your life is about to change.

We sold everything we had and left the country. The move had been brewing for months. We took a few suitcases each. My mother cried when the piano went. I wished we could have saved it. My brother and I had sung so many classics over its keyboard—"Look for the Silver Lining" and "Angels We Have Heard on High"— that it would have been nice to return to a year later, when we came straggling back. I sold my life-size doll and my toy sewing machine. I begged my mother to save her red stove for me, so I could have it when I grew up—no one else we knew had a red stove. So my mother asked some friends to save it for me in their barn.

Our parents had closed their imported-gifts stores. Our mother ran a little shop in our neighborhood in St. Louis and our father ran a bigger one in a Sheraton Hotel downtown. For years my brother and I had been sitting with them behind the counters after school, guessing if people who walked through the door would buy something or only browse. We curled up with our library books on Moroccan hassocks[1] and Egyptian camel saddles. I loved the stacks of waiting white paper bags as they lay together, and the reams of new tissue. I'd crease the folds as our smooth father in dark suit and daily

---

1. ***Moroccan hassocks*** are large, tightly stuffed cushions made in Morocco, an Arab country in North Africa.

drench of cologne counted change. Our mother rearranged shelves and penned the perfect tags with calligrapher's ink. My brother and I helped unpack the crates: nested Russian dolls, glossy mother-of-pearl earrings from Bethlehem, a family of sandalwood[2] fans nestled in shredded packaging. Something wonderful was always on its way.

But there were problems too. Sometimes whole days passed and nobody came in. It seemed so strange to wait for people to give you money for what you had. But that's what stores did everywhere. Then the stockroom filled with pre-Christmas inventory caught on fire and burned up, right when our father was between insurance policies. We could hear our parents in the living room, worrying and debating after we went to bed at night. Finally they had to give the business up. What seemed like such a good idea in the beginning—presents from around the world—turned into the sad sound of a broom sweeping out an empty space.

Our father had also been attending the Unity School for Christianity for a few years, but decided not to become a minister after all. We were relieved, having felt like imposters the whole time he was enrolled. He wasn't even a Christian, to begin with, but a gently nonpracticing Muslim. He didn't do anything like fasting or getting down on his knees five times a day. Our mother had given up the stern glare of her Lutheran ancestors, raising my brother and me in the Vedanta Society of St. Louis. When anyone asked what we were,

I said, "Hindu." We had a swami,[3] and sandalwood incense. It was over our heads, but we liked it and didn't feel very attracted to the idea of churches and collection baskets and chatty parish good will.

Now and then, just to keep things balanced, we attended the Unity Sunday School. My teacher said I was lucky my father came from the same place Jesus came from. It was a passport to notoriety. She invited me to bring artifacts for Show and Tell. I wrapped a red and white *keffiyah*[4] around my friend Jimmy's curly blond head while the girls in lacy socks giggled behind their hands. I told about my father coming to America from Palestine on the boat and throwing his old country clothes overboard before docking at Ellis Island.[5] I felt relieved he'd kept a few things, like the *keffiyah* and its black braided band. Secretly it made me mad to have lost the blue pants from Jericho with the wide cuffs he told us about.

I liked standing in front of the group, talking about my father's homeland. Stories felt like elastic bands that could stretch and stretch. Big fans purred inside their metal shells. I held up a string of olivewood[6] camels. I didn't tell our teacher about the Vedanta Society. We were growing up ecumenical, though I wouldn't know that word till a long time later in college. One night I heard my father say to my mother in the next room, "Do you think they'll be confused when they grow up?" and knew he was talking about us. My mother, bless

---

2. **Sandalwood** is the wood of several trees that grow in Asia. It has a sweet, perfumed smell.

3. **Vedanta** is a branch of the Hindu religion that studies several holy books called the Vedas. A Hindu teacher is called a **swami.**

4. A **keffiyah** is a cloth headdress for a man that is held in place by a rope.

5. **Ellis Island** in New York City was the station where immigrants entered the United States on the East Coast from 1892 until the mid-twentieth century.

6. **Olivewood** is the wood of the olive tree.

her, knew we wouldn't be. She said, "At least we're giving them a choice." I didn't know then that more clearly than all the stories of Jesus, I'd remember the way our Hindu swami said a single word three times, *"Shantih, shantih, shantih"*—peace, peace, peace.

Our father was an excellent speaker—he stood behind pulpits and podiums[7] easily, delivering gracious lectures on "The Holy Land" and "The Palestinian Question." He was much in demand during the Christmas season. I think that's how he had fallen into the ministerial swoon.[8] While he spoke, my brother and I moved toward the backs of gathering halls, hovering over and eyeing the tables of canapes and tiny tarts, slipping a few into our mouths or pockets.

What next? Our lives were entering a new chapter, but I didn't know its title yet.

We had never met our Palestinian grandmother, Sitti[9] Khadra, or seen Jerusalem, where our father had grown up, or followed the rocky, narrow alleyways of the Via Dolorosa,[10] or eaten an olive in its own neighborhood. Our mother hadn't either. The Arabic customs we knew had been filtered through the fine net of folktales. We did not speak Arabic, though the lilt of the language was familiar to us— our father's endearments, his musical blessings before meals. But that language had never lived in our mouths.

And that's where we were going, to Jerusalem. We shipped our car, a wide golden Impala, over on a boat. We would meet up with it later.

The first plane flight of my whole life was the night flight out of New York City across the ocean. I was fourteen years old. Every glittering light in every skyscraper looked like a period at the end of the sentence. Good-bye, our lives.

We stopped in Portugal for a few weeks. We were making a gradual transition. We stopped in Spain and Italy and Egypt, where the pyramids shocked me by sitting right on the edge of the giant city of Cairo,[11] not way out in the desert as I had imagined them. While we waited for our baggage to clear customs, I stared at six tall African men in brilliantly patterned dashikis[12] negotiating with an Egyptian customs agent and realized I did not even know how to say "thank you" in Arabic. How was this possible? The most elemental and important of human phrases in my father's own tongue had evaded me till now. I tugged on his sleeve, but he was busy with visas and passports. "Daddy," I said. "Daddy, I have to know. Daddy, tell me. Daddy, why didn't we ever *learn*?" An African man adjusted his turban. Always thereafter, the word *shookrun*, so simple, with a little roll in the middle, would conjure up the vast African baggage, the brown boxes looped and looped in African twine.

We stayed one or two nights at the old Shepheard's Hotel downtown but couldn't sleep due to the heat and honking traffic beneath our windows. So our father moved

---

7. A *pulpit* is the stand inside a church from which a preacher delivers a sermon. A *podium* is a raised platform used by a speaker or music conductor.

8. To *fall into the ministerial swoon* is to get enthusiastic about becoming a minister.

9. *Sitti* means grandmother.

10. The *Via Dolorosa* is the Way of Sorrow, the streets Jesus walked on the way to his death.

11. *Cairo* is the capital of Egypt.

12. A *dashiki* is a loose-fitting, colorful African shirt.

Guests of Egypt's Mena House Hotel get a bird's-eye view of the Great Pyramid of Khufu.
Analyzing the Photo How does this photo help you better understand Nye's overseas experience?

us to the famous Mena House Hotel next to the pyramids. We rode camels for the first time, and our mother received a dozen blood-red roses at her hotel room from a rug vendor who apparently liked her pale brown ponytail. The belly dancer at the hotel restaurant twined a gauzy pink scarf around my brother's astonished ten-year-old head as he tapped his knee in time to her music.

Back in our rooms, we laughed until we fell asleep. Later that night, my brother and I both awakened burning with fever and deeply nauseated, though nobody ever threw up. We were so sick that a doctor hung a Quarantine sign in Arabic and English on our hotel room door the next day. Did he know something we didn't know? I kept waiting to hear that we had malaria or typhoid,[13] but no dramatic disease was ever mentioned. We lay in bed for a week. The aged doctor tripped over my suitcase every time he entered to take our temperatures. We smothered our laughter. "*Shookrun*," I would say. But as soon as he left, to my brother, "I feel bad. How do you feel?"

"I feel really, really bad."

"I think I'm dying."

"I think I'm already dead."

At night we heard the sound and lights show[14] from the pyramids drifting across the desert air to our windows. We felt our lives stretching out across a thousand miles. The pharaohs stomped noisily through my head and churning belly. We had eaten spaghetti in the restaurant. I would not be able to eat spaghetti again for years.

Finally, finally, we appeared in the restaurant, thin and weakly smiling, and ordered the famous Mena House *shorraba*,

---

13. To *quarantine* is to separate people from everyone else to keep them from spreading diseases. *Malaria* is a disease that causes fever and chills. *Typhoid* causes intestinal problems.

---

14. A *sound and lights show* is a narrated presentation that uses sound effects and lighting effects.

lentil soup, as my brother nervously scanned the room for the belly dancer. Maybe she wouldn't recognize him now.

In those days Jerusalem, which was then a divided city, had an operating airport on the Jordanian side. My brother and I remember flying in upside down, or in a plane dramatically tipped, but it may have been the effect of our medicine. The land reminded us of a dropped canvas, graceful brown hillocks and green patches. Small and provincial, the airport had just two runways, and the first thing I observed as we climbed down slowly from the stuffy plane was all my underwear strewn across one of them. There were my flowered cotton briefs and my pink panties and my slightly embarrassing raggedy ones and my extra training bra, alive and visible in the breeze. Somehow my suitcase had popped open in the hold and dropped its contents the minute the men pried open the cargo door. So the first thing I did on the home soil of my father was re-collect my underwear, down on my knees, the posture of prayer over that ancient holy land.

Our relatives came to see us at a hotel. Our grandmother was very short. She wore a long, thickly embroidered Palestinian dress, had a musical, high-pitched voice and a low, guttural[15] laugh. She kept touching our heads and faces as if she couldn't believe we were there. I had not yet fallen in love with her. Sometimes you don't fall in love with people immediately, even if they're your own grandmother. Everyone seemed to think we were all too thin.

We moved into a second-story flat in a stone house eight miles north of the city, among fields and white stones and wandering sheep. My brother was enrolled in the Friends Girls School and I was enrolled in the Friends Boys School in the town of Ramallah[16] a few miles farther north—it all was a little confused. But the Girls School offered grades one through eight in English and high school continued at the Boys School. Most local girls went to Arabic-speaking schools after eighth grade.

I was a freshman, one of seven girl students among two hundred boys, which would cause me problems a month later. I was called in from the schoolyard at lunchtime, to the office of our counselor who wore shoes so pointed and tight her feet bulged out pinkly on top.

"You will not be talking to them anymore," she said. She rapped on the desk with a pencil for emphasis.

"To whom?"

"All the boy students at this institution. It is inappropriate behavior. From now on, you will speak only with the girls."

"But there are only six other girls! And I like only one of them!" My friend was Anna, from Italy, whose father ran a small factory that made matches. I'd visited it once with her. It felt risky to walk the aisles among a million filled matchboxes. Later we visited the factory that made olive oil soaps and stacked them in giant pyramids to dry.

"No, thank you," I said. "It's ridiculous to say that girls should only talk to girls. Did I say anything bad to a boy? Did anyone say anything bad to me? They're my friends. They're like my brothers. I won't do it, that's all."

---

15. A *guttural* laugh is a throaty laugh.

16. *Ramallah* is a town north of Jerusalem. The majority of the population is Christian.

The counselor conferred with the head-master and they called a taxi. I was sent home with a little paper requesting that I transfer to a different school. The charge: insolence. My mother, startled to see me home early and on my own, stared out the window when I told her.

My brother came home from his school as usual, full of whistling and notebooks. "Did anyone tell you not to talk to girls?" I asked him. He looked at me as if I'd gone goofy. He was too young to know the troubles of the world. He couldn't even imagine them.

"You know what I've been thinking about?" he said. "A piece of cake. That puffy white layered cake with icing like they have

Old City, Jerusalem.
Analyzing the Photo What can you learn about Jerusalem's climate and architecture from this photo?

at birthday parties in the United States. Wouldn't that taste good right now?" Our mother said she was thinking about mayonnaise. You couldn't get it in Jerusalem. She'd tried to make it and it didn't work. I felt too gloomy to talk about food.

My brother said, "Let's go let Abu Miriam's chickens out." That's what we always did when we felt sad. We let our fussy landlord's red-and-white chickens loose to flap around the yard happily, puffing their wings. Even when Abu Miriam shouted and waggled his cane and his wife waved a dishtowel, we knew the chickens were thanking us.

My father went with me to the St. Tarkmanchatz Armenian[17] School, a solemnly ancient stone school tucked deep into the Armenian Quarter of the Old City of Jerusalem. It was another world in there. He had already called the school officials on the telephone and tried to enroll me, though they didn't want to. Their school was for Armenian students only, kinder-garten through twelfth grade. Classes were taught in three languages: Armenian, Arabic and English, which was why I needed to go there. Although most Arab students at other schools were learning English, I needed a school where classes were actually taught in English—otherwise I would have been staring out the windows triple the usual amount.

The head priest wore a long robe and a tall cone-shaped hat. He said, "Excuse me, please, but your daughter, she is not an Armenian, even a small amount?"

---

17. **Armenia** is a Christian country north of Turkey and Iran. The Armenian community in Jerusalem is very old. The Armenian Apostolic Church first set up churches there in the sixth century.

"Not at all," said my father. "But in case you didn't know, there is a stipulation in the educational code books of this city that says no student may be rejected solely on the basis of ethnic background, and if you don't accept her, we will alert the proper authorities."

They took me. But the principal wasn't happy about it. The students, however, seemed glad to have a new face to look at. Everyone's name ended in -ian, the beautiful, musical Armenian ending—Boghossian, Minassian, Kevorkian, Rostomian. My new classmates started calling me Shihabian. We wore uniforms, navy blue pleated skirts for the girls, white shirts, and navy sweaters. I waited during the lessons for the English to come around, as if it were a channel on television. While other students were on the other channels, I scribbled poems in the margins of my pages, read library books, and wrote a lot of letters filled with exclamation points. All the other students knew all three languages with three entirely different alphabets. How could they carry so much in their heads? I felt humbled by my ignorance. One day I felt so frustrated in our physics class—still another language—that I pitched my book out the open window. The professor made me go collect it. All the pages had let loose at the seams and were flapping free into the gutters along with the white wrappers of sandwiches.

Every week the girls had a hands-and-fingernails check. We had to keep our nails clean and trim, and couldn't wear any rings. Some of my new friends would invite me home for lunch with them, since we had an hour-and-a-half break and I lived too far to go to my own house.

Their houses were a thousand years old, clustered bee-hive-fashion behind ancient walls, stacked and curled and tilting and dark, filled with pictures of unsmiling relatives and small white cloths dangling crocheted edges. We ate spinach pies and white cheese. We dipped our bread in olive oil, as the Arabs did. We ate small sesame cakes, our mouths full of crumbles. They taught me to say "I love you" in Armenian, which sounded like yes-kay-see-goo-see-rem. I felt I had left my old life entirely.

Every afternoon I went down to the basement of the school where the kindergarten class was having an Arabic lesson. Their desks were pint-sized, their full white smocks tied around their necks. I stuffed my fourteen-year-old self in beside them. They had rosy cheeks and shy smiles. They must have thought I was a very slow learner.

More than any of the lessons, I remember the way the teacher rapped the backs of their hands with his ruler when they made a mistake. Their little faces puffed up with quiet tears. This pained me so terribly I forgot all my words. When it was my turn to go to the blackboard and write in Arabic, my hand shook. The kindergarten students whispered hints to me from the front row, but I couldn't understand them. We learned horribly useless phrases: "Please hand me the bellows[18] for my fire." I wanted words simple as tools, simple as food and yesterday and dreams. The teacher never rapped my hand, especially after I wrote a letter to the city newspaper, which my father edited,

---

18. A **bellows** is an accordion-like tool that pumps air through a tube. It is used to blow oxygen into a fire to make it burn hotter.

protesting such harsh treatment of young learners. I wish I had known how to talk to those little ones, but they were just beginning their English studies and didn't speak much yet. They were at the same place in their English that I was in my Arabic.

From the high windows of St. Tarkmanchatz, we could look out over the Old City, the roofs and flapping laundry and television antennas, the pilgrims and churches and mosques, the olivewood prayer beads and fragrant *falafel*[19] lunch stands, the intricate interweaving of cultures and prayers and songs and holidays. We saw the barbed wire separating Jordan from Israel then, the bleak, uninhabited strip of no-man's land reminding me how little education saved us after all. People who had differing ideas still came to blows, imagining fighting could solve things. Staring out over the quiet roofs of afternoon, I thought it so foolish. I asked my friends what they thought about it and they shrugged.

"It doesn't matter what we think about it. It just keeps happening. It happened in Armenia too, you know. Really, really bad in Armenia. And who talks about it in the world news now? It happens everywhere. It happens in your country one by one, yes? Murders and guns. What can we do?"

Sometimes after school, my brother and I walked up the road that led past the crowded refugee camp of Palestinians who owned even less than our modest relatives did in the village. The little kids were stacking stones in empty tin cans and shaking them. We waved our hands and they covered their mouths and laughed.

---

19. *Falafel* are fried chickpea patties.

We wore our beat-up American tennis shoes and our old sweatshirts and talked about everything we wanted to do and everywhere else we wished we could go.

"I want to go back to Egypt," my brother said. "I sort of feel like I missed it. Spending all that time in bed instead of exploring— what a waste."

"I want to go to Greece," I said. "I want to play a violin in a symphony orchestra in Austria." We made up things. I wanted to go back to the United States most of all. Suddenly I felt like a patriotic citizen. One of my friends, Sylvie Markarian, had just been shipped off to Damascus, Syria, to marry a man who was fifty years old, a widower. Sylvie was exactly my age—we had turned fifteen two days apart. She had never met her future husband before. I thought this was the most revolting thing I had ever heard of. "Tell your parents no thank you," I urged her. "Tell them you *refuse*."

Sylvie's eyes were liquid, swirling brown. I could not see clearly to the bottom of them.

"You don't understand," she told me. "In United States you say no. We don't say no. We have to follow someone's wishes. This is the wish of my father. Me, I am scared. I never slept away from my mother before. But I have no choice. I am going because they tell me to go." She was sobbing, sobbing on my shoulder. And I was stroking her long, soft hair. After that, I carried two fists inside, one for Sylvie and one for me.

Most weekends my family went to the village to sit with the relatives. We sat and sat and sat. We sat in big rooms and little rooms, in circles, on chairs or on woven mats or brightly covered mattresses piled on the floor. People came in and out to greet my family. Sometimes even donkeys and chickens came in and out. We were like movie stars or dignitaries. They never seemed to get tired of us.

My father translated the more interesting tidbits of conversation, the funny stories my grandmother told. She talked about angels and food and money and people and politics and gossip and old memories from my father's childhood, before he emigrated[20] away from her. She wanted to make sure we were going to stick around forever, which made me feel very nervous. We ate from mountains of rice and eggplant on large silver trays—they gave us little plates of our own since it was not our custom to eat from the same plate as other people. We ripped the giant wheels of bread into triangles. Shepherds passed through town with their flocks of sheep and goats, their long canes and cloaks, straight out of the Bible. My brother and I trailed them to the edge of the village, past the lentil fields to the green meadows studded with stones, while the shepherds pretended we weren't there. I think they liked to be alone, unnoticed. The sheep had differently colored dyed bottoms, so shepherds could tell their flocks apart.

During these long, slow, smoke-stained weekends—the men still smoked cigarettes a lot in those days, and the old *taboon*, my family's mounded bread-oven, puffed billowy clouds outside the door—my crying jags began. I cried without any warning, even in the middle of a meal. My crying was usually noiseless but dramatically wet—streams of tears pouring down my cheeks, onto my collar or the back of my hand.

---

20. To **emigrate** is to leave one's country to go live somewhere else.

Analyzing the Photo Sheep graze on a hillside near Jerusalem's Old City. How does Jerusalem seem similar to or different from the cities you know?

Everything grew quiet.

Someone always asked in Arabic, "What is wrong? Are you sick? Do you wish to lie down?"

My father made valiant excuses in the beginning. "She's overtired," he said. "She has a headache. She is missing her friend who moved to Syria. She is homesick just now."

My brother stared at me as if I had just landed from Planet X.

Worst of all was our drive to school every morning, when our car came over the rise in the highway and all Jerusalem lay sprawled before us in its golden, stony splendor pockmarked with olive trees and automobiles. Even the air above the city had a thick, religious texture, as if it were a shining brocade filled with broody incense. I cried hardest then. All those hours tied up in school lay just ahead. My father pulled over and talked to me. He sighed. He kept his hands on the steering wheel even when the car was stopped and said, "Someday, I promise you, you will look back on this period in your life and have no idea what made you so unhappy here."

"I want to go home." It became my anthem. "This place depresses me. It weighs too much. I hate all these old stones that everybody keeps kissing. I'm sick of pilgrims. They act so pious and pure. And I hate the way people stare at me here." Already I'd been involved in two street skirmishes[21] with boys who stared a little too hard and long. I'd socked one in the jaw and he socked me back. I hit the other one straight in the face with my purse.

"You could be happy here if you tried just a little harder," my father said. "Don't compare it to the United States all the time. Don't pretend the United States is perfect. And look at your brother—he's not having any problems!"

"My brother is eleven years old."

I had crossed the boundary from uncomplicated childhood when happiness was a good ball and a hoard of candy-coated Jordan almonds.

One problem was that I had fallen in love with four different boys who all played in the same band. Two of them were even twins. I never quite described it to my parents, but I wrote reams and reams of notes about it on loose-leaf paper that I kept under my sweaters in my closet.

Such new energy made me feel reckless. I gave things away. I gave away my necklace and a whole box of shortbread cookies that my mother had been saving. I gave my extra shoes away to the gypsies. One night when the gypsies camped in a field down the road from our house, I thought about their mounds of white goat cheese lined up on skins in front of their tents, and the wild *oud*[22] music they played deep into the black belly of the night, and I wanted to go sit around their fire. Maybe they could use some shoes.

I packed a sack of old loafers that I rarely wore and walked with my family down the road. The gypsy mothers stared into my shoes curiously. They took them into their tent. Maybe they would use them as vases or drawers. We sat with small glasses of hot, sweet tea until a girl bellowed from deep in her throat, threw back her head, and began dancing. A long bow thrummed across the strings. The girl circled the fire, tapping and clicking, trilling a long musical wail from deep in her throat. My brother looked nervous. He was remembering the belly dancer in Egypt, and her scarf. I felt invisible. I was pretending to be a gypsy. My father stared at me. Didn't I recognize the exquisite oddity of my own life when I sat right in the middle of it? Didn't I feel lucky to be here? Well, yes I did. But sometimes it was hard to be lucky.

When we left Jerusalem, we left quickly. Left our beds in our rooms and our car in the driveway. Left in a plane, not sure where we were going. The rumbles of fighting with Israel had been growing louder and louder. In the barbed-wire no-man's land visible from the windows of our house, guns cracked loudly in the middle of the night. We lived right near the edge. My father heard disturbing rumors at the

---

21. In war, a *skirmish* is a short fight.

22. An *oud* is a stringed instrument that is plucked like a guitar.

newspaper that would soon grow into the infamous Six Day War[23] of 1967. We were in England by then, drinking tea from thin china cups and scanning the newspapers. Bombs were blowing up in Jerusalem. We worried about the village. We worried about my grandmother's dreams, which had been getting worse and worse, she'd told us. We worried about the house we'd left, and the chickens, and the children at the refugee camp. But there was nothing we could do except keep talking about it all.

My parents didn't want to go back to Missouri because they'd already said goodbye to everyone there. They thought we might try a different part of the country. They weighed the virtues of different states. Texas was big and warm. After a chilly year crowded around the small gas heaters we used in Jerusalem, a warm place sounded appealing. In roomy Texas, my parents bought the first house they looked at. My father walked into the city newspaper and said, "Any jobs open around here?"

I burst out crying when I entered a grocery store—so many different kinds of bread.

A letter on thin blue airmail paper reached me months later, written by my classmate, the bass player in my favorite Jerusalem band. "Since you left," he said, "your empty desk reminds me of a snake ready to strike. I am afraid to look at it. I hope you are having a better time than we are."

Of course I was, and I wasn't. *Home* had grown different forever. *Home* had doubled. Back *home* again in my own country, it seemed impossible to forget the place we

had just left: the piercing call of the *muezzin*[24] from the mosque at prayer time, the dusky green tint of the olive groves, the sharp, cold air that smelled as deep and old as my grandmother's white sheets flapping from the line on her roof. What story hadn't she finished?

Our father used to tell us that when he was little, the sky over Jerusalem crackled with meteors and shooting stars[25] almost every night. They streaked and flashed, igniting the dark. Some had long golden tails. For a few seconds, you could see their whole swooping trail lit up. Our father and his brothers slept on the roof to watch the sky. "There were so many of them, we didn't even call out every time we saw one."

During our year in Jerusalem, my brother and I kept our eyes cast upwards whenever we were outside at night, but the stars were different since our father was a boy. Now the sky seemed too orderly, stuck in place. The stars had learned where they belonged. Only people on the ground kept changing. ○

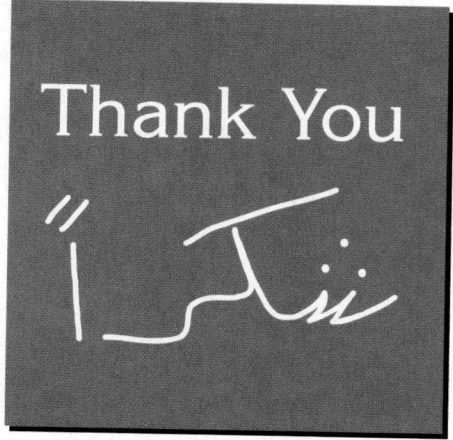

---

23. The **Six Day War** was fought in June 1967 between Israel on one side and Egypt, Syria, and Jordan on the other. Israel won and took control of the Old City of Jerusalem as well as territory from the other three countries.

24. The **muezzin** calls Muslims to prayer five times a day.

25. **Meteors** and **shooting stars** are the same thing: small heavenly bodies that burn up as they enter the earth's atmosphere from outer space.

Reading on Your Own

To read more about the Big Question, choose one of these books from your school or local library. Work on your reading skills by choosing books that are challenging to you.

Fiction

A House for Mr. Biswas
by V. S. Naipaul

A Hindu man tries to find a house of his own in the British colony of Trinidad in the Caribbean. In this humorous story he is forced to overcome people's prejudices against his culture to discover who he is inside and stick up for himself.

Slap Your Sides
by M.E. Kerr

This World War II-era story deals with issues of aggression and pacifism in the thirteen-year-old Jubal Shoemaker's Pennsylvania Quaker community. Are there times when it is wrong to fight? Are there times when it is wrong not to? Read this piece of fiction and then decide.

Of Sound Mind
by Jean Ferris

The only member of his family who can hear, Theo is frustrated by the silence in his household and by the individual demands of his high-maintenance relatives. Read this book to find out about the special friendship that helps Theo cope with the stress he has at home.

The Glory Field
by Walter Dean Myers

This novel traces the lives of an African American family, beginning with the capture and enslavement of the first member in 1753. Each generation struggles against poverty and racism. But their love for one another and for their land keeps the members of the Lewis family strong.

Nonfiction

No Body's Perfect
by Kimberly Kirberger

A collection of poems, essays, and stories written by teenagers that look at the issues surrounding body image, food, and self-esteem. The author offers insight as well as hope and helps young people think about how to stay true to themselves.

The Rose That Grew from Concrete
by Tupac Shakur

Written by Tupac when he was 19 and not yet a star, these poems bring passion to the experience of staying true to yourself.

Counting Coup: A True Story of Basketball and Honor on the Little Big Horn
by Larry Colton

Battling racism, alcoholism, and domestic violence, the girls on the Hardin High School basketball team learn how to be winners on and off the court.

And Still We Rise: The Trials and Triumphs of Twelve Gifted Inner-City High School Students
by Miles Corwin

Twelve seniors from an Advanced Placement English class in Los Angeles dream of going to college. This book deals with the hard realities of their lives and their struggle to achieve their dreams.

New York English Language Arts Test Practice

Directions

Read this passage about a young girl's thoughts on the mystery and wonder of the island on which she lives. Then answer questions 1 through 5.

from *Lizzie Bright and the Buckminster Boy*

By Gary D. Schmidt

The sea surge that had drawn up the coastal waters of Maine poured past the cliffs and tore along the ragged coast. It covered the high rocks—dry for more than three months of high tides—all the way to Small Point up past Harpswell. When it had finished its fussing, it seethed back down the New Meadows River, sluicing between the mainland and the islands. It spent its last surge on one rock-shouldered heap just a spit or two off the coast, frothing over the mudflats, setting the clam holes flapping, and carrying a small, startled crab out from its weedy hiding place. It bumbled upside down up the island shore and onto a toe stretched toward the water.

Lizzie Griffin, who belonged to the toe, grinned at the crab's frantic turnings as it tried to sort out claws and legs. Its shell was so pale that she could see the mess of the inner workings. Another almost-spent wave came up behind and tumbled it off—claws and legs all to be sorted out again. Lizzie plucked her toe and the rest of her foot out of the covering mud and slowly backed up the shore, letting a wave catch her and cover her ankles, then moving away some until she was on the thin lines of gravelly sand that marked the reach of the water.

She looked out at the thrusting tide, clenched her toes into the loose sand, and smelled the salty, piney air. At thirteen, she was, as her grandfather liked to remind her, one year older than the century, and so a good deal wiser. Too wise to stay on Malaga Island, he said, but she planned to stay there forever. Where else, after all, did the tide set a pale crab on your toe?

She turned and scrambled up the outcroppings, picking up the hatchet that was to have been splitting kindling all this time. But she could hardly help it if there was something much better to do, like watching the tide come in. She balanced the hatchet on her finger as she walked, carefully keeping herself under it while her feet guided her through the scrub and tripping roots. When she came to the pines that stood as close to the ocean as they could and still reach sweet water, she tipped the hatchet into the air, caught it by the handle, and swung it back over her shoulder. She set her eye on the heart of a youngster pine and flashed the hatchet through the scented air; it tumbled over and over itself in jerks, like a crab caught in a ripple, until it slapped high up into the trunk. Lizzie looked around to see if anyone might be nearby, half wanting to show off, half wanting to be sure that no one had seen Preacher Griffin's granddaughter throwing a hatchet around. No one had, and Lizzie slicked up the tree, her feet finding the branches easily.

She jerked out the hatchet and let it fall to the soft pine needles beneath her. Then, since she was already partway up, and since the set of the branches made it so easy, and since the pine was young enough that she could get it swaying pretty good if she got close to the top, she kept climbing until she felt the tree moving with her from side to side. She let her weight into it, back and forth, and the whole heap of Malaga Island rushed beneath her—ocean, sand, rock, scrub, mudflat, pale little crab, all rushing back and forth as the soft boughs laid their gentle, dry hands against her laughing face.

---

1 According to information in the passage, the reader can conclude that the story takes place in

A 1887
B 1901
C 1912
D 1916

2 Read this sentence from the first paragraph of the passage.

> **When it had finished its fussing, it seethed back down the New Meadows River, sluicing between the mainland and the islands.**

The word "sluicing" means about the same as

F washing
G falling
H crawling
J sneaking

3 When the author refers to a "rock-shouldered heap" in the passage, he is **most likely** referring to

A Maine
B Harpswell
C Malaga Island
D the New Meadows River

4 If an adult were to ask Lizzie what she is doing, she would probably answer that

F she is looking for crabs
G she is searching for firewood
H she is exploring the island
J she is thinking about whether to leave the island

5 The author uses personification in the passage to describe the coastal waters of Maine. If the coastal waters were a character (either a person or an animal) in the story, what type of character would it be? Use details from the passage to support your answer.

Directions

Read this passage about a boy who works in a theater during Shakespeare's time, and the adventurous scheme he has planned. Then answer questions 6 through 7.

from *The Shakespeare Stealer*

By Gary Blackwood

Everyone else in the company was occupied with some task. No one would notice. And yet, what if they *did* notice? My intentions would be obvious, and all chance of completing my mission would be lost. I turned toward the door, hesitated, turned back, started for the door again—and encountered Sander sweeping from the tiring-room dressed as Hamlet's mother.

> **Hamlet, Gertrude,** and **Laertes** are characters in the play

> **tiring-room** = theatre dressing room

"How do I look?" he asked anxiously, pushing at his voluminous wig.

Far from calm myself, I gave him a cursory look up and down. "Well enough, I wis. Wait. Your sleeve's coming off."

> **I wis** = I think

"Pin it on, would you?"

"Yes, very well," I said irritably. The task required both hands, and I glanced about, wondering what to do with the play book. "Here." I handed it to Sander.

"Make haste," he begged. "I'm due on the stage."

"I'm trying!" I snapped, fumbling with the pins. "Why don't they just sew these on?"

"You can change the dress about this way, put different sleeves on. Have you got it?"

"Almost."

There was a flourish of trumpets above the stage. "It'll have to do. There's my cue." He started for the stage entrance.

"The book!" I whispered urgently.

He shoved it into my hands and dashed for the doorway, tripped himself up in his hem, recovered, hoisted the skirts in a very unladylike fashion, and burst through the curtain onto the stage.

"Ah, Gertrude," the king said. "So glad you could join us." The audience guffawed at this spontaneous addition to the script. The king then launched into a speech that promised to be lengthy. Time to go, I thought.

> **guffawed** = laughed loudly

Suddenly the king broke off, his arm upraised, as though frozen in place. I froze, too, aware that something was amiss, but not quite sure what. A few snickers arose from the audience. The king cast a perturbed glance in my direction, and I realized he had forgotten his line.

I yanked the book open. Before I could locate the proper passage, Laertes closed the breach: "Sorry to interrupt, my lord, but I beg your leave and favor to return to France."

I looked anxiously, certain that someone would swoop down to snatch the book from my incompetent hands. But everyone was too busy to notice. If I had had the sense that God gave sheep, I would have made my escape at that moment. But the king had another attack of forgetfulness. This time I had the book open to the place. "Take thy fair hour!" I called out, too loudly, drawing another snicker from the audience. The king snatched up the cue and ran with it. Behind his back, Sander made a gesture of approval at me. I couldn't help smiling.

Ah, well, I thought; I can just as easily stay and help out here, and still slip away before the finish of the play.

---

6 Read these sentences from the beginning of the passage.

> **Everyone else in the company was occupied with some task. No one would notice. And yet, what if they *did* notice? My intentions would be obvious, and all chance of completing my mission would be lost.**

What "mission" is the narrator trying to hide?

A becoming part of the acting troupe

B stealing one of Shakespeare's plays

C memorizing all of the lines in *Hamlet*

D disguising the male actors in women's clothes

7 The passage from *The Shakespeare Stealer* offers several clues about theatrical performances during Shakespeare's time. On a separate sheet of paper, copy the graphic organizer below, list one clue (what someone said or did), and explain what the clue tells you about Shakespearean theater.

Clue	What it tells about this Shakespearean performance

*D*irections

Read this passage from a story in which a twelve-year-old boy remembers an incident that happened shortly after his eyesight was damaged. Then answer questions 8 through 11.

from *Tangerine*

By Edward Bloor

Monday, August 28

Today was the first day of school. I left the house at seven-thirty to walk to the front of the development and catch the bus. . . . I turned right at the end of Kensington Gardens Drive and walked parallel to the high gray wall. Something started to bother me almost immediately. The gray of the wall drifted along in the left side of my vision—distracting me, troubling me. What was it? Something about the wall? Something about the bus stop? Something that I needed to remember? My steps slowed down, and I came to a dead stop, frozen there like a windup toy that had run out of torque.

Then a scene came back to me. . . . Entirely on its own, a scene came back to me. *I remembered another bus stop.* And a shiny yellow school bus.

I was standing at the back of a line of kids, waiting to board the bus for one of my first days of kindergarten.

Mom had driven me to school on the actual first day. This was the first day when I would be accompanied by no one except Erik, my fifth-grade brother. But Erik did not accompany me for long. He was standing at the front of the school-bus line with his fifth-grade friends when one of them turned, made a gesture, and called to me, "Hey, Eclipse Boy, how many fingers am I holding up?"

I didn't realize at first that the boy was talking to me, and I had no idea what he meant. Erik and his friends laughed about the joke, then the bus doors opened and we all filed in. I can't put all of the details in order now, but it became clear to me later that, for some reason, the big kids on the school bus were calling me Eclipse Boy.

The fact is we did have an eclipse that summer, around three weeks before school started. Based on that, Erik was telling his friends this story: The reason for the Coke-bottle glasses on my eyes was that I had stared at the sun, unprotected, during that eclipse.

The story puzzled me then, and it puzzles me now. I do not remember doing any such thing. And yet when I search through our family photos, I can see that I never wore glasses of any kind before that summer. But right after the eclipse, I was wearing these thick lenses that I now call my regular glasses.

Puzzled or not, I went right along with the story. I even told it myself. It gave me a special kindergarten identity. It made me somebody. I was the boy who had not listened and who was now paying the price. *Look at me if you dare!* Teachers and other adults seemed to value me as an example. I was the living proof that you shouldn't look at an eclipse or you'll go blind; that you shouldn't play in an abandoned refrigerator or you'll suffocate; that you shouldn't go swimming right after you eat or you'll get stomach cramps and drown.

So there I sat on that yellow school bus—Erik Fisher's younger brother, Eclipse Boy, visually impaired and totally incapable of following in his brother's footsteps.

The scene faded. I stood still for another minute, trying to remember more, but nothing would come. Then I made myself turn away from the wall, and I made my legs move again, one step in front of the other, to the end of the street.

---

8 In the passage, the narrator is expressing his thoughts as if he were

F talking with a friend on the telephone

G relating a story to his classmates

H writing an entry in his personal journal

J composing an end-of-term paper

9 Read these sentences from the passage.

> *I remembered another bus stop.*
> **And a shiny yellow school bus.**

These sentences signal that

A the narrator is about to describe a school bus

B something bad is about to happen

C the narrator is afraid to get on the bus

D a flashback to an earlier time is about to begin

10 Read this sentence from the passage.

> **My steps slowed down, and I came to a dead stop, frozen there like a windup toy that had run out of torque.**

What does the narrator mean when he compares himself to a "windup toy that had run out of torque"?

F He is too tired to continue walking.

G Something in his mind has stopped him in his tracks.

H His thoughts have become twisted, and he cannot go on.

J A strange force has stopped all of his movements.

11 Read this sentence from the passage.

> **The story puzzled me then, and it puzzles me now.**

Why does the narrator say that the story still puzzles him? Use details from the passage to support your answer.

UNIT 6

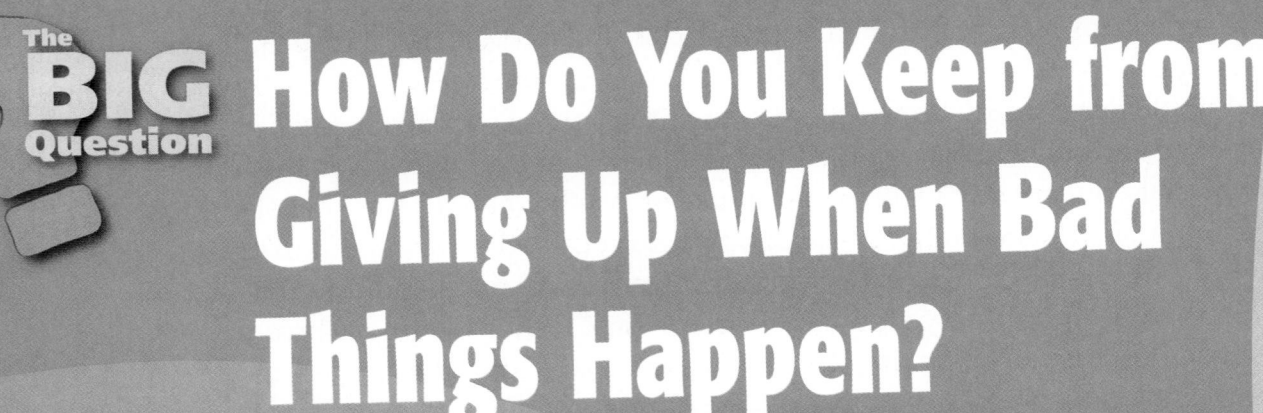

The BIG Question

How Do You Keep from Giving Up When Bad Things Happen?

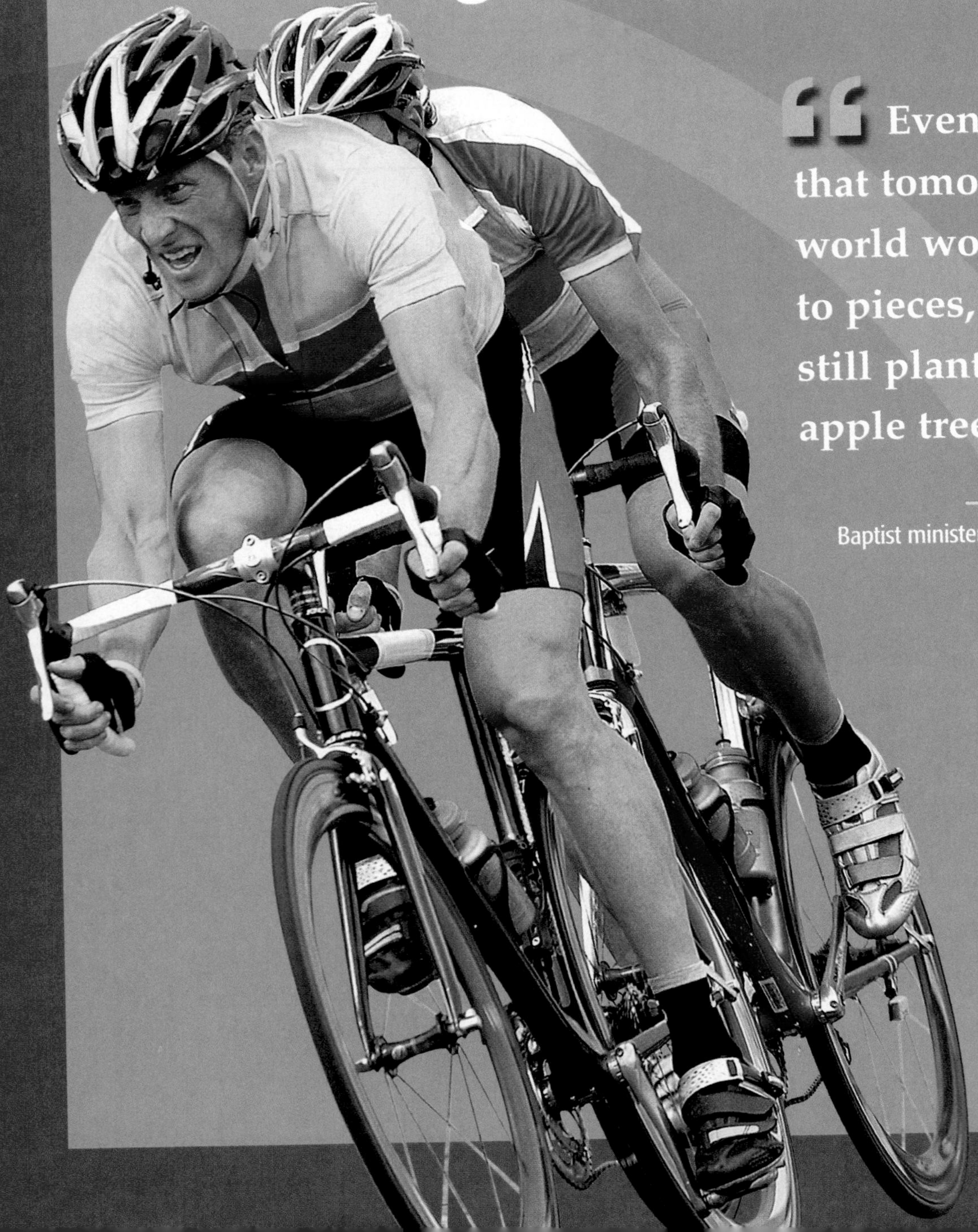

"Even if I knew that tomorrow the world would go to pieces, I would still plant my apple tree."

–Martin Luther King Jr.
Baptist minister and Civil Rights leader
(1929–1968)

LOOKING AHEAD

The skill lessons and readings in this unit will help you develop your own answer to the Big Question.

UNIT 6 WRAP-UP • Answering the Big Question

Connecting to The BIG Question

How Do You Keep from Giving Up When Bad Things Happen?

No matter how much we prepare for the future, we can't predict what will actually happen next. Unexpected events can often cause damage and hurt. But there are things we can do to help one another when we face hard times. In this unit, you'll read about how people remain hopeful when bad things happen.

Real Kids and the Big Question

NAOMI has a very close family. They've always been together on holidays, but last year Naomi's brother Kyle went away to war. This year he's still away, and Naomi is upset by the things she sees on television. She feels scared and alone. What advice would you give her?

CHRIS lives in a neighborhood with many families. A few days ago, a storm destroyed some of the houses on his block. Chris's house is still in good shape, but several families have no home or food. What can Chris and his family do to help the people on his block?

Warm-Up Activity

On your own, write a journal entry from the point of view of Naomi or Chris. Explain how you feel and why.

You and the Big Question

Reading about how other people remain hopeful during difficult times will give you ideas that will help you answer this question.

Literature Online

BIG Question Link to Web resources to further explore the Big Question at www.glencoe.com.

Plan for the Unit Challenge

At the end of the unit, you'll use notes from all your reading to complete the Unit Challenge, which will explore your answer to the Big Question.

You will choose one of the following activities:

A. Create a Newspaper Ad You'll work with classmates to write and design a newspaper ad in which you offer ways to help people in need.

B. Write a Poem Write a poem that is addressed to a person or people who have faced hard times.

- Start thinking about which activity you'd like to do so that you can focus your thoughts as you go through the unit.

- In your Learner's Notebook, write your ideas about the activity you'd like to do. Why did you choose that activity? Have you or a person you know ever gone through a difficult time?

- As you read each selection, take notes on how people act when they are faced with problems. In each case, think about what help or advice you would offer them.

Keep Track of Your Ideas

FOLDABLES™ Study Organizer

As you read, you'll make notes about the Big Question. Later, you'll use these notes to complete the Unit Challenge. See pages R8–R9 for help with making each Unit 6 Foldable. This diagram shows how each should look.

1. Make one Foldable for each workshop. Keep all of your Foldables for the unit in your Foldables folder.

2. On the bottom fold of your Foldable, write the workshop number and the Big Question.

3. Write the titles of the selections in the workshop on the front of the flaps—one title on each flap. For *Anne Frank,* add the act and scene numbers. (See page 709 for the titles.)

4. Open the flaps. At the very top of each flap, write **My Purpose for Reading.** Below each crease, write **The Big Question.**

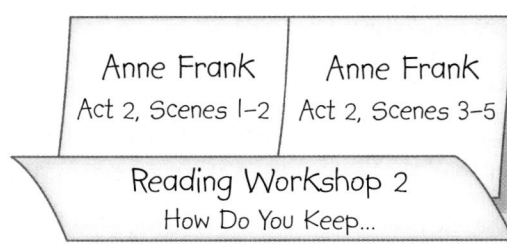

Anne Frank
Act 2, Scenes 1–2

Anne Frank
Act 2, Scenes 3–5

Reading Workshop 2
How Do You Keep...

A **drama** is any story performed for an audience. The word *drama* is used two ways. It can refer to (a) a serious play or (b) any kind of play—comedy or tragedy; musical or not; stage, TV, film, or Internet; long or short.

Why Read Drama?

When you see a play performed, the characters and their actions are right in front of you. The director, actors, and designers have already made many decisions that affect your understanding and enjoyment of the drama. Reading a play is different from seeing one. For the most part, you must "hear" it through the characters' speeches and use imagination to "see" the action. As a result, you make your own judgments.

Reading plays can help you make inferences, draw conclusions, and see how and why people grow and change. Some dramas, like *The Diary of Anne Frank*, also give you insight into historical periods and events.

How to Read Drama

Key Reading Skills

These reading skills are especially useful tools for reading and understanding drama. You'll learn more about these later in this unit.

- **Drawing Conclusions** As you read, use details about characters, ideas, and events to form general ideas. (See Reading Workshop 1.)
- **Interpreting** Using what you already know about yourself and the world, ask what the author is really saying. (See Reading Workshop 2.)
- **Paraphrasing and Summarizing** To make sure that you understand what you read, retell the main points about characters, ideas, and events in logical order and in your own words. (See Reading Workshop 3.)
- **Visualizing** Picture the characters, ideas, and events in your mind. (See Reading Workshop 4.)

Key Literary Elements

Recognizing and thinking about the following literary elements will help you understand more fully what a playwright is telling you. To learn more about them, see *The Diary of Anne Frank*.

- **Act and scene:** the major divisions of a play (See act 1, scene 3.)
- **Dialogue and monologue:** the words that the characters say to one another (See act 1, scenes 4–5.)
- **Stage directions:** descriptions of the settings, characters, sounds, and actions in a play script (See act 2, scenes 1–2.)
- **Mood:** the emotional effect a drama has on its audience (See act 2, scenes 3–5.)

Skills Focus

- Key skills for reading a drama
- Key literary elements of dramas

Skills Model

You will see how to use the key reading skills and literary elements as you read the first two scenes of

- ***The Diary of Anne Frank,*** p. 713

NY English Language Arts Core Curriculum (pp. 712–731)

R1l Draw conclusions on the basis of explicit and implied information. **R2b** Interpret characters, plot, setting, theme, and dialogue. **R2g** Compare literature to own lives. **LC R12** Combine strategies (summarize and visualize) to enhance comprehension and response. **LC R13** Use text structure and literary devices to aid comprehension and response. **R2e** Recognize how the author's use of language creates images or feelings.

For a complete description of the standards, see p. NY 11.

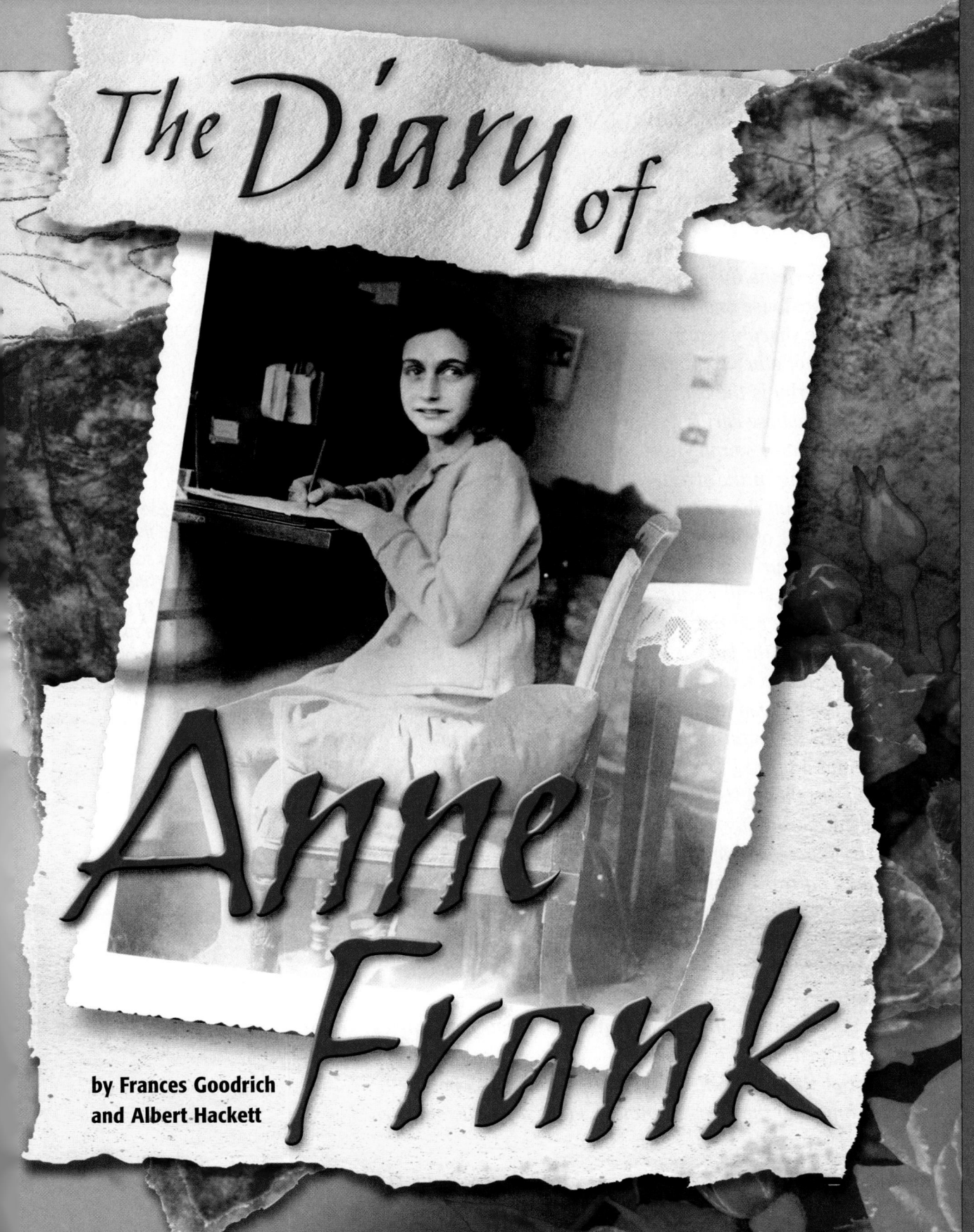

The Diary of Anne Frank

by Frances Goodrich
and Albert Hackett

CHARACTERS

Mr. Frank	Peter Van Daan	Anne Frank
Miep	Mrs. Frank	Mr. Kraler
Mrs. Van Daan	Margot Frank	Mr. Dussel
Mr. Van Daan		

ACT 1 — SCENE 1

[*The scene remains the same throughout the play. It is the top floor of a warehouse and office building in Amsterdam, Holland. The sharply peaked roof of the building is outlined against a sea of other rooftops, stretching away into the distance. Nearby is the belfry of a church tower, the Westertoren, whose carillon*[1] *rings out the hours. Occasionally faint sounds float up from below: the voices of children playing in the street, the tramp of marching feet, a boat whistle from the canal.* ❶

The three rooms of the top floor and a small attic space above are exposed to our view. The largest of the rooms is in the center, with two small rooms, slightly raised, on either side. On the right is a bathroom, out of sight. A narrow steep flight of stairs at the back leads up to the attic. The rooms are sparsely furnished with a few chairs, cots, a table or two. The windows are painted over, or covered with makeshift blackout curtains.[2] *In the main room there is a sink, a gas ring for cooking and a wood-burning stove for warmth.*

The room on the left is hardly more than a closet. There is a skylight in the sloping ceiling. Directly under this room is a small steep stairwell, with steps leading down to a door. This is the only entrance from the building below. When the door is opened we see that it has been concealed on the outer side by a bookcase attached to it.

The curtain rises on an empty stage. It is late afternoon, November, 1945.

The rooms are dusty, the curtains in rags. Chairs and tables are overturned.

The door at the foot of the small stairwell swings open. MR. FRANK *comes up the steps into view. He is a gentle, cultured*

The notes in the side columns model how to use the skills and elements you read about on page 712.

Drama

ACTIVE READING MODEL

❶ **Key Literary Element**
Stage Directions *It's "scene 1," so there are other scenes, but the directions say "the scene remains the same." I guess that must mean that the same set is used for the whole play.*

---

1. A **belfry** is the tower of a church or other building in which a bell is hung. A **carillon** (KAIR uh lawn) is a set of bells sounded by machinery, rather than rung manually.

2. **Blackout curtains** were used to hide room lights from enemy bombers.

European in his middle years. There is still a trace of a German accent in his speech.

He stands looking slowly around, making a supreme effort at self-control. He is weak, ill. His clothes are threadbare.[3]

After a second he drops his rucksack on the couch and moves slowly about. He opens the door to one of the smaller rooms, and then abruptly closes it again, turning away. He goes to the window at the back, looking off at the Westertoren as its carillon strikes the hour of six, then he moves restlessly on. From the street below we hear the sound of a barrel organ and children's voices at play. There is a many-colored scarf hanging from a nail. MR. FRANK *takes it, putting it around his neck. As he starts back for his rucksack, his eye is caught by something lying on the floor. It is a woman's white glove. He holds it in his hand and suddenly all of his self-control is gone. He breaks down, crying.*

We hear footsteps on the stairs. MIEP GIES[4] *comes up, looking for* MR. FRANK. MIEP *is a Dutch girl of about twenty-two. She wears a coat and hat, ready to go home. She is pregnant. Her attitude toward* MR. FRANK *is protective, compassionate.*] [2] [3]

MIEP. Are you all right, Mr. Frank?

MR. FRANK. [*Quickly controlling himself.*] Yes, Miep, yes.

MIEP. Everyone in the office has gone home . . . It's after six. [*Then pleading.*] Don't stay up here, Mr. Frank. What's the use of torturing yourself like this?

MR. FRANK. I've come to say good-bye . . . I'm leaving here, Miep. [4]

MIEP. What do you mean? Where are you going? Where?

MR. FRANK. I don't know yet. I haven't decided.

MIEP. Mr. Frank, you can't leave here! This is your home! Amsterdam is your home. Your business is here, waiting for you . . . You're needed here . . . Now that the war is over, there are things that . . .

[2] **Key Reading Skill**
Interpreting *Mr. Frank is really upset by this place and by the glove. Maybe it belongs to his wife or to Anne, but why does it make him sad?*

[3] **Key Literary Element**
Stage Directions *The whole section in italics is stage directions. They give really good descriptions, especially of the rooms and Mr. Frank. I didn't know stage directions would be so detailed, even about sounds.*

[4] **Key Literary Element**
Dialogue and Monologue *I see. Dialogue is like conversation in a short story, but the speeches don't have quotation marks. It's clear who's speaking because the speaker is identified at the beginning of each speech.*

---

3. Clothes that are **threadbare** are so old or worn that the threads can be seen.
4. **Miep Gies** (meep gees)

MR. FRANK. I can't stay in Amsterdam, Miep. It has too many memories for me. Everywhere there's something . . . the house we lived in . . . the school . . . that street organ playing out there . . . I'm not the person you used to know, Miep. I'm a bitter old man. [*Breaking off.*] Forgive me. I shouldn't speak to you like this . . . after all that you did for us . . . the suffering . . .

MIEP. No. No. It wasn't suffering. You can't say we suffered.

[*As she speaks, she straightens a chair which is overturned.*]

MR. FRANK. I know what you went through, you and Mr. Kraler.[5] I'll remember it as long as I live. [*He gives one last look around.*] Come, Miep.

[*He starts for the steps, then remembers his rucksack, going back to get it.*]

MIEP. [*Hurrying up to a cupboard.*] Mr. Frank, did you see? There are some of your papers here. [*She brings a bundle of papers to him.*] We found them in a heap of rubbish on the floor after . . . after you left.

MR. FRANK. Burn them. 5

[*He opens his rucksack to put the glove in it.*]

MIEP. But, Mr. Frank, there are letters, notes . . .

MR. FRANK. Burn them. All of them.

MIEP. Burn this?

[*She hands him a paperbound notebook.*]

MR. FRANK. [*Quietly.*] Anne's diary. [*He opens the diary and begins to read.*] "Monday, the sixth of July, nineteen forty-two." [*To* MIEP.] Nineteen forty-two. Is it possible, Miep? . . . Only three years ago. [*As he continues his reading, he sits down on the couch.*] "Dear Diary, since you and I are going to be great friends, I will start by telling you about myself. My name is Anne Frank. I am thirteen years old. I

5 Key Reading Skill
Drawing Conclusions
The war is over, and Mr. Frank is upset by memories that have to do with this place.

---

5. *Kraler* (KRAW lur)

was born in Germany the twelfth of June, nineteen twenty-nine. As my family is Jewish, we emigrated to Holland when Hitler came to power.⁶"

[*As* MR. FRANK *reads on, another voice joins his, as if coming from the air. It is* ANNE'S VOICE.]

MR. FRANK AND ANNE. "My father started a business, importing spice and herbs. Things went well for us until nineteen forty. Then the war came, and the Dutch capitulation, followed by the arrival of the Germans.⁷ Then things got very bad for the Jews."

[MR. FRANK'S *voice dies out.* ANNE'S VOICE *continues alone. The lights dim slowly to darkness. The curtain falls on the scene.*] **6**

ANNE'S VOICE. You could not do this and you could not do that. They forced Father out of his business. We had to wear yellow stars.⁸ I had to turn in my bike. I couldn't go to a Dutch school any more. I couldn't go to the movies, or ride in an automobile, or even on a streetcar, and a million other things. But somehow we children still managed to have fun. Yesterday Father told me we were going into hiding. Where, he wouldn't say. At five o'clock this morning Mother woke me and told me to hurry and get dressed. I was to put on as many clothes as I could. It would look too suspicious if we walked along carrying suitcases. It wasn't until we were on our way that I learned where we were going. Our hiding place was to be upstairs in the building where Father used to have his business. Three other people were coming in with us . . . the Van Daans and their son Peter . . . Father knew the Van Daans but we had never met them . . .

[*During the last lines the curtain rises on the scene. The lights dim on.* ANNE'S VOICE *fades out.*] **7**

ACTIVE READING MODEL

6 Key Literary Elements
Stage Directions; Act and Scene There are three reasons for having Anne's voice heard in darkness. First, it gives the actors and crew time to prepare the new scene. Second, a "blackout" often signals a time change, just as in a movie. Third, the blackout forces the audience to focus on Anne's words.

7 Key Reading Skill
Paraphrasing and Summarizing *Let's see if I can summarize this scene. Mr. Frank is in the place where his family hid during the war. The Franks are Jews who moved to Holland because of Hitler. When Hitler took over Holland too, things got worse. Mr. Frank's friend Miep finds a notebook. It's the diary that Mr. Frank's daughter Anne started when the family came here three years ago.*

---

6. Thousands of German Jews left the country after Adolf **Hitler** became the head of government in 1933.

7. Germany began its invasion of the Netherlands on May 10, 1940, and, within a few days, forced the Dutch army's surrender, or **capitulation** (kuh pich uh LAY shun).

8. The Nazis ordered Jews to wear **yellow stars** at all times for easy identification. The six-pointed Star of David is a religious symbol of the Jewish people.

'it is een foto.zoals
k me zou wensen,
ltijd zo te zijn.
an had ik nog we
en kans om naa
lolywood te kome
Annehank.
10 Oct

(translation)
his is a photo as I would wish ↑
self to look all the time. Then
would maybe have a chance to
me to Hollywood."
Anne Frank, 10 Oct. 1942

Anne Frank, 1942.

Analyzing the Photo In her handwritten note, Anne mentions her desire to go to Hollywood. As you read, think about how Anne's dreams are similar to or different from your own.

SCENE 2

[*It is early morning, July, 1942. The rooms are bare, as before, but they are now clean and orderly.*

MR. *VAN DAAN, a tall, portly man in his late forties, is in the main room, pacing up and down, nervously smoking a cigarette. His clothes and overcoat are expensive and well cut.*

MRS. *VAN DAAN sits on the couch, clutching her possessions, a hatbox, bags, etc. She is a pretty woman in her early forties. She wears a fur coat over her other clothes.*

PETER *VAN DAAN is standing at the window of the room on the right, looking down at the street below. He is a shy, awkward boy of sixteen. He wears a cap, a raincoat, and long Dutch trousers, like "plus fours."*[9] *At his feet is a black case, a carrier for his cat.* 🔳

🔳 **Key Literary Element**
Stage Directions *So we went back in time from November 1945 to July 1942. And there are new characters.*

---

9. ***Dutch trousers*** and ***plus fours*** are pants that end at or a few inches below the knees.

The yellow Star of David is conspicuous[10] on all of their clothes.]

MRS. VAN DAAN. [*Rising, nervous, excited.*] Something's happened to them! I know it!

MR. VAN DAAN. Now, Kerli!

MRS. VAN DAAN. Mr. Frank said they'd be here at seven o'clock. He said . . .

MR. VAN DAAN. They have two miles to walk. You can't expect . . .

MRS. VAN DAAN. They've been picked up. That's what's happened. They've been taken . . . 🖢

[*MR. VAN DAAN indicates that he hears someone coming.*]

MR. VAN DAAN. You see?

[*PETER takes up his carrier and his schoolbag, etc., and goes into the main room as MR. FRANK comes up the stairwell from below. MR. FRANK looks much younger now. His movements are brisk, his manner confident. He wears an overcoat and carries his hat and a small cardboard box. He crosses to the VAN DAANS, shaking hands with each of them.*]

MR. FRANK. Mrs. Van Daan, Mr. Van Daan, Peter. [*Then, in explanation of their lateness.*] There were too many of the Green Police[11] on the streets . . . we had to take the long way around.

[*Up the steps come MARGOT FRANK, MRS. FRANK, MIEP (not pregnant now), and MR. KRALER. All of them carry bags, packages, and so forth. The Star of David is conspicuous on all of the FRANKS' clothing. MARGOT is eighteen, beautiful, quiet, shy. MRS. FRANK is a young mother, gently bred, reserved. She, like MR. FRANK, has a slight German accent. MR. KRALER is a Dutchman, dependable, kindly. As MR. KRALER and MIEP go upstage[12] to put down their parcels, MRS. FRANK turns back to call ANNE.*]

🖢 **Key Literary Element**
Mood *It's hard to get the mood of this scene yet, but the Van Daans make me nervous for some reason.*

---

10. Something that is **conspicuous** (kun SPIK yoo us) stands out in an obvious way.

11. One branch of the Nazi police force was called the **Green Police** because its members wore green uniforms.

12. **Upstage** is toward the back of the stage; **downstage** is the front, near the audience.

MRS. FRANK. Anne?

[ANNE *comes running up the stairs. She is thirteen, quick in her movements, interested in everything, mercurial*[13] *in her emotions. She wears a cape, long wool socks and carries a schoolbag.*]

MR. FRANK. [*Introducing them.*] My wife, Edith. Mr. and Mrs. Van Daan [MRS. FRANK *hurries over, shaking hands with them.*] . . . their son, Peter . . . my daughters, Margot and Anne.

[ANNE *gives a polite little curtsy as she shakes* MR. VAN DAAN's *hand. Then she immediately starts off on a tour of investigation of her new home, going upstairs to the attic room.* MIEP *and* MR. KRALER *are putting the various things they have brought on the shelves.*]

MR. KRALER. I'm sorry there is still so much confusion. **10**

MR. FRANK. Please. Don't think of it. After all, we'll have plenty of leisure to arrange everything ourselves.

MIEP. [*To* MRS. FRANK.] We put the stores of food you sent in here. Your drugs are here . . . soap, linen here.

MRS. FRANK. Thank you, Miep.

MIEP. I made up the beds . . . the way Mr. Frank and Mr. Kraler said. [*She starts out.*] Forgive me. I have to hurry. I've got to go to the other side of town to get some ration books[14] for you.

MRS. VAN DAAN. Ration books? If they see our names on ration books, they'll know we're here.

MR. KRALER. There isn't anything . . .

MIEP. Don't worry. Your names won't be on them. [*As she hurries out.*] I'll be up later.

MR. FRANK. Thank you, Miep.

10 Key Literary Element
Mood *The mood is still pretty confused too, but I guess that's natural with everyone coming and going and unpacking.*

---

13. Anne is described as ***mercurial*** (mur KYUR ee ul) because her emotions change quickly and unpredictably, like the mercury in a thermometer.

14. ***Ration books*** contain coupons that people use to buy a limited amount of food and supplies.

MRS. FRANK. [*To* MR. KRALER.] It's illegal, then, the ration books? We've never done anything illegal.

MR. FRANK. We won't be living here exactly according to regulations.

[*As* MR. KRALER *reassures* MRS. FRANK, *he takes various small things, such as matches, soap, etc., from his pockets, handing them to her.*]

MR. KRALER. This isn't the black market, Mrs. Frank. This is what we call the white market[15] . . . helping all of the hundreds and hundreds who are hiding out in Amsterdam. **11**

[*The carillon is heard playing the quarter-hour before eight.* MR. KRALER *looks at his watch.* ANNE *stops at the window as she comes down the stairs.*]

ANNE. It's the Westertoren!

MR. KRALER. I must go. I must be out of here and downstairs in the office before the workmen get here. [*He starts for the stairs leading out.*] Miep or I, or both of us, will be up each day to bring you food and news and find out what your needs are. Tomorrow I'll get you a better bolt for the door at the foot of the stairs. It needs a bolt that you can throw yourself and open only at our signal. [*To* MR. FRANK.] Oh . . . You'll tell them about the noise?

MR. FRANK. I'll tell them.

MR. KRALER. Good-bye then for the moment. I'll come up again, after the workmen leave.

11 Key Reading Skill
Drawing Conclusions *Who is helping the hundreds of others in hiding? Miep and Mr. Kraler can't look out for them all, but they must know some of the other helpers.*

Miep Gies, 1931.
Analyzing the Photo This is Miep eleven years before she helped the Franks hide. What can you tell about her from this portrait?

---

15. In the **black market,** goods were sold illegally, usually at very high prices. In the **white market,** which also violated Nazi laws, goods were donated by people who wanted to help the Jews.

MR. FRANK. Good-bye, Mr. Kraler.

MRS. FRANK. [*Shaking his hand.*] How can we thank you?

[*The others murmur their good-byes.*]

MR. KRALER. I never thought I'd live to see the day when a man like Mr. Frank would have to go into hiding. When you think— **12**

[*He breaks off, going out.* MR. FRANK *follows him down the steps, bolting the door after him. In the interval before he returns,* PETER *goes over to* MARGOT, *shaking hands with her. As* MR. FRANK *comes back up the steps,* MRS. FRANK *questions him anxiously.*]

MRS. FRANK. What did he mean, about the noise?

MR. FRANK. First let us take off some of these clothes.

[*They all start to take off garment after garment. On each of their coats, sweaters, blouses, suits, dresses, is another yellow Star of David.* MR. *and* MRS. FRANK *are underdressed quite simply. The others wear several things, sweaters, extra dresses, bathrobes, aprons, nightgowns, etc.*]

MR. VAN DAAN. It's a wonder we weren't arrested, walking along the streets . . . Petronella with a fur coat in July . . . and that cat of Peter's crying all the way.

ANNE. [*As she is removing a pair of panties.*] A cat?

MRS. FRANK. [*Shocked.*] Anne, please!

ANNE. It's all right. I've got on three more.

[*She pulls off two more. Finally, as they have all removed their surplus clothes, they look to* MR. FRANK, *waiting for him to speak.*]

MR. FRANK. Now. About the noise. While the men are in the building below, we must have complete quiet. Every sound can be heard down there, not only in the workrooms, but in the offices too. The men come at about eight-thirty, and leave at about five-thirty. So, to be perfectly safe, from eight in the morning until six in the

12 Key Reading Skill
Drawing Conclusions
Mr. Kraler has a very good opinion of Mr. Frank. I think Mr. Kraler must be a good man to take the risk of hiding these people.

evening we must move only when it is necessary, and then in stockinged feet. We must not speak above a whisper. We must not run any water. We cannot use the sink, or even, forgive me, the w.c.[16] The pipes go down through the workrooms. It would be heard. No trash . . . [MR. FRANK *stops abruptly as he hears the sound of marching feet from the street below. Everyone is motionless, paralyzed with fear.* MR. FRANK *goes quietly into the room on the right to look down out of the window.* ANNE *runs after him, peering out with him. The tramping feet pass without stopping. The tension is relieved.* MR. FRANK, *followed by* ANNE, *returns to the main room and resumes his instructions to the group.*] . . . No trash must ever be thrown out which might reveal that someone is living up here . . . not even a potato paring. We must burn everything in the stove at night. This is the way we must live until it is over, if we are to survive. **13** **14**

[*There is silence for a second.*]

MRS. FRANK. Until it is over.

MR. FRANK. [*Reassuringly.*] After six we can move about . . . we can talk and laugh and have our supper and read and play games . . . just as we would at home. [*He looks at his watch.*] And now I think it would be wise if we all went to our rooms, and were settled before eight o'clock. Mrs. Van Daan, you and your husband will be upstairs. I regret that there's no place up there for Peter. But he will be here, near us. This will be our common room, where we'll meet to talk and eat and read, like one family. **15**

MR. VAN DAAN. And where do you and Mrs. Frank sleep?

MR. FRANK. This room is also our bedroom.

MRS. VAN DAAN. That isn't right.
We'll sleep here and you
take the room upstairs. } *Together*

MR. VAN DAAN. It's your place.

13 Key Literary Element
Dialogue and Monologue
Dialogue consists of the back-and-forth speeches between two or more people. One long speech by one character is a monologue, even when it's part of a dialogue.

14 Key Reading Skill
Drawing Conclusions *If they have to be this quiet and careful, it means there's a big risk that a worker downstairs would report them to the Nazis. I guess not all Dutch people wanted to help like Miep and Mr. Kraler.*

15 Key Literary Element
Mood *The mood lightens a little from Mr. Frank's previous, very serious speech. He makes it sound like they'll all be one happy family.*

---

16. Short for "water closet," the **w.c.** is a bathroom.

MR. FRANK. Please. I've thought this out for weeks. It's the best arrangement. The only arrangement.

MRS. VAN DAAN. [*To* MR. FRANK.] Never, never can we thank you. [*Then to* MRS. FRANK.] I don't know what would have happened to us, if it hadn't been for Mr. Frank.

MR. FRANK. You don't know how your husband helped me when I came to this country . . . knowing no one . . . not able to speak the language. I can never repay him for that. [*Going to* VAN DAAN.] May I help you with your things?

MR. VAN DAAN. No. No. [*To* MRS. VAN DAAN.] Come along, liefje.[17]

MRS. VAN DAAN. You'll be all right, Peter? You're not afraid?

PETER. [*Embarrassed.*] Please, Mother.

[*They start up the stairs to the attic room above.* MR. FRANK *turns to* MRS. FRANK.] **16**

MR. FRANK. You too must have some rest, Edith. You didn't close your eyes last night. Nor you, Margot.

ANNE. I slept, Father. Wasn't that funny? I knew it was the last night in my own bed, and yet I slept soundly.

MR. FRANK. I'm glad, Anne. Now you'll be able to help me straighten things in here. [*To* MRS. FRANK *and* MARGOT.] Come with me . . . You and Margot rest in this room for the time being.

[*He picks up their clothes, starting for the room on the right.*]

MRS. FRANK. You're sure . . . ? I could help . . . And Anne hasn't had her milk . . .

MR. FRANK. I'll give it to her. [*To* ANNE *and* PETER.] Anne, Peter . . . it's best that you take off your shoes now, before you forget.

[*He leads the way to the room, followed by* MARGOT.]

16 Key Literary Element
Stage Directions *If I read all the stage directions, I can imagine how the people move around the apartment.*

---

17. *Liefje* (LEEF yuh) is Dutch for "darling."

MRS. FRANK. You're sure you're not tired, Anne?

ANNE. I feel fine. I'm going to help Father.

MRS. FRANK. Peter, I'm glad you are to be with us.

PETER. Yes, Mrs. Frank.

[*MRS. FRANK goes to join* MR. FRANK *and* MARGOT.

During the following scene MR. FRANK *helps* MARGOT *and* MRS. FRANK *to hang up their clothes. Then he persuades them both to lie down and rest. The* VAN DAANS *in their room above settle themselves. In the main room* ANNE *and* PETER *remove their shoes.* PETER *takes his cat out of the carrier.*]

ANNE. What's your cat's name?

PETER. Mouschi.[18]

ANNE. Mouschi! Mouschi! Mouschi! [*She picks up the cat, walking away with it. To* PETER.] I love cats. I have one . . . a darling little cat. But they made me leave her behind. I left some food and a note for the neighbors to take care of her . . . I'm going to miss her terribly. What is yours? A him or a her? [17]

PETER. He's a tom. He doesn't like strangers.

[*He takes the cat from her, putting it back in its carrier.*] [18]

ANNE. [*Unabashed.*[19]] Then I'll have to stop being a stranger, won't I? Is he fixed?

PETER. [*Startled.*] Huh?

ANNE. Did you have him fixed?

PETER. No.

ANNE. Oh, you ought to have him fixed—to keep him from—you know, fighting. Where did you go to school?

PETER. Jewish Secondary.

17 Key Reading Skill
Visualizing *The stage directions and dialogue make it easy to imagine Anne and Peter handling his cat. I can even see her as she leaves her own cat at home.*

18 Key Reading Skill
Interpreting *Ouch! Maybe it's Peter who doesn't like strangers! He's not being very nice to Anne.*

---

18. **Mouschi** (MOOS kee)
19. **Unabashed** means "not ashamed; bold."

ANNE. But that's where Margot and I go! I never saw you around.

PETER. I used to see you . . . sometimes . . .

ANNE. You did?

PETER. . . . in the school yard. You were always in the middle of a bunch of kids.

[*He takes a penknife from his pocket.*]

ANNE. Why didn't you ever come over?

PETER. I'm sort of a lone wolf.

[*He starts to rip off his Star of David.*]

ANNE. What are you doing?

PETER. Taking it off.

ANNE. But you can't do that. They'll arrest you if you go out without your star.

[*He tosses his knife on the table.*]

PETER. Who's going out?

ANNE. Why, of course! You're right! Of course we don't need them any more. [*She picks up his knife and starts to take her star off.*] I wonder what our friends will think when we don't show up today? **19**

PETER. I didn't have any dates with anyone.

ANNE. Oh, I did. I had a date with Jopie to go and play ping-pong at her house. Do you know Jopie de Waal?

PETER. No.

ANNE. Jopie's my best friend. I wonder what she'll think when she telephones and there's no answer? . . . Probably she'll go over to the house . . . I wonder what she'll think . . . we left everything as if we'd suddenly been called away . . . breakfast dishes in the sink . . . beds not made . . .

19 Key Reading Skill

Interpreting I know that the Star of David is a symbol of the Jewish religion. I think it's very important that Anne takes off the star. I'm not sure why she takes it off, so I'll think about it as I read.

[*As she pulls off her star, the cloth underneath shows clearly the color and form of the star.*] Look! It's still there! [*PETER goes over to the stove with his star.*] What're you going to do with yours?

PETER. Burn it.

ANNE. [*She starts to throw hers in, and cannot.*] It's funny, I can't throw mine away. I don't know why.

PETER. You can't throw . . . ? Something they branded you with . . . ? That they made you wear so they could spit on you?

ANNE. I know. I know. But after all, it is the Star of David, isn't it? 20

[*In the bedroom, right,* MARGOT *and* MRS. FRANK *are lying down.* MR. FRANK *starts quietly out.*]

PETER. Maybe it's different for a girl.

[*MR. FRANK comes into the main room.*]

MR. FRANK. Forgive me, Peter. Now let me see. We must find a bed for your cat. [*He goes to a cupboard.*] I'm glad you brought your cat. Anne was feeling so badly about hers. [*Getting a used small washtub.*] Here we are. Will it be comfortable in that?

PETER. [*Gathering up his things.*] Thanks.

20 Key Reading Skill
Drawing Conclusions The Nazis forced Jews to wear the Star of David to identify them as Jews. Peter is eager to burn the star as a symbol of evil, but Anne sees it as a symbol of Judaism as well. How important is his Jewish heritage to Peter? How important is her Jewish heritage to Anne?

Margot, Otto, Anne, and Edith Frank (left to right), 1941.
Analyzing the Photo How would you describe the family here? Are they happy? relaxed? upset?

MR. FRANK. [*Opening the door of the room on the left.*] And here is your room. But I warn you, Peter, you can't grow any more. Not an inch, or you'll have to sleep with your feet out of the skylight. Are you hungry?

PETER. No.

MR. FRANK. We have some bread and butter.

PETER. No, thank you.

MR. FRANK. You can have it for luncheon then. And tonight we will have a real supper . . . our first supper together.

PETER. Thanks. Thanks.

[*He goes into his room. During the following scene he arranges his possessions in his new room.*]

MR. FRANK. That's a nice boy, Peter.

ANNE. He's awfully shy, isn't he?

MR. FRANK. You'll like him, I know.

ANNE. I certainly hope so, since he's the only boy I'm likely to see for months and months. **21**

[*MR. FRANK sits down, taking off his shoes.*]

MR. FRANK. Annele,[20] there's a box there. Will you open it?

[*He indicates a carton on the couch.* ANNE *brings it to the center table. In the street below there is the sound of children playing.*]

ANNE. [*As she opens the carton.*] You know the way I'm going to think of it here? I'm going to think of it as a boarding house.[21] A very peculiar summer boarding house, like the one that we—[*She breaks off as she pulls out*

21 Key Reading Skill

Interpreting *Anne doesn't sound too thrilled. She's used to having lots of friends around. I'd have a hard time too if I had only one person near my age to talk to.*

---

20. Both ***Annele*** (AWN uh luh) and ***Anneke,*** which is used later, are affectionate nicknames.

21. A ***boarding house*** is like a small hotel in a private home. The owner provides rooms and meals to people who pay a weekly or monthly rent.

some photographs.] Father! My movie stars! I was wondering where they were! I was looking for them this morning . . . and Queen Wilhelmina!²² How wonderful!

MR. FRANK. There's something more. Go on. Look further.

[*He goes over to the sink, pouring a glass of milk from a thermos bottle.*]

ANNE. [*Pulling out a pasteboard-bound book.*] A diary! [*She throws her arms around her father.*] I've never had a diary. And I've always longed for one. [*She looks around the room.*] Pencil, pencil, pencil, pencil. [*She starts down the stairs.*] I'm going down to the office to get a pencil.

MR. FRANK. Anne! No!

[*He goes after her, catching her by the arm and pulling her back.*]

ANNE. [*Startled.*] But there's no one in the building now.

MR. FRANK. It doesn't matter. I don't want you ever to go beyond that door.

ANNE. [*Sobered.*] Never . . . ? Not even at nighttime, when everyone is gone? Or on Sundays? Can't I go down to listen to the radio?

MR. FRANK. Never. I am sorry, Anneke. It isn't safe. No, you must never go beyond that door.

[*For the first time* ANNE *realizes what "going into hiding" means.*] **22**

ANNE. I see.

MR. FRANK. It'll be hard, I know. But always remember this, Anneke. There are no walls, there are no bolts, no locks that anyone can put on your mind. Miep will bring us books. We will read history, poetry, mythology. [*He gives her the glass of milk.*] Here's your milk. [*With his arm about her, they go over to the couch, sitting down side by side.*]

22 Key Reading Skill
Drawing Conclusions
It seems to me that Anne jumps into action without thinking about the possible results.

---

22. **Wilhelmina** (wil hel MEE nuh) was queen of the Netherlands from 1890 to 1948. She and her family escaped to England and then Canada at the time of the German invasion.

As a matter of fact, between us, Anne, being here has certain advantages for you. For instance, you remember the battle you had with your mother the other day on the subject of overshoes? You said you'd rather die than wear overshoes? But in the end you had to wear them? Well now, you see, for as long as we are here you will never have to wear overshoes! Isn't that good? And the coat that you inherited from Margot, you won't have to wear that any more. And the piano! You won't have to practice on the piano. I tell you, this is going to be a fine life for you! **23**

[ANNE's *panic is gone.* PETER *appears in the doorway of his room, with a saucer in his hand. He is carrying his cat.*]

PETER. I . . . I . . . I thought I'd better get some water for Mouschi before . . .

MR. FRANK. Of course.

[*As he starts toward the sink the carillon begins to chime the hour of eight. He tiptoes to the window at the back and looks down at the street below. He turns to* PETER, *indicating in pantomime*[23] *that it is too late.* PETER *starts back for his room. He steps on a creaking board. The three of them are frozen for a minute in fear. As* PETER *starts away again,* ANNE *tiptoes over to him and pours some of the milk from her glass into the saucer for the cat.* PETER *squats on the floor, putting the milk before the cat.* MR. FRANK *gives* ANNE *his fountain pen, and then goes into the room at the right. For a second* ANNE *watches the cat, then she goes over to the center table, and opens her diary.*

In the room at the right, MRS. FRANK *has sat up quickly at the sound of the carillon.* MR. FRANK *comes in and sits down beside her on the settee, his arm comfortingly around her. Upstairs, in the attic room,* MR. *and* MRS. VAN DAAN *have hung their clothes in the closet and are now seated on the iron bed.* MRS. VAN DAAN *leans back exhausted.* MR. VAN DAAN *fans her with a newspaper.*

ANNE *starts to write in her diary. The lights dim out, the curtain falls.*]

23 Key Reading Skill
Drawing Conclusions *Anne's father emphasizes positive things about their situation, but she's going to have a tough time ahead. She's too young and lively to be happy living like an animal in a cage.*

---

23. Here, *in pantomime* (PANT uh mym) means in silent gestures instead of in words.

In the darkness ANNE'S VOICE *comes to us again, faintly at first, and then with growing strength.*] **24** **25**

ANNE'S VOICE. I expect I should be describing what it feels like to go into hiding. But I really don't know yet myself. I only know it's funny never to be able to go outdoors . . . never to breathe fresh air . . . never to run and shout and jump. It's the silence in the nights that frightens me most. Every time I hear a creak in the house, or a step on the street outside, I'm sure they're coming for us. The days aren't so bad. At least we know that Miep and Mr. Kraler are down there below us in the office. Our protectors, we call them. I asked Father what would happen to them if the Nazis found out they were hiding us. Pim[24] said that they would suffer the same fate that we would . . . Imagine! They know this, and yet when they come up here, they're always cheerful and gay as if there were nothing in the world to bother them . . . Friday, the twenty-first of August, nineteen forty-two. Today I'm going to tell you our general news. Mother is unbearable. She insists on treating me like a baby, which I loathe.[25] Otherwise things are going better. The weather is . . .

[*As* ANNE'S VOICE *is fading out, the curtain rises on the scene.*]

24 Key Literary Element
Stage Directions Often, the stage directions in a published script are a record of what happened in the play's first production. In their original script, Goodrich and Hackett probably did not give such detailed descriptions of characters' actions.

25 Key Literary Element
Mood *It's almost as if it's nighttime, and everyone is getting ready for bed. Anne's diary isn't exactly a bedtime story, but the mood here is like that—calm and kind of ordinary.*

---

24. *Pim* is Anne's nickname for her father.

25. To *loathe* (lohth) is to regard with extreme disgust or hatred.

Write to Learn Anne decides to think of her time in hiding as if it were nothing more than an odd vacation. Think of a time when you used your imagination to make it easier to get through a difficult time. In your Learner's Notebook, write about what you did and whether or not it helped.

Study Central Visit www.glencoe.com and click on Study Central to review drama.

Skills Focus

You will practice using these skills when you read the following selections:

- *The Diary of Anne Frank,* Act 1, Scene 3, p. 736
- *The Diary of Anne Frank,* Act 1, Scenes 4–5, p. 766

Reading

- Drawing conclusions

Literature

- Understanding act and scene
- Understanding dialogue and monologue

Vocabulary

- Understanding historical influences on English
- Recognizing word parts

Writing/Grammar

- Using commas in series and with direct address and direct quotations

NY English Language Arts Core Curriculum (pp. 732–733)

R1l Draw conclusions on the basis of explicit and implied information.

For a complete description of the standards, see p. NY 11.

Drawing Conclusions

Learn It!

What Is It? A **conclusion** is a judgment you've made. **Drawing conclusions** means using a number of pieces of information to form a general idea of or make a general statement about people, places, ideas, or events.

Suppose, for example, that you notice that your dog has a slight limp and doesn't have much interest in eating or playing. You might—and should—draw the conclusion that your dog is sick or hurt and needs to see the vet.

Analyzing Cartoons

Baldo is daydreaming a Batman-and-Robin adventure. "Batman" quickly draws the conclusion that using the hydraulics under a tree is a bad idea.

Why Is It Important? By drawing conclusions, you make connections between ideas and events that help you see the "big picture." Noticing details is important in itself, but drawing conclusions helps you *do* something with those details.

How Do I Do It? As you read, observe details about characters, ideas, and events. If there are illustrations or photos, check them for clues. Then make a general statement on the basis of these details. Be careful, though! Make sure you have enough information to draw a reasonable and proper conclusion. Here's how one student used details from *Harriet Tubman: Conductor on the Underground Railroad* to draw conclusions.

> The masters kept hearing whispers about the man named Moses. At first they did not believe in his existence. The stories about him were fantastic, unbelievable. Yet they watched for him. They offered rewards for his capture.
>
> They never saw him. Now and then they heard whispered rumors to the effect that he was in the neighborhood. The woods were searched. The roads were watched. But there was never anything to indicate his whereabouts.

Everyone hears amazing stories about this "Moses," but no one ever sees him. There are rewards for anyone who captures him, and people try. I conclude that Moses is either very clever or very lucky.

Practice It!

Use clues from the paragraph below and your own knowledge and experience to draw all the conclusions you can.

> Manuel walked quickly but quietly. If only he could find it before anyone else got there! He didn't bother to check behind the pictures on the wall. He went directly to the dresser. He ignored the little jewelry box and the two small drawers, instead opening the large top drawer first.

Use It!

Remember to practice drawing conclusions as you continue to read *The Diary of Anne Frank*.

Before You Read

The Diary of Anne Frank, Act 1, Scene 3

Goodrich and Hackett

Meet the Authors

Frances Goodrich and her husband, Albert Hackett, spent two years writing their play, inspired by *Anne Frank: The Diary of a Young Girl*. They met with Anne's father and visited the building in which the Franks had hidden. The finished play won the Pulitzer Prize and many other awards after it was first presented in 1955. See page R2 of the Author Files for more on these playwrights.

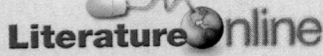

Author Search For more about Goodrich and Hackett, go to www.glencoe.com.

NY English Language Arts Core Curriculum (pp. 734–761)

Core R4 Determine the meaning of words by using structural analysis.
R1l Draw conclusions on the basis of explicit and implied information.
LC R13 Use text structure to aid comprehension and response.
For a complete description of the standards, see p. NY 11.

Vocabulary Preview

self-conscious (self KAHN shus) *adj.* too aware of one's own appearance and actions **(p. 737)** *Peter blushes and becomes self-conscious as a result of Anne's teasing.*

absurd (ub SURD) *adj.* not making sense; very silly **(p. 741)** *Mrs. Frank's fear might have been absurd in ordinary times, but now it made sense.*

vile (vyl) *adj.* very bad; extremely unpleasant **(p. 742)** *Anne had a very low opinion of math; she thought it was vile.*

mimics (MIM iks) *v.* makes fun of by imitating or copying; form of the verb mimic **(p. 743)** *Mr. Van Daan mimics his wife, showing that he's heard her tell the story many times before.*

aggravating (AG ruh vay ting) *adj.* irritating; annoying **(p. 748)** *Mr. Van Daan sees Anne as aggravating and spoiled.*

bickering (BIK ur ing) *n.* a quarrel or argument, especially about minor details **(p. 751)** *The Van Daans' endless bickering over every little thing begins to get on Mrs. Frank's nerves.*

meticulous (mih TIK yuh lus) *adj.* careful about small details **(p. 755)** *Dussel is meticulous about his appearance and his habits.*

Partner Talk With a partner, choose one of the vocabulary words and talk about all the situations you can think of in which you could use it.

English Language Coach

Word Parts In the last unit you learned about base words, roots, prefixes, and suffixes. Together, these word parts shape the meanings of many different words in the English language. For example, add a prefix to a root word, and you'll get a word that means something slightly different from the root. Look at the roots and their meanings in the following chart.

Root	Meaning	Word Example
cred	believe	incredible
graph	write	autograph
port	carry	portable
fort	strong	fortress

Partner Talk Review the word examples above. With a partner, discuss how adding prefixes and suffixes changes the meaning of the roots.

Skills Preview

Key Reading Skill: Drawing Conclusions

Drawing conclusions is similar to making inferences. You combine clues from the writing with your own knowledge and experience to figure out what the writer is saying. One meaning of *conclusion* is "the final part of something." When you draw a conclusion, you make a "final" statement that you can explain logically and with supporting details.

Try not to draw a conclusion until you have solid facts and details to support it. And don't be afraid to change a conclusion when new information comes in.

Write to Learn What conclusion(s) can you draw about Mr. Frank, based on what you've read so far? Write your answer in your Learner's Notebook.

Key Literary Element: Act and Scene

An **act** is a division of a play, which may be divided into two or more acts. An act may be divided into two or more **scenes.** *The Diary of Anne Frank* has two acts, with five scenes in each. Act 1, scene 1 introduces the setting, situation, and two characters. The remaining characters appear in scene 2.

As you read, use these tips to understand how acts and scenes work:

- Each scene usually presents action in one time and place or in one situation. The setting may change from scene to scene or stay the same throughout an entire play.
- Plays are meant to be performed. Try to imagine how an act or scene break might affect you if you were in an audience watching the play. Between scenes, you and other audience members would stay seated. At the intermission, between acts, you could get up and move around.

Interactive Literary Elements Handbook
To review or learn more about the literary elements, go to www.glencoe.com.

Get Ready to Read

Connect to Reading

Have you ever had to share a very small space with several people? What was that like? For more than two years, Anne Frank, her parents, her sister, and four other people lived together in a few small rooms.

Partner Talk With a partner, list what you'd have to give up if you shared a tiny house or apartment with others and had to be quiet most of the time.

Build Background

During World War II, many Jews in Europe were forced into hiding to avoid German labor and death camps. Most hideouts were tiny and uncomfortable—a barn, an attic, a basement, even the space under a floor.

- Anne Frank was born in 1929. She was a teenager when she and her family moved to Holland after the Nazis gained power in Germany.
- When the Germans invaded Holland, the Franks and four other Jews hid in the attic of an office building for 25 months. Sympathetic non-Jews brought them food, news, and other necessities.
- Anne "disguised" the identities of people in her diary. Those she called Van Daan were, in real life, named Herman, Auguste, and Peter van Pels. The man she calls Dr. Albert Dussel (who appears in scene 3 of the play) was actually Fritz Pfeffer.

Set Purposes for Reading

BIG Question Read the rest of act 1 to find out how Anne and the others find ways to go on despite enormous pressures and difficulties.

Set Your Own Purpose What would you like to learn from the play to help you answer the Big Question? Write your own purpose on the Workshop 1 Foldable for Unit 6.

Keep Moving

Use these skills as you read the following selection.

SCENE 3

[*It is a little after six o'clock in the evening, two months later.* ◾1
MARGOT is in the bedroom at the right, studying. MR. VAN DAAN *is lying down in the attic room above.*
The rest of the "family" is in the main room. ANNE *and* PETER *sit opposite each other at the center table, where they have been doing their lessons.* MRS. FRANK *is on the couch.* MRS. VAN DAAN *is seated with her fur coat, on which she has been sewing, in her lap. None of them are wearing their shoes.*
Their eyes are on MR. FRANK, *waiting for him to give them the signal which will release them from their day-long quiet.* MR. FRANK, *his shoes in his hand, stands looking down out of the window at the back, watching to be sure that all of the workmen have left the building below.*
After a few seconds of motionless silence, MR. FRANK *turns from the window.*]

MR. FRANK. [*Quietly, to the group.*] It's safe now. The last workman has left.

[*There is an immediate stir of relief.*]

ANNE. [*Her pent-up energy explodes.*] WHEE!

MRS. FRANK. [*Startled, amused.*] Anne!

MRS. VAN DAAN. I'm first for the w.c.

[*She hurries off to the bathroom.* MRS. FRANK *puts on her shoes and starts up to the sink to prepare supper.* ANNE *sneaks* PETER's *shoes from under the table and hides them behind her back.* MR. FRANK *goes into* MARGOT's *room.*]

MR. FRANK. [*To* MARGOT.] Six o'clock. School's over. ◾2

[*MARGOT gets up, stretching.* MR. FRANK *sits down to put on his shoes. In the main room* PETER *tries to find his.*]

PETER. [*To* ANNE.] Have you seen my shoes?

ANNE. [*Innocently.*] Your shoes?

PETER. You've taken them, haven't you?

ANNE. I don't know what you're talking about.

Practice the Skills

◾1 **Key Literary Element**

Act and Scene A new scene often signals the passage of time or a change in setting. Is there a change at the beginning of scene 3? If so, what is it?

◾2 **BIG Question**

What do Anne and the others do to make life seem more normal? Do these efforts help them keep from giving up? Explain your answers on the Workshop 1 Foldable for Unit 6.

PETER. You're going to be sorry!

ANNE. Am I?

[PETER *goes after her.* ANNE, *with his shoes in her hand, runs from him, dodging behind her mother.*]

MRS. FRANK. [*Protesting.*] Anne, dear!

PETER. Wait till I get you!

ANNE. I'm waiting! [PETER *makes a lunge for her. They both fall to the floor.* PETER *pins her down, wrestling with her to get the shoes.*] Don't! Don't! Peter, stop it. Ouch!

MRS. FRANK. Anne! . . . Peter!

[*Suddenly* PETER *becomes* **self-conscious.** *He grabs his shoes roughly and starts for his room.*]

ANNE. [*Following him.*] Peter, where are you going? Come dance with me.

PETER. I tell you I don't know how.

ANNE. I'll teach you.

PETER. I'm going to give Mouschi his dinner.

ANNE. Can I watch?

PETER. He doesn't like people around while he eats.

ANNE. Peter, please.

PETER. No!

[*He goes into his room.* ANNE *slams his door after him.*] **3**

MRS. FRANK. Anne, dear, I think you shouldn't play like that with Peter. It's not dignified.[1]

Analyzing the Photo It's hard to tell what Peter is doing, but what can you learn about him from this photo?

Practice the Skills

3 Reviewing Skills

Activating Prior Knowledge In your experience, what does it mean when a teenage girl teases a teenage boy?

---

1. **Dignified** (DIG nuh fyd) means "behaving in a calm, proper way."

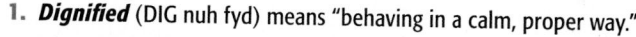

Vocabulary

self-conscious (self KAHN shus) *adj.* too aware of one's own appearance and actions

ANNE. Who cares if it's dignified? I don't want to be dignified.

[*MR. FRANK and* MARGOT *come from the room on the right.* MARGOT *goes to help her mother.* MR. FRANK *starts for the center table to correct* MARGOT's *school papers.*]

MRS. FRANK. [*To* ANNE.] You complain that I don't treat you like a grown-up. But when I do, you resent it.

ANNE. I only want some fun . . . someone to laugh and clown with . . . After you've sat still all day and hardly moved, you've got to have some fun. I don't know what's the matter with that boy.

MR. FRANK. He isn't used to girls. Give him a little time.

ANNE. Time? Isn't two months time? I could cry. [*Catching hold of* MARGOT.] Come on, Margot . . . dance with me. Come on, please.

MARGOT. I have to help with supper.

ANNE. You know we're going to forget how to dance . . . When we get out we won't remember a thing.

[*She starts to sing and dance by herself.* MR. FRANK *takes her in his arms, waltzing with her.* MRS. VAN DAAN *comes in from the bathroom.*] **4**

MRS. VAN DAAN. Next? [*She looks around as she starts putting on her shoes.*] Where's Peter?

ANNE. [*As they are dancing.*] Where would he be!

MRS. VAN DAAN. He hasn't finished his lessons, has he? His father'll kill him if he catches him in there with that cat and his work not done. [*MR. FRANK and* ANNE *finish their dance. They bow to each other with extravagant formality.*[2]] Anne, get him out of there, will you?

ANNE. [*At* PETER'S *door.*] Peter? Peter?

PETER. [*Opening the door a crack.*] What is it?

ANNE. Your mother says to come out.

Practice the Skills

4 | **Key Reading Skill**

Drawing Conclusions Why does Mr. Frank dance with Anne?

---

2. In showing **extravagant formality,** Anne and her father make deep, formal bows, exaggerating the custom of bowing to one's partner at the end of a dance.

PETER. I'm giving Mouschi his dinner.

MRS. VAN DAAN. You know what your father says.

[*She sits on the couch, sewing on the lining of her fur coat.*]

PETER. For heaven's sake, I haven't even looked at him since lunch.

MRS. VAN DAAN. I'm just telling you, that's all.

ANNE. I'll feed him.

PETER. I don't want you in there.

MRS. VAN DAAN. Peter!

PETER. [*To* ANNE.] Then give him his dinner and come right out, you hear?

[*He comes back to the table.* ANNE *shuts the door of* PETER's *room after her and disappears behind the curtain covering his closet.*]

MRS. VAN DAAN. [*To* PETER.] Now is that any way to talk to your little girlfriend?

PETER. Mother . . . for heaven's sake . . . will you please stop saying that?

MRS. VAN DAAN. Look at him blush! Look at him!

PETER. Please! I'm not . . . anyway . . . let me alone, will you?

MRS. VAN DAAN. He acts like it was something to be ashamed of. It's nothing to be ashamed of, to have a little girlfriend. **5**

PETER. You're crazy. She's only thirteen.

MRS. VAN DAAN. So what? And you're sixteen. Just perfect. Your father's ten years older than I am. [*To* MR. FRANK.] I warn you, Mr. Frank, if this war lasts much longer, we're going to be related and then . . .

MR. FRANK. *Mazeltov!*[3]

MRS. FRANK. [*Deliberately changing the conversation.*] I wonder where Miep is. She's usually so prompt. **6**

---

3. *Mazeltov* (MAW zul tawv) means "congratulations" or "best wishes" in Hebrew.

Practice the Skills

5 | **Reviewing Skills**

Analyzing Using what you've read so far in the play, describe the relationship between Peter and his mother.

6 | **Key Reading Skill**

Drawing Conclusions Why does Mrs. Frank change the subject?

[*Suddenly everything else is forgotten as they hear the sound of an automobile coming to a screeching stop in the street below. They are tense, motionless in their terror. The car starts away. A wave of relief sweeps over them. They pick up their occupations again.* ANNE *flings open the door of* PETER's *room, making a dramatic entrance. She is dressed in* PETER's *clothes.* PETER *looks at her in fury. The others are amused.*]

ANNE. Good evening, everyone. Forgive me if I don't stay. [*She jumps up on a chair.*] I have a friend waiting for me in there. My friend Tom. Tom Cat. Some people say that we look alike. But Tom has the most beautiful whiskers, and I have only a little fuzz. I am hoping . . . in time . . .

PETER. All right, Mrs. Quack Quack!

ANNE. [*Outraged—jumping down.*] Peter!

PETER. I heard about you . . . How you talked so much in class they called you Mrs. Quack Quack. How Mr. Smitter made you write a composition . . . " 'Quack, quack,' said Mrs. Quack Quack."

ANNE. Well, go on. Tell them the rest. How it was so good he read it out loud to the class and then read it to all his other classes!

PETER. Quack! Quack! Quack . . . Quack . . . Quack . . .

[ANNE *pulls off the coat and trousers.*]

ANNE. You are the most **intolerable**, **insufferable**[4] boy I've ever met! **7**

[*She throws the clothes down the stairwell.* PETER *goes down after them.*]

PETER. Quack, quack, quack!

MRS. VAN DAAN. [*To* ANNE.] That's right, Anneke! Give it to him!

ANNE. With all the boys in the world . . . Why I had to get locked up with one like you! . . .

7 **English Language Coach**

Word Parts The base words *tolerate* and *suffer* mean "to put up with (something unpleasant)." Here, *in-* means "not," and *-able* means "worthy of." If you put these exact meanings together in order, they make no sense: "not to put up with worthy of." So you juggle them a little: "not worth putting up with." And that's a good definition for both **intolerable** and **insufferable**.

---

4. Both *intolerable* and *insufferable* mean "unbearable."

PETER. Quack, quack, quack, and from now on stay out of my room! **8**

[*As* PETER *passes her,* ANNE *puts out her foot, tripping him. He picks himself up, and goes on into his room.*]

MRS. FRANK. [*Quietly.*] Anne, dear . . . your hair. [*She feels* ANNE'S *forehead.*] You're warm. Are you feeling all right?

ANNE. Please, Mother.

[*She goes over to the center table, slipping into her shoes.*]

MRS. FRANK. [*Following her.*] You haven't a fever, have you?

ANNE. [*Pulling away.*] No. No.

MRS. FRANK. You know we can't call a doctor here, ever. There's only one thing to do . . . watch carefully. Prevent an illness before it comes. Let me see your tongue.

ANNE. Mother, this is perfectly **absurd**.

MRS. FRANK. Anne, dear, don't be such a baby. Let me see your tongue. [*As* ANNE *refuses,* MRS. FRANK *appeals to* MR. FRANK.] Otto . . . ?

MR. FRANK. You hear your mother, Anne.

[ANNE *flicks out her tongue for a second, then turns away.*]

MRS. FRANK. Come on—open up! [*As* ANNE *opens her mouth very wide.*] You seem all right . . . but perhaps an aspirin . . .

MRS. VAN DAAN. For heaven's sake, don't give that child any pills. I waited for fifteen minutes this morning for her to come out of the w.c.

ANNE. I was washing my hair!

MR. FRANK. I think there's nothing the matter with our Anne that a ride on her bike, or a visit with her friend Jopie de Waal wouldn't cure. Isn't that so, Anne? **9**

Vocabulary
....

absurd (ub SURD) *adj.* not making sense; very silly

Practice the Skills

8 **Reviewing Skills**

Connecting In anger, Peter tries to mock and embarrass Anne. Have you ever done such a thing? What good did it do?

9 **Key Reading Skill**

Drawing Conclusions Why is Mrs. Frank so concerned? Why is it so important to prevent illness? What does Mr. Frank think is wrong with Anne?

[MR. VAN DAAN *comes down into the room. From outside we hear faint sounds of bombers going over and a burst of ack-ack.*[5]] **10**

MR. VAN DAAN. Miep not come yet?

MRS. VAN DAAN. The workmen just left, a little while ago.

MR. VAN DAAN. What's for dinner tonight?

MRS. VAN DAAN. Beans.

MR. VAN DAAN. Not again!

MRS. VAN DAAN. Poor Putti! I know. But what can we do? That's all that Miep brought us.

[MR. VAN DAAN *starts to pace, his hands behind his back.* ANNE *follows behind him, imitating him.*]

ANNE. We are now in what is known as the "bean cycle." Beans boiled, beans *en casserole*, beans with strings, beans without strings . . . **11**

[PETER *has come out of his room. He slides into his place at the table, becoming immediately absorbed in his studies.*]

MR. VAN DAAN. [*To* PETER.] I saw you . . . in there, playing with your cat.

MRS. VAN DAAN. He just went in for a second, putting his coat away. He's been out here all the time, doing his lessons.

MR. FRANK. [*Looking up from the papers.*] Anne, you got an excellent in your history paper today . . . and very good in Latin.

ANNE. [*Sitting beside him.*] How about algebra?

MR. FRANK. I'll have to make a confession. Up until now I've managed to stay ahead of you in algebra. Today you caught up with me. We'll leave it to Margot to correct.

ANNE. Isn't algebra **vile**, Pim!

---

5. *Ack-ack* was the slang name for antiaircraft gunfire. It was the Allies who were bombing Nazi-controlled Netherlands.

Vocabulary

vile (vyl) *adj.* very bad; extremely unpleasant

Practice the Skills

10 **Key Reading Skill**

Drawing Conclusions Earlier in the scene, everyone stopped in fear when he or she heard a car. Here, no one pays much attention to the bombers and antiaircraft fire. What accounts for the different reactions? Explain.

11 **Reviewing Skills**

Connecting There's probably some kind of food that you get tired of eating, meal after meal. How do you express your feelings about it?

MR. FRANK. Vile!

MARGOT. [*To* MR. FRANK.] How did I do?

ANNE. [*Getting up.*] Excellent, excellent, excellent, excellent!

MR. FRANK. [*To* MARGOT.] You should have used the subjunctive[6] here . . .

MARGOT. Should I? . . . I thought . . . look here . . . I didn't use it here . . .

[*The two become absorbed in the papers.*]

ANNE. Mrs. Van Daan, may I try on your coat?

MRS. FRANK. No, Anne.

MRS. VAN DAAN. [*Giving it to* ANNE.] It's all right . . . but careful with it. [ANNE *puts it on and struts with it.*] My father gave me that the year before he died. He always bought the best that money could buy.

ANNE. Mrs. Van Daan, did you have a lot of boyfriends before you were married? **12**

MRS. FRANK. Anne, that's a personal question. It's not courteous to ask personal questions.

MRS. VAN DAAN. Oh I don't mind. [*To* ANNE.] Our house was always swarming with boys. When I was a girl we had . . .

MR. VAN DAAN. Oh, God. Not again!

MRS. VAN DAAN. [*Good-humored.*] Shut up! [*Without a pause, to* ANNE. MR. VAN DAAN **mimics** MRS. VAN DAAN, *speaking the first few words in unison with her.*] One summer we had a big house in Hilversum. The boys came buzzing round like bees around a jam pot. And when I was sixteen! . . . We were wearing our skirts very short those days and I had good-looking legs. [*She pulls up her skirt, going to* MR. FRANK.] I still have 'em. I may not

---

6. The **subjunctive** (sub JUNK tiv) is the verb form used to express wishes, possibilities, or things that are opposed to fact. In the sentence, "If I were you, I wouldn't go," *were* is the subjunctive form of *to be*.

Vocabulary

mimics (MIM iks) *v.* makes fun of by imitating or copying

Practice the Skills

12 **Key Reading Skill**

Drawing Conclusions Anne jokes about beans and algebra and asks Mrs. Van Daan about boyfriends she had before she was married. What conclusions can you draw about Anne from these comments?

be as pretty as I used to be, but I still have my legs. How about it, Mr. Frank? **13**

MR. VAN DAAN. All right. All right. We see them.

MRS. VAN DAAN. I'm not asking you. I'm asking Mr. Frank.

PETER. Mother, for heaven's sake.

MRS. VAN DAAN. Oh, I embarrass you, do I? Well, I just hope the girl you marry has as good. [*Then to* ANNE.] My father used to worry about me, with so many boys hanging round. He told me, if any of them gets fresh, you say to him . . . "Remember, Mr. So-and-So, remember I'm a lady."

ANNE. "Remember, Mr. So-and-So, remember I'm a lady." **14**

[*She gives* MRS. VAN DAAN *her coat.*]

MR. VAN DAAN. Look at you, talking that way in front of her! Don't you know she puts it all down in that diary?

MRS. VAN DAAN. So, if she does? I'm only telling the truth!

[ANNE *stretches out, putting her ear to the floor, listening to what is going on below. The sound of the bombers fades away.*]

MRS. FRANK. [*Setting the table.*] Would you mind, Peter, if I moved you over to the couch?

ANNE. [*Listening.*] Miep must have the radio on.

[PETER *picks up his papers, going over to the couch beside* MRS. VAN DAAN.]

MR. VAN DAAN. [*Accusingly, to* PETER.] Haven't you finished yet?

PETER. No.

MR. VAN DAAN. You ought to be ashamed of yourself.

PETER. All right. All right. I'm a dunce. I'm a hopeless case. Why do I go on?

MRS. VAN DAAN. You're not hopeless. Don't talk that way. It's just that you haven't anyone to help you, like the girls have. [*To* MR. FRANK.] Maybe you could help him, Mr. Frank?

Practice the Skills

13 Key Reading Skill

Drawing Conclusions What does Mrs. Van Daan want the others—especially Mr. Frank—to get from her story? What do her story and her behavior tell you about her?

14 Key Reading Skill

Drawing Conclusions Why does Anne repeat these words? (Hint: See Mr. Van Daan's next speech.)

MR. FRANK. I'm sure that his father . . . ?

MR. VAN DAAN. Not me. I can't do anything with him. He won't listen to me. You go ahead . . . if you want.

MR. FRANK. [*Going to* PETER.] What about it, Peter? Shall we make our school coeducational?[7]

MRS. VAN DAAN. [*Kissing* MR. FRANK.] You're an angel, Mr. Frank. An angel. I don't know why I didn't meet you before I met that one there. Here, sit down, Mr. Frank . . . [*She forces him down on the couch beside* PETER.] Now, Peter, you listen to Mr. Frank. **15**

MR. FRANK. It might be better for us to go into Peter's room.

[PETER *jumps up eagerly, leading the way.*]

MRS. VAN DAAN. That's right. You go in there, Peter. You listen to Mr. Frank. Mr. Frank is a highly educated man.

[*As* MR. FRANK *is about to follow* PETER *into his room,* MRS. FRANK *stops him and wipes the lipstick from his lips. Then she closes the door after them.*]

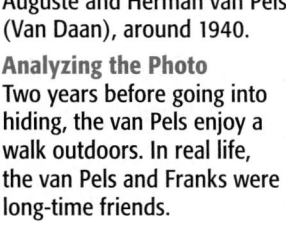

15 **Key Reading Skill**

Drawing Conclusions What conclusions can you draw about Mrs. Van Daan, Peter, and Mr. Frank from this dialogue? Explain.

Auguste and Herman van Pels (Van Daan), around 1940.

Analyzing the Photo
Two years before going into hiding, the van Pels enjoy a walk outdoors. In real life, the van Pels and Franks were long-time friends.

---

7. A *coeducational* school has both male and female students.

ANNE. [*On the floor, listening.*] Shh! I can hear a man's voice talking.

MR. VAN DAAN. [*To* ANNE.] Isn't it bad enough here without your sprawling all over the place?

[ANNE *sits up.*]

MRS. VAN DAAN. [*To* MR. VAN DAAN.] If you didn't smoke so much, you wouldn't be so bad-tempered.

MR. VAN DAAN. Am I smoking? Do you see me smoking?

MRS. VAN DAAN. Don't tell me you've used up all those cigarettes.

MR. VAN DAAN. One package. Miep only brought me one package.

MRS. VAN DAAN. It's a filthy habit anyway. It's a good time to break yourself.

MR. VAN DAAN. Oh, stop it, please.

MRS. VAN DAAN. You're smoking up all our money. You know that, don't you?

MR. VAN DAAN. Will you shut up? [*During this,* MRS. FRANK *and* MARGOT *have studiously kept their eyes down. But* ANNE, *seated on the floor, has been following the discussion interestedly.* MR. VAN DAAN *turns to see her staring up at him.*] And what are you staring at? **16**

ANNE. I never heard grown-ups quarrel before. I thought only children quarreled.

MR. VAN DAAN. This isn't a quarrel! It's a discussion. And I never heard children so rude before.

ANNE. [*Rising, indignantly.*[8]] I, rude!

MR. VAN DAAN. Yes!

MRS. FRANK. [*Quickly.*] Anne, will you get me my knitting? [ANNE *goes to get it.*] I must remember, when Miep comes, to ask her to bring me some more wool. **17**

---

8. **Indignantly** (in DIG nunt lee) means "with anger in response to an insult or injustice."

Practice the Skills

16 Reviewing Skills

Predicting Which character seems to be having the most trouble being cooped up? Could you predict anything about this character?

17 Reviewing Skills

Analyzing Mrs. Frank steps in again to change the subject. Why does she do that?

MARGOT. [*Going to her room.*] I need some hairpins and some soap. I made a list.

[*She goes into her bedroom to get the list.*]

MRS. FRANK. [*To ANNE.*] Have you some library books for Miep when she comes?

ANNE. It's a wonder that Miep has a life of her own, the way we make her run errands for us. Please, Miep, get me some starch. Please take my hair out and have it cut. Tell me all the latest news, Miep. [*She goes over, kneeling on the couch beside MRS. VAN DAAN.*] Did you know she was engaged? His name is Dirk, and Miep's afraid the Nazis will ship him off to Germany to work in one of their war plants. That's what they're doing with some of the young Dutchmen . . . they pick them up off the streets—

MR. VAN DAAN. [*Interrupting.*] Don't you ever get tired of talking? Suppose you try keeping still for five minutes. Just five minutes. **18**

[*He starts to pace again. Again ANNE follows him, mimicking him. MRS. FRANK jumps up and takes her by the arm up to the sink, and gives her a glass of milk.*]

MRS. FRANK. Come here, Anne. It's time for your glass of milk.

MR. VAN DAAN. Talk, talk, talk. I never heard such a child. Where is my . . . ? Every evening it's the same, talk, talk, talk. [*He looks around.*] Where is my . . . ?

MRS. VAN DAAN. What're you looking for?

MR. VAN DAAN. My pipe. Have you seen my pipe?

MRS. VAN DAAN. What good's a pipe? You haven't got any tobacco.

MR. VAN DAAN. At least I'll have something to hold in my mouth! [*Opening MARGOT'S bedroom door.*] Margot, have you seen my pipe?

MARGOT. It was on the table last night.

[*ANNE puts her glass of milk on the table and picks up his pipe, hiding it behind her back.*]

Practice the Skills

18 **Key Reading Skill**

Drawing Conclusions Why does Mr. Van Daan become so irritated? Is it only Anne's talking, or is something else bothering him?

MR. VAN DAAN. I know. I know. Anne, did you see my pipe? . . . Anne!

MRS. FRANK. Anne, Mr. Van Daan is speaking to you.

ANNE. Am I allowed to talk now?

MR. VAN DAAN. You're the most **aggravating** . . . The trouble with you is, you've been spoiled. What you need is a good old-fashioned spanking.

ANNE. [*Mimicking* MRS. VAN DAAN.] "Remember, Mr. So-and-So, remember I'm a lady."

[*She thrusts the pipe into his mouth, then picks up her glass of milk.*]

MR. VAN DAAN. [*Restraining himself with difficulty.*] Why aren't you nice and quiet like your sister Margot? Why do you have to show off all the time? Let me give you a little advice, young lady. Men don't like that kind of thing in a girl. You know that? A man likes a girl who'll listen to him once in a while . . . a domestic[9] girl, who'll keep her house shining for her husband . . . who loves to cook and sew and . . .

ANNE. I'd cut my throat first! I'd open my veins! I'm going to be **remarkable!** I'm going to Paris . . . **19**

MR. VAN DAAN. [*Scoffingly.*] Paris!

ANNE. . . . to study music and art.

MR. VAN DAAN. Yeah! Yeah!

ANNE. I'm going to be a famous dancer or singer . . . or something wonderful. **20**

[*She makes a wide gesture, spilling the glass of milk on the fur coat in* MRS. VAN DAAN's *lap.* MARGOT *rushes quickly over with a towel.* ANNE *tries to brush the milk off with her skirt.*]

---

9. To be *domestic* (duh MES tik) is to enjoy cooking, cleaning, and caring for the family.

Vocabulary . . . .

aggravating (AG ruh vay ting) *adj.* irritating; annoying

Practice the Skills

19 **English Language Coach**

Word Parts The root *mark* means "notice." What prefix and suffix are added to *mark* to make the word **remarkable?** What does *remarkable* mean?

20 **Reviewing Skills**

Comparing and Contrasting How does Mr. Van Daan's description of the type of girl "a man likes" differ from Anne's vision of herself?

MRS. VAN DAAN. Now look what you've done . . . you clumsy little fool! My beautiful fur coat my father gave me . . .

ANNE. I'm so sorry.

MRS. VAN DAAN. What do you care? It isn't yours . . . So go on, ruin it! Do you know what that coat cost? Do you? And now look at it! Look at it!

ANNE. I'm very, very sorry.

MRS. VAN DAAN. I could kill you for this. I could just kill you!

[MRS. VAN DAAN *goes up the stairs, clutching the coat.* MR. VAN DAAN *starts after her.*]

MR. VAN DAAN. Petronella . . . *liefje! Liefje!* . . . Come back . . . the supper . . . come back!

MRS. FRANK. Anne, you must not behave in that way.

ANNE. It was an accident. Anyone can have an accident.

MRS. FRANK. I don't mean that. I mean the answering back. You must not answer back. They are our guests. We must always show the greatest courtesy to them. We're all living under terrible tension. [*She stops as* MARGOT *indicates that* VAN DAAN *can hear. When he is gone, she continues.*] That's why we must control ourselves . . . You don't hear Margot getting into arguments with them, do you? Watch Margot. She's always courteous with them. Never familiar. She keeps her distance. And they respect her for it. Try to be like Margot.

ANNE. And have them walk all over me, the way they do her? No, thanks!

MRS. FRANK. I'm not afraid that anyone is going to walk all over you, Anne. I'm afraid for other people, that you'll walk on them. I don't know what happens to you, Anne. You are wild, self-willed. If I had ever talked to my mother as you talk to me . . .

ANNE. Things have changed. People aren't like that any more. "Yes, Mother." "No, Mother." "Anything you say, Mother." I've got to fight things out for myself! Make something of myself! **21**

Practice the Skills

21 🗨 **BIG Question**

How would you describe Anne's attitude? How is it related to her determination to survive? Write your answer on the Workshop 1 Foldable for Unit 6.

Anne (right) and a friend, playing near the Franks' apartment in Amsterdam, 1930s.

MRS. FRANK. It isn't necessary to fight to do it. Margot doesn't fight, and isn't she . . . ?

ANNE. [*Violently rebellious.*] Margot! Margot! Margot! That's all I hear from everyone . . . how wonderful Margot is . . . "Why aren't you like Margot?"

MARGOT. [*Protesting.*] Oh, come on, Anne, don't be so . . .

ANNE. [*Paying no attention.*] Everything she does is right, and everything I do is wrong! I'm the goat[10] around here! . . . You're all against me! . . . And you worst of all! **22**

[*She rushes off into her room and throws herself down on the settee, stifling[11] her sobs. MRS. FRANK sighs and starts toward the stove.*]

MRS. FRANK. [*To MARGOT.*] Let's put the soup on the stove . . . if there's anyone who cares to eat. Margot, will you take the

22 **Key Reading Skill**

Drawing Conclusions Review Anne's dialogue on pages 748–750. Can you draw any new conclusions about the type of person she is? Why or why not?

---

10. A **goat** (or scapegoat) is one who is blamed or punished for other people's mistakes.

11. **Stifling** means "smothering; holding back."

bread out? [*MARGOT gets the bread from the cupboard.*] I don't know how we can go on living this way . . . I can't say a word to Anne . . . she flies at me . . .

MARGOT. You know Anne. In half an hour she'll be out here, laughing and joking.

MRS. FRANK. And . . . [*She makes a motion upwards, indicating the* VAN DAANS.] . . . I told your father it wouldn't work . . . but no . . . no . . . he had to ask them, he said . . . he owed it to him, he said. Well, he knows now that I was right! These quarrels! . . . This **bickering!** ▨

MARGOT. [*With a warning look.*] Shush. Shush.

[*The buzzer for the door sounds.* MRS. FRANK *gasps, startled.*]

MRS. FRANK. Every time I hear that sound, my heart stops!

MARGOT. [*Starting for* PETER'S *door.*] It's Miep. [*She knocks at the door.*] Father?

[MR. FRANK *comes quickly from* PETER'S *room.*]

MR. FRANK. Thank you, Margot. [*As he goes down the steps to open the outer door.*] Has everyone his list?

MARGOT. I'll get my books. [*Giving her mother a list.*] Here's your list. [MARGOT *goes into her and* ANNE'S *bedroom on the right.* ANNE *sits up, hiding her tears, as* MARGOT *comes in.*] Miep's here.

[MARGOT *picks up her books and goes back.* ANNE *hurries over to the mirror, smoothing her hair.*]

MR. VAN DAAN. [*Coming down the stairs.*] Is it Miep?

MARGOT. Yes. Father's gone down to let her in.

MR. VAN DAAN. At last I'll have some cigarettes!

MRS. FRANK. [*To* MR. VAN DAAN.] I can't tell you how unhappy I am about Mrs. Van Daan's coat. Anne should never have touched it.

MR. VAN DAAN. She'll be all right.

▨ **Key Reading Skill**

Drawing Conclusions Both Mrs. Frank and Margot try to act as peacemaker at various times. Have they been successful in that role? Explain.

Vocabulary

bickering (BIK ur ing) *n.* a quarrel or argument, especially about minor details

MRS. FRANK. Is there anything I can do?

MR. VAN DAAN. Don't worry.

[*He turns to meet* MIEP. *But it is not* MIEP *who comes up the steps. It is* MR. KRALER, *followed by* MR. FRANK. *Their faces are grave.*[12] ANNE *comes from the bedroom.* PETER *comes from his room.*] **24**

MRS. FRANK. Mr. Kraler!

MR. VAN DAAN. How are you, Mr. Kraler?

MARGOT. This is a surprise.

MRS. FRANK. When Mr. Kraler comes, the sun begins to shine.

MR. VAN DAAN. Miep is coming?

MR. KRALER. Not tonight.

[KRALER *goes to* MARGOT *and* MRS. FRANK *and* ANNE, *shaking hands with them.*]

MRS. FRANK. Wouldn't you like a cup of coffee? . . . Or, better still, will you have supper with us?

MR. FRANK. Mr. Kraler has something to talk over with us. Something has happened, he says, which demands an immediate decision.

MRS. FRANK. [*Fearful.*] What is it?

[MR. KRALER *sits down on the couch. As he talks he takes bread, cabbages, milk, etc., from his briefcase, giving them to* MARGOT *and* ANNE *to put away.*]

MR. KRALER. Usually, when I come up here, I try to bring you some bit of good news. What's the use of telling you the bad news when there's nothing that you can do about it? But today something has happened . . . Dirk . . . Miep's Dirk, you know, came to me just now. He tells me that he has a Jewish friend living near him. A dentist. He says he's in trouble. He begged me, could I do anything for this man? Could I find him a hiding place? . . . So I've come to you . . . I know it's a terrible thing to ask of you, living as you are, but would you take him in with you?

---

12. Their faces are very serious and concerned (***grave***).

Practice the Skills

24 **Key Literary Element**

Act and Scene There is no actual scene break here, but notice the change in the "atmosphere" when Mr. Kraler makes a surprise visit.

MR. FRANK. Of course we will. **25**

MR. KRALER. [*Rising.*] It'll be just for a night or two . . . until I find some other place. This happened so suddenly that I didn't know where to turn.

MR. FRANK. Where is he?

MR. KRALER. Downstairs in the office.

MR. FRANK. Good. Bring him up.

MR. KRALER. His name is Dussel . . . Jan Dussel.[13]

MR. FRANK. Dussel . . . I think I know him.

MR. KRALER. I'll get him.

[*He goes quickly down the steps and out. MR. FRANK suddenly becomes conscious of the others.*]

MR. FRANK. Forgive me. I spoke without consulting you. But I knew you'd feel as I do.

MR. VAN DAAN. There's no reason for you to consult anyone. This is your place. You have a right to do exactly as you please. The only thing I feel . . . there's so little food as it is . . . and to take in another person . . . **26**

[*PETER turns away, ashamed of his father.*]

MR. FRANK. We can stretch the food a little. It's only for a few days.

MR. VAN DAAN. You want to make a bet?

MRS. FRANK. I think it's fine to have him. But, Otto, where are you going to put him? Where?

PETER. He can have my bed. I can sleep on the floor. I wouldn't mind.

MR. FRANK. That's good of you, Peter. But your room's too small . . . even for *you.*

13. *Jan Dussel* (yawn DOOS ul)

Practice the Skills

25 **Key Reading Skill**

Drawing Conclusions What does Mr. Frank's response show about his character?

26 **Key Reading Skill**

Drawing Conclusions What does Mr. Van Daan's response show about his character?

ANNE. I have a much better idea. I'll come in here with you and Mother, and Margot can take Peter's room and Peter can go in our room with Mr. Dussel.

MARGOT. That's right. We could do that.

MR. FRANK. No, Margot. You mustn't sleep in that room . . . neither you nor Anne. Mouschi has caught some rats in there. Peter's brave. He doesn't mind.

ANNE. Then how about this? I'll come in here with you and Mother, and Mr. Dussel can have my bed.

MRS. FRANK. No. No. No! Margot will come in here with us and he can have her bed. It's the only way. Margot, bring your things in here. Help her, Anne.

[MARGOT *hurries into her room to get her things.*]

ANNE. [*To her mother.*] Why Margot? Why can't I come in here?

MRS. FRANK. Because it wouldn't be proper for Margot to sleep with a . . . Please, Anne. Don't argue. Please.

[ANNE *starts slowly away.*]

MR. FRANK. [*To* ANNE.] You don't mind sharing your room with Mr. Dussel, do you, Anne?

ANNE. No. No, of course not. **27**

MR. FRANK. Good. [ANNE *goes off into her bedroom, helping* MARGOT. MR. FRANK *starts to search in the cupboards.*] Where's the cognac?[14]

MRS. FRANK. It's there. But, Otto, I was saving it in case of illness.

MR. FRANK. I think we couldn't find a better time to use it. Peter, will you get five glasses for me?

[PETER *goes for the glasses.* MARGOT *comes out of her bedroom, carrying her possessions, which she hangs behind a curtain in the main room.* MR. FRANK *finds the cognac and pours it into the five*

Practice the Skills

27 BIG Question

Think about the words and behavior of Peter and the four Franks in this part of the scene. How does their behavior relate to the Big Question? Write your answer on the Workshop 1 Foldable for Unit 6.

---

14. **Cognac** (KOHN yak) is an alcoholic drink.

glasses that PETER *brings him.* MR. VAN DAAN *stands looking on sourly.* MRS. VAN DAAN *comes downstairs and looks around at all the bustle.*]

MRS. VAN DAAN. What's happening? What's going on?

MR. VAN DAAN. Someone's moving in with us.

MRS. VAN DAAN. In here? You're joking.

MARGOT. It's only for a night or two . . . until Mr. Kraler finds him another place.

MR. VAN DAAN. Yeah! Yeah!

[MR. FRANK *hurries over as* MR. KRALER *and* DUSSEL *come up.* DUSSEL *is a man in his late fifties,* **meticulous,** *finicky . . . bewildered*[15] *now. He wears a raincoat. He carries a briefcase, stuffed full, and a small medicine case.*]

MR. FRANK. Come in, Mr. Dussel.

MR. KRALER. This is Mr. Frank.

DUSSEL. Mr. Otto Frank?

MR. FRANK. Yes. Let me take your things. [*He takes the hat and briefcase, but* DUSSEL *clings to his medicine case.*] This is my wife Edith . . . Mr. and Mrs. Van Daan . . . their son, Peter . . . and my daughters, Margot and Anne.

[DUSSEL *shakes hands with everyone.*]

MR. KRALER. Thank you, Mr. Frank. Thank you all. Mr. Dussel, I leave you in good hands. Oh . . . Dirk's coat.

[DUSSEL *hurriedly takes off the raincoat, giving it to* MR. KRALER. *Underneath is his white dentist's jacket, with a yellow Star of David on it.*] **28**

DUSSEL. [*To* MR. KRALER.] What can I say to thank you . . . ?

---

15. **Bewildered** (buh WIL durd) means "confused."

Vocabulary

meticulous (mih TIK yuh lus) *adj.* careful about small details

---

Practice the Skills

28 **Key Reading Skill**

Drawing Conclusions Why was Dussel wearing someone else's coat?

MRS. FRANK. [*To* DUSSEL.] Mr. Kraler and Miep . . . They're our life line. Without them we couldn't live.

MR. KRALER. Please. Please. You make us seem very heroic. It isn't that at all. We simply don't like the Nazis. [*To* MR. FRANK, *who offers him a drink.*] No, thanks. [*Then going on.*] We don't like their methods. We don't like . . .

MR. FRANK. [*Smiling.*] I know. I know. "No one's going to tell us Dutchmen what to do with our damn Jews!"

MR. KRALER. [*To* DUSSEL.] Pay no attention to Mr. Frank. I'll be up tomorrow to see that they're treating you right. [*To* MR. FRANK.] Don't trouble to come down again. Peter will bolt the door after me, won't you, Peter? **29**

PETER. Yes, sir.

MR. FRANK. Thank you, Peter. I'll do it.

MR. KRALER. Good night. Good night.

GROUP. Good night, Mr. Kraler.

We'll see you tomorrow, etc., etc.

[MR. KRALER *goes out with* MR. FRANK. MRS. FRANK *gives each one of the "grown-ups" a glass of cognac.*]

MRS. FRANK. Please, Mr. Dussel, sit down.

[MR. DUSSEL *sinks into a chair.* MRS. FRANK *gives him a glass of cognac.*]

DUSSEL. I'm dreaming. I know it. I can't believe my eyes. Mr. Otto Frank here! [*To* MRS. FRANK.] You're not in Switzerland then? A woman told me . . . She said she'd gone to your house . . . the door was open, everything was in disorder, dishes in the sink. She said she found a piece of paper in the wastebasket with an address scribbled on it . . . an address in Zurich.[16] She said you must have escaped to Zurich.

ANNE. Father put that there purposely . . . just so people would think that very thing!

DUSSEL. And you've been *here* all the time?

---

16. *Zurich* (ZOOR ik) is a city in Switzerland, a nation that remained neutral during the war.

Practice the Skills

29 **Reviewing Skills**

Analyzing Why does Mr. Frank make a joke at this point? How does Mr. Kraler respond to it? (Notice the remark about treating Dussel right. Is Mr. Kraler serious or making his own joke?)

MRS. FRANK. All the time . . . ever since July.

[*ANNE speaks to her father as he comes back.*]

ANNE. It worked, Pim . . . the address you left! Mr. Dussel says that people believe we escaped to Switzerland.

MR. FRANK. I'm glad. . . . And now let's have a little drink to welcome Mr. Dussel. [*Before they can drink, MR. DUSSEL bolts his drink. MR. FRANK smiles and raises his glass.*] To Mr. Dussel. Welcome. We're very honored to have you with us.

MRS. FRANK. To Mr. Dussel, welcome.

[*The VAN DAANS murmur a welcome. The "grown-ups" drink.*]

MRS. VAN DAAN. Um. That was good.

MR. VAN DAAN. Did Mr. Kraler warn you that you won't get much to eat here? You can imagine . . . three ration books among the seven of us . . . and now you make eight.

[*PETER walks away, humiliated.[17] Outside a street organ is heard dimly.*]

DUSSEL. [*Rising.*] Mr. Van Daan, you don't realize what is happening outside that you should warn me of a thing like that. You don't realize what's going on . . . [*As MR. VAN DAAN starts his characteristic pacing, DUSSEL turns to speak to the others.*] Right here in Amsterdam every day hundreds of Jews disappear . . . They surround a block and search house by house. Children come home from school to find their parents gone. Hundreds are being **deported** . . . people that you and I know . . . the Hallensteins . . . the Wessels . . . **30**

MRS. FRANK. [*In tears.*] Oh, no. No!

DUSSEL. They get their call-up notice . . . come to the Jewish theater on such and such a day and hour . . . bring only what

---

17. Peter is greatly embarrassed and ashamed (**humiliated**).

Practice the Skills

Fritz Pfeffer (Albert Dussel), 1930s.

30 **English Language Coach**

Word Parts The word **deport** includes the root *port* and the prefix *de–*, meaning "away." What does it mean?

you can carry in a rucksack. And if you refuse the call-up notice, then they come and drag you from your home and ship you off to Mauthausen.[18] The death camp! **31**

MRS. FRANK. We didn't know that things had got so much worse.

DUSSEL. Forgive me for speaking so.

ANNE. [*Coming to* DUSSEL.] Do you know the de Waals? . . . What's become of them? Their daughter Jopie and I are in the same class. Jopie's my best friend.

DUSSEL. They are gone.

ANNE. Gone?

DUSSEL. With all the others.

ANNE. Oh, no. Not Jopie!

[*She turns away, in tears.* MRS. FRANK *motions to* MARGOT *to comfort her.* MARGOT *goes to* ANNE, *putting her arms comfortingly around her.*]

MRS. VAN DAAN. There were some people called Wagner. They lived near us . . . ?

MR. FRANK. [*Interrupting, with a glance at* ANNE.] I think we should put this off until later. We all have many questions we want to ask . . . But I'm sure that Mr. Dussel would like to get settled before supper. **32**

DUSSEL. Thank you. I would. I brought very little with me.

MR. FRANK. [*Giving him his hat and briefcase.*] I'm sorry we can't give you a room alone. But I hope you won't be too uncomfortable. We've had to make strict rules here . . . a schedule of hours . . . We'll tell you after supper. Anne, would you like to take Mr. Dussel to his room?

ANNE. [*Controlling her tears.*] If you'll come with me, Mr. Dussel?

[*She starts for her room.*]

---

18. *Mauthausen* (MOWT how zun) was a Nazi camp in Austria.

Practice the Skills

31 **Reviewing Skills**

Comparing and Contrasting
How do problems inside the attic compare with the problems Jews on the outside are facing?

32 **Key Reading Skill**

Drawing Conclusions This time it's Mr. Frank who changes the subject. Why does he want to end this conversation?

DUSSEL. [*Shaking hands with each in turn.*] Forgive me if I haven't really expressed my gratitude to all of you. This has been such a shock to me. I'd always thought of myself as Dutch. I was born in Holland. My father was born in Holland, and my grandfather. And now . . . after all these years . . . [*He breaks off.*] If you'll excuse me.

[DUSSEL *gives a little bow and hurries off after* ANNE. MR. FRANK *and the others are subdued.*]

ANNE. [*Turning on the light.*] Well, here we are.

[DUSSEL *looks around the room. In the main room* MARGOT *speaks to her mother.*]

MARGOT. The news sounds pretty bad, doesn't it? It's so different from what Mr. Kraler tells us. Mr. Kraler says things are improving.

MR. VAN DAAN. I like it better the way Kraler tells it.

[*They resume their occupations, quietly.* PETER *goes off into his room. In* ANNE's *room,* ANNE *turns to* DUSSEL.]

ANNE. You're going to share the room with me.

DUSSEL. I'm a man who's always lived alone. I haven't had to adjust myself to others. I hope you'll bear with me until I learn. **33**

ANNE. Let me help you. [*She takes his briefcase.*] Do you always live all alone? Have you no family at all?

DUSSEL. No one.

[*He opens his medicine case and spreads his bottles on the dressing table.*]

ANNE. How dreadful. You must be terribly lonely.

DUSSEL. I'm used to it.

ANNE. I don't think I could ever get used to it. Didn't you even have a pet? A cat, or a dog?

DUSSEL. I have an allergy for fur-bearing animals. They give me asthma.

Practice the Skills

33 | **Key Reading Skill**

Drawing Conclusions Will Dussel be a good roommate? Why or why not?

ANNE. Oh, dear. Peter has a cat.

DUSSEL. Here? He has it here?

ANNE. Yes. But we hardly ever see it. He keeps it in his room all the time. I'm sure it will be all right.

DUSSEL. Let us hope so.

[*He takes some pills to* **_fortify_** *himself.*] **34**

ANNE. That's Margot's bed, where you're going to sleep. I sleep on the sofa there. [*Indicating the clothes hooks on the wall.*] We cleared these off for your things. [*She goes over to the window.*] The best part about this room . . . you can look down and see a bit of the street and the canal. There's a houseboat . . . you can see the end of it . . . a bargeman lives there with his family . . . They have a baby and he's just beginning to walk and I'm so afraid he's going to fall into the canal some day. I watch him. . . . **35**

DUSSEL. [*Interrupting.*] Your father spoke of a schedule.

ANNE. [*Coming away from the window.*] Oh, yes. It's mostly about the times we have to be quiet. And times for the w.c. You can use it now if you like.

DUSSEL. [*Stiffly.*] No, thank you.

ANNE. I suppose you think it's awful, my talking about a thing like that. But you don't know how important it can get to be, especially when you're frightened . . . About this room, the way Margot and I did . . . she had it to herself in the afternoons for studying, reading . . . lessons, you know . . . and I took the mornings. Would that be all right with you?

DUSSEL. I'm not at my best in the morning.

ANNE. You stay here in the mornings then. I'll take the room in the afternoons.

DUSSEL. Tell me, when you're in here, what happens to me? Where am I spending my time? In there, with all the people?

ANNE. Yes.

Practice the Skills

34 | **English Language Coach**

Word Parts The suffix *–ify* means "to make or cause to be." Look at the chart of roots to see the meaning of *fort*.

35 ✓ **BIG Question**

What, for Anne, is the "best part" about the room? How does it help her? Write your answer on the Workshop 1 Foldable for Unit 6. Your response will help you complete the Unit Challenge later.

DUSSEL. I see. I see.

ANNE. We have supper at half past six.

DUSSEL. [*Going over to the sofa.*] Then, if you don't mind . . . I like to lie down quietly for ten minutes before eating. I find it helps the digestion.

ANNE. Of course. I hope I'm not going to be too much of a bother to you. I seem to be able to get everyone's back up.

[*DUSSEL lies down on the sofa, curled up, his back to her.*]

DUSSEL. I always get along very well with children. My patients all bring their children to me, because they know I get on well with them. So don't you worry about that. **36**

[*ANNE leans over him, taking his hand and shaking it gratefully.*]

ANNE. Thank you. Thank you, Mr. Dussel.

[*The lights dim to darkness. The curtain falls on the scene. ANNE'S VOICE comes to us faintly at first, and then with increasing power.*] **37**

ANNE'S VOICE. . . . And yesterday I finished Cissy Van Marxvelt's latest book. I think she is a first-class writer. I shall definitely let my children read her. Monday the twenty-first of September, nineteen forty-two. Mr. Dussel and I had another battle yesterday. Yes, Mr. Dussel! According to him, nothing, I repeat . . . nothing, is right about me . . . my appearance, my character, my manners. While he was going on at me I thought . . . sometime I'll give you such a smack that you'll fly right up to the ceiling! Why is it that every grown-up thinks he knows the way to bring up children? Particularly the grown-ups that never had any. I keep wishing that Peter was a girl instead of a boy. Then I would have someone to talk to. Margot's a darling, but she takes everything too seriously. To pause for a moment on the subject of Mrs. Van Daan. I must tell you that her attempts to flirt with father are getting her nowhere. Pim, thank goodness, won't play.

[*As she is saying the last lines, the curtain rises on the darkened scene. ANNE'S VOICE fades out.*]

Practice the Skills

36 Reviewing Skills

Comparing and Contrasting Describe ways in which Anne and Dussel are different from one another. Do you see any similarities?

37 Key Literary Element

Act and Scene Each between-scenes reading provides helpful information. Sometimes, as in this one, there are details that don't relate to the action but tell us about Anne or another character. In each reading, Anne gives a date, which is the date of the next scene. Often, there's a summary of things that happened since the last scene. Why do the playwrights provide so much information in these readings?

After You Read

The Diary of Anne Frank, Act 1, Scene 3

Answering the BIG Question

1. What problems, challenges, and dangers do the characters face?
2. **Recall** Why does Peter call Anne "Mrs. Quack Quack"?
   - **Tip** Right There
3. **Describe** Tell what happened to Mrs. Van Daan's fur coat and how she reacted.
   - **Tip** Think and Search

Critical Thinking

4. **Analyze** In addition to the problems that come with hiding, Anne has to grow up with no friends her own age. What are some of the things she does to keep herself going?
   - **Tip** Think and Search
5. **Analyze** Identify one thing each of these characters does to keep from giving up: Mr. Frank, Mrs. Frank, Margot, Peter, and Mr. Kraler.
   - **Tip** Think and Search
6. **Infer** How does Peter feel about his parents? How does he feel about Anne? Explain.
   - **Tip** Author and Me
7. **Predict** Dussel describes terrible things going on in Amsterdam. How do you think this information will affect the Franks and the Van Daans?
   - **Tip** Author and Me
8. **Analyze** Review Mr. Van Daan's ideas about the kind of girl men like (p. 748). Would you say that his wife fits this description? Explain.
9. **Evaluate** Do you think Mrs. Frank and Mr. Frank would like Anne to be more like Margot? Explain.
   - **Tip** Author and Me

Talk About Your Reading

Literature Discussion Throughout the play so far, Anne shows more interest in the outside world than the other characters do. With a small group, find examples of this contrast between Anne and the other characters in the first three scenes. Then discuss possible reasons that Anne has for her interest and that the others have for not showing similar interest.

NY English Language Arts Core Curriculum (pp. 762–763)

LC R17 Demonstrate comprehension and response through a range of activities. **LC R14** Work collaboratively with peers to comprehend and respond to texts. **LC S1** Speak to share responses. **R1I** Draw conclusion on the basis of explicit and implied information. **Core R4** Determine the meaning of words by using structural analysis. **Core W7** Observe rules of punctuation.

For a complete description of the standards, see p. NY 11.

Skills Review

Key Reading Skill: Drawing Conclusions

10. By now, you should have drawn a lot of conclusions about the people living in the Annex, as well as the people who are helping them. Choose one of the characters and explain some things you have concluded about that character.

11. Do you think drawing conclusions about the people in the play helps you predict what will come next? Why or why not?

Key Literary Element: Act and Scene

12. Why do you think the play has two acts, instead of going nonstop from beginning to end?

13. In this play so far, what is the one thing that always changes when a scene changes? Explain.

Reviewing Skills: Analyzing; Comparing and Contrasting

14. Mr. Kraler's news of the "outside world" is somewhat different from Dussel's. What reasons would Mr. Kraler have for saying things are improving?

15. Compare the two sets of parents, noting at least one way they're alike as well as ways they're not.

Vocabulary Check

Match the vocabulary words with their best synonyms.

**self-conscious absurd vile mimics
aggravating bickering meticulous**

16. nasty

17. arguing

18. ridiculous

19. fussy

20. annoying

21. imitates

22. uncomfortable

23. English Language Coach What is the root of the word *demand*? (You may look it up.) What's another English word from the same root?

Grammar Link: Commas in a Series

A comma is used to separate a series of three or more words, phrases, or clauses. Place commas between items in the series.

- Clams, shrimp, and crabs are types of shellfish.
- Cioppino is a stew made with fish, clams, crabs, scallops, and a flavorful tomato-based broth.
- We collected 11 boxes of crackers, 30 cans of vegetables, and 15 cans of soup for the shelter.
- I looked in the car, outside the house, and under the deck for my bat.
- Study your lines for the play when you're in study hall, while you walk home, and after you finish dinner.

The comma before the last item in a series may be left out unless it is necessary to make the meaning clear.

> **Unclear:** I ate salad, grilled cheese and cake.
>
> **Clear:** I ate salad, grilled cheese, and cake.

You do not need commas in a series when a coordinating conjunction is repeated between items.

- The deer <u>and</u> the birds <u>and</u> the rabbits all seemed to know that a storm was coming.

Grammar Practice

Copy the paragraph below, adding three commas in the appropriate places.

> Our flight is booked the suitcases are packed and we're ready to leave for Florida. I want to taste fresh grapefruits oranges, and lemons. I love the sand and rolling waves and salt air.

Web Activities For eFlashcards, Selection Quick Checks, and other Web activities, go to www.glencoe.com.

Before You Read

The Diary of Anne Frank, Act 1, Scenes 4–5

Vocabulary Preview

makeshift (MAYK shift) *adj.* used in place of the normal or proper thing **(p. 766)** *The couch in the main room served as a makeshift bed for Mr. and Mrs. Frank.*

wallow (WAH loh) *v.* to take selfish pleasure in comfort **(p. 772)** *Anne wanted to wallow in a tub full of warm, soapy water.*

sustenance (SUS tuh nuns) *n.* food, support, and other necessities of life **(p. 773)** *Miep provided as much sustenance for the families as she could; she was their lifeline.*

jubilation (joo buh LAY shun) *n.* great joy and excitement **(p. 780)** *They all tried to show the usual holiday jubilation, despite their terrible situation.*

uncertainty (un SUR tun tee) *n.* the state of being unsure or not knowing **(p. 783)** *Even worse than being cut off from the outside world was their uncertainty about their future in that world.*

Write to Learn Use each vocabulary word correctly in a sentence about some part of your life. The sentences do not have to relate to one another.

English Language Coach

Historical Influences on English In the history of civilization, English is a fairly new language. As a new kid on the block, English has been influenced by many other languages.

Many English words have roots in Latin, Greek, and Anglo-Saxon. The following roots and their meanings can help you figure out the definitions of many words. (Sometimes the spellings of the roots change.)

Root	Origin	Meaning	Word Example
sanct	Latin	holy	sanctuary
cycle	Greek	circle	bicycle
knack	Anglo-Saxon	strike	knocking
logue	Greek	speech, word	dialogue

In literature, a dialogue (DY uh log) is a conversation between characters. The Greek prefix *dia-* means "through" or "across." A monologue (MON uh log) is a long, uninterrupted speech by one character. The Greek prefix *mono-* means "single" or "alone."

Partner Talk With a partner, talk about other word examples that come from the roots above.

NY English Language Arts Core Curriculum (pp. 764–787)

Core R4 Determine the meaning of words by using structural analysis. **R11** Draw conclusions on the basis of explicit and implied information. **LC R13** Use text structure and literary devices to aid comprehension and response.

For a complete description of the standards, see p. NY 11.

Skills Preview

Key Reading Skill: Drawing Conclusions

One of the most important steps in drawing conclusions is to read carefully. Good readers train themselves to notice details in a story. Then they think about whether those details mean more than the author is telling them. As you read further in "The Diary of Anne Frank," use these questions to help you pay attention to the details you need to draw conclusions.

- What is important to each character?
- Is anyone hiding anything?
- Does the news from outside change?

Write to Learn Who would you say is having the hardest time adjusting to life in hiding? Write your answer in a paragraph in your Learner's Notebook. Use details from the play to support your choice.

Key Literary Element: Dialogue and Monologue

Dialogue is conversation between characters. **Monologue** is a long, uninterrupted speech by one character. Like conversation in a story, dialogue and monologue in a drama provide important information about characters, events, and ideas. In a story, each speaker's part of a dialogue is enclosed in quotation marks. Since all or most of a drama is conversation, quotation marks are not used in a play script. Instead, as you've seen, the speaker's name is always given before his or her speech.

You've already read quite a lot of dialogue, of course. You've also read a few monologues. In scene 2, for example, Mr. Frank goes on for a long time about the need to avoid making noise.

At the end of each scene, Anne's voice reads from her diary. These readings represent a different sort of monologue. In them, Anne expresses thoughts and feelings that she can't or won't tell other people in conversation. These speeches also give the audience (and readers) a flavor of Anne Frank's actual diary.

Partner Work With a partner, locate every monologue spoken by a character in scene 3. (Not everyone has one in that scene.)

Get Ready to Read

Connect to the Reading

Think about a time when you had to get along with difficult people. Was it a struggle? Did you want to give up? Anne Frank knew that her hope for the future depended on her ability to get along with the other people. As you read scenes 4 and 5, think about what you might have done in her place.

Write to Learn Briefly describe a time when you had trouble getting along with someone else. Explain how you acted and why.

Build Background

Anne Frank's diary shows the awful events of the day through the eyes of a teenager.

- The diary covers the period from June 12, 1942, to August 1, 1944.
- After the war the diary was translated into more than sixty languages, making Anne one of the most memorable figures to emerge from World War II.

Set Purposes for Reading

BIG Question Read act 1, scenes 4–5, of *The Diary of Anne Frank* to discover how Anne manages to keep from giving up during hard times.

Set Your Own Purpose What would you like to learn from the play to help you answer the Big Question? Write your own purpose on the Reading Workshop 1 Foldable for Unit 6.

Literature Online

Interactive Literary Elements Handbook
To review or learn more about the literary elements, go to www.glencoe.com.

Keep Moving

Use these skills as you read the following selection.

SCENE 4

Practice the Skills

[*It is the middle of the night, several months later. The stage is dark except for a little light which comes through the skylight in* PETER'*s room.*

Everyone is in bed. MR. *and* MRS. FRANK *lie on the couch in the main room, which has been pulled out to serve as a* **makeshift** *double bed.*

MARGOT *is sleeping on a mattress on the floor in the main room, behind a curtain stretched across for privacy. The others are all in their accustomed rooms.*

From outside we hear two drunken soldiers singing "Lili Marlene." A girl's high giggle is heard. The sound of running feet is heard coming closer and then fading in the distance. Throughout the scene there is the distant sound of airplanes passing overhead. A match suddenly flares up in the attic. We dimly see MR. VAN DAAN. *He is getting his bearings.*[1] *He comes quickly down the stairs, and goes to the cupboard where the food is stored. Again the match flares up, and is as quickly blown out. The dim figure is seen to steal back up the stairs.* ◼

There is quiet for a second or two, broken only by the sound of airplanes, and running feet on the street below.

Suddenly, out of the silence and the dark, we hear ANNE *scream.*]

ANNE. [*Screaming.*] No! No! Don't . . . don't take me!

[*She moans, tossing and crying in her sleep. The other people wake, terrified.* DUSSEL *sits up in bed, furious.*]

DUSSEL. Shush! Anne! Anne, for God's sake, shush!

ANNE. [*Still in her nightmare.*] Save me! Save me!

[*She screams and screams.* DUSSEL *gets out of bed, going over to her, trying to wake her.*]

◼ Key Reading Skill

Drawing Conclusions There isn't enough solid information to draw a conclusion about what Mr. Van Daan is doing. For now, remember this part; it'll be useful in act 2.

---

1. When Mr. Van Daan is **getting his bearings,** he's figuring out his position in the dimly lit room and deciding where to go.

Vocabulary

makeshift (MAYK shift) *adj.* used in place of the normal or proper thing

Margot (left) and Anne, 1933.

DUSSEL. For God's sake! Quiet! Quiet! You want someone to hear? **2**

[*In the main room* MRS. FRANK *grabs a shawl and pulls it around her. She rushes in to* ANNE, *taking her in her arms.* MR. FRANK *hurriedly gets up, putting on his overcoat.* MARGOT *sits up, terrified.* PETER's *light goes on in his room.*]

2 | **Key Reading Skill**

Drawing Conclusions What does Dussel's reaction to Anne's cries tell you about him?

MRS. FRANK. [*To* ANNE, *in her room.*] Hush, darling, hush. It's all right. It's all right. [*Over her shoulder to* DUSSEL.] Will you be kind enough to turn on the light, Mr. Dussel? [*Back to* ANNE.] It's nothing, my darling. It was just a dream.

[DUSSEL *turns on the light in the bedroom.* MRS. FRANK *holds* ANNE *in her arms. Gradually* ANNE *comes out of her nightmare, still trembling with horror.* MR. FRANK *comes into the room, and goes quickly to the window, looking out to be sure that no one outside has heard* ANNE'S *screams.* MRS. FRANK *holds* ANNE, *talking softly to her. In the main room* MARGOT *stands on a chair, turning on the center hanging lamp. A light goes on in the* VAN DAANS' *room overhead.* PETER *puts his robe on, coming out of his room.*]

DUSSEL. [*To* MRS. FRANK, *blowing his nose.*] Something must be done about that child, Mrs. Frank. Yelling like that! Who knows but there's somebody on the streets? She's endangering all our lives.

MRS. FRANK. Anne, darling.

DUSSEL. Every night she twists and turns. I don't sleep. I spend half my night shushing her. And now it's nightmares! **3**

[MARGOT *comes to the door of* ANNE'S *room, followed by* PETER. MR. FRANK *goes to them, indicating that everything is all right.* PETER *takes* MARGOT *back.*]

MRS. FRANK. [*To* ANNE.] You're here, safe, you see? Nothing has happened. [*To* DUSSEL.] Please, Mr. Dussel, go back to bed. She'll be herself in a minute or two. Won't you, Anne?

DUSSEL. [*Picking up a book and a pillow.*] Thank you, but I'm going to the w.c. The one place where there's peace!

[*He stalks out.* MR. VAN DAAN, *in underwear and trousers, comes down the stairs.*]

MR. VAN DAAN. [*To* DUSSEL.] What is it? What happened?

DUSSEL. A nightmare. She was having a nightmare!

3 | **Key Reading Skill**

Drawing Conclusions Why is Anne having nightmares now? Do you think there's a specific cause, or is it the situation in general?

MR. VAN DAAN. I thought someone was murdering her.

DUSSEL. Unfortunately, no.

[*He goes into the bathroom.* MR. VAN DAAN *goes back up the stairs.* MR. FRANK, *in the main room, sends* PETER *back to his own bedroom.*]

MR. FRANK. Thank you, Peter. Go back to bed.

[PETER *goes back to his room.* MR. FRANK *follows him, turning out the light and looking out the window. Then he goes back to the main room, and gets up on a chair, turning out the center hanging lamp.*]

MRS. FRANK. [*To* ANNE.] Would you like some water? [ANNE *shakes her head.*] Was it a very bad dream? Perhaps if you told me . . . ?

ANNE. I'd rather not talk about it.

MRS. FRANK. Poor darling. Try to sleep then. I'll sit right here beside you until you fall asleep.

[*She brings a stool over, sitting there.*]

ANNE. You don't have to.

MRS. FRANK. But I'd like to stay with you . . . very much. Really.

ANNE. I'd rather you didn't.

MRS. FRANK. Good night, then. [*She leans down to kiss* ANNE. ANNE *throws her arm up over her face, turning away.* MRS. FRANK, *hiding her hurt, kisses* ANNE'S *arm.*] You'll be all right? There's nothing that you want?

ANNE. Will you please ask Father to come. 🔳

MRS. FRANK. [*After a second.*] Of course, Anne dear. [*She hurries out into the other room.* MR. FRANK *comes to her as she comes in.*] Sie verlangt nach Dir!

MR. FRANK. [*Sensing her hurt.*] Edith, Liebe, schau . . .

MRS. FRANK. Es macht nichts! Ich danke dem lieben Herrgott, dass sie sich wenigstens an Dich wendet, wenn sie Trost

Practice the Skills

🔳 **Key Reading Skill**

Drawing Conclusions Why does Anne respond to her mother as she does here? How do you suppose this makes Mrs. Frank feel?

braucht! Geh hinein, Otto, sie ist ganz hysterisch vor Angst. [*As* MR. FRANK *hesitates.*] Geh zu ihr.[2] [*He looks at her for a second and then goes to get a cup of water for* ANNE. MRS. FRANK *sinks down on the bed, her face in her hands, trying to keep from sobbing aloud.* MARGOT *comes over to her, putting her arms around her.*] She wants nothing of me. She pulled away when I leaned down to kiss her. **5**

MARGOT. It's a phase . . . You heard Father . . . Most girls go through it . . . they turn to their fathers at this age . . . they give all their love to their fathers.

MRS. FRANK. You weren't like this. You didn't shut me out.

MARGOT. She'll get over it . . .

[*She smooths the bed for* MRS. FRANK *and sits beside her a moment as* MRS. FRANK *lies down. In* ANNE'*s room* MR. FRANK *comes in, sitting down by* ANNE. ANNE *flings her arms around him, clinging to him. In the distance we hear the sound of ack-ack.*]

ANNE. Oh, Pim. I dreamed that they came to get us! The Green Police! They broke down the door and grabbed me and started to drag me out the way they did Jopie.

MR. FRANK. I want you to take this pill.

ANNE. What is it?

MR. FRANK. Something to quiet you.

[*She takes it and drinks the water. In the main room* MARGOT *turns out the light and goes back to her bed.*]

MR. FRANK. [*To* ANNE.] Do you want me to read to you for a while?

ANNE. No. Just sit with me for a minute. Was I awful? Did I yell terribly loud? Do you think anyone outside could have heard?

MR. FRANK. No. No. Lie quietly now. Try to sleep.

Practice the Skills

5 **Key Literary Element**

Dialogue and Monologue
Why did the playwrights have Mr. and Mrs. Frank speak in German here? How could theatergoers who don't know German (and don't have a footnoted translation) get the ideas expressed in this conversation?

---

2. The Franks' conversation in German translates as follows: MRS. FRANK. "She wanted to see you!" MR. FRANK. "Edith, dear, look . . ." MRS. FRANK. "It's all right! Thank God that at least she turns to you when she is in need of comfort. Go in, Otto, she is hysterical with fear. Go to her."

ANNE. I'm a terrible coward. I'm so disappointed in myself. I think I've conquered my fear . . . I think I'm really grown-up . . . and then something happens . . . and I run to you like a baby . . . I love you, Father. I don't love anyone but you. **6**

MR. FRANK. [*Reproachfully.*] Annele!

ANNE. It's true. I've been thinking about it for a long time. You're the only one I love.

MR. FRANK. It's fine to hear you tell me that you love me. But I'd be happier if you said you loved your mother as well . . . She needs your help so much . . . your love . . .

ANNE. We have nothing in common. She doesn't understand me. Whenever I try to explain my views on life to her she asks me if I'm constipated.

MR. FRANK. You hurt her very much just now. She's crying. She's in there crying.

ANNE. I can't help it. I only told the truth. I didn't want her here . . . [*Then, with sudden change.*] Oh, Pim, I was horrible, wasn't I? And the worst of it is, I can stand off and look at myself doing it and know it's cruel and yet I can't stop doing it. What's the matter with me? Tell me. Don't say it's just a phase! Help me.

MR. FRANK. There is so little that we parents can do to help our children. We can only try to set a good example . . . point the way. The rest you must do yourself. You must build your own character.

ANNE. I'm trying. Really I am. Every night I think back over all of the things I did that day that were wrong . . . like putting the wet mop in Mr. Dussel's bed . . . and this thing now with Mother. I say to myself, that was wrong. I make up my mind, I'm never going to do that again. Never! Of course I may do something worse . . . but at least I'll never do *that* again! . . . I have a nicer side, Father . . . a sweeter, nicer side. But I'm scared to show it. I'm afraid that people are going to laugh at me if I'm serious. So the mean Anne comes to the outside and the good Anne stays on the inside, and I keep on trying to switch them around and have the good Anne

Practice the Skills

6 **Reviewing Skills**

Connecting It's been several months since Anne heard about her friend, but the nightmare suggests that she's more upset than she realized. Do you think that makes her a "terrible coward"? How would you react to similar news?

outside and the bad Anne inside and be what I'd like to be . . . and might be . . . if only . . . only . . . **7**

[*She is asleep.* MR. FRANK *watches her for a moment and then turns off the light, and starts out. The lights dim out. The curtain falls on the scene.* ANNE'S VOICE *is heard dimly at first, and then with growing strength.*]

ANNE'S VOICE. . . . The air raids are getting worse. They come over day and night. The noise is terrifying. Pim says it should be music to our ears. The more planes, the sooner will come the end of the war. Mrs. Van Daan pretends to be a fatalist.[3] What will be, will be. But when the planes come over, who is the most frightened? No one else but Petronella! . . . **8** Monday, the ninth of November, nineteen forty-two. Wonderful news! The Allies have landed in Africa. Pim says that we can look for an early finish to the war. Just for fun he asked each of us what was the first thing we wanted to do when we got out of here. Mrs. Van Daan longs to be home with her own things, her needle-point chairs, the Beckstein piano her father gave her . . . the best that money could buy. Peter would like to go to a movie. Mr. Dussel wants to get back to his dentist's drill. He's afraid he is losing his touch. For myself, there are so many things . . . to ride a bike again . . . to laugh till my belly aches . . . to have new clothes from the skin out . . . to have a hot tub filled to overflowing and **wallow** in it for hours . . . to be back in school with my friends . . . **9**

[*As the last lines are being said, the curtain rises on the scene. The lights dim on as* ANNE'S VOICE *fades away.*]

Practice the Skills

7 Key Literary Element

Dialogue and Monologue A monologue often reveals a great deal about the speaker. Why, do you think, is Anne so open and honest about herself here?

8 Key Reading Skill

Drawing Conclusions Judging from the first few lines of this speech, who is conducting these air raids—the Allies or Germany? Why does Mr. Frank say their noise should be "music to our ears"?

9 Key Reading Skill

Drawing Conclusions What do the responses to Mr. Frank's question tell you about these characters?

---

3. A *fatalist* (FAY tul ist) is someone who believes that fate controls everything that happens.

Vocabulary

wallow (WAH loh) *v.* to take selfish pleasure in comfort

SCENE 5

[*It is the first night of the Hanukkah celebration.* MR. FRANK *is standing at the head of the table on which is the Menorah. He lights the Shamos, or servant candle, and holds it as he says the blessing. Seated listening is all of the "family," dressed in their best. The men wear hats,* PETER *wears his cap.*[4]]

MR. FRANK. [*Reading from a prayer book.*] "Praised be Thou, oh Lord our God, Ruler of the universe, who has **sanctified** us with Thy commandments and bidden us kindle the Hanukkah lights. **10** Praised be Thou, oh Lord our God, Ruler of the universe, who has wrought wondrous deliverances for our fathers in days of old. Praised be Thou, oh Lord our God, Ruler of the universe, that Thou has given us life and **sustenance** and brought us to this happy season." [MR. FRANK *lights the one candle of the Menorah as he continues.*] "We kindle this Hanukkah light to celebrate the great and wonderful deeds wrought through the zeal with which God filled the hearts of the heroic Maccabees, two thousand years ago. They fought against indifference, against tyranny and oppression, and they restored our Temple to us.[5] May these lights remind us that we should ever look to God, whence cometh our help." Amen. [*Pronounced O-mayn.*]

ALL. Amen.

[MR. FRANK *hands* MRS. FRANK *the prayer book.*]

Visual Vocabulary
The **Menorah**
(muh NOR uh) is a
candlestick with nine
branches.

10 **English Language Coach**

Historical Influences Look at the word **sanctified**. It's a form of the verb *sanctify*. The suffix *–ify* can mean "to give a certain quality." Review the chart on page 764 to remember the meaning of the root *sanct*. What do you think *sanctify* means?

---

4. The eight-day Jewish holiday **Hanukkah** (HAW nuh kuh) is celebrated in December. It honors the Jews' victory over Syrian enemies in 165 B.C. One candle of the Menorah is called the **Shamos** (SHAW mus), or **servant candle,** because it's used to light the others. Jewish males wear some sort of hat during religious services and ceremonies. In the next few speeches, Mr. and Mrs. Frank read traditional Hanukkah blessings and prayers.

5. It was the **Maccabees,** a family of Jewish patriots, who led the Jews in their fight against the Syrians' cruel and unjust use of power **(tyranny and oppression).**

Vocabulary

sustenance (SUS tuh nuns) *n.* food, support, and other necessities of life

Practice the Skills

MRS. FRANK. [*Reading.*] "I lift up mine eyes unto the mountains, from whence cometh my help. My help cometh from the Lord who made heaven and earth. He will not suffer thy foot to be moved. He that keepeth thee will not slumber. He that keepeth Israel doth neither slumber nor sleep. The Lord is thy keeper. The Lord is thy shade upon thy right hand. The sun shall not smite thee by day, nor the moon by night. The Lord shall keep thee from all evil. He shall keep thy soul. The Lord shall guard thy going out and thy coming in, from this time forth and forevermore." Amen. **11**

ALL. Amen.

[*MRS. FRANK puts down the prayer book and goes to get the food and wine. MARGOT helps her. MR. FRANK takes the men's hats and puts them aside.*]

DUSSEL. [*Rising.*] That was very moving.

ANNE. [*Pulling him back.*] It isn't over yet!

MRS. VAN DAAN. Sit down! Sit down!

ANNE. There's a lot more, songs and presents.

DUSSEL. Presents?

MRS. FRANK. Not this year, unfortunately.

MRS. VAN DAAN. But always on Hanukkah everyone gives presents . . . everyone!

DUSSEL. Like our St. Nicholas' Day.⁶

[*There is a chorus of "no's" from the group.*]

MRS. VAN DAAN. No! Not like St. Nicholas! What kind of a Jew are you that you don't know Hanukkah? **12**

MRS. FRANK. [*As she brings the food.*] I remember particularly the candles . . . First one, as we have tonight. Then the second night you light two candles, the next night three . . . and so on until you have eight candles burning. When there are eight candles it is truly beautiful.

11 **Reviewing Skills**

Monitoring Comprehension
After reading formal and difficult language, it's a good idea to monitor your comprehension. Ask yourself whether you understand what the prayers say.

12 **Key Reading Skill**

Drawing Conclusions What can you conclude from Dussel's questions and comments about his knowledge of Judaism?

---

6. In the Netherlands, Christian children receive gifts from **St. Nicholas** on December 6.

MRS. VAN DAAN. And the potato pancakes.

MR. VAN DAAN. Don't talk about them!

MRS. VAN DAAN. I make the best *latkes*[7] you ever tasted!

MRS. FRANK. Invite us all next year . . . in your own home.

MR. FRANK. God willing!

MRS. VAN DAAN. God willing.

MARGOT. What I remember best is the presents we used to get when we were little . . . eight days of presents . . . and each day they got better and better.

MRS. FRANK. [*Sitting down.*] We are all here, alive. That is present enough. **13**

ANNE. No, it isn't. I've got something . . .

[*She rushes into her room, hurriedly puts on a little hat improvised from the lamp shade, grabs a satchel bulging with parcels and comes running back.*]

MRS. FRANK. What is it?

ANNE. Presents!

MRS. VAN DAAN. Presents!

DUSSEL. Look!

MR. VAN DAAN. What's she got on her head?

PETER. A lamp shade!

ANNE. [*She picks out one at random.*] This is for Margot. [*She hands it to* MARGOT, *pulling her to her feet.*] Read it out loud.

MARGOT. [*Reading.*]

"You have never lost your temper.
You never will, I fear,
You are so good.
But if you should,
Put all your cross words here." **14**

---

7. *Latkes* (LOT kuz) are potato pancakes.

Practice the Skills

13 **BIG Question**

Do you think the characters should be celebrating Hanukkah despite their situation? What value do religion and tradition have in helping people through hard times? Write your thoughts on the Workshop 1 Foldable for Unit 6. Your response will help you complete the Unit Challenge later.

14 **Reviewing Skills**

Analyzing Anne's poem pokes fun at Margot's "perfect" behavior. What does it tell you about Anne?

[*She tears open the package.*] A new crossword puzzle book! Where did you get it?

ANNE. It isn't new. It's one that you've done. But I rubbed it all out, and if you wait a little and forget, you can do it all over again.

MARGOT. [*Sitting.*] It's wonderful, Anne. Thank you. You'd never know it wasn't new.

[*From outside we hear the sound of a streetcar passing.*]

ANNE. [*With another gift.*] Mrs. Van Daan.

MRS. VAN DAAN. [*Taking it.*] This is awful . . . I haven't anything for anyone . . . I never thought . . .

MR. FRANK. This is all Anne's idea. **15**

MRS. VAN DAAN. [*Holding up a bottle.*] What is it?

ANNE. It's hair shampoo. I took all the odds and ends of soap and mixed them with the last of my toilet water.[8]

MRS. VAN DAAN. Oh, Anneke!

ANNE. I wanted to write a poem for all of them, but I didn't have time. [*Offering a large box to* MR. VAN DAAN.] Yours, Mr. Van Daan, is really something . . . something you want more than anything. [*As she waits for him to open it.*] Look! Cigarettes!

MR. VAN DAAN. Cigarettes!

ANNE. Two of them! Pim found some old pipe tobacco in the pocket lining of his coat . . . and we made them . . . or rather, Pim did.

MRS. VAN DAAN. Let me see . . . Well, look at that! Light it, Putti! Light it.

[MR. VAN DAAN *hesitates.*]

ANNE. It's tobacco, really it is! There's a little fluff in it, but not much. **16**

---

8. **Toilet water** is a lightly scented liquid used as a perfume.

Practice the Skills

15 **Key Reading Skill**

Drawing Conclusions Why does Mr. Frank make a point of saying this?

16 **Key Literary Element**

Dialogue and Monologue In good dialogue, the characters speak in ways that suit their personalities. For example, Anne talks often, at length, and with strong feeling. How do those things match her personality? As you read, notice how the other characters speak and imagine how they sound.

[*Everyone watches intently as* MR. VAN DAAN *cautiously lights it. The cigarette flares up. Everyone laughs.*]

PETER. It works!

MRS. VAN DAAN. Look at him.

MR. VAN DAAN. [*Spluttering.*] Thank you, Anne. Thank you.

[ANNE *rushes back to her satchel for another present.*]

ANNE. [*Handing her mother a piece of paper.*] For Mother, Hanukkah greeting.

[*She pulls her mother to her feet.*]

MRS. FRANK. [*She reads.*] "Here's an I.O.U. that I promise to pay. Ten hours of doing whatever you say. Signed, Anne Frank."

[MRS. FRANK, *touched, takes* ANNE *in her arms, holding her close.*]

DUSSEL. [*To* ANNE.] Ten hours of doing what you're told? Anything you're told?

ANNE. That's right.

DUSSEL. You wouldn't want to sell that, Mrs. Frank?

MRS. FRANK. Never! This is the most precious gift I've ever had! **17**

[*She sits, showing her present to the others.* ANNE *hurries back to the satchel and pulls out a scarf, the scarf that* MR. FRANK *found in the first scene.*]

ANNE. [*Offering it to her father.*] For Pim.

MR. FRANK. Anneke . . . I wasn't supposed to have a present!

[*He takes it, unfolding it and showing it to the others.*]

ANNE. It's a muffler . . . to put round your neck . . . like an ascot, you know. I made it myself out of odds and ends . . . I knitted it in the dark each night, after I'd gone to bed. I'm afraid it looks better in the dark!

MR. FRANK. [*Putting it on.*] It's fine. It fits me perfectly. Thank you, Annele.

Practice the Skills

17 **Key Reading Skill**

Drawing Conclusions Why is Anne's gift to her mother particularly important and touching? Explain.

[ANNE *hands* PETER *a ball of paper, with a string attached to it.*]

ANNE. That's for Mouschi.

PETER. [*Rising to bow.*] On behalf of Mouschi, I thank you.

ANNE. [*Hesitant, handing him a gift.*] And . . . this is yours . . . from Mrs. Quack Quack. [*As he holds it gingerly*[9] *in his hands.*] Well . . . open it . . . Aren't you going to open it?

PETER. I'm scared to. I know something's going to jump out and hit me.

ANNE. No. It's nothing like that, really.

MRS. VAN DAAN. [*As he is opening it.*] What is it, Peter? Go on. Show it.

ANNE. [*Excitedly.*] It's a safety razor!

DUSSEL. A what?

ANNE. A razor!

MRS. VAN DAAN. [*Looking at it.*] You didn't make that out of odds and ends.

ANNE. [*To* PETER.] Miep got it for me. It's not new. It's second-hand. But you really do need a razor now.

DUSSEL. For what?

ANNE. Look on his upper lip . . . you can see the beginning of a mustache. ▊18

DUSSEL. He wants to get rid of that? Put a little milk on it and let the cat lick it off.

PETER. [*Starting for his room.*] Think you're funny, don't you?

DUSSEL. Look! He can't wait! He's going in to try it!

PETER. I'm going to give Mouschi his present!

[*He goes into his room, slamming the door behind him.*]

MR. VAN DAAN. [*Disgustedly.*] Mouschi, Mouschi, Mouschi. ▊19

9. *Gingerly* (JIN jur lee) means "lightly; cautiously."

Practice the Skills

18 Key Reading Skill

Drawing Conclusions In scene 3, Anne made fun of Peter's "little fuzz." Why does she now give him a razor? Is she mocking him again?

19 Reviewing Skills

Analyzing Why do you think Mr. Van Daan is always so disgusted about Peter and his cat?

[*In the distance we hear a dog persistently barking.* ANNE *brings a gift to* DUSSEL.]

ANNE. And last but never least, my roommate, Mr. Dussel.

DUSSEL. For me? You have something for me?

[*He opens the small box she gives him.*]

ANNE. I made them myself.

DUSSEL. [*Puzzled.*] **Capsules!** Two capsules! **20**

ANNE. They're ear-plugs!

DUSSEL. Ear-plugs?

ANNE. To put in your ears so you won't hear me when I thrash around at night. I saw them advertised in a magazine. They're not real ones . . . I made them out of cotton and candle wax. Try them . . . See if they don't work . . . see if you can hear me talk . . .

DUSSEL. [*Putting them in his ears.*] Wait now until I get them in . . . so.

ANNE. Are you ready?

DUSSEL. Huh?

ANNE. Are you ready?

DUSSEL. Good God! They've gone inside! I can't get them out! [*They laugh as* MR. DUSSEL *jumps about, trying to shake the plugs out of his ears. Finally he gets them out. Putting them away.*] Thank you, Anne! Thank you!

MR. VAN DAAN. A real Hanukkah!

MRS. VAN DAAN. Wasn't it cute of her?

MRS. FRANK. I don't know when she did it.

MARGOT. I love my present. **21**

} *Together*

ANNE. [*Sitting at the table.*] And now let's have the song, Father . . . please . . . [*To* DUSSEL.] Have you heard the Hanukkah song, Mr. Dussel? The song is the whole thing! [*She sings.*] "Oh, Hanukkah! Oh Hanukkah! The sweet celebration . . ."

Practice the Skills

20 **English Language Coach**

Historical Influences The word **capsule** came to English through French; the original Latin word meant "box or case."

21 **Key Reading Skill**

Drawing Conclusions Is Anne's gift-giving a success, particularly with those she's had conflicts with?

The Diary of Anne Frank, Act 1, Scenes 4–5 **779**

MR. FRANK. [*Quieting her.*] I'm afraid, Anne, we shouldn't sing that song tonight. [*To* DUSSEL.] It's a song of **jubilation,** of rejoicing. One is apt to become too enthusiastic.

ANNE. Oh, please, please. Let's sing the song. I promise not to shout!

MR. FRANK. Very well. But quietly now . . . I'll keep an eye on you and when . . .

[*As* ANNE *starts to sing, she is interrupted by* DUSSEL, *who is snorting and wheezing.*]

DUSSEL. [*Pointing to* PETER.] You . . . You! [PETER *is coming from his bedroom, ostentatiously*[10] *holding a bulge in his coat as if he were holding his cat, and dangling* ANNE'S *present before it.*] How many times . . . I told you . . . Out! Out!

MR. VAN DAAN. [*Going to* PETER.] What's the matter with you? Haven't you any sense? Get that cat out of here.

PETER. [*Innocently.*] Cat?

MR. VAN DAAN. You heard me. Get it out of here!

PETER. I have no cat. 🔲22

[*Delighted with his joke, he opens his coat and pulls out a bath towel. The group at the table laugh, enjoying the joke.*]

DUSSEL. [*Still wheezing.*] It doesn't need to be the cat . . . his clothes are enough . . . when he comes out of that room . . .

MR. VAN DAAN. Don't worry. You won't be bothered any more. We're getting rid of it.

DUSSEL. At last you listen to me.

[*He goes off into his bedroom.*]

---

10. When Peter holds his coat ***ostentatiously*** (aw sten TAY shus lee), he does it in a showy way that's meant to attract attention.

Practice the Skills

22 Key Reading Skill

Drawing Conclusions Why does Peter take joy in teasing Dussel? What does Peter's prank reveal about Dussel?

Vocabulary

jubilation (joo buh LAY shun) *n.* great joy and excitement

MR. VAN DAAN. [*Calling after him.*] I'm not doing it for you. That's all in your mind . . . all of it! [*He starts back to his place at the table.*] I'm doing it because I'm sick of seeing that cat eat all our food.

PETER. That's not true! I only give him bones . . . scraps . . .

MR. VAN DAAN. Don't tell me! He gets fatter every day! Damn cat looks better than any of us. Out he goes tonight!

PETER. No! No!

ANNE. Mr. Van Daan, you can't do that! That's Peter's cat. Peter loves that cat.

MRS. FRANK. [*Quietly.*] Anne.

PETER. [*To MR. VAN DAAN.*] If he goes, I go.

MR. VAN DAAN. Go! Go!

MRS. VAN DAAN. You're not going and the cat's not going! Now please . . . this is Hanukkah . . . Hanukkah . . . this is the time to celebrate . . . What's the matter with all of you? Come on, Anne. Let's have the song.

ANNE. [*Singing.*] "Oh, Hanukkah! Oh, Hanukkah! The sweet celebration."

MR. FRANK. [*Rising.*] I think we should first blow out the candle . . . then we'll have something for tomorrow night.

MARGOT. But, Father, you're supposed to let it burn itself out.

MR. FRANK. I'm sure that God understands shortages. [*Before blowing it out.*] "Praised be Thou, oh Lord our God, who hast sustained us and **permitted** us to celebrate this joyous festival." **23**

[*He is about to blow out the candle when suddenly there is a crash of something falling below. They all freeze in horror, motionless. For a few seconds there is complete silence. MR. FRANK slips off his shoes. The others noiselessly follow his example. MR. FRANK turns out a light near him. He motions to PETER to turn off the center lamp. PETER tries to reach it, realizes he cannot and gets up on a chair. Just as he is touching the lamp he loses his balance. The chair goes out from under him. He falls. The iron lamp shade*

Practice the Skills

23 **English Language Coach**

Historical Influences The word **permitted** contains the Latin root *mit,* which means "send." What other words do we get from *mit?* (No, *mitt* and *mitten* are not from this root.)

crashes to the floor. There is a sound of feet below, running down the stairs.]

MR. VAN DAAN. [Under his breath.] God Almighty! [The only light left comes from the Hanukkah candle. DUSSEL comes from his room. MR. FRANK creeps over to the stairwell and stands listening. The dog is heard barking excitedly.] Do you hear anything? **24**

MR. FRANK. [In a whisper.] No. I think they've gone.

MRS. VAN DAAN. It's the Green Police. They've found us.

MR. FRANK. If they had, they wouldn't have left. They'd be up here by now.

MRS. VAN DAAN. I know it's the Green Police. They've gone to get help. That's all. They'll be back!

MR. VAN DAAN. Or it may have been the Gestapo,[11] looking for papers . . .

MR. FRANK. [Interrupting.] Or a thief, looking for money.

MRS. VAN DAAN. We've got to do something . . . Quick! Quick! Before they come back.

MR. VAN DAAN. There isn't anything to do. Just wait.

[MR. FRANK holds up his hand for them to be quiet. He is listening intently. There is complete silence as they all strain to hear any sound from below. Suddenly ANNE begins to sway. With a low cry she falls to the floor in a faint. MRS. FRANK goes to her quickly, sitting beside her on the floor and taking her in her arms.] **25**

MRS. FRANK. Get some water, please! Get some water!

[MARGOT starts for the sink.]

MR. VAN DAAN. [Grabbing MARGOT.] No! No! No one's going to run water!

MR. FRANK. If they've found us, they've found us. Get the water. [MARGOT starts again for the sink. MR. FRANK, getting a flashlight.] I'm going down.

---

11. The **Gestapo** (guh STAW poh) were the Nazi secret police.

Practice the Skills

24 **Reviewing Skills**

Analyzing This is the second mention of the dog. (See the stage directions at the top of p. 779.) What might it mean to hear barking, silence, a crash on a floor below, then barking?

25 **Key Reading Skill**

Drawing Conclusions Why does Anne, of all people, faint? (Recall the beginning of scene 4.)

[MARGOT *rushes to him, clinging to him.* ANNE *struggles to* **consciousness**.] **26**

MARGOT. No, Father, no! There may be someone there, waiting . . . It may be a trap!

MR. FRANK. This is Saturday. There is no way for us to know what has happened until Miep or Mr. Kraler comes on Monday morning. We cannot live with this **uncertainty**.

MARGOT. Don't go, Father!

MRS. FRANK. Hush, darling, hush. [MR. FRANK *slips quietly out, down the steps, and out through the door below.*] Margot! Stay close to me.

[MARGOT *goes to her mother.*]

MR. VAN DAAN. Shush! Shush!

[MRS. FRANK *whispers to* MARGOT *to get the water.* MARGOT *goes for it.*]

MRS. VAN DAAN. Putti, where's our money? Get our money. I hear you can buy the Green Police off, so much a head. Go upstairs quick! Get the money!

MR. VAN DAAN. Keep still!

MRS. VAN DAAN. [*Kneeling before him, pleading.*] Do you want to be dragged off to a concentration camp? Are you going to stand there and wait for them to come up and get you? Do something, I tell you!

MR. VAN DAAN. [*Pushing her aside.*] Will you keep still!

[*He goes over to the stairwell to listen.* PETER *goes to his mother, helping her up onto the sofa. There is a second of silence, then* ANNE *can stand it no longer.*]

ANNE. Someone go after Father! Make Father come back!

PETER. [*Starting for the door.*] I'll go.

MR. VAN DAAN. Haven't you done enough?

Practice the Skills

26 **English Language Coach**

Historical Influences The Latin root *scientia* means "know." The words *science* and **consciousness** come from this root.

Vocabulary

uncertainty (un SUR tun tee) *n.* the state of being unsure or not knowing

The Diary of Anne Frank, Act 1, Scenes 4–5 **783**

Otto and Anne (both in light-colored coats) and friends, July 1941

[*He pushes* PETER *roughly away. In his anger against his father* PETER *grabs a chair as if to hit him with it, then puts it down, burying his face in his hands.* MRS. FRANK *begins to pray softly.*]

ANNE. Please, please, Mr. Van Daan. Get Father.

MR. VAN DAAN. Quiet! Quiet! **27**

[*ANNE is shocked into silence.* MRS. FRANK *pulls her closer, holding her protectively in her arms.*]

MRS. FRANK. [*Softly, praying.*] "I lift up mine eyes unto the mountains, from whence cometh my help. My help cometh from the Lord who made heaven and earth. He will not suffer thy foot to be moved . . . He that keepeth thee will not slumber . . ."

Practice the Skills

27 **Reviewing Skills**

Comparing and Contrasting
Compare Peter and his father as they wait for Mr. Frank to return.

[*She stops as she hears someone coming. They all watch the door tensely.* MR. FRANK *comes quietly in.* ANNE *rushes to him, holding him tight.*]

MR. FRANK. It was a thief. That noise must have scared him away.

MRS. VAN DAAN. Thank God.

MR. FRANK. He took the cash box. And the radio. He ran away in such a hurry that he didn't stop to shut the street door. It was swinging wide open. [*A breath of relief sweeps over them.*] I think it would be good to have some light.

MARGOT. Are you sure it's all right?

MR. FRANK. The danger has passed. [MARGOT *goes to light the small lamp.*] Don't be so terrified, Anne. We're safe.

DUSSEL. Who says the danger has passed? Don't you realize we are in greater danger than ever? **28**

MR. FRANK. Mr. Dussel, will you be still!

[MR. FRANK *takes* ANNE *back to the table, making her sit down with him, trying to calm her.*]

DUSSEL. [*Pointing to* PETER.] Thanks to this clumsy fool, there's someone now who knows we're up here! Someone now knows we're up here, hiding!

MRS. VAN DAAN. [*Going to* DUSSEL.] Someone knows we're here, yes. But who is the someone? A thief! A thief! You think a thief is going to go to the Green Police and say . . . I was robbing a place the other night and I heard a noise up over my head? You think a thief is going to do that?

DUSSEL. Yes. I think he will.

MRS. VAN DAAN. [*Hysterically.*] You're crazy!

[*She stumbles back to her seat at the table.* PETER *follows protectively, pushing* DUSSEL *aside.*]

DUSSEL. I think some day he'll be caught and then he'll make a bargain with the Green Police . . . if they'll let him off, he'll tell them where some Jews are hiding!

Practice the Skills

28 **Key Reading Skill**

Drawing Conclusions Do you agree with Dussel? Explain.

[*He goes off into the bedroom. There is a second of appalled silence.*]

MR. VAN DAAN. He's right.

ANNE. Father, let's get out of here! We can't stay here now . . . Let's go . . .

MR. VAN DAAN. Go! Where?

MRS. FRANK. [*Sinking into her chair at the table.*] Yes. Where?

MR. FRANK. [*Rising, to them all.*] Have we lost all faith? All courage? A moment ago we thought that they'd come for us. We were sure it was the end. But it wasn't the end. We're alive, safe. [MR. VAN DAAN *goes to the table and sits.* MR. FRANK *prays.*] "We thank Thee, oh Lord our God, that in Thy infinite mercy Thou hast again seen fit to spare us." [*He blows out the candle, then turns to* ANNE.] Come on, Anne. The song! Let's have the song! [*He starts to sing.* ANNE *finally starts falteringly to sing, as* MR. FRANK *urges her on. Her voice is hardly audible at first.*] **29**

ANNE. [*Singing.*]

"Oh, Hanukkah! Oh, Hanukkah!
 The sweet . . . celebration . . ."

[*As she goes on singing, the others gradually join in, their voices still shaking with fear.* MRS. VAN DAAN *sobs as she sings.*]

GROUP. "Around the feast . . . we . . . gather
 In complete . . . jubilation . . .
 Happiest of sea . . . sons
 Now is here.
 Many are the reasons for good cheer."

[DUSSEL *comes from the bedroom. He comes over to the table, standing beside* MARGOT, *listening to them as they sing.*]

"Together
 We'll weather
 Whatever tomorrow may bring."

[*As they sing on with growing courage, the lights start to dim.*]

Practice the Skills

29 **English Language Coach**

Historical Influences The Latin root *aud* is the basis of many words, including *audio* and *auditorium*. What does *aud* mean? What word in this paragraph can help you figure out the root's meaning?

"So hear us rejoicing
  And merrily voicing
  The Hanukkah song that we sing.
  Hoy!"

[*The lights are out. The curtain starts slowly to fall.*]

"Hear us rejoicing
  And merrily voicing
  The Hanukkah song that we sing." **30**

[*They are still singing, as the curtain falls.*]

30 🎤**BIG** Question

How does Mr. Frank respond to the others' doubts and fears? Does it work? Write your answer on the Workshop 1 Foldable for Unit 6. Your response will help you complete the Unit Challenge later.

Anne in the Franks' Amsterdam apartment, 1941.

Analyzing the Photo At age twelve, Anne is still too small for the desk and sits on a cushion to write. Notice the picture's torn corner. Most of the photos of the Franks came from the family album or from Anne's own scrapbook.

After You Read

The Diary of Anne Frank, Act 1, Scenes 4–5

Answering the BIG Question

1. In scene 5, traditions and religious faith lift the characters' spirits—until things take a very bad turn. Would they be better off at the end of the scene if they had *not* celebrated Hanukkah?

2. **Recall** What happens in the nightmare that wakes Anne?
   Tip Right There

3. **Recall** Why does Mr. Van Daan say he wants to get rid of Peter's cat?
   Tip Right There

4. **Summarize** In a paragraph, tell what Anne goes through in scenes 4 and 5. Which one event or experience do you think affects her the most?
   Tip Think and Search

Critical Thinking

5. **Interpret** What do you learn about the characters from their reactions to the thief downstairs? Explain.
   Tip Think and Search

6. **Infer** Hanukkah is a celebration of freedom. How does the group's celebration of the holiday add to the meaning of the play?
   Tip Author and Me

7. **Evaluate** How do you think Anne affects the lives of the others?
   Tip Author and Me

8. **Interpret** From your experience, is Anne's conflict with her mother normal? Explain.
   Tip Author and Me

NY English Language Arts Core Curriculum (pp. 788–789)

LC R17 Demonstrate comprehension and response through a range of activities. **LC R13** Use text structure and literary devices to aide comprehension and response. **LC W10** Engage in writing for a variety of purposes. **R11** Draw conclusion on the basis of explicit and implied information. **Core R4** Determine the meaning of words by using structural analysis. **Core W7** Observe rules of punctuation. *For a complete description of the standards, see p. NY 11.*

Write About Your Reading

Written Response At the end of scene 4, Anne's voice says that Mr. Frank asked everyone "the first thing we wanted to do when we got out of here." She then lists four responses, but there are eight main characters. She does not tell what the other four wanted. Write a sentence or two answering Mr. Frank's question for each of the following:

- Mr. Van Daan
- Mr. Frank
- Mrs. Frank
- Margot

Skills Review

Key Reading Skill: Drawing Conclusions

9. Mrs. Van Daan asks Dussel "what kind of a Jew" he is. Based on the fact that he's in hiding, what can you conclude about the "kind of a Jew" the Nazis were sending to concentration camps?

Key Literary Element: Dialogue and Monologue

10. Describe one character, based on his or her part of the dialogue. Think about how often the character speaks, how much or little he or she says, and what vocabulary he or she uses.

11. Find two monologues in scene 5. For each, list the page number and identify the speaker. Then briefly tell one thing you learned about the speaker from this monologue.

Reviewing Skills: Analyzing

12. Scene 5 begins with good feelings and a sense of togetherness. What things occur during the scene to produce bad feelings in the group?

Vocabulary Check

Rewrite each sentence, filling in the blank with the best word from the list.

> **makeshift   wallow   sustenance**
> **jubilation   uncertainty**

13. Waiting to hear from the doctor after Jason's surgery was a time of terrible ____.

14. Many hungry and homeless people depend on food pantries for ____.

15. We love to ____ on the couch, watching the Sunday football games and eating pizza.

16. You've never seen such ____ as when we won the state championship.

17. Made from a torn-up shirt, the ____ bandages would have to do until they could reach a hospital.

18. **English Language Coach** Identify the roots in *recycling, reversible,* and *science.*

Grammar Link: Commas with Direct Quotations

Use a comma and quotation marks to set off a direct quotation. A **direct quotation** gives a speaker's exact words. If it *follows* the speaker's name, place the comma directly before the opening quotation mark.

• Tito replied, "Peru is in South America."

If the quotation comes *before* the speaker's name, place the comma after the last quoted word and before the closing quotation mark.

• "Peru is in South America," Tito replied.

If the speaker's name divides the quotation, place one comma after the first part and a second comma just before the next opening quotation mark.

• "Peru," Tito replied, "is in South America."

Grammar Practice

Rewrite the sentences below, inserting commas where they are needed.

19. "This is going to be fun" she said.

20. Martina yelled "Goodbye!"

21. "Don't forget" she said "that tomorrow is Sunday."

22. Ms. DeLonga said "Unfortunately, it's too rainy for us to go on the field trip to the nature reserve."

23. "The cardboard chewing gum was a great April Fool's trick" Salina and Janine said as they giggled.

24. "Digger," Ty yelled at his dog "stop digging up the yard! It's already full of your buried bones!"

Writing Application Review your Write About Your Reading activity. If you used any direct quotations, make sure that you used commas correctly.

Web Activities For eFlashcards, Selection Quick Checks, and other Web activities, go to www.glencoe.com.

Dramatic Scene
Prewriting and Drafting

ASSIGNMENT Adapt a scene from a story and write it like a play

Purpose: To write an interesting scene about a person who doesn't give up when something bad happens

Audience: Your teacher and your classmates

Writing Rubric

As you write you should

- describe a setting
- create dialogue
- write stage directions
- develop characters

NY English Language Arts Core Curriculum
(pp. 790–793)

W2a Write original literary texts to select a genre and use appropriate conventions, such as dialogue.
Core W4 Use prewriting activities.
LC W6 Organize writing effectively to communicate ideas to an intended audience.
Core W7 Observe rules of punctuation.

For a complete description of the standards, see p. NY 11.

When you go to the movies, turn on a TV show, or see a play in a theater, you're watching people act out a story.

A play is a story performed for an audience. Actors take the roles of different characters. The stage is set up like the place where the action occurs. Often, that's a single room, but it can be any place—a farmhouse, a crater on Mars, or the Grand Canyon. And it can be as many places as the playwright wants.

A **dramatic scene** is a group of related actions or conversations that happen in a particular time and place.

In this Writing Workshop, you'll choose part of a story about what happens to someone when the going gets tough. You'll turn that story scene into a dramatic scene. You'll use the same elements you would use to write a whole play. However, you're adapting another writer's work. That means you need to try to be faithful to his or her original purpose and ideas.

Prewriting
Get Ready to Write

Choose a Story and Scene

Before you begin to write, you need to choose the story to use as the basis of your dramatic scene. Find a scene from one of the stories you've read in this book. Look for a character facing a big problem, because that's who and what your dramatic scene will be about. This checklist can help you choose. The more questions that you answer with a "yes," the better your choice will be.

Selection Checklist	Yes	No
Does the story contain a clear conflict?		
Can this conflict be acted out on a stage?		
Does the conflict occur in one particular place?		
Is it a problem that you feel strongly about?		
Is it a problem that will interest your audience?		
Does the story have characters you can use?		
Does the scene have fewer than six important characters?		
Does the story have dialogue, or can you write dialogue that will explain what is happening?		

After deciding on a story scene, reread it and focus on the main conflict. Your dramatic scene can't include every detail from the story.

The Script

A play is written in a special form called a **script.** It includes these elements:

- **Characters** A script usually provides a simple list of characters in the order they first appear onstage. Some playwrights add short descriptions, including information such as age, occupation, or physical appearance. Minor characters don't necessarily need proper names but may be given descriptive titles such as "Nurse," "Man 1," "Man 2," or "Happy Woman."

- **Setting** A script often begins with a statement of the time and place. This can be simple ("The present. A room.") or detailed ("May 4, 1921, noon, the steps in front of the Virginia County Courthouse").

- **Stage directions** These describe what the sets, lights, sound effects, and music are like, as well as how characters look, move, and sound.

- **Dialogue** This will be *most* of a script. Right before each piece of dialogue is the name of the character who will say it. Like real-life conversation, well-written dialogue can tell the audience a great deal about a character's background, personality, and motives.

Literature Online

Writing Models For models and other writing activities, go to www.glencoe.com.

Drafting
Start Writing!

It's time to start writing! Think like a playwright. Imagine how each character looks, moves, and talks. The more details you can imagine, the easier it will be to write them. (You may decide to cut some of them out later.) Also, don't get carried away with stage directions; a good playwright leaves room for the actors, designers, and directors to make creative choices too.

First Draft

Every writer begins with a first draft. That means you shouldn't worry about how things look on the page right now. You can fix it all later on. Since you're adapting a story that already exists, do the easy parts first—the character list and setting. That will help you start thinking about the harder parts.

Characters

First list every character in the story scene. If that includes a "cast of thousands," you'll have to figure out whom to keep and whom to cut. Sometimes it's possible to combine two less important characters into one. If you were adapting a story about Harriet Tubman, your list might look like this:

Harriet Tubman
Harriet's brother
John, a slave
Ten other slaves

Setting

Start by explaining the setting in the simplest, most general terms. Then add descriptive details for the benefit of the actors and director. In your final script, this information—and any other words that aren't dialogue—should be inside brackets. But now is not the time to worry about how the script looks. Now is the time to get ideas on paper. Here's a sample description:

> [The 1850s. Maryland. It's a cold, dark night on the eastern shore. Except for an occasional owl, it's quiet.]

Stage Directions: Character Descriptions

Briefly describe the characters who are onstage at the beginning. Give information to help the actors (and audience) understand why these characters are part of the scene. Putting characters' names in capital letters makes it easier for actors. Indenting the stage directions makes them look different from the dialogue.

> [HARRIET TUBMAN appears from a cluster of trees. A few of the people she is helping escape can be seen looking from behind the trees. She is in dark clothing that she pulls close for warmth and to make it easier to travel through the thick brush. Her face is alert and filled with fierce determination. She is clearly in charge of the group.]

Use directions to describe characters' important movement and actions.

> [TUBMAN peers ahead, then motions for the others to follow.]

Dialogue

At the beginning of each new speech, write the character's name in capital letters. This makes it easier to see and separates it from what the person says; but don't use all capitals for names in the speeches. Try to write dialogue that matches the character's personality.

> TUBMAN. Follow me. Don't make any noise.
>
> JOHN. Are we there yet? It'll be light soon, and we're getting tired. My wife can't keep walking much longer.
>
> WIFE. [Quietly] I'm fine, John. Don't worry about me.

Stage Directions: Action

Add directions mainly when the characters should make important movements. This will help the actors understand what to do, especially if the dialogue doesn't suggest what's going on. Keep writing directions and dialogue until your scene does what you want it to.

> [JOHN steps toward the trees. A sudden, sharp sound makes him stop suddenly. The others are frozen in shock.]

Writing Tip ▶

Audience Plays are meant to be performed for an audience. Imagine that you are the audience and "watch" the play in your imagination.

Writing Tip ▶

Conflict Discuss the scene with a friend. Ask whether the conflict is clear and, if not, what you could do to make it clearer.

Writing Tip ▶

Dialogue Write dialogue that explains the plot and action of the play. Listen to how people talk to one another to learn how to write better dialogue.

Grammar Link

Commas with Introductory Words, Phrases, and Clauses

An **introductory word** introduces a sentence. It may be an interjection, an adverb, or a present participle (a verb that ends in *-ing).*

- <u>Well</u>, it certainly took you a long time to get here!
- <u>Fortunately</u>, I found the five dollars I dropped.
- <u>Singing</u>, she went about her chores.

An **introductory phrase** begins with a preposition or a participle and introduces the sentence.

- <u>Under the maple tree</u>, Sal dozed in the hammock. (prepositional phrase)
- <u>Singing to herself</u>, she went about her chores. (participial phrase)

An **introductory clause** is a dependent clause that answers the questions *How? When? Where?*

- <u>Before the lesson began</u>, the swimming instructor checked the chlorine levels in the pool.
- <u>Whenever it thunders</u>, my dog hides.

Why Are Commas Important?

Using a comma after an introductory word, phrase, or clause clarifies meaning and prevents misreading. The comma tells the reader where to pause before reading the rest of the sentence.

Wrong: Wherever you stop Joe will begin reading.

Right: Wherever you stop, Joe will begin reading.

How Do I Do It?

Use a comma after an introductory word to introduce a sentence. A *mild* interjection must be followed by a comma. Always use a comma after an introductory participle. Use a comma after an adverb to introduce a sentence unless the meaning is clear without it. Then you can omit the comma.

- <u>Yes</u>, I know the answer. (interjection)
- <u>Giggling</u>, Jose threw the fake frog at his sister. (participle)
- <u>Clearly</u>, the field won't dry in time for the game. (adverb)
- <u>Today</u> I will finish my project. (adverb)

Some introductory phrases, such as participial phrases, require commas.

- <u>Wondering what to do</u>, she raised her hand.

Always use a comma after two or more introductory prepositional phrases or after a single long prepositional phrase.

- <u>By the end of the week</u>, I will have run 25 miles.
- <u>Throughout our great nation's history</u>, people have counted on leadership.

You may leave out the comma after a single short prepositional phrase, but it's not wrong to use one.

- <u>In 2001</u> my sister went to college in Maine.
- <u>In 2001</u>, my sister went to college in Maine.

Always use a comma after an introductory clause.

- <u>Since it snowed so much</u>, school was canceled.

Looking Ahead

Part 2 of this Writing Workshop is coming up. Keep the writing you did here, and in Part 2 you'll learn how to turn it into a really great play.

Skills Focus

You will practice these skills when you read the following selections:

- *The Diary of Anne Frank,* Act 2, Scenes 1–2, p. 798
- *The Diary of Anne Frank,* Act 2, Scenes 3–5, p. 826

Reading

- Interpreting how and why events happen

Literature

- Understanding the importance of stage directions in a play
- Identifying and analyzing mood

Vocabulary

- Understanding Anglo-Saxon roots

Writing/Grammar

- Using commas with interrupting words and with appositives

NY English Language Arts Core Curriculum
(pp. 794–795)

R2b Interpret characters, plot, setting, theme, and dialogue, using evidence from the text. **R2g** Compare literature to own lives.

For a complete description of the standards, see p. NY 11.

Skill Lesson

Interpreting

Learn It!

What Is It? Interpreting literature is using your own understanding of the world to decide the meanings of events and ideas in the work. You probably interpret people's words and actions every day. For example, your friend Joe says, "I'm glad you're here today." You could interpret this simple statement in many ways:

- Joe is the *only* one who's glad I'm here.
- Joe is glad *I'm* here because he needs my help.
- Joe is glad I'm *here* and not at the mall.

To interpret Joe's statement, you use your knowledge of Joe and the situation as well as the specific words Joe uses. You must interpret what you read in a similar way to understand what the writer is really saying.

Cornered — by Mike Baldwin

2-24 © 2004 Mike Baldwin / Dist. by Universal Press Syndicate www.cornered.com
cornered@comic.com

YOU CAN MAKE A DIFFERENCE

NOT REALLY

Fortunately there was an interpreter for those who understood sign language.

© 2004 Mike Baldwin. Reprinted with permission of UNIVERSAL PRESS SYNDICATE. All rights reserved.

Analyzing Cartoons
What is the speaker saying here? What is the woman's interpretation of his comment?

Why Is It Important? Interpreting helps you connect to what you are reading. When you interpret, you use your understanding of the world around you to create a meaning that is special to you. Interpreting can help you get closer to the author's intended meaning. Examining how other people interpret the same ideas or events can also help broaden your views.

How Do I Do It? As you read, think about what you already know about yourself and the world. Ask yourself, "What is the writer really trying to say here? What larger idea might these events be about?" Here's how one student interpreted an early passage in *The Diary of Anne Frank*.

Study Central Visit www.glencoe .com and click on Study Central to review interpreting.

> MR. FRANK. There is so little that we parents can do to help our children. We can only try to set a good example . . . point the way. The rest you must do yourself. You must build your own character.

> *Mr. Frank is talking about how parents raise their children. Sometimes my mom and dad tell me why I shouldn't do something, but I don't always listen because sometimes I have to figure things out for myself. I think Mr. Frank is saying that all parents can do is act the way they want their kids to act and then trust them.*

Practice It!

With a partner, study the sentence "I'm glad you're here today." Say the sentence aloud, stressing a different word each time. Find new ways to read the sentence. Then interpret what each reading means.

Use It!

As you read act 2 of *The Diary of Anne Frank,* use what you know about the world to interpret what the characters say and do. Ask yourself questions such as "What do the playwrights mean here?" and "What is this character really saying?"

Before You Read

The Diary of Anne Frank, Act 2, Scenes 1–2

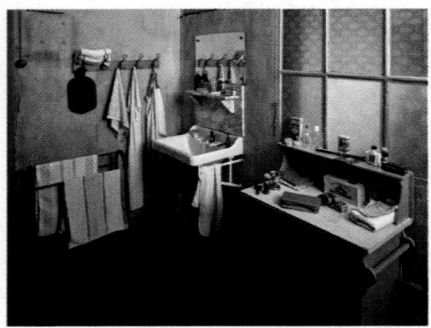

Vocabulary Preview

disgruntled (dis GRUNT uld) *adj.* not pleased; in a bad mood **(p. 799)** *Dussel was disgruntled by Anne's use of the room.*

foreboding (for BOH ding) *n.* a feeling that something bad will happen **(p. 804)** *Something in Mr. Kraler's words gives Margot a foreboding that there is bad news.*

apprehension (ap rih HEN shun) *n.* fear of what may happen **(p. 805)** *Apprehension increases after Mr. Kraler presents his bad news.*

intimate (IN tuh mit) *adj.* very close and personal; private **(p. 809)** *Anne feels she can't share intimate thoughts and feelings with anyone.*

intuition (in too ISH un) *n.* the ability to know things without having to reason them out **(p. 813)** *Anne trusts her intuition to help her through difficulties.*

poise (poyz) *n.* a calm, relaxed, and self-controlled manner **(p. 820)** *Even under great stress, Mrs. Frank shows poise.*

English Language Coach

Anglo-Saxon Roots Anglo-Saxon is the name of the language also known as Old English. It developed when the Angles and the Saxons came from what is now Germany to conquer England in the fifth century.

The Anglo-Saxons often spelled words the way they said them. For example, the word *knee* was *kuh NEE,* and *night* was *nikt.* Over the years, many pronunciations changed. Unfortunately, some of the spellings stayed the same. Fortunately, most Anglo-Saxon words that survive in modern English are fairly simple to say, spell, and use. They tend to be specific objects, actions, and relationships, like these:

bread	dinner	easy	love	old	sheep
child	earth	god	net	run	wife

Partner Talk 1 For each set of words, first guess which word comes from Anglo-Saxon. Then look up the origins of the word you chose.

1. acquaintance   associate   comrade   friend

2. alluring   beautiful   pretty   gorgeous

3. cut   divide   lacerate   sever

Partner Talk 2 Using the pronunciation cues given above, say this sentence as an Anglo-Saxon might have: *The knight's knee hurts tonight.*

NY English Language Arts Core Curriculum (pp. 796–821)

Core R4 Determine the meaning of words by using structural analysis. **R2g** Compare literature to people, events, and places in own lives. **R2b** Interpret characters, plot, setting, theme, and dialogue, using Literature from the text. **LC R13** Use text structure and literary devices to aid comprehension and response.

For a complete description of the standards, see p. NY 11.

Skills Preview

Key Reading Skill: Interpreting

The things people do are usually open to different interpretations. We make those interpretations every day. If a friend passes you in the hall without speaking, you may decide that person is angry with you. Or you may decide he or she is in a hurry and didn't see you. How you interpret actions often determines how you feel and what you do next. The same is true when you're reading. If you interpret a character's words or actions one way, you will expect certain things to happen. If you interpret them another way, you will expect other things. And if you *don't* interpret them, you won't understand what's going on at all.

Key Literary Element: Stage Directions

A playwright's original **stage directions** are likely to be general tips to help the director, actors, and designers understand what the writer has in mind. The directions in a published script are usually a record of how the play was staged in its first production. Stage directions can help readers understand the play's ideas and visualize the sets, characters, and action. Directions may give important information about:

- lighting, sets, costumes, sound effects, and music
- how characters look, sound, behave, move, and when they enter and exit
- action that takes place offstage

Small Group Work Choose eight to ten lines of dialogue from act 1 that do not have specific stage directions. Picture the scene in your head, and then write directions for the actors.

Interactive Literary Elements Handbook
To review or learn more about the literary elements, go to www.glencoe.com.

Get Ready to Read

Connect to the Reading

As the play goes on, Mr. and Mrs. Van Daan continue to argue. The others, who have nowhere to hide, must pretend not to listen. Have you ever been in the room when two people were arguing? How did you feel? As you read, think about how the others must feel when the Van Daans argue.

Partner Talk Imagine that you're a teenager growing up in a cramped living space without friends your own age. Only one other person can understand what you're going through—another teenager in the same situation. With a partner, think of one or two things that might be positive about your living arrangement.

Build Background

A year has passed since the end of act 1. In 1944 the war has begun to turn in favor of the Allies—primarily made up of the United States, Great Britain, and the Soviet Union.

- The Soviets have driven German forces out of the Soviet Union. American, British, and Canadian troops have forced the Germans out of North Africa and invaded Europe from the south.
- In June of 1944, the D-Day invasion will allow the Allies to enter Europe from the north and east. In the process, they will free much of the continent from Nazi rule.
- As act 2 begins, it is January 1, 1944, six long months before D-Day.

Set Purposes for Reading

BIG Question Read the next scenes to see how hope rises and falls for Anne and the others.

Set Your Own Purpose What would you like to learn from the story to help you answer the Big Question? Write your answer on the Workshop 2 Foldable for Unit 6.

Keep Moving

Use these skills as you read the following selection.

ACT 2 — SCENE 1

Practice the Skills

[*In the darkness we hear* ANNE'S VOICE, *again reading from the diary.*]

ANNE'S VOICE. Saturday, the first of January, nineteen forty-four. Another new year has begun and we find ourselves still in our hiding place. We have been here now for one year, five months, and twenty-five days. It seems that our life is at a standstill.

[*The curtain rises on the scene. It is late afternoon. Everyone is bundled up against the cold. In the main room* MRS. FRANK *is taking down the laundry which is hung across the back.* MR. FRANK *sits in the chair down left, reading.* MARGOT *is lying on the couch with a blanket over her and the many-colored knitted scarf around her throat.* ANNE *is seated at the center table, writing in her diary.* PETER, MR. *and* MRS. VAN DAAN, *and* DUSSEL *are all in their own rooms, reading or lying down.* ∎
As the lights dim on, ANNE'S VOICE *continues, without a break.*]

ANNE'S VOICE. We are all a little thinner. The Van Daans' "discussions" are as violent as ever. Mother still does not understand me. But then I don't understand her either. There is one great change, however. A change in myself. I read somewhere that girls of my age don't feel quite certain of themselves. That they become quiet within and begin to think of the miracle that is taking place in their bodies. I think that what is happening to me is so wonderful . . . not only what can be seen, but what is taking place inside. Each time it has happened I have a feeling that I have a sweet secret. [*We hear the chimes and then a hymn being played on the carillon outside.*] And in spite of any pain, I long for the time when I shall feel that secret within me again.

[*The buzzer of the door below suddenly sounds. Everyone is startled,* MR. FRANK *tiptoes cautiously to the top of the steps and listens. Again the buzzer sounds, in* MIEP'S *V-for-Victory[1] signal.*]

MR. FRANK. It's Miep!

∎ **Key Literary Element**

Stage Directions Beginning with act 1, scene 2, all of the main characters are onstage almost all the time. The directions at the beginning of each scene tell where the characters are and what they're doing.

---

1. The ***V-for-Victory signal*** was based on Morse Code for the letter *v*—three short buzzes followed by a long one.

[*He goes quickly down the steps to unbolt the door.* MRS. FRANK *calls upstairs to the* VAN DAANS *and then to* PETER.]

MRS. FRANK. Wake up, everyone! Miep is here! [ANNE *quickly puts her diary away.* MARGOT *sits up, pulling the blanket around her shoulders.* MR. DUSSEL *sits on the edge of his bed, listening,* **disgruntled.** MIEP *comes up the steps, followed by* MR. KRALER. *They bring flowers, books, newspapers, etc.* ANNE *rushes to* MIEP, *throwing her arms affectionately around her.*] Miep . . . and Mr. Kraler . . . What a delightful surprise!

MR. KRALER. We came to bring you New Year's greetings.

MRS. FRANK. You shouldn't . . . you should have at least one day to yourselves. **2**

[*She goes quickly to the stove and brings down teacups and tea for all of them.*]

Practice the Skills

2 Reviewing Skills

Drawing Conclusions Using Mrs. Frank's comment and what you know from act 1, what can you conclude about Mr. Kraler and Miep?

Anne's tenth birthday party, 1939.

Analyzing the Photo Can you tell which girl is Anne? What do you suppose her friends thought after Anne went into hiding?

Vocabulary

disgruntled (dis GRUNT uld) *adj.* not pleased; in a bad humor

ANNE. Don't say that, it's so wonderful to see them! [*Sniffing at* MIEP'S *coat.*] I can smell the wind and the cold on your clothes. **3**

MIEP. [*Giving her the flowers.*] There you are. [*Then to* MARGOT, *feeling her forehead.*] How are you, Margot? . . . Feeling any better?

MARGOT. I'm all right.

ANNE. We filled her full of every kind of pill so she won't cough and make a noise.

[*She runs into her room to put the flowers in water.* MR. *and* MRS. VAN DAAN *come from upstairs. Outside there is the sound of a band playing.*]

MRS. VAN DAAN. Well, hello, Miep. Mr. Kraler.

MR. KRALER. [*Giving a bouquet of flowers to* MRS. VAN DAAN.] With my hope for peace in the New Year.

PETER. [*Anxiously.*] Miep, have you seen Mouschi? Have you seen him anywhere around? **4**

MIEP. I'm sorry, Peter. I asked everyone in the neighborhood had they seen a gray cat. But they said no.

[MRS. FRANK *gives* MIEP *a cup of tea.* MR. FRANK *comes up the steps, carrying a small cake on a plate.*]

MR. FRANK. Look what Miep's brought for us!

MRS. FRANK. [*Taking it.*] A cake!

MR. VAN DAAN. A cake! [*He pinches* MIEP'S *cheeks gaily and hurries up to the cupboard.*] I'll get some plates.

[DUSSEL, *in his room, hastily puts a coat on and starts out to join the others.*]

MRS. FRANK. Thank you, Miepia. You shouldn't have done it. You must have used all of your sugar ration for weeks. [*Giving it to* MRS. VAN DAAN.] It's beautiful, isn't it?

MRS. VAN DAAN. It's been ages since I even saw a cake. Not since you brought us one last year. [*Without looking at the cake, to* MIEP.] Remember? Don't you remember, you gave us one on

Practice the Skills

3 | **Key Reading Skill**

Interpreting What does Anne mean in saying she can smell the wind and cold?

4 | **Key Reading Skill**

Interpreting What does Peter's question imply?

New Year's Day? Just this time last year? I'll never forget it because you had "Peace in nineteen forty-three" on it. [*She looks at the cake and reads.*] "Peace in nineteen forty-four!"

MIEP. Well, it has to come sometime, you know. [*As DUSSEL comes from his room.*] Hello, Mr. Dussel.

MR. KRALER. How are you?

MR. VAN DAAN. [*Bringing plates and a knife.*] Here's the knife, *liefje.* Now, how many of us are there?

MIEP. None for me, thank you.

MR. FRANK. Oh, please. You must.

MIEP. I couldn't.

MR. VAN DAAN. Good! That leaves one . . . two . . . three . . . seven of us.

DUSSEL. Eight! Eight! It's the same number as it always is!

MR. VAN DAAN. I left Margot out. I take it for granted Margot won't eat any.

ANNE. Why wouldn't she!

MRS. FRANK. I think it won't harm her.

MR. VAN DAAN. All right! All right! I just didn't want her to start coughing again, that's all.

DUSSEL. And please, Mrs. Frank should cut the cake.

MR. VAN DAAN. What's the difference?

MRS. VAN DAAN. It's not Mrs. Frank's cake, is it, Miep? It's for all of us.

DUSSEL. Mrs. Frank divides things better. **5**

MRS. VAN DAAN. [*Going to DUSSEL.*] What are you trying to say?

MR. VAN DAAN. Oh, come on! Stop wasting time!

MRS. VAN DAAN. [*To DUSSEL.*] Don't I always give everybody exactly the same? Don't I?

Practice the Skills

5 | **Key Reading Skill**

Interpreting How do you interpret Dussel's comments about cutting the cake?

MR. VAN DAAN. Forget it, Kerli.

MRS. VAN DAAN. No. I want an answer! Don't I?

DUSSEL. Yes. Yes. Everybody gets exactly the same . . . except Mr. Van Daan always gets a little bit more.

[*VAN DAAN advances on DUSSEL, the knife still in his hand.*]

MR. VAN DAAN. That's a lie!

[*DUSSEL retreats before the onslaught of the VAN DAANS.*]

MR. FRANK. Please, please! [*Then to MIEP.*] You see what a little sugar cake does to us? It goes right to our heads! **6**

MR. VAN DAAN. [*Handing MRS. FRANK the knife.*] Here you are, Mrs. Frank.

MRS. FRANK. Thank you. [*Then to MIEP as she goes to the table to cut the cake.*] Are you sure you won't have some?

MIEP. [*Drinking her tea.*] No, really, I have to go in a minute.

[*The sound of the band fades out in the distance.*] **7**

PETER. [*To MIEP.*] Maybe Mouschi went back to our house . . . they say that cats . . . Do you ever get over there . . . ? I mean . . . do you suppose you could . . . ?

MIEP. I'll try, Peter. The first minute I get I'll try. But I'm afraid, with him gone a week . . .

DUSSEL. Make up your mind, already someone has had a nice big dinner from that cat!

[*PETER is furious, inarticulate.[2] He starts toward DUSSEL as if to hit him. MR. FRANK stops him. MRS. FRANK speaks quickly to ease the situation.*]

MRS. FRANK. [*To MIEP.*] This is delicious, Miep!

MRS. VAN DAAN. [*Eating hers.*] Delicious!

MR. VAN DAAN. [*Finishing it in one gulp.*] Dirk's in luck to get a girl who can bake like this!

---

2. Peter is so angry that he becomes unable to speak (*inarticulate*).

Practice the Skills

6 **Key Reading Skill**

Interpreting How do you interpret what has just happened? Is it all about the cake?

7 **Key Literary Element**

Stage Directions The stage directions first mention the band just after Miep and Mr. Kraler arrive. What purpose could the playwrights have in including the sound of a band playing during this scene?

MIEP. [*Putting down her empty teacup.*] I have to run. Dirk's taking me to a party tonight.

ANNE. How heavenly! Remember now what everyone is wearing, and what you have to eat and everything, so you can tell us tomorrow. **8**

MIEP. I'll give you a full report! Good-bye, everyone!

MR. VAN DAAN. [*To MIEP.*] Just a minute. There's something I'd like you to do for me.

[*He hurries off up the stairs to his room.*]

MRS. VAN DAAN. [*Sharply.*] Putti, where are you going? [*She rushes up the stairs after him, calling hysterically.*] What do you want? Putti, what are you going to do?

MIEP. [*To PETER.*] What's wrong?

PETER. [*His sympathy is with his mother.*] Father says he's going to sell her fur coat. She's crazy about that old fur coat. **9**

DUSSEL. Is it possible? Is it possible that anyone is so silly as to worry about a fur coat in times like this?

PETER. It's none of your darn business . . . and if you say one more thing . . . I'll, I'll take you and I'll . . . I mean it . . . I'll . . .

[*There is a piercing scream from MRS. VAN DAAN above. She grabs at the fur coat as MR. VAN DAAN is starting downstairs with it.*]

MRS. VAN DAAN. No! No! No! Don't you dare take that! You hear? It's mine! [*Downstairs PETER turns away, embarrassed, miserable.*] My father gave me that! You didn't give it to me. You have no right. Let go of it . . . you hear?

[*MR. VAN DAAN pulls the coat from her hands and hurries downstairs. MRS. VAN DAAN sinks to the floor, sobbing. As MR. VAN DAAN comes into the main room the others look away, embarrassed for him.*] **10**

MR. VAN DAAN. [*To MR. KRALER.*] Just a little—discussion over the advisability[3] of selling this coat. As I have often reminded Mrs. Van Daan, it's very selfish of her to keep it when people

---

3. **Advisability** means "the quality of being wise, fitting, or proper."

Practice the Skills

8 **Key Reading Skill**

Interpreting How do you interpret Anne's wanting to know all about the party? Is it just curiosity?

9 **Key Reading Skill**

Interpreting How do you interpret Mrs. Van Daan's feelings about the coat? What do you think it means to her?

10 **Key Literary Element**

Stage Directions How do the stage directions in this section help to develop the Van Daans' characters?

outside are in such desperate need of clothing . . . [*He gives the coat to* MIEP.] So if you will please to sell it for us? It should fetch a good price. And by the way, will you get me cigarettes. I don't care what kind they are . . . get all you can. **11**

MIEP. It's terribly difficult to get them, Mr. Van Daan. But I'll try. Good-bye.

[*She goes.* MR. FRANK *follows her down the steps to bolt the door after her.* MRS. FRANK *gives* MR. KRALER *a cup of tea.*]

MRS. FRANK. Are you sure you won't have some cake, Mr. Kraler?

MR. KRALER. I'd better not.

MR. VAN DAAN. You're still feeling badly? What does your doctor say?

MR. KRALER. I haven't been to him.

MRS. FRANK. Now, Mr. Kraler! . . .

MR. KRALER. [*Sitting at the table.*] Oh, I tried. But you can't get near a doctor these days . . . they're so busy. After weeks I finally managed to get one on the telephone. I told him I'd like an appointment . . . I wasn't feeling very well. You know what he answers . . . over the telephone . . . Stick out your tongue! [*They laugh. He turns to* MR. FRANK *as* MR. FRANK *comes back.*] I have some contracts here . . . I wonder if you'd look over them with me . . .

MR. FRANK. [*Putting out his hand.*] Of course.

MR. KRALER. [*He rises.*] If we could go downstairs . . . [MR. FRANK *starts ahead,* MR. KRALER *speaks to the others.*] Will you forgive us? I won't keep him but a minute.

[*He starts to follow* MR. FRANK *down the steps.*]

MARGOT. [*With sudden* **foreboding**.] What's happened? Something's happened! Hasn't it, Mr. Kraler?

Vocabulary

foreboding (for BOH ding) *n.* a feeling that something bad will happen

Practice the Skills

11 **BIG** Question

How does her fur coat help Mrs. Van Daan deal with their situation? How does Mr. Van Daan's reason for selling the coat help him deal with the situation? Write your answers on the Workshop 2 Foldable for Unit 6.

[MR. KRALER *stops and comes back, trying to reassure* MARGOT *with a pretense of casualness.*]

MR. KRALER. No, really. I want your father's advice . . .

MARGOT. Something's gone wrong! I know it!

MR. FRANK. [*Coming back, to* MR. KRALER.] If it's something that concerns us here, it's better that we all hear it.

MR. KRALER. [*Turning to him, quietly.*] But . . . the children . . . ?

MR. FRANK. What they'd imagine would be worse than any reality. 🔢

[*As* MR. KRALER *speaks, they all listen with intense* **apprehension.** MRS. VAN DAAN *comes down the stairs and sits on the bottom step.*]

MR. KRALER. It's a man in the storeroom . . . I don't know whether or not you remember him . . . Carl, about fifty, heavy-set, near-sighted . . . He came with us just before you left.

MR. FRANK. He was from Utrecht?[4]

MR. KRALER. That's the man. A couple of weeks ago, when I was in the storeroom, he closed the door and asked me . . . how's Mr. Frank? What do you hear from Mr. Frank? I told him I only knew there was a rumor that you were in Switzerland. He said he'd heard that rumor too, but he thought I might know something more. I didn't pay any attention to it . . . but then a thing happened yesterday . . . He'd brought some invoices to the office for me to sign. As I was going through them, I looked up. He was standing staring at the bookcase . . . your bookcase. He said he thought he remembered a door there . . . Wasn't there a door that used to go up to the loft? Then he told me he wanted more money. Twenty guilders[5] more a week.

---

4. **Utrecht** (YOO trekt) is a city in the central Netherlands.

5. The **guilder** (GIL dur) is the monetary unit of the Netherlands.

Vocabulary

apprehension (ap rih HEN shun) *n.* fear of what may happen

Practice the Skills

🔢 **Key Reading Skill**

Interpreting Do bad things seem better or worse when they're kept secret? Explain what Mr. Frank means here and tell whether you agree with him.

MR. VAN DAAN. Blackmail! **13**

MR. FRANK. Twenty guilders? Very modest blackmail.

MR. VAN DAAN. That's just the beginning.

DUSSEL. [*Coming to* MR. FRANK.] You know what I think? He was the thief who was down there that night. That's how he knows we're here.

MR. FRANK. [*To* MR. KRALER.] How was it left? What did you tell him?

MR. KRALER. I said I had to think about it. What shall I do? Pay him the money? . . . Take a chance on firing him . . . or what? I don't know.

DUSSEL. [*Frantic.*] For God's sake don't fire him! Pay him what he asks . . . keep him here where you can have your eye on him.

MR. FRANK. Is it so much that he's asking? What are they paying nowadays?

MR. KRALER. He could get it in a war plant. But this isn't a war plant. Mind you, I don't know if he really knows . . . or if he doesn't know.

MR. FRANK. Offer him half. Then we'll soon find out if it's blackmail or not.

DUSSEL. And if it is? We've got to pay it, haven't we? Anything he asks we've got to pay!

MR. FRANK. Let's decide that when the time comes.

MR. KRALER. This may be all my imagination. You get to a point, these days, where you suspect everyone and everything. Again and again . . . on some simple look or word, I've found myself . . .

[*The telephone rings in the office below.*]

MRS. VAN DAAN. [*Hurrying to* MR. KRALER.] There's the telephone! What does that mean, the telephone ringing on a holiday?

Practice the Skills

13 **Key Reading Skill**

Interpreting Blackmail is money forced from a person in exchange for not revealing some secret. Mr. Van Daan interprets Carl's request as blackmail. Do you think it is?

MR. KRALER. That's my wife. I told her I had to go over some papers in my office . . . to call me there when she got out of church. [*He starts out.*] I'll offer him half then. Good-bye . . . we'll hope for the best! **14**

[*The group call their good-bye's half-heartedly.* MR. FRANK *follows* MR. KRALER, *to bolt the door below. During the following scene,* MR. FRANK *comes back up and stands listening, disturbed.*]

DUSSEL. [*To* MR. VAN DAAN.] You can thank your son for this . . . smashing the light! I tell you, it's just a question of time now.

[*He goes to the window at the back and stands looking out.*]

MARGOT. Sometimes I wish the end would come . . . whatever it is. **15**

MRS. FRANK. [*Shocked.*] Margot!

[ANNE *goes to* MARGOT, *sitting beside her on the couch with her arms around her.*]

MARGOT. Then at least we'd know where we were.

MRS. FRANK. You should be ashamed of yourself! Talking that way! Think how lucky we are! Think of the thousands dying in the war, every day. Think of the people in concentration camps.

ANNE. [*Interrupting.*] What's the good of that? What's the good of thinking of misery when you're already miserable? That's stupid!

MRS. FRANK. Anne!

[*As* ANNE *goes on raging at her mother,* MRS. FRANK *tries to break in, in an effort to quiet her.*]

ANNE. We're young, Margot and Peter and I! You grown-ups have had your chance! But look at us . . . If we begin thinking of all the horror in the world, we're lost! We're trying to hold onto some kind of ideals . . . when everything . . . ideals, hopes . . . everything, are being destroyed! It isn't our fault that the world is in such a mess! We weren't around when all this started! So don't try to take it out on us! **16**

Practice the Skills

14 **Reviewing Skills**

Drawing Conclusions What conclusion can you draw from Mr. Kraler's lie to his wife?

15 **BIG Question**

Has Margot given up? What do Mrs. Frank's and Anne's next few speeches indicate about how they try to keep going? Write your answers on the Workshop 2 Foldable for Unit 6.

16 **Reviewing Elements**

Dialogue and Monologue Why does Anne pause several times during this monologue? Is she struggling to find the right words? Is she struggling with her emotions?

The Diary of Anne Frank, Act 2, Scenes 1–2 **807**

[*She rushes off to her room, slamming the door after her. She picks up a brush from the chest and hurls it to the floor. Then she sits on the settee, trying to control her anger.*]

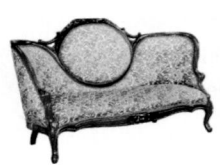

Visual Vocabulary
A *settee* (seh TEE) is a small sofa or a bench with a back.

MR. VAN DAAN. She talks as if we started the war! Did we start the war?

[*He spots* ANNE's *cake. As he starts to take it,* PETER *anticipates him.*]

PETER. She left her cake. [*He starts for* ANNE's *room with the cake. There is silence in the main room.* MRS. VAN DAAN *goes up to her room, followed by* MR. VAN DAAN. DUSSEL *stays looking out the window.* MR. FRANK *brings* MRS. FRANK *her cake. She eats it slowly, without relish.* MR. FRANK *takes his cake to* MARGOT *and sits quietly on the sofa beside her.* PETER *stands in the doorway of* ANNE's *darkened room, looking at her, then makes a little movement to let her know he is there.* ANNE *sits up, quickly, trying to hide the signs of her tears.* PETER *holds out the cake to her.*] You left this. **17**

ANNE. [*Dully.*] Thanks.

[PETER *starts to go out, then comes back.*]

PETER. I thought you were fine just now. You know just how to talk to them. You know just how to say it. I'm no good . . . I never can think . . . especially when I'm mad . . . That Dussel . . . when he said that about Mouschi . . . someone eating him . . . all I could think is . . . I wanted to hit him. I wanted to give him such a . . . a . . . that he'd . . . That's what I used to do when there was an argument at school . . . That's the way I . . . but here . . . And an old man like that . . . it wouldn't be so good. **18**

ANNE. You're making a big mistake about me. I do it all wrong. I say too much. I go too far. I hurt people's feelings . . . **19**

[DUSSEL *leaves the window, going to his room.*]

PETER. I think you're just fine . . . What I want to say . . . if it wasn't for you around here, I don't know. What I mean . . .

[PETER *is interrupted by* DUSSEL's *turning on the light.* DUSSEL *stands in the doorway, startled to see* PETER. PETER *advances toward him forbiddingly.* DUSSEL *backs out of the room.* PETER *closes the door on him.*]

Practice the Skills

17 | **Key Literary Element**

Stage Directions The details here can help you "see" the action and understand the characters' behavior.

18 | **Reviewing Elements**

Dialogue and Monologue In Peter's first monologue of the play, what is he saying about the different ways he and Anne handle problems? Why does he keep trailing off and pausing? How is this monologue similar to and different from the one Anne just gave?

19 | **Reviewing Skills**

Analyzing Do you think Anne is right about herself?

ANNE. Do you mean it, Peter? Do you really mean it?

PETER. I said it, didn't I?

ANNE. Thank you, Peter!

[*In the main room* MR. *and* MRS. FRANK *collect the dishes and take them to the sink, washing them.* MARGOT *lies down again on the couch.* DUSSEL, *lost, wanders into* PETER'S *room and takes up a book, starting to read.*]

PETER. [*Looking at the photographs on the wall.*] You've got quite a collection.

ANNE. Wouldn't you like some in your room? I could give you some. Heaven knows you spend enough time in there . . . doing heaven knows what . . .

PETER. It's easier. A fight starts, or an argument . . . I duck in there.

ANNE. You're lucky, having a room to go to. His lordship is always here . . . I hardly ever get a minute alone. When they start in on me, I can't duck away. I have to stand there and take it. **20**

PETER. You gave some of it back just now.

ANNE. I get so mad. They've formed their opinions . . . about everything . . . but we . . . we're still trying to find out . . . We have problems here that no other people our age have ever had. And just as you think you've solved them, something comes along and bang! You have to start all over again.

PETER. At least you've got someone you can talk to.

ANNE. Not really. Mother . . . I never discuss anything serious with her. She doesn't understand. Father's all right. We can talk about everything . . . everything but one thing. Mother. He simply won't talk about her. I don't think you can be really **intimate** with anyone if he holds something back, do you? **21**

Practice the Skills

20 Key Reading Skill

Interpreting Who is "his lordship"? Why does Anne call him this?

21 Reviewing Skills

Connecting Have you ever felt the things Anne and Peter are talking about?

Vocabulary

intimate (IN tuh mit) *adj.* very close and personal; private

PETER. I think your father's fine.

ANNE. Oh, he is, Peter! He is! He's the only one who's ever given me the feeling that I have any sense. But anyway, nothing can take the place of school and play and friends of your own age . . . or near your age . . . can it?

PETER. I suppose you miss your friends and all.

ANNE. It isn't just . . . [*She breaks off, staring up at him for a second.*] Isn't it funny, you and I? Here we've been seeing each other every minute for almost a year and a half, and this is the first time we've ever really talked. It helps a lot to have someone to talk to, don't you think? It helps you to let off steam.

PETER. [*Going to the door.*] Well, any time you want to let off steam, you can come into my room.

ANNE. [*Following him.*] I can get up an awful lot of steam. You'll have to be careful how you say that. **22**

PETER. It's all right with me.

ANNE. Do you mean it?

PETER. I said it, didn't I? **23**

[*He goes out. ANNE stands in her doorway looking after him. As PETER gets to his door he stands for a minute looking back at her. Then he goes into his room. DUSSEL rises as he comes in, and quickly passes him, going out. He starts across for his room. ANNE sees him coming, and pulls her door shut. DUSSEL turns back toward PETER's room. PETER pulls his door shut. DUSSEL stands there, bewildered, forlorn.*
The scene slowly dims out. The curtain falls on the scene. ANNE'S VOICE comes over in the darkness . . . faintly at first, and then with growing strength.]

ANNE'S VOICE. We've had bad news. The people from whom Miep got our ration books have been arrested. So we have had to cut down on our food. Our stomachs are so empty that they rumble and make strange noises, all in different keys. Mr. Van Daan's is deep and low, like a bass fiddle.

Practice the Skills

22 **Reviewing Skills**

Drawing Conclusions How has Anne changed since act 1? What has caused the difference? Explain.

23 **Reviewing Skills**

Predicting Did you predict that Anne and Peter would become friends? What do you predict will happen now?

Mine is high, whistling like a flute. As we all sit around waiting for supper, it's like an orchestra tuning up. It only needs Toscanini to raise his baton and we'd be off in the Ride of the Valkyries. Monday, the sixth of March, nineteen forty-four. Mr. Kraler is in the hospital. It seems he has ulcers.[6] Pim says we are his ulcers. Miep has to run the business and us too. The Americans have landed on the southern tip of Italy. Father looks for a quick finish to the war. Mr. Dussel is waiting every day for the warehouse man to demand more money. Have I been skipping too much from one subject to another? I can't help it. I feel that spring is coming. I feel it in my whole body and soul. I feel utterly confused. I am longing . . . so longing . . . for everything . . . for friends . . . for someone to talk to . . . someone who understands . . . someone young, who feels as I do . . . **24**

[*As these last lines are being said, the curtain rises on the scene. The lights dim on.* ANNE'S VOICE *fades out.*]

---

6. Arturo ***Toscanini*** (taw skuh NEE nee) was an Italian orchestra conductor. ***Ride of the Valkyries*** is a passage from an opera by Richard Wagner, a German composer. Mr. Kraler's ***ulcers*** are sores on the lining of his stomach.

Practice the Skills

24 **Reviewing Elements**

Dialogue and Monologue
Anne's speech here is a mix of funny descriptions, important news, and confused emotions. At the end she keeps referring to "someone." In your opinion, is she referring to a particular, real person or to an ideal?

Analyzing the Photo Anne posted photos of movie stars and English princesses on her bedroom wall. In what ways do these photos reflect Anne's childhood interests? How might they show her hopes and goals as a young adult?

SCENE 2

[*It is evening, after supper. From outside we hear the sound of children playing. The "grown-ups," with the exception of* MR. VAN DAAN, *are all in the main room.* MRS. FRANK *is doing some mending,* MRS. VAN DAAN *is reading a fashion magazine.* MR. FRANK *is going over business accounts.* DUSSEL, *in his dentist's jacket, is pacing up and down, impatient to get into his bedroom.* MR. VAN DAAN *is upstairs working on a piece of embroidery in an embroidery frame.*
In his room PETER *is sitting before the mirror, smoothing his hair. As the scene goes on, he puts on his tie, brushes his coat and puts it on, preparing himself meticulously for a visit from* ANNE. *On his wall are now hung some of* ANNE's *motion picture stars. In her room* ANNE *too is getting dressed. She stands before the mirror in her slip, trying various ways of dressing her hair.* MARGOT *is seated on the sofa, hemming a skirt for* ANNE *to wear. In the main room* DUSSEL *can stand it no longer. He comes over, rapping sharply on the door of his and* ANNE's *bedroom.*] **25**

ANNE. [*Calling to him.*] No, no, Mr. Dussel! I am not dressed yet. [DUSSEL *walks away, furious, sitting down and burying his head in his hands.* ANNE *turns to* MARGOT.] How is that? How does that look?

MARGOT. [*Glancing at her briefly.*] Fine.

ANNE. You didn't even look.

MARGOT. Of course I did. It's fine.

ANNE. Margot, tell me, am I terribly ugly?

MARGOT. Oh, stop fishing. **26**

ANNE. No. No. Tell me.

MARGOT. Of course you're not. You've got nice eyes . . . and a lot of animation,[7] and . . .

ANNE. A little vague, aren't you?

25 | **Key Literary Element**

Stage Directions How much time has passed since the end of scene 1? (Check the date in Anne's last monologue.) Based on the stage directions on this page, what event do you think is about to occur?

26 | **Key Reading Skill**

Interpreting What does Margot mean? What does she suggest Anne is fishing for?

---

7. Here, ***animation*** means "liveliness."

[*She reaches over and takes a brassière out of* MARGOT'*s sewing basket. She holds it up to herself, studying the effect in the mirror. Outside,* MRS. FRANK, *feeling sorry for* DUSSEL, *comes over, knocking at the girls' door.*]

MRS. FRANK. [*Outside.*] May I come in?

MARGOT. Come in, Mother.

MRS. FRANK. [*Shutting the **door** behind her.*] Mr. Dussel's impatient to get in here.

ANNE. [*Still with the brassière.*] Heavens, he takes the **room** for himself the entire day. **27**

MRS. FRANK. [*Gently.*] Anne, dear, you're not going in again tonight to see Peter?

ANNE. [*Dignified.*] That is my intention.

MRS. FRANK. But you've already spent a great deal of time in there today.

ANNE. I was in there exactly twice. Once to get the dictionary, and then three-quarters of an hour before supper.

MRS. FRANK. Aren't you afraid you're disturbing him?

ANNE. Mother, I have some **intuition.**

MRS. FRANK. Then may I ask you this much, Anne. Please don't shut the door when you go in.

ANNE. You sound like Mrs. Van Daan!

[*She throws the brassière back in* MARGOT'*s sewing basket and picks up her blouse, putting it on.*]

MRS. FRANK. No. No. I don't mean to suggest anything wrong. I only wish that you wouldn't expose yourself to criticism . . . that you wouldn't give Mrs. Van Daan the opportunity to be unpleasant. **28**

Practice the Skills

27 **English Language Coach**

Anglo-Saxon Roots Both **door** and **room** were Anglo-Saxon words with the same meanings but slightly different spellings. Oddly, *room* goes back to the Latin word *rurrus,* or "open land."

28 **Key Reading Skill**

Interpreting How do you interpret this conversation between Anne and her mother? What does it suggest about Anne and Peter?

Vocabulary

intuition (in too ISH un) *n.* the ability to know things without having to reason them out

ANNE. Mrs. Van Daan doesn't need an opportunity to be unpleasant!

MRS. FRANK. Everyone's on edge, worried about Mr. Kraler. This is one more thing . . . **29**

ANNE. I'm sorry, Mother. I'm going to Peter's room. I'm not going to let Petronella Van Daan spoil our friendship.

[*MRS. FRANK hesitates for a second, then goes out, closing the door after her. She gets a pack of playing cards and sits at the center table, playing solitaire. In ANNE's room MARGOT hands the finished skirt to ANNE. As ANNE is putting it on, MARGOT takes off her high-heeled shoes and stuffs paper in the toes so that ANNE can wear them.*]

MARGOT. [*To ANNE.*] Why don't you two talk in the main room? It'd save a lot of trouble. It's hard on Mother, having to listen to those remarks from Mrs. Van Daan and not say a word.

ANNE. Why doesn't she say a word? I think it's ridiculous to take it and take it.

MARGOT. You don't understand Mother at all, do you? She can't talk back. She's not like you. It's just not in her nature to fight back.

ANNE. Anyway . . . the only one I worry about is you. I feel awfully guilty about you.

[*She sits on the stool near MARGOT, putting on MARGOT's high-heeled shoes.*]

MARGOT. What about?

ANNE. I mean, every time I go into Peter's room, I have a feeling I may be hurting you. [*MARGOT shakes her head.*] I know if it were me, I'd be wild. I'd be desperately jealous, if it were me.

MARGOT. Well, I'm not.

ANNE. You don't feel badly? Really? Truly? You're not jealous?

MARGOT. Of course I'm jealous . . . jealous that you've got something to get up in the morning for . . . But jealous of you and Peter? No. **30**

Practice the Skills

29 **Key Reading Skill**

Interpreting Why are they nervous and upset ("on edge") about Mr. Kraler?

30 **Key Reading Skill**

Interpreting What does Margot mean when she says Anne has "something to get up in the morning for"?

[ANNE *goes back to the mirror.*]

ANNE. Maybe there's nothing to be jealous of. Maybe he doesn't really like me. Maybe I'm just taking the place of his cat . . . [*She picks up a pair of short white gloves, putting them on.*] Wouldn't you like to come in with us?

MARGOT. I have a book. **31**

[*The sound of the children playing outside fades out. In the main room* DUSSEL *can stand it no longer. He jumps up, going to the bedroom door and knocking sharply.*]

DUSSEL. Will you please let me in my room!

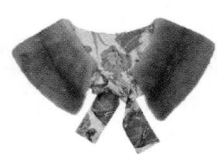

Visual Vocabulary
A *stole* is a long, wide scarf worn by women, usually across the shoulders.

ANNE. Just a minute, dear, dear Mr. Dussel. [*She picks up her Mother's pink stole and adjusts it elegantly over her shoulders, then gives a last look in the mirror.*] Well, here I go . . . to run the gauntlet.[8]

[*She starts out, followed by* MARGOT.]

DUSSEL. [*As she appears—sarcastic.*] Thank you so much. **32**

[DUSSEL *goes into his room.* ANNE *goes toward* PETER'S *room, passing* MRS. VAN DAAN *and her parents at the center table.*]

MRS. VAN DAAN. My God, look at her! [ANNE *pays no attention. She knocks at* PETER'S *door.*] I don't know what good it is to have a son. I never see him. He wouldn't care if I killed myself. [PETER *opens the door and stands aside for* ANNE *to come in.*] Just a minute, Anne. [*She goes to them at the door.*] I'd like to say a few words to my son. Do you mind? [PETER *and* ANNE *stand waiting.*] Peter, I don't want you staying up till all hours tonight. You've got to have your sleep. You're a growing boy. You hear?

MRS. FRANK. Anne won't stay late. She's going to bed promptly at nine. Aren't you, Anne?

ANNE. Yes, Mother . . . [*To* MRS. VAN DAAN.] May we go now?

---

8. To **run the gauntlet** is to endure opposition or difficulties.

Practice the Skills

31 **BIG Question**
Margot uses books as one way to escape bad times. Her conversation with Anne suggests she's developed another way as well. What is it? Write your answer on the Workshop 2 Foldable for Unit 6.

32 **Key Reading Skill**

Interpreting Sarcasm is related to irony. A sarcastic remark is a mocking statement that means the opposite of what it seems to mean. Examples are Anne's "dear, dear Mr. Dussel" (she doesn't think he's dear) and his "thank you" (he's annoyed, not grateful). Watch for several more instances of sarcasm in the next section.

MRS. VAN DAAN. Are you asking me? I didn't know I had anything to say about it.

MRS. FRANK. Listen for the chimes, Anne dear.

[*The two young people go off into* PETER's *room, shutting the door after them.*]

MRS. VAN DAAN. [*To* MRS. FRANK.] In my day it was the boys who called on the girls. Not the girls on the boys.

MRS. FRANK. You know how young people like to feel that they have secrets. Peter's room is the only place where they can talk.

MRS. VAN DAAN. Talk! That's not what they called it when I was young. **33**

[MRS. VAN DAAN *goes off to the bathroom.* MARGOT *settles down to read her book.* MR. FRANK *puts his papers away and brings a chess game to the center table. He and* MRS. FRANK *start to play. In* PETER's *room,* ANNE *speaks to* PETER, *indignant, humiliated.*]

ANNE. Aren't they awful? Aren't they impossible? Treating us as if we were still in the nursery.

[*She sits on the cot.* PETER *gets a bottle of pop and two glasses.*]

PETER. Don't let it bother you. It doesn't bother me.

ANNE. I suppose you can't really blame them . . . they think back to what they were like at our age. They don't realize how much more advanced we are . . . When you think what wonderful discussions we've had! . . . Oh, I forgot. I was going to bring you some more pictures. **34**

PETER. Oh, these are fine, thanks.

ANNE. Don't you want some more? Miep just brought me some new ones.

PETER. Maybe later.

[*He gives her a glass of pop and, taking some for himself, sits down facing her.*]

ANNE. [*Looking up at one of the photographs.*] I remember when I got that . . . I won it. I bet Jopie that I could eat five ice-cream

Practice the Skills

33 **Key Reading Skill**

Interpreting What does Mrs. Van Daan mean here?

34 **Reviewing Skills**

Analyzing In what ways might Anne and Peter be "more advanced" than their parents were as teenagers, and why?

cones. We'd all been playing ping-pong . . . We used to have heavenly times . . . we'd finish up with ice cream at the Delphi, or the Oasis, where Jews were allowed . . . there'd always be a lot of boys . . . we'd laugh and joke . . . I'd like to go back to it for a few days or a week. But after that I know I'd be bored to death. I think more seriously about life now. I want to be a journalist . . . or something. I love to write. What do you want to do? **35**

PETER. I thought I might go off some place . . . work on a farm or something . . . some job that doesn't take much brains.

ANNE. You shouldn't talk that way. You've got the most awful inferiority complex. **36**

PETER. I know I'm not smart.

ANNE. That isn't true. You're much better than I am in dozens of things . . . arithmetic and algebra and . . . well, you're a million times better than I am in algebra. [*With sudden directness.*] You like Margot, don't you? Right from the start you liked her, liked her much better than me.

PETER. [*Uncomfortably.*] Oh, I don't know. **37**

[*In the main room* MRS. VAN DAAN *comes from the bathroom and goes over to the sink, polishing a coffee pot.*]

ANNE. It's all right. Everyone feels that way. Margot's so good. She's sweet and bright and beautiful and I'm not.

PETER. I wouldn't say that.

ANNE. Oh, no, I'm not. I know that. I know quite well that I'm not a beauty. I never have been and never shall be.

PETER. I don't agree at all. I think you're pretty.

ANNE. That's not true!

PETER. And another thing. You've changed . . . from at first, I mean.

ANNE. I have?

PETER. I used to think you were awful noisy.

Practice the Skills

35 Reviewing Elements

Character What do you learn about Anne from this speech?

36 Reviewing Skills

Clarifying Do you know what an inferiority complex is? If not, look it up.

37 Key Literary Element

Stage Directions Why does Peter answer "uncomfortably"? What does this stage direction suggest about his feelings for Margot and Anne?

A view of the bathroom in the attic of the warehouse building.

Analyzing the Photo This small bathroom was shared by eight people. Could you live with all the rules and restrictions that they did?

ANNE. And what do you think now, Peter? How have I changed?

PETER. Well . . . er . . . you're . . . quieter.

[*In his room* DUSSEL *takes his pajamas and toilet articles and goes into the bathroom to change.*] **38**

ANNE. I'm glad you don't just hate me.

PETER. I never said that.

ANNE. I bet when you get out of here you'll never think of me again.

PETER. That's crazy.

ANNE. When you get back with all of your friends, you're going to say . . . now what did I ever see in that Mrs. Quack Quack.

PETER. I haven't got any friends.

Practice the Skills

38 **Key Literary Element**

Stage Directions What is the purpose of stage directions like this and the earlier one about Mrs. Van Daan polishing a coffee pot?

ANNE. Oh, Peter, of course you have. Everyone has friends.

PETER. Not me. I don't want any. I get along all right without them.

ANNE. Does that mean you can get along without me? I think of myself as your friend.

PETER. No. If they were all like you, it'd be different.

[*He takes the glasses and the bottle and puts them away. There is a second's silence and then* ANNE *speaks, hesitantly, shyly.*]

ANNE. Peter, did you ever kiss a girl?

PETER. Yes. Once.

ANNE. [*To cover her feelings.*] That picture's crooked. [PETER *goes over, straightening the photograph.*] Was she pretty?

PETER. Huh?

ANNE. The girl that you kissed.

PETER. I don't know. I was blindfolded. [*He comes back and sits down again.*] It was at a party. One of those kissing games.

ANNE. [*Relieved.*] Oh. I don't suppose that really counts, does it? **39**

PETER. It didn't with me.

ANNE. I've been kissed twice. Once a man I'd never seen before kissed me on the cheek when he picked me up off the ice and I was crying. And the other was Mr. Koophuis,[9] a friend of Father's who kissed my hand. You wouldn't say those counted, would you?

PETER. I wouldn't say so.

ANNE. I know almost for certain that Margot would never kiss anyone unless she was engaged to them. And I'm sure too that Mother never touched a man before Pim. But I don't know . . . things are so different now . . . What do you think? Do you think a girl shouldn't kiss anyone except if she's engaged or something? It's so hard to try to think what to do,

Practice the Skills

39 Key Reading Skill

Interpreting Why does Anne feel relieved?

9. **Koophuis** (KOIP hus)

when here we are with the whole world falling around our ears and you think . . . well . . . you don't know what's going to happen tomorrow and . . . What do you think? **40**

PETER. I suppose it'd depend on the girl. Some girls, anything they do's wrong. But others . . . well . . . it wouldn't necessarily be wrong with them. [*The carillon starts to strike nine o'clock.*] I've always thought that when two people . . .

ANNE. Nine o'clock. I have to go.

PETER. That's right.

ANNE. [*Without moving.*] Good night.

[*There is a second's pause, then* PETER *gets up and moves toward the door.*]

PETER. You won't let them stop you coming?

ANNE. No. [*She rises and starts for the door.*] Sometime I might bring my diary. There are so many things in it that I want to talk over with you. There's a lot about you.

PETER. What kind of things?

ANNE. I wouldn't want you to see some of it. I thought you were a nothing, just the way you thought about me.

PETER. Did you change your mind, the way I changed my mind about you?

ANNE. Well . . . You'll see . . . **41**

[*For a second* ANNE *stands looking up at* PETER, *longing for him to kiss her. As he makes no move she turns away. Then suddenly* PETER *grabs her awkwardly in his arms, kissing her on the cheek.* ANNE *walks out dazed. She stands for a minute, her back to the people in the main room. As she regains her* **poise** *she goes to her mother and father and* MARGOT, *silently kissing them. They murmur their good nights to her. As she is about to open her bedroom door, she catches sight of* MRS. VAN DAAN. *She goes*

40 **Reviewing Elements**

Dialogue and Monologue
Why is Anne talking so much?

41 **Key Reading Skill**

Interpreting What is going on—or *not* going on—between Anne and Peter in this scene?

Vocabulary

poise (poyz) *n.* a calm, relaxed, and self-controlled manner

quickly to her, taking her face in her hands and kissing her first on one cheek and then on the other. Then she hurries off into her room. MRS. VAN DAAN looks after her, and then looks over at PETER'S room. Her suspicions are confirmed.] **42**

MRS. VAN DAAN. [She knows.] Ah hah!

[The lights dim out. The curtain falls on the scene. In the darkness ANNE'S VOICE comes faintly at first and then with growing strength.]

ANNE'S VOICE. By this time we all know each other so well that if anyone starts to tell a story, the rest can finish it for him. We're having to cut down still further on our meals. What makes it worse, the rats have been at work again. They've carried off some of our precious food. Even Mr. Dussel wishes now that Mouschi was here. Thursday, the twentieth of April, nineteen forty-four. Invasion fever[10] is mounting every day. Miep tells us that people outside talk of nothing else. For myself, life has become much more pleasant. I often go to Peter's room after supper. Oh, don't think I'm in love, because I'm not. But it does make life more bearable to have someone with whom you can exchange views. No more tonight. P.S. . . . I must be honest. I must confess that I actually live for the next meeting. Is there anything lovelier than to sit under the skylight and feel the sun on your cheeks and have a darling boy in your arms? I admit now that I'm glad the Van Daans had a son and not a daughter. I've outgrown another dress. That's the third. I'm having to wear Margot's clothes after all. I'm working hard on my French and am now reading La Belle Nivernaise.[11] **43**

[As she is saying the last lines—the curtain rises on the scene. The lights dim on, as ANNE'S VOICE fades out.]

---

10. **Invasion fever** refers to the widely held belief that the Allies would soon invade and take control of areas occupied by German forces.
11. **La Belle Nivernaise** (law BEL NEE vur nayz) was a book by a nineteenth century French novelist.

Practice the Skills

42 | **Key Literary Element**

Stage Directions What were Mrs. Van Daan's suspicions, and how were they shown to be correct?

43 **BIG Question**

What new thing does Anne have to help her keep from giving up? Explain. Write your answer on the Workshop 2 Foldable for Unit 6. Your response will help you complete the Unit Challenge later.

After You Read

The Diary of Anne Frank, Act 2, Scenes 1–2

Answering the BIG Question

1. The characters in *The Diary of Anne Frank* develop routines of everyday life. How do these routines help them carry on through difficult times?

2. **Recall** What does Miep bring that causes an argument in the group?
   TIP Right There

3. **Explain** Why is Anne dressing up as scene 2 begins?
   TIP Right There

Critical Thinking

4. **Explain** Why is Mr. Kraler's news about the possible blackmail attempt so important to the group?
   TIP Author and Me

5. **Interpret** What does Anne mean when she says, "We have problems that no other people our age have ever had"? Use details from the play to support your answer.
   TIP Author and Me

6. **Evaluate** How do you think the characters are doing, given their living conditions? Are they dealing well with their situation?
   TIP Author and Me

Write About Your Reading

Letter In real life, Anne and Margot were like most sisters—laughing, loving, hurting, arguing, and sharing personal thoughts and feelings. While in hiding, they sometimes wrote letters to each other, saying things that they couldn't in person because of the crowded conditions and lack of privacy.

Imagine how Margot must have felt as she watched the relationship develop between her sister and Peter. Look again at the sisters' conversation in scene 2. Then put yourself in Margot's place. Write a letter to Anne about her friendship with Peter. Keep these things in mind:

- what kind of person Margot is
- how you think she feels, or felt, about Peter
- what she says to Anne in the play—what words she chooses, how she forms sentences, the tone she uses, and so on
- how you might feel in this situation or one like it

**NY English Language Arts
Core Curriculum** (pp. 822–823)

LC R17 Demonstrate comprehension and response through a range of activities.
W2a Write original literary texts to maintain a consistent point of view that enhances the message. **R2b** Interpret characters, plot, setting, theme, and dialogue, using evidence from the text. **LC R13** Use text structure and literary devices to aide comprehension and response.
Core R4 Determine the meaning of words by using structural analysis.
Core W7 Observe rules of punctuation.

For a complete description of the standards, see p. NY 11.

Skills Review

Key Reading Skill: Interpreting

7. How do you interpret Anne's behavior towards Peter? Do you think she's falling in love? Does she just have a crush? Is it something in between? Give details from your experience and from the play to support your interpretation.

Key Literary Element: Stage Directions

8. Some information appears only in stage directions. Find one example in act 2, scenes 1-2. Briefly state the information and identify the page where it's given.

9. In the stage directions at the end of act 2, scene 2, Anne suddenly goes over to Mrs. Van Daan and kisses her cheeks. What do you think is the purpose of this stage direction?

Reviewing Skills: Drawing Conclusions

10. In act 2, scene 1, what reason does Mr. Van Daan state for wanting to sell his wife's fur coat? Do you believe him? If so, why? If not, what do you think was his real reason for selling the coat? Support your answer with details from the play.

Vocabulary Check

Match each vocabulary word with its definition.

disgruntled **foreboding** **apprehension**
intimate **intuition** **poise**

11. a calm, relaxed, and self-controlled manner

12. fear of what may happen

13. very close and personal; private

14. not pleased; in a bad mood

15. a feeling that something bad will happen

16. the ability to know things without having to reason them out

17. **English Language Coach** The Anglo-Saxon root *side* means "edge." Explain how this root relates to the meaning of *inside*.

Grammar Link: Commas with Interrupting Words

Some words or groups of words interrupt the flow of thought in a sentence. Place commas before and after interrupting words or phrases.

- Joshua, in my opinion, has no right to question us.
- The final score, I believe, was 25 to 18.
- Eating breakfast, in fact, improves your productivity.

Some Common Interrupting Words and Phrases		
after all	I believe	moreover
by the way	I suppose	nevertheless
for example	in addition	nonetheless
furthermore	in fact	of course
however	incidentally	therefore

Grammar Practice

Copy the following sentences, inserting commas to set off the interrupting words.

18. Anne you see was a typical teenage girl.

19. The cat if you ask me is getting fatter every day!

20. It's time I think to schedule a visit to the dentist.

21. The cost nonetheless is more than I want to pay.

22. Recycled plastic milk jugs incidentally are used to make plastic pipe, drainage tile, flower pots, and more.

23. Beyoncé Knowles I believe was born in Houston, Texas.

24. Jim Carrey not surprisingly would do comedy routines for his classmates when he was a child.

Writing Application Review the letter you wrote from Margot to Anne. If any words or phrases interrupt the flow of thought, set them off with commas.

Web Activities For eFlashcards, Selection Quick Checks, and other Web activities, go to www.glencoe.com.

Before You Read

The Diary of Anne Frank, Act 2, Scenes 3–5

Vocabulary Preview

stealthily (STEL thuh lee) *adv.* in a secret or sneaky manner **(p. 826)** *People in hiding had to move stealthily during the day to avoid being caught.*

pandemonium (pan duh MOH nee um) *n.* wild disorder and uproar **(p. 832)** *There was pandemonium outside; shots were being fired in all directions, and soldiers were running down the streets.*

liberated (LIB uh ray tid) *adj.* released; freed **(p. 833)** *The idea that they would soon be liberated lifted everyone's spirits.*

downcast (DOWN kast) *adj.* sad; depressed **(p. 835)** *The lack of good news made everyone downcast.*

English Language Coach

Anglo-Saxon Roots Anglo-Saxon, or Old English, was spoken and written in England for centuries. Old English was gradually replaced by Middle English, and Middle English was gradually replaced by Modern English.

Throughout those many years, words came into English from other languages, too. We study the roots of those words more than we study Old English roots because the words Old English gave us are so simple.

Most good dictionaries include a word's history. Here are some of the special symbols and abbreviations you're likely to see:

• Brackets enclose the word's history, which might be either at the beginning of the entry or at its end.

• **OE** means "Old English," **ME** means "Middle English," and **fr** stands for "from." (Check the dictionary's table of contents for a list of all abbreviations.)

• Earlier spellings of the word are printed in *italics*.

> **knife** *n* [ME *knif,* fr OE *cnif*]
>
> **leap** *vb* [ME *lepen,* fr OE *hleapan*]

Guess the Roots Guess which word in each pair came from Old English. Then check your guesses in a dictionary.

1. chicken / poultry

2. construct / build

3. break / fracture

Skills Preview

Key Reading Skill: Interpreting

In this play, there is one thing you always need to keep in mind when you are interpreting behavior. These people hide in the Annex for more than two years. They don't see anyone else except Miep and Mr. Kraler. They don't get to go outside or listen to the radio. You can imagine how that would feel. Keep that feeling in mind as you read. It will be a very important part of your ability to interpret.

Group Discussion In a group, talk about situations where you were cut off from the outside world. They may include being grounded or sick or snowed in.

Key Literary Element: Mood

Mood is the emotional effect a piece of writing has on the reader. In most kinds of writing, the mood is created by the writer alone—and only through words. A playwright can set a mood in a script. However, when a play is performed, the mood is affected by lighting, sound effects, music, costumes, sets, direction, and acting. All of these things must work together to achieve the mood the playwright wants.

You can usually identify one general mood in a piece of writing, but each scene, chapter, or page may have a different emotional effect. The mood at the beginning of *The Diary of Anne Frank* might be described as sad and weary. That changes as characters are added and changes again as they interact.

Partner Talk Discuss act 1, scene 5, with a partner. In your Learner's Notebook, outline the important events of the scene in one column. Then, in a second column, write two or three words that describe the mood and how it changes (if it does) when each new event occurs.

Interactive Literary Elements Handbook
To review or learn more about the literary elements, go to www.glencoe.com.

Get Ready to Read

Connect to the Reading

Have you ever believed in something so much that you felt sure it would happen? In the next scene, the characters hear good news about the war and feel sure that they will soon be saved. As you read, imagine how you would react in their situation.

Group Talk In a small group, discuss a time when you really wanted something to happen. Describe your feelings as you waited. How did you react when your wish did—or did not—come true?

Build Background

Prisons are for convicted criminals. Prisoner-of-war camps are for captured soldiers. Concentration camps are for people who belong to the "wrong" ethnic groups or political parties. (*Concentration* refers to the process of gathering into one place.) The term "concentration camp" was first used in 1901.

- In the 1930s, the Nazis sent many Jews and other "enemies" and "undesirables" to camps in Germany and, later, in German-occupied countries.

- Beginning in 1942, entire communities of Jews were sent directly to extermination camps.

- It's estimated that some ten million people died in Nazi camps. Many were murdered outright. Others died of abuse, disease, and starvation.

Set Purposes for Reading

BIG Question Read the rest of *The Diary of Anne Frank* to see how people try to make the best of the most awful circumstances.

Set Your Own Purpose What would you like to learn from the play to help you answer the Big Question? Write your own purpose on the Workshop 2 Foldable for Unit 6.

Keep Moving

Use these skills as you read the following selection.

The Diary of Anne Frank, Act 2, Scenes 3–5 **825**

SCENE 3

[*It is night, a few weeks later. Everyone is in bed. There is complete quiet. In the* VAN DAANS' *room a match flares up for a moment and then is quickly put out.* MR. VAN DAAN, *in bare feet, dressed in underwear and trousers, is dimly seen coming* **stealthily** *down the stairs and into the main room, where* MR. *and* MRS. FRANK *and* MARGOT *are sleeping. He goes to the food safe and again lights a match. Then he cautiously opens the safe, taking out a half-loaf of bread. As he closes the safe, it creaks. He stands rigid.* MRS. FRANK *sits up in bed. She sees him.*] **1** **2**

MRS. FRANK. [*Screaming.*] Otto! Otto! Komme schnell!

[*The rest of the people wake, hurriedly getting up.*]

MR. FRANK. Was ist los? Was ist passiert?

[DUSSEL, *followed by* ANNE, *comes from his room.*]

MRS. FRANK. [*As she rushes over to* MR. VAN DAAN.] Er stiehlt das Essen![1]

DUSSEL. [*Grabbing* MR. VAN DAAN.] You! You! Give me that.

MRS. VAN DAAN. [*Coming down the stairs.*] Putti . . . Putti . . . what is it?

DUSSEL. [*His hands on* VAN DAAN'S *neck.*] You dirty thief . . . stealing food . . . you good-for-nothing . . .

MR. FRANK. Mr. Dussel! For God's sake! Help me, Peter!

[PETER *comes over, trying, with* MR. FRANK, *to separate the two struggling men.*]

PETER. Let him go! Let go!

[DUSSEL *drops* MR. VAN DAAN, *pushing him away. He shows them the end of a loaf of bread that he has taken from* VAN DAAN.]

---

1. The Franks' conversation in German translates as follows: mrs. frank. "Come quickly!" mr. frank. "What's the matter? What has happened?" mrs. frank. "He is stealing food!"

Vocabulary

stealthily (STEL thuh lee) *adv.* in a secret or sneaky manner

Practice the Skills

1 **English Language Coach**

Anglo-Saxon Roots The base work for **stealthily** is *stealth*. In Middle English it meant "the act of stealing." How do you think it came to mean "sneakiness"?

2 **Reviewing Skills**

Drawing Conclusions Reread the stage directions at the beginning of act 1, scene 4. Now what conclusions can you draw about Mr. Van Daan and his movements?

DUSSEL. You greedy, selfish . . . !

[*MARGOT turns on the lights.*]

MRS. VAN DAAN. Putti . . . what is it?

[*All of* MRS. FRANK*'s gentleness, her self-control, is gone. She is outraged, in a frenzy of indignation.[2]*] **3**

MRS. FRANK. The bread! He was stealing the bread!

DUSSEL. It was you, and all the time we thought it was the rats!

MR. FRANK. Mr. Van Daan, how could you!

---

2. Mrs. Frank's **frenzy of indignation** is her state of great excitement and anger.

Practice the Skills

3 **Reviewing Skills**

Character Why do the directions make such a big deal of Mrs. Frank's behavior? Think about how she has behaved up to now.

A view of the front of the warehouse building.

Analyzing the Photo The attic windows had to be covered during daylight. Can you imagine Anne or Peter looking out the window into the night?

Practice the Skills

MR. VAN DAAN. I'm hungry.

MRS. FRANK. We're all of us hungry! I see the children getting thinner and thinner. Your own son Peter . . . I've heard him moan in his sleep, he's so hungry. And you come in the night and steal food that should go to them . . . to the children!

MRS. VAN DAAN. [*Going to* MR. VAN DAAN *protectively.*] He needs more food than the rest of us. He's used to more. He's a big man.

[MR. VAN DAAN *breaks away, going over and sitting on the couch.*]

MRS. FRANK. [*Turning on* MRS. VAN DAAN.] And you . . . you're worse than he is! You're a mother, and yet you sacrifice your child to this man . . . this . . . this . . .

MR. FRANK. Edith! Edith!

[MARGOT *picks up the pink woolen stole, putting it over her mother's shoulders.*]

MRS. FRANK. [*Paying no attention, going on to* MRS. VAN DAAN.] Don't think I haven't seen you! Always saving the choicest bits for him! I've watched you day after day and I've held my tongue. But not any longer! Not after this! Now I want him to go! I want him to get out of here!

MR. FRANK. Edith!

MR. VAN DAAN. Get out of here?

MRS. VAN DAAN. What do you mean?

MRS. FRANK. Just that! Take your things and get out! 4

MR. FRANK. [*To* MRS. FRANK.] You're speaking in anger. You cannot mean what you are saying.

MRS. FRANK. I mean exactly that!

[MRS. VAN DAAN *takes a cover from the* FRANKS' *bed, pulling it about her.*]

MR. FRANK. For two long years we have lived here, side by side. We have respected each other's rights . . . we have managed to live in peace. Are we now going to throw it

4 **BIG Question**

Is Mrs. Frank just stressed out from hiding for so long? Is she right in trying to protect her family by telling Mr. Van Daan to leave? Is protecting her family one way she keeps going? Write your ideas on the Workshop 2 Foldable for Unit 6.

all away? I know this will never happen again, will it, Mr. Van Daan?

MR. VAN DAAN. No. No.

MRS. FRANK. He steals once! He'll steal again!

[*MR. VAN DAAN, holding his stomach, starts for the bathroom. ANNE puts her arms around him, helping him up the step.*]

MR. FRANK. Edith, please. Let us be calm. We'll all go to our rooms . . . and afterwards we'll sit down quietly and talk this out . . . we'll find some way . . .

MRS. FRANK. No! No! No more talk! I want them to leave!

MRS. VAN DAAN. You'd put us out, on the streets?

MRS. FRANK. There are other hiding places.

MRS. VAN DAAN. A cellar . . . a closet. I know. And we have no money left even to pay for that.

MRS. FRANK. I'll give you money. Out of my own pocket I'll give it gladly.

[*She gets her purse from a shelf and comes back with it.*]

MRS. VAN DAAN. Mr. Frank, you told Putti you'd never forget what he'd done for you when you came to Amsterdam. You said you could never repay him, that you . . .

MRS. FRANK. [*Counting out money.*] If my husband had any obligation to you, he's paid it, over and over.

MR. FRANK. Edith, I've never seen you like this before. I don't know you.

MRS. FRANK. I should have spoken out long ago.

DUSSEL. You can't be nice to some people.

MRS. VAN DAAN. [*Turning on DUSSEL.*] There would have been plenty for all of us, if you hadn't come in here!

MR. FRANK. We don't need the Nazis to destroy us. We're destroying ourselves. **5**

Practice the Skills

5 **Key Reading Skill**

Interpreting Explain Mr. Frank's statement. Do you agree?

[*He sits down, with his head in his hands.* MRS. FRANK *goes to* MRS. VAN DAAN.]

MRS. FRANK. [*Giving* MRS. VAN DAAN *some money.*] Give this to Miep. She'll find you a place.

ANNE. Mother, you're not putting Peter out. Peter hasn't done anything.

MRS. FRANK. He'll stay, of course. When I say I must protect the children, I mean Peter too.

[PETER *rises from the steps where he has been sitting.*]

PETER. I'd have to go if Father goes. **6**

[MR. VAN DAAN *comes from the bathroom.* MRS. VAN DAAN *hurries to him and takes him to the couch. Then she gets water from the sink to bathe his face.*]

MRS. FRANK. [*While this is going on.*] He's no father to you . . . that man! He doesn't know what it is to be a father!

PETER. [*Starting for his room.*] I wouldn't feel right. I couldn't stay.

MRS. FRANK. Very well, then. I'm sorry.

ANNE. [*Rushing over to* PETER.] No, Peter! No! [PETER *goes into his room, closing the door after him.* ANNE *turns back to her mother, crying.*] I don't care about the food. They can have mine! I don't want it! Only don't send them away. It'll be daylight soon. They'll be caught . . .

MARGOT. [*Putting her arms comfortingly around* ANNE.] Please, Mother!

MRS. FRANK. They're not going now. They'll stay here until Miep finds them a place. [*To* MRS. VAN DAAN.] But one thing I insist on! He must never come down here again! He must never come to this room where the food is stored! We'll divide what we have . . . an equal share for each! [DUSSEL *hurries over to get a sack of potatoes from the food safe.* MRS. FRANK *goes on, to* MRS. VAN DAAN.] You can cook it here and take it up to him. **7 8**

[DUSSEL *brings the sack of potatoes back to the center table.*]

Practice the Skills

6 **Reviewing Skills**

Character So far in the play, Peter has not seemed to like or respect his father. Why do you think he says this?

7 **Reviewing Elements**

Conflict What things have contributed to this sudden conflict? How long has it been building?

8 **Reviewing Skills**

Predicting What do you think is going to happen? Will the Van Daan's leave?

MARGOT. Oh, no. No. We haven't sunk so far that we're going to fight over a handful of rotten potatoes.

DUSSEL. [*Dividing the potatoes into piles.*] Mrs. Frank, Mr. Frank, Margot, Anne, Peter, Mrs. Van Daan, Mr. Van Daan, myself . . . Mrs. Frank . . .

[*The buzzer sounds in* MIEP's *signal.*]

MR. FRANK. It's Miep!

[*He hurries over, getting his overcoat and putting it on.*]

MARGOT. At this hour?

MRS. FRANK. It is trouble.

MR. FRANK. [*As he starts down to unbolt the door.*] I beg you, don't let her see a thing like this!

MR. DUSSEL. [*Counting without stopping.*] . . . Anne, Peter, Mrs. Van Daan, Mr. Van Daan, myself . . .

MARGOT. [*To* DUSSEL.] Stop it! Stop it! 🄨

DUSSEL. . . . Mr. Frank, Margot, Anne, Peter, Mrs. Van Daan, Mr. Van Daan, myself, Mrs. Frank . . .

MRS. VAN DAAN. You're keeping the big ones for yourself! All the big ones . . . Look at the size of that! . . . And that! . . .

[DUSSEL *continues on with his dividing.* PETER, *with his shirt and trousers on, comes from his room.*]

MARGOT. Stop it! Stop it!

[*We hear* MIEP's *excited voice speaking to* MR. FRANK *below.*]

MIEP. Mr. Frank . . . the most wonderful news! . . . The invasion has begun!

MR. FRANK. Go on, tell them! Tell them!

[MIEP *comes running up the steps, ahead of* MR. FRANK. *She has a man's raincoat on over her nightclothes and a bunch of orange-colored flowers in her hand.*]

MIEP. Did you hear that, everybody? Did you hear what I said? The invasion has begun! The invasion!

Practice the Skills

🄨 **Key Literary Element**

Mood In a few words, describe the mood of the scene up to this point.

[*They all stare at* MIEP, *unable to grasp what she is telling them.* PETER *is the first to recover his wits.*]

PETER. Where?

MRS. VAN DAAN. When? When, Miep?

MIEP. It began early this morning . . .

[*As she talks on, the realization of what she has said begins to dawn on them. Everyone goes crazy. A wild demonstration takes place.* MRS. FRANK *hugs* MR. VAN DAAN.]

MRS. FRANK. Oh, Mr. Van Daan, did you hear that?

[DUSSEL *embraces* MRS. VAN DAAN. PETER *grabs a frying pan and parades around the room, beating on it, singing the Dutch National Anthem.* ANNE *and* MARGOT *follow him, singing, weaving in and out among the excited grown-ups.* MARGOT *breaks away to take the flowers from* MIEP *and distribute them to everyone. While this* **pandemonium** *is going on* MRS. FRANK *tries to make herself heard above the excitement.*]

MRS. FRANK. [*To* MIEP.] How do you know?

MIEP. The radio . . . The B.B.C.! They said they landed on the coast of Normandy![3]

PETER. The British?

MIEP. British, Americans, French, Dutch, Poles, Norwegians . . . all of them! More than four thousand ships! Churchill spoke, and General Eisenhower![4] D-Day they call it!

MR. FRANK. Thank God, it's come!

MRS. VAN DAAN. At last! **10**

---

3. **B.B.C.** stands for British Broadcasting Corporation. **Normandy** is a region of France across the English Channel from the southern coast of England.

4. Winston **Churchill** was the prime minister of England, and Dwight D. **Eisenhower** commanded the Allied forces in Europe.

Vocabulary

pandemonium (pan duh MOH nee um) *n.* wild disorder and uproar

Practice the Skills

10 | **Key Literary Element**

Mood Now describe the mood. Why does Miep's news cause the sudden change? How will the Allied invasion affect the characters?

MIEP. [*Starting out.*] I'm going to tell Mr. Kraler. This'll be better than any blood transfusion.[5]

MR. FRANK. [*Stopping her.*] What part of Normandy did they land, did they say?

MIEP. Normandy . . . that's all I know now . . . I'll be up the minute I hear some more!

[*She goes hurriedly out.*]

MR. FRANK. [*To* MRS. FRANK.] What did I tell you? What did I tell you?

[MRS. FRANK *indicates that he has forgotten to bolt the door after* MIEP. *He hurries down the steps.* MR. VAN DAAN, *sitting on the couch, suddenly breaks into a convulsive sob. Everybody looks at him, bewildered.*] **11**

MRS. VAN DAAN. [*Hurrying to him.*] Putti! Putti! What is it? What happened?

MR. VAN DAAN. Please. I'm so ashamed.

[MR. FRANK *comes back up the steps.*]

DUSSEL. Oh, for God's sake!

MRS. VAN DAAN. Don't, Putti.

MARGOT. It doesn't matter now!

MR. FRANK. [*Going to* MR. VAN DAAN.] Didn't you hear what Miep said? The invasion has come! We're going to be **liberated!** This is a time to celebrate!

[*He embraces* MRS. FRANK *and then hurries to the cupboard and gets the cognac and a glass.*]

MR. VAN DAAN. To steal bread from children!

Practice the Skills

11 | **Key Reading Skill**

Interpreting Why does Mr. Van Daan start crying at this particular point?

---

5. A ***blood transfusion*** is the process of transferring blood from a healthy person to a sick person. Evidently, Mr. Kraler's ulcers have made him seriously ill.

Vocabulary

liberated (LIB uh ray tid) *adj.* released; freed

MRS. FRANK. We've all done things that we're ashamed of.

ANNE. Look at me, the way I've treated Mother . . . so mean and horrid to her.

MRS. FRANK. No, Anneke, no.

[*ANNE runs to her mother, putting her arms around her.*]

ANNE. Oh, Mother, I was. I was awful.

MR. VAN DAAN. Not like me. No one is as bad as me!

DUSSEL. [*To MR. VAN DAAN.*] Stop it now! Let's be happy!

MR. FRANK. [*Giving MR. VAN DAAN a glass of cognac.*] Here! Here! Schnapps! *Locheim!*[6]

[*VAN DAAN takes the cognac. They all watch him. He gives them a feeble smile. ANNE puts up her fingers in a V-for-Victory sign. As VAN DAAN gives an answering V-sign, they are startled to hear a loud sob from behind them. It is MRS. FRANK, stricken with remorse. She is sitting on the other side of the room.*]

MRS. FRANK. [*Through her sobs.*] When I think of the terrible things I said . . .

[*MR. FRANK, ANNE and MARGOT hurry to her, trying to comfort her. MR. VAN DAAN brings her his glass of cognac.*]

MR. VAN DAAN. No! No! You were right!

MRS. FRANK. That I should speak that way to you! . . . Our friends! . . . Our guests!

[*She starts to cry again.*]

DUSSEL. Stop it, you're spoiling the whole invasion! 🔟2️⃣

[*As they are comforting her, the lights dim out. The curtain falls.*]

🔟2️⃣ Key Reading Skill

Interpreting Dussel runs out of patience, but what does he mean here? How are the others "spoiling the invasion"?

---

6. *Schnapps* (shnawps) is a type of cognac, or liquor. *Locheim!* (luh KHY um) means "To life!"

On June 6, 1944, Allied troops landed on the beaches of Normandy, France. The landing was the beginning of the Allied forces' sweep through Europe that eventually defeated Nazi Germany.

ANNE'S VOICE. [*Faintly at first and then with growing strength.*] We're all in much better spirits these days. There's still excellent news of the invasion. The best part about it is that I have a feeling that friends are coming. Who knows? Maybe I'll be back in school by fall. Ha, ha! The joke is on us! The warehouse man doesn't know a thing and we are paying him all that money! . . . Wednesday, the second of July, nineteen forty-four. The invasion seems temporarily to be bogged down. Mr. Kraler has to have an operation, which looks bad. The Gestapo have found the radio that was stolen. Mr. Dussel says they'll trace it back and back to the thief, and then, it's just a matter of time till they get to us. Everyone is low. Even poor Pim can't raise their spirits. I have often been **downcast** myself . . . but never in despair. I can shake off everything if I write. But . . . and that is the great question . . . will I ever be able to write well? I want to so much. I want to go on living even after my death. Another birthday has gone by, so now I am fifteen. Already I know what I want. I have a goal, an opinion. **13** **14**

[*As this is being said—the curtain rises on the scene, the lights dim on, and* ANNE'S VOICE *fades out.*]

Vocabulary

downcast (DOWN kast) *adj.* sad; depressed

Practice the Skills

13 **Reviewing Elements**

Irony What is ironic—to a reader or theatergoer—about Anne's wondering whether she will ever be able to write well?

14 **Key Literary Element**

Mood In your own words, describe the mood of this monologue.

SCENE 4

[*It is an afternoon a few weeks later . . . Everyone but* MARGOT *is in the main room. There is a sense of great tension. Both* MRS. FRANK *and* MR. VAN DAAN *are nervously pacing back and forth,* DUSSEL *is standing at the window, looking down fixedly at the street below.* PETER *is at the center table, trying to do his lessons.* ANNE *sits opposite him, writing in her diary.* MRS. VAN DAAN *is seated on the couch, her eyes on* MR. FRANK *as he sits reading.*
The sound of a telephone ringing comes from the office below. They all are rigid, listening tensely. MR. DUSSEL *rushes down to* MR. FRANK.] **15**

DUSSEL. There it goes again, the telephone! Mr. Frank, do you hear?

MR. FRANK. [*Quietly.*] Yes. I hear.

DUSSEL. [*Pleading, insistent.*] But this is the third time, Mr. Frank! The third time in quick succession! It's a signal! I tell you it's Miep, trying to get us! For some reason she can't come to us and she's trying to warn us of something!

MR. FRANK. Please. Please.

MR. VAN DAAN. [*To* DUSSEL.] You're wasting your breath.

DUSSEL. Something has happened, Mr. Frank. For three days now Miep hasn't been to see us! And today not a man has come to work. There hasn't been a sound in the building!

MRS. FRANK. Perhaps it's Sunday. We may have lost track of the days.

MR. VAN DAAN. [*To* ANNE.] You with the diary there. What day is it?

DUSSEL. [*Going to* MRS. FRANK.] I don't lose track of the days! I know exactly what day it is! It's Friday, the fourth of August. Friday, and not a man at work. [*He rushes back to* MR. FRANK, *pleading with him, almost in tears.*] I tell you Mr. Kraler's dead. That's the only explanation. He's dead and they've closed down the building, and Miep's trying to tell us!

15 | **Key Literary Element**

Mood Even before anyone speaks, an audience would notice a sharp mood change. In reading these stage directions, what words and phrases tell you about the mood?

MR. FRANK. She'd never telephone us.

DUSSEL. [*Frantic.*] Mr. Frank, answer that! I beg you, answer it!

MR. FRANK. No.

MR. VAN DAAN. Just pick it up and listen. You don't have to speak. Just listen and see if it's Miep.

DUSSEL. [*Speaking at the same time.*] For God's sake . . . I ask you. **16**

MR. FRANK. No. I've told you, no. I'll do nothing that might let anyone know we're in the building.

PETER. Mr. Frank's right.

MR. VAN DAAN. There's no need to tell us what side you're on.

MR. FRANK. If we wait patiently, quietly, I believe that help will come.

[*There is silence for a minute as they all listen to the telephone ringing.*]

DUSSEL. I'm going down. [*He rushes down the steps.* MR. FRANK *tries ineffectually[7] to hold him.* DUSSEL *runs to the lower door, unbolting it. The telephone stops ringing.* DUSSEL *bolts the door and comes slowly back up the steps.*] Too late. [MR. FRANK *goes to* MARGOT *in* ANNE'S *bedroom.*]

MR. VAN DAAN. So we just wait here until we die.

MRS. VAN DAAN. [*Hysterically.*] I can't stand it! I'll kill myself! I'll kill myself!

MR. VAN DAAN. For God's sake, stop it!

[*In the distance, a German military band is heard playing a Viennese waltz.*] **17**

MRS. VAN DAAN. I think you'd be glad if I did! I think you want me to die!

---

7. *Ineffectually* means "without effect; uselessly."

Practice the Skills

16 | **Reviewing Skills**

Connecting Answering might give them away if the caller is not Miep. If it is Miep, she may have important information. What would you do?

17 | **Key Literary Element**

Mood Viennese waltzes are music for happy occasions. What do you think would be the effect on theatergoers of hearing a waltz in the background?

MR. VAN DAAN. Whose fault is it we're here? [*MRS. VAN DAAN starts for her room. He follows, talking at her.*] We could've been safe somewhere . . . in America or Switzerland. But no! No! You wouldn't leave when I wanted to. You couldn't leave your things. You couldn't leave your precious furniture. **18**

MRS. VAN DAAN. Don't touch me!

[*She hurries up the stairs, followed by* MR. VAN DAAN. PETER, *unable to bear it, goes to his room.* ANNE *looks after him, deeply concerned.* DUSSEL *returns to his post at the window.* MR. FRANK *comes back into the main room and takes a book, trying to read.* MRS. FRANK *sits near the sink, starting to peel some potatoes.* ANNE *quietly goes to* PETER'S *room, closing the door after her.* PETER *is lying face down on the cot.* ANNE *leans over him, holding him in her arms, trying to bring him out of his despair.*]

ANNE. Look, Peter, the sky. [*She looks up through the skylight.*] What a lovely, lovely day! Aren't the clouds beautiful? You know what I do when it seems as if I couldn't stand being cooped up for one more minute? I think myself out. I think myself on a walk in the park where I used to go with Pim. Where the jonquils and the crocus and the violets grow down the slopes. You know the most wonderful part about thinking yourself out? You can have it any way you like. You can have roses and violets and chrysanthemums all blooming at the same time . . . It's funny . . . I used to take it all for granted . . . and now I've gone crazy about everything to do with nature. Haven't you? **19**

PETER. I've just gone crazy. I think if something doesn't happen soon . . . if we don't get out of here . . . I can't stand much more of it!

ANNE. [*Softly.*] I wish you had a religion, Peter.

PETER. No, thanks! Not me!

ANNE. Oh, I don't mean you have to be Orthodox . . . or believe in heaven and hell and purgatory[8] and things . . . I just mean some religion . . . it doesn't matter what. Just to

8. The **Orthodox** branch of Judaism is the most traditional, requiring strict obedience to ancient laws and customs. **Purgatory** is, some believe, a place of temporary punishment for the souls of the dead.

Practice the Skills

18 Reviewing Skills
Character What does Mr. Van Daan reveal about himself in the way he treats his wife?

19 BIG Question
What does Anne mean by "I think myself out"? In your own words, explain what she's doing to survive this extremely tense time. Write your answer on the Workshop 2 Foldable for Unit 6.

believe in something! When I think of all that's out there . . . the trees . . . and flowers . . . and seagulls . . . when I think of the dearness of you, Peter . . . and the goodness of the people we know . . . Mr. Kraler, Miep, Dirk, the vegetable man, all risking their lives for us every day . . . When I think of these good things, I'm not afraid any more . . . I find myself, and God, and I . . .

[PETER *interrupts, getting up and walking away.*]

PETER. That's fine! But when I begin to think, I get mad! Look at us, hiding out for two years. Not able to move! Caught here like . . . waiting for them to come and get us . . . and all for what?

ANNE. We're not the only people that've had to suffer. There've always been people that've had to . . . sometimes one race . . . sometimes another . . . and yet . . .

PETER. That doesn't make me feel any better! **20**

ANNE. [*Going to him.*] I know it's terrible, trying to have any faith . . . when people are doing such horrible . . . But you know what I sometimes think? I think the world may be going through a phase, the way I was with Mother. It'll pass, maybe not for hundreds of years, but someday . . . I still believe, in spite of everything, that people are really good at heart. **21**

PETER. I want to see something now . . . Not a thousand years from now!

[*He goes over, sitting down again on the cot.*]

ANNE. But, Peter, if you'd only look at it as part of a great pattern . . . that we're just a little minute in the life . . . [*She breaks off.*] Listen to us, going at each other like a couple of stupid grown-ups! Look at the sky now. Isn't it lovely? [*She holds out her hand to him.* PETER *takes it and rises, standing with her at the window looking out, his arms around her.*] Someday, when we're outside again, I'm going to . . .

Practice the Skills

20 **Reviewing Skills**

Comparing and Contrasting
Explain the difference in the views that Anne and Peter have been expressing.

21 **BIG Question**

Do you agree with Anne? How would this belief help her—or anyone—want to keep going despite terrible times? Write your answer on the Workshop 2 Foldable for Unit 6.

[*She breaks off as she hears the sound of a car, its brakes squealing as it comes to a sudden stop. The people in the other rooms also become aware of the sound. They listen tensely. Another car roars up to a screeching stop.* ANNE *and* PETER *come from* PETER's *room.* MR. *and* MRS. VAN DAAN *creep down the stairs.* DUSSEL *comes out from his room. Everyone is listening, hardly breathing. A doorbell clangs again and again in the building below.* MR. FRANK *starts quietly down the steps to the door.* DUSSEL *and* PETER *follow him. The others stand rigid, waiting, terrified.*

In a few seconds DUSSEL *comes stumbling back up the steps. He shakes off* PETER's *help and goes to his room.* MR. FRANK *bolts the door below, and comes slowly back up the steps. Their eyes are all on him as he stands there for a minute. They realize that what they feared has happened.* MRS. VAN DAAN *starts to whimper.* MR. VAN DAAN *puts her gently in a chair, and then hurries off up the stairs to their room to collect their things.* PETER *goes to comfort his mother. There is a sound of violent pounding on a door below.*]

MR. FRANK. [*Quietly.*] For the past two years we have lived in fear. Now we can live in hope. **22**

[*The pounding below becomes more insistent. There are muffled sounds of voices, shouting commands.*]

MEN'S VOICES. Auf machen! Da drinnen! Auf machen! Schnell! Schnell! Schnell![9] etc., etc.

[*The street door below is forced open. We hear the heavy tread of footsteps coming up.* MR. FRANK *gets two school bags from the shelves, and gives one to* ANNE *and the other to* MARGOT. *He goes to get a bag for* MRS. FRANK. *The sound of feet coming up grows louder.* PETER *comes to* ANNE, *kissing her good-bye, then he goes to his room to collect his things. The buzzer of their door starts to ring.* MR. FRANK *brings* MRS. FRANK *a bag. They stand together, waiting. We hear the thud of gun butts on the door, trying to break it down.*

Practice the Skills

22 **Key Reading Skill**

Interpreting What do you think Mr. Frank means?

---

9. The voices are saying, in German: "Open up! Inside there! Open up! Quick! Quick! Quick!" The abbreviation *etc.* means "and so on." The actors are supposed to keep speaking until the curtain falls.

ANNE *stands, holding her school satchel, looking over at her father and mother with a soft, reassuring smile. She is no longer a child, but a woman with courage to meet whatever lies ahead. The lights dim out. The curtain falls on the scene. We hear a mighty crash as the door is shattered. After a second* ANNE'S VOICE *is heard.*]

ANNE'S VOICE. And so it seems our stay here is over. They are waiting for us now. They've allowed us five minutes to get our things. We can each take a bag and whatever it will hold of clothing. Nothing else. So, dear Diary, that means I must leave you behind. Good-bye for a while. P.S. Please, please, Miep, or Mr. Kraler, or anyone else. If you should find this diary, will you please keep it safe for me, because some day I hope . . .

[*Her voice stops abruptly. There is silence. After a second the curtain rises.*] **23**

Practice the Skills

23 | **Key Reading Skill**

Interpreting Why does her voice stop abruptly? What happened to Anne at this moment as she was writing?

This photograph shows the railway entrance to Auschwitz, one of the Nazi concentration camps.

The Diary of Anne Frank, Act 2, Scenes 3–5 **841**

Analyzing the Photo Describe what you see in this photo. Do you think it does a good job of representing the play's ending?

SCENE 5

[*It is again the afternoon in November, 1945. The rooms are as we saw them in the first scene.* MR. KRALER *has joined* MIEP *and* MR. FRANK. *There are coffee cups on the table. We see a great change in* MR. FRANK. *He is calm now. His bitterness is gone. He slowly turns a few pages of the diary. They are blank.*] **24**

MR. FRANK. No more.

[*He closes the diary and puts it down on the couch beside him.*]

MIEP. I'd gone to the country to find food. When I got back the block was surrounded by police . . .

MR. KRALER. We made it our business to learn how they knew. It was the thief . . . the thief who told them.

[MIEP *goes up to the gas burner, bringing back a pot of coffee.*]

Practice the Skills

24 **Key Literary Element**

Mood This scene goes back to the time of act 1, scene 1. It is more than a year since the Germans took Anne and the others away. As you read, think about the mood, or emotional effect, of this scene and of the whole play.

MR. FRANK. [*After a pause.*] It seems strange to say this, that anyone could be happy in a concentration camp. But Anne was happy in the camp in Holland where they first took us. After two years of being shut up in these rooms, she could be out . . . out in the sunshine and the fresh air that she loved.

MIEP. [*Offering the coffee to* MR. FRANK.] A little more?

MR. FRANK. [*Holding out his cup to her.*] The news of the war was good. The British and Americans were sweeping through France. We felt sure that they would get to us in time. In September we were told that we were to be shipped to Poland . . . The men to one camp. The women to another. I was sent to Auschwitz. They went to Belsen. In January we were freed, the few of us who were left. The war wasn't yet over, so it took us a long time to get home. We'd be sent here and there behind the lines where we'd be safe. Each time our train would stop . . . at a siding, or a crossing . . . we'd all get out and go from group to group . . . Where were you? Were you at Belsen? At Buchenwald? At Mauthausen?[10] Is it possible that you knew my wife? Did you ever see my husband? My son? My daughter? That's how I found out about my wife's death . . . of Margot, the Van Daans . . . Dussel. But Anne . . . I still hoped . . . Yesterday I went to Rotterdam.[11] I'd heard of a woman there . . . She'd been in Belsen with Anne . . . I know now. **25**

[*He picks up the diary again, and turns the pages back to find a certain passage. As he finds it we hear* ANNE'S VOICE.]

ANNE'S VOICE. In spite of everything, I still believe that people are really good at heart.

[MR. FRANK *slowly closes the diary.*]

MR. FRANK. She puts me to shame.

[*They are silent.*]

THE CURTAIN FALLS ○

Practice the Skills

25 Key Reading Skill

Interpreting What does Mr. Frank "know now"?

---

10. **Auschwitz** (OWSH vitz), **Belsen** (BEL zun), **Buchenwald** (BOO kun vawlt), and **Mauthausen** were the sites of Nazi concentration camps in Poland, Austria, and Germany. These camps specialized in exterminating prisoners.

11. **Rotterdam** is a city in the southwestern Netherlands.

The Diary of Anne Frank, Act 2, Scenes 3–5 **843**

After You Read

The Diary of Anne Frank, Act 2, Scenes 3–5

Answering the 💬 BIG Question

1. Anne is a good example of someone who never gives up. How do the others hiding in the attic compare with her?

2. **Recall** What does Miep bring with her when she returns to announce that the invasion has begun?
   Tip Right There

3. **Summarize** How do the others react when they catch Mr. Van Daan stealing the bread?
   Tip Think and Search

Critical Thinking

4. **Analyze** What accounts for the difference between Peter's and Anne's view of their situation? Explain your answer with details from the play.
   Tip Author and Me

5. **Explain** Are you surprised by Anne's views on the war and about people in general? Explain.
   Tip Author and Me

6. **Evaluate** Do you think Anne would have grown up as fast as she does if she hadn't gone into hiding? Would she have learned the same lessons if she had had a normal childhood?
   Tip Author and Me

7. **Interpret** At the end of the play, Mr. Frank feels shamed by the part of Anne's diary that says, "I still believe that people are really good at heart." What does his comment suggest about his own belief in people's goodness? Do you think his belief changed over the three years since the family went into hiding? Explain your answers.
   Tip Author and Me

Write About Your Reading

Monologue Imagine how this story would be different if it were told from Miep's point of view. Write a monologue from her perspective, similar to the excerpts from Anne's diary. Include these elements:

- how you feel about the actions of the Nazis
- what you think life must have been like for the Franks and the others
- why you decided to act the way you did
- how you feel about Anne and what happened to her

NY English Language Arts Core Curriculum (pp. 844–845)

LC R17 Demonstrate comprehension and response through a range of activities. **W2a** Write original literary texts to maintain a consistent point of view that enhances the message. **R2b** Interpret characters, plot, setting, theme, and dialogue, using evidence from the text. **R2e** Recognize how the author's use of language creates images or feelings. **Core R4** Determine the meaning of words by using structural analysis. **Core W7** Observe rules of punctuation.

For a complete description of the standards, see p. NY 11.

Skills Review

Key Reading Skill: Interpreting

8. "I still believe, in spite of everything, that people are really good at heart." What does this famous sentence of Anne's mean to you?

Key Literary Element: Mood

9. In two or three words, describe the mood of the last scene of the play.

10. What overall mood for the entire play do you think the playwrights wanted to create for an audience of theatergoers? Explain.

Reviewing Skills: Drawing Conclusions

11. At the end of the play, Mr. Frank knows but doesn't directly say what became of Anne. What happened to her? How do you know?

Reviewing Elements: Stage Directions

12. The second-to-last line of the script is this stage direction: [*They are silent.*] What reason(s) might the playwrights have had for including this?

Vocabulary Check

Rewrite each sentence with the best word from the list.

stealthily   pandemonium   liberated   downcast

13. ____ from the shed, the dog licked my face and then raced around the yard.

14. The robber entered ____, skillfully avoiding the guards posted at the main entrance.

15. "Don't be ____," the coach said. "Be proud that you did the very best you could."

16. There was ____ as police officers tried to control the angry protestors.

17. **English Language Coach** Below are the origins of two vocabulary words. Which word has Anglo-Saxon roots? Hint: Review the English Language Coach on page 824.

- **stealth** [ME *stelthe*, akin to OE *stelan* to steal]
- **pandemonium** [NL, fr Gk *pan-* all, every + *daimon* evil spirit]

Grammar Link: Commas with Appositives

Appositives are nouns or pronouns that rename, add more information about, or identify other nouns. Appositives can be either nonessential or essential. A nonessential appositive renames the noun or adds more information about it. The meaning of the sentence won't change if you read it without the appositive. Set off a nonessential appositive with commas.

- My sister, Maria, is the best singer. (Maria renames the noun sister. She is the speaker's only sister.)

An essential appositive identifies another noun or adds information that is necessary to the meaning of the sentence. DON'T set it off with commas.

- My sister Maria is the best singer. (Maria identifies this person as one of the speaker's sisters.)

Appositives can be phrases too. ALWAYS set off an appositive phrase with commas.

- Edison, inventor of the lightbulb, led an amazing life.

Grammar Practice

Rewrite the paragraph below. Find two nonessential appositives, and set them off with commas.

Our civics teacher Mrs. Riccio loves to read to the class. She read parts of Joan Heilbroner's book *Meet George Washington* to us. She said that Washington our first president was a great statesman.

Writing Application Review the monologue you wrote. Check that you used commas correctly with appositives.

Web Activities For eFlashcards, Selection Quick Checks, and other Web activities, go to www.glencoe.com.

Skills Focus

You will practice these skills when you read the following selections:

- Bouncing Back, p. 850
- Another Mountain, p. 856
- Standing Tall, p. 862

Reading

- Paraphrasing and summarizing

Literature

- Identifying and analyzing figurative language
- Understanding expository writing

Vocabulary

- Understanding Greek roots
- Understanding content-area words

Writing/Grammar

- Using commas with relative clauses
- Using commas with direct address

NY English Language Arts Core Curriculum (pp. 846–847)

LC R12 Combine multiple strategies (summarize) to enhance comprehension and response.

For a complete description of the standards, see p. NY 11.

Skill Lesson

Paraphrasing and Summarizing

Learn It!

What Is It? **Paraphrasing** is restating something in your own words that you've read. If a friend asks you to help him understand something from class, you probably paraphrase the teacher's words.

Summarizing is retelling the main events and ideas of a selection in your own words. You might summarize the first part of a movie for a friend who arrived late. When you summarize, it is important to put your ideas in a logical sequence. The order in which you summarize the main ideas or events should match the order in the selection.

© 1987 Watterson. Dist. By UNIVERSAL PRESS SYNDICATE. Reprinted with permission. All rights reserved.

Analyzing Cartoons

Why does Calvin want Hobbes to summarize the book? How would you summarize this cartoon if you were telling a friend about it?

Why Is It Important? Paraphrasing and summarizing are helpful when you read long selections that contain lots of details. You can paraphrase to check whether you've understood an idea, and you can summarize to make sure that you've understood a paragraph, a selection, or even an entire book. Summarizing can also help you separate main ideas from supporting information and unnecessary details.

How Do I Do It? To summarize, note major ideas and events as you read. When you come to the end of a section, ask yourself what it was about. Then put that information in an order that makes sense. To paraphrase, be on the lookout for passages that are complicated or hard to understand. When you read something that is difficult, try to restate it in your own words. Here's how one student paraphrased one of Anne's speeches in *The Diary of Anne Frank:*

> Oh, I don't mean you have to be Orthodox . . . or believe in heaven and hell and purgatory and things . . . I just mean some religion . . . it doesn't matter what. Just to believe in something! When I think of all that's out there . . . the trees . . . and flowers . . . and seagulls . . . when I think of the dearness of you, Peter . . . and the goodness of the people we know . . . Mr. Kraler, Miep, Dirk, the vegetable man, all risking their lives for us every day . . . When I think of these good things, I'm not afraid any more . . .

> *Anne is trying to explain how she keeps from giving up during difficult times. By focusing on the beauty of nature, the joy of relationships, and the goodness of people, she avoids being overcome with fear. She wants Peter to think this way too.*

Literature Online

Study Central Visit www.glencoe.com and click on Study Central to review paraphrasing and summarizing.

Practice It!

Choose a cartoon strip or an episode of a TV show that you remember well. Think about the main ideas and events and then write a summary in your Learner's Notebook. Remember to write the events in a logical sequence.

Use It!

As you read the selections in this workshop, use paraphrasing and summarizing to check whether you understand the more difficult parts.

Before You Read

Bouncing Back *and* Another Mountain

Meet the Authors

Jan Farrington is a freelance writer who contributes to *Current Health* and other publications.

Abiodun Oyewole

Abiodun Oyewole's poetry often focuses on the damage done by racism and on the need to heal after being wounded. He once said, "We have to see how we can be the greatest part of us, which is the healing part of us. . . . I'd rather that folks learn how to save themselves." See page R5 of the Author Files for more on Oyewole.

Literature Online

Author Search For more about Abiodun Oyewole, go to www .glencoe.com.

NY English Language Arts Core Curriculum (pp. 848–857)

Core R4 Determine the meaning of words by using structural analysis.
LC R12 Combine multiple strategies (summarize) to enhance comprehension and response. **R2d** Determine how the use and meaning of literary devices, such as metaphor, simile, and personification, convey the author's message or intent.

For a complete description of the standards, see p. NY 11.

Vocabulary Preview

unfulfilling (un ful FIL ing) *adj.* not satisfying **(p. 850)** *We all want to be happy in our work; nobody grows up thinking, "Gee, I hope I'll be able to find an unfulfilling career!"*

resilient (rih ZIL yunt) *adj.* able to recover from or adjust easily to misfortune or change **(p. 850)** *Some people are resilient, while others can't seem to adjust well to challenges.*

strategies (STRAT uh jeez) *n.* plans for working through a problem or activity **(p. 851)** *Fortunately, there are several good strategies for dealing with the difficulties life may present.*

phase (fayz) *n.* a step in the development of a person or thing **(p. 853)** *Most teens go through a phase in which they question the "rules."*

destitute (DES tih toot) *adj.* completely without money or possessions **(p. 853)** *For a destitute family, even macaroni and cheese can be a luxury.*

Partner Work With a partner, write four sentences about being a teenager. Use at least one vocabulary word in each sentence.

English Language Coach

Greek Roots and Combining Forms The Greek language gave English not only roots, prefixes, and suffixes, but word parts called **combining forms**. A combining form occurs only in combination with words, affixes, or other combining forms to form compounds such as *geophysics* and *geology*. In the first word, the combining form *geo-* is added to the word *physics*. In the second word, it's added to another combining form, *–logy*.

The Greek civilization was one of the earliest to form ideas about politics and education. As a result, many English words that have to do with government and learning come from the Greek roots and combining forms. Here are a few examples.

Root or combining form	Meaning	English word
arch	⟹ govern, rule	⟹ monarch
auto	⟹ self	⟹ automatic, automobile
bio	⟹ life	⟹ biology, biography
log, logy	⟹ word, study, speech	⟹ dialogue, biology

Skills Preview

Key Reading Skill: Paraphrasing and Summarizing

You probably paraphrase and summarize every day. When a friend asks about a homework assignment, you don't repeat the teacher's exact words. You paraphrase. When your parents ask what you learned in school, you don't list every single detail. You summarize.

Write to Learn Think of a story you know well. In your Learner's Notebook, summarize the story.

Literary Element: Literal and Figurative Language

Most of the time, people use words to state simple facts. When they do so, they use **literal language,** or language that uses words according to their exact definitions. "The sky at night is black with white stars" is an example of literal language.

People use **figurative language,** or language that has meaning beyond the literal definition of words, to be descriptive or imaginative. "The sky at night is a velvet blanket with sparkling diamonds" is an example of figurative language.

Three kinds of figurative language are:

- Similes and metaphors, which compare unlike things. Similes use *like* or *as*, while metaphors only imply the comparison.
- Symbolism, which uses one thing to stand for another because of a resemblance or association between the two things.
- Personification, which gives human qualities to an animal, object, or idea.

Write to Learn Use figurative language to describe an object in your classroom. Is a book a "window to the world"? Is the chalkboard "staring you down"? Perhaps the clock hands move slowly, "like students heading for class." Write two or three figurative descriptions of the object.

Get Ready to Read

Connect to the Reading

The author of "Bouncing Back" offers advice about dealing with challenges. The speaker in "Another Mountain" keeps going despite difficulties. How do you deal with challenges and hardships?

Write to Learn Think about a time when you reacted poorly to a difficult situation. Write a few sentences about how you should have acted and what you can do the next time you face a similar situation.

Build Background

"Another Mountain" is, in part, about fighting racism.

- Oyewole's group, The Last Poets, was established in 1968 after the poets read their work at a memorial for Malcolm X.
- The Last Poets were African American activists influenced by radical groups such as the Black Panthers.
- The Last Poets are considered by many to be the founders of hip-hop.

Set Purposes for Reading

BIG Question Read "Bouncing Back" and "Another Mountain" to see how people face obstacles without losing their hope or their confidence.

Set Your Own Purpose What would you like to learn from the selections to help you answer the Big Question? Write your answer on the Workshop 3 Foldable for Unit 6.

Interactive Literary Elements Handbook
To review or learn more about the literary elements, go to www.glencoe.com.

Keep Moving

Use these skills as you read the following selections.

INFORMATIONAL TEXT
MAGAZINE
Current Health

BOUNCING BACK

How to Get on Your Feet When Life Knocks You Down

by Jan Farrington

When Beth Driscoll of Denton, Texas, was in middle school, she dreamed of following her friends to a private high school. Her family didn't have the money, so she went to the local public high school. Beth made it work. But in her senior year, she got more bad news—her dad had lost his job. Her parents told her they couldn't help pay for college.

You can see where this story line might go: Beth gives up, takes an **unfulfilling** job, and maybe dives into drugs. But that didn't happen. Instead, she applied for student loans, took a part-time job, and rented a tiny room near campus, where she's now studying to be a special-education teacher.

Beth's life isn't perfect. She works too many hours to spend as much time studying as she'd like to. But Beth, now 21, is determined to earn her degree and make a good life for herself. **1**

Six Tips for Taking Charge

When life knocks you down, do you have trouble getting off the ground? Or are you a **resilient** teen with a gift for bouncing back, like Beth? **2**

"Some kids come into this world and have an easier time being happy and dealing with stress," Robert Brooks of Harvard Medical School told *Current Health*. Brooks is a

Practice the Skills

1 **Key Reading Skill**

Paraphrasing and Summarizing When you summarize, you retell the main ideas or events of a passage in a logical order. Summarize the information in the first three paragraphs about Beth Driscoll.

2 **Literary Element**

Literal and Figurative Language The phrase "life knocks you down" is figurative. Its meaning goes beyond the literal definition of the words. Explain what this expression means.

Vocabulary

unfulfilling (un ful FIL ing) *adj.* not satisfying

resilient (rih ZIL yunt) *adj.* able to recover from or adjust easily to misfortune or change

family **psychologist** and a coauthor of *The Power of Resilience: Achieving Balance, Confidence, and Personal Strength in Your Life.* But what if you don't handle stress well? Brooks says there are many things that teens can do to take charge of their own problems and build better coping skills. He suggests the strategies below. **3**

1. **Surround yourself with people who make you stronger.** Having a few close friends can be a great source of strength, says Brooks. "But some teens with low self-esteem would rather have friends who make fun of them and get them in trouble than be ignored," he added. Bottom line: Don't put up with friends who put you down.

2. **Involve adults in your life.** "Resilient people almost always say there were one or two adults who really believed in them and stood by them" when they were teens, Brooks said. For many teens, parents fit the bill.[1] For other teens, those caring adults may be relatives, family friends, or youth group leaders.

3. **Discover something you're good at.** By focusing on your strengths and talents, you can develop a sense of pride and dignity that will help you overcome obstacles in other areas of your life.

4. **Let yourself experience success.** "Success builds on success," noted Brooks. Your long-term goal may be to go to college, despite financial woes.[2] But along the way, achieving smaller goals (making a speech in public, studying for 30 minutes longer each night) can give you a taste of success that will help you cope with bigger challenges ahead. **4**

5. **Believe things will get better.** "Most of the problems that teens face are solvable," Brooks told *CH*. "But if [teens are] feeling down or incompetent,[3] it's easy for them to feel their whole life is going to be that way." Think about all the

Practice the Skills

3 **English Language Coach**

Greek Roots The Greek *psych* means "mind, soul, or spirit." Look at the chart on page 848 to see what the combining form *-logy* means. And then add the information that *-ist* means "one who has a special skill." What, then, does **psychologist** mean?

4 **Literary Element**

Literal and Figurative Language "A taste of success" is a metaphor. Explain what it means and what comparison the writer is making.

---

1. Here, to *fit the bill* means "to be right for a situation."
2. *Financial woes* are problems related to money.
3. Someone who feels *incompetent* thinks that he or she is not able to do things correctly or successfully.

Vocabulary

strategies (STRAT uh jeez) *n.* plans for working through a problem or activity

changes you've seen in your life, and you'll realize that a "rough patch" is only temporary.

6. **Put yourself out there.** Volunteer at a food bank, at a nursing home, or with the local Special Olympics program. "Teens who help others are less likely to feel depressed or angry," said Brooks. "Giving back to the community gives teens an opportunity to shine and to feel they're making a difference in the world." **5**

Classroom Heroes

What does resilience look like? Sometimes it looks like the kid sitting next to you in math class.

Robin Regan, 18, and Patricia Calderon, 19, had shared a class at their Orange County, Calif., high school. But until both girls won the 2003 Julie Inman Courage Award, neither had discussed what the other was going through.

Regan's mother had broken her neck in an accident, and Regan was helping her mom learn to walk again. Calderon had an older sister who was dying of leukemia.[4] Both teens were taking care of younger siblings, tackling household chores, and keeping up with honors classes, school commitments, and volunteer projects. But that didn't stop the two girls from graduating from high school on time. Regan and Calderon are now thriving college students.

How did they manage? "I'm not going to lie," Regan said. "After Mom's accident, I was really angry. I thought, *This isn't fair; why did it have to happen just when I need her so much?*" she said. "But my parents' dream for me always was that I go to college. So I couldn't throw away all their hard work."

Calderon says she owes her strength to her sister. "She always told me to try my hardest. She didn't get to finish [her life], so I want to succeed not just for me but for her too."

Analyzing the Photo Why is it important to choose good friends? How do your friends help you be the best you can be?

Practice the Skills

5 🔺**BIG** **Question**
Which of these six tips for taking charge do you find most helpful? Have you ever used any of these strategies? Explain your answer on the Workshop 3 Foldable for Unit 6.

---

4. *Leukemia* (loo KEE mee uh) is a deadly disease that affects blood cells.

Practice the Skills

As remarkable as their stories are, Regan and Calderon fit the profile of typical Inman award winners. The annual awards recognize teens who have earned their diplomas in spite of broken homes, illnesses, or other challenges. "Sometimes these kids are overlooked, and all we see are the athletes and scholars," said Julie Inman, the inspiration for the award. Inman herself knows a lot about resilience. After a skiing accident left her paralyzed at age 15, she went on to get a college degree with honors and has never abandoned her goal of someday walking again.

School of Hard Knocks

No one enjoys tough times. Still, there can be a surprising upside to life's downturns: They make you stronger. "I am not the same person I was before," Calderon told *CH.* "Before, I always had older sisters who looked after me. But then suddenly I had to pull myself together and take over."

"Little things don't bother me anymore," Regan added. "I had to grow up pretty quick, but in the long run, I think that will be good. When other tough things come up, I can tell myself that I've gotten through something tough before, and I can handle it." **6**

6 **Key Reading Skill**

Paraphrasing and Summarizing Paraphrase in one sentence what Regan says in this paragraph.

Tough Times of the Rich and Famous

U.S. senator Barack Obama went through a rebellious **phase** after his father left the family. Obama went so far as to experiment with alcohol and drugs. In his autobiography, *Dreams From My Father,* he writes that his mother's love and the support of some wonderful teachers and mentors[5] "pulled me out of it."

Country singer, Shania Twain grew up in a **destitute** family in a Canadian mining town. She was just 21 when her mother and stepfather were killed in a car accident. Nonetheless,

---

5. A **mentor** is a guide, coach, or role model.

Vocabulary

phase (fayz) *n.* a step in the development of a person or thing

destitute (DES tih toot) *adj.* completely without money or possessions

Twain took charge of raising her three younger siblings. "It was a difficult time," she told *Rolling Stone*. "But boy, oh boy, did I get strong."

Yankees star player Alex Rodriguez hit tough times at age 10, when his father left the family. "It was hard. I did my best to help out around the house and bring home good grades to make my mom proud," he told *Sports Illustrated for Kids.* His high school baseball coach became like a second father to him, and he found a lot of support at a Boys and Girls Club in Miami. He's now a national spokesman for the clubs. **7**

Would You Survive . . . or Thrive?

When bad things happen, feeling upset can be a normal first response. But what's your second response? Do you move in a positive direction or in a negative one?

In the situations below, think honestly about how you'd react, and circle the letter for that response. We'll help you analyze the results.

1. **The referee doesn't call pass interference when an opposing player keeps you from connecting with a pass. You**
   a) rush the ref and yell in his or her face.
   b) spend the ride home talking to your teammates about the bad call.
   c) tell yourself to get back in the game and play even harder and smarter than before.

2. **You think you did fine on your English exam, but the teacher hands it back with a grade of C minus. You**
   a) tell yourself that the test questions were confusing and blame your teacher.
   b) decide you won't study as hard for the next test, because it won't do any good.
   c) take a long walk and then ask the teacher for study suggestions.

7 **BIG Question**
Think about the personal stories in this article. What kinds of things kept these people from giving up? Have you or anyone you know ever experienced things like the people in the article? Write your answers on the Workshop 3 Foldable for Unit 6. Your response will help you complete the Unit Challenge later.

3. **You apply to three colleges but get into only your "safety" school. Your best friend gets into the one school both of you wanted to attend. You**
   a) decide not to attend college and look for a job instead.
   b) congratulate your friend but still feel jealous. You go off to college with a bad attitude.
   c) find out all you can about the college that accepted you. You ask an admissions officer to connect you with current students who can tell you what's happening on campus.

4. **Your parents divorced last year, and your dad practically disappeared from your life. Now he's e-mailed to ask if you'll have dinner with him. You've spent all year feeling hurt. You**
   a) ignore his e-mail but think a lot about what a jerk he is.
   b) send him a nasty e-mail, turning down the dinner invitation and writing things both of you will have a hard time forgetting.
   c) accept the invitation but let your dad know that he's hurt you and that it's something you need to talk about.

If you have a lot of *a* or *b* answers, you probably have a hard time letting go of negative feelings about yourself and your life. Having a lot of *c* answers means you're pretty resilient: When you hit a rough patch, you try to turn things in a more positive direction.

Do you need to work on resiliency skills? Try some of the suggestions in the article, and remember: One of the best ways to get rid of negative emotions is to get involved in something outside yourself. Do something that's worth doing—for your family, for a community group, for your school—and you'll be making yourself stronger too. 🔟 ○

🔟 **Key Reading Skill**

Paraphrasing and Summarizing Paraphrase the writer's point in the last paragraph.

Another Mountain

by Abiodun Oyewole

Sometimes there's a mountain
that I must climb **1**
even after I've climbed one already
But my legs are tired now
5 and my arms need a rest
my mind is too weary right now
But I must climb before the storm comes
before the earth rocks
and an avalanche of clouds buries me
10 and smothers my soul
And so I prepare myself for another climb
Another Mountain
and I tell myself it is nothing
it is just some more dirt and stone
15 and every now and then I should reach
another plateau* and enjoy the view
of the trees and the flowers below **2**
And I am young enough to climb
and strong enough to make it to any top
20 You see the wind has warned me
about settling too long
about peace without struggle
The wind has warned me
and taught me how to fly
25 But my wings only work
After I've climbed a mountain **3** ○

Practice the Skills

1 **Literary Element**

Literal and Figurative Language The poem's main image involves the metaphor of climbing a mountain. However, the poet also uses symbolism and personification.

2 **Key Reading Skill**

Paraphrasing and Summarizing See the footnote about *plateau* and decide what the word means here. Then paraphrase lines 15-17.

3 **BIG Question**

These lines suggest that working wings, or the ability to fly, is the speaker's reward for climbing a mountain. Is there always a reward for getting through struggle and hardship? Explain your answer on the Workshop 3 Foldable for Unit 6. Your response will help you complete the Unit Challenge later.

---

16 A *plateau* is a large, flat area of land that is higher than the surrounding land on at least one side. Figuratively, it can mean "a level of achievement."

After You Read

Bouncing Back *and* Another Mountain

Answering the **BIG** Question

1. In "Bouncing Back," the writer gives six tips for handling stress. Without looking at the article, note as many tips as you can.

2. **Recall** What important, similar thing happened in the lives of Barack Obama, Shania Twain, and Alex Rodriguez?

   TIP Right There

Critical Thinking

3. **Evaluate** In your opinion, what keeps the speaker of "Another Mountain" from giving up?

   TIP Author and Me

4. **Explain** Why does it matter what kind of people you surround yourself with when there is trouble in your life?

   TIP Think and Search

5. **Analyze** How does the speaker in "Another Mountain" prepare mentally for the challenges to be faced?

   TIP Author and Me

6. **Evaluate** Which selection do you find more helpful or inspiring? Explain your answer.

   TIP Author and Me

Write About Your Reading

Written Response Review the six strategies for "taking charge" that are suggested in the article. Choose one strategy that has helped you deal with a problem in the past, or think of a different strategy that you've used.

Write three paragraphs about how you took charge of the situation. You don't need to give personal details or names. Just explain in general terms what the problem was and how you were able to deal with it.

- In the first paragraph, briefly describe the problem.

- In the second paragraph, identify the strategy you used and how it worked for you. (Again, try to give a clear explanation, but don't reveal details that you feel are too personal.)

- In the last paragraph, explain how the strategy you used might help other people deal with their problems and with stress.

NY English Language Arts Core Curriculum (pp. 858–859)

LC R17 Demonstrate comprehension and response through a range of activities. **Core W6** Develop a personal writing style and voice. **LC R12** Combine multiple strategies (summarize) to enhance comprehension and response. **R2d** Determine how the use and meaning of literary devices, such as symbolism, metaphor and simile, and personification, convey the author's message or intent. **Core R4** Determine the meaning of words by using structural analysis. **Core W7** Observe rules of punctuation.

For a complete description of the standards, see p. NY 11.

Skills Review

Key Reading Skill: Paraphrasing and Summarizing

7. Write a brief summary of "Bouncing Back," listing the main ideas in a logical order. Then paraphrase two sentences from the selection that you believe are important to the overall idea or message.

Literary Element: Literal and Figurative Language

8. Is the title "Bouncing Back" meant to be taken literally? Explain.

9. Someone in the article says, "I had to pull myself together." Explain this figurative expression.

10. In the poem, what does the mountain (line 1) symbolize? What does Another Mountain (line 12) symbolize? Do they represent different things? Explain your answers.

11. Identify the thing that is personified in "Another Mountain," and give the line number(s) where the personification is found.

Vocabulary Check

Write the vocabulary word for each definition.

**unfulfilling   resilient   strategies
phase   destitute**

12. not satisfying

13. a step in the development of a thing

14. completely without money or possessions

15. plans for working through a problem or activity

16. able to recover from or adjust easily to misfortune or change

17. **English Language Coach** Add the Greek combining form *logy* to the word parts below, and write the definition of each word. (You may use a dictionary.)

zoo   geo   bio

Grammar Link: Commas with Relative Clauses

A **relative clause** begins with a relative pronoun like *that, who,* or *which.* If the clause is essential (necessary to make the meaning of the sentence clear) then it is not set off with commas. If the clause is nonessential (not necessary to make the meaning clear), then it is set off with commas.

Use the relative pronoun *that* or *who* to introduce an essential relative clause. Use the relative pronoun *which* or *who* to introduce a nonessential relative clause.

Essential: Jack London wrote a collection of short stories <u>that was published in 1900</u>.

Nonessential: Jack London's first book, <u>which is a collection of short stories</u>, was published in 1900.

Essential: Jack London is the author <u>who wrote *The Call of the Wild*</u>.

Nonessential: Jack London, <u>who wrote *The Call of the Wild*</u>, was the most popular novelist of his day.

Grammar Practice

Copy the following sentences and correctly add commas to set off the two relative clauses.

18. I will never forget the day that Mom brought home our first puppy.

19. The wind which was very strong brought down trees everywhere and caused a great deal of damage.

20. William Shakespeare who lived in the 1500s is the author who wrote *Romeo and Juliet*.

Writing Application Review your Write About Your Reading activity. Circle all relative pronouns. Make sure you used commas correctly with relative clauses.

Web Activities For eFlashcards, Selection Quick Checks, and other Web activities, go to www.glencoe.com.

Before You Read : Standing Tall

Meet the Author

Michael Dolan is a reporter and feature writer for *Popular Science* magazine. He frequently takes complicated, technical subjects and makes them easy for people to understand.

Author Search For more about Michael Dolan, go to www.glencoe.com.

Vocabulary Preview

tribute (TRIB yoot) *n.* evidence of some good quality **(p. 862)** *The statue of Columbus was a tribute from members of the Italian American community.*

collapse (kuh LAPS) *v.* to fall apart, cave in, or break down **(p. 862)** *We knew the chimney needed repairs, but we didn't expect it to collapse.*

stable (STAY bul) *adj.* firm and steady; long-lasting **(p. 864)** *Abigail had to shift the ladder twice before it felt stable enough to climb.*

withstand (with STAND) *v.* to resist the effect of; stand up against **(p. 865)** *This coat is designed to withstand both rain and cold.*

Sentence Challenge Use each vocabulary word in a separate sentence. Then try to use all four words in one sentence that still makes sense.

English Language Coach

Content-Area Words When you read about a certain subject, you may find words that are specific to that subject. These are called "content-area" words because they're used within a particular area, such as a job or a sport. Some words have different meanings in different content areas.

Word	Content areas	Meaning
baste	cooking, food science	to pour butter or fat over meat or fish while it's being cooked
	sewing, fashion design	to use large stitches to hold fabrics together for a short time
curveball	baseball	a particular type of pitch
extinct	environmental science	having died out completely

The structure and context of content-area words often give clues to their meanings. The next selection relates to building construction and uses the words *steel-mesh concrete.* You already know what concrete is, but what is "steel-mesh" concrete? Look for context clues to give some ideas.

Partner Talk With a partner, use clues in each sentence below to help find the meaning of the underlined word and identify the content area.

1. Mixed in with the old, fully grown trees were many **saplings**.
2. The guitarist's fingers moved over the **frets** quickly but accurately.
3. This could help people on the top floors **evacuate** to safety.

NY English Language Arts Core Curriculum (pp. 860–865)

Core R4 Determine the meaning of unfamiliar words by using context clues and structural analysis. **LC R12** Combine multiple strategies (summarize) to enhance comprehension and response. **R1f** Use knowledge of structure to understand informational text.

For a complete description of the standards, see p. NY 11.

Skills Preview

Key Reading Skill: Paraphrasing and Summarizing

"Standing Tall" discusses new methods and materials for making tall buildings stronger and safer. That was a one-sentence summary of the next selection. As you read the article, paraphrase and summarize difficult parts to help you understand the main ideas.

Partner Talk Explain to your partner something technical that you know how to do, such as creating a Web page. Or describe something you know from reading, such as a special effect in a movie. Explain the process clearly but briefly.

Text Element: Expository Writing

Descriptive writing describes a person, place, or thing. Narrative writing tells a story. Persuasive writing tries to change the reader's opinion. **Expository writing** informs and explains. An *exposition* is a detailed explanation. How-to books, newspaper and magazine articles, and instructions are some types of expository writing. Textbooks are also expository.

Most expository writing is organized using certain text structures. The following are most common.

- **Description** may be needed to help readers understand a topic.
- **Time Order** shows the stages in which something happened or should happen.
- **Compare-Contrast** writing looks at how things are similar and different.
- **Cause-Effect** text shows the relationship between outcomes and their causes.
- **Problem-Solution** writing presents a problem and one or more solutions.

Interactive Literary Elements Handbook
To review or learn more about the literary elements, go to www.glencoe.com.

Get Ready to Read

Connect to the Reading

What's your favorite skyscraper? How tall is it? Where is it? Have you been inside? Have you been in a really tall building—one that has more than sixty stories?

The Empire State Building in New York City was the world's tallest building for more than forty years after its completion in 1931. In 1974 Chicago's Sears Tower took the record. In 2005 the tallest building in the world was the Taipei Financial Center in Taiwan. Is it still?

On Your Own Search online for "world's tallest buildings." Make a chart of the ten tallest buildings, showing how tall they are and where, when, and why they were built (for offices, homes, hotels, and so on).

Build Background

- The term *skyscraper* was first used in 1883.
- The development of elevators made it practical to have buildings more than four stories tall. In 1857 a New York City store had the first passenger elevator.
- The use of iron and steel in construction allowed buildings to be taller. In 1885 the ten-story Home Insurance Building in Chicago was the first "tall" building to have steel columns and beams.
- On September 11, 2001, the World Trade Center in New York was destroyed in a terrorist attack. All over the world, people wondered whether any skyscraper could ever be safe.

Set Purposes for Reading

BIG Question Read "Standing Tall" to learn how architects today are planning safer buildings.

Set Your Own Purpose What would you like to learn from the article to help you answer the Big Question? Write your own purpose on the Workshop 3 Foldable for Unit 6.

Keep Moving

Use these skills as you read the following selection.

TIME

Standing Tall

Architects and engineers are working
with new designs and materials that can
make future skyscrapers sturdier and safer.

By MICHAEL DOLAN

The idea of building a tower to touch the sky goes back thousands of years. And during the past century, concrete, steel, and other materials have made it possible for architects and engineers to design and build structures that stand a quarter-mile high. These buildings are a **tribute** to humankind's need to both test a structure's limits and solve problems such as overcrowding in cities. **1**

But after September 11, 2001, <u>skyscrapers</u> are being seen in a whole new way. Terrorists hijacked[1] and crashed two planes into New York City's tallest buildings, causing the twin towers of the World Trade Center to **collapse.** Skyscrapers around the world suddenly gained a new label: target. **2**

That new label has inspired builders to work on a new goal—creating the safest tall building in the world. The smartest minds in architecture and structural engineering are

1. When a plane is *hijacked,* one or more people take control of it by force.

1 **Key Reading Skill**

Paraphrasing and Summarizing The last sentence is complicated and contains two ideas. Put this sentence in your own words. What is it saying?

2 **English Language Coach**

Content-Area Words
Although **skyscrapers** can be considered a content-area word, we all understand and use it.

Vocabulary

tribute (TRIB yoot) *n.* evidence of some good quality

collapse (kuh LAPS) *v.* to fall apart, cave in, or break down

working together to figure out how to construct a building that could survive threats of terrorism[2] and natural disasters.

One material that could help architects and engineers is concrete. New types of concrete are being developed to help resist the force of bomb blasts and the 2,000°F temperatures of jet fuel fires. For example, one new type of concrete contains pieces of recycled stainless steel. The stainless steel increases the concrete's strength and its ability to stand up to a bomb blast or similar forces. **3**

A skyscraper made with steel-supported concrete wouldn't shatter as much when attacked. Instead its concrete would cling together in larger chunks, making it less likely to collapse. Steel-mesh concrete was originally used as a way to keep tall buildings safe in parts of the world where

3 **Text Element**

Expository Writing Based on these first few paragraphs, which text structure appears to be the main organization of this article? Explain.

2. **Terrorism** is the use of violence, especially against civilian (non-military) targets, to try to make people or governments meet certain demands.

Farrell Grehan/Corbis

On September 11, 2001, terrorists crashed two planes into the twin towers of New York City's World Trade Center (two tallest buildings in center of photo), causing both to collapse.

earthquakes occur frequently. Now engineers are thinking of using this same material in all skyscrapers to protect against the force of airplane crashes and the fires they cause.

In addition to fire protection, various forms of concrete could make a skyscraper stronger and more **stable.** Whereas the World Trade Center towers got most of their support from steel columns around the outside of the buildings, many engineers now think every future skyscraper should have a **concrete core** that runs down the center of the building. **4**

Just as your spine supports much of your body, a concrete core would serve as a building's spine and support its weight. It would also serve as a safety zone. Designers could place emergency escape routes and fireproof elevators and stairwells in the concrete core. These features could help more people escape if a disaster were to occur.

Builders are working hard to find answers to other questions that could make skyscrapers safer. Could a building's emergency staff use sensitive laser machines to find harmful chemical materials before they even reach the building? Is it possible to create a fireproof evacuation system[3] that could help people on the top floors find safety when the middle of the building is in flames?

There's still a lot of work to be done, but the answers to these questions and many others may be coming soon to a skyscraper near you. **5**

—From *Popular Science*, July 2005

4 **English Language Coach**

Content-Area Words There are good context clues for **concrete core** here and in the next sentence.

5 **BIG Question**

How are the actions of builders and engineers an example of not giving up when bad things happen? Write your answer on the Workshop 3 Foldable for Unit 6. Your response will help you complete the Unit Challenge later.

---

3. An *evacuation system* is a way to get people out of a building when there's an emergency. To evacuate is to clear out, or leave.

Vocabulary . . . .

stable (STAY bul) *adj.* firm and steady; long-lasting

Skyscraper Self-defense

Builders are exploring new ways to make office workers feel safe. Some ideas include steel-supported concrete, escape routes that could **withstand** bomb blasts, safety floors where people could wait out a fire, and laser machines that could identify dangerous chemicals.

1. Safety areas: Spaced 15 floors apart, these concrete-supported areas would withstand high temperatures.

2. Bombproof elevator shafts: These would enable firefighters to quickly reach areas where fires have started.

3. Escape stairwells: Located in the building's concrete core, these fireproof stairwells would provide a smoke-free escape route.

4. Emergency command center: The building's security headquarters would be located on the floor above the lobby, where builders think it would be safe from car bombs.

5. Concrete core: A column of concrete at the middle of the building would support its weight and offer a fireproof zone for emergency stairs and elevators.

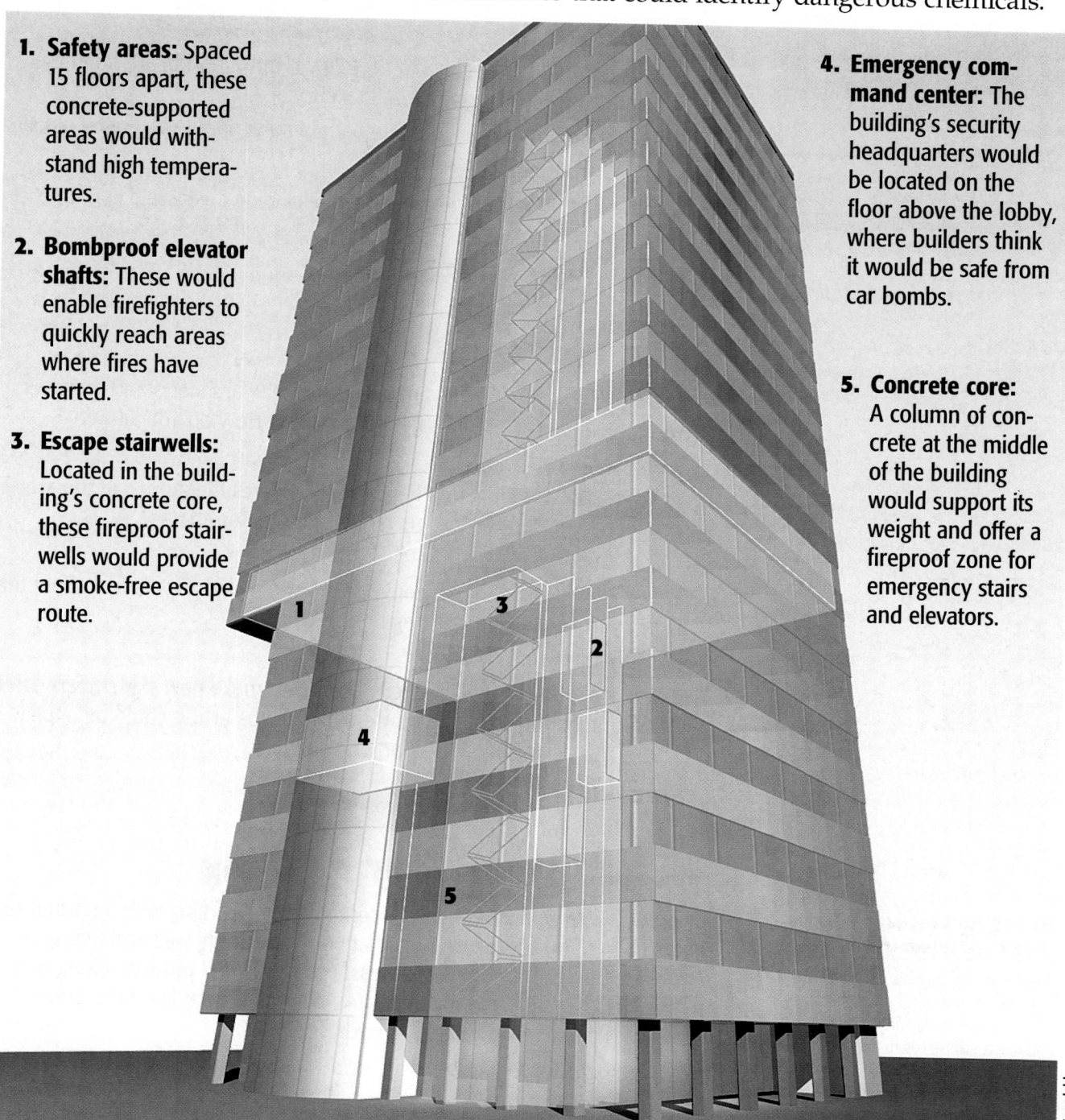

Mika Grondahl

After You Read

Standing Tall

Farrell Grehan/Corbis

Answering the BIG Question

1. Why do some people refuse to back down from a problem, no matter how much time and money it will take to face it?
2. **Recall** What event changed how people think about skyscraper safety?
   TIP Right There
3. **Summarize** What are the benefits of including a concrete core in a new skycraper?
   TIP Think and Search

Critical Thinking

4. **Infer** What is the writer's attitude toward the architects and engineers who are working to build safer skyscrapers? How do you know?
   TIP Think and Search
5. **Predict** Do you think that the safety measures mentioned in the article could really make skyscrapers less of a target for attacks?
   TIP Author and Me
6. **Infer** How do you think people who work in skyscrapers feel about the new improvements in building design? Explain.
   TIP Author and Me
7. **Evaluate** "Standing Tall" discusses how to make new skyscrapers safer. Do you think the technologies described in the article could be applied to existing skyscrapers? Why or why not?
   TIP Author and Me

Write About Your Reading

Glossary Create a glossary for a content area. Working with a partner or in a small group, choose an area that you know fairly well and that uses specialized language. Then list at least ten words and phrases, along with their parts of speech and meanings. As examples, here are three areas, along with a few terms related to each.

- Baseball: *backstop, double play, fielder's choice, infield, home plate, out, outfielder, strike, umpire*
- Education: *auditorium, etymology, grade, No Child Left Behind, middle school, standardized test*
- Theater: *act, audition, box office, dialogue, director, intermission, opening night, sound effect*

NY English Language Arts Core Curriculum (pp. 866–867)

R1m Draw conclusions on the basis of explicit and implied information. **W1h** Support ideas with examples and direct references to the text. **LC R12** Combine multiple strategies (summarize) to enhance comprehension and response. **R1f** Use knowledge of structure to understand informational text. **Core W7** Observe rules of punctuation.

For a complete description of the standards, see p. NY 11.

Skills Review

Key Reading Skill: Paraphrasing and Summarizing

8. List three ways that concrete (or new types of concrete) could make tall buildings safer. Paraphrase and summarize what the writer says about this subject.

Text Element: Expository Writing

9. The text structure of this article could be identified as either problem-solution or cause-effect. Explain why it might be either one, using details from the article to support your answer.

Reviewing Skills: Comparing and Contrasting

10. The writer uses a comparison to explain the idea of a concrete core in a building. What two things are compared?

Vocabulary Check

Rewrite each sentence with the best vocabulary word from the list. Two words will be used twice.

tribute   collapse   stable   withstand

11. There won't be a ___ peace if the two nations can't learn to live with one another.

12. Our roof cannot ___ the effects of one more winter snowstorm.

13. People meeting a king or queen are expected to bow as a ___.

14. Experts warn that the dam will ___ if it isn't strengthened before the rainy season begins.

15. Trust, patience, and work are required to build a ___ friendship.

16. It took me two weeks to build that bookcase but only a half-second for it to ___.

17. **English Language Coach** What makes **stainless steel** a good material for supporting concrete? (You may look it up.)

Grammar Link: Commas with Direct Address

A comma can be used to set off names used in **direct address.** Direct address is a name used in speaking directly to a person. It may also be a word or a phrase used in place of a name like *my dear*.

If the direct address appears at the beginning or the end of the sentence, place a comma between it and the rest of the sentence.

• <u>Josh</u>, did you get my message?

• Have you ever been skiing, <u>Majid</u>?

If the direct address is in the middle of the sentence, set it off with commas. If you remove the word between the commas, the sentence will still make sense.

• When you first came here from Greece, Mr. Pappas, was it difficult to learn English?

• I was wondering, <u>pal</u>, if you know today's date.

• Yes, Jane, I'll be glad to repeat it.

• Yes, I'll be glad to repeat it.

Grammar Practice

Rewrite the following letter, adding commas to punctuate the direct addresses correctly.

Dear Mr. Haslett:

You sir have an opportunity to own a musical pencil sharpener! Yes, my dear man imagine sharpening your pencil while listening to music in the comfort of your own office. It's yours for only $5.95 a month. Just sign the enclosed form Mr. Haslett and send it in by March 1.

Web Activities For eFlashcards, Selection Quick Checks, and other Web activities, go to www.glencoe.com.

Dramatic Scene
Revising, Editing, and Presenting

ASSIGNMENT Adapt a scene from a story and write it like a play

Purpose: To write an interesting scene about a person who doesn't give up when something bad happens

Audience: Your teacher and your classmates

Revising Rubric

Your revised scene should have

- a clear conflict
- dialogue that relates to the conflict
- characters developed through dialogue and action
- characters who don't give up

NY English Language Arts Core Curriculum
(pp. 868–871)

W2a Write original literary texts to select a genre and use appropriate conventions, such as dialogue. **Core W5** Use the writing process. **Core W6** Develop a personal writing style and voice. **Core S3** Adapt language and presentational features for the audience and purpose.

For a complete description of the standards, see p. NY 11.

Now it's time to improve your draft. You can change anything—characters, dialogue, or stage directions. Revise as much as you want. You're the editor as well as the writer. You'll keep a copy of it in a writing portfolio so that you and your teacher can evaluate your writing progress over time.

Revising
Make It Better

Reread your scene silently. In the margins, make notes about what sounds wrong. Then read the scene again, out loud this time. You may notice some dialogue that doesn't move the action along or a stage direction that isn't clear. Maybe a whole section is confusing. It's okay. Make it better.

Check the Revising Rubric to make sure your draft has all the parts you need. Ask yourself these questions, and then make any necessary changes.

- Does my scene have a clear conflict?
- Does the dialogue relate to the conflict?
- Are the characters developed through dialogue and action?
- Does the scene contain a character who doesn't give in when things go wrong?

Finally, think about making your scene even better by expanding it into a longer play. Adapt more of the original story to give the play a beginning, a middle, and an ending.

Editing and Proofreading
Finish It Up

You've done a lot of work on your scene. Now do a final edit. Proofread your work carefully, using the symbols in the chart on page R19 to mark any needed corrections. Correct any grammar, spelling, or punctuation mistakes.

Make sure that you've done the special formatting used in scripts.

- Indent the stage directions, and put brackets around them.
- Capitalize character names at the beginning of lines of dialogue and inside the stage directions but not inside the dialogue itself.
- If you added, cut, or combined characters, change the character list.

Now do something with your dramatic scene! You *could* just print a clean copy, put it in a binder, give it to your teacher, and not think about it again. The best thing, however, would be to perform it for an audience.

Literature Online

Writing Models For models and other writing activities, go to www.glencoe.com.

Applying Good Writing Traits

Analyzing Cartoons
Does Calvin's word choice show his personality? What does it tell you about him?

Word Choice

A great thing about a play is that you get to know a bunch of different people—or characters—as well as the playwright. You learn about the characters through what they do and say. You learn about the playwright from how he or she "talks" through the characters.

> MY REPORT IS ON BATS. ...AHEM...
>
> "DUSK! WITH A CREEPY, TINGLING SENSATION, YOU HEAR THE FLUTTERING OF LEATHERY WINGS! **BATS!** WITH GLOWING RED EYES AND GLISTENING FANGS, THESE UNSPEAKABLE GIANT BUGS DROP ONTO..."
>
> BATS AREN'T BUGS!!
>
> LOOK, WHO'S GIVING THE REPORT? **YOU** CHONDERHEADS ...OR **ME**?!
>
> CALVIN, I'D LIKE TO SEE YOU A MOMENT.

© 1989 Watterson. Dist. By UNIVERSAL PRESS SYNDICATE. Reprinted with permission. All rights reserved.

What Is Word Choice?

No two people sound exactly alike, choose exactly the same words, or put words together in exactly the same way. And no two people share exactly the same ideas and feelings.

It's important that each character sound like himself or herself. A character who is an English teacher probably won't say "ain't." A young person of today isn't going to say "gee whiz."

Why Is Word Choice Important in Dialogue?

Word choice is important in dialogue because that's where the audience gets most of its information. In a novel or short story, there can be descriptions of characters, telling you what they're like. In a play, everything has to come out in what the characters say and do. The writer of the play wants the audience to believe that the characters are real people, and that means making good word choices in dialogue.

How Do You Use Word Choice in Dialogue?

First, listen to the way people talk—in the lunchroom, in the halls, in the neighborhood—just listen.
- Do people use complete sentences?
- Do people from different backgrounds use different words?
- What about slang? Who uses it and who doesn't?
- What about contractions?

Now read the dialogue in your play. Does it sound the way people talk? Read it out loud. Try to imagine that you are each character. Then ask, "Would I use those words?"

Partner Work When you feel that your scene is ready, have someone else read it and
- check that the voice is clear for each character.
- underline any dialogue that sounds unnatural.
- highlight any dialogue that's unclear or unrealistic.

Go over your scene one more time, and make all the appropriate changes.

Active Writing Model

The writer provides a brief statement of the time and place, followed by a more detailed description.

The characters in the scene are listed.

The writer tells where the characters are as the scene begins. The stage directions are indented and character names capitalized for clarity.

Tubman's dialogue helps to establish her character.

John's line shows he has reached the breaking point.

The stage directions indicate necessary sounds, actions, and reactions.

The dialogue reveals Tubman's motivation.

The directions show that the conflict between Tubman and John is settled, at least for now.

Writer's Model

SETTING. The 1850s. Maryland. It's a cold, dark night along the wooded eastern shore. It's very quiet, except for the occasional cry of a hoot owl.

CHARACTERS: Harriet Tubman   Sarah, John's wife
           John, a slave   four other slaves

[TUBMAN steps out from a cluster of trees. JOHN, SARAH, and the others can be seen looking out through the trees and bushes. TUBMAN pulls her dark clothing close for warmth and to make it easier to travel through the thick brush. Her face is full of fierce determination. She is clearly in charge. She motions for her fellow travelers to come.]

TUBMAN. [Quietly] Follow me. Don't make noise.

[The others move hesitantly out from the trees.]

JOHN. Are we there? My wife can't walk much longer.

SARAH. I'm fine. Don't worry none over me.

JOHN. We're all tired, and it'll be light soon.

TUBMAN. Brother, don't cause trouble. I've told you all to keep up. I won't say it again.

[The others take a few weary steps, except for JOHN.]

JOHN. No. Let me go back. . . . It's better to be a slave than to suffer like this and be free.

[Everyone stops, and TUBMAN turns to glare at JOHN.]

TUBMAN. You'll go with us.

JOHN. [Desperately] I can't. Not anymore. I'm tired. I'm hungry. I'm cold. Let me go. Let me go back. I'm going back.

[JOHN steps toward the trees. A sharp sound from the woods makes him stop suddenly. Everyone freezes. After a moment, TUBMAN moves to JOHN.]

TUBMAN. A deer. A bear. Or maybe "Master" come looking for you. [Pause] What's the first thing Master does if he gets hold of you? He beats you until you tell him who helped you. Who you stayed with. Who fed you. It won't be just you who loses the chance for freedom, but everyone else who might want to try. [To everyone] No one goes back. Freedom isn't bought with dust. We've got to go free or die. [To JOHN] Now you go with us, or you die right here.

[JOHN hesitates, and his body sags. SARAH touches his arm. TUBMAN watches, then turns and starts walking. JOHN, SARAH, and the others follow into the night.]

Presenting
Show It Off

Now do something with your dramatic scene! You *could* just print a clean copy, put it in a binder, give it to your teacher, and not think about it again. The best thing, however, would be to perform it for an audience.

Literature Online

Writing Models For models and other writing activities, go to www.glencoe.com.

Applying Good Writing Traits

Analyzing Cartoons
Does Calvin's word choice show his personality? What does it tell you about him?

Word Choice

A great thing about a play is that you get to know a bunch of different people—or characters—as well as the playwright. You learn about the characters through what they do and say. You learn about the playwright from how he or she "talks" through the characters.

MY REPORT IS ON BATS. ...AHEM...

"DUSK! WITH A CREEPY, TINGLING SENSATION, YOU HEAR THE FLUTTERING OF LEATHERY WINGS! BATS! WITH GLOWING RED EYES AND GLISTENING FANGS, THESE UNSPEAKABLE GIANT BUGS DROP ONTO ..."

BATS AREN'T BUGS!!

LOOK, WHO'S GIVING THE REPORT? YOU CHONDERHEADS ...OR ME?!

CALVIN, I'D LIKE TO SEE YOU A MOMENT.

What Is Word Choice?

No two people sound exactly alike, choose exactly the same words, or put words together in exactly the same way. And no two people share exactly the same ideas and feelings.

It's important that each character sound like himself or herself. A character who is an English teacher probably won't say "ain't." A young person of today isn't going to say "gee whiz."

Why Is Word Choice Important in Dialogue?

Word choice is important in dialogue because that's where the audience gets most of its information. In a novel or short story, there can be descriptions of characters, telling you what they're like. In a play, everything has to come out in what the characters say and do. The writer of the play wants the audience to believe that the characters are real people, and that means making good word choices in dialogue.

How Do You Use Word Choice in Dialogue?

First, listen to the way people talk—in the lunchroom, in the halls, in the neighborhood—just listen.
- Do people use complete sentences?
- Do people from different backgrounds use different words?
- What about slang? Who uses it and who doesn't?
- What about contractions?

Now read the dialogue in your play. Does it sound the way people talk? Read it out loud. Try to imagine that you are each character. Then ask, "Would I use those words?"

Partner Work When you feel that your scene is ready, have someone else read it and
- check that the voice is clear for each character.
- underline any dialogue that sounds unnatural.
- highlight any dialogue that's unclear or unrealistic.

Go over your scene one more time, and make all the appropriate changes.

Active Writing Model

Writer's Model

The writer provides a brief statement of the time and place, followed by a more detailed description.

SETTING. The 1850s. Maryland. It's a cold, dark night along the wooded eastern shore. It's very quiet, except for the occasional cry of a hoot owl.

The characters in the scene are listed.

CHARACTERS: Harriet Tubman   Sarah, John's wife
                          John, a slave   four other slaves

The writer tells where the characters are as the scene begins. The stage directions are indented and character names capitalized for clarity.

[*TUBMAN steps out from a cluster of trees. JOHN, SARAH, and the others can be seen looking out through the trees and bushes. TUBMAN pulls her dark clothing close for warmth and to make it easier to travel through the thick brush. Her face is full of fierce determination. She is clearly in charge. She motions for her fellow travelers to come.*]

TUBMAN. [Quietly] Follow me. Don't make noise.
   [*The others move hesitantly out from the trees.*]
JOHN. Are we there? My wife can't walk much longer.
SARAH. I'm fine. Don't worry none over me.
JOHN. We're all tired, and it'll be light soon.

Tubman's dialogue helps to establish her character.

TUBMAN. Brother, don't cause trouble. I've told you all to keep up. I won't say it again.
   [*The others take a few weary steps, except for JOHN.*]

John's line shows he has reached the breaking point.

JOHN. No. Let me go back. . . . It's better to be a slave than to suffer like this and be free.
   [*Everyone stops, and TUBMAN turns to glare at JOHN.*]
TUBMAN. You'll go with us.
JOHN. [Desperately] I can't. Not anymore. I'm tired. I'm hungry. I'm cold. Let me go. Let me go back. I'm going back.

The stage directions indicate necessary sounds, actions, and reactions.

   [*JOHN steps toward the trees. A sharp sound from the woods makes him stop suddenly. Everyone freezes. After a moment, TUBMAN moves to JOHN.*]

The dialogue reveals Tubman's motivation.

TUBMAN. A deer. A bear. Or maybe "Master" come looking for you. [Pause] What's the first thing Master does if he gets hold of you? He beats you until you tell him who helped you. Who you stayed with. Who fed you. It won't be just you who loses the chance for freedom, but everyone else who might want to try. [To everyone] No one goes back. Freedom isn't bought with dust. We've got to go free or die. [To JOHN] Now you go with us, or you die right here.

The directions show that the conflict between Tubman and John is settled, at least for now.

   [*JOHN hesitates, and his body sags. SARAH touches his arm. TUBMAN watches, then turns and starts walking. JOHN, SARAH, and the others follow into the night.*]

Listening, Speaking, and Viewing

Dramatizing Literature—Performance

What Is Performance?

Performance is bringing a play to life by acting it out in front of an audience. A performance can take place on the stage of a theater, on film or videotape, or even over the radio.

Why Is Performance Important?

Plays are meant to be performed. Books can be powerful, but staged performances can affect an audience in a different way. Why else are movies and TV shows so popular? Audiences enjoy seeing actors bring a story to life.

How Do I Turn My Scene into a Performance?

Theater is a collaborative art. That means it takes a lot of people working together with the same goal. To perform your scene, you'll need some help. No matter what your dramatic scene is about, the following guidelines will help.

- You need a director to choose the actors and direct the action so that the scene is clear and interesting.

- For a full production, you need people to come up with a set, costumes, lights, and props. (Props are objects the actors use; for a meal scene, the props would include food, plates, forks, and so on.) You may also need music and sound effects. Just keep it all simple.

- For a readers' theater production, let the audience use their imaginations. Without the sets, costumes, lights, and props, the actors sit in a row and read their scripts aloud. A narrator can read stage directions to set the scene and describe the action.

Analyzing Cartoons
Is the girl in the cartoon performing? Explain.

REAL LIFE ADVENTURES by Gary Wise and Lance Aldrich

Home theater.
© 1996 GarLanco. Reprinted with permission of UNIVERSAL PRESS SYNDICATE. All rights reserved.

- For either kind of production, with the director, choose actors to play the characters.

- Have the actors read the scene aloud together, sitting down. Ask the actors to memorize and practice their roles. The more they practice, the more natural the scene will look and feel.

- Practice in the space where the scene will be performed. Stand in the back of the room. Is it clear what is going on? Can you hear everyone?

- Be prepared, as a playwright, to make changes in the script. During rehearsal, you may hear things that don't work. Ask the actors and director for ideas. You don't have to do exactly what they say, but they may inspire something wonderful. Remember that successful playmaking requires people working together.

Present Your Scene Ask your teacher if you may perform your scene for the class. A series of scenes written and performed by you and your classmates would make an interesting class project. Perhaps the scenes can be videotaped and edited with titles and music added.

Skills Focus

You will practice these skills when you read the following selections:

- "and sometimes i hear this song in my head," p. 876
- from *Sky*, p. 882

Reading

- Visualizing text descriptions

Literature

- Understanding sound devices
- Analyzing setting

Vocabulary

- Recognizing and using Latin roots

Writing/Grammar

- Using commas to prevent confusion or misreading
- Using commas with dates and addresses

Skill Lesson

Visualizing

Learn It!

What Is It? **Visualizing** is creating pictures in your mind. And it's one of the easiest "skills" there is because everybody already visualizes a thousand times a day. Look, for example, at two events in a typical day for "Max."

- Max wakes up and smells bread toasting. *In his mind, he sees the shiny toaster in the kitchen. He sees the tops of two slices of bread, with a little bit of smoke rising around them.*
- While he's eating his lightly buttered toast, Max looks at the clock. *In his mind, he sees the school bus arrive at the end of his block. He sees himself run to catch it as the bus pulls away.*

Okay, you get the idea. With reading, visualizing works the same way except that you need to focus your imagination on the images presented by the writer.

NY English Language Arts Core Curriculum (pp. 872–873)

LC R12 Combine multiple strategies (visualize) to enhance comprehension and response.

For a complete description of the standards, see p. NY 11.

Analyzing Cartoons
Is this character doing a good job of visualizing? Why or why not?

Why Is It Important? Visualizing is a great way to understand and enjoy what you read. It can help you to recall the steps in a process and to imagine how characters, rooms, and objects look. If you can visualize what you read, selections will be sharper in your mind, and you'll recall them better later on.

Study Central Visit www.glencoe .com and click on Study Central to review visualizing.

How Do I Do It? Just pay attention to what the writer is telling you, and see it in your imagination. If you have a hard time with a particular part, try sketching it on paper. Here's how one student visualized a scene from "Kamau's Finish."

> My team is the Red House, and we're squashed between the Yellow and Blue House teams. Immediately across is the three-step winners' podium. I cross my eyes three times in its direction, shooting lucky *uganga* rays.

> I'm picturing Kamau wearing a red uniform. I see his teammates are wearing red, too. To his left are runners dressed in yellow, and to his right are runners dressed in blue. Across from him is something that looks like the winners' platform at the Olympics. Kamau is doing some weird thing with his eyes to bring him good luck for the race.

Practice It!

Suppose someone is going to make a new movie version of *The Diary of Anne Frank.* (It was first filmed in 1959.) Look at the Hanukkah party in act 1. As you reread the scene, visualize the answers to the following questions:

• What actors do you see playing Anne and Peter? Who would play the other characters?

• How does the attic look? Is it decorated for the party?

• What kind of wrapping paper does Anne use for her gifts?

• How does Dussel look as he tries to remove the earplugs?

Use It!

As you read the selections in this workshop, notice the descriptive details the writers provide. Use them to visualize what's happening.

Before You Read

and sometimes i hear this song in my head

Meet the Author

Harriet Jacobs lives in the Los Angeles area. She works in the financial services industry, writing poetry "on the side." Her works have appeared in several collections, including *Spirit & Flame: An Anthology of Contemporary African American Poetry,* in which "and sometimes i hear this song in my head" appears.

Author Search For more about Harriet Jacobs, go to www.glencoe.com.

Vocabulary Preview

English Language Coach

Latin Roots Many English words come from Latin words. Latin was spoken as early as the seventh century B.C. in villages of what is now central Italy. The word *Latin* comes from the name of one village, Latium. As Rome grew into a city and then an empire, the Latin language spread too.

Eventually the Roman Empire covered much of Europe and coastal areas of northern Africa. Most people under Roman rule continued to speak their own languages in daily life. But they used Latin for literature, education, religion, and, most importantly, business.

Even after the empire fell apart around A.D. 400, Latin remained a powerful influence throughout Europe. Latin is often called "the language of knowledge." Its influence can be seen in English words for law, war, art, literature, and architecture.

Below are some examples of Latin roots:

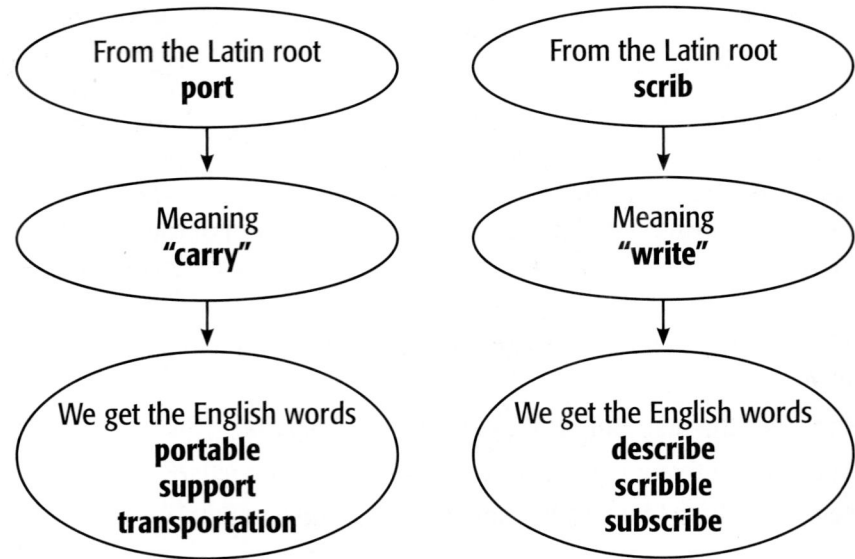

Root to Learn Fill in each blank with an English word that comes from the Latin root. (There's more than one correct answer for each blank.)

1. From the Latin root *dict,* meaning "say" or "speak," we get the English word ____.

2. From the Latin root *uni,* meaning "one," we get the English word ____.

NY English Language Arts Core Curriculum (pp. 874–877)

Core R4 Determine the meaning of unfamiliar words by using structural analysis. **LC R12** Combine multiple strategies (visualize) to enhance comprehension and response. **R2f** Identify poetic elements, such as repetition, rhythm, and rhyming patterns, to interpret poetry.

For a complete description of the standards, see p. NY 11.

Skills Preview

Key Reading Skill: Visualizing

Words can give you the outlines and colors to paint pictures in your mind. If a writer says, "Light poured through the stained glass like streams of color," you have to pay attention to the words—"poured" and "streams." Then you have to try and remember when you saw water flowing in streams. When you picture it in your mind, you can see what the colored light looked like.

Write to Learn As you read "and sometimes i hear this song in my head," pay attention to the words and what they say or suggest that would help you form a picture in your mind. In your Learner's Notebook, describe at least one image that you visualize from words in the poem.

Literary Element: Sound Devices

You already know **alliteration** was the main sound device in the oldest English poetry. It is the repetition of sounds at the beginnings of words. Most often, the repeated sounds are consonants. You've also learned about **rhyme** and **rhythm**. All of these sound devices work together to provide the music of poetry. They also support the meaning of the words.

Onomatopoeia (AHN uh MAHT uh PEE uh) occurs when a word suggests the sound it describes, like *crack* and *buzz*. It's imagery that appeals to the sense of hearing.

There are many other sound devices that poets use, even when there is no regular rhyme or rhythm. That's why it's so important to read poetry out loud.

Group Talk As a group, make a list of all the onomatopoetic words you can think of—such as *tweet* and *zip*, for example. Say them out loud and try to make them sound as much like what they describe as possible.

Get Ready to Read

Connect to the Reading

The first line in the poem is something that all readers can relate to; we all listen to music and we all hear certain songs in our minds. What songs might form a "soundtrack" to your life?

Partner Talk List the songs that would form your soundtrack, and then share them with a partner. Tell what your partner's list suggests to you about his or her life. Then listen to the ideas your partner gets from your list.

Build Background

- African American music has its roots in spirituals, which were sung by slaves.
- Spirituals gave birth to gospel and the blues. The blues formed the basis for jazz, which helped inspire most popular music that you hear today.

Set Purposes for Reading

BIG Question Read "and sometimes i hear this song in my head" to understand how music can play a positive role in difficult times.

Set Your Own Purpose What would you like to learn from the poem to help you answer the Big Question? Write your answer on the Workshop 4 Foldable for Unit 6.

Interactive Literary Elements Handbook
To review or learn more about the literary elements, go to www.glencoe.com.

Keep Moving

Use these skills as you read the following selection.

and sometimes i hear this song in my head

by Harriet Jacobs

we have always heard music
found ways to smooth back the edges
of madness
stretched our voices
5 to the slap of oar against water **1**
heard blues in the snap of cotton breaking
from stem **2**
we always been a music
people
10 sometimes lost in a jungle of tears
but we keep finding our way back
to that
clearing
at the center
15 of our selves
where the trees still talk to us

Practice the Skills

1 | **Literary Element**

Sound Devices What word in this line is an example of onomatopoeia?

2 | **Key Reading Skill**

Visualizing Don't limit your visualizing to the sense of sight. In your mind, try to hear and feel lines 4–7 as well as see them.

and our tongues keep __remembering__ the rhythm **3**
of the words we forgot
swaying on the backs of buses
²⁰ and in hot kitchens
crooning
in pool halls and shared bathrooms **4**
yeah/we carving a heartspace
and staring down the darkness some call our future
²⁵ and they saying it be just dope and more dope
and no hope **5**
and they don't even see we all the time
standing in the middle of the trees
and steady singing
³⁰ you can't
you can't
you can't
touch this **6** ○

Practice the Skills

3 | **English Language Coach**

Latin Roots The word __remember__ comes from the Latin *mem*, meaning "recall" or "keep in mind." What's another word with the same root?

4 | **Key Reading Skill**

Visualizing What mental images do you get from lines 19-22? How are they different from the images in the earlier part of the poem?

5 | **Literary Element**

Sound Devices The repetition and rhyme in lines 25-26 are there for a reason. What does the poet want to emphasize here?

6 | **BIG Question**

In the last line, what does "this" refer to? How does "this" help "we" go on? Write your answer on the Workshop 4 Foldable for Unit 6. Your answer will help you complete the Unit Challenge later.

Analyzing the Photo Can you imagine the "snap of cotton breaking" during a harvest?

After You Read

and sometimes i hear this song in my head

Answering the BIG Question

1. In what ways does music–any kind of music–help people to get through difficult times? Why do you think music has this sort of power?

2. **Recall** According to the poem's speaker, what do some people say about the future of African Americans?

   TIP Right There

Critical Thinking

3. **Interpret** This poem doesn't mention African Americans. What clues in the poem suggest that the speaker and the "we" of the poem are African American?

   TIP Think and Search

4. **Analyze** Explain the poem's title. Why do you think it begins with the word "and"? What effect does this have on how you read the poem?

   TIP Author and Me

5. **Interpret** The poem begins with "we have always heard music." Does the speaker view this as a positive or a negative thing? Explain.

   TIP Author and Me

6. **Draw Conclusions** What is the speaker's attitude toward the future of "we"? Support your answer with examples from the text.

   TIP Author and Me

Write About Your Reading

Chart Jacobs uses plenty of sensory imagery in her poem. Copy the chart below, but make the columns the length of your page. In the appropriate boxes, write words and phrases from the poem that appeal to the senses. (Some images may appeal to more than one sense.)

Sight	Sound	Touch	Smell	Taste

NY English Language Arts Core Curriculum (pp. 878–879)

LC R17 Demonstrate comprehension and response through a range of activities. **W2a** Write original literary texts to select a genre and use appropriate conventions. **LC R12** Combine multiple strategies (visualize) to enhance comprehension and response. **R2f** Identify poetic elements, such as repetition, rhythm, and rhyming patterns, to interpret poetry. **Core R4** Determine the meaning of words by using structural analysis. **Core W7** Observe rules of punctuation.

For a complete description of the standards, see p. NY 11.

Skills Review

Key Reading Skill: Visualizing

7. This poem has plenty of visual details. Which image did you find easiest to visualize, or which did you like best? Identify the line number(s) and describe the mental picture you formed.

Literary Element: Sound Devices

8. The poet uses onomatopoeia in lines 5-6 with the words *slap* and *snap*. The effect is to call attention to the senses of hearing and touch. Why might Jacobs have done this? What do these words and senses have to do with music?

9. Identify the sound device the poet uses in these phrases:
- remembering the rhythm
- on the backs of buses
- and steady singing

10. What is the effect of repeating the words "you can't" at the end of the poem? What point is the poet trying to make?

11. How might this poem benefit from being read aloud? Explain.

Reviewing Skills: Interpreting

12. In line 23, what does the speaker mean by "heartspace"? (Hint: See lines 10–15.)

Vocabulary

English Language Coach Rewrite each sentence, filling in the blank with the appropriate English word from the Latin root *scrib.*

13. In old times, a person whose job was to write or to copy writings was a ____.

14. A doctor's written order for medicine is a ____.

15. A copy of a play is a ____.

16. Certain religious writings are called ____.

17. A written or oral statement giving details of what someone or something is like is a ____.

Grammar Link: Commas to Prevent Misreading or Confusion

If the order of words in a sentence is confusing, the sentence may need a comma to prevent misunderstanding. You may even use an optional comma to make the meaning of a sentence more clear.

Unclear: Instead of writing Todd called his pen pal.

Clear: Instead of writing, Todd called his pen pal.

When a clause is introduced by the conjunction *for,* it is easy to misread *for* as a preposition. To prevent this, add a comma before the conjunction.

Unclear: She must like salad for she ate two bowls.

Clear: She must like salad, for she ate two bowls.

To prevent misreading a noun as part of the object of the preposition, add a comma after the prepositional phrase.

Unclear: Once aboard Ray put his suitcase down.

Clear: Once aboard, Ray put his suitcase down.

If a compound predicate is confusing, add a comma.

Unclear: I fell off the chair when it broke and cried.

Clear: I fell off the chair when it broke, and cried.

Grammar Practice

Rewrite the following sentences, adding commas to prevent misreading.

18. Although he saw two there were actually three cars.

19. If the window is open close it.

20. If you cut them onions will make your eyes water.

Web Activities For eFlashcards, Selection Quick Checks, and other Web activities, go to www.glencoe.com.

Before You Read : from *Sky*

Hanneke Ippisch

Meet the Author

Hanneke Ippisch was born in Holland in 1925. As a teenager, she witnessed the Nazi occupation of her country in 1940. At the age of 17, she began to help Jews escape the Nazis. After the war, she moved to Montana, where she writes and speaks to young people about her experiences.

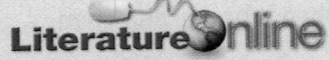

Author Search For more about Hanneke Ippisch, go to www.glencoe.com.

NY English Language Arts Core Curriculum (pp. 880–887)

Core R4 Determine the meaning of unfamiliar words by using structural analysis. **LC R12** Combine multiple strategies (visualize) to enhance comprehension and response. **R2b** Interpret setting, using evidence from the text.

For a complete description of the standards, see p. NY 11.

Vocabulary Preview

grave (grayv) *adj.* very serious; likely to produce harm or danger **(p. 882)** *The man was in grave condition for two days, and his doctors didn't know whether he would live or die.*

anticipation (an tis uh PAY shun) *n.* the act of looking forward to; expectation **(p. 883)** *My sister could barely contain her excitement in anticipation of her birthday.*

precautions (pruh KAW shunz) *n.* actions taken to prevent difficulty before it happens **(p. 884)** *Bug spray was one of the precautions Joan insisted on before she would agree to the camping trip.*

observant (ub ZUR vunt) *adj.* quick to notice or observe; alert; watchful **(p. 884)** *An observant person would have seen the sign warning "Wet cement." Unfortunately, Mr. Edwards wasn't a very observant person.*

dreaded (DRED ud) *v.* feared greatly; form of the verb *dread* **(p. 886)** *I have always dreaded heights; bridges and skyscrapers terrify me.*

Write to Learn Describe your feelings about going to places where you've never been before. Use at least four of the vocabulary words.

English Language Coach

Latin Roots The Latin root *sist* ("to stand") and prefix *re-* ("against") give us *resist.* To resist is "to stand against or fight back." The next selection uses the noun form, but it's capitalized—*Resistance.* This was a group that worked in secret against the Germans during World War II. In the selection, the narrator hears a conversation between members of the Resistance. *Conversation* is built on the Latin root *vers,* meaning "a turn." Now, what does a turn have to do with a conversation? Easy! In a conversation, each person takes a turn at talking.

Partner Conversation Many English words come from *vers.* (The spelling sometimes changes to *vert.*) With your partner, find and explain the "turn" in each word listed below. (You may use a dictionary.)

advertise	
convertible	
versatile	
version	

Skills Preview

Key Reading Skill: Visualizing

Different writers help you visualize in different ways. The author of *Sky* gives you a lot of visual details. If you use your imagination, you'll find that there are dozens of pictures in this story. One way to help yourself see these pictures is to pretend that you are an illustrator. Then try to imagine what pictures you would draw to go with the story. Illustrate it for yourself—inside your mind.

Literary Element: Setting

The time and place in which events occur in a story is its **setting.** For the most part, setting is associated with fiction, drama, and biography, but it may be important in certain other writings too. Setting can be identified in general or specific terms. For example, we can say that *Anne Frank* is set in Europe during World War II. Or we can say it's set in the attic of an office building in Amsterdam, Holland, between July 1942 and November 1945.

Understanding a story often depends on understanding its setting. To find meaning in *Anne Frank,* you don't have to know the economy of the Netherlands, but you should know the historical period—what was going on in Europe during World War II. Setting may also involve culture, religion, traditions, and spaces (rooms, buildings, landscapes, and so on).

Write to Learn Look over the fiction selections you've read so far in this book. In your Learner's Notebook, identify the settings of three stories. Remember to list both the time and place for each.

Get Ready to Read

Connect to the Reading

Most of us know about spies only from movies and novels, and very few of those stories are about teen-aged spies. In her autobiography, Hanneke Ippisch describes becoming a spy at the age of seventeen.

Write to Learn Could you be a good spy? What talents or skills do you have that a spy needs? Write your ideas in your Learner's Notebook.

Build Background

On May 12, 1940, Hanneke Ippisch learned that Germany was invading Holland when she saw German planes flying high over her home. She joined the local Resistance group but was caught eventually and kept in prison until the end of the war in 1945.

- In German-occupied countries, people formed secret, illegal groups to oppose the Germans. These groups were the Resistance, or "underground."

- Resistance members included civilians working in secret as well as armed bands fighting military-style. They included Christians, Jews, and atheists, communists and non-communists, young and old.

- Resistance activities varied widely. Members passed information about enemy forces to the Allies. They destroyed supply trains and ambushed Nazi patrols. They helped airmen whose planes had been shot down. They hid Jews or smuggled them to safety.

Set Purposes for Reading

BIG Question Read the excerpt from *Sky* to see how the writer risked her life to save others.

Set Your Own Purpose What would you like to learn from the selection to help you answer the Big Question? Write your own purpose on the Workshop 4 Foldable for Unit 6.

Interactive Literary Elements Handbook
To review or learn more about the literary elements, go to www.glencoe.com.

Keep Moving

Use these skills as you read the following selection.

from *Sky* **881**

from Sky

by Hanneke Ippisch

One night when I came home from Amsterdam during a break from my schooling, I once again overheard a conversation in my father's study, this one between him and an older woman. They were whispering, and I picked up the word "underground." Then I knew that my father was the kind of man who would be involved in the Resistance, and it made me feel very good. When the meeting ended and the woman left, I secretly followed her in the dark to her house. Maybe this was my chance to work against the enemy. **1**

She lived across a bridge, on the other side of town, in a simple room behind a small vegetable store. I knocked on her door. When she opened it just a crack, I introduced myself, and she let me in. **2**

I told her I wanted to join the underground forces. She looked at me and said, "I want you to go back to your studies and think about it for a long time. There is nothing adventurous or romantic about working against the enemy—it is incredibly hard work. Your life would not be yours anymore. Go back to your studies and maybe forget about it. You are very young." I left disappointed, her words resonating[1] in my mind, and returned to Amsterdam and my studies.

The situation became more **grave** as the war continued. We students in Amsterdam heard stories about incidents

---

1. Here, **resonating** (REZ uh nayt ing) means "echoing; repeating."

Vocabulary

grave (grayv) *adj.* very serious; likely to produce harm or danger

Practice the Skills

1 | **Reviewing Elements**

Literal and Figurative Language In this context, *underground* and *Resistance* are almost synonyms, but only one is literal language. Which word is used figuratively?

2 | **Key Reading Skill**

Visualizing The story begins with an air of mystery. What words in the first paragraph help you visualize the scene?

involving not only Jewish people, but also about students being taken to Germany against their will, and about the executions of political leaders in Holland.

About three months after my first conversation with the older woman in the vegetable store, I went back to her and told her that there was no doubt in my mind, I still wanted to join the underground.

"Very well," she said. "Tomorrow you will meet Piet in the square in front of the Protestant Church at exactly nine A.M. He will wear a brown wool hat and a gray raincoat. He will have a newspaper under his right arm and a shopping basket in his left hand. You will introduce yourself as Ellie. Good luck and be careful. Do not ever talk about what you are doing, including to your own family." **3**

After hearing those simple words, I left her. I did not sleep very well that night. I was repeating softly the things the old woman had told me: Nine A.M. in front of the Protestant Church, gray raincoat, brown hat, newspaper, shopping basket, Piet. Nine A.M. shopping basket, brown hat, Protestant Church, nine A.M. . . . . Finally I fell asleep, but woke up early and paced the floor until it was time to go. I carried my books and my tennis racket with me, so my family would think I was going back to school. **4**

Full of **anticipation** and a little bit nervous, I headed for the square and spotted Piet immediately. He was indeed in the right place at the right time, wearing a gray raincoat, a brown hat, holding a newspaper under his right arm and a shopping basket in his left hand. He gave me my first assignment: I was to bring some identification papers and food coupons[2] to a Jewish family hidden in an old house in the town of Haarlem. He also handed me a falsified I.D.: My new name was Ellie Van Dyk.

On that day my life changed completely. I rarely attended classes anymore. At night I was told where to meet my contact the next morning to receive new **instructions**, and which code words to use when approaching him or her. **5**

---

2. There were food shortages because the war limited production and imports. ***Food coupons*** were, in effect, permission slips for buying food.

Vocabulary

anticipation (an tis uh PAY shun) *n.* the act of looking forward to; expectation

Practice the Skills

3 | **Literary Element**

Setting The old woman defines the setting where Ippisch's first assignment will begin. "Protestant Church" may sound vague to us, as readers, but Ippisch appears to understand it.

4 | **Key Reading Skill**

Visualizing First visualize the narrator lying in bed repeating the old woman's words. Got it? Now visualize the church, Piet, and his shopping basket.

5 | **English Language Coach**

Latin Roots The root of **instructions** is *struct,* meaning "build." How does the English word relate to the Latin root?

Analyzing the Photo Jews had to identify themselves by wearing a star with the label "Jew" in German. The Star of David is an ancient symbol of Judaism.

I was given a different assignment each day transporting Jewish people from one place to another, safer spot. Often we had to separate the children from their parents. I traveled with the children on trains and boats to the countryside, to the safer hiding places on farms, where the Germans rarely went. Quite a few of those children—unaware of their families' fate—stayed in the countryside until the end of the war in 1945. Many farmers' families "adopted" the Jewish children and treated them as their own. They went to school with the other children in the villages. **6**

One problem was that clothing was getting scarce and the winter always seemed to get colder. Jewish people going into hiding ("underwater," as we called it) had to take the star off their coats. But cloth fades, and most old overcoats—which were so necessary during the cold winters—showed an obvious unfaded star-shaped spot. We always feared that star-shaped spot would be a dead giveaway and just hoped that it would not be noticed. Some women ingeniously took material from the inside hem of the old coats and sewed pockets over the faded spot. Others wore wool scarves over their coats, while still others held a newspaper to hide the spot. **7** Then there were people who did not take any of these **precautions** and didn't get caught. Several times, however, while walking or traveling with us, Jews were arrested by some **observant** German. If that happened, we had to pretend we did not know the arrested person. Other Resistance workers told me about tragic

Practice the Skills

6 **BIG Question**

Many Jewish parents saved their children's lives by giving them over to the Resistance. Does what those parents did demonstrate an appropriate response to the Big Question? Write your thoughts on the Workshop 4 Foldable for Unit 6.

7 **Key Reading Skill**

Visualizing First imagine the yellow star sewn on a coat—on the left side of the chest. Then, in your mind, remove the star and see the unfaded "star-shaped spot." From there, it's easy to visualize the various ways people dealt with the problem.

Vocabulary

precautions (pruh KAW shuns) *n.* actions taken to prevent difficulty before it happens

observant (ub ZUR vunt) *adj.* quick to notice or observe; alert; watchful

incidents,[3] but fortunately none of my Jewish traveling companions were ever caught.

Traveling to the Countryside, 1943 It was early in the morning and I dressed quickly and warmly. At seven A.M. I had to meet a Jewish couple, musicians who had played in the symphony in Amsterdam. I was to transport them to a village in the province of Friesland, where they were to be met and taken to a safe place on a farm. **8**

When I arrived at the given address, I knocked three times hard and twice softly (a code knock) on the door. A smiling Dutch woman opened the door and let me in. "I will miss them," she said. "They have been good company for my husband and me, but there are too many German soldiers around lately walking the streets. It is better for our guests to move on." As she spoke I followed her up two flights of stairs, through a linen closet, which had a small door inside, and into a room, where the curtains in front of the windows were closed. A Jewish man and woman, both pale and nervous, were waiting.

"Hello," I said. "Are you ready to go?" They embraced their Dutch hostess and followed me through the linen closet, down the stairs, and out into the street. Each was carrying a small shopping basket in which they had packed all their belongings.

I walked ahead, pretending not to know them, and they followed. The wind was blowing hard, and the man's hat blew off. He had lots of grayish-black, curly, rather long hair, and the wind blew his hair high around his head. He ran after his hat, grabbed it, and put it firmly on his head, holding it with one hand so he wouldn't lose it again. **9**

We rode a trolley car[4] to the Central Station, where I went to a ticket window and bought three round-trip tickets (the couple would only travel one way, but in case of a question they could say they were visiting a friend). I quickly handed their tickets to them, and we went to a platform where a train was waiting to take us to the northern part of the province of North Holland.

---

3. Ippisch is probably referring to times when Jews were caught and killed on the spot.
4. A *trolley car* runs along tracks laid in the street and is powered by electricity.

Practice the Skills

8 **Literary Element**

Setting As the subtitle and first paragraph suggest, the setting will change from city to country.

9 **Key Reading Skill**

Visualizing Use the narrator's descriptive details to visualize this man and his hat.

When we boarded the train we saw several compartments occupied by German officers. We walked through the corridors and finally found a compartment with only two older women sitting in it. The Jewish couple, immediately after sitting down, closed their eyes and pretended they were asleep. Suddenly a German officer opened the door of the compartment and hollered, "I.D. *bitte.*" ("I.D. please.") All of us pulled out our I.D. cards, he looked at them and looked at us, and compared photos with faces, and looked again. Though shaky inside, I pretended to be calm. The Jewish couple, however, seemed visibly shaken. How could the officer not detect our fear? **10**

After what seemed an eternity, the German handed our I.D. cards back to us and said with a smile, *"Danke schön und gute Reise."* ("Thank you very much and have a good trip.") Neither he nor the two older women in our compartment had noticed anything amiss.[5]

After about one hour the train stopped in the middle of some meadows. Passengers leaned out of the windows to see why the train had stopped. German soldiers were hollering and shouting commands. We heard that a small bridge had been slightly damaged, and the train could not safely cross it. We had to get out of the train and carefully walk, one after the other, over the damaged bridge. All three of us **dreaded**

10 Reading Skill

Visualizing Try to visualize this scene from the German officer's point of view. Why do you look at the I.D. cards? What do you see in this case?

This is a typical passenger train of the kind used throughout Europe in the early 1940s. Each train car was divided into small, semi-private rooms called *compartments.* Each room seated four to six passengers on a first-come, first-served basis.

---

5. *Amiss* means "wrong; not as it should be."

Vocabulary

dreaded (DRED ud) *v.* feared greatly

the watchful eyes of the German soldiers, but miraculously we crossed the bridge and boarded a waiting train on the other side without any problems.

We finally reached Enkhuizen, an ancient harbor town, where the brisk wind from the sea was blowing so hard that we had to hold on to hats, skirts, and scarves. We walked with farmers and their families to the ferry boat. The farmers were holding baskets full of chickens, purchased at the open-air market. **11**

Many fishermen who made the trip across the inland sea to sell fish at the Enkhuizen market walked toward the boat, their baskets now filled with fresh produce to bring home.

We boarded the ferry boat and settled down rather close to each other, but not together. We ate some pieces of bread, bought some imitation coffee, then closed our eyes. The wind was blowing hard, and the ferry boat bounced on the waves. The Jewish woman began to look gray-green, but never spoke. The passage on the inland sea was uneventful, and after two hours we reached the northeast coast of Holland.

We stepped ashore, again under the watchful eyes of German officers, and went to a small waiting room. I wore a bright blue scarf and red mittens and was approached by a young man who wore a red scarf and blue wool gloves. The young man said, "Did you have a good trip? I am so happy to see you again. Come on, and we will have some coffee."

I told him, "The trip was good, and I brought my aunt and uncle with me, so they can see a little bit of the countryside."

"Great!" he said. "You are very welcome."

After our coffee, the four of us left the small waiting room and climbed on a farm cart pulled by a horse. After about fifteen minutes of silent travel, the young man looked around. Nobody was in sight, and he stopped. He let me off the cart and then continued on with the Jewish couple.

I returned to the ferry boat on foot and started my long journey back to Amsterdam, very relieved that all had gone well that day. **12** ○

Practice the Skills

11 **Literary Element**

Setting Notice the many details Ippisch provides to help you see each specific setting as she guides the couple to safety.

12 **BIG Question**

Ippisch really never mentions how or why she kept from giving up. Why do you think she is so dedicated to her cause? Write your answer on the Workshop 4 Foldable for Unit 6. Your answer will help you complete the Unit Challenge later.

After You Read : from *Sky*

Answering the **BIG Question**

1. How is Hanneke Ippisch an example of someone who refuses to give up?
2. **Recall** How does the older woman respond when Ippisch goes to her house and asks to join the Resistance?
   Tip Right There
3. **Summarize** After joining the Resistance, how did Ippisch know which families to help and how to help them?
   Tip Think and Search

Critical Thinking

4. **Infer** Why do you think Ippisch decided to join the Resistance, in spite of warnings and knowing all that was at risk?
   Tip Author and Me
5. **Explain** Why was it important to get the Jews out of Amsterdam and moved to a more rural area?
   Tip Author and Me
6. **Evaluate** After the first paragraph, Ippisch never mentions her father. Do you think her father knew about her activities? If you were her father, would you approve of her joining the Resistance at such an early age? Explain your answer.
   Tip Author and Me

Talk About Your Reading

Debate Ippisch says that her life changed completely after she joined the Resistance. Looking at her life one way, you could say that she began to save people's lives. Looking at it another way, you could say that she began to tell lies, break laws, and risk lives. As a class, discuss whether it can be "right" to do "wrong." Begin by looking at the following questions.

• Apart from saving several lives, what good things came about as a result of Ippisch's choice?

• What risks were involved? Did her work for the Resistance endanger anyone other than Ippisch? If so, whom?

• When is it "right" to disobey a law? Does it matter who makes the law and why?

**NY English Language Arts
Core Curriculum** (pp. 888–889)

LC R17 Demonstrate comprehension and response through a range of activities. **S1b** Contribute to group discussions. **LC R12** Combine multiple strategies (visualize) to enhance comprehension and response. **R2b** Interpret setting, using evidence from the text. **Core R4** Determine the meaning of words by using structural analysis. **Core W7** Observe rules of punctuation

For a complete description of the standards, see p. NY 11.

Skills Review

Key Reading Skill: Visualizing

7. Choose a paragraph from the selection that you think is especially good for practicing visualizing. Identify three descriptive details and/or other information from the text to support your choice.

Literary Element: Setting

8. In general terms, identify the overall setting of this excerpt from *Sky*.

9. Which part of setting is most important in *Sky*? Which is least important? Explain your answers.

culture	economy	geography
spaces	weather	historical period

Reviewing Elements: Literal and Figurative Language

10. Explain the figurative meanings of *underground* and *underwater*, as used in this selection. Tell whom or what each term refers to.

Vocabulary Check

Rewrite each sentence, filling in the blank with the best vocabulary word from the list.

> **grave   anticipation   precautions**
> **observant   dreaded**

11. My sister always ___ the idea of walking home from the bus stop late at night.

12. "Stop, look, and listen" are ___ every child needs to learn about crossing the street.

13. Huge crowds gathered to wait in ___ of the annual fireworks display.

14. The worker who spotted the cracked beam was rewarded for being so ___.

15. The transit workers who went on strike created a ___ problem.

16. **English Language Coach** The Latin prefix *per-* means "through or throughout." What does the word *persist* mean? (For help, see the English Language Coach on page 880.)

Grammar Link: Commas with Dates and Addresses

Commas are used to set off items to prevent misreading. In a date, place a comma between the day and the year. If the date comes in the middle of a sentence, place another comma after the year. Don't use a comma if only the month and the year are given.

- The Last Poets performed at a memorial for Malcolm X on May 19, 1968.
- On May 19, 1968, the Last Poets performed at a memorial for Malcolm X.
- The Last Poets performed in May 1968.

Set off the name of a state or a country when it's used after the name of a city. Set off the name of a city when it's used after a street address. Don't use a comma after the state if it's followed by a ZIP code.
- Christian Sweerts lives in Liege, Belgium.
- Jon lived at 12 Bond Drive, Denton, Texas, for years.
- I'm moving to 229 Jamell Road, Ducks, PA 15609.

Grammar Practice

Copy each sentence, adding commas in the correct places.

17. My brother goes to college in Chicago Illinois.

18. My sister was born on February 20 1992.

19. My address is 500 Lee Avenue Boston MA 02121.

20. I was born at 2815 East Wilson Atlanta Georgia on March 14 1994 at 2:27 A.M.

Web Activities For eFlashcards, Selection Quick Checks, and other Web activities, go to www.glencoe.com.

Welcome
by Ouida Sebestyen

& Alone
by Maya Angelou

Skills Focus

You will use these skills as you read and compare the following selections:

- "Welcome," p. 893
- "Alone," p. 906

Reading

- Making connections from across texts

Literature

- Understanding literal and figurative language

Writing

- Writing to compare and contrast

NY English Language Arts Core Curriculum (pp. 890–891)

R2d Determine how the use and meaning of literary devices, such as symbolism, metaphor, simile, and personification, convey the author's message or intent. **LC R11** Respond to and comprehend various genres.

For a complete description of the standards, see p. NY 11.

Figurative language is used for descriptive effect. Writers use figures of speech to connect two things that seem different or unrelated. The narrator of "Welcome" says that her aunt "unfolded out of the car like a carpenter's ruler." In this simile, the aunt's movement reminds the narrator of a ruler that folds up to fit in the carpenter's pocket. This can help you visualize the aunt more clearly.

How to Compare Literature: Figurative Language

Here's a review of some forms of figurative language:

- A **simile** compares two unlike things using the word *like* or *as.*
  Example: The baby's blanket was soft as a cloud.
- A **metaphor** compares two unlike things without using *like* or *as.*
  Example: The baby's crib was a huge, colorful world.
- **Personification** gives a human quality to an animal, object, or idea.
  Example: Wind chimes sang the baby to sleep.
- A **symbol** is an object, person, place, or event that stands for something else.

As you read, watch for examples of figurative language. Look for

- words or phrases whose literal definitions don't make sense in their context
- objects that may represent larger ideas
- descriptions that involve comparisons

Get Ready to Compare

Writers use figurative language to communicate specific shades of meaning, or to compare unlike things. Look at the simile below:

• The fresh snow glittered like diamonds.

Snow and diamonds don't share many characteristics. You would never confuse one with the other. However, the sentence above compares their one shared quality—their glitter—to help you create a mental picture.

In your Learner's Notebook, copy the sentences below. Tell whether each sentence is an example of simile, metaphor, or personification. Then tell what two things or ideas are being compared.

• The sun smiled on Diego as he walked down the street.
• Marco was a machine, scoring nearly thirty points a game.
• Selma's cast was as hard as a rock.

Use Your Comparison

As you read each selection, keep track of examples of figurative language by using a graphic organizer like the one below. Make an organizer for each selection. You will use these organizers to compare the selections later.

In column 1, list the page number. In column 2, note the figure of speech. In column 3, identify the kind of figurative language. In column 4, explain what you think it means.

"Welcome"			
page	Figure of Speech	Kind	Explanation
894	"Aunt Dessie unfolded out of the car like a carpenter's ruler."	simile	She's stiff and sore from the long ride and has to unbend slowly.

Before You Read

Welcome

Ouida Sebestyen

Meet the Author

Ouida Sebestyen was born in Vernon, Texas in 1924. She began writing in high school, and tried to publish her first novel when she was twenty. It was not published, but she kept writing. Finally, in 1979, she published *Words by Heart,* which won several awards. Sebestyen hopes her story encourages other struggling writers to keep working on their craft. See page R6 of the Author Files for more on Sebestyen.

Author Search For more about Ouida Sebestyen, go to www.glencoe.com.

NY English Language Arts Core Curriculum (pp. 892–904)

Core R4 Determine the meaning of unfamiliar words by using structural analysis. **R2g** Compare literature to own lives.

For a complete description of the standards, see p. NY 11.

Vocabulary Preview

dismal (DIZ mul) *adj.* gloomy or depressing **(p. 893)** *Rainy and cold, the day was dismal.*

ultimatum (ul tuh MAY tum) *n.* a final demand that, if unmet, carries harsh penalties **(p. 896)** *Pedro's mother gave him an ultimatum: if he didn't clean his room, he'd be grounded for a month.*

famished (FAM ishd) *adj.* extremely hungry **(p. 900)** *After hiking for six hours, I was so famished I could have eaten a bear.*

pivoted (PIH vuh tid) *v.* turned around sharply **(p. 902)** *Hurrying to prepare dinner, Jakob's father pivoted from the stove to the refrigerator.*

coaxed (kohkst) *v.* urged gently **(p. 903)** *Suzanne coaxed the rabbit from its hiding place beneath the house.*

English Language Coach

Historical Influences on English In this unit, you've learned that many English words came from other languages. A good example of that is the word *tripod* in "Welcome." The Romans took it from the Greek *tri-* ("three") and *pod-* or *pous* ("foot"). A tripod is a three-footed stool, table, or stand (for a camera or telescope). As you read the story, watch for words that contain these roots:

vers ⟹ turn	**punct** ⟹ point, dot

Get Ready to Read

Connect to the Reading

Think of a time when you faced change or uncertainty in your own life. Did you talk about your feelings with a friend? If so, what did you say? What did you do to keep from giving up?

Set Purposes for Reading

BIG Question Read to learn more about the welcome a girl and her mother receive when their travels take them off the beaten path.

Set Your Own Purpose What would you like to learn from the selection to help you answer the Big Question? Write your own purpose on the Comparing Literature Foldable for Unit 6.

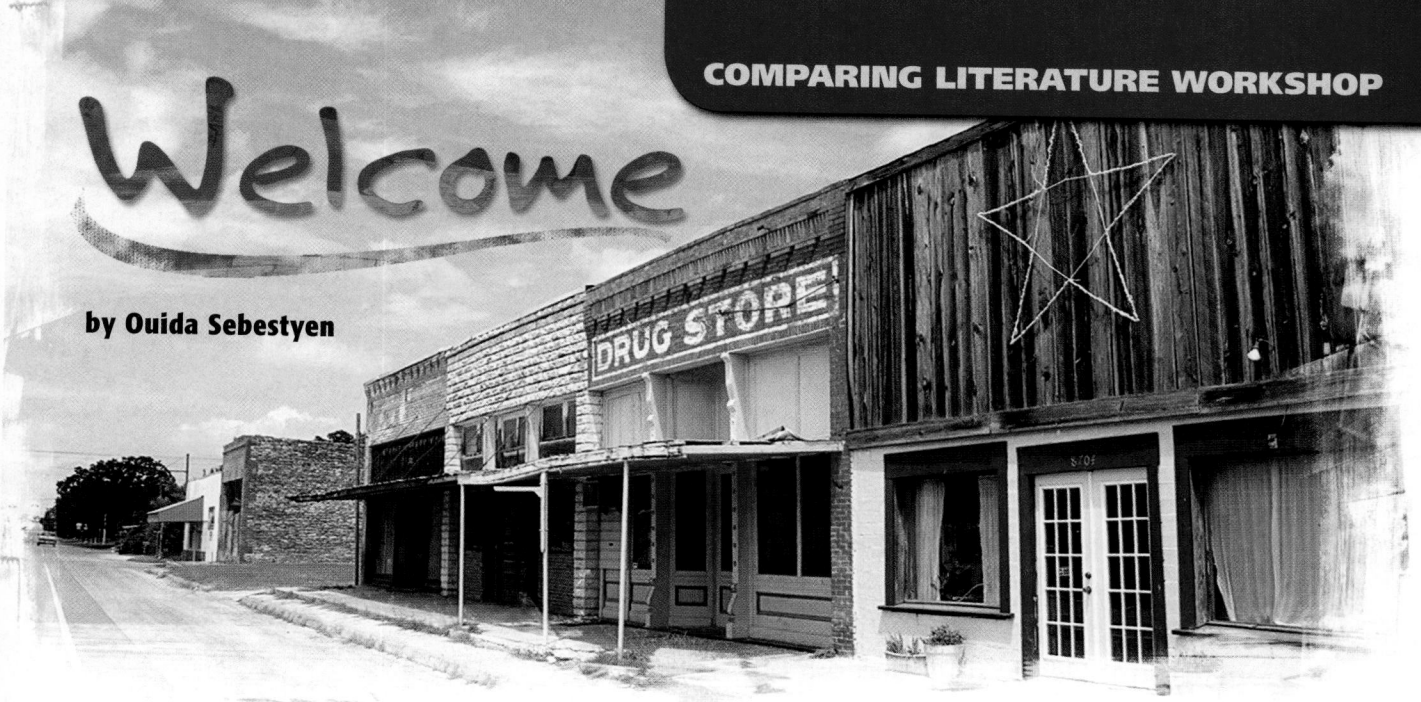

Welcome

by Ouida Sebestyen

My father's Aunt Dessie peered through the windshield at a road sign. "Slow up a little bit, Mary," she told my mother. "The last time I tried to find kinfolks I hadn't visited for a while, I got the house number and the street perfect, but I was in the wrong town." She turned to me in the back seat. "I ran across this yard yelling, 'Guess who's here, Annabelle,' and burst right in on a white lady. Perfect stranger."

I caught my mother's eyes in the rearview mirror and made a pretend smile for Aunt Dessie, thinking how I would describe her to my friend Sharon when I got home. *Picture this eighty-year-old drill sergeant? In drag? With this head of corn-row hair she must have made with a real hoe?* Sharon would double up. At least as far as she could double, now.

My mother slowed to a creep. Yesterday evening, bowling along through Texas on her way to see her parents, she had swerved off the interstate toward a **dismal** little town. **1** Before I could figure what in blazes she was doing, we were spending the night on Aunt Dessie's let-down couch between two whatnots crammed with spinster[1] junk. I had hissed, "What *is* this—I hate changes." But my mother just lay with her back

1. A **let-down couch** is a sofa that unfolds to become a bed. **Whatnots** are end tables. A **spinster** is an older, unmarried woman.

Vocabulary

dismal (DIZ mul) *adj.* gloomy or depressing

Practice the Skills

1 | **Comparing Literature**

Figurative Language When the author says "bowling along through Texas," can you imagine the car as a bowling ball?

to me, pretending to be asleep, while strange summer things from the piney woods tapped against the screens.

Aunt Dessie said, "Noella's going to be as surprised as I was. I still can't believe I'm riding along beside you, Mary. After seventeen years."

"Is it that long?" my mother said.

Aunt Dessie turned back to me. "And to finally get to see you, pretty thing. The image of your daddy."

"Are you sure this is the road?" my mother said sharply. "We've really got to keep this visit brief."

"Then why don't you stop at that little place up there and let me ask. Some of this backwoods is hazy in my mind."

We stopped. Aunt Dessie unfolded out of the car like a carpenter's ruler, and yanked open the screen door of a little grocery that had been waiting for a customer since the Depression.[2]

I murmured, "Lordy mercy, as they say down here. Are we talking hazy or crazy?"

"That's enough smart lip," my mother warned me. "You be nice to her. She took us in like royalty. She didn't have to."

"If she tells me one more time I look like my daddy—"

"You do."

"I look like me." It mattered that I was my own special leg of the proud unsteady tripod my mother and father and I had always made. "I feel very guess-who's-here-Annabelle." [2]

"Me too, a little. But suddenly I just wanted to see her and your great-aunt Noella again. I've never forgotten how they took me into the family. No questions. No testing. Just welcome." She was silent, remembering. "I guess I needed their blessing, or something. But I can't tell if Dessie knows."

She lifted the hot hair off her coffee-and-cream neck. She had always worn her hair long and straightened, to please my father. **Reverse** perm after reverse perm. [3] But now the newest inch of it had its own natural crinkle, recording almost to the day, I guess, when they stopped loving each other. Old fears began to press me like fingers finding the deep secret acupressure[3] points of pain. "What do you mean, *if she knows?* What's to know? You're going to patch all this

2 | **Comparing Literature**

Figurative Language If the narrator's family is a tripod, it has only three members. What does the rest of the metaphor suggest about the family? Make notes in your organizer.

3 | **English Language Coach**

Historical Influences How does the Latin root *vers* give meaning to **reverse**?

---

2. The **Depression** ("the Great Depression") lasted from 1929 to 1939. The stock market crashed, banks and other businesses failed, and millions of people lost their jobs and savings.

3. **Acupressure** (AK yoo preh shur) is a type of massage used to relieve tension or pain.

up. Like the other times, and everything's going to be fine again." 4

She put her hands on the wheel as if she needed to be driving.

"You are," I said.

"Tina, sometimes things—"

"No. You *are*."

Aunt Dessie came striding out, carrying a piece of paper in one hand and a bright canvas bag in the other.

"Lady in there makes these totes," she announced, handing it to me. "A souvenir."

I took it, surprised. "Thanks," I said, actually smiling in my confusion. Her old eyes studied me so long that I said too loudly, "Hey, I could embroider YUCK! on it and give it to Sharon for a diaper bag."

"Who's Sharon?" Aunt Dessie asked.

My mother started off with a jerk. "A bubble-headed little blonde Tina knows back home."

"Just my best friend," I said.

Aunt Dessie studied the scrap of paper someone had drawn a map on. "Ah," she nodded. "I see."

"Actually," my mother said, her voice accelerating with the car, "she's a strange little person who keeps trying to saddle Tina with all her problems. I hoped this trip would give them a vacation from each other."

Lie, I said to her back. *You'd rather run from that empty-feeling house than face up to your life.*

Practice the Skills

4 **Comparing Literature**

Figurative Language This paragraph begins with a meta-phor describing the color of the mother's skin. A few sentences later, the narrator uses a simile to describe "old fears." Explain both figures of speech in your organizer.

Analyzing the Photo
What experience is this picture trying to suggest?

Practice the Skills

"She didn't saddle me," I told Aunt Dessie. "Somebody has to look after Sharon, she's so casual, so inconceivably[4]—" I began to giggle crazily and couldn't stop. "I have to remind her what the doctor says to do, or she'll eat like she wants a French-fried baby with diet-cola blood."

"I think we can spare Aunt Dessie the details."

"Hey, all I did was ask if she could stay with us till the baby comes. And you went off like a ton of dynamite—rip, mangle, roar." My mother's eyes tried to grab mine in the mirror, but I wouldn't look. I wanted to give the details. Hadn't she driven miles out of her way to give her side of things to my father's aunts before he did? Okay, I wanted to tell about my friend who wasn't afraid to gulp down whole chunks of life I hadn't even dared to taste. **5**

She said, "The last thing I need is a tenth-grade dropout with a fatherless child on the way."

"There's always a father," I objected. "She just doesn't want him around." I tried to think what the slang had been in my mother's day. "He's a creep. She doesn't really like him."

"Turn left," Aunt Dessie said. My mother swerved.

"It's the baby that's important," I said. "Sharon's going to have something really truly her very own. She's glad about it."

"My God," my mother said. She bore through a tunnel of pines riddled with sunlight shafts. "But not in my house."

I braced myself carefully. "But she *is* in our house. I gave her the key before we left."

The car lurched to a stop. My mother swung around in her seat. "Tina! You knew perfectly well how I felt about that."

"Where else could she go?"

"Good heavens, she has parents."

"Oh, sure, her mother's in Florida with four stepchildren and her dad got an **ultimatum** from his girl friend. Who's she supposed to turn to besides us? I'm her friend. I thought you were, too, the way you were always nice to her and laughed when she did weird things—"

---

4. *Inconceivably* means "unbelievably."

Vocabulary

ultimatum (ul tuh MAY tum) *n.* a final demand that, if unmet, carries harsh penalties

Aunt Dessie said firmly, "Left again up there at that tree."

My mother started the car and drove past a field of sunflowers all staring at us with little happy faces. Slowly tears as hard as hailstones filled my throat. "I thought I could depend on you," I said, bumping along like the car. "To help her. But you slide out of things like a plate of noodles."

Aunt Dessie said, "I gather your daddy's away from home."

"He still travels, you know," my mother answered for me. "In his kind of work he has to, a great deal."

She slowed as the rutted road dipped for a creek. A little boy in overalls stood expectantly beside a mailbox. Suddenly I knew how my father had looked, growing up in those piney woods. Waiting for the mail carrier to come with something wonderful. I snapped my eyes shut to block him off. I didn't want to think about my father. I didn't even know how to think about him anymore. I just wanted everything to stand still, frozen like that little boy, so that nothing would ever have to arrive. **6**

"How long has he been dead?" I heard my mother say. I jerked to attention, but she added, "Noella's husband."

"I guess two years now," Aunt Dessie said. "Bless her heart, it must be hard for her." She turned around in the seat, raising her voice in case I had gone deaf. "Noella's husband was your Granddaddy Mayhew's brother, you see, and I'm from your grandmother's side, so Noella and I aren't anything like blood kin.[5]"

My mother said, "Why have you kept up with each other all these years?"

Aunt Dessie craned to read the name of a small wooden church we were passing. "I guess we just feel related." She turned back to me. "Your daddy stayed with me four years, so he could be close to a better school. I loved that boy."

I gazed at the crooked rows of her gray hair, wondering what age she had been when she stared into a mirror at her horse face and rawboned body and knew no man was ever going to love her. **7**

We passed a square unpainted house smothering under a trumpet vine. "Whoa!" Aunt Dessie commanded. "It says Mayhew on the mailbox."

---

5. Dessie and Noella are related by marriage only and are not blood relatives *(blood kin)*.

Practice the Skills

6 **Comparing Literature**

Figurative Language What does Tina tell you about her father and their relationship? Remember to explain the figures of speech in your organizer.

7 **Comparing Literature**

Figurative Language Tina is saying that her aunt's features are horse-like. How does this comparison influence your mental picture of Aunt Dessie?

"This is it?" My mother stopped and backed up. At the side of a barn two pigs lay in a juicy wallow.[6] Some little granny in **clodhopper** shoes just had to be around the corner, stewing the wash in a black pot. "Good heavens," she murmured. "I wouldn't live out here all alone for the world." 🞐

Analyzing the Photo Is this house similar to the one Tina describes?

"Well, Noella's not alone, you remember. She's still got Arley with her." Aunt Dessie flipped her stiff old hand at a hill nearby. "And the old Mayhew cemetery's up there. There's family around."

We stopped in front of the house. The screen opened and a little dried-apple woman came to the edge of the porch. Aunt Dessie unfolded and strode up the steps into her arms.

"Who do you think I brought to see you, Noella?" she demanded. "Here's Jimmie's wife. Mary."

Jimmie? I thought. My father could never have been anyone but James. Cool upwardly mobile[7] James.

"Of course it's Mary," Noella said in a quavery voice as tender as cake. "You precious thing. I'm so thankful to see you again." She wound her arms around my mother like roots. 🞐

Aunt Dessie said, "And this is Jimmie's daughter. This is Tina." Then I was inside that root-hold, as helpless as a rock being broken by long gentle pressure.

"I would have known you," Noella said. I braced myself. "You have his face, your daddy's face. I always hoped I'd get to see you." She looked beyond me at the empty car.

My mother looked, too, as if she had just recalled the trips we used to take when my father would wake up in the back

Practice the Skills

---

6. Pigs lie in a *wallow* (a puddle of thick mud) to stay cool.

7. An *upwardly mobile* person can improve his or her social status.

seat, yelling, "Hey, we've *arrived*—why didn't you tell me?" while we laughed. "James would have liked to come, I'm sure. But he's a busy man these days."

Noella took her arm. "Tell him I miss him."

"Yes," my mother said, glancing sharply at me to make sure I didn't blurt out, *How can she tell him when he moved out a month ago?*

We sat in Noella's cramped little living room while she slushed around in her slippers, bringing us iced tea. She and Aunt Dessie took big breaths and brought each other up-to-date on who had died since they last visited. They made me nervous, reminding me how life changes and the people we love fall away. **10**

I stared out the window through a bouquet of plastic flowers that was never going to die. All at once I realized that a man's bearded face was staring at me.

I screamed, giving a start that filled my lap with iced tea.

Noella said calmly, "It's just Arley, precious. He wants to see who you are, but he's shy." The face scowled, punctured by a gaping mouth, and disappeared. She patted my skirt with everyone's pink paper napkins and sent me out into the sun to dry. **11**

Aunt Dessie strolled out behind me. "Who's Arley?" I whispered, afraid I'd see that face again peeking through the beanpoles of the garden.

"Noella's son," Aunt Dessie said.

"But he's middle-aged." It sounded stupid, but I couldn't recall ever seeing a retarded adult. I guess I thought they stayed children.

"Of course he is. We grow, whether we're ready or not. We do the best we can." She picked a skinny red-pepper pod and bit off the end. "Mercy! Jalapeño.[8]" She fanned her tongue.

We walked along the garden rows while my skirt dried. Behind a hedge a bear-shaped shadow stayed even with us.

"Your mother seems very sad," Aunt Dessie said.

I shrugged. "Really?" Suddenly it would have been a relief to pour out the whole They've-split-again-and-it's-awful-and-I'm-scared story.

"Trouble at home?"

Practice the Skills

10 **Comparing Literature**

Figurative Language Of course, Tina doesn't mean that people physically fall. What does she mean? Who, in her own life, does Tina fear will "fall away"?

11 **English Language Coach**

Historical Influences Which word in this paragraph contains the root *punct?* Use the root's meaning to write a definition of this word.

---

8. The red **jalapeño** (haw luh PAY nyoh) pepper is indeed hot.

I kept shrugging. "Not exactly. Well, maybe a little, but they'll work it out. They always do."

"Ah," Aunt Dessie said.

When we went into the kitchen, my mother was setting plates around a table that practically sagged under bowls of macaroni and cheese and sliced tomatoes and fried okra and chowchow[9] and peaches that perfumed the room. All at once I was **famished.**

Noella piled food on a tray and took it to the door, saying, "Arley wants to eat on the porch. It takes him a little while to get used to new people."

I stuffed myself. Aunt Dessie kept right up with me, begging her gall bladder to forgive and forget. My mother ate in silence, watching the two old faces opposite her like a play. **12**

Noella said, "The last time Dessie came for a visit she brought me the most beautiful crocheted[10] bedspread you ever set eyes on. I'll show it to you. Are you still doing bedspreads?"

"Can't afford the thread anymore," Aunt Dessie said. "Now it's bootees and little sacques[11] and caps. I sell some for baby showers and give the rest away to whoever's expecting."

Noella asked, "What kind of projects keep you busy, Mary?"

My mother opened her mouth and nothing came out. I waited with them, curious. *Tell them your hobby is collecting little keys that lock out the things in your life that scare you. And lock you in.* **13**

A glass shattered out on the porch. We jumped again as something crashed against the wall. A blubbering growl rose and faded as footsteps pounded off the porch and away.

Noella took a broom and went out. We waited. My mother pressed a careful furrow in her food and we all studied it like a divination.[12] She asked, "Who will take care of him when she dies?"

Practice the Skills

12 **Comparing Literature**

Figurative Language People with gall bladder problems are not supposed to eat rich foods or eat too much at one time. Here, the author personifies Aunt Dessie's gall bladder, giving it the qualities of a person. What words show the author personifying Aunt Dessie's gall bladder?

13 **BIG Question**

Mary (Tina's mother) doesn't literally collect keys, of course. Tina uses this metaphor to describe how her mother deals with conflict. What exactly is she saying? Write your answer on the Comparing Foldable for Unit 6.

---

9. *Okra* is a green vegetable, and *chowchow* is a pickle relish.
10. The *crocheted* (kroh SHAYD) bedspread was made with a kind of needlework similar to knitting.
11. A *sacque* (sak) is a baby's short jacket that fastens at the neck.
12. A *divination* (dih vuh NAY shun) is an object or event that is used to predict the future.

Vocabulary

famished (FAM ishd) *adj.* extremely hungry

Aunt Dessie nodded, musing. "Yes. When he's alone. She worries terribly about that."

Unexpectedly my mother reached across the table and laid her hand on Aunt Dessie's. Aunt Dessie put her other hand on top of theirs and we all looked at the funny fragile layers of hands until Noella came back with the tray full of spilled food and broken glass.

In the hurting silence I found myself offering to do the dishes while they visited, but Noella shooed us out, saying she could do dishes when she didn't have us. I hung at the kitchen door, feeling somehow drawn to her, as she put up the food. "I'm sorry I screamed," I said. "I didn't know." **14**

"Of course you didn't, sugar." She took a dozen gorgeous peaches off the windowsill and put them in a sack. "When Arley was little and I finally knew he was never going to be right, I screamed too. Screamed and screamed." She put the sack into my hands. "Take these with you. Your mother said you're on your way to see her folks."

I wished she hadn't reminded me. "She never did this before." As if I had taken the bottom piece of fruit out of the pyramid at the market, everything began to tumble. "Left home, I mean. To go talk to her folks about it. Like this time it was—it was—" I felt silly tripping over a simple word like *serious*. **15**

"Bless your heart," Noella said.

When we went into the living room, Aunt Dessie asked us, "We do have time to go up to the cemetery a minute, don't we?"

My mother shook her head. "I'm afraid it's getting—"

"We have time," I said. I offered my arm to Noella and we went out past my mother's surprised face.

She and Aunt Dessie followed us up a shade-spattered road to the top of the hill. Noella opened a gate in a wire fence and let us into the little graveyard filled with dark cedars. "Used to be a church here, at the beginning," she said. I looked around, wondering why I had wanted so suddenly and urgently, back at the house, to stand up there with my kin.

Noella led us through the high weeds to a grave with a neat concrete cover. A jar with the stem of a rose in it stood beside the nameplate. Dried petals lay around it. "Arley comes," Noella said.

Practice the Skills

14 | **Comparing Literature**

Figurative Language How might a "hurting" silence be different from an "awkward" or "angry" silence? Think about how a figure of speech can shade the meaning of a description.

15 | **Comparing Literature**

Figurative Language What does Tina mean by *everything* here? What does the simile tell you about her feelings at this moment?

Analyzing the Photo In stories and movies, cemeteries are often scary places. What feelings do you get about this country graveyard?

Aunt Dessie pulled two weeds and brushed the nameplate with their leafy tops. "He was a good kind man, Noella." They looked down in silence. "You were fortunate."

"Oh, yes," Noella said, and put her thin arm through Aunt Dessie's bony one.

My mother walked slowly away toward a worn stone. Years of wind had scoured off all the inscription except one line. It said, *beloved wife of.*

She began to cry, with the loud surprised sound of an animal in pain.

"Oh, precious," Noella exclaimed. "Are you sick?"

My mother **pivoted** blindly into Aunt Dessie's arms. A sob broke through her fingers. They both caught her tight, not understanding. But I knew. **16**

Fear froze me. My voice made a long arc. "Nooo—you can fix it, you can work it out, you're adults!"

My mother's head rocked back and forth, her long hair sliding.

"Oh, Mary," Aunt Dessie said. "No hope at all?"

"No hope," my mother sobbed.

"What?" Noella asked. "What?"

Practice the Skills

16 **Comparing Literature**

Figurative Language What might the graveyard and grave-stone symbolize? What special meaning does the stone's inscription have for Tina and her mother?

Vocabulary

pivoted (PIH vuh tid) *v.* turned around sharply

"The marriage," Aunt Dessie said. "Over."

I whirled and ran. Before the fact could touch me. Over the humps of graves lost in the weeds. "No!" I insisted, with every gasp of breath.

But I knew the fact was right behind me, riding piggyback the way it always had, and there was no way I could ever run fast enough. My father had escaped. Oh, God, I knew it wasn't his fault that he had to keep growing. Out of the piney woods. Out of a marriage with somebody who was growing at a different speed. But I wished I could have hunted for that little boy he had been once, and **coaxed** him out, and made friends with him. **17**

The fence loomed up. I grabbed the rusty wire and hung over it, listening to myself gulping air as though nothing in me had died.

When I lifted my head, a hand was reaching toward me from behind a gravestone. I recoiled into the weeds before I saw that it was holding out a yellow flower.

Arley peeped out. "I'm nice," he whispered. "Don't cry." His soft wet mouth crumpled with anxiety. "I don't scare you." He pushed the flower closer.

I cringed away before I could stop myself. He did scare me. All the things I didn't understand scared me. Losing the people I had belonged to. Letting a special person change my life someday. Or mess it up, the way Sharon had let someone mess up hers. I had collected as many keys as my mother to lock the changes out. **18**

Carefully, Arley sniffed the flower to show me what he wanted me to do. He held it out again, smiling, with pollen on his nose.

"Don't cry," he begged. "I'm nice." He had my father's deep eyes. The family face. Mine.

"I know," I said shakily. I could see he was. A big, bearded man-child distressed to see me sad. "It's not you." A year's collection of tears tried to burst out, sweeping my breath away again. I pointed up the hill. "It's that."

He looked up and nodded solemnly, as if he knew all about divorces, and all about the key I'd given Sharon so she'd hang

Practice the Skills

17 | **Comparing Literature**

Figurative Language Again, Tina stretches her figure of speech over two paragraphs, this time personifying "the fact."

18 | **Comparing Literature**

Figurative Language Here, Tina returns to the "keys" figure of speech. What do the locks and keys symbolize for Tina?

Vocabulary

coaxed (kohkst) *v.* urged gently

out at our house like always and teach me to be brave. He smiled as if he could explain why people kept rearranging themselves into families so they could take care of each other.

I looked up the slope. My mother was walking toward me, between Aunt Dessie and Noella. Her face was calm. She held their hands. She would cut her hair, I thought. She would let it go natural.

Slowly I reached out and took Arley's flower.

I wondered if he would nod if I suddenly said that, in spite of everything, I knew I was lucky. Lucky to be able to go on from this, without too much to handle like Sharon, or starting from scratch like my mother.

Noella came to me and held me close in her root arms. She gave me a brisk pat. "I don't have a brain cell working. I forgot to show you Dessie's bedspread."

We went through the gate and down the road again. Behind me, my mother said, "Tina?" I felt the tips of her fingers brush my back. "If you're giving Sharon the diaper bag, maybe I could give her some bootees."

I stumbled around to look at her. My voice wiggled as I said, "Would you? It would mean a lot."

Aunt Dessie smiled. "What color shall they be, for this modern little mother? Purple, with orange ribbons?"

"Just a nice traditional white, I would think," my mother said. "Some things don't change." **19** ○

Practice the Skills

19 **BIG Question**

What are some of the things the four characters do to keep from giving up? In particular, how will Tina deal with her parents' breakup? Write your answers on the Comparing Foldable for Unit 6. Your answers will help you complete the Unit Challenge later.

Analyzing the Photo
Does this picture reflect how Tina and her mother might feel now? Explain.

Before You Read : Alone

Maya Angelou

Meet the Author

Maya Angelou is a writer, activist, and performer. Born in Missouri in 1928, Angelou spent much of her childhood with her grandmother in Arkansas. She writes about her experiences there in her autobiography, *I Know Why the Caged Bird Sings*. Angelou's work reflects her pride in her African American heritage and her religious faith. See page R1 of the Author Files for more on Angelou.

Author Search For more about Maya Angelou, go to www.glencoe.com.

NY English Language Arts Core Curriculum (pp. 905–907)

Core R4 Determine the meaning of unfamiliar words by using a dictionary and structural analysis. **R2g** Compare literature to own lives.

For a complete description of the standards, see p. NY 11.

Vocabulary Preview

English Language Coach

Historical Influences on English Anglo-Saxon, Greek, and Latin are the three languages that have had the greatest influence in shaping the modern English language.

- Anglo-Saxon, or Old English, was spoken and written in England for hundreds of years. Most words that come from Old English are simple objects or actions, such as *bread, knife, sit,* and *say.*
- Many Greek roots and combining forms are related to government and learning. Examples are *biology, democracy,* and *cosmos.*
- Latin is remembered as the "language of knowledge," because ancient Rome influenced the development of many things: law, war, art, science, literature, architecture, and language. Examples of words from Latin are *construct, transport,* and *dictionary.*

Get Ready to Read

Connect to the Reading

Think of a time when you depended on someone—or someone depended on you—for friendship or support. Who helps you keep going when life gets you down?

Build Background

Water is often a symbol of birth, and a raven may represent death. But a symbol's meaning is determined by the culture and experiences of both the writer and the reader. For example, an American is likely to see the bald eagle as a symbol of freedom, but a person from Egypt or Japan or Brazil might have other ideas. As you find symbols in "Alone," consider what they mean to you, what they might mean to other readers, and what they might have meant to the poet.

Set Purposes for Reading

BIG Question Read to find out why Angelou believes that people need each other.

Set Your Own Purpose What else would you like to learn from the selection to help you answer the Big Question? Write your own purpose on the Comparing Foldable for Unit 6.

Alone

by Maya Angelou

Lying, thinking
Last **night**
How to find my soul a home
Where water is not thirsty
5 And bread loaf is not stone
I came up with one thing
And I don't believe I'm wrong
That nobody,
But nobody
10 Can make it out here alone. **1** **2**

Alone, all alone
Nobody, but nobody
Can make it out here alone.

There are some millionaires
15 With money they can't use
Their wives run round like banshees*
Their children sing the blues
They've got expensive doctors
To cure their hearts of stone.
20 But nobody
No nobody
Can make it out here alone. **3**

Practice the Skills

1 **English Language Coach**

Historical Influences Middle English gave us the word **night**, which came through Old English *(niht)*, Old High German *(naht)*, Latin *(nox)*, and Greek *(nyx)*.

2 **Comparing Literature**

Figurative Language What might water and bread symbolize here? Make notes about these symbols in your organizer.

3 **Comparing Literature**

Figurative Language The speaker uses a simile in line 16 and a metaphor in line 19 to comment on people with too much money. What does each figure of speech mean? What opinion is the speaker expressing in this stanza?

---

16 In Irish folklore, a *banshee* was a female spirit whose mournful wail predicted death.

Alone, all alone
Nobody, but nobody
25 Can make it out here alone.

Now if you'll listen closely
I'll tell you what I know
Storm clouds are gathering
The wind is gonna blow
30 The race of man is suffering
And I can hear the moan,
Cause nobody,
But nobody
Can make it out here alone. 4

35 Alone, all alone
Nobody, but nobody
Can make it out here alone. 5 ○

Practice the Skills

4 **Comparing Literature**

Figurative Language What do the storm clouds represent to the speaker?

5 **BIG Question**

Think about the poem's three-line refrain. In what way is it a warning? Write your answer on the Comparing Foldable for Unit 6. Your response will help you complete the Unit Challenge later.

Cypress Maiden, 1995. Christian Pierre. Oil on canvas. Private Collection.

Analyzing the Painting Does this painting reflect the feeling you get from the poem? Why or why not?

After You Read

Welcome
by Ouida Sebestyen

& Alone
by Maya Angelou

Vocabulary Check

Rewrite each sentence below, filling in the blank with the best word from the list. Each word will be used twice.

dismal   ultimatum   famished   pivoted   coaxed

1. If you're so ___, why don't *you* cook dinner?

2. The kidnapper's ___ included serious threats that the parents couldn't bear to think about.

3. I hoped that after I ___ my bed ninety degrees the morning sun wouldn't wake me up so early.

4. No matter how much we ___ or begged, the referee simply refused to change her ruling.

5. The principal gave everyone an ___; we would arrive on time for every class, or we'd be suspended.

6. That paint is horrible! The color is too ___ even for the basement of a funeral home!

7. The doctors were worried because some of the ___ survivors had become too weak to feed themselves.

8. It took a lot of time and effort, but the twins finally ___ the babysitter into giving the answer they wanted.

9. When the woman saw the security guard approaching, she ___ and rushed out of the store.

10. With no restaurants, shops, parks, or beaches, the little village was a ___ disappointment.

English Language Coach

Rewrite each sentence below, filling in the blank with a word that comes from the root shown in parentheses. The word should make sense in the sentence.

11. Since Helena lives far from school, she has to ride her ___. *(cycle)*

12. Pedro's dog was sick, so the veterinarian ___ medication. *(scrib)*

13. When crossing the street, the ___ always has the right of way. *(ped)*

NY English Language Arts Core Curriculum (pp. 908–909)

LC R17 Demonstrate comprehension and response through a range of activities.
W3e Compare and contrast the use of literary elements in more than one genre, by more than one author.

For a complete description of the standards, see p. NY 11.

Reading/Critical Thinking
Welcome

14. **BIG Question** How does Tina keep from giving up when she realizes her family is changing?

Tip Think and Search

15. Recall What does Arley say and do to help Tina feel better?

Tip Right There

16. Summarize Explain Tina's realization after she accepts Arley's flower.

Tip Author and Me

Alone

17. Infer Why might the speaker believe that "the race of man is suffering"?

Tip Author and Me

18. Evaluate Does the speaker make a good case against trying to survive alone? Why or why not?

Tip Author and Me

19. Infer Why are the millionaires and their families in the third stanza so unhappy? What is the speaker saying about the relationship between wealth and happiness?

Tip Author and Me

Writing: Compare the Literature

Use Your Notes

Writers use figurative language to communicate specific ideas and images. No two figures of speech are exactly alike, since their meaning always depends on their context. As you compare and contrast "Welcome" and "Alone," think about how figurative language added to or changed your understanding of the selections.

As you review the notes in your graphic organizers, ask yourself:

- What purpose does figurative language serve in the short story?
- What purpose does it serve in the poem?
- How are these purposes alike and/or different?

20. Follow these steps to compare the use of figurative language in "Welcome" and "Alone."

Step 1: Look at the chart you completed for "Welcome." Circle a simile or metaphor that helped you visualize a character.

Step 2: Underline a simile or metaphor that helped you visualize a place.

Step 3: Draw a box around a simile or metaphor that helped you understand an idea or feeling.

Step 4: Put a check mark beside the story's most important symbol.

Step 5: Look at the chart you completed for "Alone." Repeat steps 1–4.

Get It on Paper

To show what you have learned about the use of figurative language in "Welcome" and "Alone," answer the questions below.

21. In "Welcome," how do similes and metaphors help you understand Tina, her mother, and her aunts? How does figurative language help you visualize these characters and their problems?

22. In "Alone," how do similes and metaphors help you understand the speaker and her concerns?

23. Were the similes and metaphors more descriptive in "Welcome" or "Alone"? Explain your answer.

24. Think about the symbols you checked above. Would the story still make sense without the symbol you chose? Would the poem? Compare the importance of the symbols you picked in "Welcome" and "Alone."

BIG Question

25. In both selections, the narrator and speaker feel alone, abandoned, or misunderstood. In "Welcome," how does Tina deal with these feelings? What does she do to make herself understood? In "Alone," what does the speaker say about surviving life alone?

Answering **The BIG Question** How Do You Keep from Giving Up When Bad Things Happen?

You've just read about people who remained positive when they were faced with hardship. Now use what you've learned to complete the Unit Challenge.

The Unit Challenge

Choose Activity A or Activity B, and follow the directions for that activity.

A. Group Activity: Create a Newspaper Ad

With three other students, imagine that a natural disaster has occurred in a nearby community. Create a newspaper advertisement explaining how people in your community can help.

1. **Discuss the Assignment** Choose one group member to be the note-keeper for the discussion. Use your Foldables to review the hardships that people faced in the selections you read in this unit. Discuss ways that they dealt with hardships and which strategies were most effective.

2. **Fill in the Details** Decide on the imaginary disaster and the needs that your ad will be concerned with. Most natural disasters have three major effects:

   • death and physical injury of people and animals
   • psychological injury to survivors
   • damage to homes, businesses, roads, bridges, trees, power lines, and so on

   Brainstorm ideas about how your community can help. Ask questions such as these:

   • What kinds of help do people need?
   • What resources are available?
   • How can your community help?
   • How can you and your classmates organize the help efforts?

3. **Write the Ad** Identify specific ways people can help, such as by

   • donating food, clothes, and furniture
   • giving money
   • volunteering to work

   Tell people how to contact disaster-relief agencies—both government and private. List each organization's phone number and location. Look in local phone books for

   • emergency services
   • gas, water, electricity, and telephone companies
   • government offices
   • the Red Cross, Salvation Army, and other private aid organizations

4. **Design the Ad** Decide how large your ad will be (full page, half page, or quarter page). Have two group members choose the fonts and do the layout. Where appropriate, they can add hand-drawn illustrations or, on a computer, digital photographs.

5. **Publish It** Make sure the ad is clear, easy to read, and simple to understand. Have two or three group members proofread it. When you're confident that it's ready, display the ad in your classroom.

B. Solo Activity: Write a Poem

Bad things can happen to people of all ages, races, nationalities, and religions. Write a poem addressed to a person or a group of people going through hard times. You may want to include advice or an encouraging message.

1. **Prepare to Write** Decide what the general idea of your poem will be and what form it will have. Ask yourself questions such as these:

   - What is the subject of the poem?
   - To whom are you addressing the poem?
   - What will the tone be?
   - How many stanzas will you write?
   - Will your poem rhyme?

2. **Create a Word Chart** Look over the notes on your Foldables. Then, brainstorm words and phrases to use in your poem. Start by choosing a word that has to do with hardship. Then write down another word that is somehow related to the first word. Continue the process, allowing your mind to wander.

Draw a blank chart based on the one below. Write your own words in the boxes as you think of them.

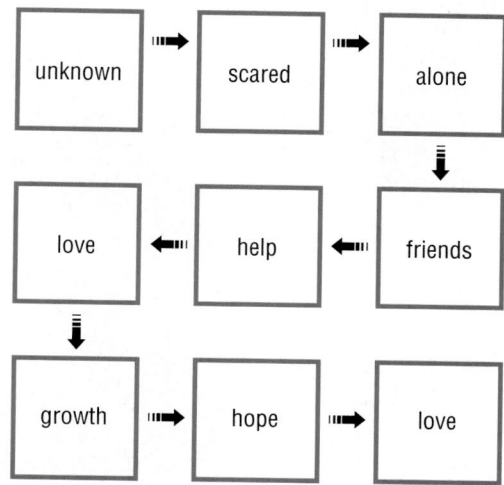

3. **Write the Poem** Use the words in your chart to write your poem. Write as if you were talking directly to someone. Use words and phrases that create mental pictures. Offer advice or sympathy to the person or people you are addressing.

4. **Present Your Poem** Read your poem aloud to yourself to make sure that it makes sense and has a clear message. Type or print it on a fresh piece of paper, and proofread it for errors. If you like, draw a picture to go along with it. Now you're ready to hand it in!

Literature Online

BIG Question Link to Web resources to further explore the Big Question at www.glencoe.com.

Naomi Shihab Nye

Meet the Author

Naomi Shihab Nye was born in 1952 to a Palestinian father and an American mother. She has lived in St. Louis, Missouri; Jerusalem, Israel; and San Antonio, Texas. She has won numerous awards for her poetry, essays, and novels. Nye often gets her inspiration from small things and everyday events. She once said, "Language can carry us to understanding and connect us to the things that matter in our lives." See page R4 of the Author Files for more on Naomi Shihab Nye.

Author Search For more about Naomi Shihab Nye, go to www.glencoe.com.

Flinn, On the Bus

by Naomi Shihab Nye

Three hours after the buildings fell,
he took a seat beside me.
Fresh out of prison, after 24 months,
You're my first hello!
5 Going home to Mom,
a life he would make better this time,
how many times
he'd been swept along before,
to things he should never have . . .
10 *drink and dope,*
but now he'd take responsibility.
Lawyers had done him wrong
and women too. He thought
about revenge, now he was out.
15 *But I'm in charge. I'll think*
before I act. I don't ever
want to go there again.
Two wrongs don't make a right.

Somehow, in his mouth, that day,
20 it sounded new.
The light came through the window
on a gentle-eyed man in a
"Focus on the Game" T-shirt,
who had given up
25 *assault** *with deadly weapons,*
no more, no good!
A man who had not seen TV in weeks,
secluding in his cell so colleagues*
wouldn't trip him up,
30 extend his stay.
Who had not heard the news.
We rolled through green Oklahoma,
the bus windows made all the trees look bent.
A trick of refraction*—
35 Flinn looked at his free hands
more than the fields,
turned them over in his lap,
no snap judgments, no quick angers,
I'll stand back, look at what happens,
40 *think calmly what my next step should be.*
It was not hard to nod,
to wish him well. But could I tell
what had happened in the world
on his long-awaited day,
45 what twists of rage greater
than we could ever guess
had savaged* skylines, thousands of lives?
I could not. He'd find out
soon enough. Flinn, take it easy.
50 Peace is rough. ○

---

25 *Assault* is any violent attack or attempt to harm someone.

28 Here, *secluding* means "keeping (himself) separated from others." *Colleagues* (KAHL eegz) are fellow workers; here, it refers to Flinn's fellow inmates.

34 *Refraction* is the bending of light waves as they pass through, in this case, glass.

47 To *savage* (SAV ij) is to destroy in a fierce, cruel, uncivilized way.

Reading on Your Own

To read more about the Big Question, choose one of these books from your school or local library. Work on your reading skills by choosing books that are challenging to you.

Fiction

Tree by Leaf
by Cynthia Voigt

Clothilde's father returns from World War I alive but disfigured and depressed. Read to find out how Clothilde's family deals with the challenges they must face.

Lupita Mañana
by Patricia Beatty

Lupita Torres is thirteen when she and her older brother decide to go to the United States. They need jobs there to support their widowed mother and younger siblings. But are they prepared for the dangers and difficulties of crossing a border illegally?

Missing May
by Cynthia Rylant

Summer has had many homes, but when she joins her aunt and uncle, she is welcomed and deeply loved. Then Aunt May dies, and Summer and Uncle Ob must come to terms with their loss.

Kira-Kira
by Cynthia Kadohata

In the 1950s a Japanese American family moves to Georgia. The adjustment is difficult for everyone, and Katie turns to her sister Lynn for help and friendship. When Lynn becomes very ill, Katie's strength is tested in almost every way. Read to find out what *kira-kira* really means to Katie and her family.

Nonfiction

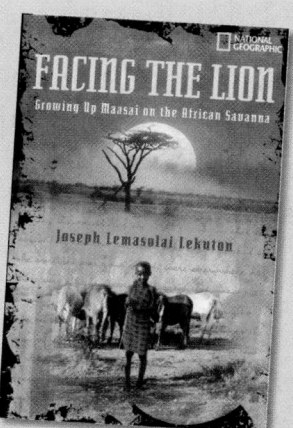

Facing the Lion: Growing Up Massai on the African Savanna
by Joseph Lemasolai-Lekuton

Joseph grew up in one of Kenya's poorest tribes. In this story of determination and courage, he describes his path from Kenya to the United States, as well as the ties that still bind him to the Africa he loves.

Jaime Escalante, Sensational Teacher
by Ann Byers

This fascinating biography discusses the challenges faced and overcome by a gifted and determined teacher. Escalante and his dedicated students proved to the world that hard work and desire can triumph over poverty and prejudice.

World History Series: The Internment of the Japanese
by Diane Yancey

This book explains how fear and hatred of Japanese Americans after the attack on Pearl Harbor led to their imprisonment in camps right here in the United States. Read about the unjust treatment of these citizens and how they managed to face racism with strength and dignity.

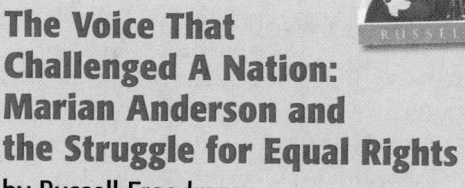

The Voice That Challenged A Nation: Marian Anderson and the Struggle for Equal Rights
by Russell Freedman

In the 1920s and 1930s, Marian Anderson became world famous for her singing voice. At home in the United States, this African American woman had to fight for the right to perform in concert halls that were restricted to whites.

New York English Language Arts Test Practice

Directions

Read this dialogue between a king and his chancellor on a day that the king's daughter is to receive a suitor. Then answer questions 1 through 5.

from *The Ugly Duckling*

By A. A. Milne

The SCENE *is the Throne Room of the Palace. . . .The* KING *is asleep on his throne with a handkerchief over his face. He is a king of any country from any story-book, in whatever costume you please. But he should be wearing his crown.*

A VOICE (*announcing*). His Excellency the Chancellor! (*The* CHANCELLOR, *an elderly man in horn-rimmed spectacles, enters, bowing. The* KING *wakes up with a start and removes the handkerchief from his face.*)

KING (*with simple dignity*). I was thinking.

CHANCELLOR (*bowing*). Never, Your Majesty, was greater need for thought than now.

KING. That's what I was thinking. (*He struggles into a more dignified position.*) Well, what is it? More trouble?

CHANCELLOR. What we might call the old trouble, Your Majesty.

KING. It's what I was saying last night to the Queen. "Uneasy lies the head that wears a crown," was how I put it.

CHANCELLOR. A profound and original thought, which may well go down to posterity.

KING. You mean it may go down well with posterity. I hope so. Remind me to tell you some time of another little thing I said to Her Majesty: something about a fierce light beating on a throne. Posterity would like that, too. Well, what is it?

CHANCELLOR. It is the matter of Her Royal Highness' wedding.

KING. Oh . . . yes.

CHANCELLOR. As Your Majesty is aware, the young Prince Simon arrives to-day to seek Her Royal Highness' hand in marriage. He has been traveling to distant lands and, as I understand, has not—er—has not—

KING. You mean he hasn't heard anything.

CHANCELLOR. It is a little difficult to put this tactfully, Your Majesty.

KING. Do your best, and I will tell you afterwards how you got on.

CHANCELLOR. Let me put it this way. The Prince Simon will naturally assume that Her Royal Highness has the customary—so customary as to be, in my

> **posterity** = future generations

own poor opinion, slightly monotonous—has what one might call the inevitable—so inevitable as to be, in my opinion, again, almost mechanical—will assume, that she has the, as I think of it, faultily faultless, icily regular, splendidly—

KING. What you are trying to say in the fewest words possible is that my daughter is not beautiful.

CHANCELLOR. Her beauty is certainly elusive, Your Majesty.

KING. It is. It has eluded you, it has eluded me, it has eluded everybody who has seen her. It even eluded the Court Painter. His last words were, "Well, I did my best." His successor is now painting the view across the water-meadows from the West Turret. He says that his doctor has advised him to keep to landscape.

elusive = hard to identify

CHANCELLOR. It is unfortunate, Your Majesty, but there it is. One just cannot understand how it can have occurred.

KING. You don't think she takes after *me*, at all? You don't detect a likeness?

CHANCELLOR. Most certainly not, Your Majesty.

KING. Good. . . . Your predecessor did.

CHANCELLOR. I have often wondered what happened to my predecessor.

KING. Well, now you know.

---

1 Which word **best** describes the king in the scene?

A dignified

B bewildered

C laughable

D humble

2 What is the main problem the king and the chancellor face in this scene?

F how long they can keep Prince Simon away from the princess

G how Prince Simon will react when he sees the princess

H what to do about the previous chancellor

J how they will be remembered

3 Read this line from the scene.

> KING. **What you are trying to say in the fewest words possible is that my daughter is not beautiful.**

In this line, the king is being

A repetitive

B indirect

C sarcastic

D inquisitive

4 Read these lines about the princess's elusive beauty.

> KING. **It is. It has eluded you, it has eluded me, it has eluded everybody who has seen her. It even eluded the Court Painter. His last words were, "Well, I did my best." His successor is now painting the view across the water-meadows from the West Turret. He says that his doctor has advised him to keep to landscape.**

The word "eluded" here means about the same as

F escaped

G struck

H impressed

J concerned

5 In the scene from *The Ugly Duckling*, the king and the chancellor engage in wordplay throughout their conversation. On a separate piece of paper, copy the chart below and list two instances in which they use words playfully and explain what each character means by his verbal wit.

Character	Wordplay	Meaning of Verbal Wit

Directions

Read this monologue delivered by the famous *Peanuts* character Charlie Brown. Then answer questions 6 through 8.

from *You're a Good Man, Charlie Brown*

CHARLIE BROWN: I think lunchtime is about the worst time of the day for me. Always having to sit here alone. Of course, sometimes mornings aren't so pleasant, either . . . waking up and wondering if anyone would really miss me if I never got out of bed. Then, there's the night, too—lying there and thinking about all the stupid things I've done during the day. And all those hours in between—when I do all those stupid things . . . Well, lunchtime is among the worst times for me. Well, I guess I'd better see what I got. (*He opens bag, unwraps a sandwich, and looks inside.*) Peanut butter. (*He bites and chews.*) Some psychiatrists say that people who eat peanut butter sandwiches are lonely. I guess they're right. And if you're really lonely the peanut butter sticks to the roof of your mouth. (*He munches quietly, idly fingering the bench.*) Boy, the PTA did a good job of painting those benches. (*He looks off to one side.*) There's that cute little red-headed girl eating her lunch over there. I wonder what she'd do if I went over and asked her if I could sit and have lunch with her. She'd probably laugh right in my face. It's hard on a face when it gets laughed in. There's an empty place next to her on the bench. There's no reason why I couldn't just go over there and sit there. I could do that right now. All I have to do is stand up. (*He stands.*) I'm standing up. (*He sits.*) I'm sitting down. I'm a coward. I'm so much a coward she wouldn't even think of looking at me. She hardly ever does look at me. In fact, I can't remember her ever looking at me. Why shouldn't she look at me? Is there any reason in the world why she shouldn't look at me? Is she so great and I'm so small that she couldn't spare one little moment just to . . . (*He freezes.*) She's looking at me! (*In terror, he looks one way, then another.*) She's looking at me! (*His head turns all around frantically trying to find something to notice.*)

---

6 Which word **best** describes how Charlie Brown feels in this scene?

A happy

B patient

C calm

D unhappy

7 What does Charlie Brown mean when he says, "It's hard on a face when it gets laughed in"?

F It's painful to be laughed at.

G It's not nice to make fun of others.

H It makes your face wrinkle.

J It's insulting to be taunted.

8 Read these sentences from the passage.

> **Is she so great and I'm so small that she couldn't spare one little moment just to . . . (*He freezes.*) She's looking at me! (*In terror, he looks one way, then another.*) She's looking at me! (*His head turns all around frantically trying to find something to notice.*)**

Why is Charlie Brown terrified?

A He can't finish his sandwich.

B He think the little red-headed girl might come talk to him.

C He thinks he looks funny.

D He can't find a place to sit.

*D*irections
Read this story told by a sad statue to a lonely bird. Then answer questions 9 through 13.

from "The Happy Prince"

By Oscar Wilde

In the middle of a large city, on a tall column, stood the statue of the Happy Prince. He was gilded all over with a layer of fine gold, for eyes he had two bright sapphires, and a large red ruby glowed on his sword-hilt. One night there flew over the city a little Swallow. His friends had gone away to Egypt six weeks before, but he had stayed behind, for he was in love with the most beautiful Reed. . . . "Where shall I put up?" he said.

Then he saw the statue on the tall column. "I will put up there," he cried; "it is a fine position with plenty of fresh air." So he alighted just between the feet of the Happy Prince.

Suddenly, the Swallow felt drops of water and thought it was raining. The Swallow looked up and saw that the statue of the Happy Prince was alive and crying. In this monologue, the Happy Prince tells the swallow why he cries.

The Character: The Happy Prince (a young man)

  "I am the Happy Prince.
  "When I was alive and had a human heart, I did not know what tears were, for I lived in the Palace of Sans-Souci, where sorrow is not allowed to enter. In the daytime I played with my companions in the garden, and in the evening I led the dance in the Great Hall. Round the garden ran a very lofty wall, but I

never cared to ask what lay beyond it, everything about me was beautiful. My courtiers called me the Happy Prince, and happy indeed I was, if pleasure be happiness. So I lived, and so I died. And now that I am dead they have set me up here so high that I can see all the ugliness and the misery of my city, and though my heart is made of lead yet I cannot choose but weep.

"Far away, far away in a little street there is a poor house. One of the windows is open, and through it I can see a woman seated on a table. Her face is thin and worn, and she has coarse, red hands, all pricked by the needle, for she is a seamstress. She is embroidering passion-flowers on a satin gown for the loveliest of the Queen's maids-of-honour to wear at the next Court-ball. In a bed in the corner of the room her little boy is lying ill. He has a fever and is asking for oranges. His mother has nothing to give him but river water, so he is crying. Swallow, Swallow, little Swallow, will you not bring her the ruby out of my sword-hilt? My feet are fastened to this pedestal and I cannot move."

---

9 Although the passage is a monologue, a speech for a single character (the Happy Prince), the swallow also plays a role in the story. In its role, the swallow serves as

A a messenger of goodwill

B a symbol of the people's misery

C an audience for the monologue

D a living thing in contrast to the statue

10 Why is the Happy Prince statue weeping?

F He misses the pleasures of his life as a prince.

G He sees the ugliness and misery of his city's people.

H His heart has turned into lead and his body into stone.

J His feet are attached to a pedestal, and he cannot move.

11 To the people who pass by his statue, the Happy Prince seems

A sad

B envious

C lonely

D content

12 Which emotion does the Happy Prince **most likely** feel that prompts him to send the ruby to the seamstress?

F loneliness

G reflection

H generosity

J compassion

13 What can you infer from the passage about the way the Happy Prince might view the use of power and wealth if he were alive today? Use details from the passage to support your answer.

The BIG Question

What's Worth Fighting For? What's Not?

> " It is easier to fight for our principles than to live up to them. "

—Alfred Adler (1870–1937), Austrian psychiatrist and author of *Understanding Human Nature*

LOOKING AHEAD

The skill lessons and readings in this unit will help you develop your own answer to the Big Question.

UNIT 7 WARM-UP • Connecting to the Big Question

GENRE FOCUS: Persuasive Writing

READING WORKSHOP 1 Skill Lesson: Distinguishing Fact from Opinion

WRITING WORKSHOP PART 1 Persuasive Essay

READING WORKSHOP 2 Skill Lesson: Questioning

READING WORKSHOP 3 Skill Lesson: Reviewing

WRITING WORKSHOP PART 2 Persuasive Essay

READING WORKSHOP 4 Skill Lesson: Clarifying

READING ACROSS TEXTS WORKSHOP

UNIT 7 WRAP-UP • Answering the Big Question

Connecting to The BIG Question

What's Worth Fighting For? What's Not?

Sometimes you want things to change, but it's difficult to figure out how *you* can change them. So you learn to sort out what really matters to you and what doesn't. You learn what's worth fighting for and what's not. Then you decide how to act to make the change you want.

Real Kids and the Big Question

SAJITHA started a video games club at her school. There are a lot of games to choose from, but one game is everyone's favorite. A few of the older kids won't even let any of the younger kids play it. As a result, some of the younger kids have decided to leave the club. Sajitha is upset, but she is also a little afraid of the older kids. What advice would you give Sajitha?

ALEJANDRO and his brother Pedro are planning to paint their room. Pedro insists that the room should be green. Alejandro wants to paint their room blue. Every time Alejandro brings it up, Pedro starts yelling, and their mother tells them to work it out. What would you say to Alejandro? What would you say to Pedro?

Warm-Up Activity

In small groups, talk about the advice you would give Sajitha, Alejandro, and Pedro. How and why might your advice help them?

You and the Big Question

Reading about what other people think is worth fighting for will help you work out your own answer to the Big Question.

Plan for the Unit Challenge

At the end of the unit, you'll use notes from all your reading to complete the Unit Challenge.

Literature Online

BIG Question

Link to Web resources to further explore the Big Question at www.glencoe.com.

You'll choose one of the following activities:

A. Make a Mural Make a poster-board mural honoring people who fought for what they believed in.

B. Propose a Change Write a proposal for a project that will help you make a change in your school or community.

- Start thinking about which activity you'd like to do, so you can focus your thoughts as you go through the unit.

- Do you want to learn about people who stood up for their beliefs? Start making a list of people and ideas.

- Is there a change you want to make in your school or community? Start thinking about how to persuade people that the change is needed.

- In your Learner's Notebook, write which activity you'd like to do.

- Each time you make notes about the Big Question, think about how your ideas will help you complete the Unit Challenge activity you chose.

Keep Track of Your Ideas

FOLDABLES™

Study Organizer

As you read, you'll make notes about the Big Question. Later, you'll use these notes to complete the Unit Challenge. See pages R8–R9 for help with making Foldable 7. This diagram shows how it should look.

1. Use this Foldable for all of the selections in this unit. On the top front flap, write the unit number and the Big Question. Label the bottom of each flap below with a title. (See page 923 for the titles.)

2. Open each flap. Near the top of each flap, write **My Purpose for Reading**.

3. Below each crease, write **the Big Question**.

```
         Unit 7
        What's Worth
        Fighting For?
        What's Not?
   Title    |    Title
   Title    |    Title
   Title    |    Title
   Title    |    Title
   Title    |    Title
```

UNIT 7 GENRE FOCUS: PERSUASIVE WRITING

The goal of **persuasive writing** is to convince readers to agree with an opinion and, in some cases, act on it. Advertisements, critical reviews, speeches, and editorials are all examples of persuasive writing.

Why Read Persuasive Writing?

Reading persuasive writing lets you see what other people think about issues and ideas. When you read persuasive writing, you do the following things:

- learn what other people think about an issue
- think about how you feel about an issue
- learn to distinguish fact from opinion

How to Read Persuasive Writing

Key Reading Skills

These reading skills are useful tools for reading and understanding persuasive writing. You'll see these skills modeled in the Active Reading Model on pages 927–929, and you'll learn more about them later in this unit.

- ■ **Distinguishing fact from opinion** To decide whether someone's arguments are trustworthy, you need to ask yourself, *Are these someone's personal beliefs, or can they be proved?* (See Reading Workshop 1.)
- ■ **Questioning** To make sure you understand a selection, ask yourself questions while you read. (See Reading Workshop 2.)
- ■ **Reviewing** Stop from time to time to go over what you've already read and to remember and organize important ideas. (See Reading Workshop 3.)
- ■ **Clarifying** Reread confusing parts, look up words you don't know, and ask questions about what you don't understand. (See Reading Workshop 4.)

Key Text Elements

Recognizing and thinking about the following literary elements will help you understand more fully what writers are saying.

- ■ **Persuasive appeals:** methods used to convince people to agree with a position. An author who appeals through the use of reason presents arguments based on facts and other kinds of evidence. An author who appeals through the use of ethics tries to show why he or she is trustworthy. An author who appeals through the use of emotion tries to spark strong feelings to get readers to care about an issue and take action. (See "Saving Water," *The Measure of Our Success,* and "All Together Now.")
- ■ **Author's bias:** an inability or unwillingness to look at all sides of an issue (See "Teen Curfews.")
- ■ **Faulty reasoning:** flawed thinking that leads to incorrect conclusions (See Rally for Better Food, student flyer and poster.)

Skills Focus
- Key skills for reading persuasive writing
- Key literary elements of persuasive writing

Skills Model
You will learn how to use the key reading skills and literary elements as you read
- *A Letter to Senator Edwards,* p. 927

NY English Language Arts Core Curriculum (pp. 926–929)

R3a Evaluate the validity and accuracy of information, ideas, themes, opinions, and experiences in texts. Identify techniques author uses to persuade (emotional and ethical appeals). Question the writer's assumptions, beliefs, intentions, and biases. Evaluate examples, details, or reasons used to support ideas. **R1h** Identify missing, conflicting, or unclear information. **LC R12** Combine multiple strategies to enhance comprehension and response.

For a complete description of the standards, see p. NY11.

A Letter to Senator Edwards

The notes in the side columns model how to use the reading skills and text elements you read about on page 926.

Persuasive Writing
ACTIVE READING MODEL

1 Key Reading Skill
Reviewing *I need to reread the introductory paragraph, so I can really understand Bill 347.9. I know it affects young drivers, but I don't remember the details.*

2 Key Reading Skill
Distinguishing Fact from Opinion *It's a fact that the bill targets one group. It's an opinion that the bill is unfair.*

Dear Senator Edwards:

I am writing to you about proposed Bill 347.9. As a result of the accident rate for young drivers, our state is thinking of issuing restricted driver's licenses to young drivers who break the traffic laws. Under Bill 347.9, a driver under eighteen who is guilty of a moving violation (for example, speeding or running a red light) would get a restricted driver's license. The license holder could then drive only during daylight hours and with an adult licensed driver. These restrictions would remain in effect until the driver's eighteenth birthday. **1**

Safe roads are everyone's concern. I doubt that anyone would oppose reasonable measures to make streets safer. The reasoning behind Bill 347.9 is admirable. The bill's purposes are to keep offending[1] drivers off the roads, to provide supervision for less-experienced young drivers, and to make the roads safer for all travelers. However, as a young driver, I urge you to vote against this bill for two reasons. First, the bill unfairly targets one group for unusually harsh punishment. **2**

---

1. *Offending* drivers break the law.

Second, the bill will make it difficult or even impossible for many students to hold part-time jobs and participate in after-school activities. **3**

   Bill 347.9 discriminates against young drivers. Don't licensed drivers over the age of eighteen also commit moving violations? Yet no one is suggesting that they get restricted licenses. There is no evidence that speeding or running a red light is a greater safety danger when the driver is under eighteen. People can be safe or reckless drivers regardless of their age. They don't automatically become better drivers once they reach eighteen. The same rules should apply to drivers of all ages. **4**

   Another factor to consider about Bill 347.9 is the effect it will have on young people who depend on their driving privileges in order to work and participate in after-school activities. Many of my classmates hold part-time jobs. Some work to save money for college. Others work to

3 Key Reading Skill
Questioning *Why will the bill make part-time jobs and after-school activities impossible?*

4 Key Text Element
Persuasive Appeals *Here, the writer appeals to readers' sense of reason by giving a logical argument in support of his opinion. He doesn't try to spark strong feelings or prove that he is a trustworthy expert on the subject.*

help out their parents. Anyone with a restricted license cannot hold a job unless he or she can walk to work, get a ride, or use public transportation. When these choices do not exist, or are not safe, many students will be forced to quit their jobs. Similar problems occur when students are unable to drive to and from after-school activities, such as music lessons, sport team practices, and games. If Bill 347.9 is passed, students will have to quit their after-school activities simply because they have had a single moving violation. **5**

Some people will argue that special rules and restrictions should apply to younger drivers, since they lack the experience and judgment of older drivers. But how will younger drivers ever gain the experience and judgment they need if they aren't allowed to drive by themselves? If Mom or Dad is always in the car, playing the role of "back-seat driver," how will a young person ever learn to drive independently out on the road? Laws already exist to restrict, suspend,[2] or take away the license of any driver who is truly reckless or a threat to public safety, regardless of age. Let's enforce the laws that already exist. Let's not pass new laws that discriminate against drivers under eighteen. **6**

In closing, I would like to thank you for considering my viewpoint. We young drivers of this state hope that we can count on you to watch out for our interests, as well as those of all citizens. In return, we will act responsibly both on and off the roads. **7** ○

---

2. Here, **suspend** means "to force to give up something for a period of time."

ACTIVE READING MODEL

5 Key Text Element
Faulty Reasoning *In the last sentence of this paragraph, the writer uses faulty "either/or" reasoning. If the bill passes, some students will still be able to get to and from activities by walking or taking public transportation.*

6 Key Reading Skill
Clarifying *I'm not sure about the difference between "suspend" and "take away." I'll read the footnote for help.*

7 Key Text Element
Author's Bias *I think the writer is a bit biased. He bases his opinion on personal experience. Since the writer is a young driver, he writes only about how the bill will affect people under eighteen.*

Partner Talk With a partner, discuss your opinion of Bill 347.9. Do you agree or disagree with the writer's opinion? Explain.

 **Study Central** Visit www.glencoe.com and click on Study Central to review persuasive writing.

Skills Focus

You will practice using these skills when you read the following selections:

- "Saving Water: Why Save Something That Covers Two-thirds of the Earth?" p. 934
- from *The Measure of Our Success,* p. 944

Reading

- Distinguishing fact from opinion

Informational Text

- Identifying persuasive appeals

Vocabulary

- Understanding connotation and denotation
- Academic Vocabulary: *ethical*

Writing/Grammar

- Using colons correctly

NY English Language Arts Core Curriculum (pp. 930–931)

R3a Evaluate the validity and accuracy of information, ideas, themes, opinions, and experiences in texts.

For a complete description of the standards, see p. NY11.

Skill Lesson

Distinguishing Fact from Opinion

Learn It!

What Is It? You can't always assume that what you read is true. It's up to you to decide whether to believe what a writer tells you. When you are deciding, distinguish facts from opinions.

- A **fact** is a piece of information that can be proved with supporting information.
- An **opinion** is a personal belief. Writers can support their opinions with facts, but an opinion cannot be proved.

© Zits Partnership. Reprinted with Permission of King Features Syndicate, Inc.

Analyzing Cartoons
These three friends can't help but share their thoughts about their classmates. Are their comments facts or opinions?

Why Is It Important? Distinguishing fact from opinion helps you decide whether to trust information that you read.

How Do I Do It? To distinguish fact from opinion, ask yourself these questions:

- *Are sources available to prove this information is correct?*
- *Does this sound like the author's view or belief?*
- *Is the writer an expert on this subject?*

Below is part of a letter to the editor about improving schools. Read how one student distinguished fact from opinion in the passage.

> I attend a school that is being run by state officials because of poor test scores. I think that a better way to improve my school, along with other American schools, is to imitate a successful school system, like Japan's. More than ninety-nine percent of adults in Japan are able to read and write. In Japan, students go to classes five and one-half days per week, do more homework than American students, and wear school uniforms.

I can do research to verify how many Japanese adults can read and write. If the research proves that about ninety-nine percent of Japanese adults are literate, that sentence is a fact. There is no way to prove whether American schools would be better if they imitated Japanese schools. That's the writer's opinion.

Practice It!

Identify each of the following statements as fact or opinion.

- Of all the water on Earth, ninety-seven percent is salt water.
- The best way to relax is a hot bath.

Use It!

Use a two-column chart in your Learner's Notebook to distinguish facts from opinions. Label the left-hand column *Facts* and the right-hand column *Opinions*. As you read "Saving Water," write key pieces of information in the appropriate column.

Literature Online

Study Central Visit www.glencoe .com and click on Study Central to review distinguishing fact from opinion.

Before You Read

Marjorie Lamb

Meet the Author

Marjorie Lamb's parents taught her that "you should always save things, you should always repair things, you should pass things on to the next person, and you should do your best to be kind to the planet in general." The following selection is from Lamb's book *2 Minutes a Day for a Greener Planet*.

Author Search For more about Marjorie Lamb, go to www.glencoe.com.

NY English Language Arts Core Curriculum (pp. 932–939)

Core R5 Distinguish between dictionary meaning and implied meaning of the author's words. **R3a** Evaluate the validity and accuracy of information, ideas, themes, opinions, and experiences in texts. Identify techniques author uses to persuade (emotional and ethical appeals).

For a complete description of the standards, see p. NY11.

Saving Water: Why Save Something That Covers Two-thirds of the Earth?

Vocabulary Preview

municipal (myoo NIS uh pul) *adj.* having to do with a city or town or its government **(p. 935)** *Water treatment is only one of many important municipal services that our local government oversees.*

distribution (dis truh BYOO shun) *n.* division into shares or portions **(p. 936)** *There would be fewer problems if the distribution of water were equal so that everyone had his or her fair share.*

contamination (kun tam uh NAY shun) *n.* pollution **(p. 936)** *Waste and contamination are two problems that we can fix.*

Partner Work In your Learner's Notebook, use each vocabulary word in a sentence. Find a partner and check each other's sentences to make sure each word is used correctly.

English Language Coach

Denotations and Connotations All words have **denotations** (dee noh TAY shunz), or dictionary definitions. But some words also have **connotations** (kon uh TAY shunz)—feelings, thoughts, and mental pictures that the words bring to mind. Take, for example, the words *thrifty* and *cheap.* Both words denote, or mean, "careful with money." Yet most people would rather be called "thrifty" than "cheap." That's because *thrifty* has positive connotations, while *cheap* has negative connotations.

Not all words have clear-cut connotations. A word like *the* does not have connotations, while a word like *thin* may have positive connotations for a successful dieter and negative connotations for someone trying to gain weight. Though connotations may differ, most are fairly clear. If you're not sure of a word's connotations, check an unabridged (complete) dictionary.

Partner Work Each of the following groups of words has about the same denotation but different connotations. With a classmate, classify the words in each group as positive, negative, or neutral. Write the words in a chart like the one shown. Use a dictionary if you need help.

- old, antique, decrepit
- spacious, big, overdone

Positive	Neutral	Negative
soft-spoken	quiet	secretive

Skills Preview

Key Reading Skill: Distinguishing Fact from Opinion

As you read the article, ask yourself whether statements are facts or opinions. Remember that opinions are not necessarily wrong. An educated person's opinion may have the force of fact.

On Your Own Which of the following statements is an opinion? Why?

• George Washington was the first U.S. president. He was also the best president.

Key Text Element: Persuasive Appeals

Writers may use a variety of techniques to persuade readers to agree with their opinions or to take action. The three major techniques, or appeals, are as follows:

• **Appeal to reason:** appeal to the "head" rather than the "heart" through the use of logic, facts, or other types of hard evidence

• **Ethical appeal:** appeal to the reader's sense of right and wrong or to the writer's claim to be a good and moral person who can be trusted

• **Emotional appeal:** appeal to the reader's "heart," or emotions, in an effort to get the reader to care about a problem or an issue

Partner Talk Discuss the following statements. Decide which appeals to reason, which appeals to ethics, and which appeals to emotions.

Vote for Jon Doe for U.S. senator because . . .

• he is a good family man and a regular church goer.

• he is tough on law and order, so you and your family won't have to live in fear.

• he is an experienced legislator who has served two terms as a state senator.

Get Ready to Read

Connect to the Reading

Think about all the water that you use in a day. Then think about where the water comes from and where it goes when you have finished using it.

Whole Class Discussion Suppose that every water source in your home had a meter. The meter would measure how much water your family used and show the total cost of using it. Would the meter change how your family uses water? Why or why not?

Build Background

Not everyone takes clean water for granted.

• Roughly one-sixth of the world's people do not have enough drinking water.

• In some African and Asian countries, people must walk nearly four miles to get water.

Set Purposes for Reading

BIG Question Read "Saving Water: Why Save Something That Covers Two-thirds of the Earth?" to find out whether conserving fresh water is a cause worth fighting for.

Set Your Own Purpose What else would you like to learn from the article to help you answer the Big Question? Write your own purpose on the "Saving Water" flap of Foldable 7.

Interactive Literary Elements Handbook
To review or learn more about the literary elements, go to www.glencoe.com.

Keep Moving

Use these skills as you read the following selection.

Saving Water:
Why Save Something That Covers Two-thirds of the Earth?
by Marjorie Lamb

Practice the Skills

All life on this planet is supported by a fixed quantity of water. We use the same water over and over again, the same water which our grandparents used for brickmaking, the same water in which Shakespeare washed his feet, the same water in which Moses floated in a basket through the bullrushes, the same water the ancient Romans transported through their aqueducts[1] to support life in their city. In fact, the water that you used to brush your teeth this morning is over four billion years old. So have a little respect.

Of all water on our planet Earth, 97% is salt water. Only 3% is fresh water, and most of that is frozen in the polar ice caps. Less than 1% of Earth's water is available for our use. 🔲

We can't make new water, any more than we can make new land. If we misuse the water we have, we can't send out for some fresh stuff. Water comes out of the tap in unlimited quantities whenever we want it. We generally assume that we have vast reserves of water available.

1 **Key Reading Skill**

Distinguishing Fact from Opinion Reread the boldface paragraph. You could prove the information is true by checking science books or encyclopedias. So the statements in this paragraph are facts.

---

1. **Aqueducts** (AK wuh dukts) are canals, tunnels, or pipelines used to move water.

Practice the Skills

And we generally assume that it's free, or almost free. But before clean water comes out of our taps, several things have to happen. We have to find a source of water, build machinery to pump it, piping to carry it, plants to treat it. Thanks to our treatment of water, chlorine[2] has become an acquired taste in millions of households. **2** We have to elect politicians who will run our **municipal** affairs, and look after our water treatment, and do the paperwork involved in supplying us with water. Once we get the water to our houses, we have to install pipes and valves and shut-offs and vents. We have to put in a separate line and a heater to heat some of the water.

Once we've got water, what do we do with it? We put it through our washing machines, toilets, sinks, dishwashers, car washes and pesticide-filled lawns. We use it to wash our windows, our sidewalks and streets. We spray it in the air for pretty fountains. We put out fires with it. We clean wounds with it. We make concrete with it. We use it in the production of plastics, steel and paper. We hose down chemical spills and industrial work sites with it. We clean paintbrushes in it. And we drink it.

What if we had water meters beside our kitchen sink? What if they read dollars and cents instead of gallons or liters?

Then we have to deal with getting rid of it. We need to build another whole network of drains to carry away our dirty water and sewage. We need to build treatment plants, and hire people to run them. And we need to elect politicians who will vow to "do something" to clean up the water that we've polluted.

The process costs billions of dollars worldwide, and still people suffer and die in many parts of the world for want of clean water, while we **blithely** open our taps and let our most precious resource pour down the drain. **3**

2. **Chlorine** (klor EEN), a green-yellow gas, is an element used to disinfect water.

2 Key Reading Skill

Distinguishing Fact from Opinion It would be impossible to prove that "chlorine has become an acquired taste in millions of households." In fact, many people drink bottled water because they dislike the taste of tap water. Therefore, the author's statement is an opinion.

3 English Language Coach

Denotations and Connotations Here, the word **blithely** means "thoughtlessly." In this context *blithely* has negative connotations. It suggests we carelessly throw away something precious.

Vocabulary

municipal (myoo NIS uh pul) *adj.* having to do with a city or town or its government

Saving Water **935**

Analyzing the Photo How does this photograph relate to what the writer says about the cycle of water use in the United States? Explain.

There's not much we can do at home about the unequal **distribution** of water in the world. But the other major problems, **contamination** and waste, we can do something about. Although most of the advice in this chapter has to do with waste (we'll deal with contamination in other chapters), these two problems are connected in ways that might not be obvious.

The more we process our water, the more chance it has to become contaminated. That's because we have one sewage system for all purposes. We put our drinking water, our toilet waste and commercially contaminated waters all down the same system. We do our best to clean it up, then we pour it all out into the same river, lake or stream, and then we drink it again. **4**

And of course, the more water we have to process, the more bleach we have to produce (which isn't a terrific thing to have around—it is, after all, a poison), and, naturally, the more we

Practice the Skills

4 **Key Text Element**

Persuasive Appeals What kind of persuasive appeal is Lamb using in this paragraph? (Hint: She is using logic to counter, or argue against, the idea that water-processing plants have solved the problem of water pollution.)

Vocabulary

distribution (dis truh BYOO shun) *n.* division into shares or portions

contamination (kun tam uh NAY shun) *n.* pollution

have to pay our governments for looking after all this stuff for us. So it's not so easy to keep cleaning our water.

Yes, we could be drinking Shakespeare's bathwater, but more to the point, will our great grandchildren be able to drink the water we used to hose down the dog? Will there be any clean water left? **5**

Does it make any sense for us to save water at home? Isn't our home usage just a drop in the bucket, compared to what agriculture and industry uses?

Household usage is about 5% to 10% of total fresh water used worldwide. Most of that is used in North America.

On average each of us consumes nearly 53 gallons of water a day at home. Some citizens of water-poor countries survive on as little as 4 gallons a day. We've grown used to seeing water flow out of our taps and down the drains. What if we had an automatic shut-off on our household water that limited us to, say, 13 gallons of water a day?

What To Do

Turn the tap on briefly to wet your toothbrush, and turn it off until it's time to rinse.

In our house, the average toothbrushing time is about a minute and 20 seconds. If we turn on the tap at the beginning of that time and don't turn it off until we're finished, we will have put down the drain approximately 2 gallons of water. In our little household of three people, we could waste over 4000 gallons of water per year just in toothbrushing. **6**

Take the test in your household. How long does it take you to brush your teeth? Multiply that by the number of times you brush your teeth each day, then multiply that by the number of people in your household, and you'll soon see that you could have a terrific amount of water rushing uselessly down the drains.

My sister, Elizabeth, spent a great deal of time traveling the earth's oceans on sailboats, where she learned to brush her teeth with ¼ cup of water. The captain brushed without any

Practice the Skills

5 **Key Text Element**

Persuasive Appeals On this page Lamb makes a strong statement in order to spark strong feelings. She points out that our grandchildren may not have clean water to drink. This statement is an emotional appeal.

6 **Key Text Element**

Persuasive Appeals Which persuasive appeal does Lamb use in this paragraph? Hint: She gives a lot of facts and figures:

- average toothbrushing time
- amount of water wasted in that time
- amount of water wasted in a year

water at all. We don't need to go that far, but we could all use less water than we do.

Keep a bottle of water in the fridge.

We use bottled water—from the tap. Have you ever let the tap run for a minute to get an ice cold drink? About 15 years ago, I filled an empty soft drink bottle with tap water and stuck it in the fridge. That same bottle is still in our fridge today. Of course it has different water in it. **7**

Our water bottle has its own spot, in one of those bottle hangers that goes under the fridge shelf (it's been in the same place for years, even when we've moved houses and changed fridges), so that we never have to run the tap for a drink of water. It's always cold and handy. If you're just starting this system, be sure to label the bottle "Drinking Water." Once, years ago, when my Dad was visiting, he took a big swig from the bottle in our fridge, only to discover that someone had put a bottle of white rum in to cool.

Take a five minute shower instead of bathing.

Abandon the bathtub, and hit the showers. Sometimes it just feels great to soak in the tub, but that tub holds between nine and 33 gallons (40 to 150 liters) of water, depending on how full we fill it. We'd have to shower for 15 minutes before we used up the quantity of water it takes to fill the tub. When we were kids, we used to share a bath. We thought it was fun, but little did we know that our smart parents were saving on water heating. My daughter Caroline still enjoys a bath with her little cousin, Lisa.

Learn the cold water hand wash.

If every time you wash your hands, you turn on the hot tap and wait for the water to get warm, you could run anywhere from a few cups to a gallon or more of water down the drain. There are two problems with that.

First, it's water that has gone through the entire system of our waterworks for nothing.

Practice the Skills

7 Key Text Element

Persuasive Appeals Here, Lamb shows that she practices what she preaches. This helps make her appear trustworthy. What kind of persuasive appeal is she using?

It's been pumped from the lake or river, using energy, it's been bleached, it's been pushed through miles of pipes, and then it just goes back down the drain to be processed all over again with our sewage, having done nothing.

Second, it's water that's already been heated in your home water heater, but has cooled before it gets to you. The energy that was used to heat it, which you pay for, has been wasted.

I even wash my face in cold water every morning and night. I'm trying to convince myself that cold water is kinder to my skin than hot, but frankly, I know of no studies that would back me up on this one. However, my partner, Barry, tells me he once read that Paul Newman soaks his face in ice water to stay young looking, so maybe I'm on to something here. Masochistic[3] as it may sound, I find it refreshing to start my day with a cold splash. I confess that so far I've made very few converts to this theory, but I still swear by it. 8

Do you get as clean with cold water as with warm? The answer is yes, although there are exceptions. If your hands are greasy or oily, warm water will help to dissolve the grease or oil more quickly than cold water. But for ordinary, garden-variety dirt or stickiness, cold water works just as well as warm.

What about germs? Ordinarily hand soap will take care of whatever germs are washable. If you wanted to be totally antiseptic, you would have to use boiling water, probably for several minutes. I think most of us would opt for just plain clean, thanks anyway.

Think of saving water this way: what if you had to carry home all the water you needed every day—in jars on your head? 9 ○

Practice the Skills

8 Key Reading Skill

Distinguishing Fact from Opinion Lamb says that washing in cold water is "kinder to . . . skin." Is that statement a fact or an opinion? How can you tell?

9 BIG Question

Do you agree that conserving the world's water is a cause worth fighting for? Explain. Write your answer on the "Saving Water" flap of Foldable 7. Your response will help you complete the Unit Challenge later.

---

3. Lamb is making a little joke here. If someone is *masochistic* (mass uh KISS tik), he or she doesn't mind pain or suffering.

After You Read

Saving Water: Why Save Something That Covers Two-thirds of the Earth?

Answering the BIG Question

1. Has reading this article changed the way you think about what is worth fighting for? Explain your answer.

2. **Recall** What is Lamb's position, or stand, on the issue of water conservation: Is she for it or against it? Support your answer by quoting a sentence or two from the selection.
   Tip Right There

3. **List** What are some changes that Lamb thinks readers should make in the way they live? List at least three things that Lamb says people should do.
   Tip Think and Search

Critical Thinking

4. **Compare and Contrast** How is U.S. water use similar to that of "water-poor" countries? How is it different?
   Tip Think and Search

5. **Analyze** On page 935 Lamb says, "We clean paintbrushes in [water]. And we drink it." Why does she put these two uses of water next to each other? What is the effect of organizing the water uses this way?
   Tip Author and Me

6. **Analyze** Reread the first paragraph of the selection. What does Lamb say to capture readers' attention and make them want to read on?
   Tip Author and Me

**NY English Language Arts
Core Curriculum** (pp. 940–941)

LC R17 Demonstrate comprehension and response through a range of activities.
LC W4 Compose mechanically grade-appropriate texts for a variety of purposes.
R3a Evaluate the validity and accuracy of information, ideas, themes, opinions, and experiences in texts. Identify techniques author uses to persuade (emotional and ethical appeals). **Core R5** Distinguish between dictionary meaning and implied meaning of the author's words.
Core R7 Use knowledge of punctuation to assist in comprehension.

For a complete description of the standards, see p. NY11.

Write About Your Reading

Fact Sheet A **fact sheet** is a short, easy-to-read summary of key facts about a subject. Use information from the selection to write a fact sheet about water use—and waste—in the United States.

• Your readers: eighth-graders who have not read "Saving Water"

• Your purpose: to inform other students about people's use and abuse of water by giving them the most important facts. Do not include opinions.

• Your format: Make a list or lists of bulleted facts. Don't write in paragraphs.

• The length: one page

Skills Review

Key Reading Skill: Distinguishing Fact from Opinion

7. Does Lamb rely mostly on facts or on opinions in her article? Explain.

8. Quote two facts and two opinions Lamb gives.

Key Text Element: Persuasive Appeals

9. Which kind of persuasive appeal does Lamb use most: reason, emotion, or ethics?

Vocabulary Check

Copy the sentences below on another sheet of paper. Fill in each blank with the right vocabulary word.

municipal • distribution • contamination

10. The Red Cross allotted the same amount of food to each flood victim so that the _____ of food would be fair and equal.

11. The U.S. president is a member of the federal government; the mayor of a city is a member of a _____ government.

12. The beach was closed because of the accidental _____ of lake water.

13. English Language Coach Explain why you must know the connotation of a word to understand its full meaning. Support your explanation with an example.

14. Academic Vocabulary If you say someone is **ethical,** what are you saying about the person?

Web Activities For eFlashcards, Selection Quick Checks, and other Web activities, go to www.glencoe.com.

Grammar Link: Colons to Introduce Items

A **colon (:)** is a punctuation mark used to introduce a list or series of items at the end of a complete thought. Sometimes the list or series is introduced by signal words such as *the following, these,* or *as follows.*

- Jamil packed <u>these</u> supplies for the trip: a tent, a lantern, sleeping bags, flashlights, clothes, and food.
- Bring <u>the following</u> items: a pen, paper, and your book.

Look out! Do not use a colon right after a verb or a preposition.

Wrong: The kids in my group <u>are:</u> Erin, Jim, and Andre.

Right: The kids in my group are Erin, Jim, and Andre.

Wrong: My family and I traveled <u>to:</u> Germany, France, and Austria.

Right: My family and I traveled to Germany, France, and Austria.

Grammar Practice

Copy the following sentences on a separate sheet of paper. Insert a colon in sentences that need one. (Some sentences don't need a colon.)

15. A variety of people traveled on the railroad the poor, the well-off, students, and more.

16. Recycle these materials glass, paper, and plastic.

17. Some of the important steps in my mother's life were the following enrolling at Alabama State University, joining CORE, and receiving a scholarship to Georgetown University.

18. The following students must report to the principal Diane Larson, Manny Greene, and Scott Freeman.

19. Many African Americans attended all-black colleges Tuskegee, Morehouse, and Spelman.

20. My favorite foods include apples, chicken, and corn.

Writing Application Review your Write About Your Reading activity. If you used colons in your fact sheet, make sure that you correctly used them.

Before You Read

from *The Measure of Our Success*

Marian Wright Edelman

Meet the Author

In 1963 Marian Wright Edelman became the first female African American lawyer in Mississippi. By 1973 Edelman had relocated to Washington, D.C., and created the Children's Defense Fund, an organization that protects the interests of poor, socially disadvantaged children.

Author Search For more about Marian Wright Edelman, go to www.glencoe.com.

NY English Language Arts Core Curriculum (pp. 942–949)

Core R5 Distinguish between dictionary meaning and implied meaning of the author's words. **R3a** Evaluate the validity and accuracy of information, ideas, themes, opinions, and experiences in texts. Identify techniques author uses to persuade (emotional and ethical appeals).

For a complete description of the standards, see p. NY11.

Vocabulary Preview

persistence (pur SIS tuntz) *n.* the act of refusing to give up **(p. 947)** *The whale watchers' persistence paid off when they saw a blue whale.*

corruption (kuh RUP shun) *n.* extreme immorality or wickedness **(p. 947)** *The government's corruption became well known after a newspaper ran a story about the scandal in city hall.*

racial (RAY shuhl) *adj.* characteristic of a race or an ethnic or cultural group **(p. 948)** *Many people would argue that racial prejudice is one of the toughest problems the United States faces.*

illiterate (ih LIT uh rit) *adj.* unable to read or write; uneducated **(p. 949)** *Although she was illiterate, Sojourner Truth spoke out powerfully in favor of women's rights and the abolition of salvery.*

Partner Talk Take turns using each vocabulary word in a sentence.

English Language Coach

Word Connotation in Persuasive Writing When an author's purpose is to persuade readers, he or she is careful to choose words with the right connotations, or emotions that come to mind. If the author wants readers to believe something is bad, he or she will choose words with negative connotations. If the author wants readers to believe that something is good, he or she will choose words with positive connotations.

Read the following ads for a car. Both describe the same car, but the words have different connotations. Which ad gives a positive description of the car?

> For sale: Vintage (1990) Arrow. The almost 100,000 miles on this slightly weathered dream mobile prove that it is truly "Old Reliable." A real bargain for the mechanically inclined!

> For sale: Aged (1990) Arrow. The almost 100,000 miles on this rusty lemon prove it is truly "Old Yeller." A real bargain if you don't count all the money it will take you to fix it!

Partner Talk With a classmate, compare and contrast the two ads. Which words have positive connotations? Negative ones?

Skills Preview

Key Reading Skill: Distinguishing Fact from Opinion

You will probably find more opinions than facts in the speech you are about to read. That's not necessarily a bad thing. Think about whether the writer establishes herself as an authority on the subject. On what does she base her opinions? Can you trust her opinions?

Write to Learn As you read, use a two-column chart to evaluate the writer's opinions. List opinions in the left-hand column. In the right-hand column, list her support for each opinion.

Key Text Element: Appeal to Ethics

People rarely listen to someone they don't trust. For this reason, authors of persuasive writing try to show that they are good, trustworthy people who know what they are talking about and have readers' best interests at heart. Together, these qualities make up an **appeal to ethics.** The ethical appeal is based on making readers trust the writer and believe that his or her position is the "right thing to do." Ethical appeals may include references to these things:

- community, family, home, parenthood
- religious or spiritual beliefs
- character, responsibility, or public service
- people whom audience members look up to

Whole Class Discussion What are some specific ways that an author can show that he or she is a good person? Well-informed? Concerned about readers' interests? As a class, discuss your ideas about ways authors make an appeal to ethics.

Get Ready to Read

Connect to the Reading

What are some of the most important lessons that your parents, family members, or guardians have taught you: To work hard? To treat others with respect? To value education? Think about what you've learned?

Write to Learn In your Learner's Notebook, write a paragraph about a person whose behavior and morals you admire. What important "life lessons" have you learned from this person?

Build Background

As founder and president of the Children's Defense League, Edelman is often asked to deliver commencement addresses (speeches for school graduations). The selection you are about to read is from a speech she made in 1992 in St. Louis, Missouri, for Washington University's spring graduation ceremony. The speech is based on her book *The Measure of Our Success: A Letter to My Children and Yours.* In the book and the speech, Edelman talks about her parents, her upbringing in a close-knit African American community, and the life lessons she learned. They are lessons she wants her children—and all children—to know.

Set Purposes for Reading

BIG Question Read the selection from *The Measure of Our Success* to find out what is worth fighting for and what is not.

Set Your Own Purpose What else would you like to learn from the speech to help you answer the Big Question? Write your own purpose on the *The Measure of Our Success* flap of Foldable 7. Your response will help you to complete the Unit Challenge later.

Literature Online

Interactive Literary Elements Handbook
To review or learn more about the literary elements, go to www.glencoe.com.

Keep Moving

Use these skills as you read the following selection.

from
THE MEASURE OF OUR SUCCESS

by Marian Wright Edelman

When I was growing up in my little rural Southern segregated[1] town, service was as essential a part of my upbringing as eating and sleeping. Caring black adults were buffers[2] against the external world that told me I, a black girl, was not important. But I did not believe it because my parents said it wasn't so. My teachers and preachers said it wasn't so. So the childhood message I internalized was that as a child of God, no man or woman could look down on me and I could look down on no man or woman. **1**

---

1. If something is **segregated** (SEG ruh gay tid) , it is separated according to race or skin color. Public facilities were segregated in the U.S. South until the Civil Rights Act was passed in 1964.

2. **Buffers** are people or objects that "soften the blow," or lessen the impact between colliding forces.

Practice the Skills

1 Key Text Element

Appeal to Ethics Edelman refers to parents, teachers, and preachers and calls herself a "child of God." These references help establish her as a good, trustworthy person. They are part of the ethical appeal.

I could not play in segregated public playgrounds or sit at drugstore lunch counters, so Daddy, a Baptist minister, built a playground and canteen behind our church. Whenever he and my mother saw a need, they tried to respond. There were no black homes for the aged in my rural segregated town, so my parents began one across the street, and all of our family had to help out. I sure did not like it a whole lot at the time, but that is how I learned that it was my responsibility to take care of elderly family members and neighbors, and that everyone was my neighbor.

Black church and community members were my watchful extended parents. They applauded me when I did well and they reported on me when I did wrong. Doing well meant being helpful to others, achieving in school and reading. The only time Daddy would not give me a chore was when I was reading, so I read a lot.

Children were taught by example that nothing was too lowly[3] to do and that the work of our hands and of our heads were both important. Our families and community made us feel useful and important. And while life was often hard and resources scarce, we always knew who we were and that the measure of our worth was inside our heads and hearts, and not outside in personal possessions or ambitions. **2**

I was taught that the world had a lot of problems, that black folk had an extra lot of problems, but that I could struggle and change them; that intellectual and material gifts brought with them the privilege and responsibility of sharing with others less fortunate; and that service is the rent that each of us pays for living—the very purpose of life—and not something you do in your spare time or after you have achieved your personal goals. . . .

Practice the Skills

2 | **Key Text Element**

Appeal to Ethics What references in this paragraph help develop a strong ethical appeal? Name at least two things.

---

3. If something is *lowly* it is common or poor.

Analyzing the Photo How does this photograph illustrate the writer's attitude toward community service?

The standard for success for too many Americans has become personal greed rather than common good. The standard for striving and achievement has become getting by rather than making an extra effort or helping somebody else. . . . **3**

. . . I also want to share a few lessons of life taken from a letter that I wrote my own three wonderful sons. Like them, I recognize that you can take or leave them, but you cannot say you were never told or reminded. Let me give you a few of them.

The first lesson is, there is no free lunch. Do not feel entitled to anything you do not sweat or struggle for. Help our nation understand that it is not entitled to world leadership based on the past or on what we say rather than how well we perform and meet changing world needs. . . .

Remember not to be lazy. Do your homework. Pay attention to detail. Take care and pride in your work. Take the initiative⁴ in creating your own opportunity and do not wait around for other people to discover you or do you a favor. Do not assume a door is closed; push on it. Do not assume if it was closed yesterday that it is closed today. And do not ever stop learning and improving your mind, because if you do, you and America are going to be left behind.

Practice the Skills

3 | **Key Reading Skill**

Distinguishing Fact from Opinion In this paragraph Edelman states opinions. You may agree or disagree with her, but you can't *prove* that the "standard of success for too many Americans has become personal greed."

Analyzing the Photo How does this young woman illustrate Edelman's "first lesson"?

---

4. *Initiative* (ih NISH uh tiv) is the action of taking responsibility for something.

Lesson two is, assign yourself. Daddy used to ask us whether the teacher gave us any homework and if we said no, he said, well, assign yourself some. Do not wait around for somebody else to direct you to do what you are able to figure out and do for yourself. Do not do just as little as you can do to get by.

Do not be a political bystander or grumbler. Vote. Democracy is not a spectator sport. Run for political office. I especially want women to run for political office. We women certainly cannot do a worse job than the men in power now. **4** But when you do run and when you do win, don't begin to think that you or your reelection are the only point. If you see a need, do not ask why doesn't somebody do something, ask why don't I do something. Hard work and **persistence** and initiative are still the non-magic carpets to success for most of us.

Lesson three: Never work just for money. Money will not **save your soul** or **build a decent family** or help you sleep at night. We are the richest nation on earth with the highest incarceration[5] and one of the **highest drug addiction and child poverty rates** in the world.

Do not confuse wealth or fame with **character.** Do not tolerate or condone[6] **moral corruption** or **violence,** whether it is found in high or low places, whatever its color or class. It is not okay to push or to use drugs even if every person in America is doing it. It is not okay to **cheat** or to **lie** even if every public- and private-sector[7] official you know does. **Be honest** and demand that those who represent you be honest. . . . **5**

Lesson four: Do not be afraid of taking risks or being criticized. If you do not want to be criticized, do not do anything, do not say anything, and do not be anything. Do not be afraid of failing. It is the way you learn to do things right. It doesn't matter how many times you fall down. All

Practice the Skills

4 █ **Key Reading Skill**

Distinguishing Fact from Opinion Is this statement a fact or an opinion? (Hint: Can you prove that "women certainly cannot do a worse job than the men in power now"?)

5 █ **English Language Coach**

Word Connotation in Persuasive Writing Notice all the words with strong emotional associations. Which of them have positive connotations? Which have negative ones?

---

5. *Incarceration* (in car ser AY shun) is the state of being imprisoned.

6. To *condone* (kuhn DOHN) is to forgive, pardon, or overlook.

7. A *sector* (SEK ter) is a particular part of society.

Vocabulary

persistence (pur SIS tuntz) *n.* the act of refusing to give up

corruption (kuh RUP shun) *n.* extreme immorality or wickedness

Practice the Skills

that matters is how many times you get up. Do not wait for everybody to come along to get something done. It is always a few people who get things done and keep things going. . . .

Lesson five: Take parenting and family life seriously, and insist that those you work for and who represent you do so. . . .

I hope that you will stress family rituals and be moral examples for your children, because if you cut corners, they will, too. If you lie, they will, too. . . . If you tell **racial** or gender jokes or snicker at them, another generation will pass on the poison that our adult generation still does not have the courage to stop doing.

Lesson six is to please remember and help America remember that the fellowship of human beings is more important than the fellowship of race and class and gender in a democratic society. Be decent and fair and insist that others do so in your presence. . . .

Lesson seven: Listen for "the sound of the genuine" within yourself. Einstein said, "Small is the number of them that see with their own eyes and feel with their own heart." Try to be one of them.

Howard Thurman, the great black theologian,[8] said, "There is in every one of us something that waits and listens for the sound of the genuine in ourselves, and it is the only true guide you'll ever have. And if you cannot hear it, you will all of your life spend your days on the ends of strings that somebody else pulls." **6**

. . . I hope that you will learn to be quiet enough to hear the sound of the genuine within yourself so that you can then hear it in other people.

Lesson eight: Never think life is not worth living or that you cannot make a difference. Never give up. I do not care how hard it gets; and it will get very hard sometimes. An old proverb[9] reminds us that when you get to your wit's end, remember that is where God lives. . . .

6 ■ Key Text Element

Appeal to Ethics Notice Edelman's reference to Howard Thurman. Why does she mention Thurman? How does quoting Thurman strengthen Edelman's ethical appeal?

---

8. A **theologian** (thee uh LOH jun) is an expert in religious studies.

9. A **proverb** is a short, traditional saying that expresses some obvious truth.

Vocabulary

racial (RAY shuhl) *adj.* characteristic of a race or an ethnic or cultural group

Analyzing the Photo What do Sojourner Truth's facial expression and posture in this photograph tell you about her? What might the writer have in common with Truth?

My role model was an **illiterate** slave woman, Sojourner Truth, who could not read or write, but she could not stand second-class treatment of women and she hated slavery. My favorite Sojourner story came one day when she was making a speech against slavery and she got heckled by a man who stood up in the audience and said, "Old slave woman, I don't care any more about your antislavery talk than for an old fleabite." And she snapped back and said, "That's all right. The Lord willing, I'm going to keep you scratching."

So often we think we have got to make a big difference and be a big dog. Let us just try to be little fleas biting. Enough fleas biting . . . can make very big dogs very uncomfortable. . . . **7** ○

Practice the Skills

7 **BIG Question**
For what cause did Sojourner Truth fight? How is Edelman's fight similar to Sojourner Truth's? Write your answers on the *Measure of Our Success* flap of the Foldable for Unit 7. Your responses will help you answer the Unit Challenge later.

Vocabulary

illiterate (ih LIT uh rit) *adj.* unable to read or write; uneducated

After You Read

from *The Measure of Our Success*

Answering the **BIG** Question

1. Now that you have read the speech, what are your ideas about causes that are worth fighting for?

2. **Quote** Copy an opinion with which Edelman wants you to agree.
   TIP **Right There**

3. **Recall** Identify the eight lessons Edelman wants to teach readers.
   TIP **Think and Search**

Critical Thinking

4. **Interpret** What does Edelman mean when she says that "service is the rent each of us pays for living"? Put the statement in your own words.
   TIP **Author and Me**

5. **Analyze** Think about the occasion for the speech—a university graduation ceremony. What do you think the purpose of Edelman's speech is?
   TIP **Author and Me**

6. **Evaluate** Do you think Edelman's lessons are still important and relevant today? Explain.
   TIP **On My Own**

Talk About Your Reading

Speech Write a short speech stating and describing two lessons that you think are important for living a good, moral life. Be sure to answer these questions in your speech:

- Why are these lessons important?
- How can people act on these lessons in their everyday lives?
- What sources support your opinions? Books? Articles? Real People?

Deliver your speech to a small group of classmates.

**NY English Language Arts
Core Curriculum** (pp. 950–951)

LC R17 Demonstrate comprehension and response through a range of activities. **S3a** Express opinions or judgments about information, ideas, opinions, issues, themes, and experiences. **R3a** Evaluate the validity and accuracy of information, ideas, themes, opinions, and experiences in texts. Identify techniques author uses to persuade (emotional and ethical appeals). **Core R5** Distinguish between dictionary meaning and implied meaning of the author's words. **Core W7** Observe rules of punctuation.

For a complete description of the standards, see p. NY11.

Skills Review

Key Reading Skill: Distinguishing Fact from Opinion

7. Does Edelman include more facts or more opinions in her speech? Why do you think that she makes this choice?

Key Text Element: Appeal to Ethics

8. What information and sources does Edelman mention to show readers that she is a good example of how to lead a moral life?

Vocabulary Check

Copy the following sentences on a separate sheet of paper. Write *T* if a sentence is true or *F* if it is false. Revise any false statement to make it true.

9. A person who gives up easily shows **persistence**.

10. **Corruption** is the opposite of goodness.

11. Someone who has **racial** pride is proud of his or her race, ethnicity, or cultural heritage.

12. A student who reads and writes well is **illiterate**.

13. **Academic Vocabulary** What are some of the **ethical** activities that Edelman's parents encouraged their children to do?

14. **English Language Coach** How does Edelman use words with positive connotations to support her opinions? Give at least two examples.

Web Activities For eFlashcards, Selection Quick Checks, and other Web activities, go to www.glencoe.com.

Grammar Link: Colons to Separate Items

The **colon** (:) is used in expressions of time. Separate the hour and the minutes with a colon when you use numerals to write the time of day.

- The movie starts at 11:15 A.M. and ends at 1:45 P.M.
- We have to be at the bus station at 3:45 P.M. today.
- At 12:00 noon, we will leave for the field trip.

Never use a colon when the time of day is written out.

- I didn't get home until one o'clock.

Also use a colon after the salutation of a business letter. (Use a comma after the salutation of a personal letter.)

- Dear Sir:
- Dear Sir or Madam:
- Dear Ms. Korsakov:
- Dear Grandma,

Grammar Practice

The following sentences make up two business letters. Copy the sentences on another sheet of paper. Add colons where needed.

15. Dear Ms. Kozar

16. I will not be able to bring snacks to the French Club meeting today at 400.

17. Mr. Fenton is tutoring me from 330 until 430.

18. Yours truly, Isabella

19. Dear Isabella

20. From 400 until 430 at today's meeting, a guest speaker will be talking about her travels to France.

21. Try to get there by 445.

22. We will serve snacks after the question-and-answer session.

23. Sincerely, Mr. Kozar

Persuasive Essay
Prewriting and Drafting

ASSIGNMENT Write a persuasive essay

Purpose: To make a case for something you think is worth fighting for

Audience: Your teacher, your classmates, and other people in your community

Writing Rubric

As you work through this writing assignment, you should

• write about something you feel strongly about

• write a clear position statement

• support your main idea with details and examples

• write a well-organized persuasive essay

See pages 996–997 in Part 2 for a model of a persuasive essay.

NY English Language Arts Core Curriculum (pp. 952–955)

Core W4 Use prewriting activities. **LC W6** Organize writing effectively to communicate ideas to an intended audience. **LC W7** Compose arguments to support points of view with relevant details. **Core W7** Observe rules of punctuation.

For a complete description of the standards, see p. NY11.

You probably already know what an essay is. It's a paper that tells a true story, explains a subject, or gives opinions. A persuasive essay also gives opinions, but the writer's goal is a little different. In a persuasive essay, the writer tries to convince readers to agree with his or her opinions. For example, if you believe that you and your classmates have too much homework, you might write a persuasive essay trying to convince teachers to agree with you. You might also go one step further and include a call to action, a statement asking readers to act on your opinions. You might, for example, ask teachers to give shorter daily assignments—ones that take no more than an hour to do.

For this workshop you may write either kind of persuasive essay. Writing a persuasive essay will help you think about the Unit 7 Big Question: What's worth fighting for? What's not?

Prewriting
Get Ready to Write

Your first step is to come up with a good topic. For this assignment you need to think of an issue that has two sides. Pick something that matters to you. The stronger your opinions, the easier it will be to write about them.

Gather Ideas

To come up with a good topic, ask yourself these questions:

• *What do I strongly believe in? Why do I think it is worth standing up for?*

• *What are some issues, ideas, or people that matter to me?*

• *What stories in the news have made me want to take a stand?*

• *What changes would I like to see made in my neighborhood or community?*

If you have trouble coming up with a topic, try looking through recent newspapers and magazines in the library or on the Internet. They often include articles about controversial issues—problems that have at least two sides to them. Or try freewriting for ten minutes about one of the issues that you think interests you. Remember that when you freewrite you jot down your thoughts quickly and freely. If you have trouble writing about the issue for ten minutes, you may want to change topics.

Generate Supporting Reasons

Once you have a topic in mind, write a position statement to be your main idea, or thesis. For your statement, write your opinion simply and clearly. For example, if you believe in protecting the environment, your position statement might be "I believe we must take steps to protect the environment." Then come up with a list of reasons why. A good way to do this is to discuss your ideas with classmates.

Group Discussion Follow these steps with a small group of classmates.

1. Read your position statement aloud to the group. Ask group members whether your opinion is clear. If it isn't, rewrite your position statement together until it is clear.

2. Give at least two reasons why you believe your opinion is right. Discuss each reason with your classmates. Ask them to help you develop your reasons with facts, examples, or other types of details. Also ask group members to add reasons of their own. Classmates who agree with your opinion may have good reasons you have overlooked.

3. Take notes on your discussion. Be sure to include all the reasons you and your group generated.

> It's important that we protect the environment
> because . . .
> 1. pollution threatens everyone's health
> 2. it's wrong to be wasteful
> 3. our children deserve a clean environment

Drafting

Start Writing!

Once you have a list of reasons, you're ready to start writing your essay. Don't worry if you don't have the whole essay worked out in your mind. Ideas will come to you as you write.

Literature Online

Writing Models For models and other writing activities, go to www.glencoe.com.

Writing Tip

Supporting Reasons
Remember that your purpose is to persuade your readers to agree with you. So keep your readers in mind when you list reasons why they should agree with your opinion. Your reasons must convince your readers, not just you.

Writing Tip

Organization Think about the order in which you present your reasons. Don't just give them in the order you thought of them. Have a strategy. For example, you might give the least important reason first and the most important reason last. That way, your essay ends on a strong note.

Develop Your Draft

To make your essay easier to write, break it down into parts. There should be three main parts to your essay: a beginning, a middle, and an end.

1. The beginning of your essay is the introduction—a paragraph that introduces your readers to your issue and your main idea, or thesis. Your introduction should also try to capture readers' attention and make readers care about your issue.

Imagine a world without trees, flowers, or animals. It could happen. Every day we pollute the air we breathe, the water we drink, and the ground we grow our food in. Slowly but surely we are ruining this planet. I believe we must take steps to protect the environment, and you should too.

2. The middle of your essay is the body. It is two or more paragraphs that explain the reasons why your readers should agree with you. Limit yourself to one reason in each paragraph. For each new reason, start a new paragraph.

We need to start taking better care of the earth because it is a healthier way to live. The environment makes life possible. If we ruin the environment, we are ruining our own bodies. Anything harmful that we put into the earth eventually harms us. When we pollute the ground where we grow our food, the pollution gets into the food. When we eat the food, the pollution gets into our bodies.

3. The end of your essay is the conclusion. It is a paragraph in which you wrap up what you have said—and, if you wish, give a call to action.

It's not too late. We can still save our environment. I ask you to stop polluting, stop wasting resources, and save the planet for our children. You and future generations will be glad you did.

Grammar Link

Apostrophes

What Is an Apostrophe?

An **apostrophe** (') is a punctuation mark used in possessive nouns, possessive indefinite pronouns, and contractions.

Why Are Apostrophes Important?

Apostrophes show when a noun is possessive.
- Bill's <u>coat</u> is on the bed.

(The apostrophe and *s* tell you that the noun *Bill* possesses, or owns, a coat.)

Apostrophes also tell when—and where—letters are missing from contractions, or shortened forms of words and numbers.
- it is = it's
- I will = I'll
- you are = you're
- is not = isn't
- 1998 = '98

How Do I Use Apostrophes?

To form the possessive of a singular noun, add an apostrophe and –s ('s).
- The girl's hat got lost on the bus.
- The dog's toy was stuck under the couch.

To form the possessive of a plural noun that does not end in *s*, use an apostrophe and –s ('s).
- The men's soccer game was canceled for the night.
- The mice's nest was under the haystack.

To form the possessive of a plural noun that ends in *s*, use an apostrophe after the final *s*.
- The boys' essays are displayed on the bulletin board.
- Both tables' legs were slightly bent.

To form the possessive of an indefinite pronoun, such as *everyone, everybody, anyone, no one,* or *nobody,* use an apostrophe and –s ('s).
- The park was everybody's to use on Saturday.

Look Out! Never use an apostrophe in the possessive personal pronouns *ours, yours, his, hers, its,* and *theirs.*
- The park was just ours on Monday.

Write to Learn Read over your draft. Check to make sure you have correctly used apostrophes. Circle any possessive nouns or possessive indefinite pronouns. Underline any contractions.

Looking Ahead

Part 2 of this Writing Workshop is coming up later. Keep the writing you did here. In Part 2 you'll learn how to turn it into an essay to be proud of.

Skills Focus

You will practice using these skills when you read the following selections:
- "All Together Now," p. 960
- from *Through My Eyes*, p. 968

Reading

- Asking questions while reading

Literature

- Identifying persuasive appeals
- Understanding point of view

Vocabulary

- Understanding extended definitions
- Understanding denotation
- Academic Vocabulary: *valid*

Writing/Grammar

- Using semicolons correctly

NY English Language Arts Core Curriculum
(pp. 956–957)

LC R12 Combine multiple strategies (question) to enhance comprehension and response.

For a complete description of the standards, see p. NY11.

Skill Lesson

Questioning

Learn It!

What Is It? **Questioning** is having a running conversation with yourself as you read. Just as you might ask yourself questions while watching a movie *(Why did he do that? What's the significance of that door they keep showing?)*, you should ask questions while you read. By asking questions, you become involved in the selection and make sure that you understand it. Feel free to question anything! For example, you might ask yourself questions like these:

- *What just happened?*
- *Is this argument* **valid**?

STONE SOUP © 1996 Jan Eliot. Reprinted with permission of UNIVERSAL PRESS SYNDICATE. All rights reserved.

Analyzing Cartoons

Here's a question to ask yourself to test your understanding of the cartoon: *What do the girls' questions show about their knowledge of jobs?*

Academic Vocabulary

valid (VAL id) *adj.* based on correct information; logical; sound

Why Is It Important? Asking questions while you read is an important part of understanding a text. To make sure you understand, ask yourself "5Ws and an H" questions: *Who? What? Where? When? Why?* and *How?*

How Do I Do It? Here are some sample questions you can ask yourself:
- *How does this event relate to other events in the text?*
- *What is this person doing and why?*
- *Why has the writer included this word, description, or piece of information?*

Below is a selection from *The Measure of Our Success.* Read how a student asked questions about the text.

Literature Online

Study Central Visit www.glencoe .com and click on Study Central to review questioning.

> Black church and community members were my watchful extended parents. They applauded me when I did well and they reported on me when I did wrong. Doing well meant being helpful to others, achieving in school and reading. The only time Daddy would not give me a chore was when I was reading, so I read a lot.
>
> Children were taught by example that nothing was too lowly to do and that the work of our hands and of our heads were both important. Our families and our community made us feel useful and important. And while life was often hard and resources scarce, we always knew who we were and that the measure of our worth was inside our heads and hearts, and not outside in personal possessions or ambitions.

> Why does the writer say that the church and community members were "extended parents"? They must have played a very important role in her childhood. Why does she mention that she read a lot? Reading may have something to do with the person she is today.

Practice It!

Reread the selection from *The Measure of Our Success* above. Then write down two additional questions that you could ask about the selection.

Use It!

As you read "All Together Now," ask yourself 5Ws and an H questions. Answer each question before going on.

Before You Read : All Together Now

Barbara Jordan

Meet the Author

Barbara Jordan was the first African American woman elected to the Texas Senate. When she was elected to the U.S. House of Representatives, she became the first African American woman to represent a former Confederate state in Congress. Jordan was also the first African American woman to give the keynote speech at a political convention.

Author Search For more about Barbara Jordan, go to www.glencoe.com.

NY English Language Arts Core Curriculum (pp. 958–963)

LC R9 Recognize multiple meanings of words and connections among meanings of words. **LC R12** Combine multiple strategies (question) to enhance comprehension and response. **R3a** Identify techniques author uses to persuade (emotional and ethical appeals).

For a complete description of the standards, see p. NY11.

Vocabulary Preview

harmonious (har MOH nee us) *adj.* getting along well together; friendly **(p. 960)** *We are all striving toward a more harmonious community.*

indispensable (in duh SPEN suh bul) *adj.* absolutely necessary **(p. 962)** *Tolerance and kindness are indispensable values.*

incurable (in KYOOR uh bul) *adj.* not likely to be changed or corrected **(p. 963)** *Racism is far from incurable; there are plenty of ways to stop it.*

optimist (OP tuh mist) *n.* a person who has a positive or cheerful outlook **(p. 963)** *If you are an optimist, those around you will think positively too.*

Write to Learn In your Learner's Notebook, write a short paragraph in which you correctly use each vocabulary word at least once.

English Language Coach

Extended Definition If you look up the word *tolerance* in the dictionary, you will find a definition similar to this one: "the willingness to let others hold opinions or follow practices that are different from one's own." This is the denotation of the word. In "All Together Now," Jordan gives her own definition of what tolerance means. Because she refers to civil rights and race relations to provide a longer, more specific definition of *tolerance,* you might say that she gives the word an **extended definition.**

Small Group Discussion With a small group of classmates, write an extended definition of *tolerance.* To begin, each group member should explain what he or she thinks *tolerance* means. The explanation could be a definition or an example. As each group member gives a definition or example, record it on a word web like the one pictured. Then use the word web to write a one- or two-paragraph extended definition of *tolerance.*

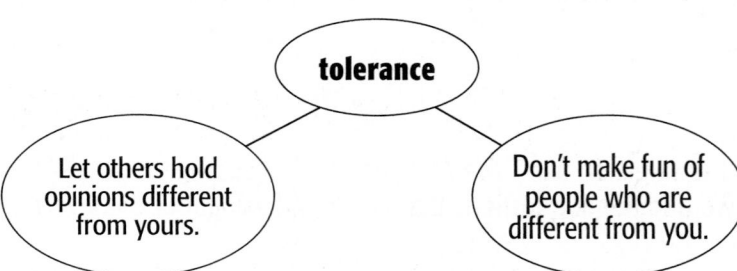

Skills Preview

Key Reading Skill: Questioning

"All Together Now" is a speech Jordan made in the 1990s. As you read the speech, ask yourself 5 Ws and an H questions to make sure you understand.

Partner Talk Jordan's speech is about the need for tolerance in the United States. What kinds of questions do you think you might ask yourself as you read the speech? Brainstorm a list with a classmate.

Key Text Element: Appeal to Emotions

Facts and figures can be very persuasive. If a writer wants to convince readers to agree with an opinion, presenting objective evidence is a good way to do so. But if the writer wants to move readers to take action, he or she may "put a human face" on facts and figures and appeal to readers' emotions.

Sometimes a writer relies only on an emotional appeal. That method is appropriate when the writer knows that readers agree with him or her but need to be persuaded to take action. Suppose, for example, that you belong to a school music club that sells candy to raise money. To move club members to sell as much as possible, you might try to inspire them with an emotional appeal. Usually, however, a writer uses all three appeals, giving facts (appeal to reason), showing why he or she is trustworthy (appeal to ethics), and trying to make readers care about the issue (appeal to emotions).

Whole Class Discussion Imagine that you want to persuade people to be more tolerant of others. As a class, think of emotional appeals you might make to move people into taking the right actions.

Get Ready to Read

Connect to the Reading

How tolerant are you of other people's opinions? When you disagree with someone, are you able to "agree to disagree," or do you continue to try to convince the other person to adopt your position?

Partner Talk With a partner, find a topic about which you disagree, such as the best subject to study in school or which performer in a musical group is best. Take turns presenting your opinions on the topic. Monitor your feelings and behavior. Can you listen to your partner's opinion calmly, or do you find yourself wanting to jump in and argue your position? Explain.

Build Background

The 1960s were a busy time for the civil rights movement in the United States.

- In June of 1963, President John Kennedy proposed civil rights legislation, but Congress failed to act.
- In August of 1963, Dr. Martin Luther King, Jr., led a march on Washington, D.C., where he delivered his famous "I Have a Dream" speech.
- In July of 1964, at the urging of President Lyndon B. Johnson, Congress adopted the Civil Rights Act, which ended legalized segregation in the United States.

Set Purposes for Reading

BIG Question Read "All Together Now" to find out whether creating a society that is tolerant in action as well as in law is a cause worth fighting for.

Set Your Own Purpose What else would you like to learn from the article to help you answer the Big Question? Write your own purpose on the "All Together Now" flap of Foldable 7.

Interactive Literary Elements Handbook
To review or learn more about the literary elements, go to www.glencoe.com.

Keep Moving

Use these skills as you read the following selection.

All Together Now

by Barbara Jordan

On August 6, 1965, President Lyndon B. Johnson celebrated signing the Voting Rights Act into law with a group including (from left) Ralph Abernathy; Dr. Martin Luther King, Jr.; and Clarence Mitchell.

When I look at race relations today I can see that some positive changes have come about. But much remains to be done, and the answer does not lie in more legislation. We *have* the legislation we need; we have the laws. Frankly, I don't believe that the task of bringing us all together can be accomplished by government. What we need now is soul force—the efforts of people working on a small scale to build a truly tolerant, **harmonious** society. And parents can do a great deal to create that tolerant society. **1**

We all know that race relations in America have had a very rocky history. Think about the 1960s when Dr. Martin Luther King, Jr., was in his heyday and there were marches and protests against segregation and discrimination. The movement culminated[1] in 1963 with the March on Washington.

Practice the Skills

1 **Key Reading Skill**

Questioning A good question to ask yourself here is, *What is Jordan's main idea?*

---

1. ***Culminated*** (KUL muh nay tid) means reached the highest point or climax.

Vocabulary

harmonious (har MOH nee us) *adj.* getting along well together; friendly

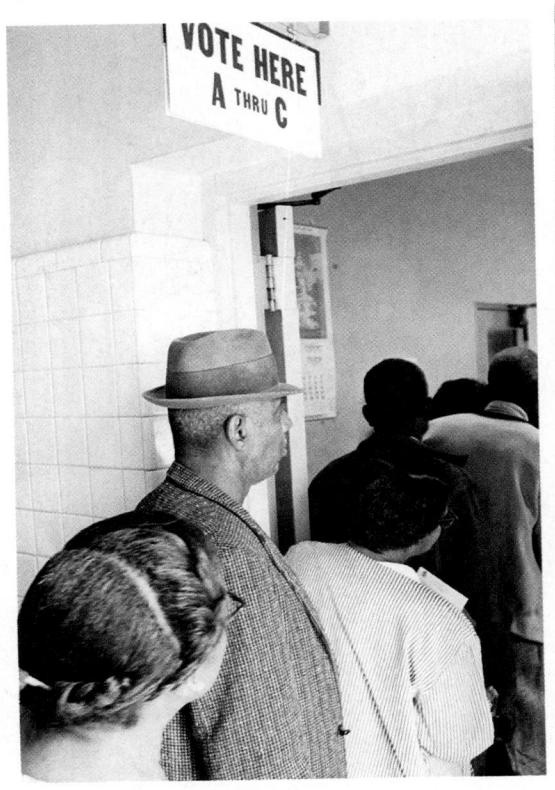

Following the enactment of the 1965 Voting Rights Act, African Americans in Alabama wait in line to vote.

Following that event, race relations reached an all-time peak. President Lyndon B. Johnson pushed through the Civil Rights Act of 1964, which remains the fundamental piece of civil rights legislation in this century. The Voting Rights Act of 1965 ensured that everyone in our country could vote. At last, black people and white people seemed ready to live together in peace.

But that is not what happened. By the 1990's the good feelings had diminished. Today the nation seems to be suffering from compassion[2] fatigue, and issues such as race relations and civil rights have never regained momentum.[3]

Those issues, however, remain crucial. As our society becomes more diverse, people of all races and backgrounds will have to learn to live together. If we don't think this is important, all we have to do is look at the situation in Bosnia[4] today. **2**

---

2. **Compassion** (kum PASH un) is sorrow for the sufferings or trouble of another.

3. **Momentum** is a strength or force that keeps growing.

4. In the early 1990s civil war erupted in **Bosnia** (BOZ nee uh) between the Serbs and the Croats. After a few months of fighting, the Serbs controlled most of the area. They attacked Sarajevo with the intent of killing all non-Serbs, a process known as *ethnic cleansing*.

Practice the Skills

2   **Key Reading Skill**

Questioning What situation is Jordan referring to? (See the note at the bottom of the page.)

How do we create a harmonious society out of so many kinds of people? The key is **tolerance**—the one value that is **indispensable** in creating community.

If we are concerned about community, if it is important to us that people not feel excluded, then we have to do something. Each of us can decide to have one friend of a different race or background in our mix of friends. If we do this, we'll be working together to push things forward.

One thing is clear to me: We, as human beings, must be willing to accept people who are different from ourselves. I must be willing to accept people who don't look as I do and don't talk as I do. It is crucial that I am open to their feelings, their inner reality. **3**

What can parents do? We can put our faith in young people as a positive force. I have yet to find a racist baby. Babies come into the world as blank as slates and, with their beautiful innocence, see others not as different but as enjoyable companions. Children learn ideas and attitudes from the adults who nurture them. I absolutely believe that children do not adopt prejudices unless they absorb them from their parents or teachers.

The best way to get this country faithful to the American dream of tolerance and equality is to start small. Parents can actively encourage their children to be in the company of people who are of other racial and ethnic backgrounds. If a child thinks, "Well, that person's color is not the same as mine, but she must be okay because she likes to play with

Analyzing the Photo How does this photograph illustrate Jordan's belief in the importance of cross-cultural friendships?

Practice the Skills

3 **English Language Coach**

Extended Definition In this paragraph and the one before, Jordan explains what she means by the word **tolerance**. Two parts of her extended definition are as follows:

- "[making] people not feel excluded"

- "decid[ing] to have one friend of a different race or background"

How else does she define the word? Quote another part of her definition.

Vocabulary

indispensable (in duh SPEN suh bul) *adj.* absolutely necessary

the same things I like to play with," that child will grow up with a broader view of humanity.

I am an **incurable** **optimist.** For the rest of the time that I have left on this planet I want to bring people together. You might think of this as a labor of love. Now, I know that love means different things to different people. But what *I* mean is this: I care about you because you are a fellow human being and I find it okay in my mind, in my heart, to simply say to you, I love you. And maybe that would encourage you to love me in return. **4**

It is possible for all of us to work on this—at home, in our schools, at our jobs. It is possible to work on human relationships in every area of our lives. **5** ◯

Practice the Skills

4 **Key Text Element**

Appeal to Emotions Notice that Jordan uses the word *love* four times. What feeling is she trying to spark in her audience? How will that help her fulfill her purpose?

5 **BIG Question**

Do you agree that a tolerant society is worth fighting for? Explain. Write your answer on the "All Together Now" flap of Foldable 7. Your response will help you answer the Unit Challenge later.

Vocabulary

incurable (in KYOOR uh bul) *adj.* not likely to be changed or corrected

optimist (OP tuh mist) *n.* a person who has a positive or cheerful outlook

After You Read

All Together Now

Answering the 🐦 BIG Question

1. After reading Jordan's speech, what are your thoughts about what is worth fighting for and what is not?
2. **Recall** Which does Jordan think is a more important force for bringing about good race relations: the government or parents? Explain.
   TIP **Right There**

3. **Recall** According to Jordan, what is the most important civil rights law of the 20th century and why?
   TIP **Right There**

Critical Thinking

4. **Interpret** What does Jordan mean when she says that the U.S. has "compassion fatigue"? Explain in your own words.
   TIP **Author and Me**

5. **Infer** Why does Jordan think that people should put their faith in children? Support your answer with examples from the selection.
   TIP **Author and Me**

6. **Evaluate** Do you think Jordan's ideas about increasing tolerance are good ones? Explain why or why not.
   TIP **Author and Me**

Talk About Your Reading

Small Group Discussion Jordan says that parents can encourage their children to have friends from other ethnic or cultural backgrounds. What do you think students and schools should do to promote a tolerant society? With a small group of classmates, come up with at least three specific ways that the students in your school can support tolerance toward others. Remember that having special awareness days and visual displays are good tools for celebrating different cultures. But also think about what students can do to bring about long-term change that lasts and makes a real difference.

NY English Language Arts Core Curriculum (pp. 964–965)

LC R17 Demonstrate comprehension and response through a range of activities. **LC S8** Participate in group discussions on a range of topics and for a variety of purposes. **LC R12** Combine multiple strategies (question) to enhance comprehension and response. **R3a** Identify techniques author uses to persuade (emotional and ethical appeals). **LC R9** Recognize multiple meanings of words and connections among meanings of words. **Core W7** Observe rules of punctuation.

For a complete description of the standards, see p. NY11.

Skills Review

Key Reading Skill: Questioning

7. Did you find it helpful to ask questions as you read? Explain your answer.

Key Text Element: Appeal to Emotions

8. Which persuasive appeal does Jordan use most often?

9. Was this type of persuasive appeal appropriate for the selection? Should Jordan have included other types of persuasive appeals? Explain.

Vocabulary Check

Match each vocabulary word on the left with its definition on the right.

10. harmonious

11. indispensable

12. incurable

13. optimist

a. a person who has a positive or cheerful outlook

b. not likely to be changed or corrected

c. getting along well together; friendly

d. absolutely necessary

14. Academic Vocabulary Are **valid** arguments logical or illogical? Explain.

English Language Coach

15. How does Jordan's extended definition of *tolerance* differ from the word's dictionary definition?

16. Write an extended (one- or two-paragraph) definition of one of these abstract words: *love, success, beauty.* Be sure to include specific examples in your definition of the word.

Web Activities For eFlashcards, Selection Quick Checks, and other Web activities, go to www.glencoe.com.

Grammar Link: Semicolons

You do not always have to use a coordinating conjuction to form a compound sentence. You can use a **semicolon** (*;*) to join two independent clauses or simple sentences to form a compound sentence.

Compound with conjunction: I like to play video games, _and_ my brother likes to play music.

Compound with semicolon: I like to play video games_;_ my brother likes to play music.

A semicolon alone works well in the example compound sentence above because the sentences are short and almost the same. When you join long or contrasting sentences, use a comma and a conjunction rather than a semicolon. A conjunction helps readers see the logical relationship between ideas.

Confusing: He takes my CDs without asking; I don't really mind. (You expect the speaker to mind, so you are surprised when he says that he doesn't.)

Better: He takes my CDs without asking, but I don't really mind. (The conjunction *but* warns you that the next idea will contrast with the first.)

Look out! Remember not to join two sentences with just a comma. You must use a semicolon or a comma and coordinating conjunction.

Grammar Practice

Copy the sentences below on another sheet of paper. Add semicolons or commas and conjunctions where they are needed.

17. We want to see a movie we can't find one we like.

18. I want to see a comedy I like to have a good laugh.

19. Renting videos is fun you can relax more at home.

20. Ogemageshig's father is Native American his mother is half white and half Latino.

Writing Application Using semicolons, combine two short, closely related sentences from the extended definition that you wrote for item 16.

Before You Read

from *Through My Eyes*

Ruby Bridges

Meet the Author

In 1960 six-year-old Ruby Bridges became the first African American student to enroll in a white elementary school in New Orleans after segregation was outlawed there. Her attendance sparked large protests. Bridges says, however, that this experience taught her that "schools can be a place to bring people together—kids of all races and backgrounds."

Literature Online

Author Search For more about Ruby Bridges, go to www.glencoe.com.

NY English Language Arts Core Curriculum (pp. 966–973)

LC R9 Recognize multiple meanings of words and connections among meanings of words. **LC R12** Combine multiple strategies (question) to enhance comprehension and response. **R1h** Identify missing, conflicting, or unclear information. **R2c** Identify the author's point of view. **LC R11** Respond to and comprehend various genres.

For a complete description of the standards, see p. NY11.

Vocabulary Preview

taunts (tawnts) *n.* hurtful or mocking remarks **(p. 968)** *The taunts of the opposing team did not distract him as he took his free throw.*

barricades (BAIR uh kaydz) *n.* barriers put up to separate or to provide defense **(p. 969)** *The peaceful protesters did not try to tear down the barricades that surrounded the political meeting.*

integrated (IN tuh grayt id) *v.* ended the separation of racial and ethnic groups, form of the verb *integrate* **(p. 971)** *The Supreme Court decision Brown v. Board of Education integrated schools across the country.*

Think-Pair-Share In your Learner's Notebook, write a sentence for each of the vocabulary words. Use context clues in each sentence to help show what the word means. Trade sentences with a classmate. Check each other's work to see if it is right.

English Language Coach

Denotation and Word Choice Word choice can provide important information about a narrator or speaker. For example, a narrator who is a child might choose words with simple denotations, or definitions.

In the selection from *Through My Eyes,* the narrator describes an experience she had when she was six years old. Even though the author was an adult when she wrote this autobiography, she uses simple words with simple definitions to show that she saw things through a child's eyes.

Read the two sentences below. Think about which one sounds more like a description that a child might give.

- "The U.S. federal marshals arrived to escort us to school and accompany us throughout the day."
- "They had come to drive us to school and stay with us all day."

The second sentence sounds like something a six-year-old would say. The narrator's word choice helps you understand what she is like.

Partner Talk With a partner, take turns reading aloud the first two paragraphs of the selection from *Through My Eyes.* After you have read the paragraphs, make a list with your partner of the words that help show that the narrator is looking back at an experience from her childhood.

Skills Preview

Reading Skill: Questioning

Have you ever been listening to a speech or a talk and wished that you could stop the speaker to ask questions? When you read, you can ask all the questions you want.

• Basic questions such as *Who? What? When? Where? Why? How?* will help you follow what is happening.

• Asking yourself why an author includes certain information and whether a detail is important will make your reading more meaningful.

Write to Learn As you read, use a two-column chart to ask questions about the selection. In the left-hand column, write any questions that you have. Write the answer to each question in the right-hand column.

Literary Element: Point of View in Nonfiction

Point of view in nonfiction is the perspective from which a real-life story is told. In the **first-person point of view,** an author calls himself or herself "I" or "me" and describes real events that he or she took part in or observed. In the **third-person point of view,** the author does not refer to himself or herself. He or she is a nameless voice that tells what happened. To identify point of view in non-fiction, ask yourself this question:

• *Does the author refer to himself or herself as "I" or "me" (first person), or is the author a nameless voice (third person)?*

Whole Class Discussion *Through My Eyes* includes different points of view of the same story. It begins with a newspaper story about what happened. Then Ruby Bridges tells what happened from her point of view. Finally, Ruby's teacher tells what happened from her point of view. What differences might you expect to find between the newspaper version of the story and Ruby Brown's? Between Ruby Brown's and her teacher's?

Get Ready to Read

Connect to the Reading

Think about your first day of school. What were your feelings as you entered the building and found yourself surrounded by strangers? Was the classroom friendly?

Write to Learn In your Learner's Notebook, write about your first day of school or your first day in a new school. Include descriptions about how you felt.

Build Background

As you read the selection, you may wonder how Ruby Bridges was chosen to be the first African American student at a newly integrated school.

• African American kindergarteners in New Orleans were tested in the spring of 1960 to determine which students would go to integrated schools in the fall. From this testing, six children were chosen to go to integrated schools.

• Two of the children decided not to go, and three of the children were sent to another school. Ruby Bridges alone enrolled in William Frantz Public School.

Set Purposes for Reading

BIG Question Read the selection from *Through My Eyes* to discover other people's ideas about what is worth fighting for and what is not.

Set Your Own Purpose What else would you like to learn from the article to help you answer the Big Question? Write your own purpose on the *Through My Eyes* flap of Foldable 7.

Literature Online

Interactive Literary Elements Handbook
To review or learn more about the literary elements, go to www.glencoe.com.

Keep Moving

Use these skills as you read the following selection.

from Through My Eyes

by Ruby Bridges

— The New York Times, November 15, 1960 *Today, hundreds of city policemen began to assemble in the mixed white and Negro residential districts of the two schools as the sun burned away the haze from the Mississippi River.*

Black squad cars cruised slowly through the narrow streets between modest white frame dwellings set among palms, oleanders, and crepe myrtle. Patrolmen in gold-striped uniforms, black boots, and white crash helmets dismounted from motorcycles to direct traffic. Police officials and detectives stationed themselves around the school buildings and inside the halls. Deputy federal marshals[1] wearing yellow armbands made a final check and drove to the homes of the four pupils. . . . ◼

Some 150 whites, mostly housewives and teenage youths, clustered along the sidewalks across from the William Frantz School when pupils marched in at 8:40 a.m. One youth chanted, "Two, four, six, eight, we don't want to integrate; eight, six, four, two, we don't want a chigeroo."

Forty minutes later, four deputy marshals arrived with a little Negro girl and her mother. They walked hurriedly up the steps and into the yellow brick building while onlookers jeered and shouted **taunts**. ◼

---

1. The U.S. Department of Justice maintains a law enforcement agency made up of **federal marshals** (FED er ul MAR shulz). Among other tasks, the marshals are charged with putting into action federal and district court orders.

Vocabulary

taunts (tawnts) *n.* hurtful or mocking remarks

Practice the Skills

◼ Literary Element

Point of View in Nonfiction
Like most newspaper stories, this story is told in the third-person point of view. You can tell because the narrator is a nameless voice describing what happened.

◼ English Language Coach

Denotation and Word Choice
You can tell that an adult is describing what happened. Does he or she use simple words or sophisticated ones? Give examples.

The girl, dressed in a stiffly starched white dress with a white ribbon in her hair, gripped her mother's hand tightly and glanced apprehensively toward the crowd. **3**

November 14, 1960

My mother took special care getting me ready for school. When somebody knocked on my door that morning, my mother expected to see people from the NAACP.[2] Instead, she saw four serious-looking white men, dressed in suits and wearing armbands. They were U.S. federal marshals. They had come to drive us to school and stay with us all day. I learned later they were carrying guns. **4**

I remember climbing into the back seat of the marshals' car with my mother, but I don't remember feeling frightened. William Frantz Public School was only five blocks away, so one of the marshals in the front seat told my mother right away what we should do when we got there.

"Let us get out of the car first," the marshal said. "Then you'll get out, and the four of us will surround you and your daughter. We'll walk up to the door together. Just walk straight ahead, and don't look back." **5**

When we were near the school, my mother said, "Ruby, I want you to behave yourself today and do what the marshals say."

We drove down North Galvez Street to the point where it crosses Alvar. I remember looking out of the car as we pulled up to the Frantz school. There were **barricades** and people shouting and policemen everywhere. I thought maybe it was Mardi Gras,[3] the carnival that takes place in New Orleans every year. Mardi Gras was always noisy.

As we walked through the crowd, I didn't see any faces. I guess that's because I wasn't very tall and I was surrounded by the marshals. People yelled and threw things. I could see the school building, and it looked bigger and nicer than my

---

2. The **NAACP,** or National Association for the Advancement of Colored People, began in 1909 with the goal of getting equal rights for African Americans.

3. **Mardi Gras** (MAR dee GRAH) is a French expression that means "Fat Tuesday." It is the name given to the celebration held the day before the fast that takes place during the Christian season of Lent.

Vocabulary

barricades (BAIR uh kaydz) *n.* barriers put up to separate or to provide defense

Practice the Skills

3 **Key Reading Skill**

Questioning Did you understand the newspaper story? To make sure, ask yourself 5Ws and an H questions. Answer these sample questions:

- *Who* is the little girl in the white dress?
- *What* is going on?
- *Where* is it happening?
- *When* is it happening?
- *Why* has a crowd gathered?
- *How* does the little girl feel?

4 **Literary Element**

Point of View in Nonfiction Who is speaking? What is the narrative point of view? Use these clues to answer:

- The narrator says her mother helped her get ready.
- The narrator calls herself "I."

5 **English Language Coach**

Denotation and Word Choice Reread the marshal's directions. Notice that he uses words with simple denotations. From his word choice, what do you think the marshall is like?

Escorted by three Deputy U.S. Marshals, Ruby Bridges enters her newly integrated public school.

Analyzing the Photo How does this photograph show the risks Ruby took to help integrate Frantz?

old school. **6** When we climbed the high steps to the front door, there were policemen in uniforms at the top. The policemen at the door and the crowd behind us made me think this was an important place.

It must be college, I thought to myself.

The First Day at William Frantz

Once we were inside the building, the marshals walked us up a flight of stairs. The school office was at the top. My mother and I went in and were told to sit in the principal's office. The marshals sat outside. There were windows in the room where we waited. That meant everybody passing by could see us. I remember noticing everyone was white.

Practice the Skills

6 **Key Reading Skill**

Questioning What does Ruby's description of the school tell you about the school system back in 1960?

All day long, white parents rushed into the office. They were upset. They were arguing and pointing at us. When they took their children to school that morning, the parents hadn't been sure whether William Frantz would be **integrated** that day or not. After my mother and I arrived, they ran into classrooms and dragged their children out of the school. From behind the windows in the office, all I saw was confusion. I told myself that this must be the way it is in a big school. **7**

That whole first day, my mother and I just sat and waited. We didn't talk to anybody. I remember watching a big, round clock on the wall. When it was 3:00 and time to go home, I was glad. I had thought my new school would be hard, but the first day was easy.

Going Home

When we left school that first day, the crowd outside was even bigger and louder than it had been in the morning. There were reporters and film cameras and people everywhere. I guess the police couldn't keep them behind the barricades. It seemed to take us a long time to get to the marshals' car.

Later on I learned there had been protestors in front of the two integrated schools the whole day. They wanted to be sure white parents would boycott⁴ the school and not let their children attend. Groups of high school boys, joining the protestors, paraded

Practice the Skills

7 | **Key Reading Skill**

Questioning How did Ruby explain away the confusion she saw?

In this November 14, 1960, photo, a crowd protests Ruby's attendance at William Frantz Public School.

Analyzing the Photo How would you describe the people in this crowd? How would you feel about the crowd if you were Ruby?

---

4. To **boycott** means to protest against something, such as an organization or a company, by refusing to do business or interact with it.

Vocabulary

integrated (IN tuh grayt id) *v.* ended the separation of racial and ethnic groups

up and down the street and sang new verses to old hymns. Their favorite was "Battle Hymn of the Republic,"[5] in which they changed the chorus to "Glory, glory, segregation, the South will rise again." Many of the boys carried signs and said awful things, but most of all I remember seeing a black doll in a coffin, which frightened me more than anything else. **8**

After the first day, I was glad to get home. I wanted to change my clothes and go outside to find my friends. My mother wasn't too worried about me because the police had set up barricades at each end of the block. Only local residents were allowed on our street. That afternoon, I taught a friend the chant I had learned: "Two, four, six, eight, we don't want to integrate." My friend and I didn't know what the words meant, but we would jump rope to it every day after school. **9**

My father heard about the trouble at school. That night when he came home from work, he said I was his "brave little Ruby."

My First White Teacher

On the second day, my mother and I drove to school with the marshals. The crowd outside the building was ready. Racists spat at us and shouted things. One woman screamed at me, "I'm going to poison you. I'll find a way." She made the same threat every morning.

I tried not to pay attention. When we finally got into the building, my new teacher was there to meet us. Her name was Mrs. Henry. She was young and white. I had not spent time with a white person before, so I was uneasy at first. Mrs. Henry led us upstairs to the second floor. As we went up, we hardly saw anyone else in the building. The white students were not coming to class. The halls were so quiet, I could hear the noise the marshals' shoes made on the shiny hardwood floors.

Mrs. Henry took us into a classroom and said to have a seat. When I looked around, the room was empty. There were rows of desks, but no children. I thought we were too early, but Mrs. Henry said we were right on time. My mother sat

Practice the Skills

8 **Key Reading Skill**

Questioning Why do you think Bridges describes the singing and chanting that she heard?

9 **Key Reading Skill**

Questioning Why do you think Ruby and her friend jump rope and chant these words?

5. The **"Battle Hymn of the Republic"** was written by Julia Ward Howe after a visit to a Union army camp during the Civil War. Howe actively supported ending slavery.

down at the back of the room. I took a seat up front, and Mrs. Henry began to teach. **10**

I spent the whole first day with Mrs. Henry in the classroom. I wasn't allowed to have lunch in the cafeteria or go outside for recess, so we just stayed in our room. The marshals sat outside. If I had to go to the bathroom, the marshals walked me down the hall.

My mother sat in the classroom that day, but not the next. When the marshals came to the house on Wednesday morning, my mother said, "Ruby, I can't go to school with you today, but don't be afraid. The marshals will take care of you. Be good now, and don't cry." **11**

I started to cry anyway, but before I knew it, I was off to school by myself.

Ruby's Teacher's Comments

— Barbara Henry, Ruby's First-Grade Teacher *Leaving the school each day seemed even more frightening than arriving in the morning.*

I always drove to work and kept my car on the playground behind the school building. The police had turned the playground into a parking lot because it was the only area they could protect.

On leaving school in the afternoon—even with a police escort— you were always fearful of how the people gathered along the sidewalks might choose to protest that day as you drove past them. The New Orleans police were supposed to be there to help us, but they very much disliked being the ones to enforce integration, so you never could be confident of their support and cooperation. ○

Practice the Skills

10 **Key Reading Skill**

Questioning Why is the classroom almost empty? Where are the other children?

11 **BIG Question**

Why is equality among races worth fighting for? How does society benefit by having equal treatment for all citizens? Write your answers on the *Through My Eyes* flap of Foldable 7. Your response will help you complete the Unit Challenge later.

After You Read

from *Through My Eyes*

Answering the 🗨️**BIG** Question

1. After reading the selection, what are your thoughts about what is worth fighting for?
2. **Recall** Why did federal marshals accompany Ruby to school?
   TIP **Right There**
3. **Recall** What did Ruby do in class her first day of school?
   TIP **Right There**

Critical Thinking

4. **Analyze** How did Ruby's age and inexperience protect her from some of the bad things that happened? Support your answer with examples.
   TIP **Author and Me**
5. **Infer** How did Ruby's teacher feel about going to school during that difficult time? How can you tell?
   TIP **Author and Me**
6. **Evaluate** In your opinion, was it wise to ask a six-year-old child to take part in such a dangerous and historic event? Explain.
   TIP **On Your Own**

Write About Your Reading

Scene from a Play With a partner, choose one of the following scenes from Ruby's story and rewrite it as a script for a play.

- Ruby and her mother at home the morning of November 14, 1960, getting ready to go to William Frantz Public School for the first time.
- Ruby, her mother, and the federal marshals arriving at William Frantz Public School on the morning of November 14, 1960, and entering the building.
- Ruby, her mother, and the federal marshals leaving William Frantz Public School on the afternoon of November 14, 1960.

To write your script, use details from the newspaper story and Ruby's story. Use your imagination to write dialogue for the characters, but make the dialogue true to what the people say they thought, saw, and felt.

NY English Language Arts Core Curriculum (pp. 974–975)

LC R17 Demonstrate comprehension and response through a range of activities. **LC W4** Compose mechanically grade-appropriate texts for a variety of purposes. **LC R12** Combine multiple strategies (question) to enhance comprehension and response. **R1h** Identify missing, conflicting, or unclear information. **R2c** Identify the author's point of view. **LC R11** Respond to and comprehend various genres. **LC R9** Recognize multiple meanings of words and connections among meanings of words. **Core W7** Observe rules of punctuation.

For a complete description of the standards, see p. NY11.

Skills Review

Key Reading Skill: Questioning

7. How did asking yourself questions as you read make the selection more meaningful for you?

Literary Element: Point of View in Nonfiction

8. Compare and contrast the newspaper version of events and Ruby's version. In what ways are they similar? Different? Put your ideas on a Venn diagram like the one pictured below.

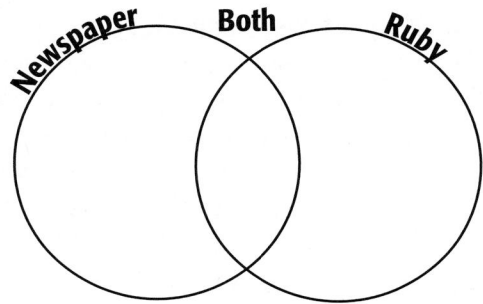

Newspaper   Both   Ruby

Vocabulary Check

Choose the vocabulary word that best completes each sentence.

taunts • barricades • integrated

9. She refused to let their _____ shake her self-confidence.

10. Public schools in New Orleans were not _____ until 1960.

11. The _____ did not keep the enemy's forces out of the castle for long.

12. **English Language Coach** How does the narrator's use of words with simple denotations help you better understand her character?

Literature Online

Web Activities For eFlashcards, Selection Quick Checks, and other Web activities, go to www.glencoe.com.

Grammar Link: Semicolons with Conjunctive Adverbs

When you join two independent clauses, or simple sentences, with a conjunctive adverb, put a **semi-colon** (;) before the conjunctive adverb and a comma after it.

Conjunctive Adverbs	What They Express
therefore, thus, consequently	cause and effect, conclusion, result
however, otherwise, still	contrast, alternative
besides, furthermore, moreover	additional information

• Ina wrote the best essay in the contest; therefore, she deserves the first place award.

• I definitely need to study the science worksheet tonight; otherwise, I won't get a good grade.

• Alika is most qualified to be student council president; furthermore, she is well liked.

Grammar Practice

Copy each sentence on a separate sheet of paper. Insert one of these conjunctive adverbs in the blank: *consequently, besides, furthermore, however, still, therefore, thus.* Correctly punctuate the sentence.

13. The teacher gave us material from Chapter 4 on the test _____ it wasn't covered in class.

14. Terry upset his father _____ his father left the room.

15. Jorge found great artwork for the group project _____ he put it together in a colorful collage.

16. Businesses require people to have computer skills _____ schools teach them to students.

17. I want some fresh air, so I'm going to walk the dog instead of going shopping _____ shopping would be fun.

Writing Application Review your Write About Your Reading activity. Combine two sentences using a semicolon, a conjunctive adverb, and a comma.

Skills Focus

You will practice using these skills when you read the following selections:
- "The Trouble with Television," p. 980
- "Teen Curfews," p. 988

Reading
- Reviewing what you read

Informational Text
- Recognizing bias

Vocabulary
- Understanding semantic slanting
- Academic Vocabulary: *concepts*

Writing/Grammar
- Using quotation marks with direct quotations

NY English Language Arts Core Curriculum
(pp. 976–977)

LC R12 Combine multiple strategies to enhance comprehension and response.

For a complete description of the standards, see p. NY11.

Skill Lesson

Reviewing

Learn It!

What Is It? If you've ever studied for a test, you've probably reviewed. **Reviewing** is going back over what you've already read to find important **concepts** and to organize ideas so you'll recall them later. You probably review various subjects in school every day. You review what you learned yesterday or last week so that you can remember important facts and ideas. Reviewing when you read helps you learn in the same way.

Reprinted with permission of King Features Syndicate.

Analyzing Cartoons
The little girl knows that reviewing will help her remember important ideas and information. What do you need to review from the last Reading Workshop?

Academic Vocabulary

concepts (KON septs) *n.* ideas; organized thoughts

Why Is It Important? Reviewing is especially helpful when you come across a lot of new information. When you review, you get the chance to find the most important ideas and organize your thoughts. Then you can think about those ideas and ask yourself, *What's this selection all about?*

How Do I Do It? As you read, pause every now and then to review. Ask yourself questions to make sure you understand what you've read. Take notes on the important points. Here's how a student reviewed the passage "November 14, 1960" from *Through My Eyes* on pages 969–970.

Study Central Visit www.glencoe .com and click on Study Central to review reviewing.

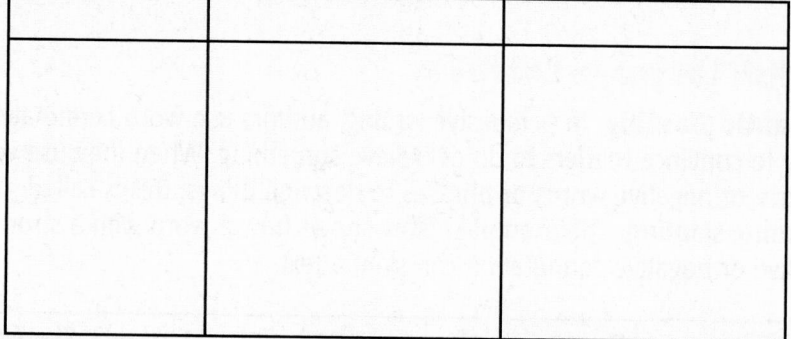

This selection is about Ruby's experience as one of the first African American children to attend an all-white school in the South, so it's important to remember the events and understand how she felt at the time. I'll use a graphic organizer to help me organize my notes.

Practice It!

Make a chart like the one above. Then review the passage "The First Day at William Frantz" on pages 970–971. Fill in the chart using your own words.

Use It!

As you read "The Trouble with Television" and "Teen Curfews," stop every now and then to think about what you've read. Then review. Take notes on the important ideas.

Before You Read

The Trouble with Television

Robert MacNeil

Meet the Author

Robert MacNeil was born and raised in Canada. His career in journalism began when he moved to London, England, after college to work for the Reuters News Agency. In 1975 he cofounded "The MacNeil/Lehrer NewsHour," a news program that discusses a single issue each night. In 1995, after twenty years as co-anchor of the show, MacNeil retired.

Author Search For more about Robert MacNeil, go to www.glencoe.com.

NY English Language Arts
Core Curriculum (pp. 978–983)

Core R5 Distinguish between dictionary meaning and implied meaning of the author's words. **LC R12** Combine multiple strategies to enhance comprehension and response. **R3a** Question the writer's assumptions, beliefs, intentions, and biases.

For a complete description of the standards, see p. NY11.

Vocabulary Preview

perpetual (per PEH choo ul) *adj.* continuing forever **(p. 981)** *Television is a perpetual display of moving images.*

passively (PASS iv lee) *adv.* not actively **(p. 981)** *Instead of passively watching television, you could exercise your brain by reading a book.*

strain (strayn) *v.* stretch to the limit; overwork **(p. 981)** *Television programmers do not want to strain your attention, so they keep programs short.*

virtually (VUR choo uh lee) *adv.* nearly **(p. 983)** *Virtually everyone, or almost the entire nation, watches television every day.*

skeptically (SKEP tik uh lee) *adv.* with doubt **(p. 983)** *The author looks at TV skeptically and questions its value to society.*

English Language Coach

Semantic Slanting In persuasive writing, authors use word connotation to try to convince readers to do or believe something. When they use very positive or negative words or phrases to describe things, this is called **semantic slanting.** The example below shows how a word with a strong positive or negative connotation can slant a text.

Sentence	Denotation of italicized word or phrase	Connotation of italicized word or phrase	Semantic Slanting
Nicole is *nosy* and likes to ask a lot of questions.	*nosy* = curious	*negative:* bothersome	suggests that Nicole is rude and does not have the right to ask questions

If you think that an author is using semantic slanting, try to paraphrase his or her words using words with neutral connotations.

Think–Pair–Share Find the negative word in each sentence. Share your results with a partner. Then discuss how the use of semantic slanting affects what you think of Andrea and "the driver of the other car."

1. Andrea likes to gossip about her neighbors.

2. As I was backing out, the driver of the other car smashed into my bumper.

Skills Preview

Key Reading Skill: Reviewing

When you read persuasive writing, it's important to understand the main points of the writing. As you read "The Trouble with Television," stop to review the author's ideas and the information he gives to support them.

On Your Own Copy this chart and use it to take notes.

Main Point	Supporting Details

Key Text Element: Author's Bias

In persuasive writing, "one-sidedness" is known as **author's bias.** Having a firm opinion is not the same as being biased. The purpose of persuasive writing is to "take sides" and argue one position over another. Bias happens when writers close their minds to opinions or viewpoints different from their own. To identify bias, ask yourself these questions. If your answer to them is "yes," the writer may be biased.

- *Does the writer fail to admit that there are two sides to the story, or issue?*

- *Does the writer **overgeneralize,** or make broad statements without including exceptions to the rule?*

- *Does the writer work for or belong to a group that might make him or her biased?*

Whole Class Discussion It's almost election time. You have to decide who gets your vote for president—Joe Doe of Party A or Moe Doe of Party B. What resources would you look into to find unbiased information about each candidate?

Literature Online

Interactive Literary Elements Handbook
To review or learn more about the literary elements, go to www.glencoe.com.

Get Ready to Read

Connect to the Reading

How often do you watch television? Take a moment to think about how many hours per week you sit in front of the TV. Do you spend as many hours doing more important activities, like homework?

On Your Own Make a list of your favorite activities. Calculate how much time you spent on each activity last week. What did you spend the most amount of time doing? What did you spend the least amount of time doing? Is there anything you would like to spend more time doing? If so, how will you find the time?

Build Background

In 1950 only 9 percent of U.S. households owned a TV. Today, over 98 percent of U.S. households have at least one TV. Viewers with cable or satellite TV may have access to more than 200 channels.

In the United States, one hour of network television usually contains between fifteen to twenty minutes of commercials advertising products and services.

Set Purposes for Reading

BIG Question Read "The Trouble with Television" to learn why the author thinks people should reduce the number of hours they spend watching television.

Set Your Own Purpose What would you like to learn from the selection to help you answer the Big Question? Write your own purpose on "The Trouble with Television" flap of Foldable 7.

Keep Moving

Use these skills as you read the following selection.

The Trouble with Television

by Robert MacNeil

It is difficult to **escape the influence** of television. If you fit the statistical averages,[1] by the age of 20 you will have been exposed to at least 20,000 hours of television. You can add 10,000 hours for each decade you have lived after the age of 20. The only things Americans do more than watch television are work and sleep. **1**

Calculate for a moment what could be done with even a part of those hours. Five thousand hours, I am told, are what a typical college undergraduate spends working on a bachelor's degree.[2] In 10,000 hours you could have learned enough to become an astronomer or engineer. You could have learned several languages fluently. If it appealed to you, you could be reading Homer in the original Greek or Dostoyevski[3] in Russian. If it didn't, you could have walked around the world and written a book about it.

The trouble with television is that it discourages concentration. **2** Almost anything interesting and rewarding

---

1. **Statistical averages** tell you about a typical person's behavior.
2. **Undergraduates** are students at a college or university who do not yet have a degree. A **bachelor's degree** is awarded to undergraduates who complete a four-year program of study.
3. **Homer** was a Greek poet who is believed to have lived around 800 B.C. Fyodor **Dostoyevski** was a Russian novelist who lived from 1821–1881.

Practice the Skills

1 English Language Coach

Semantic Slanting The opening sentence could be paraphrased as follows: *It's hard not to be affected by television.* What is the author trying to persuade you of by using the phrase **escape the influence,** which has a negative connotation? Explain.

2 Key Reading Skill

Reviewing Here, MacNeil states his main idea, or position: "The trouble with television is that it discourages concentration." Write the main idea on your chart so you remember it.

in life requires some constructive, consistently applied effort. The dullest, the least gifted of us can achieve things that seem miraculous to those who never concentrate on anything. But television encourages us to apply no effort. It sells us instant gratification. It diverts[4] us only to divert, to make the time pass without pain. **3**

Television's variety becomes a narcotic, not a stimulus. Its serial, kaleidoscopic exposures[5] force us to follow its lead. The viewer is on a **perpetual** guided tour: thirty minutes at the museum, thirty at the cathedral, then back on the bus to the next attraction—except on television, typically, the spans allotted are on the order of minutes or seconds, and the chosen delights are more often car crashes and people killing one another. In short, a lot of television usurps[6] one of the most precious of all human gifts, the ability to focus your attention yourself, rather than just **passively** surrender it. **4**

Capturing your attention—and holding it—is the prime motive of most television programming and enhances its role as a profitable advertising vehicle.[7] Programmers live in constant fear of losing anyone's attention—anyone's. The surest way to avoid doing so is to keep everything brief, not to **strain** the attention of anyone but instead to provide constant stimulation through variety, novelty, action and movement. Quite simply, television operates on the appeal to the short attention span.

It is simply the easiest way out. But it has come to be regarded as a given, as inherent in the medium itself; as an imperative, as though General Sarnoff, or one of the other

Practice the Skills

3 **Key Text Element**

Author's Bias MacNeil over-generalizes and shows bias when he says TV "diverts us only to divert, to make the time pass without pain." How about serious news programs such as the one he coanchored? Those shows aren't just entertainment, are they? What other exceptions can you think of?

4 **Key Reading Skill**

Reviewing Look back at what you have already read. What evidence does the author give to support his arguments? Write your answer on your chart.

---

4. **Instant gratification** is immediate satisfaction. **Divert** means "distract."

5. A **narcotic** is a substance that soothes. **Serial kaleidoscopic exposures** (SEER ee ul kul ide uh SKAHP ik ek SPOH zherz) are continuous and constantly changing images.

6. **Usurps** (yoo SERPS) means "takes by force or without right."

7. The author writes that the **prime motive** (goal) of television is to **enhance** (improve the value of) its role as a **profitable advertising vehicle** (a moneymaker for companies that broadcast advertisements).

Vocabulary

perpetual (per PEH choo ul) *adj.* continuing forever

passively (PASS iv lee) *adv.* not actively

strain (strayn) *v.* stretch to the limit; overwork

august pioneers of video, had bequeathed[8] to us tablets of stone commanding that nothing in television shall ever require more than a few moments' concentration.

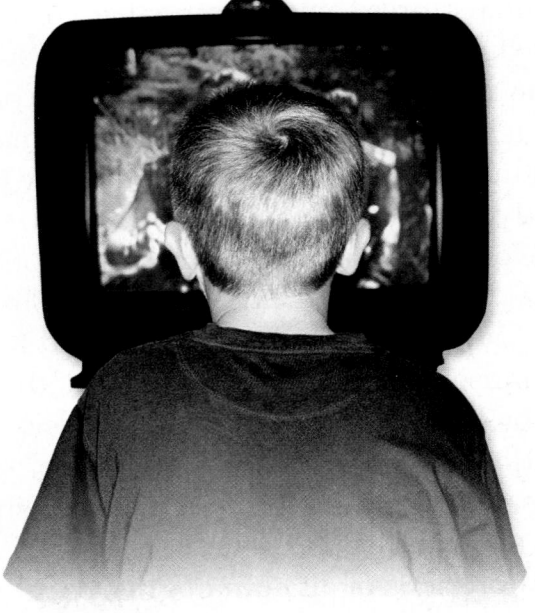

In its place that is fine. Who can quarrel with a medium that so brilliantly packages escapist entertainment as a mass-marketing tool? But I see its values now pervading[9] this nation and its life. It has become fashionable to think that, like fast food, fast ideas are the way to get to a fast-moving, impatient public.

In the case of news, this practice, in my view, results in inefficient communication. I question how much of television's nightly news effort is really absorbable and understandable. Much of it is what has been aptly described as "machine gunning with scraps." I think the technique fights coherence. I think it tends to make things ultimately boring and dismissible[10] (unless they are accompanied by horrifying pictures) because almost anything is boring and dismissible if you know almost nothing about it. **5**

I believe that TV's appeal to the short attention span is not only inefficient communication but decivilizing as well. Consider the casual assumptions that television tends to cultivate: that complexity must be avoided, that visual stimulation is a substitute for thought, that verbal precision is an anachronism.[11] It may be old-fashioned, but I was taught that thought is words, arranged in grammatically precise ways.

There is a crisis of literacy in this country. One study estimates that some 30 million adult Americans are "functionally illiterate" and cannot read or write well enough to answer a want ad or understand the instructions on a medicine bottle.

Practice the Skills

5 **Key Text Element**

Author's Bias Remember that MacNeil was once an anchor on an hour-long news program that focused on only one issue. How might this background bias him?

---

8. Here, *august* (aw GUST) means "honored." *Bequeathed* (bih KWEETHD) means "handed down."

9. The author compares television to a *mass-marketing tool,* a device used to sell products to a large number of people. *Pervading* means "spreading through all parts of."

10. *Aptly* means "correctly and accurately." *Coherence* is the quality of fitting together in a way that makes sense. Something that is *dismissible* is easily put out of one's mind.

11. *Decivilizing* is getting rid of knowledge, good taste, and social skills. *Assumptions* are beliefs that have not been proven to be true. To *cultivate* something is to encourage it to grow. An *anachronism* is something that is out of place in the present time period.

Literacy may not be an inalienable human right, but it is one that the highly literate Founding Fathers might not have found unreasonable or even unattainable.[12] We are not only not attaining it as a nation, statistically speaking, but we are falling further and further short of attaining it. And, while I would not be so simplistic as to suggest that television is the cause, I believe it contributes and is an influence. **6**

Everything about this nation—the structure of the society, its forms of family organization, its economy, its place in the world—has become more complex, not less. Yet its dominating communications instrument, its principal form of national linkage, is one that sells neat resolutions[13] to human problems that usually have no neat resolutions. It is all symbolized in my mind by the hugely successful art form that television has made central to the culture, the thirty-second commercial: the tiny drama of the earnest housewife who finds happiness in choosing the right toothpaste.

When before in human history has so much humanity collectively surrendered so much of its leisure to one toy, one mass diversion? When before has **virtually** an entire nation surrendered itself wholesale[14] to a medium for selling?

Some years ago Yale University law professor Charles L. Black, Jr., wrote: ". . . forced feeding on trivial fare is not itself a trivial matter." I think this society is being force-fed with trivial fare, and I fear that the effects on our habits of mind, our language, our tolerance for effort, and our appetite for complexity are only dimly perceived. If I am wrong, we will have done no harm to look at the issue **skeptically** and critically, to consider how we should be resisting it. I hope you will join with me in doing so. **7** ○

---

12. An *inalienable human right* is a basic right that cannot be taken away. *Unattainable* means "unable to be obtained."

13. *Dominating* means "commanding the most attention." *Resolutions* are answers or solutions.

14. In this paragraph, the author asks if there has been another time when *humanity* (the entire human race) has *collectively* (together as one) given up so much of its free time to one *mass diversion* (source of amusement), or *surrendered itself wholesale*—given itself up completely to a medium for selling.

Vocabulary

virtually (VUR choo uh lee) *adv.* nearly

skeptically (SKEP tik uh lee) *adv.* with doubt

Practice the Skills

6 **Key Reading Skill**

Reviewing Review the last two paragraphs to make sure you understand what *literacy* and *illiteracy* mean. Then write the main point of these paragraphs on your chart.

7 **BIG Question**

What does the author ask you to join him in fighting for? Write your answer on "The Trouble with Television" flap of Foldable 7. Your response will help you complete the Unit Challenge later.

After You Read

The Trouble with Television

Answering the BIG Question

1. Do you agree with the author that TV is harmful? Explain.
2. **Recall** By the age of twenty, how many hours of television has the average person watched?
   TIP Right There

3. **Recall** According to MacNeil, what are two negative effects of TV?
   TIP Think and Search

Critical Thinking

4. **Analyze** Why do you think MacNeil starts his article with statistics about the number of hours people spend watching TV? Use details from the selection to support your answer.
   TIP Author and Me

5. **Analyze** In the conclusion, MacNeil quotes Charles L. Black Jr. Why do you think he chose to quote Black?
   TIP Author and Me

6. **Evaluate** Do you think MacNeil argues his position well? Explain.
   TIP Author and Me

Talk About Your Reading

Small Group Discussion Get together with a small group of classmates and debate the pros and cons of TV. Guide your discussion with these questions:

- MacNeil says TV "discourages concentration." What examples does he give to back up his position? Is this evidence persuasive? Explain.
- MacNeil argues that TV is too simple a form of communication for today's complex world. Do you agree? Explain.
- Are there good things to be said for TV? If so, what are they?

NY English Language Arts Core Curriculum (pp. 984–985)

LC R17 Demonstrate comprehension and response through a range of activities. **LC S8** Participate in group discussions on a range of topics and for a variety of purposes. **LC R12** Combine multiple strategies to enhance comprehension and response. **R3a** Question the writer's assumptions, beliefs, intentions, and biases. **Core R5** Distinguish between dictionary meaning and implied meaning of the author's words. **Core W7** Observe rules of punctuation.

For a complete description of the standards, see p. NY11.

Skills Review

Key Reading Skill: Reviewing

7. How did reviewing help you understand this selection? Give examples.

Key Text Element: Author's Bias

8. Imagine that you're doing research to see whether television viewing harms people's ability to concentrate. To avoid bias, what other sources of information might you look into besides "The Trouble with Television?"

Vocabulary Check

Copy the following sentences on a separate sheet of paper. Fill in each blank with the correct word.

perpetual • passively • strain • virtually • skeptically

9. Turn on the light while you read so that you don't _____ your eyes.

10. After the party, _____ all the snacks were gone.

11. The doctor knew the little girl was pretending to be ill. _____, he examined her throat.

12. A person who is constantly on the go is in _____ motion.

13. Don't sit there _____ watching television; get out and do something productive!

14. **English Language Coach** Quote an example of semantic slanting from the selection. Does the word or phrase you quoted have positive connotations or negatives ones? Explain.

15. **Academic Vocabulary** List a few **concepts** you have recently studied in English class.

Web Activities For eFlashcards, Selection Quick Checks, and other Web activities, go to www.glencoe.com.

Grammar Link: Quotation Marks

Quotation marks (" ") are punctuation marks used to enclose the exact words of a speaker. When a speaker's words are not interrupted, **opening quotation marks** (") are placed before the quotation and **closing quotation marks** (") after it. The quotation may come at the end of a sentence or at the beginning.

- After they lost their lawsuit, the young women said, "We are still proud that we stood up for our beliefs."
- The reporter asked, "What will you do now?"
- "What will you do now?" asked the reporter.

A **direct quotation** states word for word what a speaker said. An **indirect quotation** does not repeat a person's exact words. It should NOT be enclosed in quotation marks.

Direct: Ms. Bosco said, "Mars has two moons."
Indirect: Ms. Bosco said that Mars has two moons.

Grammar Practice

Copy the following sentences on a separate sheet of paper. Add quotation marks where needed.

16. Please, Katelyn, would you wear white socks rather than black ones, her gym teacher said.

17. But all my socks are black, Katelyn complained.

18. The waiter apologized, We're all out of meatloaf.

19. One councilman growled, They are just taking up our precious time.

20. A student said that she thought they were brave.

21. Another student in the community said, We are grateful that the young women were willing to fight for our rights.

22. My sister said that she thinks the whole issue is ridiculous.

23. What is to be gained from all this fighting? she asked me.

24. The newspaper agrees with me that there is nothing to be gained.

Before You Read : Teen Curfews

Meet the Author

J. Todd Foster began his journalism career in 1978 as a teenage sports editor in Winchester, Tennessee. Since then he has reported on medicine, the environment, politics, crime, and human-interest stories for various publications, including *People* magazine. In 2003 Foster became managing editor of *The News Virginian*, a newspaper based out of Waynesboro, Virginia, where he lives with his family.

Author Search For more about J. Todd Foster, go to www.glencoe.com.

Vocabulary Preview

convictions (kun VIK shunz) *n.* strong beliefs or values **(p. 988)** *The young people were willing to take a risk because of their convictions.*

controversial (kon truh VUR shul) *adj.* causing disagreement **(p. 988)** *The new law was so controversial that the state's supreme court decided to hear the case and decide whether it was constitutional.*

violating (VY uh lay ting) *v.* breaking or disregarding; form of the verb *violate* **(p. 988)** *The police arrested more than fifty kids who they suspected were violating the law.*

Write to Learn Answer the following questions.

1. List and briefly explain a few of your **convictions**.
2. Name a **controversial** topic you might examine in a persuasive essay for your English class.
3. What is an antonym for *violating*?

English Language Coach

Semantic Slanting Remember that using words with strong positive or negative connotations can sway readers in one direction or another. The following two paragraphs argue for and against school uniforms. Notice the semantic slanting in each.

In favor of wearing school uniforms	*School uniforms free kids from being forced to choose a different outfit each day. Kids aren't pressured to think about whether their clothes meet the approval of their peers. They don't have to break the bank and fork out ridiculous amounts of money for expensive fads.*
Against wearing school uniforms	*School uniforms deny kids the right to make up their own minds about what they want to wear. Kids enjoy the challenge of creating outfits that earn the admiration of their peers. Trendy clothes help kids express their individuality.*

Small Group Work Form a group with a few other students. Identify the words and phrases in the paragraphs above that have strong positive or negative connotations. Discuss how they slant the texts.

NY English Language Arts Core Curriculum (pp. 986–989)

Core R5 Distinguish between dictionary meaning and implied meaning of the author's words. **LC R12** Combine multiple strategies to enhance comprehension and response. **R3a** Question the writer's assumptions, beliefs, intentions, and biases.

For a complete description of the standards, see p. NY11.

Skills Preview

Key Reading Skill: Reviewing

As you read the selection, take time to pause and review. Check your understanding of information and reread to look for anything you've missed.

Write to Learn "Teen Curfews" is a news article about a series of events that takes place in Charleston, West Virginia. You probably already know that the important points to remember in a news article are *Who, What, When, Where, Why,* and *How.* Make a graphic organizer to keep track of this information.

Key Text Element: Author's Bias

Remember that an author who unfairly slants a story is guilty of **author's bias.** To evaluate an article for bias, it's important to consider whether the author favors one side of a story over others. Ask yourself:

- *Does the author have a special interest in putting someone in a positive or negative light?*
- *Is the author's evidence reliable?*
- *What are the author's sources?*
- *Does the author stereotype, generalize, or exaggerate?*
- *What information is the author leaving out? Why?*

Write to Learn Write a short news article describing an event that caused a disagreement between you and another person. For example, you could write about a time when you wanted something that you couldn't have or when a parent set a new rule in your home. Try to be completely neutral. Leave out your personal feelings and give a fair explanation of what happened. Switch papers with a partner and ask the person to check to see if your writing shows bias.

Interactive Literary Elements Handbook
To review or learn more about the literary elements, go to www.glencoe.com.

Get Ready to Read

Connect to the Reading

Do you think teenagers should be home by a certain time in the evening? Is it safe for teens to be out at late hours in your town?

Small Group Discussion Form a group with three other students. Discuss what teenagers in your town like to do in the evenings. Do you think they should be required to be home by a certain time at night?

Build Background

A curfew is an enforced time when people must be out of public places.

- Many parents give their teenagers curfews to ensure that their children will be home at a reasonable hour.
- Some cities have curfew laws for teenagers. These laws are intended to keep young people safe as well as to stop teens from committing crimes.
- Teens are not the only targets of curfews. Members of the armed forces have to obey curfews. Some colleges have curfews too—even for students over 18. During times of war and civil unrest, governments may enforce curfews to protect all citizens, regardless of age, during evening hours.

Set Purposes for Reading

BIG Question Read the article "Teen Curfews" to see how three teenagers responded to a law that limited when they could be out in public at nighttime.

Set Your Own Purpose What would you like to learn from the article to help you answer the Big Question? Write your own purpose on the "Teen Curfews" flap of Foldable 7.

Keep Moving

Use these skills as you read the following selection.

TIME

Teen CURFEWS

Are teens unfairly targeted?

By J. TODD FOSTER

Tony Pearce

When Katelyn Kimmons was 6 years old, the precocious youngster[1] announced to her family that she was "The Woman in Black" and that from then on she planned to wear nothing but black. Later, in high school, she aced chemistry but failed physical education for refusing to wear the required white socks.

With strong **convictions** like these, Katelyn surprised no one when, at 16, she took her city to court—and brought a **controversial** youth curfew program to a grinding halt for more than a year.

Katelyn was a junior at George Washington High School in Charleston, West Virginia, when the city council passed the Youth Protection Ordinance[2] in December 1997. The ordinance stated that individuals under 18 could not be in public places after 10 p.m. on weekdays or after midnight on weekends. Officially, there were exceptions, such as for emergencies and after-school jobs—but police officers could stop anyone they thought might be **violating** the ordinance. **1**

Katelyn and classmates Anna Sale, then 18, and Lealah Pollock, then 15, agreed that the curfew violated their constitutional rights. With assistance from the West Virginia American Civil Liberties Union (ACLU), in March 1998 they

"Parents should bring up their kids," says Katelyn Kimmons, "not the establishment. I was brought up to stand up for myself."

1 **Key Reading Skill**

Reviewing Review what you have read so far. Take notes on your graphic organizer.

1. A *precocious youngster* is a child who acts like an adult.
2. An *ordinance* is a law.

Vocabulary ....

convictions (kun VIK shunz) *n.* strong beliefs or values

controversial (kon truh VUR shul) *adj.* causing disagreement

violating (VY uh lay ting) *v.* breaking or disregarding

filed a lawsuit to overturn the city ordinance, claiming it **discriminates** against teenagers because of their age. "Kids are being unfairly targeted, scapegoated,"[3] says Lealah. "If someone commits a crime, then arrest them for that." **2**

As the protest got under way, it churned up controversy in Charleston. Anna's parents got calls from friends and neighbors who complained about how much money the city was spending to defend itself against Anna's lawsuit. And many believed the curfew was necessary and important to make Charleston a better place by curbing delinquent behavior by juveniles.[4] "Parents tell me they can use this law to get their kids to come in at night," says Frederick Snuffer, the city council member who introduced the ordinance.

However, Katelyn, Anna, and Lealah stood their ground, and the city of Charleston decided to put the curfew on hold until a judge could rule on it. On July 15, 1998, the three teenagers walked past a crowd of reporters, supporters, and protesters to testify before the county circuit court about their lawsuit and the discriminatory effect of the city curfew ordinance. Mike Carey, a lawyer on the opposing side, grilled each of them for several minutes. "I was fired up and excited," recalls Katelyn. "It bothers me when people in authority positions treat me as if I'm not worth as much because I'm younger."

But Katelyn's enthusiasm was short-lived: Less than a year later, the court ruled against the girls and upheld the curfew law. Since then, more than 50 Charleston kids have been arrested or were issued warnings and sent home to their parents. "Why does the city have the right to overrule parents?" asks Lealah.

The girls appealed to the West Virginia Supreme Court of Appeals. In July 2000, the West Virginia Supreme Court voted 4–1 to uphold the law.

"This [perspective] bothers me," Anna says. "There's this thinking that kids are predators,[5] that we are to be feared. Of course, I want to cure society's ills, but not by creating a law that says if you're under 18, then we don't trust you." **3 4**

—**Updated 2005, from *Teen People*, February 2004**

---

3. To be ***scapegoated*** is to be blamed for what someone else has done.
4. ***Curbing delinquent behavior by juveniles*** means "limiting illegal behavior by teenagers." To ***curb*** is to hold back or control. ***Delinquent,*** as an adjective, refers to breaking the law or not following the rules. ***Juveniles,*** in its general meaning, refers to all children and young people. Most states define *juveniles* as being people under 18, but the age varies from state to state.
5. Among animals, a ***predator*** is one that kills and eats other animals. Among humans, a *predator* gets what he or she wants by stealing from or harming others.

2 | **English Language Coach**

Semantic Slanting The word **discriminates** (*dis KRIM uh nayts*) means "shows preference for." It is often used to highlight unfair treatment and has a negative connotation.

3 | **Key Text Element**

Author's Bias This article is from *Teen People,* a magazine whose audience is primarily teenagers. Do you think the writer had a special interest in putting one side of the story in a more positive light than the other? Explain.

4 | **BIG Question**

What would Katelyn and her friends say is worth fighting for? Write your answer on your Foldable. Your response will help you complete the Unit Challenge later.

After You Read

Teen Curfews

Tony Pearce

Answering the BIG Question

1. Would you fight a curfew for teens in your community? Why or why not?

2. **Recall** What made Katelyn stand out as an individual during her high school physical education class?
   TIP **Right There**

3. **Summarize** Sum up the teens' argument against the curfew.
   TIP **Think and Search**

Critical Thinking

4. **Analyze** What does the author do to capture readers' attention at the beginning of the selection?
   TIP **Author and Me**

5. **Interpret** What does Lealah mean when she says that the city shouldn't have the right to "overrule" parents?
   TIP **Author and Me**

6. **Evaluate** Do you think teenagers should have the right to sue their city if they disagree with its laws? Explain.
   TIP **On My Own**

Write About Your Reading

Letter to the Editor With a small group of classmates, discuss the possible pros and cons of the teen curfew law described in the selection. Take notes on what group members have to say. Decide where you stand on the issue of teen curfews—either for or against. Then, on your own, write a "letter to the editor" trying to persuade readers to agree with your position. Imagine that you're writing to the editor of your community newspaper and that your audience is grownups, not kids.

NY English Language Arts
Core Curriculum (pp. 990–991)

LC R17 Demonstrate comprehension and response through a range of activities. **LC W5** Write with voice to address varied purposes, topics, and audiences. **LC R12** Combine multiple strategies to enhance comprehension and response. **R3a** Question the writer's assumptions, beliefs, intentions, and biases. **Core R5** Distinguish between dictionary meaning and implied meaning of the author's words. **Core W7** Observe rules of punctuation.

For a complete description of the standards, see p. NY11.

Skills Review

Key Reading Skill: Reviewing

7. Using your notes, summarize the article in a paragraph. Then review the selection to make sure you included all the important information.

Key Text Element: Author's Bias

8. The author tries to give a balanced view by including the opinions of people who disagree with Katelyn, Anna, and Lealah. What "opponent" of theirs does the author quote? What is this person's opinion?

Vocabulary Check

Answer *true* or *false* to the following statements.

9. A person with **convictions** doesn't know what he or she values.

10. A **controversial** topic causes people to disagree.

11. **Violating** the law could land you in jail.

12. **English Language Coach** The teens in the selection are sometimes guilty of semantic slanting. Scan the article and reread the parts that directly quote the teens. Find at least two examples of semantic slanting in the quotations. Write the examples on a chart like the one pictured. Then complete the chart by filling in the blanks.

Word or Phrase	Denotation (Meaning)	Connotation (Associations)

Grammar Link: More Quotation Marks

Put quotation marks around both parts of a split quotation. A **split quotation** occurs when an explanatory phrase divides a quotation.

• "Today," explained Mei, "is a busy day for me."

(The explanatory phrase "explained Mei" splits the quotation "Today is a busy day for me.")

If a quotation ends with a period, the period *always* goes *inside* the quotation marks. If a quotation ends with a question mark or an exclamation point, the end mark goes *inside* the quotation marks.

• Mei whined, "The bus broke down."
• Wanda said, "Couldn't you call?"
• Mei said, "I did call!"

If a quotation appears within a question or exclamation, the question mark or exclamation point goes *outside* the quotation marks.

• Are you sure that Mei said, "Meet me at 3 p.m."?

Also put quotation marks around the titles of short works, such as poems, stories, and articles. (The titles of longer works, such as plays and novels, are italicized. If the writer does not have access to italics, underlining is used instead.)

• Read the poem "One Day" in *Ten Poems*.

(The poem title is in quotation marks; the title of the book in which the poem appears is italicized.)

Grammar Practice

Put quotation marks where needed in each sentence.

13. I wonder, Lil said, if the ice has begun to melt.

14. Joe screamed, The ice is too thin for skating!

15. Did you read the article Teen Curfews?

Web Activities For eFlashcards, Selection Quick Checks, and other Web activities, go to www.glencoe.com.

Persuasive Essay
Revising, Editing, and Presenting

ASSIGNMENT Write a persuasive essay

Purpose: To make a case for something you think is worth fighting for

Audience: Your teacher, your classmates, and other people in your community

Revising Rubric

Your revised essay should have these elements:

- a clear position statement
- a well-developed introduction, body, and conclusion
- clear reasons and supporting details and examples
- strong sentence fluency
- correct punctuation (including use of apostrophes), grammar, and spelling

NY English Language Arts Core Curriculum
(pp. 992–997)

LC W6 Organize writing effectively to communicate ideas to an intended audience. **Core W5** Use the writing process (prewriting, drafting, revising, proofreading, and editing). **LC W4** Compose mechanically grade-appropriate texts for a variety of purposes. **R3a** Identify techniques author uses to persuade. **L3b** Recognize persuasive techniques, such as emotional and ethical appeals.

For a complete description of the standards, see p. NY11.

In Writing Workshop Part 1, you developed your ideas and an early draft of your essay. Now it's time to head back to the workshop to finish your essay.

Revising

Make It Better

Revising is an important step in the writing process. It's when you figure out how to make your draft better. You may spend more time revising than you did writing the first draft. That's normal! Your goal is to make your writing as clear and strong as you can.

Use the following checklist to revise your first draft. For every question you answer "No," revise until you can answer "Yes."

Revising Checklist

Yes	No	
		Introduction
❏	❏	**1.** Is the introduction at least one paragraph long?
❏	❏	**2.** Does it begin with an attention-grabber and end with a clear position statement?
		Body
❏	❏	**3.** Are there at least two paragraphs?
❏	❏	**4.** Does each paragraph clearly state a supporting reason and details?
❏	❏	**5.** Are the reasons and details likely to convince your readers?
		Conclusion
❏	❏	**6.** Is the conclusion at least one paragraph long?
❏	❏	**7.** Does the conclusion sum up main ideas?
❏	❏	**8.** Did you remember to include a call to action if you want readers to take action?

You've checked to make sure the organization of your essay is clear and all of the important details are in place. Now revise your essay to strengthen the language. Make changes like these:

- reorder the paragraphs to make the essay easier to follow
- add transitions such as *even though, in addition,* and *however* between sentences and paragraphs
- avoid repetition by deleting unneeded words or sentences
- substitute lively, precise words for dull, unclear ones

Literature Online

Writing Models For models and other writing activities, go to www.glencoe.com.

Editing
Finish It Up

Don't let mistakes take away from the persuasive power of your essay. Before you make your final copy, read your essay one sentence at a time and use the **Editing Checklist** to help you spot errors. Use the proofreading symbols on the inside back cover of this book to mark needed corrections.

Editing Checklist

- ❏ Sentences are complete. There are no fragments or run-ons.
- ❏ All words are correctly used.
- ❏ Spelling and capitalization are correct.
- ❏ Apostrophes and other punctuation are used correctly.

> **Writing Tip**
>
> **Proofread Backwards** If you are having trouble proofreading because you are so familiar with your essay, read it backwards, from the last paragraph to the first. That will help you focus on individual words rather than ideas.

Many of us take too many things for granted, : our *~~Our~~ right to drive a big car that uses a lot of gas and our right to use as much water and power as we want. We think we don't have to be responsible for what we do. Soon* breathe *we will have no clean air to ~~breath~~, no clean water to drink, and no clean soil to grow our food in.*

Presenting
Show It Off

Once you have made your essay as good as you can, hand it in and share it with your audience. Be sure to keep a copy of your essay in your portfolio. That will help you and your teacher measure your progress.

Applying Good Writing Traits

Fluency

You know what it feels like to read something that is choppy. It is confusing *and* boring. You probably also know how pleasant it is when writing moves smoothly from one sentence to the next.

What Is Fluency?

Fluency describes how sentences "flow" in a piece of writing. One way to think about fluency is to think about how the writing *sounds.* Does it sound graceful, almost musical? That's fluency!

Sentences are the main ingredient in fluency. In good writing, sentences have different lengths. They move from one idea to the next. They should be a pleasure to read!

Why Is Fluency Important in My Writing?

Sentences that flow rhythmically interest readers and keep their attention. Choppy sentences can be confusing and distracting.

How Do I Do It?

- **Use different sentence lengths**–combine and divide sentences when needed.
- **Begin sentences in different ways**–try writing a sentence in several different ways before choosing the structure you want to use.
- **Use transitions to connect ideas and sentences**–include words such as *then, after, nevertheless, next* to move the reader smoothly.
- **Avoid too much repetition**–find other ways to emphasize ideas.

Write to Learn Look back at your persuasive essay. Read it aloud to yourself. Do the paragraphs hold together? How do the flow and rhythm sound? Are they choppy? If so, smooth out your writing by revising some of your sentences.

© Zits Partnership. Reprinted with Permission of King Features Syndicate, Inc.

Analyzing Cartoons
When a sentence is fluent, it sounds smooth. How could you change the last sentence in the cartoon to be more fluent?

Listening, Speaking, and Viewing

Understanding Persuasive Techniques

You see or hear advertisements all the time—on TV or the radio, on Web pages, on billboards, and in magazines and newspapers. These ads were made to persuade you—the viewer or listener—to do something. Usually the ads try to persuade you to buy something, but they may try to make you think a certain way. For example, they may try to get you to vote for someone.

What Are Persuasive Techniques?

Persuasive techniques are the methods advertisers and others use to convince you to agree with their opinions and take the actions they want you to take.

Why Is It Important to Understand Persuasive Techniques?

Some persuasive techniques are based on facts. For example, an ad may list the standard features on a particular model of car. Other persuasive techniques bend the truth. If you can learn to figure out how those less-than-honest persuasive techniques work, you will make better decisions.

How Do I Recognize Them?

The best way to recognize questionable persuasive techniques is to become familiar with them. Here are several common techniques:

- **Appeal to emotions:** The ad tries to get an emotional response from people, such as fear, anger, or happiness, to move the people to do something.

- **Testimonial:** A famous or important person says that he or she uses a particular product, so viewers and listeners should too—regardless of whether the product is good.

- **Transfer:** The ad connects the product to ideas that make the audience feel good but that don't necessarily have much to do with the product.

- **Repetition:** The ad repeats an idea or phrase over and over so that it sticks in the viewer's or listener's head.

- **Exaggeration:** The ad overstates a point.

- **Bandwagon:** The ad talks about how many other people use a product or act a certain way, making the viewer want to be part of the "in crowd."

Activity Bring an ad from a magazine or newspaper to school. With a small group of classmates, analyze each group member's ad. Which persuasive techniques were used?

Analyzing Cartoons
What advice would you give Curtis to help him recognize questionable persuasive techniques?

Reprinted with permission of King Features Syndicate.

Active Writing Model

Writer's Model

Save Our Planet; Save Ourselves!

The essay begins with an attention-getter and ends with a clear position statement.

Imagine a world without trees, flowers, or animals. It could happen. Every day we pollute the air we breathe, the water we drink, and the ground we grow our food in. Slowly but surely we are ruining this planet. I believe we must take steps to protect the environment, and you should too.

This paragraph gives the first reason that supports the position statement.

Many of us take too many things for granted: our right to drive a big car that uses a lot of gas and our right to use as much water and power as we want. We think we don't have to be responsible for what we do. Soon we will have no clean air to breathe, no clean water to drink, and no healthy soil to grow our food in.

In this paragraph and throughout the essay, the writer gives details to support his point.

We need to start taking better care of the earth because it is a healthier way to live. The environment makes life possible. If we ruin the environment, we are ruining our own bodies. Anything harmful that we put into the earth eventually harms us. When we pollute the ground where we grow our food, the pollution gets into the food. When we eat the food, the pollution gets into our bodies.

The writer uses an emotional appeal to persuade readers to care about the environment.

We should also remember that the world does not belong just to us. It belongs to all people, even those not yet born. We should take care of the planet so that we can pass on a healthful environment to all future generations. Isn't that an important thing to provide for our children and grandchildren? And if we don't, there may not be any future generations.

I believe the environment is the most important thing we have as human beings. If we don't have a healthful environment, we don't have anything, because we need a healthy environment to survive. There is so much that can be done to save our environment. Each of us can consider his or her actions instead of being selfish. We can start by doing simple things like these:

- Recycling newspapers and glass, aluminum, and plastic containers we don't want anymore instead of just throwing them away in the garbage

- Buying products that are made of recycled materials, like paper towels made from recycled paper

- Using less water by taking shorter showers, turning off the tap while we brush our teeth, and not watering the lawn every day during warm months

- Buying smaller cars that use less gas

- Carpooling or using public transportation instead of driving large vehicles with only one or two passengers

- Turning off lights and appliances when we aren't using them

The writer gives readers specific examples of how they can help.

We can all make better choices in the way we live today to ensure a safe and healthy tomorrow. It's not too late. We can still save our environment. Please join me in doing so.

The conclusion sums up what was said before and ends with a call to action.

READING WORKSHOP 4

Skills Focus

You will practice using these skills when you read the following selections:

- "Rally for Better Food," student flyer and poster, p. 1002
- "Stop the Sun," p. 1008

Reading

- Clarifying ideas and text

Informational Text

- Recognizing faulty reasoning
- Identifying the story climax

Vocabulary

- Understanding connotation and denotation
- Academic Vocabulary: *clarify*

Writing/Grammar

- Using dashes and parentheses correctly

NY English Language Arts Core Curriculum (pp. 998–999)

LC R12 Combine multiple strategies to enhance comprehension and response.

For a complete description of the standards, see p. NY11.

Skill Lesson

Clarifying

Learn It!

What Is It? To **clarify** is to make something clear and understandable. To clarify as you read is to clear up confusing or difficult passages. Sometimes a word, a sentence, an idea, or even a whole selection of text can be confusing. When you don't understand something you're reading, you need to clarify what it means so that you don't get "lost."

Analyzing Cartoons
What is clarified for the mother in the cartoon?

FOXTROT © 1998 Bill Amend. Reprinted with permission of UNIVERSAL PRESS SYNDICATE. All rights reserved.

Academic Vocabulary

clarify (KLAYR ih fy) *v.* make clear

Why Is It Important? Writers often build ideas on other ideas. If you don't clear up a confusing passage as you're reading, you may not understand main ideas or information that comes later.

How Do I Do It? First, figure out why you find the passage hard to understand. Then apply a strategy that will help you clear up the difficulty. Here are some ideas to get you started.

- **Unfamiliar words:** Find definitions in a dictionary or through context clues. Plug them in and reread the passage.
- **Long, complicated sentences:** Find the main ideas by looking for subjects and verbs. Put the ideas in your own words.
- **Too many unfamiliar concepts:** Find basic information by doing a quick Internet search. Or grab an encyclopedia to find basic information about the concepts.

Here's how a student clarified a difficult sentence in "The Trouble with Television" to better understand it.

> Capturing your attention—and holding it—is the prime motive of most television programming and enhances its role as a profitable advertising vehicle.

First, I reread the sentence. Then I looked up the word "vehicle," which refers to both a form of transportation and the means by which something is expressed. I realized that the author meant that television is a means by which advertising is expressed. Finally, I put the sentence in my own words: "Holding people's attention is important to TV programmers because TV makes money by getting people to watch commercials."

Practice It!

Clarify the following sentence from "The Trouble with Television" by putting the sentence in your own words: *"Forced feeding on trivial fare is not itself a trivial matter."*

Use It!

As you read the selections, note parts that need clarifying. Analyze why they are hard to understand; then strategize.

Literature Online

Study Central Visit www.glencoe.com and click on Study Central to review clarifying.

Before You Read

Rally for Better Food, student flyer and poster

Vocabulary Preview

bogus (BOH gus) *adj.* bad; not real or genuine **(p. 1002)** *The bogus money is worthless, even though it looks real.*

nutritious (noo TRIH shus) *adj.* containing or giving nourishment **(p. 1003)** *The students wanted their cafeteria to serve more nutritious food.*

Write to Learn Write a sentence correctly using each vocabulary word.

English Language Coach

Denotation and Slang Some words have both formal and informal definitions. Take the word *bookmark.* Its formal denotation is "a marker for holding a place in a book." But it also has a slang meaning. If you say to someone that you'll "bookmark" him or her, you're saying you'll save the person's telephone number or email address.

Did you know the slang meaning of *bookmark?* If not, don't feel bad. The slang meaning may no longer be in use. Most slang words go in and out quickly. In fact, one of the points of using slang is to show you're "in"—up to date and in the know.

Writers are aware of slang's power and may use it to their advantage. If a writer wants readers to see him or her as part of their group, the writer might use slang terms the group uses. If a writer has a general audience, however, he or she usually avoids slang so as not to leave anyone out.

Partner Talk With a classmate, find the slang terms in the following ad. Together, identify what age group you think the writer is trying to reach and why.

Are You a Star?

Show them who you are. Be a star. Wear Star shoes.
They come in all of today's styles.
They're all that and a bag o' chips!

NY English Language Arts Core Curriculum (pp. 1000–1003)

Core R5 Distinguish between dictionary meaning and implied meaning of the author's words. **LC R12** Combine multiple strategies to enhance comprehension and response. **R3a** Evaluate examples, details, or reasons used to support ideas.

For a complete description of the standards, see p. NY11.

Skills Preview

Key Reading Skill: Clarifying

Skim the student cafeteria flyer and poster to see if there are any words you don't know. List them in your Learner's Notebook. Then try to clarify their meanings by looking for context clues.

Write to Learn Jot down definitions for the words on your list. As you read, see if your definitions make sense.

Key Text Element: Faulty Reasoning

Faulty reasoning is flawed thinking, or thinking that has errors in it. You may find faulty reasoning in any form of persuasion such as commercials and ads, political speeches, and letters to the editor.

Though faulty reasoning may be accidental, advertisers and others may use it on purpose. That's why it's important to recognize errors in thinking. Here are some common examples:

Either/Or Fallacy: saying there are only two choices when there are actually more.

• *Example:* America—love it or leave it.

(Ask yourself, *Is there really no middle ground?*)

Faulty Cause and Effect: believing that because one event came before another, the first event caused the second event to happen

• *Example:* The last two games we won, I wore my favorite ring. That ring must be lucky.

(Ask yourself, *Did the ring actually cause the wins?*)

Bandwagon: thinking something's right because it's popular and "everybody's doing it."

• *Example:* Everybody's voting for Ed! Don't vote for Nancy. You'll just waste your vote.

(Ask yourself, *Is it true that everybody's doing it? And is something right just because it's popular?*)

Whole Class Discussion Brainstorm examples of each of the types of faulty reasoning. Are there other types you want to add to your list?

Get Ready to Read

Connect to the Reading

Have you ever felt so strongly about something that you wanted to convince others of your ideas?

Partner Talk Describe the cause of your feelings and any actions you took to persuade others.

Build Background

The student flyer and poster are examples that could have been written by eighth graders who wanted to fight for more healthful and nutritious food in their school cafeteria.

Nutrition has a major impact on your body and your mind. It can affect your health, your growth, and your ability to learn. Studies show that many school-aged children are not getting the nutrients they need. Their diets are high in sugar and fats, which can cause obesity. The number of overweight kids between the ages of six and seventeen has increased greatly in the United States in the last thirty years. This has become a serious issue because being overweight can increase the risk of illness.

Set Purposes for Reading

BIG Question Read the student flyer and poster to learn how some students might urge others to fight for more nutritious food in their school.

Set Your Own Purpose What would you like to learn from the student flyer and poster to help you answer the Big Question? Write your own purpose on the "Rally for Better Food" page of your Foldable 7.

Interactive Literary Elements Handbook
To review or learn more about the literary elements, go to www.glencoe.com.

Keep Moving

Use these skills as you read the following selection.

Practice the Skills

FRIENDS DON'T LET FRIENDS EAT THE CAFETERIA FOOD!

We demand fresher, healthier, and better-tasting food!
Come to a rally after school on March 15, 2006, outside the cafeteria to boycott the BOGUS grub we are being served!

Reasons to attend:

▶ Either you protest NOW, or you suffer for the rest of your school days! **1**

▶ Being healthy will make you happy, popular, and successful!

▶ EVERYONE will be there! **2**

REMEMBER, YOU ARE WHAT YOU EAT!

1 **Key Text Element**

Faulty Reasoning This is an example of "either/or thinking." Students want to persuade others to join the rally by claiming there are only two choices—joining the rally or suffering. Aren't there other courses of action? Explain your answer.

2 **Key Text Element**

Faulty Reasoning The writer of this flyer is trying to persuade others to join the rally by claiming, "Everyone will be there!" What type of faulty reasoning is this?

Vocabulary

bogus (BOH gus) *adj.* bad; not real or genuine

Practice the Skills

FOOD FIGHT 3

Junk the Junk
&
Come to a rally for more nutritious food

March 15, 2006
outside the cafeteria after school

NO MORE BOGUS GRUB! 4

It's your life, and you're the only one who's going to live it! 5

3 Key Reading Skill

Clarifying This attention-grabbing phrase has two meanings in this context. Can you explain them both? If the answer is "no," reread the flyer to clarify the meaning.

4 English Language Coach

Denotation and Slang What is the slang meaning of *bogus?* Of *grub?* What audience do these words appeal to?

5 BIG Question

Some of the students are unhappy with the food in their cafeteria. Do you think persuading others to participate in a rally is an effective way to get better food? Write your answer on the "Rally for Better Food" page of Foldable 7. Your response will help you answer the Unit Challenge later.

After You Read

Rally for Better Food, student flyer and poster

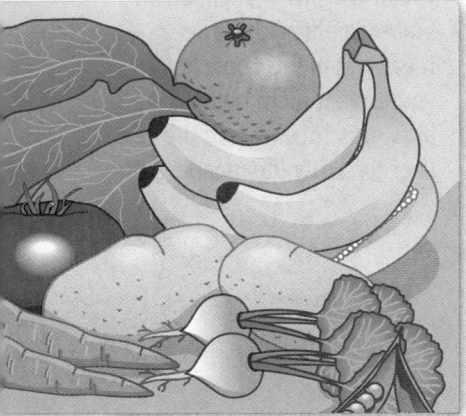

Answering the **BIG Question**

1. Do you think fighting for healthier food in the cafeteria is a worthy cause? Why or why not?

2. **Recall** What reasons does the author of the flyer give to try to persuade the students to "protest now"?

   TIP Right There

3. **Summarize** In your own words, summarize the message of the student flyer and poster.

   TIP Think and Search

Critical Thinking

4. **Analyze** Why is being healthy important to the students who created the flyer?

   TIP Author and Me

5. **Interpret** What does "junk the junk" mean? Put it in your own words.

   TIP Author and Me

6. **Evaluate** Do you think the author's reasons to rally are strong or weak? Explain your answer.

   TIP Author and Me

Write About Your Reading

Persuasive Poster What issue do you feel strongly about? Take a stand and make a persuasive poster. Follow these guidelines:

- Make the issue—and your stand on it—clear.
- Use words and pictures to capture people's attention and make them care about the issue.
- Make every word count. Don't try to squeeze too many words on to your poster. People should be able to read it easily from several feet away.
- Avoid faulty reasoning.
- Avoid semantic slanting.

NY English Language Arts Core Curriculum (pp. 1004–1005)

LC R17 Demonstrate comprehension and response through a range of activities.
LC W4 Compose mechanically grade-appropriate texts for a variety of purposes.
LC R12 Combine multiple strategies to enhance comprehension and response.
R3a Evaluate examples, details, or reasons used to support ideas. **Core R5** Distinguish between dictionary meaning and implied meaning of the author's words.
Core W7 Observe rules of punctuation.

For a complete description of the standards, see p. NY11.

Skills Review

Key Reading Skill: Clarifying

7. Clarify the expression "You are what you eat" by putting it in your own words.

Key Text Element: Faulty Reasoning

8. What form of faulty reasoning is used in this sentence: "Being healthy will make you happy, popular, and successful"?

9. What information could have been included in the flyer and poster to avoid faulty reasoning?

Vocabulary Check

Fill in each blank with a vocabulary word from the list.

bogus • nutritious

10. Fruits and vegetables are _____ food.

11. It was easy to tell that the money was _____ because it was printed on the wrong color paper.

12. English Language Coach What are some slang terms you and your friends use? How would you define the words? Make your own slang dictionary by choosing five slang terms and writing definitions for them. Use a chart like the one below.

Slang Word	Part of Speech	Definition

13. Academic Vocabulary Explain three ways that you can **clarify** the meaning of something you read.

Grammar Link: Dashes

A **dash** (–) is used in pairs to set off a long explanatory phrase or sudden break in thought.

• The books I read—*Great Aviators of the United States, What Happened to Amelia Earhart?* and *Famous Women of the 20th Century*—made me feel that Amelia Earhart was truly brave.

• I was confused—I had, after all, missed two days of school—so I asked my teacher for help.

In the first example the explanatory phrase that names the three books is set off with dashes because it is very long.

In the second example the clause *I had, after all, missed two days of school* is set off because it shows a sudden shift in thought.

Grammar Practice

Copy each of the following sentences on a separate sheet of paper. Add dashes wherever they are needed.

14. The rainforest a place I definitely hope to visit someday with my family is home to some amazing animals.

15. Flying frogs they glide through the air rather than fly, incidentally can be found in Africa.

16. There were only 30 seconds left in the game the team was down by one point when Jaquil took a jump shot and saved the day.

17. Your new shoes not the red denim sneakers but the blue leather ones are the most interesting I've ever seen!

Writing Application Look back at the persuasive poster you made. If you used dashes, make sure that you correctly used them. Also look for sentences that might need dashes.

Web Activities For eFlashcards, Selection Quick Checks, and other Web activities, go to www.glencoe.com.

Before You Read : Stop the Sun

Gary Paulsen

Meet the Author

Gary Paulsen, a young adult novelist, writes survival stories. Paulsen credits his own survival in many ways to books. Never a dedicated student, Paulsen developed a passion for reading at an early age. As a young man he met a librarian, who changed his life. "When she handed me a library card, she handed me the world," he says. See page R5 of the Author Files for more on Paulsen.

Author Search For more about Gary Paulsen, go to www.glencoe.com.

NY English Language Arts Core Curriculum (pp. 1006–1015)

LC R9 Recognize multiple meanings of words and connections among meanings of words. **LC R12** Combine multiple strategies to enhance comprehension and response. **R2b** Interpret characters, plot, setting, theme, and dialogue, using evidence from the text.

For a complete description of the standards, see p. NY11.

Vocabulary Preview

syndrome (SIN drohm) *n.* a group of symptoms that point to a certain disease **(p. 1008)** *Terry's father was not the only one to suffer from the terrible effects of Vietnam syndrome.*

dry (dry) *adj.* dull or boring; not interesting **(p. 1009)** *The history books may have made a dry history of the war, but there was nothing boring about it to Terry's father.*

foundered (FOWN durd) *v.* broke down; collapsed; form of the verb *founder* **(p. 1012)** *Terry almost foundered when he saw how much his father did not want to discuss Vietnam.*

inert (in URT) *adj.* without power to move or act; lifeless **(p. 1013)** *The father's hands lay inert on the table as he told the horrible story.*

Write to Learn Create a crossword puzzle using the vocabulary. For clues write fill-in-the-blank sentences. Exchange puzzles with a classmate.

English Language Coach

Connotation and Denotation Denotation is the literal meaning of a word. Its connotations are the thoughts, feelings, and mental pictures that the word brings to mind.

What do you picture when you hear the word *clever?* Does that picture change when you hear the word *sly?* Both words have about the same denotation. Yet the connotations of *clever* and *sly* are very different. *Clever* has positive connotations, and *sly* has negative ones.

On Your Own Copy the chart onto a separate sheet of paper. Then complete it using words with the opposite connotation. The first one has been done for you.

Positive Connotation	Negative Connotation
playful	silly
unique	
carefree	

Skills Preview

Key Reading Skill: Clarifying

Before you read the selection, make three columns in your Learner's Notebook, and fill them in as you read:

- one for new vocabulary
- one for phrases or ideas that you don't know
- one for questions you have as you read

Partner Talk With a partner, discuss what you know about the Vietnam War. Using resources like the Internet, find out why the war was fought.

Literary Element: Climax

The **climax** of a story is the point of highest interest or suspense in the plot. It is the moment at which the central, or most important, conflict comes to a head. Often the climax is the moment when a main character makes an important realization or decision that affects how—or whether—the conflict is resolved. The ending of a story is dependent upon what happens during the climax.

To identify the climax of "Stop the Sun," ask yourself these questions:

- *Who is the most important character in the story?*
- *What conflict is the main character experiencing?*
- *At what point does the character make a decision or have a realization that affects the outcome of the conflict?*

Partner Talk With a partner, review a story you read in another unit of this book. Skim the story to refresh your memory of it. Discuss what you think the climax of the story is and why.

Get Ready to Read

Connect to the Reading

Have you ever had trouble communicating with a good friend or with a member of your family? How did you feel? Think of several words or phrases to describe that feeling. As you read "Stop the Sun," ask yourself whether Terry shares some of the feelings you had.

Whole Class Discussion As a group, list some of the reasons why family members might have trouble communicating at times.

Build Background

"Stop the Sun" takes place during the 1980s, but Terry's father cannot forget his experiences as a soldier during the Vietnam War.

- From 1965 to 1973, U.S. troops fought in Vietnam alongside the South Vietnamese against Communist North Vietnam.
- Many young Americans protested the war, believing it was a war that the U.S. had no business fighting.
- In 1973 all American troops were pulled out of Vietnam.
- Many soldiers returning from Vietnam suffered from physical or psychological problems as a result of their experiences during the war.

Set Purposes for Reading

BIG Question Read "Stop the Sun" to find out what a teenage boy and his father believe is worth fighting for.

Set Your Own Purpose What would you like to learn from the story to help you answer the Big Question? Write your own purpose on the "Stop the Sun" flap of Foldable 7.

Literature Online

Interactive Literary Elements Handbook
To review or learn more about the literary elements, go to www.glencoe.com.

Keep Moving

Use these skills as you read the following selection.

Stop the Sun

by Gary Paulsen

Con Thien Run, 1967. H. Avery Chenowith. Acrylic, 3½ x 2½ ft. United States Marine Corps Art Collection.

Practice the Skills

Terry Erickson was a tall boy, 13, starting to fill out with muscle but still a little awkward. He was on the edge of being a good athlete, which meant a lot to him. He felt it coming too slowly, though, and that bothered him.

But what bothered him even more was when his father's eyes went away.

Usually it happened when it didn't cause any particular trouble. Sometimes during a meal his father's fork would stop halfway to his mouth, just stop, and there would be a long pause while the eyes went away, far away. **1**

After several minutes his mother would reach over and take the fork and put it gently down on his plate, and they would go back to eating—or try to go back to eating—normally.

They knew what caused it. When it first started, Terry had asked his mother in private what it was, what was causing the strange behavior.

"It's from the war," his mother had said. "The doctors at the veterans' hospital call it the Vietnam **syndrome**."[1]

1 Key Reading Skill

Clarifying What happens when the father's eyes "go away"? If you're not sure, read on.

---

1. ***Vietnam syndrome*** refers to physical and psychological problems that many Vietnam veterans have because of their experiences in the war. Symptoms of the psychological problems include anger, nervousness, and nightmares.

Vocabulary

syndrome (SIN drohm) *n.* a group of symptoms that point to a certain disease

"Will it go away?"

"They don't know. Sometimes it goes away. Sometimes it doesn't. They are trying to help him."

"But what happened? What actually caused it?" **2**

"I told you. Vietnam."

"But there had to be something," Terry persisted. "Something made him like that. Not just Vietnam. Billy's father was there, and he doesn't act that way."

"That's enough questions," his mother said sternly. "He doesn't talk about it, and I don't ask. Neither will you. Do you understand?"

"But, Mom."

"That's enough."

And he stopped pushing it. But it bothered him whenever it happened. When something bothered him, he liked to stay with it until he understood it, and he understood no part of this.

Words. His father had trouble, and they gave him words like Vietnam syndrome. He knew almost nothing of the war, and when he tried to find out about it, he kept hitting walls. Once he went to the school library and asked for anything they might have that could help him understand the war and how it affected his father. They gave him a **dry** history that described French involvement, Communist involvement, American involvement. But it told him nothing of the war. It was all numbers, cold numbers, and nothing of what had *happened*. There just didn't seem to be anything that could help him. **3**

Another time he stayed after class and tried to talk to Mr. Carlson, who taught history. But some part of Terry was embarrassed. He didn't want to say why he wanted to know about Vietnam, so he couldn't be specific.

"What do you want to know about Vietnam, Terry?" Mr. Carlson had asked. "It was a big war."

Terry had looked at him, and something had started up in his mind, but he didn't let it out. He shrugged. "I just want to know what it was like. I know somebody who was in it."

"A friend?"

"Yessir. A good friend."

Practice the Skills

2 **Reviewing Skills**

Predicting Do you think Terry's father's episodes will "go away" or get worse as the story progresses? Why?

3 **Key Reading Skill**

Clarifying Reread this paragraph to understand what kind of information Terry finds when he tries to research the effects of the war on veterans. Are there terms that you are unfamiliar with? Write them in your Learner's Notebook.

Vocabulary

dry (dry) *adj.* dull or boring; not interesting

Mr. Carlson had studied him, looking into his eyes, but didn't ask any other questions. Instead he mentioned a couple of books Terry had not seen. They turned out to be pretty good. They told about how it felt to be in combat. Still, he couldn't make his father be one of the men he read about.

And it may have gone on and on like that, with Terry never really knowing any more about it except that his father's eyes started going away more and more often. It might have just gone the rest of his life that way except for the shopping mall.

It was easily the most embarrassing thing that ever happened to him.

It started as a normal shopping trip. His father had to go to the hardware store, and he asked Terry to go along.

When they got to the mall they split up. His father went to the hardware store, Terry to a record store to look at albums.

Terry browsed so long that he was late meeting his father at the mall's front door. But his father wasn't there, and Terry looked out to the car to make sure it was still in the parking lot. It was, and he supposed his father had just gotten busy, so he waited.

Still his father didn't come, and he was about to go to the hardware store to find him when he noticed the commotion. Or not a commotion so much as a sudden movement of people. ◀4

Later, he thought of it and couldn't remember when the feeling first came to him that there was something wrong. The people were moving toward the hardware store and that might have been what made Terry suspicious.

There was a crowd blocking the entry to the store, and he couldn't see what they were looking at. Some of them were laughing small, nervous laughs that made no sense.

Terry squeezed through the crowd until he got near the front. At first he saw nothing unusual. There were still some

War & Peace, 1990. Tsing-Fang Chen. Acrylic on canvas, 66 x 96 in. Lucia Gallery, New York.

Analyzing the Painting How does the artist depict opposing ideas—war and peace—in this painting?

Practice the Skills

4 | **Reviewing Skills**

Predicting What do you think the commotion is? Give reasons for your prediction.

people in front of him, so he pushed a crack between them. Then he saw it: His father was squirming along the floor on his stomach. He was crying, looking terrified, his breath coming in short, hot pants like some kind of hurt animal.

It burned into Terry's mind, the picture of his father down on the floor. It burned in and in, and he wanted to walk away, but something made his feet move forward. He knelt next to his father and helped the owner of the store get him up on his feet. His father didn't speak at all but continued to make little whimpering sounds, and they led him back into the owner's office and put him in a chair. Then Terry called his mother and she came in a taxi to take them home. Waiting, Terry sat in a chair next to his father, looking at the floor, wanting only for the earth to open and let him drop in a deep hole. He wanted to disappear. **5**

Words. They gave him words like Vietnam syndrome, and his father was crawling through a hardware store on his stomach. **6**

When the embarrassment became so bad that he would cross the street when he saw his father coming, when it ate into him as he went to sleep, Terry realized he had to do something. He had to know this thing, had to understand what was wrong with his father.

When it came, it was simple enough at the start. It had taken some courage, more than Terry thought he could find. His father was sitting in the kitchen at the table and his mother had gone shopping. Terry wanted it that way; he wanted his father alone. His mother seemed to try to protect him, as if his father could break.

Terry got a soda out of the refrigerator and popped it open. As an afterthought, he handed it to his father and got another for himself. Then he sat at the table.

His father smiled. "You look serious."

"Well . . ."

It went nowhere for a moment, and Terry was just about to drop it altogether. It may be the wrong time, he thought, but there might never be a better one. He tightened his back, took a sip of pop.

"I was wondering if we could talk about something, Dad," Terry said.

Practice the Skills

5 **Literary Element**

Climax The incident in the hardware store intensifies Terry's need to understand his father. This is the rising action leading to the climax.

6 **English Language Coach**

Connotation and Denotation An older term that means about the same as "Vietnam syndrome" is *shell shock*. Which of the two terms sounds more negative? Why?

His father shrugged. "We already did the bit about girls. Some time ago, as I remember it."

"No. Not that." It was a standing joke[2] between them. When his father finally got around to explaining things to him, they'd already covered it in school. "It's something else."

"Something pretty heavy, judging by your face."

"Yes."

"Well?"

I still can't do it, Terry thought. Things are bad, but maybe not as bad as they could get. I can still drop this thing.

"Vietnam," Terry blurted out. And he thought, there, it's out. It's out and gone.

"No!" his father said sharply. It was as if he had been struck a blow. A body blow.

"But, Dad."

"No. That's another part of my life. A bad part. A rotten part. It was before I met your mother, long before you. It has nothing to do with this family, nothing. No."

So, Terry thought, so I tried. But it wasn't over yet. It wasn't started yet.

"It just seems to bother you so much," Terry said, "and I thought if I could help or maybe understand it better. . . ." His words ran until he **foundered**, until he could say no more. He looked at the table, then out the window. It was all wrong to bring it up, he thought. I blew it. I blew it all up. "I'm sorry." **7**

But now his father didn't hear him. Now his father's eyes were gone again, and a shaft of something horrible went through Terry's heart as he thought he had done this thing to his father, caused his eyes to go away.

"You can't know," his father said after a time. "You can't know this thing."

Terry said nothing. He felt he had said too much.

"This thing that you want to know—there is so much of it that you cannot know it all, and to know only a part is . . . is too awful. I can't tell you. I can't tell anybody what it was really like."

---

2. A *standing joke* is one that continues to be told or shared over time.

7 | Key Reading Skill

Clarifying When Terry "foundered," what did he do? Clarify what he did and why by putting it in your own words.

Vocabulary

foundered (FOWN durd) *v.* broke down; collapsed

It was more than he'd ever said about Vietnam, and his voice was breaking. Terry hated himself and felt he would hate himself until he was an old man. In one second he had caused such ruin. And all because he had been embarrassed. What difference did it make? Now he had done this, and he wanted to hide, to leave. But he sat, waiting, knowing that it wasn't done.

His father looked to him, through him, somewhere into and out of Terry. He wasn't in the kitchen anymore. He wasn't in the house. He was back in the green places, back in the hot places, the wet-hot places. **8**

"You think that because I act strange, that we can talk and it will be all right," his father said. "That we can talk and it will just go away. That's what you think, isn't it?"

Terry started to shake his head, but he knew it wasn't expected.

"That's what the shrinks say," his father continued. "The psychiatrists tell me that if I talk about it, the whole thing will go away. But they don't know. They weren't there. You weren't there. Nobody was there but me and some other dead people, and they can't talk because they couldn't stop the morning."

Terry pushed his soda can back and forth, looking down, frightened at what was happening. *The other dead people,* he'd said, as if he were dead as well. *Couldn't stop the morning.*

"I don't understand, Dad."

"No. You don't." His voice hardened, then softened again, and broke at the edges. "But see, see how it was. . . ." He trailed off, and Terry thought he was done. His father looked back down to the table, at the can of soda he hadn't touched, at the tablecloth, at his hands, which were folded, **inert** on the table.

"We were crossing a rice paddy in the dark," he said, and suddenly his voice flowed like a river breaking loose. "We

8 ▸ **Key Reading Skill**

Clarifying Where are the green places? How can you tell?

Analyzing the Image Here, farmers harvest rice in a Vietnamese paddy. What can you learn from this image about the place where Terry's father fought?

Vocabulary

inert (in URT) *adj.* without power to move or act; lifeless

were crossing the paddy, and it was dark, still dark, so black you couldn't see the end of your nose. There was a light rain, a mist, and I was thinking that during the next break I would whisper and tell Petey Kressler how nice the rain felt, but of course I didn't know there wouldn't be a Petey Kressler."

He took a deep, ragged breath. At that moment Terry felt his brain swirl, a kind of whirlpool pulling, and he felt the darkness and the light rain because it was in his father's eyes, in his voice. **9**

"So we were crossing the paddy, and it was a straight sweep, and then we caught it. We began taking fire from three sides, automatic weapons, and everybody went down and tried to get low, but we couldn't. We couldn't get low enough. We could never get low enough, and you could hear the rounds hitting people. It was just a short time before they brought in the mortars³ and we should have moved, should have run, but nobody got up, and after a time nobody *could* get up. The fire just kept coming and coming, and then incoming mortars, and I heard screams as they hit, but there was nothing to do. Nothing to do."

"Dad?" Terry said. He thought, maybe I can stop him. Maybe I can stop him before . . . before it gets to be too much. Before he breaks.

"Mortars," his father went on, "I hated mortars. You just heard them *wump* as they fired, and you didn't know where they would hit, and you always felt like they would hit your back. They swept back and forth with the mortars, and the automatic weapons kept coming in, and there was no radio, no way to call for artillery. Just the dark to hide in. So I crawled to the side and found Jackson, only he wasn't there, just part of his body, the top part, and I hid under it and waited, and waited, and waited.

"Finally the firing quit. But see, see how it was in the dark with nobody alive but me? I yelled once, but that brought fire again, so I shut up and there was nothing, not even the screams."

His father cried, and Terry tried to understand, and he thought he could feel part of it. But it was so much, so much and so strange to him.

Practice the Skills

9 | **Key Reading Skill**

Clarifying How can darkness and rain be in the father's eyes and voice? Explain in your own words what the author means.

---

3. *Mortars* are small, portable cannons that fire explosive shells.

"You cannot know this," his father repeated. It was almost a chant. "You cannot know the fear. It was almost dark, and I was the only one left alive out of 54 men, all dead but me, and I knew that the Vietcong were just waiting for light. When the dawn came, 'Charley'[4] would come out and finish everybody off, the way they always did. And I thought if I could stop the dawn, just stop the sun from coming up, I could make it." **10**

Terry felt the fear, and he also felt the tears coming down his cheeks. His hand went out across the table, and he took his father's hand and held it. It was shaking.

"I mean I actually thought that if I could stop the sun from coming up, I could live. I made my brain work on that because it was all I had. Through the rest of the night in the rain in the paddy, I thought I could do it. I could stop the dawn." He took a deep breath. "But you can't, you know. You can't stop it from coming, and when I saw the gray light, I knew I was dead. It would just be minutes, and the light would be full, and I just settled under Jackson's body, and hid."

He stopped, and his face came down into his hands. Terry stood and went around the table to stand in back of him, his hands on his shoulders, rubbing gently.

"They didn't shoot me. They came, one of them poked Jackson's body and went on and they left me. But I was dead. I'm still dead, don't you see? I died because I couldn't stop the sun. I died. Inside where I am—I died."

Terry was still in back of him, and he nodded, but he didn't see. Not that. He understood only that he didn't understand, and that he would probably never understand what had truly happened. And maybe his father would never be truly normal.

But Terry also knew that it didn't matter. He would try to understand, and the trying would have to be enough. He would try hard from now on, and he would not be embarrassed when his father's eyes went away. He would not be embarrassed no matter what his father did. Terry had knowledge now. Maybe not enough and maybe not all that he would need.

But it was a start. **11** ○

---

4. The **Vietcong** were the Communist forces. American soldiers often referred to them as **Charley.**

Practice the Skills

10 **Literary Element**

Climax During the climax of a story, a main character usually comes to an important realization. What does the father realize here?

11 **BIG Question**

Why does Terry believe it's so important to get his dad to talk about Vietnam? Write your answer on the "Stop the Sun" flap of your Foldable. Your response will help you complete the Unit Challenge later.

Stop the Sun **1015**

After You Read

Stop the Sun

Answering the BIG Question

1. Would you fight for a better relationship with a close family member? Why or why not?

2. **Recall** What event caused Terry's father's problems?
   TIP Right There

3. **List** List three ways Terry goes about trying to find the cause of his father's problems.
   TIP Think and Search

Critical Thinking

4. **Analyze** Why do you think Terry's father insists that Vietnam has "nothing to do with this family"? Do you agree? Explain.
   TIP Author and Me

5. **Interpret** What does the following sentence about Terry mean? "When something bothered him, he liked to stay with it until he understood it, and he understood no part of this."
   TIP Author and Me

6. **Evaluate** Is "Stop the Sun" a good title for this story? Why or why not? Explain your answer by giving details from the story.
   TIP Author and Me

Talk About Your Reading

Small Group Discussion Form a group of three or four students. Discuss the following questions. There is no right answer. Talk about the reasons behind your answers.

- How do Terry's feelings for his father change throughout the story?
- How might knowing about a family member's past affect how others feel about the person?
- What have you learned about the ways world events can affect ordinary families?

NY English Language Arts Core Curriculum (pp. 1016–1017)

LC R17 Demonstrate comprehension and response through a range of activities. **LC S8** Participate in group discussions on a range of topics and for a variety of purposes. **LC R12** Combine multiple strategies to enhance comprehension and response. **R2b** Interpret characters, plot, setting, theme, and dialogue, using evidence from the text. **LC R9** Recognize multiple meanings of words and connections among meanings of words. **Core W7** Observe rules of punctuation.

For a complete description of the standards, see p. NY11.

Skills Review

Key Reading Skill: Clarifying

7. What skills did you use to clarify as you read? Which ones were most helpful and why? Which ones were least helpful and why?

Literary Element: Climax

8. What does Terry understand, and not understand, about his father after the climax occurs?

9. How does the action of the characters at the climax affect the outcome of the story?

Reviewing Skills: Predicting

10. How do you think Terry's experiences with his father will affect Terry as he grows up? What do you think he will learn from them? How do you think they will shape him as a person?

Vocabulary Check

Answer each question with the best word from the list. Some words will be used more than once.

syndrome • dry • foundered • inert

11. Which word suggests an activity that comes to a stop?

12. Which word relates to a medical condition?

13. Which word means "unable to move"?

14. Which word could you use to describe a topic that doesn't appeal to you at all?

15. Which TWO words could be antonyms for *lively?*

16. **English Language Coach** Explain why the term *Vietnam syndrome* is confusing to Terry.

Web Activities For eFlashcards, Selection Quick Checks, and other Web activities, go to www.glencoe.com.

Grammar Link: Parentheses

Parentheses ( ) are punctuation marks used to set off words that define or explain another word. You can replace commas with parentheses to separate words more clearly from the rest of the sentence. Use them to include a) extra information about a subject, b) a reflection, or c) an afterthought.

• Marian Wright Edelman, the founder of the Children's Defense Fund, has fought for the civil rights of young Americans for more than 30 years.

• Marian Wright Edelman (the founder of the Children's Defense Fund) has fought for the civil rights of young Americans for more than 30 years.

• Neil Armstrong took his first step on the moon (who could have imagined it was possible?) on July 20, 1969.

• Spinach helps prevent anemia (as do kidney beans) because it is an excellent source of iron.

Grammar Practice

Rewrite each sentence, adding parentheses where they are needed.

17. Edelman's father a Baptist minister taught his children the importance of taking care of others.

18. Edelman's essay originally a letter to her sons gives many important life lessons we can all adopt.

19. Soccer a national sport in the United Kingdom has gained popularity in this country.

20. Violets are very hardy and beautiful, for I've seen them growing out of a crack in the sidewalk.

21. It must have been exciting although a bit scary to have traveled with Columbus in 1492.

22. Neil Armstrong the first astronaut to walk on the moon said, "One small step for man, one giant leap for mankind."

Teens Tackle
POLLUTION &
in Their Communities
by Sara Steindorf

A CHANGE IN CLIMATE
by Emily Sohn

Skills Focus

You will use these skills as you read and compare the following selections:
- "Teens Tackle Pollution in Their Communities," p. 1021
- "A Change in Climate," p. 1027

Reading

- Comparing and contrasting elements in different texts

Informational Text

- Recognizing and analyzing persuasive appeals

Writing

- Writing to compare and contrast

NY English Language Arts Core Curriculum (pp. 1018–1019)

R3a Identify techniques author uses to persuade (emotional and ethical appeals).

For a complete description of the standards, see p. NY11.

Writers often write with a single purpose: to convince their readers to think, feel, or act in a certain way. This type of writing is called persuasive writing. And it's everywhere—in advertisements, in letters to the editor, and in articles like some of the ones you've read in this unit.

How to Compare Literature: Persuasive Appeals

As you read "Teens Tackle Pollution in Their Communities" and "A Change in Climate," ask yourself the questions in the chart below to help yourself recognize persuasive appeals.

Does the writer make . . .		
an appeal to **reason?**	an **emotional** appeal?	an **ethical** appeal?
Does the writer clearly state a thesis or main point?	Does the writer use words or images that make you feel strong emotions, such as anger, sadness, sympathy, or alarm?	Does the writer seem knowledgeable and trustworthy? Is he or she fair to opponents?
Does the writer support his or her main point with facts, examples, statistics, or quotations?	Does the writer appeal to your belief in certain ideas, such as freedom, love, patriotism, or justice?	Does the writer appeal to your values and beliefs? Does he or she appeal to your sense of right and wrong?
Do the writer's points make sense?	Does the writing make you feel strongly?	Is the writer trustworthy?

Get Ready to Compare

As you read, keep track of examples of the three persuasive appeals in a chart like the one below. You will use the notes in this chart to compare the selections later.

Persuasive Appeals Comparison Chart			
	Appeals to Reason	Appeals to Emotion	Appeals to Ethics
"Teens Tackle Pollution" Writer's Position:			
"A Change in Climate" Writer's Position:			

Use Your Comparison

Have you ever tried to avoid doing chores at home, or to convince your parents to buy you something? If so, you probably used basic principles of persuasion.

Look at the list below. Pick one statement with which you strongly agree or disagree. Write a paragraph that persuades a friend to think or feel the way you do about the topic you chose. Be creative! Use at least one appeal to reason and one appeal to emotion to make your case.

- Students should not use cell phones at school.
- Video games have educational value.
- People should be able to download music from the Internet for free.
- Schools should ban junk food from cafeteria vending machines.

When you're finished, use the checklist below to revise your paragraph.

- ☑ Did I state my opinion in a clear thesis statement?
- ☑ Did I support my position with facts and examples?
- ☑ Did I include opposing viewpoints to avoid bias?
- ☑ Did I conclude with a summary of my argument, a strong appeal, or a call to action?

Before You Read

Teens Tackle Pollution in Their Communities

Did You Know?
Did you know that nearly 1.5 billion people worldwide lack safe drinking water? That's 25 percent of the planet's population! Did you know that every year, more than 500 million people die of waterborne diseases? Do you think you can take fresh water for granted in this modern age? Unfortunately, you may have to think again.

Vocabulary Preview

emit (ee MIT) *v.* to give off **(p. 1023)** *Cars emit dangerous chemicals from their tailpipes.*

buoyed (BOO eed) *adj.* supported or uplifted **(p. 1023)** *Ruiz felt buoyed by his friends' good wishes.*

English Language Coach

Denotation and Connotation A word's **denotation** expresses its literal, or dictionary, definition. When a word has implied meanings or associations in addition to its dictionary meaning, it has a **connotation.** Writers often use words with connotative meanings to influence readers' attitudes.

Look at the examples of denotation and connotation in the chart below.

Word	Denotation	Connotation
yellowed	made yellow in color	old, worn
nestled	drawn close	safe, snug

Get Ready to Read

Connect to the Reading

Think of a time when you solved a problem to make a positive difference in your world. Who or what motivated you to take action?

Build Background

Check out the list below for tips on how to make your routine more green.
- Recycle! Buy recycled products and products with less packaging.
- Bring your lunch in reusable containers.
- Carpool with friends to get to and from school and practice.

Set Purposes for Reading

BIG Question Read to see how people are fighting for the environment.

Set Your Own Purpose What else would you like to learn from this selection to help you answer the Big Question? Write your own purpose on your Foldable 7.

NY English Language Arts Core Curriculum (pp. 1020–1025)

Core R5 Distinguish between dictionary meaning and implied meaning of the author's words. **R3a** Identify techniques author uses to persuade (emotional and ethical appeals).

For a complete description of the standards, see p. NY11.

Teens Tackle POLLUTION in Their Communities

by Sara Steindorf

I bet you don't recycle your family's dryer lint. You probably don't reduce waste by reusing tuna cans as cookie cutters, either.

That's okay. The earth is packed full of plenty of areas that could stand a little improving. Take a look in your community—perhaps the pollution needs patrolling, or the sea turtles need saving. There's bound to be at least one environmental cause you find interesting and worthwhile.

To celebrate this year's Earth Day,[1] we thought you might enjoy reading about some inspiring young environmentalists. Not only did they realize the powerful effects of a little perseverance and passion, but they also proved to the government, businesses, and even their own critics that kids must be seen and heard. **1**

Barbara: Putting used oil in its place

When Barbara Brown of Victoria, Texas, was 11, her friend Kate noticed her father pouring used motor oil on a fencepost to kill weeds.

"The weeds did die, but we wanted to know: What happened to the oil?" says Barbara, who is now 17.

What Barbara and her friends Kate Klinkerman and Lacy Jones found out was that the toxic oil seeped into the soil— and eventually into the water supply. "What we were doing

Practice the Skills

1 **Reading Across Texts**

Appeal to Ethics The powerful language in this sentence appeals to the readers' sense of right and wrong. To what values or beliefs does the writer appeal here?

---

1. **Earth Day** is a day set aside each spring to celebrate the Earth and its resources. The first Earth Day was in 1970.

These teens hand out information—and recycling containers—at a used oil recycling booth. Why might efforts like this be especially important in farm communities?

on our land was possibly contaminating[2] our own water," Barbara says. **2**

So the trio set out to clean up their own backyards— literally. "We knew that we were just sixth-graders, but that didn't stop us from doing what we believe is right," Barbara says.

In 1998, they formed the program Don't Be Crude, and began educating their community about the dangers of using motor fluids as weed and insect killers. (This is a common practice in rural areas like Victoria, especially since many folks live far from car-maintenance locations, which recycle used oil.)

They also got support from the government and businesses to set up five do-it-yourself recycling units in Victoria County.

Today, Don't Be Crude has 18 units in seven counties— and protects thousands of acres of groundwater from contamination through improper fluid disposal, says Barbara.

In addition, the girls speak to audiences across the nation (some as large as 1,500 people) to encourage young people to get involved in protecting the earth. **3**

Sometimes, Barbara says, that involves getting rid of stereotypes.[3]

---

2. If something is ***contaminated,*** it has been poisoned or polluted.

3. A ***stereotype*** is an oversimplified or untrue notion about someone or something.

2 **Reading Across Texts**

Appeal to Reason A logical appeal uses facts, examples, or statistics to build a case. What fact about groundwater pollution do you learn here?

3 **Reading Across Texts**

Appeal to Reason Think about the writer's position on the topic of teen activism. How does she support her position that young environmentalists are proving that kids must be seen and heard? Take notes on your chart.

"In Texas, you're labeled a tree hugger if you do something to help the environment—but I think that's just because people aren't very educated about the environment," she says. **4**

The team also tries to teach others that there's much more to protecting the planet than recycling cans. "People usually know about recycling," she says. "But they often simply don't realize how much more they could be doing."

Amir: Reducing school-bus pollution

In December 2001, Amir Nadav was in his junior year of high school when he decided he wanted to do something more to help the environment. So he wandered into a local Sierra Club⁴ meeting. There, they were discussing new reports on the harmful effects of school-bus idling.

"I thought, this is really cool. I ride a school bus, I have friends who ride school buses, so this is an issue that clearly affects me," says the Eagan, Minn., teen. **5**

School buses **emit** diesel exhaust, and when a driver stops the bus but leaves the engine on, it creates a lot of pollution that could be easily avoided, he says.

So Amir and two friends wrote a petition calling for reduced idling and increased maintenance inspections (a well-maintained vehicle pollutes less). Then they told fellow classmates about their petition—and to their surprise, they got 500 signatures on the first day.

"I was a really shy person, and I didn't have the guts to just go up and approach people," Amir says. "But I felt really empowered because it was something I really believed in." **6**

Buoyed by their success, the petition writers and several Sierra Club members drafted a state bill calling for minimized idling of school buses.

Then they testified before the state legislature. When they ran into opposition, Amir and his co-leaders organized a rally of 150 students on the steps of the state capitol.

---

4. The **Sierra Club** is an environmental organization that works to protect both local communities and the planet as a whole.

Vocabulary

emit (ee MIT) *v.* to give off

buoyed (BOO eed) *adj.* supported or uplifted

Practice the Skills

4 **English Language Coach**

Connotation The term *tree hugger* refers to environmentalists. Do you think its connotations are positive or negative?

5 **Reading Across Texts**

Appeal to Ethics One way a writer establishes credibility is by citing knowledgeable sources. As you read about Amir Nadav, think about why the writer chose to tell his story.

6 **Reading Across Texts**

Appeal to Emotions What personal characteristic did Amir overcome to get the 500 signatures? Why do you think the writer chose to share this detail with readers?

It was a success. They gained not only media attention, but key support from the Senate majority leader. He had walked down to check out the rally, and was impressed with the students' knowledge of the topic, along with the 1,000 signatures on the petition.

Last May, the bill finally became a law.

"If you had told me a few days before I attended that Sierra Club meeting what it would amount to, I would've laughed. It's unbelievable what can happen," he says.

Another lesson Amir learned is the importance of researching a cause he felt strongly about. "It's easy to go out and say, 'I want cleaner buses,'" he says. "But I had to know stuff like: retrofits are things you can do to engines to minimize pollution. Oxidation catalysts are parts you can add to buses to reduce pollution. . . . And diesel exhaust accounts for 75 percent of soot emitted from all vehicles," he says. **7**

Such knowledge helped him feel empowered, especially in the beginning when people basically told him: "What you do won't matter—you don't even have the right to vote!" he says.

This year, the high school senior leads the Sierra Club's anti-idling campaign for students. In his free time, he travels the United States helping students get similar laws passed in their states (only about a dozen states already have bans on idling).

Gina: Paving roads with trash

Three years ago, Gina Gallant was driving with her family in Cash Creek, British Columbia—known locally as "Trash Creek" because of an overflowing landfill site nearby. Suddenly, inspiration struck: Why not use garbage to pave roads?

So the 13-year-old from Prince George, British Columbia, who has been inventing since first grade, took on the challenge.

Gina, now 15, already had some knowledge of road-building, thanks to a job at the asphalt division of Husky Oil. But she still needed to do a lot of research.

Practice the Skills

7 **Reading Across Texts**

Appeal to Ethics and Reason
Amir shows here that he really "knows his stuff." How does this make him a credible source? What facts and statistics does he use to support *his* position on the need for cleaner buses? Make notes on your chart.

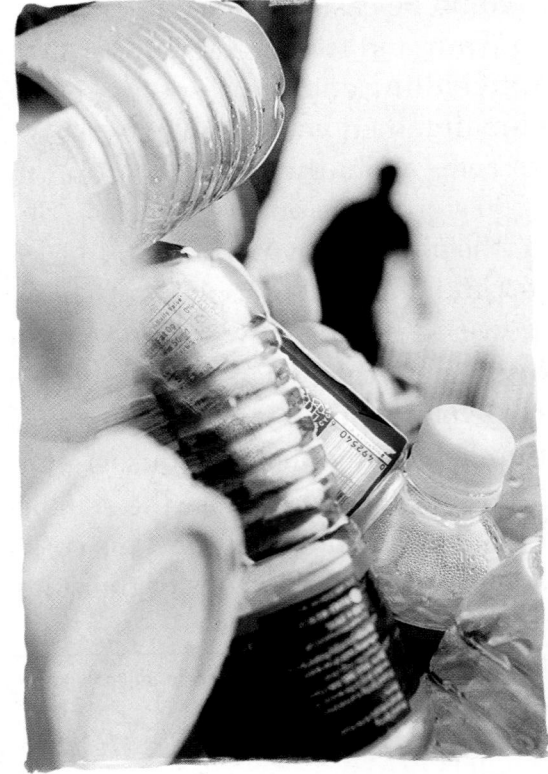

Consider the number of plastic bottles you use each week. Can you, like Gallant, think of any other uses for these landfill-bound containers?

Glass and rubber waste, Gina found, had already been tried in roads in the U.S. The materials hadn't worked well. So she turned to plastic—which takes up a whopping one-third of all landfill space around the world. (Just think of all the milk jugs, laundry-detergent containers, and water bottles that can pile up over time.) **8**

"I thought that since both plastic and asphalt are petroleum-based,[5] they might be compatible," Gina says.

Bingo.

Gina's new paving material, dubbed PAR for PolyAggreRoad, mixes ground-up plastic bottles with stone material and liquid asphalt. To take the product out of the lab and onto the streets, she tracked down companies willing to grind the plastic to her specifications and mix up enough of the compound to pave an actual road.

"At first, some of [the companies] didn't take me seriously because they thought, you know, a 13-year-old can't do something like this," Gina says. "But they finally realized I knew what I was talking about."

Finally, last October, the mayor allowed her to test PAR on a 160-foot strip of a local road. Now she's just waiting to see how her road holds up through freezes and thaws, and abuse from cars. Engineers already suspect the PAR will be able to withstand more movement without cracking than regular roads, Gina says.

"My ultimate goal is for a company to pick up my product," she says, "and to see it go all the way around the world to reduce garbage in landfill sites."

Her advice to others? "Believe in yourself and follow your heart, because if you can think of these ideas, you can do them." **9** ○

Analyzing the Photo A red maple sapling grows in recycled rubber chips. How might this image—and the possibilities it represents—symbolize hope for the future?

Practice the Skills

8 **Reading Across Texts**

Appeal to Reason Facts and examples strengthen any argument. What fact or example does the writer give here? How does it help you understand the pollution problem? Use your chart to take notes.

9 **BIG Question**

How do the teens in this article demonstrate—and fight for—their beliefs? Would you fight for clean air and water the way these young people did? Why or why not? Write your answer on the "Teens Tackle" page of Foldable 7. Your response will help you complete the Unit Challenge later.

---

5. Petroleum is oil. If something is **petroleum-based**, its major component is oil.

Before You Read : A Change in Climate

Emily Sohn

Meet the Author

Emily Sohn is a writer for *Science News for Kids*, a Web site on science news for young people. She writes about a variety of science-related topics, including archaeology, anthropology, astronomy, animals, plants, environmentalism, and more.

Author Search For more about Emily Sohn, go to www.glencoe.com.

NY English Language Arts Core Curriculum (pp. 1026–1031)

Core R5 Distinguish between dictionary meaning and implied meaning of the author's words. **R3a** Identify techniques author uses to persuade (emotional and ethical appeals).

For a complete description of the standards, see p. NY11.

Vocabulary Preview

accumulate (uh KYOOM yuh layt) *v.* gather or build up **(p. 1029)** *If you don't clean your house regularly, dust will accumulate on your tabletops.*

vulnerable (VUL nur uh bul) *adj.* exposed to danger **(p. 1030)** *Many species, large and small, are vulnerable to climate change.*

English Language Coach

Denotation and Connotation Context clues can help you understand a word's connotative meaning. In each sentence below, determine the boldface word's denotative and connotative meanings. Then use context clues to decide whether the connotations are positive or not.

• Some people like the **aroma** of freshly brewed coffee.
• The dry, wilted flowers produced a strange **aroma.**

Get Ready to Read

Connect to the Reading

Try to imagine what your community would be like if it were five degrees warmer every day. In what ways might the change in temperature affect the animals and plants in the area?

Build Background

The term *global warming* refers to an average increase in the earth's temperature. It is the result of human activities that cause pollution. For example, the earth has warmed by one degree Fahrenheit over the past 100 years. One degree doesn't sound like much, but it has already caused significant climate change in some places. Scientists fear the effects of global warming because a warmer Earth may lead to changes in rainfall patterns, a rise in sea level, and serious consequences for plants, wildlife, and people.

Set Purposes for Reading

BIG Question Read to find out how global warming is affecting plant and animal life around the world.

Set Your Own Purpose What else would you like to learn from this selection to help you answer the Big Question? Write your own purpose on your Foldable 7.

A CHANGE IN CLIMATE

by Emily Sohn

From one day to the next, weather can have a big effect on your life. When it rains, you have to stay indoors or carry an umbrella. When it's cold, you have to bundle up.

Over the course of hundreds, thousands, and millions of years, weather trends affect life on Earth in more dramatic ways. Ice ages or long droughts, for example, can wipe out certain types of plants and animals. Although many species manage to survive such extreme, long-term climate shifts, their living conditions also change.

There's lots of evidence of drastic changes in climate occurring in the distant past. Earth today may again be in the midst of such a climate change. In the last 100 years, studies show, global temperatures have risen an average of 0.6 degrees C.

That might not sound so bad. After all, what difference does half a degree make?

A growing number of studies suggest, however, that such an increase could have a big impact on life. **1**

Biologists[1] and ecologists[1] are discovering, often by accident, that climate change is forcing some plants and animals into new habitats. Others are becoming extinct. Sometimes, scientists show up at a site they've studied for years, only to discover that the organisms they've been tracking are no longer there. What's more, it now looks like this redistribution of life on Earth is sometimes happening at an alarmingly fast pace. **2**

---

1. **Biologists** study plants and animals. **Ecologists** study living things and their environments.

Practice the Skills

1 **Reading Across Texts**

Persuasive Appeals Writers of persuasive pieces take a position on an issue and then support that position with evidence. What is the writer's position on the issue of climate change?

2 **Reading Across Texts**

Appeal to Reason The writer gives two examples of the effects of climate change on some animals and plants. Note these examples on your chart.

"These little pieces of information are all warning signs that stuff is going on," says Erik Beever. He's a research ecologist with the United States Geological Survey in Corvallis, Ore. "Our world is changing more rapidly than we have observed in the recent past," he says.

Tree line

One place to look for changes in plant and animal life that may be caused by a climate shift is in the mountains.

As the globe warms up, mountaintops get warmer, too. Trees start growing at higher altitudes than before. The tree line shifts upward.

In the Alps, a mountain range in Europe, records from the last 80 to 100 years show that plants have been working their way upward at a rate of about 4 meters[2] every decade. Researchers from the University of Vienna found this trend in two-thirds of the sites they checked.

In one recent study in Nevada, Beever discovered that a type of tree called the Engleman spruce had moved its habitat upslope a dramatic 650 feet in just 9 years. "The site at the lowest elevation went from 41 individuals to just six," he says. At higher elevations, numbers increased. **3**

"When I first saw the results," Beever says, "I had a really hard time believing it because it's just too fast."

Beever's analysis of the data suggests that global warming is mainly responsible for the shift. Studies in mountain ranges from New Zealand to Spain reveal similar trends.

Global warming

What's causing today's increased temperatures?

Many scientists say that human activities, such as burning coal, oil, and other fossil fuels,[3] are largely to blame. These activities release heat-trapping gases, such as carbon dioxide, into the

---

2. **Four meters** is about 13 feet.
3. **Fossil fuels** are fuels that come from the remains of organisms preserved in rocks in the earth's crust.

Practice the Skills

3 | **Reading Across Texts**

Appeal to Reason What evidence does the writer give to support her assertion about the shifting tree line? Does it help build her case in a logical way? Make notes on your chart.

Analyzing the Photo Smoke from a fossil-fuel refinery billows into the atmosphere. How do scientists explain the relationship between air pollution and global warming?

atmosphere. The more these gases **accumulate** in the atmosphere, the hotter things get on Earth. **4**

Some experts remain skeptical. They point out that natural causes may be playing an important role in today's global temperature increases. The same factors that caused ice ages, extreme heat waves, and massive droughts[4] in the past before human activities were important could still be at work now.

In the case of rising tree lines, they say, trees may still be recovering from an unusually cool period, known as the Little Ice Age,[5] which lasted from the 1300s into the middle of the 1800s. It's even possible that efforts to put out fires allow plants to move into new habitats. **5**

Mountain islands

Scientists predict that average temperatures may go up another 1.4 to 5.8 degrees in the next 100 years. If it occurs, such a rapid increase wouldn't give plants and animals much time to adapt to new conditions. **6**

Organisms that live on mountains may face the grimmest future. That's because mountaintops are, in many ways, like islands. They're isolated clearings that poke up above the tree line.

Although it's too cold for trees to grow at such heights, these alpine environments are ideal habitats for some animals, which have become highly specialized to live there.

"A lot of populations are just little **frostings** on peaks," says James Brown. Brown is a population ecologist at the University of New Mexico, who was recently quoted in the journal *Science*. **7**

Like animals on islands, these mountaintop creatures have no escape if conditions change.

---

4. A **drought** (drowt) is a shortage of water.

5. During the **Ice Age,** glaciers covered a large part of the earth's surface.

Vocabulary

accumulate (uh KYOOM yuh layt) *v.* gather or build up

Practice the Skills

4 **Reading Across Texts**

Appeal to Reason The writer explains the relationship between human activities and today's increased temperatures. How does this explanation provide support for her position?

5 **Reading Across Texts**

Appeal to Ethics Persuasive writers can make an ethical appeal by acknowledging opposing arguments in a fair and respectful way. Does the writer do this? Explain.

6 **Reading Across Texts**

Appeal to Reason How do the facts in this paragraph provide logical support for the writer's position? Make notes on your chart.

7 **English Language Coach**

Connotation What does the word **frosting** connote in this context?

Scientists say that plants and animals that live on mountain tops like these are among the first affected by global warming. Why might this be?

Pick a pika

One of the most direct and dramatic demonstrations of the impact of global warming, Beever says, comes from a furry little creature called the pika.

Visual Vocabulary
A *pika* is a small gray mammal that lives in the mountains.

Hands down, pikas are among the most adorable animals you'll ever see in the wild. Though related to rabbits, they look like furry little gerbils. "Even as a male, I can say they're cute," Beever says. "They're pretty nifty little guys." **8**

To see pikas, you have to go high up on a mountain because they can't survive warm weather. In a famous study in the 1970s, a scientist put pikas in cages at low elevations to see what would happen. Many of the animals died, even in the shade. It was just too hot for them. **9**

Their habits make pikas particularly **vulnerable** to increased temperatures. "They don't move a lot," Beever

Vocabulary

vulnerable (VUL nur uh bul) *adj.* exposed to danger

Practice the Skills

8 Reading Across Texts

Appeal to Emotions
Emotional appeals can be serious or playful. What words here describe the pika? Does a description like this appeal to your head or your heart? Why?

9 Reading Across Texts

Appeal to Emotions How might this paragraph also appeal to your emotions? How might it provoke sympathy for the pika and for the writer's position? Make notes on your chart.

says. "A 1-mile migration for a pika would be a huge, huge deal, and a pretty rare event, as far as we know." In other words, when conditions change, pikas can't do much about it. **10**

For more than 10 years, Beever has been surveying pika populations in the mountain states of the U.S. West. By the end of 1999, he had confirmed that seven out of 25 populations that he had originally surveyed were gone. More recently, Beever found that two more populations have disappeared. **11**

Early warning

Not all species are threatened by rising temperatures. Some plants and animals like it hot and dry. Others can move or adapt to get the cold or moisture they need to survive.

Pikas are different. "Pikas are an early warning sign," Beever says. "They are very clearly vulnerable to high temperatures."

So, the case of the disappearing pikas is reason enough to wake up and take notice, he says. Something in the weather *is* changing, and the trends look alarming.

But, Beever says, there are things that you can do that may help. Choices you make every day—such as walking instead of going in a car—can add up. By reducing the levels of carbon dioxide and other "greenhouse" gases[6] in the air, we may be able to slow the warming trend.

If nothing else, do it for the pikas. The world could always use a little extra cuteness. **12** ○

Practice the Skills

10 **Reading Across Texts**

Appeal to Emotions
Innocent pikas, stranded on broiling mountaintops—how does this image appeal to the feelings you might have about cute, furry animals? Do you find this appeal effective?

11 **Reading Across Texts**

Appeal to Reason The writer makes a logical appeal when she cites Beever's work. Make notes about this appeal on your chart. Is this appeal more or less effective than her previous appeals to your emotions?

12 **BIG Question**

What does the writer fight for in "A Change in Climate"? What does she fight against? Write your answer on the "Change in Climate" page of Foldable 7. Your response will help you complete the Unit Challenge later.

---

6. A *"greenhouse" gas* is an atmospheric gas, such as methane or carbon dioxide, which contributes to the greenhouse effect. The greenhouse effect occurs when Earth's atmosphere traps solar radiation.

After You Read

Teens Tackle
POLLUTION
in Their Communities
&
A CHANGE IN
CLIMATE

Vocabulary Check

Copy the words below on a separate sheet of paper. Circle the word or phrase that most nearly means the opposite of the boldface word.

1. **emit**
   give off, reduce, take in

2. **buoyed**
   held under, supported, took away

3. **accumulate**
   build up, lose, set alongside

4. **vulnerable**
   safe, open to, excited

Now copy the sentences below. Fill in each blank with the correct vocabulary word.

emit   buoyed   accumulate   vulnerable

5. A microwave can _____ powerful rays.

6. _____ to increasing temperatures, many plants and animals are forced to migrate.

7. Gino felt _____ by her family's kindness.

8. Don't let your homework _____, Salwa's teacher warned.

English Language Coach

9. What does the word *toxic* connote?

**NY English Language Arts
Core Curriculum** (pp. 1032–1033)

LC R9 Recognize multiple meanings of words and connections among meanings of words. **R3a** Identify techniques author uses to persuade (emotional and ethical appeals). **W1g** Connect, compare, and contrast ideas and information from one or more sources.

For a complete description of the standards, see p. NY11.

Reading/Critical Thinking

Answer the following questions.

Teens Tackle POLLUTION in Their Communities

BIG Question

10. Why is a cleaner environment important to Barbara, Amir, and Gina? How do they stand up for their values and beliefs?

    Tip Think and Search

11. **Recall** Why does Amir Nadav decide to join the Sierra Club?

    Tip Right There

12. **List** List the three main sources of pollution discussed in the article.

    Tip Think and Search

A CHANGE IN CLIMATE

13. **Recall** In what two ways have mountains been affected by changes in global temperatures?

    Tip Think and Search

14. **Connect** How might global warming affect plants and animals in your community?

    Tip On My Own

15. **Interpret** What does Beever mean when she says that pikas are an "early warning sign"?

    Tip Author and Me

Writing: Reading Across Texts

Use Your Notes

As you prepare to write about "Teens Tackle Pollution in Their Communities" and "A Change in Climate," think about how the writer of each selection uses different persuasive techniques to convince you to think, feel, or act a certain way.

As you review the notes in your chart, ask yourself the following questions about each selection:

• *Did the writer state her position clearly?*

• *Did she back up her position with facts, statistics, examples, and quotations?*

• *Did she appeal to readers' emotions in an effective way?*

• *Did she address opposing viewpoints?*

• *Did she appeal to my values?*

16. Follow these steps to use the notes on your Comparison Chart to compare the appeals to reason, emotions, and ethics in "Teens Tackle Pollution in Their Communities" and "A Change in Climate."

    Step 1: Look at the notes you made for "Teens Tackle Pollution." Circle one appeal to reason that you found persuasive.

    Step 2: Underline one effective appeal to emotions.

    Step 3: Draw a box around one strong appeal to ethics. Does the example you chose rely on the writer's credibility, or does it appeal to your values?

    Step 4: Look at the notes you made for "A Change in Climate." Repeat steps 1–3.

Get It on Paper

To compare what you've learned about persuasive appeals in "Teens Tackle Pollution" and "A Change in Climate," answer the questions below.

17. Which article appealed most effectively to your sense of reason? Use examples from your chart to support your answer.

18. Which article contained more emotional appeals? Use examples from your chart to support your answer.

19. Which article contained more ethical appeals? Use examples from your chart to explain your answer.

BIG Question

20. How can you fight against pollution—and *for* clean air and water—in your community? Why is it so important to fight for the things you care about?

Answering  What's Worth Fighting For? What's Not?

As you read the selections in this unit, you thought about what's worth fighting for and what's not. Now use what you've learned to complete the Unit Challenge.

The Unit Challenge

Choose Activity A or Activity B and follow the directions for that activity.

A. Group Activity: Make a Mural

With three classmates, design a mural that honors people who took a stand for what they believed in. You won't paint your mural on a wall, but you'll use poster board and other crafts to create something just as meaningful.

1. **Discuss the Assignment** Choose a group member to take notes about your discussion. Then talk about people who have stood up for what they thought was right. Discuss people who have fought against unfair treatment, ideas, or events. The notes you made on your Foldable will help you get started. For example, think about how Ruby Bridges and her mother stood up to segregation. Maybe you have a friend, parent, or neighbor who fought for what he or she believed by not giving in or giving up.

2. **Make a List** Write a list of the people you discussed. Then use textbooks, encyclopedias, and the Internet to add more people to your list. Your list might look like this one.

3. **Create Your Mural** Work together to make a mural that honors people on your list.

   - As a group, choose the people from your list that you want to include on your mural.

   - Create a sketch (a rough idea) of what your mural will look like. Decide how you want to represent the people and their beliefs—drawings or paintings, pictures from magazines or newspapers, names and descriptions, or a combination of these. Be creative!

   - Gather all the materials you'll need (poster board, paint and paint brushes, markers, etc.). When you all agree on an idea, divide the work among group members.

4. **Present Your Mural** Make sure all the people you want to honor are in your mural. Finish all the artwork. Then hang your mural in your classroom or school so other students can view it and learn from it.

People Who Stood Up for Their Beliefs
Martin Luther King, Jr.   *Susan B. Anthony*
Cesar Chavez   *Gandhi*
George Washington   *Sitting Bull*
Rosa Parks   *Uncle Frank*

B. Solo Activity: Propose a Change

Change starts with you! Write a proposal for a change you would like to see in your school or community. A proposal is a piece of writing that suggests an idea and explains to readers why that idea is important.

1. **Brainstorm Ideas** For 10 to 15 minutes, write about your school and community. What do you like about them? What would you like to be different? Your Unit 7 Foldable notes will help you think of ideas. Make a list of things you would like to change and reasons why you would like them to be different.

2. **Choose a Change** Once you have your list, choose one thing that is most important to you. Think about how *you* can help change it. Make a list of other people who can help you change it. Then think about any obstacles that you might face as you push for change.

3. **Organize Your Ideas** Make a brief outline of your ideas. Your outline should have three main sections:

   I. Introduce your idea for change

   II. Explain how the change can happen

   III. Describe how the change will help

4. **Write a Proposal** Using your outline and the ideas in your head, write about the change you think is important. Make sure your proposal answers the following questions:

   - What do you want to change?
   - Why is the issue important? Why is change necessary?
   - What steps can you and other people take to make the change happen?
   - Is there anything that will get in the way? How will you deal with any obstacles?
   - How will your school or community benefit from the change?

5. **Perfect and Present Your Proposal**
Read and revise your proposal. Make sure that your ideas are clear. Correct any spelling or grammar mistakes. When your proposal is ready to present, read it to your class. With your classmates, discuss other ideas that may help you make the change. What is the next step?

Big Question Link to Web resources to further explore the Big Question at www.glencoe.com.

Walter Dean Myers

Meet the Author

Walter Dean Myers grew up in Harlem, a section of Manhattan in New York City. He had a speech problem as a young man, so one of his teachers encouraged him to write. Writing and reading gave Myers a whole new life. He says, "Books took me, not so much to foreign lands and fanciful adventures, but to a place within myself that I have been exploring ever since . . ." See page R4 of the Author Files for more on Walter Dean Myers.

Author Search For more about Walter Dean Myers, go to www.glencoe.com.

The Treasure of Lemon Brown

by
Walter Dean Myers

The dark sky, filled with angry swirling clouds, reflected Greg Ridley's mood as he sat on the stoop[1] of his building. His father's voice came to him again, first reading the letter the principal had sent to the house, then lecturing endlessly about his poor efforts in math.

"I had to leave school when I was 13," his father had said, "that's a year younger than you are now. If I'd had half the chances that you have, I'd. . . ."

Greg had sat in the small, pale green kitchen listening, knowing the lecture would end with his father saying he couldn't play ball with the Scorpions. He had asked his father the week before, and his father had said it depended on his next report card. It wasn't often the Scorpions took on new players, especially 14-year-olds, and this was a chance of a lifetime for Greg. He hadn't been allowed to play high school ball, which he had really wanted to do, but playing for the Community Center team was the next best thing. Report cards were due in a week, and Greg had been hoping for the best. But the principal had ended the suspense early when she sent that letter saying Greg would probably fail math if he didn't spend more time studying.

"And you want to play *basketball*?" His father's brows knitted over deep brown eyes. "That must be some kind of a joke. Now you just get into your room and hit those books."

---

1. A *stoop* is one or more steps at the entrance of a building that lead up to a raised platform or porch.

That had been two nights before. His father's words, like the distant thunder that now echoed through the streets of Harlem, still rumbled softly in his ears.

It was beginning to cool. Gusts of wind made bits of paper dance between the parked cars. There was a flash of nearby lightning, and soon large drops of rain splashed onto his jeans. He stood to go upstairs, thought of the lecture that probably awaited him if he did anything except shut himself in his room with his math book, and started walking down the street instead. Down the block there was an old tenement that had been abandoned for some months. Some of the guys had held an impromptu[2] checker tournament there the week before, and Greg had noticed that the door, once boarded over, had been slightly ajar.

Pulling his collar up as high as he could, he checked for traffic and made a dash across the street. He reached the house just as another flash of lightning changed the night to day for an instant, then returned the graffiti-scarred building to the grim shadows. He vaulted over the outer stairs and pushed tentatively[3] on the door. It was open, and he let himself in.

The inside of the building was dark except for the dim light that filtered through the dirty windows from the streetlamps. There was a room a few feet from the door, and from where he stood at the entrance, Greg could see a squarish patch of light on the floor. He entered the room, frowning at the musty[4] smell. It was a large room that might have been someone's parlor at one time. Squinting, Greg could see an old table on its side against one wall, what looked like a pile of rags or a torn mattress in the corner, and a couch, with one side broken, in front of the window.

He went to the couch. The side that wasn't broken was comfortable enough, though a little creaky. From this spot he could see the blinking neon sign over the bodega[5] on the corner. He sat awhile, watching the sign blink first green then red, allowing his mind to drift to the Scorpions, then to his father. His father had been a postal worker for all Greg's life, and was proud of it, often telling Greg how hard he had worked to pass the test. Greg had heard the story too many times to be interested now.

For a moment Greg thought he heard something that sounded like a scraping against the wall. He listened carefully, but it was gone.

Outside the wind had picked up, sending the rain against the window with a force that shook the glass in its frame. A car passed, its tires hissing over the wet street and its red tail lights glowing in the darkness.

Greg thought he heard the noise again. His stomach tightened as he held himself still and listened intently.[6] There weren't any more scraping noises, but he was sure he had heard something in the darkness—something breathing!

He tried to figure out just where the breathing was coming from; he knew it

---

2. **Impromptu** (im PRAHM too) means "made or done on the spur of the moment, without preparation."

3. As used here, **vaulted** means "jumped." **Tentatively** (TEN tuh tiv lee) means "hesitantly or uncertainly."

4. A **musty** smell is stale or moldy.

5. The Spanish word **bodega** (boh DAY guh) can refer to a bar, a restaurant, a shop, or a pantry.

6. **Intently** means "with concentration."

was in the room with him. Slowly he stood, tensing. As he turned, a flash of lightning lit up the room, frightening him with its sudden brilliance. He saw nothing, just the overturned table, the pile of rags and an old newspaper on the floor. Could he have been imagining the sounds? He continued listening, but heard nothing and thought that it might have just been rats. Still, he thought, as soon as the rain let up he would leave. He went to the window and was about to look out when he heard a voice behind him.

"Don't try nothin' 'cause I got a razor here sharp enough to cut a week into nine days!"

Greg, except for an involuntary tremor[7] in his knees, stood stock still. The voice was high and brittle, like dry twigs being broken, surely not one he had ever heard before. There was a shuffling sound as the person who had been speaking moved a step closer. Greg turned, holding his breath, his eyes straining to see in the dark room.

The upper part of the figure before him was still in darkness. The lower half was in the dim rectangle of light that fell unevenly from the window. There were two feet, in cracked, dirty shoes from which rose legs that were wrapped in rags.

"Who are you?" Greg hardly recognized his own voice.

"I'm Lemon Brown," came the answer. "Who're you?"

"Greg Ridley."

"What you doing here?" The figure shuffled forward again, and Greg took a small step backward.

"It's raining," Greg said.

"I can see that," the figure said.

The person who called himself Lemon Brown peered forward, and Greg could see him clearly. He was an old man. His black, heavily wrinkled face was surrounded by a halo of crinkly white hair and whiskers that seemed to separate his head from the layers of dirty coats piled on his smallish frame. His pants were bagged to the knee, where they were met with rags that went down to the old shoes. The rags were held on with strings, and there was a rope around his middle. Greg relaxed. He had seen the man before, picking through the trash on the corner and pulling clothes out of a Salvation Army box. There was no sign of the razor that could "cut a week into nine days."

"What are you doing here?" Greg asked.

"This is where I'm staying," Lemon Brown said. "What you here for?"

"Told you it was raining out," Greg said, leaning against the back of the couch until he felt it give slightly.

"Ain't you got no home?"

"I got a home," Greg answered.

"You ain't one of them bad boys looking for my treasure, is you?" Lemon Brown cocked his head to one side and squinted one eye. "Because I told you I got me a razor."

"I'm not looking for your treasure," Greg answered, smiling. "*If* you have one."

"What you mean, *if* I have one," Lemon Brown said. "Every man got a treasure. You don't know that, you must be a fool!"

"Sure," Greg said as he sat on the sofa and put one leg over the back. "What do you have, gold coins?"

"Don't worry none about what I got," Lemon Brown said. "You know who I am?"

---

7. A shaking movement is called a **tremor.**

"You told me your name was orange or lemon or something like that."

"Lemon Brown," the old man said, pulling back his shoulders as he did so, "they used to call me Sweet Lemon Brown."

"Sweet Lemon?" Greg asked.

"Yessir. Sweet Lemon Brown. They used to say I sung the blues so sweet that if I sang at a funeral, the dead would commence[8] to rocking with the beat. Used to travel all over Mississippi and as far as Monroe, Louisiana, and east on over to Macon, Georgia. You mean you ain't never heard of Sweet Lemon Brown?"

"Afraid not," Greg said. "What . . . what happened to you?"

"Hard times, boy. Hard times always after a poor man. One day I got tired, sat down to rest a spell and felt a tap on my shoulder. Hard times caught up with me."

"Sorry about that."

"What you doing here? How come you didn't go home when the rain come. Rain don't bother you young folks none."

"Just didn't," Greg looked away.

"I used to have a knotty-headed boy just like you." Lemon Brown had half walked, half shuffled back to the corner and sat down against the wall. "Had them big eyes like you got. I used to call them moon eyes. Look into them moon eyes and see anything you want."

"How come you gave up singing the blues?" Greg asked.

Music Lesson #1, 2000. Colin Bootman. Oil on canvas. Private Collection.

Analyzing the Painting What qualities might this man share with Lemon Brown?

"Didn't give it up," Lemon Brown said. "You don't give up the blues; they give you up. After a while you do good for yourself, and it ain't nothing but foolishness singing about how hard you got it. Ain't that right?"

"I guess so."

"What's that noise?" Lemon Brown asked, suddenly sitting upright.

Greg listened, and he heard a noise outside. He looked at Lemon Brown and saw the old man was pointing toward the window.

Greg went to the window and saw three men, neighborhood thugs, on the stoop. One was carrying a length of pipe.

---

8. **Commence** (kuh MENS) means "to begin."

Greg looked back toward Lemon Brown, who moved quietly across the room to the window. The old man looked out, then beckoned frantically for Greg to follow him. For a moment Greg couldn't move. Then he found himself following Lemon Brown into the hallway and up darkened stairs. Greg followed as closely as he could. They reached the top of the stairs, and Greg felt Lemon Brown's hand first lying on his shoulder, then probing down his arm until he finally took Greg's hand into his own as they crouched in the darkness.

"They's bad men," Lemon Brown whispered. His breath was warm against Greg's skin.

"Hey! Rag man!" A voice called. "We know you in here. What you got up under them rags? You got any money?"

Silence.

"We don't want to have to come in and hurt you, old man, but we don't mind if we have to."

Lemon Brown squeezed Greg's hand in his own hard, gnarled[9] fist.

There was a banging downstairs and a light as the men entered. They banged around noisily, calling for the rag man.

"We heard you talking about your treasure," the voice was slurred. "We just want to see it, that's all."

"You sure he's here?" One voice seemed to come from the room with the sofa.

"Yeah, he stays here every night."

"There's another room over there; I'm going to take a look. You got that flashlight?"

"Yeah, here, take the pipe too."

Greg opened his mouth to quiet the sound of his breath as he sucked it in uneasily. A beam of light hit the wall a few feet opposite him, then went out.

"Ain't nobody in that room," a voice said. "You think he's gone or something?"

"I don't know," came the answer. "All I know is that I heard him talking about some kind of treasure. You know they found that shopping bag lady with that money in her bags."

"Yeah. You think he's upstairs?"

"HEY, OLD MAN, ARE YOU UP THERE?"

Silence.

"Watch my back, I'm going up."

There was a footstep on the stairs, and the beam from the flashlight danced crazily along the peeling wallpaper. Greg held his breath. There was another step and a loud crashing noise as the man banged the pipe against the wooden banister. Greg could feel his temples throb as the man slowly neared them. Greg thought about the pipe, wondering what he would do when the man reached them—what he *could* do.

Then Lemon Brown released his hand and moved toward the top of the stairs.

---

9. Lemon Brown's fist is rough, twisted, and knotted (**gnarled**), like a tree branch.

Greg looked around and saw stairs going up to the next floor. He tried waving to Lemon Brown, hoping the old man would see him in the dim light and follow him to the next floor. Maybe, Greg thought, the man wouldn't follow them up there. Suddenly, though, Lemon Brown stood at the top of the stairs, both arms raised high above his head.

"There he is!" A voice cried from below.

"Throw down your money, old man, so I won't have to bash your head in!"

Lemon Brown didn't move. Greg felt himself near panic. The steps came closer, and still Lemon Brown didn't move. He was an eerie[10] sight, a bundle of rags standing at the top of the stairs, his shadow on the wall looming over him. Maybe, the thought came to Greg, the scene could be even eerier.

Greg wet his lips, put his hands to his mouth and tried to make a sound. Nothing came out. He swallowed hard, wet his lips once more and howled as evenly as he could.

"What's that?"

As Greg howled, the light moved away from Lemon Brown, but not before Greg saw him hurl his body down the stairs at the men who had come to take his treasure. There was a crashing noise, and then footsteps. A rush of warm air came in as the downstairs door opened, then there was only an ominous[11] silence.

Greg stood on the landing. He listened, and after a while there was another sound on the staircase.

"Mr. Brown?" he called.

"Yeah, it's me," came the answer. "I got their flashlight."

Greg exhaled in relief as Lemon Brown made his way slowly back up the stairs.

"You O.K.?"

"Few bumps and bruises," Lemon Brown said.

"I think I'd better be going," Greg said, his breath returning to normal. "You'd better leave, too, before they come back."

"They may hang around outside for a while," Lemon Brown said, "but they ain't getting their nerve up to come in here again. Not with crazy old rag men and howling spooks. Best you stay awhile till the coast is clear. I'm heading out West tomorrow, out to east St. Louis."

"They were talking about treasures," Greg said. "You *really* have a treasure?"

"What I tell you? Didn't I tell you every man got a treasure?" Lemon Brown said. "You want to see mine?"

"If you want to show it to me," Greg shrugged.

"Let's look out the window first, see what them scoundrels be doing," Lemon Brown said.

They followed the oval beam of the flashlight into one of the rooms and looked out the window. They saw the men who had tried to take the treasure sitting on the curb near the corner. One of them had his pants leg up, looking at his knee.

"You sure you're not hurt?" Greg asked Lemon Brown.

"Nothing that ain't been hurt before," Lemon Brown said. "When you get as old as me all you say when something hurts is, 'Howdy, Mr. Pain, sees you back again.' Then when Mr. Pain see he can't worry you none, he go on mess with somebody else."

---

10. Something that is *eerie* (EER ee) is weird and frightening.

11. *Ominous* (AH muh nus) means "threatening harm or evil."

Greg smiled.

"Here, you hold this." Lemon Brown gave Greg the flashlight.

He sat on the floor near Greg and carefully untied the strings that held the rags on his right leg. When he took the rags away, Greg saw a piece of plastic. The old man carefully took off the plastic and unfolded it. He revealed some yellowed newspaper clippings and a battered harmonica.

"There it be," he said, nodding his head. "There it be."

Greg looked at the old man, saw the distant look in his eye, then turned to the clippings. They told of Sweet Lemon Brown, a blues singer and harmonica player who was appearing at different theaters in the South. One of the clippings said he had been the hit of the show, although not the headliner. All of the clippings were reviews of shows Lemon Brown had been in more than 50 years ago. Greg looked at the harmonica. It was dented badly on one side, with the reed holes on one end nearly closed.

"I used to travel around and make money for to feed my wife and Jesse— that's my boy's name. Used to feed them good, too. Then his mama died, and he stayed with his mama's sister. He growed up to be a man, and when the war come he saw fit to go off and fight in it. I didn't have nothing to give him except these things that told him who I was, and what he come from. If you know your pappy did something, you know you can do something too.

"Anyway, he went off to war, and I went off still playing and singing. 'Course by then I wasn't as much as I used to be, not without somebody to make it worth the while. You know what I mean?"

"Yeah," Greg nodded, not quite really knowing.

"I traveled around, and one time I come home, and there was this letter saying Jesse got killed in the war. Broke my heart, it truly did.

"They sent back what he had with him over there, and what it was is this old mouth fiddle and these clippings. Him carrying it around with him like that told me it meant something to him. That was my treasure, and when I give it to him he treated it just like that, a treasure. Ain't that something?"

"Yeah, I guess so," Greg said.

"You *guess* so?" Lemon Brown's voice rose an octave as he started to put his treasure back into the plastic. "Well, you got to guess 'cause you sure don't know nothing. Don't know enough to get home when it's raining."

"I guess . . . I mean, you're right."

"You O.K. for a youngster," the old man said as he tied the strings around his leg, "better than those scalawags what come here looking for my treasure. That's for sure."

"You really think that treasure of yours was worth fighting for?" Greg asked. "Against a pipe?"

"What else a man got 'cepting what he can pass on to his son, or his daughter, if she be his oldest?" Lemon Brown said.

Analyzing the Art How does this picture capture the spirit of Lemon Brown's treasure?

"For a big-headed boy you sure do ask the foolishest questions."

Lemon Brown got up after patting his rags in place and looked out the window again.

"Looks like they're gone. You get on out of here and get yourself home. I'll be watching from the window so you'll be all right."

Lemon Brown went down the stairs behind Greg. When they reached the front door the old man looked out first, saw the street was clear and told Greg to scoot on home.

"You sure you'll be O.K.?" Greg asked.

"Now didn't I tell you I was going to east St. Louis in the morning?" Lemon Brown asked. "Don't that sound O.K. to you?"

"Sure it does," Greg said. "Sure it does. And you take care of that treasure of yours."

"That I'll do," Lemon said, the wrinkles about his eyes suggesting a smile. "That I'll do."

The night had warmed and the rain had stopped, leaving puddles at the curbs. Greg didn't even want to think how late it was. He thought ahead of what his father would say and wondered if he should tell him about Lemon Brown. He thought about it until he reached his stoop, and decided against it. Lemon Brown would be O.K., Greg thought, with his memories and his treasure.

Greg pushed the button over the bell marked Ridley, thought of the lecture he knew his father would give him, and smiled. ○

Reading on Your Own

To read more about the Big Question, choose one of these books from your school or local library. Work on your reading skills by choosing books that are challenging to you.

Fiction

Animal Farm
by George Orwell

In *Animal Farm,* animals work to set up a free society, only to be oppressed by a select group of animals. Read to see how deception can make you confused about what is worth fighting for.

To Kill a Mockingbird
by Harper Lee

A young girl faces racism in her own town when her father—an attorney—defends an African American man who has been wrongfully accused of a crime. Scout, the young girl, learns what is worth fighting for in a deeply divided community.

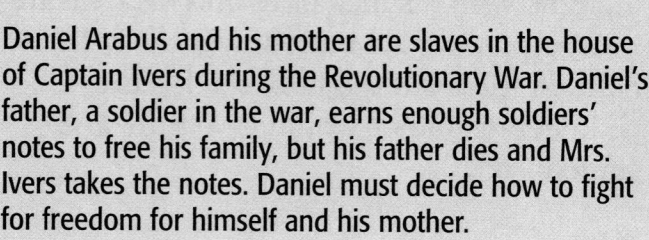

Jump Ship to Freedom
by James Collier and Christopher Collier

Daniel Arabus and his mother are slaves in the house of Captain Ivers during the Revolutionary War. Daniel's father, a soldier in the war, earns enough soldiers' notes to free his family, but his father dies and Mrs. Ivers takes the notes. Daniel must decide how to fight for freedom for himself and his mother.

Before We Were Free
by Julia Alvarez

After Anita de la Torres's aunts, uncles, and cousins suddenly leave the Dominican Republic for the United States, Anita becomes aware that her family is involved in the resistance against the Trujillo dictatorship. When Anita's father and uncle are arrested, she and her mother go into hiding.

Nonfiction

Through My Eyes
by Ruby Bridges

In 1960 Ruby Bridges was the first black student to attend an all-white New Orleans public elementary school. Nearly 40 years later, Bridges published her memoir about this historic and life-changing event. Read to find out more about the fight for civil rights.

Ryan White: My Own Story
by Ryan White and Ann Marie Cunningham

The young AIDS activist tells the story of his own life, including how he got AIDS and how he fought for the right to attend school. This moving book shares the voice of a young man who faced terrible circumstances and still stood up for tolerance.

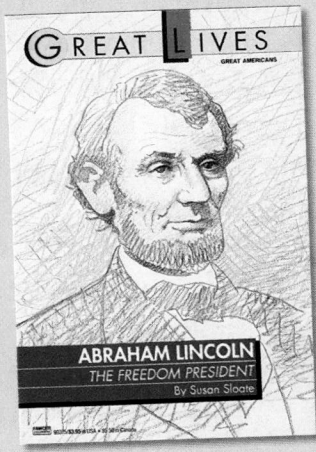

Freedom Rides
by James Haskins

In the 1960s, civil rights activists began standing up to racial segregation. The Freedom Riders were a group of individuals—some African American, some white—who fought segregation by riding buses together. In this fascinating book, one of the freedom riders describes his experiences.

Abraham Lincoln: The Freedom President
by Susan Sloate

Abraham Lincoln grew up in a poor family, but through hard work he eventually became the President of the United States. This book shows how this freedom-loving president believed in and stood up for equality.

New York English Language Arts Test Practice

Directions

Read this article about deer. Then answer questions 1 through 4.

Baby Deer Do Need Your Help
By Nate Tripp

Many people feel drawn to the beauty and gentleness of wild deer. This article about wildlife conservation explains why people need to be knowledgeable and careful about how they interact with deer in the wild.

People and deer live in overlapping worlds where they frequently encounter each other. This can lead to various problems for both deer and people.

One problem is when fawns are *saved* by well-meaning people when they do not need to be saved. We need people to spread the word that lone fawns are **not** abandoned and should **not** be touched.

During the first few weeks of its life a fawn is protected by being camouflaged, scentless and still. Fawns are what we call *"hiders."* Hiders have used hiding as their primary means of survival for thousands of years. The doe assists in her fawn's protection by staying away most of the time. She makes contact with the fawn for only a few brief periods each day to nurse and groom it. The fawn usually moves at least a short distance between visits. By staying away, the doe does not attract a predator near her fawn by either her sight or scent.

If a doe has two or more fawns, she keeps them separated for their first few weeks—usually by a distance of at least 100 yards. During these first two weeks, siblings are rarely found together. By six weeks of age, however, siblings are found fairly close together nearly 80 percent of the time.

This *"hider"* pattern of behavior works well most of the time. But with about 200,000 fawns born each year in New York State, and with a human population of 17 million, approximately 200 or more fawns get found each year.

To us, fawns are cute and helpless. And if we don't see a mother deer around, we assume the fawn is abandoned. Even the most hard-hearted person has an immediate empathetic response, and being unaware of the basic normal pattern of deer behavior we just have to "save" the fawn. However, if not returned immediately, a "captured" fawn is unlikely to become a normal deer.

So, remember, **If You Care, Leave Them There!** And help spread the word to other well-meaning people:

- It is normal for fawns to be alone.
- Do not disturb a fawn—take a quick look and leave.
- If you know of somebody else who saves a fawn, explain why the person should return it to the wild immediately.

---

1 According to the article, how does a fawn's mother help keep the fawn safe?

   A by making sure she nurses and grooms her fawn every day

   B by attracting predators to herself

   C by carefully watching for predators

   D by leaving her fawn alone

2 Which of these statements uses an emotional appeal to try persuading the reader not to "save" the fawns?

   F It is normal for fawns to be alone.

   G If you care, leave them there!

   H The "hider" pattern of behavior works well most of the time.

   J People and deer live in overlapping worlds where they frequently encounter each other.

3 Based on the article, with which opinion would the author **most likely** agree?

   A People's needs are more important than deer's needs.

   B People are invading the deer's territory.

   C People should not be allowed to hunt deer.

   D People and deer must learn to share their overlapping worlds.

4 Based on information in the article, which of these statements uses faulty reasoning?

   F The camouflage protects the fawn by keeping it hidden.

   G Because they are hidden, fawns are safer if left alone.

   H Either the fawn hides or it will be killed by a predator.

   J Fawns are not helpless, so we should not assume they need to be saved.

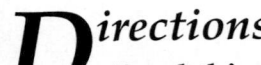
Directions

Read this passage about coon hunting. Then answer questions 5 through 8.

Coon Hunt
By LeRoy Powell

Hunting coons is a lot like eating chitterlings. If you do either of them once, you never have to do it again. It's like being vaccinated. One unpleasant dose will protect you. After one serving of chitterlings, for instance, you have an excuse that will keep you chitterling-free forever. From then on, if anybody asks you if you want some chitterlings, you can say, "No thank you, I had some already." I had my chitterlings ten years ago. I don't want any more. Coon hunting is like that too.

The raccoon is a very intelligent animal. I wish I could say the same for coon hunters. Some people around here get great pleasure out of coon hunts and go every chance they get. I figured it must hold some attraction that you can't see from a distance, so one January evening, I hooked up with a bunch of boys in Newton County, Georgia, for a night of adventure.

The way you go coon hunting is you get together with a crowd of other coon-seekers and their coon dogs and head for the woods in the middle of the night. When you get to the woods, you turn the dogs loose. Then you wait—a cluster of full-grown men wearing hip boots and hard hats with little headlights stuck to them—and listen to the dogs bark. I don't have to go to the middle of the woods to hear dogs bark. I have a dog at my house.

But coon hunters love this. They know each dog's voice. Each hunter knows what his dog is saying to him. They do not speak Dog, but they understand it fluently.

You are standing around in the woods, a pack of dogs is running around howling in the dark, and the coon hunters are having a grand old time. You, the initiate, are just freezing to death. Weather is very important in coon hunting. It has to be cold enough to be really uncomfortable or the hunters are not happy. Somewhere out in the darkness is a coon, and he is likely, when pursued by a pack of dogs, to climb a tree. The dogs report to their owners on the progress of the chase.

chitterlings = small intestines of pigs

vaccinated = made immune to a disease

5 In this passage, what is the **main** technique used by the writer to engage the reader?

 A reason

 B visual description

 C suspense

 D humor

6 According to the passage, what is the **main** reason people go coon hunting?

 F so they can hunt raccoons

 G so they can wear hip boots and hard hats

 H because they want to have stories to tell

 J because they want to stand around in the woods with their dogs

7 According to the passage, chitterlings are

 A great, but only once

 B something you should eat once every ten years

 C something you should suffer through only once

 D terrible, but good for coon hunting

8 The writer went coon hunting because

 F he wanted to understand why it was popular

 G he had always wanted to go

 H he thought it sounded fun

 J he knew it would be ridiculous

Directions
Read this passage about a temporary home for troubled city kids.
Then answer questions 9 through 14.

from *Animal Partners: Training Animals to Help People*
By Patricia Curtis

Apple Tree Farm is temporary home to ninety-odd of the most troubled, confused, and sometimes off-the-wall kids from the city. Set in rolling countryside, it was started by the state several years ago for use as a rehabilitation residence and school for disturbed children who have come to the attention of the police, courts, or social-service agencies. These youngsters need help badly. Some of them have come from horrendous family life with abusive, drunk, addicted, or violent parents. Some have no families at all.

Ranging in age from about five to fifteen, the boys and girls spend two years here in the care of a large professional staff who are determined to heal them and help them become functioning and self-controlled human beings. Our work with these difficult children sometimes seems hopeless and futile; many of them are very damaged when they arrive. . . . But inside, we are all true believers. We are really convinced that these kids can be helped—and apparently many are. We often see it happen.

The children receive special schooling, psychiatric treatment, and supervision from a hard-working bunch of educators, therapists, and counselors. I am an intern here, serving as a junior counselor while earning credit for my degree in social work.

And one of the most important parts of my job is supervising the kids with the farm animals. I was born and raised on a farm, so my background comes in handy. There are one hundred fifty cows, horses, pigs, sheep, goats, rabbits, chickens, ducks, and geese here. These animals are not pets—Apple Tree is a working farm. There are a few good-natured dogs and cats who qualify as pets. And taking care of all the animals, under supervision, is part of the youngsters' therapy.

Why does taking care of farm animals help these kids? We're not sure exactly why, we just know it does, perhaps for a combination of reasons. For one thing, these are city youngsters who have lived where starving and abandoned animals roam the streets, where pet animals are often neglected or actively abused. The idea that animals are valued and treated well is amazing to them. Learning to respect these animals' rights and needs, we think, is a step in the direction of learning to respect the rights and needs of other human beings.

9 According to the passage, one of the staff's **main** assets is that they all

    A have been growing apples for many years

    B grew up on farms

    C respect the animals

    D have faith that the children can be helped

10 According to the passage, caring for animals

    F can teach children how to respect people

    G always helps troubled children change

    H is the best therapy for troubled kids

    J helps children learn about the importance of family

11 According to the passage, what is the program's **main** goal?

    A to provide troubled kids with a home outside of the city

    B to make the children better students

    C to help the children learn how to manage themselves in society

    D to teach the children how to take care of themselves

12 The author's background is useful **most likely** because

    F the children have not spent much time around farm animals

    G Apple Tree is a working farm

    H there are 150 animals on Apple Tree Farm

    J she spends much of her time supervising the kids

13 Read this statement from the passage.

    Our work with these difficult children sometimes seems hopeless and futile.

    In this sentence, "futile" means about the same as

    A tough

    B complicated

    C useless

    D depressing

14 Write a paragraph that summarizes the main idea of the passage. Include two details from the passage to support the main idea.

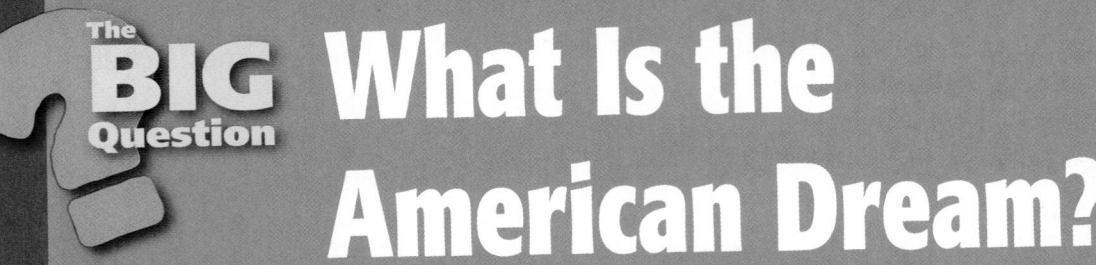

The BIG Question

What Is the American Dream?

" I have learned that if one advances confidently in the direction of his dreams, and endeavors to live the life he or she has imagined, he will meet with a success unexpected in common hours. "

—Henry David Thoreau
American Writer (1817–1862)

LOOKING AHEAD

The skill lessons and readings in this unit will help you develop your own answer to the Big Question.

UNIT 8 WRAP-UP • Answering the Big Question

Connecting to ? The BIG Question

What Is the American Dream?

The American dream means many things to many different people. One thing that many people agree on is that the American dream means that every person is free to achieve all that he or she is capable of. And every person should be recognized for who he or she is regardless of social class or ethnic background. In this unit, you'll read about different people and what the American dream means to them.

Real Kids and the Big Question

YURI and his family moved here from a country outside the United States. His family had been displaced because of wars in their county. Now Yuri and his family live in an apartment near the school. Yuri and his sisters and brothers have made many new friends. They are learning all about American culture. If you asked Yuri what the American dream means to him, what do you think he would say?

ALEXANDRA was not at all sure that she wanted to attend the new magnet school. But she took the test and was admitted. She knows that getting a good education can help her achieve her goals. Her parents always tell her that if she stays in school, she can accomplish anything. If you ask Alexandra what the American dream means to her, what do you think she would say?

Warm-Up Activity

In a small group, discuss what you think the American dream means to you, Yuri, and Alexandra. Then discuss ways in which you hope to achieve your American dream.

You and the Big Question

Reading about how other people define the American dream will help you think about how you would answer the Big Question.

Literature Online

BIG Question Link to Web resources to further explore the Big Question at www.glencoe.com.

Plan for the Unit Challenge

At the end of the unit, you'll use notes from all your reading to complete the Unit Challenge, which will explore your answer to the Big Question.

You'll choose one of the following activities:

A. The American Dream Newsletter Work in groups to write, design, and produce a newsletter about people who achieve their American dreams.

B. An American Dream Spokesperson Write a short biography or speech, or create a poster to honor your American dream spokesperson.

• Start thinking about which activity you'd like to do so that you can focus your thinking as you go through the unit.

• In your Learner's Notebook, write your thoughts about which activity you'd like to do.

• Each time you make notes about the Big Question, think about how your ideas will help you with the Unit Challenge activity you chose.

Keep Track of Your Ideas

FOLDABLES™
Study Organizer

As you read, you'll make notes about the Big Question. Later, you'll use these notes to complete the Unit Challenge. See pages R8–R9 for help with making Foldable 8. This diagram shows how it should look.

1. Use this Foldable for all of the selections in this unit. Label the stapled edge with the unit number and the Big Question.

2. Label each flap with a title. (See page 1053 for the titles.)

3. Open each flap. Near the top of the page, write **My Purpose for Reading**. Below the crease, write **The Big Question**.

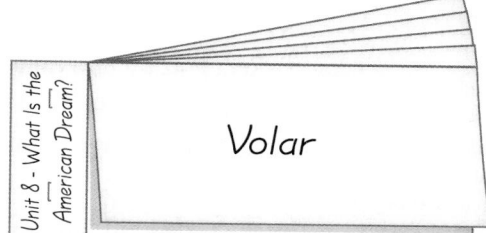

Unit 8 - What Is the American Dream?

Volar

Have you ever imagined what it might have been like to live in North America before Europeans arrived, or during the Gold Rush in the West? These times and places can be explored through a variety of historical writings. **Historical text** can take many different forms including speeches, autobiographies, biographies, and stories. It can be nonfiction or fiction. Nonfiction historical text gives a factual account of past events, places, and people. Historical fiction combines fact and fiction in a story set in the past.

Why Read Historical Text?

Historical text allows you to understand the problems and issues that people faced in the past. Often this knowledge sheds light on the problems of our own time, and helps us better understand the choices we face.

How to Read Historical Text

Key Reading Skills

These key reading skills are especially useful tools for reading and understanding historical text. You'll learn more about these skills later in the unit.

■ **Analyzing** As you read a selection, think about how its parts work together. Think about what the author is saying. Look at how the main ideas are organized. (See Reading Workshop 1.)

■ **Understanding Cause and Effect** As you read, look for what makes something happen. (See Reading Workshop 2.)

■ **Identifying Main Idea and Supporting Details** Find the most important idea in a paragraph or in a selection. Look for examples, reasons, or details that help you know it's the most important idea. (See Reading Workshop 3.)

■ **Identifying Author's Purpose** As you figure out the author's purpose, you can evaluate his or her point of view. (See Reading Workshop 4.)

Key Literary and Text Elements

Recognizing and thinking about the following literary and text elements will help you understand historical texts more fully.

■ **Chronological order:** the order in which events happen in time (See *The Century for Young People*.)

■ **Style:** an author's personal way of using language (See "The Gettysburg Address.")

■ **Cultural reference:** the mention of a value, belief, tradition, or custom practiced in a certain culture (See "I Chose Schooling.")

■ **Metaphor:** a figure of speech that compares two unlike things without using the words *like* and *as* (See "I, Too.")

Skills Focus

- Key skills for reading historical text
- Key literary elements of historical text

Skills Model

You will see how to use the key reading skills and literary elements as you read

- **"I Have a Dream,"** p. 1057

NY English Language Arts Core Curriculum
(pp. 1056–1061)

LC R12 Combine multiple strategies to enhance comprehension and response. **LC R13** Use text structure and literary devices to aid comprehension and response. **R3a** Question the writer's beliefs, intentions. **R2h** Identify social and cultural contexts to enhance understanding and appreciation of text. **R2d** Determine how literary devices, such as metaphor, convey the author's message or intent.

For a complete description of the standards, see p. NY 11.

I Have a Dream

by Martin Luther King Jr.

I am happy to join with you today in what will go down in history as the greatest demonstration for freedom in the history of our nation.[1]

Fivescore years ago, a great American, in whose symbolic shadow we stand today, signed the Emancipation Proclamation. This momentous[2] decree came as a great beacon light of hope to millions of Negro slaves who had been seared in the flames of withering injustice. It came as a joyous daybreak to end the long night of their captivity. **1**

But one hundred years later, the Negro still is not free; one hundred years later, the life of the Negro is still sadly crippled by the manacles of segregation and the chains of discrimination;[3] one hundred years later, the Negro lives on a lonely island of poverty in the midst of a vast ocean of material prosperity; one hundred years later, the Negro is still languished[4] in the corners of American society and finds himself in exile in his own land. **2**

So we've come here today to dramatize a shameful condition. In a sense we've come to our nation's capital to

Historical Text

ACTIVE READING MODEL

1 Key Text Element
Cultural Reference *The references to Lincoln and the end of slavery would have had special significance to King's audience.*

2 Key Text Element
Chronological Order *To make the order very clear, King uses signal words— "fivescore years ago" in the previous paragraph and "one hundred years later" repeatedly here.*

---

1. King gave this speech at the March for Jobs and Freedom in Washington, D.C., on August 28, 1963. The crowd was estimated at between 250,000 and 400,000 people.

2. One score is twenty, so *fivescore* is one hundred. King is echoing Abraham Lincoln's Gettysburg Address, which begins with "fourscore and seven years ago." *Momentous* (moh MEN tus) means "extremely important."

3. *Manacles* (MAN uh kuls) are handcuffs. *Segregation* is the practice of separating people because of their race or skin color. *Discrimination* is unfair treatment, especially because of people's race or skin color.

4. King uses *languished* (LANG wishd) to mean something like "suffering from neglect."

cash a check. When the architects of our republic wrote the magnificent words of the Constitution and the Declaration of Independence, they were signing a promissory note[5] to which every American was to fall heir. This note was the promise that all men, yes, black men as well as white men, would be guaranteed the unalienable[6] rights of life, liberty, and the pursuit of happiness. **3** **4**

It is obvious today that America has defaulted[7] on this promissory note in so far as her citizens of color are concerned. Instead of honoring this sacred obligation, America has given the Negro people a bad check; a check which has come back marked "insufficient funds." We refuse to believe that there are insufficient funds in the great vaults of opportunity of this nation. And so we've come to cash this check, a check that will give us upon demand the riches of freedom and the security of justice. We have also come to this hallowed spot[8] to remind America of the fierce urgency of now. This is no time to engage in the luxury of cooling off or to take the tranquilizing drug of gradualism.[9] Now is the time to make real the promises of democracy; now is the time to rise from the dark and desolate[10] valley of segregation to the sunlit path of racial justice; now is the time to lift our nation from the quicksands of racial injustice to the solid rock of brotherhood; now is the time to make justice a reality for all God's children. It would be fatal for the nation to overlook the urgency of the moment. This sweltering summer of the Negro's legitimate discontent will not pass until there is an invigorating[11] autumn of freedom and equality. **5**

3 Key Reading Skill
Identify Author's Purpose *King makes his purpose clear when he says he's "come to dramatize a shameful condition"—America's failure to live up to its promise of equality for African Americans.*

4 Key Literary Elements
Style; Metaphor *Figurative language, including metaphors, are a part of King's style. Here he introduces the check and promissory note metaphors and then explains them in the final sentence and next paragraph.*

5 Key Literary Elements
Style; Cultural Reference *References to literature are another element of King's style. Here, "summer of . . . discontent" echoes the phrase "winter of our discontent" in* Richard III *by William Shakespeare.*

---

5. A ***promissory note*** is a written promise to pay a certain amount of money to someone at a future date.

6. ***Unalienable rights,*** according to the Declaration of Independence, are rights that may not be taken away.

7. ***Defaulted*** means "failed to do what was required."

8. King spoke from the steps of the Lincoln Memorial, a place many people consider holy ***(hallowed).***

9. ***Gradualism*** is the process of trying to bring about social change gradually, or slowly.

10. ***Desolate*** (DES uh lit) means "without comfort."

11. ***Sweltering*** means "very hot and humid," and ***invigorating*** means "bringing new life and energy." King is talking about more than just seasonal changes.

King Mural, 1986. Don Miller. District of Columbia Public Library.

Nineteen sixty-three is not an end, but a beginning. And those who hope that the Negro needed to blow off steam and will now be content, will have a rude awakening if the nation returns to business as usual. There will be neither rest nor tranquility in America until the Negro is granted his citizenship rights. The whirlwinds of the revolt will continue to shake the foundations of our nation until the bright day of justice emerges.

But there is something that I must say to my people, who stand on the warm threshold which leads into the palace of justice. In the process of gaining our rightful place, we must not be guilty of wrongful deeds. Let us not seek to satisfy our thirst for freedom by drinking from the cup of bitterness and hatred. We must forever conduct our struggle on the high plain of dignity and discipline. We must not allow our creative protest to generate into physical violence. Again and again we must rise to the majestic heights of meeting physical force with soul force; and the marvelous new militancy,[12] which has engulfed the Negro community, must not lead us to a distrust of all white people. For many of our white brothers, as evidenced by their presence here today, have come to realize that their destiny is tied up with our destiny. And they have come to realize that their freedom is inextricably[13] bound to our freedom. We cannot walk alone. And as we talk, we must make the pledge that we shall always march ahead. We cannot turn back. **6**

There are those who are asking the devotees of Civil Rights, "When will you be satisfied?" We can never be satisfied as long as the Negro is the victim of the unspeakable horrors of police brutality; we can never be satisfied as long as our bodies, heavy with the fatigue of travel, cannot gain lodging in the motels of the highways and the hotels of the cities; we cannot be satisfied as long as the Negro's basic mobility is from a smaller ghetto to a larger one; we can never be satisfied as long as our children are stripped of their selfhood and robbed of their dignity by signs stating "For Whites Only"; we cannot be satisfied as long as the Negro in Mississippi cannot vote and a Negro in New York believes he has nothing for which to vote. No! no, we are not satisfied, and we will not be satisfied until "justice rolls down like waters and righteousness like a mighty stream.[14]" **7** **8**

I am not unmindful that some of you have come here out of great trials and tribulations.[15] Some of you have come fresh from narrow jail cells. Some of you have come

6 **Key Reading Skill**
Determining Main Idea *There are two main ideas in this paragraph. One is that African Americans must use peaceful methods to achieve freedom. The other is that white people who deny freedom to others are victims of their own ignorance and prejudice.*

7 **Key Reading Skill**
Identifying Cause and Effect *King states one effect (dissatisfaction) and ties it to a number of causes (police brutality and so on).*

8 **Key Literary Element**
Style *Another key part of King's style is repetition. The repetition gives the speech emotional power, just as it does in poems, song lyrics, and music.*

---

12. ***Militancy*** (MIH luh tun see) refers to being ready to fight for a cause.
13. ***Inextricably*** (ih nik STRIH kuh blee) means "in a way that cannot be separated."
14. This line is from the Old Testament's book of Amos.
15. ***Tribulation*** (trih byuh LAY shun) is a great misery or distress.

from areas where your quest for freedom left you battered by the storms of persecution and staggered by the winds of police brutality. You have been the veterans of creative suffering. Continue to work with the faith that unearned suffering is redemptive.[16] Go back to Mississippi. Go back to Alabama. Go back to South Carolina. Go back to Georgia. Go back to Louisiana. Go back to the slums and ghettos of our Northern cities, knowing that somehow this situation can and will be changed. Let us not wallow[17] in the valley of despair.

I say to you today, my friends, so even though we face the difficulties of today and tomorrow, I still have a dream. It is a dream deeply rooted in the American dream. I have a dream that one day this nation will rise up and live out the true meaning of its creed, "We hold

At the Lincoln Memorial, the crowd listens as TV cameras capture King's speech.

these truths to be self-evident, that all men are created equal." I have a dream that one day on the red hills of Georgia, sons of former slaves and the sons of former slave owners will be able to sit down together at the table of brotherhood. I have a dream that one day even the state of Mississippi, a state sweltering with the heat of injustice, sweltering with the heat of oppression, will be transformed into an oasis of freedom and justice. I have a dream that my four little children will one day

16. If something is *redemptive* (rih DEMP tiv), it brings rescue or freedom.
17. In this context, to *wallow* is to become or remain helpless.

live in a nation where they will not be judged by the color of their skin, but by the content of their character. **9**

I have a dream today!

I have a dream that one day down in Alabama— with its vicious racists, with its Governor having his lips dripping with the words of interposition and nullification[18]—one day right there in Alabama, little black boys and black girls will be able to join hands with little white boys and white girls as sisters and brothers.

I have a dream today!

I have a dream that one day "every valley shall be exalted[19] and every hill and mountain shall be made low. The rough places will be made plain and the crooked places will be made straight, and the glory of the Lord shall be revealed, and all flesh shall see it together."[20]

This is our hope. This is the faith that I go back to the South with. With this faith we shall be able to transform the jangling discords[21] of our nation into a beautiful symphony of brotherhood. With this faith we will be able to work together, to pray together, to struggle together, to go to jail together, to stand up for freedom together, knowing that we will be free one day. And this will be the day. This will be the day when all of God's children will be able to sing with new meaning, "My country 'tis of thee, sweet land of liberty, of thee I sing. Land where my fathers died, land of the pilgrim's pride, from every mountain side, let freedom ring." And if America is to be a great nation, this must become true. **10**

So let freedom ring from the prodigious[22] hilltops of New Hampshire; let freedom ring from the mighty mountains of New York; let freedom ring from the heightening Alleghenies of Pennsylvania; let freedom ring from the snowcapped Rockies of Colorado; let freedom ring from the curvaceous slopes of California.

9 Key Reading Skill
Analyzing *At the climax, or high point, of his speech, King offers his dream for a better America.*

10 Key Literary Element
Cultural Reference *Earlier, King quoted from the King James Bible. Here, building up to a powerful conclusion, he quotes a patriotic song. Finally, at the end of the speech, he borrows from another song to connect with his audience.*

---

18. George Wallace, Alabama's then-governor, opposed all efforts to end official segregation in his state. *Interposition* and *nullification* are legal arguments regarding a state's right to reject or refuse to enforce federal laws.

19. Something that is *exalted* is raised in status, dignity, power, or glory.

20. This passage is taken from the Old Testament's book of Isaiah.

21. *Discords* are disagreements or conflicts.

22. Here, *prodigious* (pruh DIJ us) means "enormous."

But not only that. Let freedom ring from Stone Mountain of Georgia; let freedom ring from Lookout Mountain of Tennessee; let freedom ring from every hill and molehill of Mississippi. From every mountainside, let freedom ring.

And when this happens, and when we allow freedom to ring, when we let it ring from every village and every hamlet, from every state and every city; we will be able to speed up that day when all God's children, black men and white men, Jews and gentiles,[23] Protestants and Catholics, will be able to join hands and sing in the words of the old Negro spiritual: "Free at last. Free at last. Thank God Almighty, we are free at last." **11** ○

---

23. People who are not Jews are known as **_gentiles_** (JEN tyls).

11 Key Reading Skill
Identifying Cause and Effect _This is really a prediction of cause and effect. King says that if we achieve equality for African Americans, the effect will be that we are all free._

Write to Learn In your Learner's Notebook, jot down some of the images you thought were full of power. How do you think these images might have affected the people in the crowd when King spoke? Explain your answer.

Partner Talk With a partner, discuss whether King's dream for America has been fulfilled since he gave this speech. Work together to come to one conclusion and give reasons for it.

 **Study Central** Visit www.glencoe.com and click on Study Central to review historical text.

Skills Focus

You will practice using these skills when you read the following selections:
- "Volar," p. 1068
- from *The Century for Young People,* p. 1076

Reading

- Analyzing

Informational Text

- Understanding imagery
- Understanding chronological order

Vocabulary

- Learning about English as a changing language

Writing/Grammar

- Using words correctly: misused and confused words

NY English Language Arts Core Curriculum
(pp. 1064–1065)

LC R12 Combine multiple strategies to enhance comprehension and response.

For a complete description of the standards, see p. NY 11.

Skill Lesson

Analyzing

Learn It!

A police detective **analyzes** a crime scene, searching for clues. A medical researcher analyzes a cancer cell, looking for a cure. A football coach analyzes last week's game, wanting to help the team improve. A student analyzes a grammar assignment, intending to master the topic and get a good grade.

When you analyze, you think critically. You think about the various elements of an object or situation in order to better understand the whole. What does that mean for reading? It means you question what you read. You break down a subject into separate parts to determine its meaning. You demonstrate awareness of a writer's technique and craft.

Reprinted with permission of King Features Syndicate.

Analyzing Cartoons

Hagar wants the guys to analyze their battle behavior so they can improve. What answer does one soldier give? Is his answer a good analysis? Why or why not?

Why Is It Important? In today's world, we're offered loads of information about all sorts of subjects. To help make sense of it all, people need critical thinking skills so that they can make smart, informed decisions. Learning to analyze information is a good way to develop those critical thinking skills. Analyzing helps you look critically at a piece of writing to discover its theme or message.

How Do I Do It? Start by thinking about the author's background, traditions, attitudes, and beliefs. To analyze fiction, think about what the author is saying through the characters, setting, and plot. For example, look at a character's words, actions, and purposes. Then use the knowledge you gain to better understand the character's behavior at other points of the story and the story as a whole.

To analyze nonfiction, look at the organization, main ideas, and supporting details. Here are some of the comments one student made in analyzing Martin Luther King's "I Have a Dream" speech.

> It's important that King spoke at the Lincoln Memorial. It makes the point that Americans gave high honor to Lincoln but treated African Americans as second-class citizens. King says that right up front.
>
> He creates images that just stick in your head. Freedom is a "beacon light of hope." Injustice is "searing flames." The promise of freedom is a "bad check."
>
> I also like his references to the Bible, Declaration of Independence, and even "My Country 'Tis of Thee." He makes me think about what the words really mean. He makes me want to make those words be true.

Literature Online

Study Central Visit www.glencoe.com and click on Study Central to review analyzing.

Practice It!

Below are some things to look for as you analyze the selections in this workshop. In your Learner's Notebook, jot down thoughts that occur to you as you read this list.

- the powers of super heroes
- the importance of family origins
- the importance of oral history
- what America means to immigrants

Use It!

As you analyze "Volar" and *The Century for Young People,* refer to your notes to help yourself focus on the important elements.

Before You Read : Volar

Judith Ortiz Cofer

Meet the Author

Judith Ortiz Cofer learned English only after her family moved to the U.S. mainland from the island of Puerto Rico. Her writing reflects the split between her two childhood homes. She has written, "The memories of [childhood and my parents] emerge in my poems and stories like time-travelers popping up with a message for me." See page R1 of the Author Files for more on Cofer.

Author Search For more about Judith Ortiz Cofer, go to www .glencoe.com.

NY English Language Arts Core Curriculum (pp. 1066–1069)

LC R9 Recognize multiple meanings of words and connections among meanings of words. **LC R12** Combine multiple strategies to enhance comprehension and response. **R2e** Recognize how the author's use of language creates images or feelings.

For a complete description of the standards, see p. NY 11.

Vocabulary Preview

avid (AV id) *adj.* very eager or enthusiastic **(p. 1068)** *The ranger, an avid hiker himself, was happy to share trail information with park visitors.*

recurring (rih KUR ing) *adj.* happening or coming back again; repeating **(p. 1068)** *It's a recurring problem that must be solved once and for all.*

adolescence (ad uh LES uns) *n.* the period between childhood and adulthood **(p. 1070)** *In adolescence, people begin to develop their abilities.*

abruptly (uh BRUPT lee) *adv.* suddenly; unexpectedly **(p. 1071)** *Our discussion ended abruptly when the fire alarm went off.*

refuse (REF yooz) *n.* trash; rubbish **(p. 1071)** *During the garbage workers' strike, great bags of refuse piled up on the street.*

Partner Talk With a partner, use each vocabulary word in a separate sentence. Then write one sentence that uses all five words correctly.

English Language Coach

English as a Changing Language There are living languages and dead ones. Latin, the language of the Roman Empire, is dead. No one uses it now in everyday life. In contrast, English is a living language. To stay alive, a language drops words and meanings that are no longer needed or wanted. It borrows words from other languages, from slang, and from culture. A living language invents terms to deal with new technologies. As an example, see how the word *program* developed new meanings to keep up with culture and technology.

Program		
1	(1633)	*n.* a printed public notice or announcement
2		*n.* a printed outline of the order of a public performance
3	(1896)	*v.* to arrange or provide a program for a performance
4		*n.* the performance of a program, especially on radio or TV
5		*n.* a plan or system for action toward a goal
6	(1940s)	*n.* the coded instructions for a computer or other machine
7		*v.* to write the instructions for a computer or other machine
8		*v.* to control as if by a program

Group Program In a group, brainstorm words and meanings that you think are recent additions to English. Look closely at words related to technology (*computer*) and culture (*hip-hop*) or borrowed from other languages (*adios*).

Skills Preview

Key Reading Skill: Analyzing

Before you read the selection, reflect on what you know about

- the feeling of flying in a dream
- sacrifices parents make for their families

Write to Learn In your Learner's Notebook, describe some of your thoughts on the topics above.

Literary Element: Imagery

An image may be a picture or statue, a copy, something reflected in a mirror, or something seen in the mind. **Imagery** is language that appeals to any or all of the senses—not just sight. Imagery helps readers hear, feel, smell, and taste, as well as see, what is described in a written text.

Imagery isn't necessarily just a description. For example, the narrator of "Volar" wants to emphasize how much she loved comic books as a child and to tell how large her collection was. Using imagery, she says that she had a stack of comics "as tall as I."

As you read, use these tips to help you learn about imagery:

- Look for language that paints a picture you can see in your mind.

  Stop and see the picture; then reread the words that created that image for you.

- Look for language that activates your other senses—hearing, touching, smelling, and tasting.

  Reread the words and think about which specific words bring these senses to mind.

Interactive Literary Elements Handbook
To review or learn more about the literary elements, go to www.glencoe.com.

Get Ready to Read

Connect to the Reading

Imagine that you had long dreamed of coming to the United States for a better life. Then imagine that, after being here for a time, you find it's not what you had hoped for. Or you miss your homeland and want to go back. As you read "Volar," imagine why the narrator's parents brought the family to the United States and how they felt about being here.

Small Group Chat In a small group, talk about a time when you hoped or wished or dreamed for something and what happened when it came true. Was it the way you imagined it? Was it really what you were wishing for? Take turns sharing your experiences.

Build Background

"Volar" is from a collection of stories and poems called *The Year of Our Revolution.* This story is not necessarily about Judith Ortiz Cofer and her family, but it could be.

- In the 1960s, many Puerto Rican families came to the mainland in search of better opportunities.
- In 1964 when the author was twelve, her family moved to Patterson, New Jersey, an industrial town very different from Puerto Rico. Cofer's mother never adjusted well to American city life.
- Comic books were a cheap and popular form of entertainment for kids growing up in the 1960s.
- The Spanish verb *volar* means "to fly."

Set Purposes for Reading

BIG Question Read "Volar" to see how two members of the same family see the American dream.

Set Your Own Purpose What would you like to learn from the selection to help you answer the Big Question? Write your own purpose on the "Volar" page of Foldable 8.

Keep Moving

Use these skills as you read the following selection.

Volar

by Judith Ortiz Cofer

Practice the Skills

At twelve I was an **avid** consumer of comic books—*Supergirl* being my favorite. I spent my allowance of a quarter a day on two twelve-cent comic books or a double issue for twenty-five. I had a stack of *Legion of Super Heroes* and *Supergirl* comic books in my bedroom closet that was as tall as I. I had a **recurring** dream in those days: that I had long blonde hair and could fly. In my dream I climbed the stairs to the top of our apartment building as myself, but as I went up each flight, changes would be taking place. Step by step I would fill out: my legs would grow long, my arms harden into steel, and my hair would magically go straight and turn a golden color. Of course, Supergirl had to be aerodynamic and sleek and hard as a supersonic missile.[1] Once on the roof, my parents safely asleep in their beds, I would get on tip-toe, arms outstretched in the position for flight, and jump out of my fifth-story-high window into the black lake of the sky. **1** From up there, over the rooftops, I could see everything, even

1 **Literary Element**

Imagery This paragraph has imagery that appeals to the senses of sight and touch (feeling). Here's a sampling:
- arms harden into steel
- hair turns golden
- sky described as black lake

---

1. To be **aerodynamic** (air oh dy NAM ik) is to be able to move through the air easily. To be **supersonic** is to be faster than the speed of sound.

Vocabulary

avid (AV id) *adj.* very eager or enthusiastic

recurring (rih KUR ing) *adj.* happening or coming back again; repeating

Visual Vocabulary
The *ermine* is a small, furry animal of the weasel family. Its fur makes luxurious and expensive coats.

beyond the few blocks of our barrio;[2] with my x-ray vision I could look inside the homes of people who interested me.

Once I saw our landlord, whom I knew my parents feared, sitting in a treasure-room dressed in an ermine coat and a large gold crown. He sat on the floor counting his dollar bills. I played a trick on him. Going up to his building's chimney, I blew a little puff of my super-breath into his fireplace, scattering his stacks of money so that he had to start counting all over again. **2**

I could more or less **program** my Supergirl dreams in those days by focusing on the object of my current obsession.[3] **3**

---

2. In the United States, **barrio** refers to a city neighborhood in which most people are Hispanic.

3. An **obsession** is an idea or feeling, especially an unreasonable one, that takes over a person's thoughts.

Practice the Skills

2 | **Key Reading Skill**

Analyzing Why do the narrator's parents fear the landlord?

3 | **English Language Coach**

A Changing Language What does **program** mean here? (If you need help, review the table on page 1066.)

Analyzing the Photo Look at the facial expression of the teenager in this photo. In what way do you think she is similar to the narrator?

Supergirl, 1984. Tristar. Movie still.

Analyzing the Photo The narrator wants certain qualities. Which of those qualities are shown in this picture from the movie *Supergirl?*

This way I saw into the private lives of my neighbors, my teachers, and in the last days of my childish fantasy and the beginning of **adolescence**, into the secret rooms of the boys I liked. In the mornings I'd wake up in my tiny bedroom with its incongruous⁴ —at least in our tiny apartment—white "princess" furniture my mother had chosen for me, and find myself back in my body; my tight curls still clinging to my head, my skinny arms and legs unchanged. ◆

---

4. Something that's ***incongruous*** (in KAHN groo us) is out of place or not working in harmony with something else. Here, the narrator feels her fancy furniture is out of place.

Vocabulary

adolescence (ad uh LES uns) *n.* the period between childhood and adulthood

Practice the Skills

◆ **Literary Element**

Imagery Notice how the narrator describes herself in the last clause. How does this picture of her compare with the image of her as Supergirl?

In the kitchen my mother and father would be talking softly over a *café con leche.*[5] She would come "wake me" exactly forty-five minutes after they had gotten up. It was their time together at the beginning of each day, and even at an early age I could feel their disappointment if I interrupted them by getting up too early. So I would stay in my bed recalling my dreams of flight, perhaps planning my next flight. In the kitchen they would be discussing events in the barrio. Actually, my father would be carrying that part of the conversation; when it was her turn to speak she would, more often than not, try shifting the topic toward her desire to see her *familia* on the Island: How about a vacation in Puerto Rico together this year, *querido?* We could rent a car, go to the beach. We could . . . And he would answer patiently, gently: *Mi amor,* do you know how much it would cost for all of us to fly there? It is not possible for me to take the time off . . . *Mi vida,*[6] please understand . . . And I knew that soon she would rise from the table. Not **abruptly.** She would look out the kitchen window. The view was of a dismal alley that was littered with **refuse** thrown from windows. The space was too narrow for anyone larger than a skinny child to enter safely, so it was never cleaned. My mother would check the time on the clock over her sink, the one with a prayer for patience and grace written in Spanish. A birthday gift. She would see that it was time to wake me. She'd sigh deeply and say the same thing the view from her kitchen window always inspired her to say: *"Ay, si yo pudiera volar.*[7]*"* **5 6** ○

---

5. *Café con leche* (kuh FAY kohn LAY chay) is Spanish for "coffee with milk."

6. *Familia* (fah MEEL ee uh) is Spanish for "family," *querido* (kay REE doh) means "darling," *mi amor* (mee ah MOR) means "my love," and *mi vida* (mee VEE dah) means "my life." Here, *mi vida* is used the same way as "darling" and "my love."

7. The mother says "Oh, if I could fly."

Vocabulary

abruptly (uh BRUPT lee) *adv.* suddenly; unexpectedly

refuse (REF yooz) *n.* trash; rubbish

Practice the Skills

5 | **Reviewing Elements**

Conflict What is the main conflict between the mother and father? What are some possible ways this conflict might be resolved?

6 **BIG** Question

How do the mother's wish and the daughter's dream reflect one another? Write your answer on the "Volar" page of Foldable 8. Your response will help you answer the Unit Challenge later.

After You Read : Volar

Answering the **BIG** Question

1. How do you think the narrator's mother would answer the question "What is the American dream?"

2. **Recall** Who was the narrator's favorite comic-book hero?
   TIP Right There

3. **Recall** According to the narrator, why does her mother want to fly to Puerto Rico?
   TIP Right There

4. **Describe** In your own words, describe the view from the kitchen window of the apartment.
   TIP Think and Search

Critical Thinking

5. **Contrast** What clues are there that the mother and father might have different attitudes toward their life in the United States? Support your answer with details from the story.
   TIP Author and Me

6. **Draw Conclusions** The title is a Spanish word, and the father and mother use Spanish words and phrases several times. Yet the narrator never uses Spanish to describe her own thoughts and dreams. What do you think accounts for the difference?
   TIP Author and Me

7. **Analyze** Each of the three characters expresses at least a thought about flying. What do you think flying represents to each person? Explain your answers, using details from the story to support your ideas.
   TIP Author and Me

Write About Your Reading

Descriptive Writing Imagine that you're a superhero in real life. What powers do you have, and what do you do with them? Write a few paragraphs describing

- your superhero self
- your most important superpowers
- how you use your powers

NY English Language Arts Core Curriculum
(pp. 1072–1073)

LC R17 Demonstrate comprehension and response through a range of activities. **LC W5** Write with voice to address varied purposes. **LC R12** Combine multiple strategies to enhance comprehension and response. **R2e** Recognize how the author's use of language creates images or feelings. **LC R9** Recognize multiple meanings of words.

For a complete description of the standards, see p. NY 11.

Skills Review

Key Reading Skill: Analyzing

8. Why does the narrator use one of her super-powers to "play a trick" on the landlord?

Literary Element: Imagery

9. List an image from the selection that appeals to each one of the five senses.

10. Explain this image from the first paragraph: "the black lake of the sky." How is the sky like a lake in the narrator's dream? Why is it black?

Reviewing Elements: Conflict

11. What is the narrator's main conflict in this story? Is it internal or external? Support your answer.

Vocabulary Check

Choose the best word from the list to complete each sentence below.

avid   recurring   adolescence   abruptly   refuse

12. She spent most of her ___ in Europe and didn't live in the United States until she was twenty.

13. Don't throw your litter on the highway! No one else wants your ___!

14. Before finishing her meal, she stood up and ___ left the room.

15. Nathan has every album the Beatles made; he's been an ___ fan for decades.

16. In this ___ nightmare, I'm always in bare feet, even in snow and freezing temperatures.

17. **English Language Coach** About when did people begin to use **program** as a verb? Find the answer in the chart on page 1066.

Web Activities For eFlashcards, Selection Quick Checks, and other Web activities, go to www.glencoe.com.

Grammar Link: Misused Words

English contains a number of confusing words, including the troublesome ones below. Some words are misused because they have *slightly* different meanings. Others are misused even though they have *very* different meanings.

between: used to talk about two people or things
• Choose **between** styles.

among: used to talk about groups of three or more
• Distribute the suits **among** the seven stores.

less: refers to a amount that you can't count
• There is **less** milk in that glass.

fewer: refers to an amount that can be counted
• I made **fewer** mistakes in this paragraph.

bring: to carry from a distant place to a closer one
• We **bring** goods into this country.

take: to carry from a closer place to a distant one
• They **take** goods to other countries.

leave: to go away
• I will **leave** on a camping trip.

let: to allow
• **Let** them bring a snack.

set: to place or to put
• They **set** our books on the desk.

sit: to place oneself in a seated position
• Let's **sit** here and talk about your problem.

Grammar Practice

Rewrite each sentence, filling in the correct word.

18. He evenly distributed the books (between, among) the four new students.

19. Rescue workers (bring, take) food to disaster sites.

20. The president will (leave, let) soon to visit Ohio.

21. The guests will (set, sit) on these chairs.

22. She has read (less, fewer) pages than I.

Writing Application Look back at your descriptive writing. If you used any of these troublesome words incorrectly, fix the mistakes.

Before You Read

from *The Century for Young People*

Alfred Levitt

Meet the Author

Alfred Levitt was born in 1894 in the Ukraine (then part of Russia). He was one of fourteen children. His family came to the United States to escape the Russian government's anti-Jewish campaigns. Here, Levitt became an artist. When he grew older, he gave this advice to a young artist: "Don't follow what other people tell you to do. [Your art] has to express who you are inside!"

Author Search For more about Alfred Levitt, go to www.glencoe.com.

NY English Language Arts Core Curriculum (pp. 1074–1077)

Core R4 Determine the meaning of words. **LC R12** Combine multiple strategies to enhance comprehension and response. **LC R13** Use text structure and literary devices to aid comprehension and response.

For a complete description of the standards, see p. NY 11.

Vocabulary Preview

literally (LIT ur uh lee) *adv.* actually; exactly **(p. 1076)** *The man couldn't even buy a pack of gum; he was literally penniless.*

accumulated (uh KYOO myuh lay tid) *v.* gathered or piled up, little by little; form of the verb *accumulate* **(p. 1077)** *The snow started slowly but soon accumulated into giant drifts that blocked the road.*

overwhelmed (oh vur WELMD) *adj.* overpowered in thought or feeling; completely covered or flooded **(p. 1077)** *Overwhelmed by the work, we fell behind schedule.*

means (meenz) *n.* methods useful for achieving a particular purpose or goal; resources **(p. 1078)** *She watched her means of getting home on time disappear as the last bus of the night left without her.*

Culture Shock Imagine that you're an immigrant just arriving in the United States. Use the vocabulary words to write a short paragraph describing your first impressions.

English Language Coach

English as a Changing Language The 12th century inhabitants of a certain island were the Engles. Where they lived was "the Engles' land," which was later reduced to "England." This simple history shows another way English language changes—in place names. Of course, names often had more complex origins. <u>America</u> was based on a mistake; here's what happened:

1492	Christopher Columbus, the Italian explorer, lands in what he believes to be India.	**India**
1498	On a second voyage, he "discovers" South America.	▼
1499–1501	Amerigo Vespucci, also Italian, explores the coast of South America. Back home, he writes letters to friends, referring to these lands as the "New World."	**New World**
1507	Martin Waldseemueller, a German mapmaker, reads Vespucci's letters, thinks Vespucci discovered the continent, and suggests naming it in his honor. He prints a map with "America" across the southern continent, and the name sticks.	▼ **America**

Naming of Names Research the name of your family, city, state, or school. Write an encyclopedia-style entry explaining its origin.

Skills Preview

Key Reading Skill: Analyzing

The selection you're about to read is an oral history. The words were spoken by one person and written down by someone else. As you read, consider its different parts to help you understand the whole selection. Think about what you already know about

- racism and religious discrimination
- what the Statue of Liberty represents
- how non-English-speaking immigrants learn English

Write to Learn In your Learner's Notebook, make a few notes about your knowledge of these topics.

Key Text Element: Chronological Order

Chronological order is a kind of sequence, a way of organizing events. The word *chronological* comes from the Greek word for *time,* and chronological order is the order in which events happen in time. In real life, events always take place in chronological order. These events are not directly related, but they're listed in the correct chronological order.

- Columbus discovers America.
- British colonies declare their independence.
- The Chicago White Sox win the 2005 World Series.

In reading, it's important to know the order of events. Time order is the clearest way to present travel directions, product instructions, and biographical narratives. Sometimes, however, writers present events in order of importance, trusting the reader to know—or figure out—the time order.

To keep track of the actual order of events, watch for signal words such as *before, first, next, then,* and *later.*

Interactive Literary Elements Handbook
To review or learn more about the literary elements, go to www.glencoe.com.

Get Ready to Read

Connect to the Reading

How would you feel if people shouted insults at you because you belonged to a particular ethnic group? How would you feel if you were not allowed to attend the same school as other students your age because of your religion? This is what happened to Alfred Levitt when he lived in Russia. As you read his selection, think about what you might have done in his place.

Partner Talk With a partner, talk about how it feels to have hurtful words used against you. Talk about how you act when you feel insulted, and explain why you act that way.

Build Background

Shortly after his 100th birthday, Alfred Levitt gave the interview that forms this oral history. As you'll see, his memories of life in Russia and his early years in America were still very clear.

- In Russia in the early 1900s, Jews were discriminated against, treated with violence, and often threatened with death. Many were killed.
- During this time, thousands of Jews and other immigrants from Europe who hoped to enter the United States came through New York City.
- Levitt's parents and their fourteen children all migrated to the United States by 1911. Levitt was then 14; he lived to the age of 105.

Set Purposes for Reading

Read the excerpt from *The Century for Young People* to think about what the American dream meant to Alfred Levitt.

Set Your Own Purpose What would you like to learn from the selection to help you answer the Big Question? Write your purpose on the "Century for Young People" page of Foldable 8.

Keep Moving

Use these skills as you read the following selection.

from The CENTURY for Young People

by Alfred Levitt

Practice the Skills

I was born in a small Russian town of about ten thousand people. We were a poor family. My father made the horse-drawn carriages that the bourgeoisie used on Sundays to promenade[1] down the street. It would take him about six months to build each carriage because he couldn't afford any tools and he had to build each one with his own ten fingers.

Visual Vocabulary
Horse-drawn carriages are wheeled vehicles that are pulled by horses and carry people.

During the six months it took my father to finish a carriage, the family starved. We had no money, and the rich people wouldn't pay my father until he finished his carriage. It was a very hard life. **1**

My family was part of a population of about two thousand Jews in our city. People yelled out "bad Jew" and "Christ-killer," and they said that we shouldn't be allowed to live. There was a pogrom[2] in 1905 where the Russians looted every store that was either owned or operated by a Jew. I remember my mother pulling me into a hiding place for fear that I would be hurt. It was this abuse against the Jews that made my two brothers decide to go to the United States. In Russia, everyone thought that America was such a rich country that you could **literally** find gold in the streets. At home there were no jobs

1 Key Reading Skill

Analyzing In these first two paragraphs, Levitt describes the situation of his family and the Jews in Russia. Explain why the Levitts decided to go to America, and tell whether you think they made a wise decision.

---

1. ***Bourgeoisie*** (burzh wah ZEE) is a French word meaning "middle class." To ***promenade*** (prawm uh NAYD) is to go for a slow, relaxed drive or stroll.

2. A ***pogrom*** (POH gruhm) was an organized attack against Jews. A great many pogroms were carried out in eastern Europe up to the early 1900s. Often, all Jews in a certain area were murdered; less often, few were killed but their homes and businesses were destroyed.

Vocabulary

literally (LIT ur uh lee) *adv.* actually; exactly

for Jews, but in America surely my brothers would find work. They went to New York, worked hard as house painters, and **accumulated** enough money to buy passage[3] for the rest of the family. **2**

I had never seen an ocean before we got on the boat for America. I looked out onto the sea and saw these huge waves crashing up against the rocks. It was a frightening experience. But then I saw the openness of the ocean, and that great body of water opened my mind to a world that I never knew existed. As we approached New York Harbor I saw the Statue of Liberty, and I was **overwhelmed** with a feeling of hope for a beautiful life in a new nation. Then we headed toward Ellis Island and I could see the big buildings of New York. It was

---

3. One meaning of *passage* is "a trip; a going across." Like most immigrants from Europe, the family crossed the Atlantic Ocean by ship.

Vocabulary

accumulated (uh KYOO myuh lay tid) *v.* gathered or piled up, little by little

overwhelmed (oh vur WELMD) *adj.* overpowered in thought or feeling; completely covered or flooded

Practice the Skills

2 **BIG Question**

How did Russians in the early 1900s picture America? Write your answer on the "Century for Young People" page of Foldable 8. Your response will help you complete the Unit Challenge later.

Analyzing the Photo Immigrants at Ellis Island see the Statue of Liberty. How does this image suggest both hope and uncertainty?

an amazing sight. The city I came from only had little shacks made of wood and stone. Here everything was big and new. At Ellis Island[4] they looked in my eyes to see if I was healthy and they checked my hair for lice. When they determined that my family and I were not sick, they put us on another boat and we were finally admitted to the United States. **3**

At first I was afraid to go in the subway. I didn't want to climb down into that dark hole. In Russia the only **means** of transportation that I knew about were horses and bicycles. When I did go in, I discovered a whole new world. There were advertisements that told me what to buy. And I saw people—blacks, yellows, all sorts of different facial looks and ethnic groups, people like I had never seen before. Most of all,

---

4. From 1892 to 1954, most European immigrants entered the United States at **Ellis Island** in New York Bay.

Vocabulary

means (meenz) *n.* methods useful for achieving a particular purpose or goal; resources

Analyzing the Photo What part of Levitt's experience does this photograph show?

Practice the Skills

3 | **Key Text Element**

Chronological Order Notice the words in this paragraph—*before, then, as, then, when,* and *finally*—that signal time order.

Practice the Skills

Analyzing the Photo Where do you think this picture was taken? What words would you use to describe this picture?

I was amazed that I could go anywhere for five cents. I was able to go all the way down to **Battery** Park, and then, if I chose, I could transfer and turn around and go all the way up to Yonkers[5] for the same nickel. **4**

My first school was on 103rd Street near Third Avenue, but when I discovered that there were too many foreign boys in the same class, I left it, because I wasn't learning the American language fast enough. I wanted to learn the American language because I wanted to understand the American people, the American mind, and the American culture. I wanted to be completely American, and that couldn't happen in a school full of foreign boys. Mostly I wanted to get a good job somewhere, and I knew if I didn't speak English, I couldn't get a good job. So I walked down to another high school in Harlem on 116th Street and asked the supervisor to give me an audience.[6] I told him I wanted to learn the American language and I wasn't getting it on 103rd Street. He said, "I will give you two questions. If you pass them, you are admitted." He asked me to spell *accident* for him, and I did right away, with two *c*'s. Then he asked me what two-thirds of fifteen was, and I said, "Ten," so he admitted me to high school. In Russia, only a small percentage of Jewish children could go to school, and then it had to be a special Jewish school. In America, I could go to school with everyone else. **5 6** ○

4 English Language Coach

A Changing Language The early meaning of **battery** is "a beating." Later, a new meaning was added: a grouping of cannons in battle. *Battery Park* got its name from the second meaning.

5 Key Reading Skill

Analyzing Why did the man ask these two questions?

6 BIG Question

In what ways did the American dream become a reality for Levitt? Write your answer on the "Century for Young People" page of Foldable 8.

---

5. **Battery Park** is a neighborhood at the southern edge of New York City, while **Yonkers** is a separate city about 25 miles north of Battery Park.
6. **Harlem** is a neighborhood of New York City. Here, **audience** means "a hearing; an interview."

After You Read

from *The Century for Young People*

Answering the **BIG** Question

1. What did the American dream mean to Alfred Levitt?

2. **Recall** How long did it take Levitt's father to build one carriage?
   Tip Right There

3. **Recall** What work did Levitt's brothers do after they came to New York?
   Tip Right There

4. **Describe** Describe Levitt's impressions of his first experiences in America.
   Tip Think and Search

Critical Thinking

5. **Compare** How was the Russian city Levitt was born in different from or similar to New York City? Give details from the oral history in your answer.
   Tip Think and Search

6. **Infer** What do you think would have happened if Levitt hadn't decided to change schools? Explain your answer.
   Tip Author and Me

7. **Interpret** In your own words, tell what Levitt means when he says he wanted to be "completely American."
   Tip Author and Me

Write About Your Reading

Postcards Pretend that you are Levitt at age 17, soon after he arrives in New York City. You're going to send two picture postcards to friends back in Russia.

First, imagine the postcard scenes Levitt might have sent. Think of two different things that impressed him or two important experiences he had. Make a few notes about each scene and what it meant to Levitt.

Second, write the message for each postcard as Levitt might have written it. Tell each friend about the picture, what it represents to Levitt, and why he chose that image for his friend. Keep each message to four or five sentences.

NY English Language Arts Core Curriculum
(pp. 1080–1081)

LC R17 Demonstrate comprehension and response through a range of activities. **LC W5** Write with voice to address varied purposes. **LC R12** Combine multiple strategies to enhance comprehension and response. **LC R13** Use text structure and literary devices to aid comprehension and response. **Core R4** Determine the meaning of words. **Core W7** Observe rules of spelling (correctly spell commonly misspelled words and homonyms).

For a complete description of the standards, see p. NY 11.

Skills Review

Key Reading Skill: Analyzing

8. What things about New York City's subway system were especially impressive to Levitt? Why do you suppose those things affected him so much?

9. Write a sentence stating the main subject of each paragraph in the selection.

Key Text Element: Chronological Order

10. Put the following events from Levitt's life in the correct chronological order.

- His mother hides him during a pogrom.
- He is admitted to a new high school.
- He sees the ocean for the first time.
- He first sees the New York skyline.
- His brothers go to New York.
- He is born in Russia.

Vocabulary Check

For each vocabulary word, choose the word or phrase that means most nearly the same thing.

11. literally
really   completely   unbelievably

12. accumulated
spent   saved up   bought

13. overwhelmed
late   undone   overcome

14. means
ways   purposes   explanations

15. English Language Coach What is the connection between these meanings of *battery?*

(a) a beating (b) a grouping of cannons in battle

Web Activities For eFlashcards, Selection Quick Checks, and other Web activities, go to www.glencoe.com.

Grammar Link: Confused Words

These words are often confused because they sound alike. Learning the correct use of these words will help you as a speaker and as a writer.

accept: to receive

except: other than
- I **accept** your nomination.
- **Except** for Lois, we all came here as immigrants.

loose: not firmly attached

lose: to misplace or to fail to win
- These jeans are too **loose.**
- If you **lose** your way, call me on your cell phone.

then: at that time

than: introduces the second part of a comparison
- **Then** I asked him his name.
- My brother is a lot taller **than** I am.

who's: contraction of *who is*

whose: possessive form of *who*
- **Who's** going to the store this afternoon?
- **Whose** book is this?

it's: contraction of *it is*

its: possessive form of *it*
- **It's** almost time to go home.
- **Its** leaves had turned crimson and began to fall.

Grammar Practice

Rewrite each sentence, filling in the correct word.

16. Will you (accept, except) my apology?

17. We have to decide (who's, whose) going to go first.

18. Did you put the camera back in (it's, its) case?

19. Texas is bigger (than, then) some countries.

Writing Application Check the postcard messages you wrote. If you used any of these troublesome words incorrectly, fix the mistakes.

Writing Rubric

As you work through this writing assignment, you should follow these guidelines:

- clearly state your opinion
- develop and support your ideas with well-chosen details
- organize your ideas in a logical order
- interview a friend, classmate, or family member

See page 1130 in Part 2 for a model of a letter.

NY English Language Arts Core Curriculum
(pp. 1082–1085)

Core W1 Understand the purpose for writing. **Core W12** Write for an authentic purpose. **Core W4** Use prewriting activities. **LC W7** Compose arguments to support points of view with relevant details. **Core L1** Adapt listening strategies to various purposes and settings. **Core W8** Use correct grammatical construction in parts of speech.

For a complete description of the standards, see p. NY 11.

People watch more television than ever before. Most comedy series are sitcoms, short for "situation comedies." In each episode, the characters deal with a new situation, or a problem, in a humorous way.

You'll evaluate the way one comedy series presents Americans, their relationships, "ordinary" life in America, and the American dream. Then you'll write a letter to the producer of that series. Your evaluation will help you think about the Unit 8 Big Question: What is the American dream?

Prewriting
Get Ready to Write

Draw from your own experience as a TV viewer and from your knowledge of the elements of fiction. Sitcoms are like ongoing short stories with characters, conflicts, dialogue, settings, and themes.

Gather Ideas

Follow these steps to generate ideas for your letter.

- List the sitcoms that you enjoy watching, and choose one to write about.
- Identify the main characters, and write a few words describing each. What are their relationships? (Are they, for example, family members, coworkers, friends, or classmates?) What does each character do? (Teacher, garbage collector, student, or store clerk?)
- Describe the setting of the show. Is it urban, suburban, or rural? What city, state, or region of the country? When does it take place? Most sitcoms are set in the present. For an older show that's set in the past, give the decade—for example, the 1960s for *The Wonder Years*.
- Describe the sort of problem the characters face in a typical episode. Do they usually solve their problems? How?
- Decide whether the characters are realistic people or stereotypes. Stereotypes are characters with traits that are supposedly shared by all members of a particular group. For example, a stereotype of old people is that they're all grumpy and hard of hearing. A stereotype of teenagers is that they only want to have fun and don't care about serious issues.
- Consider what the sitcom says about America and Americans. What impressions do you think viewers in other countries would get from it?
- What advice do you have for the people who write or produce the show?

Organize Your Thoughts

Gather your notes. Then follow these steps.

1. Decide whom to write to. You'll need to do some research to find people who work behind the scenes. Check the Web site of the channel the show is on. For example, one student liked *The Simpsons* and decided to write to its creator, Matt Groening.

2. Write one sentence that clearly states your overall opinion about the show and how it presents American life.

> I think <u>The Simpsons</u> shows both our worst and best sides.

3. Give three or more reasons for your opinion. Later, you'll develop each reason into a paragraph.

> The mix of characters is true to life.
> Springfield's problems ring true for viewers.
> The main characters have their good points.

4. Write one or two sentences that sum up your message of praise, criticism, or a combination of both.

> Thanks for making us laugh at ourselves while encouraging us to solve our problems.

Writing Models For models and other writing activities, go to www.glencoe.com.

◀ **Writing Tip**

Show Titles When you're typing the title of a TV series, you should use italics. When you're handwriting it, you can underline the title instead.

◀ **Writing Tip**

Brainstorming If you need help getting started, try freewriting for three minutes without stopping. Write down anything that comes to mind about the show. After a break, read what you've written. You may find something to use as a starting point for your letter.

Drafting
Start Writing!

You have everything you need to get started: a topic, a clear position, some organized points, and a concluding statement.

Get It on Paper

These directions can help you get started on your first draft.

- Begin by explaining your purpose for writing and briefly stating your opinion of the show.

- Write a paragraph explaining each reason for your opinion. Back up your points with specific examples from the show. You might use a quotation from a classmate or family member to support one of your points.

- Write a conclusion that explains how well or how badly you think the show portrays America and Americans.

- Finish by complimenting or criticizing the show. If you're critical, make suggestions for how to improve it.

◀ **Writing Tip**

Drafting Remember that this is only a first draft. When you go back to revise, you can add, delete, and move ideas.

Listening, Speaking, and Viewing

Conducting an Interview

As part of your evaluation, it's a good idea to ask other people what they think about the show. Interview at least two people.

What Is an Interview?

An interview is a conversation with the purpose of getting information about a particular topic. You hear, see, and read plenty of interviews, whether you realize it or not.

TV and radio shows, Web sites, newspapers, and magazines—they all make frequent use of interviews with all kinds of people, including

- government officials, crime victims, disaster survivors, and other people in the news
- movie stars, authors, coaches, athletes, and other celebrities
- sports fans, shoppers, and weather watchers

What Skills Do I Need, and Why Are They Important?

The same skills that help you talk to classmates, teachers, family members, and store clerks can help you interview them. You need to be organized and prepared. You need to be able to listen without interrupting. You need patience and understanding.

Listening to other people's ideas can reinforce or challenge your own opinions. Quoting other people can add spice to your writing.

How Do I Do an Interview?

Prepare by making a list of questions.

- Think about what supporting information you need and ask for opinions about those ideas. *Example:* If you believe the Simpson characters have their good points, you might ask, "What do you think of Bart? Why?"

Analyzing Cartoons
Is this a good interview? Why or why not?

- Don't ask leading questions. That is, don't phrase a question so that it suggests the answer you want. *Example:* Don't ask, "Do you agree that *The Simpsons* is biased against rural people?" Instead, ask, "Do you think the show portrays rural people in a fair way?"
- Phrase your questions so that the interviewee can't answer with a simple yes or no.

When you're ready to do an interview, don't rely on your memory. Write your questions down on note cards or paper. Record the conversation (only after asking permission), or take good notes.

- Start with your prepared questions, but be ready to respond to what the interviewee says.
- Try not to show your own opinions. You want people to tell you what they really think, not what they think you want to hear.
- Be a good listener. Nodding and making eye contact show that you're paying attention. Encourage people to keep talking by saying, "Go on" or "I see."
- If you don't understand something, ask the interviewee to clarify it. Paraphrase what the person said to check whether you understood correctly. *Example:* "When you said 'they,' did you mean the characters or the writers?"

Write to Learn Use your interviewees' responses in your letter. If you quote someone directly, use quotation marks and give the person's name. If you paraphrase, be sure you're presenting the interviewee's opinion accurately.

Grammar Link

Irregular Verbs

It is important to learn how to form verb tenses so you can use verbs correctly in a sentence. However, that is just the beginning. You also need to learn about irregular verbs that may be confusing.

What Are Irregular Verbs?

For regular verbs, you form the past tense and past participle by adding -d or –ed to the verb's base form.

- I want to <u>live</u> in Toledo, Ohio. (base form)
- I <u>live**d**</u> in Toledo, Ohio. (past tense)
- I <u>have live**d**</u> in Toledo, Ohio for a year. (past participle)

The past tense and past participle of irregular verbs are not formed this way.

- I am going to <u>be</u> in Toledo, Ohio. (base form)
- I <u>went</u> to Toledo, Ohio. (past tense)
- I <u>have been</u> to Toledo, Ohio. (past participle)

Several patterns are used to form irregular verbs. With time and practice, you'll remember them.

A. One vowel changes to form the past tense and the past participle. *(begin, began, have begun)*

B. The past tense and the past participle are the same. *(fight, fought, has fought)*

C. The base form and the past participle are the same. *(run, ran, had run)*

D. The past tense ends in -ew, and the past participle ends in -wn. *(draw, drew, have drawn)*

E. The past participle ends in -en. *(shake, shook, has shaken)*

F. The base form, the past tense, and the past participle are the same. *(cost, cost, have cost)*

G. The past tense and the past participle don't follow any pattern. *(be, was/were, had been)*

Why Are They Important?

When you use verbs incorrectly, it makes you sound less knowledgeable than you are. Also, you may confuse your readers if you use the wrong form or tense of a verb by treating an irregular verb as if it follows the regular pattern. For example, by using *falled* instead of *fell* or *have fell* instead of *have fallen,* you make it unclear when an action takes place.

Incorrect: I <u>have fell</u> out of a tree while climbing.
Correct: I <u>have fallen</u> out of a tree while climbing.

How Do I Use Irregular Verbs?

To express an action that happened at a fixed time in the past, use the past tense of the verb.
- The water <u>froze</u> in the pond.

To express an action that happened before another action in the past, use *had* before the past participle.
- The water <u>had frozen</u> in the pond by noon.

To express an action that will occur before a set time in the future, use *will have* before the past participle.
- The water <u>will have frozen</u> by the time we get home.

To express an action that occurred at an unspecified time in the past or an action that continues to happen into the present time, use *have* or *has* before the past participle.
- In the past, the water <u>has frozen</u> enough to allow ice skating.

Write to Learn Review your draft and fix any mistakes involving irregular verbs. If you need help, use a dictionary. The past tense and past participle of irregular verbs are usually included in the entry for the base form of the verb.

Looking Ahead

Keep the writing you've done so far. In Writing Workshop Part 2, you'll learn how to turn your writing into a strong and compelling letter.

Skills Focus

You will practice using these skills when you read the following selections:

- "Lottery Winners Who Lost Their Millions," p. 1090
- "The Gettysburg Address," p. 1098

Reading

- Understanding cause and effect

Informational Text

- Understanding theme and topic
- Identifying author's style

Vocabulary

- Learning about English as a changing language

Writing/Grammar

- Using capitalization with proper nouns, proper adjectives, and family relationships

NY English Language Arts Core Curriculum
(pp. 1086–1094)

LC R13 Use text structure and literary devices to aid comprehension and response.

For a complete description of the standards, see p. NY 11.

Understanding Cause and Effect

Learn It!

What Is It? Cause and effect is a kind of text structure that writers can use to organize information.

- A **cause** is a condition or event that makes something happen.
- What happens as the result of that condition or event is an **effect.**

For example, a person does something wrong (a cause), and a bad thing happens (an effect).

A cause-and-effect relationship can be difficult to identify exactly. Causes and effects can overlap. They may not seem directly linked. Not all events that seem to have a cause-and-effect relationship actually do.

© Zits Partnership. Reprinted with Permission of King Features Syndicate, Inc.

Analyzing Cartoons
Jeremy thinks that eating sandwiches is making Hector grow taller. Do you agree with that cause-and-effect statement? Why?

Why Is It Important? When you understand cause-and-effect relationships, you have another tool to help you think critically as a reader. You can see why characters are in the situations they're in. You can recognize when events are connected and when they aren't.

How Do I Do It? To identify cause-and-effect relationships in a selection, use your prior knowledge. Ask yourself what you know about the subject, what events may have caused it, and what events may have resulted from it.

Here's how one student used his prior knowledge about Abraham Lincoln's Gettysburg Address.

Study Central Visit www.glencoe .com and click on Study Central to review evaluating.

> I know this is one of Lincoln's most famous speeches. I know from history class that there was a huge Civil War battle at Gettysburg. And I think Lincoln spoke at a service honoring the soldiers who died there. So two effects of the battle were soldiers' deaths and Lincoln's speech.
>
> Actually, there must be a whole chain of causes and effects related to this battle and the war. I wonder what effects the Gettysburg Address had.

Practice It!

Below are some things to look for as you analyze the selections in this workshop. Jot down a few notes in your Learner's Notebook about causes and effects related to the following topics:

- the dream of being rich
- winning millions of dollars
- the Civil War
- the idea that "all men are created equal"

Use It!

As you read "Lottery Winners Who Lost Their Millions" and "The Gettysburg Address," remember the notes you made. They'll help you focus on cause and effect as you read.

Before You Read

Lottery Winners Who Lost Their Millions

Ellen Goodstein

Meet the Author

Ellen Goodstein is a freelance writer based in Florida. She contributes news stories and feature articles to both print and online publications.

Author Search For more about Ellen Goodstein, go to www .glencoe.com.

NY English Language Arts Core Curriculum
(pp. 1088–1093)

Core R4 Determine the meaning of words. **LC R13** Use text structure and literary devices to aid comprehension and response. **R2b** Interpret theme, using evidence from the text.

For a complete description of the standards, see p. NY 11.

Vocabulary Preview

siblings (SIB lingz) *n.* brothers and sisters **(p. 1091)** *My siblings and I gave our parents flowers for their anniversary.*

eventually (ih VEN choo uh lee) *adj.* happening at last; in the end **(p. 1091)** *Be patient; you'll eventually get to the front of the line.*

inevitable (in EV uh tuh bul) *adj.* sure to happen; unavoidable **(p. 1093)** *With its weak design and cheap materials, the car's failure to sell seemed inevitable.*

consequences (KAHN suh kwen suz) *n.* results or effects **(p. 1093)** *If you break the law, you will have to face the consequences.*

Write to Learn With a small group, choose a familiar board game or gameshow that involves making–and losing–money. Together, write a paragraph explaining how the game is played. Use each vocabulary word at least once.

English Language Coach

English as a Changing Language Many English words have roots in ancient, long-dead languages. The base of *lottery* is *lot*, a word that goes back more than eight hundred years. (In Old English it was spelled *hlot*, but there isn't a hlot more to say about that.)

Originally, lots were pieces of shell, bone, or wood. They were used to help decide questions or issues, just as dice are used in many modern games. You threw the lots to the ground and "read" an answer to your question. Soon people started betting on how the lots would land. From there, it was a short leap to lotteries as we now know them. Over the centuries, the word *lot* took on additional meanings, including these:

lot
a share
a portion of land
an article or group of articles sold at auction
a large quantity or amount

Small Group Discussion With your group, look again at the paragraph you wrote about a board game or gameshow. Do any of the meanings of *lot* noted above relate to the game? Is any kind of lottery (or "throwing of lots") involved? How important is chance or luck in playing the game?

Skills Preview

Key Reading Skill: Understanding Cause and Effect

A fiction writer invents causes and effects to direct a story where he or she wants it to go. A nonfiction writer doesn't need to make them up; they're right there in real life. Nonfiction writing tries to present events so that the causes and effects are clear.

The next article you'll read tells what happened to a number of people who won millions of dollars. In each case, the cause can be described as winning money in a lottery. The article focuses on

- the effects that sudden wealth can cause
- the belief that money can fix anything
- strategies for dealing with unexpected wealth

Write to Learn In your Learner's Notebook, note ideas you have about causes and effects relating to money. What are possible effects of having no money? What are possible effects of having lots of money? Add to your notes as you read the selection.

Text Element: Theme and Topic

A story's **theme** is its central message. Sometimes the theme is stated directly; sometimes it's implied, and you must figure it out.

Don't confuse theme with topic. **Topic** is the broad subject that a story is about. It can be stated in a word or phrase. For example, both "Volar" and the selection from *The Century for Young People* are about the immigrant experience. However, the theme of "Volar" involves escaping what is unpleasant in life, and the theme of *Century* involves embracing what is new and exciting.

Interactive Literary Elements Handbook
To review or learn more about the literary elements, go to www.glencoe.com.

Get Ready to Read

Connect to the Reading

Imagine becoming a millionaire overnight. Would money solve your problems? What's the first thing you'd do? Buy things? Give money to charities? How would you deal with friends and relatives who would expect you to help them out? Who would you turn to for advice?

Money Talks With a partner, talk about the problems and solutions money can bring. Draw on your own experience and the experiences of people you know or have read about.

Build Background

As of 1999, thirty-seven U.S. states operated lotteries to raise money for public services. Canada, France, Great Britain, Japan, Mexico, and other countries run national lotteries. In a modern lottery, you pay a small sum of money for a chance to win a huge sum. Your chances and your prize depend on how many people enter the lottery.

A lottery can be very profitable for its sponsor because most participants don't win anything. Since ancient times, lotteries have been used to raise money for projects including the Great Wall of China; Jamestown (the first British colony in America); and Harvard, Yale, Princeton, and Columbia universities.

Set Purposes for Reading

BIG Question Read this article to study the role of money in the American dream.

Set Your Own Purpose What would you like to learn from the article to help you answer the Big Question? Write your purpose on the "Lottery Winners" page of Foldable 8.

Keep Moving

Use these skills as you read the following selection.

Lottery Winners Who LOST Their MILLIONS

by Ellen Goodstein

INFORMATIONAL TEXT
WEB ARTICLE

Bankrate.com

For a lot of people, winning the lottery is the American dream. But for many lottery winners, the reality is more like a **nightmare**. **1**

"Winning the lottery isn't always what it's cracked up to be," says Evelyn Adams, who won the New Jersey lottery not just once, but twice (1985, 1986), to the tune of $5.4 million. Today the money is all gone and Adams lives in a trailer.

Visual Vocabulary
A *trailer* is a vehicle that can be parked and serve as a home.

"I won the American dream but I lost it, too. It was a very hard fall. It's called rock bottom," says Adams. "Everybody wanted my money. Everybody had their hand out. I never learned one simple word in the English language—'No.' I wish I had the chance to do it all over again. I'd be much smarter about it now," says Adams, who also lost money at the slot machines in Atlantic City.[1] **2**

"I was a big-time gambler," admits Adams. "I didn't drop a million dollars, but it was a lot of money. I made mistakes, some I regret, some I don't. I'm human. I can't go back now so I just go forward, one step at a time."

Living on food stamps William "Bud" Post won $16.2 million in the Pennsylvania lottery in 1988 but now lives on his Social Security.[2]

"I wish it never happened. It was totally a nightmare," says Post.

---

1. **Atlantic City,** New Jersey, offers many forms of gambling.
2. The federal **Social Security** program works like a savings account for old age. A small portion of a worker's paycheck goes to the program, along with a matching amount paid by the employer. Upon retirement, the worker receives a monthly income from the program. Most U.S. employees participate in Social Security.

Practice the Skills

1 **English Language Coach**

A Changing Language In Old English, a *mere* was either a female horse or an evil being that brought bad dreams. In modern English, the spelling has changed, and we have different ideas about what causes a **nightmare**. A *mare* is still a horse, of course.

2 **Key Reading Skill**

Understanding Cause and Effect What does Adams say was the main cause of her problems after she won the lottery? What additional cause does she identify in the next paragraph?

A former girlfriend successfully sued him for a share of his winnings. It wasn't his only lawsuit. A brother was arrested for hiring a hit man to kill him, hoping to inherit a share of the winnings. Other **siblings** pestered him until he agreed to invest in a car business and a restaurant in Sarasota, Fla.— two ventures[3] that brought no money back and further strained his relationship with his siblings.

Post even spent time in jail for firing a gun over the head of a bill collector. Within a year, he was $1 million in debt.

Post admitted he was both careless and foolish, trying to please his family. He **eventually** declared **bankruptcy**.[4] Now he lives quietly on $450 a month and food stamps. **3**

"I'm tired, I'm over 65 years old, and I just had a serious operation for a heart aneurysm.[5] Lotteries don't mean (anything) to me," says Post. **4**

Deeper in debt Suzanne Mullins won $4.2 million in the Virginia lottery in 1993. Now she's deeply in debt.

She borrowed $197,746.15, which she agreed to pay back with her yearly checks from the Virginia lottery through 2006. When the rules changed allowing her to collect her winnings in a lump sum, she cashed in the remaining amount. But she stopped making payments on the loan.

She blamed the debt on the lengthy illness of her uninsured son-in-law, who needed $1 million for medical bills.

Back to the basics Ken Proxmire was a machinist[6] when he won $1 million in the Michigan lottery. He moved to California and went into the car business with his brothers. Within five years, he had filed for bankruptcy.

"He was just a poor boy who got lucky and wanted to take care of everybody," explains Ken's son Rick. "It was a good ride for three or four years, but now he lives more simply.

---

3. **Ventures** (VEN churz) are risky business projects.
4. **Bankruptcy** is a legal status for people or businesses that are ruined financially and can't pay their debts.
5. An **aneurysm** (AN yuh rih zum) is a blocked blood vessel.
6. A **machinist** (muh SHEE nist) makes, assembles, or repairs machinery.

Vocabulary

siblings (SIB lingz) *n.* brothers and sisters

eventually (ih VEN choo uh lee) *adj.* happening at last; in the end

Practice the Skills

3 **English Language Coach**
A Changing Language The word **bankruptcy** comes from two Old Italian words—*banca*, "bank," and *rotta*, "broken."

4 **Key Reading Skill**
Understanding Cause and Effect What were some of the effects of Post's winning the lottery?

There's no more talk of owning a helicopter or riding in limos. We're just everyday folk. Dad's now back to work as a machinist," says his son.

Missourian Janite Lee won $18 million in 1993. Lee was generous to a variety of causes,[7] giving to politics, education and the community. But according to published reports, eight years after winning, Lee had filed for bankruptcy with only $700 left in two bank accounts and no cash on hand.

One Southeastern family won $4.2 million in the early '90s. They bought a huge house and gave in to repeated family requests for help in paying off debts.

The house, cars and relatives used up all their winnings. Eleven years later, the couple is divorcing, the house is sold and they have to split what is left of the lottery proceeds.[8] The wife got a very small house. The husband has moved in with the kids. Even the life insurance they bought ended up getting cashed in.

"It was not the pot of gold at the end of the rainbow," says their financial advisor.

Luck is fleeting These sad-but-true tales are not uncommon, say the experts.

"For many people, sudden money can cause disaster," says Susan Bradley, a certified financial planner in Palm Beach, Fla., and founder of the Sudden Money Institute, a resource center for people who have received large amounts of money and their advisors.

"In our culture, there is a widely held belief that money solves problems. People think if they had more money, their troubles would be over. When a family receives sudden money, they frequently learn that money can cause as many problems as it solves," she says. **5**

Winning plays a game with your head Bradley, who authored "Sudden Money: Managing a Financial Windfall,"[9] says winners get into trouble because they fail to deal with the emotional connection to their unexpected wealth.

Analyzing the Photo How does this image illustrate the fact that money management takes work?

Practice the Skills

5 **BIG Question**
According to Bradley, what role does money play in the American dream? Write your answer on the "Lottery Winners" page of Foldable 8. Your response will help you complete the Unit Challenge later.

---

7. That is, Lee gave to charities. A charity is called a **cause** because it tries to bring about some sort of change and to produce some effect.

8. Here, **proceeds** (PROH seedz) refers to the money received.

9. A **windfall** is any unearned, unexpected, or sudden gain.

"Often they can keep the money and lose family and friends—or lose the money and keep the family and friends—or even lose the money and lose the family and friends," says Bradley.

Bill Pomeroy, a certified financial planner in Baton Rouge, La., has dealt with a number of lottery winners who went broke.

"Because the winners have a large sum of money, they make the mistake of thinking they know what they're doing. They are willing to plunk down large sums on investments they know nothing about or go in with a partner who may not know how to run a business."

What if you get so (un)lucky? To avoid bad early decision-making and the **inevitable** requests of friends, relatives and strangers, Bradley recommends lottery winners start by setting up a DFZ or decision-free zone.

"Take time out from making any financial decisions," she says. "Do this right away. For some people, it's smart to do it before you even get your hands on the money.

"It's not a time to decide what stocks to buy or jump into a new house purchase or new business venture," she warns. "It's a time to think things through, sort things out and seek an advisory team to help make those important financial choices."

As an example, Bradley says that people who come into a windfall will usually put buying a house as No. 1 in list of 12 choices, whereas investing is No. 11.

"You really don't want to buy a new house before taking the time to think about what the **consequences** are. A lot of people who don't have money don't realize how much it costs to live in a big house—decorators, furniture, taxes, insurance, even utility costs are greater. People need a reality check before they sign the contract," she says.

Evelyn Adams, the N.J. lottery double-winner, learned these lessons the hard way. "There are a lot of people out there like me who don't know how to deal with money," says Adams. "Hey, some people went broke in six months. At least I held on for a few years." **6** ○

Practice the Skills

6 **Text Element**

Theme and Topic A stated theme usually appears near the beginning or ending of a work. Do you find a sentence that you think states the theme of this article?

Vocabulary

inevitable (in EV uh tuh bul) *adj.* sure to happen; unavoidable

consequences (KAHN suh kwen suz) *n.* results or effects

After You Read

Lottery Winners Who Lost Their Millions

Answering the **BIG** Question

1. Financial advisor Susan Bradley says, "In our culture, there is a widely held belief that money solves problems." Do you agree with her? Explain your answer.

2. **Recall** According to Suzanne Mullins, what caused her to go into debt?
   Tip Right There

3. **Contrast** Contrast Ken Proxmire's life today with his life after he won $1 million in the Michigan lottery.
   Tip Think and Search

Critical Thinking

4. **Interpret** Evelyn Adams says in the article, "I won the American dream but I lost it, too." What does she mean?
   Tip Author and Me

5. **Explain** According to the article, what are some of the different ways that friends and family members of a lottery winner react?
   Tip Think and Search

6. **Evaluate** According to one expert, lottery winners need to deal with the emotional connection to their unexpected wealth. What is an "emotional connection" to money? Explain your answer.
   Tip On My Own

7. **Analyze** Susan Bradley recommends that lottery winners set up a "DFZ," or decision-free zone. How would this work? Could it be effective? Could the idea apply to other areas of life? Explain your answers.
   Tip Author and Me

NY English Language Arts Core Curriculum
(pp. 1094–1095)

LC R17 Demonstrate comprehension and response through a range of activities. **S1b** Contribute to group discussions by offering comments to clarify and interpret ideas and information. **LC R13** Use text structure and literary devices to aid comprehension and response. **R2b** Interpret theme, using evidence from the text.
Core R4 Determine the meaning of words. **Core W7** Observe rules of capitalization.

For a complete description of the standards, see p. NY 11.

Talk About Your Reading

Group Discussion Buying a house and investing were two of the top twelve choices that people made after they came into a lot of money. What were the other ten choices? In a small group, discuss the possibilities, and have one person write down your ideas. As a group, pick the other ten things that you think people did with their new wealth. Then, as a class, combine all the lists to create a single list of the Top Twelve Choices. What things did every group include? What surprising choices were listed?

Skills Review

Key Reading Skill: Understanding Cause and Effect

8. Financial expert Bill Pomeroy says, "Because the winners have a large sum of money, they [think] they know what they're doing."

- What does Pomeroy identify specifically as a cause?
- What does he identify as an effect?
- What one word indicates this cause-and-effect relationship?

9. What do you think leads people in our culture to believe that money can solve all their problems?

Text Element: Theme and Topic

10. What is the topic of this article?

11. Is the article's theme stated or implied? If stated, copy the sentence in which it's given. If implied, write the theme in your own words.

12. Tell why you think the statement below is or is not a good expression of this article's theme.

"Money always causes problems."

Vocabulary Check

Rewrite each statement, filling in the blank with the best word from the list.

siblings   eventually   inevitable   consequences

13. If you delay your homework, you do it ____.

14. If you don't tell the truth, there will be ____.

15. If you are an only child, you have no ____.

16. If you can't avoid something, it is ____.

English Language Coach

17. Five meanings of the word *lot* were given on page 1088. Which two meanings are related to the modern meaning of **lottery?**

18. The *rupt* part of **bankruptcy** means "broken." How does "bank-broken" (or "broken bank") make sense with the modern meaning of *bankruptcy?*

Grammar Link: Capitalization of Proper Nouns

A **common noun** is the general name of a person, place, thing, feeling, or idea. A **proper noun** names a *particular* person, place, or thing. Common nouns are not capitalized; proper nouns are. When proper nouns name people, capitalize all parts of their names and all initials that stand for their names.

- Roy J. Wilks called the manager into his office.

Capitalize a title or its abbreviation when it comes *before* a person's name. Do *not* capitalize a title that follows a person's name or is used as a common noun.

- It was Treasurer Sanchez who gave the first report.
- Janet Molloy was promoted to vice president.

Capitalize words that show family relationships when used as titles or substitutes for a person's name. Do *not* capitalize these words when they follow an article (*a, an,* or *the*) or a possessive noun or pronoun.

- In 2000 Father and Uncle Ray participated in a reenactment of the Battle of Gettysburg.
- My aunt Lisbeth wrote an article about the experience.

Grammar Practice

Rewrite the following sentences, correcting the six capitalization errors.

19. Joe stephenson played the role of a Villager from Gettysburg.

20. My dad played Brigadier-General james j. Pettigrew.

21. The Soldiers passed by my aunt Lila's house.

22. Looking up, uncle Ray yelled, "Don't be afraid!"

Web Activities For eFlashcards, Selection Quick Checks, and other Web activities, go to www.glencoe.com.

Before You Read

The Gettysburg Address

Abraham Lincoln

Meet the Author

Abraham Lincoln, born in 1809, worked hard to educate himself and become a lawyer. While a member of the Illinois legislature, he lost a race for the U.S. Senate. Still, he earned a national reputation and, in 1860, was elected President. He is remembered as the president who saved the union.

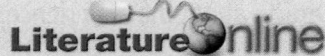

Author Search For more about Abraham Lincoln, go to www.glencoe.com.

NY English Language Arts Core Curriculum (pp. 1088–1091)

LC R5 Determine the meaning of unfamiliar words, terms, by using context, dictionaries. **LC R13** Use text structure and literary devices to aid comprehension and response. **R2e** Recognize how the author's use of language creates images or feelings.

For a complete description of the standards, see p. NY 11.

Vocabulary Preview

conceived (kun SEEVD) *adj.* formed; imagined **(p. 1098)** *As conceived by Jim, the plan would solve several problems at once.*

proposition (prahp uh ZIH shun) *n.* a plan or proposal **(p. 1098)** *Until the proposition is approved, we'll deal with things as we have in the past.*

endure (en DUR) *v.* to carry on; survive; last **(p. 1098)** *When we started out, no one thought the band would endure for three decades.*

detract (dih TRAKT) *v.* to take away from; reduce the value of **(p. 1098)** *One small flaw won't detract much from the final price.*

resolve (rih ZAHLV) *v.* to decide firmly **(p. 1099)** *It's one thing to resolve to get up earlier and another thing to actually do it.*

perish (PAIR ish) *v.* to become ruined or destroyed; die **(p. 1099)** *My garden will perish if the weather doesn't warm up soon.*

Write to Learn Pretend you're writing a speech that includes a proposition for your audience to consider. Your suggested plan involves a way to make a better school, neighborhood, or world. Don't write the speech, but write a paragraph explaining your idea and using all the vocabulary words.

English Language Coach

English as a Changing Language In Abraham Lincoln's time, the most common translation of the Bible was the King James Version. England's King James I had published this "modern" English version in 1611. It had a strong influence on Lincoln's writing style, and it has a strong influence on how speakers of English use the language today.

However, many words from the 1600s are archaic (ar KAY ik) in the twenty-first century; they're old-fashioned or out of use. For example, *score* used to be a number word, meaning "twenty," and was used like *decade* and *dozen.* If someone said "six score and five," the reader or listener had to do a bit of math (6 × 20, + 5). Now you have to do the sums. Write the numbers represented by these words:

three score	=	
four score and seven	=	
five score and two	=	

What's the Score? With a partner, research the meanings of *score,* as a noun and a verb. Note whether each meaning is archaic or still in use.

Skills Preview

Key Reading Skill: Understanding Cause and Effect

Before you read the selection, reflect on what you know about

- the causes of the Civil War
- the effects of the Civil War

Write to Learn In your Learner's Notebook, jot down some of your thoughts on the topics above.

Key Literary Element: Style

Style is a writer's personal way of using language. It includes qualities that make one writer's work unlike the work of all other writers. These qualities include

- word choice
- use of imagery
- sentence lengths
- sentence patterns
- ways of moving from one idea to the next

As you read the Gettysburg Address, use these tips to learn about Lincoln's style:

- Look at Lincoln's word choice.

  Which words seem carefully chosen? Which words are particularly effective, and why are they so effective?

- Look at the way he arranged the words and sentences.

  Can you follow his thoughts easily? Does each sentence add to the power of what he said before, yet say something new?

Interactive Literary Elements Handbook
To review or learn more about the literary elements, go to www.glencoe.com.

Get Ready to Read

Connect to the Reading

For many of us, the American dream is about working to make a good life for our families. It's easy to forget that the American dream is rooted in American history, back to the founding of our nation. Lincoln refers to this in the Gettysburg Address.

Group Discussion People often say it is important to know history. But is it really true? If so, why? Does it change anything in the present? Can it influence the future? Do we learn from our mistakes? In small groups discuss these questions.

Build Background

Nowadays, presidents have speech writers. Lincoln himself wrote the Gettysburg Address for the dedication of a cemetery.

- A major battle of the Civil War was fought near the town of Gettysburg, Pennsylvania, July 1–3, 1863. Casualties (killed and wounded) were estimated at more than 40,000 soldiers.
- The people of Gettysburg had to bury the dead. The federal government bought the battleground for a cemetery, and it provided the coffins.
- At the cemetery dedication on November 19, 1863, the main speaker went on for two hours. Lincoln spoke for two minutes. His speech is considered one of the finest speeches of all time.

Set Purposes for Reading

BIG Question Read the Gettysburg Address to see the American dream in terms of our history.

Set Your Own Purpose What would you like to learn from the speech to help you answer the Big Question? Write your own purpose on the "Gettysburg Address" page of Foldable 8.

Keep Moving

Use these skills as you read the following selection.

The Gettysburg Address

by Abraham Lincoln

Four score and seven years ago our fathers[1] brought forth on this continent a new nation, **conceived** in Liberty, and dedicated to the **proposition** that all men are created equal.

Now we are engaged in a great civil war, testing whether that nation, or any nation so conceived and so dedicated, can long **endure.** We are met on a great battlefield of that war. We have come to dedicate a portion of that field, as a final resting place for those who here gave their lives that that nation might live. It is altogether fitting and proper that we should do this. **1**

But, in a larger sense, we can not dedicate—we can not consecrate—we can not **hallow**[2]—this ground. **2** The brave men, living and dead, who struggled here, have consecrated it, far above our poor power to add or **detract.** The world will

---

1. **Four score and seven** is 87. Lincoln refers to the "founding **fathers,**" the men who wrote and adopted the Declaration of Independence and the U.S. Constitution.

2. In the first paragraph, **dedicated** meant "given completely." Here, **dedicate** means "set aside for a certain purpose." Similarly, both **consecrate** and **hallow** mean "make or honor as holy."

Vocabulary

conceived (kun SEEVD) *adj.* formed; imagined

proposition (prahp uh ZIH shun) *n.* a plan or proposal

endure (en DUR) *v.* to carry on; survive; last

detract (dih TRAKT) *v.* to take away from; reduce the value of

Practice the Skills

1 Key Literary Element

Style Pay close attention to Lincoln's word choices throughout the speech. What does he say in place of the word *cemetery?* How does he describe the dead? Does he talk about North and South?

2 English Language Coach

A Changing Language The word **hallow** is very nearly archaic. One place it is still used is in the name of a popular American holiday. Can you think of which one?

little note, nor long remember what we say here, but it can never forget what they did here. It is for us the living, rather, to be dedicated here to the unfinished work which they who fought here have thus far so nobly advanced. **3** It is rather for us to be here dedicated to the great task remaining before us—that from these honored dead we take increased devotion to that cause for which they gave the last full measure of devotion—that we here highly **resolve** that these dead shall not have died in vain[3]—that this nation, under God, shall have a new birth of freedom—and that government of the people, by the people, for the people, shall not **perish** from the earth. **4** ○

---

3. The phrase *in vain* means "for no good purpose; uselessly."

Vocabulary

resolve (rih ZAHLV) *v.* to decide firmly

perish (PAIR ish) *v.* to become ruined or destroyed; die

Practice the Skills

3 **Key Reading Skill**

Understanding Cause and Effect Lincoln is saying that the result of the Battle of Gettysburg should be—what? Rewrite this last sentence in your own words.

4 **BIG Question**

Lincoln suggests that more than the American dream is at stake. What is he talking about? Write your answers on the "Gettysburg Address" page of Foldable 8. Your response will help you complete the Unit Challenge later.

The Angle, Gettysburg, Pennsylvania, July 3, 1863, 1988. Mort Küntsler. Oil on canvas, 18 x 24 in. Collection of Mr. and Mrs. Robert L. Sharpe.

Analyzing the Painting What words or ideas in the Gettysburg Address does this painting illustrate?

After You Read : The Gettysburg Address

Answering the BIG Question

1. After reading the Gettysburg Address, how do you think Lincoln would answer the question: What is the American dream?
2. **Recall** According to Lincoln, how many years ago did the forefathers of this nation establish the country?

   Tip Right There

Critical Thinking

3. **Interpret** Lincoln says that the people attending the cemetery dedication cannot make the battleground a holy place. He says that the men who "struggled" there have already made it holy. What does he mean?

   Tip Think and Search

4. **Evaluate** Lincoln was wrong when he said, "The world will little note, nor long remember what we say here." On the contrary, the world has long remembered what he said at Gettysburg. In your own words, explain why Lincoln's speech is so memorable.

   Tip Author and Me

5. **Infer** What was Lincoln's purpose in this speech? Was he trying to persuade the crowd to think or believe or do something? Explain.

   Tip Author and Me

Write About Your Reading

Eyewitness Report Suppose you were there at Gettysburg and heard Lincoln's speech. Describe the day.

Step 1: Decide on a point of view. You might write from the point of view of one of the following: a survivor of the Battle of Gettysburg; a family member who lost someone in the battle; a newspaper reporter observing the event.

Step 2: Jot down notes for sensory details (what that person might have seen, heard, smelled, tasted, and touched on that day).

Step 3: Jot down notes about your own (or the crowd's) feelings and mood before, during, and after Lincoln's speech. Write down how you feel about Lincoln's message, and if you agree or disagree with it.

Write to Learn Use your notes to create an "eyewitness" report of the Gettysburg Address.

**NY English Language
Arts Core Curriculum**
(pp. 1100–1101)

LC R17 Demonstrate comprehension and response through a range of activities.
LC W5 Write with voice to address varied purposes. **LC R13** Use text structure and literary devices to aid comprehension and response. **R2e** Recognize how the author's use of language creates images or feelings.
LC R5 Determine the meaning of unfamiliar words, terms by using dictionaries.
Core W7 Observe rules of capitalization.

For a complete description of the standards, see p. NY 11.

Skills Review

Key Reading Skill: Understanding Cause and Effect

6. Suppose the South had won the Civil War, and the United States did *not* survive as one nation. What do you think would have been some of the effects?

Key Literary Element: Style

7. Count the number of times Lincoln uses a form of the word *dedicate.* What does this suggest about his attitude and his purpose?

8. Compare and contrast Lincoln's style with that of Martin Luther King Jr. in his "I Have a Dream" speech. How are their styles similar? How are they different? Explain your answer.

Vocabulary Check

Write the vocabulary word that each clue describes.

**conceived   proposition   endure
detract   resolve   perish**

9. make it through hard times

10. a suggestion for action

11. decide; settle

12. lessen; lower

13. die; decay

14. thought up

15. **English Language Coach** Research the word **hallow** and the origins of Halloween. How did the two originally relate to one another? What relation, if any, do they have today in common American custom?

Web Activities For eFlashcards, Selection Quick Checks, and other Web activities, go to www.glencoe.com.

Grammar Link: Capitalization of Places and Things

Capitalize the names of cities, counties, states, countries, continents, bodies of water, and geographic features.

• <u>M</u>ilwaukee, <u>W</u>isconsin, is a city on <u>L</u>ake <u>M</u>ichigan.

Capitalize a compass-point name when it refers to a specific section of the country: *the West Coast, the North.* Do NOT capitalize a compass-point name if it refers to a general direction.

• I'm from the <u>E</u>ast, and I'm heading <u>w</u>est to see the Rocky Mountains.

Capitalize the names of streets, highways, buildings, bridges, monuments, and celestial bodies.

• We live on <u>F</u>ifth <u>A</u>venue, near the <u>E</u>mpire <u>S</u>tate <u>B</u>uilding, on <u>P</u>lanet <u>E</u>arth, in the <u>M</u>ilky <u>W</u>ay.

Capitalize the names of important historical events, periods of time, documents, and holidays.

• <u>B</u>attle of <u>Y</u>orktown   • <u>B</u>ill of <u>R</u>ights
• <u>B</u>ronze <u>A</u>ge   • <u>N</u>ew <u>Y</u>ear's <u>E</u>ve

Capitalize the first word and the last word in titles. Also capitalize all other words except articles, conjunctions, or prepositions with fewer than five letters.

• *It's <u>N</u>ot <u>A</u>bout <u>M</u>e*   • *<u>W</u>ashington Post*
• "<u>T</u>he <u>R</u>aven"   • *"<u>O</u>n Top of the <u>W</u>orld"*

Grammar Practice

Rewrite these sentences, capitalizing words properly.

16. We spent thanksgiving day in columbus, ohio.

17. A southerly wind came in across the gulf coast.

18. I read about the middle ages in the *new york times.*

19. Have you read the poem "casey at the bat"?

20. The north won the american civil war.

Writing Application Make sure you capitalized proper nouns in your Gettysburg eyewitness account.

Skills Focus

You will practice using these skills when you read the following selections:
- "I Chose Schooling," p. 1106
- "The Electric Summer," p. 1114

Reading
- Identifying the main idea and supporting details

Literature
- Understanding cultural references
- Understanding the use of dialogue

Vocabulary
- Learning about English as a changing language

Writing/Grammar
- Using correct capitalization in writing

NY English Language Arts Core Curriculum
(pp. 1102–1103)

LC R12 Combine multiple strategies to enhance comprehension and response.

For a complete description of the standards, see p. NY 11.

Skill Lesson

Identifying Main Idea and Supporting Details

Learn It!

What Is It? The **main idea** is the most important idea in a paragraph or in a whole selection. It's the point, or message, the writer wants to communicate. Sometimes the writer directly states the main idea. Other times you have to figure out the main idea by looking at **supporting details**—facts that back up the author's ideas, or the actions of characters and the events in a story that support the message.

FOXTROT © 2003 Bill Amend. Reprinted with permission of UNIVERSAL PRESS SYNDICATE. All rights reserved.

Analyzing Cartoons
What's the main idea of this cartoon?

Why Is It Important? Finding the main idea helps you better understand the writer's message and reason for writing the selection. Finding details that support the idea helps you decide if that message is a good one.

How Do I Do It? Some writers directly state the main idea. When they don't and you have to figure it out, use these tips:

- In a work of nonfiction, ask yourself: *What is the writer saying about this topic?* In a short story or other work of fiction, ask: *What is the writer saying about the characters and situations?*

- To see if you've correctly identified the main idea, ask: *Do the important details explain or give evidence that supports this idea?*

One student used a diagram to figure out the main idea of this paragraph:

> "Dad, do you believe it?" Musa exclaimed. "With this paycheck, I have enough money to buy that car at Sam's Used Cars I asked you to buy me! When you told me to get a job and save for it, I wasn't sure I could do it. Thanks, Dad."

Main Idea: Hard work pays off.

Detail 1: Musa wants a car from Sam's Used Car Sales.

Detail 2: Musa's dad told him to work and save.

Detail 3: Musa has enough money to buy the car.

Practice It!

Draw your own diagram of the ideas in the paragraph below. It will help you get ready to write your response.

> "You 'n me, Darren," Isaak said. "We've finally got a chance at Friday's game. Scouts from State will be there. If we look good, we can get full scholarships. Wouldn't that be awesome? A free college education for shootin' hoops!"

Use It!

As you read "I Chose Schooling" and "The Electric Summer," use a diagram to find the main idea and supporting details. Then you can decide if the writers made their points.

Before You Read : I Chose Schooling

Jacqueling Nwaiwu

Meet the Author

Jacqueling Nwaiwu was born in Nigeria and came to the United States as a teenager. She is one of the "sisters" in *My Sisters' Voices,* a collection of writings by American teenage girls. The book was put together by 18-year-old Iris Jacob, who is biracial. In the introduction Jacob says: "We come from all different ethnic, cultural, and spiritual traditions. We are immigrants, some of us. We are beauties, inner and outer. We are heroines. . . . [W]e are the future!"

Author Search For more about Jacqueling Nwaiwu, go to www .glencoe.com.

NY English Language Arts Core Curriculum (pp. 1104–1109)

Core R4 Determine the meaning of words by using a dictionary. **LC R13** Use text structure and literary devices to aid comprehension and response. **R2h** Identify social and cultural contexts to enhance appreciation of text.

For a complete description of the standards, see p. NY 11.

Vocabulary Preview

prevailed (prih VAYLD) *v.* conquered; won; overcame; form of the verb *prevail* **(p. 1106)** *It was many years before peace finally prevailed.*

monumental (mon yuh MEN tul) *adj.* great and meaningful **(p. 1107)** *Climbing any mountain is a monumental accomplishment, if you ask me.*

attaining (uh TAY ning) *n.* the act of achieving, accomplishing, or succeeding **(p. 1107)** *Attaining a passing score will be impossible if I don't study.*

crucial (KROO shul) *adj.* extremely important **(p. 1107)** *A crucial part of every person's diet is some form of protein; it's necessary to live.*

agitated (AJ uh tay tud) *adj.* disturbed; upset **(p. 1108)** *The man wasn't harmed, but he was so agitated by the robbery that he couldn't speak.*

English Language Coach

English as a Changing Language Did you ever wonder how some words get into the English language? The chart below shows the origins of two words from "I Chose Schooling."

Word	*slacker*	*clammy*
Origin & Meaning	Old English *sleac*	Old English *claeman*
	careless in behavior	to smear or stick
Modern Meaning	someone who avoids work or responsibility	damp, soft, sticky, usually cool

There's nothing very unusual about the origins of these words, but another word in the selection—*geek*—has a more surprising history. Copy the chart below into your Learner's Notebook. Then look up *geek's* origin and meanings, and fill in the chart.

Word	geek
Origin & Meaning	
Modern Meanings	1
	2

Skills Preview

Key Reading Skill: Identifying Main Idea and Supporting Details

As you read "I Chose Schooling," pause to look for the main idea of a paragraph.

- What does the writer say is important to her?

  This could be a directly stated main idea.

- How do the details add to your understanding of the writer's ideas?

  Look for descriptions of her feelings, behavior, and actions.

To help identify the main idea of the entire selection, ask yourself these questions:

- What is the writer's most important idea or overall message?
- Which parts of the selection support this idea?

Write to Learn What was the main idea or message of a movie you've seen recently? List details (action, dialogue, and so on) that supported that idea.

Key Literary Element: Cultural Reference

Cultural references are mentions of objects, activities, products, forms of entertainment, and so on that are tied to a particular culture, place, and time. Slang is also a type of cultural reference. Notice the slang expressions as you read "I Chose Schooling." What does the slang tell you about the students' culture and time?

Partner Work *Geek* started as carnival slang, then took a different (but related) meaning in American culture. With a partner, explore the slang word *bling-bling* (or *bling*). Explain its meaning, who invented it, and why. (Your best bet is to search online for "word definitions," "online dictionaries," or something similar.)

Interactive Literary Elements Handbook
To review or learn more about the literary elements, go to www.glencoe.com.

Get Ready to Read

Connect to the Reading

In most schools, students tend to divide up into groups according to their interests and goals. There are the athletes, the musicians, the kids who study a lot, the kids who don't, and so on. These kinds of groups are called cliques. Members of a clique share similar interests and leave out those who have different interests. In this essay, the writer describes her school's cliques and offers her opinions of them.

Build Background

This essay comes from the book *My Sisters' Voices: Teenage Girls of Color Speak Out.* Published in 2001, the collection features writings by girls from Hispanic, African American, Asian American, Native American, and biracial backgrounds. Some were native-born; some were immigrants.

U.S. Census Bureau statistics for the year 2000 reveal the following information:

- Total U.S. population   281.4 million
- Hispanic or non-white   21.0%   59.1 million
- Born in other countries   11.0%   30.9 million
- Ages 13–19   10.1%   28.4 million
- Girls, ages 13–19   4.9%   13.8 million
- Girls, ages 13–19, of color   1.0%   2.9 million

Set Purposes for Reading

BIG Question   Read "I Chose Schooling" to see what a student born in another country thinks about education as part of the American dream.

Set Your Own Purpose What would you like to learn from the selection to help you answer the Big Question? Write your own purpose on the "I Chose Schooling" page of Foldable 8.

Keep Moving

Use these skills as you read the following selection.

I Chose Schooling

by Jacqueling Nwaiwu

As I walked down the crowded halls of Central High on the first day of school, I was overcome with many emotions. I was physically tired because I was not accustomed to waking up so early, and I was also scared and nervous. It was my freshman year, and above all other emotions, nervousness **prevailed.** I was trembling; my hands were clammy and sweaty. Students were greeting each other. There were clusters of students by lockers chatting away, catching up on all the summer gossip. I continued to walk through the halls observing the madness. Kids were running through the halls playing tag and ramming into each other. Bewildered, I muttered, "So this is high school. It looks more like the circus. So much for thinking that high school is exactly like the **preppy,** well-mannered students in the weekly TV show *Saved by the Bell.*[1]" **1 2 3**

I managed to find my homeroom after walking around for fifteen minutes. When I went in, I noticed that over half of the students in my homeroom were students who attended the same junior high as me. I was annoyed with that fact because I wanted to meet new people and make new friends instead of interacting with the same old students from junior high. And with that, I quickly sat down next to a girl with spiky, blue hair, whom I did not know.

---

1. *Saved by the Bell,* which first aired in 1989, was a comedy focusing on six students at the fictional Bayside High School.

Vocabulary

prevailed (prih VAYLD) *v.* conquered; won; overcame

Practice the Skills

1 **Key Reading Skill**

Identifying Main Idea The main idea of this paragraph is directly stated. Nwaiwu says she is scared and nervous on her first day of school. Her description of her "clammy and sweaty" hands is a supporting detail that shows how she felt.

2 **English Language Coach**

A Changing Language As an adjective, **preppy** describes a style of clothing. In the 1960s, as a noun, it meant a student preparing for college at a preparatory (or "prep") school.

3 **BIG Question**

TV characters often have the lives real people dream of having. Name a character or show that, to you, represents the American dream (or part of it).

Right at that moment, my blond, skinny homeroom teacher, Ms. Larsen, shouted, "Welcome to high school!" She went on, saying, "These next four years will be **monumental.** These four years will define your character; you will either choose that path of excelling in school or you will decide that socializing with friends is more important. You have two paths to choose from. Today is the first day of school, choose your path wisely."

That statement remained with me for the whole day. I kept thinking to myself, This is the beginning of my high school career, I must do well in school. I must pick the right path.

Attaining a sound education has been my goal since before I could remember. Every day from the time I was in kindergarten to the present, my parents have always said, in their thick Nigerian[2] accents, "Read hard so that you may be successful." (To my parents, "reading hard" is synonymous with studying rigorously.) I have always endeavored to excel in school and a large portion of my motivation is because of that overused quote. Whenever stress mounts, and I feel that I never want to do another paper or another homework assignment, I always remember what my parents would tell me, "Read hard so that you may be successful." **4**

Schooling is **crucial** to me. I believe that the better one does in school, the more successful he or she becomes in the real world. I define a successful person as one who is happy, has a great family, and has a great-paying job.

Over the course of the year, every student in my homeroom chose either to take school seriously or to slack off. In homeroom, cliques started to form. The **slackers** sat on one side of the room, while the studious, grade-conscious students sat on the other side. **5** Students on the slacker side of the room constantly yelled and were rowdy, while the

---

2. *Nigeria* was governed by Great Britain from the early 1900s until 1964, and most *Nigerians* speak English.

Vocabulary

monumental (mon yuh MEN tul) *adj.* great and meaningful

attaining (uh TAY ning) *n.* the act of achieving, accomplishing, or succeeding

crucial (KROO shul) *adj.* extremely important

Practice the Skills

4 **Key Reading Skill**

Identifying Main Idea
Again, Nwaiwu states the idea of the paragraph directly. What is that idea, and how does she support it?

5 **Key Literary Element**

Cultural Reference The **slackers** (a slang term) are one clique. Do you know of a slang term for the "grade-conscious" students?

students on the grade-conscious side of the room were busy trying to study or complete homework.

One day, I came into homeroom and sat in my designated spot: the studious, grade-conscious side of the room. The morning announcements were blaring while I frantically tried to complete my homework. I was completing my math problems when suddenly the bell rang, indicating that it was time for first hour. I ignored it and continued to finish the problems due that hour. Before I knew it, the second bell rang and I was late for math class.

I quickly jammed my books in my bag and ran out of my fourth-floor homeroom. I ran down the hall and up the stairs to the fifth floor. When I got to the fifth floor, I was blocked by a group of African American girls. The five **rowdy** girls stood in the entrance of the stairwell. I was so **agitated.** I wanted to push the girls out of my way so I could get to class. But instead, I maneuvered³ through the crowd. As I was doing that, one of the girls loudly said, "Who do she think she is anyway, huh?" The group of girls roared with laughter. Another girl said, "Ya'll leave her alone. She trying to get her an edgamacation." And with that, everyone laughed even more. I turned around and looked at them, but said nothing. I simply walked to my math class humiliated. 6

Black Girl with Wings, 20th century. Laura James. Acrylic on canvas, 31.8 x 43.2 cm. Private Collection.

Analyzing the Painting In what ways does the girl in the painting reflect Nwaiwu's ideas about herself?

Practice the Skills

6 **English Language Coach**

A Changing Language The word **rowdy** means "loud, rude, and rough." It most likely comes from *row,* "a noisy disturbance." (With this meaning, *row* rhymes with *how.*)

---

3. When Nwaiwu *maneuvered* (muh NOO vurd) through the crowd, she changed directions several times to get where she wanted to be.

Vocabulary

agitated (AJ uh tay tud) *adj.* disturbed; upset

At that moment, I strongly regretted running down the halls like some geek. I strongly regretted not saying something to them. I strongly regretted having the intense desire to go to my math class and do well in school. It was as if the girls were saying, "Who do she think she is, huh? A black girl trying to be white. An **oreo** black on the outside, but white on the inside. **7** Do she think she betta than us? She betta not, 'cause she ain't. School ain't that important for her to be running like that to some class. Some black girls don't know their race. Education ain't all that important. I'd rather clown wit my homies than run to class actin' like I'm white tryin' ta git an education."

"Who she think she is anyway, huh?" I was furious. What exactly did she mean by that! I was only trying to get to class. Excuse me if school means a little more to me than "hangin' out wit da homies." I couldn't believe I gave those girls so much power that they were able to ruin my day.

The next day, I went to homeroom. I mentioned the story to Meg, the girl with the spiky, blue hair. **8** Meg said, "Forget them. School is more important than trying to fit into some popular clique. Look at me. I have blue hair. I try not to fit into groups who don't accept me for me. School is much more important. Don't waste your energy on ignorant people."

Right as she said that, everything was clear. I didn't have to waste my energy on them. I chose schooling over socializing. I chose to study for tests instead of "gossiping over someone's baby's mamma." I selected education over ignorance. I thought to myself, Maybe I am not "ghetto" and maybe I do choose to speak properly. I am not any less black; I am just being me. I preferred work over play, homework instead of fitting into a crowd where I don't belong. I chose schooling.

When looking back at the experience I had with those girls, I thank God every day. That particular experience reaffirmed[5] my goal, which was to attain a sound education. I thank God for giving me the initiative to select the right path, despite all odds. **9** ○

---

5. Nwaiwu's experience supported and strengthened (**reaffirmed**) her goal.

Practice the Skills

7 **Key Literary Element**

Cultural Reference The word **oreo** is a cultural reference in two ways. Capitalized, it's the brand name of a cookie. Here, it's a slang term that suggests certain values and beliefs.

8 **Key Literary Element**

Cultural Reference Even this girl provides a cultural reference, since no one would even have thought of having "spiky, blue hair" before a certain time.

9 **BIG Question**

How does Nwaiwu's idea of the American dream compare with yours? Write your answer on the "I Chose Schooling" page of Foldable 8. Your response will help you complete the Unit Challenge later.

After You Read   I Chose Schooling

Answering the BIG Question

1. How important is education for achieving the American dream?
2. **Recall** How did Nwaiwu feel on her first day at Central High?
   TIP Right There
3. **Give Examples** Give examples of what Nwaiwu considers a successful person to be.
   TIP Right There

Critical Thinking

4. **Infer** Why does Nwaiwu sit where she does in her homeroom?
   TIP Think and Search
5. **Infer** How and why might Nwaiwu's goals have been influenced by the fact that she was the daughter of immigrants?
   TIP Author and Me
6. **Conclude** How does working toward her dream affect Nwaiwu's life?
   TIP Author and Me
7. **Analyze** Explain how the blue-haired girl's comments show that Nwaiwu does "belong to a group."
   TIP Author and Me
8. **Evaluate** Is Nwaiwu's goal worth working for?
   TIP Author and Me

Talk About Your Reading

**NY English Language Arts
Core Curriculum** (pp. 1110–1111)

LC R17 Demonstrate comprehension and response through a range of activities. **LC S8** Participate in group discussions on a range of topics and for a variety of purposes. **LC R13** Use text structure and literary devices to aid comprehension and response. **R2h** Identify social and cultural contexts to enhance appreciation of text. **Core R4** Determine the meaning of words by using a dictionary. **Core W7** Observe rules of capitalization.
For a complete description of the standards, see p. NY 11.

Literature Groups Different people have different ideas about the American dream. In a small group, compare the ideas of group members. Then discuss how your versions of the American dream compare to Nwaiwu's.

• What are your goals? How do you plan to reach them?
• What kind of life do you want for yourself ten years from now?
• How is your American dream similar to or different from Nwaiwu's dream? Why?
• How is your American dream similar to or different from the dreams of others in your group? Why?

Skills Review

Key Reading Skill: Identifying Main Idea and Supporting Details

9. What is the main idea of the selection? Is it directly stated? If so, give the page number and the first few words of the paragraph that contain the main idea. If it is not directly stated, explain how and where you identified it.

10. Name three supporting details for the main idea you identified.

Key Literary Element: Cultural Reference

11. One of the girls in Nwaiwu's class uses the slang *edgamacation* instead of the word *education.* What does her use of this term tell you about her and her values?

12. Nwaiwu mentions *Saved by the Bell.* TV shows often reflect the culture and times in which they are made. Name a show that you think reflects today's culture. Give examples that tie this show to current American culture.

13. Explain the slang expressions "hanging out with" and "homies."

Vocabulary Check

Label the following statements *true* or *false.*

14. **Attaining** an important goal means failing to meet the goal.

15. The team that **prevailed** on the soccer field won the game.

16. Finding a cure for cancer would be a **monumental** accomplishment.

17. When people are **agitated,** they're calm, cool, and confident.

18. A good diet is **crucial** to lasting good health.

19. **English Language Coach** Nwaiwu writes, "Attaining a sound education has been my goal since before I could remember." Look up the history of the word **sound** and explain how the word's origin relates to its meaning in Nwaiwu's statement.

Grammar Link: More Capitalization

Why do we capitalize the first letter of certain words? Capital letters are "look at me" flags! They tell readers that there's something special about these words.

Capitalize the first letter of a language name or a nationality. Capitalize the names of ethnic groups. In a multiple-word name, capitalize both words.

- Luc speaks <u>E</u>nglish, but his first language is <u>F</u>rench.
- Eva's an <u>A</u>merican citizen; her origins are <u>M</u>exican.
- Jose's <u>M</u>exican <u>A</u>merican family lives on one side of us, and a <u>J</u>ewish family lives on the other side.

Capitalize the names of clubs, organizations, businesses, institutions, and political parties. Capitalize brand names but not the nouns following them.

- We have an <u>I</u>nternational <u>C</u>lub meeting tomorrow.
- The <u>D</u>ata <u>C</u>orporation is expanding into Europe.
- We prefer <u>C</u>runcho peanut butter.

Grammar Practice

For each of the following, choose the sentence that shows the correct use of capitalization.

20. A. I saw a film about native Americans.
B. The Spanish weren't the first to settle the West.

21. A. One of the dialects in Louisiana is French Creole.
B. I ate french food at a restaurant yesterday.

22. A. Jorge is proud to be a canadian.
B. It will take work to preserve your Spanish heritage.

Writing Application Write a paragraph about someone you know who worked hard to achieve a dream.

Web Activities For eFlashcards, Selection Quick Checks, and other Web activities, go to www.glencoe.com.

Before You Read : The Electric Summer

Richard Peck

Meet the Author

A former high school teacher, Richard Peck began writing novels for the same age group he taught. His books focus on the problems that teens face. Peck uses the characters in his books to show young people how others their age overcome problems as they take one step closer to adulthood. His novels include *Don't Look and It Won't Hurt, Are You in the House Alone?,* and *Father Figure.* See page R5 of the Author Files for more on Peck.

Author Search For more about Richard Peck, go to www.glencoe.

NY English Language Arts Core Curriculum (pp. 1112–1115)

LC R7 Determine the meaning of unfamiliar words by using prior knowledge and context clues. **LC R13** Use text structure and literary devices to aid comprehension and response. **R2b** Interpret dialogue, using evidence from the text.

For a complete description of the standards, see p. NY 11.

Vocabulary Preview

novelty (NAH vul tee) *n.* anything new, strange, or unusual **(p. 1114)**
I grew up in the city, so seeing a cow face-to-face was a novelty.

grandeur (GRAN jur) *n.* the state of being large and impressive; greatness **(p. 1121)** *I was deeply impressed by the grandeur of the mountains.*

hovering (HUV ur ing) *adj.* remaining in or near one place in the air **(p. 1122)** *One eagle, hovering high above our heads, was the only living creature we saw as we hiked to the cabin.*

replica (REP lih kuh) *n.* a copy **(p. 1123)** *The shop had row upon row of miniature buildings, each a replica of an original structure.*

rapture (RAP chur) *n.* a feeling of great joy **(p. 1124)** *The two felt that nothing could destroy the rapture of their wedding day.*

seasoned (SEE zund) *adj.* made fit by experience; adjusted to (something) because of experience **(p. 1125)** *A more seasoned player might have been able to predict what was coming next.*

English Language Coach

English as a Changing Language In "The Electric Summer," the main character is Geneva (juh NEE vuh), which is also the name of a city in Switzerland. Some people are named for places. Many places are named for people. Two places mentioned in the story were named for kings of France—Louis IX and Louis XIV. The French don't say the *–s* at the end of Louis, but Americans are more flexible. Read the words and pronunciations in the chart below.

St. **Louis,** Missouri	LOO ee *OR* LOO us
Louisville, Kentucky	LOO ih vil *OR* LOO ih vul
Louisiana	loo ee zee AN uh *OR* loo zee AN uh

Countless other U.S. place names come from foreign languages but have peculiarly American pronunciations. Here are three examples.

	Spanish	"American"
Los Angeles, California	lohs AHN hay lays	lahs AN juh lus
Madrid, Iowa	mah DREED	MAD rid
New Berlin, Wisconsin	behr LEEN	BUR lin

Skills Preview

Key Reading Skill: Identifying Main Idea and Supporting Details

Most of the time, fiction authors don't directly state their main ideas. Instead, they provide details to help you figure them out. When you're reading fiction, use these questions to help identify the main idea:

- What points is the author trying to make about the characters' personalities and relationships?
- Which details support those points? Think about the characters' behavior and reactions to events.
- What is the main message of the story?
- What supporting details—such as events and their consequences—help the reader understand this message?

Literary Element: Dialogue

In literature, **dialogue** is the conversation between characters and it offers a great way to learn things about them. In "The Electric Summer," the dialogue gives readers a better understanding of the personalities of the major characters—Geneva, her mother, and her Aunt Elvera.

In a story with a first-person narrator, you need to be careful. It's easy to confuse what the narrator says with what the characters themselves reveal in the dialogue. Here, Geneva is the narrator, so she gives her ideas about characters and events, as well as her own thoughts and feelings. The other characters' dialogue reveals their own thoughts and feelings.

Use these tips as you read "The Electric Summer":

- What do you learn about each character's personality from what she says in the dialogue?
- What does the dialogue tell you about the events and situations?
- How does the dialogue help you understand what the characters experience in the story?

Partner Talk Have a dialogue with your partner. Choose a topic and discuss it for a couple of minutes. Then talk about your dialogue. What did you learn about your partner from what he or she said?

Get Ready to Read

Connect to the Reading

Do you recall the first time you saw a kangaroo or some other creature from a faraway place? How did you feel when you first flew in a plane or rode a roller coaster? In this story, a farm girl visits a big-city fair to see wonders from around the world.

Build Background

Long before TV and the Internet, world's fairs were held every few years in different cities around the world. Nations presented their food, art, and culture. Businesses showed off products and technologies. Visitors had the time of their lives!

At the 1904 world's fair in St. Louis, Missouri, the new products on display included everything from automatic egg boilers to pianos that played themselves. An automobile at one exhibit featured silk curtains, armchairs, a writing desk, an icebox, and a wash basin. (The car cost $18,000, a huge sum in 1904.)

Set Purposes for Reading

BIG Question Read "The Electric Summer" to find out how a girl and her mother discover new ideas about the American dream.

Set Your Own Purpose What would you like to learn from the story to help you answer the Big Question? Write your own purpose on the "Electric Summer" page of Foldable 8.

Interactive Literary Elements Handbook
To review or learn more about the literary elements, go to www.glencoe.com.

Keep Moving

Use these skills as you read the following selection.

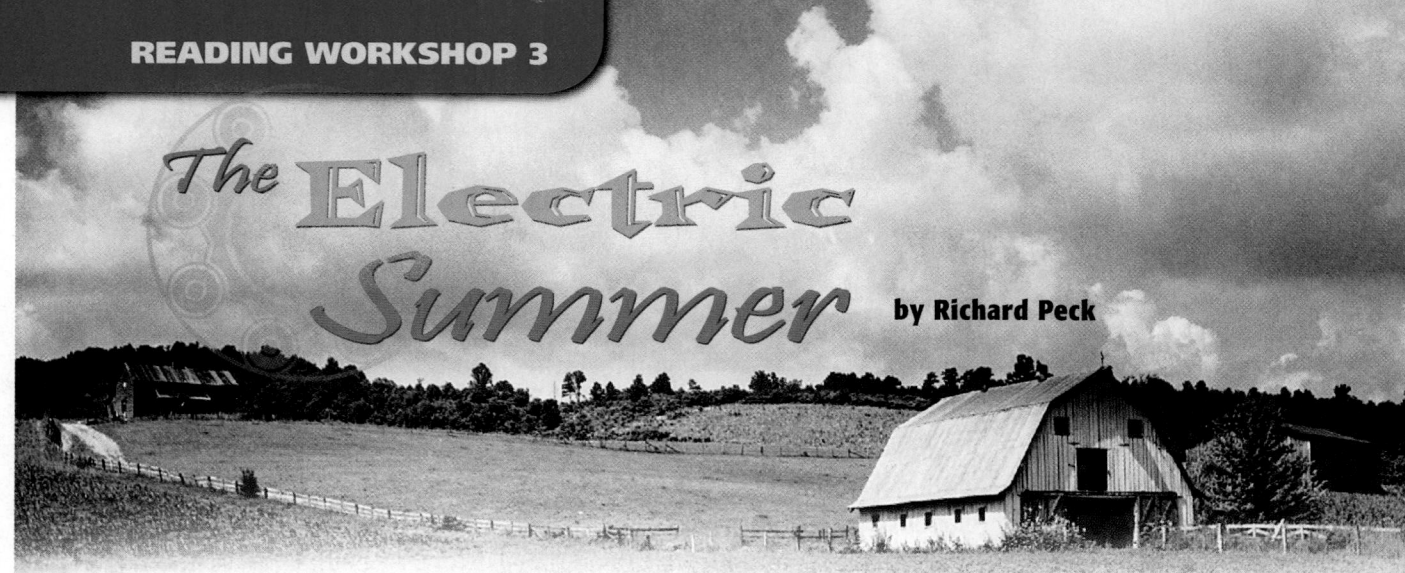

The Electric Summer

by Richard Peck

I was sitting out there on the old swing that used to hang on the back porch. We'd fed Dad and the boys. Now Mama and I were spelling each other to stir the preserves.[1] The screen door behind me was black with flies, and that smell of sugared strawberries cooking down filled all out-of-doors. A Maytime smell, promising summer.

Just turned fourteen, I was long-legged enough to push off the swing, then listen to the squeak of the chains. The swing was where I did my daytime dreaming. I sat there looking down past Mama's garden and the wind pump to the level line of long distance.[2] **1**

Like watching had made it happen, dust rose on the road from town. A black dot got bigger, scaring the sheep away from the fence line. It was an automobile. Nothing else churned the dust like that. Then by and by it was the Schumates' Oldsmobile, turning off the crown of the road and bouncing into our barn lot. There were only four automobiles in the town at that time, and only one of them driven by a woman—my aunt Elvera Schumate. She cut the motor off, but the Oldsmobile was still heaving. Climbing down, she put a gloved hand on a fender to calm it.

As Dad often said, Aunt Elvera would have been a **novelty** even without the automobile. In the heat of the day she wore

Practice the Skills

1 **Reviewing Skills**

Visualizing Take a moment to form mental pictures of Geneva and the farm. Imagine, too, the smells and sounds she describes.

---

1. In **spelling** each other, they were taking turns. Here, the **preserves** are strawberries being made into jam or jelly.

2. The **level line of long distance** refers to the horizon.

Vocabulary

novelty (NAH vul tee) *n.* anything new, strange, or unusual

a wide-brimmed canvas hat secured with a motoring veil tied under her chin. Her duster was a voluminous poplin garment,[3] leather-bound at the hem.

My cousin Dorothy climbed down from the Olds, dressed similarly. They made a business of untangling themselves from their veils, propping their **goggles** up on their foreheads, and dusting themselves down the best they could. Aunt Elvera made for the house with Dorothy following. Dorothy always held back. **2**

Behind me Mama banged on the screen door to scare the flies, then stepped outside. She was ready for a breather even if it meant Aunt Elvera. I stood up from the swing as Aunt Elvera came through the gate to the yard, Dorothy trailing. Where their goggles had been were two circles of clean skin around their eyes. They looked like a pair of raccoons. Mama's mouth twitched in something of a smile.

"Well, Mary." Aunt Elvera heaved herself up the porch steps and drew off her gauntlet gloves. "I can see you are having a busy day." Mama's hands were fire red from strawberry juice and the heat of the stove. Mine were scratched all over from picking every ripe berry in the patch.

"One day's like another on the farm," Mama remarked.

"Then I will not mince[4] words," Aunt Elvera said, overlooking me. "I'd have rung you up if you were connected to the telephone system."

"What about, Elvera?" She and Mama weren't sisters. They were sisters-in-law.

"Why, the Fair, of course!" Aunt Elvera bristled[5] in an important way. "What else? The Louisiana Purchase Exposition in St. Louis. The world will be there. It puts St. Louis at the hub of the universe." Aunt Elvera's mouth worked wordlessly.

"Well, I do know about it," Mama said. "I take it you'll be going?"

Practice the Skills

2 **English Language Coach**

A Changing Language The word **goggles** comes from the Middle English *gogolen,* which meant "to squint." Later, *goggle* came to mean "to stare at with wide eyes," which seems the opposite of its older meaning.

---

3. Early cars were open, like horse carriages, and early roads were unpaved. To protect against dirt and bad weather, drivers and passengers wore *dusters,* long coats that were large *(voluminous),* to fit over their clothes, and made of a strong, woven fabric *(poplin).* A woman was likely to wear a hat with a *motoring veil,* a long, thin scarf that tied around her face. The next paragraphs mention more of a motorist's costume: *gauntlet gloves,* which extended over the wrists, and *goggles,* which protected the eyes.

4. Here, to *mince* is to speak in an unnaturally careful or dainty way.

5. Here, *bristled* (BRIH suld) means "showed anger or annoyance."

Aunt Elvera waved her away. "My stars, yes. You know how Schumate can be. Tight as a new boot. But I put my foot down. Mary, this is the opportunity of a lifetime. We will not see such wonders again during our span.[6]"

"Ah," Mama said, and my mind wandered— took a giant leap and landed in St. Louis. We knew about the Fair. The calendar the peddler gave us at Christmas featured a different pictorial view of the Fair for every month. There were white palaces in gardens with gondolas[7] in waterways, everything electric-lit. Castles from Europe and paper houses from Japan. For the month of May the calendar featured the great floral clock on the fairgrounds. **3**

"Send us a postal,[8]" Mama said.

"The thing is . . ." Aunt Elvera's eyes slid toward Dorothy. "We thought we'd invite Geneva to go with us."

My heart liked to lurch out of my apron. Me? They wanted to take me to the Fair?

"She'll be company for Dorothy."

Then I saw how it was. Dorothy was dim, but she could set her heels like a mule. She wanted somebody with her at the Fair so she wouldn't have to trail after her mother every minute. We were about the same age. We were in the same grade, but she was a year older, having repeated fourth grade. She could read, but her lips moved. And we were cousins, not friends.

"It will be educational for them both," Aunt Elvera said. "All the progress of civilization as we know it will be on display. They say a visit to the Fair is tantamount[9] to a year of high school."

"Mercy," Mama said.

"We will take the Wabash Railroad directly to the gates of the Exposition," Aunt Elvera explained, "and we will be staying on the grounds themselves at the Inside Inn." She

Analyzing the Photo
What aspect of the fair does this photo capture?

Practice the Skills

3 | **Literary Element**

Dialogue Review the last few paragraphs of conversation between Mama and Aunt Elvera. What can you tell about Elvera's personality from this dialogue?

---

6. A *span* is a period of time; here, it's a synonym for "lifetime."

7. *Gondolas* (GAHN duh luz) are long, narrow, high-ended boats such as are used on the canals of Venice, Italy.

8. This is short for *postal* card, which we now call a postcard.

9. *Tantamount* (TAN tuh mownt) means "equal in value, importance, or effect."

leaned nearer Mama, and her voice fell. "I'm sorry to say that there will be stimulants for sale on the fairgrounds. You know how St. Louis is in the hands of the breweries." Aunt Elvera was sergeant-at-arms of the Women's Christian Temperance Union, and to her, strong drink[10] was a mocker. "But we will keep the girls away from that sort of thing." Her voice fell to a whisper. "And we naturally won't set foot on the Pike." **4**

We knew what the Pike was. It was the midway of the Fair, like a giant carnival with all sorts of goings-on.

"Well, many thanks, but I don't think so," Mama said.

My heart didn't exactly sink. It never dawned on me that I'd see the Fair. I was only a little cast down because I might never get another glimpse of the world.

"Now, you're not to think of the money," Aunt Elvera said. "Dismiss that from your mind. Schumate and I will be glad to cover all Geneva's expenses. She can sleep in the bed with Dorothy, and we are carrying a good deal of our eats. I know these aren't flush[11] times for farmers, Mary, but do not let your pride stand in Geneva's way."

"Oh, no," Mama said mildly. "Pride cometh before a fall. But we may be running down to the Fair ourselves." **5**

Aunt Elvera's eyes narrowed, and I didn't believe Mama, either. It was just her way of fending off[12] my aunt. Kept me from being in the same bed with Dorothy, too.

Aunt Elvera never liked taking no for an answer, but in time she and Dorothy made a disorderly retreat. We saw them off from the porch. Aunt Elvera had to crank the Olds to get it going while Dorothy sat up on the seat, adjusting the magneto[13] or whatever it was. We watched Aunt Elvera's rear elevation as she stooped to jerk the crank time after time. If the crank got away from you, it could break your arm, and we watched to see if it would. **6**

---

10. Here, ***stimulants*** and ***strong drink*** refer to alcoholic beverages. In the early 1900s, St. Louis ***breweries*** (beer factories) produced a large portion of the nation's beer. The ***Women's Christian Temperance Union*** (WCTU) was founded in 1874 to improve moral life, especially by encouraging people not to drink alcohol. As ***sergeant-at-arms,*** Elvera was an officer who maintained order at WCTU meetings.

11. Here, ***flush*** means "prosperous; having extra money."

12. ***Fending off*** is defending against or fighting off.

13. To start the engine, one had to turn a ***crank*** and adjust various controls, such as the ***magneto.***

Practice the Skills

4 **Reviewing Elements**

Cultural Reference The WCTU still exists, but its period of greatest influence and activity was in the early 1900s. Watch for other cultural references as you continue reading.

5 **Literary Element**

Dialogue Judging from Mama's part of this long dialogue, what would you say is her opinion of Elvera?

6 **Key Reading Skill**

Identifying Main Idea The author wants to make it clear that the automobile was an imperfect invention at this time. What details support that idea?

But at length the Olds coughed and sputtered to life. Aunt Elvera climbed aboard and circled the barn lot—she never had found the reverse gear. Then they were off back to town in a cloud of dust on the crown of the road.

I didn't want to mention the Fair, so I said, "Mama, would you ride in one of them things?"

Visual Vocabulary
A *lamp chimney* is the glass tube that surrounds the flame on an oil lamp.

"Not with Elvera running it," she said, and went back in the house.

I could tell you very little about the rest of that day. My mind was miles off. I know Mama wrung the neck off a fryer, and we had baking-powder biscuits to go with the warm jam. After supper my brothers hitched up Fanny to the trap[14] and went into town. I took a bottle brush to the lamp chimneys and trimmed the wicks. After that I was back out on the porch swing while there was some daylight left. The lightning bugs were coming out, so that reminded me of how the Fair was lit up at night with electricity, brighter than day.

Then Mama came out and settled in the swing beside me, which was unusual, since she never sat out until the nights got hotter than this. We swung together awhile. Then she said in a quiet voice, "I meant it. I want you to see the Fair." **7**

Everything stopped then. I still didn't believe it, but my heart turned over.

"I spoke to your dad about it. He can't get away, and he can't spare the boys. But I want us to go to the Fair."

Oh, she was brave to say it, she who hadn't been anywhere in her life. Brave even to think it. "I've got some egg money put back," she said. We didn't keep enough chickens to sell the eggs, but anything you managed to save was called egg money.

"That's for a rainy day," I said, being practical.

"I know it," she said. "But I'd like to see that floral clock."

Mama was famous for her garden flowers. When her glads were up, every color, people drove by to see them. And there was nobody to touch her for zinnias.

Oh, Mama, I thought, *is this just a game we're playing?* "What'll we wear?" I asked, to test her.

"They'll be dressy down at the Fair, won't they?" she said.

7 | **Key Reading Skill**

Identifying Main Idea What detail shows that Mama is serious about wanting Geneva to see the fair?

---

14. A *fryer* is a young chicken. The *trap* is a light one-horse carriage.

"You know those artificial cornflowers I've got. I thought I'd trim my hat with them. And you're getting to be a big girl. Time you had a corset.[15]"

So then I knew she meant business.

That's how Mama and I went to the Louisiana Purchase Exposition in St. Louis that summer of 1904. We studied up on it, and Dad read the Fair literature along with us. **Hayseeds** we might be, but we meant to be informed hayseeds. They said the Fair covered twelve hundred acres, and we tried to see that in our minds, how many farms that would amount to. And all we learned about the Fair filled my heart to overflowing and struck me dumb with dread.[16] 🎱

Mama weakened some. She found out when the Schumates were going, and we planned to go at the same time, just so we'd know somebody there. But we didn't take the same train. 🎱

When the great day came, Dad drove us to town, where the Wabash Cannonball stopped on its way to St. Louis. If he'd turned the trap around and taken us back home, you wouldn't have heard a peep out of me. And I think Mama was the same. But then we were on the platform with the big locomotive thundering in, everything too quick now, and too loud.

We had to scramble for seats in the day coach, lugging one straw valise between us and a gallon jug of lemonade. And a vacuum flask of the kind the Spanish-American War[17] soldiers carried, with our own well water for brushing our teeth. We'd heard that St. Louis water came straight out of the Mississippi River, and there's enough silt in it to settle at the bottom of the glass. We'd go to their fair, but we weren't going to drink their water.

When the people sitting across from us went to the dining car, Mama and I spread checkered napkins over our knees and had our noon meal out of the valise. All the while, hot wind blew clinkers and soot in the window as we raced along like a crazed horse. Then a lady flounced up and

Practice the Skills

8 **English Language Coach**

A Changing Language
Originally, **hayseeds** were bits of straw that clung to farmers' clothes. Later, city people began to use the word to refer to the farmers themselves.

9 **Key Reading Skill**

Identifying Main Idea In the next few paragraphs, notice the many details about the train trip. What idea(s) about train travel do you think the author wants to get across?

---

15. A **corset** (KOR sut) is a long, tight, girdle-like undergarment for a grown woman.

16. She is temporarily unable to speak **(dumb)** because of great fear and worry **(dread)**.

17. A **valise** (vuh LEES) is a suitcase. A **vacuum flask** (what we now call a "thermos") is used to keep liquids either hot or cold. The **Spanish-American War** was a brief conflict in 1898 between Spain and the United States over Spain's treatment of Cuba.

perched on the seat opposite. She had a full bird on the wing[18] sewed to the crown of her hat, and she was painted up like a circus pony, so we took her to be from Chicago. Leaning forward, she spoke, though we didn't know her from Adam. "Would you know where the ladies' rest room is?" she inquired.

We stared blankly back, but then Mama said politely, "No, but you're welcome to rest here till them other people come back."

The woman blinked at us, then darted away, hurrying now. I chewed on[19] that a minute, along with my ham sandwich. Then I said, "Mama, do you suppose they have a **privy** on the train?" **10**

"A *what*?" she said.

Finally, we had to know. Putting the valise on my seat and the hamper on hers, Mama and I went to explore. We walked through the swaying cars, from seat to seat, the cornflowers on Mama's hat aquiver. Sure enough, we came to a door at the end of a car with a sign reading LADIES. We crowded inside, and there it was. A water closet like you'd find in town[20] and a chain hanging down and a roll of paper. "Well, I've seen everything now," Mama said. "You wouldn't catch me sitting on that thing in a moving train. I'd fall off."

But I wanted to know how it worked and reached for the handle on the chain. "Just give it a little jerk," Mama said.

We stared down as I did. The bottom of the pan was on a hinge. It dropped open, and there below were the ties of the Wabash tracks racing along beneath us.

We both jumped back and hit the door. And we made haste back to our seats. I guess we were lucky not to have found the lady with the bird on her hat in there, sitting down.

Then before I was ready, we were crossing the Mississippi River on a high trestle.[21] There was

Practice the Skills

10 **English Language Coach**

A Changing Language The word **privy,** short for *private,* first appeared in the 14th century. But a toilet by any other name is still a toilet. And another one of those names appears in the next paragraph.

Covering nearly 16 acres, the Palace of Transportation exhibited 140 automobiles. Can you imagine Aunt Elvera in one of these cars?

---

18. ***Clinkers and soot*—**cinders and fine ashes—were from the coal burned as fuel in the locomotive. The bird, whether real or artificial, was made to look as though it were flying **(on the wing).**

19. The expression ***chewed on*** means "thought over."

20. ***Water closet*** is another word for *toilet.* In the early 1900s few farms had indoor toilets.

21. A ***trestle*** (TREH sul) is a railroad bridge, especially a high one over a river or valley.

nothing between us and the brown water. I put my hand over my eyes, but not before I glimpsed St. Louis on the far bank, sweeping away in the haze of heat as far as the eye could see.

We didn't stay at the Inside Inn. They wanted two dollars a night for a room, three if they fed you. We booked into a rooming house not far from the main gate, where we got a big square room upstairs with two beds for a dollar. It was run by a severe lady, Mrs. Wolfe, with a small, moon-faced son named Thomas clinging to her skirts. The place suited Mama, once she'd pulled down the bedclothes to check for bugs. It didn't matter where we laid our heads as long as it was clean.

We walked to the Fair that afternoon, following the crowds, trying to act like everybody else. Once again I'd have turned back if Mama had said to. It wasn't the awful **grandeur** of the pavilions[22] rising white in the sun. It was all those people. I didn't know there were that many people in the world. They scared me at first, but then I couldn't see enough. My eyes began to drink deep. **11**

We took the Intramural[23] electric railroad that ran around the Exposition grounds, making stops. The Fair passed before us, and it didn't take me long to see what I was looking for. It was hard to miss. At the Palace of Transportation stop, I told Mama this was where we got off.

There it rose before us, 250 feet high. It was the giant wheel, the invention of George Washington Gale Ferris. A great wheel[24] with thirty-six cars on it, each holding sixty people. It turned as we watched, and people were getting on and off like it was nothing to them.

"No power on earth would get me up in that thing," Mama murmured.

Analyzing the Photo How does the size of the Ferris wheel reflect the fair's grand scale?

Practice the Skills

11 **Reviewing Elements**

Figurative Language What does the last sentence mean? What kind of figurative language is used?

---

22. The **pavilions** (puh VIL yunz) are the fair's exhibit halls and other buildings.

23. The **Intramural** railroad ran only within the fairgrounds.

24. At the time, this was the only **Ferris wheel** in existence. Invented and built for the 1893 World's Columbian Exhibition in Chicago, it was moved to St. Louis in 1903. After the fair there, it was sold as scrap metal.

Vocabulary

grandeur (GRAN jur) *n.* the state of being large and impressive; greatness

But I opened my hand and showed her the extra dollar Dad had slipped me to ride the wheel. "Dad said it would give us a good view of the Fair," I said in a wobbly voice.

"It would give me a stroke," Mama said. But then she set her jaw. "Your dad is putting me to the test. He thinks I won't do it."

Gathering her skirts, she moved deliberately toward the line of people waiting to ride the wheel.

We wouldn't look up while we waited, but we heard the creaking of all that naked steel. "That is the sound of doom," Mama muttered. Then, too soon, they were ushering us into a car, and I began to **babble** out of sheer fear. **12**

"A lady named Mrs. Nicholson rode standing on the roof of one of these cars when the wheel was up at the Chicago fair, eleven years ago."

Mama turned to me. "What in the world for?"

"She was a daredevil, I guess."

"She was out of her mind," Mama said.

Now we were inside, and people mobbed the windows as we swooped up. I meant to stand in the middle of our car and watch the floor, but I looked out. In a moment we were above the roofs and towers of the Fair, a white city unfolding. There was the Grand Basin with the gondolas drifting. There was the mighty Festival Hall. Mama chanced a look.

It was cooler up there. My unforgiving Warner's Rust-Proof Corset had held me in a death grip all day, but I could breathe easier that high. Then we paused, dangling at the top. Now we were one with the birds, like hawks **hovering** over the Fair.

"How many wind pumps high are we?" Mama pondered. As we began to arch down again, we were both at a window, skinning our eyes to see the Jerusalem exhibit and the Philippine Village and, way off, the Plateau of States—a world of wonders.

Giddy when we got out, we staggered on solid ground and had to sit down on an ornamental bench. Now Mama was game for anything. "If they didn't want an arm and a leg for the fare," she said, "I'd ride that thing again. Keep the ticket stubs to show your dad we did it." **13**

Practice the Skills

12 **English Language Coach**

A Changing Language The word **babble** may come from a place name. In the Bible, the people of Babylon start to build a tower up to heaven—the Tower of Babel. They fail after God makes them "babble," or speak different languages, so that they can't communicate.

13 **Key Reading Skill**

Identifying Main Idea What is the main idea or message in this passage about the Ferris wheel ride? (Hint: What is the author saying about doing what you're afraid to do?)

Vocabulary

hovering (HUV ur ing) *adj.* remaining in or near one place in the air

Braver than before, we walked down the Pike, as it was still broad daylight. It was lined with sidewalk cafes in front of all manner of attractions: the Streets of Cairo and the Palais du Costume, Hagenbeck's Circus and a **replica** of the Galveston[25] flood. Because we were parched, we found a table at a place where they served a new drink, tea with ice in it. "How do we know we're not drinking silt?" Mama wondered, but it cooled us off.

As quick as you'd sit down anywhere at the Fair, there'd be entertainment. In front of the French Village they had a supple young man named Will Rogers doing rope tricks. And music? Everywhere you turned, and all along the Pike, the song the world sang that summer was: "Meet me in St. Louis, Louis, meet me at the fair."[26]

We sat over our tea and watched the passing parade. Some of those people you wouldn't want to meet in a dark alley. Over by the water chutes a gang of rough men waited to glimpse the ankles of women getting out of the boats. But the only thing we saw on the Pike we shouldn't have was Uncle Schumate weaving out of the saloon bar of the Tyrolean[27] Alps.

I can't tell all we saw in our two days at the Fair. We tried to look at things the boys and Dad would want to hear about—the Hall of Mines and Metallurgy, and the livestock. We learned a good deal of history: the fourteen female statues to stand for the states of the Louisiana Purchase of 1803, and the log cabin that President U. S. Grant had been born in. But most of what we saw foretold the future: automobiles and airships and moving pictures.[28] **14**

---

25. In 1900, a terrible hurricane hit **Galveston,** Texas, killing 5,000 people and destroying much of the city.

26. In the song, a woman leaves a note telling her husband Louis (LOO ee) where to meet her in St. Louis (LOO ee).

27. **Tyrolean** (tuh ROH lee un) refers to a region, mostly in Austria, of the eastern Alps Mountains.

28. Cars, planes, and movies existed in 1904; they just weren't yet widely available or easily affordable.

Vocabulary

replica (REP lih kuh) *n.* a copy

Practice the Skills

14 🗨 **BIG Question**

Geneva says that the things she saw at the fair "foretold the future." What does this tell you about the American dream in 1904? Write your answer on the "Electric Summer" page of Foldable 8.

Will Rogers (1879–1935) was one of the most popular entertainers of the time. In his live performances, he told jokes and performed rope tricks.

Our last night was the Fourth of July. Fifty bands played, some of them on horseback. John Philip Sousa, in gold braid and white, conducted his own marches. Lit in every color, the fountains played to this music and the thunder of the fireworks. And the cavalry from the Boer War[29] exhibit rode in formation, brandishing torches. **15**

Visual Vocabulary
A *minaret* is a tall, slender tower on an Islamic temple.

Mama turned away from all the army uniforms, thinking of my brothers, I suppose. But when the lights came on, every tower and minaret picked out with electric bulbs, we saw what this new century would be: all the grandeur of ancient Greece and Rome, lit by lightning. A new century, with the United States of America showing the way. But you'd have to run hard not to be left behind. **16**

We saved the floral clock for our last morning. It lay across a hillside next to the Agriculture Palace, and it was beyond anything we'd ever seen. The dial of it was 112 feet across, and each giant hand weighed 2,500 pounds. It was all made of flowers, even the numbers. Each Hour Garden had plants that opened at that time of day, beginning with morning glories. We stood in a **rapture**, waiting for it to strike the hour.

Then who appeared before us with her folding Kodak camera slung around her neck but Aunt Elvera Schumate. To demonstrate her worldliness, she merely nodded like we were all just coming out of church back home. "Well, Mary," she said to Mama, "I guess this clock shames your garden."

Mama dipped her head modestly to show the cornflowers on her hat. "Yes, Elvera," she said, "I am a humbler woman for this experience," and Aunt Elvera didn't quite know what to make of her reply. "Where's Dorothy?" Mama asked innocently.

"That child!" Aunt Elvera said. "I couldn't get her out of the bed at the Inside Inn! She complains of blistered feet. Wait till she has a woman's corns! I am a martyr to mine. I cannot get

---

29. ***Sousa*** (SOO zuh) was a popular composer and band leader. The ***cavalry*** (KAH vul ree) were soldiers on horseback. In the ***Boer War*** (1899–1902), Great Britain fought two of its former colonies in southern Africa.

Vocabulary

rapture (RAP chur) *n.* a feeling of great joy

Practice the Skills

15 **Key Reading Skill**
Identifying Main Idea Again, numerous details are given about the fair. What point is the author making?

16 **BIG Question**
What part does electricity play in the American dream of the early 1900s? Write your answer on the "Electric Summer" page of Foldable 8.

her interested in the Fair. She got as far as the bust of President Roosevelt sculpted in butter, but then she faded." Aunt Elvera cast me a baleful[30] look, as if this was all my fault. "Dorothy is going through a phase."

But there Aunt Elvera was wrong. Dorothy never was much better than that for the rest of her life. Mama didn't inquire into Uncle Schumate's whereabouts; we thought we knew.

On the train ride home we were **seasoned** travelers, Mama and I. When the candy butcher hawked his wares through our car, we knew to turn our faces away from his prices. We crossed the Mississippi River on that terrible trestle, and after Edwardsville[31] the land settled into flat fields. Looking out, Mama said, "Corn's knee high by the Fourth of July," because she was thinking ahead to home. "I'll sleep good tonight without those streetcars clanging outside the window."

But they still clanged in my mind, and "The Stars and Stripes Forever" blended with "Meet Me in St. Louis, Louis."

"But Mama, how can we just go home after all we've seen?" **17**

Thinking that over, she said, "You won't have to, you and the boys. It's your century. It can take you wherever you want to go." Then she reached over and put her hand on mine, a thing she rarely did. "I'll keep you back if I can. But I'll let you go if I must."

That thrilled me, and scared me. The great world seemed to swing wide like the gates of the Fair, and I didn't even have a plan. I hadn't even put up my hair yet. It seemed to me it was time for that, time to jerk that big bow off the braid hanging down my back and put up my hair in a woman's way.

"Maybe in the fall," said Mama, who was turning into a mind reader as we steamed through the July fields, heading for home. ○

A daily guide helped visitors choose from among hundreds of exhibits and activities.

Practice the Skills

17 🔵 **BIG** Question
How has Geneva's idea of the American dream been affected by her visit to the fair? Write your answer on the "Electric Summer" page of Foldable 8. Your responses will help you complete the Unit Challenge later.

---

30. A **martyr** (MAR tur) is someone who willingly dies for a cause. Theodore **Roosevelt** was president from 1901 to 1909. **Baleful** means "menacing; threatening harm or evil."

31. **Butcher** is an old term for someone who sells **(hawks)** products **(wares)**. **Edwardsville**, Illinois, is about 25 miles northeast of St. Louis.

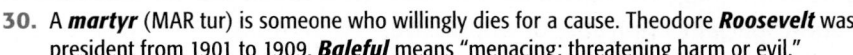

Vocabulary

seasoned (SEE zund) *adj.* made fit by experience; adjusted to (something) because of experience

After You Read : The Electric Summer

Answering the BIG Question

1. How does technology fit into the American dream?
2. **Recall** What is the first thing that Geneva wants to do after she and Mama arrive on the fairgrounds?
   TIP Right There
3. **Recall** What is the exhibit that gives Geneva and Mama such joy on their second day at the fair?
   TIP Think and Search

Critical Thinking

4. **Draw Conclusions** Geneva lives on a farm, but the story doesn't say directly where the farm is located. Identify the state, and explain how you came to this conclusion.
   TIP Think and Search
5. **Evaluate** Before visiting the fair, Geneva got her ideas about the world mostly from what she had read. How does the fair change her?
   TIP Author and Me
6. **Infer** At the end of their visit, Mama tells Geneva that the century "can take you wherever you want to go." What do you think Mama wants for Geneva?
   TIP Author and Me

Write About Your Reading

Postcards Imagine that Geneva sent herself two postcards from the fair. (If she'd sent them to her dad and brothers, she probably would have been home before the mail arrived.) Describe the postcards you think she might have chosen, and write a brief message for each one. For each of the two postcards:

- Choose an image of something Geneva saw or did at the fair that she found especially enjoyable or impressive.
- Describe the image.
- Write the message. (Keep it to about 30 words.) Remember that you're pretending to be Geneva writing to herself. What would you say to remind yourself why you liked the thing pictured on the card?

NY English Language Arts Core Curriculum
(pp. 1126–1127)

LC R17 Demonstrate comprehension and response through a range of activities. **LC W5** Write with voice to address varied purposes, topics, and audiences. **LC R13** Use text structure and literary devices to aid comprehension and response. **R2b** Interpret dialogue, using evidence from the text. **LC R7** Determine the meaning of unfamiliar words by using prior knowledge and context clues. **Core W7** Observe rules of capitalization.

For a complete description of the standards, see p. NY 11.

Skills Review

Key Reading Skill: Identifying Main Idea and Supporting Details

7. What is the main idea or message of this story?

8. It seems obvious that Geneva and Mama are not used to traveling by train. Note at least three details from the story that support this idea.

Literary Element: Dialogue

9. Choose two or more pieces of dialogue from the story that helped you understand Geneva's personality. Explain your choices.

10. How does the dialogue between Mama and Aunt Elvera show the differences in their personalities?

Reviewing Elements: Cultural Reference

11. Identify five cultural references in the story, with the page numbers where they're mentioned. List, for example, specific brand names or products, famous people, world events, or social movements that relate to the time of the story.

Vocabulary Check

Rewrite each sentence with the correct word.

> **novelty   grandeur   hovering**
> **replica   rapture   seasoned**

12. The ___ helicopter circled the air above the roof but didn't land.

13. The man couldn't resist buying a ___ of the Statue of Liberty in the gift shop.

14. Kria is a ___ soccer player. She's played in more than a hundred games this year.

15. Jesse was filled with ___ as he stood on the Olympic stand, a gold medal around his neck.

16. I enjoyed seeing Mount Rushmore, but I was more impressed by the ___ of South Dakota's Badlands.

17. That's a ___! I've never seen anything like it.

18. **English Language Coach** What does *Mississippi* mean in its original language?

Grammar Link: Capitalization of Sentences

You enter a house through a door. A capital letter is the door through which you enter a sentence. Always capitalize the first word of every sentence and the first word of every direct quotation.

- There were only four automobiles in the town.
- Looking out, Mama said, "Corn's knee high by the Fourth of July."

When a quoted sentence is interrupted by explanatory words, such as *he said,* do NOT begin the second part of the quotation with a capital letter.

- "I'd ride that thing again," she said, "if I could."

People often don't speak in complete sentences. Even if a quotation is just a single word or phrase, capitalize the first word.

- "That child!" Aunt Elvera said.

Grammar Practice

Rewrite the following paragraph, correcting the three capitalization errors.

> "it will be a fun trip," Rena thought. her class was going to see an exhibit and eat at a French restaurant. "thanks," Rena told her teacher, "for planning this!"

Writing Application Review the postcards you wrote. Make sure you capitalized the first letter in each sentence and in any quotation.

Web Activities For eFlashcards, Selection Quick Checks, and other Web activities, go to www.glencoe.com.

Revising Rubric

Your revised letter should have

- a clear beginning, middle, and end
- a clearly-stated opinion supported by relevant details
- well-organized paragraphs
- correct forms of irregular verbs
- correct business letter presentation

See page 1130 for a model of a letter.

In Writing Workshop Part 1, you generated ideas for your letter and developed a first draft. In Part 2 you'll revise and edit your draft to make your letter even better. After you've finished your letter, you'll choose a method of publishing it. Remember to keep a copy in your writing portfolio so that you and your teacher can evaluate your writing progress over time.

Revising
Make It Better

Revising is all about improving your draft. But first you have to decide what improvements it needs. You must become your own editor, evaluating your writing and deciding what to fix.

Take a Fresh Look

As you read over the draft of your letter, ask yourself the questions below. You can either make changes now or write notes to yourself so you can go back and make the changes later.

- Does the opening paragraph state your purpose for writing and your overall opinion?
- Does each paragraph in the body of your letter have a topic sentence that clearly states that paragraph's main idea?
- Does each paragraph in the body follow up the topic sentence with supporting details and specific examples from the show?
- Does your concluding paragraph provide closure by praising and/or criticizing the program and how it shows America and Americans? Do you offer suggestions to improve the show?
- Have you made your points clearly? You might want to swap letters with a partner to get a fresh perspective. Ask your partner if anything you wrote is confusing. Work together to phrase your comments in a way that's more understandable.
- Does your letter read smoothly? Read it out loud. If there are parts that you stumble over, find better ways to express them.

Editing
Finish It Up

Read the model on the next page. Look at the notes on the side to see how the writer revised and edited his letter about *The Simpsons*.

Then read your letter one sentence at a time and use the **Editing Checklist** below to help you spot errors. Use the proofreading symbols in the chart on page R19 to mark needed corrections.

If you're using a word processing program, you can use the grammar and spell-checking features to catch some kinds of mistakes. However, remember that a computer's spell-checker can't tell the difference between a misspelled word and its homophone. For example, if you meant to type "their" but accidentally typed "there," the computer won't alert you.

Editing Checklist

- ☑ Your letter is free of sentence fragments and run-on sentences.
- ☑ Verbs and subjects agree and all tenses are correct. You've used irregular verbs correctly.
- ☑ You've correctly spelled words that are easily confused, including homophones.
- ☑ You've used the proper letter format. You've correctly capitalized and punctuated direct quotations and the names of TV programs.

Publishing
Show It Off

After you've made your final revisions and corrections, make a final copy of your letter. If your letter is written by hand, it must be neat and legible. Ask someone else to make sure your handwriting can be read.

Then figure out who should receive your letter and get it ready to send! To do that, be sure you have everything in the right format for a business letter. (Follow the guidelines on page 1131 and see page R25 of the Writing Handbook for extra help.)

The best place to send the letter is in care of ("c/o") the company that distributes the program or the TV network or local station that broadcasts it. Most TV and radio stations have Web sites that give their mailing addresses.

> ◀ **Revising Tip**
>
> **Using Technology** If you're writing on a computer, save your draft and make your revisions in a new file copy. By saving the original, you're free to experiment and make mistakes. If necessary, you can open up your original draft and try again.

Literature Online

Writing Models For models and other writing activities, go to www.glencoe.com.

> ◀ **Revising Tip**
>
> **Choosing Your Audience** You could send your letter to the show's creator, director, producer, or writer. You could also write to the head of the network that runs the show or to the show's sponsors.

Active Writing Model

Writer's Model

Dear Mr. Groening:

I am in eighth grade. My English class is evaluating how TV shows portray America. In my opinion, The Simpsons shows both the good and the bad.

The introduction states the writer's purpose and his opinion.

First, the mix of characters is fairly true to life. The show revolves around a white family, but there are also African Americans (Carl and Dr. Hibbert) and immigrants (Apu and his family). Every community contains people like Police Chief Wiggum, Mayor Joe Quimby, Moe, Marge's sisters, Principal Skinner, and even greedy power-plant owner Mr. Burns.

The writer's first reason for his opinion is stated in the topic sentence. He follows up with specific details from the show to support the topic sentence. Notice how paragraphs 2–5 all follow this pattern.

Second, like many American communities today, Springfield faces a range of problems, including natural disasters (Mt. Springfield erupts), corruption (the mayor takes bribes), and schoolyard bullies.

Finally, The Simpsons shows good things about Americans too. Homer and Marge are a loving couple with a lasting marriage. Lisa is the voice of reason. Even Bart is a creative problem solver. The community takes on tough problems. The Simpsons' America is going through a lot of change, but people do their best to cope with it.

However, I have one complaint. My classmates and I agree that you don't always show both sides of an issue. Sometimes you leave out the way we feel.

The writer expresses disagreement with the way the program shows the American dream.

My classmate Ken Aya, age 14, said, "I didn't like the episode that made Milhouse's dad and all the other divorced dads in his building look so pathetic. Many divorced men cope just fine. My dad lives in an apartment building, but he's not a loser."

Thanks, Mr. Groening, for making us laugh at ourselves while encouraging us to solve our problems. But please, don't always poke fun at the characters who share my outlook on life.

The writer closes by summarizing his message in the final paragraph. He thanks the show's creator but advises him on how to fix the show's flaw.

Applying Good Writing Traits

Presentation

What Is Presentation?

A piece of writing is presented well if it's pleasing to the eye and easy to read. Its form should be right for the assignment.

Why Is Presentation Important?

No matter how hard you've worked on what you have to say, your letter will have little effect if it doesn't look good.

How Do I Use Presentation in My Writing?

Make sure your letter has the right format (the parts it contains and how they're laid out on the page). Business letters contain these elements:

- **Heading and date:** your address and the date

  Raphael Thompson
  136 Matthews Street
  Binghamton, New York 13905
  March 30, 2007

- **Inside address:** the name and address of the person to whom you're writing (Note that this example is addressed "in care of" the local Fox TV station.)

  Mr. Matt Groening
  Creator of <u>The Simpsons</u>
  c/o FOX 40 WICZ-TV
  BINGHAMTON
  4600 Vestal Parkway East
  Vestal, NY 13850

- **Greeting or salutation:** begins with "Dear," then the name of the person to whom you are writing, followed by a colon

  Dear Mr. Groening:

- **Body of the letter:** all of the text (In the student model, the body is six paragraphs.)

- **Complimentary close:** "Sincerely," "Yours truly," or a similar closing, followed by a comma

  Yours truly,

- **Signature:** your signed name, followed by your name either typed or block-printed

Present Your Letter Add a copy of your letter to a binder for a class book. Give the book a title, such as *As Seen on TV: The American Dream.* Set up a book party to discuss the shows you and your classmates wrote about. To spark the conversation, read some of the letters.

Analyzing Cartoons
Jeremy's presentation of his skills probably won't lead to a job. What kind of business card would you design for yourself?

© Zits Partnership. Reprinted with Permission of King Features Syndicate, Inc.

Skills Focus

You will practice using these skills when you read the following selections:
- "I, Too" p. 1136
- from *Dandelion Wine,* p. 1142

Reading

- Identifying author's purpose

Literature

- Identifying and understanding metaphor
- Recognizing hyperbole

Vocabulary

- Learning about English as a changing language

Writing/Grammar

- Understanding and using verbals
- Spelling and using homophones correctly

NY English Language Arts Core Curriculum
(pp. 1132–1133)

LC R13 Use text structure and literary devices to aid comprehension and response. **R3a** Question the writer's beliefs, intentions.

For a complete description of the standards, see p. NY 11.

Skill Lesson

Identifying Author's Purpose

Learn It!

What Is It? Whether it's a novel or a poem, a newspaper article or a play, a cartoon or an ad, everything you read was written for a reason. Every author has some purpose in mind when he or she sits down to write. The most common purposes are

- to entertain
- to describe
- to inform or explain
- to persuade
- a combination of the above

FOXTROT © 2002 Bill Amend. Reprinted with permissionof UNIVERSAL PRESS SYNDICATE. All rights reserved.

Analyzing Cartoons

Paige needs a bright idea. A larger bulb *might* help, but it might be more helpful for her to think about her purpose. What do you think is her purpose for writing the essay?

Why Is It Important? You read many different types of text each day. In the morning you read about prehistoric animals in your science book. Later you study a story for English. In the afternoon you do research on the Web. At home you check the directions before you microwave a snack. Before bed there's the newspaper sports section. Knowing why the authors wrote these texts can help you understand and evaluate what they say.

Study Central Visit www.glencoe .com and click on Study Central to review evaluating.

How Do I Do It? Use these tips to help you identify an author's purpose.

- Consider the audience for whom a work is intended. Persuasive writing has a different target audience than poetry. Many nonfiction works are intended for experts, not casual readers.

- Examine the author's word choices. All writers select words for their suggested meanings as well as for their definitions. But a poet might want to suggest ideas indirectly while an editorial writer tries to be specific.

- Look at the text structure. Fiction is likely to be organized in time order, and cooking and assembly instructions had better be chronological. Other nonfiction is often organized as problem-solution or cause-effect.

Here's how one student identified the author's purpose while reading the short story "The Electric Summer":

> I think Mr. Peck was writing to entertain and inform. I think he wants people to see that it was exciting to live in the early 1900s. There were new things like electricity and cars and indoor plumbing. That's kind of a funny list, but only because we're so used to those things today.
>
> Mr. Peck had a third purpose too, I think, and that was to say to keep your mind open to new ideas and experiences.

Practice It!

Look over the titles of the selections you read in Units 6 and 7. Choose five selections and, in your Learner's Notebook, briefly note what you think was the author's main purpose in each selection.

Use It!

As you read, look in the text for clues about the author's purpose. Then decide whether the author did a good job and achieved that purpose.

Before You Read : **I, Too**

Langston Hughes

Meet the Author

Langston Hughes was one of the first African American writers to make a living as a writer and public speaker. He once said he wrote about people who are "up today and down tomorrow, working this week and fired the next, beaten and baffled, but determined not to be wholly beaten." See page R3 of the Author Files for more on Hughes.

Author Search For more about Langston Hughes, go to www .glencoe.com.

NY English Language Arts Core Curriculum
(pp. 1134–1137)

Core R4 Determine the meaning of words by using a dictionary. **LC R13** Use text structure and literary devices to aid comprehension and response. **R3a** Question the writer's beliefs, intentions. **R2d** Determine how the use and meaning of literary devices, such as metaphor, convey the author's message or intent.

For a complete description of the standards, see p. NY 11.

Vocabulary Preview

English Language Coach

English as a Changing Language So what is all this stuff about "Old English" and "Middle French" and "Old High German"? It has to do with etymology (et uh MOL uh jee), the study of the origins and histories of languages. Each language has its own history, of course. Most grew out of another, older language. Some borrow from one another.

Old English was a Germanic language, meaning it grew out of an early form of German. Then, in 1066, the Normans came over from the north of France and conquered England. The Normans spoke Old French, which was a Latin language (coming out of ancient Italy). With the Normans governing, the English adopted many French words relating to law and government. In most matters relating to daily life, however, people stuck to the language they knew. So, modern English is really the offspring of Old German crossed with Old French.

The neat thing about etymology is that it shows that bits and pieces of old languages survive in modern-day English. To see them, you need to be a detective, looking for and understanding root words and their origins and meanings.

Look at the example below. You'll see this word in the selection "I, Too."

Brackets contain information about a word's etymology.

Scholars sometimes have to make educated guesses about the origins of a word.

kitchen *n.* a room or an area equipped for preparing and cooking food [Middle English *kichene,* from Old English *cycene,* probably from Vulgar Latin *cocina,* from Late Latin *coquinus,* "of cooking," from *coquus,* "cook," from *coquere,* "to cook"]

Etymology usually begins with the most recent historical influence, and traces the word back in time to its earliest roots.

Scholars have given these names to different periods in time. Vulgar Latin refers to Latin the way it was spoken by ordinary people (as opposed to the "high" language of priests and kings).

Skills Preview

Key Reading Skill: Identifying Author's Purpose

You're about to read a poem by Langston Hughes. Poetry is a very focused kind of writing. A poem is intended to make you feel a certain feeling or think about a certain idea. "I, Too" is very brief and seemingly simple, but Hughes packs a lot into it.

As you read, think about who the speaker—the "I" of the poem's title—might be. Also, look closely at Hughes's word choices. Because most poems are short, poets are very careful to use words that mean and suggest exactly the right things. Finally, to help you understand what Hughes was writing about, recall what you know about him and the times he lived in.

Write to Learn Find out what you can about the "Harlem Renaissance." In your Learner's Notebook, make notes to answer the five basic questions—who, what, when, where, and why.

Key Literary Element: Metaphor

A metaphor is a figure of speech that compares seemingly unlike things without using words such as *like* and *as*. Here's an example that makes two comparisons: "When I first arrived in the city, I was a mouse in a maze." The writer or speaker is compared to a mouse and the city to a maze.

An **extended metaphor** is continued over a passage. In a poem, it might run throughout the entire piece. In a story or essay, it might run a few paragraphs or, in a short work, throughout the whole piece.

Hughes uses an extended metaphor in "I, Too" that's implied. In the earlier example, the comparison is directly stated: "I was a mouse." In "I, Too," the speaker mentions the "kitchen" and a "table" but leaves it to the reader to decide what they represent.

Class Discussion Hughes's poem "Mother to Son" (page 472) also uses an extended metaphor. Reread the poem and talk about the crystal staircase.

Get Ready to Read

Connect to the Reading

Imagine that, because of your hair color, you aren't allowed to eat in a certain restaurant. Or imagine that you're required to sit in the back corner of the theater because you're left-handed. Imagine that you're told to leave the room whenever visitors come.

Write to Learn Write a paragraph describing your feelings when you've been treated unfairly for reasons that you couldn't control or that made no sense.

Build Background

- In 1855 American poet Walt Whitman published a poem called "I Hear America Singing."

- In the 1920s Hughes wrote "I, Too." It includes lines that echo Whitman's. The United States was still a segregated nation in which African Americans and other minorities were treated unjustly.

- Poets express their own ideas and feelings in a poem, but readers should not assume that a poem's speaker is the poet. Think of the speaker as a poem's narrator or as a character.

Set Purposes for Reading

BIG Question Read "I, Too" to see how someone who feels left out views the American dream.

Set Your Own Purpose What would you like to learn from the selection to help you answer the Big Question? Write your purpose on the "I, Too" page of Foldable 8.

Interactive Literary Elements Handbook
To review or learn more about the literary elements, go to www.glencoe.com.

Keep Moving

Use these skills as you read the following selection.

I, Too

by Langston Hughes

I, too, sing America.

I am the darker brother. **1**
They send me to eat in the kitchen
When company comes,
5 But I laugh,
And eat well,
And grow strong.

Tomorrow,
I'll be at the table
10 When company comes.
Nobody'll dare
Say to me,
"Eat in the kitchen,"
Then. **2**

15 Besides,
They'll see how beautiful I am
And be ashamed—

I, too, am America. **3** ○

Self Portrait, 1934. Malvin Gray Johnson. Smithsonian American Art Museum, Washington, D.C.

Practice the Skills

1 **Key Literary Element**

Metaphor The extended metaphor begins almost immediately. Who is the speaker?

2 **Key Reading Skill**

Identifying Author's Purpose What do you think Hughes wants his readers to understand?

3 **BIG Question**

What is the American dream to the speaker? Write your answer on the "I, Too" page of Foldable 8. Your response will help you complete the Unit Challenge later.

After You Read : I, Too

Answering the BIG Question

1. After reading "I, Too," what are your thoughts about the American dream? What are some of the restrictions people face in trying to achieve it?

2. **Recall** How is the speaker of the poem treated?

   TIP Right There

3. **Recall** How does the speaker respond to this treatment?

   TIP Right There

4. **Summarize** In one sentence, summarize what the speaker plans to do the next time there are guests.

   TIP Right There

Critical Thinking

5. **Interpret** How do you interpret "darker brother" (line 2) and "They" (line 3)? Who are they? What is their relationship? Explain.

   TIP Author and Me

6. **Analyze** What satisfaction does the speaker look forward to having "tomorrow"?

   TIP Think and Search

7. **Interpret** What does the speaker mean when he says, "I, too, sing America"? What does he mean by saying, "I, too, am America"? Why might he feel the need to say these things?

   TIP Author and Me

Talk About Your Reading

Discussion "You are what you eat," according to an old saying. It means that what you eat says things about you as a person. Change that saying to "You are *where* you eat," and discuss these questions:

• Each room in a home has one main purpose, even though it is likely used for many purposes. What is the difference between eating in a kitchen and eating in a dining room? How would you describe the sort of occasion when a meal is traditionally eaten in the dining room? What might it suggest when a meal is eaten in front of the living room TV? How does the event (not the food) of a restaurant meal differ from eating at home?

Now discuss this variation of the saying: "You are who you eat with."

NY English Language Arts Core Curriculum
(pp. 1138–1139)

LC R17 Demonstrate comprehension and response through a range of activities. **S3a** Express opinions or judgments about information, ideas, opinions, issues, themes, and experiences. **LC R13** Use text structure and literary devices to aid comprehension and response. **R2d** Determine how the use and meaning of literary devices, such as metaphor, convey the author's message or intent. **Core R4** Determine the meaning of words by using a dictionary. **Core W8** Use correct grammatical construction.

For a complete description of the standards, see p. NY 11.

Skills Review

Key Reading Skill: Identifying Author's Purpose

8. Why do you think Hughes chose *beautiful* for line 17? How would the meaning of this stanza (or the poem) be different if he had used another word, such as *powerful, angry,* or *happy*?

9. Walt Whitman's poem "I Hear America Singing" celebrates the courage, "stick-to-it" attitude, and unity of Americans. "I, Too" is a response to Whitman's work. What is that response? Does Hughes disagree about the qualities Americans possess? Is he adding something that Whitman might have overlooked? If so, what?

10. Do you think that, in this poem, Hughes is hopeful about the future? Explain.

Key Literary Element: Metaphor

11. Look at the word *brother* in line 2.

If it is used to mean "a male born of the same parents as another child," how does this word fit the metaphor? Who would be the speaker's other family members?

If it is used to mean "one who shares the same racial origin," would your interpretation of the metaphor change?

Which meaning of *brother* do you think makes the most sense, and why?

12. The table of line 9 is apparently in the dining room. Interpreting the metaphor, what might each of the two rooms—kitchen and dining room—represent?

13. Explain how the poem's extended metaphor shows the speaker's feelings about being an outsider in the house where he lives.

Vocabulary Check

14. English Language Coach The word *company* came from the Latin *com-* ("with; together") and *panis* ("bread; food"). Explain how these meanings make sense with the modern definition: "guests; visitors."

Grammar Link: Verbals

A verbal is a verb form that functions in a sentence as a noun, an adjective, or an adverb. There are three kinds of verbals: participles, gerunds, and infinitives.

A **participle** is a verb form that functions as an adjective. You form a present participle by adding *-ing* to a verb. You usually form a past participle by adding *-ed*.

• The <u>soaring</u> biplane flew 120 feet.
• The <u>awed</u> spectators watched in amazement.

A **gerund** is a verb form ending in *-ing* that is used as a noun. It can be used as the subject or the direct object of a sentence.

• <u>Moving</u> involves a lot of work. (subject)
• People enjoy <u>traveling</u>. (direct object)

An **infinitive** is made up of the word *to* and the base form of a verb. It may function as a noun and can be used as the subject or the direct object of a sentence.

• <u>To skate</u> is my ideal winter pastime. (subject)
• Many children like <u>to skate</u>. (direct object)

Grammar Practice

Copy each of the following sentences and underline the verbals. (There is only one verbal in each sentence.)

15. The girls gathered all the used containers and put them in the trash.

16. "Going home ten minutes ago will not be soon enough," the woman joked.

17. The cheering crowd rooted for the home team.

18. Drying the dishes became a sort of game.

19. To finish that novel will be an achievement.

Literature Online

Web Activities For eFlashcards, Selection Quick Checks, and other Web activities, go to www.glencoe.com.

Before You Read : from *Dandelion Wine*

Ray Bradbury

Meet the Author

Ray Bradbury was born in 1920 in Waukegan, Illinois, where he discovered the pleasure of reading comic strips and science fiction. As an adult, he often wrote from the point of view of a kid growing up in small-town America. He has said, "It is nice to be in the twenty-first century. It is like a new challenge. It is really a good and threatening new century to create for!" See page R1 of the Author Files for more on Bradbury.

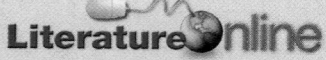

Author Search For more about Ray Bradbury, go to www.glencoe.com.

NY English Language Arts Core Curriculum (pp. 1140–1149)

LC R6 Determine the meaning of unfamiliar words by using word structure knowledge. **LC R13** Use text structure and literary devices to aid comprehension and response. **R3a** Question the writer's beliefs, intentions. **R2d** Determine the use and meaning of literary devices.

For a complete description of the standards, see p. NY 11.

Vocabulary Preview

capsize (KAP syz) *v.* to overturn or upset (especially a boat) **(p. 1142)** *He felt as if the whole place would capsize and sink beneath the ground.*

proprietor (pruh PRY uh tur) *n.* a person or firm that owns a property or a business **(p. 1145)** *The proprietor took pride in his shoe displays.*

rave (rayv) *v.* to speak about very favorably or with great enthusiasm **(p. 1146)** *How can you rave about a shoe you've never worn?*

alien (AY lee un) *adj.* strange; odd; peculiar **(p. 1147)** *The tennis shoes looked alien beneath the man's business suit.*

yielding (YEEL ding) *adj.* giving way to force or pressure **(p. 1148)** *The carpet was soft and yielding, like freshly turned soil.*

Write to Learn High-tops! Sandals! Loafers! Flip-flops! Why do some people have such strong feelings about footwear? What is it about shoes? Explain why certain people seem to have shoes "on their brains." Express your ideas in a few sentences using at least four vocabulary words.

English Language Coach

English as a Changing Language Etymology can be useful because, in learning about one word, you're actually learning about a family of words. When you come upon an unfamiliar word, you may be able to recognize the word family it belongs to. This chart shows a word from *Dandelion Wine*.

Word	*emporium*
Meaning	a retail store offering a variety of merchandise
Etymology	Latin, from Greek *emporion*, from *emporos* traveler, trader, from *em-* in + *poros* journey
Related Words	*pore, porous*

Remember, though, that a word part may be spelled the same in different words but have different meanings. For example, *portfolio* and *transport* come from the Greek *poros.* However, *corporate* and *portray* have different roots, even though they include the word part *por.*

Write to Learn Look up *pore* and *porous.* How are their modern meanings related to the original meaning of the root *poros?*

Skills Preview

Key Reading Skill: Identifying Author's Purpose

Short-story writers might have several purposes for writing. They usually want to entertain you, of course; and they usually want to make a point about life or about people. They may also want you to imagine events, people, and experiences you might not come across in your own life. To help you identify an author's purpose in a short story, think about

- word choices

  How do the author's word choices affect how you feel about the characters and events?

- intended audience

  Who is the author writing for? Which readers are most likely to make connections between the story and their own lives?

- main idea or theme

  What is the author's message?

Partner Work With a partner, identify the author's purpose in one of the short stories in this book.

Literary Element: Hyperbole

Hyperbole (hy PUR buh lee) is a figure of speech that uses exaggeration to express strong emotion, emphasize a point, or create humor. Most of us use hyperbole in ordinary conversation. (Have you ever said something "drove you crazy"?) Writers often use it too. For example, Langston Hughes says in a story that a woman carried "a large purse that had everything in it but hammer and nails."

Use these tips to help you learn about hyperbole.

- Look for any statement that may be hyperbole.

  Does the statement present a fact or an opinion? Is the exaggeration a really big one?

- Consider why the hyperbole is used.

  Does exaggeration add humor? Does it emphasize a point that's important to the speaker or writer? Does it express a strong emotion?

Get Ready to Read

Connect to the Reading

In this story, the main character spots a pair of tennis shoes in a store window—and he *has* to have them. He can't *explain* why he needs them, but he can *feel* why.

Write to Learn In your Learner's Notebook, write a paragraph or two about wanting something so badly that if you didn't get it, you'd just die. (This is the kind of situation where we all often use hyperbole.)

Build Background

This selection is an excerpt from *Dandelion Wine,* a novel first published in 1957.

- Bradbury's vision for this story is rooted in the past—his own and America's. The values he expresses are values he remembers from his childhood.

- Life in the 1950s was simple, in many ways. There were no cell phones, video games, or Internet. On TV, you probably got three channels. The only computers that existed were room-sized and belonged to the government.

Set Purposes for Reading

BIG Question Read *Dandelion Wine* to consider the American dream from the point of view of a boy growing up in a small Midwestern town.

Set Your Own Purpose What would you like to learn from the selection to help you answer the Big Question? Write your purpose on the "Dandelion Wine" page of Foldable 8.

Interactive Literary Elements Handbook
To review or learn more about the literary elements, go to www.glencoe.com.

Keep Moving

Use these skills as you read the following selection.

from Dandelion Wine

by Ray Bradbury

Late that night, going home from the show with his mother and father and his brother Tom, Douglas saw the tennis shoes in the bright store window. He glanced quickly away, but his ankles were seized, his feet suspended, then rushed. The earth spun; the shop awnings slammed their canvas wings overhead with the thrust of his body running. His mother and father and brother walked quietly on both sides of him. Douglas walked backward, watching the tennis shoes in the midnight window left behind. **1**

"It was a nice movie," said Mother.

Douglas murmured, "It was . . ."

It was June and long past time for buying the special shoes that were quiet as a summer rain falling on the walks. June and the earth full of raw power and everything everywhere in motion. The grass was still pouring in from the country, surrounding the sidewalks, stranding the houses. Any moment the town would **capsize**, go down and leave not a stir in the clover and weeds. And here Douglas stood, trapped on the dead cement and the red-brick streets, hardly able to move.

Visual Vocabulary
An *awning* is a covering over the outside of a window or door for protection from the rain and sun.

Vocabulary

capsize (KAP syz) *v.* to overturn or upset (especially a boat)

Practice the Skills

1 | **Literary Element**

Hyperbole As soon as Douglas sees the tennis shoes, what happens to him? Do you think this is actually happening, or is the author using hyperbole? Explain. Remember the reasons for using hyperbole.

"Dad!" He blurted it out. "Back there in that window, those Cream-Sponge Para Litefoot Shoes . . ."

His father didn't even turn. "Suppose you tell me why you need a new pair of sneakers. Can you do that?"

"Well . . ."

It was because they felt the way it feels every summer when you take off your shoes for the first time and run in the grass. They felt like it feels sticking your feet out of the hot covers in wintertime to let the cold wind from the open window blow on them suddenly and you let them stay out a long time until you pull them back in under the covers again to feel them, like packed snow. The tennis shoes felt like it always feels the first time every year wading in the slow waters of the creek and seeing your feet below, half an inch further downstream, with refraction,[1] than the real part of you above water. **2**

"Dad," said Douglas, "it's hard to explain."

Somehow the people who made tennis shoes knew what boys needed and wanted. They put marshmallows and coiled springs in the soles and they wove the rest out of grasses bleached and fired in the wilderness. Somewhere deep in the soft loam of the shoes the thin hard sinews[2] of the buck deer were hidden. The people that made the shoes must have watched a lot of winds blow the trees and a lot of rivers going down to the lakes. Whatever it was, it was in the shoes, and it was summer.

Douglas tried to get all this in words.

"Yes," said Father, "but what's wrong with last year's sneakers? Why can't you dig *them* out of the closet?"

Well, he felt sorry for boys who lived in California where they wore tennis shoes all year and never knew what it was to get winter off your feet, peel off the iron leather shoes all full of snow and rain and run barefoot for a day and then lace on the first new tennis shoes of the season, which was better than barefoot. The magic was always in the new pair of shoes. The magic might die by the first of September, but now in late June there was still plenty of magic, and shoes like these could jump you over trees and rivers and houses. And if you wanted, they could jump you over fences and sidewalks and dogs. **3**

1. *Refraction* is the bending of light rays as they travel through different substances. Light passing from air to water, for example, produces the effect the narrator describes here.

2. *Loam* is a rich, black soil. *Sinews* are tendons, the tissues that attach muscles to bones.

from *Dandelion Wine* **1143**

Practice the Skills

2 | **Key Reading Skill**

Identifying Author's Purpose In this paragraph, what is the author's purpose? Bradbury chooses words that create strong images to help you get a feel for how Douglas feels about the tennis shoes.

3 | **Literary Element**

Hyperbole Which parts of this paragraph would you say are hyperbole? Note those words and phrases in your Learner's Notebook.

Children Playing, Grez-sur-Loing. Alexander Harrison. Oil on canvas, 50 x 61 cm.

"Don't you see?" said Douglas. "I just *can't* use last year's pair."

For last year's pair were dead inside. They had been fine when he started them out, last year. But by the end of summer, every year, you always found out, you always knew, you couldn't really jump over rivers and trees and houses in them, and they were dead. But this was a new year, and he felt that this time, with this new pair of shoes, he could do anything, anything at all. **4**

They walked up on the steps to their house. "Save your money," said Dad. "In five or six weeks—"

"Summer'll be over!"

Lights out, with Tom asleep. Douglas lay watching his feet, far away down there at the end of the bed in the moonlight, free of the heavy iron shoes, the big chunks of winter fallen away from them.

"Reasons. I've got to think of reasons for the shoes."

Well, as anyone knew, the hills around town were wild with friends putting cows to riot, playing barometer to the

Practice the Skills

4 **Reviewing Skills**

Analyzing How does the narration help you understand why Douglas wants the shoes so badly?

atmospheric changes, taking sun, peeling like calendars each day to take more sun. To catch those friends, you must run much faster than foxes or squirrels. As for the town, it steamed with enemies grown irritable with heat, so remembering every winter argument and insult. *Find friends, ditch enemies!* That was the Cream-Sponge Para Litefoot motto. *Does the world run too fast? Want to catch up? Want to be alert, stay alert? Litefoot, then! Litefoot!*

He held his coin bank up and heard the faint small tinkling, the airy weight of money there.

Whatever you want, he thought, you got to make your own way. During the night now, let's find that path through the forest. . . .

Downtown, the store lights went out, one by one. A wind blew in the window. It was like a river going downstream and his feet wanting to go with it.

In his dreams he heard a rabbit running running running in the deep warm grass.

Old Mr. Sanderson moved through his shoe store as the **proprietor** of a pet shop must move through his shop where are kenneled animals from everywhere in the world, touching each one briefly along the way. Mr. Sanderson brushed his hands over the shoes in the window, and some of them were like cats to him and some were like dogs; he touched each pair with concern, adjusting laces, fixing tongues. Then he stood in the exact center of the carpet and looked around, nodding.

There was a sound of growing thunder.

One moment, the door to Sanderson's Shoe Emporium[3] was empty. The next, Douglas Spaulding stood clumsily there, staring down at his leather shoes as if these heavy things could not be pulled up out of the cement. **5** The thunder had stopped when his shoes stopped. Now, with painful slowness, daring to look only at the money in his cupped hand, Douglas moved out of the bright sunlight of Saturday noon. He made careful stacks of nickels, dimes, and quarters on the counter, like

Practice the Skills

5 **Literary Element**

Hyperbole Hyperbole emphasizes how heavy Douglas's shoes feel to him—as if they were stuck in cement.

---

3. An *emporium* is a store.

Vocabulary

proprietor (pruh PRY uh tur) *n.* a person or firm that owns a property or a business

someone playing chess and worried if the next move carried him out into sun or deep into shadow.

"Don't say a word!" said Mr. Sanderson.

Douglas froze.

"First, I know just what you want to buy," said Mr. Sanderson. "Second, I see you every afternoon at my window; you think I don't see? You're wrong. Third, to give it its full name, you want the Royal Crown Cream-Sponge Para Litefoot Tennis Shoes: 'LIKE **MENTHOL**[4] ON YOUR FEET!' Fourth, you want credit." 🟦6

"No!" cried Douglas, breathing hard, as if he'd run all night in his dreams. "I got something better than credit to offer!" he gasped. "Before I tell, Mr. Sanderson, you got to do me one small favor. Can you remember when was the last time you yourself wore a pair of Litefoot sneakers, sir?"

Mr. Sanderson's face darkened. "Oh, ten, twenty, say, thirty years ago. Why . . . ?"

"Mr. Sanderson, don't you think you owe it to your customers, sir, to at least try the tennis shoes you sell, for just one minute, so you know how they feel? People forget if they don't keep testing things. United Cigar Store man smokes cigars, don't he? Candy-store man samples his own stuff, I should think. So . . ."

"You may have noticed," said the old man, "I'm wearing shoes."

"But not sneakers, sir! How you going to sell sneakers unless you can **rave** about them and how you going to rave about them unless you know them?"

Mr. Sanderson backed off a little distance from the boy's fever, one hand to his chin. "Well . . ."

"Mr. Sanderson," said Douglas, "you sell me something and I'll sell you something just as valuable." 🟦7

"Is it absolutely necessary to the sale that I put on a pair of the sneakers, boy?" said the old man.

"I sure wish you could, sir!"

---

4. **Menthol** is a chemical that has the odor and cooling effect of peppermint.

Practice the Skills

6 | **English Language Coach**

A Changing Language The word **menthol** comes from German, which took it from the Latin word for *mint*.

7 | **Reviewing Skills**

Analyzing What is Douglas doing in this conversation? What does he want to "sell" to Mr. Sanderson?

Vocabulary

rave (rayv) *v.* to speak about very favorably or with great enthusiasm

The old man sighed. A minute later, seated panting quietly, he laced the tennis shoes to his long narrow feet. They looked detached and **alien** down there next to the dark cuffs of his business suit. Mr. Sanderson stood up. 🔟

"How do they *feel?*" asked the boy.

"How do they feel, he asks; they feel fine." He started to sit down.

"Please!" Douglas held out his hand. "Mr. Sanderson, now could you kind of rock back and forth a little, sponge around, bounce kind of, while I tell you the rest? It's this: I give you my money, you give me the shoes, I owe you a dollar. But, Mr. Sanderson, *but*—soon as I get those shoes on, you know what *happens?*"

"What?"

"Bang! I deliver your packages, pick up packages, bring you coffee, burn your trash, run to the post office, telegraph office, library! You'll see twelve of me in and out, in and out, every minute. Feel those shoes, Mr. Sanderson, *feel* how fast they'd take me? All those springs inside? Feel all the running inside? Feel how they kind of grab hold and can't let you alone and don't like you just *standing* there? Feel how quick I'd be doing the things you'd rather not bother with? You stay in the nice and cool store while I'm jumping all around town! But it's not me really, it's the shoes. They're going like mad down alleys, cutting corners, and back! There they go!"

Mr. Sanderson stood amazed with the rush of words. When the words got going the flow carried him; he began to sink deep in the shoes, to flex his

🔟 **English Language Coach**

A Changing Language
The word **alien** hasn't changed much from the original Latin *alienus*. The word can also refer to a person of another family, race, nation, or planet.

Vocabulary

alien (AY lee un) *adj.* strange; odd; peculiar

toes, limber his arches, test[5] his ankles. He rocked softly, secretly, back and forth in a small breeze from the open door. The tennis shoes silently hushed themselves deep in the carpet, sank as in a jungle grass, in loam and resilient[6] clay. He gave one solemn bounce of his heels in the yeasty dough, in the **yielding** and welcoming earth. Emotions hurried over his face as if many colored lights had been switched on and off. His mouth hung slightly open. Slowly he gentled and rocked himself to a halt, and the boy's voice faded and they stood there looking at each other in a tremendous and natural silence. **9**

A few people drifted by on the sidewalk outside, in the hot sun.

Still the man and boy stood there, the boy glowing, the man with revelation[7] in his face.

"Boy," said the old man at last, "in five years, how would you like a job selling shoes in this emporium?"

"Gosh, thanks, Mr. Sanderson, but I don't know what I'm going to be yet."

"Anything you want to be, son," said the old man, "you'll be. No one will ever stop you."

The old man walked lightly across the store to the wall of ten thousand boxes, came back with some shoes for the boy, and wrote up a list on some paper while the boy was lacing the shoes on his feet and then standing there, waiting.

The old man held out his list. "A dozen things you got to do for me this afternoon. Finish them, we're even Stephen, and you're fired."

"Thanks, Mr. Sanderson!" Douglas bounded away.

"Stop!" cried the old man.

Douglas pulled up and turned.

Mr. Sanderson leaned forward. "How do they *feel?*"

The boy looked down at his feet deep in the rivers, in the fields of wheat, in the wind that already was rushing him out

Practice the Skills

9 **Literary Elementl**

Hyperbole This paragraph includes figurative language, but is there any hyperbole? If so, what part(s)? If not, what kinds of figurative language are included?

---

5. Here, *flex, limber,* and *test* all mean "to bend or loosen up."

6. Anything that's *resilient* (rih ZIL yunt) is capable of returning to its original size, shape, or position.

7. Generally, a *revelation* (rev uh LAY shun) is the act of revealing something, such as a truth.

Vocabulary

yielding (YEEL ding) *adj.* giving way to force or pressure

The antelope is a swift, graceful animal with long curved horns, and the gazelle is a type of small antelope. Although they look like deer, antelopes and gazelles are in the goat family. They live in Africa and Southwest Asia.

of the town. He looked up at the old man, his eyes burning, his mouth moving, but no sound came out. **10**

"Antelopes?" said the old man, looking from the boy's face to his shoes. "Gazelles?"

The boy thought about it, hesitated, and nodded a quick nod. Almost immediately he vanished. He just spun about with a whisper and went off. The door stood empty. The sound of the tennis shoes faded in the jungle heat.

Mr. Sanderson stood in the sun-blazed door, listening. From a long time ago, when he dreamed as a boy, he remembered the sound. Beautiful creatures leaping under the sky, gone through brush, under trees, away, and only the soft echo their running left behind.

"Antelopes," said Mr. Sanderson. "Gazelles."

He bent to pick up the boy's abandoned winter shoes, heavy with forgotten rains and long-melted snows. Moving out of the blazing sun, walking softly, lightly, slowly, he headed back toward civilization. . . . **11** ○

Practice the Skills

10 **Literary Element**

Hyperbole This paragraph has a series of metaphors. Individually, the metaphors just compare the shoes' "feel" to different parts of nature. Together, they become hyperbole.

11 **BIG Question**

What would you say is Douglas's idea of the American dream? Write your purpose on the "Dandelion Wine" page of Foldable 8. Your response will help you complete the Unit Challenge later.

After You Read

from *Dandelion Wine*

Answering the BIG Question

1. Do you think life in America has changed much since Bradbury wrote his novel in 1957? Do you think the American dream has changed? Explain.

2. **Recall** To what does the author compare Old Mr. Sanderson, the shoe store proprietor?

   TIP Right There

3. **Summarize** In your own words, tell why Douglas feels he needs a new pair of tennis shoes.

   TIP Think and Search

Critical Thinking

4. **Interpret** On page 1144, find the paragraph that begins "Well, as anyone knew . . ." Tell what you think the first two sentences mean.

   TIP Author and Me

5. **Clarify** What does Douglas mean when he says to Mr. Sanderson, "you sell me something and I'll sell you something just as valuable"?

   TIP Author and Me

6. **Evaluate** The narrator says, "Somehow the people who made tennis shoes knew what boys needed and wanted." Do you think this is true? Explain.

   TIP Author and Me

7. **Explain** Why does Mr. Sanderson ask Douglas if he would like a job selling shoes in five years?

   TIP Think and Search

Write About Your Reading

Journal Entry Put yourself in Douglas's shoes. Write the journal entry that he might have written after he got home with his new Royal Crown Cream-Sponge Para Litefoot Tennis Shoes. First, think what he might have to say about getting the shoes and about his plans for the rest of the summer. Then start writing. (Don't be afraid to use some hyperbole; it's what Douglas would do.)

NY English Language Arts Core Curriculum (pp. 1150–1151)

LC R17 Demonstrate comprehension and response through a range of activities. **LC W5** Write with voice to address varied purposes, topics, and audiences. **LC R13** Use text structure and literary devices to aid comprehension and response. **R2d** Determine the use and meaning of literary devices. **LC R6** Determine the meaning of unfamiliar words by using word structure knowledge. **Core W7** Observe rules of spelling.

For a complete description of the standards, see p. NY 11.

Skills Review

Key Reading Skill: Identifying Author's Purpose

8. Who would you say is Bradbury's intended audience for *Dandelion Wine?* Why do you think this?

9. Tell what purpose(s) you think Bradbury had in mind and whether he was successful. Use details from the selection to support your answers.

Literary Element: Hyperbole

10. Explain the hyperbole in saying that "shoes like these could jump you over trees and rivers and houses."

11. Douglas says that, once he's wearing the new tennis shoes, Mr. Sanderson will "see twelve of me, in and out, in and out, every minute." Is Douglas exaggerating to express strong emotion, to emphasize a point, to create humor, or for a combination of these reasons? Explain.

Vocabulary Check

Write the vocabulary word and the word or phrase in parentheses that is its synonym.

12. capsize (straighten, tip over)

13. proprietor (salesman, owner)

14. rave (praise, scold)

15. alien (ordinary, unusual)

16. yielding (flexible, resisting)

Copy each sentence, filling in the blank with one of the vocabulary words.

17. My neighbors are so weird that even Martians would think they're ___!

18. I don't mean to ___, but you've made me the happiest person in the history of the universe!

19. If this thing were to ___, we'd sink faster than you can say "Glub!"

20. English Language Coach What do *proper, property,* and *proprietor* have in common, besides their similar spellings?

Grammar Link: Homophones

Homophones are words that sound alike but have different spellings and different meanings.

- My brother is a musician; he plays the <u>bass</u>.
- My sister is a ballplayer; she plays first <u>base</u>.

Not recognizing a homophone could result in an embarrassing spelling error. Even a computer spell-checker can't fix your mistake if you wrote *lone* when you want a *loan*. Always check a dictionary if you're unsure about which homophone to use.

Some Common Homophones	
breaks, brakes	meat, meet
by, buy	prints, prince
for, four	there, their, they're
here, hear	to, too, two
lessen, lesson	weight, wait

Grammar Practice

Copy the following sentences and circle the homophone that correctly completes each sentence. If you need help, use a dictionary.

21. Angela couldn't (wait, weight) to see the sunrise.

22. I need to (by, buy) a necktie and a pair of shoes.

23. The boys will wait in (here, hear).

24. I got my (prints, prince) from the photo shop.

25. The truck's (breaks, brakes) screeched to a stop.

26. Let's (meet, meat) at the Aerosmith concert.

Web Activities For eFlashcards, Selection Quick Checks, and other Web activities, www.glencoe.com.

Coming to AMERICA

by Joe McGowan, Marisa Wong, Vickie Bane, and Laurie Morice

& COMING to AMERICA

by Marianne Szegedy-Maszak

Skill Focus

You will use these skills as you read and compare the following selections:

- "Coming to America," p. 1155
- "Coming to America," p. 1162

Reading

- Reading and understanding informational texts
- Analyzing a writer's claims and conclusions

Writing

- Writing to compare and contrast

NY English Language Arts Core Curriculum (pp. 1152–1153)

R1j Compare and contrast information from different sources.
R3a Evaluate the validity and accuracy of information, ideas, themes, opinions, and experiences in texts.
For a complete description of the standards, see p. NY 11.

Writers help you form opinions all the time. How have the writers in this unit helped you form an opinion about the American dream?

As you read the selections in this workshop, think about how the writers view the American dream. How do their views influence yours?

How to Read Across Texts

When you read two similar texts, it's important to compare and contrast the way different writers address the same subject. To do this, ask questions about the writers' purposes for writing, their credibility (how trustworthy they are), and the evidence they use to support their opinions. Also, pay attention to point of view. Thinking about how and why writers present information helps you decide whether to believe what you read.

The selections in this workshop deal with immigration. As you read, ask yourself the following questions:

- Why is the author writing about this subject? Is the purpose to inform, to entertain, to persuade, or something else?
- Is the author credible? What makes him or her qualified to write this story about this subject?
- Does the writer support his or her ideas by providing evidence, such as facts, examples, or interviews?
- What does the evidence in these selections say about the immigrant experience in America?

Get Ready to Compare

In your Learner's Notebook, draw a graphic organizer like the one below. Use it to keep track of the details in the selections you are about to read. Your notes will help you better understand the subject and compare the selections. (By the way, *et al.* is the abbreviation of a Latin phrase that means "and others." It's used when it would be clumsy to repeat all the names in a list of people.)

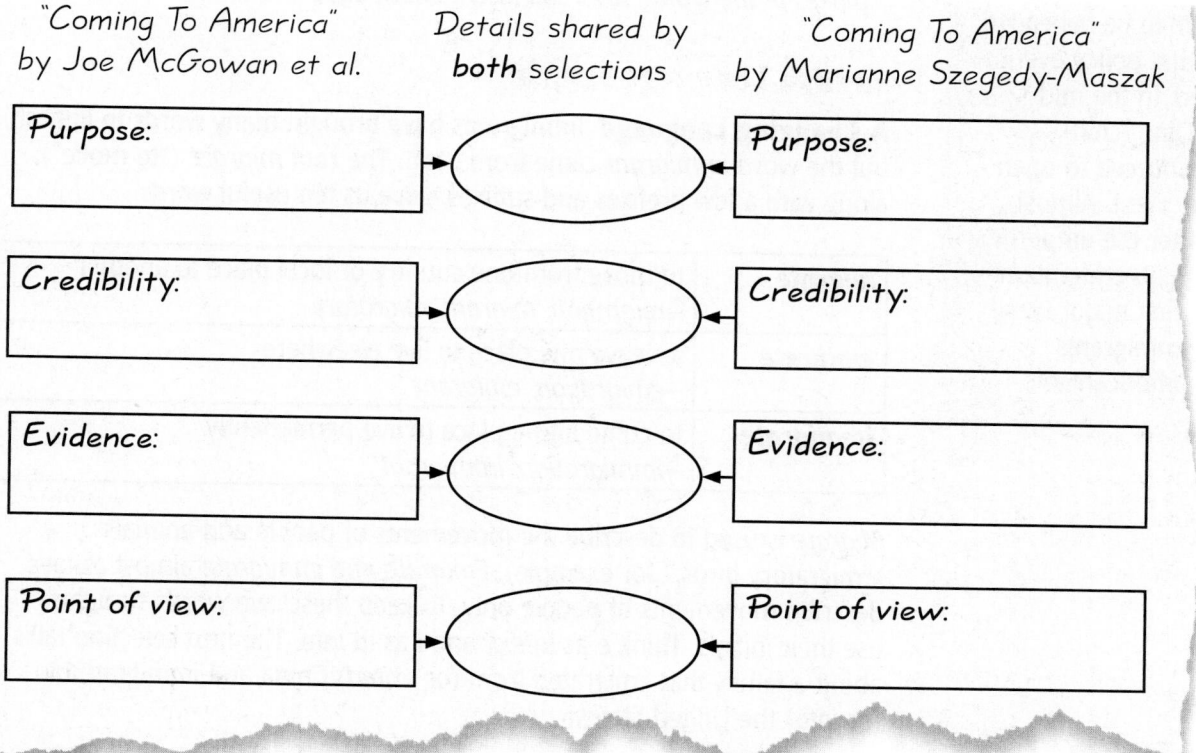

"Coming To America"
by Joe McGowan et al.

Details shared by
both selections

"Coming To America"
by Marianne Szegedy-Maszak

Purpose:

Purpose:

Credibility:

Credibility:

Evidence:

Evidence:

Point of view:

Point of view:

Use Your Comparison

Think of a time when a friend told you about something that happened to him or her. Now think of a time when a friend told you a story about something that happened to someone else. What details did you get from the first story that you didn't get from the second one? Do you trust a story told from a third-person point of view, or would you rather hear a first-person account?

The selections in this workshop deal with the same issue in different ways. Both articles are about immigration, but one relies heavily on first-person accounts. The other tells a story, but uses fewer direct quotations.

As you read, use your graphic organizer to help you answer these questions about point of view:

• What do I learn about the immigrant experience from a story told in first-person point of view?

• What do I learn from a story told in third-person?

• Is one point of view more helpful than the other, or are both equally valuable?

Before You Read

Coming to America
by Joe McGowan, Marisa Wong,
Vickie Bane, and Laurie Morice

Vocabulary Preview

toiled (toyld) *v.* worked hard **(p. 1155)** *Many immigrants toiled in factories, hoping to build a good life in America.*

discriminates (dih SKRIM uh nayts) *v.* treats unfairly **(p. 1160)** *In many places in the world, laws still discriminate against women.*

English Language Coach

A Changing Language Immigrants have brought many words to English, but the word *immigrant* came from Latin. The root *migrare* ("to move"), along with a few prefixes and suffixes, gave us ten useful words.

migrate	to move from one country or local place to another —*migration, migrant, migratory*
emigrate	to leave one place to live elsewhere —*emigration, emigrant*
immigrate	to come into a place to live permanently —*immigration, immigrant*

Migrate is used to describe the movements of people and animals ("migratory birds," for example). *Emigrate* and *immigrate* almost always describe movements of people only. To keep these two words straight, use their initials. Think *e* as in *exit* and *i* as in *into.* The next selection talks about a family that emigrated from (or *exited*) China and immigrated to (or *into*) the United States.

Get Ready to Read

Connect to the Reading

Imagine that you had to move to a new place, adjust to a new way of life, and possibly learn a new language. That is the immigrant experience.

Set Purpose for Reading

BIG Question Read to find out about three school-age immigrants and their search for the American dream.

Set Your Own Purpose What would you like to learn from this selection to help you answer the Big Question? Write your own purpose on the "Coming to America" page of Foldable 8.

NY English Language Arts Core Curriculum (pp. 1154–1160)

Core R4 Determine the meaning of words by using structural analysis.
R3a Evaluate the validity and accuracy **Vocabulary**of information, ideas, themes, opinions, and experiences in texts.

For a complete description of the standards, see p. NY 11.

TIME

Coming to AMERICA

PLEDGING ALLEGIANCE Proud, brand-new American citizens

The nation's newest immigrants share a time-honored dream with groups from the past.

By **JOE MCGOWAN, MARISA WONG, VICKIE BANE, and LAURIE MORICE**

The United States is a nation built by immigrants. From 1840 to 1870, the first wave of immigrants came from Ireland, England, Germany, and China to dig waterways and lay railroad tracks. From 1890 to 1924, a second wave crashed over Ellis Island,[1] the historic immigration station in New York Harbor, from countries such as Italy and Russia. These newcomers **toiled** in factories and built cities.

Now, a new wave of immigrants is coming to America. Over 31 million immigrants live in the U.S. They make up about 11.5% of the population. Like those who came before, these immigrants are arriving in hopes of building their own version of the American Dream. ◧

A New Era with New Challenges

Since the terrorist attacks of September 11, 2001, America has been rethinking its immigration policy. Some people want to

1. During these years, more than 20 million immigrants entered the United States through **Ellis Island,** a small island off the southern tip of Manhattan.

Vocabulary . . . .

toiled (toyld) *v.* worked hard

◧ **Reading Across Texts**

Point of View What point of view do the writers use here? How do you know? Make notes in your organizer.

limit the number of new immigrants to 300,000 a year. All foreign visitors face new delays, including high-tech screening and longer waiting periods. Still, more than 3.3 million new immigrants arrived between 2000 and 2004. On January 7, 2004, President George W. Bush proposed a plan to make it easier to track the 8 million illegal immigrants in the country. **2**

Once here, immigrants need help. "Family is always the first resource," says Lily Woo, the principal of Public School 130, in New York City, where many Chinese newcomers attend school. Extended immigrant families help one another find housing and work. Other support groups, like churches and community centers, are not as strong as they once were. As a result, about 25% of immigrant households receive government assistance, typically for health care and school for their children. Some 30% of immigrants have not graduated high school, and many have low-paying jobs.

Early immigrants quickly took on all aspects of American culture. But, today, many immigrants have one foot in the U.S. and one foot in their native land. With cell phones and the Internet, it's now easier for newcomers to keep in touch with the country they left behind.

"I'm the luckiest kid in the world," says Prudence Simon, 10, who now lives in New York. "I have two homes, Trinidad and the U.S.A."

Only the future will reveal how the new immigrants will build their American Dream. But one thing is certain, they have a rich history on which to lay a foundation. **3**

Immigrants Past and Present

They may come from different places, but immigrants share similar experiences. Starting over in a new country often takes time and can be hard. Here's a look at how three young immigrants dealt with their new American lives. **4**

2 **Reading Across Texts**

Evidence What do you learn about immigration from the facts presented here? Make notes in your organizer. How does the use of evidence build the writers' credibility?

3 **Reading Across Texts**

Purpose The writers say that new immigrants have a "rich history." What might their purpose be for writing about that history?

4 **Reading Across Texts**

Evidence Writers often use examples and direct quotations as evidence, or support, for their main idea. How does the use of examples help you find and understand the main idea in what you read? How does it build the writers' credibility?

OPEN DOORS Immigrants arrive at Ellis Island, in New York Harbor, in 1920. Nearly 14 million foreign-born people were living in the U.S. that year.

Corbis Bettmann

Jin Hua Zhang

When she was 11 years old, Jin Hua's father brought his family to New York City. Although Jin Hua has made friends and is doing well in school, she still misses her home in China.

Jin Hua shares this bedroom with her parents and older brother.

In my hometown of Ting Jiang, in southeastern China, people always said that America was very good, like some kind of wonderland. They said you could have a good life here. So when my mother, my brother, and I flew into New York City's LaGuardia Airport, I was so happy. It was night, and I thought, "This city is so good, so beautiful." I knew at that moment my life would be changing. I thought it would be great.

But then I came to my apartment. I was shocked. In China, my parents were bosses at a company that made bricks. We had a big house; it was very comfortable. Here, there were four of us squeezing into two small rooms [in Chinatown]. Everything is shared—I can't do anything in private. The next day, when I went down to the street, it was so noisy. And, oh, my gosh, so stinky! Starting school was hard too. In China, I'd been a good student—I completed every exam perfectly. Here, I didn't understand what the teacher was saying. It was the [toughest] time I've ever had. **5**

But the biggest difference between China and here was that I was lonely. Some Americans look at you differently [if you're an immigrant]; they look down on you. I had to make all new friends. In China, teenagers come together as a group and go out to play. Here, my parents didn't want me to hang out outside; they thought I could get lost or [might] hang out with bad people.

I know that my family decided to come here so my brother and I could get a better education. In China, they made money more easily, but they never felt like it was enough; they always wanted more. Now, they work all the time, every morning until midnight, [because they] want me to go to college [instead of] working in a factory like most Chinese

5 | **Reading Across Texts**

Point of View The point of view has changed. What do you learn about Jin Hua and her move to New York from this first-person account? How does this paragraph show her personality?

Erin Patrice O'Brien

immigrants [we know]. But I feel like I have less. I don't know if I consider myself an American. I feel like I'm really more Chinese. **6**

Sonia Diaz

In 1994, Sonia's family moved to Asheboro, North Carolina, from the tiny town of San Francisco de Asis, Mexico. Caught between two worlds, she struggled to stay loyal to her Hispanic <u>heritage</u> while making the most of her new life in America. 7

I wasn't ready for the racism I found when I started school here. In seventh grade, kids used to laugh at my accent when the teacher asked me to read in front of the class. By the time I was in ninth grade, my Mexican friends didn't like to talk to American people. They were scared of having people laugh. So they didn't want to get involved in anything, no clubs, no sports. I wanted to, but I never could because no other Hispanics were.

Sonia (with her little brother, Jose Luis) strikes a pose in front of her house in Asheboro, North Carolina.

6 **Reading Across Texts**

Point of View How does the point of view help you understand Jin Hua's experience? Are you surprised to learn that she feels more Chinese than American? Why or why not?

7 **English Language Coach**

A Changing Language The word <u>heritage</u> comes from Middle English, Old French, and Medieval Latin. Use a dictionary to find out more about its origins and meaning.

Then in 11th grade, I got put in mostly honors classes, because I had good grades. Back then, it was all Americans in those classes. So I needed to talk to them, and we made friends. My Hispanic friends would get mad—they'd say that I didn't know who I was. But after a while I was like, I'm going to talk to whomever I want to. And I did. I made American friends, and I had Mexican friends. I even have an American boyfriend.

Things are different at my school now. There are lots more Mexican kids, and they're more involved, more open. The soccer team used to be mostly white; now it's mostly Hispanic. Looking back, I wish I could do high school over again. I'd take every honors class, join every club. I missed so many things because I didn't want people to make fun of me. I'm glad it's not like that anymore. 🎱

Peter Deng

Peter was one of Sudan's "Lost Boys," thousands of boys who were separated from their families by the ongoing civil war in their country, and then walked by themselves for months before finally finding safety at a refugee camp in Kenya. In March 2001, he was allowed to emigrate[2] to the United States, where he's building a brand-new life.

When I first came to Denver, [Colorado,] I had never slept in a bed. I had never seen television or snow. Even women in shorts—that's not so common in Africa.

I was born in the village of Jale, in the southern part of Sudan. Our homes were huts made out of long grasses. So the first week [that the Lost Boys were in Denver], we stayed inside, not coming out.

🎱 **Reading Across Texts**

Evidence In your organizer, make notes about Sonia's experience. How is it similar to and different from Jin Hua's?

Peter stands tall at his school, the University of Colorado.

Gerard Gaskin

---

2. If you *emigrate,* you leave a country or region to live somewhere else.

There were eight of us sharing a house, two to a room. Ecumenical Refugee Services [who helped sponsor the Lost Boys] gave us a television. They also bought us clothes and groceries for the first two months and showed us how to cook. **9**

There were so many things—the stove, the refrigerator—that we didn't know how to use. I was one of the first Lost Boys to get a job, as a warehouse clerk, processing customer orders. When I got my first paycheck, I didn't know what to do with it. I kept it under the bed for two weeks—until [somebody] told me I had to put it in the bank.

Now I write checks. I've even bought a car. I love the United States. I like to watch basketball. I've started college, and I have friends—some African, some American. **10**

Sometimes we get together for parties. People are so friendly and polite, and nobody **discriminates** or takes advantage of you. My mother died in 1998, but my younger brother is still in the camp in Kenya. I want to bring him here, to get the same opportunities as me. This is a very free life. It's very, very exciting. **11**

—Updated 2005, from *TIME FOR KIDS*, January 30, 2004, and *Teen People*, March 2003

9 **Reading Across Texts**

Point of View How is Peter's story different from Jin Hua's and Sonia's? What do the first-person accounts reveal about their likes, dislikes, and hopes for the future?

10 **BIG Question**

Are Jin Hua, Sonia, and Peter living the American dream? Why or why not?

11 **Reading Across Texts**

Purpose How would you describe the writers' purpose now? Make notes in your organizer.

Vocabulary

discriminates (dih SKRIM uh nayts) *v.* treats unfairly

Before You Read : Coming to America

Marianne Szegedy-Maszak

Meet the Author

Prize-winning journalist Marianne Szegedy-Maszak has worked for several major news sources, including *Newsweek,* ABC Radio, and National Public Radio. Currently, she is a senior editor at *U.S. News and World Report.* Szegedy-Maszak taught journalism at American University in Washington, D.C., and has lived in both the United States and Europe.

Author Search For more about Marianne Szegedy-Maszak, go to www.glencoe.com.

NY English Language Arts Core Curriculum
(pp. 1161–1165)

Core R4 Determine the meaning of words by using structural analysis. **R3a** Evaluate the validity and accuracy of information, ideas, themes, opinions, and experiences in texts.

For a complete description of the standards, see p. NY 11.

Vocabulary Preview

trivial (TRIV ee ul) *adj.* of very little value or importance **(p. 1163)** *His skates appeared trivial next to larger concerns.*

incongruous (in KON groo us) *adj.* not in agreement **(p. 1164)** *The woman's dress seemed incongruous with her environment.*

immersed (ih MURSD) *v.* completely occupied mentally; form of the verb *immerse* **(p. 1165)** *He immersed himself in his studies.*

English Language Coach

A Changing Language English is the official language of the United States because the country used to be British colonies. Britain was once a part of the Roman Empire. The Latin-speaking Romans were greatly influenced by the culture and language of Greece. So let's go straight back to Greek and Latin in the next selection. Watch for these words:

Word	Roots	Meaning
architect	Greek *archi* + Greek *tekton*	master + builder
television	Greek *tele* + Latin *visio*	far + seeing

Get Ready to Read

Connect to the Reading

What challenges do you face in your daily life? What sacrifices would you be willing to make for your dreams to become a reality?

Build Background

The families in this selection came to the United States as refugees. Refugees are people who flee their homelands to escape war, oppression, persecution, or natural disaster. What does the American dream mean to refugees? It often means freedom, opportunity, and sacrifices.

Set Purpose for Reading

BIG Question Read to find out about two refugee families and their search for the American dream.

Set Your Own Purpose What else would you like to learn from this selection to help you answer the Big Question? Write your own purpose on the "Coming to America" page of Foldable 8.

INFORMATIONAL TEXT
MAGAZINE
Good Housekeeping

COMING to AMERICA!

by Marianne Szegedy-Maszak

Practice the Skills

"What day is today?" the teacher asks slowly, tossing a basketball to 11-year-old Dardan Osmani.

"Today is Monday," the boy answers with a slight accent. Then, passing the ball to a child in a Winnie-the-Pooh T-shirt, Dardan asks, "What day is tomorrow?"

"Tomorrow is **Wednesday**," the little boy starts to say, but the other children quickly interrupt with the correct answer. **1**

There are 21 children learning English in this class at Marymount College in New York City—young survivors of the genocide in Kosovo.[1] Their parents are in another classroom down the hall. They are doctors, engineers, architects—highly educated professionals now trying to learn enough English to get jobs as dishwashers, maids, janitors.

Nearly 10 percent of the U.S. population—26.3 million—was born in other countries. Mostly they've come here for the reason immigrants usually leave their homes: hoping to find a better life for themselves and their children. But a small fraction, including Dardan Osmani's family, had no choice: They were fleeing civil wars or brutal governments. Last year our TV screens showed them leaving Kosovo. Before that, we saw them running from Bosnia, Rwanda, Laos, Cambodia. And then something remarkable happened. We began to see these same people not on our televisions but in the supermarket or at school. **2**

1 **English Language Coach**

A Changing Language The Romans had named the days of the week for their gods. Much later, the English chose new names to honor their own gods, one of whom was Woden. Woden's day eventually became **Wednesday**.

2 **Reading Across Texts**

Purpose Do you think the writer's purpose is to entertain, inform, or persuade? Explain your answer in your organizer.

---

1. *Kosovo* was one of the six provinces of Yugoslavia. In the 1990s the country fought a civil war and split apart. The leader of Serbia, another former province, ordered thousands of murders in Kosovo. He was later convicted of *genocide* (JEN uh syd), the organized destruction of a racial, political, or cultural group.

Which is, perhaps, the greatest gift America can offer: the gift of an ordinary life. **3**

At the time that we're talking, the Osmanis have been in New York City just a month. But the father, Elez, 44, and his four oldest children—Dardan, his brother, Begatim, 15, and two sisters, Besarta, 14, and Dhurata, 6—move through the crowded streets like natives as they make their way from English class to an apartment in the Bronx. Nurije, a trim woman of forty, hugs her family as they enter, while baby Rrita, 13 months, wobbles happily among her sisters and brothers. **4**

Speaking through an interpreter. Elez tells the family's story. On April 1, 1999, Serbian soldiers forced them to leave their apartment. They went to Macedonia.² "Waiting for the train was tough," Elez recalls. "It was raining. The children and old people were already scared. Meanwhile, the Serbian police, trying to create a panic, kept saying they would kill us all."

Conditions at the refugee camp were even rougher. Says Elez grimly, "There was mud everywhere, little food, no showers. And a lot of sickness—twenty-three people died that first week." **5**

But the Osmanis were lucky. A week after they arrived, a friend invited the family to his home. Elez's uncle then contacted a cousin in America, who was willing to sponsor the family.

Since they left Kosovo, they've heard that their apartment has been looted. Nurije loses some of her calm self-control as she talks about the lost baby pictures. Dardan mentions his skates, then seems embarrassed that he's thinking about something so **trivial**. But Elez's encouragement keeps them all going. "I want to see my children working, learning," he says emphatically. "I want them to become citizens and not be threatened like their parents were once."

Now, that's beginning to happen. Last fall, the children started school. Elez, who was a magazine editor in Kosovo, found work as a maintenance worker. Nurije, a biology

---

2. **Macedonia** was another province of Yugoslavia.

Vocabulary

trivial (TRIV ee ul) *adj.* of very little value or importance

Practice the Skills

3 **BIG Question**
Why do you think "an ordinary life" is a part of the American dream?

4 **Reading Across Texts**
Point of View What point of view does the writer use here? Why might the writer use this point of view to tell about each member of the Osmani family?

5 **Reading Across Texts**
Evidence What information do you get from direct quotations? How do these direct quotations help you better understand the Osmanis' experience?

teacher, is at home.) He knew he'd have to take a job doing unskilled work, but it doesn't matter. All that counts, the parents agree is that this life "is better for the children." **6**

The apartment in Silver Spring, Maryland, was small, and Eva Wilson shared it with a roommate. But on the day in 1996 when Eva welcomed her four children at Newark International Airport and brought them to live with her in that too-small space, only one thing mattered: They were together. "We didn't mind being crowded, all five of us in one room," says Eva, "because where we had been was worse." **7**

"I want them to go to college, to learn all they can," says Eva Wilson of her daughters, Manny, Faith, and Peaches.

Where they'd been was Liberia, a country on Africa's west coast. A civil war had broken out there early in 1990, Eva's husband, Francis, had been killed, and she had been separated from her children—Franklin, then 12; Peaches, 8; Faith, 5; and her tiny daughter, Kimmy, only a month old.

Unbelievably, it took three and a half years for them to be reunited. Even more unbelievably, Eva then had to leave her children again. Her visa[3] to the United States had finally come through. "I knew I had to go to the U.S. if I was going to provide any kind of stable life for my family," she says. "But it was tough, I will tell you. I had to tighten my heart and be strong." She was granted asylum[4] by the United States in 1995, and her children were permitted to join her a year later. **8**

Visual Vocabulary
Town houses are houses that share walls with the houses around them.

Today, Eva, 43, is telling her story in her Gaithersburg, Maryland, home. It feels **incongruous,** this woman in a brightly printed African dress describing her ordeal amid town houses in a Washington, D.C. suburb. The adjustment has been tough, but, like so many generations of immigrants before, the Wilsons know that education is the key. Franklin, who had lost some time

---

3. A *visa* is a document that permits entry to or travel within a country.

4. Refugees who can't return to their home country can be granted *asylum*, (uh SY lum), or permission to live, work, and eventually apply for citizenship in the United States.

Vocabulary

incongruous (in KON groo us) *adj.* not in agreement

Practice the Skills

6 Reading Across Texts

Evidence What did you learn about the Osmanis? Think about how their story is similar to and different from the stories of Jin Hua, Sonia, and Peter from the first selection.

7 Reading Across Texts

Point of View and Evidence The writer uses third-person point of view. She supports her statements with direct quotations. What statement about the Wilsons does this quotation support?

8 Reading Across Texts

Point of View Do you get a better overview of events from a third-person account? Why might a writer choose this point of view to tell about several people, and the things that happen to them over time?

Analyzing the Photo In this April 1999 photo, ethnic Albanian refugees wait at a checkpoint on the Kosovo-Macedonia border. How does this photo capture the frustration and uncertainty of the refugee experience?

in school, **immersed** himself in the eleventh grade and graduated on time, winning a scholarship to a college in Florida. The older girls, too, excel at their studies, and little Kimmy, who'd never had a normal life before coming here, is now studying hard. **9**

For Eva, the challenge was work. She had a job at a school, but most days she had to be there from four in the afternoon until eight the next morning. Now, having just earned her certificate in early-childhood education, she is working at a day-care center. **10**

But the struggle has been worth it, says Eva. "Coming here was our only hope. Otherwise, we would have always been refugees." ○

Practice the Skills

9 **Reading Across Texts**

Purpose How would you describe the writer's purpose now? Make notes in your organizer.

10 **BIG Question**

Do you think the American dream means the same thing to the Wilsons as it does to the Osmanis? Why or why not?

Vocabulary

immersed (ih MURSD) *v.* completely occupied mentally

After You Read

Coming to AMERICA & COMING to AMERICA

Vocabulary Check

Each vocabulary word below is followed by a synonym. Copy each set, adding at least one synonym. (It can be a word or a phrase.) If you get stuck, use a thesaurus. Be sure to choose synonyms that are close to the meanings given on pages 1154 and 1161.

1. **discriminates:** shows prejudice
2. **incongruous:** mismatched
3. **immersed:** caught up in
4. **trivial:** insignificant
5. **toiled:** labored

Write each vocabulary word and an example of the thing described.

6. a job that requires people to **toil**
7. a hobby or activity that you find **trivial**
8. a color that you think is **incongruous** with purple
9. a recent project or activity you've had to **immerse** yourself in
10. a way that people in wheelchairs are sometimes **discriminated** against

English Language Coach

Each word below came into English from a modern foreign language with little or no change in spelling or pronunciation. Identify the original language (Spanish, for example, not the word's roots in Latin or Anglo-Saxon). If you're not sure, make a guess before you look up the word.

11. arcade
12. chili
13. confetti
14. karaoke
15. matinee
16. pretzel
17. tundra
18. wok

NY English Language Arts Core Curriculum
(pp. 1166–1167)

LC R17 Demonstrate comprehension and response through a range of activities. **R3a** Evaluate the validity and accuracy of information, ideas, themes, opinions, and experiences in texts. **R1j** Compare and contrast information from different sources. **LC W6** Organize writing effectively to communicate ideas to an intended audience.

For a complete description of the standards, see p. NY 11.

Reading/Critical Thinking

Coming to
AMERICA

19. **BIG Question** What do Jin Hua, Sonia, and Peter want to achieve in America? How are their dreams alike and different?

TIP Author and Me

20. Recall What does Sonia wish that she could do over again?

TIP Right There

21. Infer Why do you think Jin Hua feels more Chinese than American?

TIP Author and Me

COMING
to AMERICA

22. Interpret Eva uses a figure of speech when she says that she had to "tighten her heart." What does she mean?

TIP Author and Me

23. Interpret Why do you think that so many people choose to immigrate to the United States? What opportunities exist here that don't exist elsewhere?

TIP On My Own

24. Analyze Do the Osmanis and the Wilsons think their struggles have been worthwhile? Are they living their dreams?

TIP Author and Me

Writing: Reading Across Texts

Use Your Notes

What have you learned about the immigrant experience from these selections? As you review your chart and other notes, ask yourself these questions:

• *What facts and examples did I find in each selection?*

• *How did the selection's direct quotations and first-*

person accounts help me better understand the immigrant experience?

25. Use the notes in your organizer to compare and contrast what you learned from the selections in this workshop.

Step 1: Look at your notes about purpose and credibility. Did you find similarities between the selections? Write them in the appropriate circle in your organizer. How did the writers' purposes differ? Underline the differences you noted.

Step 2: Write a paragraph comparing or contrasting the writers' purposes.

Step 3: Look at your notes about evidence and point of view. Record the similarities you found in the appropriate circle in your organizer. Underline the differences you noted.

Step 4: Write a paragraph comparing or contrasting the types of evidence used in these selections. Which selection contained the most information? From which selection did you learn the most?

Step 5: Write a paragraph comparing or contrasting point of view in both selections. Which point of view was most appealing? Did you learn more about the immigrant experience from a first- or third-person account?

Get It On Paper

To compare what you've learned from these selections, answer the questions below.

26. In the first selection, the writer's purpose was ____ .

27. In the second selection, the writers' purpose was ____ .

28. I learned ____ from the first selection that I didn't learn from the second selection.

29. I learned ____ from the second selection that I didn't learn from the first selection.

30. I found the (first, second) selection more interesting because I learned ____ from it.

BIG Question

31. You've read what the American dream means to people from other parts of the world. What does the American dream mean to you?

Answering The BIG Question

What Is the American Dream?

You've just about read about the American dreams of real people and fictional characters. Now use what you've learned to do the Unit Challenge.

The Unit Challenge

Choose Activity A or Activity B and follow the directions for that activity.

A. Group Activity: American Dream Newsletter

Form a small group and create a newsletter that contains articles about people who obtain their American dreams.

1. **Talk about American Dreams** Choose one group member to be the note-keeper for the discussion. This person should make a chart with two columns labeled **Character/Person** and **American Dream/Values**. As a group, brainstorm a list of characters and real people from these Unit 8 selections whom you'd like to write about. Use your Foldable notes for ideas.

   • What versions of the American dream do the characters and people on your list have? What do they value in life?

   • What do they do or plan to do to accomplish their goals and achieve their dreams?

2. **Choose an Article** Group members can choose to write a newsletter article about a character or person from a selection or about a real person who isn't in the reading—a famous person, a friend, or a relative, for example. You can also choose to write about your version of the American dream in an opinion piece or in a persuasive essay.

First, decide on the type of article you'd like to write. Here are some ideas:

• a news article about a specific event in the person's life that helps him or her get closer to achieving the American dream

• a feature article presenting a brief biography, including what the person has done to obtain the American dream

• a feature article about the person's values and how they relate to the American dream

• an article about the people and events that have influenced the person's ideas of the American dream

• an opinion piece in which you present your idea of the American dream and why it's important to you

• an essay that tries to persuade readers of the best ways to achieve the American dream

3. **Write Your Article** Sit down and write.
- Decide what facts to include.
- Decide on a main idea and back it up with supporting details.
- Choose a text structure to help you present your ideas clearly.
- Open with an attention-getter—something that will make your readers want to keep reading.
- Create a title for your article.

4. **Create the Newsletter** Get together with your group again, and put the newsletter together.
- Decide on a name, and have someone design it for the top of the newsletter.
- Draw a rough draft of the layout, including ideas for photos and other text features.
- Exchange articles with another group member for proofreading. If you have questions, ask the writer to clarify.
- Type up or print out all the articles and cut and paste them into your newsletter. Add photos or other illustrations. Then make copies for your classmates.

B. Solo Activity: American Dream Spokesperson

You've read how people in different times and places have interpreted the American dream. Now choose someone to be an "American Dream Spokesperson."

1. **Make the Call** Review your Foldable notes, and then list the people and characters from the selections.
- Add to the list people you know personally who have in some way lived, or worked toward, the American dream.
- Choose a person or character from your list to be a spokesperson for the American dream.

2. **Speaking for Your Spokesperson** Decide how you want to honor your spokesperson. Here are some ideas:
- Write a biography. You may need to research the details of a real person's life. If you chose a fictional character, you can write his or her biography based on details you know from the selection as well as from your imagination.

- Write a speech. Have your spokesperson describe and explain his or her American dream. Be as specific as possible.
- Create a poster. Include images and words that help show your spokesperson's idea of the American Dream.

3. **Go Public!** Take your American Dream Spokesperson public. Publish your biography, speech, or poster. Display it in the classroom, read it aloud, present it to the class, or put it on your class's Web site (if you have one).

Your Turn: Read and Apply Skills

Toshio Mori

Meet the Author

Toshio Mori was born in Oakland, California, in 1910. He knew at an early age that he would become a writer. But just before his first book was published, Japan attacked the U.S. Navy base at Pearl Harbor, Hawaii. The United States entered World War II and sent 110,000 Japanese-American citizens to specially built camps. Mori's family wound up in Utah. After the war, his book was published, and Mori was recognized as an important new writer.

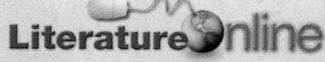

Author Search For more about Toshio Mori, go to www.glencoe .com.

by Toshio Mori

When he came to our house one day and knocked on the door and immediately sold me a copy of *The Saturday Evening Post,* it was the beginning of our friendship and also the beginning of our business relationship.

His name is John. I call him Johnny and he is eleven. It is the age when he should be crazy about baseball or football or fishing. But he isn't. Instead he came again to our door and made a business proposition.

"I think you have many old magazines here," he said.

"Yes," I said, "I have magazines of all kinds in the basement."

"Will you let me see them?" he said.

"Sure," I said.

I took him down to the basement where the stacks of magazines stood in the corner. Immediately this little boy went over to the piles and lifted a number of magazines and examined the dates of each number and the names.

"Do you want to keep these?" he said.

"No. You can have them," I said.

"No. I don't want them for nothing," he said. "How much do you want for them?"

"You can have them for nothing," I said.

"No, I want to buy them," he said. "How much do you

want for them?"

This was a boy of eleven, all seriousness and purpose.

"What are you going to do with the old magazines?"

"I am going to sell them to people," he said.

We arranged the financial matters satisfactorily. We agreed he was to pay three cents for each copy he took home. On the first day he took home an *Esquire,* a couple of *Saturday Evening Posts,* a *Scribner's,* an *Atlantic Monthly,* and a *Collier's.* He said he would be back soon to buy more magazines.[1]

When he came back several days later, I learned his name was John so I began calling him Johnny.

"How did you make out, Johnny?" I said.

"I sold them all," he said. "I made seventy cents altogether."

"Good for you," I said. "How do you manage to get seventy cents for old magazines?"

Johnny said as he made the rounds selling *The Saturday Evening Post,* he also asked the folks if there were any back numbers[2] they particularly wanted. Sometimes, he said, people will pay unbelievable prices for copies they had missed and wanted very much to see some particular articles or pictures, or their favorite writers' stories.

"You are a smart boy," I said.

"Papa says, if I want to be a salesman, be a good salesman," Johnny said. "I'm going to be a good salesman."

"That's the way to talk," I said. "And

what does your father do?"

"Dad doesn't do anything. He stays at home," Johnny said.

"Is he sick or something?" I said.

"No, he isn't sick," he said. "He's all right. There's nothing wrong with him."

"How long have you been selling *The Saturday Evening Post?*" I asked.

"Five years," he said. "I began at six."

"Your father is lucky to have a smart boy like you for a son," I said.

That day he took home a dozen or so of the old magazines. He said he had five standing orders, an *Esquire* issue of June 1937, *Atlantic Monthly* February 1938 number, a copy of December 11, 1937 issue of *The New Yorker, Story Magazine* of February 1934, and a *Collier's* of April 2, 1938. The others, he said, he was taking a chance at.

"I can sell them," Johnny said.

Several days later I saw Johnny again at the door.

"Hello, Johnny," I said. "Did you sell them already?"

"Not all," he said. "I have two left. But I want some more."

"All right," I said. "You must have good business."

"Yes," he said, "I am doing pretty good these days. I broke my own record selling *The Saturday Evening Post* this week."

"How much is that?" I said.

"I sold 167 copies this week," he said. "Most boys feel lucky if they sell seventy-five or one hundred copies. But not for me."

"How many are there in your family, Johnny?" I said.

"Six counting myself," he said. "There is my father, three smaller brothers, and two small sisters."

---

1. All the magazines named in this story are or were known for printing new works by top American writers. As of 2006, only three of the magazines were still being published: *Atlantic Monthly* (which began in 1857), *The New Yorker,* and *Esquire.*

2. **Back numbers** refers to old issues.

"Where's your mother?" I said.

"Mother died a year ago," Johnny said.

He stayed in the basement a good one hour sorting out the magazines he wished. I stood by and talked to him as he lifted each copy and inspected it thoroughly. When I asked him if he had made a good sale with the old magazines recently, he said yes. He sold the *Scribner's* Fiftieth Anniversary Issue for sixty cents. Then he said he made several good sales with *Esquire* and a *Vanity Fair* this week.

"You have a smart head, Johnny," I said. "You have found a new way to make money."

Johnny smiled and said nothing. Then he gathered up the fourteen copies he picked out and said he must be going now.

THE SATURDAY EVENING POST

An Illustrated Weekly
Founded A.º D.º 1728 by Benj. Franklin

DECEMBER 19, 1925   5cts. THE COPY

"Johnny," I said, "hereafter you pay two cents a copy. That will be enough."

Johnny looked at me.

"No," he said. "Three cents is all right. You must make a profit, too."

An eleven-year-old boy—I watched him go out with his short business-like stride.

Next day he was back early in the morning. "Back so soon?" I said.

"Yesterday's were all orders," he said. "I want some more today."

"You certainly have a good trade," I said.

"The people know me pretty good. And I know them pretty good," he said. And about ten minutes later he picked out seven copies and said that was all he was taking today.

"I am taking Dad shopping," he said. "I am going to buy a new hat and shoes for him today."

"He must be tickled," I said.

"You bet he is," Johnny said. "He told me to be sure and come home early."

So he said he was taking these seven copies to the customers who ordered them and then run home to get Dad.

Two days later Johnny wanted some more magazines. He said a Mr. Whitman who lived up a block wanted all the magazines with Theodore Dreiser's stories inside. Then he went on talking about other customers of his. Miss White, the schoolteacher, read Hemingway, and he said she would buy back copies with Hemingway stories anytime he brought them in. Some liked Sinclair Lewis, others Saroyan, Faulkner, Steinbeck, Mann, Faith Baldwin, Fannie Hurst, Thomas Wolfe.[3] So it went. It was amazing how an eleven-year-old boy could

---

3. The writers named here are among the best American short story writers. Some of them also wrote novels and nonfiction.

remember the customers' preferences and not get mixed up.

One day I asked him what he wanted to do when he grew up. He said he wanted a book shop all his own. He said he would handle old books and magazines as well as the new ones and own the biggest bookstore around the Bay Region.[4]

"That is a good ambition," I said. "You can do it. Just keep up the good work and hold your customers."

On the same day, in the afternoon, he came around to the house holding several packages.

"This is for you," he said, handing over a package. "What is this?" I said.

Johnny laughed. "Open up and see for yourself," he said.

I opened it. It was a book rest, a simple affair but handy.

"I am giving these to all my customers," Johnny said.

"This is too expensive to give away, Johnny," I said. "You will lose all your profits."

"I picked them up cheap," he said. "I'm giving these away so the customers will remember me."

"That is right, too," I said. "You have good sense."

After that he came in about half a dozen times, each time taking with him ten or twelve copies of various magazines. He said he was doing swell. Also, he said he was now selling *Liberty* along with the *Saturday Evening Posts.*

Then for two straight weeks I did not see him once. I could not understand this. He had never missed coming to the house in two or three days. Something must be wrong, I thought. He must be sick, I thought.

One day I saw Johnny at the door. "Hello, Johnny," I said. "Where were you? Were you sick?"

"No. I wasn't sick," Johnny said.

"What's the matter? What happened?" I said.

"I'm moving away," Johnny said. "My father is moving to Los Angeles."

"Sit down, Johnny," I said. "Tell me all about it."

He sat down. He told me what had happened in two weeks. He said his dad went and got married to a woman he, Johnny, did not know. And now, his dad and this woman say they are moving to Los Angeles. And about all there was for him to do was to go along with them.

"I don't know what to say, Johnny," I said.

Johnny said nothing. We sat quietly and watched the time move.

"Too bad you will lose your good trade," I finally said.

"Yes, I know," he said. "But I can sell magazines in Los Angeles."

"Yes, that is true," I said.

Then he said he must be going. I wished him good luck. We shook hands. "I will come and see you again," he said.

"And when I visit Los Angeles some day," I said, "I will see you in the largest bookstore in the city."

Johnny smiled. As he walked away, up the street and out of sight, I saw the last of him walking like a good businessman, walking briskly, energetically, purposefully. ○

---

4. The *Bay Region* is the area around San Francisco, California.

Reading on Your Own

To read more about the Big Question, choose one of these books from your school or local library. Work on your reading skills by choosing books that are challenging to you.

Fiction

Fair Weather
by Richard Peck

In 1893 Rosie Beckett's farm life has few thrills. And then her aunt invites Rosie's family to stay at her house for a week so that they can visit the Columbian Exposition, or World Fair. Now Rosie's dreams of how her life might unfold are much more exciting.

The House on Mango Street
by Sandra Cisneros

Esperanza Cordero is a young girl coming of age in a Hispanic neighborhood in Chicago. She uses poems and stories to express her feelings about growing up in an environment that she thinks is oppressive. Esperanza dreams of the house that she will own someday—a house that will not be on Mango Street.

House Made of Dawn
by N. Scott Momaday

This book tells the story of Abel, a young Native American, who journeys from a reservation and experiences the difficult environment of an American city.

Ellis Island: Land of Hope
by Joan Lowery Nixon

Rebekah Levinsky and her family are the main characters in this story of the American immigrant experience of the early 1900s. The book tells of the Levinsky family's voyage from Russia to America and their struggle to survive on New York's Lower East Side.

Nonfiction

Having Our Say: The Delany Sisters' First 100 Years
by Sarah and A. Elizabeth Delany

Two feisty African American women who each lived to be more than a century old tell their life stories. They describe the social history of the twentieth century as they saw it, from the days of Jim Crow laws to the Harlem Renaissance, the Civil Rights movement, and beyond.

Manners and Customs
By Jim Barmeier

This book is from the series *Life in America 100 Years Ago,* which tells of the effects that immigration, technological advances, and the factory system had on daily life. It also paints a picture of the confusing American lifestyle that was the dream of many immigrants.

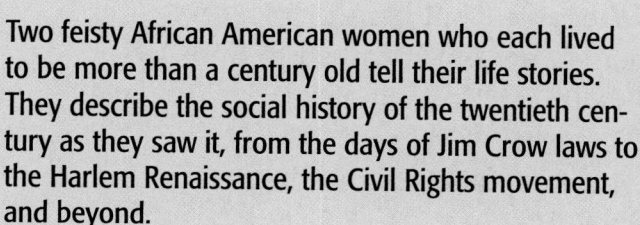

Words That Make America Great
Edited by Jerome Agel

This book presents 200 documents that have helped define America's character and ideals from its earliest days to the present. Included are many documents of the years 1750–1850, from the Declaration of Independence to the earliest rules of baseball. This is the basis of the American dream.

Stride Toward Freedom: The Montgomery Story
by Martin Luther King Jr.

Dr. King tells the story of the Montgomery bus boycott. He explains how it was conceived and organized. He describes the many violent threats on his life, and the obstacles that American society placed before those striving for their versions of the American dream.

New York English Language Arts Test Practice

*D*irections

Read this passage from a novel about Leona Vicario, a Mexican woman who helped Mexico earn its independence from Spain in the 19th century. Then answer questions 1 through 5.

from *Leona: A Love Story*
by Elizabeth Borton de Treviño

Doña Angela was reading Leona's latest composition, a four-page essay on the duties of government. It seemed a curious choice of subject, she reflected, but the girl had done her research well, and she wrote a clear and rhythmic Spanish. Still, the essay was dull.

She said so to the serious girl studying across the table from her.

"I know," agreed Leona, moving uneasily in her chair. "But I wanted to find out for myself and get it clear in my mind. That's why it is so factual, so unadorned."

Doña Angela was quick and intuitive. "Have you any doubts about the way our government here, under the Viceroy, is conducted?"

"No," protested Leona. "But sometimes I argue with Padre Anselmo. He thinks the King has too much power."

"Padre Anselmo should be reminded of his duties," said Doña Angela crisply, "which are to confess you and instruct you in religion, not to give you revolutionary ideas."

Leona wisely nodded in agreement and went on to a different subject.

"Lately," she told her chaperone, "I have been writing some poetry. Well, verse. I am not good enough to call my thoughts poetry."

Doña Angela gathered up the sheets of verses and said, "I will look these over later in my room. But meanwhile, Leona, you must be fitted for an evening dress." Don Agustín had specified a pale color, perhaps even white. But Leona was dark. Her golden-brown skin, glowing with health, showed a soft deep rose in the cheeks. Her hair, long and curly, was almost black, and with difficulty subjected to combs. Only her light brown eyes were not a part of her inheritance from native ancestors. Leona was descended on her father's side from the Mexican poet Netzahualcóyotl.

1 According to the passage, Doña Angela **most likely** disagrees with Padre Anselmo's opinions about

A religion

B Leona's education

C government

D Leona's duties

2 Which of these statements **best** describes Doña Angela's evaluation of Leona's essay?

F The essay is simply boring.

G Despite a few flaws, strong writing makes the essay interesting.

H The unusual topic results in an interesting essay.

J Although the content is not interesting, the essay is well written and well supported.

3 According to the passage, Leona's appearance

A makes her seem mysterious

B provides evidence that she is a descendent of Netzahualcóyotl's people

C leads her to wish for darker eyes

D is her only tie to her native ancestors

4 Leona's behavior toward Doña Angela shows that Leona **most likely**

F is afraid of Doña Angela

G thinks that Doña Angela is annoying

H respects Doña Angela

J is worried that Doña Angela doesn't like her

5 Read this sentence from the passage.

"That's why it is so factual, so unadorned."

In this sentence, the word "unadorned" means about the same as

A interesting

B plain

C bad

D detailed

Directions

Read this speech by President Abraham Lincoln. Then answer questions 6 through 10.

The Gettysburg Address
by Abraham Lincoln

Fourscore and seven years ago our fathers brought forth on this continent a new nation, conceived in liberty, and dedicated to the proposition that all men are created equal.

Now we are engaged in a great civil war, testing whether that nation, or any nation so conceived and so dedicated, can long endure. We are met on a great battlefield of that war. We have come to dedicate a portion of that field as a final resting-place for those who here gave their lives that this nation might live. It is altogether fitting and proper that we should do this.

But, in a larger sense, we cannot dedicate...we cannot consecrate...we cannot hallow...this ground. The brave men, living and dead, who struggled here, have consecrated it far above our poor power to add or detract. The world will little note nor long remember what we say here, but it can never forget what they did here. It is for us, the living, rather, to be dedicated here to the unfinished work which they who fought here have thus far so nobly advanced. It is rather for us to be here dedicated to the great task remaining before us...that from these honored dead we take increased devotion to that cause for which they gave the last full measure of devotion; that we here highly resolve that these dead shall not have died in vain; that this nation, under God, shall have a new birth of freedom; and that government of the people, by the people, for the people, shall not perish from the earth.

---

6 According to the speech, Lincoln feels his dedication of the field

- **F** is the only proper way to pay tribute to the dead
- **G** is a small gesture compared with what some have sacrificed
- **H** is an empty one
- **J** will declare it a great battlefield of war

7 According to the speech, the **best** way to honor the dead is

- **A** to consecrate the field
- **B** to remember what happened there
- **C** to make sure that the nation survives
- **D** to believe in freedom

8 According to the speech, what will the Civil War reveal?

F whether slavery is right

G whether a nation like the United States can survive for very long

H why these soldiers died at Gettysburg

J why liberty is the foundation of democracy

9 Study the index from a book about the Civil War.

Analyzing the War	**44–55**
Social Impact	**44–48**
casualties	45–46
divided families	46–47
poverty	44–45
rebuilding	47–48
Strategic History	**49–55**
battlefield tactics	50–51
defending the South	52–53
how the North won	54–55
supplying the front	49

Which pages would **most likely** explain why the Battle of Gettysburg was a turning point in the war?

A 50–51

B 45–46

C 52–53

D 54–55

10 The opening paragraph of the speech is **mainly** intended to

F remind people how long ago the nation was founded

G explain why all men are created equal

H help define what people are fighting for

J help define liberty

Directions

Read this letter from a novel about Harriet Jacobs, an enslaved person who escaped to the North during the 1840s. Then answer questions 11 through 15.

from *Letters from a Slave Girl*
Evening
by Mary E. Lyons

Dear Aunt Betty,

Worry sticking to me like cockleburs. The captain, he has our ticket money now. Nothing to stop him from turning us in for the reward. But Sarah says dont fret. In her three days on the ship everybody been kind.

When the captain brung me down to our little box of a cabin, Sarah just sat there with her mouth open. Harriet, is it you, she says, or your ghost? We hold each other tight, and my fears flow out in great sobs.

Then the captain comes back to shush us. For my safety and yours, he says, it would be prudent not to attract any attention. As far as the sailors know, he told us, you are Women going to meet your husbands in Philadelphia.

The boat is passing the Snaky Swamp now, and there is still enough light to make out the buildings that rim the bay. From here, Edenton is a toy town, like the ones John used to make out of sticks and sand. The wind is against us, so the boat moves slow as a giant snail. Me and Sarah, we anxious to put the miles behind us. Dont want to be playing peep squirrel with the constables who search the ships.

I am weary in my bones, but I wont sleep. Not when I can still feel Joseph pulling at my arm down by the wharf. I been looking in the Docter's window, he tells me as I climb in the rowboat, and he's at home. Good-bye, Mama, Joseph says, and waves. Don't cry, I'll come! Then my fine boy turns and runs back home.

Well, I am breaking that promise bout crying.

Harriet

Grammar

11 According to the letter, the captain tries to keep the women safe by

A hiding them in a tiny cabin

B telling them not to play peep squirrel with the constables

C staying away from Edenton

D telling the sailors that the women are going to meet their husbands in Philadelphia

12 Which of the following phrases from the letter is an example of a metaphor?

F Worry sticking to me like cockleburs

G From here, Edenton is a toy town

H the boat moves slow as a giant snail

J my fears flow out in great sobs

13 According to the letter, what problem could result from Harriet's giving the captain her ticket money?

A The sailors might steal the money.

B The sailors might discover she is a slave.

C The captain might turn her in.

D She may not have enough money for food.

14 Which of the following elements helps create Harriet's writing style?

F her fear of getting caught

G her use of everyday language

H her description of the boat

J her sadness over leaving family behind

15 According to the letter, you can conclude that Sarah

A is afraid of the captain

B is Harriet's sister

C was not expecting to see Harriet

D doesn't think they will make it to freedom

REFERENCE SECTION

AUTHOR FILES

Maya Angelou (1928–)
- was originally named Marguerite Johnson; Maya is the name her brother called her as a child
- at the age of three, was sent to live with her grandmother, who ran the only black-owned general store in the town of Stamps, Arkansas
- speaks French, Spanish, Italian, Arabic, and Fanti (a language of southern Ghana) fluently
- was the first African American woman to have a story adapted for a feature film

Ray Bradbury (1920–)
- does not like technology even though he writes about it; doesn't drive a car, use a computer, or fly in airplanes
- feels that much of his work is too fantastic to be considered science fiction, which he thinks has to be based on possibilities for the future
- has written short stories, novels, plays, screenplays, television scripts, and verse

Quote: *"The act of writing is, for me, like a fever—something I must do."*

Gwendolyn Brooks (1917–2000)
- born in Topeka, Kansas, but lived most of her life in Chicago
- in 1950 became the first African American woman to be awarded a Pulitzer Prize
- followed Carl Sandburg as poet laureate of Illinois in 1968; served until her death in 2000

Quote: *"I felt that I had to write. Even if I had never been published, I knew that I would go on writing, enjoying it, and experiencing the challenge."*

Judith Ortiz Cofer (1952–)
- grew up speaking Spanish at home, but learned English well enough to become a writer and college professor
- lives in Georgia on a farm that has been in her husband's family for generations
- believes that immigrants do not have to choose one identity over another and says she uses her art "as a bridge between my cultures . . . traveling back and forth without fear and confusion."

Meri Nana-Ama Danquah (1967–)
- was raised in the Washington, D.C., area
- has taught in schools and universities in Ghana and the United States
- appears regularly on National Public Radio to comment on a variety of issues, including the impressions Africans have about America

Quote: *"I am ever-changing, able to blend without detection into the colors and textures of my surroundings, a skill developed out of a need to belong, a longing to be claimed."*

Linnea Due (1948–)
- was born in Berkeley, California
- has worked as a graphic designer and typesetter
- locked herself in her study during a week off to write her first novel, the young adult book *High and Outside*

Quote: *"This is the joy of writing for me—when the characters assume their own identities and run away with the story, leaving my idea of the book behind."*

Nikki Giovanni (1943–)

- born Yolande Cornelia Giovanni, Jr.
- graduated early from high school and attended the historically black Fisk University
- is a University Distinguished Professor of writing and literature at Virginia Tech

Quote: *"Writers don't write from experience, though many are hesitant to admit that they don't. I want to be clear about this. If you wrote from experience, you'd get maybe one book, maybe three poems."*

Frances Goodrich (1890–1984)

- grew up in New Jersey and attended colleges in New York
- acted on Broadway before becoming a playwright
- won two Tony awards in 1956 for plays she co-wrote with her husband, Albert Hackett
- collaborated with her husband on screenplays for dozens of films, including the well-known classics *It's A Wonderful Life* and *Father of the Bride*

Albert Hackett (1900–1995)

- was the son of actors and had a brother, Raymond Hackett, who acted in silent films
- grew up in New York City
- first appeared onstage at age six, playing a girl
- acted in his first film at age twelve
- attended the Professional Children's School, a high school for young performing artists
- received four Academy Award nominations for screenplays he cowrote with his first wife, Frances Goodrich

Virginia Hamilton (1936–2002)

- was the granddaughter of a slave who escaped to rural Ohio on the Underground Railroad in the 1850s
- grew up on a farm near the homes of her large extended family
- began writing in grade school
- was influenced by her parents, who were gifted storytellers

Quote: *"I write books because I love chasing after a good story and seeing fantastic characters rising out of the mist of my imaginings."*

W. C. Heinz (1915–)

- edited the sports section of his college newspaper
- worked his way up from messenger boy to reporter at the *New York Sun*
- filed stories from Europe during World War II
- began writing about sports after the war and had a regular column about boxing
- Ernest Hemingway called Heinz's novel *The Professional* "the only good novel I've ever read about a fighter."

O. Henry (1862–1910)

- was raised by his grandmother when his mother died; his father spent all his time on an invention
- became a registered pharmacist
- fled to Honduras after being accused of stealing; came back home to Texas because his wife was dying
- published a newspaper called *Rolling Stone*
- wrote nearly 300 stories, 80 of them Westerns
- had millions of his books sold all over the world, but died poor and in debt

Langston Hughes (1902–1967)

- was elected class poet in the eighth and twelfth grades
- had lived in six different states and Mexico by the age of twelve
- worked as a truck farmer, cook, waiter, sailor, doorman and traveled extensively before the first of his books was published
- his first published poem, "The Negro Speaks of Rivers," is still one of his best known poems

Quote: *"Hughes's poems were meant to be read aloud, crooned, shouted, and sung."*

David Ignatow (1914–1997)

- was born in Brooklyn and lived most of his life in New York
- graduated from high school, but never went to college
- was known for writing in a direct and natural-sounding style
- won an award from the National Institute of Arts and Letters for "a lifetime of creative effort"

Quote: *"I want, as a poet, to speak the whole truth."*

Charlotte Foltz Jones (1945–)

- enjoyed sitting in her favorite rocking chair and coming up with story ideas when she was nine
- drew upon her experiences as an only child and the mother of an only child to write her first book, *Only Child: Clues for Coping*, which offers advice to children with no brothers and sisters
- enjoys papier-mache and sculpture

Quote: *"I write for myself—maybe for the part of me that never grew up, the part that still wonders and looks about in amazement."*

Daniel Keyes (1927–)

- joined the U.S. Maritime Service for a few years before entering college
- says he learned the craft of writing while working for a magazine publisher
- "Flowers for Algernon" was published first as a short story (1959) then as a novel (1966); it was filmed under the title "Charley" (1968).
- The short story won a Hugo Award, the novel won a Nebula Award, and the movie won a best actor Academy Award for Cliff Robertson.

Eric Kimmel (1946–)

- has wanted to be an author since kindergarten
- grew up in a neighborhood filled with Armenian, Italian, Chinese, Puerto Rican, Irish, and German families
- spoke Yiddish as a child
- draws inspiration from the stories his Ukrainian grandmother told him as a child
- is a professional storyteller
- loves bluegrass music and plays the banjo

Kathleen Krull (1952–)

- is the oldest of four children and has three younger brothers
- taught piano lessons as a teenager
- has worked in children's book publishing since the day after she graduated from college

Quote: *"I'm nosy about people . . . and [writing] the Lives of . . . series allows me to snoop behind the closed doors of some of my favorite groups of (really strange) people."*

Henry Wadsworth Longfellow (1807–1882)

- grew up in Portland, Maine
- began school at age three and showed an interest in writing at an early age
- loved music and played piano and flute
- entered Bowdoin College at fourteen
- was the most popular poet of the nineteenth century

Quote: *"You know I say just what I think, and nothing more and less. I cannot say one thing and mean another."*

Robert MacNeil (1931–)

- was born and raised in Canada; became an American citizen in 1997
- was an aspiring actor and playwright before becoming a journalist
- cofounded "The MacNeil/Lehrer News Hour," a news program on PBS
- won numerous awards for his work as a reporter and television news anchor
- retired in 1995, after twenty years as coanchor of the show

Edna St. Vincent Millay (1892–1950)

- was encouraged by her mother to be ambitious and to appreciate music and literature
- entered a poetry contest that helped her win a scholarship to Vassar College
- used modern ideas with traditional poetry styles
- was a very popular poet during her lifetime

Quote by author Thomas Hardy: *"America has two great attractions: the skyscraper and the poetry of Edna St. Vincent Millay."*

Toshio Mori (1910–1980)

- dreamed of being an artist, a Buddhist missionary, and a baseball player when he was young
- became interested in writing mostly through reading dime novels—popular fiction that sold for ten cents
- edited the literary journal *Trek* while interned in a camp during World War II
- was the first Japanese American writer to have his work published in the United States

Walter Dean Myers (1937–)

- went to live with foster parents in Harlem after his mother died when he was two
- had a speech impediment and at the suggestion of a teacher, began to write down his thoughts
- thought he could never go to college, but always kept writing, and after serving in the army was able to pay for college tuition with money from the G.I. Bill of Rights
- gets up by 5 A.M. and writes ten pages every day
- says rewriting is more fun for him than writing
- has won dozens of awards for his books

Naomi Shihab Nye (1952–)

- published her first poem at age seven
- lived in Jerusalem for a year when she was fourteen
- began keeping a journal as a child because she "wanted to remember everything"

Quote: *"In books, I hope that my characters are brave and strong. I want them to use their voices. I want young people to be reminded, always, that voices are the best tools we have."*

Dwight Okita (1958–)

- born and continues to live in Chicago
- has written poetry, plays, film scripts, and a novel
- started writing poems in first grade because he had difficulty writing stories
- earned a creative writing degree at University of Illinois at Chicago

Quote: *"I am lucky to have a diverse circle of friends—some of whom are in the arts and some who are not. I love them all equally."*

Abiodun Oyewole (1948–)

- born Charles Davis, he grew up in Queens, New York; was given the name Abiodun Oyewole by a Yoruba priest at age fifteen
- was influenced by jazz and gospel music and the poems of Langston Hughes while growing up
- cofounded The Last Poets, a musical group that is credited with being the originators of hip-hop music
- appeared with The Last Poets in the film "Poetic Justice" in 1993

Gary Paulsen (1939–)

- traveled with a carnival when he was a teenager
- has worked as a soldier, engineer, construction worker, ranch hand, truck driver, and sailor
- completed the 1,180-mile Alaskan sled dog race, the Iditarod, in 1983 and 1985
- wrote his first novel while living in a cabin in northern Minnesota
- one of the most popular writers of young adult fiction, he has written more than 175 books and even more short stories and articles

Josephine Preston Peabody (1874–1922)

- grew up in Brooklyn, New York, and Dorchester, Massachusetts
- was encouraged by her parents to paint, write, and read poetry, novels, and plays
- was one of the first women writers to achieve success as a playwright in America

Quote: *"One never learns by success. Success is the plateau that one rests upon to take breath and look down from upon the straight and difficult path, but one does not climb upon a plateau."*

Richard Peck (1934–)

- went to college in Indiana and England, was a U.S. soldier stationed in Germany, and taught English to teenagers before becoming a full-time writer for young adults
- seeks inspiration for his books by visiting schools to meet young people, teachers, and librarians

Quote: *"I want to write novels that ask honest questions about serious issues. A novel is never an answer; it's always a question."*

Ann Petry (1909–1997)

- born and grew up in a middle-class African American family that lived in a mainly white community in Connecticut
- enjoyed acting out scenes from her favorite books when she was a child
- wrote short stories while working as a pharmacist in her family's drugstore
- began her writing career after moving to New York City with her husband, mystery writer George Petry

Marge Piercy (1936–)
- was raised Jewish and has the Hebrew name Marah
- began writing when she was fifteen and had her own room for the first time
- credits her mother with making her a poet

Quote: *"As a would-be poet or fiction writer or playwright or writer of scripts, you must know what has been written in the past and what is being written right now. You have to read all the time and read a lot."*

Edgar Allan Poe (1809–1849)
- lost his parents, who were professional actors, when he was three years old
- struggled with poverty all of his life
- started writing poetry when he was a teenager
- joined the army and attended West Point
- worked as an editor of magazines
- helped develop detective mystery, science fiction, treasure hunt, and horror story formats
- has been a major influence on writers in Europe and Latin America as well as the United States

Graham Salisbury (1944–)
- grew up on the islands of Oahu and Hawaii with friends from many backgrounds, including Japanese, Chinese, Filipino, and Portuguese
- didn't wear shoes until he was in sixth grade
- saw snow for the first time at age nineteen
- is in a rock-n-roll band named *The Millennium*, which had a number-one hit in the Philippines
- says that writing is, "Magic . . . From the universe . . . A window, open to the Great Unknown."

Ouida Sebestyen (1924–)
- was an only child and had a close relationship with her father
- hated school because she had trouble making friends, but always loved to read and learn
- worked as a mechanic and repaired PT-19s (a type of airplane), cleaned houses, and owned a day-care business before becoming a writer
- writes primarily about the American West, which she calls "bleak and harsh but also beautiful, dramatic, and inspiring"

Virginia Driving Hawk Sneve (1933–)
- was the daughter of a minister
- grew up during the 1930s Great Depression
- became inspired to write when she discovered that realistic literature about Native American culture was scarce
- writes about the experiences of today's Lakota teenagers

Quote: *"In my books, I always try to write about something from the past that still affects us today and will in the future."*

Gary Soto (1952–)
- is a third-generation Mexican American
- has edited story collections and written poetry, essays, young adult and children's books and has made movies
- taught English and Chicano Studies at the University of California, Berkeley
- enjoys theater, tennis, basketball, traveling, and working in the garden

Quote: *"I discovered that reading builds a life inside the mind."*

Jerry Spinelli (1941–)

- wanted to be a cowboy until age ten
- was sixteen when he wrote a poem that was published in his hometown newspaper
- wrote several unpublished novels before his first young adult book was published
- has found material for his books from the experiences of his six kids

Quote: *"I think a person's life is a mixture of happy, sad and funny. So I try to make my books that way, too. "*

May Swenson (1919–1989)

- was born and raised in Logan, Utah
- moved to New York City after earning a bachelor's degree at the University of Utah
- was a critic, playwright, translator, and editor as well as a poet
- once said her experience of poetry was "based in a craving to get through the curtains of things as they appear, to things as they are, and then into the larger, wilder space of things as they are becoming."

Yoshiko Uchida (1921–1992)

- encouraged by her parents, became interested in books and writing at an early age
- wrote stories on pages cut from brown wrapping paper during the Depression
- started off sending stories to magazines, and, after many rejections, switched to writing for young people
- traveled to Japan in 1952 to collect folktales, which she retold in her first book, *The Dancing Kettle and Other Japanese Folktales*

Walt Whitman (1819–1892)

- worked as a printer, an editor, a newspaper reporter, and at other jobs while writing forgettable poems and novels before 1855
- published nine different editions of *Leaves of Grass* between 1855 and 1892, revising and adding new poems with each edition
- worked as a volunteer aide in hospitals, caring for sick and wounded soldiers during the Civil War
- became a strong influence on many later poets who imitated his usually rhymeless free verse

by Dinah Zike, M.Ed., Creator of Foldables™

Reading and Thinking with Foldables™

As you read the selections in each unit, the following Foldables will help you keep track of your ideas about the Big Questions. Follow these directions to make your Foldable, and then use the directions in the Unit Warm-Up for labeling your unit Foldable.

Foldable 1 and Foldable 5—For Units 1 and 5

Step 1 Fold five sheets of paper into *hamburgers*.

Step 2 Cut the sheets of paper in half along the fold lines.

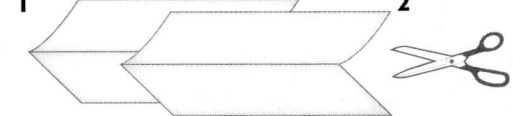

Step 3 Fold each section of paper into *hamburgers*. However, fold one side one-half inch shorter than the other side. This will form a tab that is one-half inch long.

Step 4 Fold this tab forward over the shorter side, and then fold it back the opposite way.

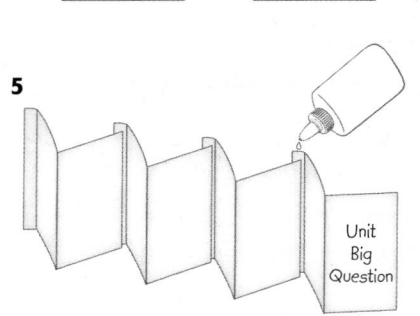

Step 5 Glue together to form an *accordion* by gluing a straight edge of one section into the *valley* of another section.

Step 6 On the front cover, write the unit number and the Big Question. Turn the page. Across the top, write the selection title. To the left of the crease, write **My Purpose for Reading**. To the right of the crease, write **The Big Question**. Repeat until you have all the titles from the Reading Workshops and the Comparing Literature Workshop in your Foldable.

Foldable 2 and Foldable 7—For Units 2 and 7

Step 1 Stack three sheets of paper so that the bottom of each sheet is one inch higher than the sheet behind it.

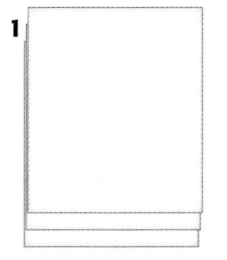
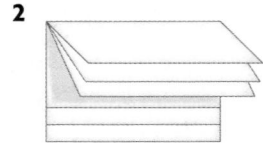

Step 2 Fold down the tops of the paper to form six tabs. Align the edges so that all of the layers are about an inch apart.

Step 3 Crease the paper to hold the layers in place and then staple them together. Cut the bottom five layers up to the crease. Do not cut the top flap.

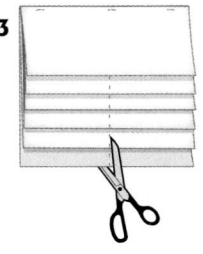

Step 4 On the top front flap, write the unit number and the Big Question. Write a selection title on the bottom of each flap. Then open each flap. Write **My Purpose for Reading** at the top of the flap and write **The Big Question** below the crease.

Foldable 3 and Foldable 6—For Units 3 and 6

Step 1 Fold a sheet of paper in half so that one side is one inch longer than the other side. Fold the one-inch tab over the short side to form a fold. On the fold, write the workshop number and the Big Question.

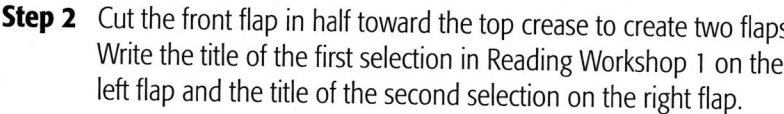

Step 2 Cut the front flap in half toward the top crease to create two flaps. Write the title of the first selection in Reading Workshop 1 on the left flap and the title of the second selection on the right flap.

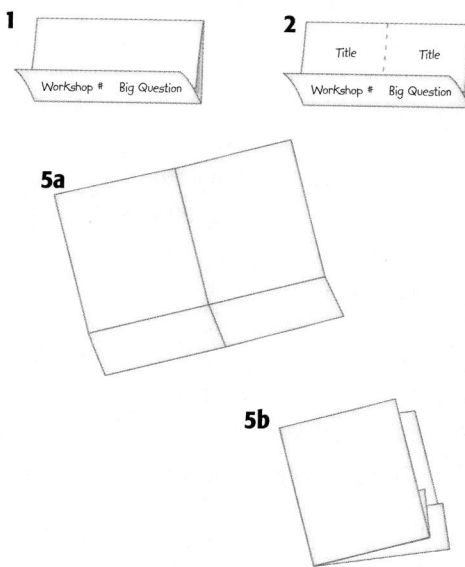

Step 3 Open the flaps. At the very top of each flap, write **My Purpose for Reading**. Below each crease, write **The Big Question**.

Step 4 Repeat these steps for each remaining Reading Workshop and the Reading Across Texts or Comparing Literature Workshop.

Step 5 Fold a 11 x 17 sheet of paper in half. Open the paper and fold up one of the long sides two inches to form a pocket. Glue the outer edges of the pocket. Refold the paper so that the pockets are on the inside. Keep your Foldables for the unit inside.

Foldable 4 and Foldable 8—For Units 4 and 8

Step 1 Fold ten sheets of paper in half from top to bottom.

Step 2 On the top flap of each folded paper, make a cut one inch from the left side (top flap only).

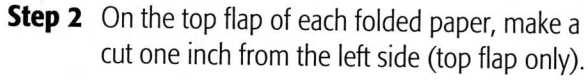

Step 3 Stack the folded papers on top of one another. Staple the ten sections together. Write the unit number and Big Question on the stapled edge.

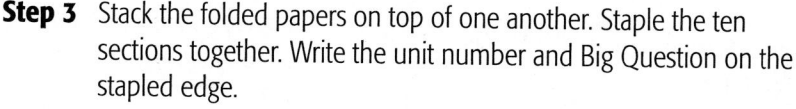

Step 4 On the top flap, write the first selection title from Reading Workshop 1. Open the flap. Near the top of the page, write **My Purpose for Reading**. Below the crease, write **The Big Question**.

Step 5 Repeat these steps for each remaining selection in the Reading Workshops and the Reading Across Texts Workshop.

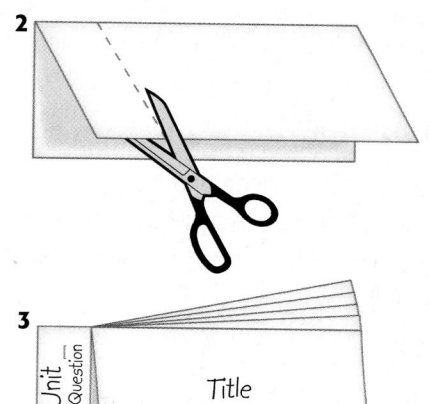

LITERARY TERMS HANDBOOK

A

Act A major unit of a drama. A play may be subdivided into several acts. Many modern plays have two or three acts. A short play can be composed of one or more scenes but only one act.

See also SCENE.

Alliteration The repitition of consonant sounds, usually at the beginnings of words or syllables. Alliteration gives emphasis to words. For example,

Over the cobbles he clattered and clashed

Allusion A reference in a work of literature to a well-known character, place, or situation in history, politics, or science or from another work of literature, music, or art.

Analogy A comparison between two things, based on one or more elements that they share. Analogies can help the reader visualize an idea. In informational text, analogies are often used to explain something unfamiliar in terms of something known. For example, a science book might compare the flow of electricity to water moving through a hose. In literature, most analogies are expressed in metaphors or similes.

See also METAPHOR, SIMILE.

Anecdote A brief, entertaining story based on a single interesting or humorous incident or event. Anecdotes are frequently biographical and reveal some aspect of a person's character.

Antagonist A person or force that opposes the protagonist, or central character, in a story or a drama. The reader is generally meant not to sympathize with the antagonist.

See also CONFLICT, PROTAGONIST.

Anthropomorphism Representing animals as if they had human emotions and intelligence. Fables and fairy tales often contain anthropomorphism.

Aside In a play, a comment made by a character that is heard by the audience but not by the other characters onstage. The speaker turns to one side, or "aside," away from the other characters onstage. Asides are common in older plays—you will find many in Shakespeare's plays—but are infrequent in modern drama.

Assonance The repetition of vowel sounds, especially in a line of poetry.

See also RHYME, SOUND DEVICES.

Author's purpose The intention of the writer. For example, the purpose of a story may be to entertain, to describe, to explain, to persuade, or a combination of these purposes.

Autobiography The story of a person's life written by that person. *I Know Why the Caged Bird Sings,* by Maya Angelou is an example of autobiography.

See also BIOGRAPHY, MEMOIR.

B

Ballad A short musical narrative song or poem. Folk ballads, which usually tell of an exciting or dramatic episode, were passed on by word of mouth for generations before being written down. Literary ballads are written in imitation of folk ballads.

See also NARRATIVE POETRY.

Biography The account of a person's life written by someone other than the subject. Biographies can be short or book-length.

See also AUTOBIOGRAPHY, MEMOIR.

C

Character A person in a literary work. (If a character is an animal, it displays human traits.) Characters who show varied and sometimes contradictory traits are called **round.** Characters who reveal only one personality trait are called **flat.** A **stereotype** is a flat character of a familiar and often-repeated type. A **dynamic** character changes during the story. A **static** character remains primarily the same throughout the story.

Characterization The methods a writer uses to develop the personality of the character. In **direct characterization,** the writer makes direct statements about a character's personality. In **indirect characterization,** the writer reveals a character's personality through the character's words and actions and through what other characters think and say about the character.

Climax The point of greatest emotional intensity, interest, or suspense in a narrative. Usually the climax comes at the turning point in a story or drama, the point at which the resolution of the conflict becomes clear. The climax in "Icarus and Daedelus" occurs when Icarus forgets his father's warnings and flies too high.

Comedy A type of drama that is humorous and has a happy ending. A heroic comedy focuses on the exploits of a larger-than-life hero. In American popular culture, comedy can take the form of a scripted performance involving one or more performers—either as a skit that is part of a variety show, as in vaudeville, or as a stand-up monologue.
See also HUMOR.

Conflict The central struggle between opposing forces in a story or drama. An **external conflict** exists when a character struggles against some outside force, such as nature, society, fate, or another person. An **internal conflict** exists within the mind of a character who is torn between opposing feelings or goals.
See also ANTAGONIST, PLOT, PROTAGONIST.

Consonance A pleasing combination of sounds, especially in poetry. Consonance usually refers to the repetition of consonant sounds in stressed syllables.
See also SOUND DEVICES.

Couplet Two successive lines of verse that form a unit and usually rhyme.

D

Description Writing that seeks to convey the impression of a setting, a person, an animal, an object, or an event by appealing to the senses. Almost all writing, fiction and nonfiction, contains elements of description.

Details Particular features of things used to make descriptions more accurate and vivid. Authors use details to help readers imagine the characters, scenes, and actions they describe.

Dialect A variation of language spoken by a particular group, often within a particular region. Dialects differ from standard language because they may contain different pronunciations, forms, and meanings.

Dialogue Conversation between characters in a literary work.
See also MONOLOGUE.

Drama A story intended to be performed by actors on a stage or before movie or TV cameras. Most dramas before the modern period can be divided into two basic types: tragedy and comedy. The script of a drama includes dialogue (the words the actors speak) and stage directions (descriptions of the action and scenery).
See also COMEDY, TRAGEDY.

E

Elegy A mournful or melancholy poem that honors someone who is dead. Some elegies are written in rhyming couplets that follow a strict metric pattern.

Epic A long narrative poem, written in a dignified style, that celebrates the adventures and achievements of one or more heroic figures of legend, history, or religion.
See also NARRATIVE POETRY.

Essay A short piece of nonfiction writing on a single topic. The purpose of the essay is to communicate an idea or opinion. A **formal essay** is serious and impersonal. A **informal essay** entertains while it informs, usually in a light conversational style.

Exposition The part of the plot of a short story, novel, novella, or play in which the characters, setting, and situation are introduced.

Extended metaphor An implied comparison that continues through an entire poem.
See also METAPHOR.

F

Fable A short, simple tale that teaches a moral. The characters in a fable are often animals who speak and act like people. The moral, or lesson, of the fable is usually stated outright.

Falling action In a play or story, the action that follows the climax.

See also PLOT.

Fantasy A form of literature that explores unreal worlds of the past, the present, or the future.

Fiction A prose narrative in which situations and characters are invented by the writer. Some aspects of a fictional work may be based on fact or experience. Fiction includes short stories, novellas, and novels.

See also NOVEL, NOVELLA, SHORT STORY.

Figurative language Language used for descriptive effect, often to imply ideas indirectly. Expressions of figurative language are not literally true but express some truth beyond the literal level. Although it appears in all kinds of writing, figurative language is especially prominent in poetry.

See also ANALOGY, FIGURE OF SPEECH, METAPHOR, PERSONIFICATION, SIMILE, SYMBOL.

Figure of speech Figurative language of a specific kind, such as **analogy, metaphor, simile,** or **personification.**

First-person narrative. *See POINT OF VIEW.*

Flashback An interruption in a chronological narrative that tells about something that happened before that point in the story or before the story began. A flashback gives readers information that helps to explain the main events of the story.

Folklore The traditional beliefs, customs, stories, songs, and dances of the ordinary people (the "folk") of a culture. Folklore is passed on by word of mouth and performance rather than in writing.

See also FOLKTALE, LEGEND, MYTH, ORAL TRADITION.

Folktale A traditional story passed down orally long before being written down. Generally the author of a folktale is anonymous. Folktales include animal stories, trickster stories, fairy tales, myths, legends, and tall tales.

See also LEGEND, MYTH, ORAL TRADITION, TALL TALE.

Foreshadowing The use of clues by an author to prepare readers for events that will happen in a story.

Free verse Poetry that has no fixed pattern of meter, rhyme, line length, or stanza arrangement.

See also RHYTHM.

G

Genre A literary or artistic category. The main literary genres are prose, poetry, and drama. Each of these is divided into smaller genres. For example: **Prose** includes fiction (such as novels, novellas, short stories, and folktales) and nonfiction (such as biography, autobiography, and essays). **Poetry** includes lyric poetry, dramatic poetry, and narrative poetry. **Drama** includes tragedy, comedy, historical drama, melodrama, and farce.

H

Haiku Originally a Japanese form of poetry that has three lines and seventeen syllables. The first and third lines have five syllables each; the middle line has seven syllables.

Hero A literary work's main character, usually one with admirable qualities. Although the word *hero* is applied only to males in traditional usage (the female form is *heroine*), the term now applies to both sexes.

See also LEGEND, MYTH, PROTAGONIST, TALL TALE.

Historical fiction A novel, novella, play, short story, or narrative poem that sets fictional characters against a historical backdrop and contains many details about the period in which it is set.

See also GENRE.

Humor The quality of a literary work that makes the characters and their situations seem funny, amusing, or ludicrous. Humorous writing can be as effective in nonfiction as in fiction.

See also COMEDY.

I

Idiom A figure of speech that belongs to a particular language, people, or region and whose meaning cannot be obtained, and might even appear ridiculous, by joining the meanings of the words composing it. You would be using an idiom if you said you *caught* a cold.

Imagery Language that emphasizes sensory impressions to help the reader of a literary work see, hear, feel, smell, and taste the scenes described in the work.

See also FIGURATIVE LANGUAGE.

Informational text One kind of nonfiction. This kind of writing conveys facts and information without introducing personal opinion.

Irony A form of expression in which the intended meaning of the words used is the opposite of their literal meaning. *Verbal irony* occurs when a person says one thing and means another—for example, saying "Nice guy!" about someone you dislike. *Situational irony* occurs when the outcome of a situation is the opposite of what was expected.

J

Journal An account of day-to-day events or a record of experiences, ideas, or thoughts. A journal may also be called a diary.

L

Legend A traditional story, based on history or an actual hero, that is passed down orally. A legend is usually exaggerated and gains elements of fantasy over the years. Stories about Daniel Boone and Davy Crockett are American legends.

Limerick A light humorous poem with a regular metrical scheme and a rhyme scheme of *aabba.*

See also HUMOR, RHYME SCHEME.

Local color The fictional portrayal of a region's features or peculiarities and its inhabitants' distinctive ways of talking and behaving, usually as a way of adding a realistic flavor to a story.

Lyric The words of a song, usually with a regular rhyme scheme.

See also RHYME SCHEME.

Lyric poetry Poems, usually short, that express strong personal feelings about a subject or an event.

M

Main idea The most important idea expressed in a paragraph or an essay. It may or may not be directly stated.

Memoir A biographical or autobiographical narrative emphasizing the narrator's personal experience during a period or at an event.

See also AUTOBIOGRAPHY, BIOGRAPHY.

Metaphor A figure of speech that compares or equates seemingly unlike things. In contrast to a simile, a metaphor implies the comparison instead of stating it directly; hence, there is no use of connectives such as *like* or *as.*

See also FIGURE OF SPEECH, IMAGERY, SIMILE.

Meter A regular pattern of stressed and unstressed syllables that gives a line of poetry a predictable rhythm.

See also RHYTHM.

Monologue A long speech by a single character in a play or a solo performance.

Mood The emotional quality or atmosphere of a story or poem.

See also SETTING.

Myth A traditional story of unknown authorship, often involving goddesses, gods, and heroes, that attempts to explain a natural phenomenon, a historic event, or the origin of a belief or custom.

N

Narration Writing or speech that tells a story. Narration is used in prose fiction and narrative poetry. Narration can also be an important element in biographies, autobiographies, and essays.

Narrative poetry Verse that tells a story.

Narrator The person who tells a story. In some cases the narrator is a character in the story.

See also POINT OF VIEW.

Nonfiction Factual prose writing. Nonfiction deals with real people and experiences. Among the categories of nonfiction are biographies, autobiographies, and essays.

See also AUTOBIOGRAPHY, BIOGRAPHY, ESSAY, FICTION.

Novel A book-length fictional prose narrative. The novel has more scope than a short story in its presentation of plot, character, setting, and theme. Because novels are not subject to any limits in their presentation of these elements, they encompass a wide range of narratives.

See also FICTION.

Novella A work of fiction shorter than a novel but longer than a short story. A novella usually has more characters, settings, and events and a more complex plot than a short story.

O

Ode A lyric poem, usually rhymed, often in the form of an address and usually dignified or lofty in subject.

See also LYRIC POETRY.

Onomatopoeia The use of a word or a phrase that actually imitates or suggests the sound of what it describes.

See also SOUND DEVICES.

Oral tradition Stories, knowledge, customs, and beliefs passed by word of mouth from one generation to the next.

See also FOLKLORE, FOLKTALE, LEGEND, MYTH.

P

Parallelism The use of a series of words, phrases, or sentences that have similar grammatical form. Parallelism emphasizes the items that are arranged in the similar structures.

See also REPETITION.

Personification A figure of speech in which an animal, object, or idea is given human form or characteristics.

See also FIGURATIVE LANGUAGE, FIGURE OF SPEECH, METAPHOR.

Plot The sequence of events in a story, novel, or play. The plot begins with **exposition,** which introduces the story's characters, setting, and situation. The plot catches the reader's attention with a **narrative hook.** The **rising action** adds complications to the story's conflict, or problem, leading to the **climax,** or point of highest emotional pitch. The **falling action** is the logical result of the climax, and the **resolution** presents the final outcome.

Plot twist An unexpected turn of events in a plot. A surprise ending is an example of a plot twist.

Poetry A form of literary expression that differs from prose in emphasizing the line as the unit of composition. Many other traditional characteristics of poetry—emotional, imaginative language; use of metaphor and simile; division into stanzas; rhyme; regular pattern of stress, or meter—apply to some poems.

Point of view The relationship of the narrator, or storyteller, to the story. In a story with **first-person point of view,** the story is told by one of the characters, referred to as "I." The reader generally sees everything through that character's eyes. In a story with a **limited third-person point of view,** the narrator reveals the thoughts of only one character, but refers to that character as "he" or "she." In a story with an **omniscient point of view,** the narrator reveals the thoughts of several characters.

Props Theater slang (a shortened form of *properties*) for objects and elements of the scenery of a stage play or movie set.

Propaganda Speech, writing, or other attempts to influence ideas or opinions, often through the use of stereotypes, faulty generalizations, logical fallacies, and/or emotional language.

Prose Writing that is similar to everyday speech and language, as opposed to poetry. Its form is based on sentences and paragraphs without the patterns of rhyme, controlled line length, or meter found in much poetry. Fiction and nonfiction are the major categories of prose. Most modern drama is also written in prose.

See also DRAMA, ESSAY, FICTION, NONFICTION.

Protagonist The central character in a story, drama, or dramatic poem. Usually the action revolves around the protagonist, who is involved in the main conflict.

See ANTAGONIST, CONFLICT.

Pun A humorous play on two or more meanings of the same word or on two words with the same sound. Today puns often appear in advertising headlines and slogans—for example, "Our hotel rooms give you suite feelings."

See also HUMOR.

R

Refrain A line or lines repeated regularly, usually in a poem or song.

Repetition The recurrence of sounds, words, phrases, lines, or stanzas in a speech or piece of writing. Repetition increases the feeling of unity in a work. When a line or stanza is repeated in a poem or song, it is called a refrain.

See also PARALLELISM, REFRAIN.

Resolution The part of a plot that concludes the falling action by revealing or suggesting the outcome of the conflict.

Rhyme The repetition of sounds at the ends of words that appear close to each other in a poem. **End rhyme** occurs at the ends of lines. **Internal rhyme** occurs within a single line. **Slant rhyme** occurs when words include sounds that are similar but not identical. Slant rhyme usually involves some variation of **consonance** (the repetition of consonant sounds) or **assonance** (the repetition of vowel sounds).

Rhyme scheme The pattern of rhyme formed by the end rhyme in a poem. The rhyme scheme is designated by the assignment of a different letter of the alphabet to each new rhyme. For example, one common rhyme scheme is *ababcb.*

Rhythm The pattern created by the arrangement of stressed and unstressed syllables, especially in poetry. Rhythm gives poetry a musical quality that helps convey its meaning. Rhythm can be regular (with a predictable pattern or meter) or irregular, (as in free verse).

See also METER.

Rising action The part of a plot that adds complications to the problems in the story and increases reader interest.

See also FALLING ACTION, PLOT.

S

Scene A subdivision of an act in a play. Each scene takes place in a specific setting and time. An act may have one or more scenes.

See also ACT.

Science fiction Fiction dealing with the impact of real science or imaginary superscience on human or alien societies of the past, present, or future. Although science fiction is mainly a product of the twentieth century, nineteenth-century authors such as Mary Shelley, Jules Verne, and Robert Louis Stevenson were pioneers of the genre.

Screenplay The script of a film, usually containing detailed instructions about camera shots and angles in addition to dialogue and stage directions. A screenplay for an original television show is called a teleplay.

See also DRAMA.

Sensory imagery Language that appeals to a reader's five senses: hearing, sight, touch, taste, and smell.

See also VISUAL IMAGERY.

Sequence of events The order in which the events in a story take place.

Setting The time and place in which the events of a short story, novel, novella, or play occur. The setting often helps create the atmosphere or mood of the story.

Short story A brief fictional narrative in prose. Elements of the short story include **plot, character, setting, point of view, theme,** and sometimes symbol and irony.

Simile A figure of speech using like or as to compare seemingly unlike things.

See also FIGURATIVE LANGUAGE, FIGURE OF SPEECH.

Sonnet A poem containing fourteen lines, usually written in iambic pentameter. Sonnets have strict patterns of rhyme and usually deal with a single theme, idea, or sentiment.

Sound devices Techniques used to create a sense of rhythm or to emphasize particular sounds in writing. For example, sound can be controlled through the use of **onomatopoeia, alliteration, consonance, assonance, and rhyme.**

See also RHYTHM.

Speaker The voice of a poem—sometimes that of the poet, sometimes that of a fictional person or even a thing. The speaker's words communicate a particular tone or attitude toward the subject of the poem.

Stage directions Instructions written by the dramatist to describe the appearance and actions of characters, as well as sets, costumes, and lighting.

Stanza A group of lines forming a unit in a poem. Stanzas are, in effect, the paragraphs of a poem.

Stereotype A character who is not developed as an individual but as a collection of traits and mannerisms supposedly shared by all members of a group.

Style The author's choice and arrangement of words and sentences in a literary work. Style can reveal an author's purpose in writing and attitude toward his or her subject and audience.

Suspense A feeling of curiosity, uncertainty, or even dread about what is going to happen next. Writers increase the level of suspense in a story by giving readers clues to what may happen.

See also FORESHADOWING, RISING ACTION.

Symbol Any object, person, place, or experience that means more than what it is. **Symbolism** is the use of images to represent internal realities.

T

Tall tale A wildly imaginative story, usually passed down orally, about the fantastic adventures or amazing feats of folk heroes in realistic local settings.

See also FOLKLORE, ORAL TRADITION.

Teleplay A play written or adapted for television.

Theme The main idea of a story, poem, novel, or play, usually expressed as a general statement. Some works have a **stated theme,** which is expressed directly. More frequently works have an **implied theme,** which is revealed gradually through other elements such as plot, character, setting, point of view, symbol, and irony.

Third-person narrative. *See POINT OF VIEW.*

Title The name of a literary work.

Tone The attitude of the narrator toward the subject, ideas, theme, or characters. A factual article would most likely have an objective tone, while an editorial on the same topic could be argumentative or satiric.

Tragedy A play in which the main character suffers a downfall. That character often is a person of dignified or heroic stature. The downfall may result from outside forces or from a weakness within the character, which is known as a tragic flaw.

V

Visual imagery Details that appeal to the sense of sight.

Voice An author's distinctive style or the particular speech patterns of a character in a story.

See also STYLE, TONE.

The Writing Process

The writing process consists of five stages: prewriting, drafting, revising, editing/proofreading, and publishing/presenting. By following the stages in order, you can turn your ideas into polished pieces of writing. Most writers take their writing through all five stages, and repeat stages when necessary.

The Writing Process

Prewriting → Drafting → Revising → Editing/ Proofreading → Publishing/ Presenting

Prewriting

Prewriting is the process of gathering and organizing your ideas. It begins whenever you start to consider what you will write about or what will interest your readers. Try keeping a small notebook with you for several days and using it to jot down possible topics. Consult the chart below for tips on using the prewriting techniques known as listing, questioning, and clustering.

Listing, Questioning, and Clustering

LISTING List as many ideas as you can—whatever comes into your head on a particular subject. This is called brainstorming. Then go back over the list and circle the ideas you like best. Eventually you'll hit on an idea you can use.

QUESTIONING If your audience is your classmates, ask yourself questions such as the following:
- *What do my friends like to learn about?*
- *What do my friends like to read about?*
- *What have I done that my friends might like to hear about?*

CLUSTERING Write your topic in the middle of a piece of paper. Organize related ideas around the topic in a cluster of circles, with lines showing how the ideas are related. Clustering can help you decide which part of a topic to write about.

When you have selected your topic, organize your ideas around the topic. Identify your main ideas and supporting ideas. Each main idea needs examples or facts to support it. Then write a plan for what you want to say.

The plan might be an organized list or outline. It does not have to use complete sentences.

Drafting

Drafting is the stage that turns your list into sentences and paragraphs. Use your prewriting notes to remember what you want to say. Begin by writing an introduction that gets the reader's attention. Move ahead through the topic, paragraph by paragraph. Let your words flow. This is the time to express yourself or try out a new idea. Don't worry about mistakes in spelling and grammar; you can correct them later. If you get stuck, try one of the tricks below.

Tips for drafting
- Work on the easiest part first. You don't have to begin at the beginning.
- Make a diagram, sketch, or drawing of the topic.
- Focus on just one sentence or paragraph at a time.
- Freewrite your thoughts and images. You can organize them later.
- Pretend that you are writing to a friend.
- Ask more questions about your topic.
- Speak your ideas into a tape recorder.
- Take a break. Take a walk or listen to music. Return to your writing later.

Revising

The goal of revising is to make your writing clearer and more interesting. When you revise, look at the whole piece of writing. Ask whether the parts go together smoothly and whether anything should be added or deleted. You may decide to organize the draft in a different way. Some writers make several revisions before they are satisfied. Ask yourself these questions:

- ☑ Did I stick to my topic?
- ☑ Did I accomplish my purpose?
- ☑ Did I keep my audience in mind?
- ☑ Does my main idea come across clearly?
- ☑ Do all the details support the main idea?
- ☑ Did I give enough information? too much?
- ☑ Did I use transition words such as *first, then* and *next* to make my sentences flow smoothly?

Tips for revising

- Step back. If you have the time, set your draft aside for a while. When you look at it again, you may see it from a new point of view. You may notice that some information is missing or that part of the paper is disorganized.
- Read your paper aloud. Listen carefully as you read your paper aloud. How does it sound?
- Have a writing conference with a peer reviewer, one of your friends or classmates. A second opinion helps. Your reader can offer a fresh point of view.

Peer review

You can direct peer responses in one or more of the following ways.

- Ask readers to tell you what they have read in their own words. If you do not hear your ideas restated, revise your writing for clarity.
- Ask readers to tell you the part they liked best and why. You may want to expand those parts.
- Repeat what the readers have told you in your own words. Ask the readers if you have understood their suggestions.
- Discuss your writing with your readers. Listen to their suggestions carefully.

As you confer, make notes of your reviewers' comments. Then revise your draft, using your own judgment and including what is helpful from your reviewers' comments.

Editing/Proofreading

When you are satisfied with the changes you've made, edit your revised draft. Replace dull, vague words with lively verbs and precise adjectives. Vary the length of your sentences. Take time to correct errors in spelling, grammar, capitalization, and punctuation. Refer to the Proofreading Checklist on page R19 and on the inside back cover of this book.

Editing for style

Use the following checklist:

- ☑ Have I avoided clichés?
- ☑ Have I avoided wordiness?
- ☑ Is the tone of my writing appropriate to my purpose?
- ☑ Have I made clear connections between ideas?
- ☑ Do my sentences and paragraphs flow smoothly?

Publishing/Presenting

Now your writing is ready for an audience. Make a clean, neat copy, and add your name and date. Check that the paper has a title. If you wish, enclose the paper in a folder or binder to give it a professional look. Hand it in to your teacher, or share it in one of the ways described below. When the paper is returned, keep it in your writing portfolio.

Ideas for presenting

- **Illustrations** A photograph, diagram, or drawing can convey helpful information.
- **Oral presentation** Almost any writing can be shared aloud. Try including music, slides, or a group oral reading.
- **Class book** A collection of class writing is a nice contribution to the school library.
- **Newspaper** Some schools have a school newspaper. Local newspapers often publish student writing, especially if it is about local people and events.
- **Literary magazine** Magazines such as *Cricket* and *MidLink* publish student writing. Some schools have a literary magazine that publishes student writing once or twice a year.
- **Bulletin board** A rotating display of student writing is an effective way to see what your classmates have written. Illustrations and photographs add interest.

Some writing, such as journal writing, is private and not intended for an audience. However, even if you don't share your paper, don't throw it away. It might contain ideas that you can use later.

Proofreading Help

Use this proofreading checklist to help you check for errors in your writing, and use the proofreading symbols in the chart below to mark places that need corrections.

- ☑ Have I avoided run-on sentences and sentence fragments and punctuated sentences correctly?
- ☑ Have I used every word correctly, including plurals, possessives, and frequently confused words?
- ☑ Do verbs and subjects agree? Are verb tenses correct?
- ☑ Do pronouns refer clearly to their antecedents and agree with them in person, number, and gender?
- ☑ Have I used adverb and adjective forms and modifying phrases correctly?
- ☑ Have I spelled every word correctly, and checked the unfamiliar ones in a dictionary?

Proofreading Symbols

Symbol	Example	Meaning
⊙	Lieut Brown	Insert a period.
∧	No one came the party.	Insert a letter or a word.
≡	I enjoyed paris.	Capitalize a letter.
/	The Class ran a bake sale.	Make a capital letter lowercase.
⌒	The campers are home sick.	Close up a space.
⯑	They visited N.Y.	Spell out.
∧ ;	Sue please come I need your help.	Insert a comma or a semicolon.
∩	He enjoyed feild day.	Transpose the position of letters or words.
#	alltogether	Insert a space.
⸜	We went to to Boston.	Delete letters or words.
ᵛ ᵛ ᵛ	She asked, Whos coming?	Insert quotation marks or an apostrophe.
/ = /	mid January	Insert a hyphen.
¶	"Where?" asked Karl. "Over there," said Ray.	Begin a new paragraph.

Writing Modes

There are four main types, or modes, of writing—expository, descriptive, narrative, and persuasive. Each mode has its own purpose and characteristics.

Expository Writing

Expository writing communicates knowledge. It provides and explains information; it may also give general directions or step-by-step instructions for an activity.

Use this checklist as you write.

- ☑ Is the opening paragraph interesting?
- ☑ Are my explanations accurate and complete? Is information clear and easy to read?
- ☑ Is information presented in a logical order?
- ☑ Does each paragraph have a main idea? Does all the information support the main idea?
- ☑ Does my essay have an introduction, a body, and a conclusion?
- ☑ Have I defined any unfamiliar terms?
- ☑ Are my comparisons clear and logical?

Kinds of expository writing

Expository writing covers a wide range of styles. The chart below describes some of the possibilities.

Descriptive Writing

Descriptive writing can make a person, place, or thing come to life. The scene described may be as unfamiliar and far away as the bottom of the sea or as familiar and close as the gym locker room. By presenting details that awaken the reader's senses, descriptive writing can help your readers see the world more clearly.

Use this checklist to help you revise your description.

- ☑ Does my introduction identify the person or place that will be described?
- ☑ Are my details vivid? Are nouns and adjectives precise?
- ☑ Do all the details contribute to the same impression?
- ☑ Is it clear why this place or person is special?
- ☑ Are transitions clear? Do the paragraphs follow a logical order?
- ☑ Does each paragraph contain a main idea?
- ☑ Have I communicated a definite impression or mood?

Kinds of Expository Writing	Examples
Instructional writing	Explain how to train for a cross-country race, how to arrange a surprise party, or how to avoid cleaning up your room.
Compare-and-contrast essay	Compare two athletes or two sports, two fictional characters, two books or movies, two places, or two kinds of vacations.
Step-by-step directions.	Give directions for building a model plane, making apple pie, or drawing on a computer screen.
Information and explanation	Explain what causes sunspots, how plants grow in the desert, or why camels have a hump.
Report or essay	Write a book report, a report on the Buddhist religion, or a report on a new wildlife center.

Narrative Writing

Narrative writing tells a story, either real or fictional. It answers the question *What happened?*

A well-written narrative holds the reader's attention by presenting interesting characters in a carefully ordered series of events.

This checklist will help you improve your narrative.

- ☑ Does my first sentence get the reader's attention?
- ☑ Are the characters and setting introduced with enough detail?
- ☑ Do the characters speak and behave realistically?
- ☑ Are the events narrated in an order clear enough for the reader to follow?
- ☑ Are there places where dialogue should be added?
- ☑ Is my ending satisfying to the reader?

Persuasive Writing

Persuasive writing presents an opinion. Its goal is to make readers feel or think a certain way about a situation or an idea. The writer includes facts and opinions often designed to urge readers to take action. Good persuasive writing can sometimes be hard to resist.

As you revise your persuasive writing, use this checklist as a guide.

- ☑ Is my main idea expressed in a clear statement?
- ☑ Have I presented good reasons to support my point of view?
- ☑ Have I supported my reasons with facts and opinions?
- ☑ Have I taken account of the opposing points of view?
- ☑ Have I addressed the interests of my audience?
- ☑ Have I ended with a strong closing statement?

Research Report Writing

When you write a research report, you explore a topic by gathering factual information from several different resources. Through your research, you develop a point of view or draw a conclusion. This point of view or conclusion becomes the main idea, or thesis, of your report.

Select a Topic

Because a research report usually takes time to prepare and write, your choice of topic is especially important. Follow these guidelines.

- Brainstorm a list of questions about a subject you would like to explore. Choose one that is neither too narrow nor too broad for the length of paper you will write. Use that question as your topic.
- Select a topic that genuinely interests you.
- Be sure you can find information on your topic from several different sources.

Do Research

Start by looking up your topic in an encyclopedia to find general information. Then find specific information in books, magazines, and newspapers, on CD-ROMs and the Internet, and from personal interviews when this seems appropriate. Use the computerized or card catalog in the library to locate books on your topic. Then search for up-to-date information in periodicals (magazines) or newspapers and from electronic sources, such as CD-ROMs or the Internet. If you need help in finding or using any of these resources, ask the librarian.

As you gather information, make sure each source you use relates closely to your topic. Also be sure that your source is reliable. Be extra careful if you are using information from the Internet. If you are not sure about the reliability of a source, consult the librarian or your teacher.

Make Source Cards

In a research report, you must document the source of your information. To keep track of your sources, write the author, title, publication information, and location of each source on a separate index card. Give each source card a number and write it in the upper right-hand corner. These cards will be useful for preparing a bibliography.

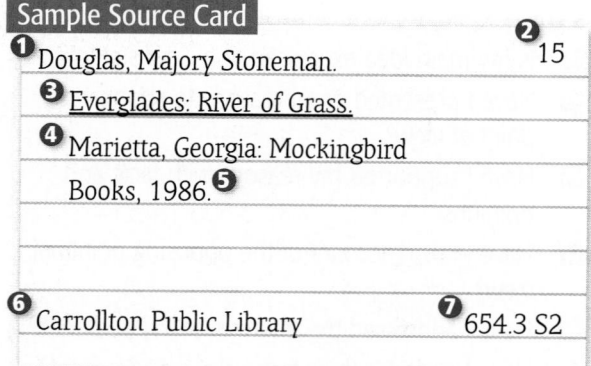

Sample Source Card

❶ Douglas, Majory Stoneman.   ❷ 15
   ❸ Everglades: River of Grass.
   ❹ Marietta, Georgia: Mockingbird
     Books, 1986. ❺

❻ Carrollton Public Library   ❼ 654.3 S2

❶ Author
❷ Source number
❸ Title
❹ City of publication/Publisher
❺ Date of publication
❻ Location of source
❼ Library call number

Take Notes

As you read, you encounter many new facts and ideas. Taking notes will help you keep track of information and focus on the topic. Here are some helpful suggestions:

- Use a new card for each important piece of information. Separate cards will help you to organize your notes.
- At the top of each card, write a key word or phrase that tells you about the information. Also, write the number of the source you used.
- Write only details and ideas that relate to your topic.
- Summarize information in your own words.
- Write down a phrase or a quote only when the words are especially interesting or come from an important source. Enclose all quotes in quotation marks to make clear that the ideas belong to someone else.

This sample note card shows information to include.

Sample Note Card

❶ Functions of Wetlands   ❷ 15
   Besides furnishing a home for a variety of
   wildlife, the wet, spongy soil of wetlands
   maintains the level of the water table.
   p. 79 ❸

❶ Write a key word or phrase that tells you what the information is about.
❷ Write the source number from your source card.
❸ Write the number of the page or pages on which you found the information.

Develop Your Thesis

As you begin researching and learning about your topic, think about the overall point you want to make. Write one sentence, your *thesis statement,* that says exactly what you plan to report on.

Sample Thesis Statement

Everglades National Park is a beautiful but endangered animal habitat.

Keep your thesis in mind as you continue to do research and think about your topic. The thesis will help you determine what information is important. However, be prepared to change your thesis if the information you find does not support it.

Write an Outline

When you finish taking notes, organize the information in an outline. Write down the main ideas that you want to cover. Write your thesis statement at the beginning of your outline. Then list the supporting details. Follow an outline form like the one on the next page.

❶ Everglades National Park is a beautiful but endangered animal habitat.

I. Special aspects of the Everglades
  ❷ A. Characteristics of wetlands
  B. Endangered birds and animals
II. Pressures on the Everglades
  A. Florida agriculture
  B. Carelessness of visitors
III. How to protect the Everglades
  A. Change agricultural practices
  B. Educate park visitors
    ❸ 1. Mandatory video on safety for individuals and environment
    2. Instructional reminders posted throughout the park

❶ The thesis statement identifies your topic and the overall point you will make.

❷ If you have subtopics under a main topic, there must be at least two. They must relate directly to your main topic.

❸ If you wish to divide a subtopic, you must have at least two divisions. Each must relate to the subtopic above it.

Document Your Information

You must document, or credit, the sources of all the information you use in your report. There are two common ways to document information.

Footnotes

To document with footnotes, place a number at the end of the information you are documenting. Number your notes consecutively, beginning with number 1. These numbers should be slightly raised and should come after any punctuation. The documentation information itself goes at the bottom of the page, with a matching number.

In-text number for note:

The Declaration of Independence was read in public for the first time on July 6, 1776.[3]

Footnote at bottom of page:

[3] John Smith, The Declaration of Independence (New York: DI, 2001) 221.

Parenthetical Documentation

In this method, you give the source for your information in parentheses at the end of the sentence where the information appears. You do not need to give all the details of the source. Just provide enough information for your readers to identify it. Here are the basic rules to follow.

- Usually it is enough to give the author's last name and the number of the page where you found the information.

  The declaration was first read in public by militia colonel John Nixon (Smith 222).

- If you mention the author's name in the sentence, you do not need to repeat it in the parentheses.

  According to Smith, the reading was greeted with wild applause (224).

- If your source does not identify a particular author, as in a newspaper or encyclopedia article, give the first word or two of the title of the piece.

  The anniversary of the reading was commemorated by a parade and fireworks ("Reading Celebrated").

Full information on your sources goes in a list at the end of your paper.

Bibliography or Works Cited

At the end of your paper, list all the sources of information that you used in preparing your report. Arrange them alphabetically by the author's last name (or by the first word in the title if no author is mentioned) as shown below. Title this list *Works Cited*. (Use the term *bibliography* if all your sources are printed media, such as books, magazines, or newspapers.)

Works Cited **❶**

❷ Bertram, Jeffrey. "African Bees: Fact or Myth?" *Orlando Sentinel* 18 Aug. 1999: D2.

❸ Gore, Rick. "Neanderthals." <u>National Geographic.</u> January 1996: 2–35. **❽**

❹ Gould, Stephen J. <u>The Panda's Thumb.</u> New York: W. W. Norton & Co., 1982.

❺ "Governor Chiles Vetoes Anti-Everglades **❾** Bills–5/13/98." <u>Friends of the Everglades.</u> May 1998. 26 Aug 1998 <http://www.everglades. org/pressrel_may28.htm>.

❻ "Neanderthal man." <u>The Columbia Encyclopedia.</u> 5th Edition. New York: Columbia University Press, 1993.

❼ Pabst, Laura (Curator of Natural History Museum), Interview. March 11, 1998.

❶ Indent all but the first line of each item.

❷ Newspaper article

❸ Magazine article

❹ Book with one author

❺ On-line article

❻ Encyclopedia

❼ Interview

❽ Include page numbers for a magazine article but not for a book, unless the book is a collection of essays by different authors.

❾ Include database (underlined), publication medium (online), computer service, and date of access.

Business Writing

Two standard formats for business letters are block style and modified block style. In block style all the parts of the letter begin at the left-hand margin.

Business Letter

The following business letter uses modified block style

❶10 Pullman Lane
Cromwell, CT 06416
January 16, 2006

❷Mr. Philip Fornaro
Principal
Cromwell School
179 West Maple St.
Cromwell, CT 06416

❸Dear Mr. Fornaro:

❹ My friends and I in the seventh grade at Brimmer Middle School feel that there is not enough to do in Cromwell during the winter vacation week. Some students can afford to go away for vacation. Many families, however, cannot afford to go away, or the parents have to work.

❺ I would like to suggest that you keep the Brimmer Middle School gym open during the vacation week. If the gym were open, the basketball teams could practice. The fencing club could meet. We could meet our friends there instead of going to the mall.

❻ Thanks for listening to my request. I hope you will think it over.

❼Sincerely,
Kim Goodwin
Kim Goodwin

❶ In the heading, write your address and the date on separate lines.

❷ In the inside address, write the name and address of the person to whom you are sending the letter.

❸ Use a colon after the greeting.

❹ In your introduction, say who you are and why you are writing.

❺ In the body of your letter, provide details concerning your request.

❻ Conclude by restating your purpose and thanking the person you are writing to.

❼ In the closing, use *Sincerely, Sincerely yours,* or *Yours truly* followed by a comma. Include both your signature and your printed or typed name.

General guidelines

Follow these guidelines when writing a business letter.

- Use correct business-letter form. Whether you write by hand, or use a computer, use 8 1/2-by-11-inch white or off-white paper. Be sure your letter is neat and clean.
- Use Standard English. Check your spelling carefully.
- Be polite, even if you are making a complaint or expressing a negative opinion.
- Be brief and to the point. State your reason for writing within the first two or three sentences.
- Include all necessary information.
- If you are making a request, be specific. Make sure what you are asking is reasonable. Express your appreciation at the end of the letter.
- Be considerate. Request only information you cannot get another way.
- When expressing an opinion or a complaint, state your reasons clearly and logically. Avoid emotional language.
- When requesting an interview, make it easy for the interviewee to meet with you. Suggest a few dates.

Writing a Memo

A memo, or memorandum, is a brief, efficient way of communicating information to another person or group of people. It begins with a header that provides basic information. A memo does not have a formal closing.

TO: *Brimmer Banner* newspaper staff
FROM: Terry Glinski
SUBJECT: Winter issue
DATE: January 18, 2006

Articles for the winter issue of the *Brimmer Banner* are due by February 1. Please see Terry about your assignment as soon as possible! The following articles or features have not yet been assigned:

Cafeteria Mess: Who Is Responsible?
Teacher Profile: Mr. Jinks, Ms. Magee
Sports roundup

Using a Computer for Writing

Using a computer offers advantages at every stage of the writing process.

Prewriting

A computer can help you gather and organize ideas and information.

Brainstorming

While brainstorming for topics or details, you can dim the computer screen and do "invisible writing." Some writers find that this technique allows their ideas to flow more freely.

Researching

Use the Internet or a CD-ROM encyclopedia to find not only text and pictures, but also sound, animated cartoons or graphics, and live-action video clips.

Outlining

Some word-processing programs offer an outlining feature that automatically indents headings and uses different type styles for main headings and subheadings.

Drafting/Revising

Most word-processing programs make it easy to do the following.

- *insert* new text at any point in your document
- *delete* or *copy* text
- *move* text from one position to another
- *undo* a change you just made
- *save* each draft or revision of your document
- *print* copies of your work-in-progress for others to read

Editing/Proofreading

You can edit and proofread directly on the computer, or you can mark your changes on a printout, or hard copy, and then input the changes on screen. The following word-processing features are helpful.

- **Grammar checker** The computer finds possible errors in grammar and suggests revisions.
- **Spelling checker** The computer finds misspellings and suggests corrections.

- **Thesaurus** If you want to replace an inappropriate or overused word, you can highlight the word and the computer will suggest synonyms.
- **Search and replace** If you want to change or correct something that occurs several times in your document, the computer can quickly make the change throughout the document.

 TIP

The grammar checker, spelling checker, and thesaurus cannot replace your own careful reading and judgment. Because English grammar is so complex, the suggestions that the grammar checker makes may not be appropriate. Also, the spelling checker will not tell you that you have typed *brake* when you meant *break,* for example, because both are valid words. The thesaurus may offer you several synonyms for a word, but you need to consider the connotations of each before deciding which, if any, fits your context.

Presenting

The computer allows you to enhance the readability, attractiveness, and visual interest of your document in many ways.

Formatting your text

The computer gives you a variety of options for the layout and appearance of your text. You can easily add or change the following elements.

- margin width
- number of columns
- type size and style
- page numbering
- header or footer (information such as a title that appears at the top or bottom of every page)

Visual aids

Some word-processing programs have graphic functions that allow you to create graphs, charts, and diagrams. Collections of *clip art,* pictures you can copy and paste into your document, are also available.

Troubleshooter

Use the Troubleshooter to recognize and correct common writing errors.

Sentence Fragment

A sentence fragment does not express a complete thought. It may lack a subject or verb or both.

- **Problem: Fragment that lacks a subject**

    The lion paced the floor of the cage. Looked hungry. *frag*

    Solution: Add a subject to the fragment to make a complete sentence.

    The lion paced the floor of the cage. He looked hungry.

- **Problem: Fragment that lacks a predicate**

    I'm painting my room. The walls yellow. *frag*

    Solution: Add a predicate to make the sentence complete.

    I'm painting my room. The walls are going to be yellow.

- **Problem: Fragment that lacks both a subject and a predicate**

    We walked around the reservoir. Near the parkway. *frag*

    Solution: Combine the fragment with another sentence.

    We walked around the reservoir near the parkway.

TIP

You can use fragments when talking with friends or writing personal letters. Some writers use fragments to produce a special effect. Use complete sentences, however, for school or business writing.

Run-on Sentence

A run-on sentence is two or more sentences written incorrectly as one sentence.

- **Problem: Two main clauses separated only by a comma**

    Roller coasters make me dizzy, I don't enjoy them. *run-on*

    Solution A: Replace the comma with a period or other end mark. Start the second sentence with a capital letter.

    Roller coasters make me dizzy. I don't enjoy them.

    Solution B: Replace the comma with a semicolon.

    Roller coasters make me dizzy; I don't enjoy them.

- **Problem: Two main clauses with no punctuation between them**

    Acid rain is a worldwide problem there are no solutions in sight. *run-on*

    Solution A: Separate the main clauses with a period or other end mark. Begin the second sentence with a capital letter.

    Acid rain is a worldwide problem. There are no solutions in sight.

    Solution B: Add a comma and a coordinating conjunction between the main clauses.

    Acid rain is a worldwide problem, but there are no solutions in sight.

- **Problem: Two main clauses with no comma before the coordinating conjunction**

    Our chorus has been practicing all month but we still need another rehearsal. *run-on*

Solution: Add a comma before the coordinating conjunction.

Our chorus has been practicing all month, but we still need another rehearsal.

Lack of Subject-Verb Agreement

A singular subject calls for a singular form of the verb. A plural subject calls for a plural form of the verb.

- **Problem: A subject that is separated from the verb by an intervening prepositional phrase**

  The two policemen at the construction site looks bored. *agr*

  The members of my baby-sitting club is saving money. *agr*

  Solution: Make sure that the verb agrees with the subject of the sentence, not with the object of the preposition. The object of a preposition is never the subject.

  The two policemen at the construction site look bored.

  The members of my baby-sitting club are saving money.

TIP ·

When subject and verb are separated by a prepositional phrase, check for agreement by reading the sentence without the prepositional phrase.

- **Problem: A sentence that begins with *here* or *there***

  Here come the last bus to Pelham Heights. *agr*

  There is my aunt and uncle. *agr*

  Solution: In sentences that begin with *here* or *there*, look for the subject after the verb. Make sure that the verb agrees with the subject.

  Here comes the last bus to Pelham Heights.

  There are my aunt and uncle.

- **Problem: An indefinite pronoun as the subject**

  Each of the candidates are qualified. *agr*

  All of the problems on the test was hard. *agr*

  Solution: Some indefinite pronouns are singular; some are plural; and some can be either singular or plural, depending on the noun they refer to. Determine whether the indefinite pronoun is singular or plural, and make sure the verb agrees with it.

  Each of the candidates is qualified.

  All of the problems on the test were hard.

- **Problem: A compound subject that is joined by *and***

  Fishing tackle and a life jacket was stowed in the boat. *agr*

  Peanut butter and jelly are delicious. *agr*

  Solution A: If the compound subjects refer to different people or things, use a plural verb.

  Fishing tackle and a life jacket were stowed in the boat.

  Solution B: If the parts of a compound subject name one unit or if they refer to the same person or thing, use a singular verb.

  Peanut butter and jelly is delicious.

- **Problem: A compound subject that is joined by *or* or *nor***

  Either my aunt or my parents plans to attend parents' night. *agr*

  Neither onions nor pepper improve the taste of this meatloaf. *agr*

  Solution: Make the verb agree with the subject that is closer to it.

  Either my aunt or my parents plan to attend parents' night.

  Neither onions nor pepper improves the taste of this meatloaf.

Incorrect Verb Tense or Form

Verbs have different tenses to show when the action takes place.

- **Problem: An incorrect or missing verb ending**

The Parks Department install a new water fountain last week. *tense*

They have also plant flowers in all the flower beds. *tense*

Solution: To form the past tense and the part participle, add *-ed* to a regular verb.

The Parks Department installed a new water fountain last week.

They have also planted flowers in all the flower beds.

- **Problem: An improperly formed irregular verb**

Wendell has standed in line for two hours. *tense*

I catched the fly ball and throwed it to first base. *tense*

Solution: Irregular verbs vary in their past and past participle forms. Look up the ones you are not sure of.

Wendell has stood in line for two hours.

I caught the fly ball and threw it to first base.

- **Problem: Confusion between the past form and the past participle**

The cast for *The Music Man* has began rehearsals. *tense*

Solution: Use the past participle form of an irregular verb, not its past form, when you use the auxiliary verb *have*.

The cast for *The Music Man* has begun rehearsals.

- **Problem: Improper use of the past participle**

Our seventh grade drawn a mural for the wall of the cafeteria. *tense*

Solution: Add the auxiliary verb *have* to the past participle of an irregular verb to form a complete verb.

Our seventh grade has drawn a mural for the wall of the cafeteria.

TIP

Because irregular verbs vary, it is useful to memorize the verbs that you use most often.

Incorrect Use of Pronouns

The noun that a pronoun refers to is called its antecedent. A pronoun must refer to its **antecedent** clearly. Subject pronouns refer to subjects in a sentence. Object pronouns refer to objects in a sentence.

- **Problem: A pronoun that could refer to more than one antecedent**

Gary and Mike are coming, but he doesn't know the other kids. *ant*

Solution: Substitute a noun for the pronoun to make your sentence clearer.

Gary and Mike are coming, but Gary doesn't know the other kids.

- **Problem: Personal pronouns as subjects**

Him and John were freezing after skating for three hours. *pro*

Lori and me decided not to audition for the musical. *pro*

Solution: Use a subject pronoun as the subject part of a sentence.

He and John were freezing after skating for three hours.

Lori and I decided not to audition for the musical.

- **Problem: Personal pronouns as objects**

Ms. Wang asked Reggie and I to enter the science fair *pro*

Ms. Wang helped he and I with the project. *pro*

Solution: Use an object pronoun as the object of a verb or a preposition.

Ms. Wang asked Reggie and me to enter the science fair.

Ms. Wang helped him and me with the project.

Incorrect Use of Adjectives

Some adjectives have irregular forms: comparative forms for comparing two things and superlative forms for comparing more than two things.

Problem: Incorrect use of *good, better, best*

Their team is more good at softball than ours. *adj*

They have more better equipment too. *adj*

Solution: The comparative and superlative forms of *good* are *better* and *best*. Do not use *more* or *most* before irregular forms of comparative and superlative adjectives.

Their team is better at softball than ours.

They have better equipment too.

Problem: Incorrect use of *bad, worse, worst*

The flooding on East Street was the baddest I've seen. *adj*

Mike's basement was in badder shape than his garage. *adj*

Solution: The comparative and superlative forms of *bad* are *worse* and *worst*. Do not use *more* or *most* or the endings *-er* or *-est* with *bad*.

The flooding on East Street was the worst I've seen.

Mike's basement was in worse shape than his garage.

Problem: Incorrect use of comparative and superlative adjectives

The Appalachian Mountains are more older than the Rockies. *adj*

Mount Washington is the most highest of the Appalachians. *adj*

Solution: Do not use both *-er* and *more* or *-est* and *most* at the same time.

The Appalachian Mountains are older than the Rockies.

Mount Washington is the highest of the Appalachians.

Incorrect Use of Commas

Commas signal a pause between parts of a sentence and help to clarify meaning.

Problem: Missing commas in a series of three or more items

Sergio put mustard, catsup, and bean sprouts on his hot dog. *com*

Solution: If there are three or more items in a series, use a comma after each one, including the item preceding the conjunction.

Sergio put mustard, catsup, and bean sprouts on his hot dog.

Problem: Missing commas with direct quotations

"A little cold water" the swim coach said, "won't hurt you." *com*

Solution: The first part of an interrupted quotation ends with a comma followed by quotation marks. The interrupting words are also followed by a comma.

"A little cold water," the swim coach said, "won't hurt you."

Problem: Missing commas with nonessential appositives

My sneakers, a new pair, are covered with mud. *com*

Solution: Determine whether the appositive is important to the meaning of the sentence. If it is not essential, set off the appositive with commas.

My sneakers, a new pair, are covered with mud.

Incorrect Use of Apostrophes

An apostrophe shows possession. It can also indicate missing letters in a contraction.

Problem: Singular possessive nouns

A parrots toes are used for gripping. *poss*

The bus color was bright yellow. *poss*

Solution: Use an apostrophe and an *s* to form the possessive of a singular noun, even one that ends in *s*.

A parrot's toes are used for gripping.

The bus's color was bright yellow.

Problem: Plural possessive nouns ending in -s

The visitors center closes at five o'clock. *poss*

The guide put several tourists luggage in one compartment. *poss*

Solution: Use an apostrophe alone to form the possessive of a plural noun that ends in *s*.

The visitors' center closes at five o'clock.

The guide put several tourists' luggage in one compartment.

Problem: Plural possessive nouns not ending in -s

The peoples applause gave courage to the young gymnast. *poss*

Solution: Use an apostrophe and an *s* to form the possessive of a plural noun that does not end in *s*.

The people's applause gave courage to the young gymnast.

Problem: Possessive personal pronouns

Jenny found the locker that was her's; she waited while her friends found their's. *poss*

Solution: Do not use apostrophes with possessive personal pronouns.

Jenny found the locker that was hers; she waited while her friends found theirs.

Incorrect Capitalization

Proper nouns, proper adjectives, and the first words of sentences always begin with a capital letter.

Problem: Words referring to ethnic groups, nationalities, and languages

Many canadians in the province of quebec speak french. *cap*

Solution: Capitalize proper nouns and adjectives that refer to ethnic groups, nationalities, and languages.

Many Canadians in the province of Quebec speak French.

Problem: Words that refer to a family member

Yesterday aunt Doreen asked me to baby-sit. *cap*

Don't forget to give dad a call. *cap*

Solution: Capitalize words that are used as part of or in place of a family member's name.

Yesterday Aunt Doreen asked me to baby-sit.

Don't forget to give Dad a call.

> **TIP**
> Do not capitalize a word that identifies a family member when it is preceded by a possessive adjective: *My father bought a new car.*

Problem: The first word of a direct quotation

The judge declared, "the court is now in session." *cap*

Solution: Capitalize the first word in a direct quotation.

The judge declared, "The court is now in session."

> **TIP**
> If you have difficulty with a rule of usage, try rewriting the rule in your own words. Check with your teacher to be sure you understand the rule.

Troublesome Words

This section will help you choose between words and expressions that are often confusing or misused.

accept, except

Accept means "to receive." *Except* means "other than."

> Phillip walked proudly to the stage to accept the award.

> Everything fits in my suitcase except my sleeping bag.

affect, effect

Affect is a verb meaning "to cause a change in" or "to influence." *Effect* as a verb means "to bring about or accomplish." As a noun, *effect* means "result."

> Bad weather will affect our plans for the weekend.

> The new medicine effected an improvement in the patient's condition.

> The gloomy weather had a bad effect on my mood.

ain't

Ain't is never used in formal speaking or writing unless you are quoting the exact words of a character or a real person. Instead of using *ain't,* say or write *am not, is not, are not;* or use contractions such as *I'm not, she isn't.*

> The pizza is not going to arrive for another half hour.

> The pizza isn't going to arrive for another half hour.

a lot

The expression *a lot* means "much" or "many" and should always be written as two words. Some authorities discourage its use in formal writing.

> A lot of my friends are learning Spanish.

> Many of my friends are learning Spanish.

all ready, already

All ready, written as two words, is a phrase that means "completely ready." *Already,* written as one word, is an adverb that means "before" or "by this time."

> By the time the fireworks display was all ready, we had already arrived.

all right, alright

The expression *all right* should be written as two words. Some dictionaries do list the single word *alright* but usually not as a preferred spelling.

> Tom hurt his ankle, but he will be all right.

all together, altogether

All together means "in a group." *Altogether* means "completely."

> The Minutemen stood all together at the end of Lexington Green.

> The rebel farmers were not altogether sure that they could fight the British soldiers.

among, between

Use *among* for three or more people, things, or groups. Use *between* for two people, things, or groups.

> Mr. Kendall divided the jobs for the car wash among the team members.

> Our soccer field lies between the gym and Main Street.

amount, number

Use *amount* with nouns that cannot be counted. Use *number* with nouns that can be counted.

> This recipe calls for an unusual amount of pepper.

> A record number of students attended last Saturday's book fair.

bad, badly

Bad is an adjective; it modifies a noun.
Badly is an adverb; it modifies a verb, an adjective, or another adverb.

> The badly burnt cookies left a bad smell in the kitchen.

> Joseph badly wants to be on the track team.

beside, besides

Beside means "next to." *Besides* means "in addition to."

> The zebra is grazing beside a wildebeest.

> Besides the zoo, I like to visit the aquarium.

bring, take

Bring means "to carry from a distant place to a closer one." *Take* means "to carry from a nearby place to a more distant one."

> Please bring a bag lunch and subway money to school tomorrow.

> Don't forget to take your art projects home this afternoon.

can, may

Can implies the ability to do something. *May* implies permission to do something.

> You may take a later bus home if you can remember which bus to get on.

TIP

Although *can* is sometimes used in place of *may* in informal speech, a distinction should be made when speaking and writing formally.

choose, chose

Choose means "to select." *Chose,* the past tense of *choose,* means "selected."

> Dad helped me choose a birthday card for my grandmother.

> Dad chose a card with a funny joke inside.

doesn't, don't

The subject of the contraction **doesn't** *(does not)* is the third-person singular (*he* or *she*). The subject of the contraction **don't** *(do not)* is *I, you, we,* or *they.*

> Tanya doesn't have any tickets for the concert.

> We don't need tickets if we stand in the back row.

farther, further

Farther refers to physical distance. *Further* refers to time or degree.

> Our new apartment is farther away from the school.

> I will not continue this argument further.

fewer, less

Fewer is used to refer to things or qualities that can be counted. *Less* is used to refer to things or qualities that cannot be counted. In addition, *less* is used with figures that are regarded as single amounts.

> Fewer people were waiting in line after lunch.

> There is less fat in this kind of peanut butter.

> Try to spend less than ten dollars on a present. [The money is treated as a single sum, not as individual dollars.]

good, well

Good is often used as an adjective meaning "pleasing" or "able." *Well* may be used as an adverb of manner telling how ably something is done or as an adjective meaning "in good health."

> That is a good haircut.

> Marco writes well.

> Because Ms. Rodriguez had a headache, she was not well enough to correct our tests.

in, into

In means "inside." *Into* indicates a movement from out-side toward the inside.

> Refreshments will be sold in the lobby of the auditorium.

> The doors opened, and the eager crowd rushed into the auditorium.

it's, its

Use an apostrophe to form the contraction of *it is.* The possessive of the personal pronoun *it* does not take an apostrophe.

> It's hard to keep up with computer technology.

> The computer industry seems to change its products daily.

lay, lie

Lay means "to place." *Lie* means "to recline."

> I will lay my beach towel here on the warm sand.

> Help! I don't want to lie next to a hill of red ants!

learn, teach

Learn means "to gain knowledge." *Teach* means "to give knowledge."

> I don't learn very quickly.

> My uncle is teaching me how to juggle.

leave, let

Leave means "to go away." *Let* means "to allow." With the word *alone,* you may use either *let* or *leave.*

> Huang has to leave at eight o'clock.

> Mr. Davio lets the band practice in his basement.

> Leave me alone. Let me alone.

like, as

Use *like,* a preposition, to introduce a prepositional phrase. Use *as,* a subordinating conjunction, to introduce a subordinate clause. Many authorities believe that *like* should not be used before a clause in formal English.

> Andy sometimes acts like a clown.

> The detective looked carefully at the empty suitcase as she examined the room.

TIP

As can be a preposition in cases like the following: *Jack went to the costume party as a giant pumpkin.*

loose, lose

Loose means "not firmly attached." *Lose* means "to misplace" or "to fail to win."

> If you keep wiggling that loose tooth, you might lose it.

raise, rise

Raise means to "cause to move up." *Rise* means "to move upward."

> Farmers in this part of Florida raise sugarcane.

> The hot air balloon began to rise slowly in the morning sky.

set, sit

Set means "to place" or "to put." *Sit* means "to place oneself in a seated position."

> I set the tips of my running shoes against the starting line.

> After running the fifty-yard dash, I had to sit down and catch my breath.

than, then

Than introduces the second part of a comparison. *Then* means "at that time" or "after that."

> I'd rather go to Disney World in the winter than in the summer.

> The park is too crowded and hot then.

their, they're

Their is the possessive form of they. *They're* is the contraction of *they are.*

> They're visiting Plymouth Plantation during their vacation.

to, too, two

To means "in the direction of." *Too* means "also" or "to an excessive degree." *Two* is the number after one.

> I bought two tickets to the concert.

> The music was too loud.

> It's my favorite group too.

who, whom

Who is a subject pronoun. *Whom* is an object pronoun.

> Who has finished the test already?

> Mr. Russo is the man to whom we owe our thanks.

who's, whose

Who's is the contraction of *who is. Whose* is the possessive form of *who.*

> Who's going to wake me up in the morning?

> The policeman discovered whose car alarm was making so much noise.

Mechanics

This section will help you use correct capitalization, punctuation, and abbreviations in your writing.

Capitalization

Capitalizing Sentences, Quotations, and Salutations

Rule: A capital letter appears at the beginning of a sentence.

> **Example:** **A**nother gust of wind shook the house.

Rule: A capital letter marks the beginning of a direct quotation that is a complete sentence.

> **Example:** Sabrina said, "**T**he lights might go out."

Rule: When a quoted sentence is interrupted by explanatory words, such as she said, do not begin the second part of the sentence with a capital letter.

> **Example:** "There's a rainbow," exclaimed Jeffrey, "**o**ver the whole beach."

Rule: When the second part of a quotation is a new sentence, put a period after the explanatory words; begin the new part with a capital letter.

> **Example:** "Please come inside," Justin said. "**W**ipe your feet."

Rule: Do not capitalize an indirect quotation.

> **Example:** Jo said that **t**he storm was getting worse.

Rule: Capitalize the first word in the salutation and closing of a letter. Capitalize the title and name of the person addressed.

> **Example:** **D**ear **D**r. **M**enino
> **D**ear **E**ditor
> **S**incerely

Capitalizing Names and Titles of People

Rule: Capitalize the names of people and the initials that stand for their names.

> **Example:** **M**alcolm **X**   **J. F. K.**
> **R**obert **E. L**ee   **Q**ueen **E**lizabeth I

Rule: Capitalize a title or an abbreviation of a title when it comes before a person's name or when it is used in direct address.

> **Example:** **D**r. **S**alinas
> "Your patient, **D**octor, is waiting."

Rule: Do not capitalize a title that follows or is a substitute for a person's name.

> **Example:** Marcia Salinas is a good **d**octor.
> He asked to speak to the **d**octor.

Rule: Capitalize the names and abbreviations of academic degrees that follow a person's name. Capitalize Jr. and Sr.

> **Example:** Marcia Salinas, **M.D.**
> Raoul Tobias, **A**ttorney
> Donald Bruns **S**r.
> Ann Lee, **P**h.**D.**

Rule: Capitalize words that show family relationships when used as titles or as substitutes for a person's name.

> **Example:** We saw **U**ncle Carlos.
> She read a book about **M**other **T**eresa.

Rule: Do not capitalize words that show family relationships when they follow a possessive noun or pronoun.

> **Example:** Your **b**rother will give us a ride.
> I forgot my **m**other's phone number.

Rule: Always capitalize the pronoun I.

> **Example:** After **I** clean my room, **I**'m going swimming.

Capitalizing Names of Places

 TIP ....

Do not capitalize articles and prepositions in proper nouns: *the Rock of Gibraltar, the Statue of Liberty.*

Rule: Capitalize the names of cities, counties, states, countries, and continents.

Example: St. Louis, Missouri
Marin County
Australia
South America

Rule: Capitalize the names of bodies of water and other geographical features.

Example: the Great Lakes   Cape Cod
the Dust Bowl

Rule: Capitalize the names of sections of a country and regions of the world.

Example: East Asia
New England
the Pacific Rim
the Midwest

Rule: Capitalize compass points when they refer to a specific section of a country.

Example: the Northwest   the South

Rule: Do not capitalize compass points when they indicate direction.

Example: Canada is north of the United States.

Rule: Do not capitalize adjectives indicating direction.

Example: western Utah

Rule: Capitalize the names of streets and highways.

Example: Dorchester Avenue   Route 22

Rule: Capitalize the names of buildings, bridges, monuments, and other structures.

Example: Empire State Building
Chesapeake Bay Bridge

Capitalizing Other Proper Nouns and Adjectives

Rule: Capitalize the names of clubs, organizations, businesses, institutions, and political parties.

Example: Houston Oilers
the Food and Drug Administration
Boys and Girls Club

Rule: Capitalize brand names but not the nouns following them.

Example: Zippo brand energy bar

Rule: Capitalize the names of days of the week, months, and holidays.

Example: Saturday   June
Thanksgiving Day

Rule: Do not capitalize the names of seasons.

Example: winter, spring, summer, fall

Rule: Capitalize the first word, the last word, and all important words in the title of a book, play, short story, poem, essay, article, film, television series, song, magazine, newspaper, and chapter of a book.

Example: *Not Without Laughter*
World Book Encyclopedia
"Jingle Bells"
Star Wars
Chapter 12

Rule: Capitalize the names of ethnic groups, nationalities, and languages.

Example: Latino   Japanese
European   Spanish

Rule: Capitalize proper adjectives that are formed from the names of ethnic groups and nationalities.

Example: Shetland pony
Jewish holiday

Punctuation

Using the Period and Other End Marks

Rule: Use a period at the end of a declarative sentence.

My great-grandfather fought in the Mexican Revolution.

Rule: Use a period at the end of an imperative sentence that does not express strong feeling.

Please set the table.

Rule: Use a question mark at the end of an interrogative sentence.

How did your sneakers get so muddy?

Rule: Use an exclamation point at the end of an exclamatory sentence or a strong imperative.

How exciting the play was!

Watch out!

Using Commas

Rule: Use commas to separate three or more items in a series.

The canary eats bird seed, fruit, and suet.

Rule: Use commas to show a pause after an introductory word and to set off names used in direct address.

Yes, I offered to take care of her canary this weekend.

Please, Stella, can I borrow your nail polish?

Rule: Use a comma after two or more introductory prepositional phrases or when the comma is needed to make the meaning clear. A comma is not needed after a single short prepositional phrase, but it is acceptable to use one.

From the back of the balcony, we had a lousy view of the stage.

After the movie we walked home. (no comma needed)

Rule: Use a comma after an introductory participle and an introductory participial phrase.

Whistling and moaning, the wind shook the little house.

Rule: Use commas to set off words that interrupt the flow of thought in a sentence.

Tomorrow, I think, our projects are due.

Rule: Use a comma after conjunctive adverbs such as *however, moreover, furthermore, nevertheless,* and *therefore.*

The skating rink is crowded on Saturday; however, it's the only time I can go.

Rule: Use commas to set off an appositive if it is not essential to the meaning of a sentence.

Ben Wagner, a resident of Pittsfield, won the first round in the golf tournament.

Rule: Use a comma before a conjunction (*and, or, but, nor, so, yet*) that joins main clauses.

We can buy our tickets now, or we can take a chance on buying them just before the show.

Rule: Use a comma after an introductory adverb clause.

Because I stayed up so late, I'm sleepy this morning.

Rule: In most cases, do not use a comma with an adverb clause that comes at the end of a sentence.

The picnic will be canceled unless the weather clears.

Rule: Use a comma or a pair of commas to set off an adjective clause that is not essential to the meaning of a sentence.

Tracy, who just moved here from Florida, has never seen snow before.

Rule: Do not use a comma or pair of commas to set off an essential clause from the rest of the sentence.

Anyone who signs up this month will get a discount.

Rule: Use commas before and after the year when it is used with both the month and the day. If only the month and the year are given, do not use a comma.

On January 2, 1985, my parents moved to Dallas, Texas.

I was born in May 1985.

Rule: Use commas before and after the name of a state or a country when it is used with the name of a city. Do not use a comma after the state if it is used with a ZIP code.

> The area code for Concord, New Hampshire, is 603.

> Please forward my mail to 6 Madison Lane, Topsham, ME 04086

Rule: Use commas or a pair of commas to set off an abbreviated title or degree following a person's name.

> The infirmary was founded by Elizabeth Blackwell, M.D., the first woman in the United States to earn a medical degree.

Rule: Use a comma or commas to set off *too* when *too* means "also."

> We, too, bought groceries, from the new online supermarket.

Rule: Use a comma or commas to set off a direct quotation.

> "My nose," exclaimed Pinocchio, "is growing longer!"

Rule: Use a comma after the salutation of a friendly letter and after the closing of both a friendly letter and a business letter.

> Dear Gary,

> Sincerely,

> Best regards,

Rule: Use a comma when necessary to prevent misreading of a sentence.

> In math, solutions always elude me.

Using Semicolons and Colons

Rule: Use a semicolon to join the parts of a compound sentence when a coordinating conjunction, such as *and, or, nor,* or *but,* is not used.

> Don't be late for the dress rehearsal; it begins at 7 o'clock sharp.

Rule: Use a semicolon to join parts of a compound sentence when the main clauses are long and are subdivided by commas. Use a semicolon even if these clauses are already joined by a coordinating conjunction.

> In the gray light of early morning, on a remote airstrip in the desert, two pilots prepared to fly on a dangerous mission; but accompanying them were a television camera crew, three newspaper reporters, and a congressman from their home state of Nebraska.

Rule: Use a semicolon to separate main clauses joined by a conjunctive adverb. Be sure to use a comma after the conjunctive adverb.

> We've been climbing all morning; therefore, we need a rest.

Rule: Use a colon to introduce a list of items that ends a sentence. Use words such as *these, the following,* or *as follows* to signal that a list is coming.

> Remember to bring the following items: a backpack, a bag lunch, sunscreen, and insect repellent.

Rule: Do not use a colon to introduce a list preceded by a verb or preposition.

> Remember to bring a backpack, a bag lunch, sunscreen, and insect repellent. (No colon is used after *bring.*)

Rule: Use a colon to separate the hour and the minutes when you write the time of day.

> My Spanish class starts at 9:15.

Rule: Use a colon after the salutation of a business letter.

> Dear Dr. Coulombe:
> Director of the Personnel Dept.:

Using Quotation Marks and Italics

Rule: Use quotation marks before and after a direct quotation.

> "Curiouser and curiouser," said Alice.

Rule: Use quotation marks with both parts of a divided quotation.

> "This gymnastics trick," explained Amanda, "took me three months to learn."

Rule: Use a comma or commas to separate a phrase such as *she said* from the quotation itself. Place the comma that precedes the phrase inside the closing quotation marks.

> "I will be late," said the cable technician, "for my appointment."

Rule: Place a period that ends a quotation inside the closing quotation marks.

> Scott said, "Thanks for letting me borrow your camping tent."

Rule: Place a question mark or an exclamation point inside the quotation marks when it is part of the quotation.

> "Why is the door of your snake's cage open?" asked my mother.

Rule: Place a question mark or an exclamation point outside the quotation marks when it is part of the entire sentence.

> How I love "The Pit and the Pendulum"!

Rule: Use quotation marks for the title of a short story, essay, poem, song, magazine or newspaper article, or book chapter.

> short story: "The Necklace"
> poem: "The Fish"
> article: "Fifty Things to Make from Bottlecaps"

Rule: Use italics or underlining for the title of a book, play, film, television series, magazine, newspaper, or work of art.

> book: *To Kill a Mockingbird*
> magazine: *The New Republic*
> painting: *Sunflowers*

Rule: Use italics or underlining for the names of ships, trains, airplanes, and spacecraft.

> ship: *Mayflower*
> airplane: *Air Force One*

Using Apostrophes

Rule: Use an apostrophe and an *s* (*'s*) to form the possessive of a singular noun.

> my brother's rock collection
> Chris's hat

Rule: Use an apostrophe and an *s* (*'s*) to form the possessive of a plural noun that does not end in *s.*

> the geese's feathers
> the oxen's domestication

TIP

If a thing is owned jointly by two or more individuals, only the last name should show possession: *Mom and Dad's car.* If the ownership is not joint, each name should show possession: *Mom and Dad's parents are coming for Thanksgiving.*

Rule: Use an apostrophe alone to form the possessive of a plural noun that ends in *s.*

> the animals' habitat
> the instruments' sound

Rule: Use an apostrophe and an *s* (*'s*) to form the possessive of an indefinite pronoun.

> everyone's homework
> someone's homework

Rule: Do not use an apostrophe in a possessive pronoun.

> The dog knocked over its dish.
> Yours is the best entry in the contest.
> One of these drawings must be hers.

Rule: Use an apostrophe to replace letters that have been omitted in a contraction.

> it + is = it's
> can + not = can't
> I + have = I've

Rule: Use an apostrophe to form the plural of a letter, a figure, or a word that is used as itself.

> Write three 7's.
> The word is spelled with two m's.
> The sentence contains three and's.

Rule: Use an apostrophe to show missing numbers in a year.

> the class of '02

Using Hyphens, Dashes, and Parentheses

Rule: Use a hyphen to show the division of a word at the end of a line. Always divide the word between its syllables.

With the new recycling program, more residents are recycling
their trash.

TIP

One-letter divisions (for example, *e-lectric*) are not permissible. Avoid dividing personal names, if possible.

Rule: Use a hyphen in a number written as a compound word.

He sold forty-six ice creams in one hour.

Rule: Use a hyphen in a fraction.

We won the vote by a two-thirds majority.

Two-thirds of the votes have been counted.

Rule: Use a hyphen or hyphens in certain compound nouns.

great-grandmother

merry-go-round

Rule: Hyphenate a compound modifier only when it precedes the word it modifies.

A well-known musician visited our school.

The story was well written.

Rule: Use a hyphen after the prefixes *all-, ex-,* and *self-* when they are joined to any noun or adjective.

all-star

ex-president

self-conscious

Rule: Use a hyphen to separate any prefix from a word that begins with a capital letter.

un-American

mid-January

Rule: Use a dash or dashes to show a sudden break or change in thought or speech.

Daniel—he's kind of a pest—is my youngest cousin.

Rule: Use parentheses to set off words that define or helpfully explain a word in the sentence.

The transverse flute (*transverse* means "sideways") is a wind instrument.

Abbreviations

Rule: Abbreviate the titles *Mr., Mrs., Ms.,* and *Dr.* before a person's name. Also abbreviate any professional or academic degree that follows a name. The titles *Jr.* and *Sr.* are *not* preceded by a comma.

Dr. Stanley Livingston (doctor)

Luisa Mendez, M.A. (Master of Arts)

Martin Luther King Jr.

Rule: Use capital letters and no periods with abbreviations that are pronounced letter by letter or as words. Exceptions are *U.S.* and *Washington, D.C.,* which do use periods.

NAACP	National Association for the Advancement of Colored People
UFO	unidentified flying object
MADD	Mothers Against Driving Drunk

Rule: With exact times use A.M. (*ante meridiem,* "before noon") and P.M. (*post meridiem,* "after noon"). For years use B.C. (before Christ) and, sometimes, A.D. (*anno Domini,* "in the year of the lord," after Christ).

| 8:15 A.M. | 6:55 P.M. |
| 5000 B.C. | A.D. 235 |

Rule: Abbreviate days and months only in charts and lists.

School will be closed on

Mon., Sept. 3

Wed., Nov. 11

Thurs., Nov. 27

Rule: In scientific writing abbreviate units of measure. Use periods with English units but not with metric units.

| inch(es) in. | yard(s) yd. |
| meter(s) m | milliliter(s) ml |

Rule: On envelopes only, abbreviate street names and state names. In general text, spell out street names and state names.

Ms. Karen Holmes

347 Grandville St.

Tilton, NH 03276

Karen lives on Grandville Street in Tilton, New Hampshire.

Writing Numbers

Rule: In charts and tables, always write numbers as numerals. Other rules apply to numbers not in charts or tables.

Student Test Scores

Student	Test 1	Test 2	Test 3
Lai, W.	82	89	94
Ostos, A.	78	90	86

Rule: Spell out a number that is expressed in one or two words.

We carried enough supplies for twenty-three days.

Rule: Use a numeral for a number of more than two words.

The tallest mountain in Mexico rises 17,520 feet.

Rule: Spell out a number that begins a sentence, or reword the sentence so that it does not begin with a number.

One hundred forty-three days later the baby elephant was born.

The baby elephant was born 143 days later.

Rule: Write a very large number as a numeral followed by the word *million* or *billion*.

There are 15 million people living in or near Mexico City.

Rule: Related numbers should be written in the same way. If one number must be written as a numeral, use numerals for all the numbers.

There are 365 days in the year, but only 52 weekends.

Rule: Spell out an ordinal number (*first, second*).

Welcome to our fifteenth annual convention.

Rule: Use words to express the time of day unless you are writing the exact time or using the abbreviation A.M. or P.M.

My guitar lesson is at five o'clock. It ends by 5:45 P.M.

Rule: Use numerals to express dates, house and street numbers, apartment and room numbers, telephone numbers, page numbers, amounts of money of more than two words, and percentages. Write out the word *percent.*

August 5, 1999

9 Davio Dr.

Apartment 9F

24 percent

Spelling

The following rules, examples, and exceptions can help you master the spelling of many words.

Spelling *ie* and *ei*

Put *i* before *e* except when both letters follow *c* or when both letters are pronounced together as an **a** sound.

believe	sieve	weight
receive	relieve	neighborhood

It is helpful to memorize exceptions to this rule. Exceptions include the following words: *species, science, weird, either, seize, leisure,* and *protein.*

Spelling unstressed vowels

Notice the vowel sound in the second syllable of the word *won-d_r-ful.* This is the unstressed vowel sound; dictionary respellings use the schwa symbol (ə) to indicate it. Because any of several vowels can be used to spell this sound, you might find yourself uncertain about which vowel to use. To spell words with unstressed vowels, try thinking of a related word in which the syllable containing the vowel sound is stressed.

Unknown Spelling	Related Word	Word Spelled Correctly
wond_rful	wonder	wonderful
fort_fications	fortify	fortifications
res_dent	reside	resident

Suffixes and the silent *e*

For most words with silent *e*, keep the *e* when adding a suffix. When you add the suffix *-ly* to a word that ends in *l* plus silent *e*, drop the *-le*. Also drop the silent *e* when you add a suffix beginning with a vowel or a *y*.

wise + ly = wisely
peaceful + ly = peacefully
skate + ing = skating
gentle + ly = gently

There are exceptions to the rule, including the following:

awe + ful = awful
judge + ment = judgment

true + ly = truly
noise + y = noisy
dye + ing = dyeing
mile + age = mileage

Suffixes and the final *y*

When you are adding a suffix to words ending with a vowel + *y*, keep the *y*. For words ending with a consonant + *y*, change the *y* to *i* unless the suffix begins with *i*. To avoid having two *i*'s together, keep the *y*.

enjoy + ment = enjoyment
merry + ment = merriment
display + ed = displayed
lazy + ness = laziness
play + ful = playful
worry + ing = worrying

Note: For some words, there are alternate spellings:

sly + er = slyer or slier
shy + est = shyest or shiest

Adding prefixes

When you add a prefix to a word, do not change the spelling of the word.

un + done = undone
re + schedule = reschedule
il + legible = illegible
semi + sweet = semisweet

Doubling the final consonant

Double the final consonant when a word ends with a single consonant following one vowel and the word is one syllable, or when the last syllable of the word is accented both before and after adding the suffix.

sit + ing = sitting
rub + ing = rubbing
commit + ed = committed
confer + ed = conferred

Do not double the final consonant if the suffix begins with a consonant, if the accent is not on the last syllable, or if the accent moves when the suffix is added.

cancel + ing = canceling
commit + ment = commitment
travel + ed = traveled
defer + ence = deference

Do not double the final consonant if the word ends in two consonants or if the suffix begins with a consonant.

climb + er = climber
nervous + ness = nervousness

import + ance = importance
star + dom = stardom

When adding -ly to a word that ends in ll, drop one l.

hill + ly = hilly full + ly = fully

Forming compound words

When forming compound words, keep the original spelling of both words.

home + work = homework
scare + crow = scarecrow
pea + nut = peanut

Forming Plurals

General Rules for Plurals		
If the noun ends in	**Rule**	**Example**
s, ch, sh, x, or z	add -es	loss→losses, latch→latches, box→boxes, bush→bushes, quiz→quizzes
a consonant + y	change y to i and add -es	ferry→ferries, baby→babies, worry→worries
a vowel + y	add -s	chimney→chimneys, monkey→monkeys, toy→toys
a vowel + o	add -s	cameo→cameos, radio→radios, rodeo→rodeos
a consonant + o	add -es but sometimes add -s	potato→potatoes, echo→echoes photo→photos, solo→solos
f or ff	add -s but sometimes change f to v and add -es	proof→proofs, bluff→bluffs sheaf→sheaves, thief→thieves, hoof→hooves
lf	change f to v and add -es	calf→calves, half→halves, loaf→loaves
fe	change f to v and add -s	knife→knives, life→lives

Special Rules for Plurals	
Rule	**Example**
To form the plural of most proper names and one-word compound nouns, follow the general rules for plurals.	Jones→Joneses, Thomas→Thomases, Hatch→Hatches
To form the plural of hyphenated compound nouns or compound nouns of more than one word, make the most important word plural.	credit card→credit cards mother-in-law→mothers-in-law district attorney→district attorneys
Some nouns have irregular plural forms and do not follow any rules.	man→men, foot→feet, tooth→teeth
Some nouns have the same singular and plural forms	deer→deer, species→species, sheep→sheep

Listening Effectively

A large part of the school day is spent either listening or speaking to others. By becoming a better listener and speaker, you will know more about what is expected of you, and understand more about your audience.

Listening to instructions in class

Some of the most important listening in the school day involves listening to instructions. Use the following tips to help you.

- First, make sure you understand what you are listening for. Are you receiving instructions for homework or for a test? What you listen for depends upon the type of instructions being given.

- Think about what you are hearing, and keep your eyes on the speaker. This will help you stay focused on the important points.

- Listen for keywords, or word clues. Examples of word clues are phrases such as *above all, most important,* or *the three basic parts.* These clues help you identify important points that you should remember.

- Take notes on what you hear. Write down only the most important parts of the instructions.

- If you don't understand something, ask questions. Then if you're still unsure about the instructions, repeat them aloud to your teacher to receive correction on any key points that you may have missed.

Interpreting nonverbal clues

Understanding nonverbal clues is part of effective listening. Nonverbal clues are everything you notice about a speaker *except* what the speaker says. As you listen, ask yourself these questions:

- Where and how is the speaker standing?
- Are some words spoken more loudly than others?
- Does the speaker make eye contact?
- Does he or she smile or look angry?
- What message is sent by the speaker's gestures and facial expression?

PRACTICE

Work with a partner to practice listening to instructions. Each of you should find a set of directions for using a simple device–for example, a mechanical tool, a telephone answering machine, or a VCR. Study the instructions carefully. If you can bring the device to class, ask your partner to try to use it by following your step-by-step instructions. If you cannot have the device in class, ask your partner to explain the directions back to you. Then change roles and listen as your partner gives you a set of directions.

Speaking Effectively

- Speak slowly, clearly, and in a normal tone of voice. Raise your voice a bit, or use gestures to stress important points.
- Pause a few seconds after making an important point.
- Use words that help your audience picture what you're talking about. Visual aids such as pictures, graphs, charts, and maps can also help make your information clear.
- Stay in contact with your audience. Make sure your eyes move from person to person in the group you're addressing.

Speaking informally

Most oral communication is informal. When you speak casually with your friends, family, and neighbors, you use informal speech. Human relationships depend on this form of communication.

- Be courteous. Listen until the other person has finished speaking.
- Speak in a relaxed and spontaneous manner.
- Make eye contact with your listeners.
- Do not monopolize a conversation.
- When telling a story, show enthusiasm.
- When giving an announcement or directions, speak clearly and slowly. Check that your listeners understand the information.

Presenting an oral report

The steps in preparing an oral report are similar to the steps in the writing process. Complete each step carefully and you can be confident of presenting an effective oral report.

Steps in Preparing an Oral Report	
Prewriting	Determine your purpose and audience. Decide on a topic and narrow it.
Drafting	Make an outline. Fill in the supporting details. Write the report.
Revising and editing	Review your draft. Check the organization of ideas and details. Reword unclear statements.
Practicing	Practice the report aloud in front of a family member. Time the report. Ask for and accept advice.
Presenting	Relax in front of your audience. Make eye contact with your audience. Speak slowly and clearly.

PRACTICE

Pretend that you have been invited to give an oral report to a group of fifth graders. Your report will tell them what to expect and how to adjust to new conditions when they enter middle school. As you plan your report, keep your purpose and your audience in mind. Include lively descriptions and examples to back up your suggestions and hold your audience's attention. As you practice giving your report, be sure to give attention to your body language as well as your vocal projection. Ask a partner to listen to your report to give you feedback on how to improve your performance. Do the same for your partner after listening to his or her report.

Viewing Effectively

Critical viewing means thinking about what you see while watching a TV program, newscast, film, or video. It requires paying attention to what you hear and see and deciding whether information is true, false, or exaggerated. If the information seems to be true, try to determine whether it is based on a fact or an opinion.

Fact versus opinion

A **fact** is something that can be proved. An opinion is what someone believes is true. **Opinions** are based on feelings and experiences and cannot be proved.

Television commercials, political speeches, and even the evening news contain both facts and opinions. They use emotional words and actions to persuade the viewer to agree with a particular point of view. They may also use faulty reasoning, such as linking an effect with the wrong cause. Think through what is being said. The speaker may seem sincere, but do his or her reasons make sense? Are the reasons based on facts or on unfair generalizations?

Commercials contain both obvious and hidden messages. Just as you need to discover the author's purpose when you read a writer's words, you must be aware of the purpose of nonverbal attempts to persuade you.

What does the message sender want, and how is the sender trying to influence you?

For example, a magazine or TV ad picturing a group of happy teenagers playing volleyball on a sunny beach expresses a positive feeling. The advertiser hopes viewers will transfer that positive feeling to the product being advertised—perhaps a soft drink or a brand of beachwear. This technique, called **transfer,** is one of several propaganda techniques regularly used by advertisers to influence consumers.

Following are a few other common techniques.

Testimonial—Famous and admired people recommend or praise a product, a policy, or a course of action even though they probably have no professional knowledge or expertise to back up their opinion.

Bandwagon—People are urged to follow the crowd ("get on the bandwagon") by buying a product, voting for a candidate, or whatever else the advertiser wants them to do.

Glittering generalities—The advertiser uses positive, good-sounding words (for example, *all-American* or *medically proven*) to impress people.

PRACTICE

Think of a television commercial that you have seen often or watch a new one and take notes as you watch it. Then analyze the commercial.

- What is the purpose behind the ad?
- What is expressed in written or spoken words?
- What is expressed nonverbally (in music or sound effects as well as in pictures and actions)?
- What methods does the advertiser use to persuade viewers?
- What questions would you ask the advertiser if you could?
- How effective is the commercial? Why?

Working in Groups

Working in a group is an opportunity to learn from others. Whether you are planning a group project (such as a class trip) or solving a math problem, each person in a group brings specific strengths and interests to the task. When a task is large, such as planting a garden, a group provides the necessary energy and talent to get the job done.

Small groups vary in size according to the nature of the task. Three to five students is a good size for most small-group tasks. Your teacher may assign you to a group, or you may be asked to form your own group. Don't work with your best friend if you are likely to chat too much. Successful groups often have a mix of student abilities and interests.

Individual role assignments give everyone in a group something to do. One student, the group recorder, may take notes. Another may lead the discussion, and another report the results to the rest of the class.

Roles for a Small Group	
Reviewer	Reads or reviews the assignment and makes sure everyone understands it
Recorder 1 (of the process)	Takes notes on the discussion
Recorder 2 (of the results)	Takes notes on the final results
Reporter	Reports results to the rest of the class
Discussion leader	Asks questions to get the discussion going; keeps the group focused
Facilitator	Helps the group resolve disagreements and reach a compromise

For a small group of three or four students, some of these roles can be combined. Your teacher may assign a role to each student in your group. Or you may be asked to choose your own role.

Tips for working in groups

- Review the group assignment and goal. Be sure that everyone in the group understands the assignment.
- Review the amount of time allotted for the task. Decide how your group will organize its time.
- Check that all the group members understand their roles in the group.
- When a question arises, try to solve it as a group before asking a teacher for help.
- Listen to other points of view. Take turns during a discussion.
- When it is your turn to talk, address the subject and help the project move forward.

Study Skills

Studying for school and doing your homework are like any other tasks—if you understand your assignment, set a goal, and make a plan, you'll save time and do great work. The tips that follow will teach you the skills you need to make schoolwork easier and more enjoyable.

Get Organized

- Keep an assignment notebook. Keep it up to date.
- Keep your notes for each course together in one place.
- Find a good place to study. Choose a place that has as few distractions as possible. Try to study in the same place each day.
- Try to study at the same time each day.
- Don't study one subject too long. If you haven't finished after thirty minutes, switch to another subject.
- Take notes on your reading. Keep your notes in one place.

Understand Your Purpose

The purpose is the reason you have been given a particular assignment. If you understand the purpose, you should be able to set a goal to work toward. With schoolwork, this means making sure you understand your assignment and you know how long you have to do it.

Set goals

These steps will help you set study goals for an assignment.

1. Listen as the teacher explains the assignment. Find out everything you need to do to finish the assignment.
2. Understand the quality of work your teacher expects from you. Are you supposed to turn in a finished paper or a rough draft?
3. Find out how much time you have. Ask: Is everything due on the same day, or are some parts due earlier?
4. In your assignment notebook, write down the assignment details and the dates when your work is due.

Homework Checklist

Goal: To understand and finish my homework assignment.

Plan: Follow these steps to reach my goal:

- ☑ Bring home the all the materials I need, including this textbook, and my notebook.
- ☑ Find a quiet space where I can concentrate. Also, make sure I have a table or other hard, flat surface to write on.
- ☑ Keep my notebook out and take notes as I read.
- ☑ Write down questions about the parts of the assignment that I don't understand. Ask my teacher or an adult at home to help me understand.
- ☑ Check this plan from time to time to make sure I stay on task.
- ☑ Take my completed homework back to school and hand it in.

Make a Plan

Making a plan is the best way to reach your goals. Try to make plans that include the work you have finish and the time you have until the assignment is due. Think about how you study best, when you might need help, and what gets in your way.

You can use a **task, obstacle, and solution chart** to show

1. what you need to do (task)
2. what might get in your way (obstacle)
3. how you can get around an obstacle (solution)

Karen's goal is to read a chapter of science before school tomorrow. Check out the chart she made, which includes **task, obstacle, and solution.**

1. (task)	I have to…	read chapter 4 tonight
2. (obstacle)	But…	after dinner I have basketball practice
3. (solution)	So I need to…	read before practice

Try it! In your **Learner's Notebook,** make your own **task, obstacle, and solution chart** for an assignment from this book. You can use Karen's plan as a model.

Take Notes

Writing notes about what you read or what you hear in a presentation will help you remember information you're expected to learn. The Cornell Note-Taking System is a way to organize the notes you take in class or the notes you take as you read. Use this system to organize your note-taking and make sense of the notes you take.

Cornell Notes

Divide the pages that you're using for notes into two sections or columns as shown below. As you read or listen, write notes in Section B. In Section A, write the highlights (main ideas and vocabulary) from Section B.

| Section A [highlights]
Use this section SECOND.
Review the notes you took in Section B and write in this section:
• Vocabulary words to remember
• Main idea statements
• Questions and other hints that will help you remember the information | Section B [notes]
Use this section FIRST.
As you read or listen, take notes in this section:
• When you're taking notes on your reading, write down the subtitles that break the text into different section. In most cases, subtitles form an outline of the information in a chapter.
• Write down the most important information: main ideas and concepts. Don't write every word or take time to write complete sentences. (Hint: if the teacher writes something on the board, it's probably important.)
• Use abbreviations and shortened word forms to get the ideas on paper quickly. (For example, POV is a good abbreviation for Point of View.)
• Define new terms and concepts in your own words so that you'll be able to under-stand them later. |

Model These are some notes one student made as she read about biographies and autobiographies.

| A.
biography

autobiography

Major elements of biog-raphy | B. Looking at the Genre: Biography
What is it?
    real people, real life
    Autobiography is about yourself
Why is it important?
    many reasons (interest, learn, entertain, etc.)
What are the important elements?
    Narrator: who tells the story
    Point of view: from who's telling the story
    Setting: time and place of a story |

Try It! Divide a sheet of paper into two columns as shown above. Practice taking notes using the Cornell system as you read your homework assignment.

Test-Taking Skills

How well you perform on a test is not a matter of chance. Some specific strategies can help you answer test questions. This section of the handbook will show how to improve your test-taking skills.

Tips for preparing for tests

Here are some useful suggestions for preparing to take a test.

- Gather information about the test. When will it be given? How long will it take? Exactly what material will it cover?
- Review material from your textbook, class notes, homework, quizzes, and handouts. Review the study questions at the end of each section of a textbook. Try to define terms in boldface type.
- Make up some sample questions and answer them. As you skim selections, try to predict what may be asked.
- Draw charts and cluster or Venn diagrams to help you remember information and to picture how one piece of information relates to another.
- Give yourself plenty of time to study. Avoid cramming for a test. Several short review sessions are more effective than one long one.
- In addition to studying alone, study with a partner or small group. Quiz one another on topics you think the test will cover.

Plan your strategy

Try following these steps:

- Read all directions carefully. Understanding the directions can prevent mistakes.
- Ask for help if you have a question.
- Answer the easier items first. By skipping the hard items, you will have time to answer all the easy ones.
- In the time that is left, return to the items you skipped. Answer them as best you can. If you won't be penalized for doing so, guess at an answer.
- If possible, save some time at the end to check your answers.

Objective Tests

An objective test is a test of factual information. The questions are usually either right or wrong; there is no difference of opinion. On an objective test, you are asked to recall information, not to present your ideas. Objective test questions include true-or-false items, multiple-choice items, fill-in-the-blanks statements, short-answer items, and matching items. At the beginning of an objective test, scan the number of items. Then budget your time.

Multiple-choice items Multiple-choice questions ask you to answer a question or complete a sentence. They are the kind of question you will encounter most often on objective tests. Read all the choices before answering. Pick the best response.

> **What is a peninsula?**
> **(a) a range of mountains**
> **(b) a circle around the moon**
> **(c) a body of land surrounded by water on three sides**

Correct answer: (c)

- Read the question carefully. Be sure that you understand it.
- Read all the answers before selecting one. Reading all of the responses is especially important when one of the choices is "all of the above" or "none of the above."
- Eliminate responses that are clearly incorrect. Focus on the responses that might be correct.
- Look for absolute words, such as *never, always, all, none*. Most generalizations have exceptions. Absolute statements are often incorrect. (Note: This tip applies to true/false items also.)

Answering essay questions

Essay questions ask you to think about what you have learned and to write about it in one or more paragraphs. Some tests present a choice of essay questions. If a test has both an objective part and an essay part, answer the objective questions first, but leave yourself enough time to work on the essay.

Read the essay question carefully. What does it ask you to do? Discuss? Explain? Define? Summarize? Compare and contrast? These key words tell what kind of information you must give in your answer.

Key Verbs in Essay Questions	
Argue	Give your opinion and supporting reasons.
Compare and contrast	Discuss likenesses and differences.
Define	Give details that show exactly what something is like.
Demonstrate	Give examples to support a point.
Describe	Present a picture with words.
Discuss	Show detailed information on a particular subject.
Explain	Give reasons.
Identify	Give specific characteristics.
List (also outline, trace)	Give details, give steps in order, give a time sequence.
Summarize	Give a short overview of the most important ideas or events.

Tips for answering essay questions

You might wish to consider the following suggestions:

- Read the question or questions carefully. Determine the kind of information required by the question.
- Plan your time. Do not spend too much time on one part of the essay.
- Make a list of what you want to cover.
- If you have time, make revisions and proofreading corrections.

Taking standardized tests

Standardized tests are taken by students all over the country. Your performance on the test is compared with the performance of other students at your grade level. There are many different kinds of standardized tests. Some measure your progress in such subjects as English, math, and science, while others measure how well you think. Standardized tests can show how you learn and what you do best.

Preparing for standardized tests

There is no way to know exactly what information will be on a standardized test, or even what topics will be covered. The best preparation is to do the best you can in your daily schoolwork. However, you can learn the *kinds* of questions that will appear on a standardized test. Some general tips will also help.

Tips for taking standardized tests

You might find the following suggestions helpful.

- Get enough sleep the night before the test. Eat a healthful breakfast.
- Arrive early for the test. Try to relax.
- Listen carefully to all test directions. Ask questions if you don't understand the directions.
- Complete easy questions first. Leave harder items for the end.
- Be sure your answers are in the right place on the answer sheet.
- If points are not subtracted for wrong answers, guess at questions that you aren't sure of.

Analogies Analogy items test your understanding of the relationships between things or ideas. On standardized tests, analogies are written in an abbreviated format, as shown below.

man : woman :: buck : doe

The symbol : means "is to"; the symbol :: means "as."

This chart shows some word relationships you might find in analogy tests.

Relationship	Definition	Example
Synonyms	Two words have a similar meaning.	huge : gigantic :: scared : afraid
Antonyms	Two words have opposite meanings.	bright : dull :: far : near
Use	Words name a user and something used.	farmer : tractor :: writer : computer
Cause-Effect	Words name a cause and its effect.	tickle : laugh :: polish : shine
Category	Words name a category and an item in it.	fish : tuna :: building : house
Description	Words name an item and a characteristic of it.	knife : sharp :: joke : funny

GLOSSARY/GLOSARIO
Academic and Selection Vocabulary

English	Español

A

abandonment (uh BAN dun mint) *n.* the state of being deserted or left alone without help **(p. 486)**

abandono *s.* estado de desolación o soledad sin poder contar con ayuda

abruptly (uh BRUPT lee) *adv.* suddenly; unexpectedly **(p. 1071)**

abruptamente *adv.* repentinamente; inesperadamente

absurd (ub SURD) *adj.* not making sense; very silly **(p. 741)**

absurdo(a) *adj.* sin sentido; disparatado

accumulate (uh KYOOM yuh layt) *v.* gather or build up **(p. 1029)**

acumular *v.* juntar y amontonar

adolescence (ad uh LES uns) *n.* the period between childhood and adulthood **(p. 1070)**

adolescencia *s.* periodo entre la niñez y la edad adulta

aggravating (AG ruh vay ting) *adj.* irritating; annoying **(p. 748)**

insoportable *adj.* molesto y enfadoso

agitated (AJ uh tay tud) *adj.* disturbed; upset **(p. 1108)**

inquieto(a) *adj.* nervioso; agitado

alien (AY lee un) *adj.* strange; odd; peculiar **(p. 1147)**

extraño(a) *adj.* raro, de naturaleza distinta a la cosa de la que forma parte

ambition (am BIH shun) *n.* a strong drive or desire to succeed **(p. 492)**

ambición *s.* deseo intenso de lograr o conseguir algo

analyzing (AN uh lyz ing) *n.* examining by separating into parts and identifying relationships between the parts **(p. 160)**

análisis *s.* examen que se hace de las partes de un todo, qué las componen y cómo se relacionan entre ellas

anthem (AN thum) *n.* the official song of a country, school, or group **(p. 590)**

himno *s.* composición musical oficial de un país, escuela o grupo

anticipation (an tis uh PAY shun) *n.* the act of looking forward to; expectation **(p. 883)**

expectativa *s.* posibilidad de que algo suceda; anticipación

appealed (uh PEELD) *v.* made a serious request **(p. 119)**

apelar *v.* recurrir a alguien o algo con autoridad para resolver una situación

apprehension (ap rih HEN shun) *n.* fear of what may happen **(p. 805)**

aprensión *s.* miedo o figuración infundada

arc (ark) *n.* a curved line between two points **(p. 453)**

arco *s.* línea continua que forma una curva

askew (uh SKYOO) *adj.* turned or twisted to one side **(p. 654)**

ladeado(a) *adj.* oblicuo; inclinado; que no es recto

attaining (uh TAY ning) *n.* the act of achieving, accomplishing, or succeeding **(p. 1107)**

logro *s.* obtención con éxito de algo que se desea

audacity (aw DAS ih tee) *n.* reckless courage **(p. 50)**

audacia *s.* osadía; valor de hacer algo nuevo y arriesgado

authentic (aw THEN tik) *adj.* real; genuine **(p. 608)**

auténtico(a) *adj.* real, genuino

available (uh VAY luh bul) *adj.* at hand; easily obtained **(p. 296)**

disponible *adj.* algo que está libre para ser utilizado

avid (AV id) *adj.* very eager or enthusiastic **(p. 1068)**

ávido(a) *adj.* ansioso, con un deseo intenso

B

barreling (BAYR ul ing) *v.* running headlong (p. 569)

barricades (BAIR uh kaydz) *n.* barriers put up to separate or for defense (p. 969)

bewilderment (bih WIL dur munt) *n.* confusion (p. 119)

bias (BY us) *n.* an opinion based on personal preferences or unfair judgments (p. 404)

bickering (BIK ur ing) *n.* a quarrel or argument, especially about minor details (p. 751)

bogus (BOH gus) *adj.* bad; not real or genuine (p. 1002)

bombardment (bom BARD mint) *n.* an attack (p. 522)

buoyed (BOO eed) *adj.* supported or uplifted (p. 1023)

precipitándose *v.* arrojarse sin prudencia a hacer o decir algo; forma del verbo *precipitar*

barricadas *s.* obstáculo improvisado para separar o defenderse

desconcierto *s.* confusión

prejuicio *s.* opinión falta de neutralidad basada en preferencias personales

riña *s.* discusión o pelea confusa

falso(a) *adj.* engañoso, que no es real

bombardeo *s.* disparo de bombas contra un objetivo, generalmente desde un avión

animado(a) *adj.* infundido de moral y alegría

C

cajoling (kuh JOHL ing) *v.* persuading, especially by using soothing words; coaxing (p. 228)

calculating (KAL kyoo layt ing) *v.* using math or logic to figure out something (p. 646)

capsize (KAP syz) *v.* to overturn or upset (especially a boat) (p. 1142)

clamor (KLA mor) *v.* to demand something in a noisy or desperate way (p. 326)

clarify (KLAYR ih fy) *v.* make clear (p. 998)

coaxed (kohkst) *v.* urged gently (p. 903)

collapse (kuh LAPS) *v.* to fall apart, cave in, or break down (p. 862)

commotion (kum OH shun) *n.* noisy, confused activity (p. 609)

compassion (kom PASH un) *n.* the feeling of sorrow or pity caused by someone else's misfortunes; sympathy (p. 59)

compiled (kum PYL ed) *v.* collected into a book or list (p. 392)

comprehension (kawm prih HEN shun) *n.* the fact or power of understanding (p. 500)

compulsory (kum PUL suh ree) *adj.* required (p. 666)

conceived (kun SEEVD) *adj.* formed; imagined (p. 1098)

engatusar *v.* persuadir o ganar la voluntad de alguien a través de halagos

calculando *v.* sacar cuentas a través de operaciones lógicas o matemáticas, forma del verbo *calcular*

volcaría *v.* torcer hacia un lado o de cabeza, forma del verbo *volcar*

clamar *v.* Exigir a voces y con vehemencia

aclarar *v.* explicar, despejar la confusión

convenció *v.* consiguió que cambiara de opinión o comportamiento, lo persuadió; forma del verbo *convencer*

colapsar *v.* producir la destrucción brusca de un cuerpo

conmoción *s.* tumulto o perturbación violenta

compasión *s.* sentimiento de pena y lástima por la desgracia ajena

compilado *v.* partes de libros reunidos en una sola obra, forma del verbo *compilar*

comprensión *s.* asimilación o entendimiento de algo

obligatorio(a) *adj.* que tiene que ser cumplido, obedecido

concebido(a) *adj.* idea o proyecto creada o imaginada

concepts (KON septs) *n.* ideas; organized thoughts **(p. 976)**

conclusive (kun KLOO siv) *adj.* definite; proven without doubt **(p. 327)**

confesses (kun FES ses) *v.* tells a truth that one rarely talks about **(p. 623)**

consciousness (KAWN shus nes) *n.* the state of being fully awake or alert **(p. 251)**

consequences (KAWN suh kwen suz) *n.* results or effects **(p. 1093)**

contamination (kun tam uh NAY shun) *n.* pollution **(p. 936)**

controversial (kawn truh VUR see ul) *adj.* causing disagreement **(p. 988)**

conversation (kahn ver SAY shun) *n.* a talk between people **(p. 584)**

convictions (kun VIK shunz) *n.* strong beliefs or values **(p. 988)**

coordinate (koh OR duh nayt) *v.* to make (things) work together smoothly **(p. 103)**

corresponded (kor uh SPON did) *v.* wrote letters to one another **(p. 109)**

corruption (kuh RUP shun) *n.* extreme immorality or wickedness **(p. 947)**

cowered (KOW erd) *v.* moved away in fear **(p. 367)**

crucial (KROO shul) *adj.* extremely important **(p. 1107)**

D

deaden (DEH dun) *v.* to make weak or dull **(p. 251)**

decades (DEK aydz) *n.* periods of ten years **(p. 306)**

deferred (dih FURD) *adj.* set aside or put off until a later time **(p. 473)**

defiance (dih FY unts) *n.* the act of challenging authority **(p. 191)**

descendants (duh SEN dunts) *n.* blood relatives of an earlier generation **(p. 611)**

descent (dih SENT) *n.* lineage; ancestry **(p. 312)**

despair (dih SPAIR) *n.* a complete loss of hope **(p. 493)**

conceptos *s.* idea o representación de algo, pensamiento expresado en palabras

concluyente *adj.* que no se puede rebatir; no admite duda o discusión

confiesa *v.* expresar voluntariamente verdades que en el fondo no se quieren contar; forma del verbo *confesar*

conocimiento *s.* cada uno de los sentidos del ser humano en la medida en que están activos

consecuencias *s.* efecto; hecho o acontecimiento que resulta de otro

contaminación *s.* alteración dañina del estado puro y normal de algo

controvertido(a) *adj.* polémico, que provoca controversia o discusión dando lugar a opiniones contrapuestas

conversación *s.* comunicación mediante palabras

convicción *s.* ideas, creencias u opiniones firmes

coordinar *v.* organizar medios y esfuerzos para una acción común

mantenían correspondencia *frase v.* se escribían cartas entre sí, forma de la frase verbal *mantener correspondencia*

corrupción *s.* perversión o vicio que estropea la moral

(se) acobardó *v.* con miedo, forma del verbo *acobardar(se)*

crucial *adj.* momento o punto decisivo o importante en el desarrollo de algo

calmará *v.* aliviar o disminuir la intensidad de algo, forma del verbo *calmar*

décadas *s.* períodos de diez años, decenas del siglo

diferido(a) *adj.* aplazado, dejado para más tarde

desafío *s.* incitación a la lucha, rivalidad

descendientes *s.* generaciones sucesivas por línea directa de personas dentro de una familia

ascendencia *s.* conjunto de antepasado de una persona, ancestros

desesperación *s.* pérdida total de la esperanza

destiny (DES tuh nee) *n.* a person's fate or fortune (p. 175)

destitute (DES tuh toot) *adj.* completely without money or possessions (p. 853)

detract (dih TRAKT) *v.* to take away from; reduce the value of (p. 1098)

disclose (dis KLOHZ) *v.* to make known; reveal (p. 227)

discriminates (dih SKRIM uh nayts) *v.* treats unfairly (p. 1160)

disgruntled (dis GRUNT uld) *adj.* not pleased; in a bad humor (p. 799)

dismal (DIZ mul) *adj.* gloomy or depressing (p. 893)

distinguished (dis TIN gwisht) *adj.* well-known for excellence and honor (p. 201)

distracted (dih STRAK tid) *adj.* losing attention easily (p. 261)

distribution (dis truh BYOO shun) *n.* division into shares or portions (p. 936)

dock (dok) *n.* a platform where boats land at the edge of a body of water (p. 479)

dormitory (DOR mi tor ee) *n.* a building with rooms for people to sleep in (p. 70)

downcast (DOWN kast) *adj.* sad; depressed (p. 835)

dramatic (druh MA tik) *adj.* showing strong emotion (p. 266)

dreaded (DRED ud) *v.* feared greatly (p. 886)

dry (dry) *adj.* dull or boring; not interesting (p. 1009)

E

eclipsed (ee KLIPSD) *v.* made to seem unimportant (p. 127)

egging (EHG ing) *adj.* urging; encouraging to take action (p. 599)

elegant (EH lih gunt) *adj.* beautiful and tasteful (p. 198)

elite (eh LEET) *adj.* the best, most talented (p. 302)

eloquence (EL uh kwunts) *n.* the ability to speak expressively (p. 226)

emerge (EE murj) *v.* to come out into view (p. 191)

eminent (IH muh nint) *adj.* of outstanding rank or quality (p. 676)

emit (ee MIT) *v.* to give off (p. 1023)

endure (en DUR) *v.* to carry on; survive; last (p. 1098)

destino *s.* fortuna, fin, punto de llegada

indigente *adj.* persona que no tiene los medios para subsistir

detraerá *v.* restarle o reducirle valor, forma del verbo *detraer*

revelar *v.* descubrir o anunciar algo ignorado o secreto

discrimina *v.* selecciona excluyendo, con prejuicio, forma del verbo *discriminar*

disgustado(a) *adj.* incomodado, descontento con algo o alguien

lúgubre *adj.* deprimente, melancólico, sombrío

distinguido(a) *adj.* ilustre, que sobresale por alguna cualidad, noble

distraído(a) *adj.* que no se da cuenta de lo que dice o hace, que no presta atención

distribución *s.* reparto entre varios asignando a cada uno una parte

muelle *s.* construcción realizada junto al agua que facilita el embarque y desembarque de embarcaciones

dormitorio *s.* lugar destinado para dormir

abatido(a) *adj.* persona desanimada, deprimida

dramático(a) *adj.* que conmueve o interesa con intensidad

temido *v.* tenerle pavor o miedo, forma del verbo *temer*

árido(a) *adj.* que no es ameno, poco interesante

eclipsó *v.* oscureció, le quitó notoriedad; forma del verbo *eclipsar*

incitar *v.* convencer o estimular a alguien para que haga algo

elegante *adj.* que tiene gracia, distinción y nobleza

elitista *adj.* que pertenece a una minoría selecta destacada en un campo

elocuencia *s.* eficacia para expresarse con viveza, persuasión y de manera conmovedora

emerger *v.* salir a la superficie, brotar

eminente *adj.* que sobresale o destaca por algún mérito

emitir *v.* arrojar, expulsar, producir, echar hacia fuera

perdurar *v.* durar mucho en un mismo estado y por un tiempo

ethical (ETH uh kul) *adj.* having to do with morals and standards of acceptable behavior **(p. 933)**

evaluate (ih VAL yoo ayt) *v.* form an opinion or make a judgment **(p. 468)**

eventually (ih VEN choo uh lee) *adj.* happening at last; in the end **(p. 1091)**

exile (EG zyl) *n.* the state of living away from one's home country **(p. 172)**

exotic (ig ZAW tik) *adj.* strangely beautiful and foreign **(p. 624)**

expectations (ek spek TAY shunz) *n.* outcomes considered likely to happen **(p. 301)**

expeditions (ek spuh DISH unz) *n.* groups that take trips for specific purposes **(p. 35)**

extinguished (ek STING wisht) *adj.* put out **(p. 520)**

F

factor (FAK tur) *n.* something that produces or contributes to a certain result **(p. 574)**

famished (FAM ishd) *adj.* extremely hungry **(p. 900)**

feat (FEET) *n.* difficult task; something that is very hard to do **(p. 32)**

fester (FES tur) *v.* to become infected; to decay **(p. 473)**

financial (fy NAN chul) *adj.* concerning money **(p. 261)**

flourishing (FLUR ish ing) *v.* thriving; doing extremely well **(p. 680)**

foreboding (for BOH ding) *n.* a feeling that something bad has happened or will happen **(p. 804)**

fortune (FOR chun) *n.* luck; riches **(p. 639)**

foundered (FOWN durd) *v.* broke down; collapsed **(p. 1012)**

furnished (FUR nisht) *v.* supplied; given **(p. 270)**

G

glistened (GLI suhnd) *v.* shone brightly **(p. 527)**

gory (GOR ee) *adj.* bloody; involving a lot of bloodshed **(p. 326)**

ético(a) *adj.* de acuerdo a las normas de conducta y de moral

evaluar *v.* estimar el valor de algo

finalmente *adv.* que sucede de último, al terminar, al fin y al cabo

exilio *s.* estado en el que la persona vive fuera de su patria

exótico(a) *adj.* extraño, desconocido, poco común

expectativas *s.* tener la esperanza, ante la posibilidad razonable, de que algo suceda

expediciones *s.* conjunto de personas que realizan un viaje o excursión con un fin determinado

extinguido(a) *adj.* se refiere a la llama o fuego cuando está apagado

factor *s.* elemento que produce o afecta a un estado determinado

hambriento(a) *adj.* que tiene mucha necesidad y ganas de comer

proeza *s.* hazaña o acción difícil y valerosa

(se) supure *v.* produce y echa pus, generalmente esto se debe a una infección; forma del verbo *supurar*

financiero(a) *adj.* concerniente a la banca o los negocios mercantiles, relativo al dinero

floreciendo *v.* prosperando, que hecha flor; forma del verbo *florecer*

presentimiento *s.* intuir un suceso del futuro gracias a señales o indicios

fortuna *s.* buena suerte, circunstancia o causa a la que se le atribuye un suceso bueno o malo

colapsó *v.* se derrumbó, fracasó; forma del verbo *colapsar*

abasteció *v.* proveer o suministrar alimentos u otras cosas necesarias; forma del verbo *abastecer*

refulgían *v.* brillaban intensamente, forma del verbo *refulgir*

sangriento(a) *adj.* teñido de sangre, manchado de sangre

grandeur (GRAN jur) *n.* the state of being large and impressive; greatness **(p. 1121)**

grave (grayv) *adj.* very serious; likely to produce harm or danger **(p. 882)**

grim (grim) *adj.* gloomy; somber **(p. 504)**

grimacing (GRIM us ing) *adj.* making a face that shows discomfort or disgust **(p. 273)**

grandeza *s.* de gran tamaño, majestad y poder

grave *adj.* muy enfermo, de mucha importancia y seriedad

ceñudo(a) *adj.* que arruga las cejas (el ceño) en señal de enfado

haciendo muecas *frase verbal.* gesticulando o contorsionando el rostro de manera burlesca; forma de la frase verbal, *hacer muecas*

H

hardships (HARD ships) *n.* things that cause pain or suffering; misfortunes **(p. 625)**

harmonious (har MOH nee us) *adj.* getting along well together; friendly **(p. 960)**

hilarious (hih LAR ee us) *adj.* very funny **(p. 250)**

hobbled (HAW buld) *v.* walked with difficulty; limped **(p. 510)**

hovering (HUV ur ing) *adj.* remaining in or near one place in the air **(p. 1122)**

humiliated (hyoo MIL ee ayt ud) *adj.* embarrassed; ashamed **(p. 110)**

hygiene (HY jeen) *n.* cleanliness; habits that lead to good health **(p. 655)**

hypocritical (hip uh KRIT i kul) *adj.* fake; pretending to be something one isn't **(p. 51)**

adversidades *s.* infortunios, situaciones desgraciadas o desfavorables

armonioso(a) *adj.* que tiene correspondencia entre sus parte

divertidísimo(a) *adj.* que inspira muchísimas ganas de reír

cojeó *v.* caminó con dificultad, forma del verbo *cojear*

planeando *v.* volando con las alas extendidas e inmóviles, suspendido en el aire

humillado(a) *adj.* con el orgullo abatido y el amor propio herido, cabizbajo

higiene *s.* cuidado de la salud a través de la limpieza y el aseo

hipócrita *adj.* que finge cualidades o sentimientos

I

identify (eye DEN tuh fy) *v.* find; recognize **(p. 322)**

illiterate (ih LIT uh rit) *adj.* unable to read or write; uneducated **(p. 949)**

illustrates (IL us trayts) *v.* shows clearly through examples **(p. 457)**

immersed (ih MURSD) *v.* completely occupied mentally **(p. 1165)**

implied (im PLYD) *adj.* expressed indirectly; suggested rather than said plainly **(p. 256)**

incompetence (in KAWMP uh tunts) *n.* lack of ability or skill **(p. 212)**

incongruous (in KONG groo us) *adj.* not in agreement **(p. 1164)**

incurable (in KYOOR uh bul) *adj.* not likely to be changed or corrected **(p. 963)**

identificar *v.* reconocer si lo buscado ha sido encontrado o no

analfabeto(a) *adj.* persona que no sabe leer ni escribir, que no tiene cultura

ilustrar *v.* aclarar un tema explicando con palabras, imágenes, ejemplos o cualquier otro modo

ensimismado(a) *v.* inmerso, abstraído, concentrado en algo, forma del verbo *ensimismar*

tácito(a) *adj.* que se sobrentiende, se infiere; algo que no está expresado porque se puede deducir

incompetencia *s.* falta de aptitud, de capacidad para hacer algo

incongruente *adj.* falta de correspondencia, de relación y lógica, carente de sentido

incurable *adj.* que no se puede sanar o corregir, no tiene remedio

indelible (in DEL ih bul) *adj.* impossible to erase, remove, or blot out **(p. 391)**

indispensable (in duh SPEN suh bul) *adj.* absolutely necessary **(p. 962)**

indomitable (in DAH mih tuh bul) *adj.* unable to be conquered or overcome **(p. 527)**

induce (in DOOS) *v.* convince to do something; influence **(p. 209)**

inert (in URT) *adj.* without power to move or act; lifeless **(p. 1013)**

inevitable (in EV uh tuh bul) *adj.* sure to happen; unavoidable **(p. 1093)**

inferring (in FUR ing) *n.* making an "educated guess" **(p. 182)**

instinctively (in STINK tiv lee) *adj.* resulting from or caused by a natural response **(p. 415)**

integrated (IN tih grayt id) *v.* ended the separation of racial and ethnic groups **(p. 971)**

intercede (in tur SEED) *v.* to help settle differences between others **(p. 410)**

interpret (in TUR prit) *v.* to find the meaning of events or ideas **(p. 482)**

intimate (IN tuh mit) *adj.* very close and personal; private **(p. 809)**

intuition (in too ISH un) *n.* the ability to know things without having to reason them out **(p. 813)**

invariably (in VAYR ee ub lee) *adv.* constantly; always **(p. 367)**

J

jubilation (joo buh LAY shun) *n.* great joy and excitement **(p. 780)**

L

liberated (LIB uh ray tid) *adj.* released; freed **(p. 833)**

lingers (LING urz) *v.* waits or is slow in leaving **(p. 189)**

literally (LIT ur uh lee) *adv.* actually; exactly **(p. 1076)**

lurching (LURCH ing) *adj.* rolling or swaying in a jerky motion **(p. 199)**

indeleble *adj.* que no se puede borrar o remover

indispensable *adj.* absolutamente imprescindible y necesario

indomable *adj.* que no se deja amansar, someter o dominar

inducir *v.* provocar, persuadir de hacer algo

inerte *adj.* sin vida, inactivo, sin capacidad de reacción

inevitable *adj.* que no puede impedirse, imposible de apartar

inferencia *s.* algo que se deduce, que se concluye a través del razonamiento

instintivamente *adj.* que se da través del sentimiento y el impulso, que no es obra de le reflexión o el juicio

integrado(a) *v.* alguien o algo pasó a formar parte de un todo; forma del verbo *integrar*

interceder *v.* mediar en favor de alguien para ayudarlo

interpretar *v.* explicar el sentido o significado de algo

íntimo(a) *adj.* los interior, profundo o reservado

intuición *s.* facultad de comprender o conocer algo rápidamente y sin necesidad de razonarlo

invariablemente *adv.* que no sufre variación; constante; siempre el mismo

júbilo *s.* viva alegría expresada

liberado(a) *adj.* eximido, puesto en libertad, sin ataduras

permanece *v.* quedarse o estar en un mismo sitio por un tiempo; forma del verbo *permanecer*

literalmente *adv.* conforme al sentido pleno de la palabra que lo acompaña; exactamente

sacudidas *s.* movimientos bruscos, violentos

M

majority (muh JOR ih tee) *n.* more than half; the greater part **(p. 575)**

makeshift (MAYK shift) *adj.* used in place of the normal or proper thing **(p. 766)**

maneuvers (muh NOO vurs) *n.* clever or skillful moves or actions **(p. 301)**

means (meenz) *n.* methods useful for achieving a particular purpose or goal; resources **(p. 1078)**

mesh (mesh) *n.* the web-like pattern of fibers in woven or knitted items **(p. 453)**

meticulous (mih TIK yuh lus) *adj.* careful about small details **(p. 755)**

migrated (MY gray tud) *v.* moved from one place to another **(p. 391)**

mimicked (MIH mikt) *v.* copied; imitated **(p. 589)**

minor (MY nur) *adj.* of little importance; not serious **(p. 511)**

minority (my NOR uh tee) *n.* the smaller group **(p. 18)**

modified (MOD i fyd) *v.* changed; altered **(p. 327)**

monumental (mon yuh MEN tul) *adj.* great and meaningful **(p. 1107)**

mournful (MORN ful) *adj.* filled with sadness or grief **(p. 505)**

municipal (myoo NIS uh pul) *adj.* having to do with a city or town or its government **(p. 935)**

mutilated (MYOO tih lay tid) *v.* damaged in a way that cannot be repaired **(p. 68)**

N

needle (NEE duhl) *v.* cause to take action by repeated stinging comments **(p. 601)**

neglected (nuh GLEK tid) *adj.* given little attention or respect **(p. 458)**

nomination (nah mih NAY shun) *n.* the act of proposing a candidate for an office or honor **(p. 487)**

novelty (NAW vul tee) *n.* anything new, strange, or unusual **(p. 1114)**

nutritious (noo TRIH shus) *adj.* containing or giving nourishment **(p. 1003)**

mayoría *s.* parte mayor, más grande o de más número de un todo

improvisado(a) *adj.* algo hecho de pronto y con los medios que se dispone en el momento

maniobra *s.* operación hecha con habilidad o astucia

medios *s.* elementos de los que se vale para alcanzar un fin

malla *s.* tejido en el que cuerdas e hilos se cruzan y anudan asemejando una red

meticuloso(a) *adj.* que tiene cuidado y detalle

migró *v.* desplazarse de un sitio de residencia a otro, forma del verbo *migrar*

imitó *v.* copió o hizo algo en semejanza a otra persona o cosa, forma del verbo *imitar*

menor *adj.* inferior o de menor importancia; pequeño

minoría *s.* parte menor, más pequeña o de menor número de un todo

modificado(a) *v.* que está transformado o cambiado; forma del verbo *modificar*

monumental *adj.* grande, espectacular

afligido(a) *adj.* con tristeza, apesadumbrado

municipal *adj.* que pertenece a un mismo término jurisdiccional, regido por el ayuntamiento o municipio; de carácter gubernamental

mutilado(a) *v.* cortado, cercenado; forma del verbo *mutilar*

provocará *v.* incitar, estimular o irritar a alguien con comentarios; forma del verbo *provocar*

descuidado(a) *adj.* desatendido, que no ha sido atendido con la diligencia que requería

nominación *s.* propuesta o selección para la obtención de un honor

novedad *s.* algo nuevo, reciente, nunca antes visto

nutritivo(a) *adj.* que aumenta la sustancia o la fuerza

O

oblivious (uh BLIV ee us) *adj.* not aware (p. 21)

obnoxious (ub NOCK shus) *adj.* very disagreeable or offensive (p. 574)

obscure (ub SKYOOR) *v.* to hide (p. 371)

observant (ub ZUR vunt) *adj.* quick to notice or observe; alert; watchful (p. 884)

offensive (uh FEN siv) *adj.* unpleasant or disagreeable, causing anger (p. 460)

oppressed (uh PRESD) *adj.* held down; held back; kept from making progress (p. 56)

optimist (AWP tuh mist) *n.* a person who has a positive or cheerful outlook (p. 963)

overwhelmed (oh vur WELMD) *adj.* overpowered in thought or feeling; completely covered or flooded (p. 1077)

P

pandemonium (pan duh MOH nee um) *n.* wild disorder and uproar (p. 832)

passively (PASS iv lee) *adv.* not actively (p. 981)

perceives (pur SEEVZ) *v.* understands something in a particular way (p. 333)

perish (PAIR ish) *v.* to become ruined or destroyed; die (p. 1099)

perpetrated (PUR pih tray tid) *v.* did something (p. 416)

perpetual (per PEH choo ul) *adj.* continuing forever (p. 981)

persecution (pur suh KYOO shun) *n.* the condition of being caused to suffer cruelty because of personal beliefs (p. 172)

perseverance (puhr suh VEER ens) *n.* persistent determination (p. 526)

persistence (pur SIS tuntz) *n.* act of refusing to give up (p. 947)

petty (PEH tee) *adj.* having or displaying a mean, narrow-minded attitude (p. 460)

phase (fayz) *n.* step in the development of a person or thing (p. 853)

pivoted (PIH vuh tid) *v.* turned around sharply (p. 902)

poise (poyz) *n.* a calm, relaxed, and self-controlled manner (p. 820)

ajeno(a) *adj.* que desconoce un asunto; carente de información

odioso(a) *adj.* desagradable, antipático

oscurecer *v.* esconder, ocultar

observador(a) *adj.* que se fija en el detalle, que mira cuidadosamente

ofensivo(a) *adj.* que molesta y falta al respeto

oprimido(a) *adj.* sometido a la tiranía y humillación

optimista *s.* que tiende a juzgar las cosas, personas y situaciones de manera favorable

abrumado(a) *adj.* inundado con una sensación

pandemónium *s.* lugar ruidoso y con mucha confusión

pasivamente *adv.* de manera inactiva, que deja transcurrir

percibe *v.* comprender o conocer algo a través de los sentidos, forma del verbo *percibir*

perecer *v.* fallecer, sufrir un gran daño, dejar de ser

perpetrado *v.* que cometió una falta grave o delito; formal del verbo *perpetrar*

perpetuo(a) *adj.* que dura para siempre

persecución *s.* acción de perseguir a una persona o grupo y castigarlos por sus ideologías

perseverancia *s.* constancia en la ejecución de propósitos y resoluciones

persistencia *s.* firmeza, constancia e insistencia

mezquino(a) *adj.* miserable, despreciable, ruin

fase *s.* cada uno de los estados sucesivos de un proceso en desarrollo o evolución

giró *v.* dar vuelta sobre un mismo eje, forma del verbo *girar*

aplomo *s.* circunspección, que muestra serenidad, seguridad

portray (por TREY) *v.* to show or represent someone or something **(p. 327)**

retratar *v.* describir con cierta fidelidad

precautions (pruh KAW shunz) *n.* actions taken to prevent difficulty before it happens **(p. 884)**

precauciones *s.* cautela, medida que se toma para evitar o prevenir inconvenientes

predicting (pree DIKT ing) *n.* using clues to guess what will happen **(p. 204)**

predicción *s.* anuncio de algo que va a suceder en el futuro

premature (pree muh CHUR) *adj.* early; before the right time **(p. 57)**

prematuro(a) *adj.* que se da antes de tiempo

prevailed (prih VAYLD) *v.* conquered; won; overcame **(p. 1106)**

prevaleció *v.* sobresalió, venció sobre los demás, superioridad y ventaja; forma del verbo *prevalecer*

prior (PRY er) *adj.* earlier; coming before **(p. 62)**

previo(a) *adj.* anterior; que viene primero

procedure (pro SEE jur) *n.* a series of steps taken to do something **(p. 124)**

procedimiento *s.* método, sistema, forma de ejecutar algo

procession (proh SEH shun) *n.* a group of individuals walking forward together in a ceremony **(p. 197)**

procesión *s.* grupo de personas que caminan de manera solemne y ordenada

promoter (pruh MOH tur) *n.* a person who organizes and pays the costs of a sporting event **(p. 271)**

promotor(a) *s.* persona que gestiona el logro de algo a través del impulso y la promoción

prone (prohn) *adj.* likely to act or be a certain way **(p. 78)**

propenso(a) *adj.* con tendencia, afición o inclinación hacia algo

proposition (prawp uh ZIH shun) *n.* a plan or proposal **(p. 1098)**

proposición *s.* idea que se expresa o manifiesta para lograr un fin

proprietor (pruh PRY uh tur) *n.* a person or firm that owns a property or a business **(p. 1145)**

propietario(a) *s.* dueño, titular de algo; persona con derecho de propiedad sobre algo

prospect (PRAH spekt) *n.* a mental picture of something to come **(p. 250)**

perspectiva *s.* idea o posibilidad de algo

publicized (PUB lih syzd) *v.* made the public aware of something **(p. 252)**

publicado(a) *v.* difundir, anunciar, dar a conocer una información; forma del verbo *publicar*

Q

quavered (KWAY verd) *v.* spoke in a shaky or trembling voice **(p. 211)**

dijo con voz trémula *frase v.* habló con voz temblorosa, forma de la frase verbal *decir con voz trémula*

quench (kwench) *v.* to satisfy a need **(p. 244)**

saciar *v.* satisfacer un deseo o necesidad

R

racial (RAY shuhl) *adj.* characteristic of a race or an ethnic or cultural group **(p. 948)**

racial *adj.* que se relaciona o pertenece la raza, grupo étnico

rage (rayj) *n.* a feeling of great anger or fury **(p. 493)**

cólera *s.* ira, enojo exaltado y violento

rapture (RAP chur) *n.* a feeling of great joy **(p. 1124)**

éxtasis *s.* arrebatamiento, estado de extremo placer

rash (rash) *adj.* reckless; done without thought or concern **(p. 243)**

precipitado(a) *adj.* que está hecho con mucha prisa y sin haberlo reflexionado

rations (RASH unz) *n.* portions of needed items **(p. 521)**

raciones *s.* parte, porción o cantidad de algo

rave (rayv) *v.* to speak about very favorably or with great enthusiasm **(p. 1146)**

elogiar *v.* ensalzar, hablar sobre algo o alguien de manera favorable

recedes (ree SEEDS) *v.*, moves or pulls back **(p. 641)**

recollections (rek uh LEK shuns) *n.* memories **(p. 125)**

recurring (rih KUR ing) *adj.* happening or coming back again; repeating **(p. 1068)**

refuse (REF yooz) *n.* trash; rubbish **(p. 1071)**

relentlessly (ruh LENT lis lee) *adv.* without stopping; without giving up **(p. 21)**

relevant (REH luh vunt) *adj.* important to the subject at hand; significant; pertinent **(p. 604)**

relish (REL ish) *n.* enjoyment or delight **(p. 109)**

reluctantly (ree LUK tunt lee) *adv.* against one's will **(p. 213)**

replica (REP lih kuh) *n.* a faithful copy **(p. 1123)**

residences (REZ uh den suz) *n.* places where one lives **(p. 79)**

resilient (rih ZIL yunt) *adj.* able to recover from or adjust easily to misfortune or change **(p. 850)**

resolve (rih ZAWLV) *v.* to decide firmly **(p. 1099)**

restrictions (ree STRIK shunz) *n.* limits to things one can and can't do **(p. 332)**

retribution (re trih BYOO shun) *n.* punishment for crimes **(p. 668)**

reveal (rih VEEL) *v.* show **(p. 662)**

ripened (RYPE und) *v.* became ready to eat **(p. 313)**

roamed (rohmd) *v.* wandered; went from place to place without purpose or direction **(p. 479)**

S

sacred (SAY krid) *adj.* holy; having to do with religion **(p. 615)**

salvaged (SAL vujd) *v.* saved from ruin; rescued **(p. 641)**

sauntered (SAWN turd) *v.* walked leisurely **(p. 682)**

scorned (skornd) *adj.* looked down upon by someone **(p. 164)**

seasoned (SEE zund) *adj.* made fit by experience; adjusted to (something) because of experience **(p. 1125)**

self-conscious (self KAWN shus) *adj.* too aware of one's own appearance and actions **(p. 737)**

(se) aleja *v.* se distancia, se pone lejos; forma del verbo *alejar*

recuerdos *s.* memoria o presencia en la mente que se tiene de algo que ya pasó

recurrente *adj.* que vuelve a pasar o aparecer de manera repetitiva

desechos *s.* residuo, basura, lo que queda de algo que ya fue usado o utilizado

implacablemente *adv.* de manera imposible de mitigar, apaciguar o suavizar

relevante *adj.* destacado, sobresaliente; significativo; pertinente

deleite *s.* con entusiasmo, con gusto

(a) regañadientes *adv.* de mala gana

réplica *s.* copia exacta del original

residencias *s.* lugar donde se vive; vivienda

resistente *adj.* que es capaz de pervivir y mantenerse sin ceder

resolver *v.* tomar una determinación

restricción(ones) *s.* reducción de los límites de algo

castigo *s.* pena impuesta por los delitos cometidos

revelar *v.* dar a conocer

maduraron *v.* alcanzaron el punto de desarrollo; forma del verbo *madurar*

deambuló *v.* recorrió; que anduvo de un lugar a otro sin rumbo fijo; forma del verbo *deambular*

sagrado(a) *adj.* santo; relativo a la religión

rescatamos *v.* salvamos de un peligro; recuperamos; forma del verbo *rescatar*

anduvo (con aire despreocupado) *frase v.* entró o salió como si estuviera relajado; forma del verbo *andar*

desdeñado(a) *adj.* persona que es despreciada por otra

avezado(a) *adj.* experimentado; acostumbrado o habituado a algo

acomplejado(a) *adj.* que siente inhibición por tener demasiada conciencia de su aspecto físico y sus actos

self-esteem (self es TEEM) *n.* a confidence and satisfaction in oneself **(p. 20)**

autoestima *s.* consideración y aprecio que se siente por uno mismo

sequence (SEE kwents) *n.* a regular order or arrangement in time, space, or importance **(p. 99)**

secuencia *s.* serie o sucesión ordenada de elementos que están relacionados entre sí

severity (sub VAIR ih tee) *n.* a state of being very dangerous or harmful **(p. 510)**

gravedad *s.* seriedad o importancia de algo, esp. enfermedad

sheepishly (SHEEP ish lee) *adv.* with embarrassment **(p. 266)**

tímidamente *adv.* con vergüenza

siblings (SIB lingz) *n.* brothers and sisters **(p. 1091)**

hermanos *s. pl.* hermanos y hermanas

significant *adj.* having meaning; having much importance **(p. 558)**

significativo(a) *adj.* que da a entender algo; que tiene mucho valor

similar (SIM uh lur): *adj.* alike, but not exactly the same **(p. 238)**

similar *adj.* parecido o semejante, pero no igual

simultaneously (sy mul TAYN ee us lee) *adv.* at the same time **(p. 671)**

simultáneamente *adv.* al mismo tiempo

skeptically (SKEP tik uh lee) *adv.* with doubt **(p. 983)**

(con) escepticismo *frase adv.* dudosamente

snarled (snarld) *v.* made tangled or knotted **(p. 166)**

enredó *v.* enmarañó o anudó; forma del verbo *enredar*

somber (SAWM bur) *adj.* dark and gloomy **(p. 187)**

sombrío(a) *adj.* oscuro y melancólico

stable (STAY bul) *adj.* firm and steady; long-lasting **(p. 864)**

estable *adj.* firme y constante; duradero

stately (STAYT lee) *adj.* grand; impressive; dignified **(p. 608)**

señorial *adj.* majestuoso; grandioso; digno

stealthy (STEL thee) *adj.* slow and secretive to avoid being seen or heard **(p. 187)**

furtivo(a) *adj.* hecho en secreto o a hurtadillas para no ser escuchado

sterile (STAIR ul) *adj.* free from germs; very clean **(p. 512)**

estéril *adj.* libre de gérmenes; muy limpio

stifled (STY fuld) *v.* held back; muffled **(p. 48)**

apagado(a) *adj.* contenido; sordo

stimulates (STIM yuh layts) *v.* makes active or more active **(p. 49)**

estimula *v.* activa o incita; forma del verbo *estimular*

stimulus (STIM yoo luss) *n.* something that causes a response **(p. 371)**

estímulo *s.* agente que provoca una reacción o respuesta

strain (strayn) *v.* stretch to the limit; overwork **(p. 981)**

esforzar *v.* someter a demasiada presión física o moral; trabajar demasiado

strategy (STRA tuh gee) *n.* a careful method or plan **(p. 43)**

estrategia *s.* planificación o técnica para obtener algo

structure (STRUK chur) *n.* the arrangement or organization of parts in a body or system **(p. 336)**

estructura *s.* distribución u orden de las partes de un cuerpo o cosa

surrender (suh REN dur) *v.* to give up ownership or control **(p. 487)**

renunciar *v.* dejar o abandonar algo

sustenance (SUS tuh nuns) *n.* food, support, and other necessities of life **(p. 773)**

sustento *s.* alimento, apoyo y demás necesidades esenciales

swaggered (SWAG urd) *v.* walked boldly or showed off **(p. 568)**

pavoneó *v.* caminó con aire arrogante o haciendo ostentación; forma del verbo *pavonear*

syndrome (SIN drohm) *n.* a group of symptoms that, together, point to a certain disease **(p. 1008)**

síndrome *s.* conjunto de síntomas que definen una enfermedad

T

tangible (TAN juh bull) *adj.* able to be seen, touched, or felt **(p. 364)**

taunts (tawnts) *n.* hurtful or mocking remarks **(p. 968)**

texts (tekts) *n.* the words and forms of written or printed works **(p. 14)**

toiled (toyld) *v.* worked hard **(p. 1155)**

tolerance (TOL ur uns) *n.* the ability to recognize and respect different beliefs **(p. 410)**

translates (TRANZ laytz) *v.* changes successfully into another form or language **(p. 658)**

treacherous (TRECH ur us) *adj.* dangerous; not reliable; not trustworthy **(p. 66)**

trekked (TREKD) *v.* walked or hiked a long distance **(p. 35)**

tribute (TRIB yoot) *n.* an action or gift that shows respect, admiration, or thanks **(p. 862)**

trivial (TRIV ee uhl) *adj.* of very little value or importance **(p. 1163)**

U

ultimatum (ul tuh MAY tum) *n.* a final demand that, if unmet, carries harsh penalties **(p. 896)**

uncertainty (un SUR tun tee) *n.* the state of being unsure or not knowing **(p. 783)**

unfulfilling (un ful FIL ing) *adj.* not satisfying **(p. 850)**

unison (YOO nih sun) *n.* at the same time; simultaneously **(p. 590)**

V

valid (VAL id) *adj.* based on correct information; logical; sound **(p. 956)**

valor (VAL or) *n.* courage **(p. 407)**

veered (veerd) *v.* suddenly changed direction **(p. 242)**

victor (VIK tor) *n.* winner; one who defeats an opponent **(p. 505)**

vile (vyl) *adj.* very bad; extremely unpleasant **(p. 742)**

violating (VY uh lay ting) *v.* breaking or disregarding a law **(p. 988)**

virtually (VUR choo uh lee) *adv.* nearly **(p. 983)**

visual (VIZH oo ul) *adj.* meant to be viewed or seen **(p. 98)**

void (voyd) *n.* empty space **(p. 22)**

---

tangible *adj.* que puede verse, tocarse o percibirse

pullas *s.* bromas o burlas hirientes

textos *s.* grupo de palabras forman un documento escrito

(se) afanó *v.* trabajó duro; forma del verbo *afanar(se)*

tolerancia *s.* respeto y consideración por las opiniones ajenas

(se) traduce *v.* se convierte o transforma en otra cosa; forma del verbo *traducir(se)*

traicionero(a) *adj.* peligroso; astuto; que no es confiable

caminaron *v.* recorrieron la distancia a pie o hicieron senderismo; forma del verbo *caminar*

tributo *s.* acción de reconocimiento como muestra de respeto, admiración o agradecimiento

trivial *adj.* de muy poco valor o importancia

ultimátum *s.* propuesta definitiva acompañada de una amenaza

incertidumbre *s.* falta de seguridad o certeza

insatisfecho(a) *adj.* que no está conforme

unísono *s.* al mismo tiempo; con el mismo sonido

válido(a) *adj.* que tiene valor porque es correcto; lógico; apropiado

valentía *s.* coraje

viró *v.* cambió de dirección; forma del verbo *virar*

vencedor(a) *s.* ganador; que derrota al oponente

repugnante *adj.* asqueroso; muy desagradable

violando *v.* quebrantando o desobedeciendo la ley; forma del verbo *violar*

prácticamente *adv.* casi

visual *adj.* que se puede ver

vacío *s.* sin contenido

vulnerable (VUL nur uh bul) *adj.* exposed to danger (p. 1030)

vulnerable *adj.* expuesto al peligro

W

wallow (WAH loh) *v.* to take selfish pleasure in comfort (p. 772)

regodear *v.* deleitarse y complacerse en un gusto

wavered (WAY vurd) *v.* became unsteady (p. 243)

tambaleó *v.* perdió el equilibrio; forma del verbo *tambalear*

withstand (with STAND) *v.* to resist the effect of; stand up against (p. 865)

soportar *v.* que soporta el efecto de algo; mantenerse sin ceder

wretched (RECH id) *adj.* very unfortunate or unhappy; terrible (p. 103)

espantoso(a) *adj.* desgraciado o desdichado; horrible

Y

yielding (YEEL ding) *adj.* giving way to force or pressure (p. 1148)

blando(a) *adj.* suave y tierno, que cede al tacto

INDEX OF SKILLS

Reading and Thinking

INDEX OF AUTHORS AND TITLES

INDEX OF ART AND ARTISTS

ACKNOWLEDGMENTS

Unit 1

Excerpt from *I Know Why the Caged Bird Sings* by Maya Angelou, copyright © 1969 and renewed 1997 by Maya Angelou. Used by permission of Random House, Inc.

"Ice" by Graham Salisbury. From *Going Where I'm Coming From: Memoirs of American Youth* edited by Anne Mazer.

Excerpt from *The Book of Rock Stars* by Kathleen Krull. Text copyright © 2003 by Kathleen Krull.

Excerpt from *Mother Jones: Fierce Fighter for Workers' Rights* by Judith Pinkerton Josephson. Copyright © 1997 by Judith Pinkerton Josephson.

From *How to Get a Job If You're a Teenager,* by Cindy Pervola and Debby Hobgood. Copyright © 1998 by Cindy Pervola and Debby Hobgood. Reprinted by permission of Highsmith Press.

Excerpt from *Young Person's Occupational Outlook Handbook.* Copyright © 2005 by JIST Publishing, Inc.

Reprinted with the permission of Simon & Schuster Books for Young Readers, an imprint of Simon & Schuster Children's Publishing Division, from *The Invisible Thread* by Yoshiko Uchida. Copyright © 1991 by Yoshiko Uchida.

Reprinted with the permission of Scribner, an imprint of Simon & Schuster Adult Publishing Group, from *A Gift of Laughter* by Allan Sherman. Copyright © 1965 by Allan Sherman

Excerpt from *Knots in My Yo-yo String: The Autobiography of a Kid* by Jerry Spinelli. Copyright © 1998 Jerry Spinelli.

"Knoxville, Tennessee" from *Black Feeling, Black Talk, Black Judgment* by Nikki Giovanni. Copyright © 1968, 1970 by Nikki Giovanni. Reprinted by permission of HarperCollins Publishers.

From *Dear Exile* by Hilary Liftin and Kate Montgomery, copyright © 1999 by Hilary Liftin and Kate Montgomery. Used by permission of Vintage Books, a division of Random House, Inc.

Unit 2

"Racing the Great Bear" from *Flying with the Eagle, Racing the Great Bear,* by Joseph Bruchac. Copyright © 1993 by Joseph Bruchac. Reprinted by permission of Barbara S. Kouts.

"The People Could Fly" from *The People Could Fly: American Black Folktales* by Virginia Hamilton, illustrated by Leo and Diane Dillon, copyright © 1985 by Virginia Hamilton. Illustrations copyright © 1985 by Leo and Diane Dillon. Used by permission of Alfred A. Knopf, an imprint of Random House Children's Books, a division of Random House, Inc.

"The Oxcart" from *Sword of the Samurai: Adventure Stories from Japan,* copyright © 1999 by Eric A. Kimmel, reprinted by permission of Harcourt, Inc.

"The Snake Chief" from *Tales from Africa* retold by Kathleen Arnott (OUP, 2000), copyright © Kathleen Arnott 1962, used by permission of Oxford University Press.

Excerpt from *Harriet Tubman: Conductor of the Underground Railroad* by Ann Petry. Reprinted by permission of Russell & Volkening as agents for the author. Copyright © 1955 by Ann Petry, renewed in 1983 by Ann Petry.

"A Dose of Medicine" from *Accidents May Happen* by Charlotte Foltz Jones, Illustrations by John O'Brien, copyright © 1996 by Charlotte Foltz Jones. Used by permission of Random House Children's Books, a division of Random House, Inc.

"Kamau's Finish" by Muthoni Muchemi, from *Memories of Sun: Stories of Africa and America*, copyright © 2004 by Jane Kurtz. Used by permission of HarperCollins Publishers.

"The Bunion Derby" by Leone Castell Anderson. Reprinted by permission of *Cricket* Magazine, May 2005, Vol. 32, No. 9, text © 2005 by Carus Publishing Company.

The Best Coon-and-Possum Dog by B. A. Botkin. From A TREASURY OF MISSISSIPPI RIVER FOLKLORE by B. A. Botkin. Copyright © 1955 by Ben A. Botkin.

Unit 3

From "Gymnasts in Pain: Out of Balance" by Scott M. Reid. *The Orange County Register,* December 19, 2004. Copyright © 2005 *The Orange County Register*. Reprinted by permission.

"In Response to Executive Order 9066," by Dwight Okita. Reprinted by permission of the author.

"The games kids play: are mature video games too violent for teens?" *Current Events*, February 7, 2003. Copyright © 2003 Weekly Reader Corporation. Reprinted by permission.

"Cruise Control," from *Teen People,* November 1, 2002.

"Flowers for Algernon," by Daniel Keyes. Copyright © 1959, 1987 by Daniel Keyes. Reprinted by permission of the author.

"Tattoos: Fad, Fashion, or Folly?" by Linda Bickerstaff, from *ODYSSEY's* May 2005 issue: *The Skin You're In*, copyright © 2005, Carus Publishing Company, published by Cobblestone Publishing, 30 Grove Street, Suite C, Peterborough, NH 03458. All rights reserved. Used by permission of the publisher.

"We Real Cool" by Gwendolyn Brooks. Reprinted by consent of Brooks Permissions.

"Market Economy" from *Circles on the Water* by Marge Piercy, copyright © 1982 by Marge Piercy. Used by permission of Alfred A. Knopf, a division of Random House, Inc.

"Wearing Hijab: Veil of Valor "by Emilia Askari from *Detroit Free Press.*

Prologue and excerpt from *Zoya's Story: An Afghan Woman's Struggle for Freedom,* by John Follain and Rita Cristofari. Copyright © 2002 by John Follain and Rita Cristofari. Reprinted by permission of HarperCollins Publishers.

"Potions from Poisons" by Andrea Dorfman. *Time*, January 15, 2001. © 2001 Time Inc. Reprinted by permission.

Unit 4

"Wishing Well" by Katherine Schmitt.

"Mother to Son" from *The Collected Poems of Langston Hughes* by Langston Hughes, copyright © 1994 by The Estate of Langston Hughes. Used by permission of Alfred A. Knopf, a division of Random House, Inc.

"Harlem" from *The Collected Poems of Langston Hughes* by Langston Hughes, copyright © 1994 by The Estate of Langston Hughes.

"Sittin' on the Dock of the Bay" by Otis Redding and Steve Cropper.

ACKNOWLEDGMENTS

Excerpt from 1988 Democratic National Convention Address by Jesse Jackson.

"Fable for When There's No Way Out," by May Swenson. Used by permission of the Literary Estate of May Swenson.

"Scorched! How to Handle Different Types of Burns" by Stephen Fraser. *Current Health*, March 2005. Copyright © 2005 Weekly Reader Corporation. Reprinted by permission.

From *Thura's Diary* by Thura Al-Windawi, translated by Robin Bray, copyright © 2004 by Thura al-Windawi. Used by permission of Viking Children's Books, A Division of Penguin Young Readers Group, A Member of Penguin Group (USA) Inc., 345 Hudson Street, New York, NY 10014. All rights reserved.

"Escaping" by Zdenko Slobodnik, from *Teen Ink: What Matters,* © 2003 The Young Authors Foundation, Inc. Reprinted by permission of Teen Ink.

David Ignatow, "Reading at Night" from *David Ignatow: Poems 1934–1969,* copyright © by David Ignatow and reprinted by permission of Wesleyan University Press.

"Wheelchairs That Kneel Down Like Elephants" Copyright © 1992 by Karen Fiser. Reprinted by permission of the author from *Words Like Fate and Pain.* Cambridge, MA: Zoland Books, 1992. Available from the author.

Unit 5

"Born Worker" from *Petty Crimes,* copyright © 1998 by Gary Soto, reprinted by permission of Harcourt, Inc.

"Cream Puff" by Linnea Due. From *Girls Got Game: Sports Stories and Poems* edited by Sue Macy.

"an african american" copyright © 1990 by Meri Nana-Ama Danquah. First published in *The Hollywood Review.* Reprinted by permission of Meri Nana-Ama Danquah.

"One Throw" by W. C. Heinz.

"The Medicine Bag" by Virginia Driving Hawk Sneve. Reprinted by permission of the author.

From "A Year of Living Bravely" by Emily Costello, published in *Scholastic Action,* October 11, 2004 by Scholastic Inc. Copyright © 2004 by Scholastic Inc. All rights reserved. Used by permission.

"The Fire Pond" by Michael Rosen. Reprinted by permission of the author.

Excerpt from *Savion!: My Life in Tap* by Savion Glover and Bruce Weber. © 2000 by Bruce Weber and Savion Glover/Maniactin, Inc.

"Thank You in Arabic" from *Going Where I'm Coming From* Copyright © 1995 by Naomi Shihab Nye. Reprinted by permission of the author.

"A Safe Space" by Joyce Hansen, from Lost and Found by M. Jerry Weiss and Helen S. Weiss, copyright © 2000 by the author and reprinted by permission of St. Martin's Press, LLC and Tom Doherty Associates, LLC.

Unit 6

The Diary of Anne Frank (Play) by Frances Goodrich and Albert Hackett, copyright © 1956 by Albert Hackett, Frances Goodrich Hackett and Otto Frank. Used by permission of Random House, Inc.

"Bouncing Back" by Jan Farrington. *Current Health*, March 2005. Copyright © 2005 Weekly Reader Corporation. Reprinted by permission.

"Another Mountain" from *The Last Poets: On a Mission: Selected Poems and a History of the Last Poets* by Abiodun Oyewole and Umar Bin Hassan with Kim Green. Copyright © Abiodun Oyewole and Umar Bin Hassan. Reprinted by permission of Henry Holt and Company, LLC.

"and sometimes I hear this song in my head" from *Catalyst.* Copyright © 1991 by Harriet Jacobs.

Reprinted with the permission of Simon & Schuster Books for Young Readers, an imprint of Simon & Schuster Children's Publishing Division, from Sky by Hanneke Ippisch. Copyright © 1996 Hanneke Ippisch.

"Welcome" by Ouida Sebestyen, copyright © 1984 by Ouida Sebestyen, from *Sixteen: Short Stories,* Donald R. Gallo, ed. Used by permission of Random House Children's Books, a division of Random House, Inc.

"Alone" from *Oh Pray My Wings Are Gonna Fit Me Well* by Maya Angelou. Copyright © 1975 by Maya Angelou.

"Flinn, on the Bus" from *19 Varieties of Gazelle: Poems of the Middle East.* Copyright © 1994, 1995, 1998, 2002 by Naomi Shihab Nye. Reprinted by permission of the author.

From "Will-o'-the-Wisp" used with permission of Sterling Publishing Co., Inc., NY, NY, from *Whodunit – You Decide!* by Hy Conrad, copyright © 1996 by Hy Conrad.

"After Agatha Christie" Copyright © 1975 by Linda Pastan, from *Carnival Evening: New and Selected Poems 1968–1998* by Linda Pastan. Used by permission of W.W. Norton & Company, Inc.

Unit 7

Excerpt from *2 Minutes a Day for a Greener Planet* by Marjorie Lamb. Copyright © 1990 by Marjorie Lamb.

From *The Measure of Our Success* by Marian Wright Edelman. Copyright © 1992 by Marian Wright Edelman. Reprinted by permission of Beacon press, Boston.

"All Together Now" by Barbara Jordan. Originally printed in *Sesame Street Parents,* July/August 1994.

From *Through My Eyes* by Ruby Bridges. Published by Scholastic Inc./ Scholastic Press. Copyright © 1999 by Ruby Bridges. Reprinted by permission. All rights reserved.

"The Trouble with Television" by Robert MacNeil. Copyright © 1984 by Robert MacNeil. Condensed from a speech delivered November 13, 1984, at the President's Leadership Forum, State University of New York at Purchase. Reprinted by permission of the author.

"Stop the Sun" copyright © 1986 by Gary Paulsen, from *Boys' Life,* January 1986.

"Teens Tackle Pollution in Their Communities" by Sara Steindorf. *Christian Science Monitor,* April 22, 2003. Copyright © 2003, The Christian Science Publishing Society. Reprinted by permission of Copyright Clearance Center.

"A Change in Climate" by Emily Sohn, from *Science News for Kids,* December 8, 2004. Reprinted with permission from *Science News for Kids,* copyright © 2004.

"The Treasure of Lemon Brown," reprinted by permission of Miriam Altshuler Literary Agency, on behalf of Walter Dean Myers. Copyright © 1983 by Walter Dean Myers.

"Baby Deer Do Need Your Help" by Nate Tripp. Reprinted by permission from the *New York State Conservationist,* April 1996.

"Take the Junk Out of Marketing Food to Kids" from *Detroit Free Press* (via *Knight-Ridder/Tribune News Service*), January 19, 2005. Copyright © 2005 by Detroit Free Press. Reprinted by permission

Unit 8

"I Have a Dream" reprinted by arrangement with the Estate of Martin Luther King Jr., c/o Writers House as agent for the proprietor New York, NY. Copyright

R82   Acknowledgments

1963 Martin Luther King Jr., copyright renewed 1991 Coretta Scott King.

"Volar: To Fly" from *The Latin Deli: Prose and Poetry* by Judith Ortiz Cofer. Reprinted by permission of The University of Georgia Press.

From *The Century for Young People* by Peter Jennings and Todd Brewster, copyright © 1999 by ABC. Used by permission of Doubleday, a division of Random House, Inc.

"8 lottery winners who lost their millions" by Ellen Goodstein, Bankrate.com. Copyright: Bankrate.com, N. Palm Beach, FL 2006. Reprinted by permission.

"I Chose Schooling" by Jacqueling Nwaiwu from *My Sisters' Voices,* edited by Iris Jacob. © 2002 by Iris Jacob. Reprinted by permission of Henry Holt and company, LLC.

"The Electric Summer" by Richard Peck, copyright © 1999 by Richard Peck, from *Time Capsule: Short Stories About Teenagers Throughout the Twentieth Century* by Donald R. Gallo. Used by permission of Dell Publishing, a division of Random House, Inc.

"I, Too" from *The Collected Poems of Langston Hughes* by Langston Hughes, copyright © 1994 by The Estate of Langston Hughes. Used by permission of Alfred A. Knopf, a division of Random House, Inc.

Excerpt from *Dandelion Wine* by Ray Bradbury, reprinted by permission of Don Congdon Associates, Inc. Copyright © 1957, renewed 1985 by Ray Bradbury.

"Coming to America" by Marianne Szegedy-Maszak. From *Good Housekeeping,* January 2000. Copyright © Hearst Magazines January 2000.

"Business at Eleven," by Toshio Mori. Reprinted by permission of Caxton Press.

Reprinted with the permission of Atheneum Books for Young Readers, an imprint of Simon & Schuster Children's Publishing Division from *Letters From a Slave Girl* by Mary E. Lyons. Copyright © 1992 by Mary E. Lyons.

Photography

Cover Hugh Gretschmer/Getty Images; IGetty Images; viii Images.com/ CORBIS; x Buzz Pictures/SuperStock ; xii Kirk Aeder/Icon SMI; xiv Julie Nicholls/CORBIS; xvi Gandee Vason/Getty Images; xviii Tim de Waele/CORBIS; xx Colin Bootman/The Bridgeman Art Library; xxii Bill Ross/CORBIS; xxiv Getty Images; xxv (tr)Clay Bennett/The Christian Science Monitor, (others)Getty Images; xxvi xxvii Getty Images; xxx Jose Luis Pelaez/Corbis; xxxvi Dinah Mite Activities; xxxvii Getty Images; RH Getty Images; RH19 (l)Klee/Corbis, (r)Corbis; 0 Images.com/CORBIS; 2 (t)Jon Feingersch/CORBIS, (b)CORBIS; 5 Images.com/CORBIS; 7 Amanita Pictures; 8 Smithsonian American Art Museum, Washington DC/Art Resource, NY; 10 CORBIS; 12 John Kaprielian/ Photo Researchers; 14 Lucky Cow/Mark Pett. Dist. By UNIVERSAL PRESS SYNDICATE; 15 John Evans; 16 Jeff Pfeffer/Random House Children's Books; 18 Tony Freeman/PhotoEdit; 19 CORBIS; 20 Kevin R. Morris/CORBIS; 21 AP/ Wide World Photos; 25 David L. Moore/Alamy Images; 26 Stephanie Maze/ CORBIS; 32 Time for Kids; 33 Royal Geographic Society; 34 (t)Royal Geographic Society, (b)BobBy Model; 35 BobBy Model; 36 Royal Geographic Society; 42 BALDO/Baldo Partnership. Dist. By UNIVERSAL PRESS SYNDICATE; 43 John Evans; 44 The Frank & Marie-Therese Wood Print Collection, Alexandria, VA; 46 The Image Bank/Getty Images; 49 Sausage International/ CORBIS; 52 The Image Bank/Getty Images; 57 Topham Picturepoint/The Image Works; 58 Eric Robert/CORBIS; 59 C Squared Studios/Getty Images; 62 Zits Partnership, Reprinted with Permission of King Features Syndicate; 63 Laura Sifferlin; 64 Judith Josephson; 66 The Newberry Library/Stock Montage; 67 CORBIS; 69 The Newberry Library/Stock Montage; 71 72 Bettmann/ CORBIS; 74 The Newberry Library/Stock Montage; 83 84 Michael Newman/ PhotoEdit; 86 Richard Klune/CORBIS; 87 through 89 Getty Images; 94 Baldo/ Baldo Partnership. Dist. By UNIVERSAL PRESS SYNDICATE; 96 Baldo/Baldo

Partnership. Dist. By UNIVERSAL PRESS SYNDICATE; 97 File photo; 98 Mary Moylan; 100 through 104 SIRIUS Entertainment; 106 George Fry/Yoshiko Uchida photograph collection, #1986.059:269--PIC The Bancroft Library; 108 CORBIS; 110 Yoshiko Uchida photograph collection, The Bancroft Library; 111 Yoshiko Uchida photograph collection, The Bancroft Library; 112 Toru Hanai/Reuters/CORBIS; 113 ImageGap/Alamy Images; 114 CORBIS; 118 Everett Collection; 119 Chris Brown/Alamy Images; 120 Tom Rosenthal/SuperStock; 122 (t)SSPL/The Image Works, (b)Comstock Images/Alamy Images; 123 (t)Gettysburg College/Random House Children's Books, (b)Judie Burstein/ Globe Photos; 124 SuperStock/Alamy Images; 125 Siede Preis/Getty Images; 126 Hulton Archive/Getty Images; 128 (t)Greg Stott/Masterfile, (b)The Bicycle Museum of America/New Bremen, OH; 129 SuperStock; 130 SuperStock/ Alamy Images; 134 136 137 Courtesy Kate Montgomery; 138 139 Eclipse Studios; 146 Buzz Pictures/SuperStock; 148 (l)Charles Gullung/Photonica/ Getty Images, (r)Photomondo/Getty Images; 151 Catherine Gehm; 152 (l)courtesy of the New York State Museum, Albany, NY, (r)Newberry Library, Chicago/SuperStock; 153 Werner Foreman/Topham/The Image Works; 154 155 157 Christie's Images; 158 blickwinkel/Alamy Images; 160 BIG TOP/ Harrell. Dist. By UNIVERSAL PRESS SYNDICATE; 161 Raoul Minsart/Masterfile; 162 Ron Rovtar; 165 Courtesy Leo & Diana Dillon; 167 Courtesy the Wyeth Collection; 168 Courtesy Leo & Diana Dillon; 173 174 176 Manuel Bauer/ Lookat; 182 Zits Partnership, Reprinted with Permission of King Features Syndicate; 183 Laura Sifferlin; 184 Bettman/CORBIS; 188 SuperStock; 190 Arthur Hoppock Hearn Fund - 1950 - The Metropolitan Museum of Art - NY (50.117) Estate of Grant Wood/Licensed By VAGA 192 SuperStock; 194 Eric Kimmel; 196 Erich Lessing/Art Resource, NY; 198 R.P. Kingston/Index Stock Imagery; 200 Brooklyn Museum of Art, NY. Frank L. Babbott Fund/Bridgeman Art Library; 201 Victoria and Albert Museum, London/AKG-Images; 202 Erich Lessing/Art Resource, NY; 204 Reprinted with permission of King Features Syndicate; 205 File photo; 208 Stapleton Collection/CORBIS; 209 Bridgeman Art Library; 210 David Else/Lonely Planet Images; 212 Inga Spence/Index Stock Imagery; 213 Ron Johnson/Index Stock Imagery; 215 Imagebroker/Alamy Images; 216 Stapleton Collection/CORBIS; 218 AP/Wide World Photos; 220 National Museum of American Art, Washington DC/Art Resource, NY; 221 R. & N. Bowers/VIREO; 222 Raymond Bial; 223 National Museum of American Art, Washington DC/Art Resource, NY; 225 Bettmann/CORBIS; 230 National Portrait Gallery, Smithsonian Institution/Art Resource, NY; 232 National Museum of American Art, Washington DC/Art Resource, NY; 238 BALDO/Baldo Partnership. Dist. By UNIVERSAL PRESS SYNDICATE; 239 File photo; 240 Radcliffe Archives, Radcliffe Institute, Harvard University; 242 Jason Hawkes/CORBIS; 244 Cindy Kassab/CORBIS; 245 Scala/Art Resource, NY; 246 Cindy Kassab/CORBIS; 248 Courtesy of Holiday House; 250 CORBIS; 251 Mary Evans Picture Library; 252 The Stapleton Collection/ Bridgeman Art Library; 253 Bettmann/CORBIS; 254 CORBIS; 258 Wallace Garland/Muthoni Garland; 259 Hubertus Kanus/SuperStock; 260 Betty Press/Woodfin Camp; 262 Knut Mueller/africa-photo/Das Fotoarchiv; 264 Rubberball/Getty Images; 267 Leone Castell Anderson; 268 Melissa Farlow/Getty Images; 269 Bettmann/CORBIS; 270 VEER Thomas Francisco/ Getty Images; 271 Bettmann/CORBIS; 272 Andreas Feininger/Time Life Pictures/Getty Images; 274 Melissa Farlow/Getty Images; 278 (l)Library of Congress/CORBIS, (r)Ace Stock Limited/Alamy Images; 280 281 Eclipse Studio; 288 Kirk Aeder/Icon SMI; 290 (t)BananaStock/SuperStock, (b)Brooke Fasani/ CORBIS; 293 Timothy A. Clary/AFP/Getty Images; 294 Lou Cappozola/Sports Illustrated; 295 (t)David N. Seelig/Icon SMI, (b)Eric Miller/Reuters/CORBIS; 296 FOXTROT/Bill Amend of UNIVERSAL PRESS SYNDICATE; 297 John Evans; 298 Nick Koon/The Orange County Register; 300 303 AP/Wide World Photos; 304 Chris Trotman/NewSport/CORBIS; 305 CORBIS; 306 Mike Powell/Getty Images; 308 AP/Wide World Photos; 310 Dwight Okita; 322 FOXTROT/Bill Amend of UNIVERSAL PRESS SYNDICATE; 323 File photo; 326 328 David Nicholls/CORBIS; 336 King Features Syndicate, Reprinted with special permission; 337 Paul Barton/CORBIS; 338 Courtesy of Daniel Keyes; 341 Spencer Grant/PhotoEdit; 343 PhotoFest; 344 Amanita Pictures; 345 Frithjof Hirdes/zefa/CORBIS; 347 Archive Pictures; 348 Erik Dreyer/Stone/

Getty Images; 350 Archive Pictures; 352 Amanita Pictures; 356 Science Museum/SSPL/The Image Works; 358 Amanita Pictures; 359 Science Museum/SSPL/The Image Works; 361 Ramon Manent/Courtesy of Museum of Textil y de la indumentaria/CORBIS; 363 Amanita Pictures; 365 Movie Still Archives; 369 George Steinmetz/CORBIS; 371 Diana Ong/SuperStock; 372 Kodansha Ltd. 1986; 373 C Squared Studios/Getty Images; 377 Imagestopshop/Alamy Images; 378 Science Museum/SSPL/The Image Works; 386 Zits Partnership, Reprinted with Permission of King Features Syndicate; 387 RubberBall/SuperStock; 388 Courtesy of Linda Bickerstaff; 390 Marc Rosenthal/eStock Photo/Alamy Images; 391 Hulton Archive/Getty Images; 392 Charles & Josette Lenars/CORBIS; 394 (t)Dr. Kessel & Dr. Kardon/Tissues & Organs/Visuals Unlimited, (b)Chris McGrath/Getty Images; 396 Marc Rosenthal/eStock Photo/Alamy Images; 398 (t)Nancy Crampton, (b)Leapfrog Press; 406 Patricia Beck/Detroit Free Press. Image courtesy of Emilia Askari; 407 Peter Turnley/CORBIS; 409 Lon C. Diehl/PhotoEdit; 410 Ingo Jezierski/Getty Images; 411 David Sacks/The Image Bank/Getty Images; 412 Susan Van Etten/PhotoEdit; 414 AP/Wide World Photos; 415 Reuters/CORBIS; 418 AP/Wide World Photos; 422 (l)Bettmann/CORBIS, (r)Eureka Productions; 423 through 433 Eureka Productions; 434 435 Eclipse Studios; 442 Julie Nicholls/CORBIS; 444 (l)Peter Barrett/Masterfile, (r)Dann Tardif/CORBIS; 447 Patrick Kennedy/Natural Selection; 448 Reprinted with Permission of King Features Syndicate; 449 DK Stock/Getty Images; 450 Courtesy of Kate Schmitt; 452 through 454 CORBIS; 459 Steve Mason/Getty Images; 460 Malcolm Piers/Photographer's Choice/Getty Images; 461 Brand X/Punchstock; 462 Steve Mason/Getty Images; 466 468 King Features Syndicate Reprinted with special permission; 469 Rob Lewine/CORBIS; 470 Schomburg Center for Research in Black Culture; 472 Amistad Research Center, Tulane University; 473 National Portrait Gallery, Smithsonian Institution; 474 (t)Amistad Research Center, Tulane University, (b)National Portrait Gallery, Smithsonian Institution; 476 AP/Wide World Photos; 478 480 David Sanger; 482 FOXTROT/Bill Amend of UNIVERSAL PRESS SYNDICATE; 483 File photo; 484 Frank Trapper/CORBIS; 487 (t)Siede Preis/Getty Images, (b)James Keyser/Time Life Pictures/Getty Images; 488 James Keyser/Time Life Pictures/Getty Images; 490 Oscar White/CORBIS; 492 494 CNAC/MNAM/Reunion des Musees Nationaux/Art Resource, NY; 499 REAL LIFE ADVENTURES/GarLanco of UNIVERSAL PRESS SYNDICATE; 500 Zits Partnership, Reprinted with Permission of King Features Syndicate; 501 File photo; 502 FPG/Getty Images; 505 Art Resources; 506 Art Resources; 510 Jason Todd/Getty Images; 511 D. Hurst/Alamy Images; 513 514 Jason Todd/Getty Images; 518 Jeff Newton/Penguin Young Readers Group; 520 Mirrorpix/Getty Images; 523 Christophe Calais/In Visu/CORBIS; 524 Joe Raedle/Getty Images; 526 F. Damm/zefa/CORBIS; 527 Liba Taylor/CORBIS; 528 (t)Joe Raedle/Getty Images, (b)Liba Taylor/CORBIS; 532 Photo By Chris Conforti. Image courtesy of Yaedi Ignatow; 533 Christie's Images/CORBIS; 534 535 Eclipse Studios; 534 Ken Krull; 542 Gandee Vason/Getty Images; 544 (t)Noel Hendrickson/Getty Images, (b)Janeart/Getty Images; 548 Howard Grey/Getty Images; 550 CORBIS; 552 Under The Light/CORBIS; 553 Ottfried Schreiter/Imagebroker/Alamy Images; 556 Harry Bartlett/Taxi/Getty Images; 558 LUCKY COW/Mark Pett. Dist. By UNIVERSAL PRESS SYNDICATE; 559 WireImageStock/Masterfile; 560 Linnea Due; 562 Mike Powell/Allsport Concepts/Getty Images; 563 Jim Cummins/CORBIS; 567 Tim Pannell/CORBIS; 568 Digital Vision/Getty Images; 569 Mike Powell/Allsport Concepts/Getty Images; 570 Jim Cummins/CORBIS; 574 Sean Murphy/Stone/Getty Images; 575 Michael Newman/PhotoEdit; 578 Sean Murphy/Stone/Getty Images; 584 Reprinted with Permission of King Features Syndicate; 585 Rubberball/SuperStock; 588 Bob Burch/Index Stock Imagery; 589 Cleve Bryant/PhotoEdit; 590 Terrence Spencer/Time Life Pictures/Getty Images; 591 Vicky Kasala/Getty Images; 592 Bob Burch/Index Stock Imagery; 594 Gayl Heinz/William Morris Agency, LLC; 596 Smithsonian American Art Museum, Washington, DC/Art Resource, NY; 598 Butler Institute of American Art, Youngstown, OH/Gift of the Friends of American Art 1975/Bridgeman Art Library; 600 Jim Arbogast/Digital Vision/Getty Images; 602 Butler Institute of American Art, Youngstown, OH/Gift of the Friends of American Art 1975/Bridgeman Art Library; 604 CALVIN AND HOBBES/Bill Watterson. Dist. By UNIVERSAL PRESS SYNDICATE; 605 File

photo; 608 David T. Vernon Collection of Native American Indian Center/Colter Bay Indian Arts Museum/Grand Teton National Park; 609 Tom Bean/CORBIS; 610 Doug Martin; 613 Christie's Images; 614 Werner Forman Archive/British Museum, London/Art Resource, NY; 615 A & L Sinibaldi/Stone/Getty Images; 617 Kam Mak/SIS; 618 David T. Vernon Collection of Native American Indian Center/Colter Bay Indian Arts Museum/Grand Teton National Park; 620 Courtesy of Emily Costello; 622 Kirk Aeder/Icon SMI/CORBIS; 623 Carlo Allegri/Getty Images; 624 Scott Gries/Getty Images; 625 CORBIS; 626 Kirk Aeder/Icon SMI/CORBIS; 629 Zits Partnership of King Features Syndicate; 633 CALVIN AND HOBBES/Bill Watterson. Dist. By UNIVERSAL PRESS SYNDICATE; 634 Zits Partnership of King Features Syndicate; 635 Brent Turner; 636 Michael J. Rosen; 638 Ric Ergenbright/CORBIS; 639 Masaaki Toyoura/Getty Images; 640 Getty Images; 642 Jeffrey Coolidge/The Images Bank; 647 Peter Johnson/CORBIS; 648 649 Wilfried Krecichwost/Getty Images; 650 Ric Ergenbright/CORBIS; 652 (t)Jamie Painter Young/CORBIS, (b)Getty Images; 654 Michael Daniel; 656 Martha Swope; 659 AP/Wide World Photos; 660 Michael Daniel; 664 Bettmann/CORBIS; 665 Douglas Grundy/Getty Images; 667 Ron Chapple/Thinkstock/JupiterImages/Comstock Images; 669 Mary Evans Picture Library; 670 MedioImages; 671 American Stock/Hulton Archive/Getty Images; 673 Mary Evans Picture Library; 674 Gary Gianni; 675 through 684 Eureka Productions; 688 American Stock Photography/Retrofile.com; 689 American Stock Photography/Retrofile.com; 692 Carl & Ann Purcell; 697 Richard T. Nowitz; 700 701 Eclipse Studios; 708 Tim de Waele/CORBIS; 710 (l)SuperStock, (r)SW Productions/Getty Images; 713 Handout/Reuters/CORBIS; 718 POPPERFOTO/Alamy Images; 721 Getty Images; 727 The Granger Collection, NY; 732 BALDO/Baldo Partnership. Dist. By UNIVERSAL PRESS SYNDICATE; 733 File photo; 734 UPI/Bettmann/CORBIS; 737 Getty Images; 745 Getty Images; 750 The Granger Collection, NY; 757 Getty Images; 762 Handout/Reuters/CORBIS; 764 AKG-images; 767 Reuters/CORBIS; 773 Michael Matisse/Getty Images; 784 AKG-images; 787 Handout/Reuters/CORBIS; 788 Reuters/CORBIS; 794 CORNERED/Mike Baldwin of UNIVERSAL PRESS SYNDICATE; 795 Rubberball/SuperStock; 796 Getty Images; 799 The Granger Collection, NY; 808 Ingram Publishing/Alamy Images; 811 The Granger Collection, NY; 815 Hugh Threlfall/Alamy Images; 818 Getty Images; 822 The Granger Collection, NY; 824 827 AKG-images; 835 Hulton-Deutsch Collection/CORBIS; 841 Bettmann/CORBIS; 842 Getty Images; 844 AKG-images; 846 CALVIN AND HOBBES/Bill Watterson. Dist. By UNIVERSAL PRESS SYNDICATE; 847 Laura Sifferlin; 848 Ray Tamarra/Getty Images; 852 Getty Images; 856 Brad Mitchell/Alamy Images; 858 (t)Getty Images, (b)Brad Mitchell/Alamy Images; 863 Farrell Grehan/CORBIS; 865 Mika Grondahl; 866 Farrell Grehan/CORBIS; 869 CALVIN AND HOBBES 1989 Bill Watterson. Dist. By UNIVERSAL PRESS SYNDICATE; 871 REAL LIFE ADVENTURES/GarLanco of UNIVERSAL PRESS SYNDICATE; 872 LUCKY COW/Mark Pett. Dist. By UNIVERSAL PRESS SYNDICATE; 873 Tim Thompson/CORBIS; 877 878 Gary Conner/Index Stock Imagery; 880 The Montana Standard/AP/Wide World Photos; 884 Bettmann/CORBIS; 886 Hulton-Deutsch Collection/CORBIS; 888 Bettmann/CORBIS; 892 Ouida Sebestyen; 893 Bob Daemmrich/The Image Works; 895 David H. Wells/CORBIS; 898 Yvonne Boyd/IPN Stock; 902 J. David Andrews/Masterfile; 904 Creatas/PhotoLibrary; 905 Yoham Kahana/Shooting Star; 907 Christian Pierre/SuperStock; 908 (t)Bob Daemmrich/The Image Works, (b)Christian Pierre/SuperStock; 911 Laura DeSantis/Getty Images; 912 (l)Matt Valentine/Valentine Photography, (r)Paul Edmondson/Getty Images; 914 915 Eclipse Studios; 922 Colin Bootman/Bridgeman Art Library; 924 CORBIS; 927 Plush Studios/Photographer's Choice/Getty Images; 928 Garry Gay/The Image Bank/Getty Images; 930 Zits Partnership of King Features Syndicate; 931 John Evans; 932 McClelland & Stewart; 934 John A Rizzo/Getty Images; 936 JW/Masterfile; 938 CORBIS; 940 John A Rizzo/Getty Images; 942 William F. Campbell/Time Life Pictures/Getty Images; 944 AP/Wide World Photos; 945 Jeff Greenberg/PhotoEdit; 946 CORBIS; 949 Hulton Archive/Getty Images; 950 AP/Wide World Photos; 956 STONE SOUP/Jan Eliot of UNIVERSAL PRESS SYNDICATE; 957 Kevin Peterson/Getty Images; 958 Wally McNamee/CORBIS; 960 CORBIS; 961 Flip Schulke/CORBIS; 962 Rosebud Pictures/Taxi/Getty Images; 963 Bryan F. Peterson; 964 CORBIS;